INTERNATIONAL BUSINESS

EIGHTH EDITION

Michael R. Czinkota
Georgetown University, University of Birmingham

Ilkka A. Ronkainen
Georgetown University

Michael H. Moffett
Thunderbird School of Global Management

WILEY

John Wiley & Sons, Inc.

Vice President & Executive Publisher: George Hoffman
Executive Editor: Lise Johnson
Production Manager: Dorothy Sinclair
Senior Production Editor: Valerie A. Vargas
Freelance Project Editor: Susan McLaughlin
Marketing Manager: Karolina Zarychta
Creative Director: Harry Nolan
Senior Designer: Madelyn Lesure
Production Management Services: Elm Street Publishing Services
Senior Illustration Editor: Anna Melhorn
Senior Photo Editor: Ellinor Wagner
Editorial Assistant: Sarah Vernon
Executive Media Editor: Allison Morris
Media Editor: Elena Santa Marie
Cover Photo Credit: © Stanislav Odyagailo/iStockphoto
Part Opener Credit: © Artville/Getty Images, Inc.

This book was set in 10.5/12.5, Goudy by Thomson Digital, India and printed and bound by Courier-Kendallville, Inc. The cover was printed by Courier-Kendallville, Inc.

ISBN-13 978-0-470-53065-8

Printed in the United States of America

10 9 8 7 6 5 4 3 2 1

To Ilona and Margaret
MRC

To Sirkka and Alpo Ronkainen
IAR

To Bennie Ruth and Hoy Moffett
MHM

We are grateful for the leadership position you, our market, have awarded to this book. Best-selling status in the international business field also imposes an obligation to deliver cutting-edge innovations and improvements in terms of content as well as presentation. We honor your trust by doing our best to delight you through our presentation of conceptually sound, reality-based knowledge and by easing your task of teaching and learning about international business. In this spirit of innovation, we offer you yet more value—*International Business*, 8th Edition.

Our textbook has always been unique in its field due to its approach to international business. But now, this eighth edition is the most special of all. International business has undergone major changes in the recent past—both in its concepts and their application. Governments are playing a new, major role in their involvement with international business. On a global scale there is an introduction of new regulations, restrictions, and ways to raise funds. Corporations and consumers are subject to new ways of thinking.

For example, the concepts of risk, competition, profit, and private property are being realigned. Some risks are no longer acceptable or require collaborative actions among many to overcome the downside. A better recognition of what it is we do not know—and the resulting uncertainty and limited ability to resolve controversial issues—requires the development of new tools and new approaches.

Many players in international business only now discover that they are but one integral component of society. Politics, security, and religion are only some of the other dimensions that are held in possibly higher esteem than business by society at large. Those who argue based on economic principles alone may increasingly find themselves on the losing side. For example, the level and structure of profits and executive compensation needs to reflect a firm's long-term best interests within an overall societal context. Small- and medium-sized firms have—thanks to changes in technology—entirely new opportunities to succeed in new global markets. At the same time, never before have they been exposed to so much unforeseen competition from distant parts of the earth. Business school programs without an emphasis on context, proportionality, and interaction must revise such shortcomings in their teaching. Legislators and government need to appreciate the direct and indirect effects their actions have on international business. What they may consider a strictly local affair may turn out to have substantial impact on global conditions.

When we originally decided to write our international business book seven editions ago, we placed our wagers on several dimensions: key of them were the strong links to government—which we expected to keep clearly addressed due to our location in Washington, DC. There was also a strong emphasis on small-and medium-sized firms—which we thought would gradually emerge as significant players in the international field. Driven by our Georgetown presence, we were fully aware of the need for the moral dimension and social responsibility by the business sector. Our research orientation helped in maintaining the focus on the truly global nature of actors and activities.

Years later, events have moved in our direction as never before. Our Washington location has given us the ability to follow, analyze, and incorporate both the role of

v

government in general, and of the U.S. government and its trade and investment posture in particular. Having held policy-making positions in the government and being called to advise both governments and elected representatives in many nations has given us the insights and social networks that enable a decisive strategic orientation of this text. Our experience in founding and running small businesses allows us to understand what the key needs and capabilities of such firms are, which in turn allows us to help such firms do better. Our advisory work for larger multinational firms permits us to share the realities of the battles in the international marketplace. Our long-term involvement with nongovernmental organizations enables us to communicate understanding of the not-for-profit world. We are, therefore, pleased to provide you with a strong theory base that also fully reflects government, managerial, and consumer concerns from around the world. We hope that you will share our view that the content, pedagogy, and presentation of this book make it fun to teach and to learn.

CHANGES IN THE EIGHTH EDITION

This new edition is even more user-friendly. Important issues, such as investment flows, are presented early in the text. The topics of transparency and governance are covered more thoroughly to echo the changing times in which we live. Multinational corporate issues, together with cooperative modes of market development, are presented in the context of international business entry and strategic planning. Countertrade is covered in conjunction with multinational financial management.

CURRENT COVERAGE

Today, change happens at breakneck speed. Keeping on top of the evolving world of international issues and their impact on international business can be difficult. This text addresses instructors' and students' needs for information with current perspectives on contemporary topics not yet available in other international business texts.

In preparing this edition, we have listened closely to our market in order to deliver an outstanding product. We begin by presenting the impact of international business on countries, corporations, and individuals.

We reflect more fully on some of the controversies in international business today, including the role of international institutions such as the World Trade Organization, the World Bank, and the International Monetary Fund. We discuss why some groups are disenchanted with increased globalization. Also presented are some of the links between and areas of friction in international business and development, such as payment for intellectual property rights, distribution of patented medication to poor countries, and development of genetically engineered foods. We address the issues of bribery and corruption and the benefit of good governance; in-depth attention is paid to the role of culture, policies, and politics. The dimensions of ethics, social responsibility, and diversity are fully reflected through examples and vignettes.

The text consistently adopts a truly global approach. Attention is given to topics that are critical to the international manager yet so far have eluded other international texts. This coverage includes chapters on supply-chain management, international service trade, and doing business with newly emerging market economies under conditions of privatization.

NEW AND IMPROVED TOPIC COVERAGE AND ORGANIZATION

International Business, 8th Edition, is organized into five parts and contains 19 chapters. These parts allow the text to flow logically from introductory material to the international environment to marketing and financial considerations in the international marketplace.

> **Part 1** deals with the impact of globalization and provides an overview of the key issues facing international business today.
>
> **Part 2** shifts to the conceptual foundations surrounding international trade and investments.
>
> **Part 3** covers the environment and focuses on the similarities and differences between cultures, as well as how global politics and laws both influence and are influenced by these same factors.
>
> **Part 4** explains strategy issues, including planning, corporate governance, marketing, and expansion.
>
> **Part 5** is devoted to international operations, investigating management issues. It concludes with a look toward the future horizons of the field and of the student.

INNOVATIVE LEARNING TOOLS

USE OF WORLDWIDE EXAMPLES

Drawing on worldwide examples, trends, and data rather than just on U.S.-based information makes this a global book. For example, many of the data sets presented and sources recommended come from Europe and Asia.

We also ensure the reality and pragmatism of our content by always addressing the issue of "What does this mean for international business?" As an example, we explain how to use cultural variables for segmentation purposes in order to create new competitive tools.

BLENDING CURRENT THEORY AND APPLICATION

Our theory section presents the latest thinking both from business researchers and leading economists. We also present the interdependence and linkages between the different theories so that students gain an appreciation of the overall context of international business thought. All tables, figures, and maps were updated to present the most current information.

RESEARCH EMPHASIS

This edition includes a greatly strengthened research chapter. An in-depth information appendix enhances the student's ability to conduct independent research, primarily by using web sites and other resources of the Internet. We devote a section to the issue of data privacy and to research on the Internet, where we highlight best practices of firms and provide a comparison of the different approaches to privacy in Europe and in the United States.

We also focus on "born global" firms, which have a global orientation from their inception, and differentiate the levels of internationalization of these firms. We offer a model of the internationalization process, reflecting the latest in research findings. We show how firms can receive export help from their governments and provide Internet information for the leading export promotion organizations from around the globe. A section highlights how leading-edge firms are developing "export complaint management systems" in order to stay close to their customers, adapt products quickly, and regain control of export channels.

TECHNOLOGY, ELECTRONIC COMMERCE, AND THE INTERNET

Issues surrounding technology in the international workplace are integrated throughout the text. In addition, Web-based questions and research exercises at the end of each chapter permit immersion in ongoing international business issues and communicate the excitement of rapid change.

We have developed a strong focus on Internet-based research, but also discuss the strengths and weaknesses of electronic databases. We highlight, for example, the fact that culture has a major effect on technology use and content expectations, and that search engines tend to pick only a small portion of actual work carried out and are still heavily biased toward English-language publications. We also show how new technology can help even very small firms reach out to international markets and compete successfully abroad.

 DISTINGUISHING PEDAGOGICAL FEATURES

GEOGRAPHY

To enhance the geographic literacy of students, the text includes many full color maps covering the social, economic and political features of the world. In addition, several chapters have maps particularly designed for this book, which integrate the materials discussed in the text and reflect a truly "global" perspective. They provide the instructor with the means to visually demonstrate concepts such as political blocs, socioeconomic variables, and transportation routes. A list of maps appears on page xxii. An appendix, dealing specifically with the impact of geography on international marketing, is part of Chapter 1. Each text is packaged with a foldout map by National Geographic Society.

CONTEMPORARY REALISM

Each chapter offers a number of Focus on Issues boxes that describe actual contemporary business situations. These issues include Politics, Ethics, e-Business, Culture, and Entrepreneurship. These boxes are intended to serve as reinforcing examples, or mini-cases. As such, they will assist the instructor in stimulating class discussion and aid the student in understanding and absorbing the text material.

CHAPTER SUMMARY AND REVIEW QUESTIONS

Each chapter closes with a chapter summary of key points that students should retain, organized by learning objective. The discussion questions are a complementary learning tool that will enable students to check their understanding of key issues, to think beyond basic concepts, and to determine areas that require further study. All these tools help students discriminate between main and supporting points and provide mechanisms for classroom activity or at-home review.

ON THE WEB

Each chapter contains several Internet exercises to involve students in the high-tech world of cyberspace. Students are asked to explore the Web to research topics related to materials covered in each chapter. This hands-on experience helps to develop Internet, research, and business skills.

TAKE A STAND!

These end-of-chapter exercises ask students to read a short paragraph outlining a situation and to make an educated decision about the outcome for the scenario. They can be used as a homework exercise, a personal assessment, or for classroom discussion.

EXEMPLARY CASE SELECTION

To further link theory and practice, we present nineteen cases, more than half of which are new or updated. We draw case materials from firms around the world to offer truly global business scenarios, ranging from Vietnam and Russia to Iceland and Turkey. The cases deal with manufacturing industries, such as automotive firms, but also with honey from New Zealand and a Soweto festival in South Africa. We present some of the controversy emanating from the diamond industry, and we also focus on the human dimension that is so highly important for expatriates. Challenging questions accompany each case. Some of our best cases from previous editions are also available on the text support site (www.wiley.com/college/czinkota) for instructor use. They encourage in-depth discussion of the material covered in the chapters and allow students to apply the knowledge they have gained and allow instructors to retain the use of favorite teaching tools.

PERSONAL SUPPORT

We personally stand behind our product, and we will work hard to delight you. Should you have any questions or comments on this book, please contact us and provide us with your feedback.

Michael R. Czinkota   Ilkka A. Ronkainen   Michael H. Moffett
Czinkotm@georgetown.edu   Ronkaii@georgetown.edu   Moffettm@t-bird.edu

ACKNOWLEDGMENTS

We are very grateful to Charles Skuba, Professor of the Practice at Georgetown University. His background as Chief of Staff for Market Access and Compliance in the U.S. Dept. of Commerce, his close linkage with industry, his dedication to students, and his willingness to share all his knowledge and experience have made him a major supporter of this book project. He is always right on track, unfailingly courteous, and deeply insightful. Most importantly, he delivers! Charlie, our hats are off to you. Thanks to Susan Ronkainen, who was able to pull together the chapter changes in marketing, culture, human resources, strategic planning, and organization and strategic planning for this edition. We thank Professor Anne Balazs of Eastern Michigan University. She was a strong motivator behind this new edition and provided meaningful insights and support. Also very helpful was Dafina Nikolova, Ph.D. candidate, who assisted in shaping some of the chapters, worked hard on many vignettes, and provided substantial research assistance—particularly with government documents.

We are grateful to many reviewers for their imaginative comments and criticisms and for showing us how to get it even more right:

Kamal M. Abouzeid
Lynchburg College

Yair Aharoni
Duke University

Zafar U. Ahmed
Minot State University

Riad Ajami
Rensselaer Polytechnic Institute

Joe Anderson
Northern Arizona University

Robert Aubey
University of Wisconsin-Madison

David Aviel
California State University

Josiah Baker
University of Central Florida

Marilynn Baker
*University of North
    Carolina—Greensboro*

Bharat B. Bhalla
Fairfield University

Julius M. Blum
University of South Alabama

Sharon Browning
Northwest Missouri State University

Peggy E. Chaudhry
Villanova University

Ellen Cook
University of San Diego

Lauren DeGeorge
University of Central Florida

Luther Trey Denton
Georgia Southern University

Dharma deSilva
Wichita State University

Gary N. Dicer
The University of Tennessee

Peter Dowling
University of Tasmania

Carol Dresden
Coastal Carolina University

Derrick E. Dsouza
University of North Texas

Massoud Farahbaksh
Salem State College

Runar Framnes
Norwegian School of Management

Anne-Marie Francesco
Pace University—New York

Esra F. Gencturk
University of Texas—Austin

Debra Glassman
University of Washington-Seattle

Raul de Gouvea Neto
University of New Mexico

Antonio Grimaldi
*Rutgers, The State University
    of New Jersey*

John H. Hallaq
University of Idaho

Daniel Himarios
University of Texas at Arlington

Veronica Horton
Middle Tennessee State University

Basil J. Janavaras
Mankato State University

Michael Kublin
University of New Haven

Diana Lawson
University of Maine

Jan B. Luytjes
Florida International University

John Manley
Iona College

David McCalman
Indiana University-Bloomington

Tom Morris
University of San Diego

James Neelankavil
Hofstra University

V. R. Nemani
Trinity College

Moonsong David Oh
*California State
    University—Los Angeles*

Sam C. Okoroafo
University of Toledo

Diane Parente
State University of New York-Fredonia

Mike W. Peng
Ohio State University

William Piper
Piedmont College

Jesus Ponce de Leon
*Southern Illinois
    University-Carbondale*

Jerry Ralston
University of Washington-Seattle

Peter V. Raven
Eastern Washington University

William Renforth
Florida International University

Martin E. Rosenfeldt
The University of North Texas

Tagi Sagafi-nejad
Loyola College

Rajib N. Sanyal
Trenton State College

Ulrike Schaede
University of California-Berkeley

John Stanbury
Indiana University-Kokomo

John Thanopoulos
University of Akron

Douglas Tseng
Portland State University

Robert G. Vambery
Pace University

C. Alexandra Van Nostrand
Palm Beach Atlantic College

Betty Velthouse
University of Michigan-Flint

Heidi Vernon-Wortzel
Northeastern University

Steven C. Walters
Davenport College

James O. Watson
Millikin University

Mindy West
Arizona State University-Tempe

George H. Westacott
SUNY-Binghamton

Jerry Wheat
Indiana University Southeast

Tim Wilkinson
University of Akron

Bill Wresch
University of Wisconsin—Oshkosh

Kitty Y. H. Young
Chinese University of Hong Kong

Many thanks to those faculty members and students who helped us in sharpening our thinking by cheerfully providing challenging comments and questions. Several individuals had particular long-term impact on our thinking. These are Professor Bernard LaLonde, of the Ohio State University, a true academic mentor; the late Professor Robert Bartels, also of Ohio State; Professor Arthur Stonehill of Oregon State University; Professor James H. Sood of American University; Professor Arch G. Woodside of Tulane University; Professor David Ricks of University of Missouri-St. Louis; Professor Brian Toyne of St. Mary's University; and Professor John Darling of Mississippi State University. They are our academic ancestors.

Many colleagues, friends, and business associates graciously gave their time and knowledge to clarify concepts; provide us with ideas, comments, and suggestions; and deepen our understanding of issues. Without the direct links to business and policy that you have provided, this book could not offer its refreshing realism. In particular, we are grateful to Secretaries Malcolm Baldrige, C. William Verity, Clayton Yeutter, and William Brock for the opportunity to gain international business policy experience and to William Morris, Paul Freedenberg, and J. Michael Farrell for enabling its implementation. We also thank William Casselman, Lew Cramer of the Utah World Trade Center, Gregory Unruh, Thunderbird School of Management, and Hannu Seristö of Aalto University. We appreciate all the horse sense shared by Professor Thomas Cooke.

Our elite team of student researchers provided valuable assistance. They made important and substantive contributions to this book. They dig up research information with tenacity and relentlessness; they organize and analyze research materials, prepare drafts of vignettes and cases, and reinforce everyone on the fourth floor of the Hariri Building with their infectious can-do spirit. They are Sugy Choi, Rebecca White, Glenn Russo, and Robert Salas, all of Georgetown University. We appreciate all of your work.

A very special thank you to the people at John Wiley & Sons. Thanks to George Hoffman, Publisher; Lisé Johnson, Executive Editor; Susan McLaughlin, Developmental Editor; Sarah Vernon, Assistant Editor; Maddy Lesure, Senior Designer; Sandra Dumas, Senior Production Editor; and Danielle Urban and Elm Street Publishing Services, for their efforts in support of this project.

Foremost, we are grateful to our families, who have had to tolerate late-night computer noises, weekend library absences, and curtailed vacations. The support and love of Ilona Vigh-Czinkota and Margaret Victoria Czinkota; Susan, Sanna, and Alex Ronkainen; Megan Murphy, Caitlin Kelly, and Sean Michael Moffett gave us the energy, stamina, and inspiration to write this book.

Michael R. Czinkota
Ilkka A. Ronkainen
Michael H. Moffett
June, 2010

Michael R. Czinkota

Michael R. Czinkota presents international business and marketing issues at the Graduate School and the Robert Emmett McDonough School of Business at Georgetown University and the Birmingham Business School in the United Kingdom. He has held professorial appointments at universities in Asia, Australia, Europe, and the Americas.

Dr. Czinkota served in the U.S. government as Deputy Assistant Secretary of Commerce. He also served as head of the U.S. Delegation to the OECD Industry Committee in Paris and as senior advisor for Export Controls.

His background includes ten years of private-sector business experience as a partner in a fur trading firm and in an advertising agency. His research has been supported by the U.S. government, the National Science Foundation, the Organization of American States, and the American Management Association. He was listed as one of the three most published contributors to international business research in the world by the *Journal of International Business Studies* and has written several books, including *Key Shifts in International Business: Adjusting to a New World*, (with I. Ronkainen and M. Kotabe, Businessexpertspress.com) and *Mastering Global Markets* (Cengage).

Dr. Czinkota has served on the Global Advisory Board of the American Marketing Association, the Global Council of the American Management Association, and the Board of Governors of the Academy of Marketing Science. He is on the editorials boards of the *Journal of Academy of Marketing Science, Journal of International Marketing*, and *Asian Journal of Marketing*. He is a contributor to the *Washington Times*, the *Korea Times*, and the *Handelsblatt* in Germany.

For his work in international business and trade policy, he was named a Distinguished Fellow of the Academy of Marketing Science, a Fellow of the Chartered Institute of Marketing, and a Fellow of the Royal Society of Arts in the United Kingdom. He has been awarded honorary degrees from the Universidad Pontificia Madre y Maestra in the Dominican Republic and the Universidad del Pacífico in Lima, Peru.

He serves on several corporate boards and has worked with corporations such as AT&T, IBM, GE, Nestlé, and US WEST. He advises the Executive Office of the President of the United States, the United Nations, and the World Trade Organization. Dr. Czinkota is often asked to testify before the United States Congress.

Dr. Czinkota was born and raised in Germany and educated in Austria, Scotland, Spain, and the United States. He studied law and business administration at the University of Erlangen-Nürnberg and was awarded a two-year Fulbright Scholarship. He holds an MBA in international business and a Ph.D. in logistics from The Ohio State University.

Ilkka A. Ronkainen

Ilkka A. Ronkainen is a member of the faculty of marketing and international business at the School of Business at Georgetown University. He has received the undergraduate teaching and research awards twice, and in 2001 and 2008, the International Executive MBA program at Georgetown recognized him as the Outstanding Professor of the Year. He is the founder and director of the MSB's summer Hong Kong program. He has been a member of the Georgetown University Faculty Senate since 1992.

Dr. Ronkainen serves as docent of international marketing at the Helsinki School of Economics. He was visiting professor at HSE during the 1988–1997 and 1991–1992 academic years and continues to teach in its Executive MBA, International MBA, and International BBA programs.

Dr. Ronkainen holds a Ph.D. and a master's degree from the University of South Carolina as well as an M.S. (Economics) degree from the Helsinki School of Economics.

Dr. Ronkainen has published extensively in academic journals and the trade press. He is a coauthor of a number of international business and marketing texts, including *Global Business: Positioning Ventures Ahead* (2010) and *Emerging Trends, Threats and Opportunities in International Marketing: What Executives Need to Know* (2009). In 1995, his co-authored text, *The Global Marketing Imperative*, was a winner of the Choice Award given to the best research books of the year. He serves on the review boards of the *Journal of Business Research*, *International Marketing Review*, and *Journal of Travel Research*, and has reviewed for the *Journal of International Marketing* and *the Journal of International Business Studies*. He served as the North American coordinator for the European Marketing Academy, 1984–1990. He was a member of the board of the Washington International Trade Association from 1981–1986 and started the association's newsletter, *Trade Trends*.

Dr. Ronkainen has served as a consultant to a wide range of U.S. and international institutions. He has worked with entities such as IBM, the Rand Organization, and the Organization of American States. He maintains close relations with a number of Finnish companies and their internationalization and educational efforts.

Michael H. Moffett

Michael H. Moffett, Ph.D., is an associate professor of finance and holds the Continental Grain Professorship in Finance at Thunderbird School of Global Management. Dr. Moffett earned his Ph.D. at the University of Colorado, Boulder in 1985. He also holds an M.A. from the University of Colorado, an M.S. from Colorado State University, and a B.A. from the University of Texas at Austin.

He has been a contributor to a number of books, including *Multinational Business Finance*, co-authored with Arthur Stonehill and David Eiteman, in its 12th edition, and *Fundamentals of Multinational Finance* with Stonehill and Eiteman in its third edition. He has authored more than 50 case studies on a variety of global business topics, and his writings have appeared in the industry's leading publications, including *Journal of Applied Corporate Finance*, *Journal of International Financial Management and Accounting*, *Journal of International Money and Finance*, *Contemporary Policy Issues*, *Brookings Discussion Papers in Economics*, and the *Journal of Financial and Quantitative Analysis*.

Prior to joining the Thunderbird faculty in 1994, Dr. Moffett was an associate professor in Oregon State University's Department of Finance and International Business. He has served as a visiting professor at a multitude of different universities including the University of Michigan, Helsinki School of Economics and Business Administration, University of Ljubljana's International Center for Public Enterprises in Slovenia, Aarhus School of Business in Denmark, University of Colorado, and University of Hawaii. In 1984–1985, Dr. Moffett was a Research Fellow at the Brookings Institute in Washington, DC. His expertise has been tapped by multinational firms in North and South America, Europe and Asia, and over the past 20-plus years, he has taught and consulted in more than 25 countries.

BRIEF CONTENTS

PART 1   IMPACT   1

1. The International Business Imperative   2

PART 2   FOUNDATIONS   31

2. Trade and Investment Polices   32
3. The Theory of Trade and Investment   62
4. The Balance of Payments   94

Part 2 Cases

Iceland 2006–A Small Country in a Global Capital Market   119
The Venezuelan Bolivar Black Market   122
Will Tire Tariffs Launch Trade Dispute?   125
The Catfish Dispute   132

PART 3   ENVIRONMENT   137

5. Culture   138
6. Politics and Law   172
7. Global Financial Markets   198
8. Economic Integration and Emerging Markets   234

Part 3 Cases

The Banana Wars   276
H1-B Visas: A High-Tech Dilemma   280
Closing the MG Rover Plant: The Aftereffects   284
The GM–AvtoVAZ Joint Venture   286
Mattel's Chinese Sourcing Crisis of 2007   292
Nine Dragons Paper   295

PART 4   STRATEGY   301

9. Strategic Planning   302
10. The Corporation: Ownership, Governance, and Sustainability   332
11. Organization, Implementation, and Control   358
12. Building the Knowledge Base   390
13. Entry and Expansion   426

Part 4 Cases

Honeyland Manuka Honey from New Zealand   455
IKEA: Furnishing the World   459
Koch Industries Acquires Georgia-Pacific   463
Petroleum Development and the Curse of Oil   466
Tao Kae Noi Seaweed Snack   469

PART 5   OPERATIONS   475

14. Marketing   476
15. Services   516
16. Logistics and Supply-Chain Management   536
17. Financial Management   570
18. Human Resource Management   600
19. New Horizons   632

Part 5 Cases

Nova International (Macedonia)   665
Porsche Changes Track   669
The Market Entry Strategy Social Approach   675
When Diamonds Weep   679

CONTENTS

Preface vii

About the Authors xv

PART 1 IMPACT 1

1. The International Business Imperative 2
Learning Objectives 2
Opening Vignette *New Challenges for International Business Managers* 3
The Need for International Business 4
A Definition of International Business 5
A Brief History 6
Global Links Today 11
The Current U.S. International Trade Position 16
The Impact of International Business on the United States 16
The Structure of the Book 18
Summary 20 / *Take a Stand* 21
Appendix 1: Geographic Perspectives on International Business 24
Location 24 / Place 25 / Interaction 26 / Movement 27 / Regions 29

PART 2 FOUNDATIONS 31

2. Trade and Investment Policies 32
Learning Objectives 32
Opening Vignette *The Global Economic Crisis and Lessons from the Depression* 33
Rationale and Goals of Trade and Investment Policies 34
Global Trade Regulation since 1945 35
Changes in the Global Policy Environment 37
Limits of Domestic Policy Influences 37 / Revitalizing International Institutions 40 / Sharpening of the Conflict between Industrialized and Developing Nations 42
Policy Responses to Changing Conditions 43
Restrictions of Imports 43 / Restrictions of Exports 49 / Export Promotion 49 / Import Promotion 51 / Investment Policies 51 / The Host-Country Perspective 52 / The Home-Country Perspective 54 / Restrictions on Investment 55 / Investment Promotion 55 / Management of the Policy Relationship 57
A Strategic Outlook for Trade and Investment Policies 58
A U.S. Perspective 58 / An International Perspective 59
Summary 60 / *Take a Stand* 61

3. The Theory of Trade and Investment 62
Learning Objectives 62

Opening Vignette *China, Trade, and the Global Recession* 63
The Age of Mercantilism 64
Classical Trade Theory 65
The Theory of Absolute Advantage 66 / The Theory of Comparative Advantage 67 / A Numerical Example of Classical Trade 67 / National Production Possibilities 68 / The Gains from International Trade 70 / Concluding Points about Classical Trade Theory 72
Factor Proportions Trade Theory 72
Factor Intensity in Production 72 / Factor Endowments, Factor Prices, and Comparative Advantage 73 / Assumptions of the Factor Proportions Theory 74 / The Leontief Paradox 74 / Linder's Overlapping Product Ranges Theory 76
International Investment and Product Cycle Theory 77
The Stages of the Product Cycle 77 / Trade Implications of the Product Cycle 78
The New Trade Theory: Strategic Trade 80
Economies of Scale and Imperfect Competition 80 / Strategic Trade 82 / The Competitive Advantage of Nations 84 / Clusters and the New Economics 85
The Theory of International Investment 86
The Foreign Direct Investment Decision 87 / The Theory of Foreign Direct Investment 88 / Firms as Seekers 88 / Firms as Exploiters of Imperfections 89 / Firms as internalizers 90
Summary 90 / *Take a Stand* 93

4. The Balance of Payments 94
Learning Objectives 94
Opening Vignette *Why Do Balance of Payments Problems Occur?* 95
Fundamentals of Balance of Payments Accounting 96
Defining International Economic Transactions 97 / The BOP as a Flow Statement 97 / BOP Accounting: Double-Entry Bookkeeping 97
The Accounts of the Balance of Payments 98
The Current Account 98 / The Capital and Financial Account 101 / Net Errors and Omissions 104 / Official Reserves Account 105
The Balance of Payments in Total 106
The Balance of Payments and Economic Crises 109
The Asian Crisis 109
Capital Mobility 113
Capital Flight 114
Summary 117 / *Take a Stand* 118
Cases 119

Iceland 2006–A Small Country in a Global Capital
Market 119
The Venezuelan Bolivar Black Market 122
Will Tire Tariffs Launch a Trade Dispute? 125
The Catfish Dispute 132

PART 3 ENVIRONMENT 137

5. Culture 138

Learning Objectives 138
Opening Vignette *Crossing Cultures: Balancing the Global
    with the Local* 139
Culture Defined 140
The Elements of Culture 144
    Language 144 / Nonverbal Language 147 / Religion 148 /
    Values and Attitudes 151 / Manners and Customs 152 /
    Material Elements 154 / Aesthetics 155 / Education 157 /
    Social Institutions 157
Sources of Cultural Knowledge 158
Cultural Analysis 161
The Training Challenge 165
Making Culture Work for Business Success 167
Summary 169 / *Take a Stand* 171

6. Politics and Law 172

Learning Objectives 172
Opening Vignette *International Trade and Elephants* 173
The Home-Country Perspective 174
    Embargoes and Sanctions 175 / Export Controls 176 / A
    New Environment for Export Controls 178 / Regulating
    International Business Behavior 180
Host-Country Political and Legal Environment 183
    Political Action and Risk 183 / Economic Risk 189 /
    Managing the Risk 190 / Legal Differences and
    Restraints 191 / The Influencing of Politics
    and Laws 192
International Relations and Laws 194
    International Politics 194 / International Law 195
Summary 196 / *Take a Stand* 197

7. Global Financial Markets 198

Learning Objectives 198
Opening Vignette *Global Capital Markets: Entering a New
    Era* 199
The Global Financial Marketplace 200
    Assets, Instruments, and Institutions 200
The Market for Currencies 201
    Exchange Rate Quotations and Terminology 202 / Size of the
    Market 205 / Market Structure 207 / The Big Three (or
    Four?) 207
Evolution of the Global Monetary System 208
    The Gold Standard 208 / The Interwar Years 1919–1939,
    209 / Bretton Woods Agreement, 1944–1971 209 / Times of
    Crisis, 1971–1973 210 / Floating Exchange Rates, 1973–
    Present 210 / The Launch of the Euro 211

The Purpose of Exchange Rates 212
    What Is a Currency Worth? 212 / The Law of One Price 213
Global Capital Markets 214
    Sources of Capital 214 / Defining International Financing 215 /
    International Money Markets 217 / International Banking and
    Bank Lending 218 / International Security Markets 219 /
    Gaining Access to International Financial Markets 221
The Financial Crisis of 2007–2009 221
    The Seeds of Crisis: Subprime Debt 221 / The Transmission
    Mechanism: Securitization of Derivatives 223 / Credit Default
    Swaps 225 / The Fallout: The Crisis of 2007 and 2008 226 /
    Global Contagion 227 / The Remedy: Prescriptions for an
    Infected Global Financial Organism 228
Summary 231 / *Take a Stand* 233

8. Economic Integration and Emerging
    Markets 234

Learning Objectives 234
Opening Vignette *Building Blocs toward Worldwide Free
    Trade* 235
Levels of Economic Integration 238
    The Free Trade Area 238 / The Customs Union 238 / The
    Common Market 239 / The Economic Union 239
Arguments Surrounding Economic Integration 239
    Trade Creation and Trade Diversion 240 / Reduced Import
    Prices 240 / Increased Competition and Economies of Scale
    241 / Higher Factor Productivity 241 / Regionalism versus
    Nationalism 242
Regional Groupings 242
    European Integration 242 / Organization of the EU 244
    North American Economic Integration 245
    Integration in Latin America 250 / Integration in Asia 251 /
    Integration in Africa and the Middle East 253
Cartels and Commodity Price Agreements 254
Emerging Markets 257
    China: Production Platform to Marketplace 260 / India: Growth
    in Services 262 / Brazil 263
Barriers to Business 264
    Infrastructure Problems 265
Transition Economies 266
The Developing Markets 267
    Research 268 / Creative Buying Power 268 / Tailoring Local
    Solutions 268 / Improving Access 268 / Shaping
    Aspirations 269
Economic Integration and the International Manager 271
    Effects of Change 271 / Strategic Planning 272 /
    Reorganization 272 / Lobbying 272
Summary 273 / *Take a Stand* 275
Cases 276
    The Banana Wars 276
    H-1B Visas: A High-Tech Dilemma 280
    Closing the MG Rover Plant: The Aftereffects 284
    The GM–AvtoVAZ Joint Venture 286
    Mattel's Chinese Sourcing Crisis of 2007 292
    Nine Dragons Paper 295

PART 4 STRATEGY 301

9. Strategic Planning 302

Learning Objectives 302
Opening Vignette *The Changing Landscape of Global
   Markets* 303
Globalization 305
   Globalization Drivers 306
The Strategic Planning Process 311
   Understanding and Adjusting the Core Strategy 311 / Formulating
   Global Strategy 314 / Global Program Development 318 /
   Implementing Global Programs 323 / Localizing Global Moves
   324 / The Local Company in the Global Environment 327
Summary 329 / *Take a Stand* 331

**10. The Corporation: Ownership, Governance, and
     Sustainability** 332

Learning Objectives 332
Opening Vignette *Treatise on the Law of
   Corporations* 333
Ownership 333
   The Corporation 334 / Corporate Stakeholders 335 / The
   Public Perspective 337
The Corporate Objective 337
   Operational Goals 338 / Publicly Traded or Privately Held 338 /
   Shareholder Wealth Maximization 339 / Separation of
   Ownership from Management 340 / Stakeholder
   Capitalism 341
Corporate Governance 342
   The Goal of Corporate Governance 342 / The Structure of
   Corporate Governance 343 / Comparative Corporate
   Governance 345 / Failures in Corporate Governance 347 /
   Good Governance and Corporate Reputation 347 / Corporate
   Governance Reform 348
Corporate Responsibility and Sustainability 352
   Triple Bottom Line 353 / Differing Perspectives on
   Responsibility 355 / A Question of Trust 355
Summary 357 / *Take a Stand* 357

**11. Organization, Implementation, and
     Control** 358

Learning Objectives 358
Opening Vignette *Organizing to Think Globally and Act
   Locally* 359
Organizational Structure 361
   Organizational Designs 361
Implementation 372
   Locus of Decision Making 372 / Factors Affecting Structure
   and Decision Making 373 / The Networked Global Organization
   374 / Promoting Global Internal Cooperation 377 / The Role
   of Country Organizations 379
Controls 381
   Types of Controls 381 / Exercising Controls 386
Summary 387 / *Take a Stand* 389

12. Building the Knowledge Base 390

Learning Objectives 390
Opening Vignette *Cool Merchandizing* 391
International and Domestic Research 393
   New Parameters 393 / New Environmental Factors 393 / The
   Number of Factors Involved 394 / Broader Definition of
   Competition 394
Recognizing the Need for International Research 394
Determining Research Objectives 395
   Going International–Exporting 395 / Going International–
   Importing 396 / Market Expansion 397
Conducting Secondary Research 397
   Identifying Sources of Data 397 / Selection of Secondary Data
   401 / Interpretation and Analysis of Secondary Data 401 /
   Data Privacy 402
Conducting Primary Research 403
   Industrial versus Consumer Sources of Data 404 / Determining
   the Research Technique 404
The International Information System 408
Summary 412 / *Take a Stand* 413
Appendix 12A: Monitors of International Issues 415
   European Union 415 / United Nations 416 / U.S. Government
   416 / Selected Organizations 417 / Indexes to Literature
   419 / Directories 419 / Encyclopedias, Handbooks, and
   Miscellaneous 420 / Periodic Reports, Newspapers,
   Magazines 420
Appendix 12B: The Structure of a Country Commercial
   Guide 423

13. Entry and Expansion 426

Learning Objectives 426
Opening Vignette *An Accidental Exporter* 427
The Role of Management 428
Motivations to Go Abroad 430
   Proactive Motivations 430 / Reactive Motivations 431
Strategic Effects of Going International 433
Entry and Development Strategies 435
   Exporting and Importing 435
International Intermediaries 436
   Export Management Companies 437 / Trading
   Companies 438 / Private-Sector Facilitators 440 /
   Public-Sector Facilitators 440 / Licensing 442 /
   Franchising 444
Local Presence 445
   Interfirm Cooperation 445 / Full Ownership 451
A Comprehensive View of International Expansion 452
Summary 453 / *Take a Stand* 454
Cases 455
   Honeyland Manuka Honey from New Zealand 455
   IKEA: Furnishing the World 459
   Koch Industries Acquires Georgia-Pacific 463
   Petroleum Development and the Curse of Oil 466
   Tao Kae Noi Seaweed Snack 469

PART 5 OPERATIONS 475

14. Marketing 476

Learning Objectives 476
Opening Vignette *Being a Good Sport Sponsorship* 477
Target Market Selection 479
Identification and Screening 479 / Concentration versus Diversification 484
Marketing Management 486
Standardization versus Adaptation 486 / Product Policy 487 / Pricing Policy 494 / Distribution Policy 498 / Promotional Policy 505
Summary 514 / *Take a Stand* 515

15. Services 516

Learning Objectives 516
Opening Vignette *Global Labor Mobility Outsourcing and the Worker of the Future* 517
Differences between Services and Goods 518
Link between Services and Goods 518 / Stand-Alone Services 519
The Role of Services in the U.S. Economy 522
The Role of Global Services in the World Economy 524
Global Transformations in the Services Sector 525
Problems in Service Trade 526
Data Collection Problems 526 / Global Regulations of Services 527
Corporations and Services Trade 528
Services and E-Commerce 528 / Typical International Services 529 / Starting to Offer Services Internationally 532 / Strategic Indications 532
Summary 534 / *Take a Stand* 535

16. Logistics and Supply-Chain Management 536

Learning Objectives 536
Opening Vignette *Supply-Chain Management Logistics in China* 537
International Logistics Defined 538
Supply-Chain Management 539
The Impact of International Logistics 540
The New Dimensions of International Logistics 542
International Transportation Issues 542 / Selecting a Mode of Transport 546 / Export Documentation 550 / Terms of Shipment and Sale 551
International Inventory Issues 553
Order Cycle Time 553 / Customer Service Levels 554 / Inventory as a Strategic Tool 555
International Packaging Issues 555
International Storage Issues 557
Storage Facilities 557 / Special Trade Zones 559
Management of International Logistics 560
Centralized Logistics Management 560 / Decentralized Logistics Management 561 / Outsourcing Logistics Services 561

The Supply Chain and the Internet 562
Logistics and Security 563
Logistics and the Environment 565
Summary 567 / *Take a Stand* 568

17. Financial Management 570

Learning Objectives 570
Opening Vignette *When International Financial Management Dictates Strategy* 571
What Is the Goal of Management? 572
Global Financial Goals 572 / Genus Corporation 573 / Multinational Management 574
Import–Export Trade Financing 576
Trade Financing Using a Letter of Credit 576
Multinational Investing 578
Captial Budgeting 578 / A Proposed Project Investment 579 / Risks in International Investments 580 / Combining Interest-Rate and Exchange-Rate Risks 580
International Cash Flow Management 582
Operating Cash Flows and Financing Cash Flows 583 / Intrafirm Cash Flows and Transfer Prices 583 / Cash Management 584
Foreign Exchange Exposure 586
Transaction Exposure 587 / Transaction Exposure Management 587 / Risk Management versus Speculation 588 / Transaction Exposure Case: Lufthansa 588 / Currency Risk Sharing 590
Economic Exposure 591
Countertrade 592
A Definition of Countertrade 593
International Taxation 595
Tax Jurisdictions 595 / Tax Types 596 / Income Categories and Taxation 598
Summary 598 / *Take a Stand* 599

18. Human Resource Management 600

Learning Objectives 600
Opening Vignette *The New Global Executive* 601
Managing Managers 603
Early Stages of Internationalization 604 / Advanced Stages of Internationalization 604 / Interfirm Cooperative Ventures 606
Sources for Management Recruitment 606
Selection Criteria for Overseas Assignments 610 / Culture Shock 615 / Repatriation 617 / Compensation 617
Managing Labor Personnel 622
Labor Participation in Management 622 / The Role of Labor Unions 626 / Human Resource Policies 628
Summary 629 / *Take a Stand* 630

19. New Horizons 632

Learning Objectives 632
Opening Vignette *Bankers See Scrooge Alive in London* 633

The International Business Environment 634
   The Increased Role of Government 634 / Terrorism 636 /
   Corruption 637 / Planned versus Market Economies 638 /
   Global Frictions 638 / The International Financial Environment
   643 / The Effects of Population Shifts 646 / The
   Technological Environment 647
Globalization and Friction 648
The Future of International Business Management 650
   International Planning and Research 650 / International Product
   Policy 652 / International Communications 654 / Distribution
   Strategies 655 / International Pricing 655
Careers in International Business 656
   Further Training 657 / Employment with a Large Firm 657 /
   Opportunities for Women in Global Management 660 /

Employment with a Small or Medium-Sized Firm 661 /
   Self-Employment 661
Summary 663 / *Take a Stand* 664
Cases
   Nova International (Macedonia) 665
   Porsche Changes Track 669
   The Market Entry Strategy Social Approach 675
   When Diamonds Weep 679

Notes 683

Glossary 701

Name Index 721

Subject Index 731

MAP CONTENTS

1. International Trade as a Percentage of Gross Domestic Product 22
2. Change of Forest Area from 1990 to 2007 44
3. Total Greenhouse Gas Emissions 45
4. Desertification Vulnerability 45
5. IMF Data Mapper 71
6. The Religions of the World 150
7. Risk Map 2010 186
8. International Free Trade Areas 235
9. International Groupings: World, Europe 256
10. Map of South America 257
11. Global Consumer Recession Index 319
12. Income Distribution: IMF Data Mapper, GDP Growth 2015 482
13. Services as a Percentage of GDP 527
14. Railway Density World Map 558
15. Labor Union Membership 624
16. Expatriate Wealth Heat Map 631
17. The Cost Per Diem in the World's Major Business Cities 662

PART 1
IMPACT

1 The International Business Imperative

The globalization of business brings new opportunities and threats to governments, firms, and individuals. The challenge is to compete successfully in the global marketplace as it exists today and develops tomorrow.

Part 1 sets the stage by introducing the effects of international business and demonstrating the need to participate in international activities.

CHAPTER 1

The International Business Imperative

CHAPTER CONTENTS & LEARNING OBJECTIVES

THE NEED FOR INTERNATIONAL BUSINESS

1. To understand the history and impact of international business

A DEFINITION OF INTERNATIONAL BUSINESS

2. To learn the definition of international business

A BRIEF HISTORY

3. To recognize the growth of global linkages today

GLOBAL LINKS TODAY

4. To understand the U.S. position in world trade and the impact international business has on the United States

THE CURRENT U.S. INTERNATIONAL TRADE POSITION

5. To appreciate the opportunities and challenges offered by international business

THE STRUCTURE OF THE BOOK

6. To identify the relationship between the text's structure and the theoretical, political, and strategic aspects of international business

APPENDIX: GEOGRAPHIC PERSPECTIVES ON INTERNATIONAL BUSINESS

The financial crisis and economic recession late in the first decade of the third millennium raised questions about the long-term viability of globalization of business and its shape in the future. Some have challenged the viability of capitalism in an internationally interconnected world. Others dispute whether the current ethical underpinnings of business are suitable in light of the global challenges that are before us.

The times are challenging: big companies depend on governments to rescue them from their unmanageable debt; firms and individuals have criminally defrauded investors; traders speculating in global commodity and currency markets have caused high dislocations and spikes in prices; there have been huge bonuses and payoffs for financial high-flyers. All these have created worldwide hostility towards capitalism and businesses. If internationalists were the subjects of popularity polls, they would probably be ranked among the lowest of the low in 2009.

Questions about capitalism are certainly not new. Back in 1942, economist Joseph Schumpeter, the champion of entrepreneurial innovation, doubted the long-term survivability of capitalism. Although capitalism and private enterprise have endured so far, their long-term future may be in question.

In his 2009 encyclical *Caritas in Veritate* ("Charity in Truth"), Pope Benedict XVI wrote: "Today's international economic scene, marked by grave deviations and failures, requires a *profoundly new way of understanding business enterprise*. Old models are disappearing, but promising new ones are taking shape on the horizon . . . . Efforts are needed—and it is essential to say this—not only to create "ethical" sectors or segments of the economy or the world of finance, but to ensure that the whole economy—the whole of finance—is ethical."

International managers are called upon to understand and handle a changing array of opportunities and challenges in the second decade of the twenty-first century. The globalization of business and economic growth that accelerated dramatically in the 1990s has created the new conditions. Now, international managers must address ethical lapses and corruption as well as the growing distrust of business among global public audiences and the stronger role of governments. In newly linked societies, governments and businesses will be increasingly interconnected.

All this highlights the importance of the study of International Business. Some suggest that there is a need for a new breed of international business executive—a new global corporate statesperson. Perhaps the manager of the future will require a broader perspective of the role of corporations in global society and a stronger moral compass. There is no doubt that corporate executives will need a solid foundation both in business area disciplines and in the international intersection of business, government, and society.

Sources: Martin Sorrell, "The Pendulum Will Swing Back," *Financial Times*, April 9, 2009; Robert J. Samuelson, "American Capitalism Besieged," *Washington Post*, March 23, 2009; Benedict XVI, Encyclical Letter, *Caritas in Veritate*, 40, 45.

THE NEED FOR INTERNATIONAL BUSINESS

1. To understand the history and impact of international business

You are about to begin an exciting, important, and necessary task: the exploration of international business. International business is exciting because it combines the science and the art of business with many other disciplines, such as economics, anthropology, geography, history, language, jurisprudence, statistics, and demography. International business is important and necessary because economic isolationism has become impossible. Failure to become a part of the global market assures a nation of declining economic influence and a deteriorating standard of living for its citizens. Successful participation in international business, however, holds the promise of improved quality of life and a better society, even leading, some believe, to a more peaceful world.

On an individual level, most students are likely to become involved with international business enterprises during their careers. Manufacturing firms, as well as service companies such as banks, insurance, or consulting firms have extensive global operations. Artwork, films, and music are already widely exposed to the international market. Many of the future professional colleagues and competitors of today's students will come from around the world. In an era of open borders, niche marketing, instant communications, and virtually free ways of reaching millions of people, there emerges an unprecedented opportunity for individuals to enter the international business arena. Start-up firms can challenge the existing, long-dominant large competition. Speed, creativity, and innovation have often become more important to international success than size. Understanding international business is therefore crucial in preparing for the opportunities, challenges, and requirements of a future career.

Not everyone agrees with the benefits of globalization.

International business offers companies new markets. Since the 1950s, the growth of international trade and investment has been substantially larger than the growth of domestic economies. Technology continues to increase the reach and the ease of conducting international business, pointing to even larger growth potential in the future. A combination of domestic and international business, therefore, presents more opportunities for expansion, growth, and income than does domestic business alone. International business causes the flow of ideas, services, and capital across the world.

As a result, innovations can be developed and disseminated more rapidly, human capital can be used better, and financing can take place more quickly. International business also offers consumers new choices. It can permit the acquisition of a wider variety of products, both in terms of quantity and quality, and do so at reduced prices through international competition. International business facilitates the mobility of factors of production—except land—and provides challenging employment opportunities to individuals with professional and entrepreneurial skills. At the same time, international business reallocates resources, makes preferential choices, and shifts activities on a global level. It also opens up markets to competition, which in many instances has been unexpected and is difficult to cope with. As a result, international business activities do not benefit everyone to the same degree. Just like Janus, the two-faced god of the Romans, international business can bring benefits and opportunity to some, while delivering drawbacks and problems to others. The international firm and its managers, as well as the consumers of international products and services, need to understand how to make globalization work for them, as well as think about how to ensure that these benefits are afforded to a wide variety of people and countries. Therefore, both as an opportunity and a challenge, international business is of vital concern to countries, companies, and individuals.

A DEFINITION OF INTERNATIONAL BUSINESS

2. *To learn the definition of international business*

International business consists of transactions that are devised and carried out across national borders to satisfy the objectives of individuals, companies, and organizations. These transactions take on various forms, which are often interrelated. Primary types of international business are export–import trade and direct foreign investment. The latter is carried out in varied forms, including wholly owned subsidiaries and joint ventures. Additional types of international business are licensing, franchising, and management contracts.

The definition of international business focuses on transactions. The use of this term recognizes that doing business internationally is an activity, not merely a passive observation. Closely linked to activity is the term "satisfaction." It is crucial that the participants in international business are satisfied. Only if they feel they are better off after the transaction than they were before, will individual business transactions develop into a business relationship. The fact that the transactions are *across national borders* highlights a key difference between domestic and international business. The international executive is subject to a new set of macroenvironmental factors, to different constraints, and to quite frequent conflicts resulting from different laws, cultures, and societies. The basic principles of business are still relevant, but their application, complexity, and intensity vary substantially.

Subject to constant change, international business is as much an art as a science. Yet success in the art of business depends on a firm grounding in its scientific aspects. Individual consumers, policymakers, and business executives with an understanding of both aspects will be able to incorporate international business considerations into their thinking and planning. They will be able to consider international issues and repercussions and make decisions related to questions such as these:

- How will our idea, good, or service fit into the international market?
- Should we enter the market through trade or through investment?
- Should I obtain my supplies domestically or from abroad?
- What product adjustments are necessary to be responsive to local conditions?
- What threats from global competition should be expected and how can these threats be counteracted?

When management integrates these issues into each decision, international markets can provide growth, profit, and needs satisfaction not available to those that limit their activities to the domestic marketplace. To aid in this decision process is the purpose of this book.

A BRIEF HISTORY

3. To recognize the growth of global linkages today

Pax Romana Two relatively peaceful centuries in the Roman Empire leading to a successful expansion of business.

Ever since the first national borders were formed, international business has been conducted by nations and individuals. In many instances, international business itself has been a major force in shaping borders and changing world history.

As an example, international business played a vital role in the formation and decline of the Roman Empire, whose impact on thought, knowledge, and development can still be felt today. Although we read about the marching of the Roman legions, it was not through military might that the empire came about. The Romans used the **Pax Romana**, or Roman peace, as a major stimulus. This ensured that merchants were able to travel safely and rapidly on roads built, maintained, and protected by the Roman legions and their affiliated troops. A second stimulus was the use of common coinage, which simplified business transactions and made them comparable throughout the empire. In addition, Rome developed a systematic law, central market locations through the founding of cities, and an effective communication system; all of these actions contributed to the functioning of the marketplace and a reduction of business uncertainty.

International business flourished within the empire, and the improved standard of living within the empire became apparent to those outside. Soon city-nations and tribes that were not part of the empire decided to join as allies. They agreed to pay tribute and taxes because the benefits were greater than the drawbacks.

Thus, the immense growth of the Roman Empire occurred mainly through the linkages of business. Of course, preserving this favorable environment required substantial effort. When pirates threatened the seaways, for example, Pompeius sent out a large fleet to subdue them. Once this was accomplished, the cost of international distribution within the empire dropped substantially because fewer shipments were lost at sea. Goods could be made available at lower prices, which in turn translated into larger demand and greater, more widely available benefits.

The fact that international business was one of the primary factors that held the empire together can also be seen in the decline of Rome. When "barbaric" tribes overran the empire, again it was not mainly through war and prolonged battles that Rome had lost ground. Rather, outside tribes were attacking an empire that was already substantially weakened at its foundations because of infighting and increasing decadence. The Roman peace was no longer enforced, the use and acceptance of the common coinage had declined, and communications no longer worked as well. Therefore, affiliation with the empire no longer offered the benefits of the past. Former allies, who no longer saw any benefits in their association with Rome, willingly cooperated with invaders rather than face prolonged battles.

While Roman authority and prosperity were firmly established in the Mediterranean, trade flourished and even extended through the Red Sea and Indian Ocean and, indirectly, as far as China, where the Han Empire provided a similar stability for nearly four centuries. After its beginnings in BC 202, Han rulers solidified the unification of China and expanded its borders westward. Under their rule, trade expanded with the development of a system of trade routes to central Asia that became known as the Silk Road.

Trade between the Roman and Chinese empires was not direct and occurred through many intermediaries in India, Arabia, and central Asia. Suppliers and recipients may not have even known of each other, even though they became highly dependent on the other. Today, many people may not know about the activities of the Deutsche Bundesbank and the European Central Bank—both located in Frankfurt, Germany—or the People's Bank of China in Beijing, but those institutions play an important role in the availability and interest rates of their student loans.

Trading routes and conditions were far more difficult and dangerous in ancient times than today. Travel by sea or land exposed traders to enormous risk of weather, disease, and piracy, and the whims of various rulers. Thus, relatively stable political conditions helped foster trade for periods. "Stable countries are trading countries . . . When Roman and Han authority finally collapsed around AD 200, trade with the East came to an almost complete standstill."[1]

Similar patterns can be seen in later eras. "Just as the stability afforded by the Pax Romana and the Han Empire encouraged the long-range and highly indirect commerce between Rome and China in the first and second centuries after Christ, the power of the early Islamic and Tang empires stimulated a far more direct intercourse between the lands of the caliphate and China during the seventh through ninth centuries."[2]

Much later, the British Empire grew mainly through its effective international business policy, which provided for efficient transportation, intensive trade, and an insistence on open markets.[3] More recently, the United States developed a world leadership position largely due to its championship of market-based business transactions in the Western world; the broad flow of ideas, goods, and services across national borders; and an encouragement of international communication and transportation. Some say that the period from 1945 to 1990 for Western countries, and since then, for the world, has been characterized by a **Pax Americana**, an American sponsored and enforced peace.

The importance of international business has not always persisted, however. For example, in 1896, the Empress Dowager Tz'u-hsi, in order to finance the renovation of the summer palace, impounded government funds that had been designated for Chinese shipping and its navy. As a result, China's participation in world trade almost came to a halt. In the subsequent decades, China operated in almost total isolation, without any transfer of knowledge from the outside, without major inflow of goods, and without the innovation and productivity increases that result from exposure to international business.

Withholding the benefits of international business has also long been a tool of national policy. The use of economic coercion by nations or groups of nations, for example, can be traced back to the time of the Greek city-states and the Peloponnesian War. In the Napoleonic Wars, combatants used naval blockades to achieve their goal of "bringing about commercial ruin and shortage of food by dislocating trade."[4] Similarly, during the Civil War period in the United States, the North consistently pursued a strategy of denying international business opportunities to the South in order to deprive it of needed export revenues.

The importance of international business linkages was highlighted during the 1930s. At that time, the **Smoot-Hawley Act** raised import duties to reduce the volume of goods coming into the United States. The act was passed in the hope that it would restore domestic employment. The result, however, was retaliation by most trading partners. The ensuing worldwide depression and the collapse of the world financial system were instrumental in bringing about the events that led to World War II.

World trade and investment have assumed a heretofore unknown importance to the global community. In past centuries, trade was conducted internationally but not at the level or with the impact on nations, firms, and individuals that it has recently

Pax Americana An American peace since 1945 that led to increased international business transactions.

Smoot-Hawley Act A 1930 act that raised import duties to the highest rates ever imposed by the United States; designed to promote domestic production, it resulted in the downfall of the world trading system.

Figure 1.1   Growth in the Volume of World Merchandise Trade and GDP, 1998–2008 (Annual percentage change)

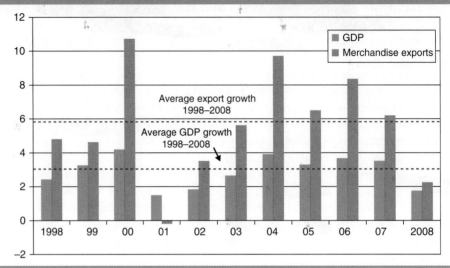

Source: World Trade Organization, World Trade Report 2009, www.wto.org/english/res_e/booksp../world_trade_report09_e.pdf, accessed August 18, 2009, p. 5.

multinational corporations
Companies that invest in countries around the globe.

achieved. Within the past 35 years alone, the volume of international trade in goods and services expanded from $200 billion to more than $19.5 trillion in 2008.[5] As Figure 1.1 shows, during almost all of the past decade, as in the preceding decades, the growth in the value of trade has greatly exceeded the level of overall world economic growth.

Concurrently, on a global level, annual foreign direct investment (FDI) inflows reached $1.8 trillion in 2007, finally exceeding the previous all-time high set in 2000, before the events of September 11, 2001, triggered a downturn.[6] FDI stock, or accumulated totals, exceeded $15 trillion in 2007. The sales by an estimated 790,000 affiliates of **multinational corporations** exceeded $31 trillion.[7] As Table 1.1 shows, these corporations have their headquarters in many of the leading economies around the world. Table 1.2 illustrates that many of these corporations have their origins in developing economies as well. Nonetheless, FDI is highly selective with a few major economies being the preferred choice of foreign investors. In 2007, developed economies received $1,248 billion, or about 68 percent of these inflows, although investment increased in developing countries and least-developed countries as well. The United States led all nations as a recipient of these inflows, followed by the United Kingdom, France, Canada, and the Netherlands.[8]

Despite the longer-term growth trends in both trade and investment, the financial crisis and economic downturn that began in 2007 resulted in the sharp volume reductions at the end of 2008 and in 2009. WTO economists assessed 2009 world trade growth as "strongly negative."[9] The major developed economies were bearing the brunt of the decline. On the other hand, developing economies such as China, India, and Brazil experienced continued growth. Individuals and firms have come to recognize that they are competing in a dynamic global marketplace, characterized by major change and where risk and opportunity must be examined not only domestically but around the world both in terms of market opportunities and global supply and sourcing chains.

Table 1.1   World's Top 25 Nonfinancial TNCs, Ranked by Foreign Assets, 2006[a] (Millions of dollars and number of employees)

Ranking by: Foreign Assets	Ranking by: TNI	Ranking by: II	Corporation	Home Economy	Industry	Assets Foreign	Assets Total	Sales Foreign	Sales Total	Employment Foreign	Employment Total
1	71	54	General Electric	United States	Electrical & electronic equipment	442,278	697,239	74,285	163,391	164,000	319,000
2	14	63	British Petroleum Company Plc	United Kingdom	Petroleum expl./ref./distr.	170,326	217,601	215,879	270,602	80,300	97,100
3	87	93	Toyota Motor Corporation	Japan	Motor vehicles	164,627	273,853	78,529	205,918	113,967	299,394
4	34	79	Royal Dutch/Shell Group	United Kingdom / Netherlands	Petroleum expl./ref./distr.	161,122	235,276	182,538	318,845	90,000	108,000
5	40	35	ExxonMobil Corporation	United States	Petroleum expl./ref./distr.	154,993	219,015	252,680	365,467	51,723	82,100
6	78	64	Ford Motor Company	United States	Motor vehicles	131,062	278,554	78,968	160,123	155,000	283,000
7	7	99	Vodafone Group Plc	United Kingdom	Tele communications	126,190	144,366	32,641	39,021	53,138	63,394
8	26	51	Total	France	Petroleum expl./ref./distr.	120,645	138,579	146,672	192,952	57,239	95,070
9	96	36	Electricite de France	France	Electricity, gas and water	111,916	235,857	33,879	73,933	17,185	155,968
10	92	18	Wal-Mart Stores	United States	Retail	110,199	151,193	77,116	344,992	540,000	1,910,000
11	37	34	Telefónica SA	Spain	Telecommunications	101,891	143,530	41,093	66,367	167,881	224,939
12	77	88	E.On	Germany	Electricity, gas and water	94,304	167,565	32,154	85,007	46,598	80,612
13	86	82	Deutsche Telekom AG	Germany	Telecommunications	93,488	171,421	36,240	76,963	88,808	248,800
14	58	65	Volkswagen Group	Germany	Motor vehicles	91,823	179,906	95,761	131,571	155,935	324,875
15	73	57	Franco Telecom	France	Telecommunications	90,871	135,876	30,448	64,863	82,148	191,036
16	90	63	ConocoPhillips	United States	Petroleum expl./ref./distr.	89,528	164,781	55,781	183,650	17,188	38,400
17	56	89	Chevron Corporation	United States	Petroleum expl./ref./distr.	85,735	132,628	111,603	204,892	33,700	62,500
18	11	75	Honda Motor Co Ltd	Japan	Motor vehicles	76,264	101,190	77,605	95,333	148,544	167,231
19	36	62	Suez	France	Electricity gas, and water	75,151	96,714	42,002	55,563	76,943	139,814
20	45	48	Siemens AG	Germany	Electrical and electronic equipment	74,585	119,812	74,858	109,553	314,000	475,000
21	10	11	Hutchison Whampoa Limited	Hong Kong, China	Diversified	70,679	87,146	28,619	34,428	182,149	220,000
22	84	85	RWE Group	Germany	Electricity, gas, and water	68,202	123,080	22,142	55,521	30,752	68,534
23	9	7	Nestle SA	Switzerland	Food and beverages	66,677	83,426	57,234	78,528	257,434	265,000
24	62	38	BMW AG	Germany	Motor vehicles	66,053	104,118	48,172	61,472	26,575	106,575
25	51	33	Procter & Gamble	United States	Diversified	64,487	138,014	44,530	76,476	101,220	138,000

[a]All data are based on the companies' annual reports unless otherwise stated. Data on affiliates are based on Dun and Bradstreet's *Who Owns Whom* database.

Source: UNCTAD, *World Investment Report 2008: Transnational Corporations and the Infrastructure Challenge,* annex table A.1.15.

Table 1.2 Top 25 Nonfinancial TNCs from Developing Countries, Ranked by Foreign Assets, 2006[a]
(Millions of dollars and number of employees)

Ranking by: Foreign Assets	TNI	II	Corporation	Home Economy	Industry	Assets Foreign	Assets Total	Sales Foreign	Sales Total	Employment Foreign	Employment Total
1	18	9	Hutchison Whampoa Limited	Hong Kong, China	Diversified	70,679	87,146	28,619	34,428	182,149	220,000
2	88	94	Petronas - Petroliam Nasional Bhd	Malaysia	Petroleum expl./ref./distr.	30,668	85,201	14,937	50,984	3,965	33,439
3	53	11	Samsung Electronics Co., Ltd.	Republic of Korea	Electrical and electronic equipment	27,011	87,111	71,590	91,856	29,472	85,813
4	21	4	Cemex S.A.	Mexico	Nonmetalic mineral products	24,411	29,749	14,595	18,114	39,505	54,635
5	86	32	Hyundai Motor Company	Republic of Korea	Motor vehicles	19,581	76,064	30,596	68,468	5,093	54,711
6	33	3	Singtel Ltd.	Singapore	Telecommunications	18,678	21,288	5,977	8,575	8,606	19,000
7	92	86	CITIC Group	China	Diversified	17,623	117,355	2,482	10,113	18,305	107,340
8	65	10	Formosa Plastic Group	Taiwan Province of China	Chemicals	16,754	75,760	13,002	50,445	67,129	89,736
9	28	18	Jardine Matheson Holdings Ltd.	Hong Kong, China	Diversified	16,704	20,378	12,527	16,281	58,203	110,125
10	57	74	LG Corp.	Republic of Korea	Electrical and electronic equipment	15,016	53,315	43,902	70,613	36,053	70,000
11	73	66	Companhia Vale do Rio Doce	Brazil	Mining and quarrying	14,974	60,954	37,063	46,746	3,982	52,646
12	94	88	Petroleo Brasileiro S.A. - Petrobras	Brazil	Petroleum expl./ref./distr.	10,454	98,680	17,845	72,347	7,414	62,266
13	69	73	China Ocean Shipping (Group) Company	China	Transport and storage	10,397	18,711	8,777	15,737	4,432	69,549
14	54	64	América Móvil	Mexico	Telecommunications	8,701	29,473	9,617	21,526	27,506	39,876
15	89	56	Petróleos De Venezuela	Venezuela, Rep. of Bol.	Petroleum expl./ref./distr.	8,534	60,305	32,773	63,736	5,373	49,180
16	50	8	Mobile Telecommunications Company	Kuwait	Telecommunications	7,968	12,027	3,373	4,185	975	12,700
17	41	85	Capitaland Limited	Singapore	Real estate	7,781	13,463	1,461	2,053	16,261	32,876
18	45	15	Hon Hai Precision Industries	Taiwan Province of China	Electrical and electronic equipment	7,606	19,223	16,801	40,507	322,372	382,000
19	80	65	China State Construction Engineering Corporation	China	Construction	6,998	15,986	4,483	18,544	25,000	119,000
20	67	5	Kia Motors	Republic of Korea	Motor vehicles	6,767	18,655	11,525	21,316	10,377	33,005
21	100	90	China National Petroleum Corporation	China	Petroleum expl./ref./distr.	6,374	178,843	3,036	114,443	22,000	1,167,129
22	72	82	New World Development Co., Ltd.	Hong Kong, China	Diversified	6,147	18,535	1,430	2,995	16,949	54,000
23	77	68	CLP Holdings	Hong Kong, China	Electricity, gas and water	6,096	15,965	1,283	4,951	1,827	6,087
24	90	40	Teléfonos De Mexico S.A. De C.V.	Mexico	Telecommunications	5,790	24,265	4,295	16,084	16,704	76,394
25	87	47	Sasol Limited	South Africa	Industrial chemicals	5,709	14,749	2,920	8,875	2,205	27,933

[a]All data are based on the companies' annual reports unless otherwise stated. Data of affiliates are from Dun and Bradstreet's *Who Owns Whom* database.

Source: UNCTAD, *World Investment Report 2008: Transnational Corporations and the Infrastructure Challenge, annex table A.1.16.*

GLOBAL LINKS TODAY

International business has forged a network of global links around the world that binds us all—countries, institutions, and individuals—much closer than ever before. These links tie together trade, financial markets, technology, and living standards in an unprecedented way. A freeze in Brazil and its effect on coffee and orange juice production are felt around the world. Just as the effects of previous financial crises in Mexico and Asia influenced stock markets, investments, and trade flows in all corners of the earth, the financial crisis that started in 2007 reverberated around the world. "Although the crisis began in the United States, it soon spread [to] financial institutions and economies throughout the developed and developing world [which] have been severely affected."[10]

These linkages have also become more intense on an individual level. Communication has built new international bridges, be it through music or the watching of international programs transmitted by CNN (http://www.cnn.com). New products have attained international appeal and encouraged similar activities around the world. For example, consumers purchase similar jeans; dance the same dances; watch the same movies; eat hamburgers, pizzas, and sushi. Transportation links let individuals from different countries see and meet each other with unprecedented ease. Common cultural pressures result in similar social phenomena and behavior—for example, more dual-income families are emerging around the world, which leads to more frequent, but due to new time constraints, also more stressful, shopping.[11]

4. To understand the U.S. position in world trade and the impact international business has on the United States

FOCUS ON CULTURE

Make That a Caffé Latte Please

If you're hungry in Hong Kong, or in São Paolo or Milan for that matter, you have many dining options beyond the local fare. Over the past three decades, perhaps one of the greatest transformations in daily life has been the global proliferation of chain restaurants and the food choices available to consumers.

You don't have to be in London to get a Slim Sandwich or a preservative-free wrap at a Pret a Manger, which has multiple locations in Hong Kong. If you prefer a burger, you might try a Tsukune Rice Burger in Kowloon at MOS Burger, the big Tokyo-based burger chain that uses Japanese ingredients and sauces. Of course, McDonald's is ubiquitous, or you can get a flame-grilled Whopper at Burger King, which opened in Hong Kong in 2007.

International business has brought diversity of choice, quality food, clean environments, and fast, efficient service to locations around the world. You can find a California Pizza Kitchen in the Dubai Mall or in Plaza Indonesia in Jakarta. Tim Hortons, the Canadian fast food chain, has brought its famous coffee and Timbits, the bite-sized donut holes, to more than 400 locations in the United States.

Some criticize restaurant franchise operations for spreading industrialized food processes and junk food to cultures that have rich cuisine and dining tradition. In 1999, José Bové, a French activist, drove a bulldozer into a McDonald's in Millau, France, to protest American cultural imperialism and "malbouffe" (bad food). While many in France were vocally supportive of Bové's sentiments, the French public proved their appreciation for Le Big Mac with their wallets. By 2007, France had become the second-most profitable market in the world for McDonald's, ranking only behind the United States.

The international restaurant business is not only about fast-food franchises, coffee, and burgers. For example, Wolfgang Puck and other celebrity chefs have opened fine dining and more casual restaurants in cities around the world. And Fogo de Chão, an upscale Brazilian churrascaria and meat lover's dream, has opened locations throughout the United States. It was an idea meant for internationalization: waiters dressed as gauchos bring a seemingly endless array of multiple cuts of beef and other meats to your table. They give you cards with green and red sides; turn the green side up and the meats keep coming. When you have had enough, flip the card to red.

But sometimes you just want a convenient espresso or cup of coffee. In 2008, Starbucks had locations in 44 countries. If you're in Milan, however, you won't find a Starbucks—but you can find a La bottega del Caffè, an Italian franchise that began in 2000 and is now spreading in Europe. Italians take their coffee seriously. If you want a caffé latte in Italy, be precise when you order. If you just ask for a latte, you'll get a cup of steamed milk.

Sources: Daniel Gross, "McSushi, Why Is American Food So Popular in Japan?" *Newsweek*, June 22, 2009; Mike Steinberger, "How McDonald's Conquered France. The fast-food chain's most surprising success," *Slate*, June 25, 2009; http://www.labottegadelcaffe.net/english, accessed August 3, 2009; http://www.mos.co.jp/english/, accessed August 3, 2009; http://www.starbucks.com/aboutus/Company_Factsheet.pdf, accessed August 3, 2009.

International business has brought a global reorientation in production strategies. Only a few decades ago, for example, it would have been thought impossible to produce parts for a car in more than one country, assemble it in another, and sell it in yet other countries around the world. Today, such global strategies, coupled with production and distribution sharing, are common. Consumers, union leaders, policymakers, and sometimes even the firms themselves are finding it increasingly difficult to define where a particular product was made, because subcomponents may come from many different nations. Firms are also linked to each other through global supply agreements and joint undertakings in research and development. Figure 1.2 gives an example of how such links result in a final consumer product.

In addition to the production of goods, service firms are increasingly part of the international scene. Consulting firms, insurance companies, software firms, and universities are participating to a growing degree in the international marketplace. As Focus on Culture explains, international franchising has changed the eating habits of global audiences with the proliferation of choices available to them.

Firms and governments are recognizing the effects that globalization of business can have on the environment common to all. For example, high sulfur emissions in one area may cause acid rain in another. Pollution in one country may result in water contamination in another. Service activities can have cross-national impacts as well. For example, weaknesses in some currencies, due to problems in a country's banking sector, can quickly spill over and affect the currency values of other nations. The deregulation of some service industries, such as air transport or telephony can, thoroughly affect the structure of these industries around the world.

All these changes have affected the international financial position of countries and the ownership of economic activities. For example, the United States, after having been a net creditor to the world for many decades, has become a world debtor since 1985. This means that overall the United States owes more to foreign institutions and individuals than is owed to the United States. China has emerged as the number one U.S. creditor. In addition, **sovereign wealth funds**, or funds owned by governments and managed specifically for investment purposes, have emerged as key international investors.

The shifts in financial flows have had major effects on **foreign direct investment** into plants as well. U.S. direct investment abroad at the end of 2008 had a market value of nearly $3.7 trillion, while foreign direct investment in the United States exceeded $2.6 trillion.[12] Plants abroad increasingly take the place of trade. All of these developments make us more and more dependent on one another.

This interdependence, however, is not stable. On an ongoing basis, realignments take place on both micro and macro levels that make past orientations at least partially obsolete. For example, for its first 200 years, the United States looked to Europe for markets and sources of supply. Despite the maintenance of this orientation by many individuals, firms, and policymakers, the reality of trade relationships has changed. U.S. two-way merchandise trade with China, Japan, Korea, Taiwan, Australia, Hong Kong, and the Association of Southeast Asian Nations totaled $993 billion in 2008, $354 billion more than trade with the 27 member-countries of the European Union (EU).[13]

At the same time, entirely new areas for international business activities have opened up as eastern Europe, Russia, and many of the countries of the former Soviet Union have eagerly pursued new trade opportunities. In 2008, Ukraine acceded to the World Trade Organization (WTO), joining Georgia, Moldova, the Kyrgyz Republic, and Mongolia, which had already become members.

sovereign wealth fund Investment vehicle containing only government financial assets, which are invested globally.

foreign direct investment The establishment or expansion of operations of a firm in a foreign country. Like all investments, it assumes a transfer of capital.

Figure 1.2   The International Burger

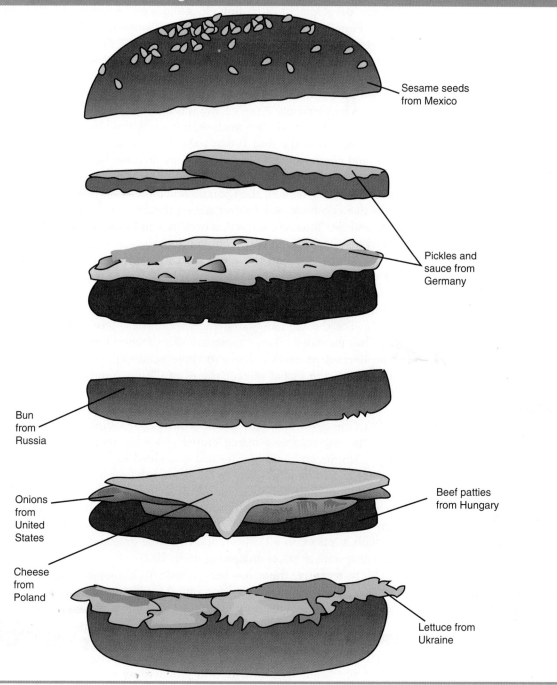

Sesame seeds
from Mexico

Pickles and
sauce from
Germany

Bun
from
Russia

Onions
from
United
States

Beef patties
from Hungary

Cheese
from
Poland

Lettuce from
Ukraine

Concurrently, a growing regionalization is taking place around the world along with the development of trading blocs and a proliferation of bilateral trade agreements. Firms must manage and navigate an increasingly complex array of trading arrangements between nations. They may find that the free flow of goods, services, and capital encounters new impediments as regions become more inward-looking and governments become more active.

Not only is the business environment changing, but the pace of technological change is accelerating. Atari's Pong was first introduced in the early 1980s; today action games and movies are made with computerized humans. The first office computers emerged in the mid 1980s; today home computers have become commonplace, and notebooks and ultraportables are favorites in the classroom.[14] E-mail was introduced to the mass market only in the 1990s; today many college students reserve "old fashioned" e-mail for their parents and professors while using blogs or social networks like Facebook and Twitter among themselves.[15] All these shifts, allow for a faster and user intense information exchange in business, leading to new approaches in advertising, production and consumption.

These changes, and the speed with which they come about, significantly affect countries, corporations, and individuals. For example, the relative participation of countries in world trade is shifting. Over the past decades, in a world of rapidly growing trade, the market share of western Europe in trade has been declining. For the United States, the export share has declined while the import share has increased. Some countries, like China, Germany, and Japan, have become dependent upon exports to drive economic growth. As their economies have grown, the global market shares of China, Southeast Asian countries, and Brazil have increased.

composition of trade The ratio of primary commodities to manufactured goods in a country's trade.

The **composition of trade** has also been changing. For example, from the 1960s to the 1990s, the trade role of primary commodities has declined precipitously while the importance of manufactured goods has increased. This has meant that those countries and workers who had specialized in commodities such as *caoutchouc* (rubber) or mining were likely to fall behind those who had embarked on strengthening their manufacturing sector. With sharply declining world market prices for commodities and rising prices for manufactured goods, their producers were increasingly unable to catch up. Some commodity-dependent countries realized temporary windfalls as prices on oil, wheat, and corn rose dramatically in 2008, only to watch them evaporate as prices dropped again in 2009.

More recently, there has been a shift in manufacturing to new nations. In the mid-1800s, manufacturing accounted for about 17 percent of employment in the United States. This proportion grew to almost 30 percent in the 1960s, only to decline at a rising rate. In mid-2009, manufacturing employment fell to about 9 percent, with the loss of some 2 million manufacturing jobs in the recession.[16] Despite this loss in employment, the U.S. manufacturing industry is in the process of significant transformation as productivity gains and skills upgrading have created a leaner and more skilled manufacturing workforce.[17] As Figures 1.3 and 1.4 show, U.S. value-added manufacturing output has been increasing as the U.S. share of global manufacturing output has remained reasonably stable at about 25 percent over the past two decades.

In the past 30 years, German manufacturing employment has dropped by 13 percentage points, while in Japan the decrease was 6.5 percentage points. All these shifts in employment reflect a transfer of manufacturing away from traditional manufacturers toward the emerging economies. During the times of large decline in the United States, Germany, and Japan, the proportion of manufacturing of gross domestic product (GDP) has more than doubled in Malaysia, Thailand, and Indonesia.[18]

Figure 1.3   U.S. Manufacturing Output and Employment, 1979–2007

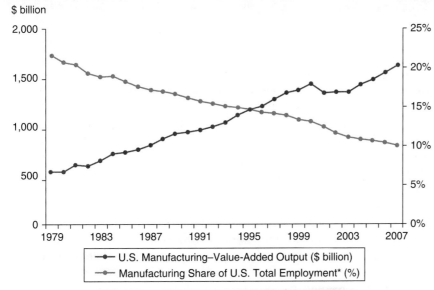

Productivity gains have led to greater output but with fewer workers.
Employment continues its long-term shift from manufacturing to services.

*Total nonfarm annual average
Sources: U.S. Bureau of Economic Analysis; U.S. Bureau of Labor Statistics; Oxford Economic Forecasting.

Increasingly, substantial shifts are also occurring in the area of services trade. Activities that were confined to specific locales have become mobile. The global transmission of radiology charts to physicians in India is a portent of shifts in trade composition in the future.

Figure 1.4   Share of Global Manufacturing Output

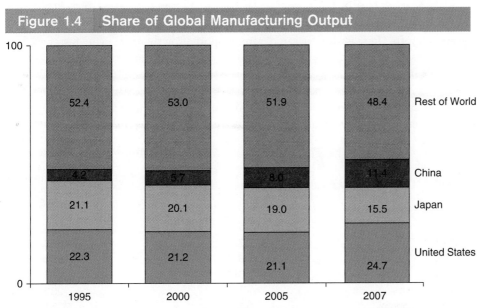

The United States is maintaining its share of global manufacturing; China is taking share from Japan.

Source: United Nations Industrial Development Organization (UNIDO; 2007 is a UNIDO estimate).

THE CURRENT U.S. INTERNATIONAL TRADE POSITION

5. To appreciate the opportunities and challenges offered by international business

From a global perspective, the United States has gained in prominence as a market for the world but has lost some of its importance as a supplier to the world. In spite of the decline in the global market share of U.S. exports, the international activities of the United States have not been reduced. On the contrary, exports have grown rapidly and successfully. However, many new participants have entered the international market. In Europe, firms in countries with war-torn economies following World War II have reestablished themselves. In Asia, new competitors have aggressively obtained a share of the growing world trade. U.S. relative export growth was not able to keep pace with the total growth of world exports.

U.S. exports as a share of the GDP have grown substantially in recent years. However, this increase pales when compared with the international trade performance of other nations. For example, Japan, which so often is maligned as the export problem child in the international trade arena, exports less than 10 percent of its GDP.[19] Table 1.3 shows the degree to which the United States comparatively "underexports and overimports" on a per capita basis.

THE IMPACT OF INTERNATIONAL BUSINESS ON THE UNITED STATES

Why should we worry about this misaligned participation in trade? Why not simply concentrate on the large domestic market and get on with it? Why should it bother us that that the U.S. Department of Commerce estimates that less than 1 percent of U.S. firms export?[20] Why should it be of concern that the United States has tens of thousands of small-business manufacturers and service sector firms that could export their goods and services but do not?[21]

macroeconomic level Level at which trading relationships affect individual markets.

U.S. international business outflows are important on the **macroeconomic level** in terms of balancing the trade account. Larger growth in imports than in exports has resulted in long-term trade deficits. In 1983, imports of products into the United States exceeded exports by more than $70 billion. In the ensuing years, exports increased at a rapid rate; import growth grew even faster. While U.S. exports grew at a significantly faster rate than imports from 2006–2008, the U.S. trade deficit in goods and services had risen to $816 billion in 2008.[22] Ongoing annual trade deficits in this range are unsupportable in the long run. Via the capital account, such deficits add to the U.S. international debt, which must be serviced and eventually repaid. Exporting is not only good in the international

Table 1.3	Exports and Imports of Goods and Services per Capita for Selected Countries (in US $)	
Country	**Exports per Capita**	**Imports per Capita**
Australia	$7,582	$7,554
Brazil	799	683
China	892	688
Japan	4,063	3,866
Kenya	115	232
United Kingdom	5,745	7,751
United States	3,241	4,707

Sources: World Factbook, http://www.cia.gov, accessed August 8, 2003, and World Bank 2002 World Development Indicators, Washington, DC, 2002.

trade picture, but a key factor in increasing employment. It has been estimated that $1 billion in exports supports the creation, on average, of 6,000 jobs.[23] Imports, in turn, bring a wider variety of products and services into a country. They exert competitive pressure for domestic firms to improve. Imports, therefore, expand the choices of consumers and improve their standard of living. Exports, in turn, are the crucial factor that makes imports possible and sustainable in the long run.

On the **microeconomic level**, participation in international business can help firms achieve economies of scale that cannot be achieved in domestic markets. Addressing a global market greatly adds to the number of potential customers. Increasing production lets firms ride the learning curve more quickly and therefore makes goods available more cheaply at home. Finally, and perhaps most important, international business permits firms to hone their competitive skills abroad by meeting the challenge of foreign products. By going abroad, firms can learn from their foreign competitors, challenge them on their ground, and translate the absorbed knowledge into productivity improvements back home. Firms that operate only in the domestic market are at risk of being surprised by the onslaught of foreign competition and thus seeing their domestic market share threatened. Research has shown that U.S. multinationals of all sizes and in all industries outperformed their strictly domestic counterparts—growing more than twice as fast in sales and earning significantly higher returns on equity and assets.[24] Workers also benefit. Typically, exporting firms of all sizes pay significantly higher wages than nonexporters.[25]

The United States as a nation and as individuals must therefore seek more involvement in the global market. The degree to which Americans can successfully do business internationally will be indicative of their competitiveness and so help to determine their future standard of living.

Most U.S. firms are affected directly or indirectly by economic and political developments in the international marketplace. Firms that refuse to participate actively are relegated to reacting to the global economy. Consider how the industrial landscape in the United States has been restructured in the past decade as a result of international business.

Many industries have experienced the need for international adjustments. U.S. farmers, because of high prices, exchange-rate inequities, increased international competition, trade-restricting government actions, and unfair foreign trade practices, have lost world market share. U.S. firms in technologically advanced industries, such as semiconductor producers, saw the prices of their products and their sales volumes drop precipitously because of global competition. As a result of competition, many industries have adjusted, but with great pain. Examples abound in the steel, automotive, and textile sectors of the U.S. economy.

Still other U.S. industries never fully recognized what had happened, and therefore, in spite of attempts to adjust, have ceased to exist or have moved manufacturing to other countries. VCRs are almost no longer produced anywhere. Only a small percentage of motorcycles are manufactured in the United States. Of the footwear purchased in the United States, less than 1 percent is manufactured in the country.[26]

These developments demonstrate that it has become virtually impossible to disregard the powerful impact that international business has on all of us. Temporary isolation may be possible and delay tactics may work for a while, but the old adage applies: you can run, but you cannot hide. Participation in the world market has become truly imperative.

microeconomic level Level of business concerns that affects an individual firm or industry.

Global activities offer many additional opportunities to business firms. Market saturation can be delayed by lengthening or rejuvenating the life of products in other countries. Sourcing policies that once were inflexible have become variable because plants can be shifted from one country to another and suppliers can be found on every continent. Cooperative agreements can be formed that enable each party to bring its major strength to the table and emerge with better goods, services, and ideas than it could on its own. Consumers all over the world can select from among a greater variety of products at lower prices, which enables them to improve their choices and lifestyles. As Focus on Ethics shows, it is also easy to stir up controversy through international business. Consumers are paying much greater attention to products and they increasingly have the resources to check whether the firms producing them are exploiting their workers or harming the environment.

All of these opportunities need careful exploration if they are to be realized. What is needed is an awareness of global developments, an understanding of their meaning, and a development of the capability to adjust to change. Judging by the global linkages found in today's market and the rapid changes taking place, a background in international business is highly desirable for business students seeking employment. **Globalization** is the watchword that increasingly looms large in all walks of life, not only in our entertainment, our fashions, and the products we buy, but also in our morals, belief systems, and our very sense of being a human species. For the first time in history, the availability of international products and services has reached beyond the elite to become the reasonable expectation of the masses. The global market is inevitable, inescapable, and here. This book will help you understand it, cope with it, and succeed in it.[27]

globalization The increased mobility of goods, services, labor, technology, and capital throughout the world.

THE STRUCTURE OF THE BOOK

6. To identify the relationship between the text's structure and the theoretical, political, and strategic aspects of international business

This book can make you a better, more successful participant in the global businessplace. It is written for both those who want to obtain more information about what is going on in international markets in order to be well-rounded and better educated and for those who want to translate their knowledge into successful business transactions. The text melds theory and practice to balance conceptual understanding and knowledge of day-to-day realities. The book, therefore, addresses the international concerns of both beginning internationalists and multinational corporations.

The beginning international manager will need to know the answers to basic, yet important, questions: How can I find out whether demand for my product exists abroad? What must I do to get ready to market internationally? These issues are also relevant for managers in multinational corporations, but the questions they consider are often much more sophisticated. Of course, the resources available to address them are also much greater.

Throughout the book, public policy concerns are included in discussions of business activities. In this way, you are exposed to both macro and micro issues. Part 1 of the book introduces the importance of international business and its global linkages. Part 2 provides the conceptual foundations by covering the theory of international trade and investment and presents balance of payments issues. Here we also cover financial markets and economic integration, as well as everyday markets. Part 3 presents the environment of international business, addressing culture, policies, politics, and law. Part 4 presents the strategy considerations surrounding international business. Planning and the organizational and control issues surrounding global market penetration are the focus. The research activities required to properly prepare for international business, and the options for market entry and expansion, are discussed subsequently. Part 5 targets the operational issues surrounding international business, using an implementation-oriented perspective. The book concludes with a focus on new horizons of the field and the reader's career.

We hope that upon finishing the book, you will not only have completed another academic subject but also be well versed in the theoretical, policy, and strategic aspects of international business and therefore will be able to contribute to improved international competitiveness and a better global standard of living.

FOCUS ON ETHICS

Students Against Sweatshops

In November 1997, students at Georgetown, Harvard, Duke, and Holy Cross universities began to look at the labels of logo merchandise in their campus bookstores to get an idea of where the clothing was made. Their goal was to find ways to improve the working conditions of people who made their caps and shirts.

In April 1998, UNITE, a union of textile workers, sponsored two workers from a Korean-owned apparel factory in the Dominican Republic for a tour of U.S. college campuses. Kenia Rodriguez and Roselio Reyes, both college-aged, described the terrible conditions at the BJ&B factory where goods featuring the logos of major American colleges like Georgetown, Brown, Duke, Harvard, and Princeton were made.

They explained that workers had to cope with rancid drinking water, locked bathrooms, sweltering conditions, and intimidation. Men and women had unequal pay scales and workers were fired when they tried to start a union. None of the workers, who all worked 75 hours a week, earned more than one-third of what the Dominican government considers sufficient for "the most basic life necessities."

In response, students at Georgetown and other universities began pressuring their administrations to adopt basic labor standards for any factories where school apparel would be made. Students wanted licensees to agree to pay workers enough to live on and disclose the locations of all of their factories. To help schools monitor factory conditions for themselves, students formed an independent organization called the Workers Rights Consortium (WRC).

Over the next two years, students used tactics such as petitions, faculty and student government resolutions, and rallies to persuade their administrations to sign on to the WRC. Some schools, such as Duke and the University of Wisconsin, held sit-ins when other tactics were not successful. At Georgetown, students occupied the office of the university's president for more than 100 hours before the administration agreed to sign on to the WRC and endorse a code of conduct that students felt was stringent enough.

In March 2003, the WRC announced a major victory at the factory where Kenia and Roselio had worked. The FEDOTRAZONAS union and the management of the BJ&B factory signed the first collective bargaining agreement in the factory's 17-year history, in part because of the WRC's efforts.

As of 2009, 186 colleges and universities in the United States had joined the WRC. In 2007–2008, the WRC carried out major investigative and remediation work at 47 factories in 16 countries, including Thailand, China, the Dominican Republic, Honduras, Bangladesh, and Nicaragua.

Also in 2009, the WRC and the Fair Labor Association investigated Russell Athletic's closing of its Jerzees de Honduras plant where workers had formed a union. On November 7, 2008, the WRC had released a report alleging that Russell managers carried out a campaign of retaliation and intimidation in order to stop workers at two of the company's Honduran factories from exercising their right to organize and bargain collectively and that animus toward worker organization played a role in Russell's decision to close the plant. Because the right to organize is protected by the codes of conduct of Russell's university business partners, Georgetown, Berkeley, Michigan, Columbia, Duke, Purdue, Rutgers, and other universities announced the end of their business relationships with Russell. Russell countered that the closing of the plant was due to "economic considerations."

Sources: http://www.workersrights.org, accessed April 26, 2003; http://www.georgetown.edu/organizations/solidarity/info.html, accessed April 26, 2003; interview with Andrew Milmore, former Solidarity Committee president, April 22, 2003 and April 26, 2003; Steven Greenhouse, "Michigan Is the Latest University to End a Licensing Deal With an Apparel Maker, *New York Times*, February 23, 2009.

SUMMARY

International business has been conducted ever since national borders were formed and has played a major role in shaping world history. Growing in importance over the past three decades, it has shaped an environment that, due to economic linkages, today presents us with a global marketplace.

In the past three decades, world trade has expanded from $200 billion to more than $19.5 trillion, while international direct investment has grown to $15 trillion. The growth of both has been far more rapid than the growth of most domestic economies. As a result, nations are much more affected by international business than in the past. Global links have made possible investment strategies and business alternatives that offer tremendous opportunities. Yet these changes and the speed of change also can represent threats to nations, firms, and individuals.

Over the past 30 years, the dominance of the U.S. international trade position has gradually eroded. New participants in international business compete fiercely for world market share. Individuals, corporations, and policymakers around the globe have awakened to the fact that international business is a major imperative and offers opportunities for future growth and prosperity. International business provides access to new customers, affords economies of scale, and permits the honing of competitive skills. Performing well in global markets is the key to improved standards of living, higher profits, and better wages. Knowledge about international business is therefore important to everyone, whether it is used to compete with foreign firms or simply to understand the world around us.

KEY TERMS

Pax Romana   6
Pax Americana   7
Smoot-Hawley Act   7
multinational corporations   8

sovereign wealth fund   12
foreign direct investment   12
composition of trade   14
macroeconomic level   16

microeconomic level   17
globalization   18

QUESTIONS FOR DISCUSSION

1. Will future expansion of international business be similar to that in the past?

2. Does increased international business mean increased risk?

3. Is it beneficial for nations to become dependent on one another?

4. Discuss the reasons for the increase in Chinese world trade market share.

5. Why do more firms in other countries enter international markets than do firms in the United States?

INTERNET EXERCISES

1. Using World Bank data for gross domestic product (shown on the Quick Reference Tables of the World Bank's web site, http://www.worldbank.org) and annual revenue information available on the web sites of individual corporations, calculate how the largest corporations might rank among countries if their annual corporate revenue were ranked as GDP. Look for ExxonMobil, Walmart, and three of the largest corporations of your choice.

2. Using World Trade Organization data shown on the International Trade page of its web site (http://www.wto.org), determine the following information: (a) the fastest growing traders; (b) the top ten exporters and importers in world merchandise trade; and (c) the top ten exporters or importers of commercial services.

TAKE A STAND

The term "globalization" describes the increased mobility of goods, services, labor, technology, and capital throughout the world. Although globalization is not a new development, its pace has increased with the advent of new technologies that make it easier for people to travel, communicate, and do business internationally as well as with the recognition of countries around the world that open trade and investment policies were beneficial for their economic growth.

For Discussion
In the July/August 2009 issue of *Foreign Affairs*, former Treasury Deputy Secretary Roger Altman contends in his article, "Globalization in Retreat": "It is now clear that the global economic crisis will be deep and prolonged and that it will have far-reaching geopolitical consequences. The long movement toward market liberalization has stopped, and a new period of state intervention, reregulation, and creeping protectionism has begun."

Given the economic dislocations and political challenges that arise with globalization of business, many agree that globalization has done more harm than good. They believe that governments need to be more involved in managing global market forces to restore and stabilize economic systems and protect domestic jobs. This has led to government "bailouts" of industries and "buy domestic" legislation. Others claim that financial crises occur regularly to correct market imbalances and that extensive government involvement impedes market growth and the benefits that globalization brings. Has globalization gone too far? Should governments enact legislation that protects domestic industries from international competition?

Source: Roger Altman, "Globalization in Retreat," *Foreign Affairs*, July/August 2009, 2–7.

MAP OF INTERNATIONAL TRADE AS A PERCENTAGE OF GROSS DOMESTIC PRODUCT

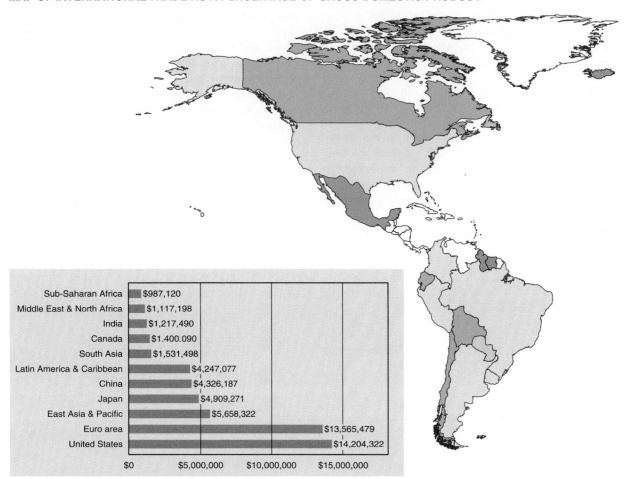

Source: Based on 2009 World Development Indicators, The World Bank.

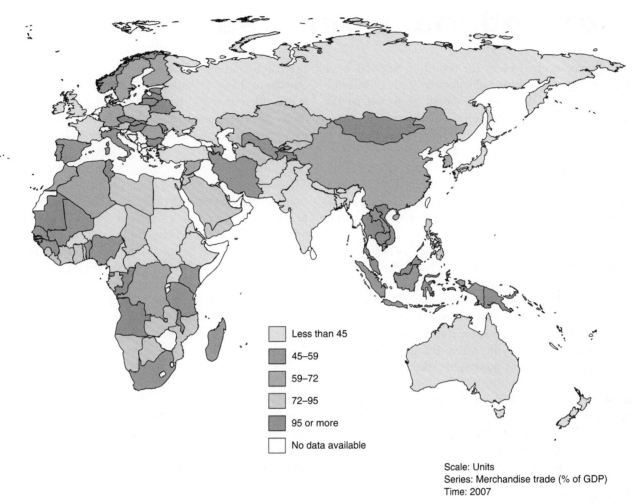

Less than 45

45–59

59–72

72–95

95 or more

No data available

Scale: Units
Series: Merchandise trade (% of GDP)
Time: 2007

Source: World Development Indicators, The World Bank.

Geographic Perspectives on International Business

The dramatic changes in the world of business have made geography indispensable for the study of international business. Without significant attention to the study of geography, critical ideas and information about the world in which business occurs will be missing.

Just as the study of business has changed significantly in recent decades, so has the study of geography. Once considered by many to be simply a descriptive inventory that filled in blank spots on maps, geography has emerged as an analytic approach that uses scientific methods to answer important questions.

Geography focuses on answering "Where?" questions. Where are things located? What is their distribution across the surface of the earth? An old aphorism holds, "If you can map it, it's geography." That statement is true, because one uses maps to gather, store, analyze, and present information that answers "Where?" questions. But identifying where things are located is only the first phase of geographic inquiry. Once locations have been determined, "Why?" and "How?" questions can be asked. Why are things located where they are? How do different things relate to one another at a specific place? How do different places relate to each other? How have geographic patterns and relationships changed over time? These are the questions that take geography beyond mere description and make it a powerful approach for analyzing and explaining geographical aspects of a wide range of different kinds of problems faced by those engaged in international business.

Geography answers questions related to the location of different kinds of economic activity and the transactions that flow across national boundaries. It provides insights into the natural and human factors that influence patterns of production and consumption in different parts of the world. It explains why patterns of trade and exchange evolve over time. And because a geographic perspective emphasizes the analysis of processes that result in different geographic patterns, it provides a means for assessing how patterns might change in the future.

Geography has a rich tradition. Classical Greeks, medieval Arabs, enlightened European explorers, and twentieth-century scholars in the United States and elsewhere have organized geographic knowledge in many different ways. In recent decades, however, geography has become more familiar and more relevant to many people because emphasis has been placed on five fundamental themes as ways to structure geographic questions and to provide answers for those questions. Those themes are (1) location, (2) place, (3) interaction, (4) movement, and (5) region. The five themes are neither exclusive nor exhaustive. They complement other disciplinary approaches for organizing information, some of which are better suited to addressing specific kinds of questions. Other questions require insights related to two or more of the themes. Experience has shown, however, that the five themes provide a powerful means for introducing students to the geographic perspective. As a result, they provide the structure for this discussion.

LOCATION

For decades, people engaged in real estate development have said that the value of a place is a product of three factors: location, location, and location. This statement also highlights the importance of location for international business. Learning the location and characteristics of other places has always been important to those interested in conducting business outside their local areas. The drive to learn about other kinds of places, and especially their resources and potential as markets, has stimulated geographic exploration throughout history. Explorations of the Mediterranean by the Phoenicians; Marco Polo's journey to China; and voyages undertaken by Christopher Columbus, Vasco de Gama, Henry Hudson, and James Cook not only improved general knowledge of the world but also expanded business opportunities.

Assessing the role of location requires more than simply determining specific locations where certain activities take place. Latitude and longitude often are used to fix the exact location of features on the Earth's surface, but to simply describe a place's coordinates

Note: This appendix was contributed by Thomas J. Baerwald. Dr. Baerwald is senior science advisor at the National Science Foundation in Arlington, Virginia. He is co-author of *Prentice Hall World Geography*—a best-selling geography textbook.

provides relatively little information about that place. Of much greater significance is its location relative to other features. The city of Singapore, for example, is between 1 and 2 degrees North latitude and is just west of 104 degrees East longitude. Its most pertinent locational characteristics, however, include its being at the southern tip of the Malay Peninsula near the eastern end of the Strait of Malacca, a critical shipping route connecting the Indian Ocean with the South China Sea. For nearly 150 years, this location made Singapore an important center for trade in the British Empire. After attaining independence in 1965, Singapore's leaders diversified its economy and complemented trade in its bustling port with numerous manufacturing plants that export products to nations around the world.

An understanding of how location influences business therefore is critical for the international business executive. Without clear knowledge of an enterprise's location relative to its suppliers, to its market, and to its competitors, an executive operates like the captain of a fog-bound vessel that has lost all navigational instruments and is heading for dangerous shoals.

PLACE

In addition to its location, each place has a diverse set of characteristics. Although many of those characteristics are present in other places, the ensemble makes each place unique. The characteristics of places—both natural and human—profoundly influence the ways that business executives in different places participate in international economic transactions.

Natural Features

Many of the characteristics of a place relate to its natural attributes. **Geologic characteristics** can be especially important, as the presence of critical minerals or energy resources may make a place a world-renowned supplier of valuable products. Gold and diamonds help make South Africa's economy the most prosperous on that continent. Rich deposits of iron ore in southern parts of the Amazon Basin have made Brazil the world's leading exporter of that commodity, while Chile remains a preeminent exporter of copper. Coal deposits provided the foundation for massive industrial development in the eastern United States, the Rhine River Basin of Europe, in western Russia, and in northeastern China. Because of abundant pools of petroleum beneath desert sands, standards of living in Saudi Arabia and nearby nations have risen rapidly to be among the highest in the world.

The geology of place also shapes its terrain. People traditionally have clustered in lower, flatter areas, because valleys and plains have permitted the agricultural development necessary to feed the local population and to generate surpluses that can be traded. Hilly and mountainous areas may support some people, but their population densities invariably are lower. Terrain also plays a critical role in focusing and inhibiting the movement of people and goods. Business leaders throughout the centuries have capitalized on this fact. Just as feudal masters sought control of mountain passes in order to collect tolls and other duties from traders who traversed an area, modern executives maintain stores and offer services near bridges and at other points where terrain focuses travel.

The terrain of a place is related to its hydrology. Rivers, lakes, and other bodies of water influence the kinds of economic activities that occur in a place. In general, abundant supplies of water boost economic development, because water is necessary for the sustenance of people and for both agricultural and industrial production. Locations like Los Angeles and Saudi Arabia have prospered despite having little local water, because other features offer advantages that more than exceed the additional costs incurred in delivering water supplies from elsewhere. While sufficient water must be available to meet local needs, overabundance of water may pose serious problems, such as in Bangladesh, where development has been inhibited by frequent flooding. The character of a place's water bodies also is important. Smooth-flowing streams and placid lakes can stimulate transportation within a place and connect it more easily with other places, while waterfalls and rapids can prevent navigation on streams. The rapid drop in elevation of such streams may boost their potential for hydroelectric power generation, however, thereby stimulating development of industries requiring considerable amounts of electricity. Large plants producing aluminum, for example, are found in the Tennessee and Columbia river valleys of the United States and in Quebec and British Columbia in Canada. These plants refine materials that originally were extracted elsewhere, especially bauxite and alumina from Caribbean nations like Jamaica and the Dominican Republic. Although the transport costs incurred in delivery of these materials to the plants is high, those costs are more than offset by the presence of abundant and inexpensive electricity.

Climate is another natural feature that has profound impact on economic activity within a place. Many activities are directly affected by climate. Locales blessed with pleasant climates, such as the Côte d'Azur of France, the Crimean Peninsula of Ukraine, Florida, and the "Gold Coast" of northeastern Australia, have become popular recreational havens, attracting tourists whose spending fuels the local economy. Agricultural production also is influenced by climate. The average daily and evening temperatures, the amount and timing of precipitation, the timing of frosts and freezing weather, and the variability of weather from one year to the next all influence the kinds of crops grown in an area. Plants producing bananas and sugar cane flourish in moist tropical areas, while cooler climates are more conducive for crops such as wheat and potatoes. Climate influences other industries as well. The aircraft manufacturing industry in the United States developed largely in warmer, drier areas where conditions for test and delivery flights were most beneficial throughout the year. In a similar way, major rocket-launching facilities have been placed in locations where climatic conditions and trajectories are most favorable. As a result, the primary launch site of the European Space Agency is not in Europe at all but rather in the South American territory of French Guiana. Climate also affects the length of the work day and the length of economic seasons. For example, in some regions of the world, the construction industry can build only during a few months of the year because permafrost makes construction prohibitively expensive the rest of the year.

Variations in **soils** have a profound impact on agricultural production. The world's great grain-exporting regions, including the central United States, the Prairie Provinces of Canada, the "Fertile Triangle" stretching from central Ukraine through southern Russia into northern Kazakhstan, and the Pampas of northern Argentina, all have been blessed with mineral-rich soils made even more fertile by humus from natural grasslands that once dominated the landscape. Soils are less fertile in much of the Amazon Basin of Brazil and in central Africa, where heavy rains leave few nutrients in upper layers of the soil. As a result, few commercial crops are grown in those areas.

The interplay between climate and soils is especially evident in the production of wines. Hundreds of varieties of grapes have been bred to take advantage of the different physical characteristics of various places. The wines fermented from these grapes are shipped around the world to consumers, who differentiate among various wines based not only on the grapes but also on the places where they were grown and the conditions during which they matured.

Human Features

The physical features of a place provide natural resources and influence the types of economic activities in which people engage, but its human characteristics also are critical. The population of a place is important

because farm production may require intensive labor to be successful, as is true in rice-growing areas of eastern Asia. The skills and qualifications of the population also play a role in determining how a place fits into global economic affairs. Although blessed with few mineral resources and a terrain and climate that limit agricultural production, the Swiss have emphasized high levels of education and training in order to maintain a labor force that manufactures sophisticated products for export around the world. In recent decades, Japan and smaller nations such as South Korea and Taiwan have increased the productivity of their workers to become major industrial exporters.

As people live in a place, they modify it, creating a **built environment** that can be as or more important than the natural environment in economic terms. The most pronounced areas of human activity and their associated structures are in cities. In nations around the world, cities have grown dramatically during the twentieth century. Much of the growth of cities has resulted from the migration of people from rural areas. This influx of new residents broadens the labor pool and creates vast new demand for goods and services. As urban populations have grown, residences and other facilities have replaced rural land uses. Executives seeking to conduct business in foreign cities need to be aware that the geographic patterns found in their home cities are not evident in many other nations. For example, in the United States, wealthier residents generally have moved outward and as they established their residences, stores and services followed. Residential patterns in the major cities of Latin America and other developing nations tend to be reversed, with the wealthy remaining close to the city center while poorer residents are consigned to the outskirts of town. A store location strategy that is successful in the United States therefore may fail miserably if transferred directly to another nation without knowledge of the different geographic patterns of that nation's cities.

INTERACTION

The international business professional seeking to take advantage of opportunities present in different places learns not to view each place separately. How a place functions depends not only on the presence and form of certain characteristics but also on interactions among those characteristics. Fortuitous combinations of features can spur a region's economic development. The presence of high-grade supplies of iron ore, coal, and limestone powered the growth of Germany's Ruhr Valley as one of Europe's foremost steel-producing regions, just as the proximity of the fertile Pampas and the deep channel of the Río de la Plata combine to make Buenos Aires the leading economic center in southern South America.

Interactions among different features change over time within places, and as they do, so does that place's character and its economic activities. Human activities can have profound impacts on natural features. The courses of rivers and streams are changed, as dams are erected and meanders are straightened. Soil fertility can be improved through fertilization. Vegetation is changed, with naturally growing plants replaced by crops and other varieties that require careful management.

Many human modifications have been successful. For centuries, the Dutch have constructed dikes and drainage systems, slowly creating polders—land that once was covered by the North Sea but that now is used for agricultural production. But other human activities have had disastrous impacts on natural features. A large area in Ukraine and Belarus was rendered uninhabitable by radioactive materials leaked from the Chernobyl reactor in 1986. In countless other places around the globe, improper disposal of wastes has seriously harmed land and water resources. In some places, damage can be repaired, as has happened in rivers and lakes of the United States following the passage of measures to curb water pollution in the past four decades, but in other locales, restoration may be impossible.

Growing concerns about environmental quality have led many people in more economically advanced nations to call for changes in economic systems that harm the natural environment. Concerted efforts are under way, for example, to halt destruction of forests in the Amazon Basin, thereby preserving the vast array of different plant and animal species in the region and saving vegetation that can help moderate the world's climate. Cooperative ventures have been established to promote selective harvesting of nuts, hardwoods, and other products taken from natural forests. Furthermore, an increasing number of restaurants and grocers are refusing to purchase beef raised on pastures that are established by clearing forests.

Like so many other geographical relationships, the nature of human-environmental interaction changes over time. With technological advances, people have been able to modify and adapt to natural features in increasingly sophisticated ways. The development of air conditioning has permitted people to function more effectively in torrid tropical environments, thereby enabling the populations of cities such as Houston, Rio de Janeiro, and Jakarta to multiply many times over in recent decades. Owners of winter resorts now can generate snow artificially to ensure favorable conditions for skiers. Advanced irrigation systems now permit crops to be grown in places such as the southwestern United States,

northern Africa, and Israel. The use of new technologies may cause serious problems over the long run, however. Extensive irrigation in large parts of the U.S. Great Plains has seriously depleted groundwater supplies. In central Asia, the diversion of river water to irrigate cotton fields in Kazakhstan and Uzbekistan has reduced the size of the Aral Sea by more than one-half since 1960. In future years, business leaders may need to factor into their decisions additional costs associated with the restoration of environmental quality after they have finished using a place's resources.

MOVEMENT

Whereas the theme of interaction encourages consideration of different characteristics within a place, movement provides a structure for considering how different places relate to each other. International business exists because movement permits the transportation of people and goods and communication of information and ideas among different places. No matter how much people in one place want something found elsewhere, they cannot have it unless transportation systems permit the good to be brought to them or allow them to move to the location of the good.

The location and character of transportation and communication systems long have had powerful influences on the economic standing of places. Especially significant have been places on which transportation routes have focused. Many ports have become prosperous cities because they channeled the movement of goods and people between ocean and inland waterways. New York became the largest city in North America because its harbor provided sheltered anchorage for ships crossing the Atlantic; the Hudson River provided access leading into the interior of the continent. In eastern Asia, Hong Kong grew under similar circumstances, as British traders used its splendid harbor as an exchange point for goods moving in and out of southern China.

Businesses also have succeeded at well-situated places along overland routes. The fabled oasis of Tombouctou has been an important trading center for centuries because it has one of the few dependable sources of water in the Sahara. Chicago's ascendancy as the premier city of the U.S. heartland came when its early leaders engineered its selection as the termination point for a dozen railroad lines converging from all directions. Not only did much of the rail traffic moving through the region have to pass through Chicago, but passengers and freight passing through the city had to be transferred from one line to another, a process that generated numerous jobs and added considerably to the wealth of many businesses in the city.

In addition to the business associated directly with the movement of people and goods, other forms of economic activity have become concentrated at critical points in the transportation network. Places where transfers from one mode of transportation to another were required often were chosen as sites for manufacturing activities. Buffalo was the most active flour-milling center in the United States for much of the twentieth century because it was the point where Great Lakes freighters carrying wheat from the northern Great Plains and Canadian prairies were unloaded. Rather than simply transfer the wheat into rail cars for shipment to the large urban markets of the northeastern United States, millers transformed the wheat into flour in Buffalo, thereby reducing the additional handling of the commodity.

Global patterns of resource refining also demonstrate the wisdom of careful selection of sites with respect to transportation systems. Some of the world's largest oil refineries are located in places like Bahrain and Houston, where pipelines bring oil to points where it is processed and loaded onto ships in the form of gasoline or other distillates for transport to other locales. Massive refinery complexes also have been built in the Tokyo and Nagoya areas of Japan and near Rotterdam in the Netherlands to process crude oil brought by giant tankers from the Middle East and other oil-exporting regions. For similar reasons, the largest new steel mills in the United States are near Baltimore and Philadelphia, where iron ore shipped from Canada and Brazil is processed. Some of the most active aluminum works in Europe are beside Norwegian fjords, where abundant local hydroelectric power is used to process imported alumina.

Favorable location along transportation lines is beneficial for a place. Conversely, an absence of good transportation severely limits the potential for firms to succeed in a specific place. Transportation patterns change over time, however, and so does their impact on places. Some places maintain themselves because their business leaders use their size and economic power to make them critical nodes in newly evolving transportation networks. New York's experience provides a good example of this process. New York became the United States's foremost business center in the early nineteenth century because it was ideally situated for water transportation. As railroad networks evolved later in that century, they sought New York connections in order to serve its massive market. During the twentieth century, a complex web of roadways and major airports reinforced New York's supremacy in the eastern United States. In similar ways, London, Moscow, and Tokyo reasserted themselves as transportation hubs for their nations through successive advances in transport technology.

Failure to adapt to changing transportation patterns can have deleterious impacts on a place. During the middle of the nineteenth century, business leaders in St. Louis discouraged railroad construction, seeking instead to maintain the supremacy of river transportation. Only after it became clear that railroads were the mode of preference did St. Louis officials seek to develop rail connections for the city, but by then it was too late; Chicago had ascended to a dominant position in the region. For about 30 years during the middle part of the twentieth century, airports at Gander, Newfoundland, Canada, and Shannon, Ireland, became important refueling points for trans-Atlantic flights. The development of planes that could travel nonstop for much longer distances returned those places to sleepy oblivion.

Continuing advances in transportation technology effectively have "shrunk" the world. Just a few centuries ago, travel across an ocean took harrowing months. As late as 1873, readers marveled when Jules Verne wrote of a hectic journey around the world in 80 days. Today's travelers can fly around the globe in less than 80 hours, and the speed and dependability of modern modes of transport have transformed the ways in which business is conducted. Modern manufacturers have transformed the notion of relationships among suppliers, manufacturers, and markets. Automobile manufacturers, for example, once maintained large stockpiles of parts in assembly plants that were located near the parts plants or close to the places where the cars would be sold. Contemporary auto assembly plants now are built in places where labor costs and worker productivity are favorable and where governments have offered attractive inducements. They keep relatively few parts on hand, calling on suppliers for rapid delivery of parts as they are needed when orders for new cars are received. This "just-in-time" system of production leaves manufacturers subject to disruptions caused by work stoppages at supply plants and to weather-related delays in the transportation system, but losses associated with these infrequent events are more than offset by reduced operating costs under normal conditions.

The role of advanced technology as a factor affecting international business is even more apparent with respect to advances in communications systems. Sophisticated forms of telecommunication that began more than 150 years ago with the telegraph have advanced through the telephone to facsimile transmissions and electronic mail networks. As a result, distance has practically ceased to be a consideration with respect to the transmission of information. Whereas information once moved only as rapidly as the person carrying the paper on which the information was written, data and ideas now can be sent instantaneously almost anywhere in the world.

These communication advances have had a staggering impact on the way that international business is conducted. They have fostered the growth of multinational corporations, which operate in diverse sites around the globe while maintaining effective links with headquarters and regional control centers. International financial operations also have been transformed because of communication advances. Money and stock markets in New York, London, Tokyo, and Frankfurt now are connected by computer systems that process transactions around the clock. As much as any other factor, the increasingly mobile forms of money have enabled modern business executives to engage in activities around the world.

REGIONS

In addition to considering places by themselves or how they relate to other places, regions provide alternative ways to organize groups of places in more meaningful ways. A region is a set of places that share certain characteristics. Many regions are defined by characteristics that all of the places in the group have in common. When economic characteristics are used, the delimited regions include places with similar kinds of economic activity. Agricultural regions include areas where certain farm products dominate. Corn is grown throughout the "Corn Belt" of the central United States, for example, although many farmers in the region also plant soybeans and many raise hogs. Regions where intensive industrial production is a prominent part of local economic activity include the manufacturing belts of the northeastern United States, southern Canada, northwestern Europe, and southern Japan.

Regions can also be defined by patterns of movement. Transportation or communication linkages among places may draw them together into configurations that differentiate them from other locales. Studies by economic geographers of the locational tendencies of modern high-technology industries have identified complex networks of firms that provide products and services to each other. Because of their linkages, these firms cluster together into well-defined regions. The "Silicon Valley" of northern California, the "Western Crescent" on the outskirts of London, and "Technopolis" of the Tokyo region all are distinguished as much by connections among firms as by the economic landscapes they have established.

Economic aspects of movement may help define functional regions by establishing areas where certain types of economic activity are more profitable than others. In the early nineteenth century, German landowner Johann Heinrich von Thünen demonstrated how different costs for transporting various agricultural goods to market helped to define regions where certain forms of farming would occur. Although theoretically simple, patterns predicted by von Thünen can still be found in the world today. Goods such as vegetables and dairy products that require more intensive production and are more expensive to ship are produced closer to markets, while less demanding goods and commodities that can be transported at lower costs come from more remote production areas. Advances in transportation have dramatically altered such regional patterns, however. Whereas a New York City native once enjoyed fresh vegetables and fruit only in the summer and early autumn when New Jersey, upstate New York, and New England producers brought their goods to market, New Yorkers today buy fresh produce year-round, with new shipments flown in daily from Florida, California, Chile, and even more remote locations during the colder months.

Governments have a strong impact on the conduct of business, and the formal borders of government jurisdictions often coincide with the functional boundaries of economic regions. The divisive character of these lines on the map has been altered in many parts of the world in recent decades, however. The formation of common markets and free trade areas in western Europe and North America has dramatically changed the patterns and flows of economic activity, and similar kinds of formal restructuring of relationships among nations likely will continue in this century. As a result, business analysts increasingly need to consider regions that cross international boundaries.

PART 2
FOUNDATIONS

2 Trade and Investment Policies
3 The Theory of Trade and Investment
4 The Balance of Payments

To achieve an understanding of the key governmental dimensions which affect international business, this part starts out by addressing the policy issues surrounding the corporate decision maker. We then progress to the theoretical background for international trade and investment activities. Classical concepts, such as absolute and comparative advantage are explained. Key emphasis rests with modern-day theoretical developments that are presented in light of the new realities of international business. In addition, the international activities of nations and the balance of payments are discussed.

CHAPTER 2

Trade and Investment Policies

CHAPTER CONTENTS & LEARNING OBJECTIVES

RATIONALE AND GOALS OF TRADE AND INVESTMENT POLICIES

1. To see how trade and investment policies have historically been a subset of domestic policies

GLOBAL TRADE REGULATION SINCE 1945

2. To examine how traditional attitudes toward trade and investment policies are changing

CHANGES IN THE GLOBAL POLICY ENVIRONMENT

3. To see the effects of global links in trade and investment on policymakers

POLICY RESPONSES TO CHANGING CONDITIONS

4. To understand that nations must cooperate closely in the future to maintain a viable global trade and investment environment

A STRATEGIC OUTLOOK FOR TRADE AND INVESTMENT POLICIES

5. To understand what polices are needed to achieve a growing, viable global trade and investment environment

In 2007, serious imbalances in the U.S. subprime mortgage market triggered a financial crisis that soon spread globally and triggered the biggest worldwide economic recession and the first contraction in global output since World War II. Unemployment climbed sharply in the United States and the major developed nations in 2008–2009 as tightened global credit flows and reduced consumer spending led to diminished industrial production.

With companies unable to access capital financing and customers nervous about making large purchases, there was a collapse in demand for durable goods and a sharp decline in the production of and global trade in manufactured goods. The World Bank noted that a "vicious circle" was operating between the financial and real sectors of the global economy in terms of global trade, investment spending, and economic growth in both high-income and developing economies.

Facing the potential of imminent collapse in the international financial system and the bankruptcy of major companies in late 2008 and early 2009, the major countries of the world created national policy responses and an infusion of liquidity that prevented serious defaults of financial institutions and stabilized financial markets. On the monetary policy side, the major central banks of countries, including the Federal Reserve Bank of the United States and the European Central Bank, responded with measures to increase money supply and provide so-called quantitative easing. At the same time, the national governments invested government capital into major banks and companies to restore lending and prevent a recurrence of the kinds of snowballing problems that resulted from bank failures and the freezing of credit in the Great Depression of the 1930s.

The severity of the problem was reflected in international trade statistics. In the summer of 2009, the World Trade Organization predicted a decrease in global merchandise trade of 10 percent in 2009 in volume terms, with the steepest decline of 14 percent for developed economies and a 7 percent decline for developing countries.

Recognizing that this was indeed a global crisis that required cooperation and coordination among the major economies of the world, the leaders of the Group of Twenty (G-20) met in April 2009 to attempt a global solution. The major result of the meeting was the leaders' pledge to make available $1.1 trillion in new resources for the International Monetary Fund, the multilateral development banks, and trade finance.

Another important result was the leaders' affirmation of their commitment to resisting protectionism and refraining from raising new barriers to trade and investment. They pledged in the Leaders' Statement: "World trade growth has underpinned rising prosperity for half a century. But it is now falling for the first time in 25 years. Falling demand is exacerbated by growing protectionist pressures and a withdrawal of trade credit. Reinvigorating world trade and investment is essential for restoring global growth. We will not repeat the historic mistakes of protectionism of previous eras."

The major concern among global leaders and economists was that globalization would go into reverse with increased protectionism and stimulus measures inconsistent with World Trade Organization commitments. Indeed, in efforts to protect domestic jobs, many countries had already enacted stimulus measures that were protectionist, such as "Buy American" or "Buy Chinese" provisions. Measures like these excluded materials and component parts from other countries and carried the potential of retaliatory actions similar to those that deepened the Great Depression. At question was whether the promises of the G-20 leaders would indeed become reality.

In a speech to the International Chamber of Commerce in February 2009, WTO Director-General Pascal Lamy warned: "We still remember the 1930 Smoot and Hawley Act sharply raising U.S. tariffs on more than 20,000 products. We also remember that many other countries retaliated, raising their tariffs on U.S. goods. The Great Depression followed. Whether it is with tariffs or with new, more sophisticated faces of Smoot and Hawley, today we run the risk of sliding down a slippery slope of tit-for-tat measures. It was Mahatma Gandhi who said, 'An eye for an eye makes the whole world blind.'"

Sources: The World Bank, Global Development Finance 2009; Martin Wolf, "The Long Road to Ruin," *Financial Times*, February 16, 2009; The G-20 Leaders' Statement, "The Slow Path to Recovery," February 17, 2009, www.g20.org; www.wto.org.

This chapter discusses the policy actions taken by countries. All nations have international trade and investment policies. The policies may be publicly pronounced or kept secret, they may be disjointed or coordinated, or they may be applied consciously or determined by a laissez-faire attitude. Trade policy actions become evident when measures taken by governments affect the flow of trade and investment across national borders.

RATIONALE AND GOALS OF TRADE AND INVESTMENT POLICIES

1. To see how trade and investment policies have historically been a subset of domestic policies

national sovereignty The supreme right of nations to determine national policies; freedom from external control.

standard of living The level of material affluence of a group or nation, measured as a composite of quantities and qualities of goods.

quality of life The standard of living combined with environmental factors, it determines the level of well-being of individuals.

foreign policy The area of public policy concerned with relationships with other countries.

Government policies are designed to regulate, stimulate, direct, and protect national activities. The exercise of these policies is the result of **national sovereignty**, which provides a government with the right and burden to shape the environment of the country and its citizens. Because they are "border bound," governments focus mainly on domestic policies. Nevertheless, many policy actions have repercussions on other nations, firms, and individuals abroad and are, therefore, a component of a nation's trade and investment policy.

Government policy can be subdivided into two groups of policy actions that affect trade and investment. One affects trade and investment directly, the other indirectly. The domestic policy actions of most governments aim to increase the **standard of living** of the country's citizens, to improve the **quality of life**, to stimulate national development, and to achieve full employment. Clearly, all of these goals are closely intertwined. For example, an improved standard of living is likely to contribute to national development. Similarly, quality of life and standard of living are closely interlinked. Also, a high level of employment will play a major role in determining the standard of living. Yet all of these policy goals will also affect international trade and investment indirectly. For example, if foreign industries become more competitive and rapidly increase their exports, employment in the importing countries may suffer. Likewise, if a country accumulates large quantities of debt, which at some time must be repaid, the present and future standard of living will be threatened.

In more direct ways, a country may also pursue policies of increased development that mandate either technology transfer from abroad or the exclusion of foreign industries to the benefit of domestic infant firms. Also, government officials may believe that imports threaten the culture, health, or standards of the country's citizens and thus the quality of life. As a result, officials are likely to develop regulations to protect the citizens.

Nations also institute **foreign policy** measures designed with domestic concerns in mind but explicitly aimed to exercise influence abroad. One major goal of foreign policy may be national security. For example, nations may develop alliances, coalitions, and agreements to protect their borders or their spheres of interest. Similarly, nations may take measures to enhance their national security preparedness in case of international conflict. Governments also wish to improve trade and investment opportunities and to contribute to the security and safety of their own firms abroad.

Policy aims may be approached in various ways. For example, to develop new markets abroad and to increase their sphere of influence, nations may give foreign aid to other countries. This was the case when the United States generously awarded Marshall Plan funds for the reconstruction of Europe. Governments may also feel a need to restrict or encourage trade and investment flows in order to preserve or enhance the capability of industries that are important to national security.

Each country develops its own domestic policies, and therefore policy aims will vary from nation to nation. Inevitably, conflicts arise. For example, full employment policies in one country may directly affect employment policies in another. Similarly, the development aims of one country may reduce the development capability of another. Even when health issues are concerned, disputes may arise. One nation may argue that its regulations are in place to protect its citizens, whereas other nations may interpret the regulations as market barriers. An example of the latter situation is the celebrated hormone dispute between the United States and the European Union. U.S. cattle are treated with growth hormones. While the United States claims that these hormones are harmless to humans, many Europeans find them scary. Given the differences in perspectives, there is much room for conflict when it comes to trade policies, particularly when the United States wants to export more beef and the European Union attempts to restrict such beef imports.

The trade disagreement between Australia and New Zealand over New Zealand–grown apples is another example. Australia closed its market to New Zealand apples in 1921 because of a fire blight disease. Since 1986, New Zealand has been fighting to have the ban removed, citing studies that have found no scientific evidence that fire blight can be transmitted through shipments of apples.[1]

Differences among national policies have always existed and are likely to erupt into occasional conflict. Yet, the closer economic links among nations have made the emergence of such conflicts more frequent and the disagreements more severe. In recognition of this development, efforts have been made since 1945 to create a multilateral institutional arrangement that can help to resolve national conflicts, harmonize national policies, and facilitate increased international trade and investments.

GLOBAL TRADE REGULATION SINCE 1945

In 1945, the United States led in the belief that international trade and investment flows were a key to worldwide prosperity. Many months of international negotiations in London, Geneva, and Lake Success (New York) culminated on March 24, 1948, in Havana, Cuba, with the signing of the Havana Charter for the **International Trade Organization (ITO)**. The charter represented a series of agreements among 53 countries. It was designed to cover international commercial policies, restrictive business practices, commodity agreements, employment and reconstruction, economic development and international investment, and a constitution for a new United Nations agency to administer the whole.[2]

Even though the International Trade Organization incorporated many farsighted notions, most nations refused to ratify its provisions. They feared the power and bureaucratic size of the new organization—and the consequent threats to national sovereignty. As a result, this most forward-looking approach to international trade and investment was never implemented. However, other organizations conceived at the time have made major contributions toward improving international business. An agreement was initiated for the purpose of reducing tariffs and therefore facilitating trade. In addition, international institutions such as the United Nations, the World Bank, and the International Monetary Fund were negotiated.

The **General Agreement on Tariffs and Trade (GATT)** has been called a "remarkable success story of a postwar international organization that was never intended to become one."[3] It started out in 1947 as a set of rules to ensure nondiscrimination, transparent procedures, the settlement of disputes, and the participation of the lesser-developed countries in international trade. To increase trade, GATT used

2. To examine how traditional attitudes toward trade and investment policies are changing

International Trade Organization (ITO) A forward-looking agreement on the approach to international trade and investment embodied in the 1948 Havana Charter; due to disagreements among sponsoring nations, its provisions were never ratified.

General Agreement on Tariffs and Trade (GATT) An international code of tariffs and trade rules signed by 23 nations in 1947; headquartered in Geneva, Switzerland; now part of the World Trade Organization with 148 members.

most-favored nation (MFN)
A term describing a GATT
clause that calls for member
countries to grant other member countries the same most
favorable treatment they accord any country concerning
imports and exports. In the
U.S. now called Normal
Trade Relations (NTR).

tariff concessions, through which member countries agreed to limit the level of tariffs they would impose on imports from other GATT members. An important tool is the **most-favored nation (MFN)** clause, which calls for each member country to grant every other member country the same most favorable treatment that it accords to any other country with respect to imports and exports.[4] MFN, in effect, provides for equal, rather than special, treatment.

The GATT was not originally intended to be an international organization. Rather, it was to be a multilateral treaty designed to operate under the International Trade Organization (ITO). However, because the ITO never came into being, the GATT became the governing body for settling international trade disputes. Gradually it evolved into an institution that sponsored various successful rounds of international trade negotiations with an initial focus on the reduction of prevailing high tariffs. Headquartered in Geneva, Switzerland, the GATT Secretariat conducted its work as instructed by the representatives of its member nations. Even though the GATT had no independent enforcement mechanism and relied entirely on moral suasion and on frequently wavering membership adherence to its rules, it achieved major progress for world trade.

Early in its history, the GATT accomplished the reduction of duties for trade in 50,000 products, amounting to two-thirds of the value of the trade among its participants. In subsequent years, special GATT negotiations such as the Kennedy Round, named after John F. Kennedy, and the Tokyo Round, named after the location where the negotiations were agreed upon, further reduced trade barriers and improved dispute-settlement mechanisms. The GATT also developed better provisions for dealing with subsidies and more explicit definitions of roles for import controls. Table 2.1 provides an overview of the different GATT rounds.

**World Trade Organization
(WTO)** The institution that
supplanted GATT in 1995 to
administer international trade
and investment accords.

In early 1995, the GATT was supplanted by a new institution, the **World Trade Organization (WTO)**, which now administers international trade and investment accords (http://www.wto.org). These accords will gradually reduce governmental subsidies to industries and will convert nontariff barriers into more transparent tariff barriers. The textile and clothing industries eventually will be brought into the WTO regime, resulting in decreased subsidies and fewer market restrictions through the General Agreement on Trade in Services (GATS). An entire new set of rules was designed to govern the service area, and agreement also was reached on new rules to encourage international investment flows.

In 2001, a new round of international trade negotiations was initiated. Since the agreement to do so was reached in the city of Doha (Qatar), the negotiations were

Table 2.1   Negotiations in the GATT

Round	Dates	Numbers of Countries	Value of Trade Covered	Average Tariff Cut	Average Tariffs Afterward
Geneva	1947	23	$10 billion	35%	n/a
Annecy	1949	33	Unavailable		n/a
Torquay	1950	34	Unavailable		n/a
Geneva	1956	22	$2.5 billion		n/a
Dillon	1960–1961	45	$4.9 billion		n/a
Kennedy	1962–1967	48	$40 billion	35%	8.7%
Tokyo	1973–1979	99	$155 billion	34%	4.7%
Uruguay	1987–1995	124	$300 billion	38%	3.9%
Doha	2001–	153	TBN[a]	TBN[a]	n/a

[a]To be negotiated

Sources: John H. Jackson, *The World Trading System* (Cambridge, Mass.: MIT Press, 1989), wto.org, accessed May 5, 2010; *The GATT: Uruguay Round Final Act Should Produce Overall U.S. Economic Gains*, U.S. General Accounting Office, Report to Congress, Washington, DC, July 1994, http://www.gao.gov.

called the **Doha Round**. The aim was to further hasten implementation of liberalization to particularly help the impoverished and developing nations. In addition, the goal was to expand the role of the WTO to encompass more of the trade activities where there were insufficient rules for its definitions and structure. This was due to either purposeful exclusion by governments in earlier negotiations or due to new technology changing the global marketplace. The issues on the negotiating table include trade in agricultural goods, nonagricultural market access (NAMA), trade in services, and trade facilitation such as customs procedures and port efficiencies. Key industries include chemicals, information technology, electronics, and environmental products.

Despite a concerted effort to reach agreement in 2008, the Doha Round has proven to be a very difficult series of negotiations. There remains considerable disagreement on the trade-off formula between agriculture and nonagricultural market access and between developed nations and developing WTO members like India and Brazil. The rewards from an agreement could be substantial. Experts predict that an agreement could bring an increase in global exports between $180 billion and $520 billion annually, as well as GDP gains of between $300 billion and $700 billion annually.[5]

The GATT and now the WTO have made major contributions to improved trade and investment flows around the world. The success of the GATT and the resulting increase in welfare has refuted the old postulate that "the strong is most powerful alone." Nations have increasingly come to recognize that international trade and investment activities are important to their own economic well-being.

Nations also have come to accept that they must generate sufficient outgoing export and incoming investment activities to compensate for the inflow of imports and outgoing investment. In the medium and long term, the balance of payments must be maintained. For short periods of time, gold or capital transfers can be used to finance a deficit. Such financing, however, can continue only while gold and foreign assets last or while foreign countries will accept the IOUs of the deficit countries, permitting them to pile up foreign liabilities. This willingness, of course, will vary. Some countries, such as the United States, can run up deficits of hundreds of billions of dollars because of political stability, acceptable rates of return, and perceived economic security. Yet, over the long term, all nations are subject to the same economic rules.

CHANGES IN THE GLOBAL POLICY ENVIRONMENT

Three major changes have occurred over time in the global policy environment: a reduction of domestic policy influence, a weakening of traditional international institutions, and a sharpening of the conflict between industrialized and developing nations. These three changes, in turn, have had a major effect on policy responses in the international trade and investment field.

LIMITS OF DOMESTIC POLICY INFLUENCES

The effects of growing global influences on a domestic economy have been significant. Policymakers have increasingly come to recognize that it is very difficult to isolate domestic economic activity from international market events. Again and again, domestic policy measures are vetoed or counteracted by the activities of global market forces. Decisions that were once clearly in the domestic purview now have to

Doha Round Currently (2010) ongoing international trade and investment liberalization negotiations within the World Trade Organization (WTO) initiated in 2001 in Doha, Quatar.

3. *To see the effects of global links in trade and investment on policymakers*

be revised due to influences from abroad. At the same time, the clash between the fixed geography of nations and the nonterritorial nature of many of today's problems and solutions continues to escalate. Nation-states may simply no longer be the natural problem-solving unit. Local government may be most appropriate to address some of the problems of individuals, while transnational or even global entities are required to deal with larger issues such as economics, resources, or the environment.[6]

Agricultural policies, for example—historically a domestic issue—have been thrust into the international realm. Any time a country or a group of nations such as the European Union contemplates changes in agricultural subsidies, quantity restrictions, or even quality regulations, international trade partners are quick to speak up against the resulting global effects of such changes. Focus on Politics shows some of the intricacies of embargoes. When countries contemplate specific industrial policies that encourage, for example, industrial innovation or collaboration, they often encounter major opposition from their trading partners, who believe that their own industries are jeopardized by such policies. Those reactions and the resulting constraints are the result of growing interdependencies among nations and a closer link between industries around the world. The following examples highlight the importance of international business and trade.

- Exports account for almost half of Germany's economy and are also very important in other large countries such as China, the United Kingdom, France, and Japan.[7]
- An expansion of the Panama Canal will double capacity and allow more traffic and longer, wider ships.[8]
- In the United States, subsidiaries of companies headquartered abroad support worker compensation that is 32 percent higher on average than compensation at U.S. companies.[9]
- Thailand exports about 10 million tons of rice per year, with Vietnam coming on strong.[10]
- China is General Motors' largest growth market. The firm has more than 20,000 employees in China, enjoys booming sales, and occupies the leading position among global automakers, with market share of about 12 percent in China.[11]

currency flows The movement of currency from nation to nation, which in turn determines exchange rates.

International business has driven dramatic changes in the world economy and continues to present governments with challenges related to the limit of their domestic policy influence. For example, trade flows used to determine **currency flows** and therefore the exchange rate. In the more recent past, currency flows have taken on a life of their own, increasing from an average global daily trading volume of $18 billion in 1980 to $3,210 billion per day in 2008.[12] Exchange rates values have become increasingly independent of trade but, in turn, have themselves begun to determine the volume of trade. Governments that want to counteract these developments with monetary policies find that currency flows outnumber trade flows by more than 60 to 1.

Also, private sector financial flows vastly outnumber the financial flows that can be marshaled by governments, even when acting in concert. The interactions between global and domestic financial flows have severely limited the freedom for governmental action. For example, if the European Central Bank or the Federal Reserve Bank of the United States changes interest rate levels, these changes will not only influence domestic activities, but also trigger international flows of capital that may reduce, enhance, or even negate the domestic effects. Similarly, rapid technological change and vast advances in communication permit firms and countries to quickly emulate innovation and counteract carefully designed plans. As a result, governments are often powerless to implement effective policy measures on their own, even when they know what to do.

Perhaps one of the lasting developments of the global financial crisis will be increased coordination of economic policy by governments. The rise of the G-20 as a forum for economic coordination reflects the need for both increased cooperation among governments and the requirement for a broader involvement than just the major developed nations represented by the G-7. The Leaders' Statement from the April 2009 summit declared: "We will conduct all our economic policies cooperatively and responsibly with regard to the impact on other countries and will refrain from competitive devaluation of our currencies and promote a stable and well-functioning international monetary system."[13]

Governments also find that domestic policy decisions often have major international repercussions. In the United States, for example, in 2009, President Barack Obama guided a restructuring plan for the "American company" General Motors involving a $30 billion investment that made U.S. taxpayers owners of 60 percent of the "new GM" along with the governments of Canada and Ontario, which owned an additional 12.5 percent. The new company would be geared to making cars for a "greener" American consumer. "Of course, GM cannot succeed solely as an American car company. Its industry is among the most competitive in the world. For any firm to prosper, global sales and operations efficiencies are a sine qua non."[14] Indeed, GM's long-term success will be largely dependent upon future sales in growing markets in Brazil, China and other Asian countries. With the divestiture of its Opel division in Europe, GM will be ceding an important car market to the competition.[15]

Legislators around the world are continually confronted with the effects of international links.

FOCUS ON POLITICS

What's Your Beef?

In 2003, after a reported case of Bovine Spongiform Encephalopathy (BSE), or mad cow disease, in the United States and Canada, the governments of Korea and Japan, and more than 30 other countries around the world, imposed bans on most imports of U.S. and Canadian beef. With Japan and Korea representing their second and third largest markets, this was a serious setback for North American beef growers. Australian beef growers quickly took advantage of the situation with Japanese imports of Australian beef increasing by 39 percent in 2004.

The U.S. and Canadian governments and industry groups took aggressive steps to isolate and contain the infection, and no serious outbreak of the disease resulted. With scientific evidence that shipments of beef could not spread BSE, the U.S. and Canadian governments protested the bans as being unreasonable barriers to trade. In 2006, U.S. beef shipments to Japan were resumed under specific provisions that all beef will come from cattle 20 months old or younger and will contain no spinal column or brain tissue. Despite the resumption, U.S. beef sales to Japan have not regained their pre-ban strength.

U.S. and Canadian officials continued to pressure Korea to resume trade in beef. In 2008, President Lee Myung-bak assumed office in Korea with a determination to improve relations with the United States and implement the stalled Korea–U.S. free trade agreement, the passage of which was jeopardized in the U.S. Congress due to the continued ban on beef. In April 2008, President Lee Myung-bak made the decision to lift the ban, triggering huge protests and violent demonstrations in Korea from a coalition of groups opposed to Lee's administration. Many of the protests were fueled by rumors spread by teenagers via text messaging and e-mail that Koreans were genetically more susceptible to BSE. Eventually, an agreement was reached limiting beef imports to come from cattle 30 months old or younger.

In 2009, the United States had become the number two beef exporter to Korea, trailing Australia. Korea's ban on Canadian beef was not lifted, and in 2009, Canada requested that a WTO panel settle the dispute.

Sources: Lauren Johnston, "New Mad Cow Rules Are Leftovers," *CBS News*, December 31, 2003; Martin Fackler, "Japan to Resume Imports of Beef from the U.S.," *New York Times*, June 21, 2006; Choe Sang-Hun, "South Korea Lifts Ban on U.S. Beef," *New York Times*, June 26, 2008.

In some countries, the implications are understood, and new legislation is devised with an understanding of its international consequences. In other nations, legislators often ignore the international repercussions and side effects of their actions. Yet, given the links among economies, this is an unwarranted and sometimes even dangerous view. It threatens to place firms at a competitive disadvantage in the international marketplace or may make it easier for foreign firms to compete in the domestic market.

Even when policymakers want to take decisive steps, they are often unable to do so. In the late 1980s, for example, the United States decided to impose **punitive tariffs** of 100 percent on selected Japanese imports to retaliate for Japanese nonadherence to a previously reached semiconductor agreement. The initial goal was clear. Yet the task became increasingly difficult as the U.S. government developed a list of specific imports to be targeted. In many instances, the U.S. market was heavily dependent on the Japanese imports, which meant that U.S. manufacturers and consumers would be severely affected by punitive tariffs. Many Japanese products are actually produced or assembled in the United States. To halt the importing of components would throw Americans out of work.

Other targeted products were not actually produced in Japan. Rather, Japanese firms had opened plants in third countries, such as Mexico. Penalizing these product imports would therefore punish Mexican workers and affect Mexican employment, an undesirable result.

More and more products were eliminated from the list before it was published. In two days of hearings, additional links emerged. For example, law enforcement agencies testified that if certain fingerprinting equipment from Japan was sanctioned, law enforcement efforts would suffer significantly. Of the $1.8 billion worth of goods initially considered for the sanctions list, the government was barely able to scrape together $300 million worth. Figure 2.1 illustrates how far such links have progressed in the aircraft industry. With so many product components being sourced from different countries around the world, it becomes increasingly difficult to decide what constitutes a domestic product. In light of this uncertainty, policy actions against foreign products become more difficult as well.

Policymakers find themselves with increasing responsibilities, yet with fewer and less effective tools to carry them out. More segments of the domestic economy are vulnerable to international shifts at the same time that they are becoming less controllable. To regain some power to influence policies, some governments have sought to restrict the influence of world trade by erecting barriers, charging tariffs, and implementing import regulations. However, these measures too have been restrained by the existence of international agreements forged through institutions such as the WTO or bilateral negotiations. World trade has therefore changed many previously held notions about the sovereignty of nation-states and extraterritoriality. The same interdependence that made us all more affluent has also left us more vulnerable.

REVITALIZING INTERNATIONAL INSTITUTIONS

The intense links among nations, the new economic environment resulting from the financial crisis, and the growing influence of developing economies have all brought into question the role that traditional international institutions should play.

The formation of the WTO provided the former GATT with new impetus. With 153 member-countries and others lined up to join, the WTO has demonstrated its appeal. The increased use of its dispute settlement mechanism is one sign of the important role that it plays for its members. However, the organization is also

punitive tariff A tax on an imported good or service intended to punish a trading partner.

Figure 2.1   Who Builds the Boeing 787?

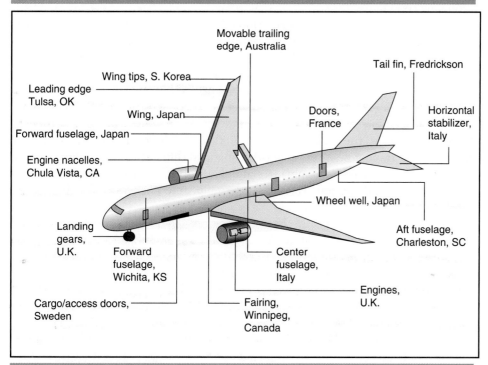

Source: Data compiled from http://www.boeing.com.

confronted with many difficulties. One of them is the result of the organization's success. Historically, a key focus of the WTO's predecessor was on reducing tariffs. With tariff levels at an unprecedented low level, however, attention now has to rest with areas such as nontariff barriers, which are much more complex and indigenous to nations. As a consequence, any emerging dispute is likely to be more heatedly contested and more difficult to resolve.

A more profound challenge to the WTO is the future of the overall multilateral trading system. With the Doha Round stalled and regional agreements multiplying, many are concerned about the future of multilateral trade liberalization and the role and focus of the WTO. With some of its members urging that the WTO introduce "social causes" into trade decisions, reducing barriers to trade would become commingled with issues such as poverty reduction, labor laws, competition, emigration freedoms, food security, provision of health care, freedom of religion, and the safety of animals. The 153 member governments have diverse perspectives, histories, relations, economies, and ambitions. Many of them fear that social causes can be used to devise new rules of protectionism against their exports. Then there is also the question of how much companies—which, after all, are the ones doing the trading and investing—should be burdened with concerns outside their scope.

To be successful, the WTO needs to be able to focus on its core mission, which is the support of international trade and investment. The addition of social causes may appear politically expedient, but it will be a cause for divisiveness and dissent, and thus will inhibit progress on further liberalization of trade and investment. Failure to achieve such progress and a successful conclusion to the Doha Round would leave the WTO without teeth and would negate much of the progress achieved in earlier rounds of negotiations. It might be best to keep the WTO free from such pressures.

Shifts in cultures, values, and ethics can then be the natural outcome of changing economic conditions.[16]

Similar problems confront international financial institutions, which have been even more the focus of criticism and reform efforts. For example, although the **International Monetary Fund (IMF)** (www.imf.org) had functioned well for decades in overseeing the international monetary system and providing macroeconomic and financial policy advice to its members, many of the developing and least-developed economies believe that its lending policies are too austere and inflexible and that the IMF does not fully understand and appreciate their situations and needs. Some critics decry the lack of authority and resources to manage imbalances in financial and trade flows. Yet, given the financial difficulties of so many nations, such as Mexico, Poland, Colombia, Iceland, Hungary, Sri Lanka, and others in sub-Saharan Africa and Central America, there simply are not enough funds to satisfy everyone's needs.

In light of this challenge, the 2009 G-20 Summit in London agreed to strengthen international financial institutions via a tripling of the IMF's lending capacity to $750 billion and provided for a $250 billion allocation of special drawing rights (SDRs), the IMF's international reserve currency. In addition, the leaders pledged "to reform and modernize the international financial institutions to ensure they can assist members and shareholders effectively in the new challenges they face" and followed through in 2010 by substantially increasing the voting shares of China.[17]

Similarly, the **World Bank** (http://www.worldbank.org) successfully met its goal of aiding the reconstruction of Europe but has been less successful in furthering the economic goals of the developing world and the newly emerging market economies in the former Soviet bloc. Some even claim that instead of alleviating poverty, misguided bank policies may have created it.[18] The G-20 appear committed to strengthening international institutions for the new array of economic challenges emanating from a more globalized world. Reforms are needed to ensure that the international financial institutions are able to carry out their important roles in furthering both stabilization and development. German Chancellor Angela Merkel has been particularly vocal in calling for a new institution that would have responsibility for increased supervision of all financial markets. What role current international financial institutions would play to that end remains to be seen.

SHARPENING OF THE CONFLICT BETWEEN INDUSTRIALIZED AND DEVELOPING NATIONS

In the 1960s and 1970s, it was hoped that the developmental gap between the industrialized nations and many countries in the less-developed world would gradually be closed. This goal was to be achieved with the transfer of technology and the major infusion of funds. Even though the 1970s saw vast quantities of petrodollars available for recycling and major growth in borrowing by some developing nations, the results have not been as expected.

Many developing nations had become highly indebted, a burden that frustrated new policies and economic development. Even with substantial debt forgiveness, the severity of the subsequent global financial crisis has caused many developing nations to become increasingly aggressive in their attempts to reshape the ground rules that apply to world trade and investment flows. The lending conditions imposed by the IMF and World Bank have been criticized for injuring developing nations through their dependence on what is termed the Washington Consensus, requiring economic liberalization, financial austerity, and privatization of national industries.[19] Although many policymakers share the view that major changes are necessary to resolve the difficulties that exist, no clear-cut solutions have emerged.

International Monetary Fund (IMF) A specialized agency of the United Nations established in 1944. An international financial institution for dealing with balance of payment problems; the first international monetary authority with at least some degree of power over national authorities.

World Bank An international financial institution created in 1944 to facilitate trade.

On top of these conflict points, an increase in environmental awareness has contributed to a further sharpening of the conflict. Developing nations, with urgent investment needs, may have a different perspective of environmental protection than their developed counterparts. If they are to take measures that will assist the industrialized nations in their environmental goals, they expect to be assisted and rewarded for these efforts. Yet, many in the industrialized world view environmental issues as a "global obligation," rather than as a matter of choice, and are reluctant to compromise.

POLICY RESPONSES TO CHANGING CONDITIONS

4. To understand that nations must cooperate closely in the future to maintain a viable global trade and investment environment

The word *policy* conjures up an image of a well-coordinated set of governmental activities. Unfortunately, in the trade and investment sector, as in most of the domestic policy areas, this is rarely the case. Policymakers need to respond too often to short-term problems, need to worry too much about what is politically salable to multiple constituencies, and in some countries, are in office too short a time to formulate a guiding set of long-term strategies. All too often, because of public and media pressures, policymakers must be concerned with current events—such as monthly trade deficit numbers and investment flow figures—that may not be very meaningful in the larger picture. In such an environment, actions may lead to extraordinarily good tactical measures but fail to achieve long-term success.

RESTRICTIONS OF IMPORTS

In the United States, Congress has a very tumultuous history of dealing with trade issues because these complex issues are often not well understood by voters. An old saying goes that you never get a parade in your home district for voting for free trade and that you might not be reelected. Voters often associate free trade agreements with manufacturers closing factories and cutting jobs. The U.S.–Central American Free Trade Agreement (CAFTA) only passed by two votes in 2005. An increasing protectionist sentiment among members of Congress led to the nonrenewal of the trade promotion authority in 2008 that Congress had provided the president to negotiate trade agreements. As a result, the power of the executive branch of government to improve international trade and investment opportunities for U.S. firms through international negotiations and the relaxation of rules, regulations, and laws has become more restricted.

Worldwide, most countries maintain at least a surface-level conformity with international principles. However, many exert substantial restraints on free trade through import controls and barriers. Some of the more frequently encountered barriers are listed in Table 2.2. They are found particularly in countries that suffer from major trade deficits or major infrastructure problems, causing them to enter into voluntary restraint agreements with trading partners or to selectively apply trade-restricting measures such as tariffs, quotas, or nontariff barriers against trading partners.

Tariffs are taxes based primarily on the value of imported goods and services. A key distinction is the difference between **bound tariffs**, those maximum duties which a country has agreed to in WTO negotiations, and **applied tariffs**, which are those duties that are actually levied by the country. In many instances, countries have, over time, reduced their applied tariffs substantially below the ones they are allowed to charge. In times of economic stress, however, many countries raise their applied tariffs. As long as the increase does not carry the charges beyond the bound tariff level, there is no violation of the WTO rules—yet, the tariff levels creep up

tariffs Taxes on imported goods and services, instituted by governments as a means to raise revenue and as barriers to trade.

bound tariff Duties agreed upon in international negotiations, often higher than those duties actually charged.

applied tariff Duty level actually charged at border crossing.

GLOBAL LAND-OCEAN TEMPERATURE INDEX

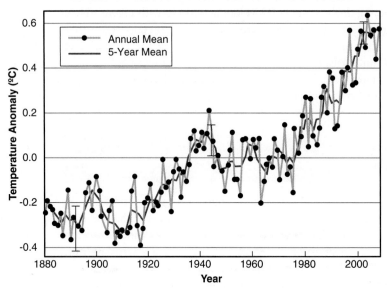

Source: NASA, Goddard Institute for Space Studies Surface Temperature Analysis.

CHANGE OF FOREST AREA FROM 1990 TO 2007

UNITS: %

- −63.33– −30.00
- −29.99–0.00
- 0.01–5.00
- 15.01–45.00
- 45.01–50.00
- No data available

0   2,000   4,000 km

Data Source: FAO
Map Source: UNIGIWG

Last Update: August 2009
Map available at: http//unstats.un.org/unsd/environment/qindicators

Sources: Food and Agriculture Organization of the United Nations (FAO);
United Nations Statistics Division/Environment Statistics.

TOTAL GREENHOUSE GAS EMISSIONS

UNITS: mio. tonnes of CO$_2$ equivalent

- 1,501–7,500
- 751–1,500
- 351–750
- 101–350
- 0–100
- No data available

*Note that data corresponds to the latest year available.

0   2,000   4,000 km

Data Source: UNFCCC/UNSD
Map Source: UNGIWG

Last Update: August 2009
Map available at: http//unstats.un.org/unsd/environment/qindicators

Sources: UN Framework Convention on Climate Change (UNFCCC) Secretariat (see: http://unfccc.int); United Nations, Department of Economic and Social Affairs, Population Division, World Population Prospects: The 2008 Revision, New York, 2009; United Nations Statistics Division/Environment Statistics.

DESERTIFICATION VULNERABILITY

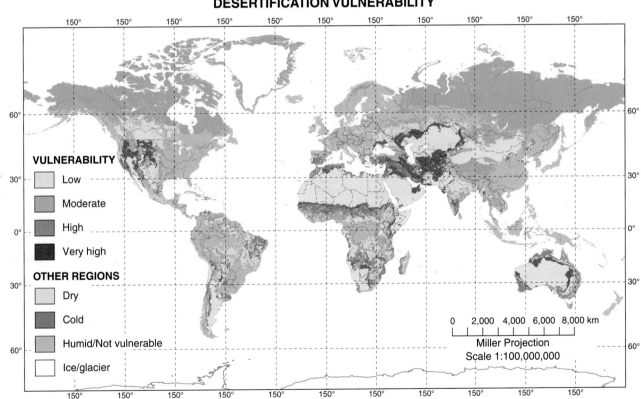

VULNERABILITY
- Low
- Moderate
- High
- Very high

OTHER REGIONS
- Dry
- Cold
- Humid/Not vulnerable
- Ice/glacier

0   2,000   4,000   6,000   8,000 km
Miller Projection
Scale 1:100,000,000

Sources: USDA–Natural Resources Conservation Service, Soil Survey Division, World Soil Resources.

Table 2.2   Trade Barriers
There are literally hundreds of ways to build a barrier. The following list provides just a few of the trade barriers that exporters face.

- Special import authorization
- Restrictions on data processing
- Voluntary export restraints
- Advance import deposits
- Taxes on foreign exchange deals
- Preferential licensing applications
- Excise duties
- Licensing fees
- Discretionary licensing
- Trade restriction on e-commerce
- Anti-competitive practices

- Country quotas
- Testing, labeling
- Seasonal prohibitions
- Health and sanitary prohibitions
- Certification
- Foreign exchange licensing
- Barter and countertrade requirements
- Customs surcharges
- Stamp taxes
- Consular invoice fees
- Taxes on transport

Source: Adapted from Office of the United States Trade Representative, 2009 National Trade Estimate Report on Foreign Trade Barriers, Washington, DC, March 2010.

quotas Legal restrictions on the import quantity of particular goods, imposed by governments as barriers to trade.

nontariff barriers Barriers to trade, other than tariffs. Examples include buy-domestic campaigns, preferential treatment for domestic bidders, and restrictions on market entry of foreign products such as involved inspection procedures.

voluntary restraint agreements Trade-restraint agreements resulting in self-imposed restrictions not covered by WTO rules; used to manage or distort trade flows. For example, Japanese restraints on the export of cars to the United States, often the direct result of trade measure threats.

antidumping Laws that many countries use to impose tariffs on foreign imports. They are designed to help domestic industries that are injured by competition from abroad due to imported products being sold at low prices.

substantially, thus increasing the cost of and barriers to trade. **Quotas** are restrictions on the number of foreign products that can be imported. **Nontariff barriers** consist of a variety of measures such as testing, certification, or simply bureaucratic hurdles that have the effect of restricting imports. All of these measures tend to raise the price of imported goods. They therefore constitute a transfer of funds from the buyers (or, if absorbed by them, the sellers) of imports to the government and—if accompanied by price increases of competing domestic products—to the domestic producers of such products. Even though there has been a global drive toward decreasing tariffs and other trade barriers, Focus on Politics demonstrates how and why some countries are slow to implement agreed-upon reductions of barriers.

Voluntary restraint agreements are designed to help domestic industries reorganize, restructure, and recapture production prominence. Even though officially voluntary, these agreements are usually implemented through severe threats against trading partners. Due to their "voluntary" nature, the agreements are not subject to any previously negotiated bilateral or multilateral trade accords.

When nations do not resort to the subtle mechanism of voluntary agreements to affect trade flows, they often impose tariffs and quotas. Many countries use **antidumping** laws to impose tariffs on imports. Antidumping laws are designed to help domestic industries that are injured by unfair competition from abroad due to products being "dumped" on them. Dumping may involve selling goods overseas at prices lower than those in the exporter's home market or at a price below the cost of production or both. The growing use of antidumping measures by governments around the world complicates the pricing decisions of exporters. Large domestic firms, on the other hand, can use the antidumping process to obtain strategic shelter from foreign competitors.[20]

For example, in 1983, the International Trade Commission imposed a five-year tariff on Japanese heavy motorcycles imported into the United States. The 49.4 percent duty was granted at the request of Harley-Davidson, which could no longer compete with the heavily discounted bikes being imported by companies such as Honda and Kawasaki. The gradually declining tariff gave Harley-Davidson the time to enact new management strategies. Within four years, Harley-Davidson was back on its feet and again had the highest market share in the heavyweight class of bikes. In 1987, Harley-Davidson officials requested that the tariff be lifted a year early. As a result, the policy was labeled a success. However, at no time were the costs of these measures to U.S. consumers even considered.

Mexican Trucks and American Safety

When the North American Free Trade Agreement (NAFTA) went into effect in 1994, an important provision was left unfulfilled. Under NAFTA, the U.S. and Mexican governments agreed to give trucks from each country equal access to deliver goods in the neighboring country and return home with new goods. However, American labor unions, environmentalists, and other activists objected to this provision, citing safety issues, environmental risks, and threats to American jobs. In 1995, the Clinton administration banned Mexican trucks outside of a 20-mile commercial zone north of the border on the grounds that Mexican trucks did not conform to U.S. safety standards. Concerns about U.S. schoolchildren being run over by Mexican trucks filled the airwaves.

Mexico appealed to a NAFTA panel in 1995 that the United States was in violation of its NAFTA commitments. That panel ruled in Mexico's favor in 2001. With the George W. Bush administration being strongly supportive of free trade and NAFTA, the White House was willing to lift the ban and comply with the panel's findings. Preemptively, the U.S. Senate voted to impose tough safety inspections on Mexican trucks at the border, generally more stringent than those required for Canadian trucks. Undaunted, in 2002, President Bush ordered the border opened to Mexican trucking, but the implementation of his decision became tied-up in court procedures brought by opponents. A 2003 ruling by the California Ninth U.S. Circuit Court of Appeals mandated an environmental impact study. In 2004, the U.S. Supreme Court, in a unanimous decision, overturned the lower court's decision, finding that the president had the power to open U.S. borders to Mexican trucks.

Yet the Bush administration still faced heated opposition on the issue from numerous groups. Some opponents of the plan accused the Bush administration of planning the construction of a "North American Super Highway" that would be filled with Mexican trucks bringing cheaper Asian imports into the country from Mexican ports. Opposition became very heated in 2006 and 2007 as some claimed that any Mexican trucks pilot program was a component of a larger political integration plan to take NAFTA further and create a North American Union.

In September 2007, a one-year pilot program, which was later extended for an additional two years, was announced. This program provided for up to 100 Mexican trucking companies approved by the U.S. Department of Transportation to operate on U.S. highways. American truckers were allowed to operate anywhere within Mexico. Proponents of the program argued that the plan would improve efficiency at the border crossings, eliminate the requirements for changing trucks within the commercial zone, and result in reduced prices for consumers.

Even though the pilot program found no significant safety issues, opposition to Mexican trucks operating in the United States remained. In March 2009, President Obama signed an omnibus spending bill that ended funding for the pilot program after Congress continued to express safety concerns. In retaliation, the government of Mexico imposed $2.4 billion in tariffs on 89 U.S. products entering Mexico, claiming that the United States' ending of the pilot program "is not, and never has been, about the safety of American roads. It is about protectionism plain and simple."

U.S. companies including Procter & Gamble, Mary Kay Cosmetics, Caterpillar, Smithfield Foods, and PepsiCo quickly organized to fight the tariffs. The Alliance to Keep U.S. Jobs pressed President Obama to end the standoff with Mexico. In an April 2009 meeting with President Calderón of Mexico, Obama promised that he would work to resolve the crisis, stating, "The last thing we want to do at a time when the global economy is contracting and trade is shrinking is to resort to protectionist measures." In a later meeting in August 2009, the two leaders again addressed the issue as Calderón told Obama that the dispute has hurt trade and jobs and raised consumer costs. Obama promised to find a solution and resolve the dispute. By March of 2010, the U.S. Congress had still not passed legislation to resolve the dispute.

Sources: Philip Shenon, "Senate Backs Strict Safety Tests for Mexican Trucks in U.S.," *New York Times*, July 27, 2001; Gretel C. Kovach, "For Mexican Trucks, a Road into the U.S.," *New York Times*, September 9, 2007; Nicholas Johnston and Jens Erik Gould, "Obama Promises Solution to U.S.-Mexico Trucking Spat (Update1)," Bloomberg.net, August 10, 2009; David Alexander, Adriana Barrera, Mica Rosenberg, and Xavier Briand, "Obama Hopeful of Fixing Truck Dispute with Mexico," *Reuters*, April 17, 2009.

Imports are also restricted by nontariff barriers. These consist of buy-domestic campaigns, preferential treatment for domestic bidders compared with foreign bidders, national standards that are not comparable to international standards, and an emphasis on the design rather than the performance of products. Such nontariff barriers are often the most insidious obstacles to free trade, because they are difficult to detect, hard to quantify, and demands for their removal are often blocked by references to a nation's cultural and historic heritage.

Another way in which imports are reduced is by tightening market access and entry of foreign products through involved procedures and inspections. Probably the most famous are the measures implemented by France. In order to stop or at least reduce the importation of foreign video recorders, the French government ruled that all of them had to be sent to the customs station at Poitiers. This customhouse was located away from major transport routes, woefully understaffed, and open only a few days each week. In addition, the few customs agents at Poitiers insisted on opening each package separately to inspect the merchandise. Within a few weeks, imports of video recorders came to a halt. Members of the French government, however, were able to point to the fact that they had not restrained trade at all; rather, they had only made some insignificant changes in the procedures of domestic governmental actions.

The Effects of Import Restriction

Policymakers are faced with several problems when trying to administer import controls. First, most of the time such controls exact a huge price from domestic consumers. Import controls may mean that the most efficient sources of supply are not available. The result is either second-best products or higher costs for restricted supplies, which in turn cause customer service standards to drop and consumers to pay significantly higher prices. Even though these costs may be widely distributed among many consumers and are less obvious, the social cost of these controls may be damaging to the economy and subject to severe attack from individuals. However, these attacks are countered by pressure from protected groups that benefit from import restrictions. For example, while citizens of the European Union may be forced by import controls to pay an elevated price for all the agricultural products they consume, agricultural producers in the region benefit from higher incomes. Achieving a proper trade-off is often difficult, if not impossible, for the policymaker.

A second major problem resulting from import controls is the downstream change in the composition of imports that may result. For example, if the importation of copper ore is restricted, through either voluntary restraints or quotas, producing countries may opt to shift their production systems and produce copper wire instead, which they can export. As a result, initially narrowly defined protectionistic measures may snowball in order to protect one downstream industry after another.

Farmers and agriculture have a major influence on the trade policy.

© Zuma/NewsCom

Another major problem that confronts the policymaker is that of efficiency. Import controls designed to provide breathing room to a domestic industry so it can either grow or recapture its competitive position often do not work. Rather than improve the productivity of an industry, such controls may provide it with a level of safety and a cushion of increased income, subsequently causing it to lag behind in technological advancements.

One must also be aware of possible responses to import restrictions. In order to protect their own industries, governments may retaliate against restrictions by erecting similar barriers at home. The result can be a gradually escalating set of trade obstacles. For example, in 2009, in **retaliation** for continued European Union restrictions on U.S. hormone-fed beef, the United States imposed punitive tariffs on Roquefort cheese from France and a list of other European products.

Corporations can also make strategic use of such barriers by incorporating them into their business plans and exploiting them in order to gain market share. For example, some multinational corporations have pressed governments to initiate antidumping actions against their competitors when faced with low-priced imports. In such instances, corporations substitute **administrative shelter** obtained through adroit handling of government relations for innovation and competitiveness.

Finally, corporations also can circumvent import restrictions by shifting their activities. For example, instead of conducting trade, corporations can shift to foreign direct investment. The result may be a drop in trade inflow, yet the domestic industry may still be under strong pressure from foreign firms. The investments of Japanese car producers in the United States serve as an example. However, due to the job-creation effects of such investment, such shifts may have been the driving desire on the part of the policymakers who implemented the import controls.

retaliation The trade or investment policy response to one nation's or group of nations' trade actions or restrictions, undertaken by another nation or group of nations in order to demonstrate displeasure or to seek retribution and change for this action.

administrative shelter Protecting firms through laws and regulations.

RESTRICTIONS OF EXPORTS

In addition to imposing restraints on imports, nations also control their exports. The reasons are short supply, national security and foreign policy purposes, or the desire to retain capital. National security and foreign policy controls are covered in Chapter 6 on politics and laws later in the book. Here, we will address export restrictions imposed for economic purposes.

Export restrictions are used by some countries to help provide local consumers with access to agricultural products and commodities at lower prices. Such actions are particularly frequent in times of shortages. Because export markets allow better pricing and profits, these actions can cause serious opposition from farmers and owners of commodities. They may even trigger resistance to such restrictions or cause production shifts to other goods for better prices. In 2008, Argentine farmers and ranchers set up road blocks to prevent grain and cattle shipments from reaching local markets to protest a new tax on soybeans and export restrictions on farm goods.

EXPORT PROMOTION

The desire to increase participation in international trade and investment flows has led nations to implement export promotion programs. These programs are designed primarily to help domestic firms enter and maintain their position in international markets and to match or counteract similar export promotion efforts by other

Table 2.3	Estimated Government Export Promotion Spending of the U.S. and Selected Major Trading Partners							
Spending per Thousand Dollars of Total Exports								
Spain	United Kingdom	Italy	France	Korea	Canada	Japan	United States	Germany
$0.83	$0.75	$0.69	$0.43	$0.34	$0.33	$0.30	$0.21	$0.11

Note: Figures exclude trade financing and agricultural trade promotion.

Source: Foreign government sources, U.S. Commercial Service estimates, and World Trade Organization data.

nations. Every day, new firms are beginning to learn about the international market and are running into barriers to international trade. For example, in any given year, a number of exporters will stop exporting, while many nonexporters will enter the global market. The most critical juncture for firms is when they begin or cease exporting, which is where export promotion has its greatest impact.

Most governments supply some support to their firms participating or planning to participate in international trade. While such support is widespread and growing, its intensity varies by country as Table 2.3 shows.

Governments have developed various approaches toward export promotion. One focus is on knowledge transfer to enable greater competence within firms. Here, governments offer either export service programs or market development programs. Service programs typically consist of seminars for potential exporters, export counseling, and "how to export" handbooks. Market development programs provide sales leads to local firms, and offer participation in foreign trade shows, preparation of market analyses and export newsletters. Within each category, program efforts can provide informational knowledge (of a "how to" nature) or experiential (how-do) knowledge that provides hands-on exposure.

A second export-promotion approach deals with direct or indirect subsidization of export activities. For example, low-cost export financing can produce an attractive and competitive offer, particularly for large sales that are paid over time, such as airplanes or power plants. Exports are also supported by lower tax rates for export earnings and favorable insurance rates. The overall focus of these subsidized activities is to increase the profitability of exporting to the firm, either by reducing the risks or by increasing the rewards.

A third approach to export promotion consists of reducing governmental red tape for exporters. For instance, the requirements for multiple export licenses or permits issued by various government agencies and the imposition of technology export controls constitute impediments to exporting, which the government can remove, thus stimulating an increase in exports. Similarly, the reduction of antitrust concerns in the export arena has led to the formation of (export) trading firms, which are able to share facilities and expertise without the threat of government intervention.[21]

Another area of activity by governments is export financing. Special export-import banks provide firms with long-term loans and loan guarantees so that they can bid on international contracts where financing is a key issue. In response to actions by foreign competitors, banks also resort to offering **mixed aid credits**. The credits, which take the form of loans composed partially of commercial interest rates and partially of highly subsidized developmental aid interest rates, result in very low interest loans to exporters.

mixed aid credits Credits at rates composed partially of commercial interest rates and partially of highly subsidized developmental aid interest rates.

The key dimensions to consider are that (potential) exporters either need a reduction in risk or an increase in rewards to be more engaged in exporting. Any promotion program needs to have these two forces in mind, which are the ones driving business. The implementation then becomes a matter of preferences, ability and resources.

Any export promotion raises several questions. One concerns the justification of the expenditure of public funds for what is essentially an activity that should be driven by profits. It appears, however, that the start-up cost for international operations, particularly for smaller firms, may be sufficiently high to warrant some kind of government support.[22] A second question focuses on the capability of government to provide such support. Both for the selection and reach of firms as well as the distribution of support, government is not necessarily better equipped than the private sector to do a good job. A third issue concerns competitive export promotion. If countries provide such support to their firms, they may well distort the flow of trade. If other countries then increase their support of firms in order to counteract the effects, all that results is the same volume of trade activity, but at subsidized rates. It is therefore important to carefully evaluate export promotion activities as to their effectiveness and competitive impact. Perhaps such promotion is only beneficial when it addresses existing market gaps.

Overall, export promotion will only comprise a small fraction of any national budget and directly support only a minute portion of exports. It cannot be the role of export promotion to directly support all export activities. Rather, export promotion needs to initiate activities, to blaze trails with new approaches and experimentation, and highlight new ways of overcoming hurdles. Perhaps one should characterize export promotion funds as the venture capital of international economic activity.

IMPORT PROMOTION

Some countries have also developed import promotion measures. The measures are implemented primarily by nations that have accumulated and maintained large balance-of-trade surpluses. They hope to allay other nations' fears of continued imbalances and to gradually redirect trade flows.

Japan, for example, has completely refurbished the operations of the Japan External Trade Organization (JETRO) (www.jetro.org). This organization, which initially was formed to encourage Japanese exports, has now begun to focus on the promotion of imports to Japan. It organizes trade missions of foreign firms coming to Japan, hosts special exhibits and fairs within Japan, and provides assistance and encouragement to potential importers.

INVESTMENT POLICIES

The discussion of policy actions has focused thus far on merchandise trade. Similar actions are applicable to investment flows and, by extension, to international trade in services. In order to protect ownership, control, and development of domestic industries, many countries attempt to influence investment capital flows. Most frequently, investment-screening agencies decide on the merits of any particular foreign investment project. Canada, for example, has "Investment Canada," an agency that scrutinizes foreign investments.[23] So do most developing nations, where special government permission must be obtained for investment projects. This permission frequently carries with it certain conditions, such as levels of ownership permitted, levels of dividends that can be repatriated, numbers of jobs that must be created, or the extent to which management can be carried out by individuals from abroad. The United States restricts foreign investment in instances where national security or related concerns are at stake. Major foreign investments may be reviewed by the **Committee on Foreign Investments in the United States (CFIUS)**.

Committee on Foreign Investments in the United States (CFIUS) A federal committee, chaired by the U.S. Treasury, with the responsibility to review major foreign investments to determine whether national security or related concerns are at stake.

Table 2.4	**Positive and Negative Impacts of Foreign Direct Investment on Host Countries**

Positive Impact

1. Capital formation
2. Technology and management skills transfer
3. Regional and sectoral development
4. Internal competition and entrepreneurship
5. Favorable effect on balance of payments
6. Increased employment

Negative Impact

1. Industrial dominance
2. Technological dependence
3. Disturbance of economic plans
4. Cultural change
5. Interference by home government of multinational corporation

Sources: Jack N. Behrman, *National Interests and the Multinational Enterprise* (Englewood Cliffs, NJ: Prentice Hall, 1970), Chapters 2 through 5; Jack N. Behrman, *Industrial Policies: International Restructuring and Transnationals* (Lexington, MA: Lexington Books, 1984), Chapter 5; and Christopher M. Korth, *International Business* (Englewood Cliffs, NJ: Prentice Hall, 1985), Chapters 12 and 13.

THE HOST-COUNTRY PERSPECTIVE

The host government is caught in a love-hate relationship with foreign direct investment. On the one hand, the host country has to appreciate the various contributions, especially economic, that the foreign direct investment will make. On the other hand, fears of dominance, interference, and dependence are often voiced and acted on. The major positive and negative impacts are summarized in Table 2.4.

The Positive Impact

Foreign direct investment has contributed greatly to world development in the past 40 years. Said Lord Lever, a British businessman who served in the cabinets of Harold Wilson and James Callaghan, "Europe got twenty times more out of American investment after the war than the multinationals did; every country gains by productive investment."[24]

Capital flows are especially beneficial to countries with limited domestic sources and restricted opportunities to raise funds in the world's capital markets. In addition, foreign direct investment may attract local capital to a project for which local capital alone would not have sufficed.

knowledge transfer The movement, communication, and implementation of insights and information across international borders between individuals, organizations, or corporate units.

Foreign direct investment is closely linked to **knowledge transfer**. Such transfer includes the introduction of not only new hardware to the market but also the techniques and skills to operate it. In industries where the role of intellectual property is substantial, such as pharmaceuticals or software development, access to parent companies' research and development provides benefits that may be far greater than those gained through infusion of capital. This explains the interest that many governments have expressed in having multinational corporations establish R&D facilities in their countries.

An integral part of knowledge transfer is managerial skills, which are the most significant labor component of foreign direct investment. With the growth of the service sector, many economies need skills rather than expatriate personnel to perform the tasks.

Foreign direct investment can be used effectively in developing a geographical region or a particular industry sector. Foreign direct investment is one of the most expedient ways in which unemployment can be reduced in chosen regions of a country.

Furthermore, the costs of establishing an industry are often too prohibitive and the time needed too excessive for the domestic industry, even with governmental help, to try it on its own. In many developing countries, foreign direct investment may be a way to diversify the industrial base and thereby reduce the country's dependence on one or a few sectors.

At the company level, foreign direct investment may intensify competition and result in benefits to the economy as a whole as well as to consumers through increased productivity and possibly lower prices. Competition typically introduces new techniques, goods and services, and ideas to the markets. It may improve existing patterns of how business is done.

Four Thai students are enjoying their cups of coffee at their Bangkok Starbucks.

The major impact of such investment on the balance of payments is long term. Import substitution, export earnings, and subsidized imports of technology and management all assist the host nation on the trade account side of the balance of payments. Not only may a new production facility substantially decrease the need to import the type of products manufactured, but it may start earning export revenue as well. Several countries, such as Brazil, have imposed export requirements as a precondition for foreign direct investment. On the capital account side, foreign direct investment may have short-term impact in lowering a deficit as well as long-term impact in keeping capital at home that otherwise could have been invested or transferred abroad. However, measurement is difficult because significant portions of the flows may miss—or evade—the usual government reporting channels.

Jobs are often the most obvious reason to cheer for foreign direct investment. In the United States, foreign companies directly employ 5.3 million Americans, and indirectly create opportunities for millions more.[25] The benefits reach far beyond mere employment. Salaries paid by multinational corporations are usually higher than those paid by domestic firms. For example, in the United States, domestic employees of the subsidiaries of foreign firms receive on average a 32 percent higher salary than do their counterparts employed by domestic firms.[26]

The creation of jobs translates also into the training and development of a skilled workforce. Consider, for example, the situation of many Caribbean states that are dependent on tourism for their well-being. In most cases, multinational hotel chains have been instrumental in establishing a pool of trained hospitality workers and managers.

All of the benefits discussed are indeed possible advantages of foreign direct investment. Their combined effect can lead to an overall enhancement in the standard of living in the market as well as an increase in the host country's access to the world market and its international competitiveness. It is equally possible, however, that the impact can be negative rather than positive.

The Negative Impact

Although some of the threats posed by multinational corporations and foreign direct investment in terms of stunted economic development, low levels of research and development, and poor treatment of local employees are exaggerated, in many countries some industrial sectors are dominated by foreign-owned entities.

Foreign direct investment most often is concentrated in technology-intensive industries. Therefore, research and development is another area of tension. Multinational corporations usually want to concentrate their R&D efforts, especially their basic research. With its knowledge transfer, the multinational corporation can assist

brain drain A migration of professional people from one country to another, usually for the purpose of improving their incomes or living conditions.

the host country's economic development, but it may leave that country dependent on flows of new and updated knowledge. Furthermore, the multinational firm may contribute to the **brain drain** by attracting scientists from host countries to its central research facility. Many countries have demanded and received research facilities on their soil, where they can better control results. They are weary of the technological dominance of the United States and Japan and view it as a long-term threat. Western European nations, for example, have joined forces in basic research and development under the auspices of the EUREKA project, which is a pan-European pooling of resources to develop new technologies with both governmental and private sector help.

The economic benefits of foreign direct investment are controversial as well. Capital inflows may be accompanied by outflows in a higher degree and over a longer term than is satisfactory to the host government. For example, hotels built in the Caribbean by multinational chains often were unable to find local suppliers. They imported supplies and thus spent much-needed foreign currency. Many officials also complain that the promised training of local personnel, especially for management positions, has never taken place. Rather than stimulate local competition and encourage entrepreneurship, multinationals with their often superior product offering and marketing skills have stifled competition. Many countries have found that even if available, multinational companies do not necessarily want to rely on local suppliers but rather bring along their own from their domestic market.

Governments may also see multinationals as a disturbance to their economic planning. Decisions are made concerning their economy over which they have little or no control. Host countries do not look favorably on a multinational that may want to keep the import content of a product high, especially when local suppliers may be available.

Multinational companies tend to be agents of change. They may alter the way business is conducted. They cause change in the lifestyles of the consumers in markets. The extent to which this is welcomed or accepted varies by country. For example, the introduction of fast-food restaurants to Taiwan dramatically altered eating patterns, especially of teenagers, who made these outlets extremely popular and profitable. Concern has been expressed about the health effects of these changes and the higher relative cost of eating in such establishments.

The multinational corporation will also have an impact on business practices. Multinationals may engage in practices that are alien to the local workforce, such as greater flexibility in work rules. Older operators in Japan, for example, may be removed from production lines to make room for more productive employees. In other countries, tradition and union rules may prevent this.

Some host nations have expressed concern over the possibility of interference, economically and politically, by the home government of the multinational corporation; that is, they fear that the multinational may be used as an instrument of political influence.[27]

Of course, the multinational firm is subject not only to the home government's political and economic directions but also to those of the host government and other groups. Fixed investments by multinationals can be held hostage by a host country in trying to win concessions from other governments.

Countries engage in informal evaluation of foreign direct investment, both outbound and inbound. Canada, for example, uses the Foreign Investment Review Agency to determine whether foreign-owned companies are good corporate citizens. Sweden reviews outbound foreign direct investment in terms of its impact on the home country, especially employment.

THE HOME-COUNTRY PERSPECTIVE

Most of the aspects of foreign direct investment that concern host countries apply to the home country as well. Foreign direct investment means increases in the home country's gross domestic product from profits, royalties, and fees remitted by affiliates. Intracompany transfers bring about additional exports. Many countries, in promoting foreign direct investment, see it as a means to stimulate economic growth—an end that would expand export markets and serve other goals, such as political motives, as well. Some countries, such as China, have tried to gain preferential access to raw materials by purchasing firms that owned the deposits. Other factors of production can be obtained through foreign direct investment as well. Companies today look to establish research and development (R&D) facilities in various global locations to take advantage of existing concentrations of intellectual excellence and skills and to be closer to markets. For example, Siemens, a German company, commits more than $5 billion and 45,000 employees to R&D in 13 corporate R&D centers in eight countries around the world.[28]

A major negative issue centers on employment. Many unions point not only to outright job loss but also to the effect on imports and exports. The most controversial have been investments in plants in developing countries that export back to the home countries. Multinationals such as electronics manufacturers, who have moved plants to southeast Asia and Mexico have justified this as a necessary cost-cutting competitive measure.

Another critical issue is that of knowledge advantage. Some critics state that, by establishing plants abroad or forming joint ventures with foreign entities, the country may be giving away its competitive position in the world marketplace. This is especially true when the recipients may be able to avoid the time and expense involved in developing new knowledge.

RESTRICTIONS ON INVESTMENT

Many nations also restrict exports of capital, because **capital flight** is a major problem for them. Particularly in situations where countries lack necessary foreign exchange reserves, governments are likely to place restrictions on capital outflow. In essence, government claims to have higher priorities for capital than its citizens. They, in turn, often believe that the return on investment or the safety of the capital is not sufficiently ensured in their own countries. The reason may be governmental measures or domestic economic factors, such as inflation. These holders of capital want to invest abroad. By doing so, however, they deprive their domestic economy of much-needed investment funds.

Once governments impose restrictions on the export of funds, the desire to transfer capital abroad only increases. Because companies and individuals are ingenious in their efforts to achieve capital flight, governments, particularly in developing countries, continue to suffer. In addition, few new outside investors will enter the country because they fear that dividends and profits will not be remitted easily.

INVESTMENT PROMOTION

Many countries also implement policy measures to attract foreign direct investment. These policies can be the result of the needs of poorer countries to attract additional foreign capital to fuel economic growth without taking out more loans that call for fixed schedules of repayment.[29] Industrialized nations also participate in these efforts since governments are under pressure to provide jobs for their citizens and have come to recognize that foreign direct investment can serve as a major means to increase employment and income. Focus on Politics reports on some of the investment promotion efforts undertaken by governments. In the United States, the Department of Commerce hosts "Invest in America," the federal initiative to promote international investment. Typically, however, most investment promotion is an area of hot competition among state and local governments.

capital flight The rapid flow of private funds abroad because investors believe that the return on investment or the safety of capital is not sufficiently ensured in their own countries.

Money Buys Investments

Once the hub of the U.S. textile industry, the southern states of Alabama, Tennessee, and Mississippi have reinvented their economies and are fast becoming the epicenter of the worldwide auto manufacturing industry. In the late 1970s, threatened changes in U.S. trade policy forced foreign carmakers selling to American consumers to relocate manufacturing operations to the United States. Eager to attract foreign auto plants, the southern states offered millions of dollars in incentives packages that include massive tax breaks, new infrastructure, and extensive job training programs. Mississippi approved a $295 million package to host Nissan and later $358 million for a new Toyota plant. Alabama offered incentives worth $158 million to Honda and $119 million to Mercedes-Benz. The reward? High-paying, skilled jobs and a thriving economy.

Individual U.S. states have investment agencies with offices in Europe and Asia that court foreign investors, offering cash incentives for job creation in their states. In 2007, Alabama granted ThyssenKrupp $810 million in subsidies to build a steel mill near Mobile that is expected to generate approximately 30,000 direct jobs and a $140 million package to Canada's National Steel Car for a railcar factory expected to create up to 1,800 jobs.

To control competition among European countries, the European Union maintains strict rules covering incentives. For example, Ireland's low corporate tax rate of 10 percent, which lured a number of firms, was seen as unfair by the rest of Europe, and Irish officials raised it to 12.5 percent. Potential investors are required to prenotify subsidies of the European Commission.

In the European Union, the competition for foreign investors is fierce. Britain lured LG, a South Korea electronics firm, by paying $48,600 for each of 6,000 jobs created. France paid more than $55,000 per job to get Mercedes-Benz's Swatch auto plant to locate in its eastern region of Lorraine. In 2008, Dell completed a new factory, bringing more than 1,800 new jobs to Lodz, Poland, but this came at the cost of 1,900 jobs in its Limerick, Ireland, operations. The European Commission is investigating a reported €52.7 million incentive package offered by Poland.

When countries such as China and Mexico offer low-cost locations for production, developed economies feel compelled to counter with other kinds of incentives, often designed to attract investment to targeted regions of the country. By offering incentive packages, Curitiba, 250 miles from São Paolo, has become Brazil's second-largest auto center. Manufacturers who invest in eastern Germany can obtain cash worth up to 50 percent of their capital investment. Changwon, South Korea, offers cheap loans and tax rebates to foreign manufacturers.

Governments engage in the hottest competition for so-called green industries and high-tech computer and electronic companies. With countries engaged in a bidding war for multinational investment, smaller nations face the prospect of being outspent by bigger competitors. Despite the high cost of the handouts, no country wants to miss the opportunity to gain job growth and modernized industry, especially when plagued by high unemployment.

Sources: Sue Anne Pressley, "The South's New Car Smell," *Washington Post*, May 11, 2001; Weld Royal, "Money for Jobs," *Industry Week*, April 3, 2000; Laura Hipp, "Toyota Package May Be a Bargain," *The Clarion-Ledger*, March 1, 2007; Andras Gergely and Gareth Jones, "In Dell Move, A Tale of Two Cities," *New York Times*, November 7, 2008; Richard Wilson, "EC to Investigate State Aid for Dell PC Plant in Poland," *Electronicsweekly.com*, December 11, 2008.

---

fiscal incentives Incentives used to attract foreign direct investment that provide specific tax measures to attract the investor.

financial incentives Monetary offers intended to motivate; special funding designed to attract foreign direct investors that may take the form of land or buildings, loans, or loan guarantees.

nonfinancial incentives Nonmonetary offers intended to motivate; special offers designed to attract foreign direct investors that may take the form of guaranteed government purchases, special protection from competition, or improved infrastructure facilities.

Incentives used by policymakers to facilitate such investments are mainly of three types: fiscal, financial, and nonfinancial. **Fiscal incentives** are specific tax measures designed to attract the foreign investor. They typically consist of special depreciation allowances, tax credits or rebates, special deductions for capital expenditures, tax holidays, and the reduction of tax burdens on the investor. **Financial incentives** offer special funding for the investor by providing, for example, land or buildings, loans, and loan guarantees. **Nonfinancial incentives** can consist of guaranteed government purchases; special protection from competition through tariffs, import quotas, and local content requirements; and investments in infrastructure facilities.

All of these incentives are designed primarily to attract more industry and therefore create more jobs. They may slightly alter the advantage of a region and therefore make it more palatable for the investor to choose to invest there. By themselves, they are unlikely to spur an investment decision if proper market conditions do not exist.

Investment promotion policies may succeed in luring new industries to a location and in creating new jobs, but they may also have several drawbacks. For example, when countries compete for foreign investment, several of them may offer more or less the same investment package. The slight advantage that the incentives of one country may have over another's package generally makes little difference in the investment site selected.[30] Moreover, investment policies aimed at attracting foreign direct investment may occasionally place established domestic firms at a disadvantage if they do not receive any support.

MANAGEMENT OF THE POLICY RELATIONSHIP

Arguments for and against foreign direct investment are endless. Costs and benefits must be weighed. Only the multinational corporation itself can assess expected gains against perceived risks in its overseas commitments. At the same time, only the host and home countries can assess benefits realized against costs in terms of their national priorities. If these entities cannot agree on objectives because their most basic interests are in conflict, they cannot agree on the means either. In most cases, the relationship between the parties is not necessarily based on logic, fairness, or equity, but on the relative bargaining power of each. Political changes may cause rapid changes in host government–MNC relations.

The bargaining positions of the multinational corporation and the host country change over time. The course of these changes is summarized in Figure 2.2. The multinational wields its greatest power before the investment is actually made; in the negotiation period, it can require a number of incentives over a period of time. Whether or not the full cycle of events takes place depends on developments in the market as well as the continued bargaining strength of the multinational.

The multinational corporation can maintain its bargaining strength by developing a local support system through local financing, procurement, and business contracts as well as by maintaining control over access to technology and markets. The first approach attempts to gain support from local market entities if discriminating actions by the government take place. The second approach aims to make the operation of the affiliate impossible without the contribution of the parent.

Host countries, on the other hand, try to enhance their role by instituting control policies and performance requirements. Governments attempt to prevent the integration of activities among affiliates and control by the parent. In this effort,

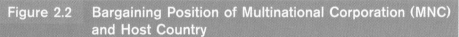

Figure 2.2   Bargaining Position of Multinational Corporation (MNC) and Host Country

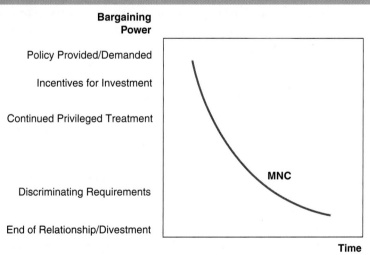

Sources: Thomas A. Poynter, "Managing Government Intervention: A Strategy for Defending the Subsidy," *Columbia Journal of World Business* 21 (winter 1986): 55–65; and Christopher M. Korth, *International Business* (Englewood Cliffs, NJ: Prentice Hall, 1985), 350.

they exclude or limit foreign participation in certain sectors of the economy and require local participation in the ownership and management of the entities established. The extent of this participation will vary by industry, depending on how much the investment is needed by the host economy. Performance requirements typically are programs aimed at established foreign investors in an economy. These often are such discriminatory policies as local content requirements, export requirements, limits on foreign payments (especially profit repatriation), and demands concerning the type of technology transferred or the sophistication and level of operation engaged in. In some cases, demands of this type have led to firms packing their bags. For example, Coca-Cola left India when the government demanded access to what the firm considered to be confidential intellectual property. Only India's free-market reforms have brought Coca-Cola and many other investors back to the country. On their part, governments can, as a last resort, expropriate the affiliate, especially if they believe that the benefits are greater than the cost.[31] Host-country policies on **intellectual property rights (IPR)** can also have an important influence on foreign investment decisions. For example, global pharmaceutical firms approach investments in China cautiously because of patent risks. It is estimated that about 97 percent of drugs produced by local Chinese companies are either generics or counterfeits.[32]

intellectual property right (IPR) Legal right resulting from industrial, scientific, literary, or artistic activity.

A STRATEGIC OUTLOOK FOR TRADE AND INVESTMENT POLICIES

5. To understand what polices are needed to achieve a growing, viable global trade and investment environment

All countries have international trade and investment policies. The importance and visibility of these policies have grown dramatically as international trade and investment flows have become more relevant to the well-being of most nations. Given the growing links among nations, it will be increasingly difficult to consider domestic policy without looking at international repercussions.

A U.S. PERSPECTIVE

protectionistic legislation A trade policy that restricts trade between (to or from) one country and another.

The U.S. need is for a positive trade policy rather than reactive, ad hoc responses to specific situations. **Protectionistic legislation** can be helpful, provided it is not enacted. Proposals in Congress, for example, can be quite useful as bargaining chips in international negotiations. If passed and signed into law, however, protectionistic legislation can result in the destruction of the international trade and investment framework.

It has been suggested that a variety of regulatory agencies could become involved in administering U.S. trade policy. Although such agencies could be useful from the standpoint of addressing narrowly defined grievances, they carry the danger that commercial policy will be determined by a new chorus of discordant voices. Shifting the power of setting trade and investment policy from the executive branch to agencies or even states could give the term *New Federalism* a quite unexpected meaning and might cause progress at the international negotiation level to grind to a halt. No U.S. negotiator can expect to retain the goodwill of foreign counterparts if he or she cannot place issues on the table that can be negotiated without constantly having to check back with various authorities.

In light of continuing large U.S. trade deficits, there is much disenchantment with past trade policies. The disappointment with previous measures, particularly trade negotiations, is mainly the result of overblown expectations. Too often, the public has mistakenly expected successful trade negotiations to affect the domestic economy in a major way, even though the issue addressed or resolved was only of minor economic importance. Yet, in light of global changes, U.S. trade policy does need to change. Rather than treating trade policy as a strictly "foreign" phenomenon, it must be recognized that domestic economic performance mainly determines global competitiveness. Trade policy must become more domestically oriented at the same time that domestic policy must become more international in vision.

Such a new approach should pursue at least six key goals. First, the nation must improve the quality and amount of information government and business share to facilitate competitiveness. Second, policy must encourage collaboration among companies in such areas as goods and process technologies. Third, U.S. industry collectively must overcome its export reluctance and its short-term financial orientation. Fourth, the United States must invest in its people, providing education and training suited to new competitive challenges.[33] Fifth, the executive branch must be given authority by Congress to negotiate international agreements with a reasonable certainty that the negotiation outcome will not be subject to minute amendments. Therefore, the existence of **trade promotion authority**, which gives Congress the right to accept or reject trade treaties and agreements but reduces the amendment procedures, is very important. Such authority is instrumental for new, large-scale trade accords to succeed. Finally, economic and trade concerns have grown in size. A new cluster of collaboration needs to enable solutions that are reflective of North American needs, accepted by the local culture and affordable with regional resources. There needs to be a drive toward closer economic tie-ins among North American neighbors to broaden the horizon of possible improvements in society.

But how to pay for the cost of policy adjustments? Currently, there is no link between governmental market openings and benefits obtained by an industry. Trade negotiations result in winners and losers, but winners have no incentive to share their bounty. The beneficiaries of protective measures do not show how they have used their revenues to help the transition of workers and communities. This must change. Private-sector winners must supplement the federal Trade Adjustment Assistance programs to help fund the cost of adjustment and become an essential engine for further trade liberalization. After all, even free trade has its price.[34]

trade promotion authority The right of the U.S. president to negotiate trade treaties and agreements with the U.S. Congress' authority to accept or reject, but not amend.

AN INTERNATIONAL PERSPECTIVE

From an international perspective, trade and investment negotiations must continue. In doing so, trade and investment policy can take either a multilateral or bilateral approach. **Bilateral negotiations** are carried out mainly between two nations, while **multilateral negotiations** are carried out among a number of nations. The approach can also be broad, covering a wide variety of products, services, or investments, or it can be narrow in that it focuses on specific problems.

In order to address narrowly defined trade issues, bilateral negotiations and a specific approach seem quite appealing. Very specific problems can be discussed and resolved expediently. However, to be successful on a global scale, negotiations need to produce winners. Narrow-based bilateral negotiations require that there be, for each issue, a clearly identified winner and loser. Therefore, such negotiations have less chance for long-term success, because no one wants to be the loser. This points toward multilateral negotiations on a broad scale, where concessions can be traded off among countries, making it possible for all participants to emerge and declare themselves as winners. The difficulty lies in devising enough incentives to bring the appropriate and desirable partners to the bargaining table.

Policymakers must be willing to trade off short-term achievements for long-term goals. All too often, measures that would be beneficial in the long term are sacrificed to short-term expediency to avoid temporary pain and the resulting political cost. Given the increasing links among nations and their economies, however, such

bilateral negotiations Negotiations carried out between two nations focusing only on their interests.

multilateral negotiations Trade negotiations among more than two parties; the intricate relationships among trading countries.

adjustments are inevitable. In the past, trade and investment volume continued to grow for everyone. Conflicts were minimized and adjustment possibilities were increased manyfold. As trade and investment policies must be implemented in an increasingly competitive environment, however, conflicts increase significantly. Thoughtful economic coordination will therefore be required among the leading trading nations. Such coordination will result to some degree in the loss of national sovereignty.

New mechanisms to evaluate restraint measure will also need to be designed. The beneficiaries of trade and investment restraints are usually clearly defined and have much to gain, whereas the losers are much less visible, which will make coalition building a key issue. The total cost of policy measures affecting trade and investment flows must be assessed, must be communicated, and must be taken into consideration before such measures are implemented.[35] The voices of retailers, consumers, wholesalers, and manufacturers all need to be heard. Only then will policymakers be sufficiently responsive in setting policy objectives that increase opportunities for firms and choice for consumers.

SUMMARY

Trade and investment policies historically have been a subset of domestic policies. Domestic policies, in turn, have aimed primarily at maintaining and improving the standard of living, the developmental level, and the employment level within a nation. Occasionally, foreign policy concerns also played a role. Increasingly, however, this view of trade and investment policies is undergoing change. While the view was appropriate for global developments that took place following World War II, changes in the current world environment require changes in policies.

Increasingly, the capability of policymakers simply to focus on domestic issues is reduced because of global links in trade and investment. In addition, traditional international institutions concerned with these policies have been weakened, and the developmental conflict among nations has been sharpened. As a result, there is a tendency by many nations to restrict imports either through tariff or nontariff barriers. Yet, all these actions have repercussions that negatively affect industries and consumers.

Nations also undertake efforts to promote exports through information and advice, production and marketing support, and financial assistance. While helpful to the individual firm, in the aggregate, such measures may only assist firms in efforts that the profit motive would encourage them to do anyway. Yet, for new entrants to the international market such assistance may be useful. Foreign direct investment restrictions are often debated in many countries. Frequently, nations become concerned about levels of foreign direct investment and the "selling out" of the patrimony. However, the bottom line is that although the restriction of investments may permit more domestic control over industries, it also denies access to foreign capital. This, in turn, can result in a tightening up of credit markets, higher interest rates, and less impetus for innovation. Governments also promote imports and foreign direct investment in order to receive needed products or to attract economic activity.

In the future, nations must cooperate closely. They must view domestic policymaking in the global context in order to maintain a viable and growing global trade and investment environment. Policies must be long term in order to ensure the well-being of nations and individuals.

KEY TERMS

national sovereignty 34
standard of living 34
quality of life 34
foreign policy 34
International Trade Organization (ITO) 35
General Agreement on Tariffs and Trade (GATT) 35

most-favored nation (MFN) 36
World Trade Organization (WTO) 36
Doha Round 37
currency flows 38
punitive tariff 40
International Monetary Fund (IMF) 42

World Bank 42
tariffs 43
bound tariff 43
applied tariff 43
quotas 46
nontariff barriers 46
voluntary restraint agreements 46
antidumping 46

retaliation   49
administrative shelter   49
mixed aid credits   50
Committee on Foreign Investments in
    the United States (CFIUS)   51
knowledge transfer   52

brain drain   54
capital flight   55
fiscal incentives   56
financial incentives   56
nonfinancial incentives   56

intellectual property right (IPR)   58
protectionistic legislation   58
trade promotion authority   59
bilateral negotiations   59
multilateral negotiations   59

QUESTIONS FOR DISCUSSION

1. Discuss the role of voluntary import restraints in international business.

2. What is meant by multilateral negotiations?

3. Discuss the impact of import restrictions on consumers.

4. Why would policymakers sacrifice major international progress for minor domestic policy gains?

5. Discuss the varying inputs to trade and investment restrictions by beneficiaries and by losers.

6. Discuss the effect of foreign direct investment on trade.

7. Do investment promotion programs of state (or provincial) governments make sense from a national perspective?

INTERNET EXERCISES

1. Go to the World Bank web site (http://www.worldbank.org) to obtain an overview of the bank's purpose and programs. Search for criticism of bank programs on other web sites and prepare a short report of the key issues accounting for the "World Bank Controversy."

2. For a country of your choice, please find the web site of its export promotion agency and identify the key programs offered to exporters. Which ones do you find most helpful to firms?

TAKE A STAND

French cheese lovers in the United States breathed a sigh of relief in May 2009 when the United States Trade Representative's office rescinded its decision of a 300 percent retaliatory tariff increase on Roquefort cheese. In return, the European Union (EU) agreed to significantly increase the amount of duty-free U.S. and Canadian hormone-free beef it allows to be imported.

The issue is not new. "For over a decade, we have been trying to resolve this dispute with the EU, but our efforts have gone nowhere," said then-U.S. Trade Representative Susan Schwab. Since the 1980s, the EU had placed increasing restrictions on imports of meat from animals that had been treated with hormones. Health safety concerns were said to be the reason. U.S. and Canadian ranchers regularly use hormones to promote animal growth and hormone-fed meat is commonly consumed in both countries. There is conflicting scientific evidence about safety.

The WTO has no enforcement arm. Typically, if a country is not complying with its WTO obligations, the WTO allows its other member countries to impose retaliatory tariffs and raise import duties in excess of bound tariff rates. Given the EU inaction over the years, the U.S. had imposed punitive tariffs on Roquefort and other products. When the United States announced the dramatic increase on Roquefort cheese tariffs in early 2009, the rationale was that the EU had not been responsive on the beef issue. The EU protested that the U.S. punitive tariffs were escalating the dispute. While there was a compromise agreement, the EU still bans many hormone-fed beef imports, and tariffs on Roquefort remain at 100 percent.

For Discussion
Are punitive tariffs effective, or do they mainly trigger retaliations? Is it better to cut the cheese or the tariff?

Sources: Matthew Dalton, "U.S. Drops Tariffs on Roquefort," Wall Street Journal, May 7, 2009; Joshua Chaffin, "US-EU Accord Ends Beef Import Rift," Financial Times, May 6, 2009; Renée Johnson and Charles E. Hanrahan, "The U.S.-EU Beef Hormone Dispute," Congressional Research Service, May 5, 2009; AFP, "U.S. Hits EU with New Tariffs in Beef Row," January 15, 2009.

CHAPTER 3

The Theory of Trade and Investment

CHAPTER CONTENTS & LEARNING OBJECTIVES

THE AGE OF MERCANTILISM

1. To understand the traditional arguments of how and why international trade improves the welfare of all countries

CLASSICAL TRADE THEORY

2. To review the history and compare the implications of trade theory from the original work of Adam Smith to the contemporary theories of Michael Porter

FACTOR PROPORTIONS TRADE THEORY

3. To examine the criticisms of classical trade theory and examine alternative viewpoints of which business and economic forces determine trade patterns between countries

INTERNATIONAL INVESTMENT AND PRODUCT CYCLE THEORY

4. To explore the similarities and distinctions between international trade and international investment

THE NEW TRADE THEORY: STRATEGIC TRADE

5. To evaluate the trade theories of Paul Krugman and Michael Porter and their relationship to business and government's approaches to trade policy

THE THEORY OF INTERNATIONAL INVESTMENT

6. To understand the theory of international investment and how it relates to firms and buyers

The global recession of 2008–2009 tested many of the theoretical principles of international trade and international economics. One such principle is that with recession comes slowed commercial and consumer spending, and slowed spending means fewer imports. The Chinese economy has enjoyed some of the largest trade surpluses in the global economy in recent years, and in the early stages of this recession, it suffered some declining export sales. But, it turns out, only for a while.

Of all the major economies, China's was the first to show true economic recovery. By late summer 2009, China's exports, and economy as a whole, was rising once again. The increasing maturity of the Chinese economy was also seen in its resurgence in domestic spending (e.g., the Chinese auto industry) as the famously penurious Chinese consumer relaxed some of the purse strings in order to buy more and more cars in what is now the world's largest automobile market.

There are a number of forces at work in the rapid turnaround of the Chinese economy. China clearly benefited from the ability of most major industrial nations to resist protectionist measures in their recessionary economies. All too often in years past, governments chose to protect their declining business environments against foreign competition when recession hit. The major trading nations today, however, have many more controls, restrictions, and general prohibitions on tariffs and quotas in place. This prevented many governments from knee-jerk reactions to calls for protectionism.

A second factor that has likely contributed to the resilience of the Chinese economy is the depth and breadth of global supply chains. Companies today do not only purchase final products from trading partners, but often an assortment of various intermediate parts and subcomponents. As a result, although specific products or services may see declining sales and trade, their constituent pieces and parts may live on in a variety of other products that are surviving or even recovering with selected global sales.

A third feature of the Chinese economy's ability to adapt to the global recession is its ability to aggressively reduce prices—and associated costs—because it possesses probably the most flexible labor market in the world. As many foreign buyers of Chinese exports have demanded price cuts in order to maintain sales in their declining country markets, Chinese manufacturers have reduced wages and employment in many of the production zones that rely on migrant workers (from the inner provinces). The flexibility in their labor markets is far above that seen in most other major industrial markets like Japan, the United States, and the European Union.

The final contributing force is the support for the export sector by the Chinese government itself. Export subsidies, major investment in logistics and export infrastructure, and the government's efforts to keep the Chinese currency undervalued all aid the support and sustenance of what is quickly becoming the engine of growth for the dragging global economy.

Sources: "Amid the Global Economic Crisis, China Rises," *The New York Times*, October 8, 2009; "Rebalancing the World Economy," *The Economist*, August 6, 2009; "China Auto Sales Jump 78 Percent in September," *The New York Times*, October 13, 2009; "China Consolidates Its Lead in Global Trade," *The New York Times*, October 14, 2009.

The debates, the costs, the benefits, and the dilemmas of international trade have in many ways not changed significantly from the time when Marco Polo crossed the barren wastelands of Eurasia to the time of the expansion of U.S. and Canadian firms across the Rio Grande into Mexico under the North American Free Trade Agreement. At the heart of the issue is what the gains—and the risks—are to the firm and the country as a result of a seller from one country servicing the needs of a buyer in a different country. If a Spanish firm wants to sell its product to the enormous market of mainland China, whether it produces at home and ships the product from Cadiz to Shanghai (international trade) or actually builds a factory in Shanghai (international investment), the goal is still the same: to sell a product for profit in the foreign market.

This chapter provides a directed path through centuries of thought on why and how trade and investment across borders occurs. Although theories and theorists come and go with time, a few basic questions have dominated this intellectual adventure:

- Why do countries trade?
- Do countries trade or do firms trade?
- Do the elements that give rise to the competitiveness of a firm, an industry, or a country as a whole, arise from some inherent endowment of the country itself, or do they change with time and circumstance?
- Once identified, can these sources of competitiveness be manipulated or managed by firms or governments to the benefit of the traders?

International trade is expected to improve the productivity of industry and the welfare of consumers. Let us learn how and why we still seek the exotic silks of the Far East and the telecommunication-linked call centers of Manila.

THE AGE OF MERCANTILISM

1. To understand the traditional arguments of how and why international trade improves the welfare of all countries

autarky Self-sufficiency: a country that is not participating in international trade.

mercantilism Political and economic policy in the seventeenth and early eighteenth centuries aimed at increasing a nation's wealth and power by encouraging the export of goods in return for gold.

The evolution of trade into the form we see today reflects three events: the collapse of feudal society, the emergence of the mercantilist philosophy, and the life cycle of the colonial systems of the European nation-states. Feudal society was a state of **autarky**, a society that did not trade because all of its needs were met internally. The feudal estate was self-sufficient, although hardly "sufficient" in more modern terms, given the limits of providing entirely for oneself. Needs literally were only those of food and shelter, and all available human labor was devoted to the task of fulfilling those basic needs. As merchants began meeting in the marketplace, as travelers began exchanging goods from faraway places at the water's edge, the attractiveness of trade became evident.

In the centuries leading up to the Industrial Revolution, international commerce was largely conducted under the authority of governments. The goals of trade were, therefore, the goals of governments. As early as 1500, the benefits of trade were clearly established in Europe, as nation-states expanded their influence across the globe in the creation of colonial systems. To maintain and expand their control over these colonial possessions, the European nations needed fleets, armies, food, and all other resources the nations could muster. They needed wealth. Trade was therefore conducted to fill the governments' treasuries, at minimum expense to themselves but to the detriment of their captive trade partners. Although colonialism normally is associated with the exploitation of those captive societies, it went hand in hand with the evolving exchange of goods among the European countries themselves: **mercantilism**. The Focus on Politics: The British East India Company, details this global expansion.

FOCUS ON POLITICS

The British East India Company

Granted an English Royal Charter by the Queen in 1600, the East India Company was one of the first joint stock companies in the world expressly created to pursue international trade. The company, although competing head to head with both Dutch and Portuguese trading companies in the East Indies, ended up dominating much of the European trade with both India (and the Indian sub-continent) and China.

The East India Company's reign of power and influence lasted nearly 200 years. It was the beneficiary of a multitude of special rights and privileges, eventually resulting in near-monopoly power in the trade of specific commodities and spices. But no right or privilege could possibly surpass the invitation and rights granted the company and its emissaries from the British government by the Mughal Emperor Nuruddin Salim Jahangir of Surat in what is India today:

Upon which assurance of your royal love I have given my general command to all the kingdoms and ports of my dominions to receive all the merchants of the English nation as the subjects of my friend; that in what place soever they choose to live, they may have free liberty without any restraint; and at what port soever they shall arrive, that neither Portugal nor any other shall dare to molest their quiet; and in what city soever they shall have residence, I have commanded all my governors and captains to give them freedom answerable to their own desires; to sell, buy, and to transport into their country at their pleasure.

For confirmation of our love and friendship, I desire your Majesty to command your merchants to bring in their ships of all sorts of rarities and rich goods fit for my palace; and that you be pleased to send me your royal letters by every opportunity, that I may rejoice in your health and prosperous affairs; that our friendship may be interchanged and eternal. Your Majesty is learned and quick-sighted as a prophet, and can conceive so much by few words that I need write no more.

Sources: James Harvey Robinson, ed., *Readings in European History*, 2 Vols. (Boston: Ginn and Co., 1904–1906), Vol. II: From the Opening of the Protestant Revolt to the Present Day, pp. 333–335.

Mercantilism mixed exchange through trade with accumulation of wealth. Since government controlled the patterns of commerce, it identified strength with the accumulation of **specie** (gold and silver) and maintained a general policy of exports dominating imports. Trade across borders—exports—was considered preferable to domestic trade because exports would earn gold. Import duties, tariffs, subsidization of exports, and outright restriction on the importation of many goods were used to maximize the gains from exports over the costs of imports. Laws were passed making it illegal to take gold or silver out of the country, even if such specie was needed to purchase imports to produce their own goods for sale. This was one-way trade, the trade of greed and power.

> **specie** Gold and silver.

The demise of mercantilism was inevitable given class structure and the distribution of society's product. As the Industrial Revolution introduced the benefits of mass production, lowering prices and increasing the supplies of goods to all, the exploitation of colonies and trading partners came to an end. However, governments still exercise considerable power and influence on the conduct of trade.

CLASSICAL TRADE THEORY

The question of why countries trade has proven difficult to answer. Since the second half of the eighteenth century, academicians have tried to understand not only the motivations and benefits of international trade, but also why some countries grow faster and wealthier than others through trade. Figure 3.1 provides an overview of the evolutionary path of trade theory since the fall of mercantilism. Although somewhat simplified, it shows the line of development of the major theories put forward over the past two centuries. It also serves as an early indication of the path of modern theory: the shifting focus from the country to the firm, from cost of production to the market as a whole, and from the perfect to the imperfect.

> **2.** To review the history and compare the implications of trade theory from the original work of Adam Smith to the contemporary theories of Michael Porter

Figure 3.1   The Evolution of Trade Theory

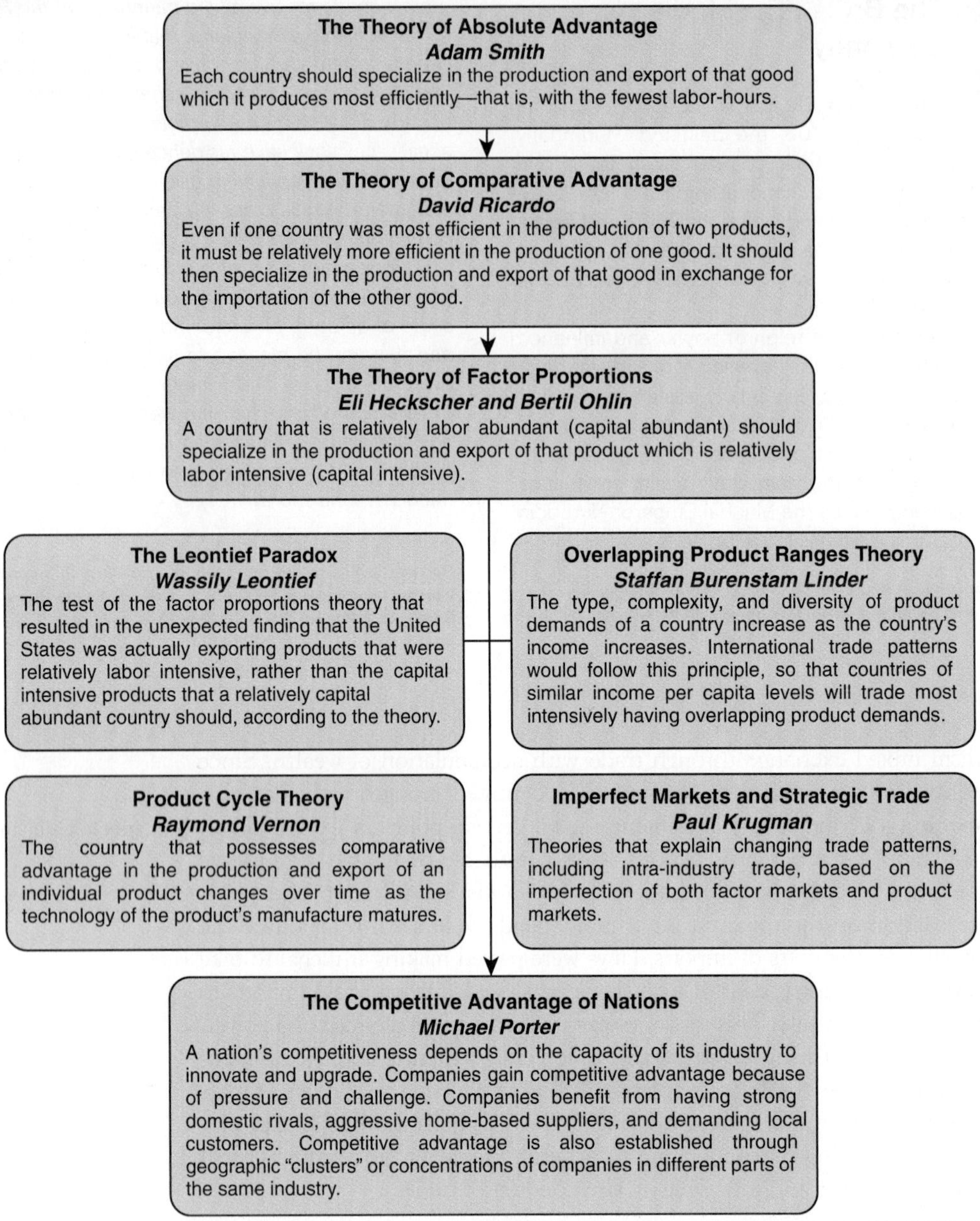

The Theory of Absolute Advantage
Adam Smith
Each country should specialize in the production and export of that good which it produces most efficiently—that is, with the fewest labor-hours.

The Theory of Comparative Advantage
David Ricardo
Even if one country was most efficient in the production of two products, it must be relatively more efficient in the production of one good. It should then specialize in the production and export of that good in exchange for the importation of the other good.

The Theory of Factor Proportions
Eli Heckscher and Bertil Ohlin
A country that is relatively labor abundant (capital abundant) should specialize in the production and export of that product which is relatively labor intensive (capital intensive).

The Leontief Paradox
Wassily Leontief
The test of the factor proportions theory that resulted in the unexpected finding that the United States was actually exporting products that were relatively labor intensive, rather than the capital intensive products that a relatively capital abundant country should, according to the theory.

Overlapping Product Ranges Theory
Staffan Burenstam Linder
The type, complexity, and diversity of product demands of a country increase as the country's income increases. International trade patterns would follow this principle, so that countries of similar income per capita levels will trade most intensively having overlapping product demands.

Product Cycle Theory
Raymond Vernon
The country that possesses comparative advantage in the production and export of an individual product changes over time as the technology of the product's manufacture matures.

Imperfect Markets and Strategic Trade
Paul Krugman
Theories that explain changing trade patterns, including intra-industry trade, based on the imperfection of both factor markets and product markets.

The Competitive Advantage of Nations
Michael Porter
A nation's competitiveness depends on the capacity of its industry to innovate and upgrade. Companies gain competitive advantage because of pressure and challenge. Companies benefit from having strong domestic rivals, aggressive home-based suppliers, and demanding local customers. Competitive advantage is also established through geographic "clusters" or concentrations of companies in different parts of the same industry.

THE THEORY OF ABSOLUTE ADVANTAGE

Generally considered the father of economics, Adam Smith published *The Wealth of Nations* in 1776 in London. In this book, Smith attempted to explain the process by which markets and production actually operate in society. Smith's two main areas of contribution, *absolute advantage* and the *division of labor* were fundamental to trade theory.

Production, the creation of a product for exchange, always requires the use of society's primary element of value: human labor. Smith noted that some countries, owing to the skills of their workers or the quality of their natural resources, could produce the same products as others with fewer labor-hours. He termed this efficiency **absolute advantage**.

absolute advantage The ability to produce a good or service more efficiently than it can be produced elsewhere.

Adam Smith observed the production processes of the early stages of the Industrial Revolution in England and recognized the fundamental changes that were occurring in production. In previous states of society, a worker performed all stages of a production process, with resulting output that was little more than sufficient for the worker's own needs. The factories of the industrializing world were, however, separating the production process into distinct stages, in which each stage would be performed exclusively by one individual, the **division of labor**. This specialization increased the production of workers and industries. Smith's pin factory analogy has long been considered the recognition of one of the most significant principles of the industrial age.

> *To take an example, therefore, from a very trifling manufacture; but one in which the division of labour has been very often taken notice of, the trade of the pin maker; a workman not educated to this business . . . could scarce, perhaps, with his utmost industry, make one pin in a day, and certainly could not make twenty. But in a way in which this business is now carried on, not only the whole work is a peculiar trade, but it is divided into a number of branches, of which the greater part are likewise peculiar trades. One man draws out the wire, another straights it, a third cuts it, a fourth points it, a fifth grinds it at the top for receiving the head: to make the head requires two or three distinct operations; to put it on is a peculiar business . . . I have seen a small manufactory of this kind where ten men only were employed, and where some of them consequently performed two or three distinct operations. But though they were very poor, and therefore but indifferently accommodated with the necessary machine, they could, when they exerted themselves, make among them about twelve pounds of pins in a day. There are in a pound upwards of four thousand pins of a middling size.*[1]

Adam Smith then extended his division of labor in the production process to a division of labor and specialized product across countries. Each country would specialize in a product for which it was uniquely suited. More would be produced for less. Thus, by each country specializing in products for which it possessed absolute advantage, countries could produce more in total and exchange products—trade— for goods that were cheaper in price than those produced at home.

division of labor The premise of modern industrial production where each stage in the production of a good is performed by one individual separately, rather than one individual being responsible for the entire production of the good.

THE THEORY OF COMPARATIVE ADVANTAGE

Although Smith's work was instrumental in the development of economic theories about trade and production, it did not answer some fundamental questions about trade. First, Smith's trade relied on a country possessing absolute advantage in production, but did not explain what gave rise to the production advantages. Second, if a country did not possess absolute advantage in any product, could it (or would it) trade?

David Ricardo, in his 1819 work entitled *On the Principles of Political Economy and Taxation*, sought to take the basic ideas set down by Smith a few steps further. Ricardo noted that even if a country possessed absolute advantage in the production of two products, it still must be relatively more efficient than the other country in one good's production than the other. Ricardo termed this the **comparative advantage**. Each country would then possess comparative advantage in the production of one of the two products, and both countries would then benefit by specializing completely in one product and trading for the other.

comparative advantage The ability to produce a good or service more cheaply, relative to other goods and services, than is possible in other countries.

A NUMERICAL EXAMPLE OF CLASSICAL TRADE

To fully understand the theories of absolute advantage and comparative advantage, consider the following example. Two countries, France and England, produce only two products, wheat and cloth (or beer and pizza, guns and butter, and so forth). The relative efficiency of each country in the production of the two products is measured

Table 3.1	Absolute Advantage and Comparative Advantage*		
Country	**Wheat**	**Cloth**	
England	2	4	
France	4	2	

- England has absolute advantage in the production of wheat. It requires fewer labor-hours (2 being less than 4) for England to produce one unit of wheat.
- France has absolute advantage in the production of cloth. It requires fewer labor-hours (2 being less than 4) for France to produce one unit of cloth.
- England has comparative advantage in the production of wheat. If England produces one unit of wheat, it is forgoing the production of 2/4 (0.50) of a unit of cloth. If France produces one unit of wheat, it is forgoing the production of 4/2 (2.00) of a unit of cloth. England therefore has the lower opportunity cost of producing wheat.
- France has comparative advantage in the production of cloth. If England produces one unit of cloth, it is forgoing the production of 4/2 (2.00) of a unit of wheat. If France produces one unit of cloth, it is forgoing the production of 2/4 (0.50) of a unit of wheat. France therefore has the lower opportunity cost of producing cloth.

*Labor-hours per unit of output.

by comparing the number of labor-hours needed to produce one unit of each product. Table 3.1 provides an efficiency comparison of the two countries.

England is obviously more efficient in the production of wheat. Whereas it takes France four labor-hours to produce one unit of wheat, it takes England only two hours to produce the same unit of wheat. France takes twice as many labor-hours to produce the same output. England has absolute advantage in the production of wheat. France needs two labor-hours to produce a unit of cloth that it takes England four labor-hours to produce. England therefore requires two more labor-hours than France to produce the same unit of cloth. France has absolute advantage in the production of cloth. The two countries are exactly opposite in relative efficiency of production.

David Ricardo took the logic of absolute advantages in production one step further to explain how countries could exploit their own advantages and gain from international trade. Comparative advantage, according to Ricardo, was based on what was given up or traded off in producing one product instead of the other. In this numerical example, England needs only two-fourths as many labor-hours to produce a unit of wheat as France, while France needs only two-fourths as many labor-hours to produce a unit of cloth. England therefore has comparative advantage in the production of wheat, while France has comparative advantage in the production of cloth. A country cannot possess comparative advantage in the production of both products, so each country has an economic role to play in international trade.

NATIONAL PRODUCTION POSSIBILITIES

production possibilities frontier A theoretical method of representing the total productive capabilities of a nation used in the formulation of classical and modern trade theory.

If the total labor-hours available for production within a nation were devoted to the full production of either product, wheat or cloth, the **production possibilities frontiers** of each country can be constructed. Assuming both countries possess the same number of labor-hours, for example 100, the production possibilities frontiers for each country can be graphed, as in Figure 3.2. If England devotes all labor-hours (100) to the production of wheat (which requires 2 labor-hours per unit produced), it can produce a maximum of 50 units of wheat. If England devotes all labor to the production of cloth instead, the same 100 labor-hours can produce a maximum of 25 units of cloth (100 labor-hours/4 hours per unit of cloth). If England did not trade with any other country, it could only consume the products that it produced itself.

Figure 3.2   Production Possibility Frontiers, Specialization of Production, and the Benefits of Trade

England

1. Initially produces and consumes at point A.
2. England chooses to specialize in the production of wheat and shifts production from point A to point B.
3. England now exports the unwanted wheat (30 units) in exchange for imports of cloth (30 units) from France.
4. England is now consuming at point C, where it is consuming the same amount of wheat but 15 more units of cloth than at original point A.

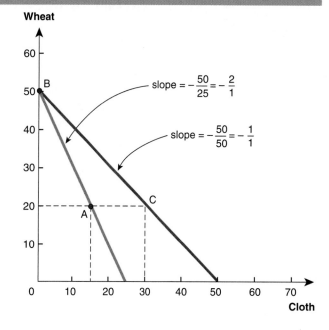

France

1. Initially produces and consumes at point D.
2. France chooses to specialize in the production of cloth and shifts production from point D to point E.
3. France now exports the unwanted cloth (30 units) in exchange for imports of wheat (30 units) from England.
4. France is now consuming at point F, where it is consuming the same amount of cloth but 15 more units of wheat than at original point D.

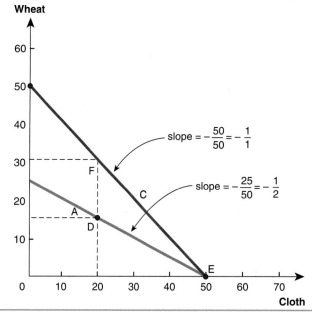

England would therefore probably produce and consume some combination of wheat and cloth such as point A in Figure 3.2 (15 units of cloth, 20 units of wheat).

France's production possibilities frontier is constructed in the same way. If France devotes all 100 labor-hours to the production of wheat, it can produce a maximum of 25 units (100 labor-hours/4 hours per unit of wheat). If France devotes all 100 labor-hours to cloth, the same 100 labor-hours can produce a maximum of 50 units of cloth (100 labor-hours/2 hours per unit of cloth). If France did not trade with other countries, it would produce and consume at some point such as point D in Figure 3.2 (20 units of cloth, 15 units of wheat).

These frontiers depict what each country could produce in isolation—without trade (sometimes referred to as *autarky*). The slope of the production possibility

opportunity costs The returns foregone on any resource or asset from using it in its next best use. The principle emphasizes that most assets or resources have alternative uses that have real value.

frontier of a nation is a measure of how one product is traded off in production with the other (moving up the frontier, England is choosing to produce more wheat and less cloth). The slope of the frontier reflects the "trade-off" of producing one product over the other; the trade-offs represent prices, or **opportunity costs**. Opportunity cost is the forgone value of a factor of production in its next-best use. If England chooses to produce more units of wheat (in fact, produce only wheat), moving from point A to point B along the production possibilities frontier, it is giving up producing cloth to produce only wheat. The "cost" of the additional wheat is the loss of cloth. The slope of the production possibilities frontier is the ratio of product prices (opportunity costs). The slope of the production possibilities frontier for England is −50/25, or −2.00. The slope of the production possibilities frontier for France is flatter, −25/50, or −0.50.

The relative prices of products also provide an alternative way of seeing comparative advantage. The flatter slope of the French production possibilities frontier means that to produce more wheat (move up the frontier), France would have to give up the production of relatively more units of cloth than would England, with its steeper sloped production possibilities frontier.

THE GAINS FROM INTERNATIONAL TRADE

Continuing with Figure 3.2, if England were originally not trading with France (the only other country) and it was producing at its own maximum possibilities (on the frontier and not inside the line), it would be producing at point A. Because it was not trading with another country, whatever it was producing it must also be consuming. So England could be said to be consuming at point A also. Therefore, without trade, you consume what you produce.

If, however, England recognized that it has comparative advantage in the production of wheat, it should move production from point A to point B. England should specialize completely in the product it produces best. It does not want to consume only wheat, however, so it would take the wheat it has produced and trade with France. For example, England may only want to consume 20 units of wheat, as it did at point A. It is now producing 50 units, and therefore has 30 units of wheat it can export to France. If England could export 30 units of wheat in exchange for imports of 30 units of cloth (a 1:1 ratio of prices), England would clearly be better off than before. The new consumption point would be point C, where it is consuming the same amount of wheat as point A, but is now consuming 30 units of cloth instead of just 15. More is better; England has benefited from international trade.

France, following the same principle of completely specializing in the product of its comparative production advantage, moves production from point D to point E, producing 50 units of cloth. If France now exported the unwanted cloth, for example 30 units, and exchanged the cloth with England for imports of 30 units of wheat (note that England's exports are France's imports), France too is better off as a result of international trade. Each country would do what it does best, exclusively, and then trade for the other product.

But at what prices will the two countries trade? Because each country's production possibilities frontier has a different slope (different relative product prices), the two countries can determine a set of prices between the two domestic prices. In the above example, England's price ratio was −2:1, while France's domestic price was −1:2. Trading 30 units of wheat for 30 units of cloth is a price ratio of −1:1, a slope, or set of prices, between the two domestic price ratios. The dashed line in Figure 3.2 illustrates this set of trade prices.

Are both countries better off as a result of trade? Yes. The final step to understanding the benefits of classical trade is to note that the point where a country

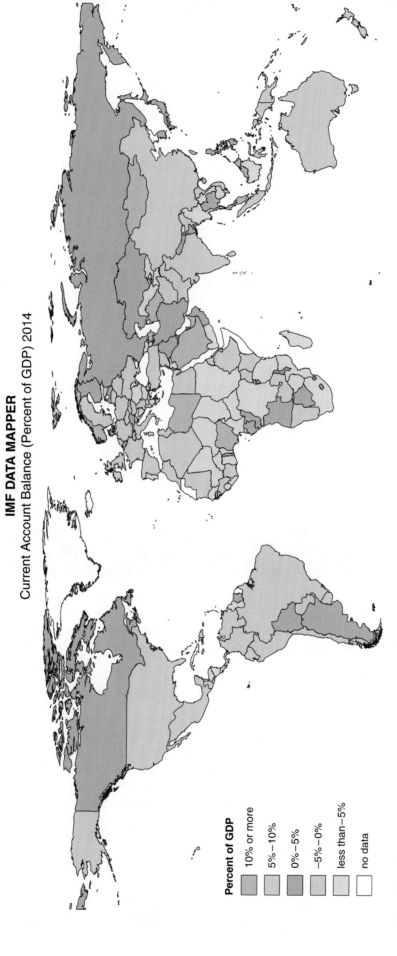

IMF DATA MAPPER
Current Account Balance (Percent of GDP) 2014

Percent of GDP

- 10% or more
- 5%–10%
- 0%–5%
- –5%–0%
- less than –5%
- no data

Source: International Monetary Fund, *World Economic Outlook*, October 2000, Data Mapper.

produces (point B for England and point E for France in Figure 3.2) and the point where it consumes are now different. This allows each country to consume beyond its own production possibilities frontier. Society's welfare, which is normally measured in its ability to consume more wheat, cloth, or any other goods or services, is increased through trade.

CONCLUDING POINTS ABOUT CLASSICAL TRADE THEORY

Classical trade theory contributed much to the understanding of how production and trade operates in the world economy. Although like all economic theories they are often criticized for being unrealistic or out of date, the purpose of a theory is to simplify reality so that the basic elements of the logic can be seen. Several of these simplifications have continued to provide insight in understanding international business.

- **Division of labor:** Adam Smith's explanation of how industrial societies can increase output using the same labor-hours as in preindustrial society is fundamental to our thinking even today. Smith extended this specialization of the efforts of a worker to the specialization of a nation.
- **Comparative advantage:** David Ricardo's extension of Smith's work explained for the first time how countries that seemingly had no obvious reason for trade could individually specialize in producing what they did best and trade for products they did not produce.
- **Gains from trade:** The theory of comparative advantage argued that nations could improve the welfare of their populations through international trade. A nation could actually achieve consumption levels beyond what it could produce by itself. To this day, this is one of the fundamental principles underlying the arguments for all countries to strive to expand and "free" world trade.

FACTOR PROPORTIONS TRADE THEORY

3. To examine the criticisms of classical trade theory and examine alternative viewpoints of which business and economic forces determine trade patterns between countries

Trade theory changed drastically in the first half of the twentieth century. The theory developed by the Swedish economist Eli Heckscher and later expanded by his former student Bertil Ohlin formed the theory of international trade that is still widely accepted today, **factor proportions theory**.

FACTOR INTENSITY IN PRODUCTION

factor proportions theory
Systematic explanation of the source of comparative advantage.

factors of production All inputs into the production process, including capital, labor, land, and technology.

factor intensity The proportion of capital input to labor input used in the production of a good.

The Heckscher-Ohlin theory considered two **factors of production**: labor and capital. Technology determines the way they combine to form a good. Different goods required different proportions of the two factors of production.

Figure 3.3 illustrates what it means to describe a good by its factor proportions. The production of one unit of good X requires 4 units of labor and 1 unit of capital. At the same time, to produce 1 unit of good Y requires 4 units of labor and 2 units of capital. Good X therefore requires more units of labor per unit of capital (4 to 1) relative to Y (4 to 2). X is therefore classified as a relatively labor-intensive product, and Y is relatively capital intensive. These **factor intensities**, or proportions, are truly relative and are determined only on the basis of what product X requires relative to product Y and not to the specific numbers of labor to capital.

It is easy to see how the factor proportions of production differ substantially across goods. For example, the manufacturing of leather footwear is still a

Figure 3.3   Factor Proportions in Production

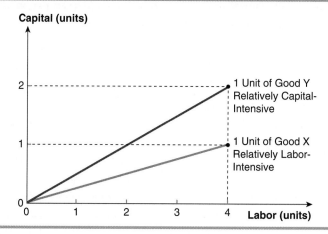

relatively labor-intensive process, even with the most sophisticated leather treatment and patterning machinery. Other goods, such as computer memory chips, however, although requiring some highly skilled labor, require massive quantities of capital for production. These large capital requirements include the enormous sums needed for research and development and the manufacturing facilities needed for clean production to ensure the extremely high quality demanded in the industry.

According to factor proportions theory, factor intensities depend on the state of technology—the current method of manufacturing a good. The theory assumed that the same technology of production would be used for the same goods in all countries. It is not, therefore, differences in the efficiency of production that will determine trade between countries as it did in classical theory. Classical theory implicitly assumed that technology or the productivity of labor is different across countries. Otherwise, there would be no logical explanation why one country requires more units of labor to produce a unit of output than another country. Factor proportions theory assumes no such productivity differences.

FACTOR ENDOWMENTS, FACTOR PRICES, AND COMPARATIVE ADVANTAGE

If there is no difference in technology or productivity of factors across countries, what then determines comparative advantage in production and export? The answer is that factor prices determine cost differences. And these prices are determined by the endowments of labor and capital the country possesses. The theory assumes that labor and capital are immobile; factors cannot move across borders. Therefore, the country's endowment determines the relative costs of labor and capital as compared with other countries.

Using these assumptions, factor proportions theory stated that a country should specialize in the production and export of those products that use intensively its relatively abundant factor.

- A country that is relatively labor abundant should specialize in the production of relatively labor-intensive goods. It should then export those labor-intensive goods in exchange for capital-intensive goods.

- A country that is relatively capital abundant should specialize in the production of relatively capital-intensive goods. It should then export those capital-intensive goods in exchange for labor-intensive goods.

ASSUMPTIONS OF THE FACTOR PROPORTIONS THEORY

The increasing level of theoretical complexity of the factor proportions theory, as compared with the classical trade theory, increased the number of assumptions necessary for the theory to "hold." It is important to take a last look at the assumptions before proceeding further.

1. The theory assumes two countries, two products, and two factors of production, the so-called $2 \times 2 \times 2$ assumption. Note that if both countries were producing all of the output they could and trading only between themselves (only two countries), both countries would have to have balances in trade!

2. The markets for the inputs and the outputs are perfectly competitive. The factors of production, labor, and capital were exchanged in markets that paid them only what they were worth. Similarly, the trade of the outputs (the international trade between the two countries) was competitive so that one country had no market power over the other.

3. Increasing production of a product experiences diminishing returns. This meant that as a country increasingly specialized in the production of one of the two outputs, it eventually would require more and more inputs per unit of output. For example there would no longer be the constant "labor-hours per unit of output" as assumed under the classical theory. Production possibilities frontiers would no longer be straight lines but concave. The result was that complete specialization would no longer occur under factor proportions theory.

4. Both countries were using identical technologies. Each product was produced in the same way in both countries. This meant the only way that a good could be produced more cheaply in one country than in the other was if the factors of production used (labor and capital) were cheaper.

Although a number of additional technical assumptions were necessary, these four highlight the very specialized set of conditions needed to explain international trade with factor proportions theory. Much of the trade theory developed since has focused on how trade changes when one or more of these assumptions is not found in the real world.

THE LEONTIEF PARADOX

One of the most famous tests of any economic or business theory occurred in 1950, when economist Wassily Leontief tested whether the factor proportions theory could be used to explain the types of goods the United States imported and exported. Leontief's premise was the following.

A widely shared view on the nature of the trade between the United States and the rest of the world is derived from what appears to be a common sense assumption that this country has a comparative advantage in the production of commodities which require for their manufacture large quantities of capital and relatively small amounts of labor. Our economic relationships with other countries are supposed to be based mainly on the export of such "capital intensive" goods in exchange for forgoing products which—if we were to make them at home—would require little capital but large quantities of American labor. Since the United States possesses a relatively large amount of capital—

so goes this oft-repeated argument—and a comparatively small amount of labor, direct domestic production of such "labor intensive" products would be uneconomical; we can much more advantageously obtain them from abroad in exchange for our capital intensive products.[2]

Leontief first had to devise a method to determine the relative amounts of labor and capital in a good. His solution, known as **input-output analysis**, was an accomplishment on its own. Input-output analysis is a technique of decomposing a good into the values and quantities of the labor, capital, and other potential factors employed in the good's manufacture. Leontief then used this methodology to analyze the labor and capital content of all U.S. merchandise imports and exports. The hypothesis was relatively straightforward: U.S. exports should be relatively capital intensive (use more units of capital relative to labor) than U.S. imports. Leontief's results were, however, a bit of a shock.

Leontief found that the products that U.S. firms exported were relatively more labor intensive than the products the United States imported.[3] It seemed that if the factor proportions theory was true, the United States is a relatively labor-abundant country! Alternatively, the theory could be wrong. Neither interpretation of the results was acceptable to many in the field of international trade.

A variety of explanations and continuing studies have attempted to solve what has become known as the **Leontief Paradox**. At first, it was thought to have been simply a result of the specific year (1947) of the data. However, the same results were found with different years and data sets. Second, it was noted that Leontief did not really analyze the labor and capital contents of imports but rather the labor and capital contents of the domestic equivalents of these imports. It was possible that the United States was actually producing the products in a more capital-intensive fashion than were the countries from which it also imported the manufactured goods.[4] Finally, the debate turned to the need to distinguish different types of labor and capital. For example, several studies attempted to separate labor factors into skilled labor and unskilled labor. These studies have continued to show results more consistent with what the factor proportions theory would predict for country trade patterns. As illustrated by the Focus on Politics: When the Numbers Don't Add Up, the Leontief Paradox is only one of the many ways in which trade theory and statistics run into confusion.

input-output analysis A method for estimating market activities and potential that measures the factor inflows into production and the resultant outflow of products.

Leontief Paradox The general belief that the United States, as a capital-abundant country, should be exporting capital-intensive products whereas its exports are labor intensive.

FOCUS ON POLITICS

When the Numbers Don't Add Up

The international trade statistics between countries, as reported by each, often do not match. As part of the continuing cooperation between the North American Free Trade Agreement (NAFTA) countries, the U.S. Department of Commerce recently concluded a study into the differences among the official trade statistics released by the United States, Mexico, and Canada in 1998 and 1999. The significance of these differences is compounded by the importance of trade among the three countries: 30 percent of all U.S. merchandise trade is with Canada and Mexico; 80 percent of Mexico's merchandise and service trade is with the United States and Canada.

The primary sources of the discrepancy in statistics include *geographic coverage, partner country attribution, nonfiling of U.S. exports,* and *low-value transactions.* An example of *geographic coverage* would be that the United States considers Puerto Rico and the U.S. Virgin Islands as part of the United States for reporting reasons, while Mexico regards them as separate trading partners. *Partner country attribution* occurs, for example, in Mexico, where the import entry form allows for the reporting of only a single country of origin. As a result, some imports are misattributed to the United States.

For more details on the study of trade statistics discrepancies, see http://www.census.gov/foreign-trade/

LINDER'S OVERLAPPING PRODUCT RANGES THEORY

The difficulties in empirically validating the factor proportions theory led many in the 1960s and 1970s to search for new explanations of the determinants of trade between countries. The work of Staffan Burenstam Linder focused not on the production or supply side, but instead on the preferences of consumers—the demand side. Linder acknowledged that in the natural resource–based industries, trade was indeed determined by relative costs of production and factor endowments.

However, Linder argued, trade in manufactured goods was dictated not by cost concerns but rather by the similarity in product demands across countries. Linder's was a significant departure from previous theory and was based on two principles:

1. As income, or more precisely per-capita income, rises, the complexity and quality level of the products demanded by the country's residents also rises. The total range of product sophistication demanded by a country's residents is largely determined by its level of income.

2. The entrepreneurs directing the firms that produce society's needs are more knowledgeable about their own domestic market than about foreign markets. An entrepreneur could not be expected to effectively serve a foreign market that is significantly different from the domestic market because competitiveness comes from experience. A logical pattern would be for an entrepreneur to gain success and market share at home first, then expand to foreign markets that are similar in their demands or tastes.

International trade in manufactured goods would then be influenced by similarity of demands. The countries that would see the most intensive trade are those with similar per-capita income levels, for they would possess a greater likelihood of overlapping product demands. The Focus on Politics: The U.S. Trade Deficit Fix highlights how demand changes when income levels drop.

So where does trade come in? According to Linder, the overlapping ranges of product sophistication represent the products that entrepreneurs would know well from their home markets and could therefore potentially export and compete with in foreign markets. For example, the United States and Canada have almost parallel sophistication ranges, implying they would have a lot of common ground, overlapping product ranges, for intensive international trade and competition. They are quite similar in their per-capita income levels. But Mexico and the United States, or

FOCUS ON POLITICS

The U.S. Trade Deficit Fix: Global Financial Crisis

It turns out that one of the fastest ways to shrink trade deficits is to have a global financial crisis. Despite years of debate and warnings from experts, analysts, politicians, and economists, trade deficits grew and grew in the United States. All cried out the same prescription, Americans needed to spend less and save more.

The global financial crisis, largely based in the United States, proved a better cure-all for spend-thrift Americans than all of the congressional hearings or warnings from Wall Street. As the financial crisis erupted in the fall of 2008, as businesses stopped, as workers lost wages and even jobs, Americans finally stopped spending. Unfortunately, that is exactly how an economic crisis in one country spreads to the business and commerce of other countries—as a halt in international trade today brings a globalized world economy to a halt.

U.S. bilateral trade deficits shrank in the first eight months of 2009 in shocking proportions: deficit with China down 14 percent; deficit with Japan down 20 percent, deficits with Mexico, Canada, and even the European Union down by nearly 40 percent. For U.S. policymakers, these would be wondrous statistics—if they weren't coming from economic recession and skyrocketing unemployment. Although the global economy appeared to be crawling out of its recession in the fall of 2009, it was still not clear whether the "rebalancing" of trade would be sustained and a permanent change in spending and saving would result.

Sources: Edmund Andrews, "As Americans Stop Buying, Trade Deficit Declines," *The New York Times*, October 10, 2009; "Rebalancing the World Economy," *The Economist*, August 6, 2009.

Mexico and Canada, would not. Mexico has a significantly different product sophistication range as a result of a different per-capita income level.

The overlapping product ranges described by Linder would today be termed **market segments**. Not only was Linder's work instrumental in extending trade theory beyond cost considerations, but it also found a place in the field of international marketing. As illustrated in the theories following the work of Linder, many of the questions that his work raised were the focus of considerable attention in the following decades.

INTERNATIONAL INVESTMENT AND PRODUCT CYCLE THEORY

A very different path was taken by Raymond Vernon in 1966 concerning what is now termed **product cycle theory**. Diverging significantly from traditional approaches, Vernon focused on the product (rather than the country and the technology of its manufacture), not its factor proportions. Most striking was the appreciation of the role of information, knowledge, and the costs and power that go hand in hand with knowledge.

> . . . *we abandon the powerful simplifying notion that knowledge is a universal free good, and introduce it as an independent variable in the decision to trade or to invest.*

Using many of the same basic tools and assumptions of factor proportions theory, Vernon added two technology-based premises to the factor-cost emphasis of existing theory:

1. Technical innovations leading to new and profitable products require large quantities of capital and highly skilled labor. These factors of production are predominantly available in highly industrialized capital-intensive countries.

2. These same technical innovations, both the product itself and more importantly the methods for its manufacture, go through three stages of maturation as the product becomes increasingly commercialized. As the manufacturing process becomes more standardized and low-skill labor-intensive, the comparative advantage in its production and export shifts across countries. Even accurately tracking exports and imports is sometimes daunting.

THE STAGES OF THE PRODUCT CYCLE

Product cycle theory is both supply-side (cost of production) and demand-side (income levels of consumers) in its orientation. Each of these three stages that Vernon described combines differing elements of each.

Stage I: The New Product

Innovation requires highly skilled labor and large quantities of capital for research and development. The product will normally be most effectively designed and initially manufactured near the parent firm and therefore in a highly industrialized market due to the need for proximity to information and the need for communication among the many different skilled-labor components required.

In this development stage, the product is nonstandardized. The production process requires a high degree of flexibility (meaning continued use of highly skilled labor). Costs of production are therefore quite high. The innovator at this stage is a

market segment Group of customers that share characteristics and behaviors.

4. To explore the similarities and distinctions between international trade and international investment

product cycle theory A theory that views products as passing through four stages: introduction, growth, maturity, decline; during which the location of production moves from industrialized to lower-cost developing nations.

monopolist and therefore enjoys all of the benefits of monopoly power, including the high profit margins required to repay the high development costs and expensive production process. Price elasticity of demand at this stage is low; high-income consumers buy it regardless of cost.

Stage II: The Maturing Product

As production expands, its process becomes increasingly standardized. The need for flexibility in design and manufacturing declines, and therefore the demand for highly skilled labor declines. The innovating country increases its sales to other countries. Competitors with slight variations develop, putting downward pressure on prices and profit margins. Production costs are an increasing concern.

As competitors increase, as well as their pressures on price, the innovating firm faces critical decisions on how to maintain market share. Vernon argues that the firm faces a critical decision at this stage, either to lose market share to foreign-based manufacturers using lower-cost labor or to invest abroad to maintain its market share by exploiting the comparative advantages of factor costs in other countries. This is one of the first theoretical explanations of how trade and investment become increasingly intertwined.

Stage III: The Standardized Product

In this final stage, the product is completely standardized in its manufacture. Thus, with access to capital on world capital markets, the country of production is simply the one with the cheapest unskilled labor. Profit margins are thin, and competition is fierce. The product has largely run its course in terms of profitability for the innovating firm.

The country of comparative advantage has therefore shifted as the technology of the product's manufacture has matured. The same product shifts in its location of production. The country possessing the product during that stage enjoys the benefits of net trade surpluses. But such advantages are fleeting, according to Vernon. As knowledge and technology continually change, so does the country of that product's comparative advantage.

TRADE IMPLICATIONS OF THE PRODUCT CYCLE

Product cycle theory shows how specific products were first produced and exported from one country but, through product and competitive evolution, shifted their location of production and export to other countries over time. Figure 3.4 illustrates the trade patterns that Vernon visualized as resulting from the maturing stages of a specific product cycle. As the product and the market for the product mature and change, the countries of its production and export shift.

The product is initially designed and manufactured in the United States. In its early stages (from time t_0 to t_1), the United States is the only country producing and consuming the product. Production is highly capital-intensive and skilled-labor intensive at this time. At time t_1, the United States begins exporting the product to other advanced countries, as Vernon classified them. These countries possess the income to purchase the product in its still new-product stage, in which it was relatively high priced. These other advanced countries also commerce their own production at time t_1 but continue to be net importers. A few exports, however, do find their way to the less-developed countries at this time as well.

As the product moves into the second stage, the maturing product stage, production capability expands rapidly in the other advanced countries. Competitive

Figure 3.4   Trade Patterns and Product Cycle Theory

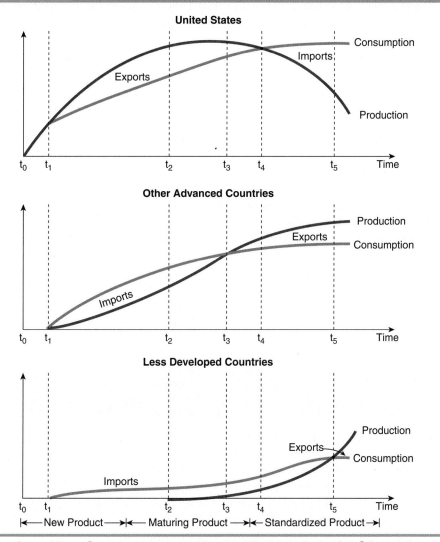

Source: Raymond Vernon, "International Investment and International Trade in the Product Cycle," *Quarterly Journal of Economics* (May 1966): 199.

variations begin to appear as the basic technology of the product becomes more widely known, and the need for skilled labor in its production declines. These countries eventually also become net exporters of the product near the end of the stage (time t_3). At time t_2 the less-developed countries begin their own production, although they continue to be net importers. Meanwhile, the lower cost of production from these growing competitors turns the United States into a net importer by time t_4. The competitive advantage for production and export is clearly shifting across countries at this time.

The third and final stage, the standardized product stage, sees the comparative advantage of production and export now shifting to the less-developed countries. The product is now a relatively mass-produced product that can be made with increasingly less-skilled labor. The United States continues to reduce domestic production and increase imports. The other advanced countries continue to produce and export, although exports peak as the less-developed countries expand production and become net exporters themselves. The product has run its course or life cycle in reaching time t_5.

A final point: Note that throughout this product cycle, the countries of production, consumption, export, and import are identified by their labor and capital levels, not firms. Vernon noted that it could very well be the same firms that are moving production from the United States to other advanced countries to less-developed countries. The shifting location of production was instrumental in the changing patterns of trade but not necessarily in the loss of market share, profitability, or competitiveness of the firms. The country of comparative advantage could change.

Although interesting in its own right for increasing emphasis on technology's impact on product costs, product cycle theory was most important because it explained international investment. Not only did the theory recognize the mobility of capital across countries (breaking the traditional assumption of factor immobility), it shifted the focus from the country to the product. This made it important to match the product by its maturity stage with its production location to examine competitiveness.

Product cycle theory has many limitations. It is obviously most appropriate for technology-based products. These are the products that are most likely to experience the changes in production process as they grow and mature. Other products, either resource-based (such as minerals and other commodities) or services (which employ capital but mostly in the form of human capital), are not so easily characterized by stages of maturity. And product cycle theory is most relevant to products that eventually fall victim to mass production and therefore cheap labor forces. But, all things considered, product cycle theory served to breach a wide gap between the trade theories of old and the intellectual challenges of a new, more globally competitive market in which capital, technology, information, and firms themselves were more mobile.

THE NEW TRADE THEORY: STRATEGIC TRADE

5. *To evaluate the trade theories of Paul Krugman and Michael Porter and their relationship to business and government's approaches to trade policy*

Global trade developments in the 1980s and 1990s led to much criticism of the existing theories of trade. First, although there was rapid growth in trade, much of it was not explained by current theory. Secondly, the massive size of the merchandise trade deficit of the United States—and the associated decline of many U.S. firms in terms of international competitiveness—served as something of a country-sized lab experiment demonstrating what some critics termed the "bankruptcy of trade theory." Academics and policymakers alike looked for new explanations.

Two new contributions to trade theory were met with great interest. Paul Krugman, along with several colleagues, developed a theory of how trade is altered when markets are not perfectly competitive, or when production of specific products possesses economies of scale. A second and very influential development was the growing work of Michael Porter, who examined the competitiveness of industries on a global basis, rather than relying on country-specific factors to determine competitiveness.

ECONOMIES OF SCALE AND IMPERFECT COMPETITION

Paul Krugman's theoretical developments once again focused on cost of production and how cost and price drive international trade. Using theoretical developments from microeconomics and market structure analysis, Krugman focused on two types of economics of scale, *internal economies of scale* and *external economies of scale*.[5]

Internal Economies of Scale

When the cost per unit of output depends on the size of an individual firm, the larger the firm the greater the scale benefits, and the lower the cost per unit. A firm possessing internal economies of scale could potentially monopolize an industry

© Blue Jean Images/SuperStock

According to the government, Chinese cell phone usage reached 200 million subscribers in 2002. As domestic spending grows, China will be able to sustain its economic growth and as a result be less dependent upon exports. This growing Chinese economy also helps China's trade partners.

(creating an *imperfect market*), both domestically and internationally. If it produces more, lowering the cost per unit, it can lower the market price and sell more products, because it *sets* market prices.

The link between dominating a domestic industry and influencing international trade comes from taking this assumption of imperfect markets back to the original concept of comparative advantage. For this firm to expand sufficiently to enjoy its economies of scale, it must take resources away from other domestic industries in order to expand. A country then sees its own range of products in which it specializes narrowing, providing an opportunity for other countries to specialize in these so-called **abandoned product ranges**. Countries again search out and exploit comparative advantage.

A particularly powerful implication of internal economies of scale is that it provides an explanation of intra-industry trade, one area in which traditional trade theory had indeed seemed bankrupt. **Intra-industry trade** is when a country seemingly imports and exports the same product, an idea that is obviously inconsistent with any of the trade theories put forward in the past three centuries. According to Krugman, internal economies of scale may lead a firm to specialize in a narrow product line (to produce the volume necessary for economies of scale cost benefits); other firms in other countries may produce products that are similarly narrow, yet extremely similar: **product differentiation**. If consumers in either country wish to buy both products, they will be importing and exporting products that are, for all intents and purposes, the same.[6]

Intra-industry trade has been studied in detail in the past decade. Intra-industry trade is measured with the Grubel-Lloyd Index, the ratio of imports and exports of the same product occurring between two trading nations. It is calculated as follows:

$$\text{Intra-industry trade index}_i = \frac{|X_i - M_i|}{(X_i + M_i)}$$

where i is the product category and $|X - M|$ is the absolute value of net exports of that product (exports–imports). For example, if Sweden imports 100 heavy machines for its forest products industry from Finland, and at the same time exports to Finland

abandoned product ranges The outcome of a firm narrowing its range of products to obtain economies of scale, which provides opportunities for other firms to enter the markets for the abandoned products.

intra-industry trade The simultaneous export and import of the same good by a country. It is of interest due to the traditional theory that a country will either export or import a good, but not do both at the same time.

product differentiation The effort to build unique differences or improvements into products.

80 of the same type of equipment, the intra-industry trade (IIT) index would be:

$$\text{IIT} = \frac{|80 - 100|}{(80 + 100)} = 1 - 0.1111 = 0.89$$

The closer the index value to 1, the higher the level of intra-industry trade in that product category. The closer the index is to 0, the more one-way the trade between the countries is, as traditional trade theory would predict.

Intra-industry trade is now thought to compose roughly 25 percent of global trade. And to its credit, intra-industry trade is increasingly viewed as having additive benefits to the fundamental benefits of comparative advantage. Intra-industry trade does allow some industrial segments in some countries to deepen their specialization while simultaneously allowing greater breadth of choices and commensurate benefits to consumers. Of course, one potentially disturbing characteristic of the growth in intra-industry trade is the potential for trade of all kinds to continue to expand in breadth and depth between the most industrialized countries (those producing the majority of the more complex manufactured goods) while those less industrialized nations do not see this added boost to trade growth.

External Economies of Scale

When the cost per unit of output depends on the size of an industry, not the size of the individual firm, the industry of that country may produce at lower costs than the same industry that is smaller in size in other countries. A country can potentially dominate world markets in a particular product, not because it has one massive firm producing enormous quantities (e.g., Boeing), but rather because it has many small firms that interact to create a large, competitive, critical mass (e.g., semiconductors in Penang, Malaysia). No one firm need be all that large, but several small firms in total may create such a competitive industry that firms in other countries cannot ever break into the industry on a competitive basis.[7]

Unlike internal economies of scale, external economies of scale may not necessarily lead to imperfect markets, but they may result in an industry maintaining its dominance in its field in world markets. This provides an explanation as to why all industries do not necessarily always move to the country with the lowest-cost energy, resources, or labor. What gives rise to this critical mass of small firms and their interrelationships is a much more complex question. The work of Michael Porter provides a partial explanation of how these critical masses are sustained.

STRATEGIC TRADE

Often criticized as being simplistic or naive, trade theory in recent years has, in the words of one critic, grown up. One fundamental assumption that both classical and modern trade theories have not been willing to stray far from is the inefficiencies introduced with governmental involvement in trade. Economic theory, however, has long recognized that government can play a beneficial role when markets are not purely competitive. This theory has now been expanded to government's role in international trade as well. This growing stream of thought is termed strategic trade. There are (at least) four specific circumstances involving imperfect competition in which strategic trade may apply, which we denote as *price, cost, repetition,* and *externalities.*

Price

A foreign firm that enjoys significant international market power—monopolistic power—has the ability to both restrict the quantity of consumption and demand higher prices. One method by which a domestic government may thwart that monopolistic power is to impose import duties or tariffs on the imported products. The monopolist, not wishing to allow the price of the product to rise too high in the target market, will often absorb some portion of the tariff. The result is roughly the same amount of product imported, and at relatively the same price to the customer, but the excessive profits (economic rent in economic theory) have been partly shifted from the monopolist to the domestic government. Governments have long fought the power of global petrochemical companies with these types of import duties.

Cost

Although much has been made in recent years about the benefits of "small and flexible," some industries still are dominated by the firms that can gain massive productive size—**scale economies**. As the firm's size increases, its per unit cost of production falls, allowing it a signficant cost advantage in competition. Governments wishing for specific firms to gain this stature may choose to protect the domestic market against foreign competition to provide a home market of size for the company's growth and maturity. This strategic trade theory is actually quite similar to the traditional arguments for the protection of infant industries, though this is a protection whose benefits accrue to firms in adolescence rather than childhood!

scale economies The increasing efficiency gains from greater size or scale, often described as lower cost per unit of output.

Repetition

Some firms in some industries have inherent competitive advantages, often efficiency based, from simply having produced repetitively for years. Sometimes referred to as "learning-by-doing," these firms may achieve competitive cost advantages from producing not only more units (as in the scale economies described above) but from producing more units *over time*. A goverment that wishes to promote these efficiency gains by domestic firms can help the firm move down the learning curve faster by protecting the domestic market from foreign competitors. Again similar in nature to the infant industry argument, the idea is not only to allow the firm to produce more, but to produce more cumulatively over time to gain competitive knowledge from the actual process itself.

Externalities

The fourth and final category of strategic trade involves those market failures in which the costs or benefits of the business process are not borne or captured by the firm itself. If, for example, the government believes that the future of business is in specific knowledge-based industries, it may be willing to subsidize the education of workers for that industry, protect that industry from foreign competition, or even aid the industry in overcoming the costs of environmental protection in order to promote the industry's development. This argument is similar to those used by governments in the 1970s and 1980s to support the development of certain industries in their countries (e.g., microelectronics in Japan and steel in Korea) which was then referred to as industrial policy. In fact, this strategic trade argument could be used in support of Michael Porter's cluster theory, in which society and industry would reap benefits of reaching critical mass in experience and interactions through promotion and protection.

Although the arguments by proponents of strategic trade are often seductive, critics charge that these theories play more to emotion than rational thought. Industries do not often learn by doing or reduce costs through scale, and governments are infamous for their inability to effectively protect (and unprotect, when the time comes) in order to promote industrial development and growth. Protection and state-supported monopolists are often some of the world's least efficient rather than most efficient. And as always, there is no assurance that foreign governments themselves will not react and retaliate, again undermining the potentially rational policies put into place in isolation. A final note of caution about strategic trade goes back to the very origins of trade theory: many of the benefits of international trade accrue to those who successfully divorce the politic from the economic.

THE COMPETITIVE ADVANTAGE OF NATIONS

The focus of early trade theory was on the country or nation and its inherent, natural, or endowment characteristics that might give rise to increasing competitiveness. As trade theory evolved, it shifted its focus to the industry and product level, leaving the national-level competitiveness question somewhat behind. Recently, many have turned their attention to the question of how countries, governments, and even private industry can alter the conditions within a country to aid the competitiveness of its firms.

The leader in this area of research has been Michael Porter of Harvard. As he states:

National prosperity is created, not inherited. It does not grow out of a country's natural endowments, its labor pool, its interest rates, or its currency's values, as classical economics insists.

A nation's competitiveness depends on the capacity of its industry to innovate and upgrade. Companies gain advantage against the world's best competitors because of pressure and challenge. They benefit from having strong domestic rivals, aggressive home-based suppliers, and demanding local customers.

In a world of increasingly global competition, nations have become more, not less, important. As the basis of competition has shifted more and more to the creation and assimilation of knowledge, the role of the nation has grown. Competitive advantage is created and sustained through a highly localized process. Differences in national values, culture, economic structures, institutions, and histories all contribute to competitive success. There are striking differences in the patterns of competitiveness in every country; no nation can or will be competitive in every or even most industries. Ultimately, nations succeed in particular industries because their home environment is most forward-looking, dynamic, and challenging.[8]

Porter argued that innovation is what drives and sustains competitiveness. A firm must avail itself of all dimensions of competition, which he categorized into four major components of "the diamond of national advantage":

1. **Factor conditions:** The appropriateness of the nation's factors of production to compete successfully in a specific industry. Porter notes that although these factor conditions are very important in the determination of trade, they are not the only source of competitiveness as suggested by the classical, or factor proportions, theories of trade. Most importantly for Porter, it is the ability of a nation to continually create, upgrade, and deploy its factors (such as skilled labor) that is important, not the initial endowment.

2. **Demand conditions:** The degree of health and competition the firm must face in its original home market. Firms that can survive and flourish in highly competitive and demanding local markets are much more likely to gain the competitive edge. Porter notes that it is the character of the market, not its size, that is paramount in promoting the continual competitiveness of the firm. And Porter translates *character* as demanding customers.

3. **Related and supporting industries:** The competitiveness of all related industries and suppliers to the firm. A firm that is operating within a mass of

Figure 3.5   Determinants of National Competitive Advantage: Porter's Diamond

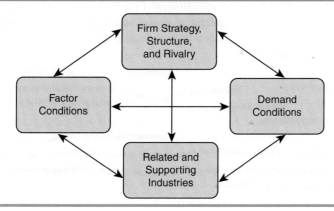

related firms and industries gains and maintains advantages through close working relationships, proximity to suppliers, and timeliness of product and information flows. The constant and close interaction is successful if it occurs not only in terms of physical proximity but also through the willingness of firms to work at it.

4. **Firm strategy, structure, and rivalry:** The conditions in the home-nation that either hinder or aid in the firm's creation and sustaining of international competitiveness. Porter notes that no one managerial, ownership, or operational strategy is universally appropriate. It depends on the fit and flexibility of what works for that industry in that country at that time.

These four points, as illustrated in Figure 3.5, constitute what nations and firms must strive to "create and sustain through a highly localized process" to ensure their success.

Porter's emphasis on innovation as the source of competitiveness reflects an increased focus on the industry and product that we have seen in the past three decades. The acknowledgment that the nation is "more, not less, important" is to many eyes a welcome return to a positive role for government and even national-level private industry in encouraging international competitiveness. Including factor conditions as a cost component, demand conditions as a motivator of firm actions, and competitiveness all combine to include the elements of classical, factor proportions, product cycle, and imperfect competition theories in a pragmatic approach to the challenges that the global markets of the twenty-first century present to the firms of today.

CLUSTERS AND THE NEW ECONOMICS

Michael Porter added an additional theoretical development to the concept of competitive advantage, that of competitive clusters.[9]*Clusters*, according to Porter, are "critical masses—in one place—of unusual competitive success in particular fields." Examples often cited are leather fashion product manufacturing in northern Italy, textiles in the Carolinas and wine in California in the United States, or semi-conductors on the Penang Peninsula in Malaysia. These geographic concentrations of competitive excellence seemingly fly in the face of modern thought on the mobility of capital and knowledge.

Porter's theoretical argument was based on his assertion that significant advantages accrue to companies from being in proximity to complementary products and services—within reach of all the suppliers and partners in the product value chain. The premise was quite simple: competitive advantages are gained through interconnected companies and institutions locally, not through the scale and scope of the firms themselves. Cluster theory suggests that competition is altered in at least three ways when clusters form successfully: (1) by increasing the productivity of the companies based in the area, (2) by driving and supporting the momentum of innovation in the area, and (3) by stimulating the creation of new companies and new configurations of business in the area. In effect, the cluster itself acts as an extended family or single firm, but flexibly and efficiently. Interestingly, the cluster's competitive sustainability is assured by the second change—the momentum gains to innovation—which is consistent with Porter's earlier work on what drives competitive advantage of the individual firm through time.

The writing of Porter and others has continued to be instrumental in the thinking of both business and government when approaching trade policy. Many, although supporting much of the findings of Porter's theories, see the true insights as being related to the complex relationships between knowledge and how knowledge is developed, shared, and transmitted within industries over time.

 ## THE THEORY OF INTERNATIONAL INVESTMENT

6. To understand the theory of international investment and how it relates to firms and buyers

Trade is the production of a good or service in one country and its sale to a buyer in another country. In fact, it is a firm (not a country) and a buyer (not a country) that are the subjects of trade, domestically or internationally. A firm is therefore attempting to access a market and its buyers. The producing firm wants to utilize its competitive advantage for growth and profit and can also reach this goal by international investment.[10]

Although this sounds easy enough, consider any of the following potholes on the road to investment success. Any of the following potholes may be avoided by producing within another country.

- Sales to some countries are difficult because of tariffs imposed on your good when it is entering. If you were producing within the country, your good would no longer be an import.
- Your good requires natural resources that are available only in certain areas of the world. It is therefore imperative that you have access to the natural resources. You can buy them from that country and bring them to your production process (import) or simply take the production to them.
- Competition is constantly pushing you to improve efficiency and decrease the costs of producing your good. You therefore may want to produce where it will be cheaper—cheaper capital, cheaper energy, cheaper natural resources, or cheaper labor. Many of these factors are still not mobile, and therefore you will go to them instead of bringing them to you.

There are thousands of reasons why a firm may want to produce in another country, and not necessarily in the country that is cheapest for production or the country where the final good is sold.

The subject of international investment arises from one basic idea: the mobility of capital. Although many of the traditional trade theories assumed the immobility of the factors of production, it is the movement of capital that has allowed foreign direct investments across the globe. If there is a competitive advantage to be gained, capital can and will get there.

THE FOREIGN DIRECT INVESTMENT DECISION

Consider a firm that wants to exploit its competitive advantage by accessing foreign markets as illustrated in the decision-sequence tree of Figure 3.6.

The first choice is whether to exploit the existing competitive advantage in new foreign markets or to concentrate its resources in the development of new competitive advantages in the domestic market. Although many firms may choose to do both as resources will allow, more and more firms are choosing to go international as at least part of their expansion strategies.

Second, should the firm produce at home and export to the foreign markets, or produce abroad? The firm will choose the path that will allow it to access the resources and markets it needs to exploit its existing competitive advantage. But it will also consider two additional dimensions of each foreign investment decision: (1) the degree of control over assets, technology, information, and operations and (2) the magnitude of capital that the firm must risk. Each decision increases the firm's control at the cost of increased capital outlays.

After choosing to produce abroad, the firm must decide how. The distinctions among different kinds of foreign direct investment (branch 3 and downward in Figure 3.6), licensing agreements to greenfield construction (building a new facility from the ground up), vary by degrees of ownership. The licensing management contract is by far the simplest and cheapest way to produce abroad. Another firm is licensed to

Figure 3.6   The Direct Foreign Investment Decision Sequence

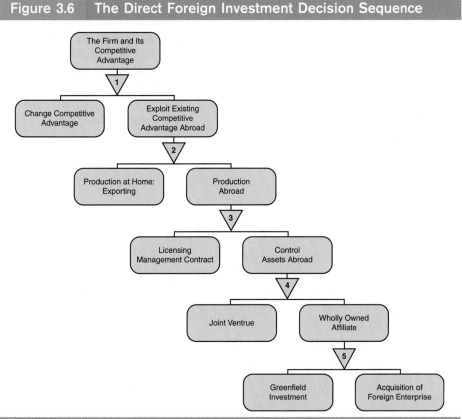

Source: Adapted from Gunter Dufey and R. Mirus, "Foreign Direct Investment: Theory and Strategic Considerations," unpublished, University of Michigan, May 1985.

produce the product, but with your firm's technology and know-how. The question is whether the reduced capital investment of simply licensing the product to another manufacturer is worth the risk of loss of control over the product and technology.

The firm that wants direct control over the foreign production process next determines the degree of equity control: to own the firm outright, or as a joint investment with another firm. Trade-offs with joint ventures continue the debate over control of assets and other sources of the firm's original competitive advantage. Many countries try to ensure the continued growth of local firms and investors by requiring that foreign firms operate jointly with local firms.

The final decision branch between a "greenfield investment"—building a firm from the ground up—and the purchase of an existing firm, is often a question of cost. A greenfield investment is the most expensive of all foreign investment alternatives. The acquisition of an existing firm is often lower in initial cost but may also contain a number of customizing and adjustment costs that are not apparent at the initial purchase. The purchase of a going concern may also have substantial benefits if the existing business possesses substantial customer and supplier relationships that can be used by the new owner in the pursuit of its own business.

THE THEORY OF FOREIGN DIRECT INVESTMENT

What motivates a firm to go beyond exporting or licensing? What benefits does the multinational firm expect to achieve by establishing a physical presence in other countries? These are the questions that the theory of foreign direct investment has sought to answer. As with trade theory, the questions have remained largely the same over time, while the answers have continued to change. With hundreds of countries, thousands of firms, and millions of products and services, there is no question that the answer to such an enormous question will likely get messy.

The following overview of investment theory has many similarities to the preceding discussion of international trade. The theme is a global business environment that attempts to satisfy increasingly sophisticated consumer demands, while the means of production, resources, skills, and technology needed become more complex and competitive. The theory of foreign direct investment is indeed eclectic, representing a collection of forces and drivers. The man responsible for the majority of the theoretical development, John Dunning, termed the theory the **eclectic paradigm**.

eclectic paradigm Representing a collection of forces or drivers.

FIRMS AS SEEKERS

A firm that expands across borders may be seeking any of a number of specific sources of profit or opportunity.

1. **Seeking resources:** There is no question that much of the initial foreign direct investment of the eighteenth and nineteenth centuries was the result of firms seeking unique and valuable natural resources for their products. Whether it be the copper resources of Chile, the linseed oils of Indonesia, or the petroleum resources spanning the Middle East, firms establishing permanent presences around the world are seeking access to the resources at the core of their business.

2. **Seeking factor advantages:** The resources needed for production are often combined with other advantages that are inherent in the country of production. The same low-cost labor at the heart of classical trade theory provides incentives for firms to move production to countries possessing these factor advantages. As noted by Vernon's product cycle, the same firms may move their own production to locations of factor advantages as the products and markets mature.

3. **Seeking knowledge:** Firms may attempt to acquire other firms in other countries for the technical or competitive skills they possess. Alternatively, companies may locate in and around centers of industrial enterprise unique to their specific industry, such as the footwear industry of Milan or the semiconductor industry of the Silicon Valley of California.

4. **Seeking security:** Firms continue to move internationally as they seek political stability or security. For example, Mexico has experienced a significant increase in foreign direct investment as a result of the tacit support of the United States, Canada, and Mexico itself as reflected by the North American Free Trade Agreement.

5. **Seeking markets:** Not the least of the motivations, the ability to gain and maintain access to markets is of paramount importance to multinational firms. Whether following the principles of Linder, in which firms learn from their domestic market and use that information to go international, or the principles of Porter, which emphasize the character of the domestic market as dictating international competitiveness, foreign market access is necessary.

FIRMS AS EXPLOITERS OF IMPERFECTIONS

Much of the investment theory developed in the past three decades has focused on the efforts of multinational firms to exploit the imperfections in factor and product markets created by governments. The work of Hymer, Kindleberger, and Caves noted that many of the policies of governments create imperfections. These market imperfections cover the entire range of supply and demand of the market: trade policy (tariffs and quotas), tax policies and incentives, preferential purchasing arrangements established by governments themselves, and financial restrictions on the access of foreign firms to domestic capital markets.

1. **Imperfections in access:** Many of the world's developing countries have long sought to create domestic industry by restricting imports of competitive products in order to allow smaller, less competitive domestic firms to grow and prosper—so-called **import substitution** policies. Multinational firms have sought to maintain their access to these markets by establishing their own productive presence within the country, effectively bypassing the tariff restriction.

2. **Imperfections in factor mobility:** Other multinational firms have exploited the same sources of comparative advantage identified throughout this chapter—the low-cost resources or factors often located in less-developed countries or countries with restrictions on the mobility of labor and capital. However, combining the mobility of capital with the immobility of low-cost labor has characterized much of the foreign direct investment seen throughout the developing world over the past 50 years.

3. **Imperfections in management:** The ability of multinational firms to successfully exploit or at least manage these imperfections still relies on their ability to gain an "advantage." Market advantages or powers are seen in international markets as in domestic markets: cost advantages, economies of scale and scope, product differentiation, managerial or marketing technique and knowledge, financial resources and strength.

import substitution A policy for economic growth adopted by many developing countries that involves the systematic encouragement of domestic production of goods formerly imported.

All these imperfections are the things of which competitive dreams are made. The multinational firm needs to find these in some form or another to justify the added complexities and costs of international investments. The Focus on Politics, Bridging the Red Sea, illustrates one of the many imperfections confronted by multinationals in real-world trade.

FOCUS ON POLITICS

Bridging the Red Sea

How can a border dispute between two of Africa's smallest countries threaten global trade? By being at the right spot at the wrong time. Djibouti and Eritrea have a long-simmering border dispute—a border that, for many miles, is nothing other than a rock wall. But more importantly, the two Horn of Africa countries are at the southern mouth of the Red Sea, and ultimately, influence shipping traffic in and out of the Suez Canal.

Djibouti has been the recipient of substantial foreign investment in recent years, particularly from Dubai, because it is seen as a major gateway for African trade in the coming decade. Although there are a variety of different shipping and logistics investments under way, it is "the Bridge" that has captured much of the world's attention. Tarek bin Laden, one of Osama bin Laden's half-brothers, is leading a project to build a 29-kilometer-long bridge from Djibouti to Yemen, traversing the Red Sea. The bridge would link Arabia and Africa and provide a base for highway, railway, and pipeline conduits—all for the nominal sum of $200 billion—linking the drought-stricken population of Djibouti, where 150,000 of its 800,000 people are today on the edge of starvation.

But all of these bridge dreams and investments could evaporate faster than water in the arid desert if Djibouti's neighbor to the north, Eritrea, stops rattling its swords and jumps the wall. Ironically, much of the border dispute dates back to a time before either existed as an independent state. The two countries are debating which colonial treaty or protocol actually defines their borders and behaviors: the 1897 Abyssinia-France treaty, the 1900–1901 France–Italy protocols, or the 1935 France–Italy treaty.

Sources: "Djibouti-Eritrea Border Tension Could Escalate, Warns UN Team," *UN News Centre*, September 18, 2008; "The Red Sea: Can It Really Be Bridged?" *Economist*, July 31, 2008; Jeffrey Gettleman, "Eritrea and Djibouti Square Off over Wasteland at the Horn of Africa," *The New York Times*, May 25, 2008.

FIRMS AS INTERNALIZERS

The question that has plagued the field of foreign direct investment is, Why can't all of the advantages and imperfections mentioned be achieved through management contracts or licensing agreements (the choice available to the international investor at step 3 in Figure 3.6)? Why is it necessary for *the firm itself* to establish a physical presence in the country? What pushes the multinational firm further down the investment decision tree?

The research of Buckley and Casson and Dunning has attempted to answer these questions by focusing on nontransferable sources of competitive advantage—proprietary information possessed by the firm and its people. Many advantages firms possess center around their hands-on knowledge of producing a good or providing a service. By establishing their own multinational operations they can internalize the production, thus keeping confidential the information that is at the core of the firm's competitiveness. **Internalization** is preferable to the use of arms-length arrangements such as management contracts or licensing agreements. They either do not allow the effective transmission of the knowledge or represent too serious a threat to the loss of the knowledge to allow the firm to successfully achieve the hoped-for benefits of international investment.

internalization Occurs when a firm establishes its own multinational operation, keeping information that is at the core of its competitiveness within the firm.

SUMMARY

The theory of international trade has changed drastically from that first put forward by Adam Smith. The classical theories of Adam Smith and David Ricardo focused on the abilities of countries to produce goods more cheaply than other countries. The earliest production and trade theories saw labor as the major factor expense that went into any product. If a country could pay that labor less, and if that labor could produce more physically than labor in other countries, the country might obtain an absolute or comparative advantage in trade.

Subsequent theoretical development led to a more detailed understanding of production and its costs. Factors of production are now believed to include labor (skilled and unskilled), capital, natural resources, and other potentially significant commodities that are difficult to reproduce or replace, such as energy. Technology, once assumed to be the same across all countries, is now seen as one of the premier driving forces in determining who holds the competitive edge or advantage. International trade is now seen as a complex combination of thousands of products, technologies, and firms that are constantly innovating to either keep up with or get ahead of the competition.

Modern trade theory has looked beyond production cost to analyze how the demands of the marketplace alter who trades with whom and which firms survive domestically and internationally. The abilities of firms to adapt to foreign markets, both in the demands and with the competitors that form the foreign markets, have required much of international trade and investment theory to search out new and innovative approaches to what determines success and failure.

Finally, as world economies grew and the magnitude of world trade increased, the simplistic ideas that guided international trade and investment theory have had to grow with them. The choices that many firms face today require them to directly move their capital, technology, and know-how to countries that possess other unique factors or market advantages that will help them keep pace with market demands. Even then, world business conditions constitute changing fortunes.

KEY TERMS

autarky   64

mercantilism   64

specie   65

absolute advantage   66

division of labor   67

comparative advantage   67

production possibilities frontier   68

opportunity costs   70

factor proportions theory   72

factors of production   72

factor intensity   72

input-output analysis   75

Leontief Paradox   75

market segment   77

product cycle theory   77

abandoned product ranges   81

intra-industry trade   81

product differentiation   81

scale economies   83

eclectic paradigm   88

import substitution   89

internalization   90

QUESTIONS FOR DISCUSSION

1. According to the theory of comparative advantage as explained by Ricardo, why is trade always possible between two countries, even when one is absolutely inefficient compared to the other?

2. The factor proportions theory of international trade assumes that all countries produce the same product the same way. Would international competition cause or prevent this from happening?

3. What, in your opinion, were the constructive impacts on trade theory resulting from the empirical research of Wassily Leontief?

4. Product cycle theory has always been a very "attractive theory" to many students. Why do you think that is?

5. If the product cycle theory were accepted for the basis of policymaking in the United States, what should the U.S. government do to help U.S. firms exploit the principles of the theory?

6. Many trade theorists argue that the primary contribution of Michael Porter has been to repopularize old ideas in new, more applicable ways. To what degree do you think Porter's ideas are new or old?

7. How would you analyze the statement that "international investment is simply a modern extension of classical trade"?

8. How can a crisis in Asia impact jobs and profits in the United States?

INTERNET EXERCISES

1. The differences across multinational firms are striking. Using a sample of firms such as those listed here, pull from their individual web pages the proportions of their incomes that are earned outside their country of incorporation.

Walt Disney	http://www.disney.com/
Nestlé S.A.	http://www.nestle.com/
Intel	http://www.intel.com/
Chrysler	http://www.chrysler.com/
Mitsubishi Motors	http://www.mitsubishi-motors.com/

Also note the way in which international business is now conducted via the Internet. Several of these home pages allow the user to choose the language of the presentation viewed. Others, like Chrysler, report financial results in two different accounting frameworks, those used in Germany and the generally accepted accounting practices (GAAP) used in the United States.

2. There is no hotter topic in business today than corporate governance, the way in which firms are controlled by management and ownership across countries. Use the following sites to view recent research, current events and news items, and other information related to the relationships between a business and its stakeholders.

Corporate Governance Net	http://www.corpgov.net/
Corporate Governance Research	http://www.irrc.org

TAKE A STAND

International trade theory has stated quite clearly for many years that countries should specialize in the production and export of products and services that intensively use a relatively cheap input that the country possesses—even if that input is labor.

A multinational company that chooses to move textile manufacturing to Central America, automobile parts manufacturing and assembly to Mexico, or pharmaceutical processing to mainland China is following the simple process of producing in the lowest cost site possible. This does not always mean low skilled jobs, but only lower cost labor, because many countries now offer highly educated and highly skilled workforces, but at very low wage rates. The economic and employment repercussions on the industrial country are well known, as workers are left unemployed, entire regions suffer economic collapse, and social infrastructures struggle to compensate.

That company, however, may be paying a wage rate that is not only less than a *living wage* back in its home country like the United States, Germany, or Japan, but may even be less than a living wage in the country in which it is now operating.

For Discussion

Should companies pay a minimum wage—a living wage—regardless of what they are required to pay by law? Or should a company pay a competitive wage with what the market demands, whether high or low?

CHAPTER 4

The Balance of Payments

CHAPTER CONTENTS & LEARNING OBJECTIVES

FUNDAMENTALS OF BALANCE OF PAYMENTS ACCOUNTING

1. To understand the fundamental principles of how countries measure international business activity, the balance of payments

THE ACCOUNTS OF THE BALANCE OF PAYMENTS

2. To examine the similarities of the current and capital accounts of the balance of payments

THE BALANCE OF PAYMENTS IN TOTAL

3. To understand the critical differences between trade in merchandise and services, and why international investment activity has recently been controversial in the United States

THE BALANCE OF PAYMENTS AND ECONOMIC CRISES

4. To review the mechanical steps of how exchange rate changes are transmitted into altered trade prices and eventually trade volumes

CAPITAL MOBILITY

5. To understand how countries with different government policies toward international trade and investment, or different levels of economic development, differ in their balance of payments

Balance of payments difficulties can arise—and, in the worst case, build into crises—even in the face of strong prevention efforts. The IMF assists countries in restoring economic stability by helping devise programs of corrective policies and providing loans to support them.

Bad luck, inappropriate policies, or a combination of the two may create balance of payments difficulties in a country—that is, a situation where sufficient financing on affordable terms cannot be obtained to meet international payment obligations. In the worst case, the difficulties can build into a crisis. The country's currency may be forced to depreciate rapidly, making international goods and capital more expensive, and the domestic economy may experience a painful disruption. These problems may also spread to other countries.

The causes of such difficulties are often varied and complex. Key factors have included weak domestic financial systems, large and persistent fiscal deficits, high levels of external and/or public debt, exchange rates fixed at inappropriate levels, natural disasters, or armed conflicts or a sudden and strong increase in the price of key commodities such as food and fuel. Some of these factors can directly affect a country's trade account, reducing exports or increasing imports. Others may reduce the financing available for international transactions; for example, investors may lose confidence in a country's prospects, leading to massive asset sales, or "capital flight." In either case, diagnoses of, and responses to, crises are complicated by linkages between various sectors of the economy. Imbalances in one sector can quickly spread to other sectors, leading to widespread economic disruption.

Source: "Factsheet, October 2008: How The IMF Helps to Resolve Balance of Payments Difficulties," http://www.imf.org/external/np/exr/facts/crises.htm, accessed September 2009.

International business transactions occur in many different forms over the course of a year. The measurement of all international economic transactions between the residents of a country and foreign residents is called the **balance of payments (BOP)**.[1] Government policymakers need such measures of economic activity to evaluate the general competitiveness of domestic industry, to set exchange-rate or interest-rate policies or goals, and for many other purposes. Individuals and businesses use various BOP measures to gauge the growth and health of specific types of trade or financial transactions by country and regions of the world against the home country.

International transactions take many forms. Each of the following examples is an international economic transaction that is counted and captured in the U.S. balance of payments.

> **balance of payments (BOP)** A statement of all transactions between one country and the rest of the world during a given period; a record of flows of goods, services, and investments across borders.

- U.S. imports of Honda automobiles, which are manufactured in Japan.
- A U.S.-based firm, Bechtel, is hired to manage the construction of a major water-treatment facility in the Middle East.
- The U.S. subsidiary of a French firm, Saint Gobain, pays profits (dividends) back to the parent firm in Paris.
- An American tourist purchases a hand-blown glass figurine in Venice, Italy.
- The U.S. government provides grant financing of military equipment for its NATO (North Atlantic Treaty Organization) military ally, Turkey.
- A Canadian dentist purchases a U.S. Treasury bill through an investment broker in Cleveland, Ohio.

These are just a small sample of the hundreds of thousands of international transactions that occur each year. The balance of payments provides a systematic method for the classification of all of these transactions. There is one rule of thumb that will always aid in the understanding of BOP accounting: Watch the direction of the movement of money.

> **current account** An account in the BOP statement that records the results of transactions involving merchandise, services, and unilateral transfers between countries.

The balance of payments is composed of a number of subaccounts that are watched quite closely by groups as diverse as investors on Wall Street, farmers in Iowa, politicians on Capitol Hill, and people in boardrooms across America. These groups track and analyze the two major subaccounts, the **current account** and the **financial account**, on a continuing basis. Before describing these two subaccounts and the balance of payments as a whole, it is necessary to understand the rather unusual features of how balance of payments accounting is conducted.

> **financial account** An account in the BOP statement that records transactions involving borrowing, lending, and investing across borders.

FUNDAMENTALS OF BALANCE OF PAYMENTS ACCOUNTING

> *1. To understand the fundamental principles of how countries measure international business activity, the balance of payments*

The balance of payments must balance. If it does not, something has either not been counted or counted properly. It is therefore improper to state that the BOP is in disequilibrium. It cannot be. The supply and demand for a country's currency may be imbalanced, but that is not the same thing. Subaccounts of the BOP, such as the merchandise trade balance, may be imbalanced, but the entire BOP of a single country is always balanced.

There are three main elements to the process of measuring international economic activity: (1) identifying what is and is not an international economic transaction; (2) understanding how the flow of goods, services, assets, and money creates debits and credits to the overall BOP; and (3) understanding the bookkeeping procedures for BOP accounting, called double entry.

DEFINING INTERNATIONAL ECONOMIC TRANSACTIONS

Identifying international transactions is ordinarily not difficult. The export of merchandise, goods such as trucks, machinery, computers, telecommunications equipment, and so forth, is obviously an international transaction. Imports such as French wine, Japanese cameras, and German automobiles are also clearly international transactions. But this merchandise trade is only a portion of the thousands of different international transactions that occur in the United States or any other country each year.

Many other international transactions are not so obvious. The purchase of a glass figure in Venice, Italy, by an American tourist is classified as a U.S. merchandise import. In fact, all expenditures made by American tourists around the globe that are for goods or services (meals, hotel accommodations, and so forth) are recorded in the U.S. balance of payments as imports of travel services in the current account. The purchase of a U.S. Treasury bill by a foreign resident is an international financial transaction and is dutifully recorded in the capital account of the U.S. balance of payments.

THE BOP AS A FLOW STATEMENT

The BOP is often misunderstood because many people believe it to be a balance sheet, rather than a cash flow statement. By recording all international transactions over a period of time, it is tracking the continuing flow of purchases and payments between a country and all other countries. It does not add up the value of all assets and liabilities of a country like a balance sheet does for an individual firm.

There are two types of business transactions that dominate the balance of payments:

1. **Real assets:** The exchange of goods (e.g., automobiles, computers, watches, textiles) and services (e.g., banking services, consulting services, travel services) for other goods and services (barter) or for the more common type of payment, money.
2. **Financial assets:** The exchange of financial claims (e.g., stocks, bonds, loans, purchases or sales of companies) in exchange for other financial claims or money.

Although assets can be separated as to whether they are real or financial, it is often easier to simply think of all assets as being goods that can be bought and sold. An American tourist's purchase of a handwoven area rug in a shop in Bangkok is not all that different from a Wall Street banker buying a British government bond for investment purposes.

BOP ACCOUNTING: DOUBLE-ENTRY BOOKKEEPING

The balance of payments employs an accounting technique called **double-entry bookkeeping**. Double-entry bookkeeping is the age-old method of accounting in which every transaction produces a debit and a credit of the same amount. Simultaneously. It has to. A debit is created whenever an asset is increased, a liability is decreased, or an expense is increased. Similarly, a credit is created whenever an asset is decreased, a liability is increased, or an expense is decreased.

An example clarifies this process. A U.S. retail store imports from Japan $2 million worth of consumer electronics. A negative entry is made in the merchandise-import subcategory of the current account in the amount of $2 million. Simultaneously, a positive entry of the same $2 million is made in the capital account for the

double-entry bookkeeping
Accounting methodology where each transaction gives rise to both a debit and a credit of the same currency amount. It is used in the construction of the balance of payments.

transfer of $2 million to the Japanese manufacturer. Obviously, the result of hundreds of thousands of such transactions and entries should theoretically result in a perfect balance.

That said, it is now a problem of application, and a problem it is. The measurement of all international transactions in and out of a country over a year is a daunting task. Mistakes, errors, and statistical discrepancies will occur. The primary problem is that although double-entry bookkeeping is employed in theory, the individual transactions are recorded independently. Current and capital account entries are recorded independent of one another, not together as double-entry bookkeeping would prescribe. It must then be recognized that there will be serious discrepancies (to use a nice term for it) between debits and credits, and the possibility in total that the balance of payments may not balance!

The following section describes the various balance of payment accounts, their meanings, and their relationships, using the United States as the example. The chapter then concludes with a discussion—and a number of examples—of how different countries with different policies or levels of economic development may differ markedly in their balance of payment accounts.

THE ACCOUNTS OF THE BALANCE OF PAYMENTS

2. To examine the similarities of the current and capital accounts of the balance of payments

The balance of payments is composed of two primary subaccounts, the *Current Account* and the *Financial/Capital Account*. In addition, the *Official Reserves Account* tracks government currency transactions, and a fourth statistical subaccount, the *Net Errors and Omissions Account*, is produced to preserve the balance in the BOP. The international economic relationships between countries do, however, continue to evolve, as the recent revision of the major accounts within the BOP discussed later indicates.[2]

THE CURRENT ACCOUNT

The *Current Account* includes all international economic transactions with income or payment flows occurring within the year, the *current* period. The *Current Account* consists of four subcategories:

1. **Goods trade:** This is the export and import of goods. Merchandise trade is the oldest and most traditional form of international economic activity. Although many countries depend on imports of many goods (as they should according to the theory of comparative advantage), they also normally work to preserve either a balance of goods trade or even a surplus.

2. **Services trade:** This is the export and import of services. Some common international services are financial services provided by banks to foreign importers and exporters, travel services of airlines, and construction services of domestic firms in other countries. For the major industrial countries, this subaccount has shown the fastest growth in the past decade.

3. **Income:** This category is predominantly *current income* associated with investments that were made in previous periods. If a U.S. firm created a subsidiary in South Korea to produce metal parts in a previous year, the proportion of net income that is paid back to the parent company in the current year (the dividend) constitutes current investment income. Additionally, wages and salaries paid to nonresident workers is also included in this category.

4. Current transfers: Transfers are the financial settlements associated with the change in ownership of real resources or financial items. Any transfer between countries that is one-way, a gift, or a grant, is termed a *current transfer*. A common example of a current transfer would be funds provided by the United States government to aid in the development of a less-developed nation. Transfers associated with the transfer of fixed assets are included in a new separate account, the Capital Account, which now follows the Current Account. The contents of what previously had been called the capital account are now included within the *Financial Account*.

All countries possess some amount of trade, most of which is merchandise. Many smaller and less-developed countries have little in the way of service trade, or items that fall under the income or transfers subaccounts.

The Current Account is typically dominated by the first component described—the export and import of merchandise. For this reason, the *balance on trade* (BOT), which is so widely quoted in the business press in most countries, refers specifically to the balance of exports and imports of goods trade only. For a larger industrialized country, however, the BOT is somewhat misleading because service trade is not included; it may be opposite in sign on net, and it may actually be fairly large as well.

Table 4.1 summarizes the Current Account and its components for the United States for the 2002–2008 period. As illustrated, the U.S. goods trade balance has consistently been negative, but has been partially offset by the continuing surplus in services trade.

Goods Trade

Figure 4.1 places the Current Account values of Table 4.1 in perspective over time by dividing the Current Account into its two major components: (1) goods trade and (2) services trade. The first and most striking message is the magnitude of the goods trade deficit in 2006, 2007, and 2008 (a continuation of a position created in the early 1980s). The balance on services and income, although not large in comparison to net goods trade, has generally run a surplus over the past two decades.

Table 4.1   The U.S. Current Account, 2002–2008 (billions of U.S. dollars)

	2002	2003	2004	2005	2006	2007	2008
Goods exports	686	717	811	898	1020	1142	1281
Goods imports	−1167	−1264	−1477	−1682	−1863	−1969	−2117
Goods trade balance (BOT)	−481	−548	−666	−783	−844	−827	−836
Services trade credits	289	301	350	385	432	501	546
Services trade debits	−231	−250	−291	−314	−349	−375	−405
Services trade balance	58	51	58	72	83	125	140
Income receipts	281	320	414	535	682	819	765
Income payments	−254	−275	−347	−463	−634	−728	−646
Income balance	27	45	67	72	48	91	118
Current transfers, credits	12	15	20	19	26	23	22
Current transfers, debits	−77	−87	−105	−109	−117	−139	−150
Net transfers	−65	−72	−84	−90	−91	−116	−128
Current Account Balance	−461	−523	−625	−729	−804	−727	−706

Source: Derived from International Monetary Fund, *International Financial Statistics*, imf.org, September 2009.

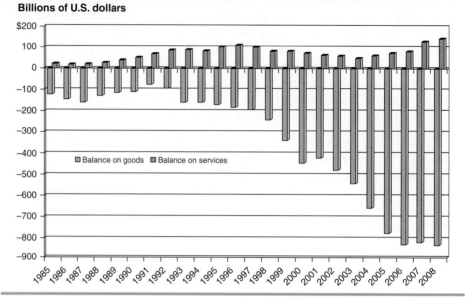

Figure 4.1   U.S. Trade Balances on Goods and Services, 1985–2008

Billions of U.S. dollars

Source: International Monetary Fund, *International Financial Statistics*, imf.org, September 2009.

The deficits in the BOT of the past decade have been an area of considerable concern for the United States. Merchandise trade is the original core of international trade. It has three major components: manufactured goods, agriculture, and fuels. The manufacturing of goods was the basis of the industrial revolution, and the focus of the theory of international trade described in the previous chapter. The U.S. goods trade deficit of the 1980s and 1990s was mainly caused by a decline in traditional manufacturing industries that have over history employed many of America's workers. Declines in the net trade balance in areas such as steel, automobiles, automotive parts, textiles, shoe manufacturing, and others caused massive economic and social disruption. The problems of dealing with these shifting trade balances will be discussed in detail in a later chapter.

The most encouraging news for U.S. manufacturing trade is the growth of exports in recent years. A number of factors contributed to the growth of U.S. exports, such as the weaker dollar (which made U.S.-manufactured goods cheaper in terms of the currencies of other countries), more rapid economic growth in Europe, and a substantial increase in agricultural exports. Understanding merchandise import and export performance is much like understanding the market for any single product. The demand factors that drive both imports and exports are income, the economic growth rate of the buyer, and price (the price of the product in the eyes of the consumer after passing through an exchange rate). For example, U.S. merchandise imports reflect the income level and growth of American consumers and industry. As income rises, so does the demand for imports.

Exports follow the same principles but in the reversed position. U.S. merchandise exports depend not on the incomes of U.S. residents, but on the incomes of the buyers of U.S. products in all other countries around the world. When these economies are growing, the demand for U.S. products will also rise. However, the recent economic crises in Asia now raise questions regarding U.S. export growth in the immediate future.

The service component of the U.S. Current Account is one of mystery to many. As illustrated in both Table 4.1 and Figure 4.1, the U.S. has consistently achieved a surplus in services trade income. The major categories of services include travel and passenger fares, transportation services, expenditures by U.S. students abroad and foreign students pursuing studies in the United States, telecommunications services, and financial services.

THE CAPITAL AND FINANCIAL ACCOUNT

The *Capital and Financial Account* of the balance of payments measures all international economic transactions of financial assets. It is divided into two major components, the *Capital Account* and the *Financial Account*.

- **The Capital Account:** The Capital Account is made up of transfers of financial assets and the acquisition and disposal of nonproduced/nonfinancial assets. The magnitude of capital transactions covered is of a relatively minor amount, and will be included in principle in all of the following discussions of the financial account.

- **The Financial Account:** The financial account consists of three components: *direct investment*, *portfolio investment*, and *other asset investment*. Financial assets can be classified in a number of different ways, including the length of the life of the asset (its maturity) and by the nature of the ownership (public or private). The Financial Account, however, uses a third way. It is classified by the degree of control over the assets or operations the claim represents: *portfolio investment*, where the investor has no control, or *direct investment*, where the investor exerts some explicit degree of control over the assets. (The contents of the Financial Account are for all intents and purposes the same as those of the Capital Account under the IMF's BOP accounting framework used prior to 1996. We will refer, from this point on, almost exclusively to the Financial Account.)

Table 4.2 shows the major subcategories of the U.S. capital account balance from 2002–2008: *direct investment*, *portfolio investment*, *financial derivatives*, and *other investment*.

Table 4.2	The U.S. Financial Account and Components, 2002–2008 (billions of U.S. dollars)						
	2002	2003	2004	2005	2006	2007	2008
Direct Investment							
Direct investment abroad	−154	−150	−316	−36	−245	−399	−332
Direct investment in the U.S.	84	64	146	113	243	276	320
Net direct investment	−70	−86	−170	76	−2	−123	−12
Portfolio Investment							
Assets, net	−49	−123	−177	−258	−499	−396	117
Liabilities, net	428	550	867	832	1127	1155	528
Net portfolio investment	379	427	690	575	628	759	645
Financial derivatives, net					30	6	−29
Other Investment							
Other investment assets	−88	−54	−510	−267	−544	−677	219
Other investment liabilities	283	244	520	303	695	699	−313
Net other investment	195	190	10	36	151	22	−94
Net Financial Account Balance	504	532	530	687	807	664	510

Source: Derived from International Monetary Fund, *International Financial Statistics*, imf.org, September 2009.

1. **Direct investment:** This is the net balance of capital dispersed out of and into the United States for the purpose of exerting control over assets. For example, if a U.S. firm either builds a new automotive parts facility in another country or actually purchases a company in another country, this would fall under *direct investment* in the U.S. balance of payments accounts. When the capital flows out of the United States, it enters the balance of payments as a negative cash flow. If, however, foreign firms purchase firms in the United States (e.g., Sony of Japan purchased Columbia Pictures in 1989) it is a capital inflow and enters the balance of payments positively. Whenever 10 percent or more of the voting shares in a U.S. company is held by foreign investors, the company is classified as the U.S. affiliate of a foreign company, and a *foreign direct investment.* Similarly, if U.S. investors hold 10 percent or more of the control in a company outside the United States, that company is considered the foreign affiliate of a U.S. company.

2. **Portfolio investment:** This is net balance of capital that flows in and out of the United States but does not reach the 10 percent ownership threshold of direct investment. If a U.S. resident purchases shares in a Japanese firm, but does not attain the 10 percent threshold, it is considered a *portfolio investment* (and in this case an outflow of capital). The purchase or sale of debt securities (like U.S. Treasury bills) across borders is also classified as *portfolio investment* because debt securities by definition do not provide the buyer with ownership or control.

3. **Financial derivatives:** Financial derivatives are financial instruments that are linked to a specific financial instrument, indicator, or commodity— the instrument's underlying asset. The value of a financial derivative derives from the price of an underlying item, such as an asset or index. Financial derivatives are used for a number of purposes, including risk management, hedging, arbitrage between markets, and speculation. Financial derivatives were previously reported as a subcategory of Portfolio Investment (section 2), but, as a result of a revision by the IMF in 2002, they are now required to be reported on their own if the country deems them to be of significant size.

4. **Other investment assets/liabilities:** This final category consists of various short-term and long-term trade credits, cross-border loans from all types of financial institutions, currency deposits and bank deposits, and other accounts receivable and payable related to cross-border trade.

Direct Investment

Figure 4.2 shows how the major subaccounts of the U.S. capital account— *net direct investment, portfolio investment,* and *other investment*—have changed since 1985.

The boom in foreign investment into the United States, or foreign resident purchases of assets in the United States, during the 1980s was extremely controversial. The source of concern over foreign investment in any country, including the United States, focuses on two topics—control and profit. Most countries possess restrictions on what foreigners may own in their country. This is based on the premise that domestic land, assets, and industry in general should be held by residents of the country. For example, up until 1990 it was not possible for a foreign firm to own more than 20 percent of any company in Finland. This rule is the norm, rather than the exception. The United States has traditionally had few restrictions on what foreign residents or firms can own or control in the United States; most restrictions that remain today are related to national security concerns. As opposed to many of the traditional debates over whether international trade should be free or not, there is not the same

Figure 4.2   The U.S. Financial Account, 1985–2008

Billions of U.S. dollars

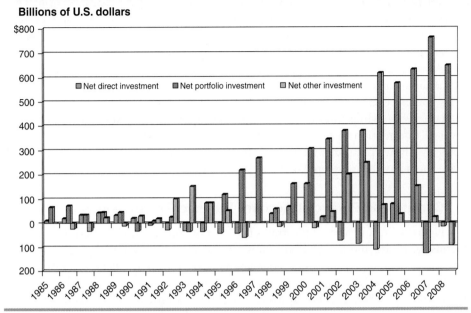

■ Net direct investment   ■ Net portfolio investment   □ Net other investment

Source: International Monetary Fund, *International Financial Statistics,* imf.org, September 2009.

consensus that international investment should necessarily be free. This is a question that is still very much a domestic political concern first, and an international economic issue second.

The second major source of concern over foreign direct investment is who receives the profits from the enterprise. Foreign companies owning firms in the United States will ultimately profit from the activities of the firms, or put another way, from the efforts of American workers. In spite of evidence that foreign firms in the United States reinvest most of the profits in the United States (in fact at a higher rate than domestic firms), the debate has continued on possible profit drains. Regardless of the actual choices made, workers of any nation feel the profits of their work should remain in the hands of their own citizens. Once again, this is in many ways a political and emotional concern rather than an economic one.

The choice of words used to describe foreign investment can also influence public opinion. If these massive capital inflows are described as "capital investments from all over the world showing their faith in the future of American industry," the net capital surplus is represented as decidedly positive. If, however, the net capital surplus is described as resulting in "the United States as the world's largest debtor nation," the negative connotation is obvious. Both are essentially spins on the economic principles at work. Capital, whether short-term or long-term, flows to where it believes it can earn the greatest return for the level of risk. Although in an accounting sense that is "international debt," when the majority of the capital inflow is in the form of direct investment and a long-term commitment to jobs, production, services, technological, and other competitive investments, the impact on the competitiveness of American industry (an industry located within the United States) is increased. The "net debtor" label is misleading in that it inappropriately invites comparison with large debt crisis conditions suffered by many countries in the past, like Mexico and Brazil.

Portfolio Investment

Portfolio investment is capital invested in activities that are purely profit-motivated (return), rather than ones made in the prospect of controlling or managing the investment. Investments that are purchases of debit securities, bonds, interest-bearing bank accounts, and the like are only intended to earn a return. They provide no vote or control over the party issuing the debt. Purchases by foreign investors of debt issued by the U.S. government (U.S. Treasury bills, notes, and bonds) constitute net portfolio investment in the United States.

As illustrated in Figure 4.2, portfolio investment has shown a much more volatile behavior than net direct investment over the past decade. Many U.S. debt securities, such as U.S. Treasury securities and corporate bonds, were in high demand in the late 1980s, while surging emerging markets in both debt and equities caused a reversal in direction in the 1990s. The motivating forces for portfolio investment flows are always the same, *return* and *risk*. This theoretical fact, however, does not make them any the more predictable.

Current and Financial Account Balance Relationships

Figure 4.3 (A, B, and C) illustrates the current and financial account balances for Germany, Japan, and the United States over recent years. What the figure shows is one of the basic economic and accounting relationships of the balance of payments: *the inverse relationship between the Current and Financial accounts.* (The only exception is Germany in 1999, the year in which the euro was introduced.) This inverse relationship is not accidental. The methodology of the balance of payments, double-entry bookkeeping, requires that the current and financial accounts be offsetting. Countries experiencing large current account deficits "finance" these purchases through equally large surpluses in the financial account and vice versa.

NET ERRORS AND OMISSIONS

net errors and omissions account Makes sure the balance of payments (BOP) actually balances.

As noted before, because Current Account and Financial Account entries are collected and recorded separately, errors or statistical discrepancies will occur. The **net errors and omissions account** (this is the title used by the International Monetary Fund) makes sure that the BOP actually balances.

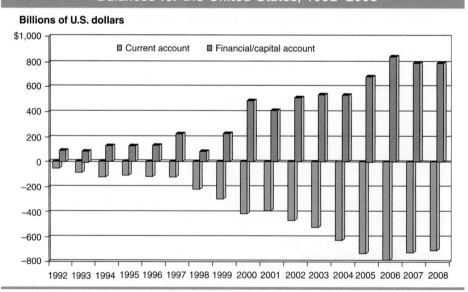

Figure 4.3(A)   Current and Combined Financial/Capital Account Balances for the United States, 1992–2008

Source: International Monetary Fund, *International Financial Statistics,* imf.org, October 2009.

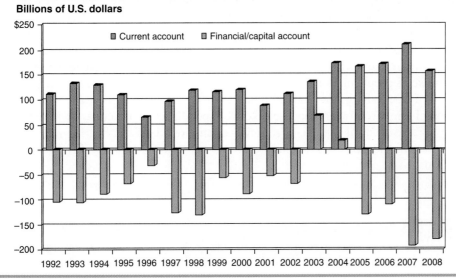

Figure 4.3(B) Current and Combined Financial/Capital Account Balances for Japan, 1992–2008

Source: International Monetary Fund, *International Financial Statistics,* imf.org, October 2009.

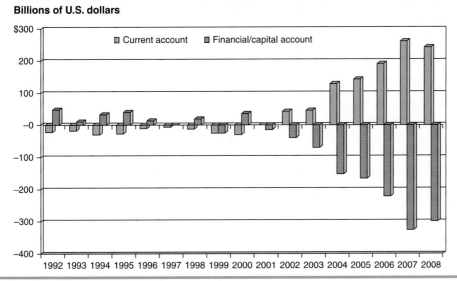

Figure 4.3(C) Current and Combined Financial/Capital Account Balances for Germany, 1992–2008

Source: International Monetary Fund, *International Financial Statistics,* imf.org, October 2009.

OFFICIAL RESERVES ACCOUNT

The **official reserves account** is the total currency and metallic reserves held by official monetary authorities within the country. These reserves are normally composed of the major currencies used in international trade and financial transactions (so-called hard currencies like the U.S. dollar, German mark, and Japanese yen) and gold.

official reserves account An account in the BOP statement that shows (1) the change in the amount of funds immediately available to a country for making international payments and (2) the borrowing and lending that has taken place between the monetary authorities of different countries either directly or through the International Monetary Fund.

fixed-exchange-rate The government of a country officially declares that its currency is convertible into a fixed amount of some other currency.

floating-exchange-rate Under this system, the government possesses no responsibility to declare that its currency is convertible into a fixed amount of some other currency; this diminishes the role of official reserves.

The significance of official reserves depends generally on whether the country is operating under a **fixed-exchange-rate** regime or a **floating-exchange-rate** system. If a country's currency is fixed, this means that the government of the country officially declares that the currency is convertible into a fixed amount of some other currency. For example, for many years the South Korean won was fixed to the U.S. dollar at 484 won equal to 1 U.S. dollar. It is the government's responsibility to maintain this fixed rate (also called *parity rate*). If for some reason there is an excess supply of Korean won on the currency market, to prevent the value of the won from falling, the South Korean government must support the won's value by purchasing won on the open market (by spending its hard currency reserves, its *official reserves*) until the excess supply is eliminated. Under a floating-rate system, the government possesses no such responsibility and the role of official reserves is diminished.

THE BALANCE OF PAYMENTS IN TOTAL

3. To understand the critical differences between trade in merchandise and services, and why international investment activity has recently been controversial in the United States

Table 4.3 provides the official balance of payments for the United States as presented by the International Monetary Fund (IMF), the multinational organization that collects these statistics for more than 160 different countries around the globe. Now that the individual accounts and the relationships among the accounts have been discussed, Table 4.3 gives a comprehensive overview of how the individual accounts are combined to create some of the most useful summary measures for multinational business managers.

The current account (line A in Table 4.3), the capital account (line B), and the financial account (line C) combine to form the *basic balance (Total, Groups A through C)*. This is one of the most frequently used summary measures of the BOP. It is used to describe the international economic activity of the nation as determined by market forces, not by government decisions (such as currency market intervention). The U.S. *basic balance* totaled a deficit of –$196 billion in 2008. A second frequently used summary measure, the overall balance, also called the official settlements balance (*Total of Groups A through D* in Table 4.3), was at a surplus of $4 billion in 2008.

The meaning of the balance of payments has changed over the past 30 years. As long as most of the major industrial countries were still operating under fixed exchange rates, the interpretation of the BOP was relatively straightforward. A surplus in the BOP implied that the demand for the country's currency exceeded the supply, and that the government should then allow the currency value to increase (*revalue*) or to intervene and accumulate additional foreign currency reserves in the Official Reserves Account. This would occur as the government sold its own currency in exchange for other currencies, thus building up its stores of hard currencies. A deficit in the BOP implied an excess supply of the country's currency on world markets, and the government would then either *devalue* the currency or expend its official reserves to support its value. But the transition to floating exchange rate regimes in the 1970s (described in the following chapter) changed the focus from the total BOP to its various subaccounts like the Current and Financial Account balances. These are the indicators of economic activities and currency repercussions to come. The crises in Mexico (1994), Asia (1997), Turkey (2001), and Argentina and Venezuela (2002) highlight the continuing changes in the role of the balance of payments.

	1998	1999	2000	2001	2002	2003	2004	2005	2006	2007	2008
A. Current Account	**-213**	**-300**	**-417**	**-385**	**-461**	**-523**	**-625**	**-729**	**-804**	**-727**	**-706**
Goods: exports fob	672	686	775	722	686	717	811	898	1020	1142	1281
Goods: imports fob	-917	-1030	-1227	-1148	-1167	-1264	-1477	-1682	-1863	-1969	-2117
Balance on Goods	-245	-344	-452	-426	-481	-548	-666	-783	-844	-827	-836
Services: credit	261	280	296	283	289	301	350	385	432	501	546
Services: debit	-181	-199	-224	-222	-231	-250	-291	-314	-349	-375	-405
Balance on Goods and Services	-165	-263	-380	-365	-424	-497	-608	-712	-760	-701	-696
Income: credit	262	294	351	291	281	320	414	535	682	819	765
Income: debit	-258	-280	-330	-259	-254	-275	-347	-463	-634	-728	-646
Balance on Goods, Services, and Income	-160	-249	-359	-333	-396	-452	-541	-639	-712	-611	-578
Current transfers: credit	10	9	11	9	12	15	20	19	26	23	22
Current transfers: debit	-63	-59	-69	-60	-77	-87	-105	-109	-117	-139	-150
B. Capital Account	**-1**	**-5**	**-1**	**-1**	**-1**	**-3**	**-2**	**-4**	**-4**	**-2**	**1**
Capital account: credit	1	1	1	1	1	1	1	1	1	2	5
Capital account: debit	-2	-6	-2	-2	-2	-4	-3	-5	-5	-4	-4
Total Groups A plus B	***-214***	***-305***	***-418***	***-386***	***-463***	***-527***	***-627***	***-733***	***-807***	***-728***	***-705***
C. Financial Account	**77**	**227**	**478**	**405**	**504**	**532**	**530**	**687**	**807**	**664**	**509**
Direct investment	36	65	162	25	-70	-86	-170	76	-2	-123	-12
Direct investment abroad	-143	-225	-159	-142	-154	-150	-316	-36	-245	-399	-332
Direct investment in United States	179	289	321	167	84	64	146	113	243	276	320
Portfolio investment assets	-130	-122	-128	-91	-49	-123	-177	-258	-499	-396	117
Equity securities	-101	-114	-107	-109	-17	-118	-85	-187	-137	-148	-1
Debt securities	-29	-8	-21	18	-32	-5	-93	-71	-362	-248	119
Portfolio investment liabilities	188	286	437	428	428	550	867	832	1127	1155	528
Equity securities	42	112	194	121	54	34	62	89	145	276	110
Debt securities	146	173	243	307	374	516	806	743	981	879	417

(continued)

Table 4.3 (Continued)

	1998	1999	2000	2001	2002	2003	2004	2005	2006	2007	2008
Financial derivatives, net	0	0	0	0	0	0	0	0	30	6	−30
Other investment assets	−74	−166	−273	−145	−88	−54	−510	−267	−544	−677	219
Monetary authorities	0	0	0	0	0	0	0	0	0	−24	−530
General government	0	3	−1	0	0	1	2	6	5	2	0
Banks	−36	−71	−133	−136	−38	−26	−359	−151	−343	−494	356
Other sectors	−38	−98	−139	−9	−50	−29	−153	−121	−207	−161	393
Other investment liabilities	57	165	280	187	283	244	520	303	695	699	−313
Monetary authorities	7	25	−11	35	70	11	13	8	2	−11	29
General government	−3	−1	−2	−2	0	−1	0	0	3	5	9
Banks	30	67	123	88	118	136	347	232	344	466	−268
Other sectors	23	74	171	66	96	98	160	62	346	238	−83
Total, Groups A through C	*−138*	*−77*	*60*	*19*	*41*	*5*	*−98*	*−46*	*−1*	*−65*	*−196*
D. Net Errors and Omissions	**144**	**69**	**−59**	**−14**	**−38**	**−6**	**95**	**32**	**−2**	**65**	**200**
Total, Groups A through D	*7*	*−9*	*0.31*	*4.88*	*3.71*	*−1.33*	*−2.80*	*−14.10*	*−2*	*0*	*4*
E. Reserves and Related Items	**−7**	**9**	**0**	**−5**	**−4**	**2**	**3**	**14**	**2**	**0**	**−5**

Note: Totals may not match original source due to rounding.

Source: International Monetary Fund, *International Financial Statistics,* imf.org, September 2009.

THE BALANCE OF PAYMENTS AND ECONOMIC CRISES

The sum of cross-border international economic activity—the balance of payments—can be used by international managers to forecast economic conditions and, in some cases, the likelihood of economic crises. The mechanics of international economic crisis often follow a similar path of development:

1. A country that experiences rapidly expanding current account deficits will simultaneously build financial account surpluses (the inverse relationship noted previously in this chapter).

2. The capital that flows into a country, giving rise to the financial account surplus, acts as the "financing" for the growing merchandise/services deficits—the constituent components of the current account deficit.

3. Some event, whether it be a report, a speech, an action by a government or business inside or outside the country, raises the question of the country's economic stability. Investors of many kinds, portfolio and direct investors in the country, fearing economic problems in the near future, withdraw capital from the country rapidly to avoid any exposure to this risk. This is prudent for the individual, but catastrophic for the whole if all individuals move similarly.

4. The rapid withdrawal of capital from the country, so-called capital flight, results in the loss of the financial account surplus, creating a severe deficit in the country's overall balance of payments. This is typically accompanied by rapid currency depreciation (if a floating-rate currency) or currency devaluation (if a fixed-rate currency).

International debt and economic crises have occurred for as long as there have been international trade and commerce. And they will occur again. Each crisis has its own unique characteristics, but all follow some of the economic fundamentals described earlier (the one additional factor that differentiates many of the crises is whether inflation is a component). The Asian economic crisis was a devastating reminder of the tenuousness of international economic relationships.

THE ASIAN CRISIS

The roots of the Asian currency crisis extended from a fundamental change in the economics of the region—the transition of many Asian nations from net exporters to net importers. Starting as early as 1990 in Thailand, the rapidly expanding economies of the Far East began importing more than they exported, requiring major net capital inflows to support their currencies. As long as the capital continued to flow in—for manufacturing plants, dam projects, infrastructure development, and even real estate speculation—the pegged exchange rates of the region could be maintained. When the investment capital inflows stopped, however, crisis was inevitable.

The most visible roots of the crisis were the excesses in capital flows into Thailand in 1996 and early 1997. With rapid economic growth and rising profits forming the backdrop, Thai firms, banks, and finance companies had ready access to capital on the international markets, finding cheap U.S. dollar loans offshore. Thai banks continued to raise capital internationally, extending credit to a variety of domestic investments and enterprises beyond the level that the Thai economy could support. Capital flows into the Thai market hit record rates, pouring into investments of all kinds, including manufacturing, real estate, and even equity market margin-lending. As the investment "bubble" expanded, some participants raised questions about the

4. To review the mechanical steps of how exchange rate changes are transmitted into altered trade prices and eventually trade volumes

economy's ability to repay the rising debt. The baht came under sudden and severe pressure.

Currency Collapse

The Thai government and central bank intervened in the foreign exchange markets directly (using up precious hard currency reserves) and indirectly (by raising interest rates to attempt to stop the continual out-flow). The Thai investment markets ground to a halt, causing massive currency losses and bank failures. On July 2, 1997, the Thai central bank, which had been expending massive amounts of its limited foreign exchange reserves to defend the baht's value, finally allowed the baht to float (or sink in this case). The baht fell 17 percent against the U.S. dollar and more than 12 percent against the Japanese yen in a matter of hours. By November, the baht had fallen from Baht25/US$ to Baht40/US$, a fall of about 38 percent. As illustrated in Table 4.4, Thailand was not alone in creating massive current account deficits in the period leading up to 1997. In fact, with the rather special exceptions of China and Singapore, all of East Asia was in current account deficit beginning in 1994.

Within days, a number of neighboring Asian nations, some with and some without characteristics similar to Thailand, came under speculative attack by currency traders and capital markets. The Philippine peso, the Malaysian ringgit, and the Indonesian rupiah all fell within months, as shown in Figure 4.4. In late October, Taiwan caught the markets off balance with a surprise competitive devaluation of 15 percent. The Taiwanese devaluation seemed only to renew the momentum of the crisis. Although the Hong Kong dollar survived (at great expense to the central bank's foreign exchange reserves), the Korean won was not so lucky. In November the historically stable Korean won also fell victim, falling from Won900/US$ to more than Won1100/US$. By the end of November the Korean government was in the process of negotiating a US$50 billion bailout of its financial sector with the International Monetary Fund (IMF). The only currency that had not fallen besides the Hong Kong dollar was the Chinese renminbi, which was not freely convertible. Although the renminbi had not been devalued, there was rising speculation that the Chinese government would devalue it for competitive reasons. Figure 4.4 shows the change in exchange rates for four of these Asian economies.

Causal Complexities

The Asian economic crisis—for the crisis was more than just a currency collapse—had many roots besides the traditional balance of payments difficulties. The causes are different in each country, yet there are specific underlying similarities that allow comparison: corporate socialism, corporate governance, and banking stability and management.

Corporate Socialism   Although Western markets have long known the cold indifference of the free market, the countries of post–World War II Asia have largely known only the good. Because of the influence of government and politics in the business arena, even in the event of failure, government would not allow firms to fail, workers to lose their jobs, or banks to close. When the problems reached the size seen in 1997, the business liability exceeded the capacities of governments to bail business out. Practices that had persisted for decades without challenge, such as lifetime employment, were now no longer sustainable. The result was a painful lesson in the harshness of the marketplace.

Corporate Governance   An expression largely unused until the 1990s, corporate governance refers to the complex process of how a firm is managed and operated,

Table 4.4 Current Account Balances of East Asian Countries, 1988–1999 (millions of U.S. dollars)

	1988	1989	1990	1991	1992	1993	1994	1995	1996	1997	1998	1999
Deficit Countries												
Indonesia	−1,397	−1,108	−2,988	−4,260	−2,780	−2,106	−2,792	−6,431	−7,663	−4,889	4,096	5,785
Korea	14,538	5,387	−1,745	−8,291	−3,944	990	−3,867	−8,507	−23,006	−8,167	40,365	24,477
Malaysia	1,867	315	−870	−4,183	−2,167	−2,991	−4,520	−8,644	−4,462	−5,935	9,529	12,606
Philippines	−390	−1,456	−2,695	−1,034	−1,000	−3,016	−2,950	−1,980	−3,953	−4,351	1,546	7,910
Thailand	−1,654	−2,498	−7,281	−7,571	−6,303	−6,364	−8,085	−13,554	−14,691	−3,021	14,243	12,428
Subtotal	**12,964**	**640**	**−15,579**	**−25,339**	**−16,194**	**−13,487**	**−22,214**	**−39,116**	**−53,775**	**−26,363**	**68,779**	**63,206**
Surplus Countries												
China	−3,802	−4,317	11,997	13,272	6,401	−11,609	6,908	1,618	7,243	36,963	31,472	15,667
Singapore	1,882	2,923	3,097	4,884	5,915	4,211	11,400	14,436	13,898	16,912	21,025	21,254
Subtotal	**−1,920**	**−1,394**	**15,094**	**18,156**	**12,316**	**−7,398**	**18,308**	**16,054**	**21,141**	**53,875**	**52,497**	**36,921**

Asian Crisis

"Deficit Countries" are those with current account balances that were negative for the 1994 to 1997 period, leading up to the Asian Crisis.
"Surplus Countries" are those with current account balances that were positive for the 1994 to 1997 period. Hong Kong and Taiwan are not listed, as they are not individually reported by the IMF.
The Asian Crisis actually began with the devaluation of the Thai baht on July 1, 1997. However, given annual balance of payments statistics, it is shown here between the 1997 and 1998 calendar years.
Source: Data abstracted from the International Monetary Fund, *Balance of Payments Statistics Yearbook 2000.*

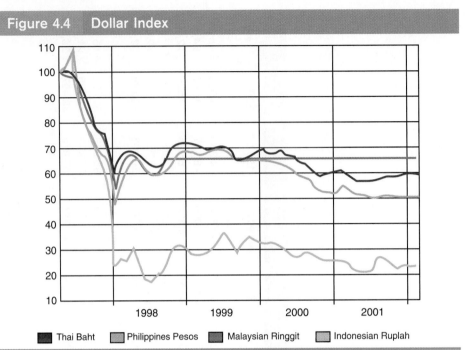

Figure 4.4   Dollar Index

Legend: Thai Baht | Philippines Pesos | Malaysian Ringgit | Indonesian Rupiah

Source: Pacific Exchange Rate Service, http://fx.sauder.ubc.ca © 2002 by Prof. Werner Antweiler, University of British Columbia, Vancouver B.C., Canada. Time period shown in diagram: April 1, 1997 through February 1, 2002. Reproduced with permission.

who it is accountable to, and how it reacts to changing business conditions. There is little doubt that many firms operating within the Far Eastern business environments were often largely controlled by either families or groups related to the governing party or body of the country. The interests of stockholders and creditors were often secondary at best to the primary motivations of corporate management. Without focusing on "the bottom line," the bottom line deteriorated.

Banking Liquidity and Management   Banking is one of those sectors that has definitely fallen out of fashion in the past two decades. Bank regulatory structures and markets have been deregulated nearly without exception around the globe. The central role played by banks in the conduct of business, however, was largely ignored and underestimated. As firms across Asia collapsed, as government coffers were emptied, as speculative investments made by the banks themselves failed, banks closed. Without banks, the "plumbing" of business conduct was shut down. Firms could not obtain the necessary working capital financing they needed to manufacture their products or provide their services. This pivotal role of banking liquidity was the focus of the International Monetary Fund's bail-out efforts.

The Asian economic crisis had global impact. What started as a currency crisis quickly became a regionwide recession (or depression, depending on definitions).[3] The slowed economies of the region quickly caused major reductions in world demand for many products, commodities especially. World oil markets, copper markets, and agricultural products all saw severe price falls as demand fell. These price falls were immediately noticeable in declining earnings and growth prospects for other emerging economies.

The post-1997 period has been one of dramatic reversal for the countries of East Asia. As Table 4.4 illustrates, beginning in 1998, every nation within East Asia listed has run a current account surplus as a result of massive recession (imports fell voluntarily, as well as being restricted by governments), significant domestic currency devaluation (resulting in significantly lower purchasing power, hence the countries could no longer afford to purchase imports), and rising exports (as currency de-valuation made their merchandise relatively cheaper for countries in other parts of the world to purchase). Unfortunately, the adjustment period has been one of massive unemployment, social disruption, and economic reconstruction with high human cost.

 ## CAPITAL MOBILITY

As we have seen, the degree to which capital moves freely cross-border is critically important to a country's balance of payments. We have already seen how the United States, while experiencing a deficit in its Current Account balance over the past 20 years, has simultaneously enjoyed a Financial Account surplus. But the ability of capital to move involves both economic and political factors. The open-ness of the U.S. economy, the depth and breadth of its financial markets, and its relative political stability, have all contributed to making the United States an attractive nation for capital investment of all kinds. Other countries, however, de-pending on their economic prospects and their political openness, may not always attract capital.

Before leaving our discussion of the balance of payments we need to gain addi-tional insights into the history of capital mobility and the contribution of capital inflows and capital outflows (so-called *capital flight*) to the balance of payments of selected countries in recent years.

Has capital always been free to move in and out of a country? Definitely not. The ability of foreign investors to own property, buy businesses, or purchase stocks and bonds in other countries has been controversial. Obstfeld and Taylor (2001) studied the globalization of capital markets and concluded that the pattern illustrated in Figure 4.5 is a fair representation of the "conventional wisdom" on the openness of

5. To understand how countries with different government policies toward international trade and investment, or differ-ent levels of economic development, differ in their balance of payments

Figure 4.5   A Stylized View of Capital Mobility in Modern History

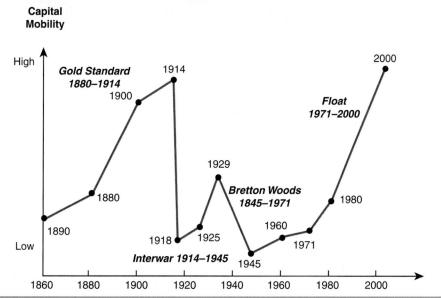

Source: "Globalization and Capital Markets," Maurice Obstfeld and Alan M. Taylor, NBER Conference Paper, May 4–5, 2001, p. 6.

global capital markets in recent history.[4] Since 1860, the gold standard in use prior to World War I and the post-1971 period of floating-exchange-rates have seen the greatest ability of capital to flow cross-border. Note that Figure 4.5 uses no specific quantitative measure of mobility. The diagram uses only a stylized distinction between "low" and "high," combining two primary factors, the exchange rate regimes and the state of international, political, and economic relations.

Obstfeld and Taylor argue that the post-1860 era can be subdivided into four distinct periods.

1. The first, 1860–1914, was a period characterized by continuously increasing capital openness as more and more countries adopted the gold standard and expanded international trade relations.

2. The second period, 1914–1945, was a period of global economic destruction. The combined destructive forces of two world wars and a worldwide depression led most nations to move toward highly nationalistic and isolationist political and economic policies, effectively eliminating any significant movement of capital between countries.

3. The third period, 1945–1971, the Bretton Woods era, saw a great expansion of international trade in goods and services. This time also saw the slow but steady recovery of capital markets. The fixed-exchange-rate regime of Bretton Woods may have failed because the sheer forces of global capital could no longer be held in check.

4. The fourth and current period, 1971–2000 [2002], is a period characterized by floating-exchange-rates and economic volatility, but rapidly expanding cross-border capital flows. The major industrial countries either no longer try, no longer need, or no longer can control the movement of capital. Because currency markets are free to reflect underlying economic fundamentals and investor sentiments about the future, capital movements increased in response to this openness.

Of course, this is a stylized global view, and the situations of the individual countries always have their own characteristics. The currency crises of the latter half of the 1990s and of the early twenty-first century may result in the reversal of this freedom of cross-border capital movement; it is still too early to tell. It is clear, however, that the ability to move instantaneously and massively cross-border has been one of the major factors in the severity of recent currency crises.

CAPITAL FLIGHT

Many recent global and financial crises have been characterized by sudden and shocking outflows of capital from the national economy, *capital flight*. Although no single accepted definition of capital flight exists, the term is traditionally used to describe sudden capital withdrawals by investors from countries in which they perceive a political, economic, or currency crisis to be forthcoming. The capital is typically portfolio investments and bank deposits (a component of "other investment" within the Financial Accounts in the balance of payments), and may be owned or controlled by both domestic and foreign investors. Much like a bank run, it is typically characterized by nearly irrational or panic behavior, as no one wants to be the last one in line to try to take their money out of a falling economy.

The rapid and sometimes illegal transfer of capital out of a country poses significant economic and political problems. Many heavily indebted countries have suffered significant capital flight, which has compounded their problems of debt service.

Five primary mechanisms exist by which capital may be moved from one country to another.

1. Transfers via the usual international payments mechanisms, regular bank transfers, are obviously the easiest and lowest cost, and are legal. Most economically healthy countries allow free exchange of their currencies, but of course for such countries "capital flight" is not a problem.

2. Transfer of physical currency by bearer (the proverbial smuggling of cash in the false bottom of a suitcase) is more costly and, for transfers out of many countries, illegal. Such transfers may be deemed illegal for balance of payments reasons or to make difficult the movement of money from the drug trade or other illegal activities.

3. The transfer of cash into collectibles or precious metals, which are then transferred across borders.

4. *Money laundering*, the cross-border purchase of assets that are then managed in a way that hides the movement of money and its ownership.

5. False invoicing of international trade transactions. Capital is moved through the underinvoicing of exports or the overinvoicing of imports, where the difference between the invoiced amount and the actually agreed-upon payment is deposited in banking institutions in a country of choice.

The concern over capital movements—both in and out of a country—has led many countries to institute a variety of capital controls at different times in history.

Capital Inflows: The Case of China

The Chinese balance of payments serves as an interesting example of one country's ongoing efforts to manage its current and financial accounts. As illustrated in Figure 4.6, China was the recipient of massive capital inflows between 1993 and 1997. This reflected a return to political norms following the Tiananmen Square events of 1989, and the perceived growing promise of the Chinese marketplace. Simultaneously, the country enjoyed a small but positive current account surplus. Both accounts, however, were heavily managed through complex Chinese regulation and intervention. Capital inflows are through a permit process, with foreign investors

---

Figure 4.6　Current and Combined Financial/Capital Account Balances for China, 1998–2008

Millions of U.S. dollars

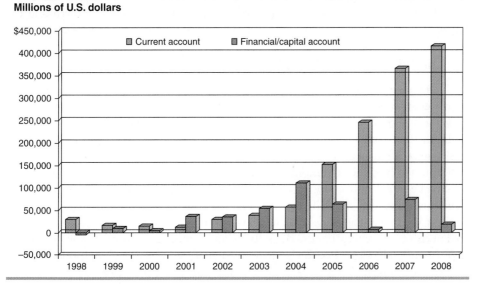

Source: International Monetary Fund, *International Financial Statistics,* imf.org, September 2009.

FOCUS ON POLITICS

MY BIG FAT GREEK DEBT (*KRISIS*)

The Greek debt crisis (*krisis* in Greek, the language which gave us the term "crisis") of 2010, and its contagious spread to the value of the euro and the members of the European Union, although not a traditional Greek tragedy, is certainly a challenge to the political economy of Europe. The problem, however, is that the problem is a bit tricky with Greece's membership within the EU.

The Greek government has for many years spent more than it took in, running a government (fiscal) deficit. And like so many other governments before it, it prints pieces of paper and sells this paper, government bonds, to the global public. These Greek government bonds, also termed sovereign debt, are denominated in euros. The growing possibility of the Greek government's inability to pay these debts in a timely manner has led to a series of loans by both the EU and the international community to Greece to allow it time to get its house in order.

The threat to Greece's balance of payments from the debt crisis arises more from the country's credit rating, however, than the actual debt service payments. Greek companies of all kinds, including those that produce products for export, need to be able to borrow money from banks to help fund their working capital—their receivables and inventories—in everyday operations. When Greece's credit rating was downgraded to junk bond status in the spring of 2010, it dramatically increased the cost of borrowing for Greece on the global market. But even more critically, it meant that Greek commercial banks could no longer use Greek bonds as collateral to borrow more money from the European Central Bank. If the banks could not borrow, they could not lend. If they could not lend, Greek businesses of all kinds, including exporters, would grind to a halt.

The European Central Bank, sensing the crisis, took the politically dangerous move of changing its rules, allowing junk bond credit quality issues to now be used as collateral, a highly controversial move to keep the Greek banks open and operating. Although all agree that it will not be enough to right the sinking Greek ship, it may save Greek business another day to fight the good fight, and give it time to cut public spending and decrease its ever-growing budget deficit.

Source: "Greek Debt Restructuring to Avoid Euro Tragedy Could Become Script," John Dizard, *Financial Times*, May 8, 2010, p. 14; "ECB Suspends Rating Limits on Greek Debt," Geoffrey T. Smith, *Wall Street Journal*, May 3, 2010; "Leaders: Acropolis Now; Europe's Soverign Debt Crisis," *The Economist*, May 1, 2010, p. 11; "Neither a Borrower nor a Lender Be: Germany and Greece," *The Economist*, May 1, 2010, p. 65; "Greek Debt Downgraded to Junk," Peter Whoriskey and Dina ElBoghdady, *The Washington Post*, April 28, 2010, p. A1.

---

being largely limited to joint venture investments within the country. At the same time, the Chinese government has aggressively promoted exports of many products while exercising extreme control over imports, both in content and quantity.

The onslaught of the Asian Crisis in 1997, however, clearly brought the capital inflows to a halt (India suffered a similar fate as well). The Chinese financial account balance fell back, suffering a deficit in 1998, and near zero balances in 1999 and 2000. But with the new millennium (remember, the official start of the new century was January 1, 2001, not 2000), China's attractiveness returned, as it was the recipient of more than $35 billion in capital inflows in 2001 alone. This massive capital injection by global investors—primarily multinational corporations—was indicative of the perceived attractiveness of the Chinese economy for future economic growth and the renewed comfort these investors felt with the current Chinese political regime.

Capital Outflows: The Case of Turkey

Turkey's economic and financial crisis of 2000–2001 serves as a prime example of how a country's balance of payments can deteriorate—or essentially collapse—in a very short period of time. Although there were a series of political, economic, and social ills that combined during the height of the crisis, a very large part of Turkey's crisis arose from capital flight. Figure 4.7 illustrates some of Turkey's financial accounts and how they deteriorated suddenly in 2001.

In the late 1990s many of Turkey's largest and most powerful banks borrowed large quantities of U.S. dollars on the international financial markets. The capital was not used for loans or development in Turkey, but rather on speculation related to Turkish government bonds. Bank funds and financing is listed in the "net other investment" subcategory of the balance of payments, and Turkey's net inflows 1997–2000 are obvious from Figure 4.7. However, a political crisis in February 2001 initiated a series of economic crises in Turkey, including the collapse of its currency. With this crisis, the capital that had so readily flowed into Turkey in the previous

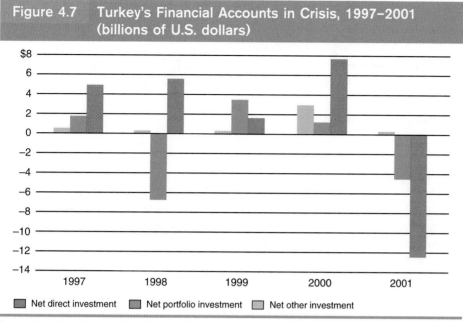

Figure 4.7   Turkey's Financial Accounts in Crisis, 1997–2001 (billions of U.S. dollars)

☐ Net direct investment   ☐ Net portfolio investment   ☐ Net other investment

Source: International Monetary Fund, *Balance of Payments Statistics Yearbook*, 2002.

years now flew out. The devastating amount in 2001, more than $12 billion, resulted in a structural collapse of the Turkish banking system.

SUMMARY

The balance of payments is the summary statement of all international transactions between one country and all other countries. The balance of payments is a flow statement, summarizing all the international transactions that occur across the geographic boundaries of the nation over a period of time, typically a year. Because of its use of double-entry bookkeeping, the BOP must always balance in theory, though in practice there are substantial imbalances as a result of statistical errors and misreporting of current account and capital account flows.

The two major subaccounts of the balance of payments, the current account and the capital account, summarize the current trade and international capital flows of the country.

Due to the double-entry bookkeeping method of accounting, the current account and capital account are always inverse on balance, one in surplus while the other experiences deficit. Although most nations strive for current account surpluses, it is not clear that a balance on current or capital account, or a surplus on current account, is either sustainable or desirable. The monitoring of the various subaccounts of a country's balance of payments activity is helpful to decision makers and policymakers at all levels of government and industry in detecting the underlying trends and movements of fundamental economic forces driving a country's international economic activity.

KEY TERMS

balance of payments (BOP)   96

current account   96

financial account   96

double-entry bookkeeping   97

net errors and omissions
  account   104

official reserves account   105

fixed-exchange-rate   106

floating-exchange-rate   106

QUESTIONS FOR DISCUSSION

1. Why must a country's balance of payments always be balanced in theory?

2. What is the difference between the merchandise trade balance (BOT) and the current account balance?

3. What is service trade?

4. Why is foreign direct investment so much more controversial than foreign portfolio investment? How did this relate to Mexico in the 1990s?

5. Should the fact that the United States may be the world's largest net debtor nation be a source of concern for government policymakers? Is the United States like Finland?

6. While the United States "suffered" a current account deficit and a capital account surplus in the 1980s, what were the respective balances of Japan doing?

7. What does it mean for the United States to be one of the world's largest indebted countries?

8. How do exchange rate changes alter trade so that the trade balance actually improves when the domestic currency depreciates?

9. How have trade balances in Asia contributed to the cause of the current Asian crisis?

INTERNET EXERCISES

1. The IMF, World Bank, and United Nations are only a few of the major world organizations that track, report, and aid international economic and financial development. Using these web sites and others that may be linked to them, briefly summarize the economic outlook for the developed and emerging nations of the world. For example, the full text of Chapter 1 of the *World Economic Outlook* published annually by the World Bank is available through the IMF's web page.

International Monetary Fund	http://www.imf.org/
United Nations	http://www.unsystem.org/
The World Bank Group	http://www.worldbank.org/
Europa (EU) Homepage	http://www.europa.eu.int/
Bank for International Settlements	http://www.bis.org/

2. Current economic and financial statistics and commentaries are available via the IMF's web page under "What's New," "Fund Rates," and the "IMF Committee on Balance of Payments Statistics." For an in-depth examination of the IMF's ongoing initiative on the validity of these statistics, termed metadata, visit the IMF's Dissemination Standards Bulletin Board listed here:

International Monetary Fund	http://www.imf.org/
IMF's Dissemination Standards Bulletin Board	http://dsbb.imf.org/

3. Visit Moody's sovereign ceilings and foreign currency ratings service site on the web to evaluate what progress is being made in the nations of the Far East on recovering their perceived creditworthiness.

Moody's Sovereign Ceilings	http://www.moodys.com/

TAKE A STAND

For years, the International Monetary Fund (IMF) has been the object of significant criticism about the way it conducts its activities in emerging markets. The IMF's primary responsibility traditionally has been to provide additional financial resources to aid countries in the grip of balance of payments crises. The IMF has, on many occasions, done just that—providing enormous quantities of capital to cash-strapped economies in the throes of crisis—but at a price. The price has been that the country must often agree to specific changes in government policies and practices before the money is provided. These policy changes frequently include the elimination of government budget deficits, removal of restrictions on capital movements, new banking standards and regulations, elimination of specific trade tariffs and quotas, to name but a few.

Critics of the IMF have argued that its job is to help those in need, and not become an advocate of specific market philosophies. The IMF's increasingly dictatorial style has turned it into an institution that is essentially a new form of capitalist imperialist, dictating the conditions upon which much-needed funds may only be made available.

For Discussion

1. The IMF should cease imposing its restrictive requirements and philosophies on the countries that need these funds so drastically. This organization was created to aid the people of the world during a time of crisis, not to take advantage of their plight to impose the IMF's increasingly right-wing philosophy on their countries and sovereignty. What the IMF so often refers to as "austerity measures" prove to be policies that place the greater burden of the bailout on the people who are already suffering.

2. The IMF is not attempting to impose its political viewpoints on countries applying for funds, but rather taking prudent measures to assure that the capital goes to good use, and does not end up being good money thrown after bad. Most countries in crisis did not get into this condition by accident, but typically as a result of significant government failure to make tough decisions regarding responsible economic management. The IMF simply wants to be assured that the right steps are being taken by government to "stop the bleeding" before providing this money that is so difficult to come by.

ICELAND 2006—A SMALL COUNTRY IN A GLOBAL CAPITAL MARKET

More than almost anything, Icelanders like a soak in hot water. Reykjavik has more thermal spas per head than any other city in the world. But lately, the North Atlantic nation has been feeling more heat than it bargained for. On February 1st Fitch, a rating agency, cut its outlook on Icelandic sovereign debt to negative from stable, drawing attention to a current-account deficit that ballooned to 15% of GDP in 2005 and fast-raising foreign debt. With only 300,000 people and an economy one-third the size of Luxembourg's, Iceland's troubles may sound like the fabled headline, "Small earthquake: not many dead." But dire warnings of contagion have flourished out of all proportion to the country's size.

"Storm in a Hot Tub," *The Economist,*
March 30, 2006

The last one or two years had been something of a shock to the Icelandic people. Long used to being ignored in the world, Iceland's economic situation and its interest rates—some of the highest in the world recently—had suddenly garnered much international attention. Now, in the spring of 2006, Iceland's central bank and governmental monetary authorities were wondering whether they were seeing the dark underside of globalization and economic growth. Is this what it felt like to be a small country in a global market?

OVERHEATING

Iceland's economy had been growing at record rates in recent years. Gross domestic product had grown at just over 8 percent in 2004, 6 percent in 2005, and was expected to be still above 4 percent by the end of the current year, 2006. While the average unemployment rate of the major economic powers was roughly 6 percent, Iceland's overheating economy had only 3 percent unemployment. But accompanying rapid economic growth in a small economy, as happens frequently in economic history, inflation raises its ugly head. And the requisite prescription for such an ailment by monetary authorities is also well known: slowing money supply growth to try and control inflationary forces. The result is always the same—increasing interest rates, as illustrated in Exhibit A.

These higher interest rates had a number of different impacts. First, Iceland was considered very stable and low risk in the international marketplace. It—the Icelandic government—had an investment grade credit rating. So foreign investors, particularly the money market investors

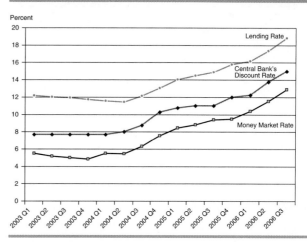

Exhibit A   Iceland's Interest Rates Continue to Rise

Source: Interest rates reported to the International Monetary Fund by Iceland; *International Financial Statistics,* monthly.

behind the carry-trade made famous in Japan, found Icelandic money market interest rates very attractive. Capital from foreign investors, American and European, flowed into the big four Icelandic banks and money market accounts of all kinds to take advantage of these higher money market rates.

But the carry-trade depends on exchange rates as well as interest rates. A foreign investor exchanging U.S. dollars or euros for Icelandic krona, and then investing in the higher yielding money market rates in Iceland, must feel relatively confident that the krona will not fall in value versus their currency by the time they need to bring the money back home. And they did. The krona had actually strengthened consistently against both the dollar and the euro in 2004 and 2005, as illustrated in Exhibit B. By the end of 2005 the krona was stronger against both the dollar and the euro than it had been since 2000.

A less desirable result of this process is that interest rates rise for everyone, including domestic Icelandic companies wishing to borrow money. Monetary policies like these have been known to bring domestic business to a standstill—which is in many ways the intent—to slow business forces driving inflation. But Iceland and many Icelandic companies were more and more global, and when borrowing rates ("lending rates") continued to rise in 2004 and 2005, they started borrowing abroad. Any company that could raise debt outside of Iceland, in Europe in euros for example, did.

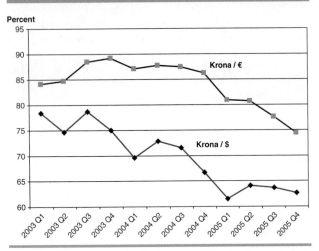

Exhibit B   The Icelandic Krona Strengthens, 2003–2005

Source: Interest rates reported to the International Monetary Fund by Iceland; *International Financial Statistics*, monthly.

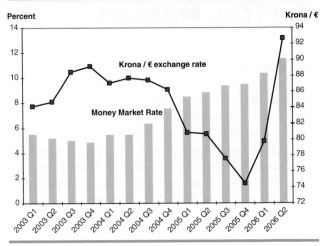

Exhibit C   Iceland's Interest and Exchange Rates Swing

Source: International Monetary Fund, *International Financial Statistics*, monthly.

THE ICELANDIC CHILL

But as the krona continued to strengthen against other major currencies, its export competitiveness declined. Iceland's current account, already in deficit, began to skyrocket in size. Iceland's current account deficit was 16 percent of its gross domestic product (GDP) at the end of 2005, and was expected to stay that high through the remainder of 2006. For comparison, the current account deficits of note of other countries were only half that of Iceland's: New Zealand (8 percent), Hungary (7 percent), and even the United States (6 percent). Not only was Iceland's current account in deficit, but the size of its outstanding debt in total, accumulated over a number of years, was troublesome.

Suddenly, in February 2006, things changed. Capital started flowing out of Iceland. The size of the country's current account deficit had become front page news, and major investors, including those in the carry trade, feared that the krona would fall undermining their interest arbitrage gains. Foreign investors dumped krona at a record rate.

Adding to "global stress," as one journalist put it, was the possibility that the fears over the Icelandic economy would spread to other countries and currencies around the world. Although in the end relatively minor, many small country and emerging market currency's suffered short-term falls as the markets feared a general spread or *contagion* as that seen during the Asian crisis in 1997. "These countries may be unrelated geographically but they are not unrelated in portfolios," said Tony Norfield, global head of FX strategy at ABN Amro. "What starts as a trimming back of a position can turn into an avalanche."

A financial crash in Iceland snowballed yesterday, setting off a series of tremors as far afield as Brazil and South

Africa. At one point the Icelandic krona was down 4.7 percent at a 15-month low of IKr69.07 to the dollar, having fallen a further 4.5 percent on Tuesday, its biggest one-day slide in almost five years. The krona's collapse meant carry trade investors who borrowed in euros to gain exposure to Reykjavik's 10 percent interest rate, saw one-and-a-half years' worth of carry trade profit wiped out in less than two days.

The collapse, which was sparked by Fitch downgrading its outlook on Iceland, citing fears over an "unsustainable" current account deficit and drawing parallels with the imbalances evident before the 1997 Asian crisis, led to a generalised sell-off in Icelandic assets. The crash sparked a sell-off among hitherto strong performing emerging market currencies across the globe, with the Brazilian real falling almost 3 percent at one point and the Turkish lira, South African rand, Mexican peso and Indonesian rupiah each losing at least 1 percent, before recovering later in the session.

Currencies markets were awash with talk of a rising tide of risk aversion, with traders exiting carry trades around the globe. However, the truth appeared to be more prosaic, with the emerging market contagion caused by investors cutting profitable positions in order to plug their Icelandic losses. "We have had a car crash in Iceland and people will have closed their winning positions in order to fund their losses," said David Bloom, currency analyst at HSBC. This trend snowballed as selling from Mexico to Indonesia exacerbated losses causing traders to cash in yet more profits to balance their positions.

"Iceland's Collapse Has Global Impact," *Financial Times*, Feb 23, 2006, p. 42

Over the following two quarters the Icelandic krona plummeted in value against the euro and the dollar, although money market interest rates were still high and attractive in relative terms. But investors were no longer convinced. Their fear of a falling krona had become a self-fulfilling prophecy. In the end, the speculators caused to happen exactly what they feared would happen: a weaker Icelandic krona.

Case Questions

1. Do you think a country the size of Iceland or New Zealand is more or less sensitive to the potential impacts of global capital movements?

2. Many countries have used interest rate increases to protect their currencies for many years. What are the pros and cons of using this strategy?

3. In the case of Iceland, the country was able to sustain a large current account deficit for several years, and at the same time have ever-rising interest rates and stronger currency. Then one day, it all changed. How does that happen?

THE VENEZUELAN BOLIVAR BLACK MARKET

Rumor has it that during the year and a half that Venezuelan President Hugo Chávez spent in jail for his role in a 1992 coup attempt against the government, he was a voracious reader. Too bad his prison syllabus seems to have been so skimpy on economics and so heavy on Machiavelli.

"Money Fun in the Venezuela of Hugo Chávez," *The Economist*, February 13, 2004

It's late afternoon on March 10, 2004, and Santiago opens the window of his office in Caracas, Venezuela. Immediately he is hit with the sounds rising from the plaza—cars honking, protesters banging their pots and pans, street vendors hawking their goods. Since the imposition of a new set of economic policies by President Hugo Chávez in 2002 such sights and sounds had become a fixture of city life in Caracas. Santiago sighed as he wished for the simplicity of life in the old Caracas.

Santiago's once-thriving pharmaceutical distribution business had hit hard times. Since capital controls were implemented in February of 2003, dollars had been hard to come by. He had been forced to pursue various methods—methods that were more expensive and not always legal—to obtain dollars, causing his margins to decrease by 50 percent. To add to the strain the Venezuelan currency, the bolivar (Bs), had been recently devalued (repeatedly). This had instantly squeezed his margins as his costs had risen directly with the exchange rate. He could not find anyone to sell him dollars. His customers needed supplies and they needed them quickly, but how was he going to come up with the $30,000—the hard currency—to pay for his most recent order?

POLITICAL CHAOS

Hugo Chávez's tenure as president of Venezuela had been tumultuous at best since his election in 1998. After repeated recalls, resignations, coups, and re-appointments, the political turmoil had taken its toll on the Venezuelan economy as a whole, and its currency in particular. The short-lived success of the anti-Chávez coup in 2001, and his nearly immediate return to office, had set the stage for a retrenchment of his isolationist economic and financial policies.

On January 21, 2003, the bolivar closed at a record low—Bs1853/$. The next day President Hugo Chávez suspended the sale of dollars for two weeks. Nearly instantaneously, an unofficial or *black market* for the exchange of Venezuelan bolivars for foreign currencies (primarily U.S. dollars) sprouted. As investors of all kinds sought ways to exit the Venezuelan market, or simply obtain the hard-currency needed to continue to conduct their businesses (as was the case for Santiago), the escalating capital flight caused the black market value of the bolivar to plummet to Bs2500/$ in weeks. As markets collapsed and exchange values fell, the Venezuelan inflation rate soared to more than 30 percent per annum.

CAPITAL CONTROLS AND CADIVI

To combat the downward pressures on the bolivar, the Venezuelan government announced on February 5, 2003, the passage of the 2003 *Exchange Regulations Decree*. The decree took the following actions:

1. Set the official exchange rate at Bs1596/$ for purchase (*bid*) and Bs1600/$ for sale (*offer*);
2. Established the Comisión de Administración de Divisas (CADIVI) to control the distribution of foreign exchange; and
3. Implemented strict price controls to stem inflation triggered by the weaker bolivar and the exchange control-induced contraction of imports.

CADIVI was both the official means and the cheapest means by which Venezuelan citizens could obtain foreign currency. In order to receive an authorization from CADIVI to obtain dollars, an applicant was required to complete a series of forms. The applicant was then required to prove that they had paid taxes the previous three years, provide proof of business and asset ownership and lease agreements for company property, and document the payment of current social security payments.

Unofficially, however, there was an additional unstated requirement for permission to obtain foreign currency: that authorizations by CADIVI would be reserved for Chávez supporters. In August 2003 an anti-Chávez petition had gained widespread circulation. One million signatures had been collected. Although the government ruled that the petition was invalid, it had used the list of signatures to create a database of names and social security numbers that CADIVI utilized to cross-check identities when deciding who would receive hard currency. President Chávez was quoted as saying "Not one more dollar for the *putschits*; the bolivars belong to the people."[1]

SANTIAGO'S ALTERNATIVES

Santiago had little luck obtaining dollars via CADIVI to pay for his imports. Because he had signed the petition calling for President Chávez's removal, he had been listed in the CADIVI database as anti-Chávez, and now could not obtain permission to exchange bolivars for dollars.

The transaction in question was an invoice for $30,000 in pharmaceutical products from his U.S.-based supplier. Santiago would then, in-turn, sell to a large Venezuelan customer who would distribute the products. This transaction, however, was not the first time that Santiago had had to search out alternative sources for meeting his U.S.-dollar obligations. Since the imposition of capital controls, the search for dollars had become a weekly activity for Santiago. In addition to the official process through CADIVI, he could also obtain dollars through the *gray market*, or the *black market*.

THE GRAY MARKET: CANTV SHARES

In May 2003, three months following the implementation of the exchange controls, a window of opportunity had opened up for Venezuelans—an opportunity that allowed investors in the Caracas stock exchange to avoid the tight foreign exchange curbs. This loophole circumvented the government-imposed restrictions, by allowing investors to purchase local shares of the leading telecommunications company CANTV on the Caracas' bourse, and to then convert them into dollar-denominated American Depositary Receipts (ADRs) traded on the NYSE.

The sponsor for CANTV ADRs on the NYSE was the Bank of New York, the leader in ADR sponsorship and management in the United States. The Bank of New York had suspended trading in CANTV ADRs in February after the passage of the decree, wishing to determine the legality of trading under the new Venezuelan currency controls. On May 26, after concluding that trading was indeed legal under the decree, trading resumed in CANTV shares. CANTV's share price and trading volume both soared in the following week.[2]

The share price of CANTV quickly became the primary method of calculating the implicit gray market exchange rate. For example, CANTV shares closed at Bs7945/share on the Caracas bourse on February 6, 2004. That same day, CANTV ADRs closed in New York at $18.84/ADR. Each New York ADR was equal to seven shares of CANTV in Caracas. The implied gray market exchange rate was then calculated as follows:

$$\text{Implicit Gray Market Rate} = \frac{7 \times \text{Bs}7945/\text{share}}{\$18.84/\text{ADR}} = \text{Bs}2952/\$.$$

The official exchange rate on that same day was Bs1597/$. This meant that the gray market rate was quoting the bolivar approximately 46 percent weaker against the dollar than what the Venezuelan government officially declared its currency to be worth. Exhibit 1 illustrates both the official exchange rate and the gray market rate (calculated using CANTV shares) for the January 2002 to March 2004 period. The divergence between the official and gray market rates beginning in February 2003 coincided with the imposition of capital controls.[3]

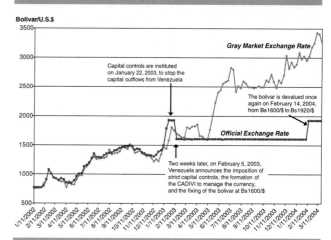

Exhibit 1   Venezuelan Official and Gray Market Exchange Rates. Venezuelan Bolivar/U.S. Dollar (January 2002–March 2004)

Note: All prices and rates are Friday closing values.

THE BLACK MARKET

A third method of obtaining hard currency by Venezuelans was through the rapidly expanding *black market*. The black market was, as is the case with black markets all over the world, essentially unseen and illegal. It was, however, quite sophisticated, using the services of a stockbroker or banker in Venezuela who simultaneously held U.S. dollar accounts offshore. The choice of a black market broker was a critical one; in the event of a failure to complete the transaction properly, there was no legal recourse.

If Santiago wished to purchase dollars on the black market, he would deposit bolivars in his broker's account in Venezuela. The agreed upon black market exchange rate was determined on the day of the deposit, and usually was within a 20 percent band of the gray market rate derived from the CANTV share price. Santiago would then be given access to a dollar-denominated bank account outside of Venezuela in the agreed amount. The transaction took, on average, two business days to settle. The unofficial black market rate was Bs3300/$.

SPRING 2004

In early 2004, President Chávez had asked Venezuela's Central Bank to give him "a little billion"—*millardito*—of its $21 billion in foreign exchange reserves. Chávez argued that the money was actually the people's, and he wished to invest some of it in the agricultural sector. The Central Bank refused. Not to be thwarted in its search for funds, the Chávez government announced on February 9, 2004, another devaluation. The bolivar was devalued 17 percent, falling in official value from Bs1600/$ to Bs1920/$ (see Exhibit 1). With all Venezuelan exports of oil being purchased in U.S. dollars, the devaluation of the bolivar meant that the country's proceeds from oil exports grew by the same 17 percent as the devaluation itself.

The Chávez government argued that the devaluation was necessary because the bolivar was "a variable that cannot be kept frozen, because it prejudices exports and pressures the balance of payments" according to Finance Minister Tobías Nóbrega. Analysts, however, pointed out that Venezuelan government actually had significant control over its balance of payments: oil was the primary export, the government maintained control over the official access to hard currency necessary for imports, and the Central Bank's foreign exchange reserves were now over $21 billion.

It's not clear whether Mr. Chávez understands what a massive hit Venezuelans take when savings and earnings in dollar terms are cut in half in just three years. Perhaps the political-science student believes that more devalued bolivars makes everyone richer. But one unavoidable conclusion is that he recognized the devaluation as a way to pay for his Bolivarian "missions," government projects that might restore his popularity long enough to allow him to survive the recall, or survive an audacious decision to squelch it.

"Money Fun in the Venezuela of Hugo Chávez,"
The Wall Street Journal (eastern edition),
February 13, 2004, p. A13

TIME WAS RUNNING OUT

Santiago received confirmation from CADIVI on the afternoon of March 10th that his latest application for dollars was approved and that he would receive $10,000 at the official exchange rate of Bs1920/$. Santiago attributed his good fortune to the fact that he paid a CADIVI insider an extra 500 bolivars per dollar to expedite his request. Santiago noted with a smile that "the Chavistas need to make money too." The noise from the street seemed to be dying with the sun. It was time for Santiago to make some decisions. None of the alternatives were *bonita*, but if he was to preserve his business, bolivars—at some price—had to be obtained.

Case Questions

1. Why does a country like Venezuela impose capital controls?

2. In the case of Venezuela, what is the difference between the gray market and the black market?

3. What would you recommend that Santiago do?

Notes

1. "Venezuela Girds for Exchange Controls," *The Wall Street Journal* (Eastern edition), February 5, 2003, p. A14.

2. In fact, CANTV's share price continued to rise over the 2002 to 2004 period as a result of its use as an exchange rate mechanism. The use of CANTV ADRs as a method of obtaining dollars by Venezuelan individuals and organizations was typically described as "not illegal."

3. Morgan Stanley Capital International (MSCI) announced on November 26, 2003, that it would change its standard spot rate for the Venezuelan bolivar to the notional rate based on the relationship between the price of CANTV Teléfonos de Venezuela D in the local market in bolivars and the price of its ADR in U.S. dollars.

WILL TIRE TARIFFS LAUNCH A TRADE DISPUTE?

Trade policy can have a powerful economic and political impact both domestically and internationally, sending a message to both domestic constituents and foreign trade partners. This is the case of a U.S. trade policy action regarding imports of Chinese rubber tires.

The ITC recommendations and USTR information led to a presidential decision in September of 2009.

A PRESIDENTIAL PROCLAMATION

THE WHITE HOUSE
Office of the Press Secretary
For Immediate Release   *September 11, 2009*

TO ADDRESS MARKET DISRUPTION FROM IMPORTS OF CERTAIN PASSENGER VEHICLE AND LIGHT TRUCK TIRES FROM THE PEOPLE'S REPUBLIC OF CHINA

BY THE PRESIDENT OF THE UNITED STATES OF AMERICA, A PROCLAMATION[1]

1. On July 9, 2009, the United States International Trade Commission (USITC) transmitted to me a report on its investigation under section 421 of the Trade Act of 1974, as amended (the "Trade Act") (19 U.S.C. 2451), with respect to imports of certain passenger vehicle and light truck tires from the People's Republic of China (China). In its report, the USITC stated that it had reached an affirmative determination under section 421(b)(1) of the Trade Act that certain passenger vehicle and light truck tires from China are being imported into the United States in such increased quantities or under such conditions as to cause or threaten to cause market disruption to the domestic producers of like or directly competitive products.

2. For purposes of its investigation, the USITC defined certain passenger vehicle and light truck tires from China as new pneumatic tires, of rubber, from China, of a kind used on motor cars (except racing cars) and on-the-highway light trucks, vans, and sport utility vehicles, provided for in subheadings 4011.10.10, 4011.10.50, 4011.20.10, and 4011.20.50 of the Harmonized Tariff Schedule of the United States (HTS).

3. The USITC commissioners voting in the affirmative under section 421(b) of the Trade Act also transmitted to me their recommendations made pursuant to section 421(f) of the Trade Act (19 U.S.C. 2451(f)) on proposed remedies that, in their view, would be necessary to remedy the market disruption and the basis for each recommendation.

4. Pursuant to section 421(a) of the Trade Act (19 U.S.C. 2451(a)), I have determined to provide import relief with respect to new pneumatic tires, of rubber, from China, of a kind used on motor cars (except racing cars) and on-the-highway light trucks, vans, and sport utility vehicles, provided for in subheadings 4011.10.10, 4011.10.50, 4011.20.10, and 4011.20.50 of the HTS.

5. Such import relief shall take the form of an additional duty on imports of the products described in paragraph 4, imposed for a period of 3 years. For the first year, the additional duty shall be in the amount of 35 percent ad valorem above the column 1 general rate of duty. For the second year, the additional duty shall be in the amount of 30 percent ad valorem above the column 1 general rate of duty, and in the third year, the additional duty shall be in the amount of 25 percent ad valorem above the column 1 general rate of duty.

6. Section 421(m) of the Trade Act (19 U.S.C. 2451(m)) provides that import relief under this section shall take effect not later than 15 days after the President's determination to provide such relief.

7. Section 604 of the Trade Act (19 U.S.C. 2483) authorizes the President to embody in the HTS the substance of the provisions of that Act, and of other acts affecting import treatment, and actions thereunder, including the removal, modification, continuance, or imposition of any rate of duty or other import restriction.

NOW, THEREFORE, I, BARACK OBAMA, President of the United States of America, acting under the authority vested in me by the Constitution and the laws of the United States of America, including but not limited to sections 421 and 604 of the Trade Act, do proclaim that:

1. In order to apply additional duties on imports of the certain passenger vehicle and light truck tires

---

*This case was prepared by Professor Michael Czinkota with assistance from Rebecca White, graduate student at Georgetown University.

from China described in paragraph 4, subchapter III of chapter 99 of the HTS is modified as provided in the Annex to this proclamation.

2. The modifications to the HTS made by this proclamation, including the Annex thereto, shall be effective with respect to goods entered, or withdrawn from warehouse for consumption, on or after 12:01 a.m. EDT on September 26, 2009, and shall continue in effect as provided in this proclamation and its Annex, unless such actions are earlier expressly modified or terminated.

3. Any provisions of previous proclamations and Executive Orders that are inconsistent with the actions taken in this proclamation are superseded to the extent of such inconsistency.

IN WITNESS WHEREOF, I have hereunto set my hand this eleventh day of September, in the year of our Lord two thousand nine, and of the Independence of the United States of America the two hundred and thirty-fourth.

Barack Obama

THE INVESTIGATION

In 2009, international competition in the production of passenger vehicle and light truck tires led to heated competition in the U.S market. In keeping with its congressional mission to identify and remedy trade injury, the U.S. International Trade Commission (ITC) conducted an investigation concerning whether China was in violation of a U.S.- China agreement relating to China's accession to the World Trade Organization.

A June 18, 2009, news release from USITC offers the following summary:

Section 421 was added to the Trade Act of 1974 by the U.S.-China Relations Act of 2000 and implements a transitional bilateral safeguard provision in the U.S.-China agreement relating to China's accession to the World Trade Organization. Domestic producers can obtain relief under this provision if the Commission finds that Chinese products are being imported into the United States in such increased quantities or under such conditions as to cause or threaten to cause market disruption to the domestic producers of like or directly competitive products. The statute states that market disruption "exists whenever imports of an article like or directly competitive with an

article produced by a domestic industry are increasing rapidly, either absolutely or relatively, so as to be a significant cause of material injury, or threat of material injury, to the domestic industry." "Significant cause" is defined by the statute as "a cause which contributes significantly to the material injury of the domestic industry, but need not be equal to or greater than any other cause." Similar to global safeguard investigations, if the Commission makes an affirmative determination, it also proposes a remedy to the President. The President makes the final decision concerning whether to provide relief to the U.S. industry and if so, the type and duration of relief.[2]

THE DETERMINATION AND REMEDY

The U.S. International Trade Commission (ITC) announced that it had made an affirmative determination, finding that certain passenger vehicle and light truck tires from China were being imported into the United States in such increased quantities or under such conditions as to cause or threaten to cause market disruption to the domestic producers of like or directly competitive products.

On June 29, 2009, the USITC announced the remedy proposals it would forward to the president and the U.S. trade representative (USTR). Four of the six members supported the following remedy proposal, while two dissenting members offered the statement found below the remedy.

Remedy Proposal of Chairman Shara L. Aranoff, Commissioner Charlotte R. Lane, Commissioner Irving A. Williamson, and Commissioner Dean A. Pinkert

In accordance with Section 421 of the Trade Act of 1974, we have determined that imports of certain passenger vehicle and light truck tires from China are being imported into the United States in such increased quantities that they are causing market disruption to the domestic industry producing such tires. Under Section 421(f) of the Act, we have the responsibility of recommending actions that will remedy the market disruption. We have considered the relevant factors set out in the statute, the written and oral submissions of all parties, and other information obtained in the investigation.

To remedy the market disruption caused by rapidly increasing subject imports, we propose that the President, for a three-year period, impose a duty, in addition to the current rate of duty, on imports of certain passenger vehicle and light truck tires from China. This duty would be

55 percent ad valorem in the first year, 45 percent ad valorem in the second year, and 35 percent ad valorem in the third year. In our opinion, these tariff levels would remedy the market disruption that we have found to exist.

Finally, we note that as a result of recent amendments to the trade adjustment assistance provisions administered by the United States Department of Labor, groups of workers who are covered by a petition for such assistance and whose firms are part of the domestic industry that is the subject of our affirmative determination of market disruption shall be certified as eligible to apply for trade adjustment assistance. If applications are filed, we recommend that the President direct the United States Department of Labor and the United States Department of Commerce to provide expedited consideration of trade adjustment assistance for workers and/or firms that are affected by subject imports.

Statement of Vice Chairman Daniel R. Pearson and Commissioner Deanna Tanner Okun Regarding Remedy

While we did not find market disruption to exist, we intend to submit views on this matter, as has been done previously under Section 421 investigations.

Briefly, our views on remedy will urge that no trade-restricting action be taken. It is our view that whereas subject imports have not been a significant cause of market disruption, any trade-restricting remedy will not benefit the domestic tire industry, its workers, the broader U.S. economy and society as a whole. This is an industry in which the trend toward gradual downsizing appears likely to continue regardless of the Commission's action today. Thus, we urge the U.S. government to be prepared to provide economic adjustment assistance to displaced tire workers. We note that Trade Adjustment Assistance already has been provided to some tire industry workers and recommend that the President utilize similar measures to help workers who find that their employment alternatives are changing. Implementing a trade restriction would be far more likely to cause market disruption than to alleviate it.[3]

SELECTED ARGUMENTS

The following excerpts from the United States Trade Representative's Trade Policy Staff Committee (TPSC) hearing offer perspectives presented by U.S. and Chinese industry representatives and economists.

Leo Gerard (International President of the Steel Workers Union):

As you consider what remedy to recommend, I urge you to keep in mind that this isn't just statistics and numbers. These are lives. These are hard working women and men, many of whom have spent their entire adult careers in the industry. Their jobs provide the income, the health insurance, and the retirement benefits that sustain a middle class family . . . These workers can make as many tires and whatever kinds of tires the market demands, but these workers cannot compete when the market is being overwhelmed by a massive flood of tires from China.

Since 2004, imports of tires from China have more than tripled, seizing a sizable share of the U.S. market almost entirely at the expense of the domestic industry.

After closing factories and slashing more than 5,100 jobs, the industry is still operating at a loss. Another 3,000 layoffs have already been announced for this year. If an effective remedy is not provided, the pain of those layoffs will continue to spread. Each of these lost jobs has a much broader impact. The industry declines. Workers and supplier firms also suffer . . . In addition, every worker directly employed in the tire industry supports many more jobs in the communities where the tire workers live and raise their families.

Mary Xu (Secretary General of the China Rubber Industry Association):

The increase of Chinese tire imports is the result, not the cause of the U.S. tire plant's closure. Since the 1990s, top tiers tire makers gradually exited the lower end market segment, and they shifted their production to other countries, such as China. After discounting the reduction of 16 million imports from Canada, Japan and Taiwan, the net increase of Chinese tire imports would be only nine million pieces from 2005 to 2008. In addition, the largest increase in part of China in year 2006 and 2007 was just after United States tire plants' closure around year 2004 and 2005. That means the increase of Chinese tires is the result not the cause.

The second point of mine is the latest trade statistics show that imports of Chinese tires have fallen in the first half of 2009 compared with 2008, and comparing 2008 and 2007, the increase in rate is only 2.7 percent. While imports may have experienced a minor bump in recent months, it's because the importers are afraid of the threat of the prohibitive tariffs. The overall change of Chinese exports is clearly downward.

My third point is the ITC has proposed a remedy in this case of a tariff rate beginning at 55 percent. A tariff rate of this size will make Chinese tires unmarketable in the United States . . . Our direct competitors in the economy segment of the U.S. tire market are producers in other countries with low production costs, such as Indonesia, South Korea, Mexico, India, Brazil. Price ultimately is often the deciding factor in whether a sale is made. The feedback our tire members received from the U.S. tire dealers . . . indicates that many U.S. consumers are delaying their tire replacement beyond the limit of minimum safety requirements.

My fourth point is the rapid development of Chinese tire industry is not a threat for the U.S. market, but meets the faster growing Chinese auto market. Earlier this year, the Chinese auto market became the largest in the world, surpassing even that of the United States. The Chinese auto market is expected to exceed 11 million new cars in 2009, and the Chinese tire industry has been gearing up production capacity just to be able to meet this surge in demand. So in closing, I would like to emphasize that the import restrictions sought by the Steel Workers Union on fairly traded goods would be protectionist, and would not provide any benefits for the U.S. tire industry or its workers. Those would simply shift to producers in other countries, while Chinese producers and the U.S. consumers would pay a very steep price.

Tom Prusu (Professor of Economics at Rutgers University):

Let me begin by reminding you that one of the most robust findings in all of international economics, namely, that a tariff always imposes costs on downstream consumers and that these costs are always larger than the benefits that accrue to the protected sector. The petitioners want you to think that the benefits exceed the costs to consumers, but that simply cannot be the case. The real question is how much larger are the costs than the benefits. Are they just a little bit bigger or are they a lot bigger? In this case, there is little doubt that the costs are far, far larger than the benefits to the tire workers. The proposed tariff will result in at least a dozen job losses for every job saved. That's the best case scenario. In fact, it is far more likely that the ratio of job losses to jobs saved will exceed 20 to one. In dollar value, consumers will pay over $300,000 per job saved.

I note that the U.S. auto companies have submitted comments which imply that the additional cost for just new car buyers will be something like $800 million per year. The auto maker estimates suggest my benchmark estimates understate the consumer cost.

In my benchmark simulation using the ITC's elasticities, I find that a 55 percent tariff will dramatically scale back imports from China. However, it will not result in any significant increase in domestic employment. Rather, in the short run, the primary effect will be higher prices, limited increase in imports from non-subject suppliers, and very high consumer costs.[4]

THE RESPONSE

Following the presidential proclamation, China immediately voiced its opposition. Foreign Ministry Spokesperson Jiang Yu offered the following comments:

We are strongly dissatisfied and resolutely opposed to the US decision on September 11 to impose special safeguard measures on passenger vehicle tire imports from China despite China's solemn position. The US decision, an abuse of trade remedies and a practice of grave trade protectionism, breached its commitments at the G-20 Financial Summit. It will not only hurt bilateral economic cooperation and trade between China and the US, but also affect an early recovery of the world economy. China has made solemn representations to the US and reserves all rights to take responsive actions.[5]

The press in both nations reported extensively on the issue. This excerpt from a *New York Times* article covered the U.S. trading relationship with China and the Chinese retaliation.

HONG KONG (September 14, 2009)—China unexpectedly increased pressure Sunday on the United States in a widening trade dispute, taking the first steps toward imposing tariffs on American exports of automotive products and chicken meat in retaliation for President Obama's decision late Friday to levy tariffs on tires from China.

The Chinese government's strong countermove followed a weekend of nationalistic vitriol against the United States on Chinese Web sites in response to the tire tariff. "The U.S. is shameless!" said one posting, while another called on the Chinese government to sell all of its huge holdings of Treasury bonds.

The impact of the dispute extends well beyond tires, chickens and cars. Both governments are facing domestic pressure to take a tougher stand against the other on economic issues. But the trade battle increases political tensions between the two nations even as they try to work together to revive the global economy and combat mutual security threats, like the nuclear ambitions of Iran and North Korea.

Mr. Obama's decision to impose a tariff of up to 35 percent on Chinese tires is a signal that he plans to deliver on his promise to labor unions that he would more strictly enforce trade laws, especially against China, which has become the world's factory while the United States has lost *millions of manufacturing jobs. The [U.S.] trade deficit with China was a record $268 billion in 2008.*[6]

THE SHORT-TERM OUTCOME

Only four months after the imposition of the tire tariff, the *Washington Post* reported that protectionist policies from both the United States and China have impacted exports as diverse as chicken, steel, nylon, autos, paper and salt. In October of 2009 China imposed duties as high as 36 percent on U.S. nylon exports, to which the U.S. retaliated with duties on Chinese-made steel pipe. The United States also launched probes into Chinese salts and glossy paper used for magazines. In November the Chinese government threatened to impose tariffs on an industrial acid used in the production of nylon and medicine, and perhaps most significantly, began an investigation of U.S.-made passenger cars, indicating that it might penalize U.S. automakers.

While academics and policy-makers differ on whether these disputes represent a normal component of a growing trade relationship or a dangerous deterioration, it appears that protectionist policies are on the rise globally. A recent study by the Global Trade Alert reports that protectionist measures have spiked, while the World Trade Organization reports that anti-dumping disputes reached 437 in 2009, more than double the 2008 figure.[7]

APPENDIX A[8]

Trading Inequality

United States imports from China dwarf its exports.

UNITED STATES TRADE WITH CHINA

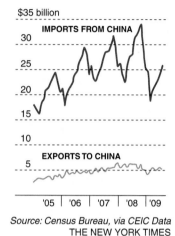

Source: Census Bureau, via CEIC Data
THE NEW YORK TIMES

Note: The U.S. buys $4.46 worth of Chinese goods for every $1 worth of American goods sold to China.

APPENDIX B

Top Three Foreign Holders of Treasury Securities[9]
(in billions of dollars)
HOLDINGS 1/AT END OF PERIOD

	2010								2009					
	Jan	Dec	Nov	Oct	Sep	Aug	Jul	Jun (New)	Jun (Old)	May	Apr	Mar	Feb	**Jan**
China, Mainland	889.0	894.8	929.0	938.3	938.3	936.5	939.9	915.8	776.4	801.5	763.5	767.9	744.2	**739.6**
Japan	765.4	765.7	754.3	742.9	747.9	727.5	720.9	708.2	711.2	677.2	685.9	686.7	661.9	**634.8**
United Kingdom	206.0	178.1	153.1	105.7	124.3	101.9	94.9	89.0	213.4	163.7	152.7	128.1	129.0	**123.9**

APPENDIX C[10]

Overall U.S. Imports from China from 2004 to 2009
(in thousands of dollars)

	Value 2004	Value 2005	Value 2006	Value 2007	Value 2008	Value 2009
TOTAL	196,682,034	243,470,105	287,774,353	321,442,867	337,772,628	296,402,134

U.S. Tire Imports from China from 2004 to 2009 (in thousands of dollars)

End-Use Code	Value 2004	Value 2005	Value 2006	Value 2007	Value 2008	Value 2009
(30220) Automotive tires and tubes	593,179	1,007,424	1,286,671	1,749,690	1,988,033	1,751,718

APPENDIX D

Cost per Job Implications of Tariffs

1. The National Center for Policy Analysis estimates that in 1994 tariffs cost the U.S. economy $32.3 billion or $170,000 for every job saved. Tariffs in Europe cost European consumers $70,000 per job saved, while Japanese consumers lost $600,000 per job saved through Japanese tariffs.[11]

2. In his essay on Free Trade at the Concise Encyclopedia of Economics, Alan Blinder states that "While the estimates differ widely across industries, they are almost always much larger than the wages of the protected workers. For example, one study in the early 1990s estimated that U.S. consumers paid $1,285,000 annually for each job in the luggage industry that was preserved by barriers to imports, a sum that greatly exceeded the average earnings of a luggage worker. That same study estimated that restricting foreign imports cost $199,000 annually for each textile worker's job that was saved, $1,044,000 for each softwood lumber job saved, and $1,376,000 for every job saved in the benzenoid chemical industry."[12]

3. In the year 2000 President Bush raised tariffs on imported steel goods between 8 and 30 percent. Economists working on behalf of the Consuming Industries Trade Action Coalition estimated that higher prices for steel products and related inefficiencies would decrease U.S. national income from between $500 million and $1.4 billion, and that while the steel producing industry would save between 4,400 and 8,900 jobs, it would be at a cost of $439,485 to $451,509 per job. In addition, for every steel job "saved" as a result of the tariff, the researchers estimated that eight jobs would be lost in all sectors of the economy.[13]

Questions for Discussion:

1. Is the ITC recommendation rational? Is it in favor of business?

2. What other political issues may have had an impact on President Obama's decision to accept the ITC remedy? Does the political context change your view on the appropriate trade action?

3. What are some alternative ways to offer relief to suffering local industries?

4. Discuss the implications of an escalating trade war between the United States and China. Does one country stand to lose more than the other?

5. Are there other industries waiting for favorable trade treatment?

Notes

1. Obama, Barack, "*To Address Market Disruption from Imports of Certain Passenger Vehicle and Light Truck Tires from the People's Republic of China.*" Office of the Press Secretary. September 11, 2009. Available at http://www.whitehouse.gov/the_press_office/Proclamation-Address-Market-Disruption-from-Imports-of-Certain-Passenger-Vehicle-and-Light-Truck-Tires/.

2. O'Laughlin, Peg, "USITC Announces Determination in China Safeguard Investigation Concerning Certain Passenger Vehicle and Light Truck Tires." United States International Trade Commission. June 18, 2009. Available at http://www.usitc.gov/press_room/news_release/2009/er0618gg1.htm.

3. O'Laughlin, Peg, "USITC Announces Determination in China Safeguard Investigation Concerning Certain Passenger Vehicle and Light Truck Tires." United States International Trade Commission. June 29, 2009. Available at http://www.usitc.gov/press_room/news_release/2009/er0629gg1.htm.

4. United States Trade Representative. "Certain Passenger Vehicle and Light Truck Tires from China," Hearing, August 7, 2009 (Serial 0017-0068). Available at http://www.regulations.gov/search/Regs/home.html#documentDetail?R=0900006480a15110.

5. Yu, Jiang, "Foreign Ministry Spokesperson Jiang Yu's Remarks on US Announcement to Impose Special Safeguard Measures on Tire Imports from China." Ministry of Foreign Affairs of the People's Republic of China. September 14, 2009. Available at http://www.fmprc.gov.cn/eng/xwfw/s2510/2535/t583898.htm.

6. Bradsher, Keith, "China Moves to Retaliate Against United States." *New York Times*. September 13, 2009. Available at http://www.nytimes.com/2009/09/14/business/global/14trade.html.

7. Eunjung Cha, Ariana, "U.S., China Locked in Trade Disputes." *Washington Post*. January 4, 2010. Available at http://www.washingtonpost.com/wp-dyn/content/article/2010/01/03/AR2010010301961.html.

8. Bradsher, Keith, "China Moves to Retaliate Against United States." *New York Times*. September 13, 2009. Available at http://www.nytimes.com/2009/09/14/business/global/14trade.html.

9. Department of the Treasury/Federal Reserve Board. "Major Foreign Holders of Treasury Securities." Available at http://www.ustreas.gov/tic/mfh.txt. Accessed March 2010.

10. Foreign Trade Statistics. U.S. Census Bureau. "U.S. Imports from China from 2004 to 2008 by 5-digit End-Use

Code." Available at http://www.census.gov/foreign-trade/statistics/product/enduse/imports/c5700.html. Accessed March 2010.

11. Moffett, Mike. "The Economic Effect of Tariffs." Available at http://economics.about.com/cs/taxpolicy/a/tariffs_2.htm.

12. Blinder, Alan. "Free Trade." *The Concise Encyclopedia of Economics*. Available at http://economics.about.com/gi/dynamic/offsite.htm?zi=1/XJ&sdn=economics&zu=http%3A%2F%2Fwww.econlib.org%2Flibrary%2FCEE.html.

13. Lafaive, Michael D. "New Steel Tariffs Will Kill Jobs." Mackinac Center for Public Policy. March 8, 2002. Available at http://www.mackinac.org/4107.

THE CATFISH DISPUTE

THE U.S. CATFISH INDUSTRY

The cultivation of water plants and animals for human use started thousands of years ago. Globally, aquaculture's growth has more than doubled in the 1990s (to more than 35 million tons a year). To meet the demand for improved quality protein sources, scallops, oysters, salmon and catfish are being raised in controlled environments. Farm raised fish has high quality and unlike ocean-caught fish is available all-year long.

U.S. aquaculture production has grown more than 49 percent since 1991.[1] Aquaculture is the fastest growing segment of agriculture in the United States. Farmed seafood makes up about a third of the seafood consumed in the United States. About two thirds of the shrimp and salmon and almost all of the catfish and trout consumed by Americans is raised in ponds.[2]

Thick-skinned, whiskered, wide-mouthed wild catfish can be found in the wild in channels and rivers of the southern United States. Wild catfish is typically described as pungent, bony and muddy. However, as a result of aquaculture technology, catfish is now an economical farm-raised species with a mild flavor. Catfish are raised in clay-based ponds filled with fresh water pumped from underground wells. They are fed an enriched, high-protein grain-based food. Their firm, white flesh can convey strong flavors and stands up to a variety of cooking techniques, which makes it suit virtually any ethnic cuisine.[3]

Americans consumed about 275 million kilograms (more than 600 million pounds) of catfish in 2000,[4] most of which came from 150,000 acres of catfish ponds in the United States, mainly located in Mississippi, Arkansas and Louisiana. The U.S. catfish industry is estimated to turn over $4 billion worth of fish product a year. Catfish is especially popular in Southern dishes, but its use has been growing also in the Midwest. Filets are now available in New York supermarkets and fish stores. One recent poll placed catfish as the country's third favorite seafood, beaten only by shrimp and lobster.[5]

THE ISSUE

The United States was the leading market for Vietnamese catfish (followed by Hong Kong, the EU, and Australia). In 2001 the United States produced 270.5 million kilograms (597 m lb) and imported about 3.7 million kilos (8.2 m lb) of catfish, out of which 90 percent, about

3.2 m kg (7 m lb), came from Vietnam. By the end of 2001 prices for U.S. catfish had dropped to 50 cents a pound, about 15 cents below the cost of production and about 30 cents below the price of 2000. U.S. producers blamed the Vietnamese for the falling prices.[6]

Vietnamese catfish exporters and importers in turn blamed U.S. producers for dragging down prices. They say that the Americans are mainly at fault for expanding inventories up to 30 percent, a figure obtained from the National Agricultural Statistics Service (www.usda.gov/nass). Vietnamese fish importers also claim that American catfish growers are to blame for their own difficulties because they sell the domestic fish in only a few states. "It is the failure to adequately market the product effectively throughout the U.S.," says Andrew Forman, president of Boston-based Infinity Seafood LLC. According to a report by Consulting Trends International, a California-based consulting firm, the price drop is "primarily the result of higher domestic catfish inventories in the U.S., which will depress prices through the end of 2001 and 2002."

The American catfish industry tripled in size from 1985 to 2001. Hugh Warren, vice president of the Catfish Institute of America, says that this growth was strictly due to the industry's marketing effort of $50 million. He feels that as importers, they get a free ride.[7] The U.S. industry offers 15,000 jobs that earn $8 an hour in the poorest parts of America. These jobs are being "stolen" by cheap Vietnamese imports.[8]

The U.S.-Vietnam Bilateral Trade Agreement (BTA), approved by Congress, was signed by the two countries on July 13, 2000. The BTA, signed by President George W. Bush in 2001, opened the door for increased bilateral trade. In the very first year, trade between the two countries doubled. The BTA reduction in tariffs resulted in an increase from 5 million pounds of frozen fillets in 1999 to 34 million pounds in 2002—capturing 20 percent of the U.S. market.

One major exception to the framework of the BTA is the lack of a formal and neutral dispute settlement mechanism. The BTA provides for a Joint Committee on Development of Economic and Trade Relations. The Committee is given the power to serve as a forum for consultation over problems regarding the agreement.

In an attempt to change this situation, American catfish farmers, industry associations and supporting organizations came to Washington, DC, to call on

Source: This case was written by Professors Michael R. Czinkota and Thomas B. Cooke, Georgetown University McDonough School of Business, assisted by graduate student Armen S. Hovhannisyan, Georgetown University School of Foreign Service.

officials at the State Department, the Commerce Department, the Food and Drug Administration and Congress for help. They waged an advertising campaign against their Vietnamese competitors in order to convince the public that Vietnamese catfish is low-quality and raised in dirty waters.[9]

CONGRESSIONAL REACTION: THE LABELING DISPUTE

The support from Congress was swift. In December 2001 an amendment was added to an appropriations bill that barred the Food and Drug Administration (FDA) from spending money "to allow admission of fish or fish products labeled in whole or in part with the term "catfish" unless the fish is from the Ictaluridae family." The senators from the South, who introduced a labeling bill, claimed Vietnamese fish to be as different scientifically from catfish "as cow from a yak."[10] Supporting a different view, Senator Phil Gramm (R-Tex.) characterized the Vietnamese catfish as follows: "Not only does it look like a catfish, but it acts like a catfish. And the people who make a living in fish science call it a catfish. Why do we want to call it anything other than a catfish?"[11] This meant that the FDA needed to identify different kinds of catfish.

In January 2002 under Congress' direction, the Food and Drug Administration (FDA) published "Guidance for Industry" regulations on how the imported fish should be labeled. Under the regulation, Flat Whiskered Fish is an acceptable substitute for the Flat Whiskered Catfish; but Katfish or Cat Fish are not. Instead, importers, restaurants and grocery stores will have to use a name such as "basa," which is one other name to call catfish from the Pangasius (Pangasiidae) family. U.S. producers were counting on such labels to discourage the sales of imported fish. The 2002 U.S. Farm Act prohibited non-ictaluridae fish from being marketed and sold as "catfish" in the U.S.

While U.S. catfish producers were counting on the labeling decision to decrease sales of Vietnamese catfish, the result was just the opposite as sales of Vietnamese "basa" or "tra" actually increased. It seemed that the term "basa" had a special market-place intrigue to it.

The amendment and the regulation were not good news for a number of concerned players (restaurants, consumers and people in the catfish industry). An article appearing in the *Far Eastern Economic Review* (December 6, 2001) noted that declining prices in the U.S. caused U.S. catfish producers to report a 30 percent (2001–2002) decline in the average earnings from a kilogram of catfish. As the owner of Piazza's Seafood World, a New Orleans based importer, put it: "Nobody in the U.S.

owns the word 'catfish'."[12] However, Vietnam was still free to export catfish to the U.S., as long as it's called something other than catfish—that is, until the special tariffs arrived.

WHEN IS A CATFISH A CATFISH?

In order to identify different kinds of catfish, the FDA sought expert help on the catfish question. Before promulgating its regulation it consulted Dr. Carl J. Ferraris of the ichthyology department at the California Academy of Sciences. Dr. Ferraris's response was that there was no scientific justification to treat or rename catfish from Vietnam differently than that of the U.S.[13]

According to U.S. catfish farmers, the only true catfish belongs to the family with the Latin name Ictaluridae. The Vietnamese variety is in the family Pangasiidae, which are "freshwater catfishes of Africa and southern Asia." Vietnamese catfish farmers claim that they have created a new agricultural industry, turning their rice and soybean fields into profitable fish farms in the poor regions of the country. By giving up crops, they gave up heavy use of chemical fertilizers and pesticides, which is good for the environment. They also gave up agriculture subsidies at a time when lawmakers wanted to get the government out of farming.[14]

U.S. catfish farmers say their catfish is raised in purified water ponds, which have to be tested by federal agencies and meet the standards of the Catfish Institute. The U.S. catfish industry must go through inspections from 17 federal agencies (including Department of Commerce, Food and Drug Administration, and Environmental Protection Agency). By contrast the Vietnamese imports have to only meet FDA approval.[15] The Vietnamese catfish are raised in cages that float in marshes in the Mekong River; some of the senators from the South talk about the possibility of toxins from Vietnam in that "dirty" river.[16]

DEPARTMENT OF COMMERCE AND INTERNATIONAL TRADE COMMISSION

Less than a year after winning the Congressional labeling ban, the Catfish Farmers of America (CFA) applied to the U.S. government for additional protection. It seems that the labeling decision was not having the desired result. By this time the Vietnamese share of the U.S. market had actually dropped to 12 percent. But, the 12 percent was seen as continuing to drive down the cost (and profits) of catfish in the U.S. The request to the International Trade Commission (ITC) was for import tariffs as high as 191 percent.

In addressing the anti-dumping complaint from the CFA, the Department of Commerce (DOC) relied on certain necessary assumptions. In assuming that Vietnam was a non-market economy (and not looking at the Vietnamese seafood industry separately), the DOC used data from India and Bangladesh to establish what would be a "fair price" for Vietnam's exports of catfish to the U.S. The initial decision of the DOC was to impose tariffs ranging from 38 percent to 64 percent on four Vietnamese exporters. The subsequent step was for the ITC to confirm DOC's actions.

In February 2003, Vietnam halted exports of catfish to the U.S. At the time of the announcement, prices of Vietnamese catfish had increased by more than 20 percent in the U.S. market. Nguyen Huu Dung, General Secretary of the Vietnamese Association of Seafood Exporters and Producers (VASEP) noted that "we are forced to stop exporting frozen catfish fillets because our U.S. importers cannot afford to pay the high tariffs."

Vietnamese seafood businesses and producers were quick to denounce the actions of the DOC. The Vietnam Ministry of Trade, Ministry of Fisheries and VASEP called the actions an "act of protectionism." Rather than wait for the ITC to confirm the decision of the DOC, VASEP offered to resolve the dispute by voluntarily offering an export quota in lieu of tariffs. The offer to settle fell of deaf ears in the U.S. and the ITC imposed tariffs of up to 64 percent on "basa" or "tra." The ITC's final vote on July 23, 2003 was 4–0.

An editorial appearing in the *New York Times* (July 26, 2003) condemned the action of the ITC by referring to the decision as "a final flourish of hypocrisy to its efforts to crush the Vietnamese catfish industry under a mountain of protectionism." In an earlier editorial (July 22) the publication noted that any decision upholding tariffs would make Vietnam become "yet another case study in the way the United States, Europe, and Japan are rigging global trade rules so they remain the only winners."

THE ISSUE AND THE FREE TRADE

Vietnam's catfish industry provides a useful example of how global cooperation can enhance participation in global business. An Australian importer, for example, taught the Vietnamese how to slice catfish fillet, French researchers worked with a local university on low-cost breeding techniques and Vietnam's leading catfish exporters depended on American industrial equipment from the U.S.[17] However, a stumbling U.S. economy has made American farmers, along with many others in a number of industries, very sensitive to surging imports, and the catfish dispute represents a case of domestic politics alignment against free market forces.[18] Critics in both Vietnam and the U.S. say that the catfish issue is an example of protectionism and hypocrisy, undermining the free-trade

policies most recently espoused by the U.S. at the World Trade Organization talks in Doha.

"After spending years encouraging the Vietnamese that open trade is a win–win situation, it would be a shame if immediately after the trade agreement is signed the U.S. shifts to a protectionist 'we win, you lose' approach on catfish," says Virginia Foote, former president of the U.S.–Vietnam Trade Council in Washington.[19]

In the ongoing dispute of how to manage global trade, agriculture and its cousin aquaculture are very sensitive issues. On the one side are industrial nations that use farm policy not only to promote their agribusinesses overseas but also to protect their markets and farmers at home. European countries have used their agricultural subsidies to defend their countryside from the urban invasion, whereas developing countries try to raise their standard of living by breaking into those markets with less expensive products.

CATFISH CONTROVERSY: UPDATE

After years of arguing that the Vietnamese catfish isn't really catfish—and getting a federal law to say as much (2002), U.S. catfish farmers are trying to create a win–win situation for themselves. The most recent game plan is (1) to have the imports labeled as catfish and (2) subject the imports to new inspection procedures. An amendment to the 2008 U.S. Farm Bill moved the regulation of catfish from the Food and Drug Administration to the Agriculture Department. Under this provision the Secretary of Agriculture would be left to define what species of "catfish" would be subject to enhanced inspection.

Any new inspection requirement would force the Vietnamese to establish a complicated and costly catfish inspection system similar to those in place in the U.S. According to Le Cong Phung, Vietnam's Ambassador to the United States, "for the U.S. to now reverse itself to prevent Vietnamese product from entering the market appears to be hypocritical." An advertisement appearing in the October 16, 2009, issue of the *Washington Post* reflects the latest strategy of the Catfish Farmers of America—go after the Vietnamese on the issue of food safety.

Despite the apparent victories (labeling, antidumping decisions, higher tariffs, etc.), the value of Vietnamese imports to the U.S. jumped from $13 million in 1999 to $77 million in 2008, according to the U.S. Commerce Department. During that same period, U.S. production fell from $488 million to $410 million.

Questions for Discussion

1. Was it fair for the Vietnamese catfish importers to step in and capture market share while the market has been expanded due to the significant efforts and investments of the domestic industry? How should quality (if quality differences exist) considerations be reconciled?

2. The label ban would probably make consumers pay a higher price than they would have paid otherwise. Is this right?

3. Can any industry in the U.S. influence lawmakers to make decisions in its favor?

Notes

1. Catfish Institute, catfishinstitute.com.

2. Elizabeth Becker, "Delta Farmers Want Copyright on Catfish," the *New York Times*, January 16, 2002, Section A1.

3. Meredith Petran, "Catfish," *Restaurant Business,* February 1, 2000.

4. Margot Cohen and Murray Hiebert, "Muddying the Waters," *Far Eastern Economic Review,* December 6, 2001.

5. "The Vietnamese Invade: Catfish in the South."

6. Philip Brasher, "When Is a Catfish Not a Catfish," *Washington Post,* December 27, 2001.

7. James Toedman, "Fighting Like Cats and Dogs Over Fish; It's U.S. vs. Vietnamese as Trade Battle Goes Global," Newsday," March 10, 2002, F02.

8. "The Vietnamese Invade: Catfish in the South."

9. "One of these negative advertisements, which ran in the national trade weekly *Supermarket News,* tells us in shrill tones, 'Never trust a catfish with a foreign accent!' This ad characterizes Vietnamese catfish as dirty and goes on to say, 'They've grown up flapping around in Third World rivers and dining on whatever they can get their fins on. . . . Those other guys probably couldn't spell U.S. even if they tried.' "—quoted in Senator John McCain's December 18, 2001, Press Release, http://mccain.senate.gov/catfish.htm.

10. Philip Brasher, "When Is a Catfish Not a Catfish."

11. Ibid.

12. Margot Cohen and Murray Hiebert, "Muddying the Waters."

13. Elizabeth Becker, "Delta Farmers Want Copyright on Catfish."

14. Ibid.

15. Tim Brown, "South and Southeast, Vietnam Embroiled in Catfish Controversy," *Marketing News,* Chicago, October 22, 2001.

16. "The Vietnamese Invade: Catfish in the South," *The Economist,* October 6, 2001.

17. Ibid.

18. Toedman, "Fighting Like Cats and Dogs Over Fish."

19. Margot Cohen and Murray Hiebert, "Muddying the Waters."

PART 3
ENVIRONMENT

5 Culture
6 Politics and Law
7 Global Financial Markets
8 Economic Integration and Emerging Markets

Operating internationally requires managers to be aware of a highly complex environment. Domestic and international environmental factors and their interactions have to be recognized and understood. In addition, ongoing changes in these environments must be appreciated.

Part 3 delineates the cultural differences as well as the political and legal dimensions which affect international business. A key global shift, namely the increasing involvement of government in the business sector, forms a core component of ongoing change. Once an understanding of cultural and political factors is in place, the workings of the international monetary system and financial markets and the consequences of economic integration around the world are highlighted.

CHAPTER 5

Culture

CHAPTER CONTENTS & LEARNING OBJECTIVES

CULTURE DEFINED

1. To define and demonstrate the effect of culture's various dimensions on business

THE ELEMENTS OF CULTURE

2. To examine ways in which cultural knowledge can be acquired and individuals and organizations prepared for cross-cultural interaction

SOURCES OF CULTURAL KNOWLEDGE

3. To illustrate ways in which cultural risk poses a challenge to the effective conduct of business communications and transactions

CULTURAL ANALYSIS

4. To suggest ways in which businesses act as change agents in the diverse cultural environments in which they operate

THE TRAINING CHALLENGE

5. To evaluate the ways in which training programs assist international managers to develop the international business skills of their employees

MAKING CULTURE WORK FOR BUSINESS SUCCESS

6. Analyzes the strategies corporations can take to work with cultural differences in order to expand their businesses internationally

The dominance of U.S. cultural exports is felt everywhere. Of the 50 worldwide highest-grossing films of 2009, all but ten were U.S. productions. *Avatar*, which came in first, has grossed $2,546 million worldwide ($707 million domestic and $1,839 million international) since its international release and has been the top earner of the time period in diverse markets, such as Lithuania ($1,358,650), Argentina ($12,835,979), and Mexico ($42,509,172). Given the marketing power of Hollywood, many are worried that diversity will not survive and that the end result of globalization will be "Americanization." Quite the opposite is actually taking place in the entertainment world and international market for popular culture.

In television, during the initial stage of the life cycle, the domestic industry has only fledgling production and cheap imports—primarily from the United States—to fill the time slots. With time, however, homegrown production develops, and its market share increases. The top TV show in South Africa is *Generations* (a soap opera); in France, it is *Julie Lescout* (a police series); and in Brazil, it is *Malhacao*. The more the world globalizes, the more people want entertainment that reflects their own culture.

U.S. shows do have their niche as well. Blockbuster Hollywood action movies, cartoons (easy to dub), and certain hit series travel well across cultural barriers. Chinese children enjoy newly introduced Mickey Mouse cartoons. However, on a broader scale, U.S. content providers are having to think about how to refashion their exports. *Art Attack,* an art show for Disney Channel (which is seen around the world), included 216 episodes shot in 26 different languages. A single format (a set that features oversized paint pots and paintbrushes, in fuchsia pink and lime green) is reshaped for each country to give it a local feel. About three-fifths of each show is made up of shared footage: close-ups of the hands of one artist (British). The rest of the show is filmed separately for each country, with the heads and shoulders of local presenters seamlessly edited in. Even though the local presenters are all flown into one central studio in the United Kingdom, the show costs just one-third of what it would take to produce separately for each country. Local viewers in each place consider the show to be theirs.

In Europe, a number of developments seem to conspire to favor U.S. films. The spread of multiplex cinemas has increased attendance, but the multiplexes tend to show more U.S. movies. Hollywood blockbusters, such as *Avatar, Indiana Jones and the Kingdom of the Crystal Skull*, *Quantum of Solace*, and *Shrek Forever After*, are made with budgets beyond the wildest dreams. Marketing spending, too, has soared—more than doubling since 2000 to an average of $36 million per movie. U.S. studios have become increasingly dependent on overseas revenues and are investing more to push their movies in foreign markets (*Indiana Jones and the Kingdom of the Crystal Skull* was the worldwide highest-grossing movie in 2008 with $470 million in foreign revenue).

Lately, French moviemakers, who have long resented the overwhelming popularity of Hollywood movies on their home turf, have begun to fight back. *Le Fabuleux Destin d'Amelie Poulain*, a French-made romantic comedy, recaptured the French box office to the tune of $37.7 million (U.S. dollars) in receipts. Édith Piaf in *La Vie en Rose* (2007) brought international acclaim with this film; she became the first actress to win an Academy Award for a French-language performance. For the first time in decades, French films stood their ground against American imports. With higher budgets and better production values, the new films were created by a wave of young directors with Hollywood experience. What is even more interesting is that films that have success in their home markets are also more acceptable to the big-money U.S. market. Warner Bros. and Overbrook Entertainment (2010) have acquired the rights to remake *Bienvenue chez les Ch'tis (Welcome to the Sticks)*, the comedy that broke box-office records in France this year. Will Smith and James Lassiter will produce the movie with Ken Stovitz. The Dany Boon–directed film grossed more than $190 million in France alone.

The trade in entertainment is no longer a one-way street, making all who watch and listen clones of one another. Much of the U.S. content going abroad is adjusted to its markets, as is the material coming into the United States. Britain's *Bob the Builder* has hammered his way into U.S. homes and the homes of 29 other countries—but with the loss of his Staffordshire accent: *Bob, o Construtor* is aired in Brazil, *Puuha-Pete* is aired in Finland, and the Welsh language version is called *Bob Y Bildar*. When being exported to Japan, it was reported that characters of *Bob the Builder* would be doctored to have five fingers instead of the original four. This was because of a practice among the Yakuza, the famed Japanese mafia, where members would "cut off their little fingers as a sign they can be trusted and have strength of character, and will stay through."

Sources: Claudia Eller, "Studios Struggle to Rein in Movie Marketing Costs," *Los Angeles Times*, April 20, 2009; Ibsen Martinez, "Romancing the Globe," *Foreign Policy* (November/December 2005), 48–56; "Score One for the PG Crowd," *The San Diego Union-Tribune*, April 10, 2005, B7; "Think Local; A Survey of Television," *The Economist*, April 13, 2002, 12–14; "Culture in Peril? Mais Oui," *Fortune*, May 13, 2002, 51; "Bob the Builder Fixed for Japan," *BBC News*, Thursday, 20 April, 2000.

International	Japanese

The ever-increasing level of world trade, opening of new markets, and intensifying competition have allowed—and sometimes forced—businesses to expand their operations. The challenge for managers is to handle the different values, attitudes, and behavior that govern human interaction. First, managers must ensure smooth interaction of the business with its different constituents, and second, they must assist others to implement programs within and across markets. It is no longer feasible to think of markets and operations in terms of domestic and international. Because the separation is no longer distinguishable, the necessity of culturally sensitive management and personnel is paramount.

As firms expand their operations across borders, they acquire new customers and new partners in new environments. Two distinct tasks become necessary: first, to understand cultural differences and the ways they manifest themselves and, second, to determine similarities across cultures and exploit them in strategy formulation as highlighted in the opening vignette. Success in new markets is very much a function of cultural adaptability: patience, flexibility, and appreciation of others' beliefs.[1]

Recognition of different approaches may lead to establishing best practice; that is, a new way of doing things applicable throughout the firm. Ideally, this means that successful ideas can be transferred across borders for efficiency and adjusted to local conditions for effectiveness. Following research, Kraft Foods learned that Chinese consumers thought the Oreo sandwich cookie was too sweet and the package size was not accommodating. Kraft tinkered with the formula of the cookies and repackaged Oreos in small and economy sizes. China is now the brand's second largest market.[2]

To take advantage of the global marketplace, companies have to have or gain a thorough understanding of market behavior, especially in terms of similarities. For example, no other group of emerging markets in the world has as much in common as those in Latin America. They share a Spanish language and heritage; the Portuguese language and heritage are close enough to allow Brazilians and their neighbors to communicate easily. The Southern Florida melting pot, where Latin Americans of all backgrounds mix in a blend of Hispanic cultures, is in itself a picture of what Latin America can be. Tapping into the region's cultural affinities through a network-scale approach (e.g., regional hubs for production and pan-Latin brands) is not only possible but advisable.[3]

Cultural competence must be recognized as a key management skill. Cultural incompetence, or inflexibility, can easily jeopardize millions of dollars through wasted negotiations; lost purchases, sales, and contracts; and poor customer relations. Furthermore, the internal efficiency of a multinational corporation may be weakened if managers and workers are not "on the same wavelength." The tendency for U.S. managers is to be open and informal, but in some cultural settings that may be inappropriate. **Cultural risk** is just as real as commercial or political risk in the international business arena.

The intent of this chapter is to analyze the concept of culture and its various elements and then to provide suggestions for not only meeting the cultural challenge but making it a base for obtaining and maintaining a competitive advantage.

cultural risk The risk of business blunders, poor customer relations, and wasted negotiations that results when firms fail to understand and adapt to the differences between their own and host countries' cultures.

CULTURE DEFINED

1. To define and demonstrate the effect of culture's various dimensions on business

Culture gives an individual an anchoring point, an identity, as well as codes of conduct. Of the more than 164 definitions of culture analyzed by Kroeber and Kluckhohn, some conceive of culture as separating humans from nonhumans, some define it as communicable knowledge, and some as the sum of historical achievements produced by human beings' social life.[4] All of the definitions have common elements: culture is learned, shared, and transmitted from one generation to the next. Culture is primarily passed on from parents to their children but also transmitted by social organizations, special interest groups, the government, schools, and churches. Common ways of thinking and behaving that are developed are then reinforced through social pressure. Geert Hofstede calls this the "collective programming of the mind."[5] Culture is also multidimensional, consisting of a number of common elements that are interdependent. Changes occurring in one of the dimensions will affect the others as well.

Mutual awareness of cultural references is essential in international business. Levels of formality vary greatly among cultures. In most situations, restraint equals respect.

For the purposes of this text, culture is defined as an *integrated system of learned behavior patterns that are characteristic of the members of any given society*. It includes everything that a group thinks, says, does, and makes—its customs, language, material artifacts, and shared systems of attitudes and feelings. The definition, therefore, encompasses a wide variety of elements from the materialistic to the spiritual. Culture is inherently conservative, resisting change and fostering continuity. Every person is acculturated into a particular culture, learning the "right way" of doing things. Problems may arise when a person acculturated in one culture has to adjust to another one. The process of **acculturation**—adjusting and adapting to a specific culture other than one's own—is one of the keys to success in international operations.

acculturation The process of adjusting and adapting to a specific culture other than one's own.

Edward T. Hall, who has made some of the most valuable studies on the effects of culture on business, makes a distinction between high- and low-context cultures.[6] In **high-context cultures**, such as Japan and Saudi Arabia, context is at least as important as what is actually said. The speaker and the listener rely on a common understanding of the context and what is not being said can carry more meaning than what is said. In **low-context cultures**, however, most of the information is contained explicitly in the words. North American cultures engage in low-context communications. Unless one is aware of this basic difference, messages and intentions can easily be misunderstood. As an example, performance appraisals are typically a human resources function. If performance appraisals are to be centrally guided or conducted in a multinational corporation, those involved must be acutely aware of cultural nuances. One of the interesting differences is that the U.S. system emphasizes the individual's development, whereas the Japanese system focuses on the group within which the individual works. In the United States, criticism is more direct and recorded formally, whereas in Japan it is more subtle and verbal.

high-context cultures Cultures in which behavioral and environmental nuances are an important means of conveying information.

low-context cultures Cultures in which most information is conveyed explicitly rather than through behavioral and environmental nuances.

Few cultures today are as homogeneous as those of Japan and Saudi Arabia. Elsewhere intracultural differences based on nationality, religion, race, or geographic areas have resulted in the emergence of distinct subcultures. The international manager's task is to distinguish relevant cross-cultural and intracultural differences and then to isolate potential opportunities and problems. Good examples are the Hispanic subculture in the United States and the Flemish and the Walloons in Belgium. On the other hand, borrowing and interaction among national cultures may narrow gaps between cultures. Here the international business entity acts as a **change agent** by introducing new products or ideas and practices. Although this may only shift consumption from one product brand to another, it may also lead to massive social change in the

change agent A person or institution who facilitates change in a firm or in a country.

manner of consumption, the type of products consumed, and social organization. Consider, for example, that the international portion of McDonald's annual sales has grown to 72 percent; 28 percent is U.S. while 72 percent is worldwide.[7] In markets such as Taiwan, one of the 118 countries on six continents entered, McDonald's and other fast-food entities dramatically changed eating habits, especially of the younger generation.

The example of Kentucky Fried Chicken in India illustrates the difficulties companies may have in entering culturally complex markets. Even though the company opened its outlets in two of India's most cosmopolitan cities (Bangalore and New Delhi), it found itself the target of protests by a wide range of opponents. KFC could have alleviated or eliminated some of the anti-Western passions by tailoring its activities to the local conditions. First, rather than opting for more direct control, KFC should have allied itself with local partners for advice and support. Second, KFC should have tried to appear more Indian rather than using high-profile advertising with Western ideas. Indians are ambivalent toward foreign culture, and its ideas may not always work well there. Finally, KFC should have planned for competition, which came from small restaurants with political clout at the local level.[8]

cultural imperialism The imposition of a foreign viewpoint, non-local perspective, or civilization on a people.

In some cases, the international business may be accused of **cultural imperialism**. There is a growing fear among many countries that globalization is bringing a surge of foreign products across their borders that will threaten their cultural heritage. Some countries, such as Brazil, Canada, France, and Indonesia, protect their cultural industries through restrictive rules and subsidies. France's measures include, for example, "prix unique du livre," a limitation on the percentage of discount on books (to support small publishing houses and help maintain small bookstores); quotas on non-French movies on French national TV channels and mandatory financing of French films by TV channels (as a provision in their license), as well as of French music on radio channels; and "avance sur recettes" or "fonds de soutien," a financial state advance on all French films.[9] Such subsidies have allowed the French to make 200 films a year, twice as many as the United Kingdom. Similar measures have been taken to protect geographic indications; that is, signs on goods that have a specific geographic origin and possess qualities or a reputation resulting from that place of origin (as seen in Focus on Politics). Some countries have started taking measures to protect their traditions in areas such as medicine, in which the concern is bio-piracy of natural remedies.[10]

Even if a particular country is dominant in a cultural sector, such as the United States in movies and television programming, the commonly suggested solution of protectionism may not work. Although the European Union has a rule that 40 percent of the programming has to be domestic, anyone wanting a U.S. program can choose an appropriate channel or rent a video. Quotas will also result in behavior not intended by regulators. U.S. programming tends to be scheduled more during prime time, while the 60 percent of domestic programming may wind up being shown during less-attractive times. Furthermore, quotas may also lead to local productions designed to satisfy official mandates and capture subsidies that accompany them. Recently, a question has been raised on whether movies produced by foreign-owned companies would be eligible for government subsidies. Many emerging markets are following suit; in Cambodia, for example, local TV stations are requested by the Information Ministry to show local films three times a week.[11]

Popular culture is not only a U.S. bastion. In many areas, such as pop music and musicals, Europeans have had an equally dominant position worldwide. Furthermore, no market is only an exporter of culture. Given the ethnic diversity in the United States (as in many other country markets), programming from around the world is made available. Many of the greatest successes of cultural products of the past five years in the United States were non-U.S.; for example, in television programming, *The X Factor* and *Pop Idol* are British concepts, as is the best-seller in children's literature, the *Harry Potter* series. In cartoons, Pokémon hails from Japan. Global

Original Taste of Place

Geography can have an impact in a variety of ways: the climate, the way the product is grown or made, culture, and tradition. As a result, the term means different things to different people. To some, it's as simple as a food or wine that hails from specific regions; to others, it requires that the products be made using high standards or traditional methods. The European Union identifies three kinds of *terroir* for wines, olive oils, butters, cheeses, meats, honeys, and breads:

- Protected designation of origin products (PDOs), such as pecorino Romano cheese and kalamata olives, are associated with a specific location and made in a traditional way.
- Protected geographic indication products (PGIs), such as Alsatian honey and bresaola (air-dried beef), have a geographic connection for at least one stage of production but not all.
- Traditional specialty guaranteed products (TSGs), such as mozzarella cheese and limbic beers, have traditional ingredients or production methods but are not linked to a specific region.

If European negotiators in the World Trade Organization get their way, food names associated with specific regions—Parma ham from Italy, Stilton cheese from the United Kingdom, and Feta wine from Greece—would be reserved solely for companies located in the respective regions. EU officials argue that mozzarella, for example, is made according to exacting standards only in that particular part of Italy, and similarly, Stilton cheese can only be produced in the three English counties of Derbyshire, Leicestershire, and Nottinghamshire.

The European Commission summarized the European point of view in this way: "Geographical indications offer the best protection to quality products which are sold by relying on their origin and reputation and other special characteristics linked to such an origin. They reward investment in quality by our producers. Abuses in other countries undermine the heritage of EU products and create confusion among consumers." Furthermore, Europeans fear that they may not be able to use their own names selling abroad in the future. A company in Canada, for example, could trademark a product named for a European place, preventing the rightful European originator from selling its goods in that market. The European Union has adopted geographic-indication laws governing more than 818 products sold inside the EU. Now the EU wants to expand such a list worldwide and establish a multilateral register to police it.

For many, the European idea is out-and-out protectionism and has no merit on protecting cultural values. "This does not speak of free trade; it is about making a monopoly of trade," said Sergio Marchi, Canada's ambassador to the WTO. "It is even hard to calculate the cost and confusion of administering such a thing." Others argue that the Europeans are merely trying to cover up for inefficient production practices. Some even make the argument that multinational companies are the ones who have built up the value of many of the product names on the list—not the small producers in the regions in question.

The debate is still in its early stages. The definition of geographic indications is not altogether clear in that some countries want to protect the adjectives found on product labels (such as "tawny" or "ruby" to describe Portuguese port wine). Other countries have their own lists as well; for example, India wants basmati rice to be protected, even though "basmati" is not a place name. Geographical indications from the United States include: "Florida" for oranges; "Idaho" for potatoes; "Vidalia" for onions; and "Washington State" for apples. Vidalia onions have a certification mark that ensures that no one outside 20 counties in Georgia is permitted to sell onions as Vidalias.

Sources: Mariann Fisher Boel, *The Green Paper on Agricultural Product Quality*, Brussels, December 2, 2008; "The Geography of Flavor," *Washington Post*, August 22, 2007, p.3; "Greek Cheese Gets EU Protection," *Marketing News*, November 15, 2005, p.15; "Food Fight!" *Time Europe*, September 8, 2003, pp. 32–33; "WTO Talks: EU Steps Up Bid for Better Protection of Regional Quality Products," *EU Institutions Press Releases*, August 28, 2003, DN:IP/03/1178; see also www.geographicindications.com.

© Hayward Gaude/iStockphoto

marketers and media have made it possible for national and regional artists to break into worldwide markets, especially the U.S. and European markets. Thailand's Tata Young has been signed by Sony BMG to be groomed for global stardom.[12]

The worst scenario for companies is when they are accused of pushing Western behaviors and values—along with products and promotions—into other cultures, and this results in consumer boycotts and even destruction of property. McDonald's, KFC, Coca-Cola, Disney, and Pepsi, for example, have all drawn the ire of anti-American demonstrators for being icons of globalization.

2. To examine ways in which cultural knowledge can be acquired and individuals and organizations prepared for cross-cultural interaction

cultural universals Similarities in the total way of life of any group of people.

The study of culture has led to generalizations that may apply to all cultures. Such characteristics are called **cultural universals**, which are manifestations of the total way of life of any group of people. These include such elements as bodily adornment, courtship rituals, etiquette, concept of family, gestures, joking, mealtime customs, music, personal names, status differentiation, and trade customs.[13] These activities occur across cultures, but they may be uniquely manifested in a particular society, bringing about cultural diversity. Common denominators can indeed be found across cultures, but cultures may vary dramatically in how they perform the same activities.[14] Even when a segment may be perceived to be similar across borders—as in the case of teenagers or the affluent—cultural differences make dealing with them challenging. For example, European teens resent being treated like Americans with an accent by U.S. companies.[15]

Observation of the major cultural elements summarized in Table 5.1 suggests that these elements are both material (such as tools) and abstract (such as attitudes). The sensitivity and adaptation to these elements by an international firm depends on the firm's level of involvement in the market—for example, licensing versus direct investment—and the good or service marketed. Naturally, some goods and services or management practices require very little adjustment, while some have to be adapted dramatically.

LANGUAGE

A total of 6,912 known living languages exist in the world, with 311 being spoken in the United States, 297 in Mexico, 13 in Finland, and 241 in China.[16] The European Union has 23 official languages for its bureaucracy. Interestingly, a total of 96 percent of the world's languages are spoken by just 4 percent of the world's population. Language has been described as the mirror of culture. Language itself is multidimensional by nature. This is true not only of the spoken word but also of what can be called the nonverbal language of international business. Messages are conveyed by the words used, by how the words are spoken (e.g., tone of voice), and through nonverbal means such as gestures, body position, and eye contact.

Very often, mastery of the language is required before a person is acculturated to a culture other than his or her own. Language mastery must go beyond technical competency, because every language has words and phrases that can be readily understood only in context. Such phrases are carriers of culture; they represent special ways a culture has developed to view some aspect of human existence.

Language capability serves four distinct roles in international business.[17]

1. Language aids in information gathering and evaluation. Rather than rely completely on the opinions of others, the manager is able to see and hear personally what is going on. People are far more comfortable speaking their own language, and this should be treated as an advantage. The best

Table 5.1 Elements of Culture	
• Language	• Manners and customs
Verbal	• Material elements
Nonverbal	• Aesthetics
	• Education
• Religion	• Social institutions
• Values and attitudes	

intelligence on a market is gathered by becoming part of the market rather than observing it from the outside. For example, local managers of a multinational corporation should be the firm's primary source of political information to assess potential risk.

2. Language provides access to local society. Although English may be widely spoken and may even be the official company language, speaking the local language may make a dramatic difference.

3. Language capability is increasingly important in company communications, whether within the corporate family or with channel members. Imagine the difficulties encountered by a country manager who must communicate with employees through an interpreter.

4. Language provides more than the ability to communicate. It extends beyond mechanics to the interpretation of contexts that may influence business operations. Curves International Inc. (owned and based in Woodway, Texas) currently has 9,468 foreign fitness franchises worldwide as of 2008. Its delivery of customized marketing tools to Curves International franchisees has not changed, but the scope and tools have. It offers more flexible, cost-effective, and dynamic solutions to its franchisees because it is now in 70 markets, and each has a unique culture and language (See Figure 5.1).

The manager's command of the national language(s) in a market must be greater than simple word recognition. Consider, for example, how dramatically different English terms can be when used in the United Kingdom or the United States. In negotiations, for U.S. delegates, "tabling a proposal" means that they want to delay a decision, while their British counterparts understand the expression to mean that immediate action is to be taken. If the British promise something "by the end of the day," this does not mean within 24 hours, but rather when they have completed the job. Additionally, they may say that negotiations "bombed," meaning that they were a success, which to an American could convey exactly the opposite message. Other

Figure 5.1   Culture and Local Language and Materials

Courtesy Curves International. Used by permission.

languages are not immune to this phenomenon either. Goodyear has identified five different terms for the word "tires" in the Spanish-speaking Americas: *cauchos* in Venezuela, *cubiertas* in Argentina, *gomas* in Puerto Rico, *neumaticos* in Chile, and *llantas* in most of the other countries in the region. The company has to adjust its communications messages accordingly.[18]

An advertising campaign presented by Electrolux highlights the difficulties in transferring advertising campaigns between markets. Electrolux's theme in marketing its vacuum cleaners, "Nothing Sucks Like an Electrolux," is interpreted literally in the United Kingdom, but in the United States, the slang implications would interfere with the intended message. Another example is the adaptation of an advertisement into Arabic. When this is carried out without considering that Arabic reads from right to left, the creative concept can be destroyed. The danger of translingual homonyms exists; an innocent word may have strong resemblance to another word not used in polite company in another country. For example, global elevator maker Kone wanted to ensure correct pronunciation of its name and added an accent aigu (Koné) to its name in French-speaking countries to avoid controversy. Toyota Motor behaved similarly in changing its MR2 model to Spider.

The role of language extends beyond that of a communication medium. Linguistic diversity often is an indicator of other types of diversity. In Quebec, the French language has always been a major consideration of most francophone governments, because it is one of the clear manifestations of the province's identity vis-à-vis the English-speaking provinces. The Charter of the French Language states that the rights of the francophone collectivity are (1) the right of every person to have the civil administration, semipublic agencies, and business firms communicate with him or her in French; (2) the right of workers to carry on their activities in French; and (3) the right of consumers to be informed and served in French. The Bay, a major Quebec retailer, spends $8 million annually on translation. It has even changed its name to La Baie in appropriate areas. Similarly, in trying to battle English as the *lingua franca*, the French government has tried to ban the use of any foreign term or expression wherever an officially approved French equivalent (e.g., *mercatique*, not *un brain-storming*, and *jeune-pousse*, not *un start-up*) exists.[19] This applies also to web sites that bear the "fr" designation; they have to be in the French language.

Other countries have taken similar measures. Germans have founded a society for the protection of the German language from the spread of "Denglish." Poland has directed that all companies selling or advertising foreign products use Polish in their advertisements. In Hong Kong, the Chinese government is promoting the use of Cantonese rather than English as the language of commerce, while some people in India—with its 800 dialects—scorn the use of English as a lingua franca since it is a reminder of British colonialism.[20]

Despite the fact that English is encountered daily by those on the Internet, the "e" in e-business does not translate into English. In a survey, European users highlighted the need to bridge the language gap. One-third of the senior managers said they will not tolerate English online, while less than 20 percent of German middle managers and less than 50 percent of French ones believe they can use English well. Being forced to use nonlocalized content was perceived to have a negative impact on productivity among 75 percent of those surveyed.[21] A truly global portal works only if the online functions are provided in a multilingual and multicultural format. Starting in late 2007, Internet users have been able to use addresses in 11 languages that do not use the Roman alphabet. Russians, for example, are able to type in web addresses entirely in the Cyrillic characters instead of having to revert to English. The change has also involved languages such as Chinese, Arabic, and Korean. There are a billion people on the Internet; this move will accelerate the incorporation of the next billion.[22]

Dealing with language invariably requires local assistance. A good local advertising agency and a good local market research firm can prevent many problems. When translation is required, as when communicating with suppliers or customers, care should be taken in selecting the translator. To make sure, the simplest method of control is **backtranslation**—translating a foreign language version back to the original language by a different person than the one who made the first translation. This approach may be able to detect only omissions and blunders, however. To assess the quality of the translation, a complete evaluation with testing of the message's impact is necessary.[23] In essence, this means that companies should translate not just words, but also emotion—which then, in turn, may well lead to the use of completely different words.

Language also has to be understood in the historic context. Nokia launched an advertising campaign in Germany for the interchangeable covers for its portable phones using a theme "*Jedem das Seine*" ("to each his own"). The campaign was withdrawn after the American Jewish Congress pointed out that the same slogan was found on the entry portal to Buchenwald, a Nazi-era concentration camp.[24] The Indian division of Cadbury-Schweppes incensed Hindu society by running an advertisement comparing its Temptations chocolate to war-torn Kashmir. The ad carried a tagline: "I'm good. I'm tempting. I'm too good to share. What am I? Cadbury's Temptations or Kashmir?" The ad also featured a map of Kashmir to highlight the point. To add insult to injury, the ad appeared on August 15th, Indian Independence Day.[25]

NONVERBAL LANGUAGE

Managers also must analyze and become familiar with the hidden language of foreign cultures.[26] Five key topics—time, space, material possessions, friendship patterns, and business agreements—offer a starting point from which managers can begin to acquire the understanding necessary to do business in foreign countries. In many parts of the world, time is flexible and not seen as a limited commodity; people come late to appointments or may not come at all. In Hong Kong, for example, it is futile to set exact meeting times, because getting from one place to another may take minutes or hours depending on the traffic situation. Showing indignation or impatience at such behavior would astonish an Arab, Latin American, or Asian. Understanding national and cultural differences in the concept of time is critical for an international business manager.

In some countries, extended social acquaintance and the establishment of appropriate personal rapport are essential to conducting business. The feeling is that one should know one's business partner on a personal level before transactions can occur. Therefore, rushing straight to business will not be rewarded, because deals are made on the basis of not only the best product or price but also the entity or person deemed most trustworthy. Contracts may be bound on handshakes, not lengthy and complex agreements—a fact that makes some, especially Western, businesspeople uneasy.

Individuals vary in the amount of space they want separating them from others. Arabs and Latin Americans like to stand close to people when they talk. If an American, who may not be comfortable at such close range, backs away from an Arab, this might incorrectly be taken as a negative reaction. Also, Westerners are often taken aback by the more physical nature of affection between Slavs—for example, being kissed squarely on the lips by a business partner, regardless of sex.

International body language must be included in the nonverbal language of international business. For example, an American manager may, after successful completion of negotiations, impulsively give a finger-and-thumb OK sign. In southern France, the manager would have indicated that the sale was worthless and in Japan,

backtranslation The retranslation of text to the original language by a different person than the one who made the first translation.

that a little bribe had been requested; the gesture would be grossly insulting to Brazilians. An interesting exercise is to compare and contrast the conversation styles of different nationalities. Northern Europeans are quite reserved in using their hands and maintain a good amount of personal space, whereas southern Europeans involve their bodies to a far greater degree in making a point.

RELIGION

In most cultures, people find in religion a reason for being and legitimacy in the belief that they are of a larger context. To define religion requires the inclusion of the supernatural and the existence of a higher power. Religion defines the ideals for life, which in turn are reflected in the values and attitudes of societies and individuals. Such values and attitudes shape the behavior and practices of institutions and members of cultures and are the most challenging for the marketer to adjust to. When Procter & Gamble launched its Biomat laundry detergent in Israel, it found reaching Orthodox Jews (15 percent of the population) a challenge because they do not own traditional media such as television sets. The solution was to focus on the segment's core belief that they should aid those less fortunate. A Biomat truck equipped with washing machines traveled around key towns. People would donate their clothing, and Biomat would wash and distribute it to the needy. As a result, the brand's share has grown 50 percent among the segment.[27]

Religion has an impact on international business that is seen in a culture's values and attitudes toward entrepreneurship, consumption, and social organization. The impact will vary depending on the strength of the dominant religious tenets. While religion's impact may be quite indirect in Protestant northern Europe, its impact in countries where Islamic fundamentalism is on the rise (such as Algeria) may be profound.

Religion provides the basis for transcultural similarities under shared beliefs and behavior. The impact of these similarities will be assessed in terms of the dominant religions of the world: Christianity, Islam, Hinduism, Buddhism, and Confucianism. Other religions may have smaller numbers of followers, such as in the case of Judaism with 14 million followers around the world, but their impact is still significant due to the centuries they have influenced world history. While some countries may officially have secularism, such as Marxism-Leninism as a state belief (e.g., China, Vietnam, and Cuba), traditional religious beliefs still remain a powerful force in shaping behavior.

International managers must be aware of the differences not only among the major religions but also within them. The impact of these divisions may range from hostility, as in Sri Lanka, to barely perceptible historic suspicion, as in many European countries where Protestant and Catholic are the main divisions. With some religions, such as Hinduism, people may be divided into groups, which determines their status and to a large extent their ability to consume.

Christianity The largest organized world religion with over 2 billion followers; Protestantism encourages work and accumulation of wealth.

Christianity has the largest following among world religions, with more than 2 billion people.[28] While there are many subgroups within Christianity, the major division is between Catholicism and Protestantism. A prominent difference between the two is the attitude toward making money. While Catholicism has questioned it, the Protestant ethic has emphasized the importance of work and the accumulation of wealth for the glory of God. At the same time, frugality was emphasized and the residual accumulation of wealth from hard work formed the basis for investment. It has been proposed that the work ethic is responsible for the development of capitalism in the Western world and the rise of predominantly Protestant countries into world economic leadership in the twentieth century.

Major holidays are often tied to religion. Holidays are observed differently from one culture to the next, to the extent that the same holiday may have different connotations. Christian cultures observe Christmas and exchange gifts on either

December 24 or December 25, with the exception of the Dutch, who exchange gifts on St. Nicholas Day, December 6. Tandy Corporation, in its first year in the Netherlands, targeted its major Christmas promotion for the third week of December with less than satisfactory results. The international manager must see to it that local holidays, such as Mexico's Día de los Muertos (October 31 to November 2), are taken into account in scheduling events ranging from fact-finding missions to marketing programs and in preparing local work schedules.

Islam, which reaches from the west coast of Africa to the Philippines and across a broad band that includes Tanzania, central Asia, western China, India, and Malaysia, has more than 1.2 billion followers. Islam is also a significant minority religion in many parts of the world, including Europe. Islam has a pervasive role in the life of its followers, referred to as Muslims, through the Sharia (law of Islam). This is most obvious in the five stated daily periods of prayer, fasting during the holy month of Ramadan, and the pilgrimage to Mecca, Islam's holy city. While Islam is supportive of entrepreneurship, it nevertheless strongly discourages acts that may be interpreted as exploitation. Islam is also absent of discrimination, except against those outside the religion. Some have argued that Islam's basic fatalism (that is, nothing happens without the will of Allah) and traditionalism have deterred economic development in countries observing the religion.

Given that Islam considers interest payments usury, bankers and Muslim scholars have worked to create interest-free banking that relies on lease agreements, mutual funds, and other methods to avoid paying interest. Banks and other financial companies have been successful in creating numerous Islamic finance instruments that have been judged as satisfying the Koran's concept of a just transaction. The market for Islamic finance has been growing at a rate of 15 percent annually and is becoming a competitive arena for Islamic banks and funds as well as global financial players. Currently there are 250 Islamic financial institutions managing funds of more than $200 billion.[29]

The role of women in business is tied to religion, especially in the Middle East, where women do not function as they would in the West. This affects the conduct of business in various ways; for example, the firm may be limited in its use of female managers or personnel in these markets, and women's role as consumers and influencers in the consumption process may be different. Access to women in Islamic countries may only be possible through the use of female sales personnel, direct marketing, and women's specialty shops.[30]

Religion affects goods and services, as well. When beef or poultry is exported to an Islamic country, the animal must be killed in the "halal" method and certified appropriately. Recognition of religious restrictions on products (for example, alcoholic beverages) can reveal opportunities, as evidenced by successful launches of several nonalcoholic beverages in the Middle East. Other restrictions may call for innovative solutions. A challenge for the Swedish firm that had the primary responsibility for building a traffic system to Mecca was that non-Muslims are not allowed access to the city. The solution was to use closed-circuit television to supervise the work.

Hinduism has 860 million followers, mainly in India, Nepal, Malaysia, Guyana, Suriname, and Sri Lanka. In addition to being a religion it is also a way of life predicated on the caste, or class to which one is born. While the caste system has produced social stability, its impact on business can be quite negative. For example, if it is difficult to rise above one's caste, individual effort is hampered. Problems in workforce integration and coordination may become quite severe. Furthermore, the drive for business success may not be important if followers place value mostly on spiritual rather than materialistic achievement.

The family is an important element of Hindu society, with extended families being a norm. The extended family structure affects the purchasing power and

Islam A religion that has over 1 billion followers from the west coast of Africa to the Philippines, as well as in the rest of the world and is supportive of entrepreneurism but not of exploitation.

Hinduism With 860 million followers, a way of life rather than a religion, with economic and other attainment dictated by the castes into which its followers are born.

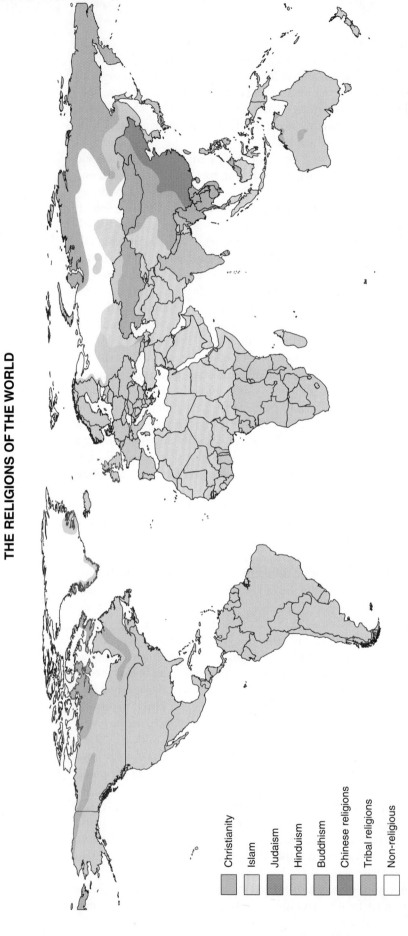

THE RELIGIONS OF THE WORLD

Christianity
Islam
Judaism
Hinduism
Buddhism
Chinese religions
Tribal religions
Non-religious

Source: The Pew Forum on Religion and Public Life, "Mapping the Global Muslim Population," October 2009.

consumption of Hindu families, and market researchers, in particular, must take this into account in assessing market potential and consumption patterns.

Buddhism, which extends its influence throughout Asia from Sri Lanka to Japan, has 360 million followers. Although it is an offspring of Hinduism, it has no caste system. Life is seen as filled with suffering, with achieving nirvana—a spiritual state marked by an absence of desire—as the solution. The emphasis in Buddhism is on spiritual achievement rather than worldly goods.

Confucianism has more than 150 million followers throughout Asia, especially among the Chinese, and has been characterized as a code of conduct rather than a religion. However, its teachings, which stress loyalty and relationships, have been broadly adopted. Loyalty to central authority and placing the good of a group before that of the individual may explain the economic success of Japan, South Korea, Singapore, and the Republic of China. It also has led to cultural misunderstandings: Western societies often perceive the subordination of the individual to the common good as a violation of human rights. The emphasis on relationships is very evident in developing business ties in Asia. Preparation may take years before understanding is reached and actual business transactions can take place.

> **Buddhism** A religion emphasizing spiritual attainment rather than worldly goods that extends through Asia from Sri Lanka to Japan and has 360 million followers.

> **Confucianism** A code of conduct, stressing loyalty and relationships with 150 million followers throughout Asia.

VALUES AND ATTITUDES

Values are shared beliefs or group norms that have been internalized by individuals. Attitudes are evaluations of alternatives based on these values. Differences in cultural values affect the way planning is executed, decisions are made, strategy is implemented, and personnel are evaluated. Table 5.2 provides examples of how U.S. values differ from other values around the world and how this, in turn, affects management functions. These cultural values have to be accommodated or used in the management of business functions.[31]

Table 5.2   Cultural Variations: Performance Appraisals

Dimensions —General	United States —Low Context	Saudi Arabia —High Context	Japan —High Context
Who does appraisal?	Supervisor.	Manager—maybe several layers up. Appraiser has to know employee well.	Mentor and supervisor. Appraiser has to know employee well.
Authority of appraiser	Presumed in supervisory role or position. Supervisor takes slight lead.	Reputation is important (prestige is determined by nationality, age, gender, family, tribe, title, education). Authority of appraiser is important—don't say "I don't know."	Respect is accorded by employee to supervisor or appraiser.
How often?	Yearly or periodically.	Yearly.	Developmental appraisal monthly. Evaluation appraisal—after first 12 years.
Assumptions	Objective appraiser is fair.	Subjective appraiser more important than objective. Connections are important.	Objective and subjective important. Japanese can be trained in anything.
Manner of communication and feedback	Criticism is direct. Criticisms may be in writing. Objective/authentic.	Criticisms are subtle. Older are more likely to be direct. Criticisms are not given in writing.	Criticisms are subtle. Criticisms are given verbally. Observe formalities.
Rebuttals	U.S. will rebut appraisal.	Saudi Arabians will retreat.	Japanese will rarely rebut.
Praise/motivators	Given individually. Money and position are strong motivators. Career development.	Given individually. Loyalty to supervisor is strong motivator.	Given to entire group. Internal excellence is strong motivator.

Source: Adapted from Robert T. Moran, Philip R. Harris, and Sarah V. Moran, *Managing Cultural Differences* (Burlington, MA: Butterworth-Heinemann, 2007), exhibit 5.2.

The more rooted values and attitudes are in central beliefs (such as religion), the more cautiously one has to move. Attitude toward change is basically positive in industrialized countries, as is one's ability to improve one's lot in life; in tradition-bound societies, however, change is viewed with suspicion—especially when it comes from a foreign entity.

The Japanese culture raises an almost invisible—yet often unscalable—wall against all *gaijin* (foreigners). Many middle-aged bureaucrats and company officials believe that buying foreign products is downright unpatriotic. The resistance is not so much to foreign products as to those who produce and market them. Similarly, foreign-based corporations have had difficulty hiring university graduates or mid-career personnel because of bias against foreign employers. Even under such adverse conditions, the race can be run and won through tenacity, patience, and drive.

Cultural attitudes are not always a deterrent to foreign business practices or foreign goods. Japanese youth, for instance, display extremely positive attitudes toward Western goods, from popular music to Nike sneakers to Louis Vuitton haute couture to Starbucks lattes. Even in Japan's faltering economy, global brands are able to charge premium prices if they tap into cultural attitudes that revere imported goods. Similarly, attitudes of U.S. youth toward Japanese "cool" have increased the popularity of authentic Japanese "manga" comics and animated cartoons. Pokémon cards, and Hello Kitty, are examples of Japanese products that caught on in the United States almost as quickly as in Japan.[32]

Dealing in China and with the Chinese, the international manager will have to realize that making deals has more to do with cooperation than competition. The Chinese believe that one should build the relationship first and, if successful, transactions will follow. The relationship, or *guanxi,* is a set of favor exchanges to establish trust.[33]

A manager must be careful not to assume that success in one market using the cultural extension ensures success somewhere else. For example, while the Disneyland concept worked well in Tokyo, it had a tougher time in Paris. One of the main reasons was that while the Japanese are fond of American pop culture, the Europeans are quite content with their own cultural heritage.[34]

MANNERS AND CUSTOMS

Changes occurring in manners and customs must be carefully monitored, especially in cases that seem to indicate a narrowing of cultural differences among peoples. Phenomena such as McDonald's and Coke have met with success around the world, but this does not mean that the world is becoming Westernized. Modernization and Westernization are not at all the same, as can be seen in Saudi Arabia, for example.

Understanding manners and customs is especially important in negotiations, because interpretations based on one's own frame of reference may lead to a totally incorrect conclusion. To negotiate effectively abroad, all types of communication should be read correctly. Americans often interpret inaction and silence as negative signs. As a result, Japanese executives tend to expect that their silence can get Americans to lower prices or sweeten a deal. Even a simple agreement may take days to negotiate in the Middle East because the Arab party may want to talk about unrelated issues or do something else for a while. The aggressive style of Russian negotiators and their usual last-minute change requests may cause astonishment and concern on the part of ill-prepared negotiators. Some of the potential ways in which negotiators may not be prepared include (1) insufficient understanding of different ways of thinking; (2) insufficient attention to the necessity to save face; (3) insufficient knowledge and appreciation of the host country—its history, culture, government, and image of foreigners; (4) insufficient recognition of the decision-making

Table 5.3 When to Give Gifts and What to Give

China	India	Japan	Mexico	Saudi Arabia	Russia
Chinese New Year (January or February)	Hindu Diwali festival (October or November)	Oseibo (January 1)	Christmas/ New Year	Id al-Fitr (December or January)	Christmas/ New Year
√ Modest gifts such as coffee table books, ties, pens	√ Sweets, nuts, and fruit; elephant carvings; candleholders	√ Scotch, brandy, Americana, round fruit such as melons	√ Desk clocks, fine pens, gold lighters	√ Fine compasses to determine direction for prayer, cashmere	√ Chocolates, cigars, good wine, or other alcohol (something other than vodka)
× Clocks, anything from Taiwan	× Leather objects, snake images	× Gifts that come in sets of four or nine	× Sterling silver items, logo gifts, food baskets	× Pork and pigskin, liquor	× Pens, lighters, cheap wine or vodka, even numbers of flowers

√ recommended
× to be avoided

Sources: Sergei Ivanchuk, "Russia–Gift Giving," *Executive Planet*, available online at: http://www.executiveplanet.com/index.php?title=Russia:_Gift_Giving, accessed September 23, 2009; Kate Murphy, "Gifts Without Gaffes for Global Clients," *BusinessWeek*, December 6, 1999, 153.

process and the role of personal relations and personalities; and (5) insufficient allocation of time for negotiations.[35]

One area where preparation and sensitivity are called for is gift giving. Table 5.3 provides examples of what and when to give. An ideal gift is one that represents the giver's own culture while being sensitive to the recipient's. For example, a Finn may give a Suunto compass to a Saudi business partner (to help him determine the direction for daily prayers). Giving gifts that are easily available in that country (e.g., chocolates to a Swiss) is not advisable. Some gifts are not suitable; clocks or other timepieces are symbols of death in China, while handkerchiefs symbolize tears in Latin America and Korea. Gifts are an important part of relationship management during visits and a way of recognizing partners during holidays. Care should be taken with the way the gift is wrapped; for example, it should be in appropriately colored paper. Always wrap the gifts you present, but remember to avoid white and brightly colored wrapping paper in Japan. If delivered in person, the actual giving has to be executed correctly; in China, this is done by extending the gift to the recipient using both hand.[36] It should be noted, however, that many companies in the United States have policies that do not allow the giving and receiving of gifts.

Managers must be concerned with differences in the ways products are used. The questions that the international manager has to ask are, "What are we selling?" "What are the benefits we are providing?" and "Who or what are we competing against?" Care should be taken not to assume cross-border similarities even if many of the indicators converge. For example, a jam producer noted that the Brazilian market seemed to hold significant potential because per capita jelly and jam consumption was one-tenth that of Argentina, clearly a difference not justified by obvious factors. However, Argentines consume jam at tea time, a custom that does not exist in Brazil. Furthermore, Argentina's climate and soil favor growing wheat, leading it to consume three times the bread Brazil does.[37]

Approaches that would not be considered in the United States or Europe might be recommended in other regions; for example, when Conrad Hotels (the international division of Hilton Hotels) experienced low initial occupancy rates at its Hong Kong facility, they brought in a *feng shui* man. These traditional "consultants" are foretellers of future events and the unknown through occult means, and are used extensively by Hong Kong businesses.[38] In Hilton's case, the *feng shui* man suggested a piece of sculpture be moved outside the hotel's lobby because one of the characters in the statue looked like it was trying to run out of the hotel. The hotel later reported a significant increase in its occupancy rate. At Disneyland Hong Kong, the feng shui master rotated the front gate, repositioned cash registers, and ordered boulders set in key locations to ensure the park's prosperity.[39]

Meticulous research plays a major role in avoiding these types of problems. Concept tests determine the potential acceptance and proper understanding of a proposed new product. **Focus groups**, each consisting of 8 to 12 consumers representative of the proposed target audience, can be interviewed and their responses used as disaster checks and to fine-tune research findings. The most sensitive products, such as consumer packaged goods, require consumer usage and attitude studies as well as retail distribution studies and audits to analyze the movement of the product to retailers and eventually to households. **In-depth studies** are also used to study consumer needs across markets. Intel, for example, has a team of 10 ethnographers traveling the world to find out how to redesign existing products or to come up with new ones to fit different cultures and demographic groups.

The adjustment to the cultural nuances of the marketplace has to be viewed as long term and may even be accomplished through trial and error. For example, U.S. retailers have found that U.S.-style retail outlets baffle overseas consumers with their size and warehouse-like atmosphere. Office Depot reduced the size of its Tokyo store by one-third, crammed the merchandise closer together, and found that sales remained at the same level as before.[40]

MATERIAL ELEMENTS

Material culture refers to the results of technology and is directly related to how a society organizes its economic activity. It is manifested in the availability and adequacy of the basic economic, social, financial, and marketing infrastructure for the international business in a market. The basic **economic infrastructure** consists of transportation, energy, and communications systems. **Social infrastructure** refers to housing, health, and educational systems prevailing in the country of interest. **Financial** and **marketing infrastructures** provide the facilitating agencies for the international firm's operation in a given market—for example, banks and research firms. In some parts of the world, the international firm may have to be an integral partner in developing the various infrastructures before it can operate, whereas in others it may greatly benefit from their high level of sophistication.

The level of material culture can aid segmentation efforts if the degree of industrialization of the market is used as a basis. For companies selling industrial goods, such as General Electric, this can provide a convenient starting point. In developing countries, demand may be highest for basic energy-generating products. In fully developed markets, time-saving home appliances may be more in demand.

While infrastructure is often a good indicator of potential demand, goods sometimes discover unexpectedly rich markets due to the informal economy at work in developing nations. In Kenya, for example, where most of the country's 30 million population live on less than a dollar a day, more than 11,444,000 cell phones (2007) have been bought; wireless providers are scrambling to keep up with demand. Leapfrogging older technologies, mobile phones are especially attractive to Kenya's thousands of small-time entrepreneurs—market-stall owners, taxi drivers, and even hustlers who sell on the sidewalks. For most, income goes unreported, creating an invisible wealth on the streets. Mobile phones outnumber fixed lines in Kenya, as

---

focus group A research technique in which representatives of a proposed target audience contribute to market research by participating in an unstructured discussion.

in-depth studies Market research tools that gather detailed data used to study consumer needs across markets.

economic infrastructure The transportation, energy, and communication systems in a country.

social infrastructure The housing, health, educational, and other social systems in a country.

financial infrastructure Facilitating financial agencies in a country; for example, banks.

marketing infrastructure Facilitating marketing agencies in a country; for example, market research firms, channel members.

well as in Uganda, Venezuela, Cambodia, South Korea, and Chile. For companies this development is attractive as well given the expense of laying land lines. Again, however, the advent of new technologies must be culturally calibrated (as seen in Focus on Telecommunication).

Technological advances have been the major cause of cultural change in many countries. Increasingly, consumers are seeking more diverse products as a way of satisfying their demand for a higher quality of life and more leisure time. For example, Chinese consumers want more than just function. This is one reason why Nokia, which has emphasized fashion over function, has seen its cell phone sales in China rocket past those of Motorola and Ericsson. If a company wants to sell vacuums or washing machines in China, it had better pay attention to emotional needs as well as physical ones. And if it's selling microwave ovens, air conditioners, and TVs, it should be sure those products are as fashionable as they are reliable (Gallup, 2006).[41] With technological advancement comes also **cultural convergence**. Black and white television sets extensively penetrated U.S. households more than a decade before similar levels occurred in Europe and Japan. With color television, the lag was reduced to five years. With video cassette recorders, the difference was only three years, but this time the Europeans and Japanese led the way while the United States was concentrating on cable systems. With the compact disc, penetration rates were equal in only one year. Today, with MTV available around the world and the use of the Internet increasing, no lag exists.[42]

Material culture—mainly the degree to which it exists and how it is esteemed— has an impact on business decisions. Many exporters do not understand the degree to which Americans are package conscious; for example, cans must be shiny and beautiful. In foreign markets, packaging problems may arise due to the lack of materials, different specifications when the material is available, and immense differences in quality and consistency of printing ink, especially in developing markets. Ownership levels of television sets, radios, personal computers, and smart phones have an impact on the ability of media to reach target audiences.

cultural convergence Increasing similarity among cultures accelerated by technological advances.

AESTHETICS

Each culture makes a clear statement concerning good taste, as expressed in the arts and in the particular symbolism of colors, form, and music. What is and what is not acceptable may vary dramatically even in otherwise highly similar markets. Sex, for example, is a big selling point in many countries. In an apparent attempt to preserve the purity of Japanese womanhood, however, advertisers frequently turn to blond, blue-eyed foreign models to make the point. In introducing the shower soap Fa from the European market to the North American market, Henkel extended its European advertising campaign to the new market. The main creative difference was to have the young woman in the waves don a bathing suit rather than be naked as in the German original.

Color is often used as a mechanism for brand identification, feature reinforcement, and differentiation. In international markets, colors have more symbolic value than in domestic markets. Black, for instance, is considered the color of mourning in the United States and Europe, whereas white has the same symbolic meaning in Japan and most of the Far East. A British bank was interested in expanding its operations to Singapore and wanted to use blue and green as its identification colors. A consulting firm was quick to tell the client that green is associated with death in that country. Although the bank insisted on its original choice of colors, the green was changed to an acceptable shade.

International firms, such as McDonald's, have to take into consideration local tastes and concerns in designing their outlets. They may have a general policy of

Mobile Payments Across the Globe?

Mobile payment services enable consumers to pay for goods and services from their bank account using their mobile phone. These services have evolved over time from using voice or short message services (SMS) to initiate and settle a transaction to the present-day use of a phone for one-step instant purchases. The convenience for consumers is significant in that they avoid using cash or credit cards, and, with prepaid services, they have no monthly bills. Services are secure in that an alphanumeric password is required for authentication. In addition, direct payments from the customer's account means that spending power is not limited to the amount of credit available on the phone account.

M-payments have taken off in Japan and Korea but failed to reach estimated potential within the European Union and the United States. Reasons for this can be found in the lack of readiness in existing technology, unwillingness of the various stakeholders (banks, credit card issuers, handset makers, and telecommunication companies) to collaborate, as well as cultural variables in terms of existing usage patterns and perceptions of risk and relative advantage of a new technology.

The chief driver of mobile innovation in Japan is NTT DoCoMo. Its market power is so significant that it can impose new systems from the top down, as it did with the introduction of the i-mode (which allowed consumers to use their phones for everything from trading stocks and checking movie times to playing games, instant messaging, and downloading *Hello Kitty* characters). While the i-mode did not include m-payments, it laid the groundwork for that continuous innovation. M-payment capability was added by using Sony's contactless chips, which allow payment by passing the phones over a sensor. Subscriptions to this service were estimated to exceed 53 million by the end of 2008. The key to success is NTT DoCoMo's dominance in the market. Customers have transitioned easily to adding making payments with their phones. Merchants want to tap into the large and growing market, especially when they were subsidized by NTT DoCoMo in buying the needed new technology. In Korea, the three big operators (SK Telecom, KTF, and LG Telecom) have collaborated with credit card companies, which are taking care of the financing and operations.

In the European Union and the United States, payment cards are already deeply embedded in consumer behavior, and consumers may not be eager to move away from a familiar system and may not have thought of using phones as payment devices. In markets where mobile diffusion is high (such as the Nordics) or in countries where cash still accounts for a majority of retail transactions (e.g., Germany and central Europe), chances may be better. In central Europe, for example, merchants may be eager to switch to cashless systems at the expense of handling currency. At the same time, all of the stakeholders need to demonstrate to mobile phone users that m-payments are much more attractive than other familiar payment schemes. The bundle of convenience items (safe, secure, available, fast, transparent) needs to be packaged and sold to target groups.

None of the North American or European players have the market power of their Asian counterparts. Cooperation among banks, credit card issuers, handset makers, and retailers will be essential. One such attempt, SIMPAY—an alliance set up by Orange, Vodafone, T-Mobile, and Telefónica Móviles—to allow consumers to charge small purchases to their mobile phone bills, closed in 2005 after 18 months of operation. One of the main reasons was the lack of sufficient volume to cover collection costs. Payforit (2006), the new payment service supported by all licensed U.K. mobile operators, was designed to make it easy to pay for low cost services on the mobile phone.

Despite uneven global acceptance, Arthur D. Little predicts a 10-fold increase in mobile payment transactions to reach $250 billion by 2012.

Sources: "Global M-Payment Report Update–2009," *Arthur D. Little's M-payment Surging Ahead* (Boston, MA: Arthur D. Little, 2009); Roman Friedrich, Johannes Bussman, Olaf Acker, and Niklas Dietrich, "Making Mobile Payment Work for Everyone," *Strategy and Business Resilience Report*, September 22, 2005, available at www.strategy-business.com; Lucy Sherriff, "Simpay Halts Mobile Commerce Project," *The Register*, June 27, 2005, available at http://www.theregister.co.uk/2005/06/27/simpay_halts_project/; "M-payments Making Inroads," *Arthur D. Little's Global M-payment Update 2005* (Boston, MA: Arthur D. Little, 2005); see also http://www.nttdocomo.com/about/facts/index.html.

uniformity in building or office space design, but local tastes often warrant modifications. Respecting local cultural traditions may also generate goodwill toward the international marketer. For example, McDonald's painstakingly renovated a seventeenth-century building in Moscow. History may also play a role. The Shanghai World Financial Center (developed largely by the Japanese Mori Building Corporation) became the tallest structure in China in 2008 at 492 meters (1,641 feet). The most distinctive feature in the design of the building is an opening at the peak (the functional reason of which is to allow airflow). The opening originally was meant to be a circular moon gate, but the intended design met with opposition from the Chinese, who saw it resemble the rising sun design of the Japanese flag. It was replaced by a trapezoidal hole featuring an observation deck on the 100th floor.

EDUCATION

Education, either formal or informal, plays a major role in the passing on and sharing of culture. Educational levels of a culture can be assessed using literacy rates, enrollment in secondary education, or enrollment in higher education available from secondary data sources. International firms also need to know about the qualitative aspects of education, namely, varying emphases on particular skills and the overall level of the education provided. Japan and South Korea, for example, emphasize the sciences, especially engineering, to a greater degree than do Western countries.

Educational levels also affect various business functions. For example, a high level of illiteracy suggests the use of visual aids rather than printed manuals. Local recruiting for sales jobs is affected by the availability of suitably trained personnel. In some cases, international firms routinely send locally recruited personnel to headquarters for training.

The international manager may also need to overcome obstacles in recruiting a suitable sales force or support personnel. For example, the Japanese culture places a premium on loyalty, and employees consider themselves members of the corporate family. If a foreign firm decides to leave Japan, its employees may find themselves stranded in midcareer, unable to find their place in the Japanese business system. Therefore, university graduates are reluctant to join any but the largest and most well-known foreign firms.

If technology is marketed, the product's sophistication will depend on the educational level of future users. Product adaptation decisions are often influenced by the extent to which targeted customers are able to use the good or service properly.

SOCIAL INSTITUTIONS

Social institutions affect the ways people relate to each other. The family unit, which in Western industrialized countries consists of parents and children, in a number of cultures is extended to include grandparents and other relatives. This affects consumption patterns and must be taken into account, for example, when conducting market research.

The concept of kinship, or blood relations between individuals, is defined in a very broad way in societies such as those in sub-Saharan Africa. Family relations and a strong obligation to family are important factors to consider in human resource management in those regions. Understanding tribal politics in countries such as Nigeria may help the manager avoid unnecessary complications in executing business transactions.

The division of a particular population into classes is termed **social stratification**. Stratification ranges from the situation in northern Europe, where most people are members of the middle class, to highly stratified societies in which the higher strata control most of the buying power and decision-making positions.

An important part of the socialization process of consumers worldwide is **reference groups**. These groups provide the values and attitudes that influence behavior. Primary reference groups include the family and coworkers and other intimate acquaintances, and secondary groups are social organizations where less-continuous interaction takes place, such as professional associations and trade organizations. In addition to providing socialization, reference groups develop a person's concept of self, which is manifested, for example, through the choice of products used. Reference groups also provide a baseline for compliance with group norms, giving the individual the option of conforming to or avoiding certain behaviors.

Social organization also determines the roles of managers and subordinates and how they relate to one another. In some cultures, managers and subordinates are

social stratification The division of a particular population into classes.

reference groups Groups such as the family, co-workers, and professional and trade associations that provide the values and attitudes that influence and shape behavior, including consumer behavior.

separated explicitly and implicitly by various boundaries ranging from social class differences to separate office facilities. In others, cooperation is elicited through equality. For example, Nissan USA has no privileged parking spaces and no private dining rooms, everyone wears the same type of white coveralls in production areas, and the president sits in the same room with a hundred other white-collar workers. Fitting an organizational culture to the larger context of a national culture has to be executed with care. Changes that are too dramatic may disrupt productivity or, at the minimum, arouse suspicion.

Although Western business has impersonal structures for channeling power and influence—primarily through reliance on laws and contracts—the Chinese emphasize personal relationships to obtain clout. Things can get done without this human political capital, or *guanxi*, only if one invests enormous personal energy, is willing to offend even trusted associates, and is prepared to see it all melt away at a moment's notice.[43] For the Chinese, contracts form a useful agenda and a symbol of progress, but obligations come from relationships. McDonald's found this out in Beijing, where it was evicted from a central building after only 2 years despite having a 20-year contract. The incomer had a strong *guanxi*, whereas McDonald's had not kept its in good repair.[44]

SOURCES OF CULTURAL KNOWLEDGE

3. To illustrate ways in which cultural risk poses a challenge to the effective conduct of business communications and transactions

experiential knowledge
Knowledge acquired through involvement as opposed to information, which is obtained through communication, research, and education.

The concept of cultural knowledge is broad and multifaceted. Cultural knowledge can be defined by the way it is acquired. Objective or factual information is obtained from others through communication, research, and education. **Experiential knowledge**, on the other hand, can be acquired only by being involved in a culture other than one's own. A summary of the types of knowledge needed by the international manager is provided in Table 5.4. Both factual and experiential information can be general or country-specific. In fact, the more a manager becomes involved in the international arena, the more he or she is able to develop a metaknowledge; that is, ground rules that apply whether in Kuala Lumpur, Malaysia, or Asunción, Paraguay. Market-specific knowledge does not necessarily travel well; the general variables on which the information is based do.

In a survey of managers on how to acquire international expertise, they ranked eight factors in terms of their importance, as shown in Table 5.5. The managers emphasized the experiential acquisition of knowledge. Written materials played an important but supplementary role, very often providing general or country-specific

Table 5.4	Types of International Information	
	Type of Information	
Source of Information	**General**	**Country Specific**
Objective	Examples:	Examples:
	Impact of GDP	Tariff barriers
	Regional integration	Government regulations
Experiential	Example:	Examples:
	Corporate adjustment	Product acceptance
	to internationalization	Program appropriateness

Table 5.5 Manager's Ranking of Factors Involved in Acquiring International Expertise

Factor	Considered Critical	Considered Important	Not Important
1. Assignments overseas	83%	17%	0%
2. Business travel	56	38	6
3. Training programs	41	51	8
4. Nonbusiness travel	9	64	27
5. Reading	28	60	12
6. Graduate courses	22	65	13
7. Precareer activities	14	55	31
8. Undergraduate courses	6	40	55

Source: Data collected by authors from 86 executives, by questionnaire, October 2009.

information before operational decisions were made. Interestingly, many of today's international managers have precareer experience in government, the Peace Corps, the armed forces, or missionary service. Although the survey emphasized travel, a one-time trip to London with a stay at a very large hotel and scheduled sightseeing tours does not significantly contribute to cultural knowledge. Travel that involves meetings with company personnel, intermediaries, facilitating agents, customers, and government officials, on the other hand, does contribute.

However, from the corporate point of view, global capability is developed in more painstaking ways: foreign assignments, networking across borders, and the use of multicountry, multicultural teams to develop strategies and programs. At Nestlé, for example, managers move around a region (such as Asia or Latin America) at four- or five-year intervals and may serve stints at headquarters for two to three years between such assignments. Such broad experience allows managers to pick up ideas and tools to be used in markets where they have not been used or where they have not been necessary before. In Thailand, where supermarkets are revolutionizing consumer-goods marketing, techniques perfected elsewhere in the Nestlé system are being put to effective use. The experiences then, in turn, are used to develop newly emerging markets in the same region, such as Vietnam.

Managers have a variety of sources and methods to extend their knowledge of specific cultures. Most of these sources deal with factual information that provides a necessary basis for market studies. Beyond the normal business literature and its anecdotal information, country specific studies are published by the U.S. government, private companies, and universities. The U.S. Department of Commerce's (http://www.ita.doc.gov) *Country Commercial Guides* cover more than 153 countries, while the Economist Intelligence Unit's (http://www.eiu.com) *Country Reports* cover 188 countries. *Culturegrams* (http://www.culturegrams.com), which detail the customs of people of 206 countries, are published by the Center for International and Area Studies at Brigham Young University. Many facilitating agencies—such as advertising agencies, banks, consulting firms, and transportation companies—provide background information on the markets they serve for their clients. These range from AIRINC (www.air-inc.com) international reports on site selections and cost of living for 125 countries; the Hong Kong Shanghai Banking Corporation's (http://www.hsbc.com) *Business Profile Series* (Dubai, Hong Kong, Singapore, South Africa, United Kingdom); to *World Trade* (http://worldtrademag.com) magazine's "Put Your Best Foot Forward" series, which covers Europe, Asia, Mexico/Canada, and Russia.

Figure 5.2   Example of Culture Consulting

Specialists who advise clients on the cultural dimensions of business are available as well. Their task is not only to help avoid mistakes but to add culture as an ingredient of success in country- or region-specific programs. An example of such a service provider is shown in Figure 5.2. InterTrend Communications guides State Farm to clients in the Asian market with some very impressive results. Personal fulfillment is derived from contributing to their family's well-being and seeing their children succeed.[45] The tagline in Chinese echoes the importance of faithfulness and reliability as valued by the customer, "with a good neighbor, you will be reassured every day."

Blunders in foreign markets that could have been avoided with factual information are generally inexcusable. A manager who travels to Taipei without first obtaining a visa and is therefore turned back has no one else to blame. Other oversights may lead to more costly mistakes. For example, Brazilians are several inches shorter than the average American, but this was not taken into account when Sears erected American-height shelves that block Brazilian shoppers' view of the rest of the store.

International business success requires not only comprehensive fact finding and preparation but also an ability to understand and fully appreciate the nuances of different cultural traits and patterns. Gaining this **interpretive cultural knowledge** requires "getting one's feet wet" over a sufficient length of time. Over the long run, culture can become a factor in the firm's overall success.

interpretive cultural knowledge An acquired ability to understand and appreciate the nuances of foreign cultural traits and patterns.

CULTURAL ANALYSIS

To try to understand and explain differences among and across cultures, researchers have developed checklists and models showing pertinent variables and their interaction. An example of such a model is provided in Figure 5.3. This model is based on the premise that all international business activity should be viewed as innovation and as producing change.[46] After all, multinational corporations introduce management practices, as well as goods and services, from one country to others, where they are perceived to be new and different. Although many question the usefulness of such models, they do bring together all or most of the relevant variables on how consumers in different cultures may perceive, evaluate, and adopt new behaviors. However, any manager using such a tool should periodically cross-check its results against reality and experience.

The key variable of the model is propensity to change, which is a function of three constructs: (1) cultural lifestyle of individuals in terms of how deeply held their traditional beliefs and attitudes are, and also which elements of culture are dominant; (2) change agents (such as multinational corporations and their practices) and strategic-opinion leaders (for example, social elites); and (3) communication about the innovation from commercial sources, neutral sources (such as government), and social sources, such as friends and relatives.

It has been argued that differences in cultural lifestyle can be explained by four dimensions of culture.[47] The dimensions consist of: (1) individualism ("I" consciousness versus "we" consciousness); (2) power distance (levels of equality in society); (3) uncertainty avoidance (need for formal rules and regulations); and (4) masculinity (attitude toward achievement, roles of men and women). Figure 5.4 presents a summary of 12 countries' positions along these dimensions. A fifth dimension has also been added to distinguish cultural differences: long-term versus short-term

4. To suggest ways in which businesses act as change agents in the diverse cultural environments in which they operate

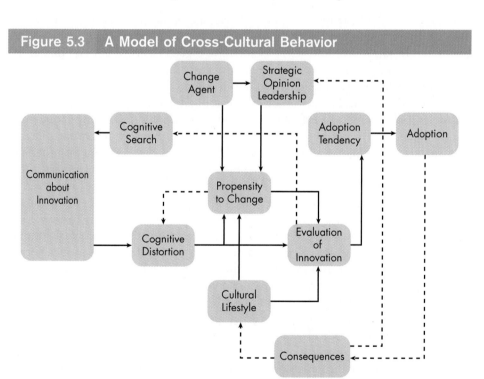

Figure 5.3   A Model of Cross-Cultural Behavior

Source: Adapted by permission of the publisher from "A Theory of Cross-Cultural Buying Behavior," by Jagdish N. Sheth and S. Prakash Sethi, in *Consumer and Industrial Buyer Behavior*, eds. Arch G. Woodside, Jagdish N. Sheth, and Petér D. Bennett, 1977, 373. Copyright 1977 by Elsevier Science Publishing Co., Inc.

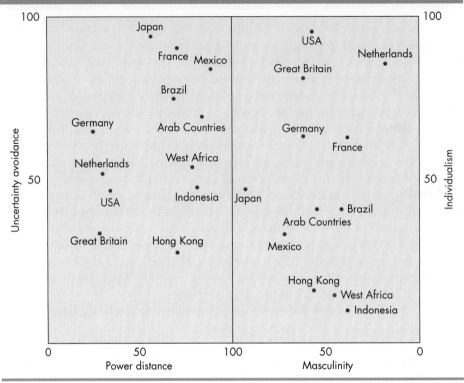

Figure 5.4   Culture Dimension Scores for 12 Countries (0 = low; 100 = high)

Source: Data for the figure derived from Geert Hofstede, "Management Scientists Are Human," *Management Science* 40, no. 1 (1994): 4–13.

orientation.[48] All of the high-scoring countries are Asian (e.g., China, Hong Kong, Taiwan, Japan, and South Korea), while most Western countries (such as the United States and Britain) have low scores. Some have argued that this cultural dimension may explain the Japanese marketing success based on market share (rather than short-term profit) motivation in market development.

Knowledge of similarities along these four dimensions allows us to cluster countries and regions and establish regional and national marketing programs.[49] An example is provided in Table 5.6, in which the global wireless communication market is segmented along cultural lines for the development of programs. Research has shown that the take-off point for new products (i.e., when initial sales turn into mass market sales) is six years on average in Europe. However, in northern Europe, new products take off almost twice as fast as they do in southern Europe. Culturally, consumers in cluster 5 are far more open to new ideas and products, and thus have remained at the forefront of technological innovation and adoption. Cluster 3, consisting of south-central Europe, Latin America, and several Asian countries, represents the youngest technology market and displays the highest level of uncertainty avoidance. It should, therefore, be targeted with risk-reducing marketing programs such as extended warranties and return privileges. It is important to position the product as a continuous innovation that does not require radical changes in consumption patterns.[50]

Understanding the implications of the dimensions helps businesspeople prepare for international business encounters. For example, in negotiating in Germany, one can expect a counterpart who is thorough, systematic, very well prepared, but also rather dogmatic and, therefore, less flexible and willing to compromise. Efficiency is emphasized. In Mexico, however, the counterpart may prefer to address problems on a

Table 5.6 Culture-Based Segmentation

	Cultural Characteristics				
	Power Distance	Uncertainty Avoidance	Individualism	Masculinity	Illustrative Marketing Implications
Cluster 1: Argentina, Italy, Belgium, Japan, Brazil, Poland, France, Spain, Germany, Turkey, Greece, United Arab Emirates	Medium	Strong	Medium	High	Early to medium technology adopters (with Japan increasingly acting as an outlier/innovator); appeal to consumer's status and power position; reduce perceived risk in product purchase and use; emphasize product functionality.
Cluster 2: Australia, Austria, United States, Ireland, Israel, Switzerland, United Kingdom	Small	Medium	High	High	Early technology adopters; preference for "high-performance" products; use "successful-achiever" theme in advertising; desire for novelty, variety, and pleasure; fairly risk-averse.
Cluster 3: Chile, Colombia, Costa Rica, El Salvador, Ecuador, Estonia, Iran, Korea, Latvia, Lithuania, Pakistan, Panama, Peru, Portugal, Romania, Slovenia, Thailand, Taiwan, Venezuela	High	Strong	Low	Medium–Low	Late technology adopters; highly risk-averse, partly due to lower discretionary income levels; emphasize product practicality, durability, and functionality.
Cluster 4: China, Hong Kong, Singapore	High	Low	Low	Medium	Medium to late technology adopters; however, rapid dissemination through imitation, once adopted; "status-symbol" themed advertising.
Cluster 5: Denmark, Finland, Netherlands, Norway, Sweden	Small	Low	High	Low	Innovators and early technology adopters; relatively weak resistance to new products; strong consumer desire for novelty and variety.

Source: Sanna Sundqvist, Lauri Frank, and Kaisu Puumalainen, "The Effects of Country Characteristics, Cultural Similarity and Adoption Timing on the Diffusion of Wireless Communications," *Journal of Business Research*, 58, no.1 (2005): 107–110.

personal and private basis rather than on a business level. This means more emphasis on socializing and conveying one's humanity, sincerity, loyalty, and friendship. Also, differences in the pace and business practices of a region have to be accepted. Boeing Airplane Company found in its annual study on world aviation safety that countries with both low individualism and substantial power distances had accident rates 2.6 times greater than those at the other end of the scale. The findings naturally have an impact on training and service operations of airlines.[51]

Communication about innovation takes place through the physical product itself (samples) or through experiencing a new company policy. If a new personnel practice, such as quality circles or flextime, is being investigated, results may be communicated in reports or through word of mouth by the participating employees. Communication content depends on the following factors: the good's or policy's relative advantage over existing alternatives; compatibility with established behavioral patterns; complexity, or the degree to which the good or process is perceived as difficult to understand and use; trialability, or the degree to which it may be experimented with without incurring major risk; and observability, which is the extent to which the consequences of the innovation are visible.

Before a good or policy is evaluated, information should be gathered about existing beliefs and circumstances. Distortion of data may occur as a result of selective attention, exposure, and retention. As examples, anything foreign may be seen in a negative light, another multinational company's efforts may have failed, or the government may discourage the proposed activity. Additional information may then be sought from any of the sources or from opinion leaders in the market.

Adoption tendency refers to the likelihood that the product or process will be accepted. Individualism has a significant positive relationship and uncertainty avoidance a negative relationship with acceptance and diffusion rates of new products.[52] Similar findings have been reached on the penetration of e-commerce in different markets.[53] If an innovation clears the hurdles, it may be adopted and slowly diffused into the entire market. An international manager has two basic choices: to adapt company offerings and methods to those in the market or to try to change market conditions to fit company programs.

In Japan, a number of Western companies have run into obstructions in the Japanese distribution system, where great value is placed on established relationships; everything is done on the basis of favoring the familiar and fearing the unfamiliar. In most cases, this problem is solved by joint ventures with a major Japanese entity that has established contacts. On occasion, when the company's approach is compatible with the central beliefs of a culture, the company may be able to change existing customs rather than adjust to them. Initially, Procter & Gamble's traditional hard-selling style in television commercials jolted most Japanese viewers accustomed to more subtle approaches. Now the ads are being imitated by Japanese competitors. However, this is not to be interpreted to mean that the Japanese will adapt to Western approaches. The emphasis in Japan is still on who speaks rather than on what is spoken. That is why, for example, Japan is a market where Procter & Gamble's company name is presented as well in the marketing communication for a brand, rather than only the product's brand name, which is customary in the United States and European markets.[54]

Although models such as the one in Figure 5.3 may aid in strategy planning by making sure that all variables and their interlinkages are considered, any analysis is incomplete without the basic recognition of cultural differences. Adjusting to differences requires putting one's own cultural values aside. James A. Lee proposes that the natural **self-reference criterion**—the unconscious reference to one's own cultural values—is the root of most international business

self-reference criterion The unconscious reference to one's own cultural values.

problems.[55] However, recognizing and admitting this is often quite difficult. The following analytical approach is recommended to reduce the influence of cultural bias:

1. Define the problem or goal in terms of the domestic cultural traits, habits, or norms.
2. Define the problem or goal in terms of the foreign cultural traits, habits, or norms. Make no value judgments.
3. Isolate the self-reference criterion influence in the problem, and examine it carefully to see how it complicates the problem.
4. Redefine the problem without the self-reference criterion influence, and solve for the optimum-goal situation.

This approach can be applied to product introduction. If Kellogg Co. wants to introduce breakfast cereals into markets where breakfast is traditionally not eaten or where consumers drink very little milk, managers must consider very carefully how to instill the new habit. The traits, habits, and norms concerning the importance of breakfast are quite different in the United States, France, and Brazil, and they have to be outlined before the product can be introduced. In France, Kellogg's commercials are aimed as much at providing nutrition lessons as they are at promoting the product. In Brazil, the company advertised on a soap opera to gain entry into the market because Brazilians often emulate the characters of these television shows.

Analytical procedures require constant monitoring of changes caused by outside events as well as the changes caused by the business entity itself. Controlling **ethnocentrism**—the tendency to consider one's own culture superior to those of others—can be achieved only by acknowledging it and properly adjusting to its possible effects in managerial decision making. The international manager needs to be prepared and able to put that preparedness to effective use.

ethnocentrism The regarding of one's own culture as superior to those of others.

THE TRAINING CHALLENGE

International managers face a dilemma in terms of international and intercultural competence. The lack of adequate foreign language and international business skills have cost U.S. firms lost contracts, weak negotiations, and ineffectual management. A UNESCO study of 10- to 14-year-old students in nine countries placed Americans next to last in their comprehension of foreign cultures. The terrorist attacks of September 11, 2001, for instance, alerted the U.S. government not only to the national lack of competence in foreign language skills, but to the nation's failure to educate its population to cultural sensibilities at home and around the world.[56]

The increase in the overall international activity of firms has increased the need for cultural sensitivity training at all levels of the organization. Further, today's training must encompass not only outsiders to the firm but interaction within the corporate family as well. However inconsequential the degree of interaction may seem, it can still cause problems if proper understanding is lacking. Consider, for example, the date 11/12/10 on a message; a European will interpret this as the 11th of December, an American as the 12th of November.

Some companies try to avoid the training problem by hiring only nationals or well-traveled Americans for their international operations. This makes sense for the management of overseas operations but will not solve the training need, especially if transfers to a culture unfamiliar to the manager are likely. International experience may not necessarily transfer from one market to another.

5. To evaluate the ways in which training programs assist international managers to develop the international business skills of their employees

To foster cultural sensitivity and acceptance of new ways of doing things within the organization, management must institute internal education programs. The programs may include: (1) culture-specific information (data covering other countries, such as videopacks and culturegrams); (2) general cultural information (values, practices, and assumptions of countries other than one's own); and (3) self-specific information (identifying one's own cultural paradigm, including values, assumptions, and perceptions about others).[57] One study found that Japanese assigned to the United States get mainly language training as preparation for the task. In addition, many companies use mentoring, whereby an individual is assigned to someone who is experienced and who will spend time squiring and explaining. Talks given by returnees and by visiting lecturers hired specifically for the task round out the formal part of training. At Samsung, several special interest groups were formed to focus on issues such as Japanese society and business practices, the Chinese economy, changes in Europe, and the U.S. economy. In addition, groups also explore cutting-edge business issues, such as new technology and marketing strategies. And for the past few years, Samsung has been sending the brightest junior employees abroad for a year.

The objective of formal training programs is to foster the four critical characteristics of preparedness, sensitivity, patience, and flexibility in managers and other personnel. The programs vary dramatically in terms of their rigor, involvement, and, of course, cost.[58] A summary of the programs is provided in Figure 5.5.

area studies Training programs that provide factual preparation prior to an overseas assignment.

Environmental briefings and cultural-orientation programs are types of **area studies** programs. The programs provide factual preparation for a manager to operate in, or work with people from, a particular country. Area studies should be a basic prerequisite for other types of training programs. Alone, area studies serve little practical purpose because they do not really get the manager's feet wet. Other, more involved, programs contribute context in which to put facts so that they can be properly understood.

Figure 5.5   Cross-Cultural Training Methods

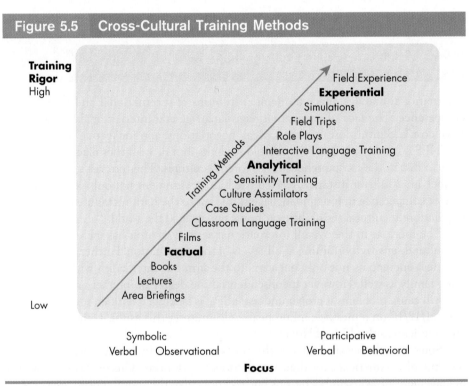

Source: J. Stewart Black and Mark Mendenhall, "A Practical but Theory-Based Framework for Selecting Cross-Cultural Training Methods," in *International Human Resource Management,* eds. Mark Mendenhall and Gary Oddou (Boston: PWS-Kent, 1991), 188.

The **cultural assimilator** is a program in which trainees must respond to scenarios of specific situations in a particular country. The programs have been developed for the Arab countries, Iran, Thailand, Central America, and Greece. The results of the trainees' assimilator experience are evaluated by a panel of judges. This type of program has been used most frequently in cases of transfers abroad on short notice.

When more time is available, managers can be trained extensively in language. This may be required if an exotic language is involved. **Sensitivity training** focuses on enhancing a manager's flexibility in situations that are quite different from those at home. The approach is based on the assumption that understanding and accepting oneself is critical to understanding a person from another culture. While most of the methods discussed are best delivered in face-to-face settings, web-based training is becoming more popular as seen in Focus on e-Business.

Finally, training may involve **field experience**, which exposes a manager to a different cultural environment for a limited amount of time. Although the expense of placing and maintaining an expatriate is high (and, therefore, the cost of failure is high), field experience is rarely used in training. One field experience technique that has been suggested when the training process needs to be rigorous is the host-family surrogate. This technique places a trainee (and possibly his or her family) in a domestically located family of the nationality to which they are assigned.[59]

Regardless of the degree of training, preparation, and positive personal characteristics, a manager will always remain foreign. A manager should never rely on his or her own judgment when local managers can be consulted. In many instances, a manager should have an interpreter present at negotiations, especially if the manager is not completely bilingual. Overconfidence in one's language capabilities can create problems.

cultural assimilator A program in which trainees for overseas assignments must respond to scenarios of specific situations in a particular country.

sensitivity training Training in human relations that focuses on personal and interpersonal interactions; training that focuses on enhancing an expatriate's flexibility in situations quite different from those at home.

field experience Experience acquired in actual rather than laboratory settings; training that exposes a corporate manager to a different cultural environment for a limited amount of time.

MAKING CULTURE WORK FOR BUSINESS SUCCESS

Culture should not be viewed as a challenge, but rather as an opportunity that can be exploited.[60] This requires, as has been shown in this chapter, an understanding of cultural differences and their fundamental determinants. Differences can quite easily be dismissed as indicators of inferiority or viewed as approaches to be changed; however, the opposite may actually be the case. Best practice knows no one particular origin, nor should it acknowledge boundaries. The following rules serve as a summary of how culture and its appreciation may serve as a tool to ensure success.

6. Analyzes the strategies corporations can take to work with cultural differences in order to expand their businesses internationally

Embrace local culture. Many corporate credos include a promise to be the best possible corporate citizens in every community operated in.[61] For the past 10 years, the Walt Disney Company has made it a priority to build its international business in television, movies, retail, and theme parks with the goal of half of their profits to come from overseas by 2010 (in 2006, the percentage was 25). Disney's theme park in Hong Kong, which opened in 2005, suffered a 30 percent drop in attendance in its second year, largely due to not appealing to mainland Chinese audiences. The first big opportunity to reverse the trend was a stroke of astrological fortune: the year 2008 was the Year of the Rat, allowing Disney to proclaim it the "Year of the Mouse." The Disneyland Chinese New Year campaign featured a logo with the Chinese character for luck flipped upside down (a New Year tradition), with mouse ears added on top. Inside the park, dumplings and turnip cakes were featured on the menus. The parade down Main Street USA was joined by the "Rhythm of Life Procession," featuring a dragon dance and puppets of birds, flowers and fish, set to traditional Chinese music.

Cultural Awareness Online

Managers heading abroad to negotiate a deal, relocating to a foreign environment, or multicultural teams working within large organizations are just some of the scenarios that benefit from cross-cultural training. Skimping on training in this area can be potentially hazardous. For example, those going to Japan unprepared for high levels of etiquette and ceremony risk offending valuable clients. Employees who move to Hong Kong are often responsible for working with multiple countries and, therefore, require the know-how to work in a variety of cultural settings.

However, it is nearly impossible to cover such complex cross-cultural training in one- or two-day training periods. Furthermore, such training costs in excess of $1,000 per person per day. Therefore, many organizations are adding online training following the face-to-face classroom training in order to gain continuous and additional training. Many of the programs use the following elements:

- *Detailed scenarios.* Training materials feature realistic business situations and events tied to elements in the learner's background. More than a briefing, sessions become a guided, narrated experience full of custom-created learning opportunities.

- *Gradual delivery.* The ability to control the flow of information to the participant supports the learning process. Not only is training flexible enough to fit into a busy schedule, but effectively mimics the real-life flow of data that informs decision making.

- *Support.* Participants have instant access to detailed materials at any time of day and from any location. They can check their perceptions against training materials or complete tailor-made exercises, reinforcing learning. They can also seek feedback on key issues.

- *Online discussions.* Sessions can be simulcast to hundreds of participants around the world. Participants benefit from the pooled learning experience, which mimics real-life decision making.

Argonaut, a cultural learning system that aims to enable international teams to work efficiently together, was conceptualized by Coghill and Beery International, U.K. A user can take the entire course—choosing the relevant culture from the base of 54 cultures—and finish it in about 15 hours. Naturally nobody would do it over that period; normally it would take about a month with breaks.

You click on the country you are interested in learning about, and you are provided with facts. Then, it gives you a questionnaire that aims to find out your impressions of that country, and it provides you with parameters to compare yourself with. From this point on, the lesson includes a simulated negotiation where you choose your partner, an issue is assigned and you start dealing with it. The software then prompts you on whether you are on the right track with a "trust meter," which measures whether you are breaking or building trust.

Argonaut software has isolated five different factors, such as the "power distance" factor, upon which the exercises are based. Expanding on this, power distance refers to the relative standing of an employee with his or her boss in different cultures. In Sweden, for example, power distance is about 30 compared to India's 95. (In India, strict obedience is found at the upper levels.) This would imply that a Swedish employee coming to India for the first time might be considered rude toward his or her employer, whereas the reverse situation might find the Swedish employer put in a distinctly uncomfortable position if he or she finds the new Indian employee giving a lot more respect than is normal.

In addition, the software also allows the user to perform a corporate culture audit or interdepartmental audit—it has feedback options, tutorials, articles, and discussions. As a result, it aims at enhancing relations overall, and not just cross-cultural efficiency.

Sources: Ross Bentley, "It Pays to Be a Cross-Culture Vulture," *Personnel Today*, January 23, 2007, p.8; Abhinav Ramnarayan, "Connect with Culture," *Business Line*, October 16, 2006, p.8; Jessica Caplan, "Innovations in Intercultural Training," *China Staff*, November 2004, pp.1, 4; www.coghillbeery.com/home.htm.

Build relationships. Each country-market has its own unique set of constituents who need to be identified and nurtured. Establishing and nurturing local ties at the various stages of the market-development cycle develops relationships that can be invaluable in expansion and countering political risk. The Hong Kong government has faced heavy public criticism for investing about HK$13.35 billion in land, equity, and debt for the construction of the Disney park, while Disney only committed HK$3.5 billion. Hong Kong Disneyland, the smallest of Disney parks, has been criticized for having too few rides and attractions. Disney has said that the expansion will focus on "universally understood" stories, adding that many of the new attractions will be unique to the Hong Kong park. One new themed area, Grizzly Trail, is set in an American frontier gold-mining town and features a roller coaster patterned after a runaway mine train. Another, Mystic Point, emphasizes supernatural and mysterious forces. The third, Toy Story Land, is based on the film series by Pixar animation studio.

Employ locals in order to gain cultural knowledge. Disney undertook major efforts to give its Hong Kong park a more Chinese character. Research was conducted in the homes of Chinese consumers, who were asked about their knowledge of the Disney brand and their lifestyles. As a result, for example, Disneyland ads now feature only one child (Chinese government rules limit most couples to just one child), two parents, and two grandparents (many households are extended ones) sharing branded Disney activities, such as watching a movie or giving a plush version of the mouse as a gift.

Help employees understand you. Employing locals will give a marketer a valuable asset in market development (i.e., acculturation). However, these employees also need their own process of adjustment (i.e., "corporatization") in order to be effective. Disney has given more power to local managers to develop completely local approaches, to adapt U.S. franchises and make local versions of them, or to build interest in U.S. shows such as *Hannah Montana* and *Kim Possible*. It is also important to help employees understand the firm better. Chinese executives and staff benefit from visits to Burbank, California, and interaction with Disney executives from around the world to combine Disney and Chinese values.

Adapting products and processes to local markets. Nowhere is commitment to local markets as evident as in product offerings. The gods of wealth, longevity, and happiness have been added to the Hong Kong Disneyland gang. To support the marketing efforts of the theme park, Disney has expanded its TV, online, and film businesses in China. The *Secret of the Magic Gourd* was the first-ever movie made just for Chinese audiences. The movie also meant a departure from Disney's obsession with going it alone in that it joined local experts (including the state-run China Film Group) to produce the culturally customized product.

Coordinate by region. The same processes are being replicated in the other emerging markets targeted by Disney. Local versions of *High School Musical* for India, Latin America, and Russia are part of Disney's $100 million investment in movies outside of the United States by 2010. *High School Musical's* cast for the Indian version was chosen in an *American Idol*–style competition. To create interest, Disney aired a dubbed version of the American movie and launched "My School Rocks," a dance competition featuring *High School Musical* songs. A CD of the movie soundtrack with Hindi lyrics and Indian instruments has been successful due to the low cost at retail. The goal of this cross-pollination is to come up with regional programs and "Asianize" or even globalize a product more quickly. Joint endeavors build cross-border esprit de corps, especially when managers may have their own markets' interests primarily at heart.[62]

SUMMARY

Culture is one of the most challenging elements of the international marketplace. This system of learned behavior patterns characteristic of the members of a given society is constantly shaped by a set of dynamic variables: language, religion, values and attitudes, manners and customs, aesthetics, technology, education, and social institutions. To cope with this system, an international manager needs both factual and interpretive knowledge of culture. To some extent, the factual knowledge can be learned; its interpretation comes only through experience.

The most complicated problems in dealing with the cultural environment stem from the fact that to truly become part of a culture, one has to live in it. Two schools of thought exist in the business world on how to deal with cultural diversity. One is that business is business the world around, following the model of Pepsi and McDonald's. In some cases, globalization is a fact of life; however, cultural differences are still far from converging.

The other school proposes that companies must tailor business approaches to individual cultures. Setting up policies and procedures in each country has been compared to an organ transplant; the critical question centers around acceptance or rejection. The major challenge to the international manager is to make sure that rejection is not a result of cultural myopia or even blindness.

The internationally successful companies all share an important quality: patience. They have not rushed into situations but rather built their operations carefully by following the most basic business principles. These principles are to know your adversary, know your audience, and know your customer.

KEY TERMS

cultural risk   140
acculturation   141
high-context cultures   141
low-context cultures   141
change agent   141
cultural imperialism   142
cultural universals   144
backtranslation   147
Christianity   148
Islam   149

Hinduism   149
Buddhism   151
Confucianism   151
focus group   154
in-depth studies   154
economic infrastructure   154
social infrastructure   154
financial infrastructure   154
marketing infrastructure   154
cultural convergence   155

social stratification   157
reference groups   157
experiential knowledge   158
interpretive cultural knowledge   160
self-reference criterion   164
ethnocentrism   165
area studies   166
cultural assimilator   167
sensitivity training   167
field experience   167

QUESTIONS FOR DISCUSSION

1. Comment on the assumption, "If people are serious about doing business with you, they will speak English."

2. You are on your first business visit to Germany. You feel confident about your ability to speak the language (you studied German in school and have taken a refresher course), and you decide to use it. During introductions, you want to break the ice by asking "Wie geht's?" and insisting that everyone call you by your first name. Speculate as to the reaction.

3. Q: "What do you call a person who can speak two languages?"
A: "Bilingual."
Q: "How about three?"

A: "Trilingual."
Q: "Excellent. How about one?"
A: "Hmmmm. . . . American!"
Is this joke malicious, or is there something to be learned from it?

4. What can be learned about a culture from reading and attending to factual materials?

5. Provide examples of how the self-reference criterion might manifest itself.

6. Is any international business entity not a cultural imperialist? How else could one explain the phenomenon of multinational corporations?

INTERNET EXERCISES

1. Many companies, such as Cultural Savvy, provide cross-cultural consulting and coaching, as well as training. Using the company's web site (www.culturalsavvy .com), assess the different ways such consultants can play an important role in mastering cultural competency.

2. In 2009, Burger King pulled an advertising campaign in the United Kingdom and Spain promoting its "Texican Whopper" because of complaints from the Mexican government of cultural insensitivity. The advertising featured an American cowboy and a "little spicy Mexican," a smaller character dressed as a Mexican wrestler wearing a cape similar to the Mexican flag. After viewing the commercial on YouTube.com, using keyword *burger king texican whopper ad*, identify why this commercial could be considered offensive. Do you agree with the decision to discontinue the advertising?

TAKE A STAND

In a vote cast as the battle between global conformity and cultural diversity waged, delegates to a UN agency turned aside strong U.S. objections and overwhelmingly approved the first international treaty designed to protect movies, music, and other cultural treasures from foreign competition. The 148-to-2 vote at the UN Educational, Scientific, and Cultural Organization emerged as a referendum on the world's love–hate relationship with Hollywood, Big Macs, and Coca-Cola. It was ratified and entered into force on March 18, 2007.

"The American delegate doesn't like to hear the word 'protection,'" Joseph Yai Olabiyi Babalola, clad in the ornate gold robes of his tiny country, Benin, told UNESCO delegates. "Not all countries are equal—some need to be protected." U.S. officials say the measure could be used to unfairly obstruct the flow of ideas, goods and services across borders. Films and music are among the United State's largest exports—the foreign box-office take for American movies was $19.3 billion in 2009. Assuring access to overseas markets for these products has been a prime U.S. goal at the World Trade Organization.

The measure passed at a time of growing fear in many countries that the world's increasing economic interdependence, known as *globalization*, is bringing a surge of foreign products across their borders that could wipe out local cultural heritage. France, for instance, has long kept measures in place to protect its film industry against imports, notably Hollywood productions. Called the Convention on the Protection and Promotion of Diversity of Cultural Expressions, the document approved recently declares the rights of countries to "maintain, adopt and implement policies and measures that they deem appropriate for the protection and promotion of the diversity of cultural expressions on their territory." Cultural expressions are defined as including music, art, language and ideas as well as "cultural activities, goods and services." Advocates say it could help small nations promote and distribute their cultural products on the world market.

What its practical effect would be remains unclear. But proponents and dissenting U.S. officials agree that it would at least allow countries to require that imported movies have subtitles or dubbing in native languages. Supporters including some of America's closest allies, such as Canada and Britain, called the document "clear, carefully balanced and consistent with the principles of international law and fundamental human rights." In the vote, only Israel sided with the United States.

The showdown came two years after the United States rejoined UNESCO following a two-decade boycott that began over objections to the organization's media policy. Many American officials said UNESCO was inherently anti-American. "Everyone would love to make this into some big U.S.-against-the-world routine. It's the standing for principles, the U.S. standing for freedom, the U.S. saying things that should be said." U.S. officials have not suggested that the United States might withdraw from UNESCO again over this issue.

For Discussion

1. Will growing fear wipe out local cultural heritage?

2. What constructive steps can governments take to protect their own cultural heritage?

Source: International Federation of Arts Councils and Culture Agencies, "The Campaign for Cultural Diversity: Why it Matters to You," April 2009, Canada, available at: http://www.ifccd.com/sites/ifccd.com/files/documents/Brochure_IFCCD_en.pdf accessed September 15, 2009; Motion Picture Association of America, "The Economic Impact of the Motion Picture & Television Industry of the United States," April 2009; Molly Moore, "U.N. Body Endorses Cultural Protection: U.S. Objections Are Turned Aside," *Washington Post*, October 21, 2005; A14. see also www.cptech.org/unesco/.

CHAPTER 6

Politics and Law

CHAPTER CONTENTS & LEARNING OBJECTIVES

THE HOME-COUNTRY PERSPECTIVE

1. To understand the importance of the political and legal environments in both the home and host countries to the international business executive

HOST-COUNTRY POLITICAL AND LEGAL ENVIRONMENT

2. To learn how governments affect business through legislation and regulations

INTERNATIONAL RELATIONS AND LAWS

3. To see how the political actions of countries expose firms to international risks

4. To examine the differing laws regulating international trade found in different countries

5. To understand how international political relations, agreements, and treaties can affect international business

International Trade and Elephants

This headline tends to make readers think of ivory and trade in elephant tusks. International trade in such products has ground to a halt. In order to protect elephants from poachers, governments around the world support restrictive measures in ivory trade.

But elephants have been an important part of international trade for millennia. Mostly, however, the trade did not focus on elephant parts, but on the entire beast itself. In many instances, elephants defined the strength of nations. In the frequent international conflicts of ancient times, elephants were the "tanks" of war. Those generals who had larger and more elephants typically won the battles. Even disciplined Roman legionnaires took to flight when confronted with the giants pachyderms from Africa. For hundreds of years, Roman mothers tried to threaten their children into obedience by calling out that "Hannibal ante portas esse." This was a reference to Roman archenemy Hannibal, from the key trading opposition city of Carthage, who had introduced elephants into warfare against the Romans, and had virtually arrived at the front doors of Rome. He and his elephant tanks had devastated multiple legions during the second Punic War (BC 218–201) and might have taken Rome itself, had he not been ordered back home by the leaders of Carthage.

Even earlier, the Egyptians were very active in elephant international trade. Their key trade priority was to acquire elephants from Ethiopia, which they transported using specially constructed boats, called *elefantegos*. After completing their training in Egypt these elephants were then used quite successfully to attack the Greek Empire in Persia.

Even though elephants no longer feature in most military conflicts today, the issue of the impact of trade in new and strong weapons continues to be with us. Millennia after Hannibal, international discussions and negotiations are ongoing, trying to assess whether nations with advanced military technology should be using the new weapons and even selling weapons systems to the world. Such sales can dramatically affect not only the trade and capital accounts of nations, but also their politics and the freedom of their citizens.

Sources: William J. Bernstein, *A Splendid Exchange: How Trade Shaped the World* (New York: Grove Press, 2008); Titus Livius (Livy), *The History of Rome* (Indianapolis, IN: Hackett Publishing, 2006); J. B. Bury, S. A. Cook, and F. E. Adcock, *The Cambridge Ancient History*, Vol. 7, (New York: Cambridge University Press, 2003).

Politics and laws play a critical role in international business. Even the best plans can go awry as a result of unexpected political or legal influences, and the failure to anticipate these factors can be the undoing of an otherwise successful business venture.

Of course, a single international political and legal environment does not exist. The business executive has to be aware of political and legal factors on a variety of levels. For example, while it is useful to understand the complexities of the host country's legal system, such knowledge may not protect against sanctions imposed by the home country. The firm, therefore, has to be aware of conflicting expectations and demands in the international arena.

This chapter will examine politics and laws from the manager's point of view. The two subjects are considered together because laws generally are the result of political decisions. The chapter discussion will break down the study of the international political and legal environment into three segments: the politics and laws of the home country; those of the host country; and the bilateral and multilateral agreements, treaties, and laws governing the relations among host and home countries.

THE HOME-COUNTRY PERSPECTIVE

1. To understand the importance of the political and legal environments in both the home and host countries to the international business executive

international competitiveness The ability of a firm, an industry, or a country to compete in the international marketplace at a stable or rising standard of living.

No manager can afford to ignore the rules and regulations of the country from which he or she conducts international business transactions. Many of the laws and regulations may not specifically address international business issues, yet they can have a major impact on a firm's opportunities abroad. Minimum-wage legislation, for example, has a bearing on the **international competitiveness** of a firm using production processes that are highly labor intensive. The cost of domestic safety regulations may significantly affect the pricing policies of firms. For example, U.S. legislation creating the Environmental Superfund requires payment by chemical firms based on their production volume, regardless of whether the production is sold domestically or exported. As a result, these firms are at a disadvantage internationally when exporting their commodity-type products. They are required to compete against firms that have a cost advantage because their home countries do not require payment into an environmental fund.

Other legal and regulatory measures, however, are clearly aimed at international business. Some may be designed to help firms in their international efforts. For example, governments may attempt to aid and protect the business efforts of domestic companies facing competition from abroad by setting standards for product content and quality.

The political environment in most countries tends to provide general support for the international business efforts of firms headquartered within the country. For example, a government may work to reduce trade barriers or to increase trade opportunities through bilateral and multilateral negotiations. Such actions will affect individual firms to the extent that they improve the international climate for free trade.

extraterritoriality An exemption from rules and regulations of one country that may challenge the national sovereignty of another. The application of one country's rules and regulations abroad.

Often governments also have specific rules and regulations that restrict international business. Such regulations are frequently political in nature and are based on governmental objectives that override commercial concerns. The restrictions are particularly sensitive when they address activities outside the country. Such measures challenge the territorial sovereignty of other governments and raise the issue of **extraterritoriality**—meaning a nation's attempt to set policy outside its territorial limits. Yet actions implying such extraterritorial reach are common, because nations often argue that their citizens and products maintain their nationality wherever they may be, and they therefore continue to be subject to the rules and laws of their home country.

Three main areas of governmental activity are of major concern to the international business manager. They are embargoes or trade sanctions, export controls, and the regulation of international business behavior.

EMBARGOES AND SANCTIONS

The terms **sanction** and **embargo** as used here refer to governmental actions that distort free flows of trade in goods, services, or ideas for decidedly adversarial and political, rather than economic, purposes. Sanctions tend to consist of specific coercive trade measures such as the cancellation of trade financing or the prohibition of high-technology trade, while embargoes are usually much broader in that they prohibit trade entirely. For example, the United States imposed sanctions against some countries by prohibiting the export of weapons to them, but it initiated an embargo against Cuba when all but humanitarian trade was banned. To understand sanctions and embargoes better, it is useful to examine the auspices and legal justifications under which they are imposed.

Trade embargoes have been used quite frequently and successfully in times of war or to address specific grievances. For example, in 1284, the Hansa, an association of north German merchants, believed that its members were suffering from several injustices by Norway. On learning that one of its ships had been attacked and pillaged by the Norwegians, the Hansa called an assembly of its members and resolved an economic blockade of Norway. The export of grain, flour, vegetables, and beer was prohibited on pain of fines and confiscation of the goods. The blockade was a complete success. Deprived of grain from Germany, the Norwegians were unable to obtain it from England or elsewhere. As a contemporary chronicler reports: "Then there broke out a famine so great that they were forced to make atonement." Norway was forced to pay indemnities for the financial losses that had been caused and to grant the Hansa extensive trade privileges.[1]

Over time, economic sanctions and embargoes have become a principal tool of the foreign policy for many countries. Often, they are imposed unilaterally in the hope of changing a country's government or at least changing its policies. Reasons for the impositions have varied, ranging from the upholding of human rights to attempts to promote nuclear nonproliferation or antiterrorism.

After World War I, the League of Nations set a precedent for the legal justification of economic sanctions by subscribing to a covenant that contained penalties or sanctions for breaching its provisions. The members of the League of Nations did not intend to use military or economic measures separately, but the success of the blockades of World War I fostered the

sanction A governmental action, usually consisting of a specific coercive trade measure, that distorts the free flow of trade for an adversarial or political purpose rather than an economic one.

embargo A governmental action, usually prohibiting trade entirely, for a decidedly adversarial or political rather than economic purpose.

The U.S. trade embargo against Cuba, imposed in 1962, deprives Americans of cigars and Cubans of export income.

opinion that "the economic weapon, conceived not as an instrument of war but as a means of peaceful pressure, is the greatest discovery and most precious possession of the League."[2] The basic idea was that economic sanctions could force countries to behave peacefully in the international community.

The idea of multilateral use of economic sanctions was again incorporated into international law under the charter of the United Nations, but greater emphasis was placed on the enforcement process. Sanctions decided on are mandatory, even though each permanent member of the Security Council can veto efforts to impose them. The charter also allows for sanctions as enforcement actions by regional agencies, such as the Organization of American States, the Arab League, and the Organization of African Unity, but only with the Security Council's authorization.

The apparent strength of the United Nations' enforcement system was soon revealed to be flawed. Stalemates in the Security Council and vetoes by permanent members often led to a shift of discussions in the General Assembly, where sanctions are not enforceable. Also, concepts such as "peace" and "breach of peace" were seldom perceived in the same context by all members, and thus no systematic sanctioning policy developed under the United Nations.[3]

Another problem with sanctions is that frequently their unilateral imposition has not produced the desired result. Sanctions may make the obtaining of goods more difficult or expensive for the sanctioned country, yet their purported objective is almost never achieved. In order to work, sanctions need to be imposed multilaterally and affect goods that are vital to the sanctioned country—goals that are clear, yet difficult to implement.

Close multinational collaboration can strengthen the sanctioning mechanism of the United Nations greatly. Economic sanctions can extend political control over foreign companies operating abroad, with or without the support of their local governments.[4] When one considers that sanctions may well be the middle ground between going to war or doing nothing, their effective functioning can represent a powerful arrow in the quiver of international policy measures.

Sanctions usually mean significant loss of business to firms. Many claim that the economic sanctions held in place by the United States annually cost the country and its firms billions of dollars in lost exports. Due to these costs, the issue of compensating the domestic firms and industries affected by these sanctions needs to be considered. Yet, trying to impose sanctions slowly or making them less expensive to ease the burden on these firms undercuts their ultimate chance for success. The international business manager is often caught in this political web and loses business as a result. Frequently, firms try to anticipate sanctions based on their evaluations of the international political climate. Nevertheless, even when substantial precautions are taken, firms may still suffer substantial losses due to contract cancellations. However, the reputation of a supplier unable to fill a contractual obligation will be damaged much more seriously than that of an exporter who anticipates sanctions and realizes it cannot offer a transaction in the first place.[5]

export-control system A system designed to deny or at least delay the acquisition of strategically important goods to adversaries; in the United States, based on the Export Administration Act and the Munitions Control Act.

EXPORT CONTROLS

Many nations have **export-control systems**, which are designed to deny or at least delay the acquisition of strategically important goods by adversaries. The legal basis for export controls varies in nations. For example, in Germany, armament exports are covered in the so-called War Weapons list which is a part of the War Weapons Control Law. The exports of other goods are covered by the German Export List.

Dual-use items, which are goods useful for both military and civilian purposes, are then controlled by the Joint List of the European Union.[6]

The United States, for example, regards trade as a privilege of the firm, granted by government, rather than a right or a necessity. U.S. legislation to control exports focuses on **national security** controls—that is, the control of weapons exports or high-technology exports that might adversely affect the safety of the nation. In addition, exports can be controlled for reasons of foreign policy and short supply. These controls restrict the international business opportunities of firms if a government believes that such a restriction would send a necessary foreign policy message to another country. Such action may be undertaken regardless of whether the message will have any impact or whether similar products can easily be supplied by companies in other nations.

In the United States, the export control system is based on the Export Administration Act and the Munitions Control Act. These laws control all export of goods, services, and ideas from the United States. The determinants for controls are national security, foreign policy, short supply, and nuclear nonproliferation.

Export licenses are issued by the Department of Commerce, which administers the Export Administration Act.[7] In consultation with other government agencies—particularly the Departments of State, Defense, and Energy—the Commerce Department has drawn up a list of commodities whose export is considered particularly sensitive. In addition, a list of countries differentiates nations according to their political relationship with the United States. Finally, a list of individual firms that are considered to be unreliable trading partners because of past trade-diversion activities exists for each country.

After an export license application has been filed, specialists in the Department of Commerce match the commodity to be exported with the **critical commodities list**, a file containing information about products that are either particularly sensitive to national security or controlled for other purposes. The product is then matched with the country of destination and the recipient company. If no concerns regarding any of the three exist, an export license is issued. Control determinants and the steps in the decision process are summarized in Figure 6.1.

This process may sound overly cumbersome, but it does not apply in equal measure to all exports. Most international business activities can be carried out under NLR conditions, which stands for "no license required." NLR provides blanket permission to export to most trading partners, provided that neither the end-user nor the end-use is considered sensitive. It therefore pays to check out the denied persons list published by the U.S. government (http://www.bis.doc.gov) to ensure that one's

dual-use items Goods and services that are useful for both military and civilian purposes.

national security The ability of a nation to protect its internal values from external threats.

export license A license provided by the government which permits the export of sensitive goods or services.

critical commodities list Governmental information about products that are either particularly sensitive to national security or controlled for other purposes.

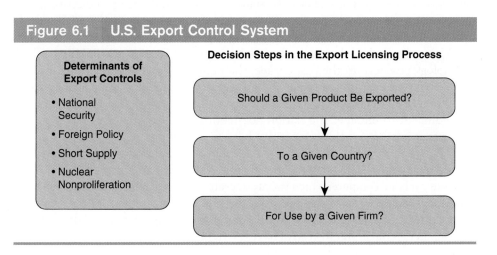

Figure 6.1　U.S. Export Control System

Determinants of Export Controls

- National Security
- Foreign Policy
- Short Supply
- Nuclear Nonproliferation

Decision Steps in the Export Licensing Process

Should a Given Product Be Exported?

↓

To a Given Country?

↓

For Use by a Given Firm?

trading partner is not a sanctioned trading party. However, the process becomes more complicated and cumbersome when products incorporating high-level technologies and countries not friendly to the United States are involved. The exporter must then apply for an export license, which consists of written authorization to send a product abroad. However, even in most of these cases, license applications can be submitted via the Internet and licensing forms can be downloaded from it. In 2007, the U.S. Department of Commerce created the Validated End-User (VEU) program for the People's Republic of China and India, which allows trusted trading partners in the U.S. and those countries a quicker way to get approvals for exports.[8]

The international business repercussions of export controls are important. It is one thing to design an export control system that is effective and that restricts those international business activities subject to important national concerns. It is, however, quite another when controls lose their effectiveness and when one country's firms are placed at a competitive disadvantage with firms in other countries whose control systems are less extensive or even nonexistent.

A NEW ENVIRONMENT FOR EXPORT CONTROLS

Terrorist attacks have again highlighted the importance of export controls. Restricting the flow of materials can be crucial in avoiding the development of weapons of mass destruction; restricting technology can limit the ability to target missiles; restricting the flow of funds can inhibit the subsidization of terrorist training.

Nowadays, the principal focus of export controls must rest on the Third World. Aggressive regimes in a number of countries want chemical and nuclear weapons and the technology to make use of them. For example, a country like North Korea, which has conducted nuclear tests, has also tested firing short- and long-range missile delivery systems in defiance of the sanctions imposed by the UN Security Council.[9] As a result, export controls have moved from a "strategic balance" to a "tactical balance" approach. Nevertheless, even though the political hot spots addressed may be less broad in terms of their geographic expanse, the peril emanating from regional disintegration and local conflict may be just as dangerous to the world community as earlier strategic concerns with the Soviet Union.[10]

A third major change consists of the loosening of mutual bonds among allied nations. For many years the United States, western Europe, and Japan, together with emerging industrialized nations, held a generally similar strategic outlook. This outlook was driven by the common desire to reduce, or at least contain, the influence of the Soviet Union. However, with the disintegration of the Soviet Union in 1991, individual national interests that had been subsumed by the overall strategic objective gained in importance. As a consequence, differences in perspectives, attitudes, and outlooks can now lead to ever-growing conflicts among the major players in the trade field.

foreign availability The degree to which products similar to those of a firm can be obtained in markets outside the firm's home country; crucial to export determination.

Major change has also resulted from the increased **foreign availability** of high technology products. In the past decade, the number of participants in the international trade field has grown rapidly. High technology products are available worldwide from many sources. The broad availability makes any denial of such products more difficult to enforce. If a nation does control the exports of widely available products, it imposes a major competitive burden on its firms.

The speed of change and the rapid dissemination of information and innovation around the world also has shifted. For example, "Moore's Law" predicts that the current life cycle of computer chips is only 2 years. More than 70 percent of the data processing industry's sales resulted from the sale of devices that did not exist two years earlier.[11] This enormous technical progress is accompanied by a radical change in computer architecture. Instead of having to replace a personal computer or a workstation with a new computer, it is possible now to simply exchange microprocessors or motherboards with new, more efficient ones. Furthermore, today's machines can be connected to more than one microprocessor and users can customize and update configurations almost at will. Export controls that used to be based largely on capacity criteria have become almost irrelevant because they can no longer fulfill the function assigned to them. A user simply acquires additional chips, from whomever, and uses expansion slots to enhance the capacity of his or her computer.

The question arises as to how much of the latest technology is required for a country to engage in "dangerous" activity. For example, nuclear weapons and sophisticated delivery systems were developed by the United States and the Soviet Union long before supercomputers became available. Therefore, it is reasonable to assert that researchers in countries working with equipment that is less than state of the art, or even obsolete, may well be able to achieve a threat capability that can result in major destruction and affect world safety.

From a control perspective, there is also the issue of equipment size. Due to their size, supercomputers and high-technology items used to be fairly difficult to hide and any movement of such products was easily detectable. Nowadays, state-of-the-art technology has been miniaturized. Much leading-edge technological equipment is so small that it can fit into a briefcase, and most equipment is no larger than the luggage compartment of a car. Given these circumstances, it has become difficult to closely supervise the transfer of such equipment.

There are several key export control problem areas for firms and policymakers. First is the continuing debate about what constitutes military-use products, civilian-use products, and dual use items. Increasingly, goods are of a dual-use nature, typically commercial products that have potential military applications. The classic example is a pesticide factory that, some years later, is revealed to be a poison gas factory.[12] It is difficult enough to clearly define weapons. It is even more problematic to achieve consensus among nations regarding dual-use goods. For example, what about quite harmless screws if they are to be installed in rockets or telecommunications equipment used by the military? The problem becomes even greater with attempts to classify and list subcomponents and regulate their exportation. Individual country lists will lead to a distortion of competition if they deviate markedly from each other. The very task of drawing up any list is itself fraught with difficulty when it comes to components that are assembled. For example, the Patriot missile consists, according to German law, only of simple parts whose individual export is permissible.

Even if governments were to agree on lists and continuously updated them, the resulting control aspects would be difficult to implement. Controlling the transfer of components within and among companies across economic areas such as NAFTA or the European Union (EU) would significantly slow down business. Even more importantly, to subject only the export of physical goods to surveillance is insufficient. The transfer of knowledge and technology is of equal or greater importance. Weapons-relevant information easily can be exported via books, periodicals, and disks, therefore their content also would have to be controlled. Foreigners would need to be prevented from gaining access to such sources during visits or from making use of data networks across borders. Attendance at conferences and symposia would have to be regulated, the flow of data across national borders would have to be controlled, and today's communication systems and highways such as the Internet would have to be scrutinized. All these concerns have led to the emergence of controls of **deemed exports**. These controls address people rather than products in those instances where knowledge transfer could lead to a breach of export restrictions. More information is available under http://www.bis.doc.gov/.

Conflicts can also result from the desire of nations to safeguard their own economic interests. Due to different industrial structures, these interests vary between

deemed exports Addresses people rather than products where knowledge transfer could lead to a breach of export restrictions.

nations. For example, Germany, with a strong world market position in machine tools, motors, and chemical raw materials, will think differently about manufacturing equipment controls than a country such as the United States, which sees computers as an area of its competitive advantage.

The terrorist attacks on Washington, DC and New York City have led to a renewal of international collaboration in the export-control field. Policies are being scrutinized as to their sensibility in light of the dangers of proliferation and international terrorism. Closer collaboration among countries has resulted in an easing of export-control policies in the technology field.[13] Increasingly, there is a feeling among the key country players in the export control field that these controls, in many instances are too onerous on businesses and the key trading countries. Therefore, there are plans to reduce unnecessary complications both through regulatory and legislative reform. The role of export controls and their sophistication can therefore be expected to decrease.

REGULATING INTERNATIONAL BUSINESS BEHAVIOR

Home countries may implement special laws and regulations to ensure that the international business behavior of firms headquartered in them is conducted within moral and ethical boundaries considered appropriate. The definition of appropriateness may vary from country to country and from government to government. Therefore, the content, enforcement, and impact of such regulations on firms may vary substantially among nations. As a result, the international manager must walk a careful line, balancing the expectations held in different countries.

One major area in which nations attempt to govern international business activities involves **boycotts**. As an example, Arab nations developed a blacklist of companies that deal with Israel. Further, Arab customers frequently demand assurance that products they purchase are not manufactured in Israel and that the supplier company does not do any business with Israel. The goal of these actions clearly is to impose a boycott on business with Israel. U.S. political ties to Israel caused the U.S. government to adopt antiboycott laws to prevent U.S. firms from complying with the boycott. The laws include a provision to deny foreign income tax benefits to companies that comply with the boycott. They also require notifying the U.S. government if boycott requests are received. U.S. firms that comply with the boycott are subject to heavy fines and to denial of export privileges. See http://www.bis.doc.gov/Antiboycott Compliance. Boycotts, however, may also spring from the reactions of disgruntled consumers or legislators.

Caught in a web of governmental activity, firms may be forced either to lose business or to pay substantial fines. This is especially true if the firm's products are competitive yet not unique, so that the supplier can opt to purchase them elsewhere. The heightening of such conflict can sometimes force companies to search for new, and possibly risky, ways to circumvent the law or to totally withdraw operations from a country.

Another area of regulatory activity affecting the international business efforts of firms is **antitrust laws**. These laws often apply to international operations as well as to domestic business. In many countries, antitrust agencies watch closely when a firm buys a company, engages in a joint venture with a foreign firm, or makes an agreement abroad with a competing firm in order to ensure that the action does not result in restraint of competition.

Given the increase in worldwide cooperation among companies, however, the wisdom of extending antitrust legislation to international activities is being questioned. Some limitations to these tough antitrust provisions were already implemented decades ago. For example, in the United States, the **Webb-Pomerene Act**

boycott An organized effort to refrain from conducting business with a particular country of origin or seller of goods or services; used in the international arena for political or economic reasons.

antitrust laws Laws that prohibit monopolies, restraint of trade, and conspiracies to inhibit competition.

Webb-Pomerene Act A 1918 statute that excludes from antitrust prosecution U.S. firms cooperating to develop foreign markets.

of 1918 excludes from antitrust prosecution firms cooperating to develop foreign markets. This law was passed as part of an effort to aid export efforts in the face of strong foreign competition by oligopolies and monopolies. The exclusion of international activities from antitrust regulation was further enhanced by the Export Trading Company Act of 1982, which ensures that cooperating firms are not exposed to the threat of treble damages. Further steps to loosen the application of antitrust laws to international business are under consideration because of increased competition from strategic alliances and global megacorporations.

Firms operating abroad are also affected by laws against **bribery** and **corruption**. In many countries, payments or favors are a way of life, and "a greasing of the wheels" is expected in return for government services. As a result, many companies doing business internationally are routinely forced to pay bribes or do favors for foreign officials in order to gain contracts. Every year, businesses pay huge amounts of money in bribes to win friends, influence, and contracts. These bribes are conservatively estimated to run to $80 billion a year—roughly the amount that the UN believes is needed to eradicate global poverty. The U.S. Commerce Department reports that, annually, bribery is believed to be a factor in commercial contracts worth $145 billion.[14]

Corruption is particularly widespread in nations where the administrative apparatus enjoys excessive and discretionary power and where there is a lack of transparency of laws and processes. Poverty, insufficient salaries of government servants, and income inequalities also tend to increase corruption.[15] Fighting corruption is therefore not only an issue of laws and ethics, but also of creating an environment that makes honesty possible and desirable.

In the 1970s, a major national debate erupted in the United States about these business practices, led by arguments that U.S. firms have an ethical and moral leadership obligation and that contracts won through bribes do not reflect competitive market activity. As a result, the **Foreign Corrupt Practices Act** was passed in

bribery The use of payments or favors to obtain some right or benefit to which the briber has no legal right; a criminal offense in the United States but a way of life in many countries.

corruption Payments or favors made to officials in return for services.

Foreign Corrupt Practices Act A 1977 law making it a crime for U.S. executives of publicly traded firms to bribe a foreign official in order to obtain business.

FOCUS ON POLITICS

Marketing Incentive or Anticompetitive Violation?

When a company controls 80 percent of an industry market, there is both a likelihood that its products or services have a strong customer appeal and that its competitive practices will attract the attention of governments. Such was the case in 2009 when the European Commission fined U.S. computer chip manufacturer Intel a record €1.06 billion for unfair business practices that violate European Union antitrust laws.

This action culminated a nine-year investigation that the EC began in 2000 after Intel's competitor, Advanced Micro Devices, another U.S.-based company, filed a complaint that Intel's practice of giving rebates to computer makers, in return for buying at least 95 percent of their chips from Intel, was anticompetitive and illegal. The practice of volume purchase rebates is, of course, a standard marketing incentive practice used for decades in many industries. Advanced Micro Devices maintained that it went too far and was a violation of EU laws.

In its action, the European Union had once again demonstrated that it will actively enforce its antitrust laws against dominant players in the technology market. In 2004, Microsoft incurred a fine of €497 million for violating EU laws by withholding information on how to make its market-dominant Windows software for office computers more interoperable with rival technologies. As of 2008, European regulators have fined Microsoft a total of almost €1.68 billion for antitrust violations or noncompliance with European Commission rulings. In 2009, they ruled that the company's practice of bundling Microsoft Windows and Internet Explorer is anticompetitive and ordered it to end. The EU statement read: "Microsoft's tying of Internet Explorer to the Windows operating system harms competition between web browsers, undermines product innovation, and ultimately reduces consumer choice."

Antitrust rulings are on the rise in other parts of the world as well. In 2009, U.S. telecom company Qualcomm received adverse rulings from both the South Korean Fair Trade Commission and Japan's Fair Trade Commission for anticompetitive behavior.

One lesson is clear: some practices may be legal in some countries but not in others. Firms need to learn to work with these differences.

Sources: Robert Wielaard, "Microsoft Loses E.U. Antitrust Case," *Washington Post*, January 17, 2009; James Kanter, "Europe Fines Intel $1.45 Billion in Antitrust Case," *New York Times*, May 14, 2009; Dylan Bushell-Embling, "Qualcomm Faces Fresh Antitrust Case in Japan," *telecomasia.net*, July 28, 2009; Mayer Brown LLP, http://www.mayerbrown.com/chinaantimonopolylaw/, accessed September 2, 2009.

1977, making it a crime for U.S. executives of publicly traded firms to bribe a foreign official in order to obtain business.

A number of U.S. firms have complained about the act, arguing that it hinders their efforts to compete internationally against companies whose home countries have no such antibribery laws. The problem is one of ethics versus practical needs and, to some extent, of the amounts involved. For example, it may be hard to draw the line between providing a generous tip and paying a bribe in order to speed up a business transaction. Many business executives believe that the United States should not apply its moral principles to other societies and cultures in which bribery and corruption are endemic. To compete internationally, executives argue, they must be free to use the most common methods of competition in the host country.

On the other hand, applying different standards to executives and firms based on whether they do business abroad or domestically is difficult to do. Also, bribes may open the way for shoddy performance and loose moral standards among executives and employees and may result in a spreading of general unethical business practices. Unrestricted bribery could result in firms concentrating on how to bribe best rather than on how to best produce and market their products. Typically, international businesses that use bribery fall into three categories: those who bribe to counterbalance the poor quality of their products or their high price; those who bribe to create a market for their unneeded goods; and, in the bulk of cases, those who bribe to stay competitive with other firms that bribe.[16] In all three of these instances, the customer is served poorly, the prices increase, and the transaction does not reflect economic competitiveness.

The international manager must carefully distinguish between reasonable ways of doing business internationally—that is, complying with foreign expectations—and outright bribery and corruption. To assist the manager in this task, the 1988 Trade Act clarifies the applicability of the Foreign Corrupt Practices legislation. The revisions outline when a manager is expected to know about violation of the act, and they draw a distinction between the facilitation of routine governmental actions and governmental policy decisions. Routine actions concern issues such as the obtaining of permits and licenses, the processing of governmental papers (such as visas and work orders), the providing of mail and phone service, and the loading and unloading of cargo.

Policy decisions refer mainly to situations in which the obtaining or retaining of a contract is at stake. While the facilitation of routine actions is not prohibited, the illegal influencing of policy decisions can result in the imposition of severe fines and penalties.

The risks inherent in bribery have grown since 1999, when the Organization for Economic Cooperation and Development (OECD) adopted a treaty criminalizing the bribery of foreign public officials, moving well beyond its previous discussions, which only sought to outlaw the tax deductibility of improper payments. The Organization of American States (OAS) has also officially condemned bribery. Similarly, the World Trade Organization has decided to place bribery rules on its agenda. In addition, nongovernmental organizations such as Transparency International are conducting widely publicized efforts to highlight corruption and bribery and even to rank countries on a Corruption Perceptions Index (http://www.transparency.de). The Foreign Corrupt Practices Act even applies to situations that some might not consider to be reasonable business transactions. For example, in 2007, Chiquita Brands International plead guilty and agreed to pay a $25 million fine for making payments to a designated foreign terrorist organization in Colombia. Chiquita had been making regular payments to a paramilitary group for "security services" in order to protect its personnel from violence.[17]

These issues place managers in the position of having to choose between home-country regulations and foreign business practices. This choice is made even more difficult because diverging standards of behavior are applied to businesses in different countries. However, the gradually emerging consensus among international organizations may eventually level the playing field.

A final, major issue that is critical for international business managers is that of general standards of behavior and ethics. Increasingly, public concerns are raised about such issues as environmental protection, global warming, pollution, and moral behavior. However, these issues are not of the same importance in every country. What may be frowned upon or even illegal in one nation may be customary or at least acceptable in others. For example, the cutting down of the Brazilian rain forest may be acceptable to the government of Brazil, but scientists and concerned consumers may object vehemently because of the effect on global warming and other climatic changes. The export of U.S. tobacco products may be legal but results in accusations of exporting death to developing nations. China may use prison labor in producing products for export, but U.S. law prohibits the importation of such products. Mexico may permit the use of low safety standards for workers, but the buyers of Mexican products may object to the resulting dangers.

International firms must understand the conflicts in standards and should assert leadership in implementing change. Not everything that is legally possible should be exploited for profit. By acting on existing, leading-edge knowledge and standards, firms will be able to benefit in the long term through consumer goodwill and the avoidance of later recriminations.

International executives are "selling" the world on two key issues: one is the benefit of market forces that results in the interplay of supply and demand. This interplay in turn uses price signals instead of government fiat to adjust activities, thrives on competition, and works within an environment of respect for profitability and private property. The second key proposition is that international marketers will do their best to identify market niches and bring their products and services to customers around the globe. Since these activities take up substantial financial resources, they provide individuals with the opportunity to invest their funds in the most productive and efficient manner.

Key underlying dimensions of both of these issues are managerial and corporate virtue, vision, and veracity. Unless the world can believe in what executives say and do, and trust their global activities, it will be hard, if not impossible, to forge a global commitment between those doing the marketing and the ones being marketed to. It is therefore of vital interest to executives to ensure that corruption, bribery, lack of transparency, and the misleading of consumers, investors, and employees are systematically relegated to the history books—where they belong. It will be the extent of openness, responsiveness, long-term thinking, and truthfulness that will determine the degrees of freedom of international business.[18]

HOST-COUNTRY POLITICAL AND LEGAL ENVIRONMENT

Politics and laws of a host country affect international business operations in a variety of ways. The good manager will understand these dimensions of the countries in which the firm operates so that he or she can work within existing parameters and can anticipate and plan for changes that may occur.

2. To learn how governments affect business through legislation and regulations

POLITICAL ACTION AND RISK

Firms usually prefer to conduct business in a country with a stable and friendly government, but such governments are not always easy to find. Managers must therefore continually monitor the government, its policies, and its stability to determine the potential for political change that could adversely affect corporate operations.

Figure 6.2   Exposure to Political Risk

Loss May Be the Result of:

Contingencies May Include:	The actions of legitimate government authorities	Events caused by factors outside the control of government
The involuntary loss of control over specific assets without adequate compensation	• Total or partial expropriation • Forced divestiture • Confiscation • Cancellation or unfair calling of performance bonds	• War • Revolution • Strikes • Extortion
A reduction in the value of a stream of benefits expected from the foreign-controlled affiliate	• Nonapplicability of "national treatment" • Restriction in access to financial, labor, or material markets • Control on prices, outputs, or activities • Currency and remittance restrictions • Value-added and export performance requirements	• Nationalistic buyers or suppliers • Threats and disruption to operations by hostile groups • Externally induced financial constraints • Externally imposed limits on imports or exports

Source: Adapted from José de la Torre and David H. Neckar, "Forecasting Political Risks for International Operations," in H. Vernon-Wortzel and L. Wortzel, *Global Strategic Management: The Essentials*, 2nd ed. (New York: John Wiley and Sons, 1990), 195.

political risk The risk of loss by an international corporation of assets, earning power, or managerial control as a result of political actions by the host country.

ownership risk The risk inherent in maintaining ownership of property abroad. The exposure of foreign owned assets to governmental intervention.

operating risk The danger of interference by governments or other groups in one's corporate operating abroad.

transfer risk The danger of having one's ability to transfer profits or products in and out of a country inhibited by governmental rules and regulations.

terrorism Illegal and violent acts toward property and people.

There is **political risk** in every nation, but the range of risks varies widely from country to country. In general, political risk is lowest in countries that have a history of stability and consistency. Political risk tends to be highest in nations that do not have this sort of history. In a number of countries, however, consistency and stability that were apparent on the surface have been quickly swept away by major popular movements that drew on the bottled-up frustrations of the population. Three major types of political risk can be encountered: **ownership risk,** which exposes property and life; **operating risk,** which refers to interference with the ongoing operations of a firm; and **transfer risk,** which is mainly encountered when attempts are made to shift funds between countries. Firms can be exposed to political risk due to government actions or even actions outside the control of governments. The type of actions and their effects are classified in Figure 6.2.

A major risk in many countries is that of conflict and violent change. A manager will want to think twice before conducting business in a country in which the likelihood of such change is high. To begin with, if conflict breaks out, violence directed toward the firm's property and employees is a strong possibility. Guerrilla warfare, civil disturbances, and **terrorism** often take an anti-industry bent, making companies and their employees potential targets. International corporations are often subject to major threats, even in countries that boast great political stability. There are a number of recent incidences where international businesses have been threatened. In July 2009, bombings killed and wounded innocent business travelers at the J.W. Marriott and Ritz Carlton hotels, both managed by Marriott, in Jakarta, Indonesia. Hundreds were killed or wounded in September 2008, when a massive explosion destroyed the Marriott in Islamabad, Pakistan. In November 2008, more than a hundred people were killed in terrorists attacks on the Taj Mahal and Oberoi, both luxury hotels favored by international managers.

International terrorists frequently target U.S. facilities, operations, and personnel abroad. Since the September 11 attacks on the World Trade Center and the

Pentagon, we know that such attacks can also take place within the United States. U.S. firms, by their nature, cannot have the elaborate security and restricted access of U.S. diplomatic offices and military bases. As a result, United States businesses are the primary target of terrorists worldwide, and remain the most vulnerable targets in the future.[19] Ironically enough, in many instances, the businesses attacked or burned are the franchisees of U.S. business concepts. Therefore, the ones suffering most from such attacks are the local owners and local employees.

Terrorist attacks often focus on international businesses.

The methods used by terrorists against business facilities include bombing, arson, hijacking, and sabotage. To obtain funds, the terrorists resort to kidnapping executives, armed robbery, and extortion.[20] To reduce international terrorism, recent experience has demonstrated that international collaboration is imperative to identify and track terrorist groups and to systematically reduce their safe havens and financial support. In spite of such efforts, terrorism is likely to continue. As former U.S. senators Hart and Rudman have written: "prudence requires we assume . . . adversaries . . . have learned from the attacks how vulnerable the U.S. and other countries are. They will also have observed that relatively low-cost terrorist operations . . . can inflict extensive damage and profound disruption . . . As long as catastrophic attacks are likely to yield tangible results in undermining our economy and way of life, undertaking these attacks will be attractive to those who regard the U.S. and its allies as their enemy."[21]

As a consequence, governments are likely to continue imposing new regulations and restrictions intended to avert terrorist acts. For example, increasingly complex customs clearance and international logistical requirements, or specific requirements imposed to enhance security systems, all combine to increase the cost of doing business internationally. Moreover, these security measures will also tend to lessen the efficiency with which international business channels can function.[22]

In many countries, particularly in the developing world, **coups d'état** can result in drastic changes in government. The new government often will attack foreign firms as remnants of a Western-dominated colonial past, as has happened in Cuba, Nicaragua, and Iran. Even if such changes do not represent an immediate physical threat, they can lead to policy changes that may have drastic effects. The past decades have seen coups in Ghana, Ethiopia, Pakistan, and Ivory Coast, for example, that have seriously impeded the conduct of international business.

coups d'état A forced change in a country's government, often resulting in attacks of foreign firms and policy changes by the new government.

Less drastic, but still worrisome, are changes in government policies that are not caused by changes in the government itself. These occur when, for one reason or another, a government feels pressured to change its policies toward foreign businesses. The pressure may be the result of nationalist or religious factions or widespread anti-Western feeling.

A broad range of policy changes is possible as a result of political unrest. All of the changes can affect the company's international operations, but not all of them are equal in weight. Except for extreme cases, companies do not usually have to fear violence against their employees, although violence against company property is quite common. Also common are changes in policy that result from a new government or a strong new stance that is nationalist and opposed to foreign investment. The most drastic public steps resulting from such policy changes are usually expropriation and confiscation.

Expropriation is the transfer of ownership by the host government to a domestic entity with payment of compensation. Expropriation was an appealing action to many countries because it demonstrated their nationalism and transferred a certain amount

expropriation The government takeover of a company with compensation, frequently at a level lower than the investment value of the company's assets.

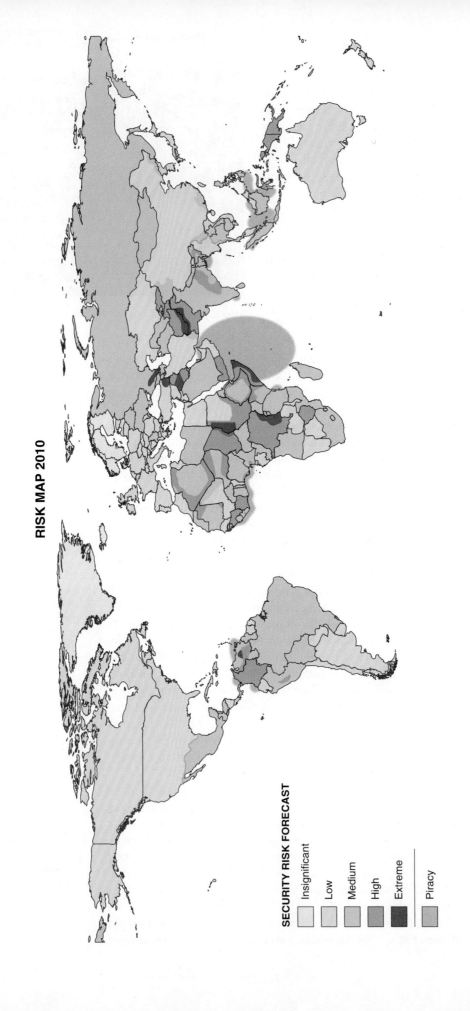

RISK MAP 2010

SECURITY RISK FORECAST

Insignificant
Low
Medium
High
Extreme

Piracy

FOCUS ON POLITICS

Pirates: Not Just in the Caribbean

Lately, there have been threats to international business emanating from ungoverned spaces. For example, government snipers had to intervene to rescue the captain of a hijacked U.S. cargo vessel. Off the coast of East Africa, piracy growth is explosive. In 2007, 41 ships were attacked; in 2008 it was 122; by mid-May 2009, 102 ships had been attacked. Often, the cargo and the crew were held hostage until a ransom payment was made. With estimated payments of more than $100 million, piracy has emerged as a very lucrative industry.

Even though it often appears as if today's governments are taken by surprise when such piracy happens, the phenomenon itself has been around for a long time and has had a major impact on international business.

During the times of Julius Caesar, Rome's carriers of wheat were so often under attack by pirates that Pompeius was issued with special powers and a fleet to end this abuse, which he accomplished successfully. In the early sixteenth century, the North African pirate Barbarossa conquered Algiers and Tunis and used them as bases to attack ocean ships. In 1661, a Chinese pirate named Koxinga led 100,000 men and seized Taiwan from the Dutch. A few decades later, a confederation of 40,000 pirates based in Canton dominated the South China Sea.

Ship owners typically try to avoid arming their ships or providing a proper defense. Rather than taking cuts in their profits, they expect their home navy and government to come to their aid. Governments, in turn, often pay large tributes in order to ensure safe passage for their ships. But even with such payments, piracy continues as a threat.

Research evidence appears to indicate that the key approach to reducing piracy is to constantly challenge the pirates. Whether a country or company sends ships of war for protection, hires private pirate hunters, offers pardons to former pirates, or chases pirates at sea and on land, it is crucial to track and intervene in piracy. The cost for the pirates must go up and their rewards must go down if a reduction of the problem is to occur.

Sources: Max Boot, "Pirates, Then and Now: How Piracy Was Defeated in the Past and Can Be Again," *Foreign Affairs*, July/August 2009, 94–107; ICC Commercial Crime Services, *IMB Piracy Map*, www.icc-ccs.org, accessed October 28, 2009.

---

of wealth and resources from foreign companies to the host country immediately. It did have costs to the host country, however, to the extent that it made other firms more hesitant to invest there. Expropriation does not relieve the host government of providing compensation to the former owners. However, these compensation negotiations are often protracted and frequently result in settlements that are unsatisfactory to the owners. For example, governments may offer compensation in the form of local, nontransferable currency or may base compensation on the book value of the firm. Even though firms that are expropriated may deplore the low levels of payment obtained, they frequently accept them in the absence of better alternatives.

In the mid-1970s, when more than 83 expropriations took place in a single year, expropriation was a serious policy tool by some governments. By 2000, the annual average had declined to fewer than three. More recently, expropriation has resurfaced, particularly among the Bolivarian socialist regimes of South America. Venezuelan President Hugo Chavez nationalized four oil projects in the Orinoco River basin in 2007, causing Exxon and ConocoPhillips to leave Venezuela. The Chavez government has also nationalized the country's largest telecommunications company, buying out Verizon's stake. In 2008, the Venezuelan government took control of the cement industry, buying out Switzerland's Holcim and reducing the stake of France's Lafarge and Mexico's Cemex. The food industry has also been targeted, with Venezuela expropriating a local unit of U.S. food giant Cargill in 2009.[23]

Confiscation is similar to expropriation in that it results in a transfer of ownership from the firm to the host country. It differs in that it does not involve compensation for the firm. Some industries are more vulnerable than others to confiscation and expropriation because of their importance to the host country's economy and their lack of ability to shift operations. For this reason, such sectors as mining, energy, public utilities, and banking have frequently been targets of such government actions.

Confiscation and expropriation constitute major political risk for foreign investors. Other government actions, however, are equally detrimental to foreign firms.

confiscation The forceful government seizure of a company without compensation for the assets seized.

domestication Government demand for partial transfer of ownership and management responsibility from a foreign company to local entities, with or without compensation.

local content Regulations to gain control over foreign investment by ensuring that a large share of the product is locally produced or a larger share of the profit is retained in the country.

Many countries are turning from confiscation and expropriation to more subtle forms of control, such as **domestication**. The goal of domestication is the same—that is, to gain control over foreign investment—but the method is different. Through domestication, the government demands transfer of ownership and management responsibility. It can impose **local content** regulations to ensure that a large share of the product is locally produced or demand that a larger share of the profit is retained in the country. Changes in labor laws, patent protection, and tax regulations are also used for purposes of domestication.

Changes in labor laws, patent protection, and tax regulations are also used for purposes of domestication. In 2006, then newly elected President Evo Morales nationalized the oil and natural gas industry in Bolivia, taking over control from companies like the Spanish/Argentine venture RepsolYPF and Brazil's PetroleoBrasiliero. "Rather than expropriation, the nationalization consisted of higher taxes on petroleum companies and renegotiated contracts. As such, the private companies chose to stay in the country and continue operations. As a result of the new policy and high gas prices, the Bolivian government's income from the country's oil and gas industry has increased dramatically, nine fold in fact between 2002 and 2007."[24]

Domestication can have profound effects on an international business operation for a number of reasons. If a firm is forced to hire nationals as managers, poor cooperation and communication can result. If domestication is imposed within a very short time span, corporate operations overseas may have to be headed by poorly trained and inexperienced local managers. Domestic content requirements may force a firm to purchase its supplies and parts locally. This can result in increased costs, less efficiency, and lower-quality products. Export requirements imposed on companies may create havoc for their international distribution plans and force them to change or even shut down operations in third countries.

Finally, domestication usually will shield an industry within one country from foreign competition. As a result, inefficiencies will be allowed to thrive due to a lack of market discipline. This will affect the long-run international competitiveness of an operation abroad and may turn into a major problem when, years later, domestication is discontinued by the government.

If government action consists of weakening or not enforcing intellectual property right (IPR) protection, companies run the risk of losing their core competitive edge. Such steps may temporarily permit domestic firms to become quick imitators. Yet, in the longer term, they will not only discourage the ongoing transfer of technology and knowledge by multinational firms, but also reduce the incentive for local firms to invest in innovation and progress.

Poor IPR legislation and enforcement in the otherwise lucrative markets of Asia illustrate a clash between international business interests and developing nations' political and legal environments. Businesses attempting to enter the markets of China, Indonesia, Malaysia, Singapore, Taiwan, Thailand, and the Philippines face considerable risk in these countries, which have the world's worst records for copyright piracy and intellectual property infringements. But these newly industrialized countries argue that IPR laws discriminate against them because they impede the diffusion of technology and artificially inflate prices. They also point to the fact that industrialized nations such as the United States and Japan violated IPR laws during earlier stages of development. In fact, the United States became a signatory to the Berne Convention on copyrights only in 1989—around one hundred years after its introduction—and Japan disregarded IPR laws in adapting Western technologies during the 1950s. Furthermore, although newly industrialized nations are becoming increasingly aware that strong IPR protection will encourage technology transfer and foreign investment, the weak nature of these countries' court structures and the slow pace of legislation often fail to keep pace with the needs of their rapidly transforming economies.[25]

Due to successful international negotiations in the Uruguay Round, the World Trade Organization now has agreement on significant dimensions of the trade-related aspects of intellectual property rights (TRIPS) (http://www.wto.org). This agreement sets minimum standards of protection to be provided by each member country for copyrights, trademarks, geographical indications, industrial designs, patents, layout designs of integrated circuits, and undisclosed information such as trade secrets and test data.[26] While not all-encompassing, these standards provide substantial assurances of protection, which, after an implementation delay for the poorest countries, will apply to virtually all parts of the world.

World Trade Organization rules do allow countries to get around intellectual property rights in the case of medical emergency, which has serious implications for pharmaceutical companies. In 2007, Thailand and Brazil issued compulsory licenses for certain anti-retroviral drugs used in treating HIV/AIDS, bypassing patents held by companies including Abbott Laboratories and Merck. This allowed the countries, both afflicted by AIDS epidemics, to purchase the drugs at cheaper prices for free distribution to their citizens.[27] This certainly seems like a humane and moral action on the part of these governments. From the companies' point of view, however, this affects their ability to realize the profits that allow further research and development for advancement in the fight against AIDS.

One might ask why companies would choose to do business in risky markets. However, as with anything international (or any business for that matter), the issue is not whether there is any risk, but rather the degree of risk that exists. Key links to risk are the dimension of reward. With appropriate rewards, many risks become more tolerable. For brave businessfolk, there may be rich returns in unexpected places.[28]

ECONOMIC RISK

Most businesses operating abroad face a number of other risks that are less dangerous, but probably more common, than the drastic ones already described. A host government's political situation or desires may lead it to impose economic regulations or laws to restrict or control the international activities of firms.

Nations that face a shortage of foreign currency will sometimes impose controls on the movement of capital into and out of the country. Such controls may make it difficult for a firm to remove its profits or investments from the host country. Sometimes **exchange controls** are also levied selectively against certain products or companies in an effort to reduce the importation of goods that are considered to be luxuries or to be sufficiently available through domestic production. Such regulations often affect the importation of parts, components, or supplies that are vital to production operations in the country. They may force a firm either to alter its production program or, worse yet, to shut down its entire plant. Prolonged negotiations with government officials may be necessary to reach a compromise on what constitutes a "valid" expenditure of foreign currency resources. Because the goals of government officials and corporate managers are often quite different, such compromises, even when they can be reached, may result in substantial damage to the international operations of the firm.

Countries may also use **tax policy** toward foreign investors in an effort to control multinational corporations and their capital. Tax increases may raise much-needed revenue for the host country, but they can severely damage the operations of foreign investors. This damage, in turn, will frequently result in decreased income for the host country in the long run. The raising of tax rates needs to be carefully differentiated from increased tax scrutiny of foreign investors. Many governments believe that multinational firms may be tempted to shift tax burdens to lower-tax countries by using artificial pricing schemes between subsidiaries. In such instances, governments are likely to take measures to obtain their fair contribution from multinational

exchange controls Controls on the movement of capital in and out of a country, sometimes imposed when the country faces a shortage of foreign currency.

tax policy A means by which countries may control foreign investors.

operations. In the United States, for example, increased focus on the taxation of multinational firms has resulted in various back-tax payments by foreign firms and the development of new corporate pricing policies developed in collaboration with the Internal Revenue Service.[29]

price controls Regulation of the prices of goods and services.

The international executive also has to worry about **price controls**. In many countries, domestic political pressures can force governments to control the prices of imported products or services, particularly in sectors considered highly sensitive from a political perspective, such as food or health care. A foreign firm involved in these areas is vulnerable to price controls because the government can play on citizens' nationalistic tendencies to enforce the controls. Particularly in countries that suffer from high inflation, frequent devaluations, or sharply rising costs, the international executive may be forced to choose between shutting down the operation or continuing production at a loss in the hope of recouping profits when the government loosens or removes its price restrictions. Price controls can also be administered to prevent prices from being too low. Because governments have enacted antidumping laws, which prevent foreign competitors from pricing their imports unfairly low in order to drive domestic competitors out of the market. Since dumping charges depend heavily on the definition of "fair" price, a firm can sometimes become the target of such accusations quite unexpectedly. Proving that no dumping took place can become quite onerous in terms of time, money, and information disclosure.

MANAGING THE RISK

Managers face the risk of confiscation, expropriation, domestication, or other government interference whenever they conduct business overseas, but ways exist to lessen the risk. Obviously, if a new government comes into power and is dedicated to the removal of all foreign influences, there is little a firm can do. In less extreme cases, however, managers can take actions that will reduce the risk, provided they understand the root causes of the host country's policies.

Adverse governmental actions are usually the result of nationalism, the deterioration of political relations between home and host country, the desire for independence, or opposition to colonial remnants. If a host country's citizens feel exploited by foreign investors, government officials are more likely to take antiforeign action. To reduce the risk of government intervention, the international firm needs to demonstrate that it is concerned with the host country's society and that it considers itself an integral part of the host country, rather than simply an exploitative foreign corporation. Ways of doing this include intensive local hiring and training practices, better pay, contributions to charity, and societally useful investments. In addition, the company can form joint ventures with local partners to demonstrate that it is willing to share its gains with nationals. Although such actions will not guarantee freedom from political risk, they will certainly lessen the exposure.

Another action that can be taken by corporations to protect against political risk is the close monitoring of political developments. Increasingly, private sector firms offer such monitoring assistance, permitting the overseas corporation to discover potential trouble spots as early as possible and to react quickly to prevent major losses.

Firms can also take out insurance to cover losses due to political and economic risk. Most industrialized countries offer insurance programs for their firms doing business abroad. In Germany, for example, Hermes Kreditanstalt (http://www.hermes.de) provides exporters with insurance. In the United States, the Overseas Private Investment Corporation (OPIC) (http://www.opic.gov) can cover three types of risk insurance: currency inconvertibility insurance, which covers the inability to convert profits, debt service, and other remittances from local currency into U.S. dollars; expropriation insurance, which covers the loss of an investment due to expropriation, nationalization, or confiscation by a foreign government; and political violence insurance, which covers the loss of assets or income due to war, revolution, insurrection, or politically motivated civil strife, terrorism, and sabotage. The cost of coverage varies by country and type of activity, but for manufacturers it averages $0.35 for $100 of coverage per year to protect against inconvertibility, $0.68 to protect against expropriation, and $0.50 to compensate for damage to business income and assets from political violence.[30] Usually the policies do not cover commercial risks and, in the event of a claim, cover only the actual loss—not lost profits. In the event of a major political upheaval, however, risk insurance can be critical to a firm's survival.

Brussels is the center of government for the European Union.

The discussion to this point has focused primarily on the political environment. Laws have been mentioned only as they appear to be the direct result of political change. However, the laws of host countries need to be considered on their own to some extent, for the basic system of law is important to the conduct of international business.

LEGAL DIFFERENCES AND RESTRAINTS

Countries differ in their laws as well as in their use of the law. For example, over the past decade, the United States has become an increasingly litigious society in which institutions and individuals are quick to initiate lawsuits. Court battles are often protracted and costly, and even the threat of a court case can reduce business opportunities. In contrast, Japan's tradition tends to minimize the role of the law and of lawyers. On a per capita basis, Japan has only about 4 percent of the number of lawyers that the United States has.[31] Whether the number of lawyers is cause or effect, the Japanese tend not to litigate. Litigation in Japan means that the parties have failed to compromise, which is contrary to Japanese tradition and results in loss of face. A cultural predisposition therefore exists to settle conflicts outside the court system.

Over the millennia of civilization, many different laws and legal systems have emerged. King Hammurabi of Babylon codified a series of decisions by judges into a body of laws. Legal issues in many African tribes were settled through the verdicts of clansmen. A key legal perspective that survives today is that of **theocracy**. Examples are Hebrew law and Islamic law (the Sharia) which are the result of the dictates of God, scripture, prophetic utterances and practices, and scholarly interpretations.[32] These legal systems have faith and belief as their key focus and are a mix of societal, legal, and spiritual guidelines.

theocracy A legal perspective based on religious practices and interpretations.

While legal systems are important to society, from an international business perspective, the two major legal systems worldwide can be categorized into common law and code law. **Common law** is based on tradition and depends less on written statutes and codes than on precedent and custom. Common law originated in England and is the system of law in the United States. **Code law** on the other hand, is based on a comprehensive set of written statutes. Countries with code law try to spell out all possible legal rules explicitly. Code law is based on Roman law and is found in the majority of the nations of the world.

common law Law based on tradition and depending less on written statutes and codes than on precedent and custom—used in the United States.

In general, countries with the code law system have much more rigid laws than those with the common law system. In the latter, courts adopt precedents and customs to fit cases, allowing a better idea of basic judgment likely to be rendered in new situations. The differences between code law and common law and their impact on international business, while wide in theory, are not as broad in practice. One

code law Law based on a comprehensive set of written statutes.

reason is that many common-law countries, including the United States, have adopted commercial codes to govern the conduct of business.

Host countries may adopt a number of laws that affect the firm's ability to do business. Tariffs and quotas, for example, can affect the entry of goods. Special licenses for foreign goods may be required.

Other laws may restrict entrepreneurial activities. In Europe for example, 11 EU member states restrict nonpharmacists from holding a majority stake in pharmacies. Spanish laws restrict pharmacy ownership to pharmacists with a limit of one location, while German laws allow a licensed pharmacist to own up to four stores. In 2009, the European Court of Justice (ECJ) upheld pharmacy ownership requirements on the grounds that its member-states should be able to take protective measures to minimize risks to human health.[33]

Specific legislation may also exist regulating what does and does not constitute deceptive advertising. Many countries prohibit specific claims that compare products to the competition, or they restrict the use of promotional devices. Even when no laws exist, regulations may hamper business operations. For example, in some countries, firms are required to join the local chamber of commerce or become a member of the national trade association. These institutions in turn may have internal sets of rules that specify standards for the conduct of business that may be quite confining.

Seemingly innocuous local regulations that may easily be overlooked can have a major impact on the international firm's success. For example, Japan had an intricate process regulating the building of new department stores or supermarkets. The government's desire to protect smaller merchants brought the opening of new, large stores to a virtual standstill. Because department stores and supermarkets serve as the major conduit for the sale of imported consumer products, the lack of new stores severely affected opportunities for market penetration of imported merchandise.[34] Only after intense pressure from the outside did the Japanese government decide to reconsider the regulations. Another example concerns the growing global controversy that surrounds the use of genetic technology. Governments increasingly devise new rules that affect trade in genetically modified products. Australia introduced a mandatory standard for foods produced using biotechnology that prohibits the sale of such products unless the food has been assessed by the Australia New Zealand Food Authority.

Other laws may be designed to protect domestic industries and reduce imports. For example, Russia assesses high excise taxes on goods such as cigarettes, automobiles, and alcoholic beverages, and provides a burdensome import licensing regime for alcohol to depress Russian demand for imports.[35]

Finally, the interpretation and enforcement of laws and regulations may have a major effect on international business activities. For example, in deciding what product can be called a "Swiss" Army knife or "French" wine, the interpretation given by courts to the meaning of a name can affect consumer perceptions and sales of products.

THE INFLUENCING OF POLITICS AND LAWS

To succeed in a market, the international manager needs much more than business know-how. He or she must also deal with the intricacies of national politics and laws. Although to fully understand another country's legal political system will rarely be possible, the good manager will be aware of its importance and will work with people who do understand how to operate within the system. To do so is particularly important for multinational corporations. These firms work in many countries and must manage relationships with a large number of governments. Often, these governments have a variety of ideologies that may require different corporate responses. To be strategically successful, the firm must therefore be able to formulate and implement political activities on a global scale.[36]

Many areas of politics and law are not immutable. Viewpoints can be modified or even reversed, and new laws can supersede old ones. Therefore, existing political and legal restraints do not always need to be accepted. To achieve change, however, some impetus for it—such as the clamors of a constituency—must occur. Otherwise, systemic inertia is likely to allow the status quo to prevail.

The international manager has various options. One is to simply ignore prevailing rules and expect to get away with it. Pursuing this option is a high-risk strategy because the possibility of objection and even prosecution exists. A second, traditional option is to provide input to trade negotiators and expect any problem areas to be resolved in multilateral negotiations. The drawbacks to this option are, of course, the quite time-consuming process involved and the lack of control by the firm.

A third option involves the development of coalitions and constituencies that can motivate legislators and politicians to consider and ultimately implement change. This option can be pursued in various ways. One direction can be the recasting or redefinition of issues. Often, specific terminology leads to conditioned, though inappropriate, responses. For example, before China's accession to the World Trade Organization in 2001, the country's trade status with the United States was highly controversial for many years. The U.S. Congress had to decide annually whether or not to grant "most-favored nation" (MFN) status to China. The debate on this decision was always very contentious and acerbic, and often framed around the question as to why China deserved to be treated the "most favored way." Lost in the debate was often the fact that the term "most favored" was simply taken from WTO terminology, and only indicated that trade with China would be treated like that with any other country. Only in late 1999 was the terminology changed from MFN to NTR, or "normal trade relations." Even though there was still considerable debate regarding China, at least the controversy about special treatment had been eliminated.[37]

Beyond terminology, firms can also highlight the direct links and their costs and benefits to legislators and politicians. For example, a manager can explain the employment and economic effects of certain laws and regulations and demonstrate the benefits of change. The picture can be enlarged by including indirect links. For example, suppliers, customers, and distributors can be asked to help explain to decision makers the benefit of change. In addition, the public at large can be involved through public statements or advertisements.

Developing such coalitions is not an easy task. Companies often seek assistance in effectively influencing the government decision-making process. Typical categories of firm-level political behavior are lobbying, public/government relations, industry alliances and associations, and political incentives.[38] Lobbying usually works best when narrow economic objectives or single-issue campaigns are involved. Typically, **lobbyists** provide this assistance. Usually, there are well-connected individuals and firms that can provide access to policymakers and legislators in order to communicate new and pertinent information.

lobbyist Typically, a well-connected person or firm that is hired by a business to influence the decision making of policymakers and legislators.

Many U.S. firms have representatives in Washington, DC, as well as in state capitals and are quite successful at influencing domestic policies. Often, however, they are less adept at ensuring proper representation abroad even though, for example, the European Commission in Brussels wields far-reaching economic power. A survey of U.S. international marketing executives found that knowledge and information about foreign trade and government officials was ranked lowest among critical international business information needs. This low ranking appears to reflect the fact that many U.S. firms are far less successful in their interactions with governments abroad and far less intensive in their lobbying efforts than are foreign entities in the United States.[39]

Many countries and companies have been effective in their lobbying in the United States. As an example, in 2005, the presidents of Costa Rica, El Salvador, Guatemala, Honduras, Nicaragua, and the Dominican Republic visited 11 U.S. cities and then came to Washington to meet with President Bush and members of Congress to push for passage of the U.S.–Central American Free Trade Agreement (CAFTA) The countries of the region retained Washington public relations and lobbying firms in the fight for CAFTA, and many Central American business leaders had also visited Capitol Hill to advocate for the free trade agreement, which was approved by Congress in July 2005. Colombia has pursued the passage of the U.S.–Colombia Free Trade Agreement very aggressively, hosting more than 50 U.S. members of Congress to demonstrate progress in social justice in Colombia. As of 2008, Colombia had paid more than $1 million to Washington lobbying firms for work to pass the agreement. Yet, by 2010 the agreement was still pending U.S. congressional approval.[40]

Political influence can be useful when it comes to general issues applicable to a wide variety of firms or industries, or when long-term policy directions are at stake. In such instances, the collaboration and power of many market actors can help sway the direction of policy.

Although representation of the firm's interests to government decision makers and legislators is entirely appropriate, the international manager must also consider any potential side effects. Major questions can be raised if such representation becomes very overt. Short-term gains may be far outweighed by long-term negative repercussions if the international firm is perceived as exerting too much political influence.

 ## INTERNATIONAL RELATIONS AND LAWS

3. To see how the political actions of countries expose firms to international risks

In addition to understanding the politics and laws of both home and host countries, the international manager must also consider the overall international political and legal environment. This is important because policies and events occurring among countries can have a profound impact on firms trying to do business internationally.

INTERNATIONAL POLITICS

The effect of politics on international business is determined by both the bilateral political relations between home and host countries and by multilateral agreements governing the relations among groups of countries.

The government-to-government relationship can have a profound influence in a number of ways, particularly if it becomes hostile. President Bush's characterization in February 2002 of Iran, Iraq, and North Korea as an "axis of evil" aggravated already unstable political relationships and threatened to set back negotiations by U.S. companies to secure lucrative oil deals.[41] In another example, although the internal political changes in the aftermath of the Iranian Revolution certainly would have affected any foreign firm doing business in Iran, the deterioration in U.S.–Iranian political relations that resulted had a significant additional impact on U.S. firms, which were injured not only by the physical damage caused by the violence, but also by the anti-American feelings of the Iranian people and their government. The resulting clashes between the two governments subsequently destroyed business relationships, regardless of corporate feelings or agreements on either side.

International political relations do not always have harmful effects. If bilateral political relations between countries improve, business can benefit. One example is the improvement in Western relations with central Europe following the official end of the Cold War. The political warming opened the potentially lucrative former Eastern bloc markets to Western firms.

The overall international political environment has effects, whether good or bad, on international business. For this reason, the manager must strive to remain aware of political currents and relations worldwide and will attempt to anticipate changes in the international political environment so that his or her firm can plan for them.

INTERNATIONAL LAW

International law plays an important role in the conduct of international business. Although no enforceable body of international law exists, certain treaties and agreements are respected by a number of countries and profoundly influence international business operations. For example, the World Trade Organization (WTO) defines internationally acceptable economic practices for its member nations. Although it does not directly deal with individual firms, it does affect them indirectly by providing some predictability in the international environment.

The World Intellectual Property Organization (WIPO), based in Geneva, is a specialized agency of the United Nations mandated to promote the protection of intellectual property globally. WIPO provides global registration systems for trademarks, industrial designs and appellations of origin, and a global filing system for patents. WIPO also works with developing countries to develop their intellectual property regimes.

The **Patent Cooperation Treaty (PCT)** provides procedures for filing one international application designating countries in which a patent is sought, which has the same effect as filing national applications in each of those countries. Similarly, the European Patent Office examines applications and issues national patents in any of its member countries. Other regional offices include the African Industrial Property Office (ARIPO), the French-speaking African Intellectual Property Organization (OAPI), and one in Saudi Arabia for six countries in the Gulf region. Negotiations for the Anti-Counterfeiting Trade Agreement are continuing among many nations, including the United States, the European Union, Japan, Korea, and Australia, to create new legal standards in the global fight against counterfeiting and piracy.

International organizations such as the United Nations and the Organization for Economic Cooperation and Development have also undertaken efforts to develop codes and guidelines that affect international business. These include the Code on International Marketing of Breast-Milk Substitutes, which was developed by the World Health Organization (WHO) (http://www.who.int/en), and the UN Code of Conduct for Transnational Corporations. Even though there are many such codes in existence, the lack of enforcement ability often hampers their full implementation.

In addition to multilateral agreements, firms are affected by bilateral treaties and conventions between the countries in which they do business. For example, a number of countries have signed bilateral Treaties of Friendship, Commerce, and Navigation (FCN). The agreements generally define the rights of firms doing business in the host country. They normally guarantee that firms will be treated by the host country in the same manner in which domestic firms are treated. While these treaties provide for some sort of stability, they can also be canceled when relations worsen.

The international legal environment also affects the manager to the extent that firms must concern themselves with jurisdictional disputes. Because no single body of international law exists, firms usually are restricted by both home and host country laws. If a conflict occurs between contracting parties in two different countries, a question arises concerning which country's laws are to be used and in which court the dispute is to be settled. Sometimes the contract will contain a jurisdictional clause that settles the matter with little problem. If the contract does not contain such a clause, however, the parties to the dispute have a few choices. They can settle the dispute by following the laws of the country in which the agreement was made, or they can resolve it by obeying the laws of the country in which the contract will have to be fulfilled. Which laws to use and in which location to settle the dispute are two different decisions. As a result, a dispute between a U.S. exporter and a French importer could be

international law The body of rules governing relationships between sovereign states; also certain treaties and agreements respected by a number of countries.

Patent Cooperation Treaty (PCT) An agreement that outlines procedures for filing one international patent application rather than individual national applications.

arbitration The procedure for settling a dispute in which an objective third party hears both sides and makes a decision; a procedure for resolving conflict in the international business arena through the use of intermediaries such as representatives of chambers of commerce, trade associations, or third-country institutions.

resolved in Paris but be based on New York State law. The importance of such provisions was highlighted by the lengthy jurisdictional disputes surrounding the Bhopal incident in India, in which an explosion of chemicals killed and maimed thousands.

In cases of disagreement, the parties can choose either arbitration or litigation. Litigation is usually avoided for several reasons. It often involves extensive delays and is very costly. In addition, firms may fear discrimination in foreign countries. Therefore, companies tend to prefer conciliation and **arbitration**, because they result in much quicker decisions. Arbitration procedures are often spelled out in the original contract and usually provide for an intermediary who is judged to be impartial by both parties. Intermediaries can be representatives of chambers of commerce, trade associations, or third-country institutions.

One key nongovernmental organization handling international commercial disputes is the International Court of Arbitration, founded in 1923 by the International Chamber of Commerce (http://www.iccwbo.org). In 2008, it handled arbitrations in some 50 different countries with arbitrators of some 74 different nationalities. Arbitration usually is faster and less expensive than litigation in the courts. In addition, the limited judicial recourse available against arbitral awards, as compared with court judgments, offers a clear advantage. Parties that use arbitration rather than litigation know that they will not have to face a prolonged and costly series of appeals. Finally, arbitration offers the parties the flexibility to set up a proceeding that can be conducted as quickly and economically as the circumstances allow.[42]

SUMMARY

The political and legal environment in the home and host countries and the laws and agreements governing relationships among nations are important to the international business executive. Compliance is mandatory in order to do business successfully abroad. To avoid the problems that can result from changes in the political and legal environment, it is essential to anticipate changes and to develop strategies for coping with them. Whenever possible, the manager must avoid being taken by surprise and letting events control business decisions.

Governments affect international business through legislation and regulations, which can support or hinder business transactions. An example is when export sanctions or embargoes are imposed to enhance foreign policy objectives. Similarly, export controls are used to preserve national security. Nations also regulate the international business behavior of firms by setting standards that relate to bribery and corruption, boycotts, and restraint of competition.

Through political actions such as expropriation, confiscation, or domestication, countries expose firms to international risk. Management therefore needs to be aware of the possibility of such risk and alert to new developments. Many private-sector services are available to track international risk situations. In the event of a loss, firms may rely on insurance for political risk or they may seek redress in court. International legal action, however, may be quite slow and may compensate for only part of the loss.

Managers need to be aware that different countries have different laws. One clearly pronounced difference is between code law countries, where all possible legal rules are spelled out, and common law countries such as the United States, where the law is based on tradition, precedent, and custom.

Managers must also pay attention to international political relations, agreements, and treaties. Changes in relations or rules can mean major new opportunities and occasional threats to international business. Even though conflict in international business may sometimes lead to litigation, the manager needs to be aware of the alternative of arbitration, which may resolve the pending matter more quickly and at a lower cost.

KEY TERMS

international competitiveness 174	embargo 175	national security 177
extraterritoriality 174	export-control systems 176	export license 177
sanction 175	dual-use items 177	critical commodities list 177

foreign availability   178
deemed exports   179
boycott   180
antitrust laws   180
Webb-Pomerene Act   180
bribery   181
corruption   181
Foreign Corrupt Practices Act   181
political risk   184
ownership risk   184
operating risk   184

transfer risk   184
terrorism   184
coups d'état   185
expropriation   185
confiscation   187
domestication   188
local content   188
intellectual property right (IPR)   188
exchange controls   189
tax policy   189

price controls   190
theocracy   191
common law   191
code law   191
lobbyist   193
international law   195
Patent Cooperation Treaty (PCT)   195
arbitration   196

QUESTIONS FOR DISCUSSION

1. Discuss this potential dilemma: "High political risk requires companies to seek a quick payback on their investments. Striving for a quick payback, however, exposes firms to charges of exploitation and results in increased political risk."

2. Discuss this statement: "The national security that our export control laws seek to protect may be threatened by the resulting lack of international competitiveness of U.S. firms."

3. Discuss the advantages and disadvantages of common law and code law.

4. Japan has been described as a nonlitigious society. How does infrequent litigation affect international business?

5. After you hand your passport to the immigration officer in country X, he misplaces it. A small "donation" would certainly help him find it again. Should you give him the money? Is this a business expense to be charged to your company? Should it be tax deductible?

INTERNET EXERCISES

1. The Bureau of Industry and Security (BIS) at the U.S. Department of Commerce is responsible for implementing and enforcing the Export Administration Regulations (EAR), which regulate the export and re-export of most commercial items. How does a company determine if it needs a commerce export license? (See http://www.bis.doc.gov.)

2. According to the anticorruption monitoring organization Transparency International, which countries have the highest levels of corruption? Which have the lowest levels? (Use the Corruption Perception Index found at http://www.transparency.de.) What problems might an exporter have in doing business in a country with high levels of corruption?

TAKE A STAND

Rowan Williams is the archbishop of Canterbury and the spiritual leader of the approximately 80 million member global Anglican Church. He stirred up some controversy when he examined the role of Sharia in British life. Sharia is the body of Islamic religious law that is based on the Koran, the words and actions of the Prophet Mohammad and the rulings of Islamic scholars. It typically finds its application mainly in Muslim countries.

The archbishop suggested that, with a population of more than 2 million Muslims in Great Britain, Sharia already figures prominently in the lives of many. For example, informal neighborhood councils provide rulings on family issues such as divorce; and banks, such as HSBC already market mortgages that comply with Sharia rules of lending. Perhaps Muslims in Britain would be more comfortable and willing to build a more constructive relationship with their fellow citizens if they could choose Sharia law for the settling of civil disputes, suggested Williams.

Many commentators, which included former British Prime Minister Gordon Brown, strongly opposed such thinking. There was the feeling that such a move would undermine British values and laws and substantially weaken the position of women. Perhaps not since Thomas Becket ran afoul of King Henry II in 1170 (and was murdered for his disagreement about the rights of church and state) was there such controversy surrounding the archbishop and the law.

For Discussion

Should there be a greater reflection of Sharia law in Britain? What are the implications for Muslims, non-Muslims U.K. citizens, and the law enforcement process?

Sources: Karla Adam, "Archbishop Defends Remarks on Islamic Law in Britain," *Washington Post,* February 12, 2008, A 11; "Archbishop of Canterbury: Sharia law unavoidable in Britain," *Christian Today,* February 7, 2008; Matthew Lynn, "Archibishop Williams Is Wrong to Back Sharia Law," Bloomberg.com, February 28, 2008.

CHAPTER 7

Global Financial Markets

CHAPTER CONTENTS & LEARNING OBJECTIVES

THE GLOBAL FINANCIAL MARKETPLACE

1. To understand how currencies are traded and quoted on world financial markets

THE MARKET FOR CURRENCIES

2. To examine the purpose of exchange rates in product, service, and capital markets

EVOLUTION OF THE GLOBAL MONETARY SYSTEM

3. To explore the primary linkage between exchange rates and money markets—LIBOR

THE PURPOSE OF EXCHANGE RATES

4. To understand the distinctions between domestic and international sources of capital

GLOBAL CAPITAL MARKETS

5. To examine how the needs of individual borrowers have changed the nature of the instruments traded on world financial markets

THE FINANCIAL CRISIS OF 2007–2009

6. To understand the origins and implications of the 2007–2009 global financial crisis and the road ahead

The current financial crisis and worldwide recession have abruptly halted a nearly three-decade-long expansion of global capital markets. From 1980 through 2007, the world's financial assets—including equities, private and public debt, and bank deposits—nearly quadrupled in size relative to global GDP. Global capital flows similarly surged. This growth reflected numerous interrelated trends, including advances in information and communication technology, financial market liberalization, and innovations in financial products and services. The result was financial globalization.

But the upheaval in financial markets in late 2008 marked a break in this trend. The total value of the world's financial assets fell by $16 trillion in 2009 to $178 trillion, the largest setback on record. In the fall of 2009, equity markets bounced back from their recent lows but remain well below their peaks. Credit markets have healed somewhat but are still impaired.

Going forward, our research suggests that global capital markets are entering a new era in which the forces fueling growth have changed. For the past 30 years, most of the overall increase in financial depth—the ratio of assets to GDP—was driven by the rapid growth of equities and private debt in mature markets. Looking ahead, these asset classes in mature markets are likely to grow more slowly, more in line with GDP, while government debt will rise sharply. An increasing share of global asset growth will occur in emerging markets, where GDP is rising faster and all asset classes have abundant room to expand.

Source: Excerpted from Charles Rosburgh, Susan Lund, Charles Atkins, Stanislas Belot, Wayne W. Hu, and Moira S. Pierce, "Global Capital Markets: Entering a New Era," McKinsey Global Institute, McKinsey & Company, September 2009, p. 7.

THE GLOBAL FINANCIAL MARKETPLACE

1. To understand how currencies are traded and quoted on world financial markets

Business—domestic, international, global—whatever the case, involves the interaction of individuals and individual organizations for the exchange of products, services, and capital through markets. The global capital markets are critical for the conduct of this exchange. The global financial crisis of 2007–2009 served as both an illustration and a warning of how tightly integrated and fragile this marketplace may be.

ASSETS, INSTRUMENTS, AND INSTITUTIONS

Figure 7.1 provides something of a map to the global capital markets. One way to characterize the global financial marketplace is through its *assets*, its *institutions*, and its *linkages*.

- **Assets.** The assets—the financial assets—that are at the heart of the global capital markets are the debt securities issued by governments, for example, U.S. Treasury bonds. These low-risk or risk-free assets then form the foundation for the creation, trading, and pricing of other financial assets like bank loans, corporate bonds, and equities (stock). In recent years a number of additional securities have been created from the existing securities—derivatives, whose value is based on market value changes in the underlying securities. The health and security of the global financial system relies on the quality of these assets.

- **Institutions.** The institutions of global finance are the central banks that create and control each country's money supply; the commercial banks that take

Figure 7.1   Global Capital Markets

The global capital market is a collection of institutions (central banks, commercial banks, investment banks, not-for-profit financial institutions like the IMF and World Bank) and securities (bonds, mortgages, derivatives, loans,etc.) that are all linked via a global network—the *interbank market*. This interbank market, in which securities of all kinds are traded, is the critical pipeline system for the movement of capital.

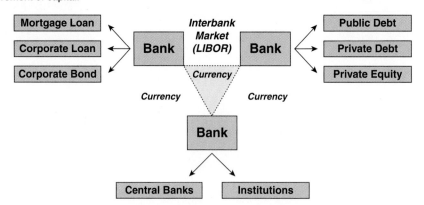

The exchange of securities—the movement of capital in the global financial system—must all take place through a vehicle—currency. The exchange of currencies is itself the largest of the financial markets. The interbank market, which must pass through and exchange securities using currencies, bases all of its pricing through the single most widely quoted interest rate in the world—LIBOR (the London Interbank Offer Rate).

deposits and extend loans to businesses, both local and global; and the multitude of other financial institutions created to trade securities and derivatives. These institutions take many shapes and are subject to many different regulatory frameworks. The health and security of the global financial system relies on the stability of these financial institutions.

- **Linkages.** The links between the financial institutions, the actual fluid or medium for exchange, are the interbank networks using currency. The ready exchange of currencies in the global marketplace is the first and foremost necessary element for the conduct of financial trading, and the global currency markets are the largest markets in the world. The exchange of currencies, and the subsequent exchange of all other securities globally via currency, is the international interbank network. This network, whose primary price is the *London Interbank Offer Rate*, or *LIBOR*, is the core component of the global financial system.

The movement of capital across borders and continents for the conduct of business has in many different forms existed for thousands of years. Yet, it is only within the past 50 years that these capital movements have started moving at the pace of an electron, either via a telephone call or more recently an e-mail. And it is only within the past 20 years that this market has been able to reach the most distant corners of the earth at any moment of the day. This market has seen an explosion of innovative products and services in the past decade, some of which proved, as in the case of the 2007–2009 crisis, somewhat toxic to the touch.

This chapter will explore the global capital market following the framework depicted in Figure 7.1, beginning with the market for currencies, and then exploring the securities and institutions making up global exchange. The final section attempts to explain in short fashion the causes and implications of the most recent global financial crisis.

THE MARKET FOR CURRENCIES

The price of any one country's currency in terms of another country's currency is called a foreign currency exchange rate. For example, the exchange rate between the U.S. dollar ($ or USD) and the European euro (€ or EUR) may be stated as "1.4565 dollar per euro" or simply abbreviated as $1.4565/€. This is the same exchange rate as when stated "EUR 1.00 = USD 1.4565." Because most international business activities require at least one of the two parties in a business transaction to either pay or receive payment in a currency that is different from their own, an understanding of exchange rates is critical to the conduct of global business.

A quick word about currency symbols. As already noted, the letters USD and EUR are often used as the symbols for the U.S. dollar and the European Union's euro. These are the computer symbols (ISO-4217 codes) used today on the world's digital networks. The field of international finance, however, has a rich history of using a variety of different symbols in the financial press, and there are a variety of different abbreviations commonly used. For example, the British pound sterling may be £ (the pound symbol), GBP (Great Britain pound), STG (British pound sterling), ST£ (pound sterling), or UKL (United Kingdom pound). This book will use the simpler common symbols throughout—the $ (dollar), the € (euro), the ¥ (yen), the £ (pound)—but be warned and watchful when reading the business press!

2. To examine the purpose of exchange rates in product, service, and capital markets

Figure 7.2   Currency Exchange Rates

Sep 10	Currency	Dollar Closing Mid	Dollar Day's Change	Euro Closing Mid	Euro Day's Change	Pound Closing Mid	Pound Day's Change
Argentina	(Peso)	3.8538	−0.0008	5.6128	−0.0076	6.4250	0.0394
Australia	(A$)	1.1634	0.0082	1.6945	0.0100	1.9396	0.0258
Bahrain	(Dinar)	0.3770	—	0.5491	−0.0007	0.6286	0.0039
Bolivia	(Boliviano)	7.0200	—	10.2243	−0.0120	11.7038	0.0740
Brazil	(R$)	1.8205	−0.0032	2.6515	0.0078	3.0351	0.0138
Canada	(C$)	1.0820	0.0062	1.5759	0.0071	1.8039	0.0216
Chile	(Peso)	553.850	2.2000	806.655	2.2664	923.379	9.4878
China	(Yuan)	6.8294	0.0006	9.9467	−0.0107	11.3860	0.0731
Colombia	(Peso)	2009.38	17.9750	2926.55	22.7944	3350.03	50.9773
Costa Rica	(Colon)	586.500	−0.1100	854.209	−1.1575	977.814	6.0051
Czech Rep.	(Koruna)	17.4977	0.0746	25.4845	0.0790	29.1721	0.3081
Denmark	(DKr)	5.1111	0.0062	7.4440	0.0002	8.5211	0.0641
Egypt	(Egypt £)	5.5190	−0.0047	8.0382	−0.0163	9.2013	0.0503
Estonia	(Kroon)	10.7429	0.0125	15.6465	—	17.9106	0.1341
Hong Kong	(HK$)	7.7506	0.0001	11.2883	−0.0130	12.9218	0.0820
Hungary	(Forint)	186.567	0.7318	271.725	0.7500	311.044	3.1807
India	(Rs)	48.6350	0.1300	70.8345	0.1069	81.0843	0.7285
Indonesia	(Rupiah)	9932.50	7.5000	14466.2	−5.9503	16559.5	117.211
Iran	(Rial)	9925.00	—	14455.3	−16.8725	16547.0	104.709
Israel	(Shk)	3.7875	0.0231	5.5163	0.0272	6.3144	0.0781
Japan	(Y)	91.7700	0.0150	133.658	−0.1341	152.999	0.9931
One Month		91.7538	0.0007	133.637	0.0030	152.956	−0.0057
Three Month		91.7187	−0.0008	133.579	−0.0023	152.892	0.0146
One Year		91.3410	0.0220	133.062	0.0192	152.194	0.0334
Kenya	(Shilling)	76.0000	—	110.690	−0.1291	126.707	0.8018
Kuwait	(Dinar)	0.2866	−0.0003	0.4174	−0.0010	0.4778	0.0026
Malaysia	(M$)	3.4990	0.0005	5.0962	−0.0052	5.8336	0.0378
Mexico	(New Peso)	13.4679	0.0937	19.6153	0.1137	22.4537	0.2972
New Zealand	(NZ$)	1.4326	0.0002	2.0865	−0.0022	2.3884	0.0155
Nigeria	(Naira)	154.270	0.1700	224.687	−0.0144	257.199	1.9092
Norway	(NKr)	5.9518	0.0615	8.6685	0.0795	9.9229	0.1647
Pakistan	(Rupee)	82.8200	−0.1300	120.623	−0.3304	138.078	0.6584
Peru	(New Sol)	2.9255	0.0063	4.2609	0.0041	4.8774	0.0412

Sep 10	Currency	Dollar Closing Mid	Dollar Day's Change	Euro Closing Mid	Euro Day's Change	Pound Closing Mid	Pound Day's Change
Philippines	(Peso)	48.3650	−0.0450	70.4412	−0.1478	80.6342	0.4357
Poland	(Zloty)	2.8467	0.0281	4.1460	0.0362	4.7460	0.0767
Romania	(New Leu)	2.9205	0.0060	4.2535	0.0038	4.8690	0.0408
Russia	(Rouble)	30.8804	−0.1232	44.9757	−0.2322	51.4837	0.1216
Saudi Arabia	(SR)	3.7502	—	5.4620	−0.0064	6.2524	−0.0396
Singapore	(S$)	1.4268	0.0030	2.0781	0.0019	2.3788	0.0200
South Africa	(R)	7.5828	0.1118	11.0439	0.1501	12.6420	0.2652
South Korea	(Won)	1224.50	−2.3000	1783.42	−5.4354	2041.49	9.1082
Sweden	(SKr)	7.0332	0.0307	10.2435	0.0328	11.7258	0.1250
Switzerland	(SFr)	1.0404	0.0003	1.5152	−0.0014	1.7345	0.0114
Taiwan	(T$)	32.6380	−0.0755	47.5356	−0.1656	54.4141	0.2192
Thailand	(Bt)	34.0050	—	49.5266	−0.0577	56.6932	0.3588
Tunisia	(Dinar)	1.3021	0.0022	1.8965	0.0010	2.1709	0.0173
Turkey	(Lira)	1.5027	0.0131	2.1886	0.0165	2.5052	0.0374
UAE	(Dirham)	3.6730	—	5.3495	−0.0062	6.1236	0.0387
UK (0.5998)*	(£)	1.6672	0.0105	0.8736	−0.0066	—	—
One Month		1.6670	−0.0001	0.8737	0.0000	—	—
Three Month		1.6670	−0.0001	0.8737	0.0001	—	—
One Year		1.6662	0.0000	0.8743	−0.0001	—	—
Ukraine	(Hrywnja)	– 8.3850	−0.0450	12.2124	12.2124	13.9795	0.0139
Uruguay	(Peso)	22.3000	—	32.4789	32.4789	37.1786	0.2353
USA	($)	—	—	1.4565	−0.0017	1.6672	0.0105
One Month		—	—	1.4565	0.0000	1.6670	−0.0001
Three Month		—	—	1.4564	0.0000	1.6670	−0.0001
One Year		—	—	1.4568	−0.0001	1.6662	0.0000
Venezuela†	(Bolivar Fuerte)	2.1473	—	3.1275	−0.0036	3.5800	0.0226
Vietnam	(Dong)	17829.5	—	25967.8	−30.3099	29725.3	188.102
Euro (0.6866)*	(Euro)	1.4565	−0.0017	—	—	1.1447	0.0086
One Month		1.4565	0.0000	—	—	1.1446	−0.0001
Three Month		1.4564	0.0000	—	—	1.1446	−0.0001
One Year		1.4568	−0.0001	—	—	1.1438	0.0001
SDR		0.6329	−0.0001	0.9217	−0.0012	1.0551	0.0065

Rates are derived from WM/Reuters at 4pm (London time). *The closing mid-point rates for the Euro and £ against the $ are shown in brackets. The other figures in the dollar column of both the Euro and Sterling rows are in the reciprocal form in line with market convention. †New Venezuelan Bolivar Fuerte introduced on Jan 1, 2008. Currency redenominated by 1000. Some values are rounded by the F.T. The exchange rates printed in this table are also available on the Internet at **http://www.FT.com/marketsdata**.

Euro Locking Rates: Austrian Schilling 13.7603, Belgium/Luxembourg Franc 40.3399, Cyprus 0.585274, Finnish Markka 5.94572, French Franc 6.55957, German Mark 1.95583, Greek Drachma 340.75, Irish Punt 0.787564, Italian Lira1936.27, Malta 0.4293, Netherlands Guilder 2.20371, Portuguese Escudo 200.482, Slovenia Tolar 239.64, Spanish Peseta 166.386.

Quotes for Thursday, September 10, published September 2009, p. 20.

Source: Financial Times, Quotes for Thursday, September 10, 2009, published September 13, 2009, p. 20.

EXCHANGE RATE QUOTATIONS AND TERMINOLOGY

Figure 7.2 lists currency exchange rates for September 10, 2009, as published by the *Financial Times*. The exchange rate listed is for a specific country's currency, for example, the Argentina peso, against the U.S. dollar (Peso 3.8538/$), the European euro (Peso 5.6128/€), and the British pound (Peso 6.4250/£). The rate listed is termed a "mid-rate" because it is the middle or average of the rates at which currency traders buy currency (bid rate) and sell currency (offer rate).

The U.S. dollar has been the focal point of most currency trading since the 1940s. As a result, most of the world's currencies have been quoted against the dollar—Mexican pesos per dollar, Brazilian real per dollar, Hong Kong dollars per dollar, etc. This quotation convention is also followed against the world's major currencies as listed in Figure 7.2. For example the Japanese yen is commonly quoted as ¥91.7700/$, ¥133.658/€, and ¥152.999/£.

Quotation Conventions

Several of the world's major currency exchange rates, however, follow a specific quotation convention that is the result of tradition and history. The rate of exchange between the U.S. dollar and the euro is always quoted as "dollars per euro" ($/€), $1.4565/€ as listed in Figure 7.2. Similarly, the exchange rate between the U.S. dollar and the British pound is always quoted as $/£, for example, the $1.6672/£ listed under "USA" in Figure 7.2. Many countries that are formerly members of the British Commonwealth will commonly be quoted against the dollar as U.S. dollars per currency like the Australian or Canadian dollars.

Spot Rates and Forward Rates

The majority of the quotes in Figure 7.2 are **spot rates**, the rate of exchange between two currencies for immediate delivery. (Although it is termed immediate, in actual practice settlement occurs two business days following the agreed-upon exchange.) Figure 7.2 also provides quotations on selected **forward rates**, rates of exchange between currencies for settlement at future dates in time. In a world in which exchange rates change constantly, basically by the minute, this is a very important contract for businesses wishing to "lock-in" a rate of exchange between two currencies at a future point in time. For example, the Japanese yen (¥) is quoted against the dollar ($) spot and for three different forward dates in Figure 7.2: one month, three months, and one year from the current point in time:

Japan (¥)	91.7700
One month	91.7538
Three months	91.7187
One year	91.3419

The forward, like the basic spot rate exchange, can be for any amount of currency. Forward contracts are available for a multitude of currencies (more than what is listed in Figure 7.2) and serve a variety of purposes in global business.

Reciprocal Quotations

Despite the common quotation conventions described above, the quotation of a rate of exchange can always be reversed—for example, quoting British pounds per U.S. dollar rather than U.S. dollars per pound—by calculating the reciprocal. The spot rate of $1.6672/£ in Figure 7.2 under "USA" can be reversed as:

$$\frac{1}{\$1.6672/£} = £0.5998/\$$$

which is the exact rate quoted for the pound in parentheses next to the "UK" listing. Depending on the exact type of business calculation being performed, one form of the same exchange rate quotation may be preferred over the other for simple clarity.

Cross Rates

Although it is common among exchange traders worldwide to quote currency values against the U.S. dollar, it is not necessary. Any currency's value can be stated in terms of any other currency. When the exchange rate of a currency is stated without using the U.S. dollar as a reference it is referred to as a **cross rate**. For example, if the Japanese yen and Mexican peso are both quoted against the U.S. dollar, they would appear as ¥91.7700/$ and Peso 13.4679/$. But if the yen per peso cross rate is needed, it can be calculated:

$$\frac{¥91.7700/\$}{\text{Peso } 13.4679/\$} = \text{Peso } 6.8140/\$$$

The yen per peso cross rate of Peso 6.8140/$ is the third side of a triangle of currencies (yen, dollar, euro) that must be true if the two exchange rates are known. If one of the exchange rates changes due to market forces, the others must adjust for the three exchange rates to again be in alignment. If they are out of alignment, it would be possible to make a profit simply by exchanging one currency for a second, the second for a third, and the third back to the first. This is known as *triangular*

spot rates Contracts that provide for two parties to exchange currencies with delivery in two business days.

forward rates Contracts that provide for two parties to exchange currencies on a future date at an agreed-upon exchange rate.

cross rates Exchange rate quotations which do not include the U.S. dollar as one of the two currencies quoted.

Figure 7.3 FT Guide To World Currencies

Sep11		£ STG	Week Change	US $	Week Change	EURO €	Week Change	Yen (× 100)	Week Change
Afghanistan	(Afghani)	79.3440	1.7005	47.5000	0.0000	69.4094	1.8003	52.4427	1.3317
Albania	(Lek)	152.900	0.7189	91.5350	−1.5650	133.756	1.2417	101.060	0.8824
Algeria	(Dinar)	121.071	2.0638	72.4800	−0.3250	105.912	2.2846	80.0221	1.6824
Andorra	(Euro)	1.1432	−0.0053	0.6843	−0.0182	1.0000	0.0000	0.7556	−0.0004
Angola	(Readj. Kwanza)	129.967	2.7855	77.8060	0.0000	113.694	2.9489	85.9023	2.1814
Antigua	(E Carib $)	4.5101	0.0966	2.7000	0.0000	3.9454	0.1024	2.9810	0.0757
Argentina	(Peso)	6.4373	0.1502	3.8538	0.0075	5.6313	0.1568	4.2548	0.1161
Armenia	(Dram)	628.070	17.5473	376.000	2.5000	549.430	17.8088	415.126	13.2318
Aruba	(Guilder)	2.9901	0.0641	1.7900	0 0000	2.6157	0.0679	1.9763	0.0502
Australia	(A $)	1.9287	−0.0050	1.1546	−0.0283	1.6872	0.0034	1.2747	0.0019
Austria	(Euro)	1.1432	−0.0053	0.6843	−0.0182	1.0000	0.0000	0.7556	−0.0004
Azerbaijan	(New Manat)	1.3444	0.0289	0.8048	0.0000	1.1760	0.0305	0.8885	0.0226
Azores	(Euro)	1.1432	−0.0053	0.6843	−0.0182	1.0000	0.0000	0.7556	−0.0004
Bahamas	(Bahama $)	1.6704	0.0358	1.0000	0.0000	1.4613	0.0379	1.1041	0.0280
Bahrain	(Dinar)	0.6298	0.0135	0.3770	0.0000	0.5509	0.0143	0.4162	0.0106
Balearic Is	(Euro)	1.1432	−0.0053	0.6843	−0.0182	1.0000	0.0000	0.7556	−0.0004
Bangladesh	(Taka)	115.349	2.4722	69.0550	0.0000	100.907	2.6172	76.2407	1.9361
Barbados	(Barb $)	3.3408	0.0716	2.0000	0.0000	2.9225	0.0758	2.2081	0.0561
Belarus	(Rouble)	4652.06	24.5114	2785.00	−46.0000	4069.58	40.0774	3074.80	28.5848
Belgium	(Euro)	1.1432	−0.0053	0.6843	−0.0182	1.0000	0.0000	0.7556	−0.0004
Belize	(B $)	3.2573	0.0698	1.9500	0.0000	2.8494	0.0739	2.1529	0.0547
Benin	(CFA Fr)	749.845	−3.4678	448.901	−11.9531	655.957	−0.0001	495.613	−0.2761
Bermuda	(Bermudian $)	1.6704	0.0358	1.0000	0.0000	1.4613	0.0379	1.1041	0.0280
Bhutan	(Ngultrum)	80.9727	1.0652	48.4750	−0.4100	70.8341	1.2537	53.5192	0.9179
Bolivia	(Boliviano)	11.7262	0.2513	7.0200	0.0000	10.2580	0.2661	7.7505	0.1968
Bosnia Herzegovina	(Marka)	2.2358	−0.0103	1.3385	−0.0357	1.9558	0.0000	1.4777	−0.0008
Botswana	(Pula)	11.1509	0.0876	6.6756	−0.0926	9.7547	0.1212	7.3702	0.0875
Brazil	(Real)	3.0192	0.0088	1.8075	−0.0450	2.6412	0.0046	1.9955	0.0023
Brunei	(Brunei $)	2.3752	0.0232	1.4219	−0.0170	2.0778	0.0297	1.5699	0.0216
Bulgaria	(Lev)	2.2363	−0.0100	1.3388	−0.0354	1.9563	0.0003	1.4781	−0.0006
Burkina Faso	(CFA Fr)	749.845	−3.4678	448.901	−11.9531	655.957	−0.0001	495.613	−0.2761
Burma	(Kyat) (o)	10.7073	0.2295	6.4100	0.0000	9.3666	0.2429	7.0770	0.1797
Burundi	(Burundi Fr)	2055.85	44.0609	1230.75	0.0000	1798.43	46.6454	1358.82	34.5060
Cambodia	(Riel)	6893.74	147.747	4127.00	0.0000	6030.58	156.413.	4556.44	115.707
Cameroon	(CFA Fr)	749.845	−3.4678	448.901	−11.9531	655.957	−0.0001	495.613	−0.2761
Canada	(Canadian $)	1.7940	0.0111	1.0740	−0.0168	1.5693	0.0169	1.1857	0.0121
Canary Is	(Euro)	1.1432	−0.0053	0.6843	−0.0182	1.0000	0.0000	0.7556	−0.0004
Cape Verde	(CV Escudo)	132.045	2.8300	79.0500	0.0000	115.512	2.9960	87.2757	2.2163
Cayman Island	(CI $)	1.3698	0.0294	0.8200	0.0000	1.1983	0.0311	0.9053	0.0230
Cent. Afr. Rep.	(CFA Fr)	749.845	−3.4678	448.901	−11.9531	655.957	−0.0001	495.613	−0.2761
Chad	(CFA Fr)	749.845	−3.4678	448.901	−11.9531	655.957	−0.0001	495.613	−0.2761
Chile	(Chilean Peso)	918.135	16.5717	549.650	−1.9000	803.176	18.1274	606.845	13.3658
China	(Yuan)	11.4072	0.2428	6.8290	−0.0010	9.9789	0.2574	7.5396	0.1904
Colombia	(Col Peso)	3310.15	14.4270	1981.65	−34.5750	2895.69	25.8924	2187.86	18.3552
Comoros	(Fr)	562.384	−2.6008	336.676	−8.9648	491.968	0.0000	371.710	−0.2071
Congo	(CFA Fr)	749.845	−3.4678	448.901	−11.9531	655.957	−0.0001	495.613	−0.2761
Congo (DemRep)	(Congo Fr)	1403.50	74.7255	840.219	27.3129	1227.77	70.7201	927.650	52.9461
Costa Rica	(Colon)	977.644	15.5178	585.275	−3.3250	855.234	17.4493	646.177	12.8313
Cote d'Ivoire	(CFA Fr)	749.845	−3.4678	448.901	−11.9531	655.957	−0.0001	495.613	−0.2761
Croatia	(Kuna)	8.3824	−0.0401	5.0182	−0.1344	7.3329	−0.0011	5.5404	−0.0039
Cuba	(Cuban Peso)	1.6704	0.0358	1.0000	0.0000	1.4613	0.0379	1.1041	0.0280
Cyprus	(Euro)	1.1432	−0.0053	0.6843	−0.0182	1.0000	0.0000	0.7556	−0.0004
Czech Rep.	(Koruna)	29.0784	−0.1919	17.4080	−0.4987	25.4375	−0.0500	19.2194	−0.0486
Denmark	(Danish Krone)	8.5083	−0.0396	5.0936	−0.1358	7.4430	−0.0002	5.6236	−0.0033
Djibouti Rep	(Djib Fr)	293.606	5.9656	175.770	−0.2000	256.844	6.3770	194.060	4.7128
Dominica	(E Carib $)	4.5101	0.0966	2.7000	0.0000	3.9454	0.1024	2.9810	0.0757
Dominican Rep	(D Peso)	60.0259	1.0985	35.9350	−0.1150	52.5101	1.1983	39.6743	0.8838
Ecuador	(Sucre)	41760.0	895.000	25000.0	0.0000	36531.3	947.500	27601.4	700.913
Egypt	(Egyptian £)	9.2190	0.1764	5.5190	−0.0130	8.0647	0.1907	6.0933	0.1408
El Salvador	(Colon)	14.6118	0.3132	8.7475	0.0000	12.7823	0.3316	9.6577	0.2453
Equat'l Guinea	(CFA Fr)	749.845	−3.4678	448.901	−11.9531	655.957	−0.0001	495.613	−0.2761
Eritrea	(Nakfa)	25.0560	0.5370	15.0000	0.0000	21.9188	0.5685	16.5609	0.4206
Estonia	(Kroon)	17.8860	−0.0827	10.7076	−0.2851	15.6465	0.0000	11.8218	−0.0066
Ethiopia	(Ethiopian Birr)	21.0150	0.4677	12.5808	0.0106	18.3837	0.4918	13.8899	0.3641
Falkland Is	(Falk £)	1.0000	0.0000	0.5987	−0.0131	0.8748	0.0040	0.6610	0.0027
Faroe Is	(Danish Krone)	8.5083	−0.0396	5.0936	−0.1358	7.4430	−0.0002	5.6236	−0.0033
Fiji Is	(Fiji $)	3.2759	0.0008	1.9612	−0 0425	2.8658	0.0140	2.1652	0.0093
Finland	(Euro)	1.1432	−0.0053	0.6843	−0.0182	1.0000	0.0000	0.7556	0.0004
France	(Euro)	1.1432	'0.0053	0.6843	−0.0182	1.0000	0.0000	0.7556	−0.004
Fr. Cty/Africa	(CFA Fr)	749.845	−3.4678	448.901	−11.9531	655.957	−0.0001	495.613	−0.2761
Fr. Guiana	(Euro)	1.1432	−0.0053	0.6843	−0.0182	1.0000	0.0000	0.7556	−0.0004
Fr. Pacific Is	(CFP Fr)	136.318	−0.6305	81.6082	−2.1731	119.250	0.0000	90.1001	−0.0502
Gabon	(CFA Fr)	749.845	−3.4678	448.901	−11.9531	655.957	−0.0001	495.613	0.2761
Gambia	(Dalasi)	44.4746	0.4221	26.6250	−0.3250	38.9059	0.5466	29.3955	0.3968
Georgia	(Lari)	2.8098	0.0572	1.6821	−0.0019	2.4580	0.0611	1.8571	0.0451
Germany	(Euro)	1.1432	−0.0053	0.6843	−0.0182	1.0000	0.0000	0.7556	−0.0004
Ghana	(Cedi)	2.4313	0.0460	1.4555	−0.0038	2.1269	0.0499	1.6070	0.0368
Gibraltar	(Gib £)	1.0000	0.0000	0.5987	−0.0131	0.8748	0.0040	0.6610	0.0027
Greece	(Euro)	1.1432	−0.0053	0.6843	−0.0182	1.0000	0.0000	0.7556	−0.0004
Greenland	(Danish Krone)	8.5083	−0.0396	5.0936	−0.1358	7.4430	−0.0002	5.6236	−0.0033
Grenada	(E Carib $)	4.5101	0.0966	2.7000	0.0000	3.9454	0.1024	2.9810	0.0757
Guadeloupe	(Euro)	1.1432	−0.0053	0.6843	−0.0182	1.0000	0.0000	0.7556	−0.0004
Guam	(US $)	1.6704	0.0358	1.0000	0.0000	1.4613	0.0379	1.1041	0.0280
Guatemala	(Quetzal)	13.8727	0.3799	8.3050	0.0505	12.1357	0.3867	9.1692	0.2872
Guinea	(Fr)	8393.77	179.895	5025.00	0.0000	7342.79	190.448	5547.89	140.884
Guinea-Bissau	(CFR Fr)	749.845	−3.4678	448.901	−11.9531	655.957	−0.0001	495.613	−0.2761
Guyana	Guyana Dollar	339.074	5.6324	202.990	−1.0000	296.619	6.2700	224.113	4.6151
Haiti	(Gourde)	66.3985	1.4231	39.7500	0.0000	58.0847	1.5066	43.8863	1.1145
Honduras	(Lempira)	31.5622	0.6765	18.8950	0.0000	27.6104	0.7162	20.8612	0.5298
Hong Kong	(HK $)	12.9459	0.2771	7.7502	−0.0003	11.3249	0.2934	8.5566	0.2170
Hungary	(Forint)	310.943	−2.5462	186.149	−5.6347	272.010	−0.9650	205.519	0.8440
Iceland	(Icelandic Krona)	207.430	−0.7443	124.180	−3.1750	181.458	0.1873	137.102	0.0652
India	(Indian Rupee)	80.9727	1.0652	48.4750	−0.4100	70.8341	1.2537	53.5192	0.9179
Indonesia	(Rupiah)	16562.0	28.0390	9915.00	−200.000	14488.3	91.1100	10946.7	62.7781
Iran	(Rial)	16628.8	372.735	9955.00	10.0000	14546.7	391.528	10990.9	289.864
Iraq	(New Iraqi Dinar)	1920.96	41.1700	1150.00	0.0000	1680.44	43.5850	1269.67	32.2420
Irish Rep	(Euro)	1.1432	−0.0053	0.6843	0.0182	1.0000	0.0000	0.7556	−0.0004
Israel	(Shekel)	6.2916	0.1578	3.7665	0.0140	5.5038	0.1627	4.1584	0.1207
Italy	(Euro)	1.1432	−0.0053	0.6843	−0.0182	1.0000	0.0000	0.7556	−0.0004
Jamaica	(Jamaican $)	147.455	2.6699	88.2750	−0.3000	128.992	2.9186	97.4607	2.1521
Japan	(Yen)	151.297	−0.6151	90.5750	−2.3600	132.353	0.0737	100.000	–
Jordan	(Jordanian Dinar)	1.1839	0.0270	0.7088	0.0010	1.0357	0.0283	0.7825	0.0210
Kazakhstan	(Tenge)	252.097	5.5664	150.920	0.1000	220.532	5.8623	166.624	4.3389
Kenya	(Kenyan Shilling)	126.566	1.9607	75.7700	−0.4600	110.719	2.2170	83.6544	1.6294
Kiribati	(Australian $)	1.9287	−0.0050	1.1546	−0.0283	1.6872	0.0034	1.2747	0.0019
Korea North	(Won)(o)	238.951	5.1212	143.050	0.0000	209.032	5.4216	157.935	4.0106
Korea South	(Won)	2040.89	11.6206	1221.80	−19.6500	1785.36	18.3374	1348.94	13.1112
Kuwait	(Kuwaiti Dinar)	0.4787	0.0094	0.2866	−0.0006	0.4187	0.0101	0.3164	0.0074
Kyrgyzstan	(Som)	73.7900	1.5406	44.1750	−0.0250	64.5508	1.6387	48.7717	1.2116
Laos	(New Kip)	14160.0	303.477	8477.00	0.0000	12387.0	321.278	9359.09	237.666
Latvia	(Lats)	0.8035	−0.0026	0.4811	−0.0121	0.7029	0.0010	0.5311	0.0005
Lebanon	(Lebanese £)	2509.78	53.7895	1502.50	0.0000	2195.53	56.9448	1658.85	42.1249
Lesotho	(Maloti)	12.4287	−0.0655	7.4405	−0.2030	10.8725	−0.0069	8.2147	−0.0098
Liberia	(Liberian $)	119.434	2.4780	71.5000	−0.0500	104.479	2.6387	78.9401	1.9508
Libya	(Libyan Dinar)	2.0429	0.0258	1.2230	−0.0110	1.7871	−0.0307	1.3503	0.0225
Liechtenstein	(Swiss Fr)	1.7301	−0.0123	1.0357	−0.0302	1.5135	−0.0037	1.1435	−0.0035
Lithuania	(Litas)	3.9471	−0.0183	2.3630	−0.0630	3.4529	−0.0000	2.6088	−0.0015
Luxembourg	(Euro)	1.1432	−0.0053	0.6843	−0.0182	1.0000	0.0000	0.7556	−0.0004
Macao	(Pataca)	13.3343	0.2854	7.9827	−0.0003	11.6647	0.3022	8.8133	0.2235
Macedonia	(Denar)	70.3239	−0.4707	42.1000	−1.2100	61.5187	−0.1267	46.4808	−0.1217
Madagascar	(Ariary)	3248.93	95.7864	1945.00	16.0000	2842.13	96.4905	2147.39	71.7474
Madeira	(Euro)	1.1432	−0.0053	0.6843	−0.0182	1.0000	0.0000	0.7556	−0.0004
Malawi	(Kwacha)	234.868	5.0339	140.606	0.0001	205.460	5.3292	155.237	3.9422
Malaysia	(Ringgit)	5.8339	0.0711	3.4925	−0.0330	5.1034	0.0854	3.8559	0.0624
Maldive Is	(Rufiyaa)	21.3812	0.4583	12.8000	0.0000	18.7040	0.4851	14.1319	0.3589
Mali Rep	(CFA Fr)	749.845	−3.4678	448.901	−11.9531	655.957	−0.0001	495.613	−0.2761
Malta	(Euro)	1.1432	−0.0053	0.6843	−0.0182	1.0000	−0.0000	0.7556	−0.0004
Martinique	(Euro)	1.1432	−0.0053	0.6843	−0.0182	1.0000	0.0000	0.7556	−0.0004
Mauritania	(Ouguiya)	439.132	14.1359	262.890	2.8900	384.149	14.0773	290.246	10.4802
Mauritius	(Maur Rupee)	51.3648	0.0384	30.7500	−0.6500	44.9335	0.2403	33.9498	0.1627
Mexico	(Mexican Peso)	22.2781	0.2821	13.3370	−0.1195	19.4887	0.3354	14.7248	0.2453
Moldova	(Leu)	18.6192	0.3362	11.1465	−0.0385	16.2879	0.3677	12.3064	0.2711
Monaco	(Euro)	1.1432	−0.0053	0.6843	−0.0182	1.0000	0.0000	0.7556	−0.0004
Mongolia	(Tugrik)	2366.37	57.4998	1416.65	4.1500	2070.08	59.5980	1564.06	44.1835
Montenegro	(Euro)(1)	1.1432	−0.0053	0.6843	−0.0182	1.0000	0.0000	0.7556	−0.0004
Montserrat	(E Carib $)	4.5101	0.0966	2.7000	0.0000	3.9454	0.1024	2.9810	0.0757
Morocco	(Dirham)	12.9712	−0.0005	7.7653	−0.1704	11.3471	0.0519	8.5733	0.0344
Mozambique	(Metical)	45.2762	−0.1249	27.1050	−0.6700	39.6072	0.0736	29.9255	0.0390
Namibia	(Dollar)	12.4287	−0.0655	7.4405	−0.2030	10.8725	−0.0069	8.2147	−0.0098
Nauru Is	(Australian $)	1.9287	−0.0050	1.1546	−0.0283	1.6872	0.0034	1.2747	0.0019
Nepal	(Nepalese Rupee)	129.556	1.7044	77.5600	−0.6560	113.335	2.0058	85.6307	1.4687
Netherlands	(Euro)	1.1432	−0.0053	0.6843	−0.0182	1.0000	0.0000	0.7556	−0.0004
N'nd Antilles	(A/Guilder)	2.9901	0.0641	1.7900	0.0000	2.6157	0.0679	1.9763	0.0502
New Zealand	(NZ $)	2.3580	−0.0305	1.4116	−0.0495	2.0628	−0.0170	1.5585	−0.0137
Nicaragua	(Gold Cordoba)	34.2993	0.7665	20.5336	0.0192	30.0047	0.8056	22.6703	0.5964
Niger Rep	(CFA Fr)	749.845	−3.4678	448.901	−11.9531	655.957	−0.0001	495.613	−0.2761
Nigeria	(Naira)	257.709	5.7031	154.280	0.1100	225.442	6.0038	170.334	4.4438
Norway	(Nor. Krone)	9.8716	−0.0223	5.9098	−0.1431	8.6356	0.0204	6.5247	0.0118
Oman	(Rial Omani)	0.6431	0.0137	0.3850	−0.0001	0.5626	0.0145	0.4251	0.0107
Pakistan	(Pak. Rupee)	138.384	2.8760	82.8450	−0.0550	121.057	3.0616	91.4656	2.2635
Panama	(Balboa)	1.6704	0.0358	1.0000	0.0000	1.4613	0.0379	1.1041	0.0280
Papua New Guinea	(Kina)	4.4840	0.1064	2.6844	0.0063	3.9225	0.1107	2.9637	0.0820
Paraguay	(Guarani)	8226.72	110.925	4925.00	−40.0000	7196.66	129.719	5437.48	95.0391
Peru	(New Sol)	4.8868	0.0851	2.9255	−0.0120	4.2749	0.0938	3.2299	0.0691
Philippines	(Peso)	80.6971	1.2146	48.3100	−0.3150	70.5930	1.3826	53.3370	1.0155
Pitcairn Is	(Sterling £)	1.0000	0.0000	0.5987	−0.0131	0.8748	0.0040	0.6610	0.0027
Poland	(Zloty)	4.7503	0.0408	2.8438	−0.0374	4.1555	0.0546	3.1397	0.0395
Portugal	(Euro)	1.1432	−0.0053	0.6843	−0.0182	1.0000	0.0000	0.7556	−0.0004
Puerto Rico	(US $)	1.6704	0.0358	1.0000	0.0000	1.4613	0.0379	1.1041	0.0280
Qatar	(Riyal)	6.0824	0.1308	3.6413	0.0003	5.3208	0.1384	4.0201	0.1024
Reunion Is. de la	(Euro)	1.1432	−0.0053	0.6843	−0.0182	1.0000	0.0000	0.7556	−0.0004
Romania	(New Leu)	4.8963	0.0132	2.9312	−0.0561	4.2833	0.0313	3.2362	0.0218
Russia	(Rouble)	51.1502	−0.6186	30.6215	−1.0491	44.7457	−0.3327	33.8079	−0.2703
Rwanda	(Fr)	950.483	21.4741	569.015	0.6750	831.474	22.5265	628.225	16.6795
St Christopher	(E Carib $)	4.5101	0.0966	2.7000	0.0000	3.9454	0.1024	2.9810	0.0757
St Helena	(£)	1.0000	0.0000	0.5987	−0.0131	0.8748	0.0040	0.6610	0.0027
St Lucia	(E Carib $)	4.5101	0.0966	2.7000	0.0000	3.9454	0.1024	2.9810	0.0757
St Pierre & Miquelon	(Euro)	1.1432	−0.0053	0.6843	−0.0182	1.0000	0.0000	0.7556	−0.0004
St Vincent	(E Carib $)	4.5101	0.0966	2.7000	0.0000	3.9454	0.1024	2.9810	0.0757
San Marino	(Euro)	1.1432	−0.0053	0.6843	−0.0182	1.0000	0.0000	0.7556	−0.0004
Sao Tome	(Dobra)	25473.6	104.608	15250.0	−270.000	22284.1	193.671	16836.9	137.032
Saudi Arabia	(Riyal)	6.2644	0.1344	3.7502	0.0001	5.4800	0.1422	4.1404	0.1052
Senegal	(CFA Fr)	749.845	−3.4678	448.901	−11.9531	655.957	−0.0001	495.613	−0.2761
Serbia	(Dinar)	106.914	−0.2336	64.0050	−1.5447	93.5274	0.2272	70.6652	0.1324
Seychelles	(Rupee)	20.4257	−0.1324	12.2280	0.3489	17.8681	−0.0331	13.5004	−0.0325
Sierra Leone	(Leone)	6029.77	222.222	3609.77	56.8900	5274.78	217.785	3985.39	162.420
Singapore	($)	2.3752	0.0232	1.4219	−0.0170	2.0778	0.0297	1.5699	0.0216
Slovakia	(Euro)	1.1432	−0.0053	0.6843	−0.0182	1.0000	0.0000	0.7556	−0.0004
Slovenia	(Euro)	1.1432	−0.0053	0.6843	−0.0182	1.0000	0.0000	0.7556	−0.0004
Solomon Is	($)	13.4178	0.5676	7.9968	0.1598	11.7378	0.5483	8.8289	0.3962
Somali Rep	(Shilling)	2333.55	82.7046	1397.00	20.000	2041.37	81.4133	1542.37	60.6875
South Africa	(Rand)	12.4287	−0.0655	7.4405	−0.2030	10.8725	−0.0069	8.2147	−0.0098
Spain	(Euro)	1.1432	−0.0053	0.6843	−0.0182	1.0000	0.0000	0.7556	−0.0004
Spanish Ports N Af.	(Euro)	1.1432	−0.0053	0.6843	−0.0182	1.0000	0.0000	0.7556	−0.0004
Sri Lanka	(Rupee)	191.804	4.1516	114.825	0.0250	167.788	4.3875	126.773	3.2462
Sudan Rep	(£)	4.0046	0.0373	2.3974	−0.0297	3.5032	0.0486	2.6469	0.0353
Surinam	(Dollar)	4.5853	0.0983	2.7450	0.0000	4.0112	0.1041	3.0306	0.0770
Swaziland	(Lilangeni)	12.4287	−0.0655	7.4405	−0.2030	10.8725	−0.0069	8.2147	−0.0098
Sweden	(Krona)	11.6828	−0.1365	6.9941	−0.2366	10.2200	−0.0718	7.7218	−0.0585
Switzerland	(Fr)	1.7301	−0.0123	1.0357	−0.0302	1.5135	−0.0037	1.1435	−0.0035
Syria	(£)	76.8384	1.6468	46.0000	0.0000	67.2175	1.7434	50.7866	1.2897
Taiwan	($)	54.4918	0.7142	32.6220	−0.2775	47.6689	0.8414	36.0166	0.6160
Tajikistan	(Somoni)	6.2264	0.1334	3.7275	0.0000	5.4468	0.1413	4.1154	0.1045
Tanzania	(Shilling)	2183.21	36.9830	1307.00	−6.0000	1909.85	40.9952	1443.00	30.1876
Thailand	(Baht)	56.7268	1.0360	33.9600	−0.1100	49.6241	1.1305	37.4938	0.8338
Togo Rep	(CFA Fr)	749.845	−3.4678	448.901	−11.9531	655.957	−0.0001	495.613	−0.2761
Tonga Is	(Pa'anga)	3.2180	0.0638	1.9260	−0.0028	2.8151	0.0685	2.1265	0.0510
Trinidad/ Tobago	($)	10.5526	0.2805	6.3174	0.0332	9.2314	0.2868	6.9748	0.2128
Tunisia	(Dinar)	2.1710	0.0074	1.2997	−0.0240	1.8991	0.0152	1.4349	0.0107
Turkey	(New Lira)	2.4957	0.0401	1.4941	−0.0082	2.1832	0.0450	1.6495	0.0331
Turkmenistan	(Manat)	23744.7	508.897	14215.0	0.0000	20771.7	538.749	15694.2	398.539
Turks & Caicos	(US $)	1.6704	0.0358	1.0000	0.0000	1.4613	0.0379	1.1041	0.0280
Tuvalu	(Australian $)	0.5185	0.0013	1.1546	−0.0283	0.5927	−0.0012	1.2747	0.0019
Uganda	(New Shilling)	3282.34	21.3090	1965.00	−30.0000	2871.36	31.7730	2169.47	22.8112
Ukraine	(Hryvnia)	14.2385	−0.2923	8.5240	−0.3655	12.4557	−0.1972	9.4110	−0.1543
UAE	(Dirham)	6.1353	0.1315	3.6730	0.0000	5.3671	0.1392	4.0551	0.1030
United Kingdom	(£)	1.0000	0.0000	0.5987	−0.0131	0.8748	0.0040	0.6610	0.0027
United States	(US $)	1.6704	0.0358	1.0000	0.0000	1.4613	0.0379	1.1041	0.0280
Uruguay	(Peso Uruguay)	36.9159	0.3826	22.1000	−0.2500	32.2937	0.4818	24.3997	0.3506
Uzbekistan	(Sum)	2499.47	55.5138	1496.33	1.1900	2186.51	58.4048	1652.03	43.2324
Vanuatu	(Vatu)	166.188	0.4641	99.4900	−1.8950	145.380	1.0733	109.843	0.7503
Vatican	(Euro)	1.1432	−0.0053	0.6843	−0.0182	1.0000	0.0000	0.7556	−0.0004
Venezuela†	(Bolivar Fuerte)	3.5800	0.0719	2.1473	0.0000	3.1275	0.0657	2.3707	0.0602
Vietnam	(Dong)	29775.7	644.692	17825.5	4.0000	26047.5	681.280	19680.4	504.069
Virgin Is-British	(US $)	1.6704	0.0358	1.0000	0.0000	1.4613	0.0379	1.1041	0.0280
Virgin Is-US	(US $)	1.6704	0.0358	1.0000	0.0000	1.4613	0.0379	1.1041	0.0280
Western Samoa	(Tala)	4.2709	0.0009	2.5556	−0.0554	3.7362	0.0180	2.8215	0.0121
Yemen (Rep of)	(Rial)	342.465	7.4297	205.020	0.0550	299.586	7.8486	226.354	5.8072
Zambia	(Kwacha)	7725.60	132.883	4625.00	−20.0000	6758.28	146.821	5106.27	108.149
Zimbabwe	($)(2)	604.017	12.9453	361.600	0.0000	528.388	13.7046	399.227	10.1380
SDR	(SDR)	1.0538	0.0068	0.6309	−0.0097	0.9219	0.0101	0.6965	0.0073

Euro Locking Rates: Austrian Schilling 13.7603. Belgium/Luxembourg Franc 40.3399, Cyprus 0.58274, Finnish Markka 5.94573, French Franc 6.55957. German Mark 1.95583, Greek Drachma 340.75. Irish Punt 0.187564, Italian Lira 1936.27, Malts 0.4293, Netherlands Guilder 2.20371. Portuguese Escudo 200.482. Slovakian Koruna 30.1260. Slovenian Tolar 239.64 Spanish Peseta 166.386. Abbrev: (o) Official rate (v) Floating rate. †Official rate set by Venezuelan government 2150 per USD; WM/Reuters rate is for valuation of capital assets. (1) Montenegro has adopted the Euro although not a formal member of the Eurozone. (2) Zimbabwe Dollar revalued on Feb 3rd. Rates derived from THE WM/REUTERS CLOSING SPOT RATES & Reuters. **FT Readers Enquiries: 020 7873 4211.**

Source: Financial Times, September 14, 2009.

arbitrage. It is, however, exceedingly rare that rates fall out of alignment for long in this world of computer-based trading and digital exchange.

Percentage Change Calculations

The quotation form is important when calculating the percentage change in an exchange rate. For example, if the spot rate between the Chinese yuan and the U.S. dollar changed from Yuan 6.8200/$ (spot 1) to Yuan 6.2000/$ (spot 2), the percentage change in the value of the Chinese yuan would be:

$$\frac{\text{Spot 1} - \text{Spot 2}}{\text{Spot 2}} \times 100 = \frac{\text{Yuan } 6.8200/\$ - \text{Yuan } 6.2000/\$}{\text{Yuan } 6.2000/\$} \times 100 = +10.00\%$$

The Chinese yuan, because it now requires fewer yuan per dollar, has risen in value versus the U.S. dollar. The rise in value is indicated by the positive sign, and the percentage increase is 10.00 percent. The same percentage change result can be achieved by using the reversed quotations, U.S. dollars per Chinese yuan, if care is taken to *also* reverse the percentage change calculation:

$$\frac{\text{Spot 2} - \text{Spot 1}}{\text{Spot 1}} \times 100 = \frac{\dfrac{1}{\text{Yuan } 6.2000/\$} - \dfrac{1}{\text{Yuan } 6.8200/\$}}{\dfrac{1}{\text{Yuan } 6.8200/\$}} \times 100 = +10.00\%$$

If the percentage changes calculated are not identical, it is normally the result of rounding errors introduced when inverting the spot rates. Both methods are identical when calculated properly. This has led to a painful lesson in many international business contracts: take special care when stating percentage changes in international business contracts including exchange rate terms.

A more comprehensive listing of the world's currencies is presented in Figure 7.3, the *FT Guide to World Currencies*. This list of 220 different currency values against the pound, the dollar, the euro, and the yen, is about as complete a listing as you will find. It is, in many respects, a reminder of the expanse and complexity of the global business environment.

SIZE OF THE MARKET

The market for foreign exchange is the largest financial market in the world. The Bank for International Settlements (BIS), which conducts a global survey of foreign exchange trading activity every three years, estimates that the spot exchange rate market alone is more than $1 trillion per day.

As illustrated by Figure 7.4, both spot and forward currency trading has been growing rapidly over the past two decades. The growth in currency trading is, in many ways, a result of the potential profits from trading alone. Although historically the trading of currencies was primarily for commercial purposes, for purchasing and payment, the size and liquidity in global currency exchange has made currencies the object of investment and speculation. Many banks and hedge funds now buy currencies in the spot markets for shorter-term speculation, moving in and out of currency holdings often in minutes and hours at the longest.

But the global currency markets are also reflecting a bit of *the old* and a bit of *the new*. Figure 7.5 shows the growth of global currency trading by city.

The old—the central role that London (United Kingdom) has played in global finance for more than *a century*, continues. London is today the absolute center of the global capital markets—which clearly includes currency trading. Second to London, New York (United States) continues to prosper as well, although the

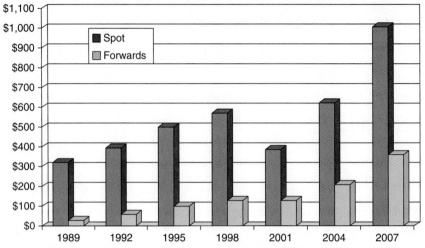

Figure 7.4   Global Foreign Exchange Market Turnover, 1989–2007
(daily averages in April, billions of U.S. dollars)

Source: Bank for International Settlements, "Triennial Central Bank Survey of Foreign Exchange and Derivatives Market Activity in April 2007: Preliminary Global Results," October 2007, www.bis.org.

long-term impacts of the global financial crisis of 2007–2009 are as yet unknown. Switzerland has always filled a rather unique role as a bastion of political stability, neutrality, and—ultimately critical for global commerce—safety. That unique position continues.

The new, however, is the growth to prominence of Hong Kong and Singapore. These two cities increasingly demonstrate the growth of the Asian marketplace, and China itself, including world currency trading activity. Whereas Japan played somewhat of a strong pivotal role throughout the 1990s, the rapid growth of the Asian

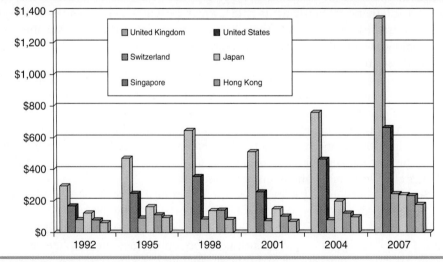

Figure 7.5   Top Six Geographic Trading Centers in the Foreign
Exchange Market, 1992–2007 (daily averages in April,
billions of U.S. dollars)

Source: Bank for International Settlements, "Triennial Central Bank Survey of Foreign Exchange and Derivatives Market Activity in April 2007: Preliminary Global Results," September 2007, www.bis.org.

Figure 7.6　Global Currency Trading: The Trading Day

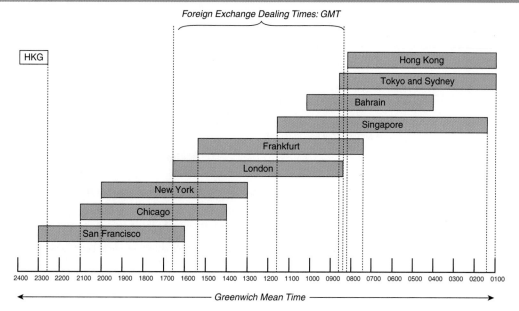

The currency trading day literally extends 24 hours per day. The busiest time of the day, however, is that period in which New York and London overlap, the world's most liquid time of day.

marketplace has clearly led a move toward prominence of Singapore and Hong Kong as centers of global finance and commerce for the coming years.

MARKET STRUCTURE

The global market for foreign currencies is an *informal market,* a market made up of hundreds of different financial institutions and trading houses. This means that is has no central place, pit, or floor like the New York Stock Exchange, where the trading takes place. The global currency market is actually thousands of telecommunications links among financial institutions in the major financial centers around the globe, and it is open nearly 24 hours a day. Someone, somewhere, is nearly always open for business. Figure 7.6 illustrates how the trading day moves with the sun across the major trading centers.

THE BIG THREE (OR FOUR?)

Although there are more than 200 currencies in the world today, different currencies have dominated global business in different combinations in recent history. Between 1950 and 1970, global currency markets were dominated by the U.S. dollar, the British pound, and several major European currencies, including the French franc, the German mark, and the Swiss franc. The 1980s and 1990s saw the growth of the Japanese yen as a pillar of size and strength. But the yen itself fell in influence follow-ing the long extended sluggish performance of the Japanese economy in the later half of the 1990s.

With the introduction of the European euro in 1999, the currency landscape changed significantly once again—but to be simpler. The dollar, the euro, and the yen now made up more than 70 percent of all global currency trading. The euro became the focal currency for Europe—eastern and western—as well as very influen-tial throughout the Mediterranean countries and Africa. The U.S. dollar continued

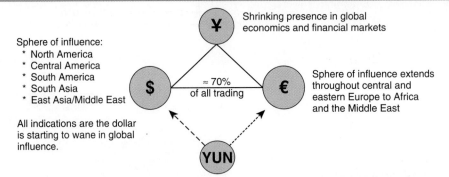

Figure 7.7   The New Global Currency Landscape

Shrinking presence in global economics and financial markets

Sphere of influence:
* North America
* Central America
* South America
* South Asia
* East Asia/Middle East

≈ 70% of all trading

Sphere of influence extends throughout central and eastern Europe to Africa and the Middle East

All indications are the dollar is starting to wane in global influence.

Chinese yuan (YUN) or renminbi (Rmb) continues to grow in influence in parallel with that of the Chinese economy.

The July 2005 restructuring of the yuan was the first major step toward making the yuan a stronger player in the world currency markets. The continuing source of debate about the yuan, however, is the Chinese government's continued control of its value, as it remains relatively undervalued according to most theories and principles of global business.

its dominance of the Western Hemisphere, with many Latin American countries continuing to peg or manage their currency values to that of the dollar. Asia, however, became an increasingly complex mix of long-term dollar linkages but strong corporate relationships between Japan (the yen) and Europe (the euro) and rapidly growing Asian enterprise.

The post-2000 global business landscape is now seeing the growth of a new currency of influence, the Chinese yuan (or renminbi—it is officially called both by the Bank of China). The historical dominance of the dollar-yen-euro framework (as depicted in Figure 7.7) may be seeing the entry of a new global player. The growing influence of the Chinese economy, as well as its "twin surpluses" noted previously, its Current Account and Capital Account surpluses, have resulted in the Chinese currency now being a money of power and influence.

EVOLUTION OF THE GLOBAL MONETARY SYSTEM

3. To explore the primary linkage between exchange rates and money markets—LIBOR

The mixed fixed/floating exchange rate system operating today is only the latest stage of a continuing process of change. The systems that have preceded the present system varied between gold-based standards (the gold standard) and complex systems in which the U.S. dollar largely took the place of gold (the Bretton Woods Agreement). To understand why the dollar, the euro, and the yen are floating today, it is necessary to return to the (pardon the pun) golden oldies.

THE GOLD STANDARD

gold standard A standard for international currencies in which currency values were stated in terms of gold.

Although there is no recognized starting date, the **gold standard** began sometime in the 1880s and extended up through the outbreak of World War I. The gold standard was premised on three basic ideas:

1. A system of fixed rates of exchange existed between participating countries.
2. "Money" issued by member countries had to be backed by reserves of gold.

3. Gold would act as an automatic adjustment, flowing in and out of countries, and automatically altering the gold reserves of that country if imbalances in trade or investment did occur.

Under the gold standard, each country's currency would be set in value per ounce of gold. For example, the U.S. dollar was defined as $20.67 per ounce, while the British pound sterling was defined as £4.2474 per ounce. Once each currency was defined versus gold, the determination of the exchange rate between the two currencies (or any two currencies) was simple:

$$\frac{\$20.67/\text{ounce of gold}}{£4.2474/\text{ounce of gold}} = \$4.8665/£$$

The use of gold as the pillar of the system was a result of historical tradition, and not anything inherently unique to the metal gold itself. It was shiny, soft, rare, and generally acceptable for payment in all countries.

INTERWAR YEARS, 1919–1939

The 1920s and 1930s were a tumultuous period. The British pound sterling, the dominant currency prior to World War I, survived the war but was greatly weakened. The U.S. dollar returned to the gold standard in 1919, but gold convertibility was largely untested across countries throughout the 1920s, as world trade took long to recover from the destruction of the war. With the economic collapse and bank runs of the 1930s, the U.S. was forced to once again abandon gold convertibility.

The economic depression of the 1930s was worldwide. As countries came under increasingly desperate economic conditions, many resorted to isolationist policies and protectionism. World trade slowed to a trickle, and with it the general need for currency exchange. It was not until the latter stages of World War II that international trade and commerce once again demanded a system for currency convertibility and stability.

BRETTON WOODS AGREEMENT, 1944–1971

The governments of 44 of the Allied Powers gathered together in Bretton Woods, New Hampshire, in 1944 to plan for the postwar international monetary system. The delegates labored long, and in the end all parties agreed that a postwar system would be stable and sustainable only if it was able to provide sufficient liquidity to countries during periods of crisis. Any new system had to have facilities for the extension of credit for countries to defend their currency values.

After weeks of debate (summarized in Focus on Politics), the Bretton Woods Agreement was reached. The plan called for the following:

1. Fixed exchange rates between member countries, termed an "adjustable peg."
2. The establishment of a fund of gold and currencies available to members for stabilization of their respective currencies (the International Monetary Fund). and
3. The establishment of a bank that would provide funding for long-term development projects (the World Bank).

Like the gold standard at the turn of the century, all participants were to establish par values of their currencies in terms of gold. Unlike the prior system, however, there was little if any convertibility of currencies for gold expected. Convertibility in this system was only against the U.S. dollar ("good as gold," pegged at $35/ounce). This reliance on the value of the dollar and on the stability of the U.S. economy led to 25 years of relative calm in the currency markets.

TIMES OF CRISIS, 1971–1973

On August 15, 1971, U.S. President Richard M. Nixon announced that "I have instructed [Treasury] Secretary [John B.] Connally to suspend temporarily the convertibility of the dollar into gold or other assets." With this simple statement, President Nixon effectively ended the fixed exchange rates established at Bretton Woods. In the weeks and months following the August announcement, world currency markets devalued the dollar, although the U.S. had only ended gold convertibility, not officially declared the dollar's value to be less. In late 1971, the Group of Ten finance ministers met at the Smithsonian Institution in Washington, DC, to try to piece together a system to keep world markets operational. First, the dollar was officially devalued to $38/ounce of gold (as if anyone had access to gold convertibility). Secondly, all other major world currencies were revalued against the dollar (the dollar was relatively devalued), and all would now be allowed to vary from their fixed parity rates by plus/minus 2.25 percent from the previous 1.00 percent.

Without convertibility of at least one of the member currencies to gold, the system was doomed from the start. Within weeks, currencies were surpassing their allowed deviation limits; revaluations were occurring more frequently; and the international monetary system was not a "system," it was chaos. Finally, world currency trading nearly ground to a halt in March 1973. After two weeks in which the world's currency markets had literally stopped, they reopened with an implicit agreement that major currencies (particularly the U.S. dollar) be allowed to float in value. In January 1976, the Group of Ten once again met, this time in Jamaica, and the Jamaica Agreement officially recognized what the markets had known for years—the world's currencies were no longer fixed in value.

FLOATING EXCHANGE RATES, 1973–PRESENT

Since March 1973 the world's major currencies have floated in value versus each other. Throughout the 1970s, if a government wished to alter the current value of its currency, or even slow or alter a trending change in the currency's value, the government would simply buy or sell its own currency in the market using its reserves of other major currencies. This process of **direct intervention** was effective as long as the government had deep pockets of foreign currency in order to keep up with the volume of trading on currency markets. For these countries—both then and today—the primary problem is maintaining adequate foreign exchange reserves.

direct intervention The process governments used in the 1970s if they wished to alter the current value of their currency. It was done by simply buying or selling their own currency in the market using their reserves of other major currencies.

By the 1980s, however, the world's currency markets were so large that the ability of a few governments (the United States, Japan, and Great Britain, to name three) to move a market simply through direct intervention was over. The major tool now left was for government, at least when operating alone, to alter economic variables such as interest rates—to alter the motivations and expectations of market participants for capital movements and currency exchange. A country that wishes to strengthen its currency versus others might raise domestic interest rates to attract capital from abroad. Although effective in many cases, the downside of this policy is that it raises interest rates for domestic consumers and investors alike, slowing the domestic economy.

coordinated intervention A currency value management method whereby the central banks of the major nations simultaneously intervene in the currency markets, hoping to change a currency's value.

There is, however, one other method of currency value management that has been selectively employed in the past 25 years, termed **coordinated intervention**. After the U.S. dollar had risen in value dramatically over the 1980–1985 period, the Group of Five, or G5, nations (France, Japan, West Germany, United States, and United Kingdom) met at the Plaza Hotel in New York in September 1985 and agreed to a set of goals and policies, the Plaza Agreement. These goals were to be accomplished through coordinated intervention among the central banks of the major nations. By the Bank of Japan (Japan), the Bundesbank (Germany), and the Federal Reserve (United States) all simultaneously intervening in the currency markets,

Hammering Out an Agreement at Bretton Woods

The governments of the Allied powers knew that the devastating impacts of World War II would require swift and decisive policies. Therefore, a full year before the end of the war, representatives of all 45 allied nations met in the summer of 1944 (July 1–22) at Bretton Woods, New Hampshire, in the United States, for the United Nations Monetary and Financial Conference. Their purpose was to plan the postwar international monetary system. It was a difficult process, and the final synthesis of viewpoints was shaded by pragmatism and significant doubt.

Although the conference was attended by 45 nations, the leading policymakers at Bretton Woods were the British and the Americans. The British delegation was led by Lord John Maynard Keynes, termed "Britain's economic heavyweight." The British argued for a postwar system that would be decidedly more flexible than the various gold standards used before the war. Keynes argued, as he had after World War I, that attempts to tie currency values to gold would create pressures for deflation (a general fall in the level of prices in a country) in many of the war-ravaged economies. And these economies were faced with enormous reindustrialization needs that would likely cause inflation, not deflation.

The American delegation was led by the director of the U.S. Treasury's monetary research department, Harry D. White, and the U.S. Secretary of the Treasury, Henry Morgenthau Jr. The Americans argued for stability (fixed exchange rates) but not a return to the gold standard itself. In fact, although the United States at that time held most of the gold of the Allied Powers, the U.S. delegates argued that currencies should be fixed in parities, but redemption of the gold should occur only between official authorities (central banks of governments).

After weeks of meetings the participants came to a three-part agreement—the *Bretton Woods Agreement*. The plan called for (1) fixed exchange rates, termed an "adjustable peg" among members; (2) a fund of gold and constituent currencies available to members for stabilization of their respective currencies, called the *International Monetary Fund* (IMF); and (3) a bank for financing long-term development projects (eventually known as the *World Bank*). One proposal resulting from the meetings that was not ratified by the United States was the establishment of an international trade organization to promote free trade. That would take many years and conferences to come.

Mount Washington Hotel, Bretton Woods, New Hampshire

they hoped to reach the combined strength level necessary to push the dollar's value down. Their actions were met with some success in that instance, but there have been few occasions since then of true coordinated intervention.

THE LAUNCH OF THE EURO

On January 4, 1999, 11 member-states of the European Union initiated the European Monetary Union and its new single currency, the *euro*. The euro replaced the individual currencies of the participating member states (Austria, Belgium, Finland, France, Germany, Ireland, Italy, Luxembourg, the Netherlands, Portugal, and Spain). The United Kingdom, Sweden, and Denmark chose to maintain their individual currencies. The euro zone has continued to grow in the years that have followed, numbering 16 euro-based countries as of 2009. On December 31, 1998, the final fixed rates among the 11 participating currencies and the euro were put into place. On January 4, 1999, the euro was officially launched.

The introduction of the euro affected markets in three ways: (1) countries within the euro zone enjoyed cheaper transaction costs, (2) currency risks and costs related to exchange rate uncertainty were reduced, and (3) all consumers and businesses both inside and outside the euro zone enjoy price transparency and increased price-based competition.

The euro has for most of the participating countries had a stabilizing influence on their general economic systems. The many different currencies have now been

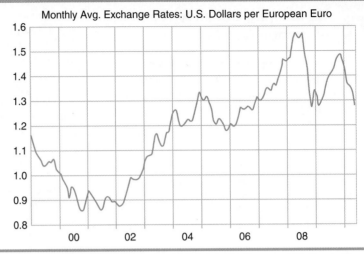

Figure 7.8   The Euro and the Dollar, 1999–2010

Monthly Avg. Exchange Rates: U.S. Dollars per European Euro

Source: © 2010 by Prof. Werner Antweiler, University of British Columbia, Vancouver BC, Canada. Time period shown in diagram: 1/Jan/1999–14/May/2010.

replaced with a single globally recognized unit of value that has, particularly against the U.S. dollar, proven strong and resilient. Figure 7.8 shows how the euro has generally increased in value against the dollar over its decade of existence.

THE PURPOSE OF EXCHANGE RATES

4. To understand the distinctions between domestic and international sources of capital

If countries are to trade, they must be able to exchange currencies. To buy wheat, or corn, or DVD players, the buyer must first have the currency in which the product is sold. An American firm purchasing consumer electronic products manufactured in Japan must first exchange its U.S. dollars for Japanese yen, then purchase the products. And each country has its own currency. (Actually, there are a few exceptions. Panama, for example, has used the U.S. dollar for many years.) The exchange of one country's currency for another should be a relatively simple transaction, but it's not.

WHAT IS A CURRENCY WORTH?

At what rate should one currency be exchanged for another currency? For example, what should the exchange rate be between the U.S. dollar and the Japanese yen? The simplest answer is that the exchange rate should equalize purchasing power. For example, if the price of a movie ticket in the U.S. is $6, the "correct" exchange rate would be one that exchanges $6 for the amount of Japanese yen it would take to purchase a movie ticket in Japan. If ticket prices are ¥540 in Japan, then the exchange rate that would equalize purchasing power would be:

$$\frac{¥540}{\$6} = ¥90/\$$$

purchasing power parity (PPP) The theory that the price of internationally traded commodities should be the same in every country, and hence the exchange rate between the two currencies of those countries should be the ratio of prices in the two countries.

Therefore, if the exchange rate between the two currencies is ¥90/$, moviegoers can purchase tickets regardless of which country they are in. This is the theory of **purchasing power parity (PPP)**, generally considered the definition of what exchange rates ideally should be. The purchasing power parity exchange rate is simply the rate that equalizes the price of the identical product or service in two different currencies:

Price in Japan (in yen) = Exchange rate (yen per dollar) × Price in U.S. (in dollars)

If the price of the same product in each currency is $P^\yen$ and $P^\$$, and the spot exchange rate between the Japanese yen and the U.S. dollar is $S^{\yen/\$}$, the price in yen is simply the price in dollars multiplied by the spot exchange rate:

$$P^\yen = S^{\yen/\$} \times P^\$$$

If this is rearranged by dividing both sides by $P^\$$, the spot exchange rate between the Japanese yen and the U.S. dollar is the ratio of the two product prices:

$$S^{\yen/\$} = \frac{P^\yen}{P^\$}$$

These prices could be the price of just one good or service, such as the movie ticket mentioned previously, or they could be price indices for each country that cover many different goods and services. Either form is an attempt to find comparable products in different countries (and currencies) in order to determine an exchange rate based on purchasing power parity. The question then is whether this logical approach to exchange rates actually works in practice.

THE LAW OF ONE PRICE

The version of purchasing power parity that estimates the exchange rate between two currencies using just one good or service as a measure of the proper exchange for all goods and services is called the **Law of One Price**. To apply the theory to actual prices across countries, we need to select a product that is identical in quality and content in every country. To be truly theoretically correct, we would want such a product to be produced entirely domestically, so that there are no import factors in its construction.

Law of One Price The theory that the relative prices of any single good between countries, expressed in each country's currency, is representative of the proper or appropriate exchange rate value.

Where would one find such a perfect product? McDonald's. Table 7.1 presents selected values from what *The Economist* magazine calls the *Big Mac Index*. What it provides is a product that is essentially the same the world over and is produced and consumed entirely domestically.

The Big Mac Index compares the actual exchange rate with the exchange rate implied by the purchasing power parity measurement of comparing Big Mac prices across countries. For example, say the average price of a Big Mac in the United States on a given date is $3.57. On the same date, the price of a Big Mac in China, in Chinese yuan, is Yuan 12.5. This then is used to calculate the PPP exchange rate, $S^{\text{Yuan}/\$}$, as before:

$$S^{\text{Yuan}/\$} = \frac{P^{\text{Yuan}}}{P^\$} = \frac{\text{Yuan } 12.5}{\$3.57} = \text{Yuan } 3.50/\$$$

The exchange rate between the Chinese yuan and the U.S. dollar should be Yuan 3.50/$ according to a PPP comparison of Big Mac prices. The actual exchange

Table 7.1	Selected Countries from the Big Mac Index				
	Big Mac Prices		Implied PPP of the Dollar	Actual Dollar Exchange Rate July 13	Under (−) or Over (+) Valuation against the Dollar (%)
	In Local Currency	In US$			
United States	$ 3.57	3.57	−	−	−
China	Yuan 12.5	1.83	3.50	6.83	−49
Euro area*	€ 3.31	4.62	1.08	1.39	+ 29
Japan	Yen 320	3.46	89.6	92.6	−3

Source: Data abstracted from *The Economist*, July 16, 2009, print edition.
*Note that the euro area exchange rate quotes are in US$/euro.

rate on the date of comparison was Yuan6.83/$. This means that each U.S. dollar was actually worth 6.83 Chinese yuan when the index indicates that each U.S. dollar should have been worth only 3.50 Chinese yuan. Therefore, if one is to believe in the Big Mac Index, the Chinese yuan was undervalued by 49 percent.

 GLOBAL CAPITAL MARKETS

5. *To examine how the needs of individual borrowers have changed the nature of the instruments traded on world financial markets*

One of the simplest, most obvious prescriptions for the growth and success of any business is ready access to affordable capital. Yet for a great proportion of the global marketplace, firms and organizations of all kinds are extremely limited in their ability to raise affordable capital for purchasing inputs, acquiring new technology, or any of the other multitude of critical components of global competitiveness. The hundreds of relatively small countries—and their companies of all sizes—often have small and illiquid capital markets from which business can draw. Globalization of capital markets, however, has changed that for many firms.

We now continue to explore the major assets, instruments, and institutions of the global capital markets depicted previously in Figure 7.1. We begin with an analysis of the needs for capital by firms globally, and follow that with a description of the international money markets and global capital markets.

SOURCES OF CAPITAL

A firm that must source its long-term debt and equity in a highly illiquid domestic securities market will probably have a relatively high cost of capital and will face limited availability of such capital, which in turn will lower its competitiveness both internationally and vis à vis foreign firms entering its home market. This category of firms includes both firms resident in emerging countries, where the capital market remains undeveloped, and firms too small to gain access to their own national securities markets. Many family-owned firms find themselves in this category because they choose not to utilize securities markets to source their long-term capital needs.

Firms resident in industrial countries with small capital markets often source their long-term debt and equity at home in these partially-liquid domestic securities markets. The firms' cost and availability of capital is better than that of firms in countries with illiquid capital markets. However, if these firms can tap the highly liquid global markets they can also strengthen their competitive advantage in sourcing capital.

Firms resident in countries with segmented capital markets must devise a strategy to escape dependence on that market for their long-term debt and equity needs. Capital markets become segmented because of such factors as excessive regulatory control, perceived political risk, anticipated foreign exchange risk, lack of transparency, asymmetric availability of information, cronyism, insider trading, and many other market imperfections. Firms constrained by any of these conditions must develop a strategy to escape their own limited capital markets and source some of their long-term capital abroad.

Capital to fund businesses comes in two varieties: debt and equity. Although the choice to add external equity—equity from outside investors—is a very difficult decision for most organizations (public versus private ownership is explored in depth in Chapter 10), the choice to take on debt from outside organizations is not. Most companies in most markets rely upon commercial banks for their debt. This debt, usually relatively short-term bank loans, is critical to the growth and ultimately international competitiveness of the firm. Bank loans are the traditional source of debt for small and medium-sized firms in all countries.

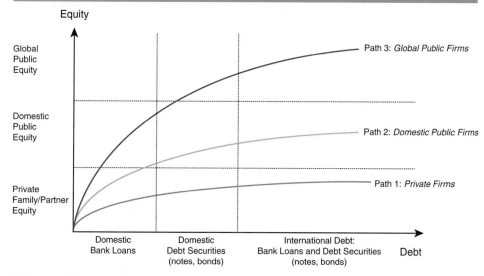

Figure 7.9   Business Evolution and Capital Access

A firm may follow any of the three generic paths in its access to capital. Although for many years it was thought that a company had to "go public" to raise enough capital to be globally competitive, that is no longer the case.

Figure 7.9 provides a map of how business evolution and access to domestic and international capital is used by companies. Firms following path 1 are firms that have chosen to remain private, to be owned and controlled by either an individual, a family, or a group of private partners. Because these firms cannot typically increase their equity capital base quickly (relying primarily on retaining profits from current period earnings), their access to debt, larger domestic markets, and possibly international debt dictates their growth potential. Path 2 is the basic capital access path for firms that have gone to the public equity markets to raise equity capital. Their increased reporting and transparency has a tendency to also increase their access to greater and greater sources of affordable debt. The third path, path 3, is simply one step further, as the publicly traded firm has its equity traded in the international equity market.

The paths of Figure 7.9 show capital access paths, not required schedules for profit or success. There are many different ways for firms to become globally competitive and potentially dominant, but the access to affordable capital is often a minimum element on a firm's road to success. Similarly, there is no requirement that a globally competitive and dominant firm be publicly traded. Path 1 may be the routing to global success for some firms, while others follow paths 2 or 3.

Just as with the money markets, the international capital markets serve as links among the capital markets of individual countries, as well as constituting a separate market of their own—the capital that flows into the **euromarkets**. Firms can now raise capital—debit or equity, fixed or floating interest rates—in any of a dozen currencies, for maturities ranging from one month to 30 years, in the international capital markets. Although the international capital markets traditionally have been dominated by debt instruments, international equity markets have shown considerable growth in recent years.

euromarkets Money and capital markets in which transactions are denominated in a currency other than that of the place of the transaction; not confined to Europe.

DEFINING INTERNATIONAL FINANCING

The definition of what constitutes an international financial transaction depends on two fundamental characteristics: (1) whether the borrower is domestic or foreign and

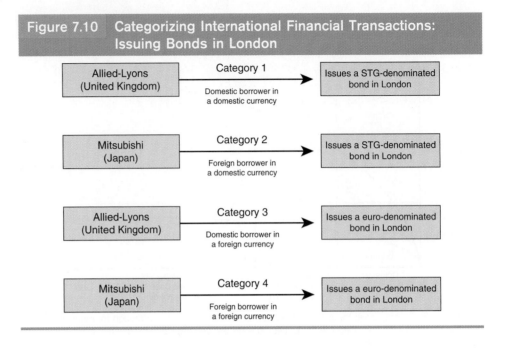

Figure 7.10   Categorizing International Financial Transactions: Issuing Bonds in London

(2) whether the borrower is raising capital denominated in the domestic currency or a foreign currency. These two characteristics form four categories of financial transactions, as illustrated in Figure 7.10.

Category 1: Domestic Borrower/Domestic Currency

This is a traditional domestic financial market activity. A borrower who is resident within the country raises capital from domestic financial institutions denominated in local currency. All countries with basic market economies have their own domestic financial markets, some large and some quite small. This is still by far the most common type of financial transaction.

Category 2: Foreign Borrower/Domestic Currency

This is when a foreign borrower enters another country's financial market and raises capital denominated in the local currency. The international dimension of this transaction is based only on who the borrower is. Many borrowers, both public and private, increasingly go to the world's largest financial markets to raise capital for their enterprises. The ability of a foreign firm to raise capital in another country's financial market is sometimes limited by that government's restrictions on who can borrow, as well as the market's willingness to lend to foreign governments and companies that it may not know as well as domestic borrowers.

Category 3: Domestic Borrower/Foreign Currency

Many borrowers in today's international markets need capital denominated in a foreign currency. A domestic firm may actually issue a bond to raise capital in its local market where it is known quite well, but raise the capital in the form of a foreign currency. This type of financial transaction occurs less often than the previous two types because it requires a local market in foreign currencies, a eurocurrency market. A number of countries, such as the United States, tightly restrict the amount and types of financial transactions in foreign currency. International financial centers such as London and Zurich have been the traditional centers of these types of transactions.

Category 4: Foreign Borrower/Foreign Currency

This is the strictest form of the traditional eurocurrency financial transaction, a foreign firm borrowing foreign currency. Once again, this type of activity may be restricted by which borrowers are allowed into a country's financial markets and which currencies are available. This type of financing dominates the activities of many banks in the offshore banking market.

Using this classification system, it is possible to categorize any individual international financial transaction. For example, the distinction between an international bond and a eurobond is simply that of a category 2 transaction (foreign borrower in a domestic currency market) and a category 3 or 4 transaction (foreign currency denominated in a single local market or many markets).

INTERNATIONAL MONEY MARKETS

A money market traditionally is defined as a market for deposits, accounts, or securities that have maturities of one year or less. The international money markets, often termed the eurocurrency markets, constitute an enormous financial marketplace that is in many ways outside the jurisdiction and supervision of world financial and governmental authorities. It is, in fact, this last characteristic that led to its central role in the financial crisis of 2007–2009.

Eurocurrency Markets

A **eurocurrency** is any foreign-currency denominated deposit or account at a financial institution outside the country of the currency's issuance. For example, U.S. dollars held on account in a bank in London are termed **eurodollars**. Similarly, Japanese yen held on account in a Parisian financial institution would be classified as euroyen. The "euro" prefix does not mean these currencies or accounts are only European; U.S. dollars on account in a Singapore financial institution would also be classified as eurocurrency—or more specifically, eurodollars.

eurocurrency A bank deposit in a currency other than the currency of the country where the bank is located; not confined to banks in Europe.

eurodollars U.S. dollars deposited in banks outside the United States; not confined to banks in Europe.

Eurocurrency Interest Rates

What is the significance of eurocurrency accounts or markets? Simply put, it is the purity of value that comes from no governmental interference or restrictions with their use. Eurocurrency accounts are not controlled or managed by governments (e.g., the Bank of England has no control, or wish to control, eurodollar accounts). As a result, these financial institutions pay no deposit insurance, hold no reserve requirements, and are typically not subject to any interest rate restrictions with respect to these foreign-currency-denominated accounts. Their interest rates are then considered as true reflections of financial and economic forces without governmental influence.

There are hundreds of different major interest rates around the globe, but the international financial markets focus on a very few, the interbank interest rates. Interbank rates charged by banks to bank in the major international financial centers such as London, New York, Tokyo, and Singapore are generally regarded as "the interest rate" in the respective currencies and markets.

The interest rate that is by far used most frequently in international loan agreements is LIBOR—the London Interbank Offer Rate. This is the eurodollar interest rate determined daily by trading between the largest and most liquid international banks. There are LIBOR rates for other currencies, like the euro and the yen, as well as city-based LIBOR rates like the interbank rate in Paris (PIBOR), Madrid (MIBOR), and Singapore (SIBOR) to name a few. While LIBOR is the offer rate—

Table 7.2	Eurocurrency LIBOR Rates				
	Overnight	1-Month	3-Month	6-Month	1-Year
US$ LIBOR	0.17875%	0.23594%	0.26188%	0.48563%	1.02000%
Euro LIBOR	0.31000	0.40375	0.67563	0.97625	1.20000
£ LIBOR	0.50375	0.51500	0.61250	0.82875	1.21125

Source: Rates are for November 23, 2009, as quoted in the *Financial Times* on November 24, 2009, p. 23.

the cost of funds "offered" to other banks for overnight or other maturity loans—the equivalent deposit rate in the euromarkets is LIBID, the London Interbank Bid Rate. This is the rate of interest other banks can earn on Eurocurrency deposits. Table 7.2 provides a sample of LIBOR rates for the dollar, the euro, and the pound on November 23, 2009.

Table 7.2 bears some discussion. First, interest rates are currency specific. They represent a percentage charge on a specific currency, and currencies are obviously not of equal value. Secondly, each LIBOR interest rate series varies over its maturity. All interest rates shown in Table 7.2 are annualized, so although they are quoted for a shorter period of time like one month, that actual interest rate is annualized for presentation. For example, the one-month US$ LIBOR rate of 0.23594 is actually $0.019662 \times 12 = 0.23594$; this is the effective annual rate for the one-month maturity. As we will see in the final section of this chapter on the global financial crisis of 2008–2009, LIBOR played a very big role in the transmission of the crisis across countries.

INTERNATIONAL BANKING AND BANK LENDING

Banks have existed in different forms and roles since the Middle Ages. Bank loans have provided nearly all of the debt capital needed by industry since the start of the Industrial Revolution. Even in this age in which securitized debt instruments (bonds, notes, and other types of tradable paper) are growing as sources of capital for firms worldwide, banks still perform a critical role by providing capital for medium-sized and smaller firms, which dominate all economies.

Similar to the direct foreign investment decision sequence discussed in Chapter 6, banks can expand their cross-border activities in a variety of ways. Like all decisions involving exports and direct investment, increasing the level of international activity and capability normally requires placing more capital and knowledge at risk to be able to reap the greater benefits of expanding markets.

correspondent bank Banks located in different countries and unrelated by ownership that have a reciprocal agreement to provide services to each other's customers.

A bank that wants to conduct business with clients in other countries but does not want to open a banking operation in that country can do so through correspondent banks or representative offices. A **correspondent bank** is an unrelated bank (by ownership) based in the foreign country. By the nature of its business, it has knowledge of the local market and access to clients, capital, and information, which a foreign bank does not.

A second way that banks may gain access to foreign markets without actually opening a banking operation there is through representative offices. A representative office is basically a sales office for a bank. It provides information regarding the financial services of the bank, but it cannot deliver the services itself. It cannot accept deposits or make loans. The foreign representative office of a U.S. bank will typically sell the bank's services to local firms that may need banking services for trade or other transactions in the United States.

If a bank wants to conduct banking business within the foreign country, it may open a branch banking office, a banking affiliate, or even a wholly owned banking subsidiary. A branch banking office is an extension of the parent bank and is not independently financed from the parent. The branch office is not independently incorporated and, therefore, is commonly restricted in the types of banking activities that it may conduct. Branch banking is by far the most common form of international banking structure used by banks, particularly by banks based in the United States.

INTERNATIONAL SECURITY MARKETS

Although banks continue to provide a large portion of the international financial needs of government and business through the international money market, it is the international security markets that have experienced the greatest growth in the two decades since their inception. The international security markets include bonds, equities, and private placements.

The International Bond Market

The international bond market provides the bulk of financing. The four categories of international debt financing discussed previously particularly apply to the international bond markets. Foreign borrowers have been using the large, well-developed capital markets of countries such as the United States and the United Kingdom for many years. These issues are classified generally as foreign bonds as opposed to eurobonds. Each has gained its own pet name for foreign bonds issued in that market. For example, foreign bond issues in the United States are called Yankee bonds, in the United Kingdom Bulldogs, in the Netherlands Rembrandt bonds, and in Japan Samurai bonds. When bonds are issued by foreign borrowers in these markets, they are subject to the same restrictions that apply to all domestic borrowers. If a Japanese firm issues a bond in the United States, it still must comply with all rules of the U.S. Securities and Exchange Commission, including the fact that they must be dollar-denominated.

Bonds that fall into categories 3 and 4 are termed eurobonds. The primary characteristic of these instruments is that they are denominated in a currency other than that of the country where they are sold. For example, many U.S. firms may issue euro-yen bonds on world markets. These bonds are sold in international financial centers such as London or Frankfurt, but they are denominated in Japanese yen. Because these eurobonds are scattered about the global markets, most are a type of bond known as a **bearer bond**. A bearer bond is owned officially by whoever is holding it, with no master registration list being held by government authorities who then track who is earning interest income from bond investments. Bearer bonds have a series of small coupons that border the bond itself. On an annual basis, one of the coupons is cut or "clipped" from the bond and taken to a banking institution that is one of the listed paying agents. The bank will pay the holder of the coupon the interest payment due, and usually no official records of payment are kept.

bearer bond A bond owned officially by whoever is holding it.

International Equity Markets

Firms are financed with both debt and equity. Although the debt markets have been the center of activity in the international financial markets over the past three decades, there are signs that international equity capital is becoming more popular.

Again using the same categories of international financial activities, the category 2 transaction of a foreign borrower in a domestic market in local currency is the predominant international equity activity. Foreign firms often issue new shares in foreign markets and list their stock on major stock exchanges such as those in New York, Tokyo, or

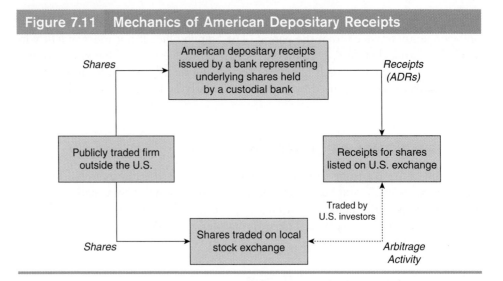

Figure 7.11   Mechanics of American Depositary Receipts

London. The purpose of foreign issues and listings is to expand the investor base in the hope of gaining access to capital markets in which the demand for equities is strong.

A foreign firm that wants to list its shares on an exchange in the U.S. does so through American depositary receipts (ADRs). As illustrated in Figure 7.11, these are the receipts to bank accounts that hold shares of the foreign firm's stock in that firm's country. The equities are actually in a foreign currency, so by holding them in a bank account and listing the receipt on the account on the American exchange, the shares can be revalued in dollars and redivided so that the price per share is more typical of that of the U.S. equity markets ($20 to $60 per share frequently being the desired range).

There was considerable growth in the 1990s in the euro-equity markets. A euro-equity issue is the simultaneous sale of a firm's shares in several different countries, with or without listing the shares on an exchange in that country. The sales take place through investment banks. Once issued, most euro-equities are listed at least on the computer screen quoting system of the International Stock Exchange (ISE) in London.

Private Placement Market

One of the largest and largely unpublicized capital markets is the private placement market. A private placement is the sale of debt or equity to a large investor. The sale is normally a one-time-only transaction in which the buyer of the bond or stock purchases the investment and intends to hold it until maturity (if debt) or until repurchased by the firm (if equity). How does this differ from normal bond and stock sales? The answer is that the securities are not resold on a secondary market such as the domestic bond market or the New York or London stock exchanges. If the security was intended to be publicly traded, the issuing firm would have to meet a number of disclosure and registration requirements with the regulatory authorities. In the United States, this would be the Securities and Exchange Commission.

Historically, much of the volume of private placements of securities occurred in Europe, with a large volume being placed with large Swiss financial institutions and large private investors. But in recent years the market has grown substantially across all countries as the world's financial markets have grown and as large institutional investors (particularly pension funds and insurance firms) have gained control over increasing shares of investment capital.

GAINING ACCESS TO INTERNATIONAL FINANCIAL MARKETS

Although the international markets are large and growing, this does not mean they are for everyone. For many years, only the largest of the world's multinational firms could enter another country's capital markets and find acceptance. The reasons are information and reputation.

Financial markets are, by definition, risk averse. This means they are very reluctant to make loans to or buy debt issued by firms that they know little about. Therefore, the ability to gain access to the international markets is dependent on a firm's reputation and its ability to educate the markets about what it does, how successful it has been, and its patience. The firm must, in the end, be willing to expend the resources and effort required to build a credit reputation in the international markets. If successful, the firm may enjoy the benefits of new, larger, and more diversified sources of the capital it needs.

The individual firm—whether it be a chili dog stand serving the international tastes of office workers at the United Nations Plaza or a major multinational firm such as McDonald's or Honda of Japan—is affected by the workings of the international financial markets. Although the owner of the chili dog stand probably has more important and immediate problems to deal with, it is clear that firms such as Honda see the movements in these markets as critically important to their long-term competitiveness.

 THE FINANCIAL CRISIS OF 2007–2009

Confidence in markets and institutions, it's a lot like oxygen. When you have it, you don't even think about it. Indispensable. You can go years without thinking about it. When its gone for five minutes, it's the only thing you think about. The confidence has been sucked out of the credit markets and institutions.

—Warren Buffett, October 1, 2008

6. To understand the origins and implications of the 2007–2009 global financial crisis and the road ahead

Beginning in the summer of 2007, the United States, followed by the European and Asian financial markets, incurred financial crises. The impacts on global business have been significant and lasting. No student of global business should be without a clear understanding of the causes and consequences of this breakdown in global financial markets. This section will trace the seeds of the crisis and the transmission mechanisms for its expansion across the globe (including LIBOR) and will look briefly at possible solutions.

THE SEEDS OF CRISIS: SUBPRIME DEBT

The origins of the 2007 crisis lie within the ashes of the equity bubble and subsequent collapse of the equity markets at the end of the 1990s. As the so-called *dotcom bubble* collapsed in 2000 and 2001, capital flowed increasingly toward the real estate sectors in the United States. Some economists have argued that much of the wealth accumulated from the equity markets during the period was now used to push housing prices and general real estate demands upward. Although corporate lending was still relatively slow, the U.S. banking sector found mortgage lending rapidly expanding and highly profitable. The following years saw investment and speculation in the real estate sector increase rapidly. As prices rose and speculation increased, a growing number of the borrowers were of lower and lower credit quality. These borrowers and their associated mortgage agreements, *subprime debt*, now carried higher debt service obligations with lower and lower income and cash flow capabilities.

Repeal of Glass-Steagall

The market was also more competitive than ever, as a number of deregulation efforts in the United States in 1999 and 2000 now opened these markets up to more and more financial organizations and institutions than ever before. One of the major openings was the passage of the Gramm-Leach-Bliley Financial Services Modernization Act of 1999 by the U.S. Congress, which repealed the last vestiges of the Glass-Steagall Act of 1933, eliminating the barriers between commercial and investment banks. The Act now allowed commercial banks to enter into riskier activities like underwriting and proprietary dealing.

The Housing Sector and Mortgage Lending

One of the key outcomes of this new openness was that many borrowers who in previous times could not have qualified for mortgages now could. Borrowers often borrowed at floating rates, often priced at LIBOR plus a small interest rate spread. The loans would then reset at much higher fixed rates within two to five years. Other forms included loan agreements that were interest-only in the early years, requiring complete refinancing at later dates.

Credit Quality

Mortgage loans in the U.S. marketplace are normally categorized as *prime* (or A-paper), *Alt-A* (Alternative-A paper), and *subprime*, in increasing order of riskiness. Alt-A mortgages would be considered a relatively low risk loan and the borrower creditworthy, but for some reason not initially conforming for prime. Investors wishing to buy homes for resale purposes, *flipping*, would typically qualify for an Alt-A mortgage, but not a prime. The growth in financial assets of all kinds, measured as a percentage of gross domestic product, more than doubled between 1980 and 2008, rising from 400 percent to more than 1,000 percent.

International Asset Values

One of the key financial elements of this growing debt was the value of the assets collateralizing the mortgages—the houses and real estate themselves. As the market demands pushed up prices, housing assets rose in market value. The increased values were then used as collateral in refinancing, and in some cases, additional debt in the form of second mortgages based on the rising equity value of the home.

Mortgage debt as a percentage of household disposable income continued to rapidly climb in the United States in the post-2000 business environment. But it was not a uniquely American issue; as debt obligations were rising in a variety of countries including Great Britain, France, Germany, and Australia. Figure 7.12 illustrates the rising household debt levels for three selected countries through mid-2008. In the end, Great Britain was significantly more indebted in mortgage debt than even the United States.

The U.S. Federal Reserve, at the same time, intentionally aided the debt growth mechanism by continuing to lower interest rates. The Fed's monetary policy actions were predictably to lower interest rates to aid the U.S. economy in its recovery from the 2000–2001 recession. These lower rates provided additional incentive and aid for borrowers of all kinds to raise new and ever-cheaper debt.

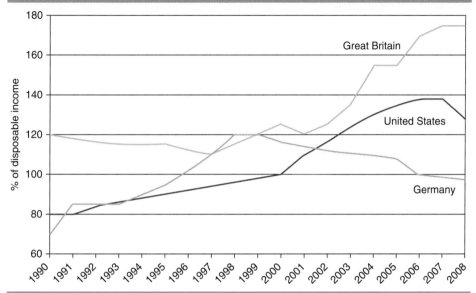

Figure 7.12   Household Debt in the United States, Great Britain, and Germany

Source: Deutsche Bundesbank, U.K. Statistics Authority, U.S. Federal Reserve, *The Economist.*

THE TRANSMISSION MECHANISM: SECURITIZATION OF DERIVATIVES

If subprime debt was malaria, then securitization was the mosquito carrier, the airborne transmission mechanism of the protozoan parasite. The transport vehicle for the growing lower quality debt was a combination of securitization and repackaging provided by a series of new financial derivatives.

Securitization

Securitization has long been a force of change in global financial markets. Securitization is the process of turning an illiquid asset into a liquid saleable asset. The key element is in the interpretation of the word *liquid.* Liquid, in the field of finance, is the ability to exchange an asset for cash instantly, at fair market value.[1] In its purest form, securitization essentially bypasses the traditional financial intermediaries, typically banks, to go directly to investors in the marketplace in order to raise funds. As a result, it may often reduce the costs of lending and borrowing, while possibly raising the returns to investors, as the financial middleman is eliminated.

The growth in subprime lending and Alt-A lending in the post-2000 U.S. debt markets depended on this same securitization force. Financial institutions extended more and more loans of all kinds—mortgage, corporate, industrial, and asset-backed—and then moved these loan and bond agreements to the ever-growing liquid markets using securitization. The securitized assets took two major forms: *mortgage-backed securities* (MBSs) and *asset-backed securities* (ABSs). ABSs included second mortgages and home-equity loans based on mortgages, in addition to credit card receivables, auto loans, and a variety of others. Of the $1.3 trillion in Alt-A debt outstanding at the end of 2008, more than $600 billion of it had been securitized, roughly the same as the outstanding subprime securities outstanding.

The credit crisis of 2007–2008 renewed much of the debate over the use of securitization. By securitizing the debt, portfolios of loans and other debt instruments could be resold into a more liquid market, freeing up the originators to make more new loans. The problem is that securitization may degrade credit quality. As long as the lender held the loan, the lender was keen to ensure the quality of the loan and the capability of the borrower to repay in a timely manner. Securitization severed that link. Now the originator could originate and sell, not being held accountable for the ultimate capability of the borrower to fulfill the loan obligation.

Collateralized Debt Obligations (CDOs)

One of the key instruments in this new growing securitization was the *collateralized debt obligation*, or CDO. Banks originating mortgage loans, and corporate loans and bonds, could now create a portfolio of these debt instruments and package them as an asset-backed security. Once packaged, the bank passed the security to a *special-purpose vehicle* (SPV), often located in an offshore financial center like the Cayman Islands for legal and tax advantages.

The CDO now became the preferred asset *du jour*, as financial institutions of all kinds, from pension funds to hedge funds, purchased the assets and earned the relatively high rates of interest and returns as the economy, real estate, and mortgage lending markets boomed from 2001 to 2007. These markets, aided substantially by slowly performing equity markets and relatively low interest rates, benefitted from investors moving rapidly towards real estate investment and speculation. By 2007 the CDO market had reached a record level of more than $600 billion.

Regardless of the CDO's weaknesses, it became a mainstay of investment banking activity globally by 2007. By the time the first real cracks in the market appeared in 2007, the CDO had spread far and wide within the global financial marketplace. Many would later argue that it would act as a cancer to the future of the system's health. The beginning of the end was the collapse of two Bear Stearns' hedge funds in July 2007. Both funds were made up nearly entirely of CDOs. Within a month, the market for CDOs was completely illiquid. Anyone trying to liquidate a CDO was met with bids approaching eight cents on the dollar. The market effectively collapsed, as illustrated in Figure 7.13.

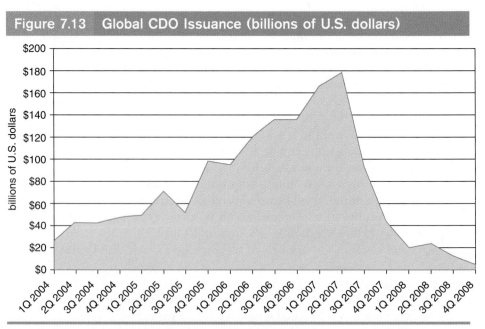

Figure 7.13   Global CDO Issuance (billions of U.S. dollars)

Source: Data drawn from "Global CDO Market Issuance Data," Securities Industry and Financial Market.

CREDIT DEFAULT SWAPS

Despite its forbidding name, the CDS is a simple idea: it allows an investor to buy insurance against a company defaulting on its debt payments. When it was invented, the CDS was a useful concept because more people felt comfortable owning corporate debt if they could eliminate the risk of the issuer failing. The extra appetite for debt helped lower the cost of capital.

—"Derivatives: Giving Credit Where It Is Due," *The Economist*,
November 6, 2008

The second derivative of increasing note—or concern—was the *credit default swap* (CDS). The credit default swap was a contract, a derivative, that derived its value from the credit quality and performance of any specified asset. The CDS was new, invented by a team at JPMorgan in 1997, and designed to shift the risk of default to a third party. In short, it was a way to bet whether a specific mortgage or security would either fail to pay on time or fail to pay at all. In some cases, for hedging, it provided insurance against the possibility that a borrower might not pay. In other instances, it was a way in which a speculator could bet against the increasingly risky securities (like the CDO), to hold their value. And, uniquely, you could make the bet without ever holding or being directly exposed to the credit instrument itself.

As seen in Figure 7.14, the market boomed. New proposals for regulation of the market have centered on first requiring participants to have an actual exposure to a credit instrument or obligation This eliminated the outside speculators simply wishing to take a position in the market. Also needed was the formation of some type of clearinghouse to provide systematic trading and valuation of all CDS positions at all times.

Critics of regulation argue that the market has weathered many challenges, such as the failures of Bear Stearns and Lehman Brothers (at one time estimated to have been a seller of 10 percent of global CDS obligations), the near-failure of AIG, and the defaults of Freddie Mac and Fannie Mae. Despite these challenges, the CDS

Figure 7.14   Credit Default Swap Market Growth

Amount outstanding in trillions of U.S. dollars

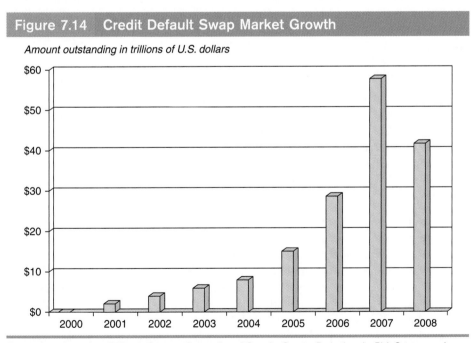

Source: Data drawn from Table 19: Amounts Outstanding of Over-the-Counter Derivatives, by Risk Category and Instrument, *BIS Quarterly Review*, June 2009, bis.org.

market continues to function and may have learned its lessons. Proponents argue that increased transparency of activity alone might provide sufficient information for growing market resiliency and liquidity.

THE FALLOUT: THE CRISIS OF 2007 AND 2008

The housing market began to falter in late 2005, with increasing signs of collapse throughout 2006. The bubble finally burst in the spring of 2007. The United States was not alone, as housing markets in the United Kingdom and Australia followed similar paths. What followed was a literal domino effect of collapsing loans and securities, followed by the funds and institutions that were their holders. In July 2007 two hedge funds at Bear Stearns holding a variety of CDOs and other mortgage-based assets failed. Soon thereafter, Northern Rock, a major British banking organization, was rescued from the brink of collapse by the Bank of England. In early September 2007, global financial markets turned to near-panic, as a multitude of financial institutions on several continents suffered bank runs. Interest rates rose, equity markets fell, and the first stages of crisis rolled through the global economy.

Then, 2008 proved even more volatile than 2007. Crude oil prices—as well as nearly every other commodity price—rose at astronomical rates in the first half of the year. The massive growth in the Chinese and Indian economies, and, in fact, in many emerging markets, globally, continued unabated. And just as suddenly, it stopped. Crude oil peaked at $147/barrel in July, then plummeted, as did nearly every other commodity price, including copper, nickel, timber, concrete, and steel.

As mortgage markets faltered in the United States, a series of failures followed. On September 7, 2008, the U.S. government announced that it was placing Fannie Mae (the Federal National Mortgage Association) and Freddie Mac (the Federal Home Loan Mortgage Corporation) into conservatorship. In essence, the government was taking over the institutions as result of their near-insolvency. Over the following week, Lehman Brothers, one of the oldest investment banks on Wall Street, struggled to survive. Finally on September 14, 2008, Lehman filed for bankruptcy.

On Monday September 15, equity markets plunged. In many ways much more important for the financial security of multinational enterprises, U.S. dollar LIBOR rates shot skyward, as illustrated in Figure 7.15, as a result of the growing international perception of financial collapse by U.S. banking institutions. The following day, American International Group (AIG), the U.S. insurance conglomerate, received an $85 billion injection from the U.S. Federal Reserve in exchange for an 80 percent equity interest. AIG had extensive credit default swap exposure. Although dollar markets seemingly calmed, the following weeks saw renewed periods of collapse and calm as more and more financial institutions failed.

The credit crisis now began in full force. Beginning in September 2008 and extending into the spring of 2009, the world's credit markets—lending of all kinds—nearly stopped. The corporate lending markets now demonstrated a complex combination of crisis conditions.

- In the end, the risky investment banking activities undertaken post-deregulation, especially in the mortgage market, overwhelmed the banks' commercial banking activities. Traditional commercial bank lending for working capital financing, automobile loans, student loans, and credit card debt were squeezed out by the huge losses from the investment banking activities. Thus began the credit squeeze worldwide, a decline of asset prices, burgeoning real estate foreclosures, and a general global malaise.

- The indebtedness of the corporate sector was tiered, with the biggest firms actually being extremely well positioned to withstand the crisis. The middle- and

Figure 7.15   U.S. Dollar and Japanese Yen LIBOR Rates

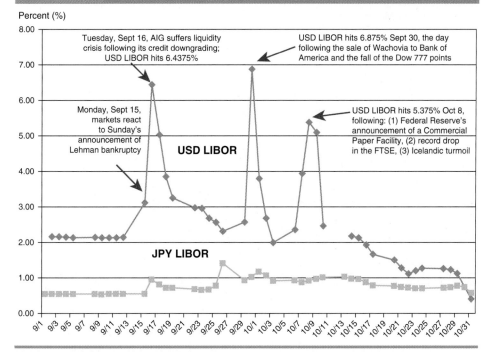

Source: British Bankers Association (BBA). Overnight Lending Rates, September–October 2008.

lower-tier companies by size, however, were heavily dependent on debt, particularly short-term debt for working capital financing. Many were now having trouble in both servicing existing debt and gaining access to new debt to continue business.

• The commercial paper market nearly ceased to operate in September and October. Although the commercial paper market had always been a short-term money market, more than 90 percent of all issuances in September 2008 were overnight. The markets no longer trusted the credit quality of any counterparty—whether they be hedge funds, money market funds, mutual funds, investment banks, commercial banks, or corporations.

GLOBAL CONTAGION

Although it is difficult to ascribe causality, the rapid collapse of the mortgage-backed securities markets in the United States definitely spread to the global marketplace. Capital invested in equity and debt instruments in all major financial markets fled not only for cash, but for cash in traditional safe-haven countries and markets. Equity markets fell worldwide, while capital fled many of the world's most promising emerging markets. Figure 7.16 illustrates clearly how markets fell in September and October 2008.

The impact was felt immediately in the currencies of a multitude of the more financially open emerging markets. Many currencies now fell against the traditional three safe-haven currencies, the dollar, the euro, and the yen: the Icelandic krona, Hungarian forint, Pakistani rupee, Indian rupee, South Korean won, Mexican peso, Brazilian real, to name but a few.

As financial institutions and markets faltered in many industrial countries, pressure of all kinds—business, market, and political—increased to focus on the needs of "their own." A new form of antiglobalization force arose, the differentiation of the

Figure 7.16   Selected Stock Markets and the Crisis

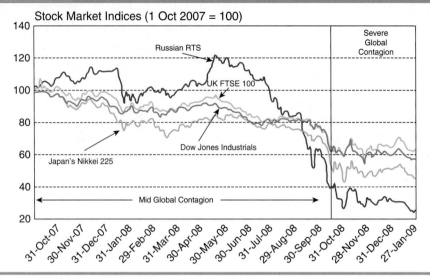

Source: Dick K. Nanto, "The U.S. Financial Crisis: The Global Dimension with Implications for U.S. Policy," Congressional Research Service, Washington DC, January 29, 2009, p. 11.

financial mercantilism
Government policy to protect and promote the home-country financial and non-financial companies first.

domestic from the multinational. This new form of **financial mercantilism** focused on supporting the home-country financial and nonfinancial firms first, all others second. Multinational companies, even in emerging markets, now saw increasing indicators that they were being assessed higher credit risks and lower credit qualities, even though they theoretically had greater business diversity and the wherewithal to withstand the onslaught. The financial press categorized the credit dynamics as *homeward flow*. Credit conditions and a variety of new government bailout plans were under way in Australia, Belgium, Canada, France, Germany, Iceland, Ireland, Italy, Luxembourg, Spain, Sweden, the United Kingdom, and the United States.

The credit crisis now moved to a third stage. The first stage had been the failure of specific mortgage-backed securities. These had caused the fall of specific funds and instruments. The second stage had seen the crisis spread to the very foundations of the organizations at the core of the global financial system, the commercial and investment banks on all continents. This third new stage had been feared from the beginning—a credit-induced global recession of potential depression-like depths. Not only had lending stopped, but in many cases borrowing and investing. Although interest rates in U.S. dollar markets hovered little above zero, the price was not the issue. The prospects for investment returns of all types were now dim. The corporate sector did not see economic opportunities and returns to new investment. Budgets were slashed, layoffs continued, and the economies of the industrial world retrenched.

THE REMEDY: PRESCRIPTIONS FOR AN INFECTED GLOBAL FINANCIAL ORGANISM

The new system evolved over the past three decades and saw explosive growth in the past few years thanks to three simultaneous but distinct developments: deregulation, technological innovation and the growing international mobility of capital.

—"The World Economy: Taming The Beast," *The Economist*, October 8, 2008

So where now for the global financial markets? Dismissing the absolute extremes, on one end that capitalism has failed and on the other end that extreme regulation is the only solution, what practical solutions fall in between? What if we return to the sequence of events that has led to the most recent global credit crisis?

Debt

Was the mortgage boom itself the problem? The market largely boomed as a result of the combination of few competing investments (equity markets had fallen) with the low cost and great availability of capital. Of greater concern was the originate-to-distribute behavior combined with questionable credit assessments and classifications. New guidelines for credit quality and access to mortgages are already under way.

As illustrated by Focus on Business there were a number of additional surprises—unintended consequences—from the financial bailout.

Securitization

Was the financial technique of combining assets into packaged portfolios for trading the problem, or the lack of transparency and accountability for the individual elements within the portfolio? Although portfolio theory itself has been used for risk reduction since the 1960s, it was always used in the construction of assets with uncorrelated movements. In the case of mortgage-backed securities, however, the portfolio components were so similar that the only benefit was that the holder "hoped" that all the same securities would not fall into delinquency simultaneously. This was not the premise of portfolio theory.

Derivatives

This is not the first time that derivatives have been the source of substantial market failures, and it will most likely not be the last. They are the core of financial technological innovation. But derivatives are only devices and tools, and they are no better or worse than those using them. The creation of complex mortgage-backed assets and derivative structures, which ultimately made the securities nearly impossible to value, particularly in thin markets, was in hind-sight a very poor choice.

FOCUS ON BUSINESS

Refinancing Opportunities and the Credit Crisis

One of the more unusual outcomes of the credit crisis in the fall of 2008 was the opportunity for many companies to buy back their own debt at fractions of face value. The crisis had driven secondary market prices of debt, particularly speculative-grade debt, extremely low. In some cases, outstanding debt was trading at 30 percent of face value. Now, if the issuing company had available cash, or access to new lower cost sources of debt, it could repurchase its outstanding debt at fire-sale prices. The actual repurchase could be from the public market or via a debt tender, where an offer would be extended directly to all current debtholders.

A multitude of companies, including FreeScale, First Data, GenTek, and Weyerhause, have all taken advantage of the opportunity to retire more costly debt at discount prices.

Many companies currently held by private equity investors, who have access to additional financial resources, have moved aggressively to repurchase. Firms have focused particularly on debt issuances that are coming due in the short term, particularly if they feared difficulty in refinancing.

There have been a number of unintended consequences, however. A number of the distressed financial institutions have used some of the government funds provided under bailout lending to repurchase their own debt. Morgan Stanley reported earnings of more than $2.1 billion in the fourth quarter of 2008 from just buying back $12 billion of its own debt. Although this does indeed shore-up the balance sheets, the primary intent of the government-backed capital had been to renew lending and financing by the banks to the nonbank financial sector—commercial businesses—in hopes of restarting general business activity, not to generate bank profits from the refinancing of its own portfolio.

Renewed regulatory requirements, increasing reporting, and greater degrees of transparency in pricing and valuation will aid in pulling derivatives back from the brink.

Deregulation and Reregulation

Regulation itself is complex enough in today's rapidly changing financial marketplace, and domestic financial deregulation has the tendency to put very dangerous tools and toys in the hands of the uninitiated. Certain corrections have clearly been needed from the beginning. There are many today who argue that financial markets do indeed need to be regulated, but of course the degree and type is unclear. There are new voices now calling for a new world order of regulation on the movement of capital and the trading of currencies—all in pursuit of preventing a recurrence of the financial crisis. This regulatory initiative has followed financial crises for decades, but little has been accomplished. Time will tell, once again.

Capital Mobility

Capital is more mobile today than ever before. The combination of global capital markets of size never seen before with more and more economic systems around the globe that are pursuing market economic solutions to both wealth and social ills means capital will continue to act as the elephant in the row boat. Many countries and regulatory authorities are now considering restrictions on the movement of capital, a measure that would potentially be a major setback for globalization.

Illiquid Markets

This, finally, will be the most troublesome. Most of the mathematics and rational behavior behind the design of today's sophisticated financial products, derivatives, and investment vehicles are based on principles of orderly and liquid markets. When the trading of highly commoditized securities as clean as overnight bank loans between banks becomes the core source of instability in the system, then all traditional knowledge and assumptions of finance have indeed come into question.

As the long-term impacts of the global financial crisis are still under study, it is also clear that the sheer size of the crisis may have been even larger than suspected. Figure 7.17 presents the results of a recent study by McKinsey, which estimated that

Figure 7.17 The Global Financial Crash

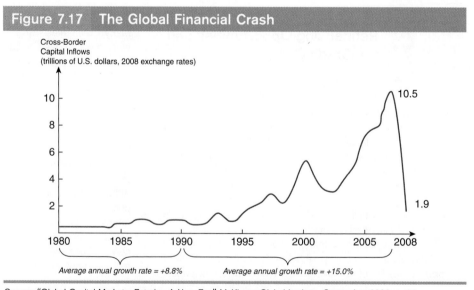

Cross-Border
Capital Inflows
(trillions of U.S. dollars, 2008 exchange rates)

Average annual growth rate = +8.8%

Average annual growth rate = +15.0%

Source: "Global Capital Markets: Entering A New Era," McKinsey Global Institute, September 2009, p. 14.

international capital flows plummeted in 2008 to levels not seen since 2002. Despite the collapse in cross-border capital movements, the global economy today continues its recovery and capital is once more flowing to fund the innovation and imagination of global entrepreneurs.

SUMMARY

This chapter has spanned the breadth of the global capital markets—the currencies, the assets, the institutions—that provide the core of funding for global business. The world's single largest capital market, the market for foreign exchange, was shown to be growing at an ever-faster rate in recent years. And although globalization forces have seen the expansion of currency trading to every corner of the earth, the center of activity remains London and New York. One major change, however, is clearly on the horizon: the ascendency of the Chinese currency, the yuan, to being one of the top four or five currencies of the world.

The global capital markets used for funding business growth, the debt and equity that are traded in the traditional global financial centers, are still largely accessible via commercial banks. Banks play a pivotal role in the trading and pricing of international securities. It is this critical linkage, however, that was so influential with the onset of the global financial crisis of 2007–2009. The very trust in trading between banks, the so-called counterparty risk, and the fundamental interest rate between banks—LIBOR—was at the core of the crisis. Although the global capital markets and global economy itself are showing signs of recovery, the long-term impacts of the global financial crisis are still unknown.

KEY TERMS

spot rates   203
forward rates   203
cross rates   203
gold standard   208
direct intervention   210

coordinated intervention   210
purchasing power parity
   (PPP)   212
Law of One Price   213
euromarkets   215

eurocurrency   217
eurodollars   217
correspondent banks   218
bearer bond   219
financial mercantilism   228

QUESTIONS FOR DISCUSSION

1. What is the role of banks in the international capital markets?

2. What is the purpose of an exchange rate?

3. How should an exchange rate change over time?

4. How are currencies traded today?

5. What is a forward exchange rate?

6. Is the Big Mac a good or bad measure of purchasing power parity?

7. How do firms use the international capital markets?

8. What is traditionally more "global," debt or equity?

9. What were the major causes of the global financial crisis of 2007–2009?

10. Was securitization to blame for the global financial crisis or simply a vehicle for trading debt?

11. What role did LIBOR play in the global financial crisis?

12. What do you think should be done to prevent another global financial crisis?

INTERNET EXERCISES

1. The online version of the *New York Times* has a special section entitled "Times Topics"—issues of continuing interest and coverage by the publication. The current financial crisis is covered and updated regularly here.

   http://topics.nytimes.com/topics/reference/timestopics/subjects/c/credit_crisis/

2. The British Bankers Association (BBA), the author of LIBOR, provides both current data for LIBOR of varying maturities as well as timely studies of interbank market behavior and practices.

   http://www.bba.org.uk/bba/jsp/polopoly.jsp?d=141

3. The Bank for International Settlements (BIS) publishes regular assessments of international banking activity. Use the BIS website to find up to date analysis of the ongoing credit crisis.

http://www.bis.org/

4. The New York Federal Reserve Bank maintains an interactive map of mortgage and credit card delinquencies for the United States. Use the following web site to view the latest in default rates according to the Fed.

http://data.newyorkfed.org/creditconditionsmap/

TAKE A STAND

The global financial crisis has led to a serious debate over the performance and reward system used in the financial sector. Whether it be the loan originators who were rewarded with fee-based bonuses for the mortgage loans they could initiate, or the CDOs or CDSs that investment banking and hedge funds could create and sell, many market analysts believe it is a system that is motivated to create and trade securities that are ultimately of questionable value. They are generally rewarded for the initiation of the asset, not on the basis of whether it proves the test of time in its creditworthiness and ability to repay.

For Discussion

1. The current fee and bonus income generated in the investment banking community is needed to attract and retain the intellectual and entrepreneurial talent to sustain one of the most innovative markets in the world. Without these rewards, the global capital markets will fall into a sluggish system of archaic banking that will prevent the true possibilities of globalization to be realized.

2. The current system of enormous rewards for origination—but not sustainability of creditworthiness over time—has led to a short-term trading culture, which created the global credit crisis. The returns to the developers and originators of the many financial derivatives at the heart of the credit crisis need to be tied to the demonstrated ability of the derivatives to be secure and sound investments over time.

CHAPTER 8

Economic Integration and Emerging Markets

CHAPTER CONTENTS & LEARNING OBJECTIVES

LEVELS OF ECONOMIC INTEGRATION

　1. To review types of economic integration among countries

ARGUMENTS SURROUNDING ECONOMIC INTEGRATION

　2. To compare and contrast the costs and benefits to advancing economic integration

REGIONAL GROUPINGS

　3. To suggest corporate response to advancing economic integration

CARTELS AND COMMODITY PRICE AGREEMENTS

　4. To examine how an organization tries to control the price and quantity supplied of a particular commodity

EMERGING MARKETS

　5. To survey the vast opportunities for trade offered by emerging market economies

BARRIERS TO BUSINESS

　6. To understand the scope of barriers to business and infrastructure challenges

TRANSITION ECONOMIES

　7. To define economies that are changing from a centrally planned economy to a free market

THE DEVELOPING MARKETS

　8. To illustrate growth in developing countries by encouraging potential markets

ECONOMIC INTEGRATION AND THE INTERNATIONAL MANAGER

　9. To suggest corporate response to advancing economic integration

Building Blocs toward Worldwide Free Trade

Regional groupings based on economics became increasingly important in the last ten years. Thirty-two such groupings are estimated to be in existence: three in Europe, four in the Middle East, five in Asia, and ten each in Africa and the Americas. Trade within the three major blocs, the American, European, and Asian, has grown rapidly, while trading among these blocs or with outsiders is either declining or growing far more moderately.

Some of these groupings around the world have the superstructure of nation-states (such as the European Union), some (such as the ASEAN Free Trade Area) are multinational agreements that may be more political arrangements than cohesive **trading blocs** at present. Increasingly, new blocs are made up of several independent blocs; for example, the European Economic Area is composed of the EU member-nations and the nations belonging to the European Free Trade Area. Some arrangements are not trading blocs per se, but work to further them. The Free Trade Area of the Americas (FTAA) is a policy initiative to bring together five major blocs in the Western Hemisphere to compete more effectively against Europe and Asia. It was supposed to go into effect in 2005, but due to political changes in South America and disputes over agriculture and intellectual property rights, there is little chance for a comprehensive trade agreement in the foreseeable future. As a matter of

fact, an alternative has arisen in opposition to the U.S.–led FTAA. The Bolivarian Alternative for the People of Our Americas (led by Venezuela) focuses more on social welfare and economic aid than trade liberalization. When the Free Trade Area of the Americas stalled, the United States only has free trade arrangements with Chile, Colombia, Panama, and Peru. The Central America–Dominican Republic–United States Free Trade Agreement (CAFTA –DR) includes seven signatories. Regional economic integration in Asia has been driven more by market forces than by treaties and by a need to maintain balance in negotiations with Europe and North America. Broader formal agreements are in formative stages; for example, the Asia Pacific Economic Cooperation (APEC) initiated in 1989 would bring together partners from multiple continents and blocs. APEC members are joined by such economic powerhouses as China, Japan, South Korea, Taiwan, and the United States.

Regional groupings are constantly being developed in multiple ways either internally, by adding new dimensions to the existing ones, or by creating new blocs. In 1995 and 2007, informal proposals were made to create a new bloc between NAFTA and EU members called TAFTA, the Transatlantic Free Trade Area. Since the elimination of the Soviet Union, 12 former republics have tried to forge common economic policies, but thus far only

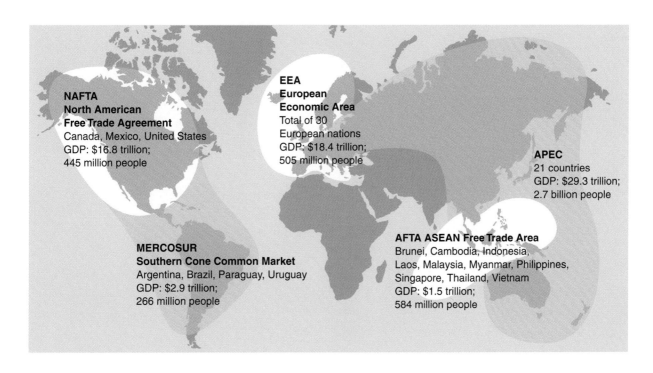

NAFTA
North American
Free Trade Agreement
Canada, Mexico, United States
GDP: $16.8 trillion;
445 million people

EEA
European
Economic Area
Total of 30
European nations
GDP: $18.4 trillion;
505 million people

APEC
21 countries
GDP: $29.3 trillion;
2.7 billion people

MERCOSUR
Southern Cone Common Market
Argentina, Brazil, Paraguay, Uruguay
GDP: $2.9 trillion;
266 million people

AFTA ASEAN Free Trade Area
Brunei, Cambodia, Indonesia,
Laos, Malaysia, Myanmar, Philippines,
Singapore, Thailand, Vietnam
GDP: $1.5 trillion;
584 million people

Belarus, Kazakhstan, and Russia are signatories. In 2002, 16 EU countries adopted the euro as a common currency and eliminated their respective national currencies. More than 175 million people worldwide use currencies that are pegged to the euro, including more than 150 million people in Africa.

Companies are facing ever-intensifying competition within these blocs but, at the same time, can take advantage of emerging opportunities. As new countries join blocs, fears that these blocs are nothing but protectionism on a grander scale are allayed. As governments liberalize their industrial sectors and allow for competition, they give birth to companies that are not only competitive regionally but globally as well.

Sources: "Leaders: Doing Doha Down; Trade," *Economist*, September 5, 2009, 15; "Building Blocks Asia. View," *Econmist.com/ Global Agenda*, February 27, 2008, 1; "Kazakhstan Ratifies Eurasec Customs Union Agreement," *Regional Trade Agreements in the ECE*, June 3, 2008; "The Morning Brief: Free Trade Draws Even More Fire," *Wall Street Journal*, October 4, 2007, online edition; "Merkel Ponders Atlantic Free Trade Zone," *Financial Times*, September 16, 2006; "Politics & Economic Nationalism, Is Outmaneuvered by Paris," *Wall Street Journal*, May 25, 2006, A8; and Ilkka A. Ronkainen, "Trading Blocs: Opportunity or Demise for International Trade?" *Multinational Business Review*, 1 (Spring 1993): 1–9.

The **Group of Five** (the United States, Britain, France, Germany and Japan) consists of the major industrialized countries of the world. This group is sometimes expanded to the **Group of Seven** (by adding Italy and Canada) and the **Group of Ten** (by adding Sweden, the Netherlands, and Belgium). It may also be expanded to encompass the members of the Organization for Economic Cooperation and Development, OECD (which consists of 30 countries: western Europe, the United States, Australia, Canada, Czech Republic, Hungary, Japan, Mexico, New Zealand, Poland, Slovakia, South Korea, and Turkey). In 2009, the **Group of Twenty** (the Group of Seven plus Argentina, Australia, Brazil, China, India, Indonesia, Mexico, Russia, Saudi Arabia, South Africa, South Korea, and Turkey) has been prominent in dealing with the economic crisis.

Important among the middle-income developing countries are the newly industrialized countries (NICs), which include Singapore, Taiwan, Korea, Hong Kong, Brazil, and Mexico (some propose adding Malaysia and the Philippines to the list as well). Some of these NICs will earn a new acronym, RIC (rapidly industrializing country). Over the past 20 years, Singapore has served as a hub, providing critical financial and managerial services to the Southeast Asian markets. Singapore has successfully attracted foreign investment, mostly regional corporate headquarters and knowledge-intensive industries, and has served as one of the main gateways for Asian trade. Its exports have reached well over 300 percent of GDP.[1]

The major oil-exporting countries, in particular the eleven members of the Organization of Petroleum Exporting Countries (OPEC) and countries such as Russia, are dependent on the price of oil for their world market participation. A relatively high dollar price per barrel (as high as $140 in 2008) works very much in these countries' favor, while lower prices (as low as $40 in 2009) cause significant economic hardship.[2]

Many of the emerging economies will depend on the success of their industrialization efforts in the years to come, even in the case of resource-rich countries that may find commodity prices being driven down by human-made substitutes. This applies especially to the Brazil, Russia, India, and China (BRIC) group. China has become the world's largest exporter of textiles since beginning to increase production in the 1980s. Despite an image of hopeless poverty, India has nearly 300 million middle-class consumers, more than Germany. These countries, which constitute the majority of the world's population, may also provide the biggest potential market opportunity for marketers in the twenty-first century.[3] Even if they lack the scale of the BRIC, 11 (also known as the "Next 11") countries can rival the G7 in time. These include Bangladesh, Egypt, Indonesia, Iran, Korea, Mexico, Nigeria, Pakistan, Philippines, Turkey, and Vietnam.[4]

In less-developed countries, debt problems and falling commodity prices make market development difficult. Africa, the poorest continent, owes the rest of the world $200 billion, an amount equal to three-quarters of its gross domestic product (GDP) and nearly four times its annual exports. Another factor contributing to the challenging situation is that only 1 percent of the world's private investment goes to sub-Saharan Africa.[5]

In the former centrally planned economies, dramatic changes have been under way for the past 15 years. A hefty capital inflow has been key to modernizing the newly emerging democracies of both central and eastern Europe. Desperately needed will be Western technology, management, and marketing know-how to provide better jobs and put more locally made and imported consumer goods in the shops. Within the groups, prospects vary: the future for countries such as Hungary, the Baltics, the Czech Republic, and Poland looks far better than it does for Russia, as they reap the benefits of membership in the European Union.

Group of Five Name given to the five industrialized nations that meet periodically to achieve a cooperative effort on international economic and monetary issues. The **Group of Seven**, the **Group of Ten**, and the **Group of Twenty** are forums for member nations to discuss key issues related to the global economy.

LEVELS OF ECONOMIC INTEGRATION

1. To review types of economic integration among countries

A trading bloc is a preferential economic arrangement among a group of countries. The forms it may take are shown in Table 8.1. From least to most integrative, they are the free trade area, the customs union, the common market, and the economic union.[6] It should be noted that countries (or groups of countries) may give preferential treatment to other countries on the basis of historic ties or due to political motivations. Examples include the European Union granting preferential access for selected products from their former colonies under the Cotenou Agreement, or similar treatment by the United States of Caribbean nations (the Caribbean Basin Initiative). Since the benefits are unidirectional, these arrangements are not considered to be part of economic integration.

THE FREE TRADE AREA

free trade area An area in which all barriers to trade among member countries are removed, although sometimes only for certain goods or services.

The **free trade area** is the least restrictive and loosest form of economic integration among countries. In a free trade area, all barriers to trade among member countries are removed. Therefore, goods and services are freely traded among member countries in much the same way that they flow freely between, for example, South Carolina and New York. No discriminatory taxes, quotas, tariffs, or other trade barriers are allowed. Sometimes a free trade area is formed only for certain classes of goods and services. An agricultural free trade area, for example, implies the absence of restrictions on the trade of agricultural products only. The most notable feature of a free trade area is that each country continues to set its own policies in relation to nonmembers. In other words, each member is free to set any tariffs, quotas, or other restrictions that it chooses on trade with countries outside the free trade area. Among such free trade areas the most notable are the European Free Trade Area (EFTA) and the North American Free Trade Agreement (NAFTA). As an example of the freedom members have in terms of their policies toward nonmembers, Mexico has signed a number of bilateral free trade agreements with other blocs (the European Union) and nations (Chile) to both improve trade and to attract foreign direct investment. The United States has free trade agreements in force with 17 countries: Australia, Bahrain, Canada, Chile, Costa Rica, Dominican Republic, El Salvador, Guatemala, Honduras, Israel, Jordan, Mexico, Morocco, Nicaragua, Oman, Peru, and Singapore. The United States has signed free trade agreements with Colombia, Korea, and Panama, but Congress must enact legislation to approve and implement each individual agreement in order for them to go into effect.[7]

THE CUSTOMS UNION

customs union Collaboration among trading countries in which members dismantle trade barriers among members and also establish a common trade policy with respect to nonmembers.

The **customs union** is one step further along the spectrum of economic integration. Like the members of a free trade area, members of a customs union dismantle barriers to trade in goods and services among themselves. In addition, however, the customs union establishes a common trade policy with respect to nonmembers. Typically, this takes the form of a common external tariff, where imports from nonmembers are subject to the

Table 8.1	Forms of International Economic Integration			
Stage of Integration	Abolition of Tariffs and Quotas Among Members	Common Tariff and Quota System	Abolition of Restrictions on Factor Movements	Harmonization and Unification of Economic Policies and Institutions
Free trade area	Yes	No	No	No
Customs union	Yes	Yes	No	No
Common market	Yes	Yes	Yes	No
Economic union	Yes	Yes	Yes	Yes

same tariff when sold to any member country. Tariff revenues are then shared among members according to a prespecified formula. The Southern African Customs Union is the oldest (1910) and most successful example of economic integration in Africa.

THE COMMON MARKET

Further still along the spectrum of economic integrations is the **common market**. Like the customs union, a common market has no barriers to trade among members and has a common external trade policy. In addition, however, factors of production are also mobile among members. Factors of production include labor, capital, and technology. Thus restrictions on immigration, emigration, and cross-border investment are abolished. The importance of **factor mobility** for economic growth cannot be overstated. When factors of production are freely mobile, then capital, labor, and technology may be employed in their most productive uses. To see the importance of factor mobility, imagine the state of the U.S. economy if unemployed steelworkers in Pittsburgh were prevented from migrating to the growing Sunbelt in search of better opportunities. Alternatively, imagine that savings in New York banks could not be invested in profitable opportunities in Chicago.

Despite the obvious benefits, members of a common market must be prepared to cooperate closely in monetary, fiscal, and employment policies. Furthermore, while a common market will enhance the productivity of members in the aggregate, it is by no means clear that individual member countries will always benefit. Because of these difficulties, the goals of common markets have proved to be elusive in many areas of the world, notably South America and Asia.

THE ECONOMIC UNION

The creation of a true **economic union** requires integration of economic policies in addition to the free movement of goods, services, and factors of production across borders. Under an economic union, members would harmonize monetary policies, taxation, and government spending. In addition, a common currency would be used by all members. This could be accomplished de facto, or in effect, by a system of fixed exchange rates. Clearly, the formation of an economic union requires nations to surrender a large measure of their national sovereignty to supranational authorities in communitywide institutions such as the European Parliament. The ratification of the Maastricht Treaty by all of the then 12 member-countries created the European Union, effective January 1, 1994. The treaty (jointly with the Treaty of Amsterdam, which took effect in 1999) set the foundation for an **economic and monetary union (EMU)** with the establishment of the euro (€) as a common currency by January 1, 1999. A total of 16 of the EU countries are currently part of "Euroland" (Austria, Belgium, Cyprus, Finland, France, Germany, Greece, Holland, Ireland, Italy, Luxembourg, Malta, Portugal, Slovakia, Slovenia, and Spain). The Treaty of Nice (February 1, 2003) reformed the institutional structure of the European Union to withstand eastward expansion. In addition, moves would be made toward a **political union** with common foreign and security policy, as well as judicial cooperation.[8] The Lisbon Treaty (December 1, 2009) makes an attempt to streamline EU institutions to make the enlarged bloc of 27 states function better.

ARGUMENTS SURROUNDING ECONOMIC INTEGRATION

A number of arguments surround economic integration. They center on (1) trade creation and diversion; (2) the effects of integration on import prices, competition, economies of scale, and factor productivity; and (3) the benefits of regionalism versus nationalism.

---

common market A group of countries that agrees to remove all barriers to trade among members, to establish a common trade policy with respect to nonmembers, and also to allow mobility for factors of production—labor, capital, and technology.

factor mobility The ability to freely move factors of production across borders, as among common market countries.

economic union A union among trading countries that has the characteristics of a common market and also harmonizes monetary policies, taxation, and government spending and uses a common currency.

economic and monetary union (EMU) The ideal among European leaders that economic integration should move beyond the four freedoms; specifically, it entails (1) closer coordination of economic policies to promote exchange rate stability and convergence of inflation rates and growth rates, (2) creation of a European central bank, and (3) replacement of national monetary authorities by the European Central Bank and adoption of the euro as the European currency.

political union A group of countries that have common foreign policy and security policy and that share judicial cooperation.

2. To compare and contrast the costs and benefits to advancing economic integration

TRADE CREATION AND TRADE DIVERSION

Either negative or positive effects may result when a group of countries trade freely among themselves but maintain common barriers to trade with nonmembers.[9]

In 1986, Spain formally entered the European Union (EU) as a member. Prior to membership, Spain—like all nonmembers such as the United States, Canada, and Japan—traded with the EU and suffered the common external tariff. Imports of agricultural products from Spain or the United States had the same tariff applied to their products, for example, 20 percent. During this period, the United States was a lower-cost producer of wheat compared to Spain. U.S. exports to EU members may have cost $3.00 per bushel, plus a 20 percent tariff of $0.60, for a total of $3.60 per bushel. If Spain at the same time produced wheat at $3.20 per bushel, plus a 20 percent tariff of $0.64 for a total cost to EU customers of $3.84 per bushel, its wheat was more expensive and therefore less competitive.

But when Spain joined the EU as a member, its products were no longer subject to the common external tariffs; Spain had become a member of the "club" and therefore enjoyed its benefits. Spain was now the low-cost producer of wheat at $3.20 per bushel, compared to the price of $3.60 from the United States. Trade flows changed as a result. The increased export of wheat and other products by Spain to the EU as a result of its membership is termed **trade creation**. The elimination of the tariff literally created more trade between Spain and the EU. At the same time, because the United States was still outside of the EU, its products suffered the higher price as a result of tariff application. U.S. exports to the EU fell. When the source of trading competitiveness is shifted in this manner from one country to another, it is termed **trade diversion**.

Whereas trade creation is distinctly positive in moving toward freer trade and therefore lower prices for consumers within the EU, the impact of trade diversion is negative. Trade diversion is inherently negative because the competitive advantage has shifted away from the lower-cost producer to the higher-cost producer. The benefits of Spain's membership are enjoyed by Spanish farmers (greater export sales) and EU consumers (lower prices). The two major costs are reduced tariff revenues collected and costs borne by the United States and its exports as a result of lost sales. In such cases, the injured party may seek compensation based on global trade rules. As a result of the European Union's expansion in 2004, the Japanese government argued that its exporters would lose sales of $22 million in the new member countries in product categories such as autos and consumer electronics. The EU argued that the Union's expansion would benefit Japanese companies in the long term.[10]

From the perspective of nonmembers such as the United States, the formation or expansion of a customs union is obviously negative. Most damaged will naturally be countries that may need to have trade to build their economies, such as the countries of the Third World. From the perspective of members of the customs union, the formation or expansion is only beneficial if the trade creation benefits exceed trade diversion costs. When Finland and Sweden joined the EU, the cost of an average food basket decreased by 10 percent. The only major item with a significant price increase was bananas due to the quota and tariff regime that the EU maintained in favor of its former colonies and against the major banana-producing nations in Latin America.

REDUCED IMPORT PRICES

When a small country imposes a tariff on imports, the price of the goods will typically rise because sellers will increase prices to cover the cost of the tariff. This increase in price, in turn, will result in lower demand for the imported goods. If a bloc of countries imposes the tariff, however, the fall in demand for the imported goods will be substantial. The exporting country may then be forced to reduce the price of the

trade creation A benefit of economic integration; the benefit to a particular country when a group of countries trade a product freely among themselves but maintain common barriers to trade with nonmembers.

trade diversion A cost of economic integration; the cost to a particular country when a group of countries trade a product freely among themselves but maintain common barriers to trade with nonmembers.

goods. The possibility of lower prices for imports results from the greater market power of the bloc relative to that of a single country. The result may then be an improvement in the trade position of the bloc countries. Any gain in the trade position of bloc members, however, is offset by a deteriorating trade position for the exporting country. Again, unlike the win–win situation resulting from free trade, the scenario involving a trade bloc is instead win–lose.

INCREASED COMPETITION AND ECONOMIES OF SCALE

Integration increases market size and therefore may result in a lower degree of monopoly in the production of certain goods and services.[11] This is because a larger market will tend to increase the number of competing firms, resulting in greater efficiency and lower prices for consumers. Moreover, less energetic and productive economies may be spurred into action by competition from the more industrious bloc members.

Many industries, such as steel and automobiles, require large-scale production in order to obtain economies of scale in production. Therefore, certain industries may simply not be economically viable in smaller, trade-protected countries. However, the formation of a trading bloc enlarges the market so that large-scale production is justified. The lower per-unit costs resulting from scale economies may then be obtained. These lower production costs resulting from greater production for an enlarged market are called **internal economies of scale**. This is evident if the region adopts common standards, thus allowing not only for bigger markets for the companies but enabling them to become global powerhouses. Ericsson and Nokia both benefited from the EU adopting the Global System for Mobile (GSM) standard for wireless communication to build scale beyond their small domestic markets.

internal economies of scale Lower production costs resulting from greater production for an enlarged market.

In a common market, **external economies of scale** may also be present. Because a common market allows factors of production to flow freely across borders, the firm may now have access to cheaper capital, more highly skilled labor, or superior technology. These factors will improve the quality of the firm's good or service or will lower costs or both.

external economies of scale Lower production costs resulting from the free mobility of factors of production in a common market.

HIGHER FACTOR PRODUCTIVITY

When factors of production are freely mobile, the wealth of the common market countries, in aggregate, will likely increase. The theory behind this contention is straightforward: factor mobility will lead to the movement of labor and capital from areas of low productivity to areas of high productivity. In addition to the economic gains from factor mobility, there are other benefits not so easily quantified. The free movement of labor fosters a higher level of communication across cultures. This, in turn, leads to a higher degree of cross-cultural understanding; as people move, their ideas, skills, and ethnicity move with them.

Again, however, factor mobility will not necessarily benefit each country in the common market. A poorer country, for example, may lose badly needed investment capital to a richer country, where opportunities are perceived to be more profitable. Another disadvantage of factor mobility that is often cited is the brain-drain phenomenon. A poorer country may lose its most talented workers when they are free to search out better opportunities. More-developed member countries worry that companies may leave for other member countries where costs of operation, such as social costs, are lower. Nokia's decision to close down a major production facility for mobile devices in Bochum, Germany, and to move its manufacturing to more cost-competitive regions in Europe (such as Cluj in Romania) met with a hailstorm of protests from the German government and individual citizens.[12]

REGIONALISM VERSUS NATIONALISM

Economists have composed elegant and compelling arguments in favor of the various levels of economic integration. It is difficult, however, to turn these arguments into reality in the face of intense nationalism. The biggest impediment to economic integration remains the reluctance of nations to surrender a measure of their autonomy. Integration, by its very nature, requires the surrender of national power and self-determinism. American firms are contributing aggressively to the reverse brain drain. For decades, they shifted blue-collar manufacturing jobs to parts of the world with low labor costs and acceptable quality standards. Now, firms are outsourcing knowledge work—engineering, software, and product design and development—to such countries as China, India, and Russia and already have as many as 250 million to 500 million knowledge workers—the kind of highly educated, technologically skilled employees who can write computer code, design sophisticated products, and manage high-end production processes.[13]

REGIONAL GROUPINGS

3. To suggest corporate response to advancing economic integration

EUROPEAN INTEGRATION

The first steps toward European integration were taken following the devastation of World War II, when a spirit of cooperation began to emerge across Europe. Established in 1948 to administer Marshall Plan aid from the United States, the Organization for European Economic Cooperation (OEEC) set the stage for more ambitious integration programs. Over the following years, several cooperative treaties and coalitions contributed to the eventual development of the European Union. Most notably, in 1957, the European Economic Community (EEC) was formally established by the **Treaty of Rome**. The cooperative spirit apparent throughout the treaty was based on the premise that the mobility of goods, services, labor, and capital—the "four freedoms"—was of paramount importance for the economic prosperity of the region. Founding members envisioned that the successful integration of the European economies would result in an economic power to rival that of the United States. Table 8.2 shows the founding members of the community in 1957 and members who have joined since, as well as those invited to join early in the twenty-first century.

Some countries were reluctant to embrace the ambitious integrative effort of the Treaty of Rome. In 1960, a looser, less integrated philosophy was endorsed with the formation of the European Free Trade Association (EFTA) by eight countries:

Treaty of Rome The original agreement that established the foundation for the formation of the European Economic Community.

Table 8.2	Membership of the European Union					
1957	**1993**	**1995**	**2004**		**2007**	
France*	Great Britain (1973)	Austria (1995)*	Czech Republic	Latvia	Bulgaria	
West Germany*	Ireland (1973)*	Finland (1995)*	Cyprus*	Lithuania	Romania	
Italy*	Denmark (1973)	Sweden (1995)	Estonia	Malta*		
Belgium*	Greece (1981)*		Hungary	Slovakia*		
Netherlands*	Spain (1986)*		Poland			
Luxembourg*	Portugal (1986)*		Slovenia*			

*Euro users

United Kingdom, Norway, Denmark, Sweden, Austria, Finland, Portugal, and Switzerland. Barriers to trade among member countries were dismantled, although each country maintained its own policies with nonmember states. Because all but Norway, Switzerland, and newer members Iceland and Liechtenstein have joined or plan to join the EU, EFTA has lost much of its significance. Since 1994, the European Economic Area (EEA) agreement between the EU and three EFTA countries allows these EFTA countries to participate in the European Single Market without joining the EU. Switzerland is linked to the EU by Swiss–EU bilateral agreements, with a different content from that of the EEA agreement.[14]

Perhaps the most important implication of the four freedoms for Europe is the economic growth that is expected to result. First, there will be growth resulting from the elimination of transaction costs associated with border patrols, customs procedures, and so forth. Second, economic growth will be spurred by the economies of scale achieved when production facilities become more concentrated. For example, Procter & Gamble in Lodz, Poland, focuses on blades and razor products for EU and other international markets. Third, there will be gains from more intense competition among EU companies. Firms that hold monopolies in one country will now be subject to competition from firms in other EU countries. The introduction of the euro is expected to add to the efficiencies, especially in terms of consolidation of firms across industries and across countries. Furthermore, countries in euroland will enjoy cheaper transaction costs and reduced currency risks, and consumers and businesses will enjoy price transparency and increased price-based competition. Economic growth in Europe has important implications for firms within and outside the EU. There will be substantial benefits for those firms already operating in Europe. Those firms will gain because their operations in one country can now be freely expanded into others, and their products may be freely sold across borders. In a border-free Europe, firms will have access to a total of 505 million consumers. In addition, the free movement of capital will allow the firms to sell securities, raise capital, and recruit labor throughout Europe.

Progress toward the goal of free movement of goods has been achieved largely due to the move from a "common standards approach" to a "mutual recognition approach." Under the common standards approach, EU members were forced to negotiate the specifications for literally thousands of products, often unsuccessfully. For example, because of differences in tastes, agreement was never reached on specifications for beer, sausage, or mayonnaise. Under the mutual recognition approach, the laborious quest for common standards is, in most cases, no longer necessary. Instead, as long as a product meets legal and specification requirements in one member-country, it may be freely exported to any other, and customers serve as the final arbiters of success. Less progress toward free movement of people in Europe has been made than toward free movement of goods.

The primary difficulty is that EU members have been unable to agree on a common immigration policy. As long as this disagreement persists, travelers between countries must pass through border checkpoints. Some countries—notably Germany—have had relatively lax immigration policies, while others—especially those with higher unemployment rates—favor strict controls. The member-states have agreed to develop a common immigration policy at EU level by a coordinated approach that takes into account the economic and demographic situation of the EU.[15] A second issue concerning the free movement of people is the acceptability of professional certifications across countries. In 1993, the largest EU member-countries passed all of the professional worker directives. This means that workers' professional qualifications will be recognized throughout the EU, guaranteeing them equal treatment in terms of employment, working conditions, and social protection in the host country.

Attaining free movement of capital within the EU entails several measures. First, it requires that citizens be free to trade in EU currencies without restrictions. Second, the regulations governing banks and other financial institutions would be harmonized. In addition, mergers and acquisitions would be regulated by the EU rather than by national governments. Finally, securities would be freely tradable across countries.

A key aspect of free trade in services is the right to compete fairly to obtain government contracts. Under the guidelines, a government should not give preference to its own citizens in awarding government contracts. However, little progress has been made in this regard. Public procurement accounts for 10 to 25 percent of world trade but is mostly restricted to national companies.[16]

common agricultural policy (CAP) An integrated system of subsidies and rebates applied to agricultural interests in the European Union.

Another source of difficulty that intensified in the 1980s and continues today was the administration of the community's **common agricultural policy (CAP)**. Most industrialized countries, including the United States, Canada, and Japan, have adopted wide-scale government intervention and subsidization schemes for agriculture. In the case of the EU, however, these policies have been implemented on a communitywide, rather than national, level. The CAP includes (1) a price-support system, whereby EU agriculture officials intervene in the market to keep farm product prices within a specified range; (2) direct subsidies to farmers; and (3) rebates to farmers who export or agree to store farm products rather than sell them within the community. The implementation of these policies absorbs about 48 percent of the annual EU budget. The CAP has caused problems both within the EU and in relationships with nonmembers. Within the EU, the richer, more industrialized countries resent the extensive subsidization of the more agrarian economies. Outside trading partners, especially the United States, have repeatedly charged the EU with unfair trade practices in agriculture.[17]

Single European Act The legislative basis for the European Integration.

ORGANIZATION OF THE EU

© Guy Vanderelst/Taxi/Getty Images, Inc.

The European Union has several governing bodies, one of which is the EU Parliament. The Parliament has 751 members elected by popular vote in their home nations. The Parliament has power to veto membership applications and trade agreements with non-EU countries. The Commission must enjoy the confidence of the Parliament.

The executive body of the EU is the European Commission, headquartered in Brussels. The commission may be likened to the executive branch of the U.S. government. It is composed of 27 commissioners and headed by a president. The commissioners oversee more than 30 directorates-general (or departments), such as agriculture, transportation, and external relations. The commissioners are appointed by the member states, but according to the Treaty of Rome, their allegiance is to the community, not to their home countries. The commission's staff in Brussels numbers over 25,000. Because the EU has 23 official languages, 20 percent of the staff are interpreters and translators.

The Council of Ministers has the final power to decide EU actions. The votes are allocated to the representatives of member countries on the basis of country size. With the reweighting of votes to accommodate new members, the United Kingdom has 29 votes, while Finland has 7. Some of the most important provisions of the **Single European Act** expanded the ability of the Council to pass legislation. The number of matters requiring unanimity was reduced, and countries' ability to veto legislation was weakened substantially. Most decisions are taken by qualified majority vote. The presidency of the Council rotates among the member states every six months.

Figure 8.1   The Institutions of the European Union

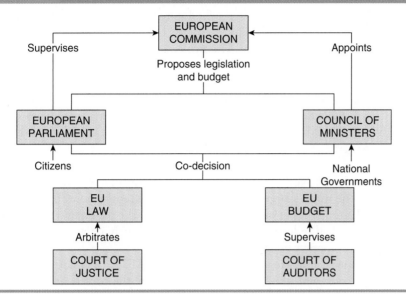

Source: Web sites of the major institutions of the European Union can be found at http://news.bbc.co.uk/2/hi/europe/7840766.stm; http://www.europarl.europa.eu/addresses/institutions/websites.htm.

The Court of Justice is somewhat analogous to the judicial branch of the U.S. government. The court is composed of 27 judges and is based in Luxembourg. The court adjudicates matters related to the European Constitution, especially trade and business disputes. Judicial proceedings may be initiated by member countries, as well as by firms and individuals.

The European Parliament is composed of 751 members elected by popular vote in member countries for a five-year term. The Parliament started essentially as an advisory body with relatively little power. The fact that the only elected body of the EU had little policymaking power led many to charge that the EU suffered from a "democratic deficit." In other words, decisions are made bureaucratically rather than democratically. However, the Single European Act empowered the Parliament to veto EU membership applications as well as trade agreements with non-EU countries. The Maastricht and Amsterdam Treaties empowered the Parliament to veto legislation in certain policy areas and confer with the Council to settle differences in their respective drafts of legislation. Furthermore, the Parliament can question the Commission and Council, amend and reject the budget, and dismiss the entire Commission.[18] The entities and the process of decision making are summarized in Figure 8.1. Not shown are the Court of Auditors (who are to ensure the sound financial management of the EU) and the European Central Bank, which is responsible for monetary policy and the euro.

NORTH AMERICAN ECONOMIC INTEGRATION

Although the EU is undoubtedly the most successful and well-known integrative effort, integration efforts in North America, although only a few years old, have gained momentum and attention. What started as a trading pact between two close and economically well-developed allies has already been expanded conceptually to include Mexico, and long-term plans call for further additions. However, in North American integration the interest is purely economic; there are no constituencies for political integration.

North American Free Trade Agreement

After three failed tries this century, the United States and Canada signed a free trade agreement that went into effect January 1, 1989. The agreement created a $ 15.8 trillion continental economy. The two countries had already had sectoral free trade arrangements; for example, one for automotive products had existed for over 20 years. Even before the agreement, however, the United States and Canada were already the world's largest trading partners, and there were relatively few trade barriers. The new arrangement eliminated duties selectively in three stages over the 1989–1999 period.[19] It has also added as much as 1 percent in growth to both countries' economies. Trade between the United States and Canada exceeded $601 billion in 2008.

Negotiations on a North American Free Trade Agreement (NAFTA) began in 1994 to create the world's largest free market, with currently more than 445 million consumers and a total output of nearly 16.8 trillion.[20] The pact marked a bold departure: never before had industrialized countries created such a massive free trade area with a developing country neighbor.

Because Canada stands to gain very little from NAFTA (its trade with Mexico is 1 percent of its trade with the United States), much of the controversy has centered on the gains and losses for the United States and Mexico. Proponents have argued that the agreement will give U.S. firms access to a huge pool of relatively low-cost Mexican labor at a time when demographic trends are indicating labor shortages in many parts of the United States. At the same time, many new jobs will be created in Mexico. The agreement will give firms in both countries access to millions of additional consumers, and the liberalized trade flows will result in faster economic growth in both countries. The top 20 exports and imports between Mexico and the United States are in virtually the same industries, indicating intra-industry specialization and building of economies of scale for global competitiveness.[21] Overall, the corporate view toward NAFTA is overwhelmingly positive.

Opposition to NAFTA has been on issues relating to labor and the environment. Unions in particular worried about job loss to Mexico given lower wages and work standards, some estimating that six million U.S. workers were vulnerable to job loss. A distinctive feature of NAFTA is the two side agreements that were worked out to correct perceived abuses in labor and in the environment in Mexico. The North American Agreement on Labor Cooperation (NAALC) was set up to hear complaints about worker abuse. Similarly, the Commission on Environmental Compliance was established to act as a public advocate on the environment. The side agreements have, however, had little impact, mainly because the mechanisms they created have almost no enforcement power.[22]

After a remarkable start in increased trade and investment, NAFTA suffered a serious setback due to significant devaluation of the Mexican peso in early 1995 and the subsequent impact on trade. Critics of NAFTA argued that too much was expected too fast of a country whose political system and economy

Trucks from Mexico cross the border into the United States. Mexican truckers are subjected to increased inspections, insurance, and other requirements before entering the United States.

© Sandy Huffaker/Getty Images, Inc.

were not ready for open markets. In response, advocates of NAFTA argued that there was nothing wrong with the Mexican real economy and that the peso crisis was a political one that would be overcome with time.

Trade among Canada, Mexico, and the United States has increased dramatically since NAFTA took effect, with total trade exceeding $994.8 billion in 2008.[23] Reforms have turned Mexico into an attractive market in its own right. Mexico's gross domestic product has been expanding by more than 3 percent every year since 1989, and exports to the United States have risen 20 percent a year to $215.9 billion in 2008. By institutionalizing the nation's turn to open markets, the free trade agreement has attracted considerable new foreign investment. The United States has benefited from Mexico's success. U.S. exports to Mexico are nearly double those to Japan at $151.5 billion in 2008. While the surplus of $1.3 billion in 1994 has turned to a deficit of $64.4 billion in 2008, these imports have helped in Mexico's growth and will, therefore, strengthen NAFTA in the long term. Furthermore, U.S. imports from Mexico have been shown to have much higher U.S. content than imports from other countries.[24] At present, cooperation between Mexico and the United States is taking new forms beyond trade and investment; for example, binational bodies have been established to tackle issues such as migration, border control, and drug trafficking.[25]

Among the U.S. industries to benefit are computers, autos, petrochemicals, financial services, and aerospace. Aerospace companies such as Boeing, Honeywell, Airbus Industrie, and GE Aircraft Engines have recently made Mexico a center for both parts manufacture and assembly. Aerospace is now one of Mexico's largest industries, second only to electronics, with 20,000 workers employed.[26] In Mexico's growth toward a more advanced society, manufacturers of consumer goods will also stand to benefit. NAFTA has already had a major impact in the emergence of new retail chains, many established to handle new products from abroad.[27] Not only have U.S. retailers, such as Walmart, expanded to and in Mexico, but Mexican retailers, such as Grupo Gigante, have entered the U.S. market.[28] Walmart's use of lower tariffs, physical proximity, and buying power is changing the Mexican retail landscape as shown in the Focus on Entrepreneurship.

Free trade does produce both winners and losers. Although opponents concede that the agreement is likely to spur economic growth, they point out that

FOCUS ON ENTREPRENEURSHIP

NAFTA: Reshaping the Retail Market in Mexico and United States

Walmart International operates in 15 markets, and their focus is quite singular—deliver price leadership to customers. "Save money, live better" may translate differently into many languages where Walmart operates, but the message behind the mission is universal: Walmart has 3,859 locations, 694,000 people, and total sales of $24.6 billion worldwide.

Walmart saw the promise of the Mexican market in 1991 when it stepped outside of the United States for the first time and launched Sam's Clubs in 50-50 partnership with Cifra, Mexico's largest retailer. The local partner was needed to provide operational expertise in a market of significant culture and income differences from Walmart's domestic one. Within months the first outlet—a bare-bones unit that sold bulk items at just above wholesale prices—was breaking all Walmart records in sales. While tariffs still made imported goods pricey, "Made in the USA" merchandise also started appearing on the shelves.

After NAFTA took effect in 1994, tariffs tumbled, unleashing pent-up demand in Mexico for U.S.-made goods. The trade treaty also helped eliminate some of the transportation headaches and government red tape that had kept Walmart from fully realizing its competitive advantage. NAFTA resulted in many European and Asian manufacturers setting up plants in Mexico, giving the retailer cheaper access to more foreign brands.

Walmart's enormous buying power has kept it ahead of its Mexican competitors who are making similar moves. Because Walmart consolidates its orders for all goods it sells outside of the United States, it can wring deeper discounts from

(continued)

suppliers than can its local competitors. Walmart Mexico has repeatedly exploited NAFTA and other economic forces to trigger price wars. For example, rather than pocket the windfall that resulted when tariffs on Lasko brand floor fans fell from 20 percent to 2 percent, price cuts took place equal to the tariff reductions.

Behind Walmart's success are increasingly price-conscious consumers. The greater economic security of NAFTA has helped tame Mexico's once fierce inflation. The resulting price stability has made it easier for Mexican consumers to spot bargains. In addition, Walmart's clean, brightly lit interiors, orderly and well-stocked aisles, and consistent pricing policies are a relief from the chaotic atmosphere that still prevails in many local stores.

Walmart's aggressive tactics have resulted in complaints as well. In 2002, Mexico's Competition Commission was asked to probe into reports that Walmart exerts undue pressure on suppliers to lower their prices. Local retailers, such as Comerci, Gigante, and Soriana, have seen their profits plummet but are forced to provide prices competitive to Walmart's. In addition, they have engaged in aggressive rehauls of their operations. Soriana took out ads in local newspapers warning about "foreign supermarkets" when regulators fined a Walmart in Monterrey because a shelf price did not match the price on the checkout receipt.

Mexican retailers are not only playing a defensive game either. Gigante has opened nine stores in the Los Angeles area and aims to become the most popular supermarket among California's 11 million Latinos, most of whom are from Mexico and connect with the stores. Latinos boast a collective disposable income of $450 billion a year, with much of it going toward food. "The big chains gave Gigante the opportunity to come in here," said Steven Soto, head of the Mexican-American Grocers Association, a trade group that represents some 18,000 Latino store managers and owners. "The chains did not understand how to market to our community." Given that food tastes are the last things to change with immigrants, Gigante's product choices (e.g., chorizo and carnitas), placements (e.g., produce close by the entrance), and décor have made it a success. Some local players are focusing on relatively uncontested rural markets in a similar fashion to the way Walmart was able to grow in the United States against Kmart and Sears in its time. Soriana and Chedraui have avoided Mexico City until recently, opting instead to build a presence and refine their approaches in rural areas, where their knowledge of the customer are most valuable.

Sources: Walmart, 2009 Annual Report, www.wal-mart.com; Dante Di Gregorio, Douglas Thomas, and Fernán González de Castilla, "Competition Between Emerging Market and Multinational Firms: Wal-Mart and Mexican Retailers," *International Journal of Management* 25 (September 2008): 532–545; "Grocer Grande," *Time Inside Business*, April 2003, A3–A10; "War of the Superstores," *Business Week*, September 23, 2002, 60; "How Well Does Walmart Travel?" *BusinessWeek*, September 3, 2001, 82–84; "How NAFTA Helped Wal-Mart Reshape the Mexican Market," *Wall Street Journal*, August 31, 2001, A1–A2; and Vijay Govindarajan and Anil K. Gupta, "Taking Wal-Mart Global: Lessons from Retailing's Giant," *Strategy and Business* (Fourth Quarter, 1999): 45–56.

Customers leaving the Walmart in Mexico City. Walmart has stores across the U.S. and recently opened operations in Canada, Puerto Rico, Brazil, Germany and Asia.

Albertson's brand as seen competing against Bimbo, Mexican-brand bread, on a shelf of a California Super Savers market. Super Savers, owned by Albertson's, are focused toward the growing Hispanic market. Mexico-based Gigante has opened five Southern California stores in an effort to attract that same demographic.

segments of the U.S. economy will be harmed by the agreement. Overall wages and employment for unskilled workers in the United States will fall because of Mexico's low-cost labor pool. U.S. companies have been moving operations to Mexico since the 1960s. The door was opened when Mexico liberalized export restrictions to allow for more so-called **maquiladoras**, plants that make goods and parts or process food for export back to the United States. The supply of labor is plentiful, the pay and benefits are low, and the work regulations are lax by U.S. standards. In the past two decades, maquiladoras evolved from low-end garment or small-appliance assembly outfits to higher-end manufacturing of big-screen TVs, computers, and auto parts. The factories shipped $100 billion worth of goods (half of all Mexican exports), almost all of it to the United States. Wages have also been rising to $2.10 an hour resulting in some low-end manufacturers of apparel and toys moving production to Asia. While the Mexican government is eager to attract maquiladora investment, it is also keen to move away from using cheap labor as a central element of competitiveness. Mexico also stands to benefit from a subtle but steady shift in strategic thinking by U.S. manufacturers, who are reassessing their reliance on Asia and focusing more on near-shore options. Rising Chinese costs and fears of higher trans-Pacific shipping prices if oil spikes again are part of it. With capital scarce and markets hard to forecast, companies do not want to tie up cash in inventory as they wait for their cargo to arrive.[29] Such reasons are driving precision manufacturers like GKN Aerospace, a maker of aircraft engine components, to cluster close to the border in cities like Mexicali.

Despite U.S. fears of rapid job loss if companies send business south of the border, recent studies have put job gain or loss as almost a washout. The good news is that free trade has created higher-skilled and better-paying jobs in the United States as a result of growth in exports. As a matter of fact, jobs in exporting firms tend to pay 10 to 15 percent more than the jobs they replace. Losers have been U.S. manufacturers of auto parts, furniture, and household glass; sugar, peanut, and citrus growers; and seafood and vegetable producers. The U.S. Labor Department has certified 316,000 jobs as threatened or lost due to trade with Mexico and Canada. At the same time, the U.S. economy has added some 20 million jobs in the years since NAFTA. The fact that job losses have been in more heavily unionized sectors has made these losses politically charged. In most cases, high Mexican shipping and inventory costs will continue to make it more efficient for many U.S. industries to serve their home market from U.S. plants. Outsourcing of lower-skilled jobs is an unstoppable trend for developed economies such as the United States. However, NAFTA has given U.S. firms a way of taking advantage of cheaper labor while still keeping close links to U.S. suppliers. Mexican assembly plants get 82 percent of their parts from U.S. suppliers, while factories in Asia are using only a fraction of that.[30] Without NAFTA, entire industries might be lost to Asia rather than just the labor-intensive portions.

Integration pains extend to other areas as well. Approximately 85 percent of U.S.–Mexican trade moves on trucks. Under NAFTA, cross-border controls on trucking were to be eliminated by the end of 1995, allowing commercial vehicles to move freely in four U.S. and six Mexican border states. But the U.S. truckers, backed by the Teamsters Union, would have nothing of this, arguing that Mexican trucks were dangerous and exceeded weight limits. The union also worried that opening of the border would depress wages, because it would allow U.S. trucking companies to team up with lower-cost counterparts in Mexico. In 2001, however, the NAFTA Arbitration Panel ruled that Mexican trucks must be allowed to cross U.S. borders and the U.S. Senate approved a measure that allows Mexican truckers to haul cargo provided they meet strict inspection and safety rules.[31] Yet, even ten years later, the

maquiladoras Mexican border plants, with lower labor costs, make goods and parts or process food for export back to the United States.

trading issue continues to be controversial and a source of trade conflict. On the Mexican side, truckers are worried that if the border opens, U.S. firms will simply take over the trucking industry in Mexico.

Countries dependent on trade with NAFTA countries are concerned that the agreement will divert trade and impose significant losses on their economies. Asia's continuing economic success depends largely on easy access to the North American markets, which account for more than 25 percent of annual export revenue for many Asian countries. Lower-cost producers in Asia are likely to lose some exports to the United States if they are subject to tariffs while Mexican firms are not and may, therefore, have to invest in NAFTA[32] Similarly, many in the Caribbean and Central America fear that the apparel industries of their regions will be threatened, as would much-needed investments.

INTEGRATION IN LATIN AMERICA

Mercado Común del Sur (MERCOSUR)—was created in 1991 and includes Brazil, Argentina, Paraguay, and Uruguay. Bolivia, Chile, Colombia, Ecuador, Peru, and Venezuela have joined this South American trading bloc as associate members. MERCOSUR has three main objectives: (1) establishment of a free trade zone; (2) creation of a common external tariff system (i.e., a customs union); and (3) free movement of capital, labor, and services.

It has been likened to the European Union, but with an area of 4.6 million square miles (12 million square kilometers), it is four times as big. The bloc's combined market encompasses more than 266 million people and accounts for more than three-quarters of the economic activity on the continent. MERCOSUR is the world's fourth-largest trading bloc.[33]

Of the four MERCOSUR countries, Brazil is the most advanced in manufacturing and technology. São Paulo is one of the world's major industrial cities and is home to the affiliates and subsidiaries of many foreign corporations. Even with its significant industrial base, vast interior areas of Brazil and their rich resources remain virtually untapped. Major infrastructure improvements are under way to permit these resources to be brought to market in a cost-efficient manner. Infrastructure and transportation improvements throughout member nations and in other parts of South America are an important outgrowth of MERCOSUR. Intra-MERCOSUR exports now account for only 13 percent of its members' total exports (intra-EU exports are 60 percent). Brazil's exports to Argentina, for example, its main partner in the MERCOSUR bloc, amount to only about 1 percent of its GDP.

EU-MERCOSUR trade represents as much as EU trade with the rest of Latin America taken together. The EU is MERCOSUR's second largest trading partner after the United States. The EU and MERCOSUR plan to build a transatlantic free trade zone in the early part of the twenty-first century. Since 1995, when South America began to open up its markets, Europeans have won many of the top privatization deals. Spain's Telefónica de España spent $5 billion buying telephone companies in Brazil, Chile, Peru, and Argentina, where French Telecom and STET of Italy are active as well. In Brazil, seven of the ten largest private companies are European-owned, while just two are controlled by U.S. interests. Europeans dominate huge sectors in the economy, from automakers Volkswagen and Fiat to French supermarket chain Carrefour to Anglo-Dutch personal-care products group Lever.

The Andean Common Market (ANCOM) was founded in 1969 and currently comprises four countries that straddle the Andes: Bolivia, Colombia, Ecuador, and Peru. ANCOM and MERCOSUR leaders have discussed the possibility of allying to form a South American Community of Nations, modeled on the European Union, but those talks have not progressed quickly. The Andean Trade Preference Act (ATPA) was enacted to help four Andean countries in their fight against drug production and trafficking by expanding their economic alternatives.[34]

As a matter of fact, an alternative has arisen in opposition to the U.S.-led Free Trade Area of the Americas (FTAA). ALBA, the Bolivarian Alternative for the People of Our America (led by Cuba and Venezuela) focuses more on social welfare and economic aid than trade liberalization. Ideally, the larger countries would have agreed to consider giving smaller and lesser-developed countries more time to reduce tariffs; to open their economies to foreign investment; and to adopt effective laws in areas such as antitrust, intellectual property rights, bank regulation, and prohibitions on corrupt business practices. At the same time, the less-developed countries would agree to include labor and environmental standards in the negotiations.

The Central American Common Market (CACM) was formed by the Treaty of Managua in 1960. Its members are Costa Rica, El Salvador, Guatemala, Honduras, and Nicaragua. The group anticipates the eventual liberalization of interregional trade and the establishment of a free-trade zone. The CACM has often been cited as a model integrative effort for other developing countries. By the end of the 1960s, the CACM had succeeded in eliminating restrictions on 80 percent of trade among members. A continuing source of difficulty, however, is that the benefits of integration have fallen disproportionately to the richer and more developed members. Political difficulties in the area have also hampered progress. However, the member-countries renewed their commitment to integration in 1990. A major change occurred in 2005 with the signing of the Central America–Dominican Republic–United States Free Trade Agreement. CAFTA–DR created the second-largest U.S. export market in Latin America, behind only Mexico, and the 13th largest U.S. export market in the world. The United States exported $24.5 billion in goods to the five Central American countries and the Dominican Republic in 2008—more than all exports to Russia, India, and Indonesia combined. At the same time, U.S. imports amounted to $19.3 billion.

Integration efforts in the Caribbean have focused on the Caribbean Common Market (CARICOM) formed in 1968. Its primary mandate is to provide a framework for regional political and economic integration. The following 15 nations make up the Caribbean community: Antigua and Barbuda, Bahamas, Barbados, Belize, Dominica, Grenada, Guyana, Haiti, Jamaica, Montserrat, St. Kitts-Nevis, St. Lucia, St. Vincent and the Grenadines, Suriname, and Trinidad and Tobago. Among CARICOM's objectives are the strengthening of the economic and trade regulations among member-states, the expansion and integration of economic activities, and the achievement of a greater measure of economic independence for member-states. Before NAFTA, CARICOM members (excluding Suriname) benefited from the **Caribbean Basin Initiative (CBI)**, which, since 1983, extended trade preferences and granted access to the U.S. market. Under NAFTA, such preferences were lost, which means that the member-countries have to cooperate more closely.

Caribbean Basin Initiative (CBI) Extended trade preferences to Caribbean countries granting them special access to the markets of the United States.

INTEGRATION IN ASIA

The development in Asia has been quite different from that in Europe and in the Americas. While European and North American arrangements have been driven by political will, market forces may compel politicians in Asia to move toward formal integration. Also, in terms of economic and political distance, the potential member countries are far from each other, especially compared to the EU. However, Asian interest in regional integration is increasing for pragmatic reasons. First, European and American markets are significant for the Asian producers, and some type of organization or bloc may be needed to maintain leverage and balance against the two other blocs. Second, given that much of the growth in trade for the nations in the region is from intra-Asian trade, having a common understanding and policies will become necessary. A future arrangement will most likely use the frame of the most established arrangement in the region, the Association of Southeast Asian Nations (ASEAN). In the past, ASEAN had no real structures, and consensus was reached through information consultations. In October 1991, ASEAN members (Brunei, Indonesia, Malaysia, Philippines, Singapore, Thailand, Vietnam and, since 1997, Cambodia, Myanmar, and Laos) announced the formation of a customs union called ASEAN Free Trade Area (AFTA). The ten member-countries have agreed to reduce tariffs to a maximum level of 5 percent by 2005 and to create a customs union by 2020.[35] Even a common currency has been proposed. Skepticism about the lofty targets have been raised about the group's ability to follow the example of the European Union, given the widely divergent levels of economic development (e.g., Singapore versus Laos) and the lack of democratic institutions (especially in Myanmar). ASEAN has also agreed to economic cooperation with China, Japan, and South Korea (the so-called ASEAN+1 and ASEAN+3 arrangements), as well as with India, Australia and New Zealand.

The Malaysians have pushed for the formation of the East Asia Economic Group (EAEG), which would add Hong Kong, Japan, South Korea, and Taiwan to the list. This proposal makes sense; without Japan and the rapidly industrializing countries of the region such as South Korea and Taiwan, the effect of the arrangement would be small. Japan's reaction has been generally negative toward all types of regionalization efforts, mainly because it has had the most to gain from free trade efforts. However, part of what has been driving regionalization has been Japan's reluctance to foster some of the elements that promote free trade, such as reciprocity. Should the other trading blocs turn against Japan, its only resort may be to work toward a more formal trade arrangement in the Asia-Pacific area.

Another formal proposal for cooperation would start building bridges between two emerging trade blocs. Some individuals have publicly called for a U.S.–Japan common market. Given the differences on all fronts between the two, the proposal may be quite unrealistic at this time. Negotiated trade liberalization will not open Japanese markets due to major institutional differences, as seen in many rounds of successful negotiations but totally unsatisfactory results. The only solution for the U.S. government is to forge better cooperation between the government and the private sector to improve competitiveness.

In 1989, Australia proposed the Asia Pacific Economic Cooperation (APEC) as an annual forum. The proposal called for ASEAN members to be joined by Australia, New Zealand, Japan, China, Hong Kong, Taiwan, South Korea, Canada, and the United States. It was initially modeled after the Organization for Economic Cooperation and Development (OECD), which is a center for research and high-level discussion. Since then, APEC's goals have become more ambitious. At present, APEC has 21 members with a combined GDP of $29.3 trillion, nearly 44 percent of global trade, and is the third largest economy of the world. The key objectives of APEC are to liberalize trade by 2020, to facilitate trade by harmonizing standards, and to build human capacities for realizing the region's ambitions. The trade-driven economies of the region have the world's largest pool of savings, the most advanced technologies, and fastest growing markets.[36]

Economic integration has also taken place on the Indian subcontinent. In 1985, seven nations of the region (India, Pakistan, Bangladesh, Sri Lanka, Nepal, Bhutan, and the Maldives) launched the South Asian Association for Regional Cooperation (SAARC). Cooperation is limited to relatively noncontroversial areas, such as agriculture and regional development, and hampered by political disagreements. Elements such as the formation of a common market have not been included.

INTEGRATION IN AFRICA AND THE MIDDLE EAST

Africa's economic groupings range from currency unions among European nations and their former colonies to customs unions among neighboring states. In addition to wanting to liberalize trade among members, African countries want to gain better access to European and North American markets for farm and textile products. Given that most of the countries are too small to negotiate with the other blocs, alliances have been the solution. In 1975, 16 West African nations attempted to create a megamarket large enough to interest investors from the industrialized world and reduce hardship through economic integration. The objective of the Economic Community of West African States (ECOWAS) was to form a customs union and eventual common market. Although many of its objectives have not been reached, its combined population of 160 million represents the largest economic entity in sub-Saharan Africa. Other entities in Africa include the Common Market for Eastern and Southern Africa (COMESA), the Economic Community of Central African States (CEEAC), the Southern African Customs Union, the Southern African Development Community (SADC), and some smaller, less globally oriented blocs such as the Economic Community of the Great Lakes Countries, the Mano River Union, and the East African Community (EAC). Most member countries are part of more than one bloc (for example, Tanzania is a member in both the EAC and SADC). The blocs, for the most part, have not been successful due to the small size of the members and lack of economic infrastructure to produce goods to be traded inside the blocs. Moreover, some of the blocs have been relatively inactive for substantial periods of time while their members endure internal political turmoil or even warfare amongst each other. In 2002, African nations established the African Union (AU) for regional cooperation. Eventually, plans call for a pan-African parliament, a court of justice, a central bank, and a shared currency by 2023.[37]

Countries in the Arab world have made some progress in economic integration. The Arab Maghreb Union ties together Algeria, Libya, Mauritania, Morocco, and Tunisia in northern Africa. The Gulf Cooperation Council (GCC) is one of the most powerful, economically speaking, of any trade groups. The per capita income of its six member states (Bahrain, Kuwait, Oman, Qatar, Saudi Arabia, and the United Arab Emirates) is in the 90th percentile in the world. Significant progress has already been made in regional economic integration. The GCC countries have largely unrestricted intraregional mobility of goods, labor, and capital; regulation of the banking sector is being harmonized; and in 2008 the countries established a common market. Further, most of the convergence criteria established for entry into a monetary union have already been achieved. In establishing a monetary union, however, the GCC countries must decide on the exchange rate regime for the single currency.[38] A proposal among GCC members calls for the creation of a common currency by 2013. This area has some of the fastest-growing economies in the world, mostly due to a boom in oil and natural gas revenues coupled with a building and investment boom backed by decades of saved petroleum revenues. In an effort to build a tax base and economic foundation before the reserves run out, the UAE's Abu Dhabi Investment Authority retained more than $875 billion in assets. In recent years, the ratio of private-to-government expenditure in GCC countries has been below the OECD average, suggesting strong potential for more private-sector involvement in infrastructure development. GCC governments have already made efforts to encourage that investment—privatizing government assets and completing initial public offerings of public-sector infrastructure companies.[39]

A listing of the major regional trade agreements is provided in Table 8.3.

Table 8.3   Major Regional Trade Agreements

AFTA   **ASEAN Free Trade Area**
Brunei, Cambodia, Indonesia, Laos, Malaysia, Myanmar, Philippines, Singapore, Thailand, Vietnam

ANCOM   **Andean Common Market**
Bolivia, Colombia, Ecuador, Peru

APEC   **Asia Pacific Economic Cooperation**
Australia, Brunei, Canada, Chile, China, Hong Kong, Indonesia, Japan, Malaysia, Mexico, New Zealand, Papua New Guinea, Peru, Philippines, Russia, Singapore, South Korea, Taiwan, Thailand, United States, Vietnam

CACM   **Central American Common Market**
Costa Rica, Dominican Republic, El Salvador, Guatemala, Honduras, Nicaragua, Panama

CARICOM   **Caribbean Community**
Antigua and Barbuda, Bahamas, Barbados, Belize, Dominica, Grenada, Guyana, Haiti, Jamaica, Montserrat, St. Kitts-Nevis, St. Lucia, St. Vincent and the Grenadines, Suriname, Trinidad-Tobago

ECOWAS   **Economic Community of West African States**
Benin, Burkina Faso, Cape Verde, Gambia, Ghana, Guinea, Guinea-Bissau, Ivory Coast, Liberia, Mali, Mauritania, Niger, Nigeria, Senegal, Sierra Leone, Togo

EFTA   **European Free Trade Association**
Iceland, Liechtenstein, Norway, Switzerland

EU   **European Union**
Austria, Belgium, Bulgaria, Cyprus, Czech Republic, Denmark, Estonia, Finland, France, Germany, Greece, Hungary, Ireland, Italy, Latvia, Lithuania, Luxembourg, Malta, Netherlands, Poland, Portugal, Romania, Slovakia, Slovenia, Spain, Sweden, United Kingdom

GCC   **Gulf Cooperation Council**
Bahrain, Kuwait, Oman, Qatar, Saudi Arabia, United Arab Emirates

LAIA   **Latin American Integration Association**
Argentina, Bolivia, Brazil, Chile, Colombia, Cuba, Ecuador, Mexico, Paraguay, Peru, Uruguay, Venezuela

MERCOSUR   **Southern Common Market**
Argentina, Brazil, Paraguay, Uruguay

NAFTA   **North American Free Trade Agreement**
Canada, Mexico, United States

SAARC   **South Asian Association for Regional Cooperation**
Afghanistan, Bangladesh, Bhutan, India, Maldives, Nepal, Pakistan, Sri Lanka

SACU   **Southern African Customs Union**
Botswana, Lesotho, Namibia, South Africa, Swaziland

For information see http://www.aseansec.org; http://www.apec.org; http://www.caricom.org; http://www.eurounion.org; http://www.mercosur.int; http://www.nafta-customs.org.

4. To examine how an organization tries to control the price and quantity supplied of a particular commodity

CARTELS AND COMMODITY PRICE AGREEMENTS

An important characteristic that distinguishes developing countries from industrialized countries is the nature of their export earnings. While industrialized countries rely heavily on the export of manufactured goods, technology, and services, the developing countries rely chiefly on the export of primary products and raw materials— for example, copper, iron ore, and agricultural products. This distinction is important for several reasons. First, the level of price competition is higher among sellers of primary goods because of the typically larger number of sellers and also because primary goods are homogeneous. This can be seen by comparing the sale of computers with, for example, copper. Only three of four countries are competitive forces in the computer market, whereas at least a dozen compete in the sale of copper. Furthermore, while goods differentiation and therefore brand loyalty are likely to exist in the market for computers, buyers of copper are likely to purchase on the basis of price

INTERNATIONAL GROUPINGS: WORLD

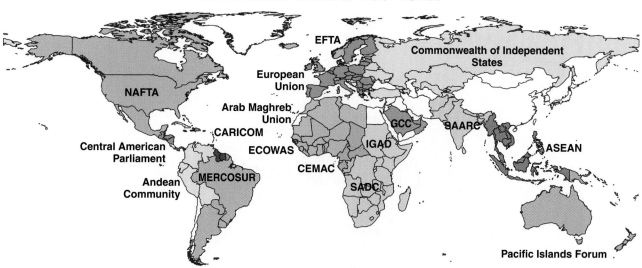

INTERNATIONAL GROUPINGS: EUROPE

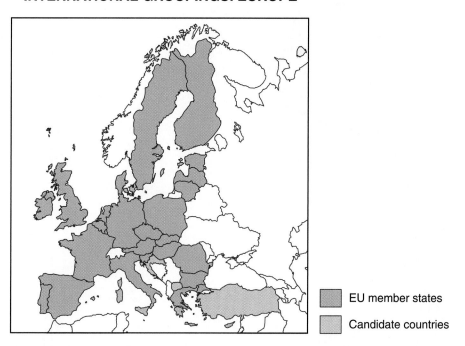

EU member states

Candidate countries

Countries with EU membership application: Croatia, Former Yugoslav Republic of Macedonia, Turkey

MAP OF SOUTH AMERICA

Table 8.4 MPI for 2009

Countries	Market Size		Market Growth Rate		Market Intensity		Market Consumption Capacity		Commercial Infrastructure		Economic Freedom		Market Receptivity		Country Risk		Overall index	
	Rank	Index	Rank	Index	Rank	Index	Rank	Index	Rank	Index	Rank	Index	Rank	Index	Rank	Index	Rank	Index
Singapore	26	1	12	28	2	73	15	57	3	94	6	77	1	100	1	100	1	100
China	1	100	1	100	26	1	13	60	19	34	26	1	18	4	10	55	2	97
Hong Kong	24	1	14	27	1	100	18	48	1	100	2	93	2	69	2	89	3	93
Korea, South	7	10	23	12	6	64	1	100	4	92	5	77	8	15	6	87	4	69
Czech Rep.	22	1	21	17	15	45	2	94	2	94	3	85	9	14	3	77	5	61
Israel	23	1	24	12	3	68	9	74	7	70	7	77	4	23	4	74	6	54
Poland	15	4	13	27	7	63	5	78	6	78	8	70	15	6	8	61	7	53
Hungary	25	1	26	1	4	67	3	90	5	82	4	81	5	16	15	43	8	48
Russia	3	25	8	38	21	29	8	75	8	65	24	7	21	3	12	48	9	40
Malaysia	19	3	17	26	22	27	10	73	9	64	16	45	3	24	9	55	10	36
India	2	38	3	54	23	25	11	60	25	2	17	44	24	3	23	24	11	36
Turkey	8	7	9	38	5	66	14	58	12	49	13	51	19	4	19	35	12	33
Chile	21	2	15	27	12	49	23	24	13	49	1	100	10	13	7	63	13	33
Mexico	6	10	22	16	10	58	22	38	15	46	10	63	6	15	11	51	14	31
Saudi Arabia	13	4	7	39	25	12	7	75	10	59	23	19	11	12	5	72	15	31
Brazil	4	21	11	29	17	44	24	20	14	47	12	54	25	1	14	46	16	26
Egypt	14	4	6	40	11	54	6	75	20	32	22	19	13	6	20	34	17	24
Argentina	12	4	4	53	13	47	20	42	11	56	15	48	20	3	24	14	18	23
Thailand	16	4	10	31	24	22	17	52	16	48	20	38	7	15	17	40	19	18
Pakistan	10	6	5	52	6	61	4	79	24	4	21	28	26	1	26	1	20	18
Peru	20	2	2	56	18	42	21	39	26	1	11	61	17	5	16	40	21	17
Indonesia	5	11	16	26	20	37	16	55	21	30	18	43	22	3	21	27	22	16
Philippines	11	5	25	12	9	59	19	48	22	26	19	38	16	6	22	25	23	15
Venezuela	17	3	18	24	19	37	12	60	18	41	25	5	12	7	25	13	24	8
South Africa	9	6	19	21	16	45	26	1	23	13	9	65	14	6	13	47	25	3
Colombia	18	3	20	17	14	46	25	9	17	41	14	47	23	3	18	35	26	1

Market Intensity = private consumption as a percent of GDP
Market Consumption Capacity = share of middle-class income
Commercial Infrastructure = composite of factors such as mobile subscribers and Internet hosts
Market Receptivity = trade as a percent of GDP

Source: Global Edge, available at http://www.globaledge.msu/edu/resourcedesk/mpi/.

Table 8.5	Most Populous Countries, 2008 and 2050		
2008		**2050**	
Country	Population (millions)	Country	Population (millions)
China	1,324.7	India	1,755.2
India	1,149.3	China	1,437.0
United States	304.5	United States	438.2
Indonesia	239.9	Indonesia	343.1
Brazil	195.1	Pakistan	295.2
Pakistan	172.8	Nigeria	282.2
Nigeria	148.1	Brazil	259.8
Bangladesh	147.3	Bangladesh	215.1
Russia	141.9	Congo, Dem. Rep.	189.3
Japan	127.7	Philippines	150.1

Source: 2008 World Population Data Sheet, 2008 Population Reference Bureau, http://www.prb.org/Publications/Datasheets/2008/2008wpds.aspx, retrieved October 8, 2009.

CHINA: PRODUCTION PLATFORM TO MARKETPLACE

A major key to China's phenomenal economic growth was its rapid transformation from a largely agrarian socialist state to an export-driven platform for global manufacturing. When Deng Xiao Ping began the liberalization of China in 1979, he famously said: "Poverty is not socialism. We should make economic development

Figure 8.2	The 15 Most Attractive Economies for the Location of FDI, 2009–2011

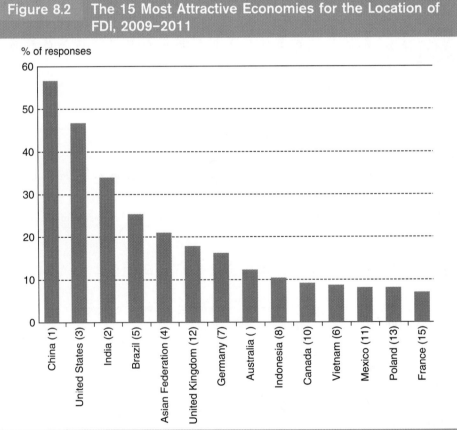

Source: UNCTAD Survey World Investment Prospects 2009–2011, p. 54.

Figure 8.3   Forecasts for real GDP

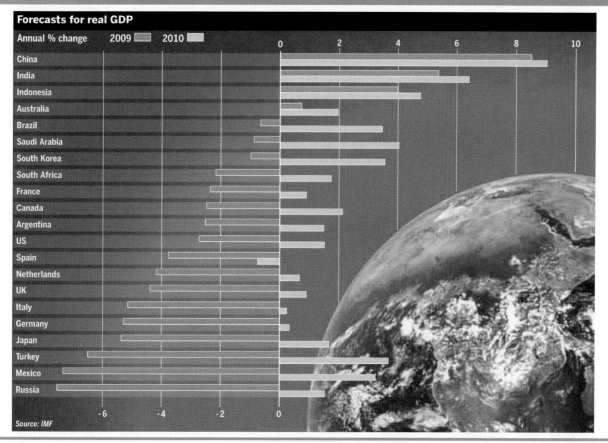

Forecasts for real GDP

Annual % change   2009 ☐   2010 ☐

Source: IMF

Source: Ralph Atkins, "Global Strengths and Weaknesses Are Exposed," *Financial Times*, October 6, 2008; IMF data.

the top priority of all priorities."[49] Deng opened the doors to Chinese participation in capitalism and encouraged international companies to invest in China. Much of the early investment by international firms focused on the creation of a production base to capitalize on inexpensive factors of production, particularly low-cost labor. Over time, the Chinese production platform increased its attractiveness though improvements in production facilities, infrastructure, access to ports, and skilled labor. "Much of the world's commerce has connected with China because the Chinese government has spared no incentive in wooing foreign companies to build factories there. China's modernization drive has combined its developing-world, low-cost labor with nearly state-of-the-art technology and an export-friendly infrastructure. Meanwhile, China's huge population has provided companies with a giant pool of low-wage workers in the same place where they have found a potentially large set of new customers, enabling mass-market factories to produce both for the export market and for the growing Chinese market."[50]

Rapid economic development and rising standards of living in China, along with the rise of new, lower-cost production platforms in countries like Indonesia, Malaysia, Vietnam and Bangladesh, has caused international businesses to focus on China more as a marketplace. For example, China was the largest automobile market in the world in 2009 and is General Motors' fastest growing market while sales in the United States have slumped.[51] In a press conference at the time of the 2009 restructuring of General Motors, GM's Chairman Fritz Henderson said, "Our ventures in China are a critical part of the new GM—unequivocally. Our business in China continues to grow at a very fast—even torrid—pace and remains a critical part of GM going forward."[52]

INDIA: GROWTH IN SERVICES

Napoleon Bonaparte is attributed to have described China as a "sleeping giant" and cautioned his European audience: "Let her sleep, for when she wakes she will shake the world." With China now seemingly fully awake and, indeed, shaking the world of international business, perhaps Napoleon's observation can now also be applied to India. In the middle of a currency crisis and shortly after the assassination of Prime Minister Rajiv Gandhi in 1991, India, under the guidance of then Finance Minister and currently Prime Minister Manmohan Singh, initiated a series of economic reform measures that propelled India from a long stagnation into sustained economic growth and participation in the global economy. Reflecting the feeling of optimism that fuels India's thriving private sector, Alan Rosling of Tata Sons, India's largest company, noted in 2005, "India has been a perennial underperformer for 50 years; it has been held back by bad politics, bad policy choices, and bad infrastructure. It is my belief that over the next 50 years India will at last begin to capitalize on its abundant advantages: of democracy and the rule of law; of cheaply available, skilled, English-speaking manpower; and, above all, of a thriving, well-managed and competitive private sector."[53] That optimism appears to have been well founded as India's economy has grown by an average of 9 percent from 2004 to 2008 and is on solid footing in 2009 with projected growth of approximately 6 percent.[54]

India has grown differently from China, with an emphasis on its domestic economy and the service sector rather than export-oriented manufacturing. Gurcharan Das, former CEO of Procter & Gamble India described this aptly: "The notable thing about India's rise is not that it is new, but that its path has been unique. Rather than adopting the classic Asian strategy—exporting labor-intensive, low-priced manufactured goods to the West—India has relied on its domestic market more than exports, consumption more than investment, services more than industry, and high-tech more than low-skilled manufacturing."[55] The World Trade Organization found India to lead all other economies in the growth of commercial services between 2000 and 2007 (see Figure 8.4).

In its guide to doing business in India, FedEx identifies what is causing companies to favor the Indian market:

Indian Prime Minister Manmohan Singh and Chinese premier Wen Jiabao in Beijing, China, January 14, 2008. Xinhua Photo

Figure 8.4   Leading Exporters of Commercial Services, Growth 2000–2007

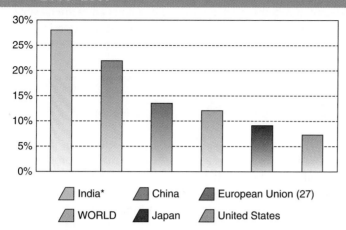

India*   China   European Union (27)
WORLD   Japan   United States

* Growth of India for 2004–2005 is partly affected by a break in a series following an improved coverage of other business services exports.

Source: World Trade Organization, International Trade Statistics 2008, p. 5.

"Favorable demographics coupled with rising income levels are fueling growth across many product segments and industries in India. One result of India's newfound prosperity has been the swelling of the country's middle class to more than 250 million, which in turn has fueled demand for consumer products such as televisions, refrigerators, washing machines and air conditioners."[56]

BRAZIL

Brazil's population of more than 190 million people and the world's ninth largest economy, with GDP of more than $1.5 trillion, makes it a leading country not only in South America but in the world.[57] While not experiencing the same dramatic economic growth rates of India and China in the first decade of the twenty-first century, Brazil nonetheless grew at consistently steady rates in the 3.9 to 5 percent range. This was mainly due to President Lula da Silva's implementation of economic liberalization policies and the avoidance of inflation problems that have plagued Argentina, its neighbor to the south. Because of its history of alternating between economic disciplines and more interventionist policy and a succession of economic crises, many observers have been cautious in assessing Brazil's ability to continue to grow. However, Brazil's economic performance in 2008 demonstrated great resiliency in the midst of the recession and international companies show increased interest in doing business there. Indeed, the UNCTAD World Investment Prospects Survey identified Brazil as the fourth most attractive country for foreign direct investment for 2009–2011.[58]

Brazil's attractiveness will certainly be enhanced by the city of Rio de Janeiro being selected as the site for the 2016 Olympic Summer Games. In addition to the existing incentives for infrastructure, building launched as a part of the growth acceleration program in 2007, investment in infrastructure to prepare for the Olympics is certain to be significant and should act as a stimulus for further foreign direct investment and trade.

Many Brazilian companies are already competing at the highest level in international business. Embraer, the Brazilian aircraft manufacturer, is one of the largest companies in the world aircraft industry and one of Brazil's leading exportes; 95 percent of Embraer's 2008 sales were to international customers.[59] A study by Brazil's Institute for Applied Economics found that 1,200 Brazilian companies are capable of competing internationally in terms of innovation and product differentiation instead of price.[60]

BARRIERS TO BUSINESS

6. To understand the scope of barriers to business and infrastructure challenges

Despite their attractiveness to business, the large emerging markets are not easy places to conduct business. Consider the World Bank's "Doing Business 2010" report, which examines and ranks 183 countries on the basis of ten factors emanating from the regulatory environment in which businesses operate. According to this report, China ranked 89, Brazil ranked 129, and India ranked 133.[61] The World Bank looks at factors such as registering a business, labor flexibility, construction permit requirements, protecting investors, taxation, access to credit, enforcement of contracts, and trade across borders. Related barriers exist as well for international companies and vary by country. These include sectoral restrictions on foreign investment, government subsidization of local industries, local procurement requirements, technology standards that differ from international standards, transparency issues in government procurement and judicial proceedings, vague regulations, burdensome port and customs procedures, high-tariff barriers in certain categories, and insufficient protection for intellectual property rights.

An example of Chinese legislation that represents a barrier to entry is the Chinese Postal Law that went into effect in October 2009. China's new postal law provides exclusivity to state-owned post offices for some categories of express delivery services. This means that private-sector companies, including FedEx and UPS, are barred from competing in what some estimate as 80 percent of the express delivery market.[62] China also maintains significant barriers to foreign financial services companies through mechanisms such as caps on investment; lack of authorization to compete in electronic payments services, third-party liability automobile insurance, and political risk insurance; limited licenses to participate in some markets such as enterprise annuities services; local incorporation requirements for banks; and requirements that foreign financial information services must operate through Chinese-designated agents.[63]

Internet services companies confront ongoing problems in China, where that country's authorities conduct extensive filtering of content that they consider to be objectionable for political, social, or religious reasons.[64] In 2009, China implemented its Green Dam-Youth Escort censorship program that requires PC makers to preinstall Internet filtering software on PCs used in schools, Internet cafés, and other public places.[65]

Problems with intellectual property rights protection remains a serious issue regarding China, Brazil, and India. The problem is so serious that companies must approach these markets very carefully and some have chosen not to compete in them. In its 2007 report on "Issues of Importance to American Business in the U.S.-China Commercial Relationship," the U.S. Chamber of Commerce stressed the issue of the need to improve intellectual property protection: "Counterfeiting and piracy constitute a fundamental blight on China's economic progress that will lead political leaders in the United States and other countries to call into question China's status as a responsible global power."[66] In 2007, Brazil issued a compulsory license to produce a lower-cost, generic version of Merck's anti-HIV drug Efavirenzne.[67] At the same time, in the 2008 Piracy Study, the Business Software Alliance noted improvements in the piracy rates and stepped-up education and enforcement efforts in China, India, and Brazil.[68]

Foreign companies can sometimes be subject to capricious government actions at the national or local levels. In 2006, India's Kerala province banned the bottling of Pepsi and Coca-Cola products and their sales in state schools, hospitals, and other buildings after a study was released showing that the products contained high levels of pesticides. An Indian court quickly lifted the ban after finding scientific inconsistencies in the study.[69]

Some barriers to entry come in the form of traditional tariff structures. India maintains tariffs on American wine, which, when combined at the federal and provincial levels, can amount to 400 percent and more. The Indian government allowed the import of Harley-Davidson motorcycles in 2007 by allowing international emissions and testing requirements, but the iconic American bikes still face a 100 percent tariff coming into India.[70]

In August 2009, Harley Davidson announced that its plans to formally enter the Indian market in 2010. India is the second largest motorcycle market in the world.

Corruption remains a significant problem in emerging markets. In the 2009 Transparency International Global Corruption Report, China ranked 72, Brazil 80, and India 85 in the Corruption Perceptions Index, not very good—although better than Russia, which ranked 147.[71] The Chinese government has been very aggressive in prosecuting corruption, but it remains a persistent problem that is sometimes aggravated by excessive layers of government bureaucracy and powerful regional authorities as well as the presence of gangsters.[72] In India, the government is stepping up its efforts to fight corruption, including the prosecution of the founder and chairman of Satyam Computer Systems, who confessed in 2009 to falsifying $1 billion in the company's balance sheet.[73]

INFRASTRUCTURE PROBLEMS

A significant challenge to international companies in emerging markets is the lack of infrastructure. Poor roads, outdated port facilities, the lack of refrigeration capacity, and inefficient distribution systems make it difficult to bring products to the marketplace. Special packaging consideration is required to prevent deterioration of product in situations with high variations in temperature and inadequate storage. Market intermediaries often do not exist, and significant amounts of retail sales are made through relatively informal distribution channels like kiosks. Payments and funds-transfer systems are often inadequate.

The state of infrastructure development varies among the major emerging markets. China continues a program of infrastructure development that may be unparalleled in history with the construction and modernization of cities, highways, ports, and airports across the country. In the 2008 U.S. presidential campaign, then-candidate Barack Obama stated at a campaign event: "Think about the money that China has spent on infrastructure. Their ports, their train systems, their airports are all vastly superior to us now. Which means if you're a corporation deciding where to do business, you're starting to think Beijing looks like a pretty good option."[74]

India, however, is a different situation and requires significant future infrastructure investment in order to make its market more competitive globally. "A lot depends on how soon India modernizes its infrastructure. Until more roads are built to connect factories and farms with ports and railways, neither factories nor farmers are likely to see a Chinese style export boom that would create hundreds of millions of jobs."[75] This is not lost on the Indians as annual investments, with private sector participation, in highways, energy, and telecommunications infrastructure doubled in 2006 and 2007 over the annual amount in any previous year and over the total of all infrastructure investment in the 1990s.[76] A source of great pride in India is the new Golden Quadrilateral (GQ), a 3,633-mile expressway between the country's major population centers of Delhi, Mumbai, Chennai, and Kolkata.[77] In Brazil, a second phase of the country's Growth Acceleration Project that began in 2007 is expected to improve transportation and energy infrastructure by 2011.

TRANSITION ECONOMIES

7. To define economies that are changing from a centrally planned economy to a free market

Since the end of the Soviet Union, enormous change has occurred throughout central and eastern Europe as the new nations that emerged underwent a process of transition from central planning to market orientation. With the expansion of the European Union eastward and the embrace of market economics by the majority of central and eastern European countries, established trading patterns shifted as many of these countries looked westward for business. During the time of the Soviet bloc, trade took place within the political organization. That meant, for example, that more than 35 percent of Czech trade took place with the Soviet Union, and only 20 percent with western Europe. In 2008, only 6 percent of Czech trade was with Russia and Ukraine, while 77 percent was with EU countries and 29 percent with Germany alone.[78]

The major economies that remain in transition are Russia and Ukraine, along with smaller economies such as Armenia, Azerbaijan, Georgia, Belarus, Croatia, Serbia, Albania, Moldova, and the new countries of central Asia. In many of these countries, privatization is ongoing, and the increasing transition of economic activity from government ownership into private hands presents a substantial shift in market orientation and offers new opportunities for trade and investment. Entire industries have either privatized or closed down. While some realized success and increasing prosperity, others experienced economic difficulties and hardship. Some segments of the population still have a desire for a return to the "good old days" of dependence upon government for their welfare. Old ways of thinking and the strong role of government remain resistant to change in many transition countries. Also, strong feelings of nationalism may sometimes take the shape of resentment against foreign nations and businesses.

Despite impressive economic growth in the first decade of the twenty-first century, high levels of foreign investment, and significant accumulation of wealth, Russia has yet to diversify its economy and remains highly dependent on the fuel and minerals sectors. With oil and gas playing such a large role in the Russian economy, many observers in the West were concerned about hardball Russian tactics with energy companies and neighboring customer countries. After Western oil and gas companies like Shell, BP, and ExxonMobil had acquired major holdings in Russia, and after energy profits rose, they were subjected to severe pressure from the national governments and local Russian partners to sell back ventures to the state-controlled Gazprom and other energy groups at low prices.[79] With the downturn in fuel prices in 2008, Russia's eight years of sustained, strong economic growth came to an end and concerns mounted over Russia's true commitment to liberalization. Yet, Russian Prime Minister Vladimir Putin asserted to Western investors in 2009, "There will be no return to the past. Russia will remain a liberal market economy."[80]

For Western firms, the political and economic shifts converted latent but closed markets into markets offering very real and vast opportunities. Yet the shifts are only part of a process of change. The announcement of an intention or commitment to change does not automatically result in change itself. For example, the abolition of a centrally planned economy does not create a market economy. Laws permitting the emergence of private-sector entrepreneurs do not create entrepreneurship. The reduction of price controls does not immediately make goods available or affordable. Deeply ingrained systemic differences between the transition economies and Western firms continue. Highly prized, fully accepted fundamentals of the market economy—such as the reliance on competition, support of the profit motive, and the willingness to live with risk on a corporate and personal level—are not yet fully accepted, Major changes still need to take place. In addition, issues of corruption, gangster activities, and counterfeiting continue to present Western businesses with serious challenges. Yet, Western firms adapt. The French-owned energy company Total, for example, despite its problems in Russia, completed a 2009 deal with Gazprom, which owns 19 percent of Novatek, its local partner. Total CEO Christophe de Margerie remarked about the deal, "I don't think it's difficult to work in Russia. One only needs to learn to work efficiently with Gazprom, Novatek, and Rosneft."[81]

Firms doing business with transition economies often encounter interesting demand conditions. Buyers' preferences can still be vague and undefined as consumers are exposed to new and expanded choices in products and services. Market research is only slowly catching up to what is available in the United States or European Union. Distribution channels and pricing structures are still evolving, and information about demand and channel supply can often be frustratingly limited. Yet, the market potential keeps international firms committed to transition economies as well as emerging markets. Michael White, CEO of PepsiCo International, sums it up well: "Between Brazil, Russia, India and China, you've probably got half of the world's population and the average age for the most part is well below what it is in developed countries. So you've got very young consumers in many of those countries, which, for our products, is our target consumer."[82]

THE DEVELOPING MARKETS

The time may have come to look at the 4 billion people in the world who live in poverty, subsisting on less than $2,000 a year.[83] Not only is this segment a full two-thirds of the current marketplace, but it is expected to grow to 6 billion by 2040. Despite initial skepticism about access and purchasing power, marketers are finding that they can make profits while having a positive effect on the sustainable livelihoods of people not normally considered potential customers.[84] However, it will require radical departures from the traditional business models, for example, new partnerships (ranging from local governments to nonprofits) and new pricing structures (allowing customers to rent or lease rather than buy and

8. To illustrate growth in developing countries by encouraging potential markets

providing new financing choices for purchases). Hewlett-Packard has an initiative called World e-Inclusion that, working with a range of global and local partners, aims to sell, lease, or donate a billion dollars' worth of satellite-powered computer products and services to markets in Africa, Asia, eastern Europe, Latin American, and the Middle East.[85] To engage with beta communities in Senegal, Hewlett-Packard partnered with Joko Inc., a company founded by revered Senegalese pop star Youssou n'Dour.

Five elements of success are required for an international marketer to take advantage of and thrive in developing markets.[86]

RESEARCH

The first order of business is to learn about the needs, aspirations, and habits of targeted populations for whom traditional intelligence gathering may not be the most effective. For example, just because the demand for land lines in developing countries was low, it would have been wrong to assume that little demand for phones existed. The real reasons were that land lines were expensive, subscribers had to wait for months to get hooked up, and lines often went down due to bad maintenance, flood, and theft of copper cables. Mobile phones have been a solution to that problem. Subscriptions increased 67 percent in sub-Saharan Africa in 2004, as compared with 10 percent in western Europe.[87]

CREATIVE BUYING POWER

microfinance The provision of financial services to low-income clients, including consumers and the self-employed, who traditionally lack access to banking and related services.

Without credit, it is impossible for many of the developing-country consumers to make major purchases. Programs in **microfinance** have allowed consumers, with no property as collateral, to borrow sums averaging $100 to make purchases and have retail banking services available to them. Lenders such as Grameen Bank in Bangladesh and Compartamos in Mexico have helped millions of families escape poverty. Excellent payment records (e.g., only 0.56 percent of the loans are even days late at Compartamos) have started attracting companies such as Citicorp to microfinancing, through underwriting microfinance bonds in markets such as Peru.[88]

TAILORING LOCAL SOLUTIONS

In the product area, companies must combine advanced technology with local insights. Hindustan Lever (part of Unilever) learned that low-income Indians, usually forced to settle for low-quality products, wanted to buy high-end detergents and personal-care products, but could not afford them in the quantities available. In response, the company developed extremely low-cost packaging material and other innovations that allowed for a product priced in pennies instead of the $4 to $15 price of the regular containers. The same brand is on all of the product forms, regardless of packaging. Given that these consumers do not shop at supermarkets, Lever employs local residents with pushcarts who take small quantities of the sachets to kiosks.[89]

IMPROVING ACCESS

Due to economic and physical isolation of poor communities, providing access can lead to a thriving business. In Bangladesh (with income levels of $200), Grameen Phone Ltd. leases access to wireless phones to villagers. Every phone is used by an average of 100 people and generates $90 in revenue a month—two or three times the revenues generated by wealthier users who own their phones in urban areas.[90]

Founded in 1996 to bring mobile telephone service to the broad population of Bangladesh, Grameen Phone had become the largest tax-generating company in Bangladesh, with more than 16 million subscribers by 2007.[91]

Similarly, the Jhai Foundation, an American-Lao foundation, is helping villagers in Laos with Internet access. The first step, however, was to develop an inexpensive and robust computer. The computer has no moving, and very few delicate, parts. Instead of a hard disk, it relies on flash-memory chips, and instead of an energy-guzzling glass cathode ray tube, its screen is a liquid-crystal display.[92] The XO-1, previously known as the $100 Laptop, is an inexpensive laptop computer intended to be distributed to 150 million children in developing countries around the world. The laptop was developed by One Laptop Per Child (OLPC), a nonprofit organization, and manufactured by Quanta Computer. Originally intended to run on open-source software, OLPC has reached an agreement for the use of Microsoft's Windows XP operating system. The agreement with OLPC underscores Microsoft's eagerness to market its software in emerging markets, where it has tried to seed Windows in schools—the target of OLPC's machines. The $3 price represents a big discount to what the company charges in the United States. Recently, Microsoft has also done $3 software deals in Russia, Libya, and Egypt.[93]

SHAPING ASPIRATIONS

The biggest challenges in developing markets are in providing essential services. In this sense, developing markets can be ideal settings for commercial and technological innovation. With significant demand for mobile handsets in developing countries, both Nokia and Motorola have developed models that sell for as little as $25. They are ideally suited to match consumer demand for inexpensive phones with the features, quality, and brand names consumers want. Emerging low-cost producers from China cannot match the volume or the brand franchises of the global players. While gross margins on these phones may be as little as 15 percent (as compared with 33 percent at the high end), the big volumes and scale economies reduce costs even for high-end models.[94] Global marketers are very often the only ones that can realistically make a difference in solving some of the problems in developing markets. Developing new technologies or products is a resource-intensive task and requires knowledge transfer from one market to another. Without multinationals as catalysts, nongovernmental organizations, local governments, and communities will continue to flounder in their attempts to bring development to the poorest nations in the world.[95]

The emergence of these markets presents a great growth opportunity for companies. It also creates a chance for business, government, and civil society to join together in a common cause to help the aspiring poor to join the world market economy. An example of such an approach is provided in Focus on Technology. Lifting billions of people from poverty may help avert social decay, political chaos, terrorism, and environmental deterioration that is certain to continue if the gap between the rich and poor countries continues to widen. For example, Coca-Cola has introduced "Project Mission" in Botswana to launch a drink to combat anemia, blindness, and other afflictions common in poorer parts of the world. The drink, called Vitango, is like the company's Hi-C orange-flavored drink, but it contains 12 vitamins and minerals chronically lacking in the diets of people in developing countries. The project satisfies multiple objectives for the Coca-Cola Company. First, it could help boost sales at a time when global sales of carbonated drinks are slowing, and, second, it will help in establishing relationships with governments and other local constituents that will serve as a positive platform for the Coca-Cola brand. The market for such nutritional drinks may be limited, but they are meant to show Coca-Cola in a role of good corporate citizen at a time when being perceived as such is increasingly important for multinational corporations.[96]

Connect the World

Early in the twenty-first century, Cisco (which sells everything from million-dollar routers to $300,000 videoconferencing systems to set-top boxes for cable TV) approached emerging markets in the same simplistic way as most developed-market companies did: it had a few sales offices and distributors but no specialized effort. Today, more than $4.5 billion of its total $36 billion in sales come from emerging markets, such as Saudi Arabia, Turkey, and Poland.

Win the Government, Business Will Follow

Cisco CEO John Chambers and emerging-markets chief Paul Mountford focus on selling "country transformation" plans to heads of state and top ministers. Governments often drive these massive investment initiatives, and success there converts into equipment sales at companies building the nation's infrastructure. "We have been good on corporate social responsibility, we're almost always in the top ten places to work, which we are in every major country in the world. But also, the better in corporate social responsibility, it's amazing how it transfers over to business success."

Sell More Than Technology

Rather than just peddle its wide array of products, Cisco focuses on working with governments on broad issues. In Saudi Arabia, for example, the government had trouble managing the many pilgrims who visit Mecca. Cisco brought in consultants and partners to build an online system that allows travelers to secure a visa and hotel room in hours rather than weeks.

Charity Pays

Cisco won big points in the Middle East and elsewhere by getting involved in philanthropic efforts. In Jordan, the company helped launch training programs to boost the skills of the poverty stricken. It is also giving away its high-end videoconferencing systems, which can cost up to $300,000 per location, to all Middle Eastern heads of state, including Israel's prime minister.

Hire Well-Connected Locals

Cisco doesn't just hire locals: it recruits top power brokers. In Turkey, it recently brought in the former chairman of Türk Telekom, the dominant phone carrier in the country. In Saudi Arabia, Mountford hired Badr Al Badr, a well-known entrepreneur and son of a leading adviser to the king, as the country's chief.

Create Jobs

With half of its population under 21, Saudi Arabia needs to create millions of jobs to absorb those entering the labor force and build a modern economy. Cisco has agreed to

invest $265 million in the country over five years. Most of that is going to establish Networking Academy training centers, where locals learn everything from repairing routers to network design. The Saudi centers have had 13,700 students so far.

Create and Adapt Products For Local Needs

Cisco has a campus in Bangalore, India, from which teams of engineers can be dispatched to deliver to different market needs. For example, a web site in Turkey allows small textile companies to bid on a variety of contracts. The customized products are then marketed to potential buyers in others, similar countries.

Sources: "McKinsey Conversations with Global Leaders: John Chambers of Cisco," McKinsey & Company, July 2009; "Cisco Raises More than $4.6 Million to Support Global Hunger Relief," Cisco Systems, February 11, 2009; Burrows, Peter, "Cisco's Emerging-Markets Gambit," *BusinessWeek*, November 13, 2008, online; "Cisco: 'The Best Company for the World,'" *BusinessWeek*, November 13, 2008, online; and Jeff Borden, "Cisco Humanizes Technology and Connects the World," *Marketing News*, September 2008, 14–17.

ECONOMIC INTEGRATION AND THE INTERNATIONAL MANAGER

Regional economic integration creates opportunities and challenges for the international manager. Economic integration may have an impact on a company's entry mode by favoring direct investment, since one of the basic rationales for integration is to generate favorable conditions for local production and inter-regional trade. By design, larger markets are created with potentially more opportunity. Harmonization efforts may result in standardized regulations, which can positively affect production and marketing efforts.

Decisions regarding integrating markets must be assessed from four different perspectives: the range and impact of changes resulting from integration, development of strategies to relate to these changes, organizational changes needed to exploit these changes, and strategies to influence change in a more favorable direction.[97]

9. To suggest corporate response to advancing economic integration

EFFECTS OF CHANGE

The first task is to create a vision of the outcome of the change. Change in the competitive landscape can be dramatic if scale opportunities can be exploited in relatively homogeneous demand conditions. This could be the case, for example, for industrial goods and consumer durables, such as cameras and watches, as well as for professional services. The international manager will have to take into consideration varying degrees of change readiness within the markets themselves; that is, governments and other stakeholders, such as labor unions, may oppose the liberalization of competition, especially when national champions such as airlines, automobiles, energy, and telecommunications are concerned. The rapidly emerging economies consist of the so-called BRIC nations (Brazil, Russia, India, and China) and a group of other relatively wealthy developed nations. The lower-growth economies (compared to the REEs) consist of about 100 nations with relatively impoverished populations and poor economic prospects. These countries may become markets for motorized transportation after 2020. The mature economies include the established industrialized nations in North America and Europe, as well as Japan. Competition is also becoming much more intense.[98]

STRATEGIC PLANNING

The international manager will have to develop a strategic response to the new environment to maintain a sustainable long-term competitive advantage. Those companies already present in an integrating market should fill in gaps in goods and market portfolios through acquisitions or alliances to create a regional or global company. It is increasingly evident that even a regional presence is not sufficient and sights need to be set on a presence beyond that. In industries such as automobiles, mobile telephony, and retailing, blocs in the twenty-first century may be dominated by two or three giants leaving room only for niche players. Those with currently weak positions, or no presence at all, will have to create alliances for market entry and development with established firms. Tesco entered the $270 billion-a-year (in U.S. dollars) grocery market in China in 2004 through a joint venture with Taiwan's Hymall, of which it now owns 90 percent. Today, Tesco operates 60 stores in China, with 95 percent of products sourced within the country. Global reach is key to local effectiveness: Tesco believes that, in China, it can use the experience it has gained from operating around the world to localize its food offerings.[99]

REORGANIZATION

Whatever the changes, they will call for company reorganization.[100] Structurally, authority will have to be more centralized so that regional programs can be executed. In staffing, focus will have to be on individuals who understand the subtleties of consumer behavior across markets and therefore are able to evaluate the similarities and differences among cultures and markets. In developing systems for the planning and implementation of regional programs, adjustments will have to be made to incorporate views throughout the organization. If, for example, decisions on regional advertising campaigns are made at headquarters without consultation with country operations, resentment by the local staff will lead to less-than-optimal execution. The introduction of the euro will mean increased coordination in pricing as compared to the relative autonomy in price setting enjoyed by country organizations in the past. Companies may move corporate or divisional headquarters from the domestic market to be closer to the customer or centers of innovation. "Forum Nokia," a portal available in English, Chinese, and Japanese, gives outside developers access to resources to help them design, test, certify, market, and sell their own applications, content, services, or web sites to mobile user via Nokia devices.[101]

LOBBYING

The international manager, as a change agent, must constantly seek ways to influence the regulatory environment in which they must operate. Economic integration will involve various powers and procedures, such as the EU's Commission and its directives. The international manager is not powerless to influence both of them; a passive approach may result in competitors gaining an advantage or a disadvantageous situation emerging for the company. For example, it was very important for the U.S. pharmaceutical industry to obtain tight patent protection as part of the NAFTA agreement and substantial time and money was spent on lobbying both the executive and legislative branches of the U.S. government in the effort to meet its goal. Often policymakers rely heavily on the knowledge and experience of the private sector in carrying out its own work. Influencing change will therefore mean providing policymakers with industry information such as test results. Lobbying will usually have to take place at multiple levels simultaneously; within the EU, this means the European Commission in Brussels, the European Parliament in Strasbourg, or the national governments within the EU. Managers with substantial resources have established their own lobbying offices in Brussels, while smaller companies get their voices heard through joint offices or their industry associations. In terms of lobbying, U.S. firms have been at an advantage given their experience in their home market; however, for many non-U.S. firms, lobbying is a new, yet necessary, skill to be acquired. Culture does play a role in lobbying in Brussels versus lobbying in Washington, DC. One does not have to grapple with 20 different languages in Washington as you do in Brussels. Although English is increasingly imposing itself as the *lingua franca* in Brussels, significantly, many Members of the European Parliament (MEP) still value being approached in their native language. Internal political cultures are starkly different too. While U.S.-style politics tend to be polarized around bi-partisanship and be highly adversarial, Brussels politics draw on a wider array of parties and specific national issues that are often deeply rooted in a country's governance culture (e.g., British laissez-faire versus French command and control).[102] At the same time, managers in two or more blocs can work together to produce more efficient trade through, for example, mutual recognition agreements (MRAs) on standards.

SUMMARY

Economic integration involves agreements among countries to establish links through the movement of goods, services, and factors of production across borders. These links may be weak or strong, depending on the levels of integration. Levels of integration include the free trade area, customs union, common market, and full economic union.

The benefits derived from economic integration include trade creation, economies of scale, improved terms of trade, the reduction of monopoly power, and improved cross-cultural communication. However, a number of disadvantages may also exist. Most important, economic integration may work to the detriment of nonmembers by causing deteriorating terms of trade and trade diversion. Of course, no guarantee exists that all members will share the gains from integration.

The most successful example of economic integration is the European Union. The EU has succeeded in eliminating most barriers to the free flow of goods, services, and factors of production as well as in creating a central bank, and establishing the euro as a strong common currency among most of the member nations. In the Americas, based on its success with NAFTA, the United States has created free trade agreements with ten countries, while MERCOSUR eliminates barriers among Brazil, Argentina, Paraguay, and Uruguay. ASEAN is increasingly successful in Asia. The international manager must analyze the increasingly complex effects of these and other regional agreements to determine how economic integration affects trade and investment decisions.

Businesses are increasingly looking to emerging markets for sources of growth and competitive advantage because parts of the developing world have outpaced the developed countries in economic growth in the first decade of the twenty-first century. With their large population base and records of economic growth, China, India, and Brazil continue to attract the attention of international businesses.

Emerging markets also present the international managers with barriers to market entry in the form of restrictions on foreign investment, programs that favor domestic companies, vague regulations, burdensome port and customs procedures, high-tariff barriers in certain categories, and insufficient protection for intellectual property rights. Lack of infrastructure development can also present international managers significant challenges in bringing products and services to emerging markets.

Markets like Russia that are still in transition from centrally planned economies to market-oriented economies also represent significant opportunity for international businesses. As the international manager develops strategies to succeed in transition markets, deeply ingrained systemic differences between the transition economies and Western firms must be considered. Developing markets, where poverty still remains a large problem, also offer opportunities for the strategic manager to combine positive social benefits with profitable ventures. Firms must develop creative solutions for these markets based on good research and local knowledge.

KEY TERMS

Group of Five   237

free trade area   238

customs union   238

common market   239

factor mobility   239

economic union   239

economic and monetary
    union (EMU)   239

political union   239

trade creation   240

trade diversion   240

internal economies
    of scale   241

external economies
    of scale   241

Treaty of Rome   242

common agricultural policy
    (CAP)   244

Single European Act   244

maquiladoras   249

Caribbean Basin Iritiative
    (CBI)   251

cartel   257

commodity price
    agreements   257

buffer stock   257

microfinance   268

QUESTIONS FOR DISCUSSION

1. Explain the difference between a free trade area and a common market. Speculate why negotiations were held for a North American Free Trade Agreement rather than for a North American Common Market.

2. Are economic blocs building blocks or stumbling blocks as far as worldwide free trade is concerned?

3. In addition to Brazil, Russia, India, and China, identify three other emerging markets that make sense for international business growth. Why?

4. The China-ASEAN Free Trade Area went into effect in 2010. Low wages have encouraged local and foreign manufacturers to phase out their operations in relatively high-wage Southeast Asia and move them to China. For its Southeast Asian partners, what are the benefits of this current situation?

5. What are the advantages and disadvantages of global businesses outsourcing customer service functions to countries like India?

6. In 2009, Tata Motors introduced the Nano, a fuel-efficient, two-cylinder-engine automobile that has the lowest CO_2 emission of all cars in India. What other countries might be potential markets for the Nano?

INTERNET EXERCISES

1. Compare and contrast two different points of view on expanding trade by accessing the web site of the U.S. Chamber of Commerce, an industry coalition promoting world markets (http://www.uschamber.com), and the AFL-CIO, American Federation of Labor-Congress of Industrial Organizations (http://www.aflcio.org).

2. Alibaba.com (http://www.alibaba.com) is a business-to-business e-commerce company. It operates two marketplaces: the first is an international marketplace based in English, tailored to global importers and exporters in China; the second is a Chinese marketplace that focuses on suppliers and buyers trading domestically in China. Is a company able to operate in both capacities?

TAKE A STAND

Turkey has aspired to join what is today's European Union since 1959, when it applied for associate membership, which it gained in 1963. Turkey signed a customs union agreement with the EU in 1995 and was officially recognized as a candidate for full membership in 1999. Negotiations were started in 2005, and the process is likely to take at least a decade to complete. Almost immediately thereafter, the EU froze negotiations on eight policy areas because of Turkey's refusal to open its ports and airports to vessels and aircraft from Cyprus. Overall, the membership bid has become the central controversy of the enlargement of the European Union.

Institutionally and commercially, Turkey is deeply integrated into Europe. For example, nearly 60 percent of its exports and more than 50 percent of its imports are with European Union members. Turkey's membership would bolster the EU's economy by $635 billion (PPP basis) and add a member that is part of the OECD and G-20. Arguments in favor of Turkey joining include the belief that this would bolster democratic institutions in Turkey and enable further improvements in human rights. Many fear that if Turkey is not granted membership in the EU, the winners will be the country's ultranationalists, and the West would lose an important ally.

The concerns are many as well. If Turkey joined the EU in 2015, it would become its most populous state within a decade, due to strong population growth in the predominantly Muslim republic and low fertility rates in the European Union. As population size largely determines voting power in the EU, it would leapfrog Germany to become the state with the greatest political clout. Despite the fact that Europe already has more than 15 million Muslims (3.5 million of whom are Turkish),

critics have argued that Turkey is "in permanent contrast to Europe." Turkey is considerably poorer than EU states, with a per-capita gross domestic product equal to a quarter of the EU average. Many fear that more Turks would emigrate into European territories, which might result in tensions both on the labor side and on the level of society.

While many of the EU member-states are in favor of membership, the mood among the general population is more negative, with nearly 60 percent of respondents being against and less than 30 percent in favor. A new cloud gathered over EU–Turkish relations in May, 2007, when Nicolas Sarkozy, an opponent of Turkey's EU aspirations, was elected French president. Sarkozy proposed an alternative "Mediterranean Union," which would combine various EU and non-EU countries around the Mediterranean Sea. "I want to say that Europe must give itself borders, that not all countries have a vocation to become members of Europe, beginning with Turkey, which has no place inside the European Union."

For Discussion

1. Are Turkey's culture and values too different from those of the European Union as a whole?

2. What are the different barriers of culture and values to Iceland's (2012) quick membership to the European Union?

Sources: "Turkey's EU Talks Inch Forward," *Financial Times*, December 20, 2007, 8; "The Slow Move Towards Accession," *Business Europe*, November 1–15, 2007, 8; "Don't Go Cold on Turkey," *Wall Street Journal*, March 3, 2007, A8; "Turkey Has No Place Inside the European Union," *TurkishPress.com*, January 15, available at http://www.turkishpress.com/news.asp?id=159133; "The West's Eastern Front," *Wall Street Journal*, November 28, 2006, A14.

THE BANANA WARS

The European Union (EU) is the main market in the world for bananas, constituting 33.3 percent of all world trade (see Figure 1).

That is why a decision by the EU Farm Council in December of 1992 attracted attention among banana-producing nations. Up until the decision, different EU countries had different policies regarding imports of bananas. While Germany, for example, had no restrictions at all, countries such as the United Kingdom, France, and Spain restricted their imports to favor those from their current and former African, Caribbean, and Pacific (ACP) colonies. (This preferential trading agreement is known as the Lomé Convention.) The decision called for a quota of 2.2 million tons with a 20 percent tariff for all banana imports from Latin America ($126 per ton), rising to 170 percent for quantities over that limit ($1,150 per ton). Because Latin American exports to Europe were approximately 2.7 million tons in 1992, the quota has effectively cut almost 25 percent of the countries' exports to the EU.

The main stated reason for imposing the quota and the tariffs is to protect former colonies by allowing them to enjoy preferential access to the EU market. Other reasons implied have been the $300 million in tariff revenue resulting from the measures, as well as moving against the "banana dollar" (reference to the U.S. control of the Latin American banana trade through its multinationals). Belgium, Germany, and Holland have objected to the measures not only because of the preference given to higher-cost, lower-quality bananas from current and former colonies, but also because of the economic impact. The Belgians estimated an immediate loss of 500 jobs in their port cities, which traditionally have handled substantial amounts of Latin American banana imports. Twice, the European Court of Justice has rejected Germany's challenge to the EU's banana policy. Even in the United Kingdom, where the preferential treatment has enjoyed widespread support, there has been criticism of the decision.

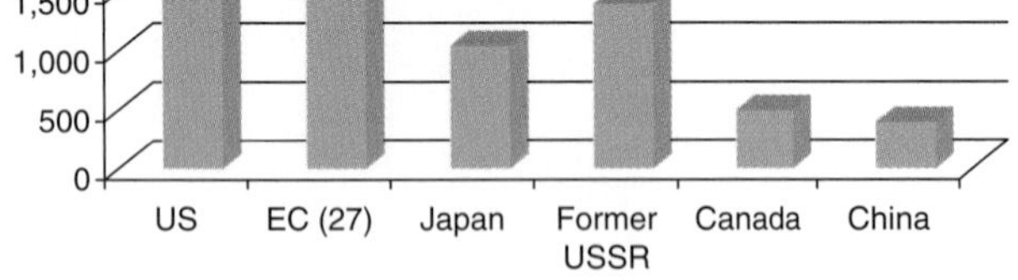

On two separate occasions in 1993 and 1994 panels of the General Agreement on Tariffs and Trade (GATT) found EU banana rules to be unfair and tried to convince the EU to reform its discriminatory and burdensome banana rules. As a result of the EU's failure to do anything, a case was initiated with GATT's successor, the World Trade Organization (WTO), in 1996. The WTO agreed in 1997 with the complaint and turned down a subsequent EU appeal later in the same year. In 1999, the WTO authorized the United States to impose $191.4 million in trade sanctions on the EU. The last WTO ruling, again upholding the complaint, was issued in early 2008. Trade ministers tried, and failed, to secure a deal as part of the Doha Round of trade talks. Finally, the four groups involved found common ground in a separate deal. Delegates from the EU, United States, former EU colonies, and the Latin American banana powers met in Geneva more than 100 times for a total of 400 hours of talks. The settlement means less-expensive bananas for Europeans, more profit for U.S. fruit companies, and lower revenue for some former EU colonies. The EU will reduce tariffs on bananas from Latin American countries to $167 a ton in 2017 from $252 today, in return for Latin American countries dropping their WTO case. The EU's former colonies will

Figure 1   Banana Imports, Major Countries 2006–2008 Average (thousand tonnes)

Sources: This case was written by Ilkka Ronkainen. "Info-Comm," *UNCTAD*, December 22, 2009; John W. Miller, "World News: EU Ends 16-Year Banana Trade Battle, Agreement to Cut Tariffs Will Benefit U.S. Fruit Companies," *The Wall Street Journal*, December 16, 2009, A12; "Food Outlook," *FAO*, December 2009; Alan M. Field, "Bananas: Battered and Bruised," *Journal of Commerce*, May 26, 2008, 1A: Guy Ellis, "St. Lucia's Declining Banana Trade," *BBC*, August 2, 2005; "Caribbean, U.S. Blame Each Other in Banana Split," *Journal of Commerce*, October 15, 1997, 4A.

The help of Gladys Navarro with an earlier version of this case is appreciated. For more information on bananas and trade in bananas, see http://www.chiquita.com; http://www.delmonte.com/company/; http://www.dole.com; and http://www.fyffes.com. For different points of view on the banana dispute, http://www.bananalink.org.uk/content/view/61/21/lang,en/; http://www.cbea.org; http://www.sice.oas.org; and http://www.ustr.gov/reports/index.html.

Figure 2   Banana Exports, Major Countries 2006–2008 Average (thousand tonnes)

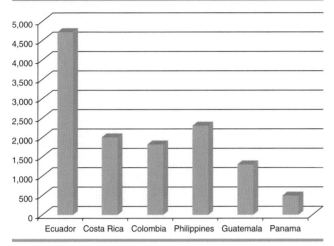

started only in earnest with the introduction of the steam engine and refrigeration, enabling quicker transportation and arrival in better condition to Europe and North America. As late as the Victorian era, bananas were not widely known in Europe, although they were available via merchant trade. Consumers in the United States were first introduced to bananas at the Philadelphia Centennial Exhibition in 1876. In the early twentieth century, bananas began forming the basis of large commercial empires, for example, by the United Fruit Company, which created immense banana plantations especially in Central and South America.

The Latin American Position

Bananas are the world's most-traded fruit, and the $14.6 million tons (2008) in banana trade make it second only to coffee among foodstuffs. For countries such as Ecuador, Costa Rica, Colombia, and Honduras, the restrictions would cost $1 billion in revenues and 170,000 jobs. For countries such as Costa Rica, banana exports are vital. Bananas represent 8 percent of the country's domestic product, bring in $500 million in hard-currency earnings, and employ one-fifth of the labor force.

The presidents of Colombia, Costa Rica, Ecuador, Guatemala, Honduras, Nicaragua, Panama, and Venezuela held a summit February 11, 1993, in Ecuador and issued a declaration rejecting the EU banana-marketing guidelines as a violation of GATT and principles of trade liberalization. However, following the formal adoption of the banana decision by the EU in July 1993, the EU and four Latin American nations (Costa Rica, Colombia, Nicaragua, and Venezuela) cut a deal in March 1994. The four countries agreed to drop their GATT protest in exchange for modifications in the restrictions they face. Guatemala refused to sign the agreement, and Ecuador, Panama, and Mexico lodged protests.

The economics of production are clearly in favor of the Latin producers. The unit-cost of production in the Caribbean is nearly 2.5 times what it is for Latin American producers. For some producers, such as Martinique and Guadeloupe, the cost difference is even higher. The EU quota therefore results in major trade diversion.

The affected Latin nations have used various means at the international level to get the EU to modify its position. In addition to the summit, many are engaged in lobbying in Brussels as well as the individual EU-member capitals. They have also sought the support of the United States, given its interests both in terms of U.S. multinational corporations' involvement in the banana trade as well as its investment in encouraging economic growth in the developing democracies of Latin America.

continue to receive virtually tariff-free access for its EU banana shipments, and will get a one-time cash payment of $300 million. Ecuador, the world's largest banana exporter, hailed the deal as a victory for all Latin American nations (see Figure 2).

History of the Conflict

1993: The EU offers special low banana tariffs to its most recent colonies. Colombia, Costa Rica, Guatemala, Nicaragua, and Venezuela file a complaint at the World Trade Organization.

1994: WTO rules against the EU.

1997: WTO rules the EU was failing to comply.

1999: WTO authorizes U.S. trade sanctions against the EU.

2007: In a new complaint, WTO again rules the EU must stop its subsidies.

2008: Trade ministers at a global summit in Geneva fail to find a compromise.

2009: After 400 hours of meetings, all parties agree to a new tariff regime.

HISTORY OF THE BANANA

Bananas can be traced back thousands of years to ancient manuscripts by the Chinese and Arabs. European experience starts in 327 BC with Alexander the Great's conquest of India. Bananas were introduced to the Americas by Spanish explorers in 1516. From that point on, many tropical regions with average temperatures of 80°F (25°C) and annual rainfall of 78 to 98 inches (2,300 to 2,900 mm) have benefited from bananas as a source of food and, increasingly, trade. Trade in bananas

The U.S. Position

Initial U.S. reaction was that of an interested observer. The United States provided support and encouragement for the Latin Americans in their lobbying efforts in Geneva, Brussels, and the European capitals. However, in October 1994, the U.S. announced plans to start a year-long investigation of the EU's banana restrictions, with sanctions against European imports as a possibility. This action broke new ground in trade disputes. While governments traditionally have started trade wars as a means of protecting domestic jobs and key industries, the banana dispute involves U.S. investment and overseas markets more than it does jobs at home. The probe was requested by Chiquita and the Hawaii Banana Industry Association, whose 130 small family farms constitute the entire banana-growing contingent. Although only 7,000 of the company's 45,000 employees are in the United States, Chiquita officials argued that the value added by the company's U.S. workers—marketers, shippers, and distributors—make it a major agricultural priority.

The U.S. challenge was "not politically prudent," because the United States does not even export bananas. However, 12 senators sent a letter to Mr. Mickey Kantor (U.S. trade representative, 1993 to 1996) warning against the dangerous precedent if the EU banana regime went unchallenged. Unless deterred, the EU could possibly employ similar measures for other agricultural products, especially those that the United States does export.

The United States is, however, in favor of a WTO waiver to the EU to provide support to its former colonies. The contention is that the EU feels that it can, within this waiver, take any measures it deems necessary regardless of the impact on other WTO members. The United States and the other four countries filing the complaint argued for a more narrow interpretation, which would mean a simple system of tariff protection supported by aid to increase the efficiency of some producers and help the remainder to retire or diversify. The tariff would, in effect, offset some of the cost differences in the EU markets.

The United States argues that many ACP producers are not competitive because of their special circumstances (such as small average farm size of five acres/two hectares) as well as EU preferences, which have given the ACP nations a disincentive to become competitive or to diversify.

The Caribbean Position

For many nations, banana exports are the mainstay of their economies (see Figure 3). Therefore, it was not

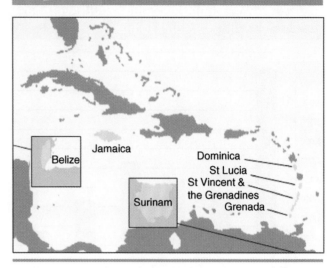

Figure 3   The Caribbean

surprising that heads of government of the 13-member Caribbean Community (CARICOM) approved a resolution February 24, 1993, supporting the EU guidelines. "No one country in this hemisphere is as dependent on bananas for its economic survival as the Windward Islands," declared Ambassador Joseph Edsel Edmunds of St. Lucia. Referring to the criticism of the EU decision by the Latin nations, he added: "Are we being told that, in the interest of free trade, all past international agreements between the Caribbean and friendly nations are to be dissolved, leaving us at the mercy of Latin American states and megablocs?" He noted that Latin American banana producers command 95 percent of the world market and more than two-thirds of the EU market.

Ambassador Kingsley A. Layne of St. Vincent and the Grenadines asserted that the issue at stake "is nothing short of a consideration of the right of small states to exist with a decent and acceptable standard of living, self-determination, and independence. The same flexibility and understanding being sought by other powerful partners in the WTO in respect of their specific national interests must also be extended to the small island developing states." The highest levels of dependence on banana exports can be found in the Windward Islands countries: St. Lucia (19.7 percent), St. Vincent and Grenadines (22.3 percent), and Dominica (18.1 percent).

After the WTO decision was rendered, the Caribbean nations have tried to strengthen alliances with European parliamentarians and have mobilized international opinion to continue to challenge the WTO ruling. "The decision represents a failure by the WTO, in its blind pursuit of free trade, to take into account the interests of small developing countries," said Marshall Hall, chairman of the Caribbean Banana Exporters

Association. The Windward Islands, especially, are worried that the WTO ruling will further discourage farmers in the region who are already reducing quantities of fruit for export.

St. Lucia's banana exports have declined from 132,000 tons in 1992 to just 42,000 tons in 2009. The number of banana farmers has also fallen from 10,000 to 1,800 today, as the industry is forced to produce the quality fruit the market demands while facing stronger competition and lower prices. The country's exports of bananas (known locally as "green gold") have dropped more than 60 percent in the past decade. The minister of tourism estimates that every acre of land used for tourism is three times as profitable as one used for growing bananas. Those farmers who have stayed in the business, he describes as "hard core and genuine." It is they, he said, who are now producing the quality of bananas that the market is demanding. The future of the industry now seems to lie in exporting under the "fair trade" label. Caribbean bananas are grown mainly on small family farms, with intensive and justly paid labor and low usage of agro-chemical inputs. That inevitably results in lower yields and higher average cost. But many consumers are willing to pay a fair, if slightly higher, price for such an ethical and quality product—as they do for free-range and fair trade products.

The Corporate Position

The two largest producer and marketers of bananas are both U.S.-based companies: Dole Food Company and Chiquita Brands International. Each accounts for just over a quarter of all bananas traded internationally. Then comes Fresh Del Monte Produce, controlled by the Chilean-based IAT Group (capital held in the United Arab Emirates), which controls approximately 16 percent of the banana trade. Fresh Del Monte Produce headquarters is Miami, Florida. The fourth biggest banana export company is Exportadora Bananera Noboa (Bonita brand), part of the largest Ecuadorian conglomerate, Grupo Noboa, which controls a quarter of Ecuador's exports and, therefore, about 13 percent of total world trade. In fifth place is the Irish fruit company Fyffes, with an estimated 7 percent share (see Figure 4).

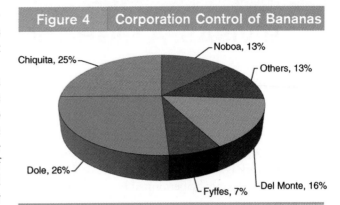

Figure 4   Corporation Control of Bananas

Chiquita, 25%
Noboa, 13%
Others, 13%
Dole, 26%
Fyffes, 7%
Del Monte, 16%

The dispute has also pitted U.S. multinationals (Chiquita, Dole, and Del Monte) against the Europeans (Fyffes). Since 1996, the European group controls virtually all of the banana shipping and marketing from such markets as Belize, Suriname, Jamaica, and the Windward Islands. Chiquita, in particular, complains that the EU is arranging insider deals for Fyffes to exempt them from export licensing fees imposed by Latin American nations that have agreed with the EU, or even to secure them a slice of the export business from Latin American markets where they have no foothold at present. The EU's licensing system has transferred 50 percent or more of U.S. or Latin American companies' import rights principally to EU firms. The Caribbean nations and the EU assert that the United States is taking its action solely to support the world's largest banana trader, Chiquita, because it wields great political influence.

Questions for Discussion

1. If you were a member of the Organization of American States (of which all of the Caribbean and Latin American countries mentioned in the case are members) and its Permanent Council (which must react to two opposing statements concerning the EU decision), with which one would you side?

2. Given the WTO's decision, what are the alternatives for the EU and the Caribbean banana growers?

3. What types of strategic moves will an international marketing manager of a Latin American banana exporter make?

H-1B VISAS: A HIGH-TECH DILEMMA

INTRODUCING THE DEBATE

The public face of the immigration debate in the United States has typically revolved around illegal workers filling low-wage/low-skill jobs. Traditional wisdom dictates that some work is so labor-intensive and poorly compensated that it can only be performed by desperate foreigners with limited options. However, there is another aspect of the immigration debate that generates no less controversy but receives far less public scrutiny. The H-1B temporary worker visa program has long been a thorn in the side of U.S. companies looking to attract highly skilled foreign labor. The high-tech industry has been particularly impacted and has sought to liberalize the rules and regulations governing H-1B. Opponents of the program have characterized its current form as the present-day version of indentured servitude. Some domestic labor groups have argued that temporary workers are an unnecessary evil that depresses wages and takes American jobs away from Americans.

The H-1B is a visa program that allows foreign individuals with highly specialized knowledge and skills to work in the United States for a maximum of six years. It was initiated in the 1950s to attract mathematicians, physicists, and engineers from behind the Iron Curtain. H1-B has undergone many revisions since its inception. However, it has not been able to keep pace with the changing needs of American employers. This is best illustrated by the information technology sector, where historically robust labor demand is projected to grow by approximately 40 percent by 2016. The industry's growth long ago outpaced the domestic supply of skilled workers, leaving IT companies to navigate the murky waters of securing H-1B visas for qualified foreigners.

Keeping up with legislative changes to the program is a full-time job in itself. In 2000, Congress approved a three-year increase in the H-1B allotment from 115,000 to 195,000. The bill passed, largely because high-tech lobbyists were successful in positioning the visas as protection for the U.S. competitive edge in technology. However, when the three years were up, the allotment was scaled back drastically under pressure from domestic interest groups, using the dot-com bubble burst and resulting temporary sector contraction as partial

justification. Currently, there are only 65,000 H1-B visas available, with an additional 20,000 reserved for foreign holders of U.S. advanced degrees. That number's inadequacy is plainly obvious, when one considers that for the 2008 tranche, there were 123,480 applications filed in the first two days after the offer date. The Bureau of Citizenship and Immigration Services resorted to a lottery to determine who would get a visa and who would not.

As Table 1 demonstrates, demand for H1-B visas has long outpaced supply. Do note that the data includes visas given to employers exempt from the cap, such as colleges, universities, and nonprofit research organizations. It is plainly obvious that even amidst a global downturn, the program has not been able to accommodate demand both from American employers and willing immigrants. This limits the country's human capital growth and, consequently, its productivity and overall economic expansion. Experts predict that as the economy rebounds, demand for H-1B visas will spike, further exposing the program's inadequacies. Simultaneously, growing domestic concerns over unemployment, irrespective of the uneven distribution of job losses across sectors, have led to accusations of H-1B abuses and calls for increased oversight and more stringent controls.

In response to these political pressures, Congress passed a measure in February of 2009, limiting the use of H-1B visas by financial firms that have received bailouts. The mainstream media response was largely negative. The *Washington Post* characterized the provision as "antithetical to innovation and domestic prosperity." *The Wall Street Journal* published a critical editorial, titled "Turning Away Talent," and *New York Times* columnist Thomas Friedman called it "S-T-U-P-I-D." However, it is important to recognize that the labor market has indeed managed to find ways of circumventing the stringent H-1B regulations. For example, use of L-1 visas, or short-term visas for intra-company transfer increased by 34 percent from 2004 (62,700) to 2008 (84,078). Such visas have no annual cap and no requirement to pay holders the prevalent wage, and hence companies find them less politically sensitive and more user-friendly. However, they make it hard to retain the best and the brightest, since L-1s represent only a temporary

Sources: This case was written by Dafina Nikolova, Ilkka Ronkainen, and Beverly Reusser. It is based on publicly available materials, such as Moira Herbst, "The H-1B Visa Lull Is Only Temporary," November 2, 2009, *BusinessWeek*, http://www.businessweek.com/bwdaily/dnflash/content/nov2009/db2009112_270880.htm; Ron Hira, "It's Time to Overhaul H-1B Visas," *BusinessWeek*, April 2, 2009, http://www.businessweek.com/magazine/content/09_15/b4126063331942.htm; "White Collar Sweatshops," *The Economist*, April 1 2008, 51–52; and Julia Preston, "Visa Application Period Opens for Highly Skilled Workers," *The New York Times*, April 1, 2008, http://www.nytimes.com/2008/04/01/washington/01visa.html?_r=1&ref=us.

Table 1	H-1B Facts, 2006–2008			
Year	Total Petitions Filed	Total Petitions Approved	Initial Employment	Continuing Employment
2006	295,915	270,981	109,614	161,367
2007	304,877	281,444	120,031	161,413
2008	288,764	276,252	109,335	166,917

Source: U.S. Citizenship and Immigration Services, Fiscal Year 2008 Annual Report, "Characteristics of Specialty Occupation Workers (H-1B)," http://www.uscis .gov/USCIS/New%20Structure/2nd%20Level%20%28Left%20Nav%20Parents%29/Resources%20-%202nd%20Level/h1b_fy08_characteristics_report_01may09 .pdf, p. 4.

fix. There also are some flagrant abuses of the system, exemplified by one company that filed numerous H-1B petitions for Iowa, where prevalent wages are lower than the national average, and then transferred approved workers to higher-wage areas.

THE CRITIC'S POSITION

Examples, such as the one above, provide justification for interest groups that seek a complete overhaul of the H-1B system. Their main grievance is that employers are not required by law to demonstrate a shortage of U.S. workers in their field. They point to the Labor Department's 2006–2011 Strategic Plan, which states that "H-1B workers may be hired even when a qualified U.S. worker wants the job, and a U.S. worker can be displaced from the job in favor of the foreign worker." This critique is predicated on the assumption that employers exaggerate labor shortages in order to hire cheaper workers from abroad. There are some numbers to support such claims. The median annual wage for new H-1B holders in the IT industry, including those with advanced degrees and years of experience, was $50,000 in 2005 (the last year for which USCIS provided such demographic statistics). Simultaneously, entry-level U.S. workers with only a bachelor's degree in the field made, on average, $51,000.

However, even if this line of argument is correct in the majority of cases, basic economic theory would suggest that the macroeconomic effects might actually be beneficial. The H1-B program is designed to increase the supply of skilled workers, and hence reduces wages for the most affected occupations. Companies are able to secure lower paid labor, which reduces costs and increases the overall economy's profit potential. This argument has been previously used for using cheaper imports in the textile and steel industries, which have translated into lower consumer prices and economic expansion. In other words, increasing America's knowledge base and stock of human capital would escalate long term growth and the earning potential of all workers.

Other critics question whether H-1B attracts the best and the brightest. They argue that truly exceptional workers constitute the minority of the visa holders and point out that the minimum degree requirements for H-1B are rather low—a bachelor's or equivalent experience. The implication is that H-1B is becoming obsolete, given that there are plenty of capable Americans, eager and willing to work, especially in the wake of the global economic collapse and rising unemployment rates. However, this criticism does not take into account long-term processes or current and future differences in labor supply and demand across industries.

There are some key economic and demographic trends that need to be considered, chief among them, the rapidly aging American workforce. The U.S. Census projects that the number of Americans 65 and older will increase by 26 percent in the next five years, while the 25 to 39 age group will grow by only 6 percent. One example of the potential impact of an aging workforce is the healthcare industry, which is already grappling with persistent labor shortages. The average nurse in the United States is 42 years old. Once the baby-boomers retire, replacing them will be difficult without the help of qualified foreign workers. Another important concern is the decline in domestic workforce readiness, as graduation rates for the nation's colleges and universities have been steadily declining. In 2002, 51 percent of college students graduated within five years of initial enrollment, compared to a rate of 55 percent in 1988. Analysts are predicting that the next decade will result in a 33 percent shortfall in graduates of four-year or higher degree programs. A recent Harvard study has identified the main reason for the increasing wage gap as the sharp decline in the growth of U.S.-born skilled labor since 1980, driven by a slowdown in the rise of educational attainment levels. College-age students in the United States are faced with the double-whammy of rising tuition rates and contracting credit. Of those who do pursue higher education, fewer are entering "hard" science and technology-oriented tracks. For example, enrollment in key courses for computer majors has dropped by 10 to 30 percent since 2001. Simultaneously, the American economy is gradually shifting away from manufacturing and toward services, as exemplified by the ever-expanding technology sector. This trend will increase demand for science, math, and computer skills, which are in increasingly short supply.

What would happen if technology companies were unable to find enough skilled workers domestically, either by using local talent or importing from abroad? In a word—outsourcing. Expediting the move of America's technology sector overseas is not a desirable outcome, especially from a political point of view. Some policymakers have proposed a comprehensive approach to permanent skilled immigration, similar to the merit-based point systems of Canada and the United Kingdom. This could ensure expedited processing for potential immigrant workers in needed occupations. However, because of pressures from domestic interest groups, the political will for such a comprehensive overhaul has remained in short supply.

THE VISA HOLDER'S PERSPECTIVE

A political solution to the skilled labor and immigration debate is crucially important. However, many analysts operate under the mistaken assumption of "if you build it, they will come." In other words, there will never be a shortage of highly skilled employees, willing to move to America, so immigration reform is not pressing. The incentives for international labor mobility are well-established and straightforward—better wages and standard of living, coupled with job security and possibilities for career advancement. From the immigrant's perspective, the H1-B system fails on almost all counts. The visa represents a temporary work permit, held by the employer and not by the worker. Because the number of available foreign workers has traditionally exceeded the H1-B allotment (refer to Table 1), employment-based

green card holders have little bargaining power with their employers and can be stuck in a less-than-ideal job for as long as ten years, with no possibility to switch companies or get a promotion. As previously discussed, they are also paid less than their American counterparts, irrespective of experience and educational attainment.

At the same time, developing countries like China, India, and South Korea have implemented policies aimed at fostering return migration and retaining domestic talent. They have made massive investments in innovation, infrastructure, and R&D (research and development), with some measurable results. According to a 2009 report by the Kauffman Foundation, 50,000 highly skilled immigrants have left the United States in the past two decades for China and India. These two countries coincidentally account for the majority of H1-B visa holders (see Figure 1); 100,000 more are predicted to make the return trip over the next five years, so the trend is gathering momentum. A survey of 1,203 Indian and Chinese workers who had studied or worked in the United States for a year or more before returning home cited growing demand for their skills and lucrative career opportunities back home as the primary motivator for repatriation. Most of these individuals were in their early 30s and nearly 90 percent had master's or doctoral degrees. Beyond returning home, in-demand workers also have more opportunities to move to developed countries other than the United States Over the past decade, many OECD [Organization for Economic Cooperation and Development] governments have recognized the looming global demographic and skill redistribution trends and have stepped up efforts to attract skilled foreign employees. For example, Germany has implemented a special visa/incentive program for information

| Figure 1 | Percentages of U.S. Immigrants with H-1B Visas from Various Nations |

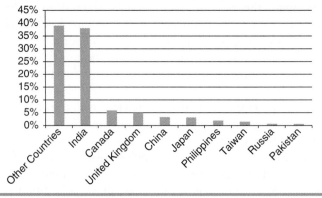

Source: Department of Homeland Security, Office of Immigration Statistics, "Statistical Yearbook, 2008" http://www.dhs.gov/xlibrary/assets/statistics/yearbook/2008/ois_yb_2008.pdf, accessed January, 28, 2010, pp. 89–94.

Table 2	Companies with the Largest Number of Approved H-1B Petitions for Fiscal 2009
Wipro	1,964
Microsoft	1,318
Intel	723
IBM India	695
Patni Americas	609
Larsen & Toubro Infotech	602
Ernst & Young	481
Infosys Technologies	440
UST Global	344
Deloitte Consulting	328

Source: U.S. Citizenship & Immigration Services.

technology workers, while Australia and Ireland have adopted fast-track work authorization for in-demand professions. The skilled workers of the future are likely to truly have the world as their oyster, with lucrative employment opportunities across the globe.

THE BALANCE

In order to meet the growing needs of many of its industries, such as information technology and healthcare, the United States would have to completely reevaluate its immigration philosophy. Similar to the "Arms Race" and "Space Race" of the not-so-distant past, the global economic future likely holds an equally challenging and important "Brain Race." The ability to attract and retain skilled foreign workers in key developing industries should not be taken for granted, but fostered through functional immigration policies and incentives. The current H1-B system provides a temporary and imperfect fix (Table 2). On the domestic front, the knowledge base needs to be expanded through increased investment in education and industry-specific career development. Some have suggested that the market might evolve its own measures to combat employment shortages. "Microsoft University" and "Comcast Institute of Technology" could well be part of the future American academic community. However, without a comprehensive plan to restructure America's workforce, such piecemeal solutions will not guarantee continued economic expansion and prosperity.

Questions for Discussion

1. Comment on the following statement: "The firms of the New Economy seem to be awfully fond of the Old Economy of 200 years ago, when indentured servitude was in vogue."

2. Identify some measures that could attract American college students to the technology and "hard sciences" fields. Should companies in these industries bear a greater responsibility for expanding the knowledge base and reinvesting some of their profits in, for example, scholarships and loan-repayment programs?

3. Should the cap for H-1B visas be eliminated altogether? Should no such provision exist at all and efforts be directed at domestic supply?

CLOSING THE MG ROVER PLANTS: THE AFTEREFFECTS

BACKGROUND

The closure of the MG Rover plant at Longbridge, Birmingham, England in April 2005 was one of the largest industrial failures seen in the U.K. for some 20 years, with around 6,300 workers losing their jobs when MG Rover went into administration, and several thousand more affected in the supply chain. The scale of the job losses in an already economically disadvantaged region and the loss of the last remaining British-owned car manufacturer combined to highlight the consequences of the ongoing decline of manufacturing and the associated human costs of structural change.

By February 2006, of the 6,300 unemployed resulting directly from the collapse, around 4,300 were back at work (90% of whom were working full-time). A further 667 were in training or awaiting training, 398 had received training but were still not working, 530 were not working and had not received any training, 443 had unknown destinations, and 257 had claimed alternative benefits after claiming Job Seekers' Allowance (RTF, 2006).

THIS REPORT

This report presents findings on where people now live and work relative to before the closure. It also provides a survey that investigates their lives.

KEY FINDINGS

Key points from the report's findings are:

- Most workers are now in full-time employment on permanent contracts;
- Most employees have witnessed a significant drop in salary relative to their MG Rover wage, on average a decrease of £5,640 (adjusted for inflation), but post MG Rover salaries are highly differentiated;
- Managers are earning about the same as they were at MG Rover, just £1,280 more (adjusted for inflation). Those now working in some service sectors took average cuts of more than £6,000 per annum compared to their final salaries at MG Rover;

- 25% reported being in debt or needing to draw on savings and 36% were "just about managing;"
- 66% of all ex-MG Rover workers reporting being financially worse off now;
- Those who found re-employment sooner use similar skills to those they used at MG Rover and earn more than other ex-MG Rover workers;
- Of those who were still unemployed eight months post closure, 80% underwent some forms of training;
- Overall, 60% of workers received some form of training or educational support, with 40% taking up the offer of free training;
- Workers who took up training reported higher satisfaction and less of a decline in health than those who did not receive any form of training;
- Workers re-employed sooner reported higher levels of overall job quality with higher life satisfaction and lower anxiety levels.

Overall, the vast majority of ex-workers surveyed (90%) are back at work, with most in full-time work on permanent contracts. Behind this "success story," workers nevertheless reported difficulties in finding a job, with the main perceived barriers being age, skills and experience, and the simple fact that there were too many people applying for the same jobs (not a surprise given the scale of job losses at MG Rover and the level of unemployment in parts of Birmingham when the plant closed). In overcoming such barriers to find work, personal initiative and networks have been the key to ex-workers finding jobs.

The jobs that ex-MG Rover workers have found are highly diversified, with only 30% working in manufacturing and a mix of both lower and higher occupational status. The gross average salary of workers has decreased (on average by £5,640, adjusted for inflation, for workers in full-time employment) even three years after closure. A third of respondents have actually reported an increase in salary. People who found work in four sectors—wholesale and retail, real estate and business services, education, and health and social work—took average cuts of more than £6,000 in annual income (adjusted for inflation).

Source: This case was derived from: David Bailey, Caroline Chapin, Michelle Mahdon, and Rebecca Fauth, "Life after Longbridge: Three Years on: Pathways to re-employment in a restructuring economy," *University of Birmingham Economic & Social Research Council* (November 2008): 1-66. http://www.theworkfoundation .com/assets/does/MG_Rover_2008.pdf, accessed June 1, 2010.

Job satisfaction was higher for those who had received some form of training relative to those in our sample who had not. Only a third of ex-workers surveyed felt that their current job was better than the one they had at MG Rover. Nearly half felt that their job was worse than the one they had at MG Rover. Nevertheless, a majority of workers still like the work that they do and expected to be doing it for the foreseeable future.

Some Policy Implications

Much work was done by the RDA Advantage West Midlands and other agencies before the MG Rover closure in diversifying the supply chain and economy. This work may have "saved" as many as 10,000–12,000 jobs in the supply chain (Bailey and MacNeill, 2008).

When MG Rover finally closed in 2005, the MG Rover Task Force Mark II was able to hit the ground running on the day of the announcement of the closure. Such advance preparation could work well in future closure situations, since it is unlikely that a future closure would happen without at least some prior warning. This lesson points toward the need for good "institutional memory" of how to work in such a situation and having a permanent capacity to deal with such situations. Keeping knowledge available would help with advanced planning and avoid "fire fighting" in the future.

Our research has identified three "pathways" back into re-employment, looking at different groups of workers (those employed by three months after the closure, those employed eight months on, and those still unemployed at eight months but in employment by three years after the closure). The impact of the closure across these groups has varied, suggesting that a greater degree of differentiation in support may be appropriate in similar situations in the future. Such tailored support would combine to help psychologically, in making training and education available and accessible, enabling mobility (both in occupational and physical terms), counseling and support regarding finance and debt, and help for partners to retrain and/or enter work.

Questions for Discussion

1. How do you evaluate the outcomes described in this case?

2. Should workers be forced to change industries?

3. What key dimensions would you evaluate to determine success?

4. Compare these findings with more recent changes in Detroit and Toyota City.

THE GM–AvtoVAZ JOINT VENTURE*

Moscow–General Motors Corp., the world's largest automaker has sealed a $332 million deal to build cars in Russia, a move seen as a show of confidence that Western companies are ready to take a chance here again, three years after the financial crisis that drove many of them away. GM's president, Rick Wagoner, flew to Moscow to meet Prime Minister Mikhail Kasyanov of Russia and then signed documents Wednesday creating a joint venture with AvtoVAZ, Russia's largest domestic car manufacturer, culminating years of difficult negotiations.

— "GM Joint Venture Shows Confidence in Russia," *The Washington Post*, June 28, 2001.

"It's the beginning of Russia's integration into the world's car market. We cannot live in isolation anymore, and we think our buyers should be able to take advantage of the world's experience."

— Vladimir Kadannikov, Chairman of AvtoVAZ, June 28, 2001

General Motors Corporation (U.S.), the world's largest automobile company, had reached agreement on its joint venture (JV) with GAO AvtoVAZ (Russia). The JV had been GM's solution to the problem that had confronted all Western automakers in Russia: how to penetrate a market which desired and appreciated higher quality, but could not pay for it. The problem for Russian automakers was how to gain the knowledge and technical know-how to produce higher quality and yet keep costs down. These were the forces that had driven the two parties to enter into the JV in the spring of 2001. But the subsequent ups and downs of the JV, still running in 2007, is a complex story.

GM'S INTERESTS

GM had made some small efforts on penetrating the Russian auto market throughout the 1990s with little success. Although the market was expected to grow rapidly, doubling in the 2001–2006 period, GM did not think the market could support an automobile which would be priced much above $10,000. GM traditionally had serviced low-price markets like this through the use of complete knockdown (CKD) or semi-knockdown (SKD) car kits, where the auto was manufactured largely at an existing facility in, say, Germany, and then the major components shipped to a final assembly facility in-country. After initial studies, however, GM had concluded that even this mechanism would not result in a cheap-enough automobile for the Russian market.

The Russian automobile market had never been successfully penetrated by a Western automaker. The reasons were many and nearly insurmountable. The entire auto infrastructure was undeveloped, with few suppliers meeting even minimal quality standards. Dealership networks were controlled by management of the automakers themselves. There was no credit-check system for individuals in Russia, to provide the basis for credit sales. This required all auto purchases to be for cash. And that was *before* the crisis of 1998 impoverished the country.

GM's conclusion had been to enter into a joint venture with the dominant automobile manufacturer in Russia, AvtoVAZ. AvtoVAZ held a commanding 65% market share, had existing plant and facilities which could be instantly leveraged, and most importantly of all, possessed an existing product, the Niva, which GM felt could be highly commercial after significant reengineering and higher quality assembly.

AvtoVAZ'S INTERESTS

AvtoVAZ, originally called "VAZ" for Volzhsky Avtomobilny Zavod (Volga Auto Factory), produced nearly 700,000 autos in 2000. AvtoVAZ was the builder of the infamous *Lada*. The Lada itself was nothing other than a Fiat. Fiat of Italy had built a factory along the Volga River in 1970 under contract. It turned over the facility, once constructed for ownership and operation, to AvtoVAZ. The company was privatized in 1993, and had shown spurts of growth and some success.

The financial crisis of August 1998 with the fall of the rouble from Rbl 11/$ to over Rbl 25/$, had actually bolstered AvtoVAZ's market position. Imports were now prohibitively expensive for most Russians, and the management of AvtoVAZ knew it months before it happened.

"It's cynical to say, but in the case of a devaluation, the situation at AvtoVAZ would be better. There would be a different effectiveness of export sales, and demand would be different. Seeing that money is losing value, people would buy durable goods in the hopes of saving at least something."

—Vladimir Kadannikov,
Chairman of the Board, AvtoVAZ, May 1998

But the collapse of the rouble and the purchasing power of the Russian populace had a larger and more complex repercussion on the market—unfulfilled demand. The average Russian needed and wanted an automobile of higher quality than was available in the domestic market, but could no longer afford Western autos. Whatever they bought had to cost less than the equivalent of $10,000. If, however, a Western automaker could figure out a way to produce a high quality auto in Russia at an affordable price, the market was waiting.

THE JOINT VENTURE AGREEMENT

On June 26, 2001, GM and AvtoVAZ reached final agreement on the JV. AvtoVAZ would offer its Niva platform and engineering design for joint production with GM in Russia of a new Niva—the Chevy Niva. By using AvtoVAZ design and facilities the costs would be local, and by using GM's knowledge of manufacturing excellence, the product quality could be improved significantly. The total investment of $338.2 million was divided between three parties: General Motors, $99.1 million by cash and equipment (41.61%); AvtoVAZ, $99.1 million by intellectual property (patents and Niva 2121), buildings, etc. (41.61%); and the European Bank for Reconstruction and Development (EBRD), $40 million in cash and $100 million loan facility (16.78%).

The Chevy Niva would carry both the AvtoVAZ and Chevrolet badge. The badge alone was worth an additional $1,500 per car according to market surveys. The market was willing to pay, but not too much, for what it perceived as superior Western quality. Much of the business case behind the JV was for roughly one-half of the 75,000 annual units to be exported. Both GM and AvtoVAZ believed that Russia would serve as a very effective low-cost country of production for a moderately priced small SUV like the Chevy Niva. Exports would please AvtoVAZ, generate substantial hard-currency earnings, and simultaneously add significantly to the JV's profitability. All parties expected the Russian ruble to continue to fall in value over time against both the dollar and the euro, adding to the competitiveness of the exportable product.

The new Chevy Niva produced by the JV would have to be upgraded, however, in order to be exported to eastern or western Europe. The export version would need a larger engine (GM proposed the Open F-1 engine), better emissions control for compliance with EU standards, and additional safety features. Although this would require a bit more investment, it was thought easily doable over the following years with initial JV profitability. The exports would assure GM of reaching its minimum rate of return on the investment (lowered to 11% from a normal 22% as a result of strong lobbying by GM's Russian team).

One of the major expectations of both parties was a large and rapid transfer of technology between GM and AvtoVAZ on state-of-the-art automobile manufacturing and assembly. Although AvtoVAZ really did not see an additional 75,000 units per year as a big addition to its existing 700,000 units per year, the technology transfer component made the JV attractive in terms of its long-term benefits.

A final component of the agreement was important. As the new Chevy Nivas began rolling off the production line in Togliatti, AvtoVAZ would begin phasing-out the older Niva, eventually ceasing production of the 77,000 units per year currently sold. This would preserve the margins and competitiveness of the new Chevy Niva's uniqueness.

PRODUCTION BEGINS

Production of the Chevy Niva began as scheduled on September 23, 2001. It would be priced at $8,000, and the production and marketing plan was for annual sales to reach 75,000 units by 2004. Of that total, approximately 40,000 were targeted for the export market. The primary export markets were expected to be eastern and central Europe, in addition to Mexico and other countries in Latin America. The joint venture production facility was housed within one corner of the massive existing AvtoVAZ facility in Togliatti, Russia. The new Niva (seen in Exhibit 1) was well-received by the Russian press, with many eyes from around the world watching with interest the performance of this high-profile Western investment in post-perestroika Russia.

Much of the early attention focused on the JV's efforts at creating a quality culture in the facility. But despite intensive effort, quality was a problem. The Chevy-Niva managing director was quoted as saying that the quality of parts delivered to the plant was a major concern and that as much as 20 percent were defective. But a Chevy-Niva employee said the situation was much worse. The employee, who worked in quality control and asked not to be identified, said "99 percent of

Exhibit 1   The New Chevrolet Niva

© Zinin Vladimir/ITAR-TASS /Landov

the parts do not fit or are damaged and have to be sent back to the supplier. There are a lot of problems." Chevy Niva sales were sluggish in 2003, with total production at 25,235 cars and sales of 22,442 units.

Used car imports also continued to impact new car sales. Used cars brought into Russia *by individuals*, although still subject to import duties on automobiles, were not subject to the 20% Value Added Tax (VAT), making it difficult for new Russian-manufactured autos to compete. Finally in late 2003 the Russian government heeded the arguments of many (including Heidi McCormack) and this loophole was closed.

In the spring of 2004 the relations between the JV partners came under increasing strain. In May a Moscow arbitration court upheld a decision by the Russian Antimonopoly Service that required the elimination of a clause from the original JV agreement.[1] The clause had required that AvtoVAZ gradually phase-out the original Niva, introduced in the early 1990s, from the marketplace in order to reduce competition in the Russian market for the Chevy Niva. Since the original Niva and the new Chevy Niva were the only domestically manufactured (not assembled) sport utility vehicles sold in Russia, the court deemed the clause anti-competitive.

In September 2004, exactly two years after the introduction of the Chevy Niva, the JV introduced the Chevrolet Viva. The hopes of both partners were that the Viva would give a boost to JV sales by expanding the product-line breadth with a higher-priced model to take advantage of growing consumer purchasing power

in the Russian market. The Viva was based on the sedan version of the GM Opel and was sold under the Chevrolet brand in Russia. The Viva was essentially an assembly operation, with 90% of the components imported in the initial production. In less than a year the imported components were scheduled to fall to 57%. The Viva was equipped with a 1.8-liter 125-horse power Opel engine, and was available in two different trim levels. It met Euro-4 emissions standards, making it possible for export to central and western Europe.

The starting price of the Viva-L entry model—offered with ABS, electro-hydraulic power steering, electronic traction control and engineering adaptation to Russian road and climate conditions—was 333,333 rubles (US$11,400). In less than a year, however, the Viva's production plan was scaled-back as sales of the new higher priced model proved slow. The explanations, as seen in Exhibit 2, focused on pricing. The JV closed 2004 with $45 million in net profit, and for the first time distributed dividends to the three owners.

In April of 2005 General Motors surprisingly canceled the introduction of the Niva to western European showrooms (the 1.8 liter engine had been slated for commercial introduction) with no explanation. In October 2005 Vladimir Kadannikov announced his retirement from AvtoVAZ, ending his 17-year tenure as the CEO of Russia's largest automaker. In early November 2005 Rosoboronexport, a state defense agency, seized control of AvtoVAZ, removing management rather forcefully.

Exhibit 2   GM-AvtoVAZ Scales Back Viva Production Outlook, August 31, 2005

VIENNA—Russia's ZAO GM-AvtoVAZ says it will manufacture less than half the number of Chevrolet Viva cars initially expected this year due to sluggish demand for the new model. Production of the Viva, based on the Opel Astra II, officially was launched at GM-AvtoVAZ in September 2004. Original plans for 2005 called for production of 7,500 units. However, only 1,196 units were sold between January and July, and GM-AvtoVAZ Chairman Vladimir Kadannikov now says the production schedule is being cut to 3,000 Vivas for this year.

The problem appears to be the car's high price. "We asked a marketing company to conduct market research whether a car with that price tag would be popular," Kadannikov says. "They said yes—and they made the mistake, not us."

According to Kadannikov, the joint venture, owned by General Motors Corp., OAO AvtoVAZ and the European Bank for Reconstruction and Development (EBRD), is considering whether to ask the Russian government to begin implementing a new law that reduces or eliminates tariffs on key car components. This would allow GM-AvtoVAZ to slash the production costs and price of the Viva. The Chevrolet Niva SUV remains GM-AvtoVAZ's main model.

First, though, the old management team had to be persuaded to leave peacefully. After Mr. Kadannikov resigned in October, a team of police investigators and prosecutors was airlifted in to begin the process. "To impose order . . . the state had to bring in 300 policemen from outside," says Mr. Chemezov [AvtoVAZ spokesman]. "Over the next few months, we had to replace virtually the entire police force, both in Togliatti and in the factory itself." Soon, three of AvtoVAZ's senior accountants found themselves facing charges of theft and tax evasion. The charges were dropped a few weeks later.

—*"Kremlin Capitalism," Wall Street Journal, May 19, 2006, p. A1*

Rosoboronexport, controlled by Sergey Chemezov, a close friend of Russian President Vladimir Putin, announced a plan to restructure the company to improve both its profitability and its international potential.

AvtoVAZ's shareholders approved the new Board and management team unanimously on December 22, although the new team was the only choice on the ballot.

The JV closed 2005 with sales of less than 50,000 Chevy Nivas and about $10 million in net profit. AvtoVAZ's new management also announced that it was suing its JV partner, General Motors, for 1,680 rubles ($60)—a token sum—the purported damages sustained by AvtoVAZ after the JV stopped the assembly line in a dispute over the quality of parts delivered by AvtoVAZ in December. The suit was largely a test of the Russian courts' willingness to enter into the fray between the two disgruntled parties.

MARKET & JV CHALLENGES: 2006

Less than a decade ago, owning a foreign car in Russia was privilege for the rich and powerful. Last year, nearly every second car sold in Russia was foreign. This change testifies to the sharp growth in consumer demand in Russia and the

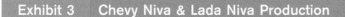

Exhibit 3   Chevy Niva & Lada Niva Production

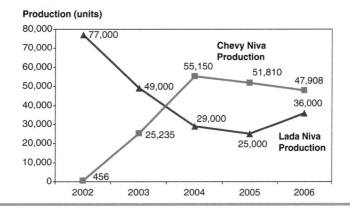

squeeze which foreign companies—from east and west—are putting on Russian car plants. Russian car makers, who once enjoyed a monopoly in their home market, last year accounted for less than 50% of it for the first time. The appreciation of the rouble, and rising incomes in Russia, are expected to drive market share to about 36% in one year's time as foreign makers conquer Russia's potholed roads.

The company suffering most from this squeeze is AvtoVAZ, the maker of Lada cars. It has the country's largest vertically integrated car plant—a site that has now become a poignant symbol of its industrial decline. It still makes more than 900,000 cars a year—most assembled on old production lines little changed since the 1960s. It has one new production line filled with new, shining German and Italian equipment, producing the modern Kalina model. But the Kalina—with an unmistakably Lada-like engine and gear-box—forms only 10% of units produced by AvtoVAZ.
—"Cars: Consumer Demand Alters Russia's Car Map," *Financial Times*, April 20, 2006.

In February 2006 the production line of the JV came to a halt for 10 days. The shutdown was a result of a disagreement between the two partners over the prices of parts sold to the JV by AvtoVAZ. AvtoVAZ's new management believed that the JV was not paying high enough prices for the parts supplied by AvtoVAZ, and demanded higher prices immediately. The price dispute was resolved in a little more than one week with what both parties called a "short-term solution." The JV was once again operating.

GM ST. PETERSBURG

"With Order 166 the government has consciously promulgated legislation that is conducive to investment and that will stimulate growth of the auto industry. But, the proof is in the pudding."
—Heidi McCormack (of GM-Russia), "Car Queues Stage Comeback," *Financial Times*, October 20, 2006, p. 4

In June 2006 GM announced the completion of an agreement with local authorities in St. Petersburg for the construction of a new automobile assembly facility in the St. Petersburg suburb of Shushary. The facility, near the new Toyota automobile assembly plant, would assemble between 20,000 and 25,000 cars a year, employ 700 Russian workers, and represent an initial investment of $115 million. The facility would produce the Chevrolet Capitva SUV from complete knockdown (CKD) kits. Depending on market conditions, GM said the facility could be expanded in the near future, potentially doubling the capital investment.

The new GM venture was designed to take advantage of the new Russian law, Government Order N166, passed in 2005, which provides import duty relief on imported components for foreign investors in Russia and a variety of other tax incentives for foreign investors. GO166 eliminates import duties for 8 years but requires that the investor reduce import costs by 10% every two years over the 8 year period. GM described the St. Petersburg investment as being the "third-leg" of GM's presence in the Russian market (the JV being the first leg and a Kaliningrad facility the second leg). Starting in September 2006 GM would begin assembling Chevrolet Capitvas from kits at a separate St. Petersburg facility.

NEAR THE END?

In July and August 2006 a series of additional rumors swept through the joint venture. In late July AvtoVAZ rejected a preliminary proposal by Renault of France to take a 25% interest in all of AvtoVAZ. Despite the rejection, the CEO of AvtoVAZ, Igor Yesipovsky, resigned the following week. The rumors surrounding his resignation focused on his continuing opposition to a major equity interest in AvtoVAZ being sold to Renault. There was also growing speculation that AvtoVAZ would buy GM's stake in what was increasingly called the "failed JV." The chairman of the board at AvtoVAZ, Vladimir Artyakov, was quoted as saying, "If GM offers favorable terms, we will accept them and will buy out their stake."[2] However, the two parties had yet to meet and neither party had officially made such an offer or other termination agreement.

By the end of 2006 the relationship between AvtoVAZ and General Motors had once again stabilized, the new management team from Rosboronexport expressing a more cooperative stance with their American counterpart. And there was progress. The parties had finally managed to agree on the introduction of the Opel Family-1 (F1) engine into the Chevy Niva for early 2007, a significant improvement for potential market share growth both domestically and possibly internationally. And the GM-AvtoVAZ dealership network, which had started with only 15 outlets in 2002, ended 2006 with more than 130 dealerships throughout Russia. As illustrated by Exhibit 4, the production of the Chevy Niva, however, did not seem to be rising, and in the eyes of some, was losing ground to the rejuvenated Lada 4x4, the original Niva which AvtoVAZ continued to produce and sell but not under the traditional Niva name. Many analysts of both GM and AvtoVAZ continue to debate the future of the joint venture.

Case Questions

1. How did the original JV agreement balance out strategic needs versus financial needs for the two JV partners? Do you believe the JV partners were aligned in terms of the strategic interests?

2. Why do you think the kit-assembly approach was not more successful in Russia? It was a common automaker production/distribution strategy employed in much of the world's emerging markets, but was not working in Russia.

3. All things considered, do you believe that the JV parties would consider the JV successful? Although it never exported and it never reached its production goal (at least to date), would the leadership teams of GM and AvtoVAZ consider what they gained sufficient to cover what it cost them?

Notes

1. The clause had been a part of the original agreement signed by the joint venture parties in 2001, but had only been reviewed by the Antimonopoly Service as a result of a request by AvtoVAZ.

2. "Russian's AvtoVAZ Ready to Buy Out GM Stake in Failed JV," *Mosnews.com*, July 24, 2006.

MATTEL'S CHINESE SOURCING CRISIS OF 2007*

Mattel was forced to deliver a humiliating public apology to "the Chinese people" on Friday over the damaging succession of product recalls of China-made toys that the U.S. toy maker has announced in recent months. In a carefully stage-managed meeting in Beijing with a senior Chinese official, which, unusually, was open to the media, Thomas Debrowski, Mattel's executive vice-president for worldwide operations, read out a prepared text that played down the role of Chinese factories in the recalls.

"Mattel takes full responsibility for these recalls and apologises personally to you, the Chinese people, and all of our customers who received the toys," Mr. Debrowski said. The apology was in stark contrast to recent comments from Robert Eckert, Mattel's chief executive. In testimony to the U.S. Senate last week, he suggested that the fault for the group's recent product recalls lay with outside contractors. "We were let down, and so we let you down," he said.

—"Mattel in Apology to Chinese," Financial Times, September 22, 2007, p. 15

Bob Eckhart, CEO of Mattel (U.S.), had a problem—a big problem. Mattel had discovered on July 30 that a number of its toys manufactured in China contained lead paint. The following month had seen a series of recalls, rising political tensions between the United States and Chinese governments, and a suicide. But no company had been in China longer than Mattel; the original Barbie had been created there in 1959. Mattel had a depth of experience and a longevity of relationships which should have prevented the problem. In the end it was those relationships and that longevity that may have contributed to the product safety failures.

MATTEL'S SOURCING

Mattel had long known the risks associated with a toy product's value stream. Toys were based on a global supply chain which was highly sensitive to petrochemical (plastics) and labor input costs, environmental and human rights sensitivities to socially responsible and sustainable business practices, transportation and logistic disruptions, border crossings, and cost and time to market—all of which added to risk.

Growing concerns and controversies over labor practices had led Mattel to establish its *Global Manufacturing Principles* in 1997, in which it established principles and practices for all companies and sites that manufactured Mattel products, either company owned or licensed manufacturing. The *Global Manufacturing Principles* (GMP) were established to confirm the company's commitment to responsible manufacturing practices around the world. To support the GMP standards the company created the Mattel Independent Monitoring Council (MIMCO). Mattel was highly regarded as the first global consumer products company to apply the system to both its own facilities and core contractors on a worldwide basis. But the problems had still happened.

The crisis had actually begun in June when U.S. toy maker RC2 recalled 1.5 million Thomas the Tank Engine products made in Guangdong, the Chinese province adjacent to Hong Kong and long the center for contract manufacturing by Western firms. Mattel had then followed with a disturbing series of three product recalls in less than one month.

- The first recall of 1.5 million toys of 83 different models was made on August 2, most of which were produced by Lee Der Industrial, a Mattel supplier for 15 years. The toys were found to contain high levels of lead paint, a chemical banned many years ago but still secretly used by manufacturers around the globe in an effort to reduce costs (paint with lead often dried glossier and faster). Lee Der Industrial had knowingly used paint that was not approved by Mattel.

- The second recall, amounting to more than 18 million toys worldwide, was announced on August 14, only two weeks following the first recall. Products recalled were primarily products of The Early Light Industrial company in China, a Mattel partner for 20 years. The recall included just 436,000 Pixar toy cars over lead paint concerns, but nearly 18 million over the concern that small magnets on some products could be ingested. Early Light had sub-contracted components of the Pixar cars to Hong Li Da, another Chinese company, which had actually used lead paint. This second announcement resulted in an immediate 6% drop in Mattel's share price on the New York Stock Exchange.

- The third recall, announced on September 4, was for 800,000 toys, most of which were accessories for Barbie dolls. Mattel explained that further product testing had indicated they possessed "impermissible levels" of lead paint. The products originated from seven different Chinese factories. This third announcement had prompted the European Union to announce a two-month review of toy product safety for toys sold within the EU, regardless of the source of their manufacture.

Chinese manufacturers were the source of 65% of Mattel's toys. Of those 65%, about one-half were owned by Mattel, and one-half manufactured product for the company under a variety of licensed manufacturing agreements. Mattel still owns the 12 factories which make the majority of its core products like Barbie and Hot Wheels. But for the other roughly 50% of its product lines it relies on a set of vendors, which had included Lee Der Industrial and Early Light. For long-standing relationships like those with Lee Der and Early Light, Mattel allowed the companies to do most of their own product testing as a result of the trust between the two parties. But regardless of who owned the actual manufacturing facility, many of the non-Mattel vendors had in-turn out-sourced many components and parts to other businesses. All of the businesses in the complex supply chain were facing the same competitive cost pressures in China—rising wage rates, a shortage of skilled labor in coastal provinces, escalating material and commodity prices—some of which may have been the motivation for suppliers to cut corners and costs.

It was, therefore, not clear that outsourced manufacturing was really the culprit in this case, or simply the fact that much of the manufacturing and material industries operating throughout China were relatively fragmented, newly developed, under heavy cost pressures, and generally unregulated. Mattel had long held a very high reputation as being one of the very best at assuring healthy and safe product manufacturing, and had worked diligently with its suppliers to assure their conformity with manufacturing specifications and product safety. The resulting problem was that a number of suppliers in China had used lead paint instead of the paint that Mattel had specified and approved for use. They had done it to cut costs.

On September 5th Mattel had told an American Congressional committee that its recall of 17.4m toys containing a small magnet that could be swallowed by children was due to a flaw in the toys' design, rather than production flaws in China. As for some other toys recalled because of allegedly hazardous levels of lead in their paint, Mattel admitted that it had been overzealous and is likely to have recalled toys that did not contravene American regulations on lead content.

CHINA BEARS THE COST OF DEVELOPMENT

> As Beijing cracks down on unsafe toy exports and demands more testing, many small toy producers in China are feeling a financial squeeze. The increased testing "has created real havoc for some . . . manufacturers" in China, says Ron Rycek, vice-president of toy sales at Hilco Corp., which sells toys such as Sonic Skillball to Toys "R" Us and Amazon.com.
>
> Even some companies that are able to keep operating feel the pinch. Manufacturers generally don't get paid until they ship their products, and they usually take out loans to buy materials, pay wages, and cover other expenses until customers transfer funds. With toys now waiting in warehouses while samples are sent to labs, producers can't repay those loans as quickly as they had expected. The testing "is holding up our capital and our warehouse space," says Leona Lam, CEO of Leconcepts Holdings, a Hong Kong–based subcontractor that supplies parts to factories making plastic toys for the likes of Mattel Inc. and Fisher-Price.
>
> —"Bottlenecks in Toyland," *BusinessWeek*, October 15, 2007, p. 52

But regardless of how it had been presented in the press, a multitude of foreign firms selling everything from toothpaste to pet foot to mobile phones had discovered a variety of product defects and health and safety risks in their Chinese-based manufacturing and supplier bases. The question remained, however, as to how much of this risk was inherently "Chinese" and how much was "low-cost country sourcing" in origin.

The rising anxieties over Chinese products and their associated risks and returns in 2007 reflected a multitude of different political, economic, and business difficulties. The rapid growth of the Chinese economy was already well-known and well-documented: approximately 5% of all manufactured goods in the world were now Chinese;

Exhibit 1　China-Manufactured Products Recalled by the U.S. Consumer Products Safety Commission between August 3 and September 6, 2007

Company	Product	Number of Units Affected
Fisher-Price	Sesame Street, Geotrax, other toys	1 million
Mattel	Barbie accessories, Sarge toys	925,000
Springs Windows Fashions	Basic Blindz windows blinds	140,000
Wal-Mart (Sam's Club)	Outdoor torches	138,000
Hayes	Outdoor candles	83,000
Jo-Ann Stores	Children's watering cans	6,000
Raleigh America	Bicycles	1,200
Life Is Good	Children's hooded sweatshirts	400

Source: "Supply Chain: Thomas and His Washington Friends," *CFO*, October 2007, p. 18; and the Consumer Products Safety Commission (CPSC).

25 percent of all products sold in the United States had significant Chinese content; global commodity prices of oil, copper, molybdenum, steel, and others, were seeing record levels as the rate of infrastructure and business development in China caused global shortages and market pressures. But the costs of such rapid economic development were only now starting to become painfully apparent.

The rate of manufacturing growth had far surpassed the ability of the Chinese government on all levels to manage the growth. Regulatory shortfalls—health, safety, and environmental—were now obvious. Although Mattel and other companies were now confessing their own guilt and accepting responsibility for managing their own product risks, the Chinese government was scurrying to not only close regulatory gaps and protect the export customers who were not protecting themselves, but trying to preserve the reputation of Chinese manufacturing and avoid increasing trade restrictions or barriers to their products in foreign markets.

The human costs were already high. Zheng Xiaoyu, a former boss of the Chinese State Food and Drug Administration (SFDA), had been executed earlier in the year for taking bribes to approve inferior drugs and certificates claiming that the paint used by Mattel's suppliers was lead-free. Mr. Zhang Shuhong, the CEO of Lee Der Industrial, the firm which had been the supplier for many of the products included within Mattel's first product recall, had committed suicide on August 14. Political pressure continued to build between the Chinese government and the United States as the list of products which had been banned by the Consumer Protection Council of the United States continued to grow (see Exhibit 1).

The costs of increased regulation were already rising. A survey of consumers in the United Kingdom in September, for example, had found that 37% of the people surveyed noted that the crisis had affected their view of Chinese products overall. As a result, many stated they were much less likely to purchase products made in China. The fall-out from the crisis was indeed no single company, regulatory agency, or government's fault. But the damage was significant and lasting.

Case Questions

1. Mattel's global sourcing in China, like all other toy manufacturers, was based on low-cost manufacturing, low-cost labor, and a growing critical mass of factories competitively vying for contract manufacturing business. Do you think the product recalls and product quality problems are separate from or part of pursuing a low-cost country strategy?

2. Whether it is lead paint on toys or defective sliding sides on baby cribs, whose responsibility do you think it is to assure safety—the company, like Mattel, or the country, in this case China?

3. Many international trade and development experts argue that China is just now discovering the difference between being a major economic player in global business and its previous peripheral role as a low-cost manufacturing site on the periphery of the world economy. What do you think?

NINE DRAGONS PAPER*

NINE DRAGONS DENIES REPORT OF BANKRUPTCY

China's Nine Dragons Paper (Holdings) Limited is denying media reports that it would declare bankruptcy at the end of 2008 and says its finances are fine, Bloomberg reports. The Guangzhou, China based Times Weekly reported on Dec. 25 that an unidentified Nine Dragons official said in an unidentified web posting that the company would declare bankruptcy because it couldn't repay a loan worth $75 million.

"Such articles have no basis in fact," Nine Dragons said in a Hong Kong stock exchange filing on Dec. 29. "The company is not involved in any bankruptcy, liquidation, or winding up proceedings and the company's financial situation is sound and stable. Operations are normal."

Nine Dragon's profit for the six months ended June 30 fell 22 percent from the same period a year earlier.

—Official Board Markets, 3 Jan 2009, p. 13

THE GLOBAL RECESSION

"This time is really different. Large and small are all affected. In the past, the big waves would only wash away the sand and leave the rocks. Now the waves are so big, even some rocks are being washed away."

—Cheung Yan, co-founder and Chairwoman of Nine Dragons Paper[1]

Incorporated in Hong Kong in 1995, Nine Dragons Paper (Holdings) Limited, had become an international powerhouse in the paper industry. The company's primary product was linerboard, with a product line including kraftlinerboard, testlinerboard and white top linerboard in a portfolio of paperboard products used to manufacture consumer product packaging. The company had expanded rapidly and spent extensively.

But by January 2009 the world economy was spiraling downward. Squeezed by market conditions and burdened by debt, Nine Dragons Paper (NDP), the largest paperboard manufacturer in Asia and second largest in the world, saw its share price drop to HK$ 2.33, 90% off its high and less than half of book value. As the economic crisis of 2007 bled into 2009, export-oriented industries suffered. Rumors had been buzzing since October that NDP was on the ropes. It was carrying so much debt that more than one analyst was asking, "Will they go bust?" Was the financial crisis of 2008 about to claim another victim, or had friction between the global economic crisis and the company's debt ignited jittery nerves in the global markets?

THE CHAIRLADY

Cheung Yan, or Mrs. Cheung as she preferred, was the visionary force behind NDP's success. Her empire had been built from trash—discarded cardboard cartons, to be precise. The cartons were collected in the U.S. and Europe, shipped to China, then pulped and re-manufactured into paperboard. NDP customers then used the paperboard to package goods that were shipped back to the U.S. and Europe where the cycle was repeated. "Wastepaper is a forest," a former boss once told Mrs. Cheung. NDP had worked to perfect the harvesting of that forest.

Born in 1957, Mrs. Cheung came from a modest family background yet through hard work, perseverance and savvy business strategy she built a company that was a dominant force in the industry. She had started as an accountant for a Chinese trading company in Hong Kong; after her employer failed, she started her own company to deal in scrap paper. In 1990 she moved to the U.S. to start another company, American Chung Nam Incorporated (ACN), to capture the waste paper stream there.

ORIGINS

It is the largest of scaly animals, and it has the following nine characteristics. Its head is like a camel's, its horns like a deer's, its eyes like a hare's, its ears like a bull's, its neck like an iguana's, its belly like a frog's, its scales like those of a carp, its paws like a tiger's, and its claws like an eagle's. It has nine times nine scales, it being the extreme of a lucky number.

—www.ninedragonbaguazhang.com/ dragons.htm

One of the first companies to export waste paper from the U.S. to China, ACN started by collecting waste paper from dumps, then expanded its network to include grocery stores, waste haulers and waste paper collectors. Mrs. Cheung negotiated favorable contracts with shipping companies whose ships were returning to China empty after unloading goods in North America. ACN soon expanded abroad and became a leading exporter of recovered paper from Europe and Asia to China. By 2001, ACN had become the largest exporter, by volume, of freight from the United States. "In other words, nobody in America was shipping more of anything each year anywhere in the world."[2]

The Chinese economic miracle which began in the late 1990s rose on the back of exports of consumer goods which required massive quantities of packaging material. Within a few years, the demand for packaging outgrew what domestic suppliers could provide. Seizing the opportunity, Mrs. Cheung founded Nine Dragons Paper Industries Company in Dongguan, China in 1995. By 1998, the first papermaking machine (PM1) was installed and running. NDP expanded rapidly and by 2008 it had 22 paperboard manufacturing machines at five locations in China and Vietnam producing 7.85 million tonnes annually.

EXPANSION

"The market waits for no one. If I don't develop today, if I wait for a year, or two or three years, to develop, I will have nothing for the market, and I will miss the opportunity."[3]
— Cheung Yan, co-founder and Chairwoman of Nine Dragons Paper

Even with capacity expansion across the Chinese paperboard industry, the demand for paperboard surpassed production. In 2005 Chinese manufacturers produced nearly 28 million tonnes of containerboard, yet consumption equaled 30 million tonnes. The output gap had narrowed over the past decade, yet despite its standing as the largest containerboard manufacturing country in the world, China remained a net importer.

Since its founding, NDP had expanded production capacity rapidly, as illustrated in Exhibit 1. The company had three paperboard manufacturing plants in China: (1) Dongguan, in Guangdong Province in the Pearl River Delta; (2) Taicang, in Jiangsu Province in the Yangtze River Delta region; and (3) Chongqing, in Sichuan Province in western China. All three were strategically located close to consumer goods manufacturers and shipping ports. NDP also had three other major investments to support its paperboard manufacturing: (a) a specialty board producer in Sichuan Province; (b) a joint venture in a pulp manufacturer in Inner Mongolia (55% interest); and (c) a joint venture in a pulp manufacturer and paper mill in Binh Duong Province, Vietnam (60% interest). NDP by 2008 was the largest paperboard manufacturer in Asia. If planned expansion was completed, NDP would become the largest paperboard manufacturer in the world by the end of 2009.

Mrs. Cheung believed that expansion and its resultant economies of scale were the primary drivers in increasing profit margins. And in fact, looking at the company's sales and profit growth over the previous years (Exhibit 2), this did not appear to be a company that should be on the brink of bankruptcy. In papermaking, expansion required significant capital outlay and a long term outlook. For example, a papermaking machine cost $100 to $200 million to purchase and setup, and even then it might take up to two years before it reached

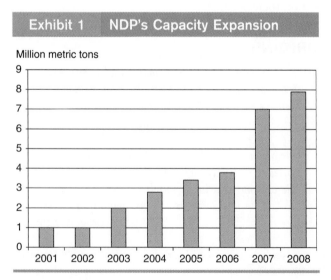

Exhibit 1   NDP's Capacity Expansion

Million metric tons

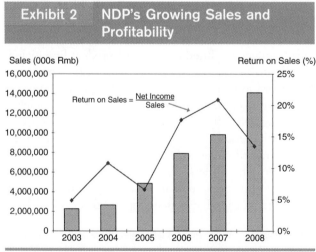

Exhibit 2   NDP's Growing Sales and Profitability

Exhibit 3   NDP's Capex and Operating Cash Flow

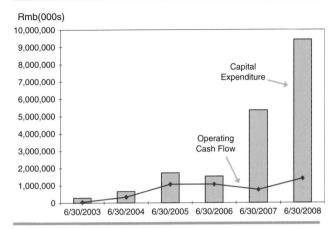

optimal productivity. But all things considered, sales had continued to grow—even faster, although the rate of profitability had fallen in 2008.

FINANCING EXPANSION

"Why are we in debt?" she asked. "I didn't misuse this money on derivatives or something! I took a high level of risk because that is the preparation for the future, so that we will be first in the market when things change."[4]

—Cheung Yan, co-founder and Chairwoman of Nine Dragons Paper

Historically, NDP had funded capital expenditure with a combination of operating cash flow and bank borrowings. But the increasing rate of expansion, as illustrated in Exhibit 3, meant that the company needed a sizeable injection of outside capital. In March 2006, NDP offered 25% of the company's equity, one billion shares, at an

Exhibit 4   NDP's Changing Financial Structure, 2005–2008

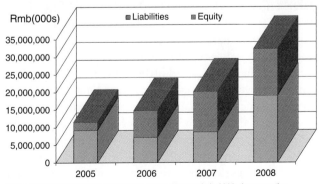

Although both liabilities and equities had grown once again in 2008, the proportion of the company's funding base made up of debt (liabilities) had declined.

offer price of HK$ 3.40 per share. Within six months the stock (HK:2689) was a constituent stock of the Hang Seng Composite Index and by the end of the year the price had increased nearly 400%, to HK$ 13.28, making Mrs. Cheung, who had retained 72% interest, the richest woman in China.

The proceeds from the IPO allowed NDP to retire a large portion of its accumulated debt. But as Mrs. Cheung increased the rate of asset growth, capital expenditure outpaced operating cash flow, generating a negative free cash flow. (*Free cash flow* is generally defined in industry practice as operating cash flow less capital expenditure, *capex*.) When financial markets ground to a halt in the fall of 2008 and the economic crisis spread around the globe, export orders dropped 50%, sales revenue plummeted, and the debt burden became noticeably heavier.

In April 2008 NDP had issued $300 million in senior unsecured notes, notes that Fitch rated BBB-. This was the very edge of *investment grade*, and typical for the industry. Fitch had cited many factors common to the industry in its initial rating: the current economy, raw material price increases and supply risk—but specific to NDP, it noted the aggressive capital expenditure program. As price pressure from raw materials continued and the company's leverage increased, Fitch downgraded NDP to BB+ in October 2008, *speculative grade*, and as markets tumbled, to BB- in December.[5] NDP's management team had argued that by the end of 2008 the company's financial structure had improved, not worsened, as shown in Exhibit 4.

OPERATIONS AND INNOVATION

"We only have a certain number of opportunities in our lifetime. Once you miss it, it's gone forever."[6]

—Cheung Yan, co-founder and Chairwoman of Nine Dragons Paper

From the beginning, the company had invested in the most advanced equipment available, importing papermaking machines from the U.S. and Italy. Each plant was constructed with multiple production lines, allowing flexible configuration. This allowed the company to offer a diversified product portfolio to its customers with options including product types, sizes, grades, burst indices, stacking strengths, basis weights and printability. Five principal products were available in over 60 basis weights and over 1,000 different sizes and type specifications. This flexibility allowed responsiveness to customer demand. NDP had become an innovation leader in the industry. Equipment utilization rates consistently averaged 94%, surpassing the industry average.

Containerboard manufacture demands an uninterrupted supply of electricity, consumes large quantities of water and generates noxious waste products. NDP constructed water treatment plants, waste treatment facilities, coal fired cogeneration power plants and transportation infrastructure to support its operations. These facilities generated operational efficiencies and cost controls while also reducing their environmental impact as much as possible in an historically dirty industry. The Chinese government had imposed increasingly strict regulations to limit environmental impact and compliance was costly: expenses associated with environmental compliance had led to the closing of more than 550 small paper mills in 2008 alone.

Water was used as efficiently as possible. At all of its plants, NDP had constructed its own water conservation and recycling system. The system reduced consumption by taking advantage of differences in water quality requirements of different production lines. For example, water used by one production line was treated and reused before being treated again and discharged into the environment. This innovation resulted in water usage of 6 to 15 tonnes per tonne of production, less than half the international standard. NDP also found that if it controlled the saline levels in the water, it could provide a consistently high quality product to customers. Waste treatment facilities were constructed at all manufacturing plants. Their purposes were three-fold: to capture part of the waste stream for reuse, to re-enter paper pulp into the production stream, and to channel remaining waste into an energy boiler for incineration.

Coal fired co-generation power plants were constructed to supply the plants in Dongguan, Taicang and Chongqing. The cost of power was reduced by approximately one third, steam generated as a by-product was redirected to the production line for use in the drying process and surplus electricity was sold to the regional power grid. In the future, this surplus power could support additional capacity expansion. Also, the power plants were equipped with particulate filtration and desulphurization equipment to reduce pollution.

The company also owned and operated its own transportation infrastructure, including piers and unloading facilities, railway spurs, and truck fleets. The company received shipments of raw materials, including recovered paper, chemicals and coal, at its self-owned piers in Taicang and Chongqing and at the Xinsha Port in Dongguan. These facilities took advantage of ocean and inland waterway transportation, reducing port loading and unloading charges, and allowed the company to avoid transportation bottlenecks.

RAW MATERIALS

"Wastepaper is like a forest. Paper recycles itself, generation after generation."[7]
—Cheung Yan, co-founder and Chairwoman of Nine Dragons Paper

Recovered paper and kraft pulp are the principal raw materials used in the manufacture of paperboard; therefore, the ability to consistently source large volumes of high quality recovered paper is critical to success in the industry. To ensure supply of manufacturing inputs, NDP had secured long-term contracts with American Chung Nam to supply up to 80% of its recovered paper needs. To establish a secure source of wood pulp, NDP entered into a joint venture with China Inner Mongolia Forestry Industry Company, a state owned enterprise, in 2004. In 2008 NDP acquired a wood and bamboo pulp/specialty paper project in Leshan, Sichuan, and in May 2008 acquired Sichuan Rui Song Paper Company which would provide additional supplies of kraft and bamboo pulp.

PAPERBOARD AND THE PACKAGING INDUSTRY

The paper industry in China mirrored the global paper industry—resource hungry and dominated by large domestic players. Lee & Man Paper Manufacturing Limited was NDP's strongest competitor in China. Also founded in 1995, it also focused on containerboard and also added capacity rapidly, producing 2.88 million tonnes in 2008. Together, NDP and Lee and Man Paper accounted for 24% of domestic production in 2008.[8] Other paper manufacturers in China were generally smaller, older, and more diversified. International companies, though large enough to compare with NDP, typically had a broader focus and were vertically integrated into other paper related market segments. Because production in the industry was not labor intensive, the low labor cost advantage in China added little value; and because shipping costs were high on a value-to-volume basis, it was not cost effective to manufacture far from customers.

Global demand for consumer goods had been the primary driver of China's manufacturing and export-led growth over the past decade. Conversely, given the manufacturing slowdown resulting from the 2007 global economic crisis, some industry experts expected that future demand might not match the anticipated capacity

Exhibit 5 NDP's Growing Gap in Free Cash Flow (FCF)

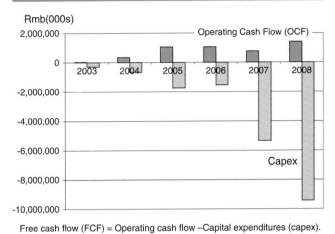

Free cash flow (FCF) = Operating cash flow −Capital expenditures (capex).

increase in the paperboard industry. Already, production had slowed. In fact, the demand for raw materials had decelerated so rapidly that scrap paper was "backing up in America like a clogged drain."[9]

PROSPECTS

Our future path of development may remain thorny ahead, but armed with the shared confidence and courage throughout the Group to overcome and conquer, we are poised to act even more diligently and powerfully to prepare for the next global economic recovery.
—"Chairlady's Statement," 2008/09 Interim Report, Nine Dragons Paper (Holdings) Limited

Nine Dragons Paper was being squeezed by declining markets, burdensome debt—and possibly—just possibly, some market hysteria. As the economic crisis of 2007 continued into 2009, many of NDP's customers simply disappeared. Mrs. Cheung's focused determination had guided NDP to its present industry leadership position. NDP's management team wondered if the growing gap between operating cash flow and capex in recent years was dominating the market's thinking. That gap, as seen in Exhibit 5, was indeed large, but it was a gap that had always been filled opportunistically with debt. Would this time be different? More than 670,000 Chinese businesses had failed in 2008. Would NDP be next?

Case Questions

1. How would you characterize the way in which Mrs. Cheung has gone about building NDP?

2. In your opinion, do you believe NDP's approach to rapid capacity expansion is too risky?

3. What actions would you recommend to NDP to stop the market's attack on its financial viability?

Notes

1. "Wastepaper Queen: Letter from China," *New Yorker,* March 30, 2009, p. 4.

2. Wastepaper Queen: Letter from China," *New Yorker,* March 30, 2009, p. 4.

3. Ibid., 2009, p. 2.

4. "Wastepaper Queen: Letter from China," *New Yorker,* March 30, 2009, p. 2.

5. Fitch Ratings, market announcement, April 14, 2008.

6. "Wastepaper Queen: Letter from China," *New Yorker,* March 30, 2009, p. 2.

7. "Blazing a Paper Trail in China: A Self-Made Billionaire Wrote Her Ticket on Recycled Cardboard," *New York Times,* January 16, 2007.

8. Deutsche Bank AG/Hong Kong, August 24, 2009.

9. "Wastepaper Queen: Letter from China," *New Yorker,* March 30, 2009, p. 7.

PART 4
STRATEGY

9 Strategic Planning
10 The Corporation: Ownership, Governance, and Sustainability
11 Organization, Implementation, and Control
12 Building the Knowledge Base
13 Entry and Expansion

This section deals with the strategic dimensions both within and outside of the corporation. In order to assure longer term direction, management must engage in substantial strategic planning. Particularly in a new age of social awareness and corporate responsibility, there is a growing need to monitor corporate performance on a variety of dimensions and to engage in ongoing reform in order to develop societally responsive corporate governance. Such steps, however, only bear fruit if there are efforts for coordination, implementation and control.

In order to operate abroad successfully, firms must prepare for their market entry. Key in such preparation is the use of research in order to build a knowledge base of country-specific issues and market-specific opportunities and concerns.

Once such a base is established, firms can enter international markets, initially often through exporting, franchising and international intermediaries. Over time, expansion can continue through foreign direct investment. Eventually, ongoing growth can lead to the formation of the multinational corporation.

CHAPTER 9

Strategic Planning

CHAPTER CONTENTS & LEARNING OBJECTIVES

GLOBALIZATION

1. To outline the process of strategic planning in the context of the global marketplace

THE STRATEGIC PLANNING PROCESS

2. To examine both the external and internal factors that determine the conditions for development of strategy and resource allocation

3. To illustrate how best to utilize the environmental conditions within the competitive challenges and resources of the firm to develop effective programs

4. To suggest how to achieve a balance between local and regional/global priorities and concerns in the implementation of strategy

Global markets for everything from banks to beer have witnessed major consolidations in the last five years. Companies are playing the global game by being in all major, and even minor, markets of the world to gain competitive advantage. They are doing so by acquiring local players and by consolidating their own businesses to focus on key opportunities for growth, realizing efficiencies at the same time.

The food and beverage industry is one of the most competitive businesses in the world, with about ten large companies fighting it out for global advantage. Every year brings news of new acquisitions, divestitures, mergers, and strategic partnerships. For example, in 2008, Unilever entered a partnership with PepsiCo for marketing and distribution of Lipton tea products internationally. In 2009, Kraft announced its intention to acquire Cadbury Schweppes. As the major global food and beverage players set their global strategies, a huge challenge confronting them is how to allocate resources across global geographies and broad business portfolios for maximum business results. Inevitably, this means that companies must focus on specific business categories and brands in key country markets.

An example of this focus is Kraft's 5-10-10 strategy for global growth, which lays out Kraft's emphasis on five categories, ten brands, and ten countries. In 2008, Sanjay Khosla, president of Kraft International, identified five categories for growth (biscuits, chocolate, powdered beverages, coffee, and cream cheese) in which the company had strong share positions across the globe. Among these categories, Kraft was the global leader in biscuits

with brands like Oreo cookies and Tuc/Club Social crackers. Biscuits and chocolate represent about half of Kraft International's sales, and Kraft has been deliberate in growing this business with moves like the $7.6 billion purchase of Groupe Danone S.A.'s cracker and cookie businesses in 2007. The ten brands that Kraft will concentrate on overseas include Oreos, Tuc/Club Social, Milka, Côte d'Or, Toblerone and Lacta chocolates, Jacobs and Carte Noire coffees, Philadelphia cream cheese, and Tang. Outside of North America, the company announced its focus on four growth engine markets (Brazil, Russia, China, and the ASEAN countries) and six scale markets (France, Germany, the United Kingdom, Italy, Spain, and Australia). Mr. Khosla explained: "Instead of planting Kraft flags all over the world and trying to be all things to all people, we are now focusing where we can win."

Nestlé, the global leader in the food and beverage category, has a different approach and country selection strategy than Kraft. In addition to Nestlé's strong brands in categories like powdered and liquid beverages (Nescafé and Nestea), milk products and ice cream (Häagen Dazs), prepared foods (Hot Pockets, Stouffer's, and Lean Cuisine), and confectionary (KitKat and Baci), the company is focusing on growth drivers in emerging markets and the developing world. These include the categories of nutrition, health and wellness (with brands like NaturNes 100% natural baby food, Nido nutritional milk powders, and Nestlé Pure Life natural water beverages) and popularly positioned products (PPPs), which brings lower income consumers brands like Maggi instant

noodles at affordable prices. Nestlé sees growth opportunity in serving developing markets. Nestle's reach is broader with PPPs sold in 72 countries and more than 100 confectionary products.

Similar to Nestlé, Danone is also placing emphasis on penetrating markets in developing countries as well as in the developed world. Dairy and new geographical markets have been identified as growth engines for Danone, which sees opportunity in bringing affordably priced dairy brands like Danette, Activia, and NutriDay to developing countries. On the beverage side of the industry, The Coca-Cola Company is the world's largest beverage company, with operations in more than 200 countries.

Sources: David Sterrett, "Kraft Hones Its International Strategy with Oreos, Tang," *Crain's Chicago Business*, September 3, 2008; Brad Dorfman, "Kraft to Focus on 10 Brands Overseas: International Chief," *Reuters*, September 3, 2008; Kraft Foods Inc. Press Release, "Kraft Highlights Strategic and International Growth Progress at Lehman Brothers Back-to-School Consumer Conference," presentation, September 3, 2008; The Coca-Cola Company 2008 Annual Review, http://www.thecoca-colacompany.com; "Danone Back to School Conference" presentation by Emmanuel Faber, September 9–10, 2009, http://www.danone.com; Nestlé S.A. "Bernstein Pan-European Strategic Conference," presentation by James Singh, September 2009, http://www.nestle.com.

GLOBALIZATION

The transformations in the world marketplace have been extensive and, in many cases, rapid. Local industries operating in protected national economies are challenged by integrated global markets contested by global players. National borders are becoming increasingly irrelevant as liberalization and privatization take place. This has then led to such phenomena as the growing scale and mobility of the world's capital markets and many companies' ability to leverage knowledge and talent across borders.[1] Even the biggest companies in the biggest home markets cannot survive by taking their situation as a given if they are in global industries such as automobiles, banking, consumer electronics, entertainment, pharmaceuticals, publishing, travel services, home appliances, or the food and beverage industry as shown in the opening vignette for the chapter. Rather than seeking to maximize their share of the pie in home markets, they have to seek to maximize the size of the pie by having a presence in all of the major markets of the world. They have to be in all major markets to survive the shakeouts expected to leave three to five players per industry at the beginning of the twenty-first century.[2]

Companies from emerging markets, such as China, have entered the megamarkets of North America and Europe not only to gain necessary size but also to gain experience in competing against global players in their home markets.[3] Sometimes that may involve partnering with global companies in third markets. For example, General Motors and SAIC Motor Corp, China's largest auto manufacturer, are partnering in China to manufacture Chevrolets, Cadillacs, and Buicks. The two companies are also working together in Korea, with GM owning 51 percent of GM Daewoo and SAIC owning 9.8 percent. Now the two partners are investigating a joint venture to manufacture vehicles in India.[4]

Globalization reflects a business orientation based on the belief that the world is becoming more homogeneous and that distinctions between national markets are not only fading but, for some products, will eventually disappear. As a result, companies need to globalize their international strategy by formulating it across markets to take advantage of underlying market, cost, environmental, and competitive factors.

As shown in Figure 9.1, globalization can be seen as the culmination of a process of international market entry and expansion. Before globalization, companies utilized, to a great extent, a country-by-country **multidomestic strategy** with each country organization operated as a profit center. Each national entity markets a range of different products and services targeted to different customer

1. To outline the process of strategic planning in the context of the global marketplace

multidomestic strategy A business strategy where each individual country organization is operated as a profit center.

Figure 9.1   Evolution of Global Strategy

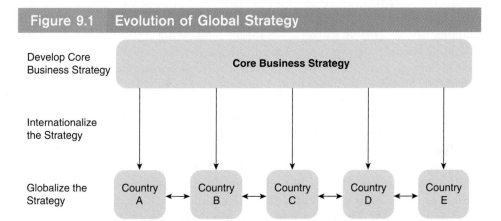

Source: George S. Yip, *Total Global Strategy II* (Upper Saddle River, NJ: Prentice Hall, 2002), 4.

segments, utilizing different strategies with little or no coordination of operations between countries.

However, as national markets become increasingly similar and scale economies become increasingly important, the inefficiencies of duplicating product and program development and manufacture in each country become more apparent and the pressure to leverage resources and coordinate activities across borders gains urgency.[5] Similarly, the number of customers operating globally, as well as the same or similar competitors faced throughout the major markets, adds to the need for strategy coordination and integration.[6]

GLOBALIZATION DRIVERS

Both external and internal factors will create the favorable conditions for development of strategy and resource allocation on a global basis. These factors can be divided into market, cost, environmental, and competitive factors.[7]

Market Factors

The world customer identified by Ernst Dichter more than 40 years ago has gained new meaning today.[8] For example, Kenichi Ohmae has identified a new group of consumers emerging in the triad of North America, Europe, and the Far East whom marketers can treat as a single market with the same spending habits.[9] Approximately a billion in number, these consumers have similar educational backgrounds, income levels, lifestyles, use of leisure time, and aspirations. One reason given for the similarities in their demand is a level of purchasing power (ten times greater than that of the developing markets or even emerging economies) that translates into higher diffusion rates for certain products. Another reason is that developed infrastructures—diffusion of telecommunication and common platforms such as Microsoft Windows and the Internet—lead to attractive markets for other goods and services. Emerging and developing markets have been able to leapfrog into the newest technologies, closing significant gaps of the past. Products can, therefore, be designed to meet similar demand conditions throughout the triad and beyond. These similarities also enhance the transferability of other marketing elements. For example, mobile subscribers in BRIC countries rank entertainment, gaming, and music sites among their top categories while European and U.S. users rank e-mail, weather and news, and sports highest. The reason for the difference is that BRIC residents often do not have the home PCs, cable TV, and iPods that Westerners do, thus using phones for entertainment purposes.[10]

At the same time, channels of distribution are becoming more global; that is, a growing number of retailers are now showing great flexibility in their strategies for entering new geographic markets.[11] Some are already world powers (e.g., Benetton and McDonald's), whereas others are pursuing aggressive growth (e.g., ALDI, Toys 'Я' Us, Subway, and IKEA). Also noteworthy are cross-border retail alliances, which expand the presence of retailers to new markets quite rapidly. Under the brand name of Best Price Modern Wholesale, Walmart and Bharti opened their first "cash-and-carry joint venture wholesale store" in Armritsar, India, in 2009—the first of at least 15 planned store openings before 2012.[12]

Technology is changing the landscape of markets as well. As Internet penetration continues to increase globally, so will e-commerce. According to the 2008 Nielsen global survey, Trends in Online Shopping, more than 85 percent of the world's online population has used the Internet to make a purchase, a 40 percent increase from 2006. The report found that more than half of Internet users make online purchases at least once a month.[13]

Cost Factors

Avoiding cost inefficiencies and duplication of effort are two of the most powerful globalization drivers. A single-country approach may not be large enough for the local business to achieve all possible economies of scale and scope as well as synergies, especially given the dramatic changes in the marketplace. Take, for example, pharmaceuticals. In the 1970s, developing a new drug cost about $16 million and took four years. The drug could be produced in Britain or the United States and eventually exported. Now, developing a drug costs from $500 million to $1 billion and takes as long as 12 years, with competitive efforts close behind. For the leading companies, annual R&D budgets can run to $5 billion. Only a global product for a global market can support that much risk.[14]

Size has become a major asset, which partly explains the many mergers and acquisitions in industries such as aerospace, pharmaceuticals, and telecommunications. The paper industry underwent major regional consolidation between 2000 and 2009, as shown in Table 9.1. International Paper Company won Champion International in a tense bidding contest with Finland's UPM-Kymmene to protect its home market position. As a result, UPM immediately targeted Sappi Ltd., a South African magazine-paper maker with significant North American operations and two U.S.-based paper makers, Mead and Bowater.[15] In the heavily contested consumer goods sectors, launching a new brand may cost as much as $100 million, meaning that companies such as Unilever and Procter & Gamble are not necessarily going to spend precious resources on one-country projects.

When GE announced it would spin off its appliance unit for up to $8 billion, five possible buyers emerged, each wanting to boost its global position: LG, a South Korean electronics and telecommunications giant; Haier, already the second largest maker of refrigerators in the world, ranked sixth in overall appliance sales; Controladora Mabe, a successful Mexico-based appliance firm that is partly owned by GE, and that already makes appliances for other brand-name firms (including GE); Electrolux AB, a Stockholm-based company that parlayed its success in high-end vacuum cleaners into a broader success in home appliances; and Arcelik Anonim Sirketi, an Istanbul, Turkey–based appliance maker that does business throughout the world—

Table 9.1 Consolidation in the Paper Industry, 2000–2009			
Acquirer	**Target**	**Value**	**Date Announced**
Sappi (South Africa)	**M-Real** (Finland)	$1.1 billion	9/29/08
Abitibi-Consol (Canada)*	**Bowater** (United States)*	$8 billion	10/29/07
Koch Industries (United States)	**Georgia-Pacific** (United States)	$13.2 billion	11/13/05
Chuetsu Pulp & Paper (Japan)	**Mitsubishi Paper** (Japan)	$2.4 billion	1/31/05
Semapa (Portugal)	**Portucel** (Portugal)	$1.9 billion	7/6/04
Weyerhaeuser (United States)	**Willamette Industries**	$6.2 billion	1/28/02
MeadWestvaco (United States)	**Mead** (United States)	$3.2 billion	8/29/01
Norske Skogindustrier (Norway)	**Fletcher Challenge Paper** (New Zealand)	$2.5 billion	4/03/00
Smurfir-Stone (United States)	**St. Laurent Paperboard** (Canada)	$1.0 billion	2/23/00
Stora Enso (Finland)	**Consolidated Papers** (United States)	$3.9 billion	2/22/00
Int'l Paper (United States)	**Champion Int'l** (United States)	$7.3 billion	5/12/00
Abitibi-Consol. (Canada)	**Donohue** (Canada)	$4.0 billion	2/11/00

*Merger of equals

Sources: "Sappi Acquires Coated Graphic Paper Business from M-Real," *PR Newswire*, September 29, 2008; Donald Granholm, "Industry Consolidation, Escalating Cost of Materials Push Paper Prices Higher," Nashua Corporation, available at www.nashua.com; "Koch Industries Agrees to Buy Georgia-Pacific," *Wall Street Journal*, November 14, 2005, A3; "Paper Merger Attains Size Without Adding Huge Debt," *Wall Street Journal*, August 30, 2001, B4; "International Paper Has Its Work Cut Out for It," *Wall Street Journal*, May 15, 2000, A4; and "Stora Enso to Buy Consolidated Papers," *Wall Street Journal*, February 23, 2000, A3, A8.

including in the United States. Even if GE does spin off the consumer unit, it does not mean that it will become a small company. While the consumer group is perhaps the most widely recognized part of its business, the unit actually accounted for just 7.4 percent of its $174 billion in sales last year.[16]

Environmental Factors

As shown earlier in this text, government barriers have fallen dramatically in the last years to further facilitate the globalization of markets and the activities of companies within them. For example, the forces pushing toward a pan-European market are very powerful: the increasing wealth and mobility of European consumers (favored by the relaxed immigration controls), the accelerating flow of information across borders, the introduction of new products where local preferences are not well established, and the publicity surrounding the integration process itself all promote globalization.[17] Also, the resulting removal of physical, fiscal, and technical barriers is indicative of the changes that are taking place around the world on a greater scale.

At the same time, rapid technological evolution is contributing to the process. With operations spread across different continents, companies regularly use teleconferencing, videoconferencing, knowledge networks, as well as travel, and are always on the lookout for innovative methods to share information and knowledge. IBM was named one of *CIO* magazine's 2009 CIO 100 award winners for its IBM Virtual Event Space, which allows more IBM employees to virtually attend company events. IBM estimates that this technology saved the company approximately $1 million, including travel, meeting, and venue costs in 2008.[18] Newly emerging markets will benefit from advanced communications by being able to leapfrog stages of economic development. Places that until recently were incommunicado in China, Vietnam, Hungary, or Brazil are rapidly acquiring state-of-the-art telecommunications that will let them foster both internal and external development.[19]

A new group of global players is taking advantage of today's more open trading regions and newer technologies. **Mininationals** or **born globals** (newer companies with sales between $200 million and $1 billion), are able to serve the world from a handful of manufacturing bases, compared with having to build a plant in every country as the established multinational corporations once had to do. Their smaller bureaucracies have also allowed these mininationals to move swiftly to seize new markets and develop new products—a key to global success.[20]

The lessons from these new-generation global players are to (1) keep focused and concentrate on being number one or two in a niche; (2) stay lean by having small headquarters to save on costs and to accelerate decision making; (3) take ideas and solutions to and from wherever they can be found; (4) take advantage of employees, regardless of nationality, to globalize thinking; and (5) solve customers' problems by involving them rather than pushing standardized solutions on them.[21] For example, Cochlear, an Australian firm specializing in implants for the profoundly deaf, exports 95 percent of its output and maintains its technological lead through strong links with hospitals and research units around the world.[22]

An example of this phenomenon in the area of social sustainability is provided in Focus on Entrepreneurship.

mininationals Newer companies with sales between $200 million and $1 billion that are able to serve the world from a handful of manufacturing bases.

born global Newly founded firm that, from its inception, is established as an international business.

Competitive Factors

Many industries are already dominated by global competitors that are trying to take advantage of the three sets of factors mentioned earlier. To remain competitive, a company may have to be the first to do something or to be able to match or preempt competitors' moves. Products are now introduced, upgraded, and distributed at

How Social Entrepreneurs Think Global

Companies that embrace the mission of social entrepreneurship utilize business practices in the solution of societal evils, such as disease, malnutrition, poverty, and illiteracy. According to Labdesk, a nonprofit organization that certifies these purpose-driven operations, there are currently more than 30,000 socially conscious companies around the globe that account for more than $40 billion in revenue. One of the pioneers in this field was the Ashoka Foundation, which since its inception in 1981, has granted living stipends to more than 2,000 fellows who are dedicated to eradicating social evils through entrepreneurship. The number of universities, institutes, and organizations that focus on socially sustainable business has grown exponentially over the past two decades, according to observers and leaders in the social venture community.

The concept of building a profitable business model in which doing good is an essential part of the business and not just a philanthropic sideline has grown in popularity, especially in light of turbulence in the global economy. Both governments and the private sector have been searching for innovative ways to bring back prosperity, and many regard these entrepreneurs as a powerful tool for change. According to Bo Fishback, vice president for entrepreneurship at the Kauffman Foundation in Kansas City, Missouri, "Many social entrepreneurs have shown they can accomplish their mission. They can deliver on the social good and report a cash flow."

Atsumasa Tochisako is an example of what a successful merging of social responsibility and business acumen can accomplish. Tochisako experienced firsthand the widespread poverty in Latin America, when he was stationed there with the Bank of Tokyo–Mitsubishi from 1979 to 1989 in a variety of positions. He realized that microlending has the potential to be both a commercially profitable business and to serve as a form of high-impact developmental assistance. He also knew that remittances from immigrants in the industrialized world provide the largest source of capital to many developing countries, often exceeding any other source of capital inflow and representing up to 20 percent of GDP. For example, Latin American immigrants send some $69 billion back to their native homes annually.

Applying his banking experience and the world-renowned financial expertise of the team he assembled, Tochisako designed a business model that links remittances with microfinance for the benefit of immigrants in the United States and their families in developing countries. In 2003, he founded Microfinance International (MFI), which markets its remittance, check cashing, microloans, and other services to people in the United States, helping them build financial knowledge and a credit history. MFI was global from its birth, with operations in the United States and El Salvador. Since then, it has expanded to more than ten Latin American countries and further extended its reach by allowing international financial institutions to use its proprietary Internet-based settlement platform. Currently, MFI operates ten microfinance service centers in the mid-Atlantic, with new branches scheduled to open in California and Texas. Tochisako, who was named an Ashoka Global Fellow in 2007, has big plans to further expand internationally and serve immigrants from many regions in the world, including Africa. Since its inception, the 80-employee operation has served about 70,000 immigrants living in the United States. Last year, the firm generated $9.7 million in sales from a variety of revenue streams.

Social enterprises are born global for three reasons. First, social problems exist on a large scale in many developing countries. Second, the resources (funds, institutions, and governance systems) are mainly in the developed world. Third, global for-profit social enterprises that tackle specific conditions can often be adapted to other similar countries and situations. For example, the Lapdesk Company with the support of corporations, international agencies, and nongovernmental organizations, is tackling classroom desk shortages. In contrast to the conventional school desk, which is expensive and unsuited to outside schooling and overcrowded classrooms, the portable Lapdesk offers a cost-effective, creative, and proven solution suitable to any type of environment where schooling is conducted. The program has been extended from its African origins to India and Latin America.

Sources: Stacy Perman, "Making a Profit and a Difference," *BusinessWeek*, April 3, 2009; Daniel J. Isenberg, "How Social Entrepreneurs Think Global," *Harvard Business Review* 86 (December 2008): 110; www.mfi-corp.com; and www.lapdesk.co.za.

rates unimaginable a decade ago. Without a global network, carefully researched ideas may be picked off by other global players. This is what Procter & Gamble and Unilever did to Kao's Attack concentrated detergent, which they mimicked and introduced into the United States and Europe before Kao could react.

With the triad markets often both flat in terms of growth and fiercely competitive, many global marketers are looking for new markets and zeroing in on the best product categories for growth. Pepsi, for example, sees strong opportunity to drive sales in emerging and developing markets where per capita consumption of their products is still relatively low. In 2008, the company announced significant investments, capacity expansion, and business building in key countries like Brazil,

India, Mexico, and China. Pepsi expanded its beverage business in 2008 by acquiring Lebedyansky, the number one juice brand in Russia, and V Water in the United Kingdom as well its snack business by acquiring Bulgaria's leading nuts and seeds producer and introducing new extensions of global brands in Russia, China, and India.[23]

Market presence may be necessary to execute global strategies and to prevent others from having undue advantage in unchallenged markets. Caterpillar faced mounting global competition from Komatsu but found out that strengthening its products and operations was not enough to meet the challenge. Although Japan was a small part of the world market, as a secure home base (no serious competitors), it generated 80 percent of Komatsu's cash flow. To put a check on its major global competitor's market share and cash flow, Caterpillar formed a heavy-equipment joint venture with Matsushita to serve the Japanese market.[24] Similarly, when Unilever tried to acquire Richardson-Vicks and Gillette in the United States, Procter & Gamble saw this as a threat to its home market position and outbid its archrival for the company.

Sara Lee received a binding offer of $1.75 billion from Unilever for its Global Body Care business. The global body care and European detergents businesses encompass a wide variety of popular brands, including *Sanex*, *Radox*, and *Duschdas*. P&G is mainly interested in the division's hair-care business, which makes Ambi Pur air fresheners. Sara Lee's units may also draw interest from companies including Godrej Consumer Products Ltd.; India's second-biggest soap maker may acquire some of Sara Lee's international businesses, including the U.S. company's stake in its Indian joint ventures.[25] With Google owning about 65 percent of the Internet search engine category, Microsoft announced a potential search and advertising partnership with Yahoo! in 2009 to create a stronger challenge to Google's dominance.[26]

The Outcome

The four globalization drivers have affected countries and sectors differently. While some industries are truly globally contested, such as paper and pulp and soft drinks, some sectors, such as government services, are still quite closed and will open up as a decades-long evolution. Commodities and manufactured goods are already in a globalized state, while many consumer goods are accelerating toward more globalization. Similarly, the leading trading nations of the world display far more openness than low-income countries, thus advancing the state of globalization in general.

The expansion of the global trade arena is summarized in Figure 9.2. Emerging countries are increasingly moving toward more globalization as they liberalize their trading environment. At the same time, low-income markets may be financially unattractive. For example, while financially unattractive in the short- to medium term, low-income markets may be attractive for learning the business climate, developing relationships, and building brands for the future. Hewlett-Packard is looking at speech interfaces for the Internet, solar applications, and cheap devices that connect with the web.[27] Danone works with Grameen in Bangladesh in their Grameen Danone Foods joint venture to produce and sell an enriched yogurt product at a price affordable to the very poor.[28] Nestlé is rolling out a variety of affordable, fortified milk products, with brands like Nido and Ideal, in developing and emerging markets that address local nutrition needs. "Nestlé has various approaches for making these milks affordable, such as sourcing milk from local farmers, manufacturing products locally, and using local distribution networks."[29]

Leading companies by their very actions drive the globalization process. There is no structural reason why soft drinks should be at a more advanced stage of globalization while beer and spirits remain more local except for the opportunistic behavior of

Figure 9.2   The Global Landscape by Industry and Market

Industry

Country	Commodities and scale-driven goods	Consumer goods and locally delivered goods and services	Government services
Triad*	Old arena Globalized in 1980s		
Emerging countries†	Growing arena Globally contestable today		
Low-income countries‡	Closed arena Still blocked or lacking significant opportunity		

Global ←——————————————————→ Local

More globalized ↑ ↓ Less globalized

* 30 OECD countries from North America, western Europe, and Asia, Japan and Australia included

† 70 countries with middle income per capita, plus China and India

‡ 100 countries of small absolute size and low income per capita

Source: Adapted and updated from Jagdish N. Sheth and Atul Parkatiyar, "The Antecedents and Consequences of Integrated Global Marketing," *International Marketing Review* 18, 1 (2001): 16–29; and Jane Fraser and Jeremy Oppenheim, "What's New About Globalization?" *McKinsey Quarterly* 2 (1997), 173.

Coca-Cola. Similarly, Nike and Reebok have driven their business in a global direction by creating global brands, a global customer segment, and a global supply chain.

THE STRATEGIC PLANNING PROCESS

Given the opportunities and challenges provided by the new realities of the marketplace, decision makers have to engage in strategic planning to match markets with products and other corporate resources more effectively and efficiently to strengthen the company's long-term competitive advantage. While the process has been summarized as a sequence of steps in Figure 9.3, many of the stages can occur in parallel. Furthermore, feedback as a result of evaluation and control may restart the process at any stage.

It has been shown that for globally committed marketers, formal strategic planning contributes to both financial performance and nonfinancial objectives.[30] These benefits include raising the efficacy of new-product launches, increasing cost-reduction efforts, and improving product quality and market-share performance. Internally, these efforts increase cohesion and improve understanding of different units' points of view. The process will have to keep three broad dimensions in mind: (1) the potential benefits for the company in the short versus the long-term, (2) the costs in terms of management time and process realignment, and (3) the presence of the necessary management resources to undertake the endeavor.[31]

UNDERSTANDING AND ADJUSTING THE CORE STRATEGY

The planning process has to start with a clear definition of the business for which strategy is to be developed. Generally, the strategic business unit (SBU) is the unit around which decisions are based. In practice, SBUs represent groupings with product-market similarities based on: (1) needs or wants to be met, (2) end-user customers to be targeted, or (3) the good or service used to meet the needs of specific customers. For a global company such as Black & Decker, the options may be to

2. To examine both the external and internal factors that determine the conditions for development of strategy and resource allocation

3. To illustrate how best to utilize the environmental conditions within the competitive challenges and resources of the firm to develop effective programs

4. To suggest how to achieve a balance between local and regional/global priorities and concerns in the implementation of strategy

Figure 9.3   Global Strategy Formulation

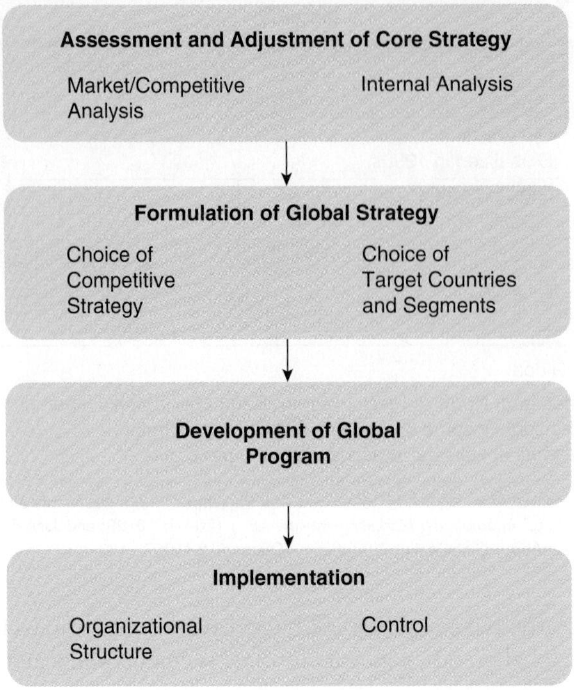

Assessment and Adjustment of Core Strategy

Market/Competitive   Internal Analysis
Analysis

Formulation of Global Strategy

Choice of   Choice of
Competitive   Target Countries
Strategy   and Segments

Development of Global Program

Implementation

Organizational   Control
Structure

The authors appreciate the contributions of Robert M. Grant in the preparation of this figure.

define the business to be analyzed as the home improvement business, the do-it-your-self business, or the power tool business. Ideally, each of these SBUs should have primary responsibility and authority in managing its basic business functions.

This phase of the planning process requires the participation of executives from different functions, especially marketing, production, finance, logistics, and procurement. Geographic representation should be from the major markets or regions as well as from the smaller, yet emerging, markets. With appropriate members, the committee can focus on product and markets as well as competitors whom they face in different markets, whether they are global, regional, or purely local. Heading this effort should be an executive with highest-level experience in regional or global markets. For example, one global firm called on the president of its European operations to come back to headquarters to head the global planning effort. This effort calls for commitment by the company itself, both in calling on the best talent to participate in the planning effort and later in implementing their proposals.

It should be noted that this assessment against environmental realities may mean a dramatic change in direction and approach. For example, the once-separate sectors of computing and mobile telephony will be colliding and the direction of future products is still uncertain. The computer industry believes in miniaturizing the general-purpose computer, while the mobile-phone industry believes in adding new features (such as photo-messaging, gaming, and location-based information) to its existing products and downloads. Facebook is the world's largest social network, while Opera Mini offers fast mobile Web browsers that do not cost anything to use on your smartphone.[32]

Market and Competitive Analysis

Planning on a country-by-country basis can result in spotty worldwide market performance. The starting point for global strategic planning is to understand the underlying forces that determine business success are common to the different countries in which the firm competes. Planning processes that focus simultaneously across a broad range of markets provide global marketers with tools to help balance risks, resource requirements, competitive economies of scale, and profitability to gain stronger long-term positions.[33] On the demand side, this requires an understanding of the common features of customer requirements and choice factors. In terms of competition, the key is to understand the structure of the global industry in order to identify the forces that will drive competition and determine profitability.[34]

Strategy begins not with individual national markets, but with understanding trends and sources of profit in the global automobile market, for example. What are the trends in world demand? What are the underlying trends in lifestyles and transportation patterns that will shape customer expectations and preferences with respect to safety, economy, design, and performance? What is the emerging structure of the industry, especially with regard to consolidation among both auto makers and their suppliers? What will determine the intensity of competition among the different auto makers? The level of excess capacity (in the worldwide auto industry, the total global capacity for light vehicles was 87 million in 2008, with actual utilization at 76 percent) is likely to be a key influence. If competition is likely to intensify, which companies will emerge the winners? An understanding of scale economies, state of technology, and the other factors that determine cost efficiency is likely to be critically important. Hybrid vehicles sold worldwide within two years, while global cumulative sales have topped more than 2 million as of 2009.[35] Governments have offered trade-in incentives for older gas-guzzlers traded for new fuel-efficient vehicles.[36]

Internal Analysis

Organizational resources have to be used as a reality check for any strategic choice in that they determine a company's capacity for establishing and sustaining competitive advantage within global markets. Industrial giants with deep pockets may be able to establish a presence in any market they wish, while more thinly capitalized companies may have to move cautiously. Human resources may also present a challenge for market expansion. A survey of multinational corporations revealed that good marketing managers, skilled technicians, and production managers were especially difficult to find. This difficulty is further compounded when the search is for people with cross-cultural experience to run future regional operations.

At this stage it is imperative that the company assess its own readiness for the moves necessary. This means a rigorous assessment of organizational commitment to global or regional expansion, as well as an assessment of the good's readiness to face the competitive environment. In many cases this has meant painful decisions to focus on certain industries and to leave others.

For example, Nokia, one of the world's largest manufacturers of cellular phones, started its rise in the industry when a decision was made at the company in 1992 to focus on digital cellular phones and to sell off dozens of other product lines (such as PCs, automotive tires, and toilet tissue). By focusing its efforts on this line, the company was able to bring new products to market quickly, build scale economies into its manufacturing, and concentrate on its customers, thereby communicating a commitment to their needs. Nokia's current 39 percent share allows it the best global visibility of and by the market.[37] Its size also allows it to deal with low-cost challengers in an aggressive manner. In China, which is the company's single largest market, Nokia faced a challenge from Ningbo Bird, which was able to provide appealing new designs for the country's young target audience. In response, Nokia developed new, far more trendy phones for the market and, in order to sell them, radically expanded its sales and distribution network.[38]

FORMULATING GLOBAL STRATEGY

The first step in the formulation of global strategy is the choice of competitive strategy to be employed, followed by the choice of country markets to be entered or to be penetrated further.

Choice of Competitive Strategy

In dealing with the global markets, the manager has three general choices of strategies, as shown in Figure 9.4 (1) cost leadership, (2) differentiation, and (3) focus.[39] A focus strategy is defined by its emphasis on a single industry segment within which the orientation may be either toward low cost or differentiation. Any one of these strategies can be pursued on a global or regional basis, or the manager may decide to mix and match strategies as a function of market or product dimensions.

In pursuing **cost leadership**, the company offers an identical product or service at a lower cost than the competition. This often means investment in scale economies and strict control of costs, such as overheads, research and development, and logistics. **Differentiation**, whether it is industrywide or focused on a single segment, takes advantage of the company's real or perceived uniqueness on elements such as design or after-sales service. It should be noted, however, that a low-price, low-cost strategy does not imply a commodity situation.[40]

Although Japanese, U.S., and European technical standards differ, mobile phone manufacturers like Motorola, Nokia, and Samsung design their phones to be as similar as possible to hold down manufacturing costs. As a result, they can all be made on the same production line, allowing the manufacturers to shift rapidly from one model to another to meet changes in demand and customer requirements. In the case of IKEA, the low-price approach is associated with clear positioning and a unique brand image focused on a clearly defined target audience of "young people of all ages." Similarly, companies that opt for high differentiation cannot forget the monitoring of costs. One common denominator of consumers around the world is their quest for value for their money. With the availability of information increasing and levels of education improving, customers are poised to demand even more of their suppliers.

Most global companies combine high differentiation with cost containment to enter markets and to expand their market shares. Flexible manufacturing systems using mostly standard components and total quality management, reducing the occurrence of defects, are allowing companies to customize an increasing amount of their production, while at the same time saving on costs. Global activities will in themselves permit the exploitation of scale economies not only in production but also in marketing activities, such as promotion.

cost leadership A pricing tactic where a company offers an identical product or service at a lower cost than the competition.

differentiation Takes advantage of the company's real or perceived uniqueness on elements such as design or after-sales service.

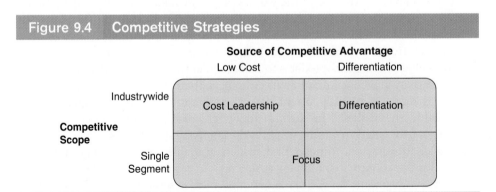

Figure 9.4   Competitive Strategies

		Source of Competitive Advantage	
		Low Cost	Differentiation
Competitive Scope	Industrywide	Cost Leadership	Differentiation
	Single Segment	Focus	

Source: Michael Porter, *Competitive Advantage* (New York: The Free Press, 1987), ch. 1.

Country-Market Choice

A global strategy does not imply that a company should serve the entire globe. Critical choices relate to the allocation of a company's resources among different countries and segments. The usual approach is first to start with regions and further split the analysis by country. Many managers use multiple levels of regional groupings to follow the organizational structure of the company—for example, splitting Europe into northern, central, and southern regions, which display similarities in demographic and behavioral traits. An important consideration is that data may be more readily available if existing structures and frameworks are used.[41]

Various **portfolio models** have been proposed as tools for this analysis. They typically involve two measures—internal strength and external attractiveness.[42] As indicators of internal strength, the following variables have been used: relative market share, product fit, contribution margin, and market presence, which would incorporate the level of support by constituents as well as resources allocated by the company itself. Country attractiveness has been measured using market size, market growth rate, number and type of competitors, governmental regulation, as well as economic and political stability. An example of such a matrix is provided in Figure 9.5.

The 3 × 3 matrix on country attractiveness and company strength is applied to the European markets. Markets in the invest/grow position will require continued commitment by management in research and development, investment in facilities, and the training of personnel at the country level. In cases of relative weakness in growing markets, the company's position may have to be strengthened (through acquisitions or strategic alliances) or a decision to divest may be necessary. For example, General Mills signed a complementary marketing arrangement with Nestlé to enter the European market dominated by its main global rival, Kellogg's. This arrangement allowed General Mills effective market entry and Nestlé more efficient utilization of its distribution channels in Europe, as well as entry to a new product market. The alliance has since resulted in the formation of Cereal Partners

portfolio models Tools that have been proposed for use in market and competitive analysis. They typically involve two measures—internal strength and external attractiveness.

Figure 9.5   Example of a Market-Portfolio Matrix

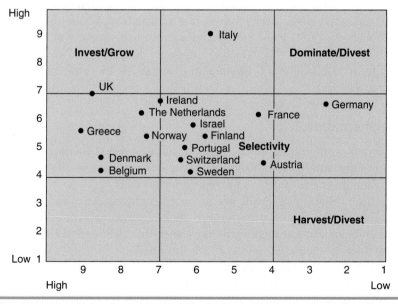

Source: Adapted from Gilbert D. Harrell and Richard O. Kiefer, "Multinational Market Portfolios in Global Strategy Development," *International Marketing Review* 10 (1993): 60–72.

Worldwide, which has a combined worldwide market share of 21 percent and sells its products in more than 130 countries.[43]

In choosing country markets, a company must make decisions beyond those relating to market attractiveness and company position. A market expansion policy will determine the allocation of resources among various markets. The basic alternatives are concentration on a small number of markets and diversification, which is characterized by growth in a relatively large number of markets. With high and stable growth rates only in certain markets, the firm will likely opt for a concentration strategy, which is often the case for innovative products early in their life cycle. If demand is strong worldwide, as the case may be for consumer goods, diversification may be attractive. If markets respond to marketing efforts at increasing rates, concentration will occur; however, when the cost of market share points in any one market becomes too high, marketers tend to begin looking for diversification opportunities.

The uniqueness of the product offering with respect to competition is also a factor in expansion strategy. If lead time over competition is considerable, the decision to diversify may not seem urgent. Very few products, however, afford such a luxury. In many product categories, marketers will be affected by spillover effects. Consider, for example, the impact of satellite channels on advertising in Europe or in Asia, where ads for a product now reach most of the market. The greater the degree to which marketing mix elements can be standardized, the more diversification is probable. Overall savings through economies of scale can then be utilized in marketing efforts. Finally, the objectives and policies of the company itself will guide the decision making on expansion. If extensive interaction is called for with intermediaries and clients, efforts are most likely to be concentrated because of resource constraints.

The conventional wisdom of globalization requires a presence in all of the major triad markets of the world. In some cases, markets may not be attractive in their own right but may have some other significance, such as being the home market of the most demanding customers, thereby aiding in product development, or being the home market of a significant competitor (a preemptive rationale). European PC makers, such as Germany's Maxdata and Britain's Tiny, are taking aim at the U.S. market based on the premise that if they can compete with the big multinationals (Dell, Hewlett-Packard, and Acer) at home, there is no reason why they cannot be competitive in North America.[44]

Therefore, for global companies, three factors should determine country selection: (1) the stand-alone attractiveness of a market (e.g., China in consumer products due to its size), (2) global strategic importance (e.g., Finland in shipbuilding due to its lead in technological development in vessel design), and (3) possible synergies (e.g., entry into Latvia and Lithuania after success in the Estonian market, given market similarities).

Segmentation

Effective use of segmentation—that is, the recognition that groups within markets differ sufficiently to warrant individual approaches—allows global companies to take advantage of the benefits of standardization (such as economies of scale and consistency in positioning) while addressing the unique needs and expectations of a specific target group. This approach means looking at markets on a global or regional basis, thereby ignoring the political boundaries that define markets in many cases. The identification and cultivation of such intermarket segments is necessary for any standardization of programs to work.[45]

The emergence of segments that span across markets is already evident in the world marketplace. Global companies have successfully targeted the teenage segment, which is converging as a result of common tastes in sports and music fueled by their computer literacy, travels abroad, and, in many countries, financial independence.[46] Furthermore, a media revolution is creating a common fabric of attitudes and tastes among teenagers. Today, satellite TV and global network concepts such as MTV are both helping create this segment and providing global companies an access to the teen audience around the world. Similarly, two other distinct segments have been detected to be ready for a panregional approach, especially in Europe. One includes trendsetters who are wealthier and better educated and tend to value independence, refuse consumer stereotypes, and appreciate exclusive products. The second one includes Europe's businesspeople who are well-to-do, regularly travel abroad, and have a taste for luxury goods.

Despite convergence, global marketers still have to make adjustments in some of the marketing mix elements for maximum impact. For example, while Levi's jeans are globally accepted by the teenage segment, European teens reacted negatively to the urban realism of Levi's U.S. ads. Levi's converted its ads in Europe, drawing on images of a mythical America.[47] Similarly, segment sizes vary from one market to another even in cohesive regions such as Europe. The value-oriented segment in Germany accounts for 32 percent of grocery sales but only 9 percent in the United Kingdom and 8 percent in France.

The greatest challenge for the global company is the choice of an appropriate base for the segmentation effort. The objective is to arrive at a grouping or groupings that are substantial enough to merit the segmentation effort (e.g., there are nearly 560 million teenagers in the Americas, Europe, and the Asia-Pacific region, with the teenagers spending nearly $100 billion of their own money yearly) and are reachable as well by the marketing effort (e.g., the majority of MTV's audience consists of teenagers).

The possible bases for segmentation are summarized in Figure 9.6. Managers have traditionally used environmental bases for segmentation. However, using geographic proximity, political system characteristics, economic standing, or cultural

---

Figure 9.6   Bases for Global Market Segmentation

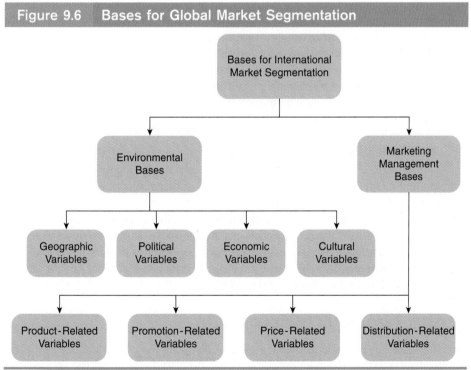

Source: Imad B. Baalbaki and Naresh K. Malhotra, "Marketing Management Bases for International Market Segmentation: An Alternate Look at the Standardization/Customization Debate," *International Marketing Review* 10, 1 (1993): 19–44.

traits as stand-alone bases may not provide relevant data for decision making. Using a combination of them, however, may produce more meaningful results. One of the segments pursued by global companies around the world is the middle-class family. Defining the composition of this global middle class is tricky, given the varying levels of development among nations in Latin America and Asia. However, some experts estimate that 23 percent of the world population enjoy middle-class lives—some 300 million in India alone.[48] Using household income alone may be quite a poor gauge of class. Income figures ignore vast differences in international purchasing power. Chinese consumers, for example, spend less than 5 percent of their total outlays on rent, transportation, and health, while a typical U.S. household spends 45 to 50 percent. Additionally, income distinctions do not reflect education or values—two increasingly important barometers of middle-class status. A global segmentation effort using cultural values is presented in Focus on Economy.

It has also been proposed that markets that reflect a high degree of homogeneity with respect to marketing mix variables could be grouped into segments and thereby targeted with a largely standardized strategy.[49] Whether bases related to product, promotion, pricing, or distribution are used, their influence should be related to environmentally based variables. Product-related bases include the degree to which products are culture-based, which stage of the life cycle they occupy, consumption patterns, attitudes toward product attributes (such as country of origin), as well as consumption infrastructure (for example, telephone lines for modems). The growth of microwave sales, for example, has been surprising in low-income countries; however, microwaves have become status symbols and buying them more of an emotional issue. Many consumers in these markets also want to make sure they get the same product as available in developed markets, thereby eliminating the need in many cases to develop market-specific products. Adjustments will have to be made, however. Noticing that for reasons of status and space, many Asian consumers put their refrigerators in their living rooms, Whirlpool makes refrigerators available in striking colors such as red and blue.

With promotional variables, the consumers' values and norms may necessitate local solutions rather than opting for a regional approach. Similar influences may be exerted by the availability, or lack, of media vehicles or government regulations affecting promotional campaigns. On the pricing side, dimensions such as customers' price sensitivity may lead the manager to go after segments that insist on high quality despite high price in markets where overall purchasing power may be low to ensure global or regional uniformity in the marketing approach.

Affordability is a major issue for customers, whose buying power may fall short for at least the time being. Offering only one option may exclude potential customers of the future who are not yet part of a targeted segment. Companies like Procter & Gamble and Unilever offer an array of products at different price points to attract customers and to keep them as they move up the income scale.[50] As distribution systems converge, for example, with the increase of global chains, markets can also be segmented by outlet types that reach environmentally defined groups. For example, toy manufacturers may look at markets not only in terms of numbers of children but by how effectively and efficiently they can be reached by global chains such as Toys 'Я' Us, as opposed to purely local outlets.

GLOBAL PROGRAM DEVELOPMENT

Decisions need to be made regarding how best to utilize the conditions set by globalization drivers within the framework of competitive challenges and the resources of the firm. Decisions will have to be made in four areas: (1) the degree of standardization in the product offering, (2) the marketing program beyond the product variable,

FOCUS ON ECONOMY

Global Extremes

All signs point to the global economic crisis coming to an end. Banks are returning to profitability, government stimulus programs are in effect, and the IMF has revised a more positive forecast for growth and recovery for the next year. And, in many countries, people are feeling more positive about the state of their financial affairs and the economy in general. But according to a new report, some consumers may find it hard to shake recessionary habits. The severity of the recession has brought about a change in consumer values, spending habits, and lifestyle choices in some parts of the world, and the indication is that some consumers in the West will continue to refrain from excessive or unnecessary spending across all aspects, at least in the short term.

Based on GfK Roper Consulting's 2009 GfK Roper Mood of the World® Study, the Index was created by averaging, weighting, and combining the following three measures to calculate an overall score in terms of how consumers are feeling:

- **Distress.** Consumers indicate which positive and negative financial-related events they have experienced from a list of eight. Globally, 62 percent say they faced a negative event (e.g., losing their job or having difficulty paying their bills) in the past 12 months; the United States clocked in higher at 77 percent with Canada not far behind at 72 percent. Americans are also among the most distressed, following only Turkey.
- **Reaction.** Participants report where they have cut back from a list of 26 items and activities as well as which of 10 money-saving strategies they have employed. Consumers in English-speaking nations such as the United States, Australia, Canada, and the United Kingdom are the most likely to be doing things to cut back and save money.
- **Concern.** Respondents list their top-three worries from a selection of 21 economic, social, and political issues. "Recession" ranked as the top concern globally. Regarding the highest levels of economic concern, Asian consumers topped the list, while the United States landed in 15th place, just behind its northern neighbor, Canada (14th).

Major global markets surveyed as part of the Nielsen Global Consumer Confidence Index 2009 indicate that consumers around the world might be expected to return to their previous spending patterns. Indonesia and India have the highest consumer confidence scores while, the lowest scores are in Korea and Japan.

- One in six Russians said that they would not retain any of their recessionary habits once the economy improves, and they are particularly eager to spend their money on clothing.
- Chinese remain the most confident of an economic rebound in the near future, and sales of consumer goods products remained robust last year—up 21 percent.
- Technology such as home computers and mobile phones look to be early winners: consumers in Japan, Korea, and the Philippines are looking forward to upgrading their current gear.

GLOBAL CONSUMER RECESSION INDEX

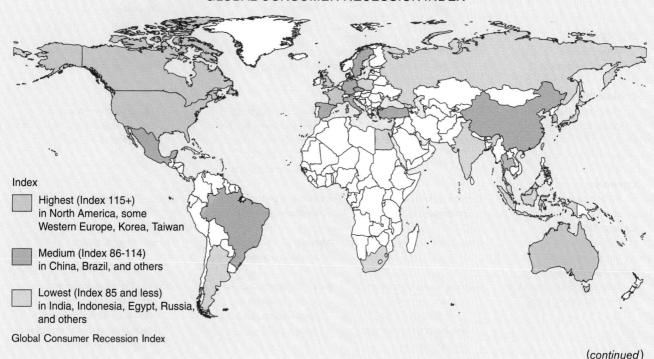

Index

Highest (Index 115+) in North America, some Western Europe, Korea, Taiwan

Medium (Index 86-114) in China, Brazil, and others

Lowest (Index 85 and less) in India, Indonesia, Egypt, Russia, and others

Global Consumer Recession Index

(continued)

(continued)

- More than 40 percent of Americans say they expect to increase their spending on travel and holidays, dining out, and out-of-home entertainment in the coming months.
- One in six global consumers will continue to cut back on take-away meals, with 22 percent of Australians indicating that this is one area in which they will continue to reduce spending. Significant numbers of New Zealanders, Japanese, Irish, South Africans, Brazilians, and Americans also indicated that they would stay away from take-away.
- One in six global consumers says that they will continue purchasing cheaper grocery products, spend less on new clothes, and cut down on out-of-home entertainment.

As economic recovery gathers pace, consumption and spending will increase, but the post-recession consumer is likely to consume very differently. She or he will think twice—and maybe thrice—about making purchases big or small. It's now fashionable in the West to be frugal and trendy to be thrifty. But marketers that are able to convey the value of their products and services will likely continue to grow and prosper. This time, however, emerging Asia is providing unexpected locomotion, with the result that recovery in Europe now appears to be leading the latent one in the United States.

Sources: "The Global Consumer in a Post-Recession World," *NielsenWire*, October 9, 2009; "Investment Management," *ING*, August 17, 2009; and "GfK Roper Consulting Introduces Global Consumer Recession Index; Reveals Most and Least Affected Countries," GfK Research, North America, June 1, 2009.

(3) location and extent of value-adding activities, and (4) competitive moves to be made.

This development effort has to combine three elements: (1) adaptation, by maximizing the marketer's local relevance; (2) aggregation, by leveraging cross-border resources; and (3) arbitrage, by exploiting differences between local and regional markets by placing marketing activities where they are most efficiently executed and by making competitive moves where they deliver the maximum impact.[51] See Table 9.2 below.

Table 9.2   Adaptation, Aggregation, and Arbitrage

	ADAPTATION	AGGREGATION	ARBITRAGE
Competitive Advantage Why should we globalize at all?	To achieve scale and scope economies through international standardization	To achieve scale and scope economies through international standardization	To achieve absolute economies through international specialization
Configuration Where should we locate operations overseas?	Mainly in foreign countries that are similar to the home base, to limit the effects of cultural, administrative, geographic, and economic distance		In a more diverse set of countries, to exploit some elements of distance
Coordination How should we connect international operations?	By country, with emphasis on achieving local presence within borders	By business, region, or customer, with emphasis on horizontal relationships for cross-border economies of scale	By function, with emphasis on vertical relationships, even across organizational boundaries
Controls What types of extremes should we watch for?	Excessive variety or complexity	Excessive standardization, with emphasis on scale	Narrowing spreads
Change Blockers Whom should we watch out for internally?	Entrenched country chiefs	All-powerful unit, regional, or account heads	Heads of key functions
Corporate Diplomacy How should we approach corporate diplomacy?	Address issues of concern, but proceed with discretion, given the emphasis on cultivating local presence	Avoid the appearance of homogenization or hegemonism; be sensitive to any backlash	Address the exploitation or displacement of suppliers, channels, or intermediaries, which are potentially most prone to political disruption

Source: Adapted from Pankaj Ghamawat, "Managing Differences: The Central Challenge of Global Strategy," *Harvard Business Review*, March 2007: 58–69.

Product Offering

Globalization is not equal to standardization except in the case of the core product or the technology used to produce the product. The need to localize varies by product. Fashion or fashion products depend on their appeal on sameness. Information technology products are susceptible to power requirements, keyboard configurations (e.g., Europe alone may require 20 different keyboards), instruction-manual language, and warning labels compliant with local regulations.[52] Product standardization may result in significant cost savings upstream. For example, Stanley Works' compromise between French preferences for handsaws with plastic handles and "soft teeth" and British preferences for wooden handles and "hard teeth"—to produce a plastic-handled saw with "hard teeth"—allowed consolidation for production and resulted in substantial economies of scale. Most automakers have reduced the number of platforms they offer worldwide to achieve greater economies of scale. For example, Jaguar Land Rover has reduced the number of its platforms from 6 to 2. This is not to reduce variety but to deliver it more cost effectively.[53] Shania Twain's double CD *Up!* is an example of catering to multiple segments at the same time: both discs contain the same 19 tracks, but one with the effects pop fans appreciate, the other with country dimensions. A third disc with "an Asian Indian vibe" replaces the country disc in Europe.[54]

Marketing Approach

Nowhere is the need for the local touch as critical as in the execution of the marketing program. Uniformity is sought especially in elements that are strategic (e.g., positioning) in nature, whereas care is taken to localize necessary tactical elements (e.g., distribution). This approach has been called **glocalization**. For example, Unilever achieved great success with a fabric softener that used a common positioning, advertising theme, and symbol (a teddy bear) but differing brand names (e.g., Snuggle, Cajoline, Kuschelweich, Mimosin, and Yumos) and bottle sizes. P&G scored a huge success with its Fusion and MACH3 shavers when they were rolled out in the United States, Europe, and Asia with a common approach based on the premise that men everywhere want the same thing in a shave. The TV commercials for the Gillette Champions, offering the theme "the best a man can get," languages varied (with Michael Clarke representing Australia; Derek Jeter, United States; Kaka, Brazil; Park Ji-sung, Korea; and Yasser Saeed Al-Qahtani, Saudi Arabia), but most of the footage was the same. United Technologies' corporate advertising campaign known as "Cross Section" is designed to run in targeted financial, business and thought leader publications. Later, UTC modified these ads with regionally appropriate and culturally relevant details. The campaign defines how energy-efficient products meet the fast growing needs of a rapidly urbanizing and increasingly environmentally-aware China (Figure 9.7).

glocalization A term coined to describe the networked global organization approach to an organizational structure.

Location of Value-Added Activities

Globalization strives at cost reductions by pooling production or other activities or exploiting factor costs or capabilities within a system. Rather than duplicating activities in multiple, or even all, country organizations, a firm concentrates its activities. Nokia's more than 39,350 research & development people work in centers in 16 different countries, including China, Finland, Germany, and Hungary. The company has also entered into development agreements with operators (such as France Telecom and Vodafone) to bring innovations to market more efficiently.[55] Many global companies have established R&D centers next to key production facilities so that concurrent engineering can take place every day on the factory floor.

Figure 9.7   Corporate Advertising Campaign

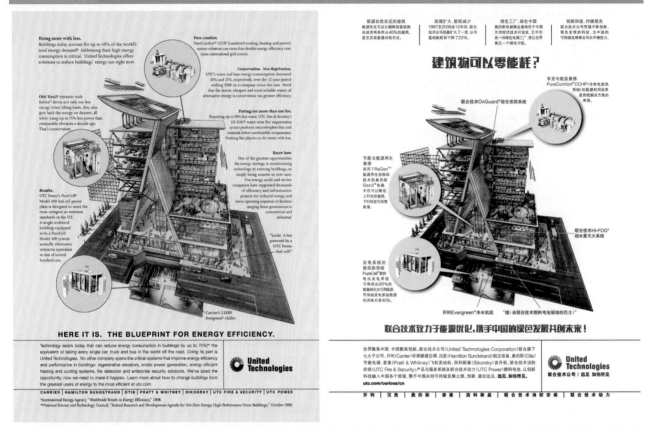

Source: http://www.utc.com

To enhance the global exchange of ideas, the centers have joint projects and are in real-time contact with each other.

The quest for cost savings and improved transportation methods has allowed some companies to concentrate customer service activities rather than having them present in all country markets. For example, Sony used to have repair centers in all of the Scandinavian countries and Finland; today, all service and maintenance activities are actually performed in a regional center in Stockholm, Sweden. Similarly, MasterCard has teamed up with Mascon Global in Chennai, India, where Master-Card's core processing functions—authorization, clearing, and settlement—for worldwide operations are handled.[56]

To show commitment to a given market, both economically and politically, centers may be established in these markets. Philips Electronics has chosen China as their Asian center for global product research and development.[57]

Competitive Moves

A company with regional or global presence will not have to respond to competitive moves only in the market where it is being attacked. A competitor may be attacked in its profit sanctuary to drain its resources, or its position in its home market may be challenged.[58] When Fuji began cutting into Kodak's market share in the United States, Kodak responded by drastically increasing its penetration in Japan and created a new subsidiary to deal strictly with that market. In addition, Kodak solicited the support of the U.S. government to gain more access to Japanese distribution systems that Kodak felt were unfairly blocked from them.

cross-subsidization The use of resources accumulated in one part of the world to fight a competitive battle in another.

Cross-subsidization, or the use of resources accumulated in one part of the world to fight a competitive battle in another, may be the competitive advantage needed for the long term.[59] One major market lost may mean losses in others, resulting in a domino effect. Jockeying for overall global leadership may result in competitive action in any part of the world. This has manifested itself in the form of "wars" between major global players in industries such as soft drinks, automotive tires, computers, and mobile devices. The new markets often signal a new battle, as happened in the 1990s in Russia, in Mexico after the signing of the North American Free Trade Agreement, and in Vietnam after the normalization of relations with the United States. Imbedded in this planning has to be the selection of the types of power the company wants to exercise in the global marketplace. In business, *hard power* refers to the use of scale, financial might, or the use of low-cost position to win market access and share. Increasingly, marketers will also have to incorporate **soft power** into their tool kits. Soft power refers to the capability of attracting and influencing all stakeholders, whether through energetic brands, heroic missions, distinctive talent development, or an inspirational corporate culture.[60] In light of business and reputation risks that may arise from doing business with countries designated as State Sponsors of Terrorism by the U.S. Department of State (Cuba, Iran, North Korea, Sudan, and Syria), companies will not accept business in any of these countries, except activity that is authorized by the U.S. government for humanitarian or public policy purposes.

Given their multiple bases of operation, global companies may defend against a competitive attack in one country by countering in another country or, if the competitors operate in multiple businesses, countering in a different product category altogether. In the mobile devices category, the winners in the future will be those who can better attack less-mature markets with cheaper phones, while providing Internet-based devices elsewhere. In a study of how automakers develop strategies that balance the conflicting pressures of local responsiveness and regional integration in Europe and the United States, Japanese marketers were found to practice standardization in model offerings but selectively respond to differences in market conditions by manipulating prices and advertising levels.[61]

soft power The ability to obtain what one wants through co-option and attraction.

IMPLEMENTING GLOBAL PROGRAMS

The successful global companies of the future will be those that can achieve a balance between the local and the regional/global concerns. Companies that have tried the global concept have often run into problems with local differences. Especially early on, global programs were seen as standardized efforts dictated to the country organizations by headquarters. For example, when Coca-Cola reentered the Indian market, it invested most heavily in its Coke brand, using its typical global positioning, and had its market leadership slip to Pepsi. Recognizing the mistake, Coke reemphasized a popular local cola brand (Thums Up) and refocused the Coke brand advertising to be more relevant to the local Indian consumer.[62] In the past ten years, Coca-Cola has been acquiring local soft-drink brands such as Inca Cola in Peru and making it available in Peru, Chile, Ecuador, and the United States.[63]

Challenges

Pitfalls that handicap global programs and contribute to their suboptimal performance include market-related reasons, such as insufficient research and a tendency to overstandardize, as well as internal reasons, such as inflexibility in planning and implementation.

If a product is to be launched on a broader scale without formal research as to regional or local differences, the result may be failure. An example of this is Lego A/S, the Danish toy manufacturer, which decided to transfer sales promotional tactics successful in the U.S. market unaltered to other markets, such as Japan. This promotion included approaches such as "bonus packs" and gift promotions. However,

Japanese consumers considered these promotions wasteful, expensive, and not very appealing.[64] Going too local has its drawbacks as well. With too much customization or with local production, the marketer may lose its import positioning.

Globalization by design requires a balance between sensitivity to local needs and deployment of technologies and concepts globally. This means that neither headquarters nor independent country managers can alone call the shots. If country organizations are not part of the planning process, or if adoption is forced on them by headquarters, local resistance in the form of the **not-invented-here (NIH) syndrome** may lead to the demise of the global program or, worse still, to an overall decline in morale. Subsidiary resistance may stem from resistance to any idea originating from the outside or from valid concerns about the applicability of a concept to that particular market. Without local commitment, no global program will survive.

not-invented-here (NIH) syndrome A defensive, territorial attitude that, if held by managers, can frustrate effective implementation of global strategies.

LOCALIZING GLOBAL MOVES

The successful global companies of the twenty-first century will be those that can achieve a balance between country managers and global product managers at headquarters. This balance may be achieved by a series of actions to improve a company's ability to develop and implement global strategy. These actions relate to management processes, organization structures, and overall corporate culture, all of which should ensure cross-fertilization within the firm.

Management Processes

In the multidomestic approach, country organizations had very little need to exchange ideas. Globalization, however, requires transfer of information not only between headquarters and country organizations but also between the country organizations themselves. By facilitating the flow of information, ideas are exchanged and organizational values strengthened. Information exchange can be achieved through periodic meetings of marketing managers or through worldwide conferences to allow employees to discuss their issues and local approaches to solving them. The IBM Institute for Business Value is comprised of more than 50 consultants who conduct research and analysis across multiple industries and functional disciplines. The institute has a worldwide presence, drawing on consultants in 11 countries to identify issues of global interest and to develop practical recommendations with local relevance.[65] IBM has found that some country organizations find it easier to accept input of other country organizations than that coming directly from headquarters.

Part of the preparation for becoming global has to be personnel interchange. Many companies encourage (or even require) mid-level managers to gain experience abroad during the early or middle stages of their careers. The more experience people have in working with others from different nationalities—getting to know other markets and surroundings—the better a company's global philosophy, strategy, and actions will be integrated locally.

The role of headquarters staff should be that of coordination and leveraging the resources of the corporation. For example, this may mean activities focused on combining good ideas that come from different parts of the company to be fed into global planning. Many global companies also employ world-class staffs whose role should be to consult subsidiaries by upgrading their technical skills and focusing their attention not only on local issues but also on those with global impact.

Globalization calls for the centralization of decision-making authority far beyond that of the multidomestic approach. Once a strategy has been jointly developed, headquarters may want to permit local managers to develop their own programs within specified parameters and subject to approval rather than forcing them to adhere strictly to the formulated strategy. For example, Colgate Palmolive allows local units to use their own approaches, but only if they can prove they can beat the global "benchmark" version. With a properly managed approval process, effective control can be exerted without unduly dampening a country manager's creativity.

Overall, the best approach against the emergence of the NIH syndrome is utilizing various motivational policies such as (1) ensuring that local managers participate in the development of strategies and programs, (2) encouraging local managers to generate ideas for possible regional or global use, (3) maintaining a product portfolio that includes local as well as regional and global brands, and (4) allowing local managers control over their budgets so that they can respond to local customer needs and counter global competition (rather than depleting budgets by forcing them to participate only in uniform campaigns). Acknowledging this local potential, global companies can pick up successful brands in one country and make them cross-border stars. Since Nestlé acquired British candy maker Rowntree Mackintosh, it has increased its exports by 60 percent and made formerly local brands, such as After Eight Dinner mints, pan-European hits. When an innovation or a product is deemed to have global potential, rolling it out in other regions or worldwide becomes an important consideration.

Organization Structures

Various organization structures have emerged to support the globalization effort. Some companies have established global or regional product managers and their support groups at headquarters. Their task is to develop long-term strategies for product categories on a worldwide basis and to act as the support system for the country organizations. This matrix structure focused on customers, which has replaced the traditional country-by-country approach, is considered more effective in today's global marketplace according to companies that have adopted it.

Whenever a product group has global potential, firms such as Procter & Gamble, 3M, and Henkel create strategic-planning units to work on the programs. These units consist of members from the country organizations that market the products, managers from both global and regional headquarters, as well as technical specialists. Within P&G, the technology entrepreneurs work out of six connect-and-develop hubs, in China, India, Japan, western Europe, Latin America, and the United States. Each hub focuses on finding products and technologies that, in a sense, are specialties of its region: the China hub, for example, looks in particular for new high-quality materials and cost innovations (products that exploit China's unique ability to make things at low cost). The India hub seeks out local talent in the sciences to solve problems in manufacturing processes, for instance, using tools like computer modeling.[66]

To deal with the globalization of customers, companies such as Hewlett-Packard and Unilever are extending national account management programs across countries, typically for the most important customers.[67] In a study of 165 multinational companies, 13 percent of their revenue came from global customers (revenue from all international customers was 46 percent). While relatively small, these 13 percent come from the most important customers, who cannot be ignored.[68] AT&T, for example, distinguishes between international and global customers and provides the global customers with special services including a single point of contact for domestic and international operations and consistent worldwide service. Honeywell provides global account services to multinational customers who want to centrally specify the types of process control equipment installed in their facilities worldwide in order to ensure common quality standards and to minimize variations in operating and training procedures.

Executing **global account management** programs not only builds relationships with important customers but also allows for the development of internal systems and interaction. It will require, however, a new organizational overlay and demands new ways of working for anyone involved in marketing to international customers. One of

global account management Global customers of a company may be provided with a single point of contact for domestic and international operations and consistent worldwide service.

FOCUS ON CULTURE

Staffing Creatively

Companies are sending more people abroad than ever before, but they are trying to keep down the costs of doing so. The traditional business-class expatriate, usually male and Western, is steadily being replaced by an economy version who may well come from any country in the organization. Companies are trying hard to reduce their reliance on the traditional sort of expatriates, not only because firms want to avoid the expense of sending people abroad, but because companies are also increasingly aware that having locals in top jobs can be a boon in foreign markets.

Many expatriates are charged with finding their replacements as quickly as they can. Promising local candidates are often sent to the head office to learn the ropes before returning with the prospect of taking over an expatriate's job. Increasingly, employees from developing countries are being sent to developed ones rather than the other way around. Well-educated Indians, Chinese, Brazilians, or Mexicans, often with degrees from foreign universities, are perfect candidates for many European or American firms that want them to gain experience in the head office before they take on greater responsibility in their home markets.

Tetra-Pak is a case in point. It used to send an army of expatriates, once all Swedes, to open and manage its factories around the world. Now it is encouraging more local executives to step up into important roles. One way it is doing this is by building up talent and experience in local clusters. This involves frequent transfers of employees within certain regions, such as Latin America and Southeast Asia. The best performers are groomed to make bigger geographic moves.

Given the importance of families in making expatriate decisions, some employers are offering new types of foreign postings. More people are being sent on short-term "commuter" assignments, where they do not need to uproot their families. The commuting trend is particularly common in Europe: a banker from Vienna, for instance, may spend Monday to Friday working in Dresden and then fly home for the weekend. In some cases, where the locations are not that far from each other, a daily commute may be feasible.

Sources: David G. Collings, Hugh Scullion, and Michael J. Morley, "Changing Patterns of Global Staffing in the Multinational Enterprise: Challenges to the Conventional Expatriate Assignment and Emerging Alternatives," *Journal of World Business* 42, no. 2 (2007): 198–214; "Travelling More Lightly–Staffing Globalization," *Economist*, June 24, 2006, 99–101.

the main challenges is in evaluating and rewarding for sales efforts. If Nokia sells equipment to Telefónica in Brazil, should the sale be credited to the sales manager in Brazil or to the global account manager for Telefónica? The answer in most cases is to double-count the credit.[69]

Technology has allowed companies to take unique advantage of strengths that are present in different parts of the world. A powerful new business model for organizations may be emerging, as shown in Focus on Culture.

Corporate Culture

Corporate culture affects and is affected by two dimensions: the overall way in which the company holds its operations together and makes them a single entity as well as the commitment to the global marketplace. For example, Panasonic (formerly Matshushita) has a corporate vision of being a "possibility-searching company" with four specific objectives: (1) business that creates new lifestyles based on creativity and convenience; (2) technology based on artificial intelligence, fuzzy logic, and networking technology; (3) a culture based on heterogeneity and diversity; and (4) a structure to enable both localization and global synergy. Overall, this would mean a company in which individuals with rich and diversified knowledge share similar ideals and values.[70]

An example of a manifestation of the global commitment is a global identity that favors no specific country (especially the "home country" of the company). The management features several nationalities, and whenever teams are assembled, people from various country organizations get represented. The management development system has to be transparent, allowing nonnational executives an equal chance for the fast track to top management.[71]

Whirlpool's corporate profile states the following: "Beyond selling products around the world, being a global home-appliance company means identifying and respecting genuine national and regional differences in customer expectations, but also recognizing and responding to similarities in product development, engineering, purchasing, manufacturing, marketing and sales, distribution, and other areas. Companies which exploit the efficiencies from these similarities will outperform others in terms of market share, cost, quality, productivity, innovation, and return to shareholders."[72] In truly global companies, very little decision making occurs that does not support the goal of treating the world as a single market. Planning for and execution of programs takes place on a worldwide basis.

The pressure to be global and, at the same time, local has to be addressed in developing talent. Leading companies systematically identify global talent sources, including making the company's name known in the labor market. Second, they develop global training programs and manage careers carefully over many years, including expatriate assignments. Finally, the companies have to implement appropriate compensation and mobility policies to ensure that the best talent is always available, regardless of the destination of the task.[73]

For marketers from emerging markets, finding a balance of cultures may be a daunting task for global integration. Many Chinese managers have limited fluency in English, which is increasingly the language of global business. Second, Chinese cultural traits, such as avoiding direct confrontation, few boundaries between work and personal life, as well as emphasis on seniority and relationships have to be approached through tactics such as regular meetings and training programs.[74]

THE LOCAL COMPANY IN THE GLOBAL ENVIRONMENT[75]

The global marketplace presents significant challenges—but also opportunities—for local firms. As global marketers such as Boeing, Honda, McDonald's, and Volkswagen expand their presence, there are local companies that must defend their positions or lose out. They can no longer rely on the government to protect or support them. If selling out or becoming a part of a bigger global entity is not an acceptable option, the local marketer will have to build on an existing competitive advantage or adopt a creative growth strategy globally. To counter the significant resources of global marketers (such as powerful brands and sizable promotional budgets), the local company can compete successfully in the local market by emphasizing the perceived advantages of its product and marketing.[76] More proactively, the local company can pursue its own globalization strategy through segments that have similar features to the local marketer's home market or segments that global marketers have not catered to.

Strategies available to the local company depend on both external and internal realities. The degree and strength of globalization in an industry will determine the pressure that the local marketer will be under. Internally, the extent to which the company's assets are transferable (as opposed to having only local relevance) will determine the opportunity dimension. Figure 9.8 provides a summary of the options to be considered.

In markets where a local company has enjoyed government protection, the liberalization of markets as a result of economic integration or WTO membership may mean hardship for the local company. A **dodger** may have to rethink its entire strategy. With the collapse of communism and the introduction of free-market reforms, the Czech carmaker Škoda found its models to be outdated and with little appeal in comparison to Western makes that became available for consumers. The company became part of the largest privatization deal in eastern Europe in its sale to Volkswagen in 1991. Rather than being merged with VW's operations, Škoda has followed VW's formula for success: performance-oriented management, cooperative labor relations, utilitarian marketing, and an emphasis on design. It has benefited from wholesale implementation of the latest technologies and working practices and has been able to leapfrog into leaner and more intelligent supply and distribution networks. With sales in 85 countries, Škoda is a leading emerging global brand in one of the most competitive industries.[77] Robust

dodger A local company that sells out to a global player or becomes part of an alliance.

| Figure 9.8 | Competitive Strategies for Local Companies |

Competitive Assets

		Customized to home market	Transferable abroad
Pressures to Globalize in the Industry	High	**Dodger** Sells out to a global player or becomes part of an alliance	**Contender** Upgrades capabilities to match globals in niches
	Low	**Defender** Leverages local assets in segments where globals are weak	**Extender** Expands into markets similar to home base

Source: Adapted from Niraj Dawar and Tony Frost, "Competing with the Giants: Survival Strategies for Local Companies in Emerging Markets," *Harvard Business Review* 77 (March–April 1999): 119–129.

Group used to be a leading brand of healthy food and drink in China. In early 2000, facing the fierce competition from other Chinese manufacturers and declining profit, the company was sold to Danone, the French food and drink giant.

defender A local company that has assets that give it a competitive advantage only in its home market.

A **defender** is a local company that has assets that give it a competitive advantage only in its home market. Ideally, this asset is something that an entering global marketer cannot easily replicate, for example, channel penetration or a product line that has a strong local-customer franchise. Many believed that small local retailers in Latin America would be swept away with the sector's consolidation and the entry of global players such as Carrefour. This has been the case in developed markets, where small retailers have retained only 10 to 20 percent of the consumer-packaged-goods market as large retailers have expanded. In Latin America, their share has remained at 45 to 61 percent because they are not only meeting the needs of emerging consumers, but, in many ways, are serving them better. For emerging-market consumers, price is not the determining factor of retailer choice; it is the total cost of purchases (including cost of transportation, time, the burden of carrying purchases, and ability to store purchased items).[78] Similarly, U.S. chocolate companies Mars and Hershey's have established only a marginal presence in Latin America with their larger chocolate bars; Arcor and Nacional de Chocolates have maintained their businesses selling bite-sized chocolates that are affordable to low-income consumers, cater to their tastes, and can be bought in remote rural stores.[79]

contender A local company whose assets are transferable, allowing it to compete head-on with established global players worldwide.

If a local company's assets are transferable, the company may be able to compete head-on with the established global players worldwide. While Airbus and Boeing have competed by developing and launching ever-bigger aircraft, the niche for jets that carry 70 to 110 passengers has been left open for others. In the past ten years, the number of regional-jet routes has grown 1,000 percent in Europe and 1,400 percent in North America. Much of that increase has come from commuter airlines that the majors own or contract with to connect smaller markets with their hubs. The **contender** that has taken advantage of the increased demand is Brazil's Embraer, which has challenged the market leader, Canada's Bombardier. When demand took off faster than expected, Bombardier could not meet demand, thus opening the door for Embraer. Currently, Brazil's lower labor costs allow Embraer to undercut its competitor on prices.[80]

extender A company that is able to exploit its success at home as a platform for expansion elsewhere.

Extenders are able to exploit their success at home as a platform for expansion elsewhere. This calls for markets or segments that are similar in terms of customer preferences (e.g., sizable expatriate communities). The number of Indians in the United States has doubled in the past ten years to 2.5 million, making them the largest and fastest-growing Asian minority.[81] This will provide an opportunity for Bollywood to extend its marketing beyond India. Televisa from Mexico, Venevisión from Venezuela, and Globo TV in Brazil have emerged as leading producers and marketers of *telenovelas*, especially to culturally close markets in Europe.[82] Some local marketers are seasoned in competing against global players and have subsequently extended their market presence to new markets abroad. Jollibee Foods Corporation challenged McDonald's in its home market of the Philippines, with its products and services customized to local tastes, and has subsequently expanded its presence to other markets with sizable Filipino communities, such as Hong Kong and California. Jollibee now has 50 restaurants operating in five countries and continues to grow.[83]

Multiple strategies are available to the local marketers when global markets and marketers challenge them. The key is to innovate, rather than imitate, and exploit the inherent competitive advantages over global players. A six-part strategy for success has been proposed.[84] First, given that local companies have an inherent familiarity with their own marketplace, they should create customized products and services. E-commerce site Dangdang edged out Amazon in China by recognizing the country's poor credit-card payment infrastructure and developing the best cash-settlement system. Second, the local marketer can develop approaches that overcome key obstacles. Grupo Elektra, a leading Mexican retailer, provides consumer financing to cater to low-income Mexican consumers. The retailer has 4,000 loan officers to visit prospective borrowers' homes to establish creditworthiness. Third, local companies can utilize the latest technologies for advantage. Brazil Gol airline issues e-tickets and promotes online sales for cost efficiency. Customers without Internet access can use kiosks or approach attendants with wireless-enabled pocket PCs to process check-ins. Fourth, local companies are able to scale up swiftly. This occurs not only locally, but also regionally, even globally. Chinese auto parts company Wanxiang has used its production know-how it gained in China to revive a number of U.S. producers. Fifth, local companies can often exploit low-cost labor. Chinese dairy companies such as Mengniu and Yili are examples of success in categories where a relatively high proportion of the cost structure and capital goes to production and logistics, and where customer needs change less frequently. Finally, local companies need to invest in talent to sustain their growth and expansion. The successful players promise and deliver accelerated careers, a chance to contribute meaningfully, and a meritocratic corporate culture.[85]

SUMMARY

Globalization continues to be one of the most important strategy issues for managers. Many forces, both external and internal, are driving companies to further globalize their markets and operations. As companies look to expand and coordinate their participation in foreign markets, they must consider various factors such as where they will find markets for accelerated growth or opportunities to realize scale efficiencies. Standardization, although attractive to managers for its cost benefits, is not the answer. Managers may indeed occasionally be able to take identical concepts and approaches around the world, but most often, they must be customized to local tastes. Internally, companies must make sure that country organizations around the world are ready to launch global products and programs as if they had been developed only for their markets. Firms that are able to exploit commonalities across borders and to do so with competent marketing managers in country organizations are able to see the benefits in their overall performance.[86]

Managers need to engage in strategic planning to better adjust to the realities of the new marketplace. Understanding the firm's core strategy (i.e., what business they are really in) starts the process, and this assessment may lead to adjustments in what business the company may want to be in. In formulating global strategy for the chosen business, the decision makers have to assess and make choices about markets and competitive strategy to be used in penetrating them. This may result in the choice of one particular segment across markets or the targeting of multiple segments in which the company has a competitive advantage. Managers must decide how to allocate resources across the most desirable countries and segments. Once that focus is achieved, the old adage, "think globally, act locally," becomes a critical guiding principle both as far as customers are concerned and in terms of country organization motivation.

KEY TERMS

multidomestic strategy   305
mininationals   308
born global   308
cost leadership   314
differentiation   314
portfolio models   315

glocalization   321
cross-subsidization   322
soft power   322
not-invented-here (NIH) syndrome   324

global account management   325
dodger   327
defender   328
contender   328
extender   328

QUESTIONS FOR DISCUSSION

1. What is the danger in oversimplifying the globalization approach? Would you agree with the statement that "if something is working in a big way in one market, you better assume it will work in all markets"?

2. What are the critical ways in which globalization and standardization differ?

3. In addition to teenagers as a global segment, are there possibly other groups with similar traits and behaviors that have emerged worldwide?

4. Why is the assessment of internal resources critical as early as possible in developing a global strategic plan?

5. Outline the basic reasons why a company does not necessarily have to be large and have years of experience to succeed in the global marketplace.

6. What are the basic reasons why country operations would not embrace a new regional or global plan (i.e., why the not-invented-here syndrome might emerge)?

INTERNET EXERCISES

1. In little more than two decades, two-thirds of all Chinese—1 billion people—will probably be living in cities (Janamitra Devan, Stefano Negri, and Jonathan Woetzel, "Meeting the Challenges of China's Growing Cities," *McKinsey Quarterly* 3 (2008): 107–116; https://www .mckinseyquarterly.com/Video/Chinas_urbanization_challenge_ 2204). National and local officials must take steps now to ensure that this unprecedented transformation unfolds as smoothly as possible. What problems do you see as the benefits and harm with development of large cities so quickly?

2. Using the material available at their web sites (http:// www2.dupont.com/DuPont_Home/en_US/index.html; http:// www.ogilvy.com/#/The-Work/Galleries/DuPont.aspx/), suggest ways in which DuPont's business groups can take advantage of global and regional strategies due to interconnections in production and marketing.

TAKE A STAND

Cruise Ship Building: Asia Invades Europe

For a long time now, Italy, France, Germany, and Finland—and very occasionally Japan—have been the only serious builders in the world to produce large cruise ships. But with recent ship-building takeovers, this may now be changing.

© Tom Paiva/Getty Images, Inc.

In Italy, three of Fincantieri's biggest customers are Carnival Cruise Lines, Holland America Line, and Princess Cruises, all of whom have taken most of their new deliveries from the Italian ship-builders. To these can now be added Cunard and P&O. Carnival's new 130,000-ton Carnival Dream will be Finantieri's largest product when she delivers next year. Fincantieri, one of the largest ship-builders in the world, designs and produces cruise ships, ferries, naval vessels, offshore units, and mega yachts. With nine shipyards (eight in Italy), it has 10,000 employees. The company's order book at the end of 2007 stood at 49 ships. Over the past 18 years, it has built and delivered 82 cruise ships and ferries.

Weyer Werft built a series of ships for Celebrity, Royal Caribbean, Star Cruises/NCL, and Aida. Its last delivery will be this year's Celebrity Solstice, its largest ship yet at 122,000 tons. Lloyd Werft has delivered and refit ships such as Costa Victoria, Norwegian Sky, Norwegian Sun, and Pride of America; this Bremerhaven shipyard will learn by the end of this year, however, whether Italian shipbuilding group Fincantieri will increase its stake in it to a majority 51 percent. At present, Fincantieri holds 21 percent of the German yard's equity.

STX Group, the South Korean conglomerate, made a daring swoop last year on Aker Yards (a Finnish-based company) that will see it take two-thirds of Aker Yards and leave the French with 34 percent—25 percent is already held by Alstom, and 9 percent will now be sold to the French government. The buyout will cost STX about $1.3 billion. Aker Yards gives STX Group a conglomerate involved in shipbuilding and energy production, specialized cruise ships, and offshore vessel capabilities. STX is presently the sixth largest shipbuilder worldwide, with strength in bulk carriers and container ships. Aker Yards, meanwhile, controls 13 shipyards and has 15 cruise and ferry-type vessels on its order book. However, Aker Yards has suffered losses, and building cruise ships is not only vulnerable to the economic downturn but also to changes in the dollar-euro exchange rates. STX competes with three bigger firms in South Korea: Hyundai Heavy Industries Co, Samsung Heavy Industries Co, and Daewoo Shipbuilding. But Aker Yards' advanced technologies in cruise ships, icebreakers, and specialized ships should put it less head-on-head with its national competitors.

Following the acquisition, STX Group plans to rename the company STX Europe, while Aker Yards' French unit will become STX France Cruise, focusing on cruise and defense businesses. French trade unions, meanwhile, have expressed fears that powerful Asian shipbuilders will push traditional European industry leaders out of the business.

For Discussion

1. Will the new lower-cost Asian yards be able to capture the market from the European shipbuilding?

2. Aker Yards offers a wide variety of ships, including ice-breakers: Will this allow it to retain its market share?

Source: Robert Anderson, "Korea's STX Takes Control of Aker Yards," *Financial Times*, August 19, 2008, 17; http://www.cybercruises.com/cruisecolumn_sep2 .htm.

The Corporation: Ownership, Governance, and Sustainability

CHAPTER CONTENTS & LEARNING OBJECTIVES

OWNERSHIP

1. To explore how the differing ownership structures of organizations around the world alter the way in which those same organizations respond to stakeholder interests

THE CORPORATE OBJECTIVE

2. To examine how corporations, both publicly traded and privately held firms, conduct their activities to pursue both operational and financial goals and objectives

CORPORATE GOVERNANCE

3. To review, in detail, goals, structures, and participants in corporate governance across the globe, and how good and bad corporate governance affects an organization's reputation

CORPORATE RESPONSIBILITY AND SUSTAINABILITY

4. To differentiate between corporate governance, corporate responsibility, and corporate sustainability, and what attributes society increasingly expects from responsible organizations

A Corporation, then, or a body politic, or body incorporate, is a collection of many individuals united into one body, under a special denomination, having perpetual succession under an artificial form, and vested, by policy of the law, with the capacity of acting, in several respects, as an individual, particularly of taking and granting property, of contracting obligations, and of suing and being sued, of enjoying privileges and immunities in common, and of exercising a variety of political rights, more or less extensive, according to the design of its institution, or the powers conferred upon it, either at the time of its creation, or at any subsequent period of its existence.

—Stewart Kyd, *A Treatise on the Law of Corporations*, 1793, p. 13

Global business is conducted by many different types of organizations for many different purposes. Although it may appear at times that global business is dominated by the publicly traded corporation, and for the sole purpose of profit, these are only large parts of a much more complex global business environment. This chapter will explore the different forms of business organizations used today around the world, their governance and goals, and ultimately their ability to pursue sustainability. We begin our discussion by deepening our understanding of ownership, the legal construct so often associated with global business—the **corporation**, and then ultimately the roles and responsibilities of corporations by and for their major stakeholders.

> **corporation** The most common form of business organization, which has all of the rights and responsibilities of an individual, while possessing limited liability to its owners.

OWNERSHIP

1. To explore how the differing ownership structures of organizations around the world alter the way in which those same organizations respond to stakeholder interests

A business may be owned by a single individual (sole proprietorship, corporation sole), a few private individuals (partnership), a multitude of private owners who may exchange their ownership portions (publicly traded company or corporation), or even partially or wholly by government. A quick survey of the businesses operating up and down the street of any major city in most countries will likely yield a mixture of these ownership forms. Businesses in all parts of the globe cover the extremes of the ownership spectrum, from the owner-operator of a fruit cart on the corner, to a publicly traded Anglo-Dutch mining concern, to a publicly traded Russian oil company largely controlled by the Russian government.

Most companies begin as the creations of entrepreneurs, individuals or a small number of individual partners, with an idea. Whether those individuals or their families can retain control over time is a different story for every company. Consider the following businesses found around the globe today:

- **Porsche** (Germany). Founded in the 1930s, the company in recent years has been both publicly traded and yet controlled by only two families, the Porsche and Piëch families; then. The inter-related and often feuding families maintained their control by holding all of the voting shares in the company, while the publicly traded shares carried no voting power and therefore little influence on the company. In 2008, Porsche attempted to take control of Volkswagen (VW), another European automaker controlled by Ferdinand Piëch of the same Piëch family; then VW attempted to take control of Porsche! After two years of inter-family feuding, the two companies have agreed to work toward a merger slated for completion in 2011.

- **Rosneft** (Russia). One of the largest natural gas companies in the world, Rosneft is owned by both the Russian government (88 percent) and public stockholders (12 percent). Created from a number of different government-controlled businesses, Rosneft sold a portion of its ownership to the public market in 2006 in order to raise capital to repay debt obligations. It continues, however, to be operated and controlled by the Russian government.

- **Microsoft** (United States). One of the largest and sometimes most profitable companies in the world in recent years, Microsoft began as a partnership of two private individuals, Bill Gates and Paul Allen. The partners eventually sold the majority of the company's ownership to the public marketplace, although both retained small shares. The company today is led by professional management, which holds a relatively small stake in the company.

- **Cargill, Incorporated** (United States). Thought by many to be the largest privately held company in the world, Cargill is a diversified multinational company with more than $120 billion in sales. Although operating in nearly 70 countries and employing more than 160,000 people worldwide, the company is still owned by descendants of the founders (85 percent), with the remaining shares (15 percent) held by employees. Like Microsoft, Cargill is led by non-family management.

These four companies serve as examples of how ownership and control may diverge. Do the owners of the company run the company? Can a government-owned and -controlled company gain access to capital in the public marketplace? Can a family-owned and -run company be globally competitive? Can professional management successfully create value for a privately held business? These are just a few of the questions that a deeper understanding of the modern corporation can potentially resolve.

THE CORPORATION

The people who own a business and the people who operate a business may, however, be very different groups. The creation of the corporation, as described by Stewart Kyd in 1793 in the opening quote, solved a number of fundamental dilemmas faced by small businesses created by individuals.

- A corporation is legally separated from its owner(s). If it loses money, acquires debts, or incurs legal liabilities, the individual owners can lose no more than what they have invested in the company. The owners are, therefore, not legally liable for debts or obligations to creditors beyond their ownership investment. This is what is meant by the oft-used phrase "limited liability."

- A corporation is perpetual. As opposed to individuals or families, which may die, a corporation cannot die in the normal human sense of the word. A corporation may go bankrupt, it may be acquired, or it may be intentionally closed. But it can continue to operate in perpetuity, beyond the lives of its creators or immediate owners.

- A corporation is a legal creation but is deemed to have rights and responsibilities like a person, sometimes described as having a "legal personality."[1] As such, a corporation can buy or sell, sue or be sued, borrow and lend, conduct business— all as a member of society. With these legal rights, it has the responsibility to follow all laws of the state and can be held accountable for failing to act in a legal manner. Unlike human beings, however, it has no moral conscience.

The creation of the corporation had an enormously powerful influence on the growth of global commerce. The creation of a legally separate but legally responsible entity allowed the organization to raise capital independent of the financial health of any of the individual owners, to contract for purchasing and sale, and to survive the working life spans of its human creators. It may also have freed the business entity to act as if a machine, devoid of the multitude of social, cultural, and moral concerns of the human individual.

Figure 10.1   Stakeholders in the Firm

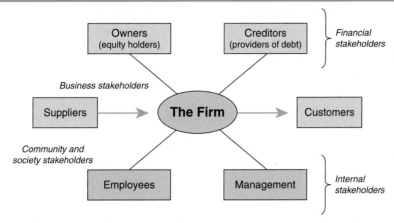

Differences in ownership, law, country of incorporation activity, and culture lead to differences in interest and power among stakeholder groups (*business, financial, internal, and society.*)

CORPORATE STAKEHOLDERS

So who are the **stakeholders** in the corporation, and what is the nature of their interests?[2] A stake, in theory, is an interest or a share in some organization or undertaking. Stakes themselves may be differentiated as to whether they are interests, rights, or ownership stakes. Figure 10.1 provides an overview of the potential stakeholders in the firm.

An *interest* is when a person or group is potentially affected by the actions of an organization or firm. The community in which a company operates, employing many of the people in the community, frequently opposes the closing of the firm citing its interest. A *right* is when a person or group has a legal claim, a contract, or some other existing arrangement to be treated in a certain way or have a particular right protected. This may be expressed in a variety of ways, including a right to be treated fairly, or an expectation that a firm will stand behind the quality of a product purchased from it. Ownership, the strongest form of stake, is when a person or group holds legal title to an asset such as a firm. Of course, this then raises the question of whether the owner of a firm has dictatorial power or must also consider the interests of nonowners.

Any analysis of corporate stakeholders must include all three levels of stakeholder interest. Depending on the country and culture of the firm itself, however, they may have very different voices in the vision, strategy, and operation of the firm. As described in the following sections, the power and influence of those having an interest versus a right versus legal title (ownership) often serves to differentiate the business environments of countries.

Financial Stakeholders

The two primary financial stakeholders of the firm, the providers of capital for both investment and operation, are shareholders and creditors. Shareholders are the actual owners of the firm, holding title to the firm's assets and operations as a result of their capital investment. Creditors, typically bank loans (Europe and Asia) or debt markets (Anglo-American markets), lend capital to the firm in exchange for promised repayment of both the principal amount and a return (interest). In the event that the firm cannot repay its debt obligations in a timely manner, the creditors hold a legal right over specific assets of the firm. Note that there is no assumption that the owners are the operators of the firm; the two groups are often completely separate. Financial stakeholders hold ownership stakes.

stakeholders All persons or groups which may affect or be affected by the activities of an organization like a corporation.

Business Stakeholders

The business stakeholders in the firm, its suppliers and customers, are the core of what business strategists term the *value chain*. The company purchases products and services from its suppliers, then combines, alters, and creates its own products and services from those and, in turn, sells its finished products and services to its customers. Most of these transactions are conducted under contract. How the company conducts its business, including its financial health, the ethics of its business practices, and its business development prospects, all affect the operations and livelihood of its business stakeholders.

Within the business stakeholders, customers have always enjoyed an area of particular focus. One influential academic and writer, Peter Drucker, in one of his earliest writings, advocated that the customer—not the stockholder—should be the focus of management action:

If we want to know what business is, we have to start with its purpose. And the purpose must lie outside the business itself. In fact, it must lie in society, since a business enterprise is an organ of society. There is only one valid definition of business purpose: to create a customer. The customer is the foundation of a business and keeps it in existence. He alone gives employment. And it is to supply the customer that society entrusts wealth-producing resources to the business enterprise.[3]

This belief in the customer as the focal point of management action has a long list of believers. One of the more recent advocates was the former CEO of Porsche, who stated:

Yes, of course we have heard of shareholder value. But that does not change the fact that we put customers first, then workers, then business partners, suppliers and dealers, and then shareholders.[4]

Advocates for a customer focus are, in principle, arguing that the best way to run and grow the business is focusing solely on the needs and satisfaction of the customer, and not the corporate owner. They are not, however, arguing that the benefits of the on-going business are for distribution to the customer.

Internal Stakeholders

The internal stakeholders of the firm are all those employed by the firm, including management and leadership. Workers and managers are hired to conduct the product and service procurement, purchasing, processing, production, and distribution of the company's products and services. Leadership and management may also provide most of the strategic vision and direction of the operations of the firm. Leadership may hold no ownership, partial ownership, or even complete ownership in the firm. Internal stakeholders hold both rights and interest stakes.

Social Stakeholders

The corporation may be a legal construction, but it also has a great influence and impact on the local community and society as a whole. Community and society are the social stakeholders. Although more distant from the actual operations and transactions of the firm and its business, social stakeholders may be severely affected by the success or failure of the corporation, its investments and divestments, its employment and involvement, and its longevity and environmental stewardship. Social stakeholders hold interest stakes.

Even with this multitude of participants, there are others who may be stakeholders in specific organizations, including many different government organizations and

Figure 10.2   Stakeholder Interests and CEO Decisions

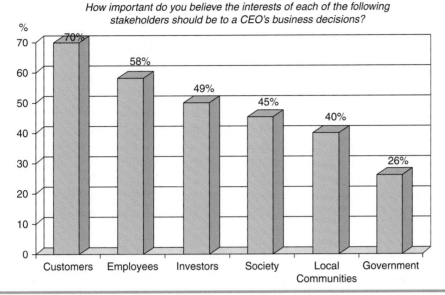

How important do you believe the interests of each of the following stakeholders should be to a CEO's business decisions?

Source: "2009 Special Midyear Trust Survey," Edelman Trust Barometer, August 3, 2009, p.14. Survey of 1,675 people In the United States, China, India, France, Germany, and the United Kingdom, between May 26 and July 3, 2009.

regulators, equity exchanges, and social and environmental interest groups. As discussed in the following section, depending on the cultural and business culture in which the corporation operates, the voices of different stakeholder groups are more and less pronounced.

THE PUBLIC PERSPECTIVE

In addition to what any individual country's law thinks, or what the individual stakeholders in any specific organization think, there is also what society thinks about the interests of stakeholders and the governance of the corporation. Figure 10.2 presents 2009 survey results on how important the interests of specific stakeholder groups should be in the business decisions by corporate CEOs.

The clear "winner" in Figure 10.2 is the customer. In the eyes of the public, the customer's interests should come first in a CEO's business decisions (70 percent). But what is striking is the public's ranking of employee interests second (58 percent), ahead of that of investors (49 percent). This is an area of growing debate, particularly in times of global recession, when the corporation is often seen to lay off workers in order to preserve profitability of ownership.

 THE CORPORATE OBJECTIVE

So what is the goal—the objective—of the corporation? If the answer is "to earn a profit," then it has to be made very clear: For whom? An introductory course in business often states that the objective of the corporation, and therefore the goal of management, is the **maximization of shareholder value**. This would then imply that the stockholder is the primary stakeholder and all other stakeholders are of lesser priority. This is not, however, accepted globally as the objective of the corporation, meaning that the interests of other stakeholders carry significant weight as well

maximization of shareholder value The pursuit of the interests of corporate shareholders, primarily the profitability of the organization, over and above the interests of other stakeholders. (Also commonly referred to as *shareholder wealth maximization*.)

2. To examine how corporations, both publicly traded and privately held firms, conduct their activities to pursue both operational and financial goals and objectives

stakeholder capitalism The operation of a firm or organization in a manner that attempts to balance the interests of all stakeholders of the organization (stockholders, employees, creditors, suppliers, customers, and community).

in many other cultures. In many countries and cultures, **stakeholder capitalism** is the predominant business philosophy, in which the interests of multiple stakeholders are pursued by the corporation and its management. Before we move on to discuss the different possible objectives of the corporation, we need to first explore how profit may be derived from the corporation—the operational goals of the corporation.

OPERATIONAL GOALS

It is one thing to say "maximize value," but it is quite another to do it. The management objective of maximizing profit is not as simple as it sounds, because the measure of profit used by ownership/management differs between the privately held firm and the publicly traded firm. In other words, is management attempting to maximize current income, capital appreciation, or both?

The return to a shareholder in a publicly traded company combines current income in the form of dividends and capital gains from the appreciation of share price:

$$\text{Shareholder return} = \frac{\text{Dividend}}{\text{Price}_1} + \frac{\text{Price}_2 - \text{Price}_1}{\text{Price}_1}$$

where the initial price, P_1, is equivalent to the initial investment by the shareholder, and P_2 is the price of the share at the end of period (keeping in mind that the owners of the company expect P_2 to be bigger than P_1). The shareholder theoretically receives income from both components. For example, over the past 60 years in the U.S. marketplace, a diversified investor may have received an average annual return of 14 percent, split roughly between dividends, 2 percent, and capital gains, 12 percent. Because capital gains make up such a greater proportion of the return, more and more emphasis has been placed by corporate management on the share price rather than on the distribution of profits in the form of dividends.

dividend yield The dividend paid per share to shareholders as a percent of the current share price.

Management generally believes it has the most direct influence over the first component—the **dividend yield**. Management makes strategic and operational decisions that grow sales and generate profits, and then distributes those profits to ownership in the form of dividends. **Capital gains**—the change in the share price as traded in the equity markets—is much more complex, and reflects many forces that are not in the direct control of management. Despite growing market share, profits, or any other traditional measure of business success, the market may not reward these actions directly with share price appreciation. Many top executives believe that stock markets move in mysterious ways and are not always consistent in their valuations.

capital gains Profits that arise from the increase in the value of an asset, such as a publicly traded share, over what was paid for that same asset.

PUBLICLY TRADED OR PRIVATELY HELD

One of the biggest misconceptions about global business is that most companies are publicly traded.[5] In fact, the reality is the opposite. Most of the world's businesses are privately held, either by an individual, a family, or by partnership. It is estimated that more than 70 percent of the world's publicly traded companies are U.S. or British. Most other countries have publicly traded companies, but their markets are dominated by private firms, many of which are family owned. For example, in a study of 5,232 corporations in 13 western European countries, family-controlled firms represented 44 percent of the sample compared to 37 percent that were widely held.[6]

A privately held firm has a much simpler shareholder return objective function: maximize current and sustainable income. The privately held firm does not have a share price (it does have a value, but this is not a publicly visible, market-determined value in the way in which we see share price markets work every day). It, therefore, simply focuses on generating current income, primarily dividend income, to generate the returns to its ownership. If ownership is a family, the family may also place great emphasis on the ability to sustain those earnings over time while maintaining a slower rate of growth that can be managed by the family and for the family. It is, therefore, critical that we understand the nature of ownership's financial interests from the start if we are to understand the strategic and financial goals of management.

Over time, however, some firms may choose to go public via an **initial public offering (IPO)**. Typically, only a relatively small percentage of the company is initially sold to the public, resulting in a company that may still be controlled by a small number of private investors but also has public shares outstanding that are generating a market-based share price on a daily basis.

Whether the ownership structure ever actually moves from private to even partially public is very case specific. Some companies may sell more and more of their equity interests into the public marketplace, with their private founders no longer holding any ownership or control. Or the private owner or family may choose to retain a major share but not maintain explicit control. Possibly, as has been the case in recent years, a firm that has moved from being privately held to publicly traded may move back to being privately held. For example, in late 2005, a very large private firm, Koch Industries (U.S.), acquired Georgia-Pacific (U.S.), a very large publicly traded firm; Koch took Georgia-Pacific private.

An added consideration is that even when the firm's ownership is publicly traded, it may still be controlled by a single investor or a small group of investors, including major institutional investors. This means that the control of the company is much like the privately held company and, therefore, reflects the interests and goals of the individual investor. As discussed in Focus on Culture, family-controlled firms all over the world may outperform publicly traded firms in terms of financial performance.

Something else of significance results from the initial sale of shares to the public: the firm becomes subject to many of the increased legal, regulatory, and reporting requirements in most countries surrounding the sale and trading of securities. In the United States, for example, going public means the firm will now have to disclose a sizable degree of financial and operational detail, publish this information at least quarterly, comply with Securities and Exchange Commission (SEC) rules and regulations, and comply with all the specific operating and reporting requirements of the specific exchange on which it is traded. Obviously, the move to public trading of shares comes with a lot of baggage!

initial public offering (IPO) The first sale or issuance of shares of ownership (stock) in an organization to the market. A private firm that issues its shares to the public market would henceforth be classified as publicly traded.

SHAREHOLDER WEALTH MAXIMIZATION

The social responsibility of business is to increase its profits.
—Milton Friedman, *The New York Times Magazine*, September 13, 1970

The Anglo-American markets (primarily the United Kingdom and the United States) have a philosophy that a firm's objective should follow the shareholder wealth

---

FOCUS ON CULTURE

The Benefits of Family

Research indicates that as opposed to popular belief, family-owned firms in some highly developed economies typically outperform publicly owned firms. This is true not only in western Europe, but also in the United States. A recent study of firms included in the S&P500 found that families are present in fully one-third of the S&P500 and account for 18 percent of its outstanding equity. An added insight is that firms possessing a CEO from the family also perform better than those with outside CEOs. Interestingly, it seems that minority shareholders are actually better off, according to this study, when part of a family-influenced firm.

Source: Ronald C. Anderson and David M. Reeb, "Founding Family Ownership and Firm Performance from the S&P500," *Journal of Finance*, June 2003: 1301.

maximization model. More specifically, the management of the firm should strive to maximize the return to shareholders while enduring acceptable levels of risk. According to this model, the firm exists for the benefit of its stockholders (owners of equity), and the pursuit of profit on their part is the primary motivation for all of management's activities. The interests of all other stakeholders are secondary to the primary purpose of creating shareholder value. In fact, in a number of countries, by law, the company's managers must consider the interests of stockholders over and above all other interests in its conduct of the business—a **fiduciary responsibility**.[7]

fiduciary responsibility A relationship between two parties whereby one party has the trust and legal and ethical duty to act in the best interests of the other.

The strength of the shareholder wealth maximization model is its clear focus on the returns to a specific stakeholder, the stockholder. The stockholder is the provider of the equity capital for the creation and sustenance of the corporation, and the "returns" to the stockholder are traditionally refined even further to focus on the financial returns to shareholders, as measured by the sum of capital gains (the change in share price) and dividends (distributions of income to shareholders).

SEPARATION OF OWNERSHIP FROM MANAGEMENT

One of the biggest weaknesses of the shareholder wealth maximization model has long been considered the failure of management to always act in the best interest of shareholders. This is a strong possibility when the business is not managed by the owner, but by hired professionals. This field of thought, known as **agency theory**, is the study of how shareholder and management's interests may diverge (the agency problem) and how a firm can motivate management to act like owners when managing the corporation (agency interests).[8]

agency theory The question of whether the principals of an organization, ownership and management, may not be aligned in terms of strategy, interests, and risk-taking.

One example of the agency problem is risk taking. Because management's total income arises from the company's operations, it may be reluctant to undertake any risky activity that may endanger its own income. Ownership—the stockholder who owns a part of the business but whose income does not come just from that business—may wish management to take on more risky activities in the hope of driving the share price upward. One solution used frequently in the past two decades has been to give the management of the corporation stock options (financial derivatives that increase in value as the share price rises) as part of its compensation, the rewards and motivations for management are then more aligned with those of the stockholder. Whether these inducements succeed has been hotly debated.

A second issue arising from the separation of ownership and management is share concentration. The U.S. and U.K. stock markets have been characterized by widespread ownership of shares, many investors holding shares, but no real strength of concentrated ownership. Management owns only a small proportion of stock in its own firms. In contrast, in the rest of the world, ownership is usually characterized by controlling shareholders. Typical controlling shareholders are:

1. Government (e.g., privatized utilities)
2. Institutions (such as banks in Germany)
3. Family (such as in France and Italy in Europe and increasingly, Asia)
4. Consortiums (such as *keiretsus* in Japan and *chaebols* in South Korea)

Control is enhanced by ownership of shares with dual voting rights, interlocking directorates, staggered election of the board of directors, takeover safeguards, and other techniques not used in the Anglo-American markets. However, the recent emergence of huge equity funds and hedge funds in the United States and the United Kingdom has led to the privatization of some very prominent publicly traded firms.

An added dimension to shareholder wealth maximizing firms is the discipline of the market. If management deviates too much from stockholder interests, the board of directors should replace it. In cases where the board is too weak or ingrown to take this action, the discipline of the equity markets could do it through a takeover. This discipline is made possible by the one-share–one-vote rule that exists in most Anglo-American markets.

STAKEHOLDER CAPITALISM

Corporations have neither bodies to be punished, nor souls to be condemned; they therefore do as they like.
—Edward Thurlow (1st Baron Thurlow), 1731–1806, as quoted by
John Poynder in *Literary Extracts*, 1844, vol. 1, p. 2.

In countries like Germany and Japan, the management of the corporation strives to operate the firm in the interest of multiple stakeholders, not just the shareholders. It is generally referred to as stakeholder capitalism. It does indeed try to earn returns for its stockholders—so it is a capitalist structure, but it also takes into consideration the interests of many of the other stakeholders when making strategic and operating decisions about the company. Depending on the country, the two stakeholder groups that generally gain a larger voice are employees and creditors, while government is seen to intervene more often in the workings of the firm. Many have argued that by pursuing the interests of multiple stakeholders, the corporation is exhibiting a type of moral character not found in purely shareholder wealth–focused enterprises. The Focus on Culture, German Stakeholder Practices, illustrates how that system reacted differently to the recent global recession.

Although stakeholder capitalism may avoid the flaw of shareholder wealth maximization's singular focus on short-term profitability, it has its own set of challenges. First and foremost, finding common ground between multiple stakeholder interests often proves daunting, slowing decision making and often the ability to move quickly enough to remain competitive.

Both models have their strengths and weaknesses, and two trends in recent years have led to a growing focus on the shareholder wealth form. First, as more of the non–Anglo-American markets privatized industry, a shareholder wealth focus was believed to attract capital from outside investors, many of whom are in other countries. Second, and still quite controversial, many analysts believe that shareholder-based multinationals are increasingly dominating their global industry segments. Success wins followers.

FOCUS ON CULTURE

German Stakeholder Practices

German companies have frequently been used as examples of stakeholder capitalism, in which the voices of workers and community have near-equal volume to those of owners. As a result, German stakeholder practices have the reputation as being a strength of the German business sector, taking a longer-term focus on competitiveness and employment consistent with the interests of the multitude of stakeholders.

First and foremost, German companies are required by law to consider and act in the interest of all stakeholders. Second, German companies structurally have two boards: (1) a supervisory board, in which worker representatives hold half the seats and the board itself monitors all general interest issues and activities and (2) a managerial board, which is charged with the oversight of the ongoing operations of the company, in which the voting equity ownership holds power. As with all systems of corporate governance, there will be occasions in which the interests of different stakeholder groups diverge—traditionally characterized as profits versus jobs.

Many of the inherent behaviors of the German corporate governance system were evident during the 2007–2009 recession. As corporate sales and profitability fell, management was under increasing pressure to cut costs and employment to protect shareholder interests. As opposed to the shareholder-wealth–maximizing firms of the Anglo-American markets, many German firms cut their dividends, not their employment.

CORPORATE GOVERNANCE

3. To review, in detail, goals, structures, and participants in corporate governance across the globe, and how good and bad corporate governance affects an organization's reputation

corporate governance The relationship among stakeholders that is used to determine and control the strategic direction and performance of the corporation.

Corporate governance represents the relationship among stakeholders that is used to determine and control the strategic direction and performance of the corporation. Although the governance structure of any company—domestic, international, or multinational—is fundamental to its very existence, this very subject has become the lightning rod of political and business debate in the past few years as failures in governance in a variety of forms have led to corporate fraud and failure. Abuses and failures in corporate governance have dominated global business news in recent years. Beginning with the accounting fraud and questionable ethics of business conduct at Enron (culminating in its bankruptcy in the fall of 2001), failures in corporate governance have raised issues about the very ethics and culture of the conduct of business.

THE GOAL OF CORPORATE GOVERNANCE

The single overriding objective of corporate governance in the Anglo-American markets is the optimization over time of the returns to shareholders. To achieve this, good governance practices should focus the attention of the board of directors of the corporation on this objective by developing and implementing a strategy for the corporation that ensures corporate growth and improvement in the value of the corporation's equity. At the same time, it should ensure an effective relationship with stakeholders.[9]

One of the most widely accepted statements of good corporate governance practices is that established by the Organization for Economic Cooperation and Development (OECD):[10]

- **The rights of shareholders.** The corporate governance framework should protect shareholders' rights.
- **The equitable treatment of shareholders.** The corporate governance framework should ensure the equitable treatment of all shareholders, including minority and foreign shareholders. All shareholders should have the opportunity to obtain effective redress for violation of their rights.
- **The role of stakeholders in corporate governance.** The corporate governance framework should recognize the rights of stakeholders as established by law and encourage active cooperation between corporations and stakeholders in creating wealth, jobs, and the sustainability of financially sound enterprises.
- **Disclosure and transparency.** The corporate governance framework should ensure that timely and accurate disclosure is made on all material matters regarding the corporation, including the financial situation, performance, ownership, and governance of the company.
- **The responsibilities of the board.** The corporate governance framework should ensure the strategic guidance of the company, the effective monitoring of management by the board, and the board's accountability to the company and the shareholders.

These principles obviously focus on several key areas—shareholder rights and roles, disclosure and transparency, and the responsibilities of boards—that we will discuss in more detail later. On a more general level, however, corporate governance of any organization, publicly traded or not, must focus on four basic principles: (1) accounting and reporting; (2) board structure, composition, and reward; (3) executive ethics; and (4) executive and management compensation. Many of the corporate governance failures in the past decade, including those at the core of the global

Figure 10.3   The Structure of Corporate Governance

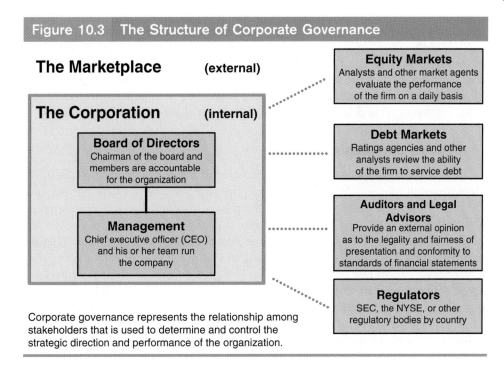

Corporate governance represents the relationship among stakeholders that is used to determine and control the strategic direction and performance of the organization.

financial crisis from 2007–2009 at some of the world's largest financial institutions, involved failures in one or more of these elements.

THE STRUCTURE OF CORPORATE GOVERNANCE

Our first challenge is to try and capture what people mean when they use the expression "corporate governance." Figure 10.3 provides an overview of the various parties and their responsibilities associated with the governance of the modern corporation. The modern corporation's actions and behaviors are directed and controlled by both internal forces and external forces.

The internal forces, the officers of the corporation (such as the chief executive officer) and the board of directors of the corporation (including the chairman of the board), are those directly responsible for determining both the strategic direction and the execution of the company's future. But they are not acting within a vacuum; they are subject to the constant prying eyes of the external forces in the marketplace who question the validity and soundness of their decisions and performance. These include the equity markets in which the shares are traded, the analysts who critique their investment prospects, the creditors and credit agencies who lend them money, the auditors and legal advisors who testify to the fairness and legality of their reporting, and the multitude of regulators who oversee their actions in order to protect the investment public.

The Board of Directors

The legal body that is accountable for the governance of the corporation is its board of directors. The board is composed of both employees of the organization (inside members) and senior and influential nonemployees (outside members). Areas of debate surrounding boards include the following: (1) the proper balance between inside and outside members, (2) the means by which board members are compensated for their service, and (3) the actual ability of a board to adequately monitor and manage a corporation when board members are spending sometimes less than five days a year in board activities. Outside members, very often the current or retired chief executives of other major companies, may bring with them a healthy sense of distance and impartiality, which although refreshing, may also result in limited understanding of the true issues and events within the company. In German companies, the distinction between the governing board and the management board provides a different set of dilemmas on these same internal versus external trade-offs.

Officers and Management

The senior officers of the corporation—the chief executive officer (CEO), the chief financial officer (CFO), and the chief operating officer (COO)—are not only the most knowledgeable of the business, but the creators and directors of its strategic and operational direction. The management of the firm is, according to theory, acting as a contractor—as an agent—of shareholders to pursue value creation. They are motivated by salary, bonuses, and stock options (positively) or the risk of losing their jobs (negatively). They may, however, have biases of self-enrichment or personal agendas that the board and other corporate stakeholders are responsible for overseeing and policing. Interestingly enough, in more than 80 percent of the companies in the U.S. *Fortune* 500, the CEO is also the chairman of the board. This is, in the opinion of many, a conflict of interest and not in the best interests of the company and its shareholders. British-based corporations are more aggressive and consistent in separating these roles.

Equity Markets

The publicly traded company, regardless of country of residence, is highly susceptible to the changing opinion of the marketplace. The equity markets themselves, whether they be the New York Stock Exchange (NYSE), London Stock Exchange, or Mexico City Bolsa, should reflect the market's constant evaluation of the promise and performance of the individual company. The analysts are those self-described experts employed by the many investment banking firms who also trade in the client company shares. They are expected (sometimes naively) to evaluate the strategies, plans for execution of the strategies, and financial performance of the firms on a real-time basis. Analysts depend on the financial statements and other public disclosures of the firm for their information.

Debt Markets

Although the debt markets (banks and other financial institutions providing loans and various forms of securitized debt, like corporate bonds) are not specifically interested in building shareholder value, they are indeed interested in the financial health of the company. Their interest, specifically, is in the company's ability to repay its debt in a timely and efficient manner. These markets, like the equity markets, must rely on the financial statements and other disclosures (public and private in this case) of the companies with which they work.

Auditors and Legal Advisors

Auditors and legal advisors are responsible for providing an external professional opinion as to the fairness, legality, and accuracy of corporate financial statements. In this process, they attempt to determine whether the firm's financial records and practices follow what in the United States is termed *generally accepted accounting principles (GAAP)* with regard to accounting procedures. Auditors and legal advisors are hired by the firms they are auditing, leading to a rather unique practice of policing their employers. The additional difficulty that has arisen in recent years is that the major accounting firms pursued the development of large consulting practices, often leading to a conflict of interest. An auditor not giving a clean bill of health to a client could not expect to gain many lucrative consulting contracts from that same firm in the near future.

Regulators

Publicly traded firms in the United States and elsewhere are subject to the regulatory oversight of both governmental organizations and nongovernmental organizations. In the United States, the Securities and Exchange Commission (SEC) is a careful watchdog of the publicly traded equity markets, both in the behavior of the companies themselves in those markets and of the various investors participating in those markets. The SEC and other authorities like it outside of the United States require a regular and orderly disclosure process of corporate performance in order that all investors may evaluate the company's investment value with adequate, accurate, and fairly distributed information. This regulatory oversight is often focused on when and what information is released by the company, and to whom.

A publicly traded firm in the United States is also subject to the rules and regulations of the exchange upon which it is traded (NYSE, American Stock Exchange, and NASDAQ being the largest). These organizations, typically categorized as "self-regulatory" in nature, construct and enforce standards of conduct for both their member companies and themselves in the conduct of share trading.

COMPARATIVE CORPORATE GOVERNANCE[11]

The origins of the need for a corporate governance process arise from the separation of ownership from management, and from the varying views by culture of who the stakeholders are and of what significance. This assures that corporate governance practices will differ across countries, economies, and cultures. As described in Table 10.1, the various corporate governance systems may be classified by regime. The regimes in turn reflect the evolution of business ownership and direction within the countries over time.

Market-based regimes, like those of the United States, Canada, and the United Kingdom, are characterized by relatively efficient capital markets in which the ownership of publicly traded companies is widely dispersed. Family-based systems, like those characterized in many of the emerging markets, Asian markets, and Latin

Table 10.1 Comparative Corporate Governance Regimes

Regime Basis	Characteristics	Examples
Market based	Efficient equity markets; dispersed ownership	United States, United Kingdom, Canada, Australia
Family based	Management and ownership is combined; family/majority and minority shareholders	Hong Kong, Indonesia, Malaysia, Singapore, Taiwan, France
Bank based	Government influence in bank lending; lack of transparency; family control	Korea, Germany
Government affiliated	State ownership of enterprise; lack of transparency; no minority influence	China, Russia

Source: Based on J. Tsui and T. Shieh, "Corporate Governance in Emerging Markets: An Asian Perspective," in Frederick D. S. Chol, ed., International Finance and Accounting Handbook, 3rd ed., (New York: Wiley, 2004), 24.4–24.6.

American markets, not only started with strong concentrations of family ownership (as opposed to partnerships or small investment groups, which are not family based), but have continued to be largely controlled by families even after going public. Bank-based and government-based regimes are those reflecting markets in which government ownership of property and industry has been the constant force over time, resulting in only marginal "public ownership" of enterprise, and even then, subject to significant restrictions on business practices.

These regimes are, therefore, a function of at least four major factors in the evolution of corporate governance principles and practices globally: (1) financial market development, (2) the degree of separation between management and ownership, (3) the concept of disclosure and transparency, and (4) the historical development of the legal system.

Financial Market Development

The depth and breadth of capital markets is critical to the evolution of corporate governance practices. Country markets that have had relatively slow growth (as in the emerging markets) or have industrialized rapidly utilizing neighboring capital markets (as is the case of western Europe) may not form large public equity market systems. Without significant public trading of ownership shares, high concentrations of ownership are preserved and few disciplined processes of governance develop.

Separation of Management and Ownership

In countries and cultures in which the ownership of the firm has continued to be an integral part of management, agency failures have been less of a problem. In countries like the United States, in which ownership has become largely separated from management (and widely dispersed), aligning the goals of management and ownership is much more difficult.

Disclosure and Transparency

The extent of disclosure regarding the operations and financial results of a company vary dramatically across countries. Disclosure practices reflect a wide range of cultural and social forces, including the degree of ownership that is public, the degree to which government feels it needs to protect investors' rights, and the extent to which family-based and government-based business remains central to the culture. Transparency, a parallel concept to disclosure, reflects the visibility of decision-making processes within the business organization.

Historical Development of the Legal System

Investor protection is typically better in countries in which English common law is the basis of the legal system, compared to the codified civil law that is typical in France and Germany (the so-called *Code Napoleon*). English common law is typically the basis of the legal systems in the United Kingdom and former colonies of the United Kingdom, including the United States and Canada. The Code Napoleon is typically the basis of the legal systems in former French colonies and the European countries that Napoleon once ruled, such as Belgium, Spain, and Italy. In countries with weak investor protection, controlling shareholder ownership is often a substitute for a lack of legal protection.

Note that the word *ethics* has not been used. All of the principles and practices described so far have assumed that the individuals in roles of responsibility and leadership pursue them truly and fairly. That, however, has not always been the case.

FAILURES IN CORPORATE GOVERNANCE

Failures in corporate governance have become increasingly visible in recent years. In addition to Enron, other firms that have revealed major accounting and disclosure failures, as well as executives looting the firm, are WorldCom, Parmalat, Global Crossing, Tyco, Adelphia, and HealthSouth.

In each case, prestigious auditing firms, such as Arthur Andersen, missed the violations or minimized them—possibly because of lucrative consulting relationships or other conflicts of interest. Moreover, security analysts and banks urged investors to buy the shares and debt issues of these and other firms that they knew to be risky or even close to bankruptcy. Even more egregious, most of the top executives responsible for the mismanagement that destroyed their firms walked away (initially) with huge gains on shares sold before the downfall, and even overly generous severance payments.

It appears that the day of reckoning has come. The first to fall was Arthur Andersen, one of the former "Big Five" U.S. accounting firms, due to its involvement with Enron. However, many more legal actions against former executives are under way. Although the corruption scandals were first revealed in the United States, they have spread to Canada and the European Union countries.

GOOD GOVERNANCE AND CORPORATE REPUTATION

Does good corporate governance matter? This is actually a difficult question, and, historically, the realistic answer has been largely dependent on outcomes. For example, as long as Enron's share price continued to rise dramatically throughout the 1990s, questions over transparency, accounting propriety, and even financial facts were largely overlooked by many of the stakeholders of the corporation. Yet, eventually, the fraud, deceit, and failure of the multitude of corporate governance practices resulted in the bankruptcy of the firm. It not only destroyed the wealth of investors, but the careers, incomes, and savings of so many of its basic stakeholders—its own employees. Ultimately, *yes*, good governance does matter. A lot.

Good corporate governance is dependent on a variety of factors, one of which is the general governance reputation of the country of incorporation and registration. Figure 10.4 presents selected recent country rankings compiled by Governance Metrics International (GMI) as of September 2008. Studies by many different

Figure 10.4   Country Governance Rankings

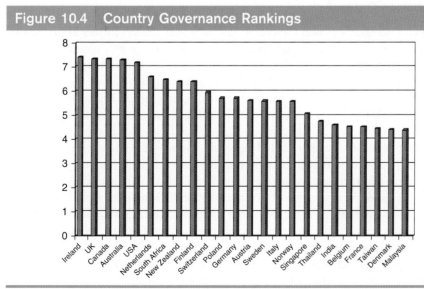

Source: Governance Metrics International, http://www.gmiratings.com. Top 24 Rankings as of September 23, 2009.

organizations and academics, including GMI, have continued to show a number of important linkages between good governance (at both the country and corporate levels) and the cost of capital, returns to shareholders, and corporate profitability. An added dimension of interest is the role of country governance because it may influence the country in which international investors may choose to invest. Early studies indicate that good governance does indeed attract international investor interest.

A second way of valuing good governance is by measuring the attitudes and tendencies of the large global institutional investors, who ultimately decide where capital may go. A recent McKinsey study surveyed more that 200 institutional investors as to the value they placed on good governance. The survey results indicated that institutional investors would be willing to pay a premium for companies with good governance within specific country markets. Although this is not exactly equivalent to saying who has "good" or "bad" corporate governance globally, it does provide some insight as to which countries institutional investors see good governance as scarce. It is again important to note that most of the emerging market nations have relatively few publicly traded companies even today.

CORPORATE GOVERNANCE REFORM

Within the United States and United Kingdom, the main corporate governance problem is the one treated by agency theory: with widespread share ownership, how can a firm align management's interest with that of the shareholders? Because individual shareholders do not have the resources or the power to monitor management, the U.S. and U.K. markets rely on regulators to assist in the agency theory monitoring task. Outside the United States and United Kingdom, large controlling shareholders are in the majority (including Canada). They are able to monitor management in some ways better than regulators. However, controlling shareholders pose a different agency problem. How can minority shareholders be protected against the controlling shareholders?

In recent years, reform in the United States and Canada has been largely regulatory. Reform elsewhere has been largely in the adoption of principles rather than stricter legal regulations. The principles approach is softer, less costly, and less likely to conflict with other existing regulations.

Sarbanes-Oxley Act

The U.S. Congress passed the Sarbanes-Oxley Act (SOX) in July 2002. Named after its two primary congressional sponsors, SOX had four major requirements: (1) CEOs and CFOs of publicly traded firms must vouch for the veracity of the firm's published financial statements, (2) corporate boards must have audit and compensation committees drawn from independent (outside) directors, (3) companies are prohibited from making loans to corporate officers and directors, and (4) companies must test their internal financial controls against fraud.

The first provision—the so-called signature clause—has already had significant impacts on the way in which companies prepare their financial statements. The provision was intended to instill a sense of responsibility and accountability in senior management (and, therefore, fewer explanations of "the auditors signed-off on it"). The companies themselves have pushed the same procedure downward in their organizations, often requiring business unit managers and directors at lower levels to sign their financial statements. Severe penalties were enacted in case of noncompliance.

SOX has been much more expensive to implement than was originally expected. Apart from the obvious costs of filling out more forms, many critics argue that too much time is consumed in meeting the new regulations, modifying internal controls to combat fraud, and restating past earnings, rather than running the companies. This cost may be disproportionately high for smaller firms that must meet the same regulatory requirements as large firms. In particular, auditing and legal fees have skyrocketed.

Everyone is afraid of following in the footsteps of Arthur Andersen, which collapsed as a result of the Enron scandal. (The "Big Five" accounting firms became the "Big Four" overnight!) The net result may lead to more small but growing firms choosing to sell out to larger firms instead of going the initial public offering (IPO) route. Other firms may simply choose to stay private, feeling that the costs of public offerings outweigh the benefits. Moreover, many firms may become more risk averse. Lower-level employees might pass all risky decisions up the line to a more central risk assessment level. Such an action would slow down decision making and potentially growth.

SOX has been quite controversial internationally. Its "one size fits all" style conflicts with a number of the corporate governance practices already in place in markets that view themselves as having better governance records than the United States. A foreign firm wishing to list or continue listing their shares on a U.S. exchange must comply with the law. Some companies, such as Porsche, withdrew plans for a U.S. listing specifically in opposition to SOX. Other companies, however, including many of the largest foreign companies traded on U.S. exchanges such as Unilever, Siemens, and ST Microelectronics, have stated their willingness to comply—if they can find acceptable compromises between U.S. law and the governance requirements and principles in their own countries. One example is Germany, where supervisory board audit committees must include employee representatives. According to U.S. law, employees are not independent. Many of these firms have concluded they need access to the U.S. capital market and therefore must comply.

Board Structure and Compensation

Many critics have argued for the United States to move more toward structural reforms more consistent with European standards (e.g., prohibiting CEOs from also being chairs). Although this is increasingly common, there is no regulatory or other legal requirement to force the issue. Second, and more radically, would be to move toward the two-tiered structure of countries like Germany, in which there is a supervisory board (largely outsiders and many in number—e.g., Siemens has 18 members) and a management board (predominantly insiders and smaller—Siemens has 8 members).

Although SOX addresses the agency theory problem of transparency, it does not address the agency theory problem of aligning the goals of boards and managers with the interests of shareholders. In the past, the United States was characterized by compensation schemes to reward directors and management with a combination of an annual stipend or salary with significant stock options. However, when stock options go underwater (become essentially valueless because they are so far out-of-the-money), it does not cost the recipient any direct cost, only the loss of a potential future benefit. Indeed, some firms simply rewrite the options so that they have higher values immediately. It now appears that many firms are changing their compensation schemes to replace options with restricted stock. Restricted stock cannot be sold publicly for some specified period of time. If the price of the firm's shares falls, the recipient has actually lost money and is normally not recompensed by receiving more restricted shares.

Table 10.2 describes the current practices of the top 100 U.S. companies in regard to director independence. Director independence is the subject of continuing debate when reviewing board structure.

Table 10.2　Director Independence in the United States

Selected results from Shearman & Sterling's latest survey of U.S. corporate governance practices at the 100 largest publicly traded companies.

Independence Policies

Both the New York Stock Exchange (NYSE) and the NASDAQ listing standards require that a majority of a listed company's directors be independent. Of the Top 100 Companies, 51 have adopted and disclosed stricter standards for the minimum number of independent directors than required by the NYSE and NASDAQ listing standards.

Actual Number of Independent Directors

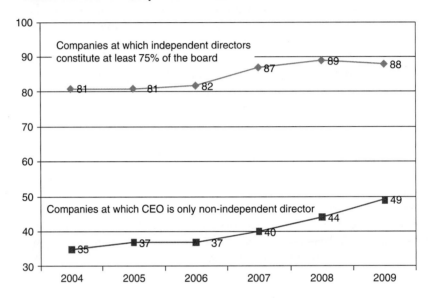

Independent directors constitute 75 percent or more of the boards of 88 of the Top 100 Companies surveyed this year. The CEO is the only non-independent director at 49 of the Top 100 Companies. Of the Top 100 Companies, six companies included CFOs and eight companies included COOs as members of the board. Fifteen of the Top 100 Companies had directors who were not independent because of commercial relationships. Approximately a quarter of the Top 100 Companies had directors who were not independent because they were former or current officers or employees of the company.

Source: "2009 Trends in Corporate Governance of the Largest U.S. Public Companies: Director & Executive Compensation," Shearman & Sterling LLP, www.shearman.com, accessed April 7, 2010, pp. 10–11.

Transparency, Accounting, and Auditing

transparency The open and public disclosure and reporting of the activities of an organization, including financial, civil, and environmental impacts and concerns.

The concept of **transparency** is also one that has been raised in a variety of different markets and contexts. Transparency is a rather common term used to describe the degree to which an investor—either existing or potential—can discern the true activities and value drivers of a company from the disclosures and financial results reported. For example, Enron was often considered a "black box" when it came to what the actual operational and financial results and risks were for its multitude of business lines. The consensus of corporate governance experts is that all firms, globally, should work toward increasing the transparency of the firm's risk–return profile.

The accounting process itself has now come under debate. The U.S. system is characterized as strictly rule based, rather than conceptually based as is common in western Europe. Many critics of U.S. corporate governance practices point to this as a fundamental flaw, in which constantly more clever accountants find ways to follow the rules, yet not meet the underlying purpose for which the rules were intended. An extension of the accounting process debate is that of the role and remuneration associated with auditing. This is the process of using third parties, paid by the firm, to vet their reporting practices as being consistent with generally accepted accounting principles. As the collapse of Arthur Andersen illustrated following the Enron debacle, serious questions remain as to the validity of this current practice.

Minority Shareholder Rights

Finally, the issue of minority shareholder rights continues to rage in many of the world's largest markets. Many of the emerging markets are still characterized by the family-based corporate governance regime, where the family remains in control even after the firm has gone public. But what of the interests and voices of the other shareholders? How are their interests preserved in organizations where families or controlling investors make all true decisions, including the boards? As Focus on Culture points out, minority shareholder rights are an issue in all markets today, including China.

Poor performance of management usually requires changes to management, ownership, or both. And that change can be effected through a variety of paths. In times gone by, and depending on the culture and accepted practices of the country and corporate culture, shareholders who believed management was consistently underperforming might have either simply remained quietly disgruntled or, at the opposite

---

FOCUS ON CULTURE

Corporate Governance Reform in China

China has made many positive improvements to its corporate governance structure in recent times by revising its securities and company laws. Notable changes include greater financial disclosure requirements, improved protection of minority shareholders' rights, and clearer guidelines on the role of supervising boards.

Significant progress has also been made in improving corporate governance in both the banking and equity markets. Foreign banks are now allowed to invest in People's Republic of China (PRC) banks and to bring with them their corporate governance concepts. The government has also introduced a share reform program, making it mandatory for nontradable shares in state-owned enterprises (SOEs) to be converted into tradable shares. Efforts have also been made to decrease financial risk in China's banking system by reducing the large number of nonperforming loans held by local banks.

While there have been significant improvements in the corporate governance structure in China, it still lags behind that of many developed countries. What are the shortcomings in China's corporate governance system? China has a two-tier board governance structure for companies that is very similar to the German system, with a board of directors and a supervisory board. Unfortunately, in reality, supervisory boards in China usually just rubber-stamp decisions taken by the board of directors. This duplication in the system does not do any good except to create redundancy and increase administrative costs for companies. Also, although Chinese companies are required

to have at least a third of their boards constitute independent directors, in practice these directors have very limited ability to influence how their companies are run.

Moreover, the financial disclosure requirements of Chinese listed companies are still weak compared to those of many developed jurisdictions. The continued uncertain reform of SOEs' share structures and the lack of good financial information make it extremely difficult for China's equity markets to grow and function properly.

The PRC government has been encouraging companies to improve their awareness of good corporate governance. One method adopted by the government has been to actively encourage local companies to list on the Hong Kong stock exchange, which has a more internationally accepted corporate governance system for listed companies. However, this plan could backfire and hinder the development of China's equity markets, because it creates the perception that the local stock exchanges in Shanghai and Shenzhen—and the companies listed on them—are weaker and less professionally managed.

Another corporate governance problem for big PRC companies (most of which are majority government owned) is that of the government trying to exert a strong management influence on them. Many of the senior management of these majority stated-owned companies see their role as that of keeping the government happy at all costs. Clearly, there is plenty of room to improve China's corporate governance system.

Source: J. Cheung, "Shortcomings in China's Corporate Governance Regime," *China Law & Practice*, February 2007: 1.

extreme, sold their shares. Over the past decade in many of the world's larger markets, however, shareholder activism has resulted in a number of more direct and aggressive actions. Now disgruntled shareholders may actively seek the board's and other shareholders' support in removing and replacing management. Activist shareholders, although still considered a troublesome element by many existing management teams, are actually an increasingly powerful device in getting shareholder concerns heard through annual meetings, online ballots and voting, and general public disclosure of concern and unhappiness.

Executive Pay

The financial crisis of 2007–2009 raised many questions over executive pay and compensation in the corporate sector, particularly in many of the world's largest and most recognizable financial institutions. With the emergency sale of Bear Stearns, the failure of Lehman Brothers, and the government-financed bailouts of corporations like AIG in the United States, what was seen as excessive compensation for many in these corporations became the object of much debate. Issues spanned the full spectrum of the role compensation plays in business, from the financial incentives for individuals and organizations to originate and securitize what ultimately proved to be bad real estate loans, to the bonuses paid executives in companies that were failing or about to fail or had failed but been bailed out.

Executive pay differs dramatically across countries. Many analysts believe that the roots of the recent global financial crisis involving the Lehman Brothers and AIGs of the world resulted from U.S. executive pay. It is estimated that the average senior executive in the United States today receives 400 times the pay of the company's lowest paid worker. This is a significant difference from the ten times estimate for workers in Japan and western European firms. That income differential, combined with the focus on stock option–based compensation in the U.S. marketplace, may have led to an extreme short-term focus of business and financial decision making in recent years.

Market for Corporate Control

An external force is also at work in effecting management change—the market for corporate control. A firm that is underperforming, particularly for an extended period, may become the subject of either friendly or hostile takeover activities. Depending on the marketplace, an outside investor may conduct what is termed a "creeping takeover," slowly accumulating shares over time, gradually gaining more and more relative equity and voting strength. In some markets, like that of the countries of the European Union, an outside investor is limited to an accumulation of shares to 30 percent. After that point, the aggressor must offer all remaining investors a single, across-the-board price for their shares, offering to buy all remaining outstanding shares. This is intended to protect the minority shareholders' interest.

CORPORATE RESPONSIBILITY AND SUSTAINABILITY

4. To differentiate between corporate governance, corporate responsibility, and corporate sustainability, and what attributes society increasingly expects from responsible organizations

Sustainable development is development that meets the needs of the present without compromising the ability of future generations to meet their own needs.
—Brundtland Report, 1987, p. 54

What is the purpose of the corporation? This basic question, which we defined earlier as creating value for either the stockholder or for all stakeholders, has grown in importance in the twenty-first century. It is increasingly accepted that the purpose of the corporation is to certainly create profits and value for its stakeholders, but the responsibility of the corporation is to do so in a way that inflicts no costs on the environment and society. As a result of globalization, this growing responsibility and role of the corporation in society has added an additional level of complexity to the modern corporation never seen before.

The discussion has been somewhat hampered to date by a lot of conflicting terms and labels—corporate goodness, corporate responsibility, **corporate social responsibility (CSR)**, corporate philanthropy, and **corporate sustainability**, to list but a few. We will try to simplify the confusion along a number of different principles, one being that sustainability is often described as a goal, while responsibility is an obligation of the corporation. If it is differentiable, the obligation is to pursue profit, social development, and the environment along sustainable principles.

The term *sustainable* has evolved greatly within the context of global business in the past decade. One of the traditional primary objectives of the family-owned business was the "sustainability of the organization"—the long-term ability of the company to remain commercially viable and provide security and income for future generations of the family. Although narrower in scope than the concept of environmental sustainability, it does share a common core thread—the ability of a company, a culture, or even the earth to survive and renew over time. As documented by Focus on Ethics, there is considerable confusion, even among consumers, on what sustainability really means.

TRIPLE BOTTOM LINE

. . . balancing economic growth, social development, and environmental protection, so that future generations are not compromised by actions taken today.
—2008 Sustainability Report, ExxonMobil Corporation

Nearly two decades ago, a number of large corporations began to refine their publicly acknowledged corporate objective as "the pursuit of the triple bottom line." This triple bottom line—profitability, social responsibility, and environmental sustainability—was considered an enlightened development of modern capitalism. What some critics referred to as a softer and gentler form of market capitalism was a growing acceptance on the part of the corporation for doing something more than generating a financial profit.

There are a variety of theoretical rationalizations for this more expanded view of corporate responsibilities, one of which divides the arguments along two channels, the economic channel and the moral channel:

corporate social responsibility (CSR) To operate an organization in a manner which will both assure a profitable and sustainable future for the organization's primary stakeholders while having positive and managed impacts on both society and the environment. (Also frequently referred to as *corporate responsibility*.)

corporate sustainability The corporate pursuit of long-term profitability and viability while making positive contributions to both society and the environment.

FOCUS ON ETHICS

Consumers Are Confused by Sustainability

- Nearly half of consumers (44 percent) are confused by the term *sustainability*.
- Close to three-quarters of consumers do not know which products (75 percent) or companies (71 percent) are sustainable.
- About one-third of consumers (34 percent) are willing to pay a premium for sustainable goods despite the economic downturn.
- About one in five consumers (21 percent) are actually buying more sustainability.

Source: Sustainability: The Rise of Consumer Responsibility, The Harman Group Inc., January 2009.

- The economic channel argues that by pursuing corporate sustainability objectives the corporation is actually still pursuing profitability, but is doing so with a more intelligent longer-term perspective—sometimes referred to as "enlightened self-interest." It has realized that a responsible organization must ensure that its actions over time, whether or not required by law or markets, conduct its business in a way which does not reduce future choices.

- The moral channel argues that because the corporation has all the rights and responsibilities of a citizen, it also has the moral responsibility to act in the best interests of society and society's future, regardless of its impacts on profitability. It is recognizing that in some instances doing the right thing may have explicit costs, even to shareholders. Focus on Ethics provides one company's explanation as to why it thinks that it should be doing the right thing.

FOCUS ON ETHICS

Corporate Responsibility at Intel

"Our commitment to corporate responsibility is unwavering, even during economic downturns. Taking a proactive, integrated approach to managing our impact on local communities and the environment not only benefits people and our planet, but is good for our business. Making corporate responsibility an integral part of Intel's strategy helps us mitigate risk, build strong relationships with our stakeholders, and expand our market opportunities."

Source: Letter from our CEO, *Intel 2008 Corporate Responsibility Report*, 3.

Consider the case of a manufacturing plant that produces effluents and that can disperse those to the environment through the land, water, and air, with no real legal liabilities or requirements. It may still choose to intentionally spend the additional capital to remove the effluents in-house. Although it may have no actual legal responsibility to do so, it may choose to remove the effluents because it knows that it would be imposing an environmental cost on society that is real. It is correcting, on its own, a market failure.[12]

But is this the purpose of the corporation, or is this a reflection of a market failure being righted by an agency failure, in which the leaders of the company are undertaking personal agenda items at the expense of the stockholder (or possibly other stakeholders)? It might be doing it because the leadership of the corporation believes it is the right thing to do. Alternatively, if society increasingly expects the corporation to act in this way, it makes economic sense for the firm to pursue these activities in increasing its corporate reputation, the value of its brand, and its general image in the eyes of the potential customer. These two arguments both could represent an enlightened self-interest.

A second debate is whether the corporation itself is actually competent in this arena. Does it possess any core competency to pursue specific social and environmental objectives that are not traditional fields of organizational experience and expertise? This has been debated in a number of specific industrial sectors. For example, would a large multinational integrated oil and gas company really be expected to pursue wind or biofuels research and development when it has no experience or competence in these scientific or technology areas? Should that same oil and gas company, when developing oil fields in sub-Saharan Africa, also be expected to build schools and hospitals and provide ongoing educational or medical services? Although its business activities in no way altered these sectors, should it still invest the capital and incur the expenses of providing these services because it is capable of it?

Table 10.3 Ranking Corporate Responsibility Issues

Rank	Issue	United States	Britain	Germany	China	Brazil
1	The environment	21	2	2	1	
2	Safer products	5	4	6	3	2
3	Retirement benefits	42	1	4	7	
4	Health-care benefits	15	8	1	8	
5	Affordable products	6	3	3	5	3
6	Human-rights standards	88	9	9	4	
7	Workplace conditions	9	10	4	7	6
8	Job losses from outsourcing	3	6	5	13	13
9	Privacy and security	77	7	6		10
10	Ethically produced products	10	9	10	8	9
11	Investment in developing countries	16	11	14	12	5
12	Ethical advertising and marketing	12	12	16	11	11
13	Political influence of companies	11	14	12	14	14
14	Executive pay	151	61	11	1	5
15	Other	131	31	51	51	2
16	Opposition to free trade	14	15	13	15	16

Source: McKinsey Global Survey, September 2007.

DIFFERING PERCEPTIONS ON RESPONSIBILITY

The goals, governance, and responsibilities of the corporation today go far beyond the simple concept of financial profit. Firms are responsible not only for their impact on the environment; the impact and safety of their products, services, and activities on human health and the quality of life of their employees both during and after employment—and may even extend beyond their own direct activities—but the resulting changes and affects of their business on social and environmental systems. If at times it seems a bit overwhelming—well, you are probably right.

One example of differing perceptions on corporate responsibility is presented in Table 10.3. This survey indicated a very different ranking of the corporation's responsibilities across countries. Clearly, the environment is either first or second in importance across countries. But after that, the differences are dramatic. Health-care benefits, retirement benefits, and product safety all rank in the top two across the countries surveyed. Note, however, that the top issues of agreed-upon corporate responsibility focus on the company's business (the customer), its people, and the environment.

A QUESTION OF TRUST

The current and future role and responsibilities of business—and the corporation—are in many ways ultimately dependent on the degree of trust that the people have in business. If the people believe that business can largely be trusted to act in the best interests of both society and their principal stakeholders, then business will receive society's support and less of society's restrictions and regulations. If, however, society increasingly questions business's ability to consistently do the right thing, then business will most likely find itself under increasing scrutiny. That scrutiny may result in the rise of more regulatory oversight of business and the rise of perceived society interest over the interests of individual interests in pursuit of profit and competitiveness in the recently trumpeted advance of market economics.

One interesting indicator of where this question currently rests is in surveys of attitudes and trust such as those conducted by Edelman and others. Figure 10.5 presents the results of Edelman's Trust Barometer, mid-year 2009. The results for the

Figure 10.5   Survey Results on Trust in Business

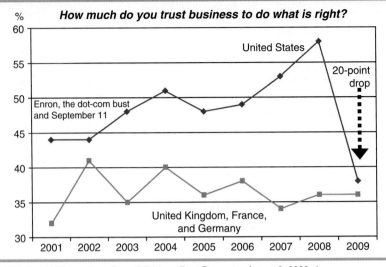

How much do you trust business to do what is right?

Source: "2009 Special Midyear Trust Survey," Edelman Trust Barometer, August 3, 2009, 1.

public surveys of trust by residents of the United States compared to other major western European countries is interesting, in that although trust in business in the United States fell to a very low level in January 2009 following the major financial crises and bank failures in the fall of 2008, trust in the United States was still just above that of the average for the United Kingdom, France, and Germany. That said, the fall in the trust in the ability of business in the United States to do the right thing was remarkably lower than that seen even following the Enron debacle in 2000 and 2001, the period of crisis which led directly to the passage of Sarbanes-Oxley.

The differing perceptions of different cultures to the trustworthiness of business is obvious in Figure 10.6. Here it is clear that, at least for two emerging market cultures—India and China—the public holds greater faith in business to do what is right (for society) than in the United States and United Kingdom.

Figure 10.6   Trust in Business Across Cultures

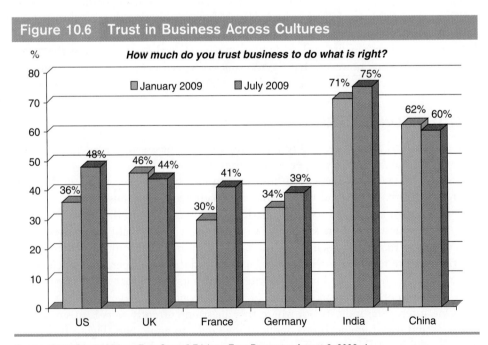

How much do you trust business to do what is right?

Source: "2009 Special Midyear Trust Survey," Edelman Trust Barometer, August 3, 2009, 4.

SUMMARY

The global recession of the past few years posed a major test for the corporation's true commitment to corporate responsibility. Society, and actually the corporate sector itself, watched closely what would happen to corporate responsibility activities during hard times. Although there was clearly a reduction in financial resources devoted to responsibility, to the corporate sector's credit, it was not abandoned. In fact, there was a rather surprising resiliency of corporate activities on both environmental (carbon emissions reductions particularly) and community concerns.

There is a growing belief that there is an emerging consensus on the critical role corporate responsibility plays in the long-term success of the firm. Although a core of good business capability—core competency in its business line—is a requirement for long-term success, it may not be sufficient. In coming years it may be also necessary that the corporation establish a proven commitment to corporate responsibility. Both elements—business acumen and corporate responsibility—may be the required elements for the corporation's long-term success in the new era of globalization.

KEY TERMS

corporation   333
stakeholders   335
maximization of shareholder
    value   337
stakeholder capitalism   338

dividend yield   338
capital gains   338
initial public offering (IPO)   339
fiduciary responsibility   340
agency theory   340

corporate governance   342
transparency   350
corporate social responsibility
    (CSR)   353
corporate sustainability   353

QUESTIONS FOR DISCUSSION

1. How would you describe, technically, a *corporation*?

2. Who are the stakeholders of a corporation? How would you either rank or prioritize their interests?

3. How do corporations profit their owners? How is this different between publicly traded companies and privately held companies?

4. What is *shareholder wealth maximization*?

5. What is *stakeholder capitalism*? How does it differ from *shareholder wealth maximization*?

6. The term *corporate governance* is used frequently, but few people truly understand what it means. How would you define it to aid in their understanding?

7. What is the difference between *internal forces* and *external forces* in corporate governance?

8. What factors or forces have led to the development of different corporate governance regimes around the world?

9. Does good governance really matter? Does it have value?

10. What principles in governance have been the focus of governance reform?

11. How would you differentiate between *corporate responsibility* and *corporate sustainability*?

TAKE A STAND

A corporation has a multitude of stakeholders, including employees and owners. During major downturns in business like that of the global recession of 2008–2009, companies suffer losses in sales and, ultimately, profits. One regular response by businesses during bad economic times is to reduce costs, which may include laying off workers to reduce wage and other labor-related expenses.

For Discussion

1. In order for a company to stay competitive and produce returns for its stockholders over time, it needs to reduce employment during downturns in business cycles. This is done to try and preserve minimal profit margins for ownership, and in the case of publicly traded companies, keep a higher share price.

2. A company can choose, even during economic downturns, to try and preserve employment of its workers even if it means reduced profits for the company's owners. Although the company's cost structure may be higher than some other competitors during bad business times, it may enjoy increased employee commitment over time which will yield greater returns in the long run.

CHAPTER 11

Organization, Implementation, and Control

CHAPTER CONTENTS & LEARNING OBJECTIVES

ORGANIZATIONAL STRUCTURE

1. To describe alternative organizational structures for international operations

IMPLEMENTATION

2. To highlight factors affecting decisions about the structure of international organizations

3. To indicate roles for country organizations in the development of strategy and implementation of programs

CONTROLS

4. To outline the need for and challenges of controls in international operations

Globalization is at the heart of Procter & Gamble's structuring of its organization. This global structure replaced a region-driven apparatus with the goal of making employees stretch themselves and speed up innovation as well as moving products and processes across borders.

Four pillars—global business units, market development organizations, global business services, and corporate functions—form the heart of P&G's organizational structure:

- Global business units (GBU) build major global brands with robust business strategies.
- Market development organizations (MDO) build local understanding as a foundation for marketing campaigns.
- Global business services (GBS) provide business technology and services that drive business success.
- Corporate functions (CF) work to maintain our place as a leader of our industries.

How the new organization works can be highlighted with an example. The GBUs define the equity, or what a brand stands for. The Pantene brand, for example, gives a customer healthy, shiny hair, and a Pantene Team within the Health and Beauty Care GBU is charged with building on this. It starts with product initiatives or upgrades, which ideally would be launched simultaneously around the world. It includes a marketing campaign that communicates the same fundamental benefit around the world, and it includes manufacturing the product against global formula and package specifications.

The MDOs then ensure Pantene excels in their region. In the United States, this could mean focusing on club stores, which might entail partnering with the GBU to develop large-size packaging the outlet demands to maximize value for their shoppers. Conversely, the focus in Latin America might be to develop the smallest possible package, like a sachet, because consumers in that region want to minimize their out-of-pocket costs. The outcome should be the same overall brand equity, but very different executions by region. The GBS center in Costa Rica would be providing support for both the U.S. and Latin America MDOs in this example (and for any other brand business team from these regions). Some of the services would include accounting, employee benefits and payroll, order management and product logistics, and systems operations. Those working directly on the business teams would likely determine the amount of corporate function support. Each function would want to ensure that it is capitalizing on the latest thinking or methodologies for each discipline. In this capacity, think of CFs as a consulting group ready to provide service if called upon.

Changes to P&G's culture should create an environment that produces bolder, mind-stretching goals and plans bigger innovations with greater speed. For example, the reward system has been redesigned to better link executive compensation with new business goals and results. Collaborative technologies, including chat rooms on the company's intranet, are transforming the company's conservative culture to one that encourages employees to be candid, test boundaries, and take chances.

Sources: Procter & Gamble Annual Report, 2009; A. G. Lafley, "What Only the CEO Can Do," *Harvard Business Review* 87 (May 2009): 54–62; "It Was a No-Brainer," *Fortune*, February 21, 2005, 96–102; "P&G Profits by Paradox," *Advertising Age*, February 24, 2004, 18–19, 31; Sonoo Singh, "P&G Opens Up Its Doors and Its Ears," *Marketing Week*, February 13, 2003.

	Global Business Units (GBU)	Market Development Organizations (MDO)	Global Business Services (GBS)	Corporate Functions (CF)
Philosophy:	Think Globally	Act Locally	Minimize Administrative Costs	Be the Smartest/Best
General Role:	Create strong brand equities, robust strategies, and ongoing innovation in product and marketing to build major global brands.	Interface with customers to ensure marketing plans fully capitalize on local understanding, to seek synergy across programs to leverage corporate scale, and to develop strong programs that change the game in our favor at point of purchase.	Bring together transactional activities such as accounting and order management in a single organization to provide services to all P&G units at best-in-class quality, cost, and speed.	Ensure that the functional capability integrated into the rest of the company remains on the cutting edge of the industry. We want to be the thought leader within each CF.
There Are:	**Three GBUs:** • Beauty • Health and Well-Being • Household Care	**Seven MDO Regions:** • North America • ASEAN/Australia/India/Korea • Japan • Greater China • Central-Eastern Europe/Middle East/Africa • Western Europe • Latin America	**Three GBS Centers:** • GBS Americas located in Costa Rica • GBS Asia located in Manila • GBS Europe, Middle East & Africa located in Newcastle	**Nine CFs:** • Customer Business Development • Finance and Accounting • Human Resources • Information Technology • Legal • Marketing • Consumer and Market Knowledge • Product Supply • Research and Development

As companies evolve from purely domestic to multinational, their organizational structure, implementation, and control systems must change to reflect new strategies. With growth comes diversity in terms of products and services, geographic markets, and people in the company itself, bringing along a set of challenges for the company. Three critical issues are basic to all of these challenges: (1) the type of organization that provides the best framework for operational effectiveness; (2) the optimal approach to implementing corporate strategy globally, regionally, and locally; and (3) the type and degree of control to be exercised from headquarters to maximize total effort. [1] Organizational structures, organizations' abilities to implement strategies, and control systems have to be adjusted as market conditions change, as seen in the chapter's opening vignette. While some units are charged with the development of global strategies, others are charged with local adaptation and creating synergies across programs.

ORGANIZATIONAL STRUCTURE

The basic functions of an organization are to provide (1) a route and locus of decision making and coordination and (2) a system for reporting and communications. Increasingly, the coordination and communication dimensions have to include learning from the global marketplace through the company's different units. [2] These networks are typically depicted in the organizational chart.

1. To describe alternative organizational structures for international operations

ORGANIZATIONAL DESIGNS

The basic configurations of international organizations correspond to those of purely domestic ones; the greater the degree of internalization, the more complex the structures can become. The types of structures that companies use to manage foreign activities can be divided into three categories, based on the degree of internationalization:

1. Little or no formal organizational recognition of international activities of the firm. This category ranges from domestic operations handling an occasional international transaction on an ad hoc basis to firms with separate export departments.
2. International division. Firms in this category recognize the ever-growing importance of the international involvement.
3. Global organizations. These can be structured by product, area, function, process, or customer, but ignore the traditional domestic–international split.

Hybrid structures may exist as well, in which one market may be structured by product, another by areas. Matrix organizations have merged in large multinational corporations to combine product-specific, regional, and functional expertise. As worldwide competition has increased dramatically in many industries, the latest organizational response is networked global organizations in which heavy flows of hardware, software, and personnel take place between strategically interdependent units to establish greater global integration.

The ability to identify and disseminate best practices throughout the organization is an important competitive advantage for global companies. For example, a U.S. automaker found that in the face of distinctive challenges presented by the local environment, Brazilian engineers developed superior seals, which the company then incorporated in all its models worldwide. [3] The increasing enthusiasm for outsourcing has put new demands on managing relationships with independent partners. Boeing, for example, holds a partners' council meeting every six weeks and has set up a network that makes it possible for designers (both at Boeing and suppliers) to work on the same up-to-the-minute database. Virtual meetings with colleagues in different time zones take place throughout the day.[4]

Little or No Formal Organization

In the very early stages of international involvement, domestic operations assume responsibility for international activities. The role of international activities in the sales and profits of the corporation is initially so minor that no organizational adjustment takes place. No consolidation of information or authority over international sales is undertaken or is necessary. Transactions are conducted on a case-by-case basis, either by the resident expert or quite often with the help of facilitating agents, such as freight forwarders.

As demand from the international marketplace grows and interest within the firm expands, the organizational structure will reflect it. An export department appears as a separate entity. This may be an outside export management company—that is, an independent company that becomes the de facto export department of the firm. This is an indirect approach to international involvement in that very little experience is accumulated within the firm itself.

Alternatively, a firm may establish its own export department, hiring a few seasoned individuals to take responsibility for international activities. Organizationally, the department may be a subdepartment of marketing (as shown in Figure 11.1) or may have equal ranking with the various functional departments. The choice will depend on the importance assigned to overseas activities by the firm. The export department is the first real step toward internationalizing the organizational structures. It should be a full-fledged marketing organization and not merely a sales organization; i.e., it should have the resources for market research and market-development activities (such as trade show participation).

Headquartered in Hong Kong, TAL is an innovative garment manufacturer for the world's leading brands, including Banana Republic, Calvin Klein, Giordano, and L. L. Bean. The United States has traditionally been TAL's main market, taking 80 percent of its production, but emerging markets are now playing a larger role with demand for

Figure 11.1   The Export Department Structure (TAL)

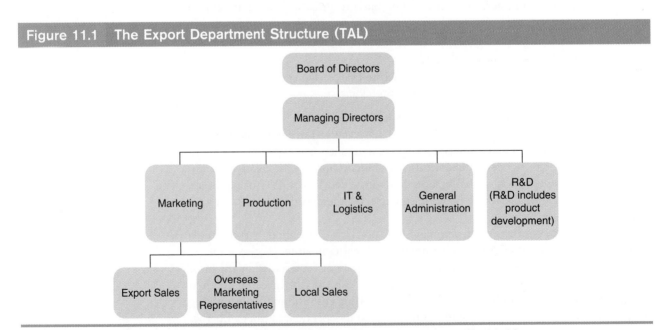

Note: TAL is centrally managed in Hong Kong, with operations in China, Indonesia, Malaysia, Thailand, Vietnam, and the United States.
Source: Hong Kong Chamber of Commerce

branded garments increasing dramatically in China and other countries. Presently, its customers in the United States and other countries report back to TAL's sales team on what has been sold on a daily basis. Within the week, garments are delivered directly to stores to replenish their stocks. TAL is centrally managed in Hong Kong with operations in the United States, China, Thailand, Indonesia, Vietnam, and Malaysia.

Licensing as an international entry mode may be assigned to the R&D function despite its importance to the overall international strategy of the firm. A formal liaison among the export, marketing, production, and R&D functions has to be formed for the maximum utilization of licensing.[5] If licensing indeed becomes a major activity for the firm, a separate manager should be appointed.

The more the firm becomes involved in foreign markets, the more quickly the export department structure will become obsolete. For example, the firm may undertake joint ventures or direct foreign investment, which require those involved to have functional experience. The firm therefore typically establishes an international division.

Some firms that acquire foreign production facilities pass through an additional stage in which foreign subsidiaries report directly to the president or to a manager specifically assigned the duty. However, the amount of coordination and control that are required quickly establish the need for a more formal international organization in the firm.

The International Division

The international division centralizes in one entity, with or without separate incorporation, all of the responsibility for international activities, as illustrated in Figure 11.2 (Timberland is a global leader in the design and marketing of premium-quality footwear, apparel, and accessories throughout North America, Europe, Asia, Latin America, South Africa and the Middle East). The approach aims to eliminate a possible bias against international operations that may exist if domestic divisions are allowed to serve international customers independently. In some cases, international markets have been treated as secondary to domestic markets. The international division concentrates international expertise, information flows concerning foreign market opportunities, and authority over international activities. However, manufacturing and other related functions remain with the domestic divisions to take advantage of economies of scale.

To avoid putting the international division at a disadvantage in competing for products, personnel, and corporate services, coordination between domestic and international operations is necessary. Coordination can be achieved through a joint staff or by requiring domestic and international divisions to interact in strategic planning and to submit the plans to headquarters. Further, many corporations require and encourage frequent interaction between domestic and international personnel to discuss common problems in areas such as product planning. Coordination is also important because domestic operations are typically organized along product or functional lines, whereas international divisions are geographically oriented.

International divisions best serve firms with few products that do not vary significantly in terms of their environmental sensitivity and with international sales and profits that are still quite insignificant compared with those of the domestic divisions.[6] Companies may outgrow their international divisions as their sales outside of the domestic market grow in significance, diversity, and complexity. European companies have traditionally used international divisions far less than their U.S. counterparts due to the relatively small size of their domestic markets. Timberland divides its operations between two U.S. divisions and an international division. With Timberland's North American share of sales decreasing from 55.5 percent in 2006 to 47.8 percent in 2008, Timberland may see a need for a different structure in the future.[7] International divisions were once quite popular among U.S. companies, but globalization of markets and increased shares of overseas sales have made them less suitable

Figure 11.2 The International Division Structure (Timberland)

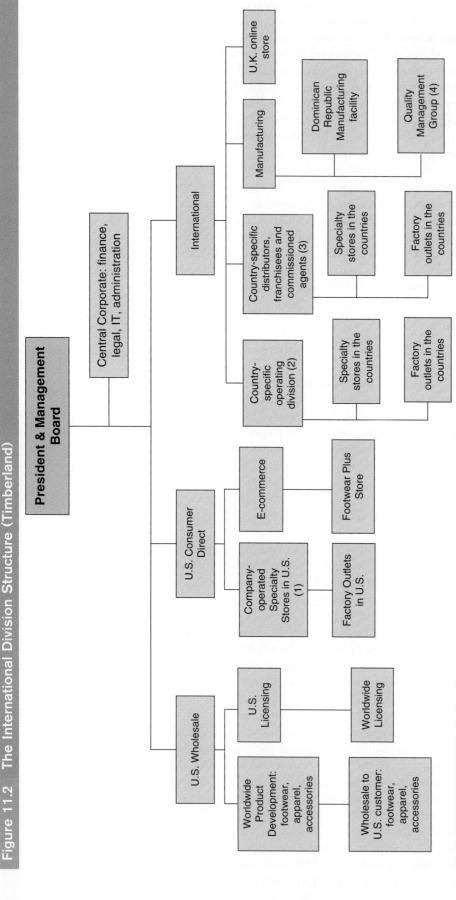

* Timberland has operating divisions in the United Kingdom, Italy, France, Germany, Switzerland, Spain, Japan, Hong Kong, Taiwan, Singapore, Malaysia, and Canada.

The distribution covers Europe, Asia, Middle East, Africa, Central America and South America. Products are sold to Chinese and Russian market through distributors in the countries.

The quality management group has offices in Bangkok, Thailand; Zhu Hai, China; Hong Kong; Ho Chi Minh City, Vietnam; Istanbul, Turkey; and Chennai, India. These offices are responsible for supervising the sourcing activities in the Asia-Pacific region.

than more global structures. Kraft Foods, a notable exception among consumer goods companies, was still using the international division structure in 2009, with sales from international customers at approximately 40 percent. Kraft's successful acquisition of Cadbury Schweppes will most likely result in a complete transformation of the combined company's structure because international sales will probably exceed U.S. sales.

Global Organizational Structures

Global structures have grown out of competitive necessity. In many industries, competition is on a global basis, with a result that companies must have a high degree of reactive capability.

Six basic types of global structures are available:

1. Global product structure, in which product divisions are responsible for all manufacture and marketing worldwide.
2. Global area structure, in which geographic divisions are responsible for all manufacture and marketing in their respective areas.
3. Global functional structures, in which functional areas (such as production, marketing, finance, and personnel) are responsible for the worldwide operations of their own functional area.
4. Global customer structures, in which operations are structured based on distinct worldwide customer groups.
5. Mixed—or hybrid—structures, which may combine the other alternatives.
6. Matrix structures, in which operations have reporting responsibility to more than one group (typically, product, functions, or area).

Product Structure   Some form of a **product structure** is most commonly used by multinational corporations whether in its pure form or as the driver in a more complex matrix structure.[8] The pure product structure approach gives worldwide responsibility to strategic business units for the marketing of their product lines, as shown in Figure 11.3. Most consumer-product firms use some form of this approach, mainly because of the diversity of their product lines. One of the major benefits of this approach is improved cost efficiency through centralization of manufacturing facilities. This is crucial in industries in which competitive position is determined by world market share, which in turn is often determined by the degree to which manufacturing is rationalized.[9]

Adaptation to this approach has historically been associated with consolidation of operations and plant closings. A good example is Black & Decker, which groups its brands under consumer products, industrial products, and fastening and assembly systems groups and which rationalized many of its operations in its worldwide competitive effort against Makita, the Japanese power-tool manufacturer.

In a similar move, Ford merged its large and culturally distinct European and North American auto operations by vehicle platform type to make more efficient use of its engineering and product development resources against rapidly globalizing rivals.[10] The Ford Focus, Ford's compact car was designed by one team of engineers for worldwide markets. With competitive pressures on the automotive industry intensifying, many automotive companies have consolidated and reorganized for greater efficiency. Emerging from Chapter 11 reorganization in 2008, U.S.–based Dura Automotive Systems announced its shift from a regional organization structure to four global business units, each headquartered in either the United States or Germany. These four units were organized around product lines for sales to global automakers including cable systems, shifter systems, glass and trim systems, and structural and safety systems.[11]

product structure An organizational structure in which product divisions are responsible for all manufacturing and marketing.

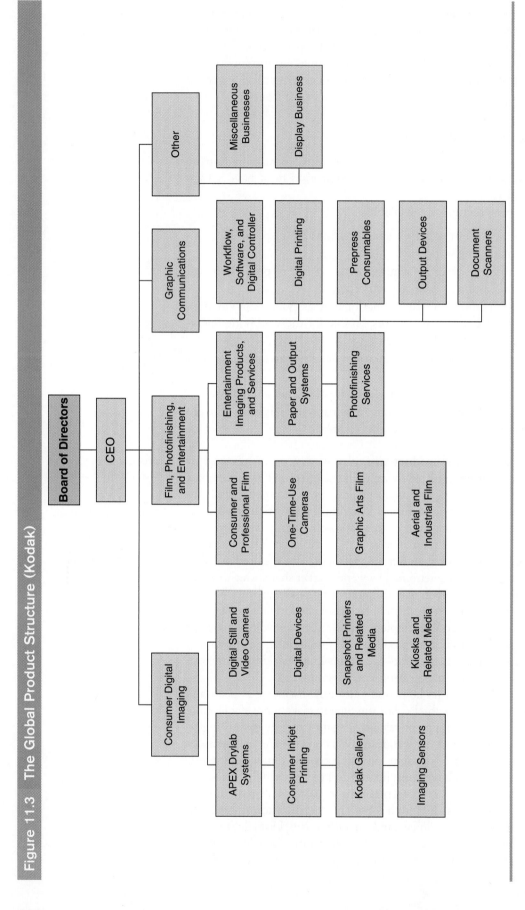

Figure 11.3 The Global Product Structure (Kodak)

Other benefits of the product structure are the ability to balance the functional inputs needed for a product and the ability to react quickly to product-specific problems in the marketplace. Even smaller brands receive individual attention. Product-specific attention is important because products vary in terms of the adaptation they need for different foreign markets. All in all, the product approach is ideally suited to the development of a global strategic focus in response to global competition.

At the same time, the product structure fragments international expertise within the firm because a central pool of international experience no longer exists. The structure assumes that managers will have adequate regional experience or advice to allow them to make balanced decisions. Coordination of activities among the various product groups operating in the same markets is crucial to avoid unnecessary duplication of basic tasks. For some of these tasks, such as market research, special staff functions may be created and then filled by the product divisions when needed. If they lack an appreciation for the international dimension, product managers may focus their attention only on the larger markets or only on the domestic, and fail to take the long-term view.

Area Structure   The second most used approach is the **area structure**. Such firms are organized on the basis of geographical areas; for example, operations may be divided into those dealing with Asia-Pacific, North America, Latin America, and Europe. Ideally, no special preference is given to the region in which the headquarters is located—for example, North America or Europe. Central staffs are responsible for providing coordination support for worldwide planning and control activities performed at headquarters.

area structure An organizational structure in which geographic divisions are responsible for all manufacturing and marketing in their respective areas.

Regional integration continues to play a major role in area restructuring; for example, many multinational corporations have located their European headquarters in Brussels, where the EU has its headquarters. Brussels is a top choice for law and lobbying firms, consulting companies, accounting firms, and nongovernmental organizations. For some companies, economic integration as a result of NAFTA has led to the formation of North American divisions in place of specific U.S. divisions. German manufacturing companies like Schneider Electric and Trumpf have created North American operational units that operate across the United States, Mexico, and Canada.

The driver of structural choices may also be cultural similarity, such as in the case of Asia, or historic connections between countries, such as in the case of combining Europe with the Middle East and Africa. As new markets emerge, they may be first delegated to an established country organization for guidance with the ultimate objective of having them be equal partners with others in the organization.

The area approach follows the marketing concept most closely because individual areas and markets are given concentrated attention. If market conditions with respect to product acceptance and operating conditions vary dramatically, the area approach is the one to choose. Companies opting for this alternative typically have relatively narrow product lines with similar end uses and end users. However, expertise is needed in adapting the product and its marketing to local market conditions. Once again, to avoid duplication of effort in product management and in functional areas, staff specialists—for product categories, for example—may be used.

Without appropriate coordination from the staff, essential information and experience may not be transferred from one regional entity to another. Also, if the company expands its product lines and if end markets begin to diversify, the area structure may become inappropriate.

Some managers may feel that going into a global product structure may be too much, too quickly, and opt, therefore, to have a regional organization for planning and reporting purposes. The objective may also be to keep profit or sales centers of similar size at similar levels in the corporate hierarchy. If a group of countries has small sales as compared with other country operations, it may be consolidated into a region. The benefit of a regional operation and regional headquarters would be the more efficient coordination of programs across the region (as opposed to globally), a more sensitized management to country-market operations in the region, and the ability to have the region's voice heard more clearly at global headquarters (as compared to what an individual, especially smaller, country operation could achieve).[12]

functional structure An organizational structure in which departments are formed on the basis of functional areas such as production, marketing, and finance.

Functional Structure   Of all the approaches, the **functional structure** is the simplest from the administrative viewpoint because it emphasizes the basic tasks of the firm—for example, manufacturing, sales, and research and development. The approach works best when both products and customers are relatively few and similar in nature. Coordination is typically the key problem, therefore, staff functions have been created to interact between the functional areas. Otherwise, the company's operational and regional expertise may not be exploited to the fullest extent possible.

process structure A variation of the functional structure in which departments are formed on the basis of production processes.

A variation of the functional approach is one that uses processes as a basis for structure. The **process structure** is common in the energy and mining industries, where one corporate entity may be in charge of exploration worldwide and another may be responsible for the actual mining operations.

customer structure An organizational structure in which divisions are formed on the basis of customer groups.

Customer Structure   Firms may also organize their operations using the **customer structure**, especially if the customer groups they serve are dramatically different—for example, consumers and businesses and governments. Catering to such diverse groups may require concentrating specialists in particular divisions. The product may be the same, but the buying processes of the various customer groups may differ. Governmental buying is characterized by bidding, in which price plays a larger role than when businesses are the buyers. However, increasingly products and solutions are developed around capabilities, such as networked communications, that can be used by more than one service or agency.[13] Similarly, in financial institutions, it is important to know whether customers who signed up for one service are already customers for other services being provided by the institution.[14]

mixed structure An organizational structure that combines two or more organizational dimensions; for example, products, areas, or functions.

Mixed Structure   In some cases, mixed, or hybrid, organizations exist. A **mixed structure** combines two or more organizational dimensions simultaneously. It permits adequate attention to product, area, or functional needs as is needed by the company. The approach may only be a result of a transitional period after a merger or an acquisition, or it may come about due to unique market characteristics or product line. It may also provide a useful structure before the implementation of a worldwide matrix structure.

Naturally, organizational structures are never as clear-cut and simple as presented here. Whatever the basic format is, product, functional, and area inputs are needed. Alternatives could include an initial product structure that would subsequently have regional groupings or an initial regional structure with subsequent product groupings. However, in the long term, coordination and control across such structures become tedious.

matrix structure An organizational structure that uses functional and divisional structures simultaneously.

Matrix Structure   Many multinational corporations, in an attempt to facilitate planning for, organizing, and controlling interdependent businesses, critical resources, strategies, and geographic regions, have adopted the **matrix structure**.[15] Business is driven by a worldwide business unit (e.g., photographic products or commercial and information systems) and implemented through a geographic unit (e.g., Europe or Latin America). The geographical units, as well as their country subsidiaries, serve as "the glue" between autonomous product operations.

Organizational matrices integrate the various approaches already discussed, as the example in Figure 11.4 illustrates. Matrices vary in terms of their areas of emphasis and the number of dimensions. For example, Dow Chemical's structure reflects its diversified

Figure 11.4 Global Matrix Structure

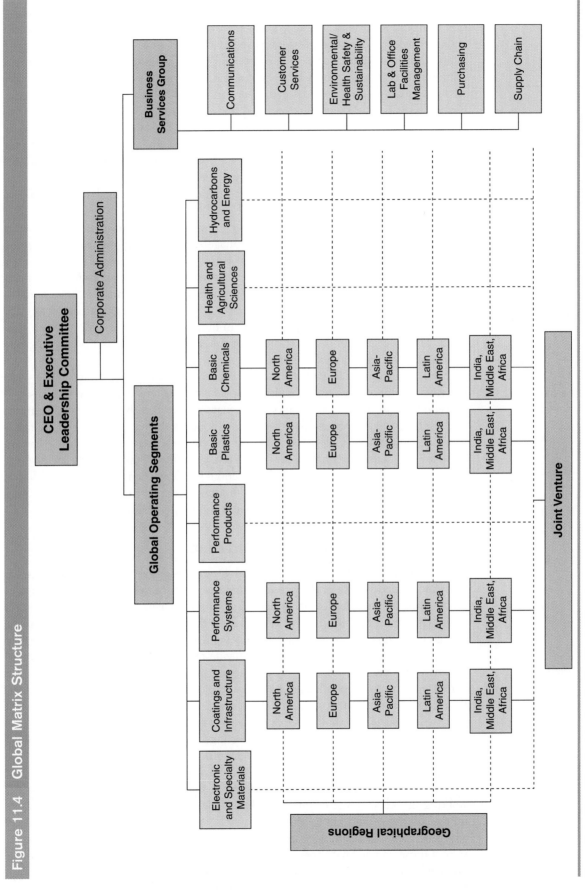

Source: Derived from information taken from the Dow Chemical Company.

chemicals business and global spread that became even more so with the 2009 acquisition of Rohm and Haas. In 2008, Dow employed approximately 46,000 people in 35 countries, while Rohm and Haas employed 15,000 people in 30 countries. Dow has a multidimensional matrix consisting of five geographic areas, eight operating segments that include both wholly owned operations and joint ventures, and the new Dow business services group that provides global support capabilities to the operating segments. Each of the operating segments has sales and marketing, research and development, engineering and manufacturing, and finance functions. The business services group consists of four operating units: the business process service center, project and support centers, asset operations, and consulting and expertise services. These provide operational support in focused service functions that include communications, customer service, environment/health safety and sustainability, information systems, lab and office facilities management, purchasing, and supply chain.[16]

The matrix approach helps cut through enormous organizational complexities in making business managers, functional managers, and strategy managers cooperate. However, the matrix requires sensitive, well-trained middle managers who can cope with problems that arise from reporting to two bosses—possibly a product-line manager and an area manager. For example, every management unit may have a multidimensional reporting relationship that may cross functional, regional, or operational lines. On a regional basis, group managers in Europe, for example, report administratively to a vice president of operations for Europe, but report functionally to group vice presidents at global headquarters.

Most companies have found the matrix arrangement problematic.[17] The dual-reporting channel easily causes conflict, complex issues are forced into a two-dimensional decision framework, and even minor issues may have to be solved through committee discussion. Ideally, managers should solve the problems themselves through formal and informal communication; however, physical and psychic distance often makes that impossible. The matrix structure, with its inherent complexity, may actually increase the reaction time of a company—a potentially serious problem when competitive conditions require quick responses. As a result, the authority has started to shift in many organizations from area to product, although the matrix still may officially be used.

Evolution of Organizational Structures

Companies have been shown to develop new structures in a pattern of stages as their products diversify and share of foreign sales increases.[18] At the first stage of autonomous subsidiaries reporting directly to top management, the establishment of an international division follows. As product diversity and the importance of the foreign marketplace increase, companies develop global structures to coordinate subsidiary operations and to rationalize worldwide production. As multinational corporations have been faced with simultaneous pressures to adapt to local market conditions and to rationalize production and globalize competitive reactions, many have opted for the matrix structure. The matrix structure probably allows a corporation to best meet the challenges of global markets (to be global and local, big and small, decentralized with centralized reporting) by allowing the optimizing of businesses globally and maximizing performance in every country of operation.[19] The evolutionary process is summarized in Figure 11.5.

Whatever the organizational arrangement may be, the challenge of employees working in "silos" remains. Employee knowledge tends to be fragmented, with one unit's experience and know-how inaccessible to other units. Therefore, the wheel gets reinvented each time—at considerable cost to the company and to the frustration of those charged with tasks. Information technology can be used to synchronize knowledge across even the most complicated and diverse organizations.[20] At Procter & Gamble, for example, brand managers use a standardized, worldwide ad-testing

Figure 11.5   Evolution of International Structures

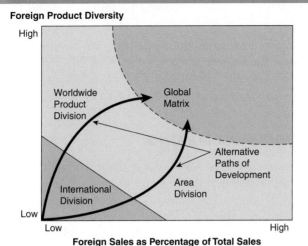

Source: From Christopher A. Bartlett, "Building and Managing the Transnational: The New Organizational Challenge," in *Competition in Global Industries*, ed. Michael E. Porter (Boston: Harvard Business School Press, 1986), 368.

system that allows them to access every ad the company has ever run, providing examples of how to meet particular needs at a particular time. Once knowledge transfer is established, what may be needed is a form of organization in which individuals and teams decide for themselves what to do, but are accountable for the results.[21] (See the Focus on Management box for more information.)

FOCUS ON MANAGEMENT

Organizing for Growth

With global corporations increasingly finding revenue growth in emerging markets and scale in the developed countries, they are adapting their geographic organizational structures to fit the new scenario. Each company must decide what locations make the most sense for efficient management and operations given their unique businesses and customer distribution patterns.

Some companies group growth markets as a whole category. In 2008, IBM formed a "Growth Markets" organization based in Shanghai, with regional headquarters in Dubai and São Paulo, to address high potential markets globally. This unit covers about 50 countries across Asia, Africa, eastern Europe, and Latin America.

Traditionally, companies that organize regionally, even within matrix structures, have followed reasonably predictable patterns in establishing international management centers. Usually, companies will organize with a central corporate headquarters and regional headquarters set up to handle specific geographic regions such as North America, Latin America, Europe, Asia, the Middle East, and Africa. In addition to its Bentonville, Arkansas, corporate and U.S. headquarters, Walmart Stores has a regional headquarters for the Americas in Miami, one for Asia in Hong Kong, and one for Europe in Leeds, England.

A gateway model to reduce the tension between global integration and local responsiveness has been proposed. As new markets emerge, the need to manage increased complexity is necessary. For example, ten gateway countries could serve as hubs for the developed markets (United States, Japan, Germany, the United Kingdom, France, Italy, Spain, Canada, Australia, and the Netherlands), and another ten countries would perform the same role for emerging markets (China, India, Brazil, Russia, Mexico, South Korea, Indonesia, Turkey, South Africa, and Thailand). Each hub would serve the gateway market as well as other similar markets. For example, the German hub would manage Austria, Hungary, and Switzerland; Brazil would support Argentina, Bolivia, Chile, Paraguay, and Uruguay. The non-hub countries would usually feature only customer contact and service. Some countries would cover all aspects of corporate activity, while some others might gradually build capabilities beyond sales. The executive committee of the company would consist of leaders from all of the hubs, with diverse experience across the key countries of the developed and developing world.

Of course, non-gateway hub countries still offer significant advantages. A late 2007 survey by Spire Research and Consulting among Asia-Pacific manufacturing companies found that Singapore, China, and Hong Kong were preferred, in order, as the best locations for regional headquarters. Singapore was number one mainly because of its economic policies, infrastructure, and political stability. In the Western Hemisphere, many companies, and many Latin American executives, value Miami as a regional headquarters location for the same kind of qualities.

Sources: C. K. Prahalad and Hrishi Bhattacharyya, "Twenty Hubs and No HQ," *Strategy and Business*, Spring 2008, 1–6; IBM press release, "IBM Signs Technology Infrastructure and Services Agreements Across Asia Pacific," October 17, 2008; Press release, Spire Research and Consulting, November 9, 2007, accessed November 5, 2009, from http://www.spireresearch.com/pdf/archive/press/PR-Nov:7RHQ.pdf.

IMPLEMENTATION

2. *To highlight factors affecting decisions about the structure of international organizations*

3. *To indicate roles for country organizations in the development of strategy and implementation of programs*

decentralization The granting of a high degree of autonomy to subsidiaries.

centralization The concentrating of control and strategic decision making at headquarters.

Organizational structures provide the frameworks for carrying out decision-making processes. However, for that decision making to be effective, a series of organizational initiatives are needed to develop strategy to its full potential, that is, to secure implementation both at the national level and across markets.[22]

LOCUS OF DECISION MAKING

Organizational structures themselves do not indicate where the authority for decision making and control rests within the organization nor will it reveal the level of coordination between the units. The different levels of coordination between country units are summarized in Table 11.1. Once a suitable structure is found, it has to be made to work by finding a balance between the center and country organizations.

If subsidiaries are granted a high degree of autonomy, the system is called **decentralization**. In decentralized systems, controls are relatively loose and simple, and the flows between headquarters and subsidiaries are mainly financial; that is, each subsidiary operates as a profit center. On the other hand, if controls are tight and the strategic decision making is concentrated at headquarters, the system is described as **centralization**. Firms are typically neither completely centralized nor decentralized. Increasingly, companies do not want constituents to think they are from anywhere in particular or want to be perceived as having a home base in each of the markets in which they operate. For example, Lenovo's main corporate functions are divided between Beijing, Singapore, and Raleigh, North Carolina.[23] Some functions of the firm—such as finance—lend themselves to more centralized decision making; others—such as promotional decisions—do so far less. Research and development in organizations is typically centralized, especially in cases of basic research work. Some companies have, partly due to governmental pressures, added R&D functions on a regional or local basis. In many cases, however, variations are product and market based; for example, in Unilever's new organization launched in 2005, managers of global business units are responsible for brand management and product development, and managers of regional market development organizations are responsible for sales, trade marketing, and media choices.[24]

The basic advantage of allowing maximum flexibility at the country-market level is that subsidiary management knows its market and can react to changes more quickly. Problems of motivation and acceptance are avoided when decision makers are also the

Table 11.1   Levels of Coordination

Level	Description
5. Central control	No national structures
4. Central direction	Central functional heads have line authority over national functions
3. Central coordination	Central staff functions in coordinating role
2. Coordinating mechanisms	Formal committees and systems
1. Informal cooperation	Functional meetings: exchange of information
0. National autonomy	No coordination between decentralized units, which may even compete in export markets

Level 5 = highest; Level 0 = lowest. Most commonly found levels are 1–4.

Source: Norman Blackwell, Jean-Pierre Bizet, Peter Child, and David Hensley, "Creating European Organizations That Work," Michael R. Czinkota and Ilkka A. Ronkainen, eds., *Readings in Global Marketing* (London: The Dryden Press, 1995): 376–385.

implementers of the strategy. On the other hand, many multinationals faced with global competitive threats and opportunities have adopted global strategy formulation, which by definition requires a higher degree of centralization. What has emerged as a result can be called **coordinated decentralization**. This means that overall corporate strategy is provided from headquarters, while subsidiaries are free to implement it within the range agreed on in consultation between headquarters and the subsidiaries.

However, companies moving into this new mode may face significant challenges. Among these systemic difficulties are a lack of widespread commitment to dismantling traditional national structures, driven by an inadequate understanding of the larger, global forces at work. Power barriers from perceived threats to the personal roles of national managers, especially if their tasks are under the threat of being consolidated into regional organizations, can lead to proposals being challenged without valid reason. Finally, some organizational initiatives (such as multicultural teams or corporate chat rooms) may be jeopardized by the fact the people do not have the necessary skills (e.g., language ability) or that an infrastructure (e.g., intranet) may not exist in an appropriate format.[25]

One particular case is of special interest. Organizationally, the forces of globalization are changing the country manager's role significantly. With profit-and-loss responsibility, oversight of multiple functions, and the benefit of distance from headquarters, country managers enjoyed considerable decision-making autonomy as well as entrepreneurial initiative when country operations were largely stand-alone. Today, however, many companies have to emphasize global and regional priorities, which means that the power has to shift at least to some extent from the country manager to worldwide strategic business unit and product-line managers. Many of the local decisions are now subordinated to global strategic moves. However, regional and local programs still require an effective local management component. Therefore, the future country manager will have to wear many hats in balancing the needs of the operation for which the manager is directly responsible with those of the entire region or strategic business unit.[26] To emphasize the importance of the global/regional dimension in the country manager's portfolio, many companies have tied the country manager's compensation to how the company performs globally or regionally, not just in the market for which the manager is responsible.

FACTORS AFFECTING STRUCTURE AND DECISION MAKING

The organizational structure and locus of decision making in a multinational corporation are determined by a number of factors, such as (1) its degree of involvement in international operations, (2) the products the firm markets, (3) the size and importance of the firm's markets, and (4) the human resource capability of the firm.[27]

The effect of the degree of involvement on structure and decision making was discussed earlier in the chapter. With low degrees of involvement, subsidiaries can enjoy high degrees of autonomy as long as they meet their profit targets. The same situation can occur even with the most globally oriented companies, but within a different framework. Consider, for example, Alcatel Lucent, which generates 30 percent of its worldwide revenues from North America, mostly from the United States. The company is organized into three geographies (Americas, Europe–Middle East–Africa, and Asia-Pacific) and three corporate functions (customer care, solutions and marketing, and quality assurance). However, its United States–based Bell Labs, the company's "innovation engine," enjoys considerable autonomy because it is at the leading edge of communications technology development, although it is still within the parent company's planning and control system.

The firm's country of origin and the political history of the area can also affect organizational structure and decision making. For example, Swiss-based Nestlé, with

coordinated decentralization Direction of overall corporate strategy by headquarters while granting subsidiaries the freedom to implement strategy within established ranges.

only 3 to 4 percent of its sales from its small domestic market, has traditionally had a highly decentralized organization. Moreover, European history for the past 80 years—particularly the two world wars—has often forced subsidiaries of European-based companies to act independently to survive.

The type and variety of products marketed will affect organizational decisions. Companies that market consumer products typically have product organizations with high degrees of decentralization, allowing for maximum local flexibility. On the other hand, companies that market technologically sophisticated products—such as GE, which markets turbines—display centralized organizations with worldwide product responsibilities.

Going global has recently meant transferring world headquarters of important business units abroad. For example, Halliburton opened a second corporate headquarters office in Dubai, United Arab Emirates, in 2007 to align with the the oil and gas business moving its focus to the Eastern Hemisphere in order to "provide new manufacturing capacity, move closer to key markets, and help reduce the costs of moving materials, products, tools, and people."[28]

Apart from situations that require the development of an area structure, the unique characteristics of particular markets or regions may require separate and specific considerations for the firm. For example, Yum Brands has a structure that emphasizes its individual brands—including KFC, Pizza Hut, Taco Bell, and Long John Silver's—but it also has three operational units—one for the U.S. market, an international division, and a separate China division (covering mainland China, Thailand and KFC Taiwan)—because of the size and strategic importance of China.[29]

The human factor in any organization is critical. Managers at both headquarters and the country organizations must bridge the physical and cultural distances separating them. If country organizations have competent managers who rarely need to consult headquarters about their challenges, they may be granted high degrees of autonomy. In the case of global organizations, local management must understand overall corporate goals in that decisions that meet the long-term objectives may not be optimal for the individual local market.

THE NETWORKED GLOBAL ORGANIZATION

No international structure is ideal, and some have challenged the wisdom of even looking for one. They have recommended attention to new processes that would, in a given structure, help to develop new perspectives and attitudes that reflect and respond to the complex, opposing demands of global integration and local responsiveness. The question thus changes from which structural alternative is best to how the different perspectives of various corporate entities can better be taken into account when making decisions. In structural terms, little may change. Philips, for example, has not changed its basic matrix structure, yet major changes have occurred in its functional sectors and its internal relations. In 2008, Philips organized on an operating sector basis with each of its three sectors—health care, consumer lifestyle, and lighting—responsible for the management of its businesses globally. In addition, Philips created an innovation and emerging businesses sector to invest in future-oriented projects outside of the operating sectors and the group management and services sector to provide support in areas such as brand management for the operating sectors. Philips operates as a networked global organization, rather than a decentralized federation model, as depicted in Figure 11.6.

Many of the most successful global companies have adopted an organizational approach that provides clear global strategic direction along with the flexibility to adapt to local opportunities and requirements. The term **glocal** has been coined to

glocal Refers to an individual, group, division, unit, organization, or community that is willing and able to think globally and act locally.

Figure 11.6   The Networked Global Organization

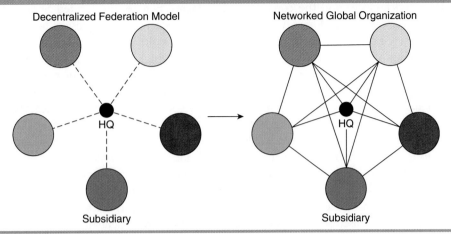

Decentralized Federation Model   Networked Global Organization

HQ   HQ

Subsidiary   Subsidiary

Source: Thomas Gross, Ernie Turner, and Lars Cederholm, "Building Teams for Global Operations," *Management Review*, June 1987 (New York: American Management Association), 34.

describe this approach. Kraft International describes the company's strategy as "to win locally and leverage globally." A Dow Chemical executive explained his company's approach, "You simply cannot develop or initiate a market penetration strategy, in an emerging country from a location thousands of miles away in which no one has seen and still be successful . . . period. You need to 'Think and Act Globally but Implement Locally.'"[30]

Companies that have adopted this approach have incorporated the following three dimensions into their organizations: (1) the development and communication of a clear corporate vision, (2) the effective management of human resource tools to broaden individual perspectives and develop identification with corporate goals, and (3) the integration of individual thinking and activities into the broad corporate agenda.[31] The first dimension relates to a clear and consistent long-term corporate mission that guides individuals wherever they work in the organization. IBM has established three values for the twenty-first century: dedication to every client's success, innovation that matters (for the company and the world), and trust and personal responsibility in all relationships.[32] Examples of this are Johnson & Johnson's corporate credo of customer focus, Coca-Cola's mission of leveraging global beverage brand leadership "to refresh the world," and Nestlé's vision to make the company the "reference for nutrition, health, and wellness."[33]

The second relates both to the development of global managers who can find opportunities in spite of environmental challenges as well as creating a global perspective among country managers. The last dimension relates to the development of a cooperative mind-set among country organizations to ensure effective implementation of global strategies. Managers may believe that global strategies are intrusions on their operations if they do not have an understanding of the corporate vision, if they have not contributed to the global corporate agenda, or if they are not given direct responsibility for its implementation. Defensive, territorial attitudes, can lead to the emergence of the "not-invented-here" syndrome, that is, country organizations objecting to or rejecting an otherwise sound strategy.[34]

For example, in an area structure, units (such as Europe and North America) may operate quite independently, sharing little expertise and information with the other units. While they are supposed to build links to headquarters and other units, they may actually be building walls. To tackle this problem, Nissan established four management committees that meet once a month to supervise regional operations. Each committee includes representatives of the major functions (e.g., manufacturing, marketing, and finance) and the committees (for Japan, Europe, the United States, and general overseas markets) are chaired by the Nissan executive vice presidents based in Japan. The CEO attends the committee meetings periodically but regularly.[35]

The network avoids the problems of effort duplication, inefficiency and resistance to ideas developed elsewhere by giving subsidiaries the latitude, encouragement, and tools to pursue local business development within the framework of the global strategy. Headquarters considers each unit a source of ideas, skills, capabilities, and knowledge that can be utilized for the benefit of the entire organization. This means that subsidiaries must be upgraded from mere implementers and adapters to contributors and partners in the development and execution of worldwide strategies. Efficient plants may be converted into international production centers, innovative R&D units converted into centers of excellence (and thus role models), and leading subsidiary groups given the leadership role in developing new strategies for the entire corporation. These centers of excellence are discussed in this chapter's Focus on Entrepreneurship.

FOCUS ON ENTREPRENEURSHIP

Centers of Excellence

Local markets are absorbing bigger roles as marketers scan the world for ideas that will cross borders. The consensus among marketers is that many more countries are now capable of developing products and product solutions that can be applied on a worldwide basis. This realization has given birth to centers of excellence. A *center of excellence* is defined as an organizational unit that incorporates a set of capabilities that has been identified as an important source of value creation with the explicit intention that these capabilities be leveraged by and/or disseminated to other parts of the firm.

Colgate-Palmolive has set up centers of excellence around the world, clustering countries with geographic, linguistic, or cultural similarities to exploit the same marketing plans. Unilever is extending the innovation centers it opened for personal care products to its food businesses, starting with ice cream. In addition to innovation centers for oral care in Milan and hair care in Paris, there are now similar centers for developing product ideas, research, technology, and marketing expertise for ice cream products in Rome, Hamburg, London, Paris, and Green Bay, Wisconsin as well as in Bangkok for the Asian market.

Countries have an edge if there is strong local development in a particular product category, such as hair care in France and Thailand, creating an abundance of research and development talent. Local management or existing products with a history of sensitivity to the core competence also helps win a worldwide role for a country unit. For example, ABB Stromberg in Finland was assigned as a worldwide center of excellence for electric drivers, a category for which it is a recognized world leader.

Ford's centers of excellence have been established with two key goals in mind: to avoid duplicating efforts and to capitalize on the expertise of specialists on a worldwide basis. Located in several countries, the centers will work on key components for cars. One will, for example, work on certain kinds of engines. Another will engineer and develop common platforms—the suspension and other undercarriage components—for similar-sized cars. Designers in each market will then style exteriors and passenger compartments to appeal to local tastes. Each car will usually be built on the continent where it is sold. Ford of Europe introduced the Focus, originally intended to replace the Escort. The one-year time lag between the two continents was to allow the same team of engineers to direct factory launches in both Europe and North America. Five Ford design studios had to compromise on design proposals that ranged from a soft, rounded body to a sharply angular one. Although European operations maintained a leadership role, key responsibilities were divided. The U.S. side took over automatic transmissions, with Europe handling the manual version.

Centers of excellence do not necessarily have to be focused on products or technologies. For example, Corning has established a Center for Marketing Excellence, where sales and marketing staff from all Corning's businesses, from glass to television components to electronic communications displays, will be able to find help with marketing intelligence, strategies, new product lines, and e-business. Procter & Gamble has six development hubs that are focused on finding products and technologies that are specialties of their regions. The China hub looks for new high-quality materials and cost innovations, while the India hub seeks out local talent in the sciences to solve problems, using tools such as computer modeling.

Whatever the format, centers of excellence have, as the most important tasks, to leverage and/or transfer their current leading-edge capabilities and to continually fine-tune and enhance those capabilities so that they remain state of the art. Centers of excellence provide country organizations with a critical tool by which to develop subsidiary-specific advantages to benefit the entire global organization.

Sources: Larry Huston and Nabil Sakkab, "Connect and Develop: Inside Procter & Gamble's Model for Innovation," *Harvard Business Review* 84 (March 2006): 58–66; Tony Frost, Julian Birkinshaw, and Prescott Ensign, "Centers of Excellence in Multinational Corporations," *Strategic Management Journal* 23 (November 2002): 997–1018; Karl J. Moore, "A Strategy for Subsidiaries: Centers of Excellence to Build Subsidiary-Specific Advantages," *Management International Review* 41 (third quarter, 2001): 275–290; http://www.colgate.com; http://www.abb.com; http://www.ford.com; http://www.pg.com; and http://www.corning.com.

PROMOTING GLOBAL INTERNAL COOPERATION

In today's environment, the global business entity can be successful only if it is able to move intellectual capital within the organization, that is, transmit ideas and information in real time. If there are impediments to the free flow of information across organizational boundaries, important updates about changes in the competitive environment might not be communicated in a timely fashion to those tasked with incorporating them into strategy.[36]

One of the tools is teaching through educational programs and executive development. The focus is on teachable points of view, that is, an explanation of what a person knows and believes about what it takes to succeed in his or her business. For example, Procter & Gamble makes recruitment and teaching future leaders a priority for its top executives. All of the top officers at the company teach in the company's executive education programs and act as mentors and coaches for younger managers. P&G takes global executive development seriously and grooms its top management prospects through a series of career-building assignments across business units and geographies; eighty-five percent of the company's top management has had one or more international assignments.[37] WPP, the global marketing services group, has developed a graduate marketing fellowship program for promising global managers, comprising three one-year rotations with individual companies within the group's global network and requiring an international assignment.

Former GE CEO Jack Welch coined the term "boundarylessness," which means that people can act without regard to status or functional loyalty and can look for better ideas from anywhere. Top leadership of GE spends considerable time at GE training centers interacting with up-and-comers from all over the company. Each training class is given a real, current company problem to solve, and the reports can be career makers (or breakers). In 2009, GE claimed that its 191 top executives had spent at least one year in training and development programs in their first 15 years at GE.[38] With this approach, a powerful teachable point of view can reach the entire company within a reasonable period by having students become teachers themselves. At PepsiCo, the CEO passed one teachable point to 110 executives, who then passed it to 20,000 people within 18 months.

Another method to promote internal cooperation for global strategy implementation is the use of international teams or councils. In the case of a new product or program, an international team of managers may be assembled to develop strategy. While final direction may come from headquarters, it has been informed of local conditions, and implementation of the strategy is enhanced because local-country managers were involved in its development. The approach has worked even in cases involving seemingly impossible market differences. Both Procter & Gamble and Henkel have successfully introduced pan-European brands for which strategy was developed by European teams. These teams consisted of country managers and staff personnel to smooth eventual implementation and to avoid unnecessarily long and disruptive discussions about the fit of a new product to individual markets.

On a broader and longer-term basis, companies use councils to share **best practices**, for example, an idea that may have saved money or time or a process that is more efficient than existing ones. Most professionals at the leading global companies are members of multiple councils. In some cases, it is important to bring in members of other constituencies (e.g., suppliers, intermediaries, service providers) to such meetings to share their views and experiences and make available their own best practice for benchmarking. In some major production undertakings, technology allows ongoing participation by numerous internal and external team members. For the production of the Boeing 787, Boeing created the Global Collaborative Environment (GCE), a set of computer and networking capabilities made available via the

best practice An idea which has saved money or time, or a process that is more efficient than existing ones.

Web to every member of the 787 team around the world.[39] The Swiss-Swedish engineering firm ABB created two group R&D laboratories—Global Lab Automation and Global Lab Power—to link and integrate its global R&D operations in Germany, Switzerland, Sweden, the United States, Poland, China, and India with universities and other external partners in a fully networked online environment.[40]

While technology has made such teamwork possible wherever the individual participants may be, relying only on technology may not bring about the desired results; "high-tech" approaches inherently mean "low touch," at the expense of results. Human relationships are still paramount. A common purpose is what binds team members to a particular task, which can only be achieved through trust, achievable through face-to-face meetings.[41]

The term *network* also implies two-way communications between headquarters and subsidiaries themselves. This translates into intercultural communication efforts focused on developing relationships.[42] While this communication has traditionally taken the form of newsletters, traveling executive "road shows," or regular and periodic meetings of appropriate personnel, new technologies are allowing businesses to link far-flung entities and eliminate the traditional barriers of time and distance.

Companies now use regular **podcasts** to transmit seminars and conferences to employees globally. Streaming media technology allows live **webcasts** for important company meetings. TBWA Worldwide, *Advertising Age's* Global Agency of the Year in 2008, conducts three live webcasts every year, showing recent creative work and taking questions from agency employees around the world. TBWA does the webcast three times during the day to allow staffers from different time zones the ability to conveniently participate.[43]

Intranets integrate a company's information assets into a single, globally accessible system that allows more efficient collaboration and the formation of **virtual teams**. For example, employees at Levi Strauss & Co. can join an electronic discussion group with colleagues around the world, watch the latest Levi's commercials, or comment on the latest business programs or plans. The benefits of intranets include (1) increased productivity, in that there is no longer a time lag between an idea and the information needed to assess and implement it; (2) enhanced knowledge capital, which is constantly updated and upgraded; (3) facilitated teamwork enabling online communication at insignificant expense; and (4) incorporation of best practice at a moment's notice by allowing managers and functional-area personnel to make to-the-minute decisions anywhere in the world. For consumer goods companies, intranets allow global brand management teams access to consumer research, product development timelines, international creative concepts, individual country campaigns, media planning and buying information, international pricing structures, new packaging ideas, and much more. The challenge becomes one of efficient design interface and usage stimulation and training.[44]

As can be seen from the discussion, the networked approach is not a structural adaptation but a procedural one, calling for a change in management mentality. It requires adjustment mainly in the coordination and control functions of the firm. And while there is still considerable disagreement as to which of the approaches work best, some measures have been shown to correlate with success. Of the many initiatives developed to enhance the workings of a networked global organization, such as cross-border task forces and establishment of centers of excellence, the most significant was the use of electronic networking capabilities.

Further adjustment in organizational approaches is required as businesses face new challenges such as emerging markets, global accounts, the digitization of business, and cyber-security.[45] Emerging markets present the company with unique opportunities but also challenges such as product counterfeiters and informal competitors who ignore local labor and tax laws. How these issues are addressed may require organizational rethinking. Increasingly, companies are organizing their business not just regionally but

podcasts A series of digital media files that are released episodically and often downloaded through web syndication.

webcasts A media file distributed over the Internet using streaming media technology to distribute a single content source to many simultaneous listeners/viewers.

intranet A process that integrates a company's information assets into a single accessible system using Internet-based technologies such as e-mail, news groups, and the World Wide Web.

virtual team A team of people who are based at various locations around the world and communicate through intranet and other electronic means to achieve a common goal.

also to focus on emerging markets as a group. Global account managers need to have skills and the empowerment to work across functional areas and borders to deliver quality service to the company's largest clients. Also, digital business, such as business-to-business and business-to-consumer Internet-based activities, will continue to be brought into the mainstay of the business's activities and structures and not just segregated as a separate activity.

Finally, cyber-security has surfaced as an issue of critical importance as increased global team collaboration can expose the company to risks from hackers and spies. In 2008, U.S. government agencies and defense contractors were "the victims of an unprecedented rash of (sic) cyber attacks over the last two years," and those attacks were linked to Chinese sources.[46] A 2009 Accenture report related this problem to a corporate organizational issue as it discussed the tendencies of young "millennial generation" workers within corporations to ignore corporate CIO policies about data protection and to share work outside of corporate "firewalls" through e-mail, Google applications, and other networking practices because it is easier and faster. Companies must adapt to new technologies and networking options to balance the need for easy and fast with that of security.[47]

THE ROLE OF COUNTRY ORGANIZATIONS

Country organizations should be treated as a source of supply as much as a source of demand. Quite often, however, headquarters managers see their role as the coordinators of key decisions and controllers of resources and perceive subsidiaries as implementers and adaptors of global strategy in their respective local markets. Furthermore, they may see all country organizations as the same. This view severely limits utilization of the firm's resources and deprives country managers of the opportunity to exercise their creativity.[48]

The role that a particular country organization can play naturally depends on that market's overall strategic importance as well as its organizational competence. Using these criteria, four different roles emerge, as shown in Figure 11.7.

Figure 11.7   Roles for Country Organizations

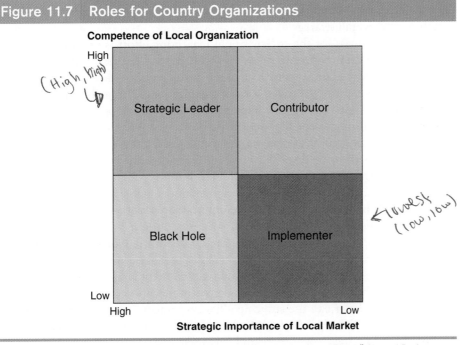

Source: Christopher Bartlett and Sumantra Ghoshal, "Tap Your Subsidiaries for Global Reach," *Harvard Business Review* 64, November–December 1986 (Boston: Harvard Business School Publishing Division), 87–94.

strategic leader A highly competent firm located in a strategically critical market.

The role of a **strategic leader** can be played by a highly competent national subsidiary located in a strategically critical market. Such a country organization serves as a partner of headquarters in developing and implementing strategy. Procter & Gamble's brand teams, which analyze opportunities for greater product and marketing program standardization, are chaired by a brand manager from a "lead country." For example, a strategic leader market may have products designed specifically with it in mind. Nissan's Z-cars have always been designated primarily for the U.S. market, starting with the 240Z in the 1970s to the 350Z and 370Z. The new model was designed by the company's La Jolla, California, studio. Mercedes-Benz Design Studios regularly shares ideas among Sindelfingen (Germany), Irvine (California), and Yokohama (Japan); a fourth studio in Como (Italy) focuses exclusively on interior vehicle design. They function as a seismograph for influences emerging from art, culture and architecture.[49] Global automotive companies like GM and Volkswagen have joint ventures with Chinese auto manufacturer SAIC to produce cars specifically for the Chinese market. Because China is the largest automobile market in the world in 2009, it is logical that the country's management team play an important strategic role in the company's global planning.

contributor A national subsidiary with a distinctive competence, such as product development.

A **contributor** is a country organization with a distinctive competence, such as product development. Increasingly, country organizations are the source of new products. IBM scientists (Zurich), were the first to image the "anatomy" of a molecule, which opens new possibilities for exploring the building blocks of future microprocessors and other nanodevices.[50] Procter & Gamble's country team in Turkey developed new seal-tight polyethylene bags for shipping Ariel that are entirely recyclable and use significantly less packing material. P&G is expanding the use of these shipping materials across different regions.[51] A contributor designation may be a function of geography as well. The development of new markets such as the "Stans" (e.g., Kazakhstan and Azerbaijan) has been delegated to country organizations in Russia, Turkey, and Dubai. For products or technologies with multiple applications, leadership may be divided among different country operations. For example, INVISTA delegates responsibility for each different application of Lycra to managers in a country where the application is strongest, that is, Brazil for swimwear and France for fashion. The global brand manager for Lycra ensures that those applications come together in an overall strategy.[52]

implementer The typical subsidiary role, which involves implementing strategy that originates with headquarters.

The critical mass for the international marketing effort is provided by **implementers**. These country organizations may exist in smaller, less-established markets in which corporate commitment to market development is less. The presence in these markets is typically through a sales organization. Although most entities fill this role, it should not be slighted: implementers provide the opportunity to capture economies of scale and scope that are the basis of a global strategy. With a few notable exceptions, most subsidiary managers would argue they do not get the level of attention they need or deserve. But it is important nonetheless, because it provides clear evidence that parent companies can view initiative-taking and profile-building efforts positively (rather than as unnecessary or annoying lobbying).[53]

black hole The situation that arises when an international marketer has a low-competence subsidiary—or none at all—in a highly strategic market.

The **black hole** is a situation that an international marketer has to work out of. A company may be in a "black hole" situation because it has read the market incorrectly (e.g., Philips focused its marketing efforts in the North American market on less-expensive items instead of the up-market products that have made the company's reputation worldwide)[54] or because government may restrict its activities (e.g., Citibank being restricted in terms of activities and geography in China). If possible, the marketer can use strategic alliances or acquisitions to change its competitive position. Whirlpool established itself in the European Union by acquiring Philips's "white goods" operation and has used joint ventures to penetrate the

Chinese market. If governmental regulations hinder the scale of operations, the firm may use its presence in a major market as an observation post to keep up with developments before a major thrust for entry is executed. Meanwhile, the Indian government has been careful to limit foreign investment in single-brand retailers. Sweden's IKEA, the world's biggest furniture retailer, recently called off a $1 billion investment plan due to the restrictions.[55]

Depending on the role, the relationship between headquarters and the country organization will vary from loose control based mostly on support to tighter control in making sure strategies are implemented appropriately. Yet in each of these cases, it is imperative that country organizations have enough operating independence to cater to local needs and to provide motivation to the country managers. For example, an implementer should provide input in the development of a regional or a global strategy or program. Strategy formulation should ensure that appropriate implementation can be achieved at the country level.

Good ideas can, and should, come from any country organization. To take full advantage of this, individuals at the country level have to feel that they have the authority to pursue ideas in the first place and that they can see their concepts through to commercialization.[56] In some cases, this may mean that subsidiaries are allowed to experiment with projects that would not be seen as feasible by headquarters. For example, developing products for small-scale power generation using renewable resources may not generate interest in Honeywell's major markets and subsidiaries but may well be something that one of its developing-country subsidiaries should investigate.

CONTROLS

The function of the organizational structure is to provide a framework in which objectives can be met. A set of instruments and processes is needed, however, to influence the performance of organizational members so as to meet the goals. Controls focus on means to verify and correct actions that differ from established plans. Compliance needs to be secured from subordinates through different means of coordinating specialized and interdependent parts of the organization.[57] Within an organization, control serves as an integrating mechanism. Controls are designed to reduce uncertainty, increase predictability, and ensure that behaviors originating in separate parts of the organization are compatible and in support of common organizational goals despite physical, psychic, and temporal distances.

The critical issue here is the same as with organizational structure: What is the ideal amount of control? On the one hand, headquarters needs controls to ensure that international activities contribute the greatest benefit to the overall organization. On the other hand, they should not be construed as a code of laws and subsequently allowed to stifle local initiative.

This section will focus on the design and functions of control instruments available for international business operations, along with an assessment of their appropriateness. Emphasis will be placed on the degree of formality of controls used by firms.

4. To outline the need for and challenges of controls in international operations

TYPES OF CONTROLS

Most organizations display some administrative flexibility, as demonstrated by variations in how they apply management directives, corporate objectives, or measurement systems. A distinction should be made, however, between variations that have emerged by design and those that are the result of autonomy. The first is the result of a management decision, whereas the second typically has grown without central direction and are based on emerging practices. In both instances, some type of control will be exercised. Controls that result from headquarters initiative rather than those that are the consequences of tolerated practices will be discussed here. Firms that wait for self-emerging controls often experience rapid international growth but subsequent problems in product-line performance, program coordination, and strategic planning.[58]

Whatever the system, it is important in today's competitive environment to have internal benchmarking. This relates to organizational learning and sharing of best practices throughout the corporate system to avoid the costs of reinventing solutions that have already been discovered. Three critical features are necessary in sharing best practice. First, there needs to be a device for organizational memory. For example, at Xerox, contributors to solutions can send their ideas to an electronic library where they are indexed and provided to potential adopters in the corporate family. Second, best practice must be updated and adjusted to new situations. For example, best practice adopted by a company's China office will be modified and customized, and this learning should then become part of the database. Finally, best practice must be legitimized. This calls for a shared understanding that exchanging knowledge across units is organizationally valued and that these systems are important mechanisms for knowledge exchange. Use can be encouraged by including an assessment in employee performance evaluations of how effectively employees share information with colleagues and utilize the databases.

In the design of the control systems, a major decision concerns the object of control. Two major objects are typically identified: output and behavior.[59] Output controls include balance sheets, sales data, production data, product-line growth, and performance reviews of personnel. Measures of output are accumulated at regular intervals and forwarded from the foreign locale to headquarters, where they are evaluated and critiqued based on comparisons to the plan or budget. Behavioral controls require the exertion of influence over behavior after—or, ideally, before—it leads to action. Behavioral controls can be achieved through the preparation of manuals on such topics as sales techniques to be made available to subsidiary personnel or through efforts to fit new employees into the corporate culture.

To institute either of these measures, instruments of control have to be decided upon. The general alternatives are either bureaucratic/formalized control or cultural control. Bureaucratic controls consist of a limited and explicit set of regulations and rules that outline the desired levels of performance. Cultural controls, on the other hand, are much less formal and are the result of shared beliefs and expectations among the members of an organization. Table 11.2 provides a schematic explanation of the types of controls and their objectives.

Table 11.2 Comparison of Bureaucratic and Cultural Control Mechanisms

| Object of Control | TYPE OF CONTROL | | |
	Pure Bureaucratic/ Formalized Control	Pure Cultural Control	Characteristics of Control
Output	Formal performance reports	Shared norms of performance	HQ sets short-term performance target and requires frequent reports from subsidiaries
Behavior	Company policies, manuals	Shared philosophy of management	Active participation of HQ in strategy formulation of subsidiaries

Sources: Peter J. Kidger, "Management Structure in Multinational Enterprises: Responding to Globalization," *Employee Relations*, August 2001, 69–85; and B. R. Baliga and Alfred M. Jaeger, "Multinational Corporations: Control Systems and Delegation Issues," *Journal of International Business Studies* 15 (Fall 1984): 25–40.

Bureaucratic/Formalized Control

The elements of a bureaucratic/formalized control system are (1) an international budget and planning system, (2) the functional reporting system, and (3) policy manuals used to direct functional performance.

Budgets refers to shorter-term guidelines regarding investment, cash, and personnel policies, while *plans* refers to formalized plans with more than a one-year horizon. The budget and planning process is the major control instrument in headquarters-subsidiary relationships. Although systems and their execution vary, the objective is to achieve as good a fit as possible with the objectives and characteristics of the firm and its environment.

The budgetary period is typically one year, since it is tied to the accounting systems of the multinational. The budget system is used for four main purposes: (1) allocation of funds among subsidiaries; (2) planning and coordination of global production capacity and supplies; (3) evaluation of subsidiary performance; and (4) communication and information exchange among subsidiaries, product organizations, and corporate headquarters.[60] Long-range plans vary dramatically, ranging from two years to ten years in length, and are more qualitative and judgmental in nature. However, shorter periods such as two years are the norm, considering the added uncertainty of diverse foreign environments.

Although firms strive for uniformity, achieving it may be as difficult as trying to design a suit to fit the average person. The processes themselves are very formalized in terms of the schedules to be followed.

Control can also be seen as a mechanism to secure cooperation of local units. For example, while a company may grant substantial autonomy to a country organization in terms of strategies, headquarters may use allocation of production volume as a powerful tool to ensure compliance. Some of the ways for headquarters to gain cooperation of country organizations are summarized in Figure 11.8. Some of the methods used are formal, such as approval of strategic plans and personnel selection, while some are more informal, including personal contact and relationships, as well as international networking.[61]

Because the frequency of reports required from subsidiaries is likely to increase due to globalization, it is essential that subsidiaries see the rationale for the often

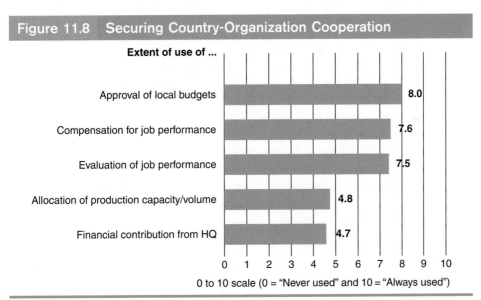

Figure 11.8   Securing Country-Organization Cooperation

Extent of use of ...

Approval of local budgets	8.0
Compensation for job performance	7.6
Evaluation of job performance	7.5
Allocation of production capacity/volume	4.8
Financial contribution from HQ	4.7

0 1 2 3 4 5 6 7 8 9 10

0 to 10 scale (0 = "Never used" and 10 = "Always used")

Source: Henry P. Conn and George S. Yip, "Global Transfer of Critical Capabilities," in Michael R. Czinkota and Ilkka A. Ronkainen, eds., *Best Practices in International Business* (Mason, OH: South-Western, 2001): 256–274.

time-consuming exercise. Two approaches, used in tandem, can facilitate the process: participation and feedback. The first refers to avoiding the perception at subsidiary levels that reports are "art for art's sake" by involving the preparers in the actual use of the reports. When this is not possible, feedback about their consequences is warranted. Through this process, communication is enhanced as well.

On the behavioral front, headquarters may want to guide the way in which subsidiaries make decisions and implement agreed-upon strategies. U.S.-based multinationals tend to be far more formalized than their Japanese and European counterparts, with a heavy reliance on manuals for all major functions.[62] The manuals discuss such items as recruitment, training, motivation, and dismissal policies. The use of manuals is in direct correlation with the required level of reports from subsidiaries, discussed in the previous section.

Cultural Control

As seen from the country comparisons, less emphasis is placed outside the United States on formal controls, as they are viewed as too rigid and too quantitatively oriented. Rather, multinational corporations (MNCs) in other countries emphasize corporate values and culture, and evaluations are based on the extent to which an individual or entity fits in with the norms.

Cultural controls require an extensive socialization process to which informal, personal interaction is central. Substantial resources have to be spent to train the individual to share the corporate cultures, or "the way things are done at the company." Adding to this need is the increasing cultural diversity at companies. For example, 120 different nationalities work at Nokia, and 45 percent of senior management comes from a non-Finnish ethnicity.[63] To build common vision and values, managers spend a substantial share of their first months at Matsushita in what the company calls "cultural and spiritual training." They study the company credo, the "Seven Spirits of Matsushita," and the philosophy of the founder, Konosuke Matsushita and learn how to translate the internalized lessons into daily behavior and operational decisions. Although more prevalent in Japanese organizations, many Western entities have similar programs, such as Philips's "organization cohesion training" and Unilever's "indoctrination." This corporate acculturation will be critical to achieve the acceptance of possible transfers of best practice within the organization as seen in Focus on Ethics.[64]

The primary instruments of cultural control are the careful selection and training of corporate personnel and the institution of self-control. The choice of cultural controls can be justified if the company enjoys a low turnover rate; they are thus applied when companies can offer and expect lifetime or long-term employment, as many firms do in Japan.

In selecting home-country nationals and, to some extent, third-country nationals, MNCs are exercising cultural control. The assumption is that the managers have already internalized the norms and values of the company and they tend to run a country organization with a more global view. In some cases, the use of headquarters personnel to ensure uniformity in decision making may be advisable; for example, Volvo uses a home-country national for the position of chief financial officer. Expatriates are used in subsidiaries not only for control purposes but also to effect change processes. Companies control the efforts of management specifically through compensation and promotion policies, as well as through policies concerning replacement.

When the expatriate corps is small, headquarters can still exercise its control through other means. Management training programs for overseas managers as well as time at headquarters will indoctrinate individuals to the company's ways of doing

FOCUS ON ETHICS

Corporate Acculturation

Toyota has 27 different companies with 320,808 employees around the world and 53 factories outside of Japan, and it sells 8,913,000 cars in more than 170 countries. What holds these operations together and makes them part of a cohesive entity is a strong corporate culture.

The "Toyota Way" has seven distinct elements: (1) *kaizen*, the process of continuous improvement that has Toyota employees coming back to work each day determined to perform better than the day before; (2) *genchi genbustu*, which expects fact-based consensus building on defining challenges; (3) *kakushin*, which focuses on radical innovation in terms of technologies and models; (4) a *challenge*, which helps employees see obstacles not as something undesirable but as way to help reach improvements; (5) *teamwork*, sharing knowledge with others in the team and putting the company's interests before those of the individual; (6) *respect* for other people, not just as people but for their skills and special knowledge; and (7) *customers first, dealers second—and manufacturer last*, with the realization that customers pay the salaries not the company.

Ultimately, employees reach a point of "emotional fortitude," where their behavior is consistent with the organization's objectives. In the West, where individualism is at a higher level, it is more difficult for employees to absorb this. Emulating Toyota is not about copying any one practice, it is about creating a culture.

It was during this time, when the term *hybrid* was not yet in common use, that Toyota launched a project to investigate what type of vehicles would be best for the twenty-first century. The scope of research was expanded to include areas such as ease of boarding and exiting, body size, design, and fuel efficiency, as well as twenty-first-century themes including societal issues and a process of reviewing from the very beginning what a vehicle is and its manufacturing processes.

A short time later, global environmental issues, including global warming and the limits of fossil fuels, became increasingly prominent. The hybrid system, which combines an engine and a motor, is one of the responses to those serious problems that humanity was facing for the first time. The hybrid system presented to the planet, and the people who inhabit it, the

Third-generation Prius launched in 2009.

completely new value of "amenability that takes the environment into consideration."

In 2009–10, after two separate recalls covering 7.5 million vehicles, Toyota was forced to announce it was suspending the sale of eight of its best-selling vehicles, a move that cost the company and its dealers a minimum of $54 million a day in lost sales revenue. How did a company that became the world's largest and most profitable automaker on the back of a rock-solid reputation for quality and dependability find itself at the center of the biggest product recall?

The challenge is created by two elements of culture: firstly, an obsession with quality, which means that anything less than perfection is seen as shameful and embarrassing. As a consequence, problems with quality are literally inconceivable and denial takes over. The second interlinked element of culture is a hierarchical approach to management and a lack of open communication. Where this exists, junior employees who are best placed to spot early sins of crisis feel unable to point out flaws. As a result, problems go unnoticed and unresolved until they explode into a major crisis.

Sources: Jonathan Hemus, "Accelerating Towards Crisis: a PR View of Toyota's Recall," *Guardian*, February 9, 2010, 25; Angus MacKenzie and Scott Evans, "The Toyota Recall Crisis," *Motor Trend*, January, 2010; Hirotaka Takeuchi, Emi Osono, and Norihiko Shimizu, "The Contradictions that Drive Toyota's Success," *Harvard Business Review* 86 (June 2008): 96–105; Thomas A. Stewart and Anand P. Raman, "Lessons from Toyota's Long Drive," *Harvard Business Review* 85 (July/August 2007): 74–82; "Inculcating Culture," *Economist*, January 21, 2006, 11; see also http://www.toyota.co.jp/en/index_company.html.

things. Similarly, formal visits by headquarters teams (for example, for a strategy audit) or informal visits (perhaps to launch a new product) will enhance the feeling of belonging to the same corporate family. Some of the innovative global companies assemble temporary teams of their best talent to build local skills. IBM, for example, drafted 50 engineers from its facilities in Italy, Japan, New York, and North Carolina to run three-week to six-month training courses on all operations carried on at its Shenzhen facility in China. After the trainers left the country, they stayed in touch by e-mail, so whenever the Chinese managers have a problem, they know they can reach someone for help. The continuation of the support has been as important as the training itself.[65]

Corporations rarely use one pure control mechanism. Rather, most use both quantitative and qualitative measures. Corporations are likely, however, to place different levels of emphasis on different types of performance measures and on how they are taken. To generate global buy-in, annual bonuses have shifted away from the employee's individual unit toward the company as a whole. This sends a strong signal in favor of collaboration across all boundaries. Other similar approaches to motivate and generate changes in thinking exist. For example, in the past Kraft has provided incentive to the general manager of a country (e.g., China) based on the total performance. Now, bonuses are calculated by weighing the performance of their individual businesses (e.g., China) at 70 percent and the next higher level of aggregation (e.g., Asia-Pacific) at 30 percent. That is just enough to encourage the managers to support the greater good, not just their own individual performance.[66] At BP, for example, individual performance assessments exclude the effects of the price of oil and foreign exchange because they are outside of the employee's control.[67]

EXERCISING CONTROLS

Within most corporations, different functional areas are subject to different guidelines because they are subject to different constraints. For example, the marketing function has traditionally been seen as incorporating many more behavioral dimensions than manufacturing or finance. As a result, many multinational corporations employ control systems that are responsive to the needs of the function. Yet such differentiation is sometimes based less on appropriateness than on personalities. It has been hypothesized that manufacturing subsidiaries are controlled more intensively than sales subsidiaries because production more readily lends itself to centralized direction, and technicians and engineers adhere more firmly to standards and regulations than do salespeople.[68]

Similarly, the degree of control imposed will vary by subsidiary characteristics, including location. For example, because Malaysia is an emerging economy in which managerial talent is in short supply, headquarters may want to participate more in all facets of decision making. If a country-market witnesses economic or political turmoil, controls may also be tightened to ensure the management of risk.[69]

In their international operations, U.S.-based multinationals place major emphasis on obtaining quantitative data. Although this allows for good centralized comparisons against standards and benchmarks or cross-comparisons among different corporate units, it entails several drawbacks. In the international environment, new dimensions—such as inflation, differing rates of taxation, and exchange rate fluctuations—may distort the performance evaluation of any given individual or organizational unit.

For the global corporation, measurement of whether a business unit in a particular country is earning a superior return on investment relative to risk may be irrelevant to the contribution an investment may make worldwide or to the long-term results of the firm. In the short term, the return may even be negative.[70] Therefore, the control mechanism may quite inappropriately indicate reward or punishment. Standardizing the information received may be difficult if the various environments involved fluctuate and require frequent and major adaptations. Further complicating the issue is the fact that although quantitative information may be collected monthly, or at least quarterly, environmental data may be acquired annually or "now and then," especially when a crisis seems to loom on the horizon.

To design a control system that is acceptable not only to headquarters but also to the organization and individuals abroad, great care must be taken to use only relevant data. Major concerns, therefore, are the data collection process and the analysis and utilization of data. Evaluators need management information systems that provide for greater comparability and equity in administering controls. The more behaviorally-based and culture-oriented controls are, the more care needs to be taken.

In designing a control system, management must consider the costs of establishing and maintaining it versus the benefits to be gained. Any control system will require investment in a management structure and in systems design. Consider, for example, costs associated with cultural controls: personal interaction, use of expatriates, and training programs are all quite expensive. Yet these expenses may be justified by cost savings through lower employee turnover, an extensive worldwide information system, and an improved control system.[71] Moreover, the impact goes beyond the administrative component. If controls are misguided or too time-consuming, they can slow or undermine the strategy implementation process and thus the overall capability of the firm. The result will be lost opportunities or, worse yet, increased threats. In addition, time spent on reporting takes time from everything else, and if the exercise is seen as mundane, it results in lowered motivation. A parsimonious design is therefore imperative. The control system should collect all the information required and trigger all the intervention necessary; however, it should not lead to the pulling of strings by a puppeteer.

The impact of the environment has to be taken into account as well, in two ways. First, the control system must measure only those dimensions over which the organization has actual control. Rewards or sanctions make little sense if they are based on dimensions that may be relevant to overall corporate performance but over which no influence can be exerted, such as price controls. Neglecting the factor of individual performance capability would send wrong signals and severely harm motivation. Second, control systems have to be in harmony with local regulations and customs. In some cases, however, corporate behavioral controls have to be exercised against local customs even though overall operations may be affected negatively. This type of situation occurs, for example, when a subsidiary operates in markets in which unauthorized facilitating payments are a common business practice.

Corporations are faced with major challenges in the area of appropriate and adequate control systems in today's business environment. Given increased local government demands for a share in companies established, controls can become tedious, especially if the MNC is a minority partner. Even if the new entity is a result of two companies' joining forces through a merger—such as the one between Ciba and Sandoz to create Novartis—or two companies joining forces to form a new entity—such as Siecor established by Siemens AG and Corning Incorporated—the backgrounds of the partners may be different enough to cause problems in devising the required controls.

SUMMARY

This chapter discussed the structure, implementation and control mechanisms needed to operate in the international business field. These elements define relationships between the entities of the firm and provide the channels through which the relationships develop. The fundamental tests of organizational design are whether there is a fit with the company's overall marketing strategy and whether it reflects the strengths of the entities within the organization.[72]

International firms can choose from a variety of organizational structures, ranging from a domestic organization that handles ad hoc export orders to a full-fledged global organization. The choice will depend heavily on the degree of internationalization of the firm, the diversity of international activities, and the relative importance of product, area, function, and customer variables in the process. Whatever the choice on structure may be, implementation of the planned strategies is a critical factor determining success. Companies typically realize only 60 percent of their strategies potential value due to factors such as organizational silos and culture blocking execution.[73] What is critical is that the framework establish a common language for the dialogue between the corporate center and the units; one that the strategy, marketing, and finance teams all understand and use.

The control function is of increasing importance because of the high variability in performance that results from divergent local environments and the need to reconcile local objectives with the corporate goal of synergism. It is important to grant autonomy to country organizations so that they can be responsive to local markets' needs, but it is equally important to ensure close cooperation between units.

Control can be exercised through bureaucratic means, which emphasize formal reporting and evaluation of benchmark data or through cultural means, in which norms and values are understood by the individuals and entities that make up the corporation. U.S. firms typically rely more on bureaucratic controls, while MNCs from other countries frequently run operations abroad through informal means and rely less on stringent measures.

The implementation of controls requires great sensitivity to behavioral dimensions and the environment. The measurements used must be appropriate and reflective of actual performance rather than marketplace vagaries. Similarly, entities should be judged only on factors over which they have some degree of control.

KEY TERMS

product structure   365
area structure   367
functional structure   368
process structure   368
customer structure   368
mixed structure   368
matrix structure   368

decentralization   372
centralization   372
coordinated decentralization   373
glocal   374
best practices   377
podcasts   378
webcasts   378

intranets   378
virtual teams   378
strategic leader   380
contributor   380
implementers   380
black hole   380

QUESTIONS FOR DISCUSSION

1. Firms differ, often substantially, in their organizational structures even within the same industry. What accounts for the differences in their approaches?

2. Discuss the benefits gained by adopting a matrix form of organizational structure.

3. What changes in the firm and/or in the environment might cause a firm to abandon the functional approach?

4. Is there more to the not-invented-here syndrome than simply hurt feelings on the part of those who believe they are being dictated to by headquarters?

5. "Implementers are the most important country organizations in terms of buy-in for a global strategy." Comment.

6. How can systems that are built for global knowledge transfer be used as control tools?

INTERNET EXERCISES

1. Internal cooperation in terms of best-practices transfer, for example, is a key objective for global organizations. Using the web site of Lotus (http://www-01.ibm.com/software/solutions/ smartwork/smartercollaboration/) and the section on case studies, outline how companies have used Lotus Notes and Domino to facilitate the interactive sharing of information.

2. Every big company has in-house experts. So why don't they use them more? Search systems that apply social-computing tools such as internal blogs, wikis and social networks can fill these critical gaps. Posted comments and communication between users help reveal not only who knows what, but who is approachable.

TAKE A STAND

After deciding to enter a market and finding a route to their customers, companies can still discover that their products fail to find a niche, either because of local competition or because they do not understand the market's distinctive characteristics. High-performance businesses avoid this fate by identifying and isolating important regional differences and tailoring products and services to chosen consumer segments.

Lack of available customer data, especially in emerging markets, can make it difficult to identify consumer preferences and trends. High-performance businesses get around these difficulties by hiring and partnering locally to get closer to customers.

U.S.–headquartered consumer electronics retailer Best Buy partnered with the Carphone Warehouse, Europe's leading mobile phone retailer, in 2006 to serve European consumers with its Geek Squad services (agents who make help-desk house calls). The companies agreed to a joint venture granting Best Buy a 50 percent share of European retail stores and other businesses. This mode of market entry fits with Best Buy's careful expansion strategy because it enables the company to benefit from the Carphone Warehouse's understanding of European consumers before launching its own branded stores. Best Buy has agreed to acquire a majority interest in Jiangsu Five Star Appliance, China's fourth largest appliance and consumer electronics retailer. This transaction, consistent with the company's previously announced strategy for global expansion, will provide Best Buy with an immediate retail presence in China through Five Star's 136 stores throughout 8 of China's 34 provinces. Together with Five Star's knowledgeable, established management team, Best Buy hopes to accelerate its understanding of customers and retail operations in the world's fastest-growing market.

High performers also use their market insight to tailor products and services to meet local tastes and requirements. Local consumption patterns, for example, are rarely the same everywhere. Based in the United Kingdom, Tesco is the world's third-largest grocer, operating more than 3,900 stores in 14 countries. There are culturally specific tastes and preferences, varying income levels, disparate modes of shopping for goods and services, and uneven retail infrastructures. Because Chinese consumers traditionally buy groceries on a daily basis at "wet" markets and prefer fresh produce, many of Tesco's stores in China have large, waterfilled tanks of live turtles and toads. This approach of tailoring offerings to accommodate local shopping habits has proved so successful that Tesco now operates 71 stores in China.

In addition, companies need to improvise around the constraints imposed by physical isolation and inadequate infrastructure in many markets. In terms of reaching customers, mobile devices will be both a business opportunity and a business necessity. In the developed world, mobile phones will augment personal computers as e-commerce and customer support channels. In the emerging world, where there are more than 1 billion new consumers, mobile devices are likely to be the sole electronic channel for most people. Nearly 4 billion people—or 60 percent of the world's population—are mobile customers. More than 500 million new customers were added in 2008 alone. Seventy-five percent of subscribers are located in emerging markets, where the mobile phone is their sole means of electronic communication. Nearly all the devices have Short Message Service (SMS) texting capability, and an increasing number have some rudimentary Internet connectivity. Norwegian telecommunications company Telenor has brought mobile banking to migrant workers who might otherwise have insufficient access to regular banking services.

In a partnership with Citibank, Telenor's DiGiREMIT service allows customers in Malaysia to transfer money securely to Bangladesh, Indonesia, and the Philippines. Subscribers to Telenor's TeleDoctor service in Pakistan receive easy access to experienced physicians, who provide medical advice and symptom diagnosis in eight languages, eliminating the need to travel to an appointment.

For Discussion

1. Local leadership in particular helps businesses plant deep roots in local talent markets. Talent pools can be shallower than they first appear, with business-ready skills often in short supply. Which of these attributes can be harder to find in emerging markets?

2. What should companies do if headquarters–subsidiary conflicts emerge?

Source: http://www.accenture.com/Global/Consulting/globalchallenge.htm.

Building the Knowledge Base

CHAPTER CONTENTS & LEARNING OBJECTIVES

INTERNATIONAL AND DOMESTIC RESEARCH

1. To gain an understanding of the need for research

RECOGNIZING THE NEED FOR INTERNATIONAL RESEARCH

2. To explore the differences between domestic and international research

DETERMINING RESEARCH OBJECTIVES

3. To learn where to find and how to use sources of secondary information

CONDUCTING SECONDARY RESEARCH

4. To gain insight into the gathering of primary data

CONDUCTING PRIMARY RESEARCH

5. To examine the need for international management information systems

THE INTERNATIONAL INFORMATION SYSTEM

6. To examine the role importance of international information systems for corporate decision processes and strategic planning

APPENDIX 12A: MONITORS OF INTERNATIONAL ISSUES

APPENDIX 12B: THE STRUCTURE OF A COUNTRY COMMERCIAL GUIDE

Cool Merchandising

The ability to predict the next hot trend could translate into a large competitive advantage and boost a company's bottom line. Conventional wisdom dictates that teenagers are the population segment that generates most of these hot new trends, which has given rise to a new marketing research segment—*coolhunting*.

Many large international brands, such as Reebok, Adidas, Nike, Coca-Cola, Levi's, Converse, Nokia, Gap, and Pepsi, have invested in the quest for cool—either by employing outside consultants or by conducting their own in-house teenager focus groups. Forecasting what kids would want to wear, eat, listen to, and play with has evolved into a multibilliondollar industry, especially considering that they are the population segment with the most disposable income. Without worries about mortgages and pension funds, teenagers are free to spend their allowances or babysitting money on whatever they choose. Ensuring that they choose a particular brand or product is the coolhunter's job.

Coolhunters roam city streets, clubs, and schools in the search of hot new trends. For example, in the design development of sneakers, market researches might drive around inner-city neighborhoods, taking pictures of "cool kid" footwear, or take a shoe, find the coolest kids they can, and ask them if they like it. Some analysts have characterized this type of work as a form of cultural anthropology—observing teenagers in their natural habitat. Others have described it as a sophisticated recruitment process—identifying the trendiest kids and harnessing their knowledge. However, "cool" by its very nature is unidentifiable, and recognizing it has more to do with personal preferences than any explicit methodology.

If a brand is successful in capturing the next hot trend, it needs to be aware of the limited window of opportunity, before it spreads to the general public and ceases to be "cool." Sprite's research, for example, indicated that because of the pervasiveness of advertising, kids had become inundated, and ads frequently achieved the opposite of their intended purpose. The more a product was advertised, the less likely teenagers were to buy it. Therefore, Sprite embarked on an innovative ad campaign that poked fun at traditional advertising. Famous athletes were seen extolling the drink's virtues, while at the bottom of the screen there was a cartoon of the athlete collecting large bags of money. Kids responded positively and sales skyrocketed. However, once other brands

Young consumers are often international trendsetters.

started catching on to this new trend of "cynical advertising," it stopped being cool, and Sprite had to develop a new marketing strategy. Its next move was to establish relationships with hip-hop artists and sponsor their concerts and merchandise. Teenagers and sales again responded well. Yet, Sprite executives are aware that this approach also will eventually outlive its "coolness" and are searching for the next big trend. This is the nature of the coolhunting game—it is driven by an endless quest for novelty. In the words of Douglas Rushkoff, "The paradox of 'cool hunting' is that it kills what it finds."

Sources: Nick Southgate, "Coolhunting with Aristotle," *International Journal of Marketing Research* 45, no. 2 (June 1, 2003): 167–189. "The Merchants of Cool," *Frontline*, PBS, http://www.pbs.org/wgbh/pages/frontline/shows/cool/, accessed November 13, 2009; John F. Sherry Jr., "The Ethnographer's Apprentice: Trying Consumer Culture from the Outside In," *Journal of Business Ethics* 80, no. 1 (June 2008): 85–95.

The single most important cause of failure in international business is insufficient preparation and information. The failure of managers to comprehend cultural disparities, the failure to remember that customers differ from country to country, and the lack of investigation into whether or not a market exists prior to market entry has made international business a high-risk activity.[1] International business research is therefore instrumental to international business success because it permits the firm to take into account different environments, attitudes, and market conditions. Fortunately, such research has become less complicated. As the opening vignette shows, information from around the globe can be obtained quite easily.

This chapter discusses data collection and provides a comprehensive overview of how to obtain general screening information on international markets, to evaluate business potential, and to assess current or potential opportunities and problems. Data sources that are low cost and that take little time to accumulate—in short, secondary data—are considered first. The balance of the chapter is devoted to more sophisticated forms of international research, including primary data collection and the development of an information system.

 ## INTERNATIONAL AND DOMESTIC RESEARCH

The tools and techniques of international research are the same as those of domestic research. The difference is in the environment to which the tools are applied. The environment determines how well the tools, techniques, and concepts work. Although the objectives of research may be the same, the execution of international research may differ substantially from that of domestic research. The four primary reasons for this difference are new parameters, new environmental factors, an increase in the number of factors involved, and a broader definition of competition.

1. To gain an understanding of the need for research

NEW PARAMETERS

In crossing national borders, a firm encounters parameters not found in domestic business. Examples include duties, foreign currencies and changes in their value, different modes of transportation, and international documentation. New parameters also emerge because of differing modes of operating internationally. For example, the firm can export, license its products, engage in a joint venture, or carry out foreign direct investment. The firm that has done business only domestically will have had little or no experience with the requirements and conditions of these types of operations. Managers must therefore obtain information in order to make good business decisions.

NEW ENVIRONMENTAL FACTORS

When going international, a firm is exposed to an unfamiliar environment. Many of the domestic assumptions on which the firm and its activities were founded may not hold true internationally. Management needs to learn the culture of the host country, understand its political systems and level of stability, and comprehend the existing differences in societal structures and language. In addition, it must understand pertinent legal issues in order to avoid violating local laws. The technological level of the society must also be incorporated in the business plan. In short, all the assumptions that were formulated over the years based on domestic business activities must now be reevaluated. This crucial point is often neglected because most managers are born in the environment of their domestic operations and only subconsciously learn to understand the constraints and opportunities of their business activities. The situation is analogous to learning one's native language. Being born to a language makes speaking it seem easy. Only when attempting to learn a foreign language does one begin to appreciate the structure of language and the need for grammatical rules.

THE NUMBER OF FACTORS INVOLVED

Environmental relationships need to be relearned whenever a firm enters a new international market. The number of changing dimensions increases geometrically. Coordination of the interaction among the dimensions becomes increasingly difficult because of their sheer number. Such coordination, however, is crucial to the international success of the firm for two reasons. First, in order to exercise some central control over its international operations, a firm must be able to compare results and activities across countries. Otherwise, any plans made by headquarters may be inappropriate. Second, the firm must be able to learn from its international operations and must find ways to apply the new lessons learned to different markets. Without coordination, such learning cannot take place in a systematic way. The international research process can help in this undertaking.

BROADER DEFINITION OF COMPETITION

The international market exposes the firm to a much greater variety of competition than that found in the home market. For example, a firm may find that ketchup competes against soy sauce. Similarly, firms that offer labor-saving devices domestically may encounter competition abroad from cheap manual labor. Therefore, firms must determine the breadth of the competition, track competitive activities, and evaluate their actual and potential impact on company operations on an ongoing basis.

RECOGNIZING THE NEED FOR INTERNATIONAL RESEARCH

2. To explore the differences between domestic and international research

Many firms do little research before they enter a foreign market. Often, decisions concerning entry and expansion in overseas markets and selection and appointment of distributors are made after a cursory, subjective assessment of the situation. The research done is often less rigorous, less formal, and less quantitative than for domestic activities.

A major reason managers are reluctant to engage in international research is their lack of sensitivity to differences in culture, consumer tastes, and market demands. Often managers assume that their methods are both best and acceptable to all others. Fortunately, this is not true. What a boring place the world would be if it were!

A second reason is a limited appreciation for the different environments abroad. Often managers are insufficiently informed about the effect of geographic boundaries and do not understand that even national boundaries need not always coincide with culturally homogenous societies.[2] In addition, they are not prepared to accept that labor rules, distribution systems, the availability of media, or advertising regulations may be entirely different from those in the home market. Due to pressure to satisfy short-term financial goals, managers are unwilling to spend money to find out about the differences.

A third reason is lack of familiarity with national and international data sources and inability to use international data once it is obtained. As a result, the cost of conducting international research is perceived to be prohibitively high and therefore not a worthwhile investment relative to the benefits to be gained.[3] However, the Internet makes international research much easier and much less expensive. Data that are hard to find now become accessible at a click of a mouse. As the availability of the Internet grows around the world, so does the availability of research information.

Finally, firms often build their international business activities gradually, frequently based on unsolicited orders. Over time, actual business experience in a country or with a specific firm may then be used as a substitute for organized research.

Despite the reservations firms have, research is as important internationally as it is domestically. Firms must learn where the opportunities are, what customers want, why they want it, and how they satisfy their needs and wants so that the firm can serve them efficiently. Firms must obtain information about the local infrastructure, labor market, and tax rules before making a plant location decision. Doing business abroad without the benefit of research places firms, their assets, and their entire international future at risk.

Research allows management to identify and develop international strategies. The task includes the identification, evaluation, and comparison of potential foreign business opportunities and the subsequent target market selection. In addition, research is necessary for the development of a business plan that identifies all the requirements necessary for market entry, market penetration, and expansion. On a continuing basis, research provides the feedback needed to fine-tune various business activities. Finally, research can provide management with the intelligence to help anticipate events, take appropriate action, and adequately prepare for global changes.

 ## DETERMINING RESEARCH OBJECTIVES

As a starting point for research, research objectives must be determined. They will vary depending on the views of management, the corporate mission of the firm, the firm's level of internationalization, and its competitive situation. These objectives must be embedded in a firm's internal level of readiness to participate in the global market. A review of corporate capabilities such as personnel resources and the degree of financial exposure and risk that the firm is willing and able to tolerate also needs to be conducted. Existing diagnostic tools can be used to compare a firm's current preparedness on a broad-based level.[4] Knowing its internal readiness, the firm can then pursue its objectives with more confidence.

3. To learn where to find and how to use sources of secondary information

GOING INTERNATIONAL—EXPORTING

A frequent objective of international research is that of **foreign market opportunity analysis**. When a firm launches its international activities, it will usually find the world to be uncharted territory. Fortunately, information can be accumulated to provide basic guidelines. The aim is not to conduct a painstaking and detailed analysis of the world on a market-by-market basis, but instead to utilize a broad-brush approach. Accomplished quickly and at low cost, this approach will narrow the possibilities for international business activities.

foreign market opportunity analysis Broad-based research to obtain information about the general variables of a target market outside a firm's home country.

Such an approach should begin with a cursory analysis of general variables of a country, including total and per capita GDP, mortality rates, and population figures. Although these factors in themselves will not provide any detailed information, they will enable the researcher to determine whether corporate objectives might be met in the market. For example, the offering of computer software services in Ethiopia may be of little value because that country has one of the lowest global rates of computer usage. Similarly, high-priced consumer products are unlikely to be successful in Tajikistan because their price may well exceed the customer's annual salary.[5] Such a cursory evaluation will help reduce the number of markets to be considered to a more manageable number—for example, from 225 to 25.

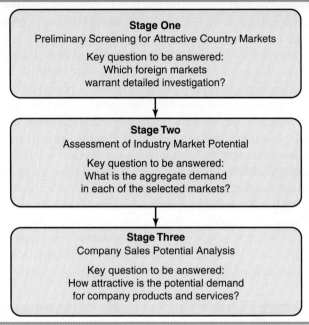

Figure 12.1   A Sequential Process of Researching Foreign Market Potentials

Stage One
Preliminary Screening for Attractive Country Markets

Key question to be answered:
Which foreign markets
warrant detailed investigation?

Stage Two
Assessment of Industry Market Potential

Key question to be answered:
What is the aggregate demand
in each of the selected markets?

Stage Three
Company Sales Potential Analysis

Key question to be answered:
How attractive is the potential demand
for company products and services?

Source: S. Tamer Cavusgil, "Guidelines for Export Market Research," *Business Horizons* 28 (November–December 1985): 29. © Copyright 1985 by the Foundation for the School of Business at Indiana University. Reprinted by permission.

As a next step, the researcher will require information on each individual country for a preliminary evaluation. Information will highlight the fastest growing markets, the largest markets for a particular category of product or service, demand trends, and business restrictions. Although precise and detailed information on individual products may not be obtainable, information is available for general product categories or service industries. Again, this overview will be cursory but will serve to quickly evaluate markets and further reduce the number to be considered.

At this stage, the researcher must select appropriate markets for in-depth evaluation. The focus will now be on opportunities for a specific type of service, product, or brand, and will include an assessment as to whether demand already exists or can be stimulated. Even though aggregate industry data may have been obtained previously, this general information is insufficient to make company-specific decisions. For example, the demand for sports equipment should not be confused with the potential demand for a specific brand. The research now should identify demand and supply patterns and evaluate any regulations and standards. Finally, a **competitive assessment** needs to be made, matching markets to corporate strengths and providing an analysis of the best potential for specific offerings. A summary of the various stages in the determination of market potential is provided in Figure 12.1.

competitive assessment A research process that consists of matching markets to corporate strengths and providing an analysis of the best potential for specific offerings.

GOING INTERNATIONAL—IMPORTING

When importing, the major focus shifts from supplying to sourcing. Management must identify markets that produce supplies or materials desired or that have the potential to do so. Foreign firms must be evaluated in terms of their capabilities and competitive standing.

Just as management would want to have some details on a domestic supplier, the importer needs to know, for example, about the reliability of a foreign supplier, the consistency of its product or service quality, and the length of delivery time. Information obtained through the subsidiary office of a bank or an embassy can prove very helpful. Information from business rating services and recommendations from current customers are also very useful in evaluating the potential business partner.

In addition, foreign government rules must be scrutinized as to whether exportation from the source country is possible. As examples, India may set limits on the cobra handbags it allows to be exported, and laws protecting a nation's cultural heritage may prevent the exportation of pre-Columbian artifacts from Latin American countries.

The international manager must also analyze domestic restrictions and legislation that may prohibit the importation of certain goods into the home country. Even though a market may exist at home for foreign umbrella handles, for example, quotas may restrict their importation to protect domestic industries. Similarly, even though domestic demand may exist for ivory, its importation may be illegal because of legislation enacted to protect wildlife worldwide.

MARKET EXPANSION

Research objectives include obtaining more detailed information for business expansion or monitoring the political climate so that the firm successfully can maintain its international operation. Information may be needed to enable the international manager to evaluate new business partners or assess the impact of a technological breakthrough on future business operations. The better defined the research objective is, the better the researcher will be able to determine information requirements and thus conserve the time and financial resources of the firm.

CONDUCTING SECONDARY RESEARCH

IDENTIFYING SOURCES OF DATA

4. To gain insight into the gathering of primary data

Typically, the information requirements of firms will cover both macro information about countries and trade, as well as micro information specific to the firm's activities. Table 12.1 provides an overview of the types of information that are most crucial for international business executives. If each firm had to go out and collect all the information needed on-site in the country under scrutiny, the task would be unwieldy and far too expensive. On many occasions, however, firms can make use of **secondary data**, that is, information that already has been collected by some other organization. A wide variety of sources present secondary data. The principal ones are governments, international institutions, service organizations, trade associations, directories, and other firms. This section provides a brief review of major data sources. Details on selected monitors of international issues are presented in Appendix 12A at the end of the chapter.

secondary data Data originally collected to serve another purpose than the one in which the researcher is currently interested.

Table 12.1 Critical International Information

Macro Data	Micro Data
• Tariff information	• Local laws and regulations
• U.S. export/import data	• Size of market
• Nontariff measures	• Local standards and specifications
• Foreign export/import data	• Distribution system
• Data on government trade policy	• Competitive activity

Governments

Most countries have a wide array of national and international trade data available. Typically, the information provided by governments addresses either macro and micro issues or offers specific data services. Macro information includes data on population trends, general trade flows among countries, and world agriculture production. Micro information includes materials on specific industries in a country, their growth prospects, and the extent and direction to which they are traded.

Unfortunately, the data are often published only in their home countries and in their native languages. However, the publications mainly present numerical data and so the translation task is relatively easy. In addition, the information sources are often available at embassies and consulates, whose missions include the enhancement of trade activities. The commercial counselor or commercial attaché can provide the information as can government-sponsored web sites. The user should be cautioned that the printed information is often dated and that the industry categories used abroad may not be compatible with industry categories used at home. Increasingly, government data are available on the Internet—often well before they are released in printed form. Closer collaboration between governmental statistical agencies also makes the data more accurate and reliable, because it is now much easier to compare data such as bilateral exports and imports to each other. Nonetheless, there are also occasional problems with government data, as discussed in Focus on Politics.

While many of the current data are available at no charge, governments often charge a fee for the use of data libraries. Given the depth of information such data can provide, the cost usually is a worthwhile expenditure for firms in light of the insights into trade patterns and reduction in risk they can achieve.

International Organizations

International organizations often provide useful data for the researcher. The United Nations (UN) *Statistical Yearbook* (http://unstats.un.org/unsd/syb/default.htm) is an annual publication of economic, social, and environmental statistics for more than 200 countries. It is compiled using a wide variety of sources, including UN agencies and other international, national, and specialized organizations. However, because of the time needed for the collection of such a large amount of information, the *Yearbook* does not always present the most current data. More up-to-date additional

---

FOCUS ON POLITICS

Government Reports Are Doubted in Argentina: Economists Dispute Inflation Numbers

During the past 50 years, Argentina has consistently been among the countries with the highest inflation rates in the world. Apparently, the government hoped to improve the economic reputation of the country by reporting better numbers.

In early 2007, several statisticians, clerks, and field workers who collect consumer prices were replaced, and lower inflation figures started to be reported. Before the personnel changes, the reported inflation rate was about 25 percent; afterwards, inflation had dropped to 8.5 percent. If something went up more than 15 percent, it was taken off the inflation basket.

Controversies erupted about the government's official poverty figures. Official calculations are about 15.3 percent, while social aid organizations claim that it is near 40 percent.

All these disputes have decreased the trustworthiness of government in the eyes of Argentine citizens. Economists and political analysts say the allegations also hurt the country's credibility in terms of investments. "It is very difficult to analyze a country as a result of statistics that can't be believed," said Fergus McCormick, a senior vice president at DBRS, a New York credit-rating agency that tracks Argentina.

Sources: http://www.washingtonpost.com/wp-dyn/content/article/2009/08/15/AR2009081502758.html, accessed November 11, 2009; http://commons.globalintegrity.org/2009/03/argentina-inflation-is-low-because-i.html, accessed November 11, 2009.

information is made available by specialized substructures of the United Nations, such as the UN Conference on Trade and Development (http://www.unctad.org/) and the International Trade Center (http://www.intracen.org/). The World Bank (http://econ .worldbank.org/) provides a wealth of country-specific economic data, including detailed development reports, research books, and policy papers. The World Trade Organization (http://www.wto.org/) and the Organization for Economic Cooperation and Development (http://www.oecd.org/home/) also publish quarterly and annual trade data on their member-countries. The International Monetary Fund (https:// www.imf.org/external/data.htm) is another useful source of information. Its publications include the World Economic Outlook databases, international trade statistics, and financial data by country. Additionally, there are many industry-specific international organizations, such as the International Air Transport Association (http://www .iata.org/index.htm) and the Federation of International Trade Associations (http:// www.fita.org/), which provide a wealth of data to researchers.

Service Organizations

A wide variety of service organizations that provide information include banks, accounting firms, freight forwarders, airlines, international trade consultants, research firms, and publishing houses located around the world. Frequently they are able to provide information on business practices, legislative or regulatory requirements, and political stability, as well as trade and financial data.

Trade Associations

Associations such as world trade clubs and domestic and international chambers of commerce (such as the American Chamber of Commerce abroad) can provide good information on local markets. Often files are maintained on international trade flows and trends affecting international managers. Valuable information can also be obtained from industry associations. These groups, formed to represent entire industry segments, often collect a wide variety of data from their members that are then published in an aggregate form. Most of these associations represent the viewpoints of their member firms to the government, so they usually have one or more publicly listed representatives in the capital. The information provided is often quite general, however, because of the wide variety of clientele served.

Directories and Newsletters

A large number of industry directories are available on local, national, and international levels. The directories primarily serve to identify firms and to provide very general background information, such as the name of the chief executive officer, the level of capitalization of the firm, the location, the address and telephone number, and some description of the firm's products. A host of newsletters discuss specific international business issues, such as international trade finance, legislative activities, countertrade, international payment flows, and customs news. Usually these newsletters cater to narrow audiences but can provide important information to the firm interested in a specific area.

Electronic Information Services

When information is needed, managers often cannot spend a lot of time, energy, or money finding, sifting through, and categorizing existing materials. Consider laboring through every copy of a trade publication to find out the latest news on how environmental concerns are affecting marketing decisions in Mexico. With electronic information services, search results can be obtained almost immediately. International online computer database services, numbering in the thousands, can be purchased to supply information external to the firm, such as exchange rates, international news, and import restrictions. Most database hosts do not charge any sign-up fee and request payment only for actual use. The selection of initial database hosts depends on the choice of relevant databases, taking into account their product and market limitations, language used, and geographical location. A large number of databases, developed by analysts who systematically sift through a wide range of periodicals, reports, and books in different languages, provide information on given products and markets. Many of the main news agencies now have information available through online databases, providing information on events that affect certain markets. Some databases cover extensive lists of companies in given countries and the products they buy and sell. Figure 12.2 provides an example.

The development of digital technology and online data-carrying communications systems has transformed computers into gateways to almost unlimited volumes

Figure 12.2   An Advertisement for International Information Services

Instant access to just what you need.

In order to thrive in today's rapidly changing marketplace you need access to timely, relevant and global business intelligence. The Economist Intelligence Unit can now deliver exactly what you need, when you need it. It's all part of our new EIU Online Store.

At the EIU Online Store you can gain instant access to the latest analysis of more than 180 countries, industry trends, and global best practices. You can select from any one of over 200 subscription titles and research reports or search our entire database for the specific "byte-sized" article or record you require. With the EIU Online Store, take just what you need, and download it instantly to your desktop.

As a customer of the EIU Online Store, **you benefit from:**
- Access to our entire database, archived up to two years
- Quick and easy navigation by category
- Expenses tracked on a per-project basis
- Special announcements and trial offers
- An up-to-date complete catalogue of EIU publications

Whether you need to keep track of business developments in a particular country every quarter or you need GDP figures for a whole region, the EIU Online Store has got what you're looking for. There's no minimum purchase, so there's no reason not to try it right now. Log on to www.eiu.com, and using a credit card, get instant access to the precise intelligence you need.

Byte-size global business intelligence from the EIU: *The EIU Online Store.*

www.eiu.com

 E·I·U The Economist Intelligence Unit

Courtesy Economist Intelligence Unit.

of information content. An online service widely used in the United States is the National Trade Data Bank (NDTB), offered by the U.S. Department of Commerce's Economics and Statistics Administration (http://www.stat-usa.gov/tradtest.nsf). The NTDB includes more than 200,000 current and historical documents—including trade releases, international market research, country analysis, and trade and procurement leads—compiled from 40 federal agencies and offices.[6] Another example of valuable on-line information is the Country Commercial Guides (http://www.buyusainfo.net/adsearch.cfm?search_type=int&loadnav=no), offered by the U.S. Foreign Commercial Service, an example of which is shown in Appendix 12B of this chapter.

Using data services for research means that professionals do not have to leave their offices, going from library to library to locate the facts they need. Many online services have late-breaking information available on a real-time basis to the user. These techniques of research are cost-effective as well. Stocking a company's library with all the books needed to have the same amount of data that is available online or with CD-ROM would be too expensive and space-consuming.

In spite of the ease of access to data on the Internet, it must be remembered that search engines only cover a portion of international publications. Also, they are heavily biased towards English-language publications. As a result, sole reliance on electronic information may let the researcher lose out on valuable input.[7] Electronic databases should therefore be seen as only one important dimension of research scrutiny. A listing of selected databases useful for international business is presented in Appendix 12A of this chapter.

SELECTION OF SECONDARY DATA

Just because secondary information has been found to exist does not mean that it must be used. Even though one key advantage of secondary data over primary research is that they are available relatively quickly and inexpensively, the researcher should still assess the effort and benefit of using them. Secondary data should be evaluated regarding the quality of their source, their recency, and their relevance to the task at hand. Clearly, because the information was collected without the current research requirements in mind, there may well be difficulties in coverage, categorization, and comparability. For example, an "engineer" in one country may differ substantially in terms of training and responsibilities from a person in another country holding the same title. It is therefore important to be careful when getting ready to interpret and analyze data.

The ease of access to information through online searches has raised concerns about information usage. As Focus on Ethics shows, governments and private-sector organizations are analyzing the effects of declassification programs that may place sensitive information into the hands of dangerous people.

INTERPRETATION AND ANALYSIS OF SECONDARY DATA

Once secondary data have been obtained, the researcher must creatively convert them into information. Secondary data were originally collected to serve another purpose than the one in which the researcher is currently interested. Therefore, they can often be used only as **proxy information** in order to arrive at conclusions that address the research objectives. For example, the market penetration of DVD players may be used as a proxy variable for the potential demand for Blu-ray players. Similarly, in an industrial setting, information about plans for new port facilities may be useful in determining future container requirements.

The researcher must often use creative inferences, and such creativity brings risks. Therefore, once interpretation and analysis have taken place, a consistency

proxy information Data used as a substitute for more desirable data that are unobtainable.

To Share, or Not to Share, That Is the Question

Many believe that scientific knowledge is a public good that should be freely shared within the global research community for the betterment of humanity. Breakthroughs in the treatment and containment of infectious disease, improved water purification techniques, and the genetic modification of crops to increase yields are all examples of real-life applications of scientific innovation. However, issues of data ownership, security concerns, and general lack of consensus within the research community have erected barriers that prohibit the free flow of scientific information around the world. There are two main sources of obstacles to research sharing—private industry and government policies.

Private industry finances the majority of global research and development (R&D). For example, in the United States, businesses account for roughly 60 percent of all R&D spending. Most of the increase in private research finance is attributed to the development of the telecommunications and biotechnology industries. Because companies' primary goal is profit maximization, it is in their best interest to keep any scientific innovations that emerge from the research they fund proprietary. This allows for the monetarization of patents and the establishment and maintenance of competitive advantages. One issue that has generated tremendous controversy is the relationship between intellectual property law and global health. For example, the avian flu pandemic led to public pressure for Roche to relax its patent on Oseltamivir, a drug used to treat bird influenza. Such situations have contributed to the debate over whether companies should be forced to share their proprietary research in times of global crises, such as viral pandemics.

However, governmental efforts to legislate patent restrictions could be interpreted as disingenuous, because most national governments place their own restrictions on the dissemination of the scientific innovations, developed within their academic communities. The areas of nuclear physics and biotechnology face the most regulation, especially in light of the global counterterrorism effort. Simultaneously, governments are keenly aware that by limiting the free flow of scientific ideas, they could be stunting future innovation, and they have sought to develop compromise solutions.

In the United States, the National Research Council and the National Academy of Sciences established the Panel on Data Access for Research Purposes in order to examine the trade-off between the risks and benefits of access to research data and to make recommendations about how data "should optimally (from a societal standpoint) be made available to researchers." The United Kingdom is a signatory to the OECD's Declaration on Access to Research Data from Public Funding and has demonstrated a strong policy commitment to supporting the free flow of research to support science and innovation. In Australia, the government has provided $24 million (in Australian dollars) toward the establishment of a National Australian Data Service (ANDS). Germany's Alliance of Science Organizations has identified the sharing of research data as a major focus area in its Priority Initiative on Digital Information.

This trend confirms that governments realize that the free flow of research is an accelerant to any scientific field. However, there still is a lack of consensus over how to manage this flow for the sake of national security. Additionally, regulators continue to struggle with issues of free enterprise versus "the greater good." Until international norms for the sharing of scientific research are established and globally accepted, the unimpeded flow of international scientific innovation remains a mirage.

Sources: Eleanor Singer, "Access to Research Data: Reconciling Risk and Benefits," *Journal of Law and Policy* 14 (2006): 85; Neil Beagrie, Robert Beagrie, and Ian Rowlands, "Research Data Preservation and Access: The Views of Researchers," *Ariadne* 60 (July 30, 2009), http://www.ariadne.ac.uk/issue60/beagrie-et-al/, accessed November 16, 2009; Michael Westerhaus and Arachu Castro, "How Do Intellectual Property Law and International Trade Agreements Affect Access to Antiretroviral Therapy?" *PLoS Medicine* 3, no. 8 (August 2006): 332.

check must be conducted. The researcher should always cross-check the results with other possible sources of information or with experts. Yet, if properly implemented, such creativity can open up one's eyes to new market potential.

DATA PRIVACY

data privacy Electronic information security that restricts secondary use of data according to laws and preferences of the subjects.

The attitude of society toward obtaining and using both secondary and primary data must be taken into account. Many societies are increasingly sensitive to the issue of **data privacy**, and the concern has grown exponentially as a result of e-business. Readily accessible databases may contain information valuable to marketers, but they may also be considered privileged by individuals who have provided the data.

In 1995, the European Union adopted a stringent data-privacy directive, which restricts access to lifestyle information and its use for segmentation purposes. Companies are permitted to collect personal data only if the individuals consent to the collection, know how the data will be used, and have access to databases to correct or erase their information. Additionally, the directive contains an extraterritorial clause, which bars the transfer of customer information to countries that fail to adopt "adequate" protections. This represents a distinctly different approach to data privacy than the one adopted in the United States, where personal information is often treated as a conventional good and commoditized.

The fundamental differences in EU and U.S. privacy laws led to what many analysts have identified as the first big trade and security conflict of the information age. After 9/11, the United States sought to expand its international data collection, as part of its effort to combat terrorism and was thwarted by EU privacy rules, which have become the de facto international norm, with more than 30 countries following the European example. The EU has made some concessions in support of the U.S. antiterror effort, such as the "Terrorist Finance Tracking Programme," which transmits financial transaction records from Europe to the U.S. Treasury Department. However, when it comes to access to voter rolls, birth records, or mortgage information for international marketing purposes, companies looking to do business in the EU are still out of luck.[8]

Increasingly, however, the desire for personal privacy, particularly in the context of business contacts, is growing in value in the United States. Firms must inform their customers of privacy policies and inform them of the right to deny the use of their personal information. Therefore, the gap in policies is likely to shrink.

CONDUCTING PRIMARY RESEARCH

Even though secondary data are useful to the researcher, on many occasions primary information will be required. **Primary data** are obtained by a firm to fill specific information needs. Although the research may not be conducted by the company with the need, the work must be carried out for a specific research purpose in order to qualify as primary research. Typically, primary research intends to answer such clear-cut questions as:

- What is the sales potential for our measuring equipment in Malaysia?
- How much does the typical Greek consumer spend on fast food?
- What effect will our new type of packaging have on our green consumers in Norway?
- What service standards do industrial customers expect in Japan?

The researcher must have a clear idea of what the population under study should be and where it is located before deciding on the country or region to investigate. Conducting research in an entire country may not be necessary if, for example, only urban centers are to be penetrated. Multiple regions of a country need to be investigated, however, if a lack of homogeneity exists because of different economic, geographic, or behavioral factors. One source reports of the failure of a firm in Indonesia due to insufficient geographic dispersion of its research. The firm conducted its study only in large Indonesian cities during the height of tourism season, but projected the results to the entire population. When the company set up large production and distribution facilities to meet the expected demand, it realized only limited sales to city tourists.[9]

The discussion presented here will focus mainly on the research-specific issues. Application dimensions such as market choice and market analysis will be covered in Chapter 15.

5. To examine the need for international management information systems

primary data Data obtained directly for a specific research purpose through interviews, focus groups, surveys, observation, or experimentation.

INDUSTRIAL VERSUS CONSUMER SOURCES OF DATA

The researcher must decide whether research is to be conducted in the consumer or the industrial product area, which in turn determines the size of the universe and respondent accessibility. Consumers usually are a very large group, whereas the total population of industrial users may be limited. Cooperation by respondents may also vary. In the industrial setting, differentiation between users and decision makers may be important because their personalities, their outlooks, and their evaluative criteria may differ widely. Determining the proper focus of the research is therefore of major importance to its successful completion.

DETERMINING THE RESEARCH TECHNIQUE

unstructured data
Information collected for analysis with open-ended questions.

Selection of the research technique depends on a variety of factors. First, the objectivity of the data sought must be determined. Standardized techniques are more useful in the collection of objective data than of subjective data. **Unstructured data** will require more open-ended questions and more time than structured data. Whether the data are to be collected in the real world or in a controlled environment must be determined. Finally, it must be decided whether to collect historical facts or information about future developments. This is particularly important for consumer research, because firms frequently want to determine the future intentions of consumers about buying a certain product.

Once the desired data structure is determined, the researcher must choose a research technique. As in domestic research, the types available are interviews, focus groups, observation, surveys, and the use of web technology. Each one provides a different depth of information and has its own unique strengths and weaknesses.

Interviews

interview A face-to-face research tool to obtain in-depth information.

Interviews with knowledgeable people can be of great value for the corporation that wants international information. Bias from the individual may slant the findings, so the intent should be to obtain not a wide variety of data, but rather in-depth information. When specific answers are sought to very narrow questions, interviews can be particularly useful.

Focus Groups

Focus groups are a useful research tool resulting in interactive interviews. A group of knowledgeable people is gathered for a limited period of time (two to four hours). Usually, seven to ten participants is the ideal size for a focus group. A specific topic is introduced and thoroughly discussed by all group members. Because of the interaction, hidden issues are sometimes raised that would not have been detected in an individual interview. The skill of the group leader in stimulating discussion is crucial to the success of a focus group. Like in-depth interviews, focus groups do not provide statistically significant information; however, they can be helpful in providing information about perceptions, emotions, and attitudinal factors. In addition, once individuals have been gathered, focus groups are a highly efficient means of rapidly accumulating a substantial amount of information.

When planning international research using focus groups, the researcher must be aware of the importance of language and culture in the interaction process. Major differences may exist already in preparing for the focus group. In some countries, participants can simply be asked to show up at a later date at a location where they will join the focus group. In other countries, participants have to be brought into the group immediately because commitments made for a future date have little meaning. In some nations, providing a payment to participants is sufficient motivation for them to open up in discussion. In other countries, one first needs to host a luncheon or dinner for the group so that members get to know each other and are willing to interact.

Once the focus group is started, the researcher must remember that not all societies encourage frank and open exchange and disagreement among individuals. Status consciousness may result in the opinion of one participant being reflected by all others. Disagreement may be seen as impolite, or certain topics may be taboo. Unless a native focus group leader is used, it also is possible to completely misread the interactions among group participants and to miss out on nuances and constraints participants feel when commenting in the group situation. One of this book's authors, for example, used the term *group discussion* in a focus group with Russian executives, only to learn that the translated meaning of the term was *political indoctrination session*.[10] As Focus on Culture explains, the use of different languages in research makes it necessary to check one's translations very carefully.

Observation

Observation requires the researcher to play the role of a nonparticipating observer of activity and behavior. In an international setting, observation can be extremely useful in shedding light on practices not previously encountered or understood. This aspect is especially valuable to the researcher who has no knowledge of a particular market or market situation. It can help in understanding phenomena that would have been difficult to assess with other techniques. For example, Toyota sent a group of its engineers and designers to southern California to nonchalantly observe how women get into and operate their cars. They found that women with long fingernails have trouble opening the door and operating various knobs on the dashboard. Toyota engineers and designers were able to comprehend the women's plight and redesign some of their automobile exteriors and interiors, producing more desirable cars.[11] This is an example of **empathic design**, or a user-centered design approach that observes customers in their normal environment in order to see how they use products and better identify their needs.[12]

All the research instruments discussed so far are useful primarily for the gathering of **qualitative information**. The intent is not to amass data or to search for statistical significance, but rather to obtain a better understanding of given situations, behavioral patterns, or underlying dimensions. The researcher using these instruments must be cautioned that even frequent repetition of the measurements will not lead to a statistically valid result. However, statistical validity often may not be the major focus of corporate research. Rather, it may be the better understanding, description, and prediction of events that have an impact on decision making. When **quantitative data** are desired, surveys and experimentation are more appropriate research instruments.

Surveys

Survey research is useful in quantifying concepts. **Surveys** are usually conducted via questionnaires that are administered personally, by mail, or by telephone. Use of the survey technique presupposes that the population under study is accessible and able to comprehend and respond to the questions posed through the chosen medium. Particularly for mail and telephone surveys, a major precondition is the feasibility of using the postal system or the widespread availability of telephones. Obviously, this is not a given in all countries. In many nations only limited records about dwellings, their locations, and their occupants are available. In Venezuela, for example, most houses are not numbered but rather are given individual names such as Casa Rosa or El Retiro. In some countries, street maps are not even available. As a result, reaching respondents by mail is virtually impossible. In other countries, obtaining a correct address may be easy, but the postal system may not function well.

observation A research tool where the subject's activity and behavior are scrutinized.

empathic design A user-centered design approach that observes customers in their normal environment in order to see how they use products and better identify their needs.

qualitative information Data that are not amenable to statistical analysis, but provide a better understanding, description, or prediction of given situations, behavioral patterns, or underlying dimensions.

quantitative data Information based on numeric and statistical relationships.

surveys The use of questionnaires to obtain quantifiable research information.

FOCUS ON CULTURE

The Business Tower of Babel

All sorts of comical things can go wrong when a company translates its advertising into foreign languages. Managers at one American car manufacturer marketed their new car—the Matador—based on an image of courage and strength. However, in Puerto Rico the name means "killer" and was very unpopular on the country's hazardous roads. Kellogg renamed its Bran Buds cereal in Sweden when it discovered that it roughly translated to "burned farmer." PepsiCo's innocuous-sounding "Come Alive with Pepsi" campaign led not only to one but to two translation blunders. The slogan was translated in Chinese as "Pepsi brings your ancestors back from the dead," and in German as "Come Alive from the Grave." Advertising mistakes receive a fair amount of attention in the media and the international business world when they occur, but many people never stop to think about what would happen if a company unknowingly committed translation errors much earlier—in the research phase.

The possibility of disaster due to such errors is in many ways even greater than in the advertising stage because research findings are often used to determine a firm's strategy or for new product development. A translation blunder that goes undiscovered at this stage could set a company on the wrong track entirely. Imagine spending millions of dollars to develop a new product or to enter a new market only to find that your company's surveys had asked the wrong questions!

Researchers at the Pew Research Center for the People and the Press in Washington, DC, are not new to international research. They have been conducting public opinion research around the globe for more than a decade. Their findings related to attitudes toward the press, politics, and public policy issues are regularly cited in the media. However, the company received an unwelcome surprise when it translated one of its worldwide polls into 63 languages and then back into English. As it turns out, the ride to the foreign languages and back again was a bit bumpier than they had imagined.

For example, in Ghana, the original phrase "married or living with a partner" was first translated into one of the country's tribal languages as "married but have a girlfriend," and the category "separated" became "There's a misunderstanding between me and my spouse." The original version of a questionnaire to be used in Nigeria had similar problems: "American ideas and customs" came out "the ideology of America and border guards" (get it, customs? border guards?) and the phrase "success in life is pretty much determined by forces outside our control" initially read, "Goodness in life starts with blessings from one's personal god." In the original Nigerian Yoruba version, "fast food" had been translated to "microwave food" and "the military" became "Herbalist/medicine man." Not quite the same thing, is it?

Fortunately, the meanings were corrected in the final translations of the questionnaire, said the Center's director Andrew Kohut. The lesson? Multinational researchers, check your translations!

Sources: "Results of Poor Cultural Awareness," Kwintessential Ltd., http://www.kwintessential.co.uk/cultural-services/articles/Results%20of%20Poor%20Cross%20Cultural%20Awareness.html, accessed November 15, 2009; David A. Ricks, *Blunders in International Business*, 4th ed. (Malden, MA: Wiley-Blackwell, 2006).

Telephone surveys may also be inappropriate if telephone ownership is rare. In such instances, any information obtained would be highly biased even if the researcher randomized the calls. In some cases, inadequate telephone networks and systems, frequent line congestion, and a lack of telephone directories may also prevent the researcher from conducting surveys.

Since surveys deal with people who in an international setting display major differences in culture, preference, education, and attitude, just to mention a few factors, the use of the survey technique must be carefully examined. For example, in some regions of the world, recipients of letters may be illiterate. Others may be very literate, but totally unaccustomed to some of the standard research scaling techniques used in the United States and therefore may be unable to respond to the instrument. Survey respondents in different countries may have different extreme response styles. If members of one culture are much more likely than those of another culture to agree very much or very little with a question, for example, then the researcher must adjust the findings in order to make them comparable to each other.[13] Other recipients of a survey may be reluctant to respond in writing, particularly when sensitive questions are asked. This sensitivity, of course, also varies by country. In some nations, any questions about income, even in categorical form, are considered highly proprietary; in others the purchasing behavior of individuals is not readily divulged.

The researcher needs to understand such constraints and prepare a survey that is responsive to the subjects. For example, surveys can incorporate drawings or even

Surveys are key to learning more about consumer wants and needs.

© Image Bank/Getty Images, Inc.

cartoons to communicate better. Personal administration or collaboration with locally accepted intermediaries may improve the response rate. Indirect questions may need to substitute for direct ones in sensitive areas. Questions may have to be reworded to ensure proper communication. Figure 12.3 provides an example of a rating scale developed by researchers to work with a diverse population with relatively little education. In its use, however, it was found that the same scale aroused negative reactions among better-educated respondents, who considered the scale childish and insulting to their intelligence.

Figure 12.3   The Funny Faces Scale

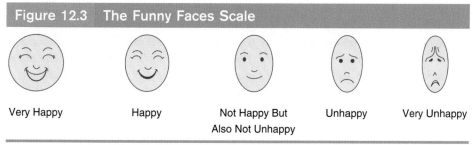

| Very Happy | Happy | Not Happy But Also Not Unhappy | Unhappy | Very Unhappy |

Source: C. K. Corder, "Problems and Pitfalls in Conducting Marketing Research in Africa," *Marketing Expansion in a Shrinking World*, ed. Betsy Gelb. Proceedings of American Marketing Association Business Conference (Chicago: AMA, 1978), pp. 86–90.

In spite of all the potential difficulties, the survey technique remains a useful one because it allows the researcher to rapidly accumulate a large quantity of data amenable to statistical analysis. With constantly expanding technological capabilities, international researchers will be able to use this technique even more in the future.

Web Technology

The growing use of technology has given rise to new marketing research approaches that allow consumers to be heard much more and permit firms to work much harder at their listening skills. Two primary research approaches are rapidly growing in their use: web-based research and e-mail-based surveys.

The increasing degree to which the World Wide Web truly lives up to its name is making it possible for international marketers to use this medium in their research efforts. The technology can reach out in a low-cost fashion and provide innovative ways to present stimuli and collect data. For example, on a web site, product details, pictures of products, brands, and the shopping environment can be portrayed with integrated graphics and sound—thus bringing the issues to be researched much closer to the respondent. In addition, the behavior of visitors to a site can be traced and interpreted regarding the interest in product, services, or information.[14]

Surveys can be administered either through a web site or through e-mail. If they are posted on a site, surveys can be of the pop-up nature, where visitors can be specifically targeted. An e-mail survey eliminates the need for postage and printing. As a result, larger and geographically diverse audiences can be the focus of an inquiry. Research indicates that there is a higher and faster response rate to such electronic inquiries. In addition, the process of data entry can be automated so that responses are automatically fed into data-analysis software.[15]

However, it would be too simplistic to assume that the digitalization of survey content is all that it takes to go global on the web. There are cultural differences that must be taken into account by the researcher. Global visitors to a site should encounter research that matches their own cultural values, rituals, and symbols, and testimonials or encouragement should be delivered by culture-specific heroes. For example, a web site might first offer a visitor from Korea the opportunity to become part of a product-user community. A low-context visitor from the United States may in turn be exposed to product features immediately.[16]

In addition, such electronic research suffers from a lack of confidentiality of the participants since e-mails disclose the identity of the sender. This issue, in turn, triggers concerns and rules of data privacy, which may limit the use of these tools in some nations or regions. Also, the opportunity to overuse a tool may result in the gradual disenchantment of its audience. Therefore, current high response rates may well decline over time.

Some have also questioned the value of online research tools. For example, industry observers have identified the growing phenomenon of the "professional online respondent"—an individual who is significantly less likely than the norm to be employed full time and far more likely to spend disproportionately higher amounts of his or her time online. In other words, the typical online research respondent might not be very typical of the general population that the marketer would like to target. A simple online search of "earn survey money" demonstrates the extent of this problem.

However, as long as the researcher is aware of the limitations of online survey research and takes proactive steps to control for them (e.g., preventing repeat respondents to surveys through standard methods of IP address validation and assignment), the Internet offers international marketers an entire array of new opportunities that will grow rather than diminish. As stated by a leading marketing research expert, in the not-too-distant future, web-based survey research will become the norm, not the exception.[17]

information system Can provide the decision maker with basic data for most ongoing decisions.

6. To examine the role importance of international information systems for corporate decision processes and strategic planning

THE INTERNATIONAL INFORMATION SYSTEM

Many organizations have data needs that go beyond specific international research projects. Most of the time, daily decisions must be made for which there is neither time nor money for special research. An **information system** can provide the decision maker with basic data for most ongoing decisions. Defined as "the systematic and continuous gathering, analysis, and reporting of data for decision-making purposes,"[18] such a system serves as a mechanism to coordinate the flow of information to corporate managers.

To be useful to the decision maker, the system must have certain attributes. First of all, the information must be *relevant*. The data gathered must have meaning for the manager's decision-making process. Only rarely can corporations afford to spend large amounts of money on information that is simply "nice to know." Any information system will have to continuously address the balance to be struck between the expense of the research design and process and the value of the information to ongoing business activities. Second, the information must be *timely*. Managers derive little benefit if decision information needed today does not become available until a month from now. To be of use to the international decision maker, the system must therefore feed from a variety of international sources and be updated frequently. For multinational corporations, this means a real-time link between international subsidiaries and a broad-based ongoing data input operation. Third, information must be *flexible*—that is, it must be available in the form needed by management. An information system must therefore permit manipulation of the format and combination of the data. Fourth, information contained in the system must be *accurate*. This is especially important in international research because information quickly becomes outdated as a result of major environmental changes. Fifth, the system's information bank must be reasonably *exhaustive*. Factors that may influence a particular decision must be appropriately represented in the information system because of the interrelationships among variables. This means that the information system must be based on a wide variety of factors. Sixth, the collection and processing of data must be *consistent*. This is to hold down project cost and turnaround time, while ensuring that data can be compared regionally. This can be achieved by centralizing the management under one manager who oversees the system's design, processing, and analysis.[19] Finally, to be useful to managers, the system must be *convenient* to use. Systems that are cumbersome and time-consuming to reach and to use will not be used enough to justify corporate expenditures to build and maintain them.

One area where international firms are gradually increasing the use of information system technology is in the export field. In order to stay close to their customers, proactive firms are developing **export complaint systems**. These systems allow customers to contact the original supplier of a product in order to inquire about products, to make suggestions, or to present complaints. Firms are finding that about 5 percent of their customers abroad are dissatisfied with their products. By establishing direct contact via e-mail, a toll-free telephone number, or a web site, firms do not need to rely on the filtered feedback from channel intermediaries abroad and can learn directly about product failures, channel problems, or other causes of customer dissatisfaction.

export complaint systems Allow customers to contact the original supplier of a product in order to inquire about products, make suggestions, or present complaints.

The development of such an export complaint system requires substantial resources, intensive planning, and a high degree of cultural sensitivity. Customers abroad must be informed of how to complain, and their cost of complaining must be minimized, for example, by offering an interactive web site. The response to complaints must also be tailored to the culture of the complainant. For example, to some customers, the speed of reply matters most, while to others the thoughtfulness of the reply is of key concern. As a result, substantial resources must be invested into personnel training so the system works in harmony with customer expectations. Most important, however, is a firm's ability to aggregate and analyze complaints and to make use of them internally. Complaints are often the symptom for underlying structural problems of a product or a process. If used properly, an export complaint system can become a rich source of information for product improvement and innovation.

Increasingly, the Internet enables customers to provide feedback on their experiences with a firm. Online reputation can have an important effect on a firm's prospects and can even preclude individuals from participating in business transactions. A symposium sponsored by the National Science Foundation and the Massachusetts Institute of Technology created the Reputation Research Network (http://databases .si.umich.edu/reputations/), an electronic database of studies on reputation systems and their importance for businesses seeking to preserve customer loyalty.[20]

To build an information system, corporations use the internal data that are available from divisions such as accounting and finance and also from various subsidiaries. In addition, many organizations put mechanisms in place to enrich the basic data flow to information systems. Three such mechanisms are environmental scanning, Delphi studies, and scenario building.

Environmental Scanning

Any changes in the business environment, whether domestic or foreign, may have serious repercussions on the activities of the firm. Corporations therefore understand the necessity for tracking new developments. Although this can be done implicitly in the domestic environment, the remoteness of international markets requires a continuous information flow. For this purpose, some large multinational organizations have formed environmental scanning groups.

environmental scanning Obtaining ongoing data about a country.

Environmental scanning activities provide continuous information on political, social, and economic affairs internationally; on changes of attitudes of public institutions and private citizens; and on possible upcoming alterations. Environmental scanning models can be used for a variety of purposes, such as the development of long-term strategies, getting managers to broaden their horizons, or structuring action plans. Obviously, the precision required for environmental scanning varies with its purpose. The more immediate and precise the application will be within the corporation, the greater the need for detailed information. On the other hand, heightened precision may reduce the usefulness of environmental scanning in strategic planning, which is long term.

Environmental scanning can be performed in various ways. One consists of obtaining factual input on a wide variety of demographic, social, and economic characteristics of foreign countries. Frequently, managers believe that factual data alone are insufficient for their information needs. Particularly when forecasting future developments, other methods are used to capture underlying dimensions of social change. One significant method is that of **content analysis**. A wide array of newspapers, magazines, and other publications are scanned worldwide in order to pinpoint over time the gradual evolution of new views or trends. Corporations also use the technique of media analysis to pinpoint upcoming changes in their line of business. This is especially important in the field of communications and information technology, where innovations create a rapidly changing business environment. For example, when Google announced the development of new software that consumers could download to their mobile phones and receive free turn-by-turn directions, investors fled traditional global positioning system (GPS) makers like TomTom and Garmin. Within hours after Google's announcement, Garmin's shares had dropped by 17 percent and TomTom's by 21 percent.[21]

content analysis Systematic evaluation of communication for frequency of expressions.

Content analysis is also useful in identifying consumer attitudes about environmental and ethical issues, such as pollution, preservation of natural resources, and animal testing, which allows firms to locate new opportunities for expanding their operations while remaining within changing moral and environmental boundaries.

Environmental scanning is conducted by a variety of groups within and outside the corporation. Quite frequently, small corporate staffs are created at headquarters to coordinate the information flow. In addition, subsidiary staff can be used to provide occasional intelligence reports. Groups of volunteers are also formed to gather and analyze information worldwide and feed their individual analyses back to corporate headquarters, where the "big picture" can then be constructed. Rapidly growing use of the Internet also allows firms to find out about new developments in their fields of interest and permits them to gather information through bulletin boards and discussion groups. For example, some firms use search engines to comb through thousands of newsgroups for any mention of a particular product or application. If they find frequent references, they can investigate further to see what customers are saying.[22]

Finally, it should be kept in mind that internationally there may be a fine line between tracking and obtaining information and the misappropriation of corporate secrets. With growing frequency, governments and firms claim that their trade secrets are being obtained and abused by foreign competitors. The perceived threat from economic espionage has led to legislation[23] and accusations of government spying networks trying to undermine the commercial interests of companies.[24] Information gatherers must be sensitive to these issues in order to avoid conflict.

Delphi Studies

To enrich the information obtained from factual data, corporations and governments frequently resort to the use of creative and highly qualitative data-gathering methods. One approach is through **Delphi studies**. These studies are particularly useful in the international environment because they are "a means for aggregating the judgments of a number of . . . experts . . . who cannot come together physically."[25] This type of research clearly aims at qualitative measures by seeking a consensus from those who know, rather than average responses from many people with only limited knowledge.

Delphi studies A research tool using a group of experts to rank major future developments.

Typically, Delphi studies are carried out with groups of about 30 well-chosen participants who possess expertise in an area of concern, such as future developments of the international trade environment. The participants are asked to identify the major issues in the given area of concern. They are also requested to rank order their statements according to importance and explain the rationale behind the order. The aggregated information and comments are then sent to all participants in the Delphi group. Group members are encouraged to agree or disagree with the various rank orders and the comments. This allows statements to be challenged. In another round, the participants respond to the challenges. Several rounds of challenges and responses result in a reasonably coherent consensus.

The Delphi technique is particularly valuable because it uses mail, facsimile, or electronic communication to bridge large distances and therefore makes experts quite accessible at a reasonable cost. It avoids the drawback of ordinary mail investigations, which lack interaction among participants. Several rounds may be required, however, so substantial time may elapse before the information is obtained. Also, a major effort must be expended in selecting the appropriate participants and in motivating them to participate in the exercise with enthusiasm and continuity. When carried out on a regular basis, Delphi studies can provide crucial augmentation of the factual data available for the information system. For example, a large portion of this book's last chapter was written based on an extensive Delphi study carried out by the authors.

Scenario Building

The information obtained through environmental scanning or Delphi studies can then be used to conduct a scenario analysis. One approach involves the development of a series of plausible scenarios that are constructed from trends observed in the environment. Another method consists of formally reviewing assumptions built into existing business plans and positions.[26] Subsequently, some of these key assumptions such as economic growth rates, import penetration, population growth, and political stability, can be varied. By projecting variations for medium- to long-term periods, completely new environmental conditions can emerge. The conditions can then be analyzed for their potential domestic and international impact on corporate strategy.

The identification of crucial variables and the degree of variation are of major importance in **scenario building**. Scenario builders also need to recognize the nonlinearity of factors. To simply extrapolate from currently existing situations is insufficient, since extraneous factors often enter the picture with significant impact. The possibility of **joint occurrences** must be recognized as well, because changes may not come about in isolated fashion but instead may spread over wide regions. For example, given large technological advances, the possibility of wholesale obsolescence of current technology must be considered. Quantum leaps in computer development and new generations of computers may render obsolete the entire technological investment of a corporation.

For scenarios to be useful, management must analyze and respond to them by formulating contingency plans. Such planning will broaden horizons and may prepare managers for unexpected situations. Through the anticipation of possible problems, managers hone their response capability and in turn shorten response times to actual problems.

The development of an international information system is of major importance to the multinational corporation. It aids the ongoing decision process and becomes a vital tool in performing the strategic planning task. Only by observing global trends and changes will the firm be able to maintain and improve its competitive position. Much of the data available are quantitative in nature, but researchers must also pay attention to qualitative dimensions. Quantitative analysis will continue to improve as the ability to collect, store, analyze, and retrieve data increases as a result of computer development. Nevertheless, the qualitative dimension will remain a major component for corporate research and planning activities.

scenario building The identification of crucial variables and determining their effects on different cases or approaches.

joint occurrence Occurrence of one or several shifts affecting the business environment in several locations simultaneously.

SUMMARY

Constraints of time, resources, and expertise are the major inhibitors to international research. Nevertheless, firms need to carry out planned and organized research in order to explore foreign market opportunities and challenges successfully. Such research must be linked closely to the decision-making process.

International research differs from domestic research in that the environment—which determines how well tools, techniques, and concepts apply—is different abroad. In addition, the international manager must deal with duties, exchange rates, and international documentation; a greater number of interacting factors; and a much broader definition of the concept of competition.

When the firm is uninformed about international differences in consumer tastes and preferences or about foreign market environments, the need for international research is particularly great. Research objectives need to be determined based on the corporate mission, the level of international expertise, and the business plan. These objectives will enable the research to identify the information requirements.

Given the scarcity of resources, companies beginning their international effort must rely on data that have already been collected. These secondary data are available from sources such as governments, international organizations, or electronic information services. It is important to respect privacy laws and preferences when making use of secondary data.

To fulfill specific information requirements, the researcher may need to collect primary data. An appropriate research technique must be selected to collect the information. Sensitivity to different international environments and cultures will aid the researcher in deciding whether to use interviews, focus groups, observation, surveys, or web technology as data-collection techniques.

To provide ongoing information to management, an information system is useful. Such a system will provide for the continuous gathering, analysis, and reporting of data for decision-making purposes. Data gathered through environmental scanning, Delphi studies, or scenario building enable management to prepare for the future and hone its decision-making abilities.

KEY TERMS

foreign market opportunity analysis   395
competitive assessment   396
secondary data   397
proxy information   401
data privacy   402
primary data   403

unstructured data   404
interview   404
observation   405
empathic design   405
qualitative information   405
quantitative data   405
surveys   405

information system   408
export complaint systems   409
environmental scanning   410
content analysis   410
Delphi studies   411
scenario building   412
joint occurrence   412

QUESTIONS FOR DISCUSSION

1. You are employed by National Engineering, a firm that designs subways. You are responsible for exploring international possibilities for the company. How will you go about this task?

2. What are some of the products and services the World Bank offers to firms doing business in the developing world? Refer to the Bank's Business Center through http://web .worldbank.org/WBSITE/EXTERNAL/OPPORTUNITIES/0,, pagePK:95647~theSitePK:95480,00.html.

3. Among all the OECD countries, which derives the largest share of its GDP from the service sector? From agriculture? From industry? (Refer to www.oecd.org.)

4. To which group of countries are NAFTA members most likely to export (use the Inter-American Development Bank's export tables, located in the Research and Data section of its webpage, http://www.iadb.org/research/)?

INTERNET EXERCISE

1. Show macro aggregate changes in international markets by listing the total value of three commodities exported from your country to five other countries for the last four years. For each of the countries, provide a one paragraph statement in which you identify positive or negative trends. Give your opinion on whether or not these trends are relevant or reflect the reality of today's international business environment. What are the dangers of relying on perceived trends? You are encouraged to conduct research on products from your hometown or region.

TAKE A STAND

Business research, especially the collection and manipulation of consumer data, is not without its critics. With the rapid development of information technology and the rise of e-business, consumers and analysts alike are increasingly concerned about personal privacy. Most search engines, for example, keep track of the web pages visited by users. This allows both for targeted online marketing by partners, and, in some instances, for direct marketing offline, either through mailers or that old favorite—the telemarketer call.

Questions For Discussion

1. Should search engines be prohibited from storing and disseminating their users' online activity, in order to protect their privacy? Should governments introduce tighter controls for direct marketing?

2. Considering that more consumer data allows businesses to employ more targeted marketing, which saves money and boosts sales, which in turn creates jobs and stimulates the economy, should governments encourage customer research?

SUGGESTED READINGS

Sheila Keegan, *Qualitative Research: Good Decision Making through Understanding People, Cultures and Markets (Market Research in Practice)* (London: Kogan Page, 2009).

C. Samuel Craig and Susan P. Douglas, *International Marketing Research*, 3rd ed. (New York: Wiley, 2005).

Gilbert A. Churchill, Tom J. Brown, and Tracy A. Suter, *Basic Marketing Research*, 7th ed. (Mason, OH: South-Western, 2009).

Gale Directory of Online, Portable, and Internet Databases, http://library.dialog .com/bluesheets/html/bl0230.html, accessed November 15, 2009.

GreenBook 2009, Worldwide Directory of Marketing Research Companies and Services, 47th ed. (New York: American Marketing Association, 2009).

Jan vom Brocke and Michael Rosemann, eds., *Handbook on Business Process Management 1: Introduction, Methods and Information Systems (International Handbooks on Information Systems)* (New York: Springer, 2010).

Monitors of International Issues

EUROPEAN UNION

- **EUROPA**

  The umbrella server for all institutions

  http://www.europa.eu

- **ISPO (Information Society Project Office)**

  Information on telecommunications and
    information market developments

  Information Society

  European Commission

  Directorate General Information Society

  BU 24 O/74

  Rue de la Loi 200

  B-1049 Brussels

  http://ec.europa.eu/information_society

- **CORDIS**

  Information on EU research programs

  http://www.cordis.lu

- **EUROPARL**

  Information on the European Parliament's activities

  http://www.europarl.eu.int

- **Delegation of the European Commission to
  the U.S.**

  Press releases, EURECOM: Economic and
    Financial News, EU-US relations, information
    on EU policies and delegation programs

  European Union

  Delegation of the European Commission to the
    United States

  2300 M Street, NW

  Washington, DC 20037

  http://www.eurunion.org

- **Citizens Europe**

  Covers rights of citizens of EU member states

  www.ecas-citizens.eu

- **EURLEX (European Union Law)**

  Bibliographic database

  http://eur-lex.europa.eu/en/index.htm

- **Euro**

  The Single Currency

  http://www.euro.ecb.int

- **European Agency for the Evaluation of
  Medicinal Products**

  Information on drug approval procedures and
    documents of the Committee for Proprietary
    Medicinal Products and the Committee for
    Veterinary Medicinal Products

  http://www.emea.eu

- **European Central Bank**

  Kaiserstrasse 29

  D-60311 Frankfurt am Main

  Germany

  Postal:

  Postfach 160319

  D-60066 Frankfurt am Main

  Germany

  http://www.ecb.int

- **European Centre for the Development of
  Vocational Training**

  Under construction with information on the
    Centre and contact information

  Cedefop

  Europe 123

  GR-57001 Thessaloniki

  (Pylea)

  Mailing Address:

  PO Box 22427

  Thessaloniki

  GR-55102 Thessaloniki

  http://www.cedefop.europa.eu

- **European Environment Agency**

  Information on the mission, products and
    services, and organizations and staff of the EEA

  http://www.eea.eu.int

- **European Investment Bank**

  Press releases and information on borrowing and
    loan operations, staff, and publications

  100, boulevard Konrad Adenauer

  L-2950 Luxembourg

  http://www.eib.org

- **European Union Internet Resources**

  Main Library, 2nd Floor

The Library
University of California
Berkeley, CA 94720-6000
http://www.lib.berkeley.edu/doemoff/gov_eu.html

- **Office for Harmonization in the Internal Market**

  Guidelines, application forms and other
  information to register an EU trademark

  http://oami.europa.eu

- **Council of the European Union**

  Information and news from the Council with
  sections covering Common Foreign and
  Security Policy (CFSP) and Justice and Home
  Affairs Under Construction

  http://ue.eu.int

- **Court of Justice**

  Overview, press releases, publications, and
  full-text proceedings of the court

  http://curia.eurpa.eu/jcms/jcms

- **Court of Auditors**

  Information notes, annual reports, and other
  publications

  http://www.eca.eu.int/en/menu.htm

- **European Community Information Service**

  200 Rue de la Loi
  1049 Brussels, Belgium
  and
  2100 M Street NW, 7th Floor
  Washington, DC 20037

- **European Bank for Reconstruction and Development**

  One Exchange Square
  London EC2A 2JN
  United Kingdom
  http://www.ebrd.com

- **European Union**

  200 Rue de la Loi
  1049 Brussels, Belgium
  and
  2100 M Street NW 7th Floor
  Washington, DC 20037
  http://www.eurunion.org

UNITED NATIONS

  http://www.un.org

- **Conference of Trade and Development**

  Palais des Nations
  1211 Geneva 10

Switzerland
http://www.unctad.org

- **Department of Economic and Social Affairs**

  1 United Nations Plaza
  New York, NY 10017
  http://www.un.org/esa

- **Industrial Development Organization**

  1660 L Street NW
  Washington, DC 20036
  and
  Post Office Box 300
  Vienna International Center
  A-1400 Vienna, Austria
  http://www.unido.org

- **International Trade Centre**

  UNCTAD/WTO
  54–56 Rue de Mountbrillant
  CH-1202 Geneva
  Switzerland
  http://www.intracen.org

- **UN Publications**

  Room 1194
  1 United Nations Plaza
  New York, NY 10017
  http://www.un.org/Pubs/

- **Statistical Yearbook**

  1 United Nations Plaza
  New York, NY 10017
  http://www.un.org/Pubs/

- **Yearbook of International Trade Statistics**

  United Nations Publishing Division
  1 United Nations Plaza
  Room DC2-0853
  New York, NY 10017
  http://www.un.org/Pubs/

U.S. GOVERNMENT

- **Agency for International Development**

  Office of Business Relations Washington, DC
  20523
  http://www.usaid.gov

- **Customs and Border Protection**

  1300 Pennsylvania Ave. NW
  Room 6.3D
  Washington, DC 20229
  www.cbp.gov

- **Department of Agriculture**

  12th Street and Jefferson Drive SW
  Washington, DC 20250
  http://www.usda.gov

- **Department of Commerce**

  Herbert C. Hoover Building
  14th Street and Constitution Avenue NW
  Washington, DC 20230
  http://www.commerce.gov

- **Department of Homeland Security**

  http://www.whitehouse.gov/homeland

- **Department of State**

  2201 C Street NW
  Washington, DC 20520
  http://www.state.gov

- **Department of the Treasury**

  15th Street and Pennsylvania Avenue NW
  Washington, DC 20220
  http://www.ustreas.gov

- **Federal Trade Commission**

  6th Street and Pennsylvania Avenue NW
  Washington, DC 20580
  http://www.ftc.gov

- **International Trade Commission**

  500 E Street NW
  Washington, DC 20436
  http://www.usitc.gov

- **Small Business Administration**

  409 Third Street SW
  Washington, DC 20416
  http://www.sbaonline.sba.gov

- **Trade Information Center**

  International Trade Administration
  U.S. Department of Commerce
  Washington, D.C. 20230
  www.export.gov/exportbasics

- **U.S. Trade and Development Agency**

  1621 North Kent Street
  Rosslyn, VA 22209
  http://www.tda.gov

- **World Trade Centers Association**

  60 East 42nd Street, Suite 1901
  New York, NY 10169
  world.wtca.org

- **Council of Economic Advisers**—http://www.whitehouse.gov/cea

- **Department of Defense**—http://www.dod.gov
- **Department of Energy**—http://www.osti.gov
- **Department of Interior**—http://www.doi.gov
- **Department of Labor**—http://www.dol.gov
- **Department of Transportation**—http://www.dot.gov
- **Environmental Protection Agency**—http://www.epa.gov
- **National Trade Data Bank**—http://www.stat-usa.gov
- **National Economic Council**—http://www.whitehouse.gov/nec
- **Office of the U.S. Trade Representative**—http://www.ustr.gov
- **Office of Management and Budget**—http://www.whitehouse.gov/omb
- **Overseas Private Investment Corporation**—http://www.opic.gov

SELECTED ORGANIZATIONS

- **American Bankers Association**

  1120 Connecticut Avenue NW
  Washington, DC 20036
  http://www.aba.com

- **American Bar Association**

  750 N. Lake Shore Drive
  Chicago, IL 60611
  and
  1800 M Street NW
  Washington, DC 20036
  http://www.abanet.org/intlaw/home.html

- **American Management Association**

  440 First Street NW
  Washington, DC 20001
  http://www.amanet.org

- **American Marketing Association**

  311 S. Wacker Drive, Suite 5800
  Chicago, IL 60606
  http://www.marketingpower.com

- **American Petroleum Institute**

  1220 L Street NW
  Washington, DC 20005
  http://www.api.org

- **Asia-Pacific Economic Cooperation Secretariat**

  438 Alexandra Road
  #41-00, Alexandra Road
  Singapore 119958
  http://www.apecsec.org.sg

- **Asian Development Bank**

  2330 Roxas Boulevard

  Pasay City, Philippines

  http://www.adb.org

- **Association of Southeast Asian Nations (ASEAN)**

  Publication Office

  c/o The ASEAN Secretariat

  70A, Jalan Sisingamangaraja

  Jakarta 11210

  Indonesia

  www.aseansec.org

- **Canadian Market Data**

  http://www.strategis.ic.gc.ca

- **Chamber of Commerce of the United States**

  1615 H Street NW

  Washington, DC 20062

  http://www.uschamber.org

- **Commission of the European Communities to the United States**

  2100 M Street NW

  Suite 707

  Washington, DC 20037

  http://www.eurunion.org

- **Conference Board**

  845 Third Avenue

  New York, NY 10022

  and

  1755 Massachusetts Avenue

  NW Suite 312

  Washington, DC 20036

  http://www.conference-board.org

- **Deutsche Bundesbank**

  Wilhelm-Epstein-Str. 14

  P.O.B. 10 06 02

  D-60006 Frankfurt am Main

  http://www.bundesbank.de

- **Electronic Industries Alliance**

  2001 Pennsylvania Avenue NW

  Washington, DC 20004

  http://www.eia.org

- **Export-Import Bank of the United States**

  811 Vermont Avenue NW

  Washington, DC 20571

  http://www.exim.gov

- **Federal Reserve Bank of New York**

  33 Liberty Street

  New York, NY 10045

  http://www.ny.frb.org

- **The Federation of International Trade Associations**

  11800 Sunrise Valley Drive, Suite 210

  Reston, VA 20191

  http://www.fita.org

- **Inter-American Development Bank**

  1300 New York Avenue NW

  Washington, DC 20577

  http://www.iadb.org

- **International Bank for Reconstruction and Development (World Bank)**

  1818 H Street NW

  Washington, DC 20433

  http://www.worldbank.org

- **International Monetary Fund**

  700 19th Street NW

  Washington, DC 20431

  http://www.imf.org

- **International Chamber of Commerce**

  38, Cours Albert ler

  7800 Paris, France

  http://www.iccwbo.org

- **International Telecommunication Union**

  Place des Nations

  Ch-1211 Geneva 20

  Switzerland

  http://www.itu.int

- **International Trade Law Monitor**

  http://lexmercatoria.org

- **Michigan State University Center for International Business Education and Research**

  http://www.globaledge.msu.edu

- **Marketing Research Society**

  111 E. Wacker Drive, Suite 600

  Chicago, IL 60601

- **National Association of Manufacturers**

  1331 Pennsylvania Avenue

  Suite 1500

  Washington, DC 20004

  http://www.nam.org

- **National Federation of Independent Business**
  600 Maryland Avenue SW
  Suite 700
  Washington, DC 20024
  http://www.nfib.org
- **Organization for Economic Cooperation and Development**
  2 rue Andre Pascal
  75775 Paris Cedex Ko, France
  and
  2001 L Street NW, Suite 700
  Washington, DC 20036
  http://www.oecd.org
- **Organization of American States**
  17th and Constitution Avenue NW
  Washington, DC 20006
  http://www.oas.org
- **Society for International Development**
  1401 New York Avenue NW
  Suite 1100
  Washington, DC 20005
  http://www.sidint.org
- **Transparency International**
  Otto-Suhr-Allee 97-99
  D-10585 Berlin
  Germany
  http://www.transparency.de

INDEXES TO LITERATURE

- **Business Periodical Index**
  H.W. Wilson Co.
  950 University Avenue
  Bronx, NY 10452
- **New York Times Index**
  University Microfilms International
  300 N. Zeeb Road
  Ann Arbor, MI 48106
  http://www.nytimes.com
- **Reader's Guide to Periodical Literature**
  H.W. Wilson Co.
  950 University Avenue
  Bronx, NY 10452
  http://www.tulane.edu/~horn/rdg.html
- **Wall Street Journal Index**
  University Microfilms International
  300 N. Zeeb Road
  Ann Arbor, MI 48106
  http://www.wsj.com

DIRECTORIES

- **American Register of Exporters and Importers**
  38 Park Row
  New York, NY 10038
- **Arabian Year Book**
  Dar Al-Seuassam Est.
  Box 42480
  Shuwahk, Kuwait
- **Directories of American Firms Operating in Foreign Countries**
  World Trade Academy Press
  Uniworld Business Publications Inc.
  50 E. 42nd Street
  New York, NY 10017
- **The Directory of International Sources of Business Information**
  Pitman
  128 Long Acre
  London WC2E 9AN, England
- **Encyclopedia of Associations**
  Gale Research Co.
  Book Tower
  Detroit, MI 48226
- **Polk's World Bank Directory**
  R.C. Polk & Co.
  2001 Elm Hill Pike
  P.O. Box 1340
  Nashville, TN 37202
- **Verified Directory of Manufacturer's Representatives**
  MacRae's Blue Book Inc.
  817 Broadway
  New York, NY 10003
- **World Guide to Trade Associations**
  K.G. Saur & Co.
  175 Fifth Avenue
  New York, NY 10010
- **Market research Library**
  http://www.buyusainfo.net

ENCYCLOPEDIAS, HANDBOOKS, AND MISCELLANEOUS

- **A Basic Guide to Exporting**
  U.S. Government Printing Office
  Superintendent of Documents
  Washington, DC 20402

- **Doing Business In . . . Series**
  Price Waterhouse
  1251 Avenue of the Americas
  New York, NY 10020

- **Economic Survey of Europe**
  United Nations Publishing Division
  1 United Nations Plaza
  Room DC2-0853
  New York, NY 10017

- **Economic Survey of Latin America**
  United Nations Publishing Division
  1 United Nations Plaza
  Room DC2-0853
  New York, NY 10017

- **Encyclopedia Americana, International Edition**
  Grolier Inc.
  Danbury, CT 06816

- **Encyclopedia of Business Information Sources**
  Gale Research Co.
  Book Tower
  Detroit, MI 48226

- **Europa Year Book**
  Europa Publications Ltd.
  18 Bedford Square
  London WCIB 3JN, England

- **Export Administration Regulations**
  U.S. Government Printing Office
  Superintendent of Documents
  Washington, DC 20402

- **Exporters' Encyclopedia—World Marketing Guide**
  Dun's Marketing Services
  49 Old Bloomfield Rd.
  Mountain Lake, NJ 07046
  Stat-USA
  www.Stat-Usa.gov

- **Export-Import Bank of the United States Annual Report**

  U.S. Government Printing Office
  Superintendent of Documents
  Washington, DC 20402

- **Exporting for the Small Business**
  U.S. Government Printing Office
  Superintendent of Documents
  Washington, DC 20402

- **Exporting to the United States**
  U.S. Government Printing Office
  Superintendent of Documents
  Washington, DC 20402

- **Export Shipping Manual**
  U.S. Government Printing Office
  Superintendent of Documents
  Washington, DC 20402

- **Foreign Business Practices: Materials on Practical Aspects of Exporting, International Licensing, and Investing**
  U.S. Government Printing Office
  Superintendent of Documents
  Washington, DC 20402

- **A Guide to Financing Exports**
  U.S. Government Printing Office
  Superintendent of Documents
  Washington, DC 20402

- **Handbook of Marketing Research**
  McGraw-Hill Book Co.
  1221 Avenue of the Americas
  New York, NY 10020

PERIODIC REPORTS, NEWSPAPERS, MAGAZINES

- **Advertising Age**
  Crain Communications Inc.
  740 N. Rush Street
  Chicago, IL 60611
  http://www.adage.com

- **Advertising World**
  Directories International Inc.
  150 Fifth Avenue, Suite 610
  New York, NY 10011
  http://advertising.utexas.edu/world/

- **Agricultural Outlook**
  U.S. Department of Agriculture
  Economic Research Service

http://www.ers.usda.gov/publications/AgOutlook/
Archives/

- **Arab Report and Record**
84 Chancery Lane
London WC2A 1DL, England

- **Barron's**
University Microfilms International
300 N. Zeeb Road
Ann Arbor, MI 48106
http://www.barrons.com

- **Business America**
U.S. Department of Commerce
14th Street and Constitution Avenue NW
Washington, DC 20230
http://www.doc.gov

- **Business International**
Business International Corp.
One Dag Hammarskjold Plaza
New York, NY 10017

- **BusinessWeek**
McGraw-Hill Publications Co.
1221 Avenue of the Americas
New York, NY 10020
http://www.businessweek.com

- **Commodity Trade Statistics**
United Nations Publications
1 United Nations Plaza
Room DC2-0853
New York, NY 10017

- **Conference Board Record**
Conference Board Inc.
845 Third Avenue
New York, NY 10022
http://www.conference-board.org

- **Customs Bulletin**
U.S. Customs Service
1301 Constitution Avenue NW
Washington, DC 20229

- **The Economist**
Economist Newspaper Ltd.
25 St. James Street
London SWIA 1HG, England
http://www.economist.com

- **The Financial Times**
Bracken House

10 Cannon Street
London EC4P 4BY, England
www.ft.com

- **Forbes**
Forbes Inc.
60 Fifth Avenue
New York, NY 10011
http://www.forbes.com

- **Fortune**
Time Inc.
Time & Life Building
1271 Avenue of the Americas
New York, NY 10020
http://www.fortune.com

- **International Financial Statistics**
International Monetary Fund
Publications Unit
700 19th Street NW
Washington, DC 20431
www.imfstatistics.org

- **Investor's Business Daily**
Box 25970
Los Angeles, CA 90025
Journal of Commerce
110 Wall Street
New York, NY 10005
http://www.investors.com

- **Journal of Commerce**
100 Wall Street
New York, NY 10005
http://www.joc.com

- **Sales and Marketing Management**
Bill Communications Inc.
633 Third Avenue
New York, NY 10017

- **Wall Street Journal**
Dow Jones & Company
200 Liberty Street
New York, NY 10281
http://www.wsj.com

- **Pergamon Press Inc.**
Journals Division
Maxwell House
Fairview Park
Elmsford, NY 10523

- **World Trade Center Association (WTCA) Directory**
  World Trade Centers Association
  60 East 42nd Street, Suite 1901
  New York, NY 10169

- **International Encyclopedia of the Social Sciences**
  Macmillan and the Free Press
  866 Third Avenue
  New York, NY 10022

- **Marketing and Communications Media Dictionary**
  Media Horizons Inc.
  50 W. 25th Street
  New York, NY 10010

- **Market Share Reports**
  U.S. Government Printing Office
  Superintendent of Documents
  Washington, DC 20402
  http://www.access.gpo.gov

- **Media Guide International: Business/ Professional Publications**

Directories International Inc.
150 Fifth Avenue, Suite 610
New York, NY 10011

- **Overseas Business Reports**
  U.S Government Printing Office
  Superintendent of Documents
  Washington, DC 20402
  http://www.access.gpo.gov

- **Sales and Marketing Management**
  http://www.salesandmarketing.com

- **Trade Finance**
  U.S. Department of Commerce
  International Trade Administration
  Washington, DC 20230
  http://www.commerce.gov

- **World Economic Conditions in Relation to Agricultural Trade**
  U.S. Government Printing Office
  Superintendent of Documents
  Washington, DC 20402
  http://www.access.gpo.gov

The Structure of a Country Commercial Guide

Country Commercial Guide for Austria

TABLE OF CONTENTS

Chapter 1 Introduction to the Austrian Market

A. Market Overview
B. Market Challenges
C. Market Opportunities
D. Market Entry Strategy

Chapter 2 The Political and Economic Environment in Austria

(Link to U.S. Department of State Background Notes, http://www.state.gov/r/pa/ei/bgn)

Chapter 3 Selling U.S. Products and Services in Austria

A. Using an Agent or Distributor
B. Establishing an Office
C. Franchising
D. Direct Marketing
  ◦ Processing Customer Data
E. Distance Selling Rules
  ◦ Distance and Door-to-Door Sales
  ◦ Distance Selling of Financial Services
  ◦ Direct Marketing Over the Internet
F. Joint Ventures and Licensing
G. Selling to the Government
H. Distribution and Sales Channels
I. Selling Factors and Techniques
J. Electronic Commerce
K. Trade Promotion and Advertising
  ◦ General EU Legislation
  ◦ Medicine
  ◦ Food
  ◦ Food Supplements
  ◦ Tobacco
L. Pricing

M. Sales Service and Customer Support
  ◦ Product Liability
  ◦ Product Safety
  ◦ Legal Warranties and After-sales Service
N. Protecting Your Intellectual Property
  ◦ Copyright
  ◦ Patents
  ◦ Trademarks
  ◦ Designs
  ◦ Trademark Exhaustion
O. Due Diligence
P. Local Professional Services
Q. Web Resources

Chapter 4 Leading Sectors for U.S. Exports and Investment

A. Agricultural Sectors
  ◦ Agricultural Fish and Forestry Sector Total
  ◦ Dried Fruits and Nuts
  ◦ Wine
  ◦ Fish and Seafood
B. Commercial Sectors
  ◦ Computer Software and Services (CSP)
  ◦ Drugs and Pharmaceuticals (DRG)
  ◦ Medical Devices (MED)
  ◦ Aircraft and Parts (AIR)
  ◦ Computers and Peripherals (CPT)
  ◦ Dental Equipment (DNT)
  ◦ Audiovisual Equipment (AV)
  ◦ Electrical Power Systems (ELP)
  ◦ Oil and Gas Field Equipment (OGM)

Chapter 5 Trade Regulations, Customs, and Standards

A. Import Tariffs
B. Trade Barriers
C. Import Requirements and Documentation
  ◦ Import Licenses
  ◦ Import Documentation

D. U.S. Export Controls

E. Temporary Entry

F. Labeling and Marking Requirements

G. Prohibited and Restricted Imports

H. Customs Regulations and Contact Information

I. Standards

J. Standard Organizations

K. Conformity Assessment

L. Product Certification

M. Accreditation

N. Labeling and Marking
  ○ The Eco-label

O. Contact Information

P. Trade Agreements

Q. Web Resources

Chapter 6 The Investment Climate in Austria

A. Introduction

B. Openness to Foreign Investment

C. Conversion and Transfer Policies

D. Expropriation and Compensation

E. Dispute Settlement

F. Performance Requirements/Incentives

G. Right to Private Ownership and Establishment

H. Protection of Property Rights

I. Transparency of the Regulatory System

J. Efficient Capital Markets and Portfolio Investment

K. Political Violence

L. Corruption

M. Bilateral Investment Agreements

N. OPIC and Other Investment Insurance Programs

O. Labor

P. Foreign Trade Zones/Free Ports

Q. Foreign Direct Investment Statistics

R. List of Major Foreign Investors:

S. Web Resources

Chapter 7 Trade and Project Financing

A. How do I get paid? (Method of Payment)

B. How does the banking system operate?

C. Foreign-Exchange Controls

D. U.S. Banks and Local Correspondent Banks
  ○ Commercial and private
  ○ Corporate and investment banking—no retail services
  ○ Consumer financial services

E. Austrian Banks with Subsidiaries in the U.S.
  ○ Erste Bank der oesterreichischen Sparkassen AG
  ○ Raiffeisen Zentralbank AG

F. Project Financing
  ○ Tendering for European public procurement contracts

G. Web Resources

Chapter 8 Business Travel

A. Business Customs

B. Tipping

C. Travel Advisory

D. Electrical voltage

E. Safety

F. Arrival at Vienna International Airport

G. Visa Requirements

H. Telecommunication
  ○ Direct Long Distance
  ○ Internet Calling
  ○ Call-Back Long Distance Services
  ○ Cellular phones
  ○ Internet

I. Transportation

J. Language

K. Health
  ○ Water
  ○ Emergencies
  ○ Pharmacies

L. Local Time, Business Hours, and Holidays

M. Temporary Entry of Materials and Personal Belongings

N. Web Resources

Chapter 9 Contacts, Market Research, and Trade Events

A. Contacts
  ○ Austrian Government Agencies
  ○ Austrian Trade Associations/Chambers of Commerce
  ○ Austrian Commercial Banks/Branch Offices of Austrian Banks in the U.S.
  ○ U.S. Commercial Service
  ○ U.S.-based Associations
  ○ Washington-based U.S. Government Contacts

B. Market Research

C. Trade Events

Chapter 10 Guide to Our Services

The U.S. Commercial Service offers customized solutions to help your business enter and succeed in markets worldwide. Our global network of trade specialists will work one-on-one with you through every step of the exporting process, helping you to:

- Target the best markets with our world-class research.
- Promote your products and services to qualified buyers.
- Meet the best distributors and agents for your products and services.
- Overcome potential challenges or trade barriers.

For more information on the services the U.S. Commercial Service offers U.S. businesses, please see http://www.buyusa.gov/austria/en/

Chapter 11 Tariffs and Other Barriers to Trade

Austria is a member of the European Union (EU), thus the Austrian customs regime is based on the "TARIC" (integrated tariff of the EU), determined in Brussels.

EU Import tariffs vary depending on the product, however, for most U.S. exports the tariffs are relatively low. In fact, over half of all products from non-EU countries enter without any tariff.

Tariff inquiries online are available at http://europa.eu.int/comm/taxation_customs/dds/en/tarhome.htm.

Chapter 12 Frequently Asked Questions

A. REACH FAQs
B. WEEE/RoHS
C. Pharmaceuticals

Chapter 13 Finding Business Partners in Austria

A. Gold Key Matching Service
B. International Partner Search
C. Contact List
D. Feature Your Company on Our Website
E. Platinum Key Service

Chapter 14 Promote Your Company in Austria

A. Single Company Promotion
B. Promotional Seminars
C. Feature Your Company on Our Website

Chapter 15 Market Research on Austria

Chapter 16 Austrian Business Service Providers

A. Business Consulting (4)
B. Hotels and Meeting Facilities (1)
C. Human Resources (2)
D. Legal Services (5)
E. Marketing, Public Relations and Sales (1)
F. Real Estate Services (1)
G. Regional Economic Development (1)
H. Relocation services (4)
I. Translation and Interpretation (1)
J. Transportation, Freight Forwarder and Storage Services (4)
K. Other Business Services (1)

Chapter 17 Contact Us

A. Staff Directory

Chapter 18 Links

A. U.S. Embassy
B. State Department Information
C. CITRA: Center for International Regulatory Assistance
D. American Chamber of Commerce
E. Austrian Federal Economic Chamber
F. Austrian Trade Commission
G. Austrian Federal Association of Independent Commercial Agents and Negotiators
H. Virtual Vienna
I. Austrian Press and Information Service
J. Rechtsfreund

Chapter 19 Events

Source: U.S. Department of Commerce, The Commercial Service, Washington, DC, 2009, http://www.buyusa.gov/austria/en/

CHAPTER 13

Entry and Expansion

CHAPTER CONTENTS & LEARNING OBJECTIVES

THE ROLE OF MANAGEMENT

1. To learn how firms gradually progress through an internationalization process

MOTIVATIONS TO GO ABROAD

2. To understand the strategic effects of internationalization on the firm

STRATEGIC EFFECTS OF GOING INTERNATIONAL

3. To study the various modes of entering international markets

ENTRY AND DEVELOPMENT STRATEGIES

4. To understand the role and functions of international intermediaries

INTERNATIONAL INTERMEDIARIES

5. To learn about the opportunities and challenges of cooperative market development

LOCAL PRESENCE

6. To understand how firms can overcome market barriers by either building competitive capabilities abroad from scratch or acquiring them from local owners.

A COMPREHENSIVE VIEW OF INTERNATIONAL EXPANSION

7. To observe a model linking managerial commitment, international expansion and corporate concerns

In 2005, two former co-workers—Sab Jhooti and Robin Parker—tried to start their own business, streaming home closed-circuit television (CCTV) footage. It did not do well. However, in the process of researching this venture, the partners developed the idea of marketing helmets with built-in cameras for adventure sport enthusiasts. It turned out to be extremely profitable.

Jhooti and Parker established their new company, Action Cameras, in January 2006. A month later, it had already gone international. This caught the newly minted entrepreneurs by surprise. According to Jhooti, "We ran the business from my bedroom, and on one day we were shipping goods to the U.S., Israel, South Africa, and Australia. We'd done no marketing but they were coming to us."

More and more orders were coming in from overseas. A large percentage of them were from French-speaking customers. Concerned about losing them to local competitors, Jhooti and Parker decided to create a French language web site. The company also established a public presence in France, advertising at extreme sports events, such as the French Moto GP. This turned out to be an extremely profitable decision. By 2009, sales generated by the French-language web site accounted for a quarter of Action Camera's total revenue.

Jhooti and Parker know their consumers well. Most adventure sports aficionados are young and tech-savvy.

In addition to translating their web site, (which has since been replicated in Spanish, Portuguese, and Italian) the partners have engaged in other forms of e-marketing, including the use of social networking sites. For example, Action Cameras has its own Facebook page with an ever-growing number of "friends." However, savvy advertising alone cannot account for international success. It needs to be based on product quality and technological innovation. Over the past three years, nearly every model of helmet camera sold in Europe was pioneered by Action Cameras. They have provided camera systems to Formula 1 teams, Red Bull air racers, Super Bike teams, Rally Teams, production companies, the BBC, and thousands of action sports enthusiasts across Europe.

In the world of the Internet, where word-of-mouth advertising can be amplified many-fold through weblogs, social networking sites, and consumer reviews, any company that identifies a promising market niche, provides a quality product, and maintains a technological lead on its competitors could find itself in the position of an international firm engaged in exporting.

Sources: Jamie Oliver, "Trade Month: Exports Click for Action Cameras after a Shaky Start in France," *The Telegraph*, October 5, 2009; Action Cameras company web site, http://www.actioncameras.co.uk/, accessed October 10, 2009.

International business holds out the promise of large new market areas, yet firms cannot simply jump into the international marketplace and expect to be successful. They must adjust to needs and opportunities abroad, have quality products, understand their customers, and do their homework to comprehend the vagaries of international markets. The rapid globalization of markets, however, reduces the time available to adjust to new market realities.

This chapter is concerned with firms preparing to enter international markets and companies expanding their current international activities. Initial emphasis is placed on export activities with a focus on the role of management in starting up international operations and a description of the basic stimuli for international activities. Entry modes for the international arena are highlighted, and the problems and benefits of each mode are discussed. The roles of facilitators and intermediaries in international business are described. Finally, alternatives that involve a local presence by the firm are presented.

THE ROLE OF MANAGEMENT

1. To learn how firms gradually progress through an internationalization process

Management dynamism and commitment are crucial to a firm's first steps toward international operations. Managers of firms with a strong international performance typically are active, aggressive, and display a high degree of international orientation.[1] Such an orientation is indicated by substantial global awareness and cultural sensitivity.[2] Conversely, the managers of firms that are unsuccessful or inactive internationally usually exhibit a lack of determination or devotion to international business.

managerial commitment
The desire and drive on the part of management to act on an idea and to support it in the long run.

The issue of **managerial commitment** is a critical one because foreign market penetration requires a vast amount of market development activity, sensitivity toward foreign environments, research, and innovation. Regardless of what the firm produces or where it does business internationally, managerial commitment is crucial for enduring stagnation and sometimes even setbacks and failure. After all, it is top management that determines the willingness to take risk, to introduce new products, to seek new solutions to problems, and to continuously strive to succeed abroad.[3] To achieve such a commitment, it is important to involve all levels of management early on in the international planning process and to impress on all players that the effort will only succeed with a commitment that is companywide.[4]

Initiating international business activities takes the firm in an entirely new direction, quite different from adding a product line or hiring a few more people. Going international means that a fundamental strategic change is taking place. Companies that initiate international expansion efforts and succeed with them, typically begin to enjoy operational improvements—such as positioning strengths in competition—long before financial improvements appear.[5]

The decision to export usually comes from the highest levels of management, typically the owner, president, chairman, or vice president of marketing.[6] The carrying out of the decision—that is, the implementation of international business transactions—is then the primary responsibility of marketing personnel. It is important to establish an organizational structure in which someone has the specific responsibility for international activities. Without such a responsibility center, the focus necessary for success can easily be lost. Such a center need not be large. For example, just one person assigned part time to international activities can begin exploring and entering international markets.

The first step in developing international commitment is to become aware of international business opportunities. Management must then determine the degree and timing of the firm's internationalization. For instance, a German corporation that expands its operation into Austria, Switzerland, Belgium, and the Netherlands is less international than a German corporation that launches operations in Japan and Brazil. Moreover, if a German-based corporation already has activities in the United States, setting up a business in Canada does not increase its degree of internationalization as much as if Canada was the first "bridgehead" in North America.[7] Management must decide the timing of when to start the internationalization process and how quickly it should progress. For example, market entry might be desirable as soon as possible because clients are waiting for the product or because competitors are expected to enter the market shortly. In addition, it may be desirable to either enter a market abroad selectively or to achieve full market coverage from the outset. Decisions on these timing issues will determine the speed with which management must mobilize and motivate the people involved in the process.[8]

It must be kept in mind that a firmwide international orientation does not develop overnight, but rather needs time to grow. Internationalization is a matter of learning, of acquiring experiential knowledge. A firm must learn about foreign markets and institutions, but also about its own internal resources in order to know what it is capable of when exposed to new and unfamiliar conditions.[9] Planning and execution of an export venture must be incorporated into the firm's strategic management process. A firm that sets no strategic goals for its export venture is less likely to make the venture a long-term success.[10] As markets around the world become more linked and more competitive, the importance of developing and following a strategy becomes increasingly key to making things better.[11]

Management is often much too preoccupied with short-term, immediate problems to engage in sophisticated long-run planning. As a result, many firms are simply not interested in international business. Yet certain situations may lead a manager to discover and understand the value of going international and to decide to pursue international business activities. One trigger factor can be international travel, during which new business opportunities are discovered. Alternatively, the receipt of information can lead management to believe that international business opportunities exist. **Unsolicited orders** from abroad are an example. In the United States, for example, such unsolicited orders have been found to account for more than half of all cases of export initiation by small and medium-sized firms.

With the growth of corporate web sites, firms can become unplanned participants in the international market even more often. For example, customers from abroad can visit a web site and place an international order, even though a firm's plans may have been strictly domestic. Of course, a firm can choose to ignore foreign interest and lose out on new markets. Alternatively, it can find itself unexpectedly an exporter. Such firms can be called **accidental exporters**. While good fortune may have initiated the export activity, over the longer term the firm must start planning how to systematically increase its international expansion or, at least, how to make more of these accidents happen.[12]

Managers who have lived abroad and have learned foreign languages or are particularly interested in foreign cultures are more likely to investigate whether international business opportunities would be appropriate for their firms. Countries or regions with high levels of immigration may, over time, benefit from greater export success due to more ties, better information, and greater international business sensitivity by their new residents.

New management or new employees can also introduce an international orientation. For example, managers entering a firm may already have had some international business experience and may use this experience to further the business activities of their new employer.

unsolicited order An unplanned business opportunity that arises as a result of another firm's activities.

accidental exporters Firms which participate in international trade due to initiative of active outside demand rather than based on gradual inside planning.

MOTIVATIONS TO GO ABROAD

2. *To understand the strategic effects of internationalization on the firm*

Normally, management will consider international activities only when stimulated to do so. A variety of motivations can push and pull individuals and firms along the international path. An overview of the major motivations that have been found to make firms go international is provided in Table 13.1. Proactive motivations represent stimuli for firm-initiated strategic change. Reactive motivations describe stimuli that result in a firm's response and adaptation to changes imposed by the outside environment. In other words, firms with proactive motivations go international because they want to; those with reactive motivations go international because they have to.

PROACTIVE MOTIVATIONS

Profits are the major proactive motivation for international business. Management may perceive international sales as a potential source of higher profit margins or of

Licensing and franchising are important methods of internationalization.

more added-on profits. Of course, the profitability expected when planning to go international is often quite different from the profitability actually obtained. Profitability is often linked with international growth—yet many corporate international entry decisions are made based on expectations of market growth rather than on actual market growth.[13] Particularly in start-up operations, initial profitability may be quite low due to the cost of getting ready for going international, and the losses resulting from early mistakes.[14] The gap between expectation and reality may be especially large when the firm has not previously engaged in international business. Even with thorough planning, unexpected influences can change the profit picture substantially. Shifts in exchange rates, for example, may drastically affect profit forecasts.

© Feng Li/Getty Images, Inc.

Table 13.1 Major Motivations to Firms

Proactive Motivations	Reactive Motivations
Profit advantage	Competitive pressures
Unique products	Overproduction
Technological advantage	Stagnant or declining domestic sales
Exclusive information	Excess capacity
Tax benefit	Saturated domestic markets
Economies of scale	Proximity to customers and ports

Unique products or a technological advantage can be another major stimulus. A firm may produce goods or services that are not widely available from international competitors. Again, real and perceived advantages must be differentiated. Many firms believe that they offer unique products or services, even though this may not be the case internationally. If products or technologies are unique, however, they certainly can provide a competitive edge. What needs to be considered is how long such an advantage will last. The length of time is a function of the product, its technology, and the creativity of competitors. In the past, a firm with a competitive edge could often count on being the sole supplier to foreign markets for years to come. This type of advantage has shrunk dramatically because of competing technologies and the frequent lack of international patent protection.

Special knowledge about foreign customers or market situations may be another proactive stimulus. Such knowledge may result from particular insights by a firm, special contacts an individual may have, in-depth research, or simply from being in the right place at the right time (e.g., recognizing a good business situation during a vacation trip). Although such exclusivity can serve well as an initial stimulus for international business, it will rarely provide prolonged motivation because competitors can be expected to catch up with the information advantage. Only if firms build up international information advantage as an ongoing process through, for example, broad market scanning or special analytical capabilities, can prolonged corporate strategy be based on this motivation.

Tax benefits can also play a major motivating role. Many governments use preferential tax treatment to encourage exports. As a result of such tax benefits, firms either can offer their product at a lower cost in foreign markets or can accumulate a higher profit. However, international trade rules make it increasingly difficult for governments to use tax subsidies to encourage exports. For example, to counteract the value added tax refund provided to exporters by the European Union, the United States attempted to provide tax deferment to its exporters. The deferment, originally called the Domestic International Sales Corporation (DISC) and subsequently renamed the Extraterritorial Income Tax Exclusion (ETI), was challenged by the European Union before the World Trade Organization (WTO). Following a long series of hearings and appeals, the WTO ruled definitively against the ETI, subjecting it to abolishment or retaliatory tariffs by trading partners. In 2004, the European Union put into effect a number of countervailing duties, forcing then President George W. Bush to repeal the FSC-ETI legislation in favor of broader (nonexporter specific) tax relief.[15]

A final major proactive motivation involves economies of scale. International activities may enable the firm to increase its output and therefore rise more rapidly on the learning curve. The Boston Consulting Group has shown that the doubling of output can reduce production costs up to 30 percent. Additionally, studies have shown that the benefits of centralized production are substantial enough to offset any increases in transportation costs. Therefore, increased production for international markets can help reduce the cost of production and make the firm more competitive domestically.[16]

REACTIVE MOTIVATIONS

Reactive motivations influence firms to respond to environmental changes and pressures rather than blaze new trails. Competitive pressures are one example. A company may worry about losing domestic market share to competing firms that have benefited from the economies of scale gained through international business activities. Further, it may fear losing foreign markets permanently to competitors that have decided to focus on these markets. Because market share usually is most easily retained by firms that initially obtain it, some companies may enter the international market head over heels. Quick entry, however, may result in equally quick withdrawal once the firm recognizes that its preparation has been inadequate.

Similarly, overproduction may represent a reactive motivation. During downturns in the domestic business cycle, foreign markets can provide an ideal outlet for excess inventories. International business expansion motivated by overproduction usually does not represent full commitment by management, but rather a temporary safety valve. As soon as domestic demand returns to previous levels, international business activities are curtailed or even terminated. Firms that have used such a strategy once may encounter difficulties when trying to employ it again because many international customers are not interested in temporary or sporadic business relationships.

Declining domestic sales, whether measured in sales volume or market share, have a similar motivating effect. Goods marketed domestically may be at the declining stage of their product life cycle. Instead of attempting to push back the life cycle process domestically, or in addition to such an effort, firms may opt to prolong the product life cycle by expanding the market. Such efforts often meet with success, particularly with high–technology products that are outmoded by the latest innovation. Such "just-dated" technology may enable vast progress in manufacturing or services industries and, most importantly, may make such progress affordable. For example, a hospital without any imaging equipment may be much better off acquiring a "just-dated" MRI machine, rather than waiting for enough funding to purchase the latest state-of-the-art equipment.

Excess capacity can also be a powerful motivator. If equipment for production is not fully utilized, firms may see expansion abroad as an ideal way to achieve broader distribution of fixed costs. Alternatively, if all fixed costs are assigned to domestic production, the firm can penetrate foreign markets with a pricing scheme that focuses mainly on variable cost. Yet such a view is feasible only for market entry. A market-penetration strategy based on variable cost alone is unrealistic because, in the long run, fixed costs have to be recovered to replace production equipment.

The reactive motivation of a saturated domestic market has similar results to that of declining domestic sales. Again, firms in this situation can use the international market to prolong the life of their good and even of their organization.

A final major reactive motivation is that of proximity to customers and ports. Physical and psychological closeness to the international market can often play a major role in the international business activities of the firm. For example, a firm established near a border may not even perceive itself as going abroad if it does business in the neighboring country. Except for some firms close to the Canadian or Mexican borders, however, this factor is much less prevalent in the United States than in many other nations. Most European firms automatically go abroad simply because their neighbors are so close.

psychological distance A measure resulting from the combination of physical and mental distance.

In this context, the concept of psychic or **psychological distance** needs to be understood. Geographic closeness to foreign markets may not necessarily translate into real or perceived closeness to the foreign customer. Sometimes complex cultural variables, such as language, religion, legal, and political systems, make a geographically close foreign market seem psychologically distant. Some research has suggested that these intangibles also account for concrete differences in health, education, and consumption patterns.[17] For example, research has shown that U.S. firms perceive Canada to be much closer psychologically than Mexico. Even England, mainly because of the similarity in language, is perceived by many U.S. firms to be much closer than Mexico or other Latin American countries, despite the geographic distances. However, in light of the reduction of trade barriers as a result of the North American Free Trade Agreement (NAFTA), and a growing proportion of the U.S. population with Hispanic backgrounds, this long-standing perception may be changing rapidly.

It is important to remember two major issues in the context of psychological distance. First, some of the distance seen by firms is based on perception rather than

FOCUS
ON
ENTREPRENEURSHIP

An International Bug

How did a small Phoenix-based environmental cleanup company boost international sales from zero to 25 percent of annual revenues? By proactively going for the world!

First, Dan Kelley, CEO of Tierra Dynamic Company, and his 30 employees had to discover a very special "bug." Tierra Dynamic patented a discovery called the *bio sparge*, a naturally occurring bacteria that Tierra cultivates, then induces to eat spilled hydrocarbons at an accelerated rate. According to Kelley, "this technique remediates soil three times faster than other methods now on the market, a significant advantage when you're concerned about carcinogens that can cause cancers and other health problems."

Second, Kelley discovered a gaping hole in the international market for his product—and leaped to fill that hole. Kelley comments, "The environmental industry is new to many developing countries and we can compete better over there than we can in more developed countries . . . . There's a big void in the market and we're happy to fill it."

Third came the identification of locations that required environmental cleanup. Kelley focused on Brazil and Argentina, as well as Indonesia, Malaysia, and Singapore. His market analysis was based primarily on the environmental regulation enforcement priorities of a given country.

Next came the practical issue of setting up shop on foreign soil. Kelley prefers working with a local partner, one who has the necessary local contacts, but who lacks the requisite technology. In the span of a few years, Tierra Dynamic has developed businesses overseas that account for one-quarter of its annual revenues. In addition to technological innovation and the identification and use of an international market niche, Tierra has successfully utilized outside sources of information and support, such as the Inter-American Development Bank and the U.S. Department of Commerce. According to Dan Kelley, "Our success in penetrating two of the largest markets in South America is a direct result of the substantial help and assistance provided by the Commercial Service." He hopes that the rise of new technologies will continue to protect the health of families worldwide and that Tierra will remain an important innovation driver in the industry.

Sources: Doug Barry, "Have Microbes, Will Travel: Small Sun Belt Company Finds Niche in Cleaning Up After Others," *Export America*, Vol. 3, No. 2, February 2002; "Global Environmental Technologies: Trends, Markets, and Prospects," Office of Environmental Technologies Industries, *Trade Development*, July 3, 2007, http://www.ad-mkt-review.com/public_html/govdocs/wmfs/wmfs02114.html, accessed October 11, 2009.

reality. For example, many U.S. firms may see the United Kingdom as psychologically very close due to the similarity in language. However, the attitudes and values of managers and customers may vary substantially between markets. Too much of a focus on the similarities may let the firm lose sight of the differences. Many Canadian firms have incurred high costs in learning this lesson when entering the United States. Second, closer psychological proximity does make it easier for firms to enter markets. Therefore, for firms new to international business it may be advantageous to begin this new activity by entering the psychologically closer markets first in order to gather experience before venturing into markets that are farther away.

In general, firms that are most successful in international business are usually motivated by proactive—that is, firm internal—factors. Proactive firms are also frequently more service oriented than reactive firms. Further, proactive firms tend to be more marketing and strategy oriented than reactive firms, which have as their major concern operational issues. Focus on Entrepreneurship describes the proactive efforts of an exporter. The clearest differentiation between the two types of firms can probably be made after the fact by determining how they initially entered international markets. Proactive firms are more likely to have solicited their first international order, whereas reactive firms frequently begin international activities after receiving an unsolicited order from abroad.

STRATEGIC EFFECTS OF GOING INTERNATIONAL

Going international presents the firm with new environments, entirely new ways of doing business, and a host of new problems. The problems have a wide range. They can consist of strategic considerations, such as service delivery and compliance with

3. To study the various modes of entering international markets

government regulations. In addition, the firm has to focus on start-up issues, such as how to find and effectively communicate with customers and operational matters, such as information flows and the mechanics of carrying out an international business transaction. This involves a variety of new documents, including commercial invoices, bills of lading, consular invoices, inspection certificates, and shipper's export declarations. The paperwork is necessary to comply with various domestic, international, or foreign regulations. The regulations may be designed to control international business activities, to streamline the individual transaction, or, as in the case of the shipper's export declaration, to compile trade statistics.

The firm needs to determine its preparedness for internationalization by assessing its internal strengths and weaknesses. This preparedness has to be evaluated in the context of the globalization of the industry within which the firm operates, since this context will affect the competitive position and strategic options available to the firm.[18] Unusual things can happen to both risk and profit. Management's perception of risk exposure grows in light of the gradual development of expertise, the many concerns about engaging in a new activity, and uncertainty about the new environment it is about to enter. Domestically, the firm has gradually learned about the market and therefore managed to decrease its risk. In the course of international expansion, the firm now encounters new and unfamiliar factors, exposing it to increased risk. At the same time, because of the investment needs required by a serious international effort, immediate profit performance may slip. In the longer term, increasing familiarity with international markets and the diversification benefits of serving multiple markets will decrease the firm's risk below the previous "domestic only" level and increase profitability as well. In the short term, however, managers may face an unusual, and perhaps unacceptable, situation: rising risk accompanied by decreasing profitability. In light of this reality, which is depicted in Figure 13.1, many executives are tempted to either not initiate international activities or to discontinue them.[19]

Understanding the changes in risk and profitability can help management overcome the seemingly prohibitive cost of going international, since the negative developments may only be short-term. Yet, success does require the firm to be a risk taker, and firms must realize that satisfactory international performance will take time.[20] Satisfactory performance can be achieved in three ways: effectiveness, efficiency, and competitive strength. Effectiveness is characterized by the acquisition of market share abroad and by increased sales. Efficiency is manifested later by rising profitability. Competitive strength refers to the firm's position compared to other firms in the

Figure 13.1   Profit and Risk During Early Internationalization

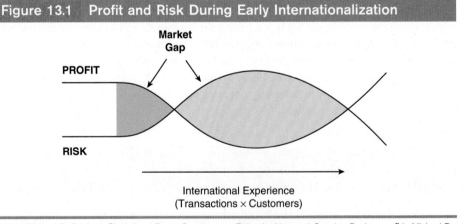

Source: Michael R. Czinkota, "A National Export Development Policy for New and Growing Businesses," in Michael R. Czinkota, I. Ronkainen, and M. Kotabe, eds., *Emerging Trends, Threats and Opportunities in International Marketing: What Executives Need to Know* (New York: Business Expert Press, 2010).

industry, and, due to the benefits of international experience, is likely to grow. The international executive must appreciate the time and performance dimensions associated with going abroad in order to overcome short-term setbacks for the sake of long-term success.

ENTRY AND DEVELOPMENT STRATEGIES

Here we will present the most typical international entry and expansion strategies. These are exporting and importing, licensing, and franchising. Another key way to expand is through a local presence, either via interfirm cooperation or foreign direct investment. These can take on many forms such as contractual agreements, equity participation and joint ventures, or direct investment conducted by the firms alone.

4. To understand the role and functions of international intermediaries

EXPORTING AND IMPORTING

Firms can be involved in exporting and importing in an indirect or direct way. **Indirect involvement** means that the firm participates in international business through an intermediary and does not deal with foreign customers or firms. **Direct involvement** means that the firm works with foreign customers or markets with the opportunity to develop a relationship. Firms typically opt for direct involvement based on cost decisions. **Transaction cost theory** postulates that firms will evaluate and compare the costs of integrating an operation internally, as compared to the cost of using an external party to act for the firm abroad.[21] Once it becomes easier and more efficient for a firm to conduct all the research, negotiations, shipping, and monitoring itself, rather than paying someone else to do it, the firm is likely to become a direct exporter or importer.

The end result of exporting and importing is similar whether the activities are direct or indirect. In both cases, goods and services either go abroad or come to the domestic market from abroad, and goods may have to be adapted to suit the targeted market. However, the different approaches have varying degrees of impact on the knowledge and experience levels of firms. The less direct the involvement of the firm, the less likely is the internal development of a storehouse of information and expertise on how to do business abroad, information that the firm can draw on later for further international expansion. Therefore, while indirect activities represent a form of international market entry, they may not result in growing management commitment to international markets or increased capabilities in serving them.

Many firms are indirect exporters and importers, often without their knowledge. As an example, merchandise can be sold to a domestic firm that in turn sells it abroad. This is most frequently the case when smaller suppliers deliver products to large multinational corporations, which use them as input to their foreign sales. Foreign buyers may also purchase products locally and then send them immediately to their home country. While indirect exports may be the result of unwitting participation, some firms also choose this method of international entry as a strategic alternative that conserves effort and resources while still taking advantage of foreign opportunities.

At the same time, many firms that perceive themselves as buying domestically may in reality buy imported products. They may have long-standing relations with a domestic supplier who, because of cost and competitive pressures, has begun to source products from abroad rather than to produce them domestically. In this case, the buyer firm has become an indirect importer.

indirect involvement
Participation by a firm in international business through an intermediary, in which the firm does not deal with foreign customers or firms.

direct involvement
Participation by a firm in international business in which the firm works with foreign customers or markets to establish a relationship.

transaction cost theory
The thought that the carrying out of an interaction (typically in business an exchange) takes resources and will cause expenses.

Firms that opt to export or import directly have more opportunities ahead of them. They more quickly learn the competitive advantages of their products and can therefore expand more rapidly. They also have the ability to control their international activities better and can forge relationships with their trading partners, which can lead to further international growth and success.

However, the firms also are faced with obstacles. These hurdles include indentifying and targeting foreign suppliers and/or customers and finding retail space, all of which are processes that can be very costly and time-consuming. Some firms are overcoming such barriers through the use of mail-order catalogs or electronic commerce ("storeless" distribution) networks. In Japan, for example, "high-cost rents, crowded shelves, and an intricate distribution system have made launching new products via conventional methods an increasingly difficult and expensive proposition. Direct marketing via e-commerce eliminates the need for high-priced shop space."[22] In addition, particularly in industry sectors characterized by very thin profit margins, survival is determined by sales volume. Under such conditions, a large market size is essential for success—pointing many firms in the direction of international markets reached through electronic business.[23]

As a firm and its managers gather experience with exporting, they move through different levels of commitment, ranging from awareness, interest, trial, evaluation, and finally, adaptation of an international outlook as part of corporate strategy. Of course, not all firms will progress with equal speed through all these levels. Some will do so very rapidly, perhaps encouraged by success with an electronic commerce approach, and move on to other forms of international involvement such as foreign direct investment. Others may withdraw from exporting, due to disappointing experiences or as part of a strategic resource allocation decision.[24]

Increasingly, there are many new firms that either start out with an international orientation or develop one shortly after their establishment. Such born global firms emerge particularly in industries that require large numbers of customers, and in countries that only offer small internal markets. They tend to be small and young[25] and often make heavy use of electronic commerce in reaching out to the world. In some countries more than one third of new companies have been reported to export within two years.[26] Firms, managers, and governments therefore will need to be much quicker than they have been in the past, when it comes to introducing firms to and preparing them for the international market.

INTERNATIONAL INTERMEDIARIES

5. To learn about the opportunities and challenges of cooperative market development

Both direct and indirect importers and exporters frequently make use of intermediaries who can assist with troublesome yet important details such as documentation, financing, and transportation. The intermediaries also can identify foreign suppliers and customers and help the firm with long- or short-term market penetration efforts. Major types of international intermediaries are export management companies and trading companies. Together with export facilitators, the intermediaries can bring the global market to the domestic firm's doorstep and help overcome financial and time constraints. Table 13.2 shows those areas in which intermediaries have been found to be particularly helpful.

It is the responsibility of the firm's management to decide how to use the intermediaries. Options range from using their help for initial market entry to developing a long-term strategic collaboration. It is the degree of corporate involvement in and control of the international effort that determines whether the firm operates as an indirect or direct internationalist.

Table 13.2 How a Trade Intermediary Can Offer Assistance

1. Knows foreign market competitive conditions
2. Has personal contacts with potential foreign buyers
3. Evaluates credit risk associated with foreign buyers
4. Has sales staff to call on current foreign customers in person
5. Assumes responsibility for physical delivery of product to foreign buyer

Source: Richard M. Castaldi, Alex F. De Noble, and Jeffrey Kantor, "The Intermediary Service Requirements of Canadian and American Exporters," *International Marketing Review* 9, 2 (1992): 21–40; Patrick K. O. Fung, Ivy S. N. Chen, and Leslie S. C. Yip, "Relationships and Performance of Trade Intermediaries: An Exploratory Study," *European Journal of Marketing* 41, no. 1/2 (2007): 159–180.

EXPORT MANAGEMENT COMPANIES

Firms that specialize in performing international business services as commission representatives or as distributors are known as **export management companies (EMCs)**. Most EMCs are quite small. Many were formed by one or two principals with experience in international business or in a particular geographic area. Their expertise enables them to offer specialized services to domestic corporations.

export management companies (EMCs) Domestic firms that specialize in performing international business services as commission representatives or as distributors.

EMCs have two primary forms of operation: they take title to goods and distribute internationally on their own account, or they perform services as agents. They often serve a variety of clients, thus their mode of operation may vary from client to client and from transaction to transaction. An EMC may act as an agent for one client and as a distributor for another. It may even act as both for the same client on different occasions.

When working as an **agent**, the EMC is primarily responsible for developing foreign business and sales strategies and establishing contacts abroad. Because the EMC does not share in the profits from a sale, it depends heavily on a high sales volume, on which it charges commission. The EMC may therefore be tempted to take on as many products and as many clients as possible to obtain a high sales volume. As a result, the EMC may spread itself too thin and may be unable to adequately represent all the clients and products it carries. The risk is particularly great with small EMCs.

agent A representative or intermediary for the firm that works to develop business and sales strategies and that develops contacts.

EMCs that have specific expertise in selecting markets because of language capabilities, previous exposure, or specialized contacts appear to be the ones most successful and useful in aiding client firms in their international business efforts. For example, they can cooperate with firms that are already successful in international business but have been unable to penetrate a specific region. By sticking to their area of expertise and representing only a limited number of clients, such agents can provide quite valuable services.

When operating as a **distributor**, the EMC purchases products from the domestic firm, takes title, and assumes the trading risk. Selling in its own name, it has the opportunity to reap greater profits than when acting as an agent. The potential for greater profit is appropriate, because the EMC has drastically reduced the risk for the domestic firm while increasing its own risk. The burden of the merchandise acquired provides a major motivation to complete an international sale successfully. The domestic firm selling to the EMC is in the comfortable position of having sold its merchandise and received its money without having to deal with the complexities of the international market. On the other hand, it is less likely to gather much international business expertise.

distributor A representative or intermediary for the firm that purchases products from the firm, takes title, and assumes the selling risk.

Compensation of EMCs

The mechanism of an EMC may be very useful to the domestic firm if such activities produce additional sales abroad. However, certain activities must take place and must be paid for. As an example, a firm must incur market development expenses to enter foreign markets. At the very least, product availability must be communicated, goods must be shown abroad, visits must be arranged, or contacts must be established. These activities must be funded.

One possibility is a fee charged to the manufacturer by the EMC for market development, sometimes in the form of a retainer and often on an annual basis. The retainers vary and are dependent on the number of products represented and the difficulty of foreign market penetration. Frequently, manufacturers are also expected to pay all or part of the direct expenses associated with foreign market penetration. These expenses may involve the production and translation of promotional product brochures, the cost of attending trade shows, the provision of product samples, or trade advertising.

Alternatively, the EMC may demand a price break for international sales. In one way or another, the firm that uses an EMC must pay the EMC for the international business effort. Otherwise, despite promises, the EMC may simply add the firm and product in name only to its product offering and do nothing to achieve international success.

Power Conflicts between EMCs and Clients

The EMC faces the continuous problem of retaining a client once foreign market penetration is achieved. Many firms use an EMC's services mainly to test the international arena, with the clear desire to become a direct participant once successful operations have been established. Of course, this is particularly true if foreign demand turns out to be strong and profit levels are high. The conflict between the EMC and its clients, with one side wanting to retain market power by not sharing too much international business information, and the other side wanting to obtain that power, often results in short-term relationships and a lack of cooperation. Because international business development is based on long-term efforts, this conflict frequently leads to a lack of success.

For the concept of an export management company to work, both parties must fully recognize the delegation of responsibilities, the costs associated with those activities, and the need for information sharing, cooperation, and mutual reliance. Use of an EMC should be viewed just like a domestic channel commitment, requiring a thorough investigation of the intermediary and the advisability of relying on its efforts, a willingness to cooperate on a relationship rather than on a transaction basis, and a willingness to properly reward its efforts. The EMC in turn must adopt a flexible approach to managing the export relationship. As access to the Internet is making customers increasingly sophisticated and world-wise, export management companies must ensure that they continue to deliver true value added. They must acquire, develop, and deploy resources such as new knowledge about foreign markets or about export processes in order to lower their client firm's export-related transaction costs and therefore remain a useful intermediary.[27] By doing so, the EMC lets the client know that the cost is worth the service and thereby reduces the desire for circumvention.

TRADING COMPANIES

Another major intermediary is the trading company. The concept was originated by the European trading houses such as the Fuggers of Augsburg, Germany. Later on, monarchs chartered traders to form corporate bodies that enjoyed exclusive trading rights and protection by the naval forces in exchange for tax payments. Examples of such early trading companies are the Oost-Indische Compagnie of the Netherlands, formed in 1602, followed shortly by the British East India Company and La

Compagnie des Indes chartered by France.[28] Today, the most famous trading companies are the **sogoshosha** of Japan. Names such as Mitsubishi, Mitsui, and C. Itoh have become household words around the world. The nine trading company giants of Japan act as intermediaries for about one third of the country's exports and two fifths of its imports.[29] The general trading companies play a unique role in world commerce by importing, exporting, countertrading, investing, and manufacturing. Their vast size allows them to benefit from economies of scale and perform their operations at high rates of return, even though their profit margins are less than 2 percent.

Four major reasons have been given for the success of the Japanese sogoshosha. First, by concentrating on obtaining and disseminating information about market opportunities and by investing huge funds in the development of information systems, the firms have the mechanisms and organizations in place to gather, evaluate, and translate market information into business opportunities. Second, economies of scale permit the firms to take advantage of their vast transaction volume to obtain preferential treatment by, for example, negotiating transportation rates or even opening up new transportation routes and distribution systems. Third, the firms serve large internal markets, not only in Japan but also around the world, and can benefit from opportunities for countertrade. Finally, sogoshosha have access to vast quantities of capital, both within Japan and in the international capital markets. They can therefore carry out transactions that are too large or risky to be palatable or feasible for other firms.[30] In spite of changing trading patterns, these giants continue to succeed by shifting their strategy to expand their domestic activities in Japan, entering more newly developing markets, increasing their trading activities among third countries, and forming joint ventures with non-Japanese firms.

Expansion of Trading Companies

For many decades, the emergence of trading companies was commonly believed to be a Japan-specific phenomenon. Japanese cultural factors were cited as the reason that such intermediaries could operate successfully only from that country. In the last few decades, however, many other governments have established trading companies. In countries as diverse as Korea, Brazil, and Turkey, trading companies handle large portions of national exports.[31] The reason these firms have become so large is due, in good measure, to special and preferential government incentives, rather than market forces alone. Therefore, they may be vulnerable to changes in government policies.

In the United States, trading companies in which firms could cooperate internationally were initially permitted through the Webb-Pomerene associations established in 1918. While in the 1930s these collaborative ventures accounted for about 12 percent of U.S. exports, their share had dropped to less than 1 percent by 2009. Another governmental approach to export trade facilitation was **export trading company (ETC)** legislation designed to improve the export performance of small and medium-sized firms. Bank participation in trading companies was permitted, and the antitrust threat to joint export efforts was reduced through precertification of planned activities by the U.S. Department of Commerce. Businesses were encouraged to join together to export or offer export services.

Permitting banks to participate in ETCs was intended to allow ETCs better access to capital and therefore permit more trading transactions and easier receipt of title to goods. The relaxation of antitrust provisions in turn was meant to enable firms to form joint ventures more easily. The cost of developing and penetrating international markets would then be shared, with the proportional share being, for many small and medium-sized firms, much easier to bear. As an example, in case a warehouse is needed in order to secure foreign market penetration, one firm alone does not have to bear all the costs. A consortium of firms can

sogoshosha A large Japanese general trading company.

export trading company (ETC) The result of 1982 legislation to improve the export performance of small- and medium-sized firms, the export trading company allows businesses to band together to export or offer export services. Additionally, the law permits bank participation in trading companies and relaxes antitrust provisions.

jointly rent a foreign warehouse. Similarly, each firm need not station a service technician abroad at substantial cost. Joint funding of a service center by several firms makes the cost less prohibitive for each one. The trading company concept also offers a one-stop shopping center for both the firm and its foreign customers. The firm can be assured that all international functions will be performed efficiently by the trading company, and at the same time, the foreign customer will have to deal with few individual firms.

"Although ETCs seem to offer major benefits to U.S. firms wishing to penetrate international markets, they have not been used very extensively. As of 2009, certificates were held by 75 individuals, companies, and associations. Yet these certificates cover more than 3,000 firms, mainly because the various trade associations have applied for certification for all of their members.[32]

PRIVATE-SECTOR FACILITATORS

Facilitators are entities outside the firm that assist in the process of going international. They supply knowledge and information but do not participate in the transaction. Such facilitators can come both from the private and the public sector.

Major encouragement and assistance can result from the statements and actions of other firms in the same industry. Information that would be considered proprietary if it involved domestic operations is often freely shared by competing firms when it concerns international business. The information not only has source credibility but is viewed with a certain amount of fear, because a too-successful competitor may eventually infringe on the firm's domestic business.

A second influential group of private-sector facilitators is distributors. Often a firm's distributors are engaged, through some of their business activities, in international business. To increase their international distribution volume, they encourage purely domestic firms to participate in the international market. This is true not only for exports but also for imports. For example, a major customer of a manufacturing firm may find that materials available from abroad, if used in the domestic production process, would make the product available at lower cost. In such instances, the customer may approach the supplier and strongly encourage foreign sourcing.

Banks and other service firms, such as accounting and consulting firms, can serve as major facilitators by alerting their clients to international opportunities. While these service providers historically follow their major multinational clients abroad, increasingly they are establishing a foreign presence on their own. Frequently, they work with domestic clients on expanding market reach in the hope that their service will be used for any international transaction that results. Given the extensive information network of many service providers—banks, for example, often have a wide variety of correspondence relationships—the role of these facilitators can be major. Like a mother hen, they can take firms under their wings and be pathfinders in foreign markets.

Chambers of commerce and other business associations that interact with firms can frequently heighten their interest in international business. Yet, in most instances, such organizations function mainly as secondary intermediaries, because true change is brought about by the presence and encouragement of other managers.

PUBLIC-SECTOR FACILITATORS

Government efforts can also facilitate the international efforts of firms. In the United States, for example, the Department of Commerce provides major export assistance, as do other federal organizations such as the Small Business Administration and the Export-Import Bank. Most countries maintain similar export support organizations. Table 13.3 provides the names of selected export promotion agencies from around

Table 13.3 Selected Export Promotion Agencies Around the Globe

Australia: Australian Trade Commission
http://www.austrade.gov.au
Canada: Export Development Corporation
http://www.edc.ca/
France: Centre Français du Commerce Extérieur
http://www.ubifrance.fr/default.html
Germany: Germany Trade and Invest
http://www.gtai.de/web_de/startseite
India: India Trade Promotion Organisation (ITPO)
http://www.indiatradepromotion.org
Japan: Japan External Trade Organization (JETRO)
http://www.jetro.go.jp
Singapore: International Enterprise Singapore
http://www.iesingapore.gov.sg/wps/portal
South Korea: Trade-Investment Promotion Agency (KOTRA)
http://www.kotra.or.kr/wps/portal/dk
United Kingdom: Department of Business Innovation and Skills
http://www.bis.gov.uk
United Nations/World Trade Organization: International Trade Centre
http://www.intracen.org
United States: Export-Import Bank
http://www.exim.gov
International Trade Administration
http://www.ita.doc.gov
Foreign Agricultural Service
http://www.fas.usda.gov

the globe, together with their web addresses. Employees of these organizations typically visit firms and attempt to analyze their international business opportunities. Through rapid access to government resources, these individuals can provide data, research reports, counseling, and financing information to firms. Government organizations can also sponsor meetings that bring interested parties together and alert them to new business opportunities abroad. Key governmental support is also provided when firms are abroad. By receiving information and assistance from their embassies, many business ventures abroad can be made easier. The ad on the next page provides an example of active government involvement in investment promotion.

Increasingly, organizations at the state and local level also are active in encouraging firms to participate in international business. Many states and provinces have formed agencies for economic development that provide information, display products abroad, conduct trade missions, and sometimes even offer financing. Similar services can also be offered by state and local port authorities and by some of the larger cities. State and local authorities can be a major factor in facilitating international activities because of their closeness to firms.

Educational institutions such as universities and community colleges can also be major international business facilitators. They can act as trade information clearinghouses, facilitate networking opportunities, provide client counseling and technical assistance, and develop trade education programs.[33] They can also develop course projects that are useful to firms interested in international business. For example, students may visit a firm and examine its potential in the international market as a course requirement. With the skill and supervision of faculty members to help the students develop the final report, such projects can be useful to firms with scarce resources, while they expose students to real-world problems.

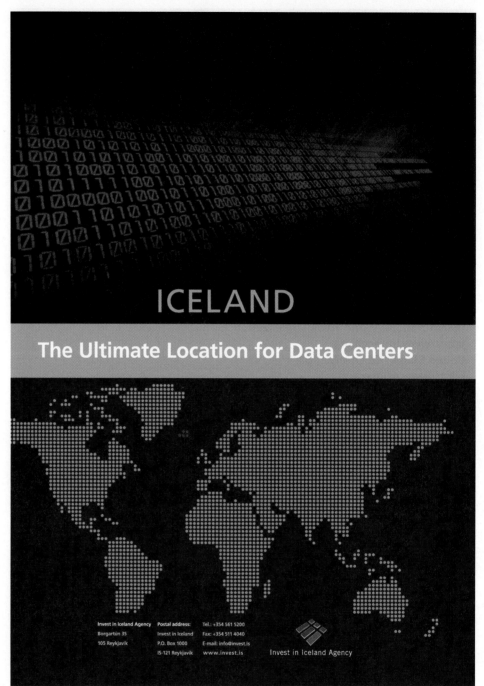

ICELAND

The Ultimate Location for Data Centers

Invest in Iceland Agency	Postal address:	Tel.: +354 561 5200
Borgartún 35	Invest in Iceland	Fax: +354 511 4040
105 Reykjavík	P.O. Box 1000	E-mail: info@invest.is
	IS-121 Reykjavík	www.invest.is Invest in Iceland Agency

© Courtesy Invest In Iceland

LICENSING

licensing agreement An agreement in which one firm permits another to use its intellectual property in exchange for compensation.

royalty The compensation paid by one firm to another under an agreement.

Under a **licensing agreement**, one firm permits another to use its intellectual property for compensation designated as **royalty** The recipient firm is the licensee. The property licensed might include patents, trademarks, copyrights, technology, technical know-how, or specific business skills. For example, a firm that has developed a bag-in-the-box packaging process for milk can permit other firms abroad to use the same process. Licensing therefore can also be called the export of intangibles.

Licensing has intuitive appeal to many would-be international managers. As an entry strategy, it requires neither capital investment nor detailed involvement with foreign customers. By generating royalty income, licensing provides an opportunity to exploit research and development already conducted. After initial costs, the licensor can reap benefits until the end of the license contract period. Licensing also reduces the risk of expropriation because the licensee is a local company that can provide leverage against government action.

Licensing may help to avoid host-country regulations applicable to equity ventures. It also may provide a means by which foreign markets can be tested without major involvement of capital or management time. Similarly, licensing can be used as a strategy to preempt a market before the entry of competition, especially if the licensor's resources permit full-scale involvement only in selected markets. Licensing also relieves the originating company from having to come up with culturally responsive changes in every market. As Focus on Culture shows, the local licensees can worry about that part.

A special form of licensing is **trademark licensing**, which has become a substantial source of worldwide revenue for companies that can trade on well-known names and characters. Trademark licensing permits the names or logos of designers, literary characters, sports teams, or movie stars to appear on clothing, games, foods and beverages, gifts and novelties, toys, and home furnishings. Licensors can make millions of dollars with little effort, while licensees can produce a brand or product that consumers will recognize immediately. Trademark licensing is possible, however, only if the trademark name conveys instant recognition.

trademark licensing
Providing someone the right to use an established brand symbol in exchange for payment.

Licensing is not without disadvantages. It is a very limited form of foreign market participation and does not in any way guarantee a basis for future expansion. As a matter of fact, quite the opposite may take place. In exchange for the royalty, the

FOCUS ON CULTURE

TV Program Licenses Are International

For most of the history of television, American programming has dominated the airwaves in the United States and abroad. The most popular shows in any given country were likely to be American concepts produced by American firms. The cop show, the sitcom, and the western are all television concepts developed in the United States.

The privatization of many state-run television enterprises during the 1980s created more competition and increased demand for American programming. The new commercial stations lacked the expertise needed to produce hit shows in a cost-effective way, so they filled their many open hours of airtime by purchasing programming from the United States.

American companies took advantage of high demand and prices skyrocketed. The trend continued through the 1990s as prices increased fivefold. During a bidding war in Britain, for example, the price of each episode of the *Simpsons* went up to $1.5 million. American companies also bundled their offerings and forced television stations to buy less popular programming along with popular shows.

Over time, the situation abroad has changed. Local stations have become more adept at developing and producing their own programming. Tastes also changed as consumers demanded television shows more reflective of their own cultural values and preferences. All this means that stations no longer rely on American programming to win prime-time ratings battles.

In addition to claiming a larger share of their domestic markets, European production companies have turned the tables with licensing agreements. Now they develop winning television shows and license the idea to other companies for production in their own country.

Some very successful U.S. reality series were pioneered overseas. One example is the Dutch hit show *Big Brother*. New concepts are being developed, tested in foreign markets, and exported all the time. The British television hit *Pop Idol* gave rise to licensed versions in Poland, South Africa, and the United States. In the new international television market, winning ideas can come from any country.

Therefore, it is surprising that the European Union has preserved its antiquated 1989 "Television Without Frontiers" directive, which mandates that EU television channels are required to reserve at least 50 percent of their output for European-made content. In a global cultural environment, where ideas originate from Mumbai to Memphis and are transformed as they travel around the world, government intervention and culture by legislation are more of an obstacle than a facilitator of human creativity.

Sources: http://www.endemol.com, accessed May 14, 2003; Bill Brioux, "Excuse Me, Is that a Canadian Idol?" *Edmonton Sun*, October 23, 2002; "Television Broadcasting Activities: 'Television Without Frontiers'" (TVWF) Directive, European Commission, September 9, 2008, http://europa.eu/legislation_summaries/audiovisual_and_media/124101_en.html, accessed October 2, 2009; Jean K. Chalaby, *Transnational Television in Europe: Reconfiguring Global Communications Networks* (London: I. B. Tauris, 2009).

licensor may create its own competitor not only in the market for which the agreement was made but for third-country markets as well.

Licensing has also come under criticism from many governments and supra-national organizations. They have alleged that licensing provides a mechanism for corporations in industrialized countries to capitalize on older technology. These accusations have been made even though licensing offers a foreign entity the opportunity for immediate market entry with a proven concept. It therefore eliminates the risk of R&D failure, the cost of designing around the licensor's patents, or the fear of patent-infringement litigation.

FRANCHISING

franchising A form of licensing that allows a distributor or retailer exclusive rights to sell a product or service in a specified area.

Franchising is the granting of the right by a parent company (the franchisor) to another, independent entity (the franchisee) to do business in a prescribed manner. The right can take the form of selling the franchisor's products, using its name, production, and marketing techniques, or using its general business approach.[34] Usually franchising involves a combination of many of those elements. The major forms of franchising are manufacturer-retailer systems (such as car dealerships), manufacturer-wholesaler systems (such as soft drink companies), and service-firm retailer systems (such as lodging services and fast-food outlets).

The expansion or contraction of franchising results from the global economic climate. When financing is readily available and product demand is soaring, companies are eager to expand their franchise operations. The reverse is also true. For example, during the global credit crunch in 2009, the number of franchise establishments in the United States declined by 1.2 percent, from nearly 865,000 to less than 855,000—a net loss of approximately 10,000. Jobs in the franchise sector fell by 2.1 percent, for a loss of 207,000. Overall economic output, the gross value of goods and services produced by franchises, declined by 0.5 percent—an annual loss of $4.2 billion. However, once credit markets and demand stabilize, franchising should rebound. After the recession of 2000–2001 and the terrorist attacks of September 11, 2001, the U.S. franchise industry expanded by more than 140,000 new businesses and created 1.2 million new jobs over a five-year period.[35]

Chicken tastes good everywhere.

© Eric Nathan/Alamy

Typically, to be successful in international franchising, the firm must be able to offer unique products or unique selling propositions. A franchise must also offer a high degree of standardization, which does not require 100 percent uniformity, but rather, international recognizability. Concurrent with this recognizability, the franchisor can and should adapt to local circumstances. Food franchisors, for example, will vary the products and product lines offered, depending on local market conditions and tastes.

Key reasons for the international expansion of franchise systems are market potential, financial gain, and saturated domestic markets. From a franchisee's perspective, the franchise is beneficial because it reduces risk by implementing a proven concept. There are also major benefits from a governmental perspective. The source country does not see a replacement of exports or an export of jobs. The recipient country sees franchising as requiring little outflow of foreign exchange, since the bulk of the profits generated remains within the country.[36]

Franchising has been growing rapidly, but government intervention, or lack thereof, continues to be a major problem. Many multinational corporations (MNCs) attempting to establish franchises in China, for example, have encountered the People's Republic's reluctance to protect their intellectual property rights. Intellectual piracy is still quite common in the country, even after its accession to the WTO. Franchisors are advised to register their brands in Chinese characters. Otherwise, they could be registered by someone else. In China, recovering a trademark after it has been registered by another party (including a franchisee) can be a complex undertaking. In 2003, Starbucks Corporation began a protracted legal battle against a local competitor that had registered its Chinese name—Xingbake—and was even using the Seattle-based company's green logo. The case was not resolved until 2007, when the Shanghai Municipal Higher People's Court finally ruled in Starbucks' favor.[37]

Selection and training of franchisees represents another problem area. Many franchise systems have run into difficulty by expanding too quickly and granting franchises to unqualified entities. Although the local franchisee knows the market best, the franchisor still needs to understand the market for product adaptation and operational purposes. The franchisor, in order to remain viable in the long term, needs to coordinate the efforts of individual franchisees—for example, to share ideas and engage in joint undertakings, such as cooperative advertising.

LOCAL PRESENCE

INTERFIRM COOPERATION

6. *To understand how firms can overcome market barriers by either building competitive capabilities abroad from scratch or acquiring them from local owners.*

The world is too large and the competition too strong for even the largest companies to do everything independently. Technologies are converging and markets are becoming integrated, thus making the costs and risks of both goods and market development ever greater. Partly as a reaction to and partly to exploit the developments, management in multinational corporations has become more pragmatic about what it takes to be successful in global markets. The result has been the formation of **strategic alliances** with suppliers, customers, competitors, and companies in other industries to achieve multiple goals.

strategic alliances A new term for collaboration among firms, often similar to joint ventures.

A strategic alliance (or partnership) is an informal or formal arrangement between two or more companies with a common business objective. It is something more than the traditional customer-vendor relationship but something less than an outright acquisition. The alliances can take forms ranging from informal cooperation to joint ownership of worldwide operations. For example, Texas Instruments has reported agreements with companies such as IBM, Hyundai, Fujitsu, Alcatel, and L. M. Ericsson using such terms as "joint development agreement," "cooperative technical effort," "joint program for development," "alternative sourcing agreement," and "design/exchange agreement for cooperative product development and exchange of technical data."[38]

Reasons for Interfirm Cooperation

Strategic alliances are used for many different purposes by the partners involved. Market development is one common focus. Penetrating foreign markets is a primary objective of many companies. In Japan, Motorola is sharing chip designs and manufacturing facilities with Toshiba to gain greater access to the Japanese market. Some alliances aim to defend home markets. With no orders coming in for nuclear power plants, Bechtel Group has teamed up with Germany's Siemens to service existing U.S. plants. Another key focus is to either share the risk of engaging in a particular activity in a particular market, or to share the resource requirements of an activity.[39] The costs of developing new jet engines are so vast that they force aerospace companies into collaboration. One such consortium was formed by United Technologies' Pratt & Whitney division, Britain's Rolls-Royce, Motoren-und-Turbinen Union from Germany, Fiat of Italy, and Japanese Aero Engines (made up of Ishikawajima Heavy Industries and Kawasaki Heavy Industries).[40] Some alliances are formed to block and co-opt competitors.[41] For example, Caterpillar formed a heavy equipment joint venture with Mitsubishi in Japan to strike back at its main global rival, Komatsu, in its home market.

The most successful alliances are those that match the complementary strengths of partners to satisfy a joint objective. Often the partners have different product, geographic, or functional strengths that the partners build on, rather than use to fill gaps.[42] Some of the major alliances created on this basis are provided in Figure 13.2.

Types of Interfirm Cooperation

Each form of alliance is distinct in terms of the amount of commitment required and the degree of control each partner has. The equity alliances—minority ownership, joint ventures, and consortia—feature the most extensive commitment and shared control. The types of strategic alliances are summarized in Figure 13.3, using the extent of equity involved and the number of partners in the endeavor as defining characteristics.

Figure 13.2   Complementary Strengths Create Value

Partner *Strength...*	+ Partner *Strength...*	= Joint Objective
PepsiCo *marketing clout for canned beverages*	**Lipton** *recognized tea brand and customer franchise*	*To sell canned iced tea beverages jointly*
Philips *consumer electronics innovation and leadership*	**Levi Strauss** *fashion design and distribution*	*Outdoor wear with integrated electronic equipment for fashion-conscious consumers*
KFC *established brand and store format, and operations skills*	**Mitsubishi** *real estate and site-selection skills in Japan*	*To establish a KFC chain in Japan*
Siemens *presence in range of telecommunications markets worldwide and cable-manufacturing technology*	**Corning** *technological strength in optical fibers and glass*	*To create a fibre-optic-cable business*
Ericsson *technological strength in public telecommunications networks*	**Hewlett-Packard** *computers, software, and access to electronics-channels*	*To create and market network management systems*

Sources: "Portable Technology Takes the Next Step: Electronics You Can Wear," *Wall Street Journal*, August 22, 2000, B1, B4; Joel Bleeke and David Ernst, "Is Your Strategic Alliance Really a Sale?" *Harvard Business Review* 73 (January–February 1995): 97–105. See also (Melanie Wells, "Coca-Cola Proclaims Nestea Time for CAA," *Advertising Age*, January 30, 1995, 2. See also http://www.pepsico.com; http://www.lipton.com; http://www.kfc.com; http://w1.siemens.com/entry/cc/en/; http://www.ericsson.com; http://www.hp.com; Susanne Royer and Roland Simons, "Evolution of Cooperation and Dynamics of Expectations–Implications for Strategic Alliances," *International Journal of Strategic Business Alliances* 1, no. 1, 2009: 73–88.

Figure 13.3   Forms of Interfirm Cooperation

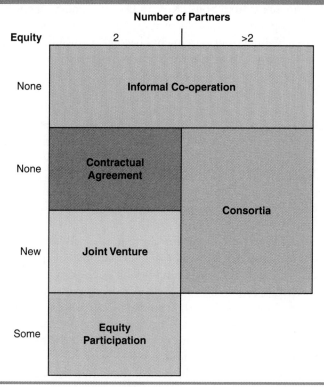

Source: Adapted with permission from Bernard L. Simonin, *Transfer of Knowledge of International Strategic Alliances: A Structural Approach*, unpublished dissertation (Ann Arbor: University of Michigan, 1991).

Informal Cooperation   In informal cooperative deals, partners work together without a binding agreement. This arrangement often takes the form of visits to exchange information about new products, processes, and technologies or may take the more formal form of the exchange of personnel for limited amounts of time. Often such partners are of no real threat in each other's markets and are of modest size in comparison to the competition, making collaboration necessary.[43] The relationships are based on mutual trust and friendship, and may lead to more formal arrangements, such as contractual agreements or joint projects.

Contractual Agreements   Strategic alliance partners may join forces for joint R&D, joint marketing, or joint production. Similarly, their joint efforts might include **licensing**, cross-licensing, or **cross-marketing activities**. Nestlé and General Mills had an agreement whereby Honey Nut Cheerios and Golden Grahams were made in General Mills's U.S. plants and shipped in bulk to Europe for packaging by Nestlé. Such an arrangement—complementary marketing (also known as piggybacking)—allows firms to reach objectives that they cannot reach efficiently by themselves.[44] The alliance between General Mills and Nestlé evolved into a joint venture, Cereal Partners Worldwide, which markets both companies' products in Europe and Asia. Firms also can have a reciprocal arrangement whereby each partner provides the other access to its market. The New York Yankees and Manchester United sell each others' licensed products and develop joint sponsorship programs. International airlines share hubs, coordinate schedules, and simplify ticketing. Alliances such as Star (joining United and Lufthansa), Oneworld (British Airways and American Airlines), and Sky Team (Delta and Air France) provide worldwide coverage for their customers both in the travel and shipping communities.

licensing A firm gives a license to another firm to produce, package, or market its product.

cross-marketing activities A reciprocal arrangement whereby each partner provides the other access to its markets for a product.

contract manufacturing
Outsourcing the actual production of goods so that the corporation can focus on research, development, and marketing.

Contractual agreements also exist for outsourcing. For example, General Motors buys cars and components from South Korea's Daewoo, and Siemens buys computers from Fujitsu. As corporations look for ways to simultaneously grow and maintain their competitive advantage, outsourcing has become a powerful new tool for achieving those goals. **Contract manufacturing** allows the corporation to separate the physical production of goods from the research and development and marketing stages, especially if the latter are the core competencies of the firm. Benefits of such contracting are to improve company focus on higher value-added activities, to gain access to world-class capabilities, and to reduce operating costs. Contract manufacturing has been criticized because of the pressure it puts on the contractors to cut prices and, thereby, labor costs. However, such work does provide many companies, especially in developing countries, the opportunity to gain the necessary experience in product design and manufacturing technology to allow them to function in world markets. Some have even voiced concerns that the experience eventually may make future competitors of current partners.

management contract An international business alternative in which the firm sells its expertise in running a company while avoiding the risk or benefit of ownership.

In some parts of the world and in certain industries, governments insist on complete or majority ownership of firms. There, multinational companies offer **management contracts**, selling their expertise in running a company while avoiding the risk or benefit of ownership. Depending on the contract, doing so may even permit some measure of control. As an example, the manufacturing process may have to be relinquished to local firms, yet international distribution may be required for the product. A management contract could maintain a strong hold on the operation by ensuring that all distribution channels remain firmly controlled.

A management contract may be the critical element in the success of a project. For example, financial institutions may gain confidence in a project because of the existence of a management contract and may even make it a precondition for funding.[45]

turnkey operation A specialized form of management contract between a customer and an organization to provide a complete operational system together with the skills needed for unassisted maintenance and operation.

One specialized form of management contract is the **turnkey operation**. Here, the arrangement permits a client to acquire a complete international system, together with skills sufficient to allow unassisted maintenance and operation of the system following its completion.[46] The client need not search for individual contractors or subcontractors or deal with scheduling conflicts or with difficulties in assigning responsibilities or blame. Instead, a package arrangement focuses responsibility on one entity, thus greatly easing the negotiation and supervision requirements and subsequent accountability. When the project is running, the system will be totally owned, controlled, and operated by the customer. Companies such as AES are part of consortia building electric power facilities around the world, operating them, and, in some cases, even owning parts of them.

Management contracts have clear benefits for the client. They provide organizational skills not available locally, expertise that is immediately available, and management assistance in the form of support services that would be difficult and costly to replicate locally. For example, hotels managed by the Sheraton Corporation have access to Sheraton's worldwide reservation system. Management contracts today typically involve training locals to take over the operation after a given period.

Similar advantages exist for the supplier. The risk of participating in an international venture is substantially lowered, while significant amounts of control are still exercised. Existing know-how that has been built up through substantial investment can be commercialized, and frequently the impact of fluctuations in business volume can be reduced by making use of experienced personnel who otherwise would have to be laid off. Accumulated service knowledge should be used internationally. Management contracts permit firms to do so.

Equity Participation   Many multinational corporations have acquired minority ownerships in companies that have strategic importance for them to ensure supplier ability and build formal and informal working relationships. An example is the 2009 equity swap between China's Unicom and Spain's Telefónica. The partners continue operating as separate entities, but each enjoys the strengths that the other provides. For example, both telecom giants were motivated by a desire to stay competitive and gain market share in the midst of a global economic downturn. The agreement ensured cooperation in infrastructure and equipment sharing, research and development, and the provision of roaming and other services for multinational customers. The deal gave both companies access to a combined 550 million customers worldwide. Equity ownership in an innovator may also give the investing company first access to any newly developed technology.

Another significant reason for equity ownership is market entry and support of global operations. For example, Telefónica has acquired varying stakes in Latin American telecommunications systems—a market that is the fastest-growing region of the world after Asia. As of 2009, Telefónica had evolved into the third-largest global telecom operator and one of the largest in Latin America, with a subscriber base of 124.65 million.[47]

Joint Ventures A joint venture can be defined as the participation of two or more companies in an enterprise in which each party contributes assets, has some equity, and shares risk.[48] The venture is also considered long term. The reasons for establishing a joint venture can be divided into three groups: (1) government policy or legislation; (2) one partner's needs for other partners' skills; and (3) one partner's needs for other partners' attributes or assets.[49] Equality of the partners or of their contribution is not necessary. In some joint ventures, each partners' contributions—typically consisting of funds, technology, plant, or labor—also vary.

The key to a joint venture is the sharing of a common business objective, which makes the arrangement more than a customer-vendor relationship but less than an outright acquisition. The partners' rationales for entering into the arrangement may vary. An example is New United Motor Manufacturing Inc. (NUMMI), the joint venture between Toyota and GM. Toyota needed direct access to the U.S. market, while GM benefited from the technology and management approaches provided by its Japanese partner. NUMMI also represents an important example of how changes in a partner's business objectives and environment can lead to the dissolution of a joint venture. GM was severely battered by the global economic recession of 2007–2009, leading to the need for an emergency government bailout in April 2009. Consequently, GM was forced to pull out of NUMMI in June 2009 and effectively dissolved the partnership. Toyota indicated that it planned to pull out by March 2010.[50]

Joint ventures may be the only way in which a firm can profitably participate in a particular market since many governments restrict equity participation in local operations by foreigners. Other entry modes may be limited; for example, exports may be restricted because of tariff barriers. Joint ventures are valuable when the pooling of resources results in a better outcome for each partner than if each were to conduct its activities individually. This is particularly true when each partner has a specialized advantage in areas that benefit the venture. For example, a firm may have new technology yet lack sufficient capital to carry out foreign direct investment on its own. Through a joint venture, the technology can be used more quickly and market penetration achieved more easily. Similarly, one of the partners may have a distribution system already established or have better access to local suppliers, either of which permits a greater volume of sales in a shorter period of time.

Joint ventures also permit better relationships with local government and other organizations such as labor unions. Government-related reasons are the main rationale for joint ventures to take place in less-developed countries. If the local partner is politically influential, the new venture may be eligible for tax incentives, grants, and government support. Negotiations for certifications or licenses may be easier because authorities may not perceive themselves as dealing with a foreign firm. Relationships between the local partner and the local financial establishment may enable the joint venture to tap local capital markets. The greater experience (and therefore greater familiarity) with the local culture and environment of the local partner may enable the joint venture to benefit from greater insights into changing market conditions and needs.

Many joint ventures fall short of expectations and/or are disbanded. The reasons typically relate to conflicts of interest, problems with disclosure of sensitive information, and disagreements over how profits are to be shared. There is also often a lack of communication before, during, and after formation of the venture. In some cases, managers have been more interested in the launching of the venture than the actual running of the enterprise. Many of the problems stem from a lack of careful consideration in advance of how to manage the new endeavor. A partnership works on the basis of trust and commitment or not at all.

Typical disagreements cover the whole range of business decisions, including strategy, management style, accounting and control, marketing policies and strategies, research and development, and personnel. The joint venture may, for example, identify a particular market as a target only to find that one of the partners already has individual plans for it. U.S. partners have frequently complained that their Japanese counterparts do not send their most competent personnel to the joint venture; instead, because of their lifetime employment practice, they get rid of less competent managers by sending them to the new entities.

Similarly, the issue of profit accumulation and distribution may cause discontent. If one partner supplies the joint venture with a good, the partner will prefer that any profits accumulate at headquarters and accrue 100 percent to one firm rather than at the joint venture, where profits are divided according to equity participation. Such a decision may not be greeted with enthusiasm by the other partner. Once profits are accumulated, their distribution may lead to dispute. For example, one partner may insist on a high payout of dividends because of financial needs, whereas the other may prefer the reinvestment of profits into a growing operation.

Consortia   A new drug can cost $500 million to develop and bring to market; a mainframe computer or a telecommunications switch can require $1 billion. Some $7 billion goes into creating a new generation of computer chips. To combat the high costs and risks of research and development, research consortia have emerged in the United States, Japan, and Europe. For example, Ericsson, Panasonic, Samsung, Siemens, Sony, Motorola, Nokia, and Psion have formed Symbian to develop technologies for wireless communication. Headquartered in the U.K., the firm also has offices in Japan, Sweden, and the United States.

Joint Research and Development Act A 1984 law that allows both domestic and foreign firms to participate in joint basic-research efforts without fear of U.S. antitrust action.

Since the passage of the **Joint Research and Development Act** of 1984 (which allows both domestic and foreign firms to participate in joint basic research efforts without the fear of antitrust action), well over 100 consortia have been registered in the United States. The consortia pool their resources for research into technologies ranging from artificial intelligence to semiconductor manufacturing. (The major consortia in those fields are MCC and Sematech.) The European Union has five megaprojects to develop new technologies registered under the names EUREKA, ESPRIT, BRITE, RACE, and COMET. Japanese consortia have worked on producing the world's highest-capacity memory chip and advanced computer technologies. On the manufacturing side, the formation of Airbus Industries secured European production of commercial jets. The consortium, now backed by the European Aeronautic Defence and Space Company (EADS), which emerged from the link-up of the German DaimlerChrysler Aerospace AG, the French Aerospatiale Matra, and CASA of Spain,[51] has become a prime global competitor especially in the development of megaliners.

Managerial Considerations   The first requirement of interfirm cooperation is to find the right partner. Partners should have an orientation and goals in common and should bring complementary and relevant benefits to the endeavor. The venture makes little sense if the expertise of both partners is in the same area; for example, if both have production expertise but neither has distribution know-how. Patience should be exercised; a deal should not be rushed into, nor should the partners expect immediate results. Learning should be paramount in the endeavor while at the same time, partners must try not to give away core secrets to each other.[52]

Second, the more formal the arrangement, the greater the care that needs to be taken in negotiating the agreement. In joint venture negotiations, for example, extensive provisions must be made for contingencies. The points to be explored should include: (1) clear definition of the venture and its duration; (2) ownership, control, and management; (3) financial structure and policies; (4) taxation and fiscal obligation; (5) employment and training; (6) production; (7) government assistance; (8) transfer of technology; (9) marketing arrangements; (10) environmental protection; (11) record keeping and inspection; and (12) settlement of disputes. [53] These issues have to be addressed before the formation of the venture; otherwise, they eventually will surface as points of contention. A joint venture agreement, although comparable to a marriage agreement, should contain the elements of a divorce contract. In case the joint venture cannot be maintained to the satisfaction of partners, plans must exist for the dissolution of the agreement and for the allocation of profits and costs. Typically, however, one of the partners buys out the other partner(s) when partners decide to part ways.

A strategic alliance, by definition, also means a joining of two corporate cultures, which can often be quite different than a joint venture. To meet this challenge, partners must have frequent communication and interaction at three levels of the organization: the top management, operational leaders, and workforce levels. Trust and relinquishing control are difficult not only at the top but also at levels where the future of the venture is determined. A dominant partner may determine the corporate culture, but even then the other partners should be consulted. The development of specific alliance managers may be advised to forge the net of relationships both within and between alliance partners and, therefore, to support the formal alliance structure.[54]

Strategic alliances operate in a dynamic business environment and must therefore adjust to changing market conditions. The agreement between partners should provide for changes in the original concept so that the venture can flourish and grow. The trick is to have a prior understanding as to which party will take care of which pains and problems so that a common goal is reached.

Government attitudes and policies have to be part of the environmental considerations of corporate decision makers. While some alliances may be seen as a threat to the long-term economic security of a nation, in general, links with foreign operators should be encouraged. For example, the U.S. government urged major U.S. airlines to form alliances with foreign carriers to gain access to emerging world markets, partly in response to the failure to achieve free access to all markets through the negotiation of so-called open-skies agreements.[55]

FULL OWNERSHIP

For some firms, foreign direct investment requires, initially at least, 100 percent ownership. The reason may have an ethnocentric basis; that is, management may believe that no outside entity should have an impact on corporate decision making. Alternatively, it may be based on financial concerns. For example, in 2009, Starbucks Coffee Company assumed full control of the Starbucks business in France, which was previously operated through a joint venture with Sigla S.A. (Grupo Vips) of Spain. The ownership switch was motivated by potential increases in profitability and operational efficiency in the growing French market. Starbucks had opened its first location at the Paris Opera House in 2004.[56] In order to make a rational decision about the extent of ownership, management must evaluate the extent to which total control is important to the success of its international marketing activities. Often, full ownership may be a desirable, but not a necessary, prerequisite for international success. At other times it may be essential, particularly when strong links exist within the corporation. Interdependencies between and among local operations and headquarters may be so strong that nothing short of total coordination will result in an acceptable benefit to the firm as a whole.[57]

Increasingly, however, the international environment is hostile to full ownership by multinational firms. Government action through outright legal restrictions or discriminatory actions is making the option less attractive. There seems to be a distinct "liability of foreignness" to which multinational firms are exposed. Such disadvantages can result from government resentment of greater opportunities by multinational firms. But they can also be the consequence of corporate actions such as the decision to have many expatriates rotate in top management positions, which may weaken the standing of a subsidiary and its local employees.[58]

To overcome market barriers abroad, firms can either build competitive capabilities from scratch or acquire them from local owners.[59] The choice is often to accept a reduction in control or to lose the opportunity to operate efficiently in a country. In addition to formal action by the government, the general conditions in the market may make it advisable for the firm to join forces with local entities.

A COMPREHENSIVE VIEW OF INTERNATIONAL EXPANSION

7. To observe a model linking managerial commitment, international expansion and corporate concerns

The central driver of internationalization is the level of managerial commitment. This commitment will grow gradually from an awareness of international potential to the adaptation of international business as a strategic business direction. It will be influenced by the information, experience, and perception of management, which in turn is shaped by motivations, concerns, and the activities of change agents.

Management's commitment and its view of the capabilities of the firm will then trigger various international business activities, which can range from indirect exporting and importing to more direct involvement in the global market. Eventually, the firm may then expand further through measures such as joint ventures, strategic alliances, or foreign direct investment.

Figure 13.4   A Comprehensive Model of International Market Entry and Development

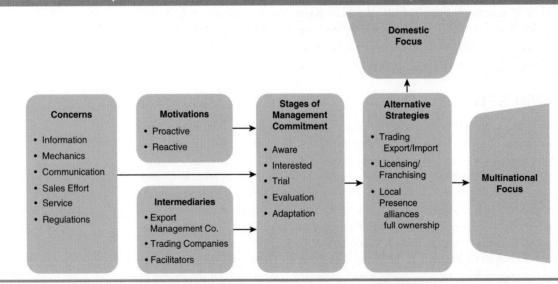

All of the developments, processes, and factors involved in the overall process of going international are linked to each other. A comprehensive view of these links is presented schematically in Figure 13.4.

SUMMARY

Firms do not become experienced in international business overnight, but rather progress gradually through an internationalization process. The process is triggered by different motivations to go abroad. The motivations can be proactive or reactive. Proactive motivations are initiated by aggressive management, whereas reactive motivations are the defensive response of management to environmental changes and pressures. Firms that are primarily stimulated by proactive motivations are more likely to enter international business and succeed.

In going abroad, firms encounter multiple problems and challenges, which range from a lack of information to mechanics and documentation. In order to gain assistance in its initial international experience, the firm can make use of either intermediaries or facilitators. Intermediaries are outside companies that actively participate in an international transaction. They are export management companies or trading companies. In order for these intermediaries to perform international business functions properly, however, they must be compensated. This will result in a reduction of profits.

International facilitators do not participate in international business transactions, but they contribute knowledge and information. Increasingly, facilitating roles are played by private-sector groups, such as industry associations, banks, accountants, or consultants, and by universities and federal, state, and local government authorities.

Apart from exporting and importing, alternatives for international business entry are licensing, franchising, and local presence. The basic advantage of licensing is that it does not involve capital investment or knowledge of foreign markets. Its major disadvantage is that licensing agreements typically have time limits, are often proscribed by foreign governments, and may result in creating a competitor. The use of franchising as a means of expansion into foreign markets has increased dramatically. Franchisors must learn to strike a balance between adapting to local environments and standardizing to the degree necessary to maintain international recognizability.

Full ownership is becoming more unlikely in many markets as well as industries, and the firm has to look at alternative approaches. The main alternative is interfirm cooperation, in which the firm joins forces with other business entities, possibly even a foreign government. In some cases, when the firm may not want to make a direct investment, it will offer its management expertise for sale in the form of management contracts.

KEY TERMS

managerial commitment 428	agent 437	strategic alliances 445
unsolicited order 429	distributor 437	licensing 447
accidental exporters 429	sogoshosha 439	cross-marketing activities 447
psychological distance 432	export trading company (ETC) 439	contract manufacturing 448
indirect involvement 435	licensing agreement 442	management contract 448
direct involvement 435	royalty 442	turnkey operation 448
transaction cost theory 435	trademark licensing 443	Joint Research and Development
export management companies (EMCs) 437	franchising 444	Act 450

QUESTIONS FOR DISCUSSION

1. Why is management commitment so important to export success?

2. Explain the benefits that international sales can have for domestic business activities.

3. Comment on the stance that "licensing is really not a form of international involvement because it requires no substantial additional effort on the part of the licensor."

4. What is the purpose of export intermediaries?

5. How can an export intermediary avoid circumvention by a client or customer?

6. Comment on the observation that "a joint venture may be a combination of Leonardo da Vinci's brain and Carl Lewis's legs; one wants to fly, the other insists on running."

7. Why would an internationalizing company opt for a management contract over other modes of operation? Relate your answer especially to the case of hospitality companies such as Hyatt, Marriott, and Sheraton.

INTERNET EXERCISES

1. What forms of export assistance are offered by the Small Business Administration (www.sba.gov) and the Export-Import Bank (www.exim.gov)?

2. Prepare a one-page memo to a foreign company introducing your product or service. Include a contact listing of ten foreign businesses looking to import your particular product. Cite the sources you used.

Sample sources of trade leads:

http://www.trade.gov/
http://www.tradematch.co.uk/
http://www.mnileads.com/

3. Using Nike's Code of Conduct (see http://www.nikebiz .com/responsibility/documents/Nike_Code_of_Conduct .pdf), assess how the company is addressing public criticism of working conditions in its subcontract factories.

TAKE A STAND

The European Union (EU) has implemented an agriculture policy that heavily subsidizes local producers. As a result, European farmers have increased their production capacity and are able to export large quantities of cheap foodstuffs to the international market. The EU has come under heavy scrutiny for these subsidies. Critics claim that the policy is harming agriculture in the developing world by cutting out suppliers in poor countries, where governments are unable or unwilling to dole out assistance.

Questions For Discussion

Conversely, others believe that cheaper food for the poor is better than the alternative. EU agriculture subsidies are funded through the higher prices paid by European consumers. Therefore, Europeans are paying a portion of the food costs for consumers in the developing world. Is there a way to make cheap food available in poor countries, without forcing people in rich countries to pay artificially high prices for it and unfairly cutting out suppliers in the developing world? Does it matter that the EU is a generous international aid donor? Under what circumstances are government subsidies justified?

SUGGESTED READINGS

Andrew Humphries and Richard Gibbs, *Strategic Alliances and Marketing Partnerships: Gaining Competitive Advantage Through Collaboration and Partnering* (London: Kogan Page, 2009).

Jati K, Sengupta, *Dynamics of Entry and Market Evolution* (New York: Palgrave Macmillan, 2007).

Gerald I. Susman (ed.), *Small and Medium-Sized Enterprises and the Global Economy* (Cheltenlam, U.K. Edward Elgar Publishing, 2007).

Alexander S. Konigsberg, *International Franchising*, 3rd ed. (New York: Juris Publishers, 2008).

Sandy Piderit, Ronald Fry, and David Cooperrider (eds.), *Handbook of Transformative Cooperation: New Designs and Dynamics* (Stanford, CA: Stanford Business Books, 2007).

Dirk Holtbrügge and Jones F. Puck, *Geschäftserfolg in China* (Heidelberg, Germany: Springer, 2008).

HONEYLAND MANUKA HONEY FROM NEW ZEALAND

AN INTERNATIONAL NEW VENTURE

NEW ZEALAND'S ECONOMIC ENVIRONMENT

New Zealand is a small island nation in the South Pacific south-east of Australia. Its landmass of 268 million square kilometers compares with the size of Oregon. With a slightly higher population than Oregon—just over four million (4.36 million in 2010)—New Zealand's domestic market is small. GDP per capita is about US$30.045 per year (2010), slightly more than half of that of the United States, with an annual economic growth rate of 3 percent in 2010. Virtually free access of overseas competitors to New Zealand's home market forces its numerous small and medium enterprises (SME[1]) to seek and develop international markets. Australia is its most important trading partner, accounting for 22 percent of New Zealand's exports, followed by the United States (11.5 percent) and Japan (9.2 percent). New Zealand relies for its economic viability mainly on the success of its SMEs, since these constitute up to 90.7 percent of all firms and provide about 50 percent of New Zealanders with work and income (Ministry of Economic Development, 2004). A 2002 report initiated by the New Zealand Treasury identified the two major constraints for economic growth in New Zealand: the distant geographic location from international markets and the difficulty of raising sufficient capital.

THE MAKING OF HONEYLAND AND ITS PRODUCTS

Honeyland is an export business specializing in native New Zealand honeys. It was established in Palmerston North, a small town in the New Zealand Manawatu region in July 1986. The business started exporting right from its beginnings and has, in effect, never operated in the domestic New Zealand market, focusing on one international market only. The company supplies exclusively to the lucrative Japanese market. The company is, even by New Zealand's standards, very small. It is literally a one (wo)man enterprise. That does not limit the success, though. From modest beginnings the enterprise

has grown into a reasonable business that turns over more than NZ$500,000 (about US$275,000) operating from a small office in the family home.

New Zealand honey is positioned as a health-promoting product, using New Zealand's clean and green image. The company strategically targets quality-conscious customers, especially those who have been to New Zealand for a holiday and know its spectacular landscape. New Zealand has a reputation for its beautiful and rather unspoilt natural environment, including its exotic plants. The majority of New Zealand's plants are indigenous, found growing naturally only in that part of the world. In particular, New Zealand has many flowering trees, such as the pohutukawa, kamahi, manuka, tawari, and rewarewa. Native bush and forest honey, which is produced in this environment, has a reputation for being healthy and beneficial to human well-being. The honey that bees collect from the flowers of the New Zealand tea or manuka tree is said to have a great taste and very beneficial healing properties.

The owner of Honeyland, Sue, a trained school teacher, became aware of the good reputation and health benefits of New Zealand honey early on. In the 1970s, she raised a young family while keeping bees in a few beehives in the back of her garden around the family home. Sue has always kept a friendly open home and entertained the many international friends of her teenage children and business partners of her husband. *"When I look back, our home was always an open home, long before other people actually were in the international world."* Many of these visitors were Japanese because Palmerston North has strong links to Japan through its Japanese-based International Pacific College and Massey University. Many young Japanese students complete their high school and university education there. Attracted to the cultivated polite Japanese people, Sue chose her preferred market destination long before she started the company. Her interest in Japan and Japanese culture grew during visits when she accompanied her husband, a successful wool merchant, on his business trips. Soon Sue started looking for a business idea that would enable her to visit Japan on a regular basis

Source: This case was contributed by Sabina Jaeger, Lecturer in International Business, AUT University, New Zealand, sabina.jaeger@aut.ac.nz.

without having to depend on her husband. The hobby of producing honey grew into a business idea.

EXPORT MARKET JAPAN

The contacts with Japanese friends exposed her to their culture, way of life, and work. While on her trips in Japan she gradually built up an extensive network of friends and business partners. *"We had a real network of friends and acquaintances in Japan. I think that probably has been one of the great advantages, because some of them are students, some of them are old, they range from 15 years old to 90 years old. "They are all around Japan and they enjoy different sorts of lifestyles. So that is a wonderful way of getting a feel for what a country is like."* Additionally, Sue undertook further preparation before starting up the enterprise. She began to learn the Japanese language because she understood the importance of language skills when doing business in Japan. It did not take long before she became convinced that New Zealand speciality honeys would be a suitable export product. Sue applied great care to understanding the specifics of the Japanese market. One major hurdle she had to overcome was gaining access to Japanese distributors and retail businesses. She said that in the 1980s this was not easy for a businesswoman. Speaking the language, and with some support from her friends, she eventually overcame this difficulty. Sue modifies and markets her products to the special Japanese requirements.

MARKETING STRATEGY

Honeyland's market can be categorized into three different segments. One third of the business comes from sales through a supermarket chain that operates a "fixed price" strategy. Quality branded products are sold at a discount: *"It is a discount type store. Unbelievable, their whole layout is similar to the one of the "two dollar" shop.[2] Like 1 dollar, 2 dollar, 3 dollar shop! It is primarily liquor. . . . So they use good brands to bring people in and sell them cheaply."* Another third of her business involves supplying a Japanese honey company with New Zealand comb honey. This company brands the product under its own name. The third and most important segment of Honeyland's business derives from sales to a firm that is associated with Japan Travel Business (JTB). It targets the top range of the gift product industry with high returns selling gifts of various

honeys in small gift packaging to returning travelers. Sue says: *"The third part of my market is very much a niche market, a very top shelf specialty honey. . . . The niche market is going through my representative in Japan."* Japanese tourists spend their short holidays in New Zealand's surroundings. They experience the great outdoors enjoying the scenery doing bush walks and encountering many exotic plants among New Zealand's wild flora. It is part of Japanese culture that travellers take home a small gift to friends and family. Others like to have a piece of New Zealand as a memory for themselves. Honeyland provides a solution for those tourists who do not want to worry about purchasing presents when holidaying. Honeyland products are available in Japanese airport stores for tourists to pick up upon arrival back in Japan. Packaged in small, beautifully labeled containers, the distinctive New Zealand honeys have become a much appreciated gift in Japan.

EXPORT BARRIERS

One of the biggest obstacles to Honeyland's growth is sourcing and securing the supply of quality honey. Thus, the New Zealand supply determines the extent of the company's involvement in the international market and limits business expansion. Annual variations in quality and quantity are natural occurrences of the product. Sue solved the supply difficulties by developing and maintaining a very good relationship with her domestic supplier. Its loyal commitment guarantees preferential supply even when overall stocks are low and it cannot deliver to other clients. Another problem is the management of organic export products. New Zealand has entered into an international treaty to protect plants and natural vegetation that requires strict export controls. New Zealand's Ministry of Agriculture and Fisheries (MAF) is the official body that looks after the treaty's enforcement. Export operations are difficult because MAF requires strict compliance with its phyto-sanitary and bio-security regulations, including the inspection of all exported organic products and detailed documentation. Careful planning and organization on the part of Honeyland is necessary to be able to meet the export deadlines. These problems have been solved through close attention to MAF regulations at the planning and strategy stages. Thus, Honeyland now organizes international trade around these requirements and uses the MAF certificates for quality differentiation.

Table 1	Approximate Exchange Rates for the New Zealand Dollar						
1 NZ $ buys	Mar-10	Nov-08	Jan-08	Jul-07	Jan-07	Jan-06	Jan-05
U.S. $	0.71	0.55	0.78	0.74	0.70	0.68	0.72
Japan Yen	64	52	85	95	82	80	74

Source: New Zealand Reserve Bank.

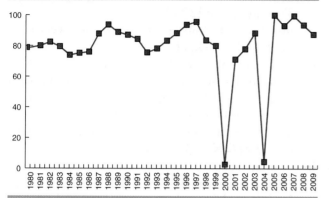

Figure 1   New Zealand's Real Effective Exchange Rate, 1980–2004 (Index 2000 = 100)

Source: International Monetary Fund, International Financial Statistics, 2010.

LOGISTICS

Access to reliable and cost-effective transportation is another issue with which Honeyland has to deal. New Zealand is far off the main shipping routes and transport costs are high compared to countries that are in the center of the world trade network. The large geographical distance between New Zealand and Japan is a big obstacle in itself. The normal shipping time to Japan is ten days on average. However, in reality it takes much longer for a shipment to arrive safely to the customer. Why is this? Honeyland usually ships out of Napier, a small rural town with international harbor facilities. Napier has turned out to be a convenient location since most of the honey is sourced and packaged regionally. The supplier loads the honey into sea containers onsite so transport costs and time inside New Zealand are minimized. However, using a small regional port also has disadvantages. Most of the drawbacks are related to capacity and frequency of transportation services, particularly during times when the general harvest season is underway. Around harvest time a variety of produce exporters usually compete for limited container space and shipping facilities.

There are other problems concerning logistics. The size of Honeyland's export unit is on average just one container load. The shipping of a "20 foot" standard container to Japan costs about NZ$4000 (US$2,200). This price includes the basic paperwork such as customs declaration. There may be times when customers require a more frequent delivery mode and then the size of the shipment can be less than one container. If containers are shared, the projected arrival time is less predictable than normal because a suitable load going to the same destination to fill up the remainder of the container has to be found. When shipping smaller quantities of high-priced niche products, Honeyland employs the services of a reliable international freight forwarder. Although utilizing the services of freight forwarders is more costly than organizing the shipping with the shipping company directly, it has the advantage that professional logistics services take care of all the formalities, including the customs declaration and the documentation of the bio-security requirement. It also ensures the necessary import license that is only valid for one year and has to be renewed in a timely fashion. If need be, it organizes the clearing of customs at port in Japan swiftly, which reduces the order cycle time considerably.

EXPORT PRICING

For the setting of export prices it is important to remember that Honeyland has no domestic sales and that only one export market is involved. Therefore, the price decision is straightforward since the export prices are based on the costs of sourcing the honeys as well as logistics. The prices for the Japanese customers are quoted and paid for in NZ$. Sue acknowledges that sufficiently large profit margins are critical to manage foreign exchange risk. Frequent currency fluctuations of the NZ$ affect profits and in the long term the business itself.

RISK MANAGEMENT

Sue believes in the benefits of maintaining long-term relationships with her clients. One factor that will most certainly upset Japanese clients is the renegotiating of prices. Sue knows this sensitivity. Therefore, she attempts to keep her prices fairly constant in spite of the New Zealand currency volatility. She does so even if that means that sometimes losses occur. Another important aspect of good business relationships is that it minimizes general risks, lowers transaction costs, and helps to avoid lengthy negotiations. For example, Honeyland experiences reliable payments on time and payment to the full amount. The company's excellent networks and culturally appropriate business practices practically guarantee that default situations hardly arise.

For Honeyland, the existing three Japanese business segments are a sufficiently large market because they account for Honeyland's entire export volume. A prerequisite for sustained good business relations with Japanese companies is that size and quality of the export ventures have to match expectations in order to create a good business fit and sustainability. Sue explains: *"Just from the beginning I realized three main factors in dealing with Japan: one is quality and guaranty of quality; two is supply ability—you must be able to guarantee supply and that was very important with maintaining this relationship with this catalogue company. . . . And the third one was stability in price—so you have to take losses sometimes."*

INTERNATIONAL COMMUNICATIONS

Over the years, Honeyland has maintained mutually beneficial and trusting relationships with the same networks. Information technology, Internet access, and email have allowed Sue to keep in regular contact with her network partners in between her regular visits to Japan. Often she is also busy with answering customers' queries and requests directly. She explains: *"There are daily e-mails from business partners; they have a habit of sending vast numbers of e-mails with queries, such as potential benefits of treating race horses with NZ Manuka honey to prevent stomach ulcers."* These kinds of queries have given Sue food for thought if she ever wanted to expand her business and develop other products. It is not astonishing that Honeyland has its own website for general information and marketing.

CONCLUSION

Sue says that she is very content with her business. She operates a lean and efficient enterprise with only minimal expenses and overheads. She does so single-handedly (no employees) from a small office room in her own home, and she has no immediate plans to change it. Honeyland is now one of the long-time successful "international new venture" businesses in New Zealand.

Questions for Discussion

1. Imagine that you are in charge of logistics for a small exporting business such as Honeyland. What are the difficulties you need to think about?

2. What are the specific contextual requirements when exporting from New Zealand?

3. Considering that Sue is under a significant time constraint, do you think that outsourcing the entire logistics would be a good move for Honeyland?

4. What would have been an alternative entry strategy for the Japanese market?

5. Do you think the company should expand or diversify?

ADDITIONAL RESOURCES FOR RESEARCH

For further information, please see the following websites:

General information about New Zealand, including socio-economic details, supplied by the New Zealand Trade & Enterprise web site which is government sponsored http://www.marketnewzealand.com/MNZ/aboutNZ/sectors/14436.aspx?Buyer= true.

Economic overview, including some detailed economic data on the New Zealand economy, New Zealand Treasury Report (2008) http://www.treasury.govt.nz/economy/overview/2008/nzefo-08-3.pdf.

Report about New Zealand's export barriers, New Zealand Treasury Working Paper 02/10, *Growing Pains: New Zealand, Qualitative Evidence on Hurdles to Exporting Growth*, by Simmons, G. http://www.treasury.govt.nz/publications/research-policy/ wp/2002/02-10/twp02-10.pdf.

Information about bio-security regulations for New Zealand's exporters exporting products of organic origin http://www.biosecurity.govt.nz/commercial-exports/animal-exports/export-requirements-omars/omars-list.

Information about New Zealand specialty food and beverages destined for export http://www.marketnewzealand.com/MNZ/aboutNZ/sectors/14413.aspx.

Information about New Zealand's quality assurance program for bee products, including its certification http://www.asurequality.com/auditing_and_inspection/apiary.cfm.

Information about Japanese customs requirements concerning import into Japan http://www.customs.go.jp/english/summary/import.htm.

Information about the port facilities of Napier and useful details concerning transport and shipping vessels http://www.portofnapier.co.nz/.

Notes

1. In New Zealand small and medium sized enterprises (SMEs) are firms with between 0 and 20 employees. This makes the New Zealand SME much smaller than its counterpart in the USA.

2. A "two dollar shop" is a retail outlet where all sales items are offered at the same ($2) price. These types of shops appeared in New Zealand in the late 1990s and have become very popular. They attract a lot of customers, especially bargain hunters or those with little disposable income. Most sales items are perceived as worth more than the purchase price.

IKEA: FURNISHING THE WORLD

IKEA, the world's largest home furnishings retail chain, was founded in Sweden in 1943 as a mail-order company and opened its first showroom ten years later. From its headquarters in Almhult, Sweden, IKEA has since expanded to worldwide sales of $30 billion from 301 outlets in 38 countries (see Table 1). In fact, the second store that IKEA built was in Oslo, Norway. The IKEA Group owns 267 stores in 25 countries: Australia, Austria, Belgium, Canada, China, Czech Republic, Denmark, Finland, France, Germany, Hungary, Italy, Japan, Netherlands, Norway, Poland, Portugal, Russia, Slovakia, Spain, Sweden, Switzerland, the United Kingdom, and the United States. The other 34 stores are owned and run by franchisees outside the IKEA Group in 16 countries/territories: Australia, the United Arab Emirates, Cyprus, Greece, Hong Kong, Iceland, Israel, Kuwait, Malaysia, the Netherlands, Romania, Saudi Arabia, Singapore, Spain, Taiwan, and Turkey. IKEA first appeared on the Internet in 1997 with the World Wide Living Room Web site. IKEA attracted 561 million visits (2009). The IKEA Group's new organization has three regions: Europe, North America, and Asia-Pacific.

The international expansion of IKEA has progressed in three phases, all of them continuing at the present time: Scandinavian expansion, begun in 1963; West European expansion, begun in 1973; and North American expansion, begun in 1976. Of the individual markets, Germany is the largest, accounting for 16 percent, followed by the U.S. at 15 percent of company sales. The phases of expansion are detectable in the worldwide sales shares depicted in Figure 1. "We want to bring the IKEA concept to as many people as possible," IKEA officials have said. The company estimates that over 590 million people visit its showrooms annually.

THE IKEA CONCEPT

Ingvar Kamprad, the founder, formulated as IKEA's mission to "offer a wide variety of home furnishings of good design and function at prices so low that the majority of people can afford to buy them." The principal target market of IKEA, which is similar across countries and regions in which IKEA has a presence, is composed of people who are young, highly educated, liberal in their cultural values, white-collar workers, and not especially concerned with status symbols.

IKEA follows a standardized product strategy with a universally accepted assortment around the world. Today, IKEA carries an assortment of thousands of different home furnishings that range from plants to pots, sofas to soup spoons, and wine glasses to wallpaper. The smaller items are carried to complement the bigger ones. IKEA has very limited manufacturing of its own, but designs all of its furniture. The network of subcontracted manufacturers numbers 1,220 in 55 different countries. The top five purchasing countries are China (20 percent), Poland (18 percent), Italy (8 percent), Germany (6 percent), and Sweden (5 percent). IKEA had 31 trading service offices in 26 countries with 28 distribution centers and 11 customer distribution centers in 16 countries.

IKEA's strategy is based on cost leadership secured by contract manufacturers, many of which are in low-labor-cost countries and close to raw materials, yet accessible to logistics links. Extreme care is taken to match manufacturers with products. Ski makers—experts in bent wood—have been contracted to make armchairs, and producers of supermarket carts have been contracted for durable sofas. High-volume production of standardized items allows for significant economies of scale. In exchange for long-term contracts, leased equipment, and technical support from IKEA, the suppliers manufacture exclusively at low prices for IKEA. IKEA's designers work with the suppliers to build savings-generating features into the production and products from the outset. If sales continue at the forecasted rate, by 2010 IKEA will need to source twice as much material as today. Because Russia is a major source of lumber, IKEA aims to turn it into a major supplier of finished products in the future.

IKEA has some of its production as well, constituting 12 percent of its total sales. IKEA has operations and offices in Sweden, Russia, Latvia, Lithuania, Poland, Germany, Slovakia, Hungary, Ukraine, Portugal, China, and the United States. The Swedwood Group is a fully integrated international industrial group of IKEA, which consists of more than 50 production units and offices in 12 countries across three continents.

IKEA consumers have to become "prosumers"—half producers, half consumers—because most products have to be assembled. The final distribution is the customer's

Sources: This case, prepared by Ilkka Ronkainen, is based on "First IKEA Furniture Manufacturing Facility to Open in Danville," *Reuters*, April 30, 2008; Kerry Capell, "How a Swedish Retailer Became a Global Cult Brand," *BusinessWeek*, November 14, 2005, 96–106; "What a Sweetheart of a Love Seat," *BusinessWeek*, November 14, 2005, 102; "Create IKEA. Make Billions, Take Bus," *Fortune*, May 3, 2004, 44; http://www.ikea.com/; and http://www.ikea.com/ms/en_US/about_ikea/facts_and_figures/index.html.

Table 1   IKEA International Expansion

Year	Outlets[a]	Countries	Coworkers	Catalog[b]	Turnover[c]
1954	1	1	15	0.3	1
1964	2	2	250	2	25
1974	9	5	1,500	13	169
1984	52	17	8,300	35	1,216
1994	114	27	30,500	72	4,396
2004	201	33	90,000	145	13,570
2006	237	34	100,000	174	17,658
2008	285	37	127,800	199	22,498
2009	301	38	123,000	199	22,713

[a]Stores/countries being opened by 2009.
[b]Millions.
[c]In euros.

Sources: http://www.ikea.com/; http://www.ikea.com/ms/en_US/about_ikea/facts_and_figures/index.html.

responsibility as well. Although IKEA expects its customers to be active participants in the buy-sell process, it is not rigid about it. There is a "moving boundary" between what consumers do for themselves and what IKEA employees will do for them. Consumers save the most by driving to the warehouses themselves, putting the boxes on the trolley, loading them into their cars, driving home, and assembling the furniture. Yet IKEA can arrange to provide these services at an extra charge. For example, IKEA cooperates with car rental companies to offer vans and small trucks at reasonable rates for customers needing delivery service. Additional economies are reaped from the size of the IKEA outlets; the blue-and-yellow buildings average 300,000 square feet (28,000 square meters) in size. IKEA stores include babysitting areas and cafeterias and are therefore intended to provide the value-seeking, car-borne consumer with a complete shopping destination. IKEA managers state that their competitors are not other furniture outlets but all attractions vying for the consumers'

Figure 1   IKEA Worldwide Sales

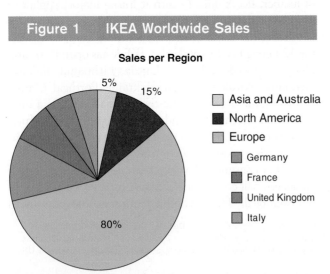

Sales per Region

- Asia and Australia
- North America
- Europe
- Germany
- France
- United Kingdom
- Italy

Figure 2   IKEA's Value Chain

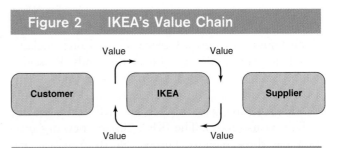

Source: Richard Norman and Rafael Ramirez, "From Value Chain to Value Constellation: Designing Interactive Strategy." *Harvard Business Review 71* (July/August 1993): 72.

free time. By not selling through dealers, the company hears directly from its customers.

Management believes that its designer-to-user relationship affords an unusual degree of adaptive fit. IKEA has "forced both customers and suppliers to think about value in a new way in which customers are also suppliers (of time, labor, information, and transportation), suppliers are also customers (of IKEA's business and technical services), and IKEA itself is not so much a retailer as the central star in a constellation of services." Figure 2 provides a presentation of IKEA's value chain.

Although IKEA has concentrated on company-owned, larger-scale outlets, franchising has been used in areas in which the market is relatively small or where uncertainty may exist as to the response to the IKEA concept. These markets include Hong Kong and the United Arab Emirates. IKEA uses mail order in Europe, North America, and Australia.

IKEA offers prices that are 30 to 50 percent lower than fully assembled competing products. This is a result of large-quantity purchasing, low-cost logistics, store locations in suburban areas, and the do-it-yourself approach to marketing. IKEA's prices do vary from market to market, largely because of fluctuations in exchange rates and

Table 2	The IKEA Concept
Target market:	"Young people of all ages"
Product:	IKEA offers the same products worldwide. The number of active articles is 9,500. The countries of origin of these products are: Europe (67 percent), Asia (30 percent), and North America (3 percent). Most items have to be assembled by the customer. The furniture design is modern and light.
Distribution:	IKEA has built its own distribution network. Outlets are outside the city limits of major metropolitan areas. Products are not delivered, but IKEA cooperates with car rental companies that offer small trucks. IKEA offers mail order in Europe North America, and Australia.
Pricing:	The IKEA concept is based on low price. The firm tries to keep its price-image constant.
Promotion:	IKEA's promotional efforts are mainly through its catalogs. IKEA has developed a prototype communications model that must be followed by all stores. Its advertising is attention-getting and provocative. Media choices vary by market.

differences in taxation regimes, but price positioning is kept as standardized as possible. IKEA's operating margins of approximately 10 percent are among the best in home furnishings (as compared to 5 percent at U.S. competitor Pier 1 Imports and 7.7 percent at Target). This profit level has been maintained while the company has cut prices steadily. For example, the Klippan sofa's price has decreased by 40 percent since 1999.

IKEA's promotion is centered on the catalog. A total of 198 million copies of the catalog have been printed in 56 editions and 27 languages. The catalogs are uniform in layout except for minor regional differences. The company's advertising goal is to generate word-of-mouth publicity through innovative approaches. The IKEA concept is summarized in Table 2.

IKEA Food Services reported sales of $1.5 billion. The IKEA restaurant and Swedish food market are the two elements that together make up IKEA food services. Both encourage people to visit the IKEA store and spend more time there; in this way, they support the store's total home furnishing sales.

IKEA IN THE COMPETITIVE ENVIRONMENT

IKEA's strategy positioning is unique. As Figure 3 illustrates, few furniture retailers anywhere have engaged in

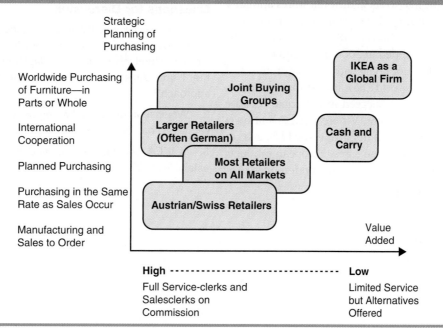

Figure 3   Competition in Furniture Retailing

Source: Rita Martenson, "Is Standardization of Marketing Feasible in Culture-Bound Industries? A European Case Study," *International Marketing Review* 4 (Autumn 1987), 14.

long-term planning or achieved scale economies in production. European furniture retailers, especially those in Sweden, Switzerland, Germany, and Austria, are much smaller than IKEA. Even when companies have joined forces as buying groups, their heterogeneous operations have made it difficult for them to achieve the same degree of coordination and concentration as IKEA. Because customers are usually content to wait for the delivery of furniture, retailers have not been forced to take purchasing risks.

The value-added dimension differentiates IKEA from its competition. IKEA offers limited customer assistance but creates opportunities for consumers to choose (for example, through informational signage), transport and assemble units of furniture. The best summary of the competitive situation was provided by a manager at another firm: "We can't do what IKEA does, and IKEA doesn't want to do what we do."

IKEA IN THE UNITED STATES

After careful study and assessment of its Canadian experience, IKEA decided to enter the U.S. market in 1985 by establishing outlets on the East Coast and, in 1990, in Burbank, California. In 2009, a total of 37 stores (12 in the Northeast, 8 in California, and others in Arizona, Florida, Georgia, Illinois, Michigan, Minnesota, Ohio, Oregon, Texas, Utah, and Washington State) generated sales of more than $4 billion. The overwhelming level of success in 1987 led the company to invest in a warehousing facility near Philadelphia that receives goods from Sweden as well as directly from suppliers around the world. Plans call for five to six additional stores annually over the next 25 years, concentrating on the northeastern United States and California. IKEA's first U.S. manufacturing operation opened in 2008 in Virginia.

Success today has not come without compromises. If you are going to be the world's best furnishings company, you have to show you can succeed in America, because there is so much to learn here. Whereas IKEA's universal approach had worked well in Europe, the U.S. market proved to be different. In some cases, European products conflicted with American tastes and preferences. For example, IKEA did not sell matching bedroom suites that consumers wanted. Kitchen cupboards were too narrow for the large dinner plates needed for pizza. Some Americans were buying IKEA's flower vases for glasses.

Adaptations were made. IKEA managers adjusted chest drawers to be an inch or two deeper because consumers wanted to store sweaters in them. Sales of chests increased immediately by 40 percent. In all, IKEA has redesigned approximately one-fifth of its product range in North America. Today, 45 percent of the furniture in the stores in North America is produced locally, up from 15 percent in the early 1990s. In addition to not having to pay expensive freight costs from Europe, this has also helped to cut stock-outs. And because Americans hate standing in lines, store layouts have been changed to accommodate new cash registers. IKEA offers a more generous return policy in North America than in Europe, as well as next-day delivery service.

In hindsight, IKEA executives are saying they behaved like exporters, which meant not really being in the country. IKEA's adaptation has not meant destroying its original formula. Its approach is still to market the streamlined and contemporary Scandinavian style to North America by carrying a universally accepted product—range but with attention to product lines and features that appeal to local preference. The North American experience has caused the company to start remixing its formula elsewhere as well. Indeed, now that Europeans are adopting some American furnishing concepts (such as sleeper sofas), IKEA is transferring some American concepts to other markets such as Europe.

Questions for Discussion

1. What has allowed IKEA to be successful with a relatively standardized product and product line in a business with strong cultural influence? Did adaptations to this strategy in the North American market constitute a defeat of its approach?

2. Which features of the "young people of all ages" are universal and can be exploited by a global/regional strategy?

3. Is IKEA destined to succeed everywhere it cares to establish itself?

KOCH INDUSTRIES ACQUIRES GEORGIA-PACIFIC

The forest products industry, an umbrella for a broadly diverse output ranging from paper and packaging to building and other wood products, is rapidly becoming a strategic misnomer. That is a key reason why the industry has been executing a marathon restructuring, that most recently included the $21 billion acquisition of Georgia-Pacific by privately owned industrial titan Koch Industries, Inc. Although few private companies have the clout of a Koch to engineer comparable megadeals, the acquisition could serve as a model for private equity firms to buy forest products and other diverse raw material companies and over haul them without investors looking on.

"Georgia-Pacific Buys Spurs Paper Shake-Out,"
Mergers and Acquisitions, January 2006, p. 32

We rate the shares of Georgia-Pacific Corporation BUY/ HIGH RISK (1H). Georgia-Pacific is one of the most profitable companies in the U.S. paper and forest industry, and it remains one of our preferred stocks. The company has heavy exposure to our favorite commodity businesses, wood products and containerboard. We have believed the stock's valuation is clearly out of step with the fundamental forces affecting the company.

Georgia-Pacific Group, Citigroup,
November 15, 2005, p. 3

It was January 2006, and A. D. "Pete" Correll, CEO of Georgia-Pacific, had finally reached an agreement which would take his industry leading U.S.-based forest products conglomerate private. In a deal totaling $13 billion, Koch (pronounced "coke") Industries, a privately held enterprise with more than $60 billion in annual sales, would become the sole owner. Both boards had approved the friendly acquisition in November 2005, and now all regulators in both the United States and Europe had approved the sale. After Koch's acquisition of Georgia-Pacific, the combined company would become the largest privately held company in the United States (and possibly the world), with more than $80 billion in sales. With the stroke of a pen, Pete Correll would, in his words, "never have to talk to a 22 year-old analyst again." And he would never have to argue that the company's strategic moves were *intended to increase shareholder value.*

GEORGIA-PACIFIC TAKEN PRIVATE

Under the buy-out agreement, Georgia-Pacific would become a privately held wholly owned subsidiary of Koch Industries. Koch's final offer of $48 per share had been a convincing 39 percent premium over Georgia-Pacific's recent market price. The premium had been so large—most acquisitions in recent years had involved premiums of between 22 percent and 28 percent—that even Correll's loudest critics among his shareholders had been quieted. Correll had made it no secret that he was unhappy with the market's valuation of Georgia-Pacific, and that he was tired of hearing from unhappy shareholders. The 39 percent premium had seemed to finally make them all happy, at least until they discovered that he would pocket roughly $92 million personally on the sale.

The transaction would involve all of Georgia-Pacific's assets, including its North American and international consumer products segments, its building products, packaging, paper, and bleached board segments. All together, the deal would have an equity value of $12.7 billion and a total enterprise value of $20.6 billion, including Koch's assumption of $7.8 billion of Georgia-Pacific debt (see Exhibit 1). The cash purchase was funded by Citigroup, which was providing an $11 billion bridge loan to Koch.

Many of Georgia-Pacific's creditors had originally been quite unhappy to learn that their debt was being transferred to a private company. An ad hoc Committee of Note holders had put Georgia-Pacific on notice that the members of the group held more than $2 billion of

Exhibit 1	Koch Acquisition of Georgia-Pacific
Georgia-Pacific share price (11/11/05)	$34.65
Koch tender price	$48.00
Tender share price premium	39%
Shares outstanding (diluted)	266,000,000
Transaction equity value	$12,768,000,000
Assumed net debt	7,826,000,000
Transaction enterprise value	$20,594,000,000

Source: Credit Suisse First Boston, Georgia-Pacific Corporation, November 28, 2005, p. 5.

Georgia-Pacific's debt. The committee argued that they collectively held more than the required amount of debt to be able to give the company a notice of default under the debt indentures. An agreement with Koch was reached quickly.

Many industry experts believed that Koch was in the midst of testing out a controversial new investment philosophy based on the idea that stock markets tend to punish traditional companies in cyclical industries. Koch's management felt that companies with heavily cyclical operations are often undervalued in the market because of the market's failure to see trends and cycles appropriately, "treating companies more like statistical data sets than living breathing organisms with tendencies and behaviors which may not always be perfectly predictable, but did demonstrate patterns for those brave enough to embrace them."[1]

Correll had grown increasingly frustrated in recent years with the market's valuation of Georgia-Pacific. It seemed that no matter what the company did to try and please the market, nothing worked. For example, Georgia-Pacific had reduced its debt by roughly $10 billion over the past four years, an arduous task that ended up having nearly no impact on Georgia-Pacific's stock price. The company had also sold-off a number of what were considered "non-core" business lines in recent years in-line with what many of its analyst critics thought appropriate. Again, there had been little appreciation shown in the share price. Although the company was obviously subject to the risks of interest rates and the construction and pulp and paper industries, Correll had argued repeatedly that it was appropriately diversified to protect itself and its earnings and cash flows against a downtrend in any of the individual segments. Despite all moves and efforts, the company had ended up with a beta of 1.62 over recent years, and the prospects were no better.

Koch on the other hand, evidently saw great value in Georgia-Pacific's future as evidenced by the $48 a share the company was willing to pay. Koch had also made it clear that it believed in the company's current management and strategy, and had already committed publicly to reinvesting 90 percent of Georgia-Pacific's profits back into the business—a practice which Koch had used for many years to build its own business.

GEORGIA-PACIFIC

Georgia-Pacific (GP) was the world's largest manufacturer and marketer of consumer paper products and the second largest forest products company in the United States. Its tissue paper products include Brawny paper towels, Angel Soft and Quilted Northern bath tissue,

and Mardi Gras napkins as well as the extensive Dixie line of paper products. Georgia-Pacific expected to reach $18.99 billion in sales in 2006; earnings before interest, taxes, depreciation and amortization (EBITDA) of $2.42 billion; and earnings after tax of $794 million. The company had been traded on the New York Stock Exchange since 1967 under the symbol "GP".

Georgia-Pacific had its roots in Augusta, Georgia, where Owen Cheatham started the Georgia Hardwood Lumber Company in 1927. During WWII the company was the largest supplier of lumber to the U.S. armed forces. In 1951 Cheatham acquired the company's first timberlands, and subsequently moved the company's headquarters to Olympia, Washington, adopting the name Georgia-Pacific. In 1954 the headquarters was once again moved, this time to Portland, Oregon. The company went public in 1967, and in 1972 became so large that the U.S. Federal Trade Commission forced it to sell 20 percent of its assets, fearing that the company was effectively becoming a forest products monopoly. In 1982 the headquarters was moved to Atlanta, Georgia, where it remains today.

Recently, GP had been working to reduce its debt and improve its return on assets. This effort included exiting non-strategic business areas and focusing on high value-added business segments that would bring it closer to the customer. GP sold pulp mills and a short line railroad in Georgia and Mississippi for $610 million to Koch Industries. In the same year it sold its building products distribution business for $810 million to Cerebrus Capital Management, a private investment group. GP then sold a controlling stake in a printing and imaging paper distributor, Unisource Worldwide, to Bain Capital for $850 million.

In early October of 2005, GP announced that it would be eliminating 1,000 jobs as part of its restructuring effort to save $100 million a year and retain a yearly operating profit of $1.2 billion in North America. The restructuring effort was expected to cost $100 million over the next two years. Rising energy costs, raw materials costs, industry overcapacity, and Asian competition are said to have been factors in this decision.

KOCH INDUSTRIES

In 1928 Fred Koch, graduate of MIT, developed a process to refine more gasoline from crude oil. When he tried to market his invention, however, the major oil companies sued him for patent infringement. After 15 years of legal battles, Koch finally won the right to his patent. In 1940 Koch launched Wood River Oil & Refining in Illinois and bought the Rock Island refinery in

Oklahoma in 1947. After Koch's death in 1967, his son Charles took charge, and renamed the company Koch Industries. The company then undertook a series of acquisitions, adding petrochemical and oil trading service operations.

Today, Charles Koch continues as chairman and chief executive officer of Koch Industries. Under his leadership Koch has expanded and diversified globally. The privately owned company, based in Wichita, Kansas, owns a diverse group of companies engaged in trading, investment and operations, with nearly 30,000 employees in more than 50 countries. Koch had grown from a modest privately held American company into a global conglomerate of more than $60 billion in annual sales. These companies are involved in industries such as petroleum, chemicals, energy, fibers, intermediates and polymers, minerals, fertilizers, chemical technology equipment, pulp and paper, ranching, trading, and securities and finance, as well as in other ventures and investments. Koch's continued financial strength can be attributed to the fact that historically its ownership has continued to reinvest 90 percent of earnings back into the company each and every year.

GOING PRIVATE

Public companies, and their senior leadership, feel enormous pressure to generate value for their shareholders, primarily through share price appreciation. The larger and more successful of these firms then generate increasing interest, the result of which is more analyst coverage and more access to affordable capital. The constant focus on top-line sales growth and profitability (primarily measured in earnings per share) often is criticized as encouraging leadership to focus too much on short-term results. Many publicly traded companies have been accused of under investing in the long term, forgoing good long term investments in exchange for preserving short-

term profitability. However, if shareholders' interests are to be maximized and preserved, many argue that the company must find a proper balance of keeping profitability and market value up (allowing investors to exit the company without loss at their choice) while pursuing long-term competitiveness.

Georgia-Pacific's financial returns in recent years had been "dodgy" in the words of one analyst. Although the dividend had been sustained at its current $0.70/share rate for some time, and would probably stay there for years to come, the share price itself had been up and down—mostly down. The current price of $34.65 (just prior to the announced acquisition tender) was down nearly $6.00 from its two-year high, although several analysts thought that it could regain $3 to $4 of that in the coming year. In a market that was now expected to yield roughly 12 percent across the S&P500 for the coming year, Georgia-Pacific had been an underachiever. The current dividend yield was substantially below the U.S. Treasury Bond rate which was currently hovering at 6.00 percent.

The sale would go through. On December 23, 2005, Georgia-Pacific became the 337th company in the United States to de-list that year.

Questions for Discussion

1. Why does Koch Industries believe the market has "undervalued" Georgia-Pacific?

2. What has been the recent rate of return to stockholders of Georgia-Pacific?

3. Why are publicly traded firms often accused of being short-sighted and focusing on short-term results rather than building long-term value? Do you believe that is true?

Note

1. Extracted from the press releases of Koch Industries.

PETROLEUM DEVELOPMENT AND THE CURSE OF OIL

An unusual meeting took place in October at St. Matthew's church in Baltimore. After the sermon, some parishioners stayed behind to hear two emissaries from Africa explain the harm that America's gasoline guzzling does to the poor in far-away lands. An elderly parishioner raised his hand: "I know Africa is very rich in diamonds, gold and oil, but the people are very poor. Why are your governments so bad at managing that wealth?" Austin Onuoha, a human-rights activist from Nigeria, smiled and conceded, "You hit the nail right on the head."

"The Curse of Oil: The Paradox of Plenty," *The Economist*, December 20, 2005, print edition

One of the most controversial of topics related to the development of petroleum resources around the globe is what is commonly referred to as *the curse of oil* or *the paradox of plenty*. The *curse of oil* is the argument that the development of oil and gas resources in many emerging market countries results in a slower rate of economic development, increasing both poverty and income inequality, while increasing corruption and fraud. Proponents of the curse point to countries such as Angola and Nigeria as examples of how the development of oil and gas over several decades have resulted in lower levels of economic development despite the country earning billions of dollars from their oil.

THE ECONOMICS OF THE CURSE

There are at least three different principles at work in the curse. The first is that most petroleum developments in emerging markets are done under contract or license (fiscal regimes) with foreign companies. These companies possess the managerial and technical knowledge necessary for development. They do not typically pass this knowledge to a local or in-country partner for both business and skill reasons. They generate income which, like the oil and gas, is extracted from the country. Employment benefits for national residents are usually limited to the construction phase (three years or less in most cases). Therefore there are limited long-term human resource development benefits.

The second argument behind the curse is a derivative argument of what the *Economist* magazine labeled *Dutch Disease* many years ago—the impact of a natural resource development on the country's exchange rate. Dutch Disease, named after the development of North Sea gas properties by the Netherlands in the 1970s, means that the rapid growth of natural resource for export purposes may drive the value of the country's currency up as the demand for the natural resource rises. The appreciation of the domestic currency then makes other export products and commodities from the country increasingly expensive, and reduces the health, earnings, investment in, and future of those other industries.

In recent years the Dutch Disease phenomena has been altered fundamentally, moving away from the impact on exchange rates and focusing more specifically on the economic opportunities—or lack thereof—in competing sectors. For example, in Nigeria, a country that at one time was a major exporter of a number of highly profitable agricultural commodities, the agricultural sector has largely been disassembled as a result of the movement of all labor and capital to the oil industry and its development. In the end, when the oil and gas have been fully developed and largely depleted, the country is left with little in the way of an internationally competitive industry.

The third principle at work in the curse is the impact major increases in income and wealth have on the government and politically powerful entities in the country. The income earned by the government of any country as a result of the development of a new oil or gas field may be enormous. Money flows from *big oil* to the *big man*, as government is frequently labeled in Africa. The sudden surge in income then may result in enrichment of the people currently in power in the country politically and personally. The inflow of earnings from concessions or production sharing agreements (PSAs) used for oil development then often fill the government's coffers independently of the health of the domestic economy (independent of sales, excise or corporate income taxes) or the income of the people themselves (personal income taxes). The result is a government which is increasingly distant from its own people.

Within this complex web of petroleum development—the international oil companies, the sovereign states, the national oil companies, the people of the states—lies the problem. And for many people, their attitudes and information may be a bit out of date. The power no longer lies with the IOCs, the power has shifted—onshore.

NATIONAL OIL COMPANIES

WHEN activists, journalists and others speak of "Big Oil," you know exactly what they mean: companies such as ExxonMobil, Chevron, BP and Royal Dutch Shell. These titans have been making lots of money for their shareholders; their bosses enjoy vast pay packets; and their actions affect us all.

Yet Big Oil is pretty small next to the industry's true giants: the national oil companies (NOCs) owned or controlled by the governments of oil-rich countries, which manage over 90% of the world's oil, depending on how you count. Of the 20 biggest oil firms, in terms of reserves of oil and gas, 16 are NOCs. Saudi Aramco, the biggest, has more than ten times the reserves that Exxon does. Those with misgivings about oil—that its price is too high, that reserves are running out, that it damages the environment, that it is more a curse than an asset for countries that produce it—must look to NOCs for reassurance.

"National Oil Companies: Really Big Oil," *The Economist*, August 10, 2006, print edition.

Since the mid-1950s the power of oil, its development and proceeds, have been shifting from the IOCs to the countries owning the oil, their governments, and their national oil companies. In most of the world, the oil and gas that lies beneath the surface of the earth is owned by the state (the United States is one of the last countries in which a private citizen may own natural resources). And as a resource owned by the state, the oil and its development is now subject to a varied list of priorities different from the traditional stockholder wealth or corporate stakeholder wealth maxims of the capitalist markets.

Since the future of any oil or gas company is its reserves in the ground, the control of the resource itself by the state has had enormous implications for the goals and strategies of the true oil majors of today. The oil and gas produced by a country today is often one of the largest, if not the largest, sources of export revenues and hard-currency earnings. In many instances, like that of Mexico and Venezuela, oil makes up more than 70 percent of the government's budget revenues. So when oil prices fall, like the precipitous declines of 2008, the government budgets and governments themselves are not

prepared for their reduced budgetary resources. It is a problem that members of the Organization of Petroleum Exporting Countries (OPEC) has been dealing with since the 1970s.

One continuing conundrum of national oil companies and emerging market development is the fact that many of these same countries still need the IOCs as much as they ever did. The managerial and technical expertise and the access of the IOCs to the international capital markets make their continuing role a valuable one. As one oil company executive noted, "*The continuing need of oil governments for the big international companies is the difference between economics and business. In economics, all firms are the same. In business—in the real world—all firms are not created equal.*"

Ironically, this continuing relationship has put many of the world's IOCs in the forefront of the battle over the curse of oil. Whereas the governments of the producing states are not 'reachable' in a political sense, the publicly traded IOCs are. And they continue to bear the brunt of growing concern over the curse of oil and are increasingly expected to act in some fashion to solve the problem. That is a difficult task given that a sovereign state is just that – sovereign, and if it has a standing elected government, that government speaks for the people of that country. At least in theory.

PROPOSED SOLUTIONS

This report argues that transparency in revenues, expenditure and wealth management from extractive industries, is crucial to defeating the resource curse. Achieving transparency requires a higher profile in U.S. diplomacy and foreign policy. When oil revenue in a producing country can be easily tracked, that country's elite are more likely to use revenues for the vital needs of their citizens and less likely to squander newfound wealth for self-aggrandizing projects.

"The Petroleum Poverty Paradox: Assessing U.S. and International Community Efforts to Fight the Resource Curse," Report of the Minority Staff of the U.S. Senate, Foreign Relations Committee, September 9, 2008, draft, p. 3

The government of any country, elected or not, does not exist and operate in isolation. Any organization that chooses to operate in that country must, however, be subject to the laws and regulations imposed by that sovereign state. That organization, however, is also subject to the laws and rules and regulations and expectations of the various stakeholders it possesses in its home country and the variety of country-markets in which it operates. For example, a specific government may not only condone bribery payments for access to resources or markets, it may require it. But that same company cannot, typically under the laws of its own foreign incorporation, make those payments whether it is requested or required. This is a lesson learned all too well by many IOCs over the past century.

Transparency—the exposure of all payments to all parties involved in petroleum development to the light of day (and the global press), has been the primary proposal. Two of the more visible transparency initiatives, the *Extractive Industries Transparency Initiative* (EITI), a voluntary program combining governments, IOCs and NOCs, as well as the *Publish What You Pay* (PYP) program, supported by global philanthropist George Soros have achieved some degree of success.

But the solutions to the curse of oil have stressed not only transparency, but the removal of temptation from the hands of the sovereign. A number of oil and gas developments in the past 15 years around the globe have been designed to require the state to either distribute oil proceeds in a specific mix which includes the needs of the people, or set-aside large portions of the wealth for future projects and generations. One such development, the Chad-Cameroon Petroleum Development in Africa (organized between the states, a consortium of IOCs, and the World Bank), has shown some success. Strangely, and probably unfortunately, the World Bank withdrew in August 2008 (after five full years of petroleum production), requesting that the Chadian government pay off its obligation, which it promptly did, so that the World Bank could in essence get out of the oil business. In the eyes of many, that was a confusing and disappointing outcome (though the project itself continues to reap benefits for all remaining parties).

At the heart of the issue is what power or influence external parties, like the British or American governments or the United Nations, have over the sovereign states of concern. In a number of key oil developments in the past decade these distribution/saving arrangements were requirements for gaining access to the capital, debt and equity, for petroleum development. But in many cases this has proven to be a very blunt instrument for global policy results. The results have been mixed at best.

Questions for Discussion

1. Why are the governments of many countries falling victim to the *curse of oil*? Why aren't their people requiring it or demanding it of them?

2. What, in your opinion, is the responsibility of the IOCs for how a government spends the money it earns from the development of its own oil and gas?

3. How will transparency in the payments associated with oil and gas development work to reduce the detrimental impacts of the *curse of oil*?

TAO KAE NOI SEAWEED SNACK

"I like to eat seaweed and chestnut and that's why I am in this business. But you can't think just for today or tomorrow when doing business, you have to look much further than that," said Aitthipat who founded a seaweed snack business, Tao kae noi, in 2004 when he was only 19 years old. Tao kae noi headquarters is located on a small plot on the outskirts of Bangkok, Thailand. The machines to produce the snacks cost almost 10 million baht. He became a millionaire at a tender age when his trade volume reached 75 million baht in 2005.

BRIEF COUNTRY BACKGROUND

Known as Siam in the past, Thailand is in the center of Southeast Asia surrounded by Laos, Myanmar (Burma), Cambodia, and Malaysia. Thailand is about the size of France and its total population in 2009 was 66 million. As a tropical country its temperature ranges from 23°C to 32°C.

Thailand's population is relatively homogeneous with Thais as the majority followed by Chinese and other ethnic groups. Chinese and other ethic groups have assimilated into the Thai culture although the Chinese are more likely to reside in urban areas and engage in business. Thais are predominantly Buddhists.

The country is comprised of 76 provinces divided into 4 regions: Central, North, Northeast, and South. Situated in the Central region, Bangkok is the capital city and is the center of political, commercial, industrial and financial activities. The unit of currency is the baht at 33 baht per U.S. dollar.

BACKGROUND OF THE ENTREPRISE AND THE ENTREPRENEUR

Tao kae noi was established in 2004 by Atthipot Kulapngvanich. His initial capital came from trading characters and points earned from playing on-line games. He dropped out during his freshmen year in a private university to start a business. He invested part of his money into selling the first product—baked ready-to-eat Chinese chestnuts—targeting women who did not want to get their hands dirty cracking the chestnut shells. Previously, the only place for people to get Chinese chestnuts was Chinatown. His franchise was located in department stores convenient for the customers. He named this new venture "Tao kae noi" or "Young Boss" because his father teased him that his son was going to be a boss. Within a little over more than a year, the business had expanded to more than 30 units. In addition to baked chestnuts, Tob tried to add other product lines, including pickled plums, dried fruit, and fried seaweed to be sold at his outlets. Since the revenue from selling fried seaweed exceeded that of other products, including chestnuts, his business interest turned to the fried seaweed snack.

However, expanding the snack business turned out to be harder than he anticipated. Tob was turned down by several outlets, including the 7-Eleven convenience store chain, because of the snack's unattractive packages and its short shelf life. After studying packages of potato chip brands of international firms, he launched a modern attractive package based on a Japanese-style design. In addition to the health appeal due to low calories and high nutrition, the product was positioned as cute and friendly with an attractive logo of a playful cartoon character of a Chinese boy in traditional Chinese garb.

In 2004, the 7-Eleven convenience chain, the largest outlet for snack items, accepted Tao kae noi into the store. Tob expanded his production capacity rapidly to serve the huge demand generated from selling at the stores. Due to his youth and lack of experience, no bank would lend him money for this expansion. Therefore, he had to sell his baked chestnut franchise to finance a new factory. Obtaining initial access to the convenience stores seemed to be easier than keeping his snack on the shelf since the stores would drop any products if their sales volume did not meet expectations. To stimulate initial product trial, Tao kae noi used a low price strategy of 10 baht (about 35 cents) per unit and allocated 40 percent of total output as free samples distributed at schools, universities, and BTS Sky Trains stations for three months. This tactic turned out to be successful as seen when the sales of his snack at the convenience stores increased dramatically. (See Exhibit 1). Eventually, his snack was distributed in all major convenience stores and modern trade outlets throughout Thailand.

PRODUCT LINE

Tao kae noi seaweed snack is made of seaweed imported from Korea and is processed using modern production systems similar to those of global brands. The company

Source: This case study was contributed by Prof. Nittaya Wongtada of NIDA Business School in Thailand.

Exhibit 1   Financial Performance of the
Tao Kae Noi Company

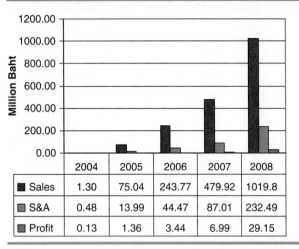

	2004	2005	2006	2007	2008
■ Sales	1.30	75.04	243.77	479.92	1019.8
■ S&A	0.48	13.99	44.47	87.01	232.49
■ Profit	0.13	1.36	3.44	6.99	29.15

Source: Department of Business Development, Ministry of Commerce, Thailand.

was awarded with ISO 9001, GMP, and HACCP in recognition of its quality. Seaweeds contain fiber, protein, iron, and calcium, making it suitable for positioning the snack as a healthy choice.

The original product line of Tao kae noi fried seaweed has four flavors—classic, hot and spicy, wasabi, and shrimp soup. The hot and spicy and wasabi varieties are for those customers who prefer a salty and intense flavor. The original product line aims at the youth market covering 15 to 25-year olds of both genders. The tempura line is for students in the age range of 4 to 17 years. The spicy shrimp soup variety is for the export market because the soup is well-known to those who prefer Thai food.

The "Curve" seaweed was introduced in 2008 to meet the needs of female consumers 18 to 28 years old, who were health conscious and concerned about their weight. It uses premium grade seaweed *Ajinsuke Nori*, which is processed in thin sheets that melt quickly when eaten, contains only 15 calories, and has a high fiber content.

Brand building is important to Tao kae noi. Working with Ogilvy & Mather in creating its distinctive brand story and DKSH in distributing the snack, had helped the company to develop a competitive edge over its competitors. The company has invested a large sum of its earnings on this long-term investment (see Exhibit 2).

THE SNACK MARKET IN THAILAND

Thailand's snack foods market is one of the largest and most diverse in the Asia-Pacific region, with an estimated total value of 21.8 billion baht in 2009 and more than 2,000 competing brands. The industry growth rate in 2009 was 7 percent in value. Main customers are children and teenagers who want to try new snacks.

Although there are many varieties of snacks, extruded snack and potato chips account for over 65 percent of the total market. The competition is intense because new products and operators have entered the market. Typically an excessive promotional budget brings a spurt in market share but does not gain customer loyalty. Frito-Lay Thailand Co. Ltd, the manufacturer of Lay's, Tawan, Doritos, Twisties, and Cheetos, maintained its leadership in 2008 with a 27 percent share of retail value sales. However, the increased awareness of health and wellness trends among Thai consumers helps perceived healthier snacks such as seaweed, fish, fruit, and nuts to grow faster than other fried processed snacks.

Seaweed snacks accounted for 900 million baht in 2008 with an annual growth rate of 50 to 60 percent. In this market, fried seaweed snacks represented 60 percent, tempura 25 percent, and baked seaweed 15 percent. Tao kae noi controlled about 84 percent of the fried seaweed segment, 52 percent of the tempura segment, and 30 percent of the baked seaweed segment. The success of Tao kae noi has brought several competitors who imitated its strategy. The names of competing brands purport to be of the same corporate family e.g., Tao Kae Nie (Woman Boss), Tee Leek (Younger Brother). Other competing brands such as Taberu, Mtaro, Yuki, Shogune, Slimi, and Khun Film also employ similar strategies as Tao kae noi in positioning the product as a Japanese-style seaweed snack appealing to young consumers. Only Seleco was a real challenge to Tao kae noi since it has been on the market long before the entrance of Tao kae noi and is backed up by a large conglomerate. Seleco has invested in continuous marketing campaigns in an attempt to replace Tao kae noi as number one in the market. Tob welcomes the competition in the market in order to keep his staff from being complacent. At the same time, the advertising activities of competitors maintains the public interest in seaweed snacks. (See Exhibit 3.)

FIRST STEP IN EXPORTING

After noticing a large volume purchase from a buyer, Tob found that the snack was shipped to Singapore. Having never been to the country, he bought a package tour and went with his parents. While in Singapore, he and his sister did not join the group tour but visited open trade markets where he was informed that his snack was sold. He found only one store that prominently displayed his products. There the owner told him that Tao kae noi sold well but was often out-of-stock. Returning to his hotel, he was encouraged to see that the Singaporean consumers with a high disposable income could afford Tao kae noi seaweed at 80 baht per pack while it was sold in Thailand at only 30 baht.

Exhibit 2   The Product Line of Tao Kae Noi

	Size	Retail price per unit	Flavor
Crispy seaweed	20 grams	10 baht	Classic
	50 grams	20 baht	Hot & Spicy
	85 grams	29 baht	Wasabi
			Prawn soup
Big Sheet	4 grams	5 baht	Classic
			Hot & Spicy
			Garlic
Tempura 	10 grams	10 baht	Classic
	40 grams	20 baht	Hot & Spicy
	80 grams	40 baht	
Curve 	4.5 grams	12 baht	

Source: Company information

Setting up a trading company in Singapore was out of reach since his business in Thailand was growing rapidly and consumed most of his time and effort. He needed a trader to open the Singaporean market. Finding potential trading partners through trade shows was impractical since the desired trade show was scheduled for the next year. By then, he realized that his product might have fallen out of favor or the competitors might already have entered the market. Thus, he went back to Singapore to observe different retail outlets. After several days and several attempts in making appointments with buyers of large retail stores, he had a meeting with a purchaser of the 7-Eleven convenience chain, but was told that regulations in Singapore prohibited manufacturers from dealing

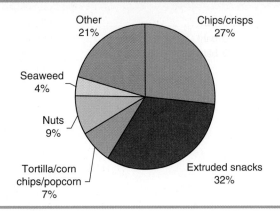

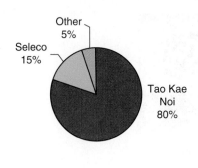

Source: http://www.euromonitor.com, 2010.

Source: Company information

directly with retailers. After receiving the list of potential distributors from the outlet, he contacted them and sent product samples. Unfortunately, none paid attention to his business proposal. Undeterred, Tob went to large supermarkets in Singapore in a search for imported snacks. At that time, he found names and addresses of local distributors printed on the packages. Again he called them up and sent them his product sample.

Despite the fact that he presented them with information about his product success in Thailand and Singapore, none were receptive. Only San SeSan Global, a smaller distributor, showed some interest in discussions with him. They were a good match in their long-term orientation toward brand building. Both worked together in adapting the snack to meet the local need. Initially the label was in Thai, which Singaporeans did not understand, and so the package had to use both Chinese and English. The Singaporean market preferred tomato sauce flavor and a more mild flavor. It took Tao kae noi almost nine months to adjust its snack to meet the need of this new market. The trader conducted several field tests before launching a six-month marketing blitz. (See Exhibit 4.)

The snack was positioned as healthy food for a modern lifestyle. Both Japanese and Chinese seaweed snacks were available in the Singaporean market. However, Japanese brands were too expensive while Chinese brands were cheaper but of inferior quality. By positioning Tao kae noi in an affordable price range but with high quality and catering better to the local taste, the snack was well accepted by Singaporean consumers.

This well-planned effort had helped Tao kae noi to become a mainstay on convenience store shelves all over the island. Two years after it was launched, Tao kae noi

| Thailand | Export Market |

Source: Company information

was displayed in the front of many shops. Tao kae noi and its trader were willing to invest in outlets to control the best product display area. Running an island-wide contest led people to buy the products, so retailers had to put them up front.

Crediting the entry success to his collaboration with his trader, Tob also believed that a superior product was a key factor and that brand building helped to differentiate his brands from others. Tob stressed that "The product must have a story to tell, not just the tangible product itself. Consumers will appreciate the effort that we put in making this snack."

EXPORT EXPANSION

After the initial success in Singapore, Tob had realized the vast opportunity in the export market. The market was more lucrative and payment was more rapid because buyers sent him a letter of credit before he shipped out the order. By comparison, in Thailand he had to wait to receive payments and had to follow the strict guidelines of large retail operators.

Thus, when a relative, who was a trader sending Thai food items to Hong Kong, approached him in 2006 to export his snack to Hong Kong, Tob was delighted. After sending a few boxes, orders expanded rapidly and Tob went to Hong Kong to investigate the market. Similar to Singapore, the snack was sold in only one traditional retail shop and was not available in the main stream market. He employed the same technique in searching and screening local representatives. After finding one trader matching his criteria, they developed a marketing plan to launch the snack in Hong Kong.

Finding traders in Hong Kong was easier than in Singapore. The sales volume in Thailand had reached over 200 million baht within three years. That success, combined with the initial market entry in Singapore had convinced several Hong Kong traders to be interested in representing his snack. After he selected one of the traders, the others approached his competitors in Thailand. However, the competing Thai companies were more concerned with making an immediate profit and, therefore, were not interested in cooperating with traders in investing in brand building. Hong Kong has turned out to be the largest export market for Tao kae noi because it is also served as a gateway to China.

After entering the Hong Kong market, Tao kae noi has expanded its exports to countries in Asia Pacific including Indonesia, Philippines, Taiwan, Malaysia, and Brunei. Eventually, the snack was sold in the United States, Canada, and England. Currently, the company relies on trade shows to meet potential partners since it is more cost effective than visiting individual countries. During a trade show in Hong Kong, for instance, Tao kae noi was able to meet with buyers from all over the world.

Tao kae noi snack is now available in 16 countries, and accounts for 30 percent of the company's total revenue. Hong Kong is its largest market, accounting for 25 percent of its export revenue, followed by Singapore (15 percent), and Taiwan and Indonesia (5 percent each). After exporting for a few years, Tob realizes that Asian consumers are more receptive to his snack now that they are more familiar with having seaweed as an ingredient in foods and snacks. Even when the snack is distributed in the United States, Canada, and England, the main buyers are still Asians residing in these countries. Thus the company plans to concentrate on the Asian market, especially China where the sales volume is well below its market potential. The Chinese market, particularly Shanghai, generates higher profit than selling in Thailand because the price in this market is double that in Thailand. The company has worked with DKSH in distributing Tao kae noi in Hong Kong and planning its market expansion in China.

CHALLENGES IN THE INTERNATIONAL MARKET

Even though exporting was viable for Tao kae noi, Tob faced numerous obstacles. When starting to enter into Singapore, his company spent nine months to adapt the snack to meet the local needs and so did not earn any revenue from this market. Furthermore it had to invest heavily in introducing the brand to Singaporean consumers. If he had borrowed from a bank, it would have reduced his chance at success since it would have taken a long time to get a loan approved. Uncertainties in venturing into exporting for the first time and the risk of failure were serious concerns. Tob wished that the Thai government could alleviate the financial risk and provide consultation from specialists who could cater specifically to his needs. Moreover, the country image being reflected in "Made in Thailand" signified to many buyers inferior quality compared to products from other countries. If the government invested in promoting a positive country image, his task would be easier and his bargaining power would be higher since foreign traders would seek out Thai products.

With his current success in exporting, Tob no longer has problems with financing the company's export activities. The exchange rate fluctuation does not affect him very much, because a stronger baht reduces his cost of seaweed imports. On the other hand, since his price quoted to foreign buyers is in baht, any currency depreciation has no impact on his revenue.

However Tob is facing other problems. Exporting to more countries requires his company's ability to adapt to diverse needs and regulations. For instance, Japan has restrictive rules for imported food. One lot of Tao kae noi snack being shipped to Japan contained a food color that was prohibited by the Japanese government. The Japanese custom informed him that the product would be destroyed or shipped back to Thailand. Deciding to send the snack back to Thailand incurred additional and unnecessary costs. Another difficulty occurred when dealing with a Chinese trader. The trader did not follow the distribution and marketing rules initially agreed upon, causing some friction in their relationship. Tob believes that this conflict resulted from different business cultures.

The most difficult task facing him now is how to penetrate the Chinese market successfully. Tao kae noi snacks can reach only a small fraction of the market because due to import duties of 30 percent, his retail price was higher than that of goods produced in China.

Building a factory in China is also next to impossible since foreigners cannot solely own a factory. Tob would have to form a join investment with a Chinese partner, leading to his loss of control. Finding a suitable partner is also rather difficult because he wants a partner interested in long-term success. Doing so will not generate immediate large profits because much capital will have to be invested in brand building.

In addition, setting up a factory in China is a very complicated process; each province has its own set of regulations in addition to those from the central government. Many Thai manufacturers have failed after building operations in China, which deters others from such a venture. Unlike the Japanese government, the Thai government has not negotiated with the Chinese government to reduce this complexity. Moreover if Tao kae noi brand is well-known in the Chinese market, Tob fears that the brand will be counterfeited.

BACK TO THE CLASSROOM

While busy managing his business, Tob has been back to a private university to pursue his BA in business administration and, even more important, to take subjects that will help him run his business successfully. He is an avid reader. In addition to reading textbooks in management, finance, and marketing, studies of business success and failure provide valuable lessons. University life teaches him social skills which are essential in business dealings. At age 24, Tob still has big dreams ahead of him. He wants to build his business into a multinational snack company.

Questions for Discussion

1. What does it take to make a new small business a successful exporter? Is it important to be successful in the domestic market before expanding overseas? Discuss the importance of brand building even in the early stage of exporting.

2. Which type of market expansion did Tao kae noi use in exporting? Discuss the appropriateness of market diversification versus concentration on expanding a company's export markets. What conditions are suitable for these options?

3. In order for a government to encourage more young entrepreneurs to export, how should the government set up its export program? How should the assistance services from the government be reflecting different stages in exporting?

PART 5
OPERATIONS

14 Marketing
15 Services
16 Logistics and Supply-Chain Management
17 Financial Management
18 Human Resource Management
19 New Horizons

Once the firm has entered and established itself in international markets, new concerns rest primarily with operational issues in order to develop and maintain a competitively advantageous position. Part five focuses on overarching dimensions such as services and supply chain management, as well as on the traditional areas of marketing, finance, and human resources management.

We differentiate in each chapter between smaller firms and multinational corporations (MNCs). Low cost and low resource approaches are presented for firms with little international experience. Subsequently, a globally oriented perspective with a major focus on MNCs is offered.

The book concludes with a chapter focusing on New Horizons. Based on global research conducted by the authors, the chapter covers the newest developments, knowledge and speculations about international business, as well as information about employment options in the international business field.

CHAPTER 14

Marketing

CHAPTER CONTENTS & LEARNING OBJECTIVES

TARGET MARKET SELECTION

1. *To suggest how markets for international expansion can be selected, their demand assessed, and appropriate strategies for their development devised*

2. *To describe how environmental differences generate new challenges for the international marketing manager*

MARKETING MANAGEMENT

3. *To compare and contrast the merits of standardization versus localization strategies for country markets and of regional versus global marketing efforts*

4. *To discuss market-specific and global challenges facing the marketing functions: product, price, distribution, and promotion within both the traditional and e-business dimensions*

All around the world, the majority of corporate sponsorship is allocated to sports. Global sports sponsorship has gradually grown over the past decade to approximately $30 billion per year. At the same time, the number of big annual international sporting events has also increased exponentially—from 20 in 1912 to more than 1,000 in 2009, or an average of almost three per day. Companies seek to align themselves with—and create—meaningful sports-related memories for consumers. Because of the positive association of sports with leadership, teamwork, and the pursuit of excellence, marketers are eager to develop relationships with teams, organizers, and individual superstars, such as David Beckham and Roger Federer.

Marketers have employed a wide variety of strategies, such as attaching a company's name to a stadium, sponsoring Little League baseball tournaments, and using famous sport personalities in their advertising. However, in today's age of information technology, the bulk of corporate attention is concentrated on the sports broadcasting market. There are three basic forms of sports broadcasting: (1) a monopoly with only one organizer supplying an exclusive event to competing TV channels (e.g., the International Olympic Committee offering the Olympic Games); (2) an oligopsonistic monopoly, where only one organizer is facing very few potential buyers (e.g., regional soccer championships); and (3) a bilateral monopoly with a single public TV channel or a cartel of public channels monopolizing the demand side of a domestic market.

The monopolistic market is the most highly competitive, because it allows the organizer to charge high broadcasting fees. It is also the norm with most large international events, such as the Olympic Games and the World Soccer Cup. Coincidentally, these are the events that guarantee marketers the largest amount of exposure to the largest number of potential customers.

For multinationals, crafting a successful global sports marketing strategy involves finding the right combination of expensive, "big-ticket" international competitions, as well as smaller-scale local and regional events. Anheuser-Busch InBev NV—the world's largest brewer—has been particularly successful in using sports sponsorships to promote its global brand. The bulk of the corporation's advertising spending (about 85 percent) is allocated to sponsorship of and advertising during sporting events. In addition to the large-scale sponsorships listed here, Anheuser-Busch has thousands of smaller regional contracts. Even though most industry observers agree that the company is doing a good job of targeting its consumer base and promoting its brand globally, the big problem with sports sponsorships and advertising is that their benefits are tough to quantify. In other words, their contributions to Anheuser-Busch's bottom line are impossible to measure. Additionally, it is generally hard to account for the exact cost of sponsorships and broadcasting deals because, over time, most corporate sponsors spend about three times as much promoting the sponsorship as they do on the deal itself.

Sports sponsorship might be a case of the "dog that did not bark"—more conspicuous in its absence than its presence. If Anheuser-Busch were to withdraw from one of the big sporting events that it currently sponsors, a competitor would step in. Additionally, the company's long-standing relationships with the broadcasters and organizers could be damaged. There also are some positive measurements of investment return. Evaluating the number of new corporate customers that sell Anheuser-Busch products in their stores, the incremental amount of promotional/display activity, new vending placements, and so forth, could provide useful benchmarks of success.

Anheuser-Busch InBev NV's Sports Sponsorships
Baseball
- Official beer sponsor of Major League Baseball and 26 teams.

Basketball
- Official beer sponsor of the National Basketball Association and 26 teams.
- Official beer sponsor of the National Basketball Association in China and Mexico.

Football (American)
- Official beer sponsor of 28 National Football League teams.
- Official beer sponsor of the National Football League in Canada.
- Exclusive alcohol beverage of the Super Bowl through 2012.
- Exclusive beverage of the collegiate Bowl Championship Series (Orange, Sugar, Fiesta, and National Championship Games) through 2010.

Football (Soccer)
- Official beer sponsor of the 2010 FIFA World Cup™ in South Africa and the 2014 FIFA World Cup™ in Brazil.
- Official beer sponsor of the English Premier League and Manchester United football club.
- Official beer sponsor of Major League Soccer and each of its 13 teams.
- Official sponsor of the U.S. men's and women's National and Olympic teams.

- Official beer of the InterLiga tournament.
- Official beer of the SuperLiga Tournament between Mexican First Division and MLS teams.
- Official beer sponsor of the 2009 FIFA Confederations Cup™ in South Africa.

Mixed Martial Arts
- Official beer sponsor of the Ultimate Fighting Championship (UFC) and World Extreme Cagefighting (WEC).

NASCAR
- Primary team sponsor of Gillett Evernham Motorsports, the No. 9 Budweiser Dodge, and driver Kasey Kahne (Budweiser).
- Official beer sponsor of Daytona International Speedway and the Daytona 500.
- Title sponsor of the Budweiser Shootout at Daytona.

Olympics
- Official international beer sponsor of the 2008 Olympic Games in Beijing, China.
- Official malt beverage sponsor of the U.S. Olympic Team through 2008 (Anheuser-Busch).
- Exclusive alcohol and nonalcohol malt-based beverage of the 2008 Beijing Olympic Games telecast on NBC, Telemundo, and all cable properties (Anheuser-Busch).
- Official beer sponsor of the China Olympic Team through 2008 (Budweiser).
- Official beer sponsor of Team Great Britain.
- Official beer sponsor of the National Olympic Teams in 25 countries.

© Julian Finney /Getty Images, Inc.

Manchester United's Wayne Rooney.

Sources: Darren Rovell, "Anheuser-Busch: Will It Continue to 'Brew' Sports Advertising?" *CNBC*, Monday, July 14, 2008; "A Look at Anheuser-Busch's Sports Marketing," *USAToday*, July 17, 2008; Wladimir Andreff, "Globalization of the Sports Economy," *Rivista Di Diritto Ed Economia Dello Sport* IV, no. 3 (2008); Molly Neal, "Stressed Advertisers Blow the Whistle on Sports Sponsorship Deals," *The Wall Street Journal*, December 10, 2008; Paul Thomasch and Ben Klayman, "Anheuser-Busch Ending Sponsorship of Hot Rod Racing," *Reuters*, March 17, 2009.

Marketing is the activity, set of institutions, and processes for creating, communicating, delivering, and exchanging offerings that have value for customers, clients, partners, and society at large.[1] The concepts of exchange, value, satisfaction, and exchange are at the core of marketing. For an exchange to take place, two or more parties have to come together physically or electronically and they must communicate and deliver things of perceived value. Customers should be perceived as information seekers who evaluate marketers' offerings in terms of their own drives and needs. When the offering is consistent with their needs, they tend to choose the good or service; if it is not, other alternatives are chosen. A key task of the marketer is to recognize the ever-changing nature of needs and wants. Marketing techniques apply not only to goods but to ideas and services as well. Further, well over 50 percent of all marketing activities are business marketing—directed at other businesses, governmental entities, and various types of institutions.

The marketing manager's task is to plan and execute programs that will ensure a long-term competitive advantage for the company. This task has two integral parts: (1) the determining of specific target markets and (2) marketing management, which consists of manipulating marketing mix elements to best satisfy the needs of the individual target markets. Regardless of geographic markets, the basic tasks do not vary; they have been called the technical universals of marketing.[2]

This chapter will focus on the formulation of marketing strategy for international operations. The first section describes target market selection and how to identify pertinent characteristics of the various markets. The balance of the chapter is devoted to adjusting the elements of the marketing program to a particular market for maximum effectiveness and efficiency, while attempting to exploit global and regional similarities, as highlighted in the opening vignette.

TARGET MARKET SELECTION

The process of target market selection involves narrowing down potential country markets to a feasible number of countries and market segments within them. Rather than try to appeal to everyone, firms best utilize their resources by (1) identifying potential markets for entry and (2) expanding selectively over time to those deemed attractive.

IDENTIFICATION AND SCREENING

A four-stage process for screening and analyzing foreign markets is presented in Figure 14.1. It begins with very general criteria and ends with product-specific market analyses. The data and the methods needed for decision making change from secondary to primary as the steps are taken in sequence. Although presented here as a screening process for choosing target markets, the process is also applicable to change of entry mode or even divestment.

If markets were similar in their characteristics, the international marketer could enter any one of the potential markets. However, differences among markets exist in three dimensions: physical, psychic, and economic.[3] Physical distance is the geographic distance between home and target countries; its impact has decreased as a result of recent technological developments. Psychic, or cultural, distance refers to differences in language, tradition, and customs between two countries. Economic

1. To suggest how markets for international expansion can be selected, their demand assessed, and appropriate strategies for their development devised

2. To describe how environmental differences generate new challenges for the international marketing manager

Figure 14.1   The Screening Process in Target Market Choice

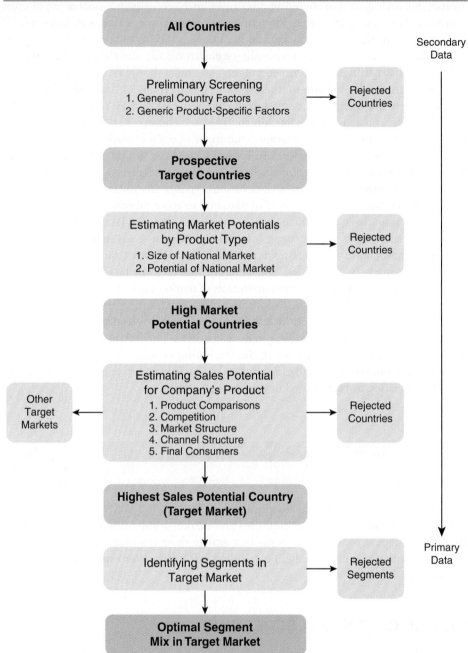

Source: Adapted from Franklin R. Root, *Entry Strategies for International Markets* 40 (San Francisco: Jossey-Bass, 1994), 40.

distance translates into the target's ability to pay. Generally, the greater the overall distance—or difference—between the two countries, the less knowledge the marketer has about the target market. The amount of information that is available varies dramatically. For example, although the marketer can easily learn about the economic environment from secondary sources, invaluable interpretive information may not be available until the firm actually operates in the market. In the early stages of this assessment, international marketers can be assisted by numerous online data sources as shown in Chapter 12.

The four stages in the screening process are preliminary screening, estimation of market potential, estimation of sales potential, and identification of segments. Each stage should be given careful attention. The first stage, for example, should not merely reduce the number of alternatives to a manageable few for the sake of reduction, even though the expense of analyzing markets in depth is great. Unless care is taken, attractive alternatives may be eliminated.

Preliminary Screening

The preliminary screening process must rely chiefly on secondary data for country-specific factors as well as product- and industry-specific factors. Country-specific factors typically include those that would indicate the market's overall buying power—for example, population, gross national product in total and per capita, total exports and imports, and production of cement, electricity, and steel.[4] Product-specific factors narrow the analysis to the firm's specific areas of operation. A company such as Motorola, manufacturing for the automotive aftermarket, is interested in the number of passenger cars, trucks, and buses in use. The statistical analyses must be accompanied by qualitative assessments of the impact of cultural elements and the overall climate for foreign firms and products. A market that satisfies the levels set becomes a prospective target country.

Estimating Market Potential

Total market potential is the sales, in physical or monetary units, that might be available to all firms in an industry during a given period under a given level of industry marketing effort and given environmental conditions.[5] The international marketer needs to assess the size of existing markets and forecast the size of future markets. A number of techniques, both quantitative and qualitative, are available for this task.

Income elasticity of demand is the relationship between demand and economic progress. The share of income spent on necessities reflects the level of development of the market as well as monies left for other purchases. When consumption per capita of a product category is mapped against GNP per capita, it reflects a diminishing rate in consumption as incomes rise. For the majority of goods, consumption rises most quickly between $3,000 and $10,000 per capita, bringing in new consumers to the market while those who are already in the market may be trading into higher-value substitutes.[6] This points out the attractiveness of emerging markets in spite of their volatility.

income elasticity of demand A means of describing change in demand in relative response to a change in income.

If the data are available for product-specific analysis, the simplest way to establish a market-size estimate is to conduct a **market audit**, which adds together local production and imports with exports deducted from the total. However, in many cases, data may not exist, be current, or be appropriate. In such cases, market potentials may have to be estimated by methods such as **analogy**. This approach is based on the use of proxy variables that have been shown (either through research or intuition) to correlate with the demand for the product in question. The market size for a product (such as mobile advertising) in country A is estimated by comparing a ratio for an available indicator (e.g., smartphones) for country A and country B, and using this ratio in conjunction with market data available on mobile advertising for country B. In some cases, a time lag in demand patterns may be seen, thus requiring a **longitudinal analysis**. For example, it is suggested that the use of wireless communication in southern Europe lags northern Europe by two years and that wireless phone use overall is tied to the state of the economy (e.g., GNP per capita). Therefore, to estimate wireless use in southern

market audit A method of estimating market size by adding together local production and imports, with exports subtracted from the total.

analogy A method for estimating market potential from similar products when data for the specific products do not exist.

longitudinal analysis A longitudinal analysis that involves repeated observations of the same items over long periods of time.

Europe, the following formula could be used:

$$WC_{SE}^{2013} = GNP_{SE}^{2013} * \left(\frac{WC_{NE}^{2011}}{GNP_{NE}^{2011}} \right)$$

In similar fashion, a country or a group of countries may be used as a proxy for an entire region. For example, Coca-Cola Company launched Georgia, a ready-to-drink coffee brand developed in Japan, available in the following locations: Bahrain, India, Oman, Qatar, Republic of Korea, Saudi Arabia, and United Arab Emirates. In 2008, the Coca-Cola Company expanded the availability of its Jugos del Valle® fruit juice brands developed in Mexico and Brazil to new markets, including Colombia, Costa Rica, Panama, and Spain.[7]

Despite the valuable insight generated through these techniques, caution should be used in interpreting the results. All of the quantitative techniques are based on historical data that may be obsolete or inapplicable because of differences in cultural and geographic traits of the market. Further, with today's technological developments, lags between markets are no longer at a level that would make all of the measurements valid. Moreover, the measurements look at a market as an aggregate; that is, no regional differences are taken into account. In industrialized countries, the richest 10 percent of the population consumes 20 percent of all goods and services, whereas the respective figure for the developing countries may be as high as 45 percent.[8] Therefore, even in the developing countries with low GNP figures, segments exist with buying power rivaled only in the richest developed countries.

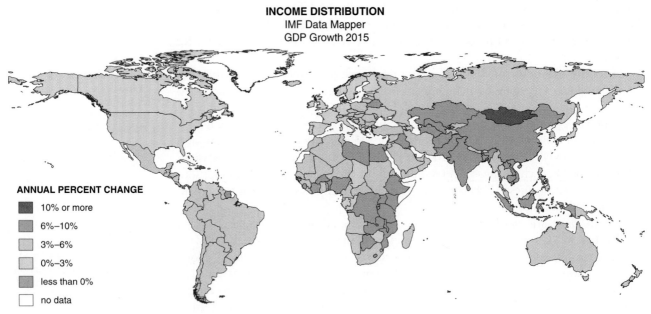

INCOME DISTRIBUTION
IMF Data Mapper
GDP Growth 2015

ANNUAL PERCENT CHANGE
- 10% or more
- 6%–10%
- 3%–6%
- 0%–3%
- less than 0%
- no data

Source: International Monetary Fund, *World Economic Outlook*, April 2010.

In addition to these quantitative techniques that rely on secondary data, international marketers can use various survey techniques. They are especially useful when marketing new technologies. A survey of end-user interest and responses may provide a relatively clear picture of the possibilities in a new market. Surveys can also be administered through a web site or through e-mail.[9]

Comparing figures for market potential with actual sales will provide the international marketer with further understanding of his or her firm's chances in the market. If the difference between potential and reality is substantial, the reasons can be evaluated using **gap analysis**. The differences can be the result of usage, distribution, or product line gaps.[10] If the firm is already in the market, part of the difference between its sales and the market potential can be explained through the competitive gap. Usage gaps indicate that not all potential users are using the product or that those using it are not using as much as they could, which suggests mainly a promotional task. Distribution gaps indicate coverage problems, which may be vertical (concentrating only on urban markets) or horizontal (if the product is only available at large-scale international retailers and not local ones). Product line gaps typically suggest latent demand. Global fashion designers and retailers pay close attention to what trendy teenagers are wearing on the streets of Tokyo's Shibuya and Harajuku districts in order to spot emerging trends and develop new products for sales opportunities in other countries.

gap analysis Analysis of the difference between market potential and actual sales.

Estimating Sales Potential

Even when the international marketer has gained an understanding of markets with the greatest overall promise, the firm's own possibilities in those markets are still not known. Sales potential is the share of the market potential that the firm can reasonably expect to get over the longer term. To arrive at an estimate, the marketer needs to collect product- and market-specific data. The data will have to do with:

1. Competition—strength, likely reaction to entry
2. Market—strength of barriers
3. Consumers—ability and willingness to buy
4. Product—degree of relative advantage, compatibility, complexity, trialability, and communicability
5. Channel structure—access to retail level

In 2009, Russia's market for new cars was one of the fastest growing in the world. It had gone from annual sales of less than 1.5 million in 2005 to nearly 3 million in 2008 and was poised to overtake Germany as the fourth-biggest car market in the world. Credit Suisse confidently predicted that sales would grow by at least 12 percent a year until 2012, and that by then the foreign car firms that had rushed to build factories in Russia would be producing more than 1.5 million cars a year. How wrong were they? Credit Suisse, which was used to finance the purchase of about half of all new cars, disappeared almost instantly because Russian banks were unusually dependent on shuttered wholesale markets. Thanks to the economy's reliance on exports of oil and gas, slumping energy prices immediately hit both earnings and the rouble. The tumbling rouble also meant that foreign car brands suddenly became much less affordable, including those made in Russia, because most of their components are still imported. In addition, foreign multinational corporations such as Renault, Ford, and General Motors amended their production plans for year 2009 in Russia and delayed their production of new models.[11] The marketer's questions can never be fully answered until the firm has made a commitment to enter the market and is operational. The mode of entry has special significance in determining the firm's sales potential.

Identifying Segments

Within the markets selected, individuals and organizations will vary in their wants, resources, geographical locations, buying attitudes, and buying practices. Initially, the firm may cater to one or only a few segments and later expand to others, especially if the product is innovative. Segmentation is indicated when segments are indeed different enough to warrant individualized attention, are large enough for profit potential, and can be reached through the methods that the international marketer wants to use. The number of China's wealthy households, which hit 1.6 million in 2008, will climb to more than 4.4 million by 2015, trailing only the United States, Japan, and the United Kingdom in sheer size (with definitions of wealth adjusted for purchasing power parity). One of the factors distinguishing China's wealthy consumers from their foreign counterparts is their youth: some 80 percent are under 45 years of age (with 30 percent in the United States). China's wealthy value the functional benefits of any particular purchase (the quality, material, design, or craftsmanship, for instance) more than wealthy consumers elsewhere do. The BMW offers its full line of products (with design changes catering to wealthy Chinese) and advertises them across a range of channels (such as glossy magazines, television, and the Internet) to create wide brand awareness. Annual BMW Experience Days rotating from city to city offer groups of buyers a first look at the coming year's models, giving these customers a luxurious experience, along with an opportunity to test-drive the new cars.[12]

Once the process is complete for a market or group of markets, the international marketer may begin it again for another one. When growth potential is no longer in market development, the firm may opt for market penetration.

CONCENTRATION VERSUS DIVERSIFICATION

concentration strategy The market expansion policy that involves concentrating on a small number of markets.

diversification A market expansion policy characterized by growth in a relatively large number of markets or market segments.

Choosing a market expansion policy involves the allocation of effort among various markets. The major alternatives are **concentration strategy** on a small number of markets or **diversification**, which is characterized by growth in a relatively large number of markets in the early stages of international market expansion.[13] For example, the German hub would manage Austria, Hungary, and Switzerland; Brazil would support Argentina, Bolivia, Chile, Paraguay, and Uruguay; and Mexico might cover Colombia, Venezuela, Peru, and Ecuador.[14]

Expansion Alternatives

Either concentration or diversification is applicable to market segments or to total markets, depending on the resource commitment the international marketer is willing and able to make. One option is a dual-concentration strategy, in which efforts are focused on a few segments in a limited number of countries. Another is a dual-diversification strategy, in which entry is to most segments in most available markets. The first is a likely strategy for small firms or firms that market specialized products to clearly definable markets, for example, ocean-capable sailing boats. The second is typical for large consumer-oriented companies that have sufficient resources for broad coverage. Market concentration/segment diversification opts for a limited number of markets but for wide coverage within them, putting emphasis on company acceptance. Market diversification/segment concentration usually involves the identification of a segment, possibly worldwide, to which the company can market without major changes in its marketing mix.

Factors Affecting Expansion Strategy

Expansion strategy is determined by the factors relating to market, mix, and company that are listed in Table 14.1. In most cases, the factors are interrelated.

Market-Related Factors   These factors are the ones that were influential in determining the attractiveness of the market in the first place. In the choice of expansion strategy, demand for the firm's products is a critical factor. With high and stable growth rates in certain markets, the firm will most likely opt for a concentration strategy. If the demand is strong worldwide, diversification may be attractive.

Table 14.1 Factors Affecting the Choice between Concentration and Diversification Strategies

Factor	Diversification	Concentration
Market growth rate	Low	High
Sales stability	Low	High
Sales response function	Concave	S curve
Competitive lead time/response	Short	Long
Spillover effects	High	Low
Need for product adaptation	Low	High
Need for communication adaptation	Low	High
Economies of scale in distribution	Low	High
Extent of constraints	Low	High
Program control requirements	Low	High

Source: Adapted from Igal Ayal and Jehiel Zif, "Marketing Expansion Strategies in Multinational Marketing," *Journal of Marketing* 43 (Spring 1979): 89.

A forecast of the sales response function can be used to predict sales at various levels of marketing expenditure. Two general response functions exist: concave and S curve. When the function is concave, sales will increase at a decreasing rate because of competition and a lowering adoption rate. The function might involve a unique, innovative product or marketing program. An S-curve function assumes that a viable market share can be achieved only through sizable marketing efforts. This is typical for new entrants to well-established markets.

The uniqueness of the firm's offering with respect to competition is also a factor in the expansion strategy. If lead time over competition is considerable, the decision to diversify may not seem urgent. However, complacency can be a mistake in today's competitive environment; competitors can rush new products into the market in a matter of days. Competition may present other challenges as well. For products in which fast-changing technology and service offerings can provide only temporary and sometimes questionable competitive advantage, competitive superiority claims, either explicit or implicit, will often face immediate challenge. In 2008, the United Kingdom's Advertising Standards Authority (ASA) found that Vodafone's mobile broadband advertising that touted "the fastest, most reliable mobile broadband in the galaxy" was misleading after receiving complaints from rival mobile operators Hutchison and T-Mobile.[15]

In many product categories marketers, knowingly or unknowingly, will be affected by spillover effects. Consider, for example, the impact that satellite channels have had on advertising in Europe or Asia, where ads for a product now reach most of the markets. Where geographic (and psychic) distances are short, spillover is likely, and marketers are most likely to diversify.

Government constraints—or the threat of them—can be a powerful motivator in a firm's expansion. While government barriers may naturally prevent new-market entry, marketers may seek access through using new entry modes, adjusting marketing programs, or getting into a market before entry barriers are erected.

Mix-Related Factors   These factors relate to the degree to which marketing mix elements—primarily product, promotion, and distribution—can be standardized. The more that standardization is possible, the more diversification is indicated. Overall savings through economies of scale can then be utilized in marketing efforts.

Depending on the product, each market will have its own challenges. Whether constraints are apparent (such as tariffs) or hidden (such as tests or standards), they will complicate all of the other factors. Nevertheless, regional integration has allowed many marketers to diversify their efforts.

Company-Related Factors   These include the objectives set by the company for its international operations and the policies it adopts in those markets. As an example, the firm may require—either by stated policy or because of its goods—extensive interaction with intermediaries and clients. When this is the case, the firm's efforts will likely be concentrated because of resource constraints.

The opportunity to take advantage of diversification is available for all types of companies, not only the large ones. The identification of unique worldwide segments for which a customized marketing mix is provided has proven to be successful for many small and medium-sized companies. For example, Logitech, the global leader in the computer mouse, diversified its product portfolio to include a wide range of personal peripherals beyond the PC to include digital music and home-entertainment control. Upon its founding in 2005, Joby became known for its Gorillapod camera tripods but now has expanded to the design and development of numerous products that solve problems in the consumer electronics market such as the Gorillatorch, a flexible, hands-free flashlight.[16]

MARKETING MANAGEMENT

3. To compare and contrast the merits of standardization versus localization strategies for country markets and of regional versus global marketing efforts

4. To discuss market-specific and global challenges facing the marketing functions: product, price, distribution, and promotion within both the traditional and e-business dimensions

After target markets are selected, the next step is the determination of marketing efforts at appropriate levels. A key question in international marketing concerns the extent to which the elements of the marketing mix—product, price, place, and distribution—should be standardized. The marketer also faces the specific challenges of adjusting each of the mix elements in the international marketplace.

STANDARDIZATION VERSUS ADAPTATION

The international marketer must first decide what modifications in the mix policy are needed or warranted. Three basic alternatives in approaching international markets are available:

1. Make no special provisions for the international marketplace but, rather, identify potential target markets and then choose products that can easily be marketed with little or no modification.
2. Adapt to local conditions in each and every target market (the multidomestic approach).
3. Incorporate differences into a regional or global strategy that will allow for local differences in implementation (globalization approach).

In today's environment, standardization usually means cross-national strategies rather than a policy of viewing foreign markets as secondary and therefore not important enough to have products adapted for them. Ideally, the international marketer should think globally and act locally, focusing on neither extreme: full standardization or full localization. Global thinking requires flexibility in exploiting good ideas and products on a worldwide basis regardless of their origin. Factors that encourage standardization or adaptation are summarized in Table 14.2.

The adaptation decision will also have to be assessed as a function of time and market involvement. The more companies learn about local market characteristics in individual markets, the more they are able to establish similarities and, as a result,

Table 14.2 Standardization versus Adaptation

Factors Encouraging Standardization	Factors Encouraging Adaptation
• Economies in product R&D	• Differing use conditions
• Economies of scale in production	• Government and regulatory influences
• Economies in marketing	• Differing buyer behavior patterns
• Control of marketing programs	• Local initiative and motivation in implementation
• "Shrinking" of the world marketplace	• Adherence to the marketing concept

standardize their approach. This market insight will give them legitimacy with local constituents in developing a common understanding of the extent of standardization versus adaptation.[17] For example, for years Mattel marketed Barbie dolls around the world that featured local characteristics. In 2009, however, the company's new superstore in Shanghai featured the classic Barbie. According to the general manager of Barbie Shanghai, "our research shows that Chinese women want a blond doll, that they expect a blond doll because Barbie is American."[18] In 2009, Haier Appliances India, a division of the Chinese appliance maker Haier, introduced a new range of electric spa water heaters designed specifically for Indian consumers after extensive research of the Indian market and consumer needs there.[19]

Factors Affecting Adaptation

Even when marketing programs are based on highly standardized ideas and strategies, they depend on three sets of variables: (1) the market(s) targeted; (2) the product and its characteristics; and (3) company characteristics, including factors such as resources and policy.

Questions of adaptation have no easy answers. Marketers in many firms rely on decision-support systems to aid in program adaptation, while others consider every situation independently. All goods must, of course, conform to environmental conditions over which the marketer has no control. Further, the international marketer may use adaptation to enhance its competitiveness in the marketplace.

PRODUCT POLICY

Goods or services form the core of the firm's international operations. Its success depends on how well goods satisfy needs and wants and how well they are differentiated from those of the competition. This section focuses on product and product-line adaptation to foreign markets as well as product counterfeiting as a current problem facing international marketers.

Factors in Product Adaptation

Factors affecting product adaptation to foreign market conditions are summarized in Figure 14.2. The changes vary from minor ones, such as translation of a user's manual, to major ones, such as a more economical version of the product. Many of the factors have an impact on product selection as well as product adaptation for a given market.

Studies of product adaptation show that the majority of products have to be modified for the international marketplace one way or another. Changes typically affect packaging, measurement units, labeling, product constituents and features, usage instructions, and, to a lesser extent, logos and brand names.[20]

Figure 14.2   Factors Affecting Product Adaptation Decisions

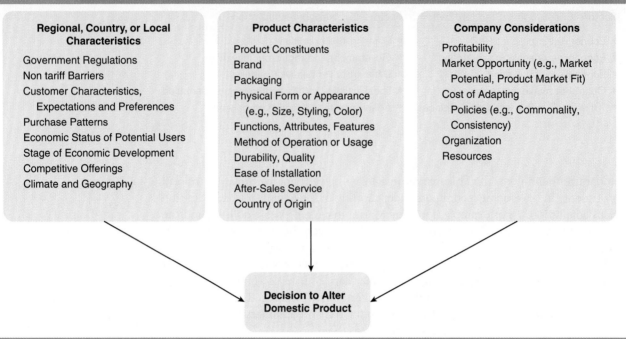

Regional, Country, or Local Characteristics

Government Regulations
Non tariff Barriers
Customer Characteristics, Expectations and Preferences
Purchase Patterns
Economic Status of Potential Users
Stage of Economic Development
Competitive Offerings
Climate and Geography

Product Characteristics

Product Constituents
Brand
Packaging
Physical Form or Appearance (e.g., Size, Styling, Color)
Functions, Attributes, Features
Method of Operation or Usage
Durability, Quality
Ease of Installation
After-Sales Service
Country of Origin

Company Considerations

Profitability
Market Opportunity (e.g., Market Potential, Product Market Fit)
Cost of Adapting
Policies (e.g., Commonality, Consistency)
Organization
Resources

Decision to Alter Domestic Product

Source: Adapted from V. Yorio, *Adapting Products for Export* (New York: The Conference Board, 1983), 7.

Regional, Country, or Local Characteristics   Typically, the market environment mandates the majority of product modifications. However, the most stringent requirements often result from government regulations. Some of the requirements may serve no purpose other than a political one (such as protection of domestic industry or response to political pressures). Because of the sovereignty of nations, individual firms must comply, but they can influence the situation either by lobbying directly or through industry associations to have the issue raised during trade negotiations. Government regulations may be spelled out, but firms need to be ever vigilant for changes and exceptions.

The member countries of the European Economic Area are imposing standards in more than 10,000 product categories ranging from toys to tractor seats. While companies such as Murray Manufacturing have had to change their products to comply with the standards (in Murray's case, making its lawnmowers quieter), they will be able to produce one European product in the future. Overall, U.S. producers may be forced to improve quality of all their products because some product rules require adoption of an overall system approved by the International Standards Organization (ISO).[21] By December 2009, ISO had more than 162 member-countries and 17,500 international standards and similar documents governing a broad range of activities, products, services, and practices.[22]

Product decisions made by marketers of consumer products are especially affected by local behavior, tastes, attitudes, and traditions—all reflecting the marketer's need to gain the customer's approval. A knowledge of cultural and psychological differences may be the key to success. For example, Brazilians rarely eat breakfast or they eat it at home; therefore, Dunkin' Donuts markets doughnuts as snacks, as dessert, and for parties. To further appeal to Brazilians, doughnuts are made with local fruit fillings such as papaya and guava.[23] While China's Kentucky Fried Chicken menu features its signature "Original Recipe" fried chicken, it also creates products that appeal to local tastes such as the Spicy Dragon Twister, Pi Dan Congee (rice porridge), Fu Young Vegetable

Soup, and Egg Tart (signature dessert). Pizza Hut restaurants display upscale decor to satisfy their customers' preference for "five-star service and atmosphere at a three-star price." The casual dining atmosphere is centered around an extensive menu that covers soup, salads, appetizers, and a range of pizzas such as Seafood Catch (seafood mix, crab sticks, green pepper, pineapple), and The Hot One (chili pepper, onion, tomato, beef, spicy chicken). Even with the success of KFC and Pizza Hut in China, the company is not resting on its laurels. Yum! China is testing East Dawning, the company's first Chinese quick-service restaurant brand to provide affordable, great-tasting, authentic quick-service Chinese food to the Chinese consumer.[24] As discussed in Focus on Culture, food is arguably one of the most culture-sensitive categories.

Chinese and Western consumers share similar standards when it comes to evaluating brand names. Both appreciate a brand name that is catchy, memorable,

FOCUS ON CULTURE

Anyone for Flatbread?

Food is arguably one of the most culture-sensitive categories. How is it possible for a company whose main line of business is in the production of corn flour and related products to be a player in markets beyond Mexico, where corn is plentiful and tortillas are a staple? Gruma, a company headquartered in Monterrey, Mexico, is a $2.5 billion international powerhouse transcending to markets as diverse as the United States, Mexico, Central America, Venezuela, and, more recently, Europe. The company began operations in Mexico in 1949. Its objective was to modernize the traditional Mexican masa and tortilla industry, which is an activity of huge economic and social significance, through an industrial, ecological, and more efficient process. Because of its constant research and development efforts, Gruma developed proprietary technology that allowed the company to position itself as the worldwide leader in corn flour and tortilla production, in both production costs and product quality.

Gruma's success has come in part from the realization that its product is a *carrier* of local tastes and that it is the company's job to adapt that carrier to local tastes. Ultimately, Gruma's most versatile and marketable product has proven to be not a food, but a process—more specifically, the ability to roll any kind of flour, from corn to wheat to rice, into salable flatbread. Most people from India do not eat corn tortillas, but they do eat a flatbread called *naan*, made from wheat, which Gruma sells in the United Kingdom and plans to sell in India. The Chinese don't have much taste for corn tortillas either, but they buy wraps made by Gruma for Peking duck and plum sauce.

At the same time, Gruma is using a combination of psychographics and "chefmanship" to establish market potential, in particular to know if consumers are willing to try something new, and specifically, if they are willing to try *their* new product. People in certain markets are looking for healthier, less fattening foods, and are thus open to products like Gruma's wheat flour sandwich wraps. Other markets are becoming faster paced, so flatbread, which can be eaten on the run without utensils, is a good fit. In still other areas, such as China, people seem predisposed to experimentation. They want to try new things. Tortillas are more expensive in China than traditional sandwich bread, but they are growing in popularity nonetheless.

In many European countries, however—such as Portugal, Spain, Italy, Greece, and France—where the food is healthy and the eating habits are good, it is harder to make inroads. Because Italians have very traditional eating habits, quick-serve restaurants that offer flatbread were not successful for many years. But when these quick-serve restaurants appeared in tourist destinations such as Rome, Venice, and Florence, local resistance ebbed. Tourists frequented the restaurants and ate the flatbread, and the local Italians became curious and wanted to try it themselves, particularly the younger Italians.

Flatbread

Similar sensitivities have to be applied in single-market efforts as well. In Texas, for example, people generally like fluffier tortillas than those sold in the rest of the United States. In California they like elastic tortillas, and in Arizona they like chewy tortillas. Through research, Gruma marketers learned that each of those areas had been settled predominantly by Mexicans from a particular region, where variations in the local quality of tortilla manufacturing ingrained certain preferences.

Sources: Jairo Senise, "Who Is Your Next Customer?" *eNews of Strategy and Business*, September 28, 2007, 1–4; Alonzo Martinez and Ronald Haddock, "The Flatbread Factor," *Strategy and Business*, Spring 2007, 1–14; "Gruma Opens First Tortilla Plant in China," *Business Wire*, September 30, 2006; see also www.gruma.com.

© Joe Raedle/Getty Images, Inc.

distinct, and says something indicative of the product. But, because of cultural and linguistic factors, Chinese consumers expect more in terms of how the names are spelled, written, and styled, and whether they are considered lucky. PepsiCo Inc. introduced Cheetos in the Chinese market under a Chinese name, *qi duo*, roughly pronounced "chee-do," that translates as "many surprises."[25]

positioning The perception by consumers of a firm's product in relation to competitors' products.

Often no concrete product changes are needed, only a change in the product's **positioning**. Positioning is the perception by consumers of the firm's brand in relation to competitors' brands; that is, the mental image a brand, or the company as a whole, evokes. Coca-Cola took a risk in marketing Diet Coke in Japan because the population is not overweight by Western standards. Further, Japanese women do not like to drink anything clearly labeled as a diet product. The company changed the name to Coke Light and subtly shifted the promotional theme from "weight loss" to "figure maintenance."

Nontariff barriers include product standards, testing or approval procedures, subsidies for local products, and bureaucratic red tape. The nontariff barriers affecting product adjustments usually concern elements outside the core product. The U.S. Department of Commerce estimates that a typical machine manufacturer can expect to spend between $50,000 and $100,000 a year complying with foreign standards. For certain exports to the European Union, that figure can reach as high as $200,000.[26] Because nontariff barriers are usually in place to keep foreign products out or to protect domestic producers, getting around them may be the single toughest problem for the international marketer.

The monitoring of competitors' product features, as well as determining what has to be done to meet and beat them, is critical to product-adaptation decisions. Competitive offerings may provide a baseline against which resources can be measured—for example, they may help to determine what it takes to reach a critical market share in a given competitive situation. With a 14 percent share of the Chinese market compared to market leader Lenovo's 28.5 percent share, Hewlett-Packard (HP) adjusted its urban-oriented strategy and marketing to respond to a 2009 Chinese government price rebate program for rural buyers of PCs. Both HP and Lenovo adapted the PCs to function through the electric voltage fluctuations common in rural areas and loaded the machines with software programs such as agricultural databases for farmers.[27]

reverse innovation Refers to an innovation seen first, or likely to be used first, in the developing world before spreading to the industrialized world.

Management must take into account the stage of economic development of the overseas market. As a country's economy advances, buyers are in a better position to buy and to demand more sophisticated products and product versions. Many companies have described how they have adapted to the new global era through a process they call **reverse innovation**. For example, in India, General Electric has developed a handheld electrocardiogram device that it sells for $1,000, about one-tenth of the price of the original (and much bulkier) U.S.-developed machine. Similarly, in China, the company has introduced a portable ultrasound machine with a price tag of $15,000, again vastly cheaper than the model GE used to try to sell to the Chinese market. Both these innovations have not only been successful in emerging markets, but they have also found new customers back in the United States, with ambulance teams and in emergency rooms.[28] There is also a great need to develop new products for people with little money who aspire to a taste of the better life. For example, Tata Motors' $2,200 Nano (a small vehicle analogous to the American SMART car) is specifically designed for India's poor. Similarly, fewer than one in five Indian homes has a refrigerator; thus, a company could attract a huge new group of consumers if it could get the price right. By keeping it small and reducing the number of parts to around 20 instead of the 200 that go into regular refrigerators, Godrej Little Cool Refrigerator has been able to sell it for only $70, which is less than one-third of the price of a regular bottom-of-the-line fridge. It also consumes only half the power, so it keeps electricity bills at a level the poor can afford.[29]

Product Characteristics   Product characteristics are the inherent features of the product offering, whether actual or perceived. The inherent characteristics of products, and the benefits they provide to consumers in the various markets in which they are marketed, make certain products good candidates for standardization—and others not.

The international marketer has to make sure that products do not contain ingredients that might violate legal requirements or religious or social customs. DEP Corporation, a Los Angeles manufacturer with $19 million in annual sales of hair and skin products, takes particular pains to make sure that no Japan-bound products contain formaldehyde, an ingredient commonly used in the United States but illegal in Japan. Where religion or custom determines consumption, ingredients may have to be replaced for the product to be acceptable. In Islamic countries, for example, vegetable shortening has to be substituted for animal fats. In deference to Hindu and Muslim beliefs, McDonald's Maharaja Mac is made with chicken or lamb in India. There is also a vegetarian burger, the McAloo Tikki.

Packaging is an area where firms generally do make modifications. Due to the longer time that products spend in channels of distribution, international companies, especially those marketing food products, have used more expensive packaging materials and/or more expensive transportation modes for export shipments. Food processors have solved the problem by using airtight, reclosable containers that seal out moisture and other contaminants.

The promotional aspect of packaging relates primarily to labeling. The major adjustments concern legally required bilinguality, as in Canada (French and English), Belgium (French and Flemish), and Finland (Finnish and Swedish). Other governmental requirements include more informative labeling of products for consumer protection and education. Inadequate identification, failure to use the required languages, or inadequate or incorrect descriptions printed on the labels may all cause problems. Increasingly, environmental concerns are having an impact on packaging decisions. On the one hand, governments want to reduce the amount of packaging waste by encouraging marketers to adopt the four environmentally correct Rs: redesign, reduce, reuse, and recycle.[30] The EU has strict policies on the amounts of packaging waste that are generated and the levels of recycling of such materials. Depending on the packaging materials (20 percent for plastics and 60 percent for glass), producers, importers, distributors, wholesalers, and retailers are held responsible for generating the waste. In Germany, which has the toughest requirements, all packaging must be reusable or recyclable, and packaging must be kept to a minimum needed for proper protection and marketing of the product. Exporters to the EU must find distributors that can fulfill such requirements and must agree how to split the costs of such compliance.

The product offered in the domestic market may not be operable in the foreign market. One of the major differences faced by appliance manufacturers is electrical power systems. In some cases, variations may exist within a country, such as Brazil. Some companies have adjusted their products to operate in different systems; for example, video equipment can be adjusted to record and play back on different systems.

When a product that is sold internationally requires repairs, parts, or service, the problems of obtaining, training, and holding a sophisticated engineering or repair staff are not easy to solve. If the product breaks down and the repair arrangements are not up to standard, the product image will suffer. In some cases, products abroad may not even be used for their intended purpose and thus may require not only modifications in product configuration but also in service frequency. For instance, snowplows exported from the United States are used to remove sand from driveways in Saudi Arabia.

The country of origin of a product, typically communicated by the phrase "made in (country)," has considerable influence on quality perceptions. The perception of products manufactured in certain countries is affected by a built-in positive or negative assumption about quality. For example, many consumers around the world perceive

Nokia as a Japanese brand, which does not have a negative impact on the company despite the incorrect appropriation, and has led to no action by Nokia. However, a Japanese carmaker, Daihatsu, suffered in the U.S. market at the time of its launch because it was perceived as a Korean brand. For this and other reasons, Daihatsu is no longer in the United States but concentrates its efforts in Latin America. These types of findings indicate that steps must be taken by the international marketer to overcome or at least neutralize biases. The issue is especially important to developing countries that need to increase exports, and for importers who source products from countries different from where they are sold.[31] Some countries have started promotional campaigns to improve their overall images in support of exports and investment.[32]

Company Considerations   Company policy will often determine the presence and degree of adaptation. Discussions of product adaptation often end with the question, "Is it worth it?" The answer depends on the company's ability to control costs, to correctly estimate market potential, and, finally, to secure profitability. The decision to adapt should be preceded by a thorough analysis of the market. Formal market research with primary data collection and/or testing is warranted. From the financial standpoint, some companies have specific return-on-investment levels (e.g., 25 percent) to be satisfied before adaptation. Others let the requirement vary as a function of the market considered and also the time in the market—that is, profitability may be initially compromised for proper market entry.

India is a country of more than a billion people with different cultures, languages, geographies, food habits, traditions, and sociocultural behaviors. No one can successfully do business in India by reading its potential from quantitative market reports. Understanding the psychological, sociological, and historical backgrounds is fundamental to hit the bull's eye. Maggi has managed to enter Indian homes to change the traditional food habits of Indian children based on its promise of convenience. This brand has understood the psychology of Indian mothers and positioned itself for mother–child indulgence. Nokia produced a cell phone with a dust-resistant keypad, anti-slip grip, and a built-in flashlight; truck drivers and rural consumers enjoyed these simple-yet-useful features.[33]

Most companies aim for consistency in their market efforts. This means that all products must fit in terms of quality, price, and user perceptions. Consistency may be difficult to attain, for example, in the area of warranties. Warranties can be uniform only if use conditions do not vary drastically and if the company is able to deliver equally on its promise anywhere it has a presence.

Brand Strategy Decisions

The goal of many marketers currently is to create consistency and impact, both of which are easier to manage with a single worldwide identity.[34] **Global brands** are a key way of reaching this goal (Table 14.3). Global brands are those that reach the world's mega-markets and are perceived as the same brand by consumers and internal constituents.[35] While some of the global brands are completely standardized, some elements of the product may be adapted to local conditions. These adjustments include brand names (e.g., Tide, Whisper, and Clairol in North America are Ariel, Allways, and Wella in Europe), positioning (e.g., Ford Fiesta as a small car in Germany but a family vehicle in Portugal), or product versions sold under the same brand name (e.g., 9 to 13 different types of coffee sold under the Nescafé name in northern Europe alone).[36]

Consumers all over the world associate global brands with three characteristics and evaluate their performance on them when making purchase decisions.[37] Global brands carry a strong quality signal suggested by their success across markets. Part of this is that great brands often represent great ideas and leading-edge technological

global brands Brands that reach the world's mega-markets and are perceived as the same brand by consumers and internal constituents.

Table 14.3 25 Most Valuable Global Brands

Rank			Brand Value ($ Millions)		Country of Ownership
2009	2008	Brand	2009	2008	
1	1	Coca-Cola	$68,734	$66,667	United States
2	2	IBM	60,211	59,031	United States
3	3	Microsoft	56,647	59,007	United States
4	4	GE	47,777	53,086	United States
5	5	Nokia	34,864	35,942	Finland
6	8	McDonald's	32,275	31,049	United States
7	10	Google	31,980	25,590	United States
8	6	Toyota	31,330	34,050	Japan
9	7	Intel	30,636	31,261	United States
10	9	Disney	28,447	29,251	United States
11	12	Hewlett-Packard	24,096	23,509	United States
12	11	Mercedes-Benz	23,867	25,577	Germany
13	14	Gillette	22,841	22,069	United States
14	17	Cisco	22,030	21,306	United States
15	13	BMW	21,671	23,298	Germany
16	16	Louis Vuitton	21,120	21,602	France
17	18	Marlboro	19,010	21,300	United States
18	20	Honda	17,803	19,079	Japan
19	21	Samsung	16,796	17,518	South Korea
20	24	Apple	15,443	13,724	United States
21	22	H&M	15,375	13,840	Sweden
22	15	American Express	14,971	21,940	United States
23	26	Pepsi	13,706	13,249	United States
24	23	Oracle	13,699	13,831	United States
25	28	Néscafe	13,317	13,055	Switzerland

Source: "Best Global Brands," BusinessWeek, September 28, 2009.

solutions. Second, global brands compete on emotion, catering to aspirations that cut across cultural differences. Global brands may cater to needs to feel cosmopolitan, something that local brands cannot deliver. Global brands may also convey that their user has reached a certain status both professionally and personally. This type of recognition represents both perception and reality, enabling brands to establish credibility in markets.[38] The third reason consumers choose global brands is involvement in solving social problems linked to what they are marketing and how they conduct their business. Expectations that global marketers use their monetary and human resources to benefit society are uniform from developed to developing markets.

There are three main implications for the marketing manager to consider:

1. **Don't hide globality.** Given the benefits of globality, marketers should not be shy in communicating this feature of a brand. Creatively this may mean referring to the leadership position of the brand around the world or referring to the extent of innovation or features that are possible only for a brand with considerable reach. Marketers intent on scaling down their brand portfolios and focusing on global offerings are able to invest in more marketing muscle and creative effort behind the sleeker set of offerings.

2. **Tackle home-country bias.** One of the marketing mantras is "being local on a global scale." Because some markets feature substantial preference for home-grown brands, it is imperative to localize some features of the marketing approach, possibly even including the brand name. One approach could be where a brand has a consistent global positioning but the name varies according to

country language. An example is Mr. Clean becoming Mr. Propre in France. Many global brands have already localized to neutralize the home-country effect.

3. **Satisfy the basics.** Global brands signal quality and aspiration. However, taking a global approach to branding is not in itself the critical factor. What is critical is creating differentiation and familiarity as well as the needed margins and growth. The greater esteem that global brands enjoy is not sufficient in itself for pursuing this strategy; however, this dimension may tip the balance in ultimate strategy choice. At the same time, it is evident that globality should not be pursued at the cost of alienating local consumers by preemptively eliminating purely local brands or converging them under a global brand.[39]

Product Counterfeiting

About $250 billion in domestic and export sales are estimated to be lost by companies worldwide annually because of product counterfeiting and trademark patent infringement of consumer and industrial products.[40] The hardest hit are software, entertainment, and pharmaceutical sectors. Counterfeit goods are any goods bearing an unauthorized representation of a trademark, patented invention, or copyrighted work that is legally protected in the country where it is marketed.

The practice of product counterfeiting has spread to high technology and services from the traditionally counterfeited products: high-visibility, strong brand-name consumer goods. In addition, a new dimension has emerged to complicate the situation. Previously, the only concern was whether a firm's product was being counterfeited; now, management has to worry about whether raw materials and components purchased for production are themselves real.

Four types of action that can be taken against counterfeiting are legislative action, bilateral and multilateral negotiations, joint private sector action, and measures taken by individual firms. Governments have enacted special legislation and set country-specific negotiation objectives for reciprocity and retaliatory options for intellectual property protection.[41]

In today's environment, firms are taking more aggressive steps to protect themselves. Victimized firms are not only losing sales but also goodwill in the longer term if customers, believing they are getting the real product, unknowingly end up with a copy of inferior quality. In addition to the normal measures of registering trademarks and copyrights, firms are taking steps in product development to prevent the copying of trademarked goods. For example, new authentication materials in labeling are virtually impossible to duplicate. Jointly, companies have formed organizations to lobby for legislation and to act as information clearinghouses.

PRICING POLICY

Pricing is the only element in the marketing mix that is revenue generating; all of the others are costs. It should therefore be used as an active instrument of strategy in the major areas of marketing decision making. Pricing in the international environment is more complicated than in the domestic market, however, because of such factors as government influence, different currencies, and additional costs. International pricing situations can be divided into four general categories: export pricing, foreign market pricing, price coordination, and intracompany, or transfer, pricing.

Export Pricing

Three general price-setting strategies in international marketing are a standard worldwide price; dual pricing, which differentiates between domestic and export prices; and market-differentiated pricing.[42] The first two are cost-oriented pricing methods that are relatively simple to establish, are easy to understand, and cover all of the necessary costs. **Standard worldwide pricing** is based on average unit costs of fixed, variable, and export-related costs.

In **dual pricing**, domestic and export prices are differentiated, and two approaches are available: the **cost-plus method** and the **marginal cost method** The cost-plus strategy involves the actual costs, that is, a full allocation of domestic and foreign costs to the product. Although this type of pricing ensures margins, the final price may put the product beyond the reach of the customer. As a result, some exporters resort to flexible cost-plus strategy, wherein discounts are provided when necessary as a result of customer type, intensity of competition, or size of order. The marginal cost method considers the direct costs of producing and selling for export as the floor beneath which prices cannot be set. Fixed costs for plants, R&D, domestic overhead, and domestic marketing costs are disregarded. An exporter can thus lower export prices to be competitive in markets that otherwise might have been considered beyond access.

On the other hand, **market-differentiated pricing** is based on a demand-oriented strategy and is thus more consistent with the marketing concept. This method also allows consideration of competitive forces in setting export price. The major problem is the exporter's perennial dilemma: lack of information. Therefore, in most cases, marginal costs provide a basis for competitive comparisons, on which the export price is set.

In preparing a quotation, the exporter must be careful to take into account unique export-related costs and, if possible, include them. They are in addition to the normal costs shared with the domestic side. They include:

1. The cost incurred in modifying the good for foreign markets.
2. Operational costs of the export operation. Examples are personnel, market research, additional shipping and insurance costs, communications costs with foreign customers, and overseas promotional costs.
3. Costs incurred in entering foreign markets. These include tariffs and taxes; risks associated with a buyer in a different market (mainly commercial credit risks and political risks); and dealing in other than the exporter's domestic currency—that is, foreign exchange risk.

The combined effect of both clear-cut and hidden costs results in export prices far in excess of domestic prices. This is called **price escalation**. Management must take into account the stage of economic development and buying power of the market. For example, Nestlé was able to double the sales of their Bono cookies in Brazil after shrinking the package from 200 grams to 140 grams with a commensurate price decrease.[43] Economic conditions may shift rapidly, thus warranting change in the product or the product line. In the midst of the global economic recession in 2009, Avon switched its product emphasis to its lower-priced "smart value" products.[44] The exporter has many alternatives under these circumstances, such as stretching out payment terms, cutting prices, or bringing scaled-down, more affordable products to the affected markets.[45]

Inexpensive imports often trigger accusations of **dumping**—that is, selling goods overseas for less than in the exporter's home market, at a price below the cost of production, or both. Dumping ranges from predatory to unintentional. Predatory dumping is the tactic of a foreign firm that intentionally sells at a loss in another country to increase its market share at the expense of domestic producers. This amounts to an international price war. Unintentional dumping is the result of time lags between the date of sales transactions, shipment, and arrival. Prices, including exchange rates, can change in such a way that the final sales price is below the cost of production or below the price prevailing in the exporter's home market.

---

standard worldwide pricing Price-setting strategy based on average unit costs of fixed, variable, and export-related costs.

dual pricing Price-setting strategy in which the export price and domestic price are differentiated.

cost-plus method A pricing policy in which there is a full allocation of foreign and domestic costs to the product.

marginal cost method This method considers the direct costs of producing and selling goods for export as the floor beneath which prices cannot be set.

market-differentiated pricing Price-setting strategy based on demand rather than cost.

price escalation The establishing of export prices far in excess of domestic prices—often due to a long distribution channel and frequent markups.

dumping Selling goods overseas at a price lower than in the exporter's home market, or at a price below the cost of production, or both.

In the United States, domestic producers may petition the government to impose antidumping duties on imports alleged to be dumped. The remedy is a duty equal to the dumping margin. International agreements and U.S. law provide for countervailing duties. They may be imposed on imports that are found to be subsidized by foreign governments. They are designed to offset the advantages imports would otherwise receive from the subsidy.

Foreign Market Pricing

Pricing within the individual markets in which the firm operates is determined by (1) corporate objectives, (2) costs, (3) customer behavior and market conditions, (4) market structure, and (5) environmental constraints. All of these factors vary from country to country, and pricing policies of the multinational corporation must vary as well. As the Danone example in Focus on Management illustrates, marketers can respond to changing market conditions with carefully calibrated price

---

FOCUS ON MANAGEMENT

Danone's Price Reset

Fluctuations in commodity pricing can create havoc in consumer markets for food companies with the price of some packaged goods brands occasionally rising above broad consumer acceptance. This situation became apparent to Danone in the dairy business in 2008. Beginning in the second half of 2007, commodity milk prices rose dramatically, reaching a peak in early 2008 before eventually declining at the end of 2008. With the global economy deteriorating, Danone was facing significant challenges in maintaining dairy product revenue streams in 2009.

With sales revenues declining, Danone initiated a program of price cuts, advertising, packaging revisions, new-product introductions, and consumer promotion to boost volume growth in international markets. Referred to internally as "the price reset program," Danone launched a broad marketing initiative behind brands in its health and fresh dairy business such as Activia, Danacol, Danette, Actimel, Danonino, and NutriDay in countries like Poland, Hungary, Germany, France, Ukraine, Mexico, and the United States. For Danone in 2008, the major European markets represented more than half of dairy product sales, while the United States and other Western Hemisphere countries accounted for another 25 percent. Based on success in the early markets, Danone extended the program to other countries like Spain and Russia.

A key element of the price reset program was the use of advertising to create broad consumer awareness. In addition to lowered prices, the program also involved tactics in some countries such as a switch from sampling to couponing and the use of hard discounts for six-packs of products like Danette in France.

The program worked with sales of Danone's dairy products increasing 7 percent in volume in the third quarter of 2009, the group's largest increase since mid-2007. Activia resumed strong growth particularly in Germany, the United States, and Brazil, while Actimel realized strong performance in France and Spain. "We gained market share in the three quarters of our markets," said Peter Andre Térisse, Danone's CFO.

Danone yogurt

Sources: Thompson Reuters, Q3 2009 Danone Earnings Conference Call Transcript, October 23, 2009; Emmanuel Faber presentation, Barclay's Capital Back-to-School Conference, September 9–10, 2009; Franck Ribaud presentation, Sanford Bernstein Strategic Decisions Conference, September 15, 2009; Reuters, Danone: Third Quarter and Nine Month Sales 2009, October 23, 2009; www.danone.com, accessed November 13, 2009.

adjustments in individual countries accompanied and integrated with other elements of the marketing mix. Despite arguments in favor of uniform pricing in multinational markets, price discrimination is an essential characteristic of the pricing policies of firms conducting business in differing markets. In a study of 42 U.S.-based multinational corporations, the major problem areas they reported in making pricing decisions were meeting competition, cost, lack of competitive information, distribution and channel factors, and governmental barriers.[46]

Studies have shown that non-U.S. based companies allow their U.S. subsidiaries considerable freedom in pricing due to the size and unique features of the market. Further, it has been argued that these subsidiaries control the North American market and that distances create a natural barrier against arbitrage practices (i.e., customers going for the lowest price) that would be more likely to emerge in Europe. However, many argue that price coordination has to be worldwide as a result of increasing levels of economic integration efforts around the world.

Price Coordination

The issue of standard worldwide pricing may be mostly a theoretical one because of the influence of environments, but if standardization is sought, it relates more to price levels and the use of pricing as a positioning tool.

Calls for price coordination have increased, especially after the introduction of the euro in 16 EU countries. The single currency will make prices completely transparent for all buyers. If discrepancies are not justifiable due to market differences such as consumption preferences, competition, or government interference, cross-border purchases will occur. The simplest solution would be to have one euro-based price throughout the market. However, given significant differences up to 100 percent, that solution would lead to significant losses in sales and/or profits, as a single price would likely be closer to the lower-priced countries' level. The recommended approach is a pricing corridor that considers existing country-specific prices while optimizing the profits at a pan-European level.[47] Such a corridor defines the maximum and minimum prices that a country organization can charge—enough to allow flexibility as a result of differences in price elasticities and competition, but not enough to attract people to engage in cross-border shopping that starts at price differences of 20 percent or higher.[48] This approach moves pricing authority away from country managers to regional management and requires changes in management systems and incentive structures.

Significant price gaps lead to the emergence of **gray markets**/parallel importation. The term refers to brand-name imports that enter a country legally but outside regular, authorized distribution channels. The industrial technology (IT) industry estimates that gray market sales of IT products account for more than $40 billion in revenue each year, collectively costing IT manufacturers up to $5 billion annually in lost profits.[49] The gray market is fueled by companies that sell goods in foreign markets at prices that are far lower than prices charged to, for example, U.S. distributors, and by one strong currency, such as the dollar or the yen. The gray market has flourished in mobile phones, cars, watches, and even baby powder, cameras, and chewing gum. This phenomenon not only harms the company financially but also may harm its reputation, because authorized distributors often refuse to honor warranties on items bought through the gray market. Cars bought through the gray market in the United States, for example, may not pass EPA inspections and thus may cause major expense to the unsuspecting buyer.[50]

The proponents of gray marketing argue for their right to "free trade" by pointing to manufacturers who are both overproducing and overpricing in some markets. The main beneficiaries are consumers, who benefit from lower prices, and discount

gray market Marketing of products through unauthorized channels.

distributors, who now have access to the good. Companies can combat gray marketing through strategic interference. For example, companies can make sure authorized dealers do not engage in transshipments. Companies can also promote the deficiencies in gray-marketed goods, which may not carry a full warranty or after-sales service.[51]

Transfer Pricing

Transfer, or intracompany, pricing is the pricing of sales to members of the corporate family. The overall competitive and financial position of the firm forms the basis of any pricing policy. In this, transfer pricing plays a key role. Intracorporate sales can easily change consolidated global results because they often are one of the most important ongoing decision areas in a company.

arm's length price A price that unrelated parties would have reached.

Four main transfer-pricing possibilities have emerged over time: (1) transfer at direct cost; (2) transfer at direct cost plus additional expenses; (3) transfer at a price derived from end-market prices; and (4) transfer at an **arm's length price**, or the price that unrelated parties would have reached on the same transaction. Doing business overseas requires coping with complexities of environmental peculiarities, the effect of which can be alleviated by manipulating transfer prices. Factors that call for adjustments include taxes, import duties, inflationary tendencies, unstable governments, and other regulations.[52] For example, high transfer prices on goods shipped to a subsidiary and low ones on goods imported from it will result in minimizing the tax liability of a subsidiary operating in a country with a high income tax. Tax liability thus results not only from the absolute tax rate but also from differences in how income is computed. On the other hand, a higher transfer price may have an effect on the import duty, especially if it is assessed on an ad valorem basis. Exceeding a certain threshold may boost the duty substantially and thus have a negative impact on the subsidiary's posture.

Quite often the multinational corporation is put in a difficult position. U.S. authorities may think the transfer price is too low, whereas the foreign entity (especially a less-developed country) may perceive it to be too high. Since 1991, the Internal Revenue Service has been signing "advance pricing" agreements (APAs) with multinational corporations to stem the tide of unpaid U.S. income taxes. By 2009, a total of 841 such agreements were completed and 123 were under negotiation. Since 1998, special provisions have been made for small and medium-sized companies to negotiate such arrangements.[53]

In the host environments, the concern of the multinational corporation is to maintain its status as a good corporate citizen. Many corporations, in drafting multinational codes of conduct, have specified that intracorporate pricing will follow the arm's length principle. Multinationals have also been found to closely abide by tax regulations governing transfer pricing.[54] The OECD has issued transfer pricing guidelines including methodology and documentation scenarios to assist in the compliance process.[55]

DISTRIBUTION POLICY

Channels of distribution provide the essential links that connect producers and customers. The channel decision is the longest term of the marketing mix decisions in that it cannot be readily changed. In addition, it involves relinquishing some of the control the firm has over the marketing of its products. The two factors make choosing the right channel structure a crucial decision. Properly structured and staffed, the distribution system will function more as one rather than as a collection of often quite different units.

Channel Design

channel design The length and width of the distribution channel.

The term *channel design* refers to the length and width of the channel employed. **Channel design** is determined by factors that can be summarized as the 11 Cs:

customer, culture, competition, company, character, capital, cost, coverage, control, continuity, and communication. While there are no standard answers to channel design, the international marketer can use the 11 Cs as a checklist to determine the proper approach to reach target audiences before selecting channel members to fill the roles. The first three factors are givens in that the company must adjust its approach to the existing structures. The other eight are controllable to a certain extent by the marketer.

1. Customers   The demographic and psychographic characteristics of targeted *customers* will form the basis for channel-design decisions. Answers to questions such as what customers need as well as why, when, and how they buy are used to determine ways in which products should be made available to generate a competitive advantage. In the three rapidly growing cities of Mumbai, Rio de Janeiro, and Accra (Ghana), Nokia's design team set up open studios where members of the local community could sketch their dream phones. The team gleaned information on participants' tastes, styles, personalities, professions, religions, sense of heritage, and communities.

2. Culture   The marketer must analyze existing channel structures, or what might be called the distribution *culture* of a market. Many believed small retail players in Latin America would be swept away by the sector's consolidation and the rapid entry of new hypermarkets and supermarkets, as was the case in the United States and Europe, where small retailers have retained only 10 to 20 percent of the consumer packaged-goods market as large retailers have grown. So far, this has not occurred in Latin America. Small-scale independent supermarkets and traditional stores together still account for between 45 and 61 percent of consumer-goods retailing in Latin American countries.

3. Competition   Channels used by *competitors* may make up the only distribution system that is accepted both by the trade and by consumers. In this case, the international marketer's task is to use the structure more effectively and efficiently. Wal-Mart's investments outside North America have had mixed results: its operations in the United Kingdom, South America, and China are highly successful, while it was forced to pull out of Germany and South Korea when ventures there were unsuccessful. An alternate strategy is to use a totally different distribution approach from the competition and hope to develop a competitive advantage in that manner as IKEA has been able to do with its use of supermarketing concepts in furniture retail.

4. Company Objectives   Sometimes, management goals may conflict with the best possible channel design. Fast-food chains have typically rushed into newly opened markets to capitalize on the development. The companies have attempted to establish mass sales as soon as possible by opening numerous restaurants in the

H&M store in Japan

busiest sections of several cities. Unfortunately, control has proven to be quite difficult because of the sheer number of openings over a relatively short period of time. Starbucks invests very little capital in international expansion ($\leq$5 percent of revenue), and local partners bear all business risk.

5. Character The type or *character* of the good will have an impact on the design of the channel. Rules of thumb aside, particular products may be distributed in a number of ways even to the same target audience for the PC industry. A dual channel may be used in which both intermediaries and a direct contact with customers are used. In some cases, a channel may extend beyond having one tier of distributors and resellers to include importers or agents. Another alternative—hybrid channels—features sharing of marketing functions, with the manufacturer handling promotion and customer generation, and the intermediaries handling sales and distribution. The hybrid strategy is based more on cooperation and partnership, while the dual channel may result in conflict if disagreements arise as to who is to handle a specific customer. In either case, multiple channels are used to enhance sales performance in a foreign market.

6. Capital The term *capital* is used to describe the financial requirements in setting up a channel system. The international marketer's financial strength will determine the type of channel and the basis on which channel relationships will be built. The stronger the marketer's finances, the more able the firm is to establish channels it either owns or controls. Intermediaries' requirements for beginning inventories, selling on a consignment basis, preferential loans, and need for training will all have an impact on the type of approach chosen by the international marketer. Coca-Cola, which usually visits its smallest retailers once or twice weekly, has proposed that these retailers receive three to four weeks of consigned inventory in return for exclusivity. When Coca-Cola returns at the end of the period, the retailers pay only for the product sold during that time. For cash-strapped small shop owners, this is extremely attractive. Coca-Cola wins increased sales at the expense of displaced competition and a much lower cost-to-serve, with delivery visits cut by a factor of three or more.

7. Cost Closely related to the capital dimension is *cost*—that is, the expenditure incurred in maintaining a channel once it is established. Costs will naturally vary over the life cycle of the relationship as well as over the life cycle of the product marketed. An example of the costs involved is promotional monies spent by a distributor for the marketer's product. Costs may also be incurred in protecting the company's distributors against adverse market conditions. A number of European manufacturers helped their distributors maintain competitive prices through subsidies when the high rate for the U.S. dollar caused pricing problems.

8. Coverage The term *coverage* is used to describe both the number of areas in which the marketer's products are represented and the quality of that representation. Coverage, therefore, is two-dimensional in that both horizontal and vertical coverage need to be considered in channel design. The number of areas to be covered depends on the dispersion of demand in the market and also the time elapsed since the product's introduction to the market. A company typically enters a market with one local distributor, but, as volume expands, the distribution base often has to be adjusted. Benetton's plan was abandoned because of concerns about oversaturation of certain urban areas and overprojection of retail sales. Rather, more emphasis is being put on customer service, and the number of stores in major North American cities was 50 in 2009.

9. Control The use of intermediaries will automatically lead to loss of some *control* over the marketing of the firm's products. The looser the relationship is between the marketer and the intermediaries, the less control can be exerted. The longer the channel, the more difficult it becomes for the marketer to have a final say over pricing, promotion, and the types of outlets in which the product will be made available. Sales at TaoBao, China's largest online retailer, have soared to more than $14 billion annually since it was launched in 2003. Lancôme reports that its partnership with Baidu, China's largest search engine, helped lift online sales in China by 30 percent. And Amway has become one of China's largest consumer packaged-goods companies by selling its products door-to-door through a network of 300,000 sales representatives.[56]

10. Continuity Nurturing *continuity* rests heavily on the marketer because foreign distributors may have a more short-term view of the relationship. For example, Japanese wholesalers believe that it is important for manufacturers to follow up initial success with continuous improvement of the product. If such improvements are not forthcoming, competitors are likely to enter the market with similar, but lower-priced, products and the wholesalers of the imported product will turn to the Japanese suppliers.[57]

11. Communication Proper communication will perform important roles for the international marketer. It will help convey the marketer's goals to the distributors, help solve conflict situations, and aid in the overall marketing of the product. Communication is a two-way process that does not permit the marketer to dictate to intermediaries. Sometimes the planned program may not work because of a lack of communication. Prices may not be competitive; promotional materials may be obsolete or inaccurate and not well received overall. It is for this reason that Dell formed the company Customer Experience Council, a group that is scrutinizing every aspect of how Dell interacts with customers.[58]

Selection and Screening of Intermediaries

Once the basic design of the channel has been determined, the international marketer must begin a search to fill the defined roles with the best available candidates. Choices will have to be made within the framework of the company's overall philosophy on distributors versus agents, as well as whether the company will use an indirect or direct approach to foreign markets.

Firms that have successful international distribution attest to the importance of finding top representatives. For companies such as Loctite, whose adhesives require high levels of technical selling skills, only the best distributors in a given market will do. The undertaking should be held in the same regard as recruiting and hiring within the company because an ineffective foreign distributor can set you back years; it is almost better to have no distributor than a bad one in a major market.

Various sources exist to assist the marketer in locating intermediary candidates. One of the easiest and most economical ways is to use the service of governmental agencies. The U.S. Department of Commerce has various services that can assist firms in identifying suitable representatives abroad; some have been designed specifically for that purpose. A number of private sources are also available to the international marketer. Trade directories, such as those by Dun & Bradstreet (D&B), usually list foreign representatives geographically and by product classification. D&B's products and services are drawn from a global database of more than 130 million companies. It maintains global data coverage on business records in more than 190 countries. Telephone directories, especially the yellow page sections or editions, can provide distributor lists. Although not detailed, the listings will give addresses and an indication of the products sold. The firm can solicit the support of some of its facilitating agencies, such as banks, advertising agencies, shipping lines, and airlines. The marketer can take an even more direct approach by buying advertising space to

Figure 14.3   Providers of International Intermediary Information

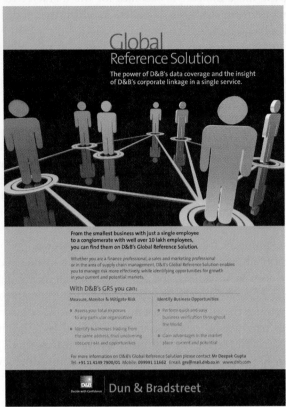

Source: Courtesy of the U.S. Commercial Service (http://www.usatrade.gov); copyright © Dun & Bradstreet and The Guild Group.

solicit representation. The advertisements typically indicate the type of support the marketer will be able to give to its distributor.

Intermediaries can be screened on their performance and professionalism. An intermediary's performance can be evaluated on the basis of financial standing and sales as well as the likely fit it would provide in terms of its existing product lines and coverage. Professionalism can be assessed through reputation and overall standing in the business community. Information on these dimensions can be secured either from governmental or private-sector sources as shown in Figure 14.3.

Managing the Channel Relationship

A channel relationship can be likened to a marriage in that it brings together two independent entities that have shared goals. For the relationship to work, each party has to be open about its expectations and openly communicate changes perceived in the other's behavior that might be contrary to the agreement. A framework for managing channel relationships is provided in Table 14.4.

The complicating factors that separate the two parties fall into three categories: ownership, geographic and cultural distance, and different rules of law. Rather than lament their existence, both parties must take strong action to remedy them. Often the first major step is for both parties to acknowledge that differences exist.

E-Commerce

e-commerce The ability to offer goods and services over the Web.

E-commerce, the ability to offer goods and services over the Web, continues to experience rapid growth around the globe as Internet penetration has increased.

Table 14.4 Managing Relations with Overseas Distributors

High Export Performance Inhibitors ———→	Bring ———————→	Remedy Lies In
Separate ownership	• Divided loyalties • Seller-buyer atmosphere • Unclear future intentions	Offering good incentives, helpful support schemes, discussing plans frankly, and interacting in a mutually beneficial way
Geographic and cultural separation	• Communication blocks • Negative attitudes toward foreigners • Physical distribution strains	Making judicious use of two-way visits, establishing a well-managed communication program
Different rules of law	• Vertical trading restrictions • Dismissal difficulties	Complying fully with the law, drafting a strong distributor agreement

Source: Adapted from Philip J. Rosson, "Source Factors in Manufacture–Overseas Distributor Relationships in International Marketing," in Erdener Kaynak, ed., *International Marketing Management* (New York: Praeger, 1984), 95.

Global Internet penetration grew at a rate of 380 percent from 2000 to 2009, with further penetration projected as relatively inexpensive mobile 3G devices allow more access in developing countries. This, in turn, has facilitated, the growth of **m-commerce**, the exchange of goods and services via the use of smart mobile handheld devices that allow Web browsing. In 2009, Internet penetration in North America exceeded all other regions at 74.2 percent, followed by Oceania/Australia at 60.4 percent and Europe at 52 percent. Latin America (30.5 percent), Asia (19.4 percent), and Africa (6.8 percent) lag behind, but Asia exceeds all other regions in Internet users with 42.6 percent of the worldwide total.[59] As shown in Table 14.5, worldwide e-commerce revenue is projected to grow at a rate of 18 percent between 2008 and 2013, with the fasted rates of growth occurring in Japan, Asia-Pacific, and in parts of the world outside of the United States and western Europe. The United States, however, is projected to remain the largest market for e-commerce, followed by western Europe.

Many companies entering e-commerce choose to use marketplace sites, like eBay, that bring together buyers, sellers, distributors, and transaction payment processors in one single marketplace, making convenience the key attraction. Amazon.com has broadened its offerings from books and music to include tools, clothing, shows, jewelry, health and beauty, and electronics among others. Walmart.com has 1,000,000 products available online and continues to develop new online services such as music downloads and photo developing. For companies that choose to operate their own e-commerce sites, transaction payment processors like PayPal offer services to facilitate payments around the world. In 2009, PayPal opened its global

m-commerce Any transaction involving the transfer of ownership or rights to use goods and services, which is initiated and/or completed by using mobile access to computer-mediated networks with the help of an electronic device.

Table 14.5 Worldwide E-Commerce Revenue by Region ($ billions)

	2009	2011	2013	CAGR (%)
Worldwide	$8,016,573,619,602	$11,652,895,721,406	$15,941,552,833,377	18.0
United States	$2,907,434,372,206	$4,104,922,634,218	$5,223,773,311,655	15.3
Western Europe	$2,639,388,626,919	$3,448,263,278,747	$4,185,002,407,239	11.8
Rest of World	$582,398,213,596	$1,032,304,996,534	$1,841,525,754,972	32.1
Japan	$711,473,814,527	$1,186,456,656,559	$1,862,455,335,939	26.3
Asia-Pacific	$1,175,878,592,355	$1,880,948,155,348	$2,828,796,023,572	23.9
Share of business-to-business market	$90.1	$90.6	$90.9	

Source: IDC's Worldwide Digital Marketplace Model and Forecast, November 2009.

payments platform with capabilities that include currency conversion and mobile applications.[60]

To fully serve the needs of its customers via e-commerce, the company itself must be prepared to provide 24-hour order taking and customer service; have the regulatory and customs-handling expertise to deliver internationally; and have an in-depth understanding of marketing environments, as well as customer habits and preferences, for the further development of the business relationship. The instantaneous interactivity users experience will also be translated into an expectation of expedient delivery of answers and products ordered. Many people living outside the United States, who purchase online expect U.S.-style service. However, in many cases, these shoppers may find that shipping is not even available.

The challenges faced in terms of response and delivery capabilities can be overcome through outsourcing services or by building international distribution networks. Air express carriers, such as FedEx and UPS, offer full-service packages that leverage their own Internet infrastructure with customs clearance and e-mail shipment notification. If a company needs help in order fulfillment and customer support, logistics centers offer warehousing and inventory management services as well as same-day delivery from in-country stocks. UPS, for example, has 901 supply chain facilities in more than 120 countries and serves more than 200 countries and territories.[61] Some companies elect to build their own international distribution networks, especially as they open country-specific web sites. Amazon.com, for example, now has country web sites in the United States, the United Kingdom, Germany, France, Japan, China, and Canada. As the company broadens its product categories, it will require additional facilities to fulfill the orders generated locally more quickly and cheaply. As of 2009, Amazon was offering free shipping options in each of these countries except Canada and China.

Transactions and the information they provide about the buyer allows for greater customization and for service by region, market, or even by individual customer. Dell Computer does 30 percent of its business via the Web; this adds up to $18 million worth of hardware, software, and accessories per day. Dell offers thousands of its corporate customers a premier page site with procurement and support designed to save these customers money with their IT process. Iglu.com, a leading U.K. online ski holiday retailer, needed to ensure that its main database, containing details of availability and pricing from more than 200 suppliers, could scale up to cope at times of peak traffic. Its existing technology was struggling to process customer searches quickly enough and the company was concerned that this would inevitably have an impact on its profitability. Iglu can buy products directly from Dell, so it does not have to waste time dealing with third-party resellers. It could have been complicated working with Microsoft, Intel, and Dell together, but communication between the companies was seamless.[62]

Although English was originally perceived as the *lingua franca* of the Web, increased global Internet penetration has made localization of web content and e-commerce a requirement. In targeting international markets, it is prudent to use a company located in the specific geographic area, as seen in Focus on e-Business. It has been shown that web users are three times more likely to buy when the offering is made in their own language.[63] True to the marketing concept, smart marketers will seek to customize commercial web sites to meet customer convenience and ease-of-use needs in different countries, starting with language localization. Numerous service providers can assist international businesses with this process, and reliable localization guidance can be found at the Localization Industry Standards Association, www.lisa.org, or the Globalization and Localization Association, www.gala-global.org.

The marketer has to be sensitive to the governmental role in e-commerce with regard to local regulations and taxation implications. Some countries require businesses to have a "permanent establishment" or taxable entity established before they will hold the company responsible for taxes. The U.S. Commercial Services offers good counsel for prospective international online merchants: "Electronically delivered goods should be treated like any other sale to a foreign customer. It generally is the responsibility of the customer/importer to declare their purchase and pay any taxes." In addition, marketers should anticipate that a foreign country may require value-added taxes (VATs) on sales. For example, the EU requires that e-commerce merchants must register with tax authorities in their member-states and comply with the VAT regime and rates where the customer is located.[64]

Privacy issues have grown exponentially as a result of e-business as businesses collect and process personally identifiable information. Many countries, including the United States and the member-states of the European Union, have specific privacy laws requiring strict compliance by online businesses. In 1998, the EU passed a Directive on Data Protection that introduced high standards of data privacy to ensure the free flow of data throughout its member-states. Each individual has the right to review personal data, correct them, and limit their use. But, and more important, the directive also requires member-states to block transmission of data to countries, including the United States, if those countries' domestic legislation does not provide an adequate level of protection.

The comprehensive requirements of the EU directive involved particularly restrictive government approval of databases and data processing, which can pose significant barriers for non-EU firms. To avoid these barriers, the U.S. Department of Commerce and the European Commission created a "safe harbor" process that allows participating companies a simpler and easier means of complying with the requirements of the directive. Information on "safe harbor" can be found at http://www.export.gov/safeharbor/. In addition, in 2009, the United States and Switzerland completed negotiations on a U.S.–Swiss Safe Harbor data protection framework.

For industries such as music and motion pictures, the Internet has proven to be both an opportunity and a threat. The Web provides a new efficient method of distribution and customization of products that has been enthusiastically embraced by music and film lovers. At the same time, it can be a channel for intellectual property violation through unauthorized distribution methods that threaten the revenue streams to artists and creative industries.[65]

PROMOTIONAL POLICY

The international marketer must choose a proper combination of the various promotional tools—advertising, personal selling, sales promotion, and publicity—to create images among the intended target audience. The choice will depend on the target audience, company objectives, the product or service marketed, the resources available for the endeavor, and the availability of promotional tools in a particular market. The focus may not only be on a product or service but the company's overall image.

Advertising

The key decision-making areas in advertising are (1) media strategy, (2) the promotional message, and (3) the organization of the promotional program.

Media strategy is applied to the selection of media vehicles and the development of a media schedule. Worldwide media spending, which totaled approximately $494 billion in 2008, varies dramatically around the world.[66] The largest media spenders in 2008 were Procter & Gamble ($9.7 billion), Unilever ($5.7 billion), L'Oréal ($4.0 billion), General Motors ($3.7 billion), Toyota ($3.2 billion), Coca-Cola ($2.7 billion), Johnson & Johnson ($2.6 billion), and Ford ($2.4 billion). The top 100 global advertisers spent 62 percent of their measured media spending outside

media strategy Strategy applied to the selection of media vehicles and the development of a media schedule.

The International Pay-per-Click Market

Pay-per-click (PPC) is an Internet advertising model used on search engines, advertising networks, and content web sites (such as blogs), where advertisers only pay when a user actually clicks on an advertisement to visit the advertisers' web sites. It has become a battlefield between global players and their local challengers.

China

In China, e-commerce and online payment platforms are well developed and have a large number of users. The numbers will soon surpass U.S. figures, and in 2008 alone, Chinese marketers continued to grow spending at approximately 8 percent. The Chinese search engine market is expected to see a compound annual growth of 30+ percent from 2006 to 2010. Within ten years, China is expected to be the most important online ad and commerce market in the world. In China, Baidu is considered the leading search engine. Market shares for 2008 are Baidu, 60.9 percent; Google, 27 percent; and Sogou, 3.1 percent.

Baidu's early success is attributed to its MP3 search engine. With Baidu, there are various well-known controversies regarding corruption. One of the big ones is that strong players must have strong governmental relations—which may translate to foreign companies (like Google) never having equal footing in the Chinese market. With Baidu, issues related to poor search quality have also been documented.

Japan

Japan has one of the highest Internet penetrations worldwide at 67.7 percent (with the United States at approximately 70 percent). Japan has approximately $5.7 billion in the online advertising market out of a global market estimated at $45 billion. By 2011, Internet advertising is projected to grow to $7.5 billion, including $1.28 billion for mobile ads and $2.26 billion for PPC ads. In Japan, Yahoo! is predominant. The Japanese market share breakdown is Yahoo!, 56.5 percent; and Google, 33.7 percent.

In January 2009, searchers in Japan conducted an average of 100 searches per searcher during the month. Yahoo! sites captured 51 percent of all search queries, followed by Google sites with 38 percent and Rakuten Inc. with 2 percent.

Yahoo! sites had the highest frequency of searches per searcher at 62, followed by Google sites at 55 searches per searcher. In terms of search volume, one can only speculate as Japanese search engines do not disclose search volume figures. In Japan, more than half of the Internet users access the Web via mobile devices. Japan is ranked number three in terms of total Web population at 94 million. This is the same as the Web populations of Germany and the United Kingdom combined.

Russia

Internet penetration in Russia is about 25 percent. The Russian Internet market has been experiencing rapid development, with its audience growing 25 percent during the past year. In Russia, search-related ads revenue is expected to rise from $200 million in 2007 to approximately $1 billion by 2010. In Russia, the largest search engine is called the Yandex (contained within a Web portal). The two predominant players in the Russian market are Yandex, 47.4 percent, and Google, 34 percent. In 2006, Google had a 5 percent market share and has since managed to capture one-third of the Russian paid search market.

Marketing Considerations for International PPC

In targeting international markets, it is prudent to use a company located in the specific geographic area. A company with "boots on the ground" will have knowledge of language, culture, and marketing jargon and will be able to localize content and not just translate it from one language to another.

Currently, there are good deals to be had in other countries. For example, click costs are cheaper on the Yandex and Baidu than on Google in the United States and United Kingdom. In markets like China and Russia, the government is an important consideration because both countries have been known to interfere in business. Having said this, China's government seems to be encouraging and supporting Internet- and technology-related industries.

Sources: "Yahoo! Attracts More Than Half of All Searches Conducted in Japan in January 2009," *comScore*, March 10, 2009; Mona Elesseily, "Getting to Know International PPC Markets," *Search Engine Land*, November 3, 2008, available at http://searchengineland.com/getting-to-know-international-ppc-markets-14955.php; and Nick Wilsdon, ed., Global Search Report 2007, available at http://www.e3internet.com/downloads/global-search-report-2007.pdf.

the United States. In 2009, advertising spending decreased dramatically, with some estimates identifying a drop of approximately 10 percent. Remarkably, the top 100 global advertisers actually increased spending slightly in 2008, which may be a sign that sophisticated marketing companies do not cut media spending in a recession as much as their less marketing-oriented counterparts.[67]

In 2008, the United States remained the largest single media market in the world, with $170 billion in measured media spending. The other large media markets were

Japan ($44.9 billion), Germany ($27.5 billion), the United Kingdom ($22.8 billion), and China ($18.9 billion).[68] China is increasingly the emerging market of choice, although it only represents 3 to 4 percent of total spending. Five global marketers—Procter & Gamble, Yum Brands, Pernod Ricard, Avon Products, and Colgate-Palmolive—already invest more than 10 percent of their budgets in China.[69]

The makeup of media spending varies considerably by region and market. For example, television is projected to retain 61.4 percent of media spending in Latin America and 57.8 percent in central and eastern Europe in 2011, compared to only 30.2 percent in western Europe, 34.9 percent in North America, and 41.1 percent in Asia-Pacific. Television is projected to remain very dominant in some individual countries like Serbia (82.8 percent), Slovakia (79 percent), and Ecuador (77 percent), as opposed to countries like Denmark (17.2 percent) and Finland (19.7 percent). While radio remains an important medium in some markets like Canada, the United States, and New Zealand, its share of spending is generally below 15 percent in each country. However, radio is projected to grow in Colombia (24.9 percent) and the Philippines (23.7 percent) by 2011. Internet advertising is the fastest-growing major media category and is projected to attain even more significant market share in some European and Asian countries by 2011, like Denmark (29.5 percent), the United Kingdom (27 percent), Japan (21.6 percent), and Taiwan (22 percent). Print advertising has been diminishing in its share of advertising due to the growth of digital media. Nonetheless, newspaper advertising is projected to retain 27.7 percent of measured media advertising spending in western Europe and 21.8 percent in Asia-Pacific by 2011, compared to 19.1 percent in North America and 16 percent in Latin America. In central and eastern Europe, where advertising supported newspapers do not have a long tradition, newspaper advertising is projected to account for only 8.5 percent of media spending in 2011.[70]

Media regulations also vary. Some regulations include limits on the amount of time available for advertisements; in the EU, for example, the Audiovisual Media Services Directive (AVMSD) replaced the Television without Frontiers Directive in 2007 in defining a set of common rules for advertising in all audiovisual media services for its member-states. The new rules provide advertisers and broadcasters with more flexibility to insert spot advertising and remove the old 20-minutes-between-advertising-break-periods rule. The amount of advertising commercials in the EU remains limited to 12 minutes in any given hour. Furthermore, films, current affairs programs, and news programs, as well as children's programs longer then 30 minutes, may be interrupted only once in each 30-minute period by advertising. Product placement is generally prohibited in the EU with some exception.[71] Marketers must be cautious in the use of comparative advertising, avoiding denigrating the competition, and in the use of superlatives such as "best," which can be illegal in countries like Germany. Although the German courts have been less stringent in cases as recent as 2009, the courts can find comparative advertising to be illegal if as little as 15 percent of consumers are "misled" by the advertising.

Global media vehicles have been developed that have target audiences on at least three continents and for which the media buying takes place through a centralized office. These media have traditionally been publications that, in addition to the worldwide edition, have provided advertisers the option of using regional editions. For example, *Time* publishes regional editions for the United States, Asia, South Pacific, Europe, the Middle East, and Africa. For each region, *Time* publishes subregional editions. In Asia, for example, there are 19 geographic subeditions available for advertisers to reach country-specific audiences. Other global publications include the *International Herald Tribune*, *The Wall Street Journal* (as well as the *Asian Wall Street Journal*), the *Financial Times*, and *The Economist*. The Internet provides the international marketer with an extremely versatile global medium. Online editions of publications, as well as mobile editions and podcasts, can be used in tandem with print publications and broadcast media or separately. Advertisers who want to reach business travelers, for example, can buy advertising packages from CNN that may include CNN regional programming in Africa, the Middle East, Europe, the United States, Latin America (CNN en Español), or Asia; CNN.com; and CNN mobile services. Advertisers in the Middle East might look to Al Jazeera as a very attractive medium. Aljazeera TV claims 40 million viewers, and Aljazeera.net is the most visited web site in the Arab world.[72] National Geographic Channel is available in over 143 countries, seen in more than 160 million homes and in 25 languages (see Figure 14.4).

A smart approach to global marketing over the Internet might start with search engine optimization or paid placement in search marketing. In 2009, Google sites dominated global search properties with a 67.3 percent share, followed by Yahoo! sites with a 7.9 percent share. Baidu, the Chinese search engine, was third with 3.5 percent of global searches.[73] In Japan, however, Yahoo! continues to be the lead search engine, with 56.5 percent of the Japanese market compared to Google's 33.7 percent share. Yahoo! has proven particularly adept at customizing its product to the needs of the Japanese consumer, while Google has had a more difficult time in penetrating the market.[74]

With the rapid growth in the use of social media such as Facebook, LinkedIn, Twitter, YouTube, and blogs, marketers are increasingly integrating public relations and viral marketing ideas into their media planning. Word-of-mouth and grassroots-brand advocacy can have a powerful effect, particularly for the launch of new products and services or a new marketing push. In 2009, T-Mobile staged an event in Liverpool Station, where 350 hired dancers began dancing to popular music to amplify the launch of T-Mobile's "Life's for Sharing" television campaign. Hidden cameras captured the reactions of surprised commuters, many of whom joined in the fun. The news quickly spread through social media and was covered by multiple news organizations.[75]

Developing the promotional message is referred to as *creative strategy*. The marketer must determine what the consumer is really buying—that is, the consumer's motivations. They will vary, depending on:

1. The diffusion of the product, service, or concept into the market. For example, to enter China with online sales requires an understanding of the variances in Internet penetration and online shopping by region. Overall Internet penetration in China was approximately 25 percent and online shopping penetration at less than 7 percent in 2009. Half of Beijing and Shanghai Internet users are online shoppers, while only 35 percent of users in Guangzhou and 29 percent in Chengdu shop online.[76]

2. The criteria on which the consumer will evaluate the product. For example, Hyundai Motors spent considerable time researching its Indian customers. After determining that Indian consumers valued most the lifetime ownership cost of a vehicle, Hyundai integrated that value into its Santro automobile with a reduced engine output, keeping the car fuel efficient. Hyundai also considered India's less-than-optimum road conditions when designing the car. Hyundai also priced its spare parts reasonably and tailored dozens of more product specifications to the Indian market. As a result, the Santro has been a success with Indian consumers, far outselling the other foreign brands.[77]

3. The product's positioning. For example, Parker Pen's upscale image may not be profitable enough in a market that is more or less a commodity business. The solution is to create an image for a commodity product and make the public pay for it. In 2008, FIJI Water received *Elle Magazine*'s Green Award and Oracle Corporation's "Empower the Green Enterprise" Award.[78]

Figure 14.4   Example of Panregional Medium

We've got it covered

We are a unique brand that delivers factual entertainment at its best. With our five channels including HD, Wild, Adventure and Music we are able to offer documentary programming that spans the globe.
For more information go to **media.ngceurope.com**.

PROGRAM SALES:
Germaine Deagan Sweet, gdeagans@ngs.org, +1 202 912 6674
Shirley Bowers, shbowers@ngs.org +1 202 912 6775
MIPCOM Stand #R29.40

Courtesy: National Geographic Channels International.

The ideal situation in developing message strategy is to have a world brand—a product that is manufactured, packaged, and positioned the same around the world. However, a number of factors will force companies to abandon identical campaigns in favor of recognizable campaigns. The factors are culture, of which language is the main manifestation, economic development, and lifestyles. Consider, for example, the campaign for Marriott International presented in Figure 14.5. International marketers customized the advertising copy to appeal to the local market. While retaining similar graphic elements, these Marriott ads were uniquely designed and written to appeal to the Arabic, French and Italian cultures.

Many multinational corporations are staffed and equipped to perform the full range of promotional activities. In most cases, however, they rely on the outside expertise of advertising agencies and other promotions-related companies such as media-buying companies and specialty marketing firms. In a study of 40 multinational marketers, 32.5 percent are using a single agency worldwide, 20 percent are using two, 5 percent are using three, 10 percent are using four, and 32.5 percent are using more than four agencies. Euro RSCG Worldwide, McCann Worldgroup, and Ogilvy Group are top global marketers as well as large networks with major clients

Figure 14.5   Global Advertising Campaign Approaches

Courtesy of Marriott.

(in at least in five countries). Euro RSCG Worldwide has 55 global client companies, McCann Worldgroup has 46 global clients.[79] Local agencies will survive, however, because of governmental regulations. In Peru, for example, a law mandates that any commercial aired on Peruvian television must be 100 percent nationally produced. Local agencies tend to forge ties with foreign ad agencies for better coverage and customer service, and thus become part of the general globalization effort. Marketers are choosing specialized interactive shops over full-service agencies for Internet advertising. However, a major weakness with the interactive agencies is their lack of international experience.

Personal Selling

Although advertising is often equated with the promotional effort, in many cases promotional efforts consist of personal selling. In the early stages of internationalization, exporters rely heavily on personal contact. The marketing of industrial goods, especially of high-priced items, requires strong personal selling efforts. In some cases, personal selling may be truly international; for example, Boeing or Northrop Grumman salespeople engage in sales efforts around the world. However, in most cases, personal selling takes place at the local level. The best interests of any company in the industrial area lie in establishing a solid base of dealerships staffed by local people. Personal selling efforts can be developed in the same fashion as advertising. For the multinational company, the primary goal again is the enhancement and standardization of personal selling efforts, especially if the product offering is standardized. When distribution is intensive, channels are long, or markets have tradition-oriented distribution, headquarters' role should be less pronounced and should concentrate mostly on offering help and guidance. A pivotal role is played by the field sales manager as the organizational link between headquarters and the salespeople.[80]

As an example, Eastman Kodak has developed a line-of-business approach to allow for standardized strategy throughout a region.[81] In Europe, one person is placed in charge of the entire copier-duplicator program in each country. That person is responsible for all sales and service teams within the country. Typically, each customer is served by three representatives, each with a different responsibility. Sales representatives maintain ultimate responsibility for the account; they conduct demonstrations, analyze customer requirements, determine the right type of equipment for each installation, and obtain orders. Service representatives install and maintain the equipment and retrofit new-product improvements to existing equipment. Customer service representatives are the liaison between sales and service. They provide operator training on a continuing basis and handle routine questions and complaints. Each team is positioned to respond to any European customer within four hours.

Sales Promotion

Sales promotion has been used as the catchall term for promotion that is not advertising, personal selling, or publicity. Sales promotion directed at consumers involves such activities as couponing, sampling, premiums, consumer education and demonstration activities, cents-off packages, point-of-purchase materials, and direct mail. The success in Latin America of Tang, Kraft Foods' presweetened powder juice substitute, is for the most part traceable to successful sales promotion efforts. One promotion involved trading Tang pouches for free popsicles from Kraft Foods' Brazilian subsidiary. The company also placed coupons for free groceries in Tang pouches. In Puerto Rico, General Foods ran Tang sweepstakes. In Argentina, in-store sampling featured Tang poured from Tang pitchers by girls in orange Tang dresses. Decorative Tang pitchers were a hit throughout Latin America.

For sales promotion to work, the campaigns planned by manufacturers or their agencies have to gain the support of the local retailer population. As an example, retailers must redeem coupons presented by consumers and forward them to the manufacturer or to the company handling the promotion. A. C. Nielsen tried to introduce cents-off coupons in Chile and ran into trouble with the nation's supermarket union, which notified its members that it opposed the project and recommended that coupons not be accepted. The main complaint was that an intermediary, such as Nielsen, would unnecessarily raise costs and thus the prices to be charged to consumers. Also, some critics felt that coupons would limit individual negotiations, because Chileans often bargain for their purchases. Global marketers are well advised to take advantage of local regional opportunities in Brazil: gas delivery people are used to distribute product samples to households by companies such as Nestlé, Johnson & Johnson, and Unilever. The delivery people are usually assigned to the same district for years and have, therefore, earned their clientele's trust. For the marketers, distributing samples this way is not only effective, it is very economical: they are charged 5 cents for each unit distribution. The gas companies benefit as well in that their relationship with customers is enhanced through these "presents."[82]

Sales promotion directed at intermediaries, also known as trade promotion, includes activities such as trade shows and exhibits, trade discounts, and cooperative advertising. For example, attendance at an appropriate trade show is one of the best ways to make contacts with government officials and decision makers, work with present intermediaries, or attract new ones.

Public Relations

Public relations is the marketing communications function charged with executing programs to earn public understanding and acceptance, which means both internal and external communication. Internal communication is important, especially in multinational companies, to create an appropriate corporate culture. External campaigns can be achieved through the use of corporate symbols, corporate advertising, customer relations programs, the generation of publicity, as well as getting a company's view to the public via the Internet. Some material on the firm is produced for special audiences to assist in personal selling.

A significant part of public relations activity focuses on portraying multinational corporations as good citizens of their host markets. General Electric's policies of good corporate citizenship are summarized in the Focus on Ethics. Cisco Systems' Networking Academy is an example of how a marketer can link philanthropic strategy, its competitive advantage, and broader social good. To address a chronic deficit in IT job applicants, the company created the Network Academy concept, whereby it contributes networking equipment to schools. Cisco now operates 10,000 academies in secondary schools, community colleges, and community-based organizations in 150 countries, with more than 1.5 million students currently enrolled. As the leading player in the field, Cisco stands to benefit the most from this improved labor pool. At the same time, Cisco has attracted worldwide recognition for this program, boosted its employee morale and partner goodwill, and has generated a reputation for leadership in philanthropy.[83]

Increasingly, the United Nations is promoting programs to partner multinationals and NGOs to tackle issues such as healthcare, energy, and biodiversity. For example Merck and GlaxoSmithKline have partnered with UNICEF and the World Bank to improve access to AIDS care in the hardest hit regions of the world.[84]

Public relations activity includes anticipating and countering criticism. The criticisms range from general ones against all multinational corporations to specific complaints. First-party certification is the most common variety, whereby a single firm develops its own rules and reports on compliance. This certification includes prohibitions on child labor and forced labor guarantee of nondiscrimination in the workplace. Second-party certification involves an industry or trade association fashioning a code of conduct and implementing reporting mechanisms. The chemical industry's global Responsible Care® program developed environmental, health, and safety principles and codes; required participating firms to submit implementation reports; and reported aggregate industry progress. Third-party certification involves an external group, often a nongovernmental organization (NGO), imposing its rules and compliance methods onto a particular firm or industry. The Council on Economic Priorities (CEP), the pioneering New York–based NGO, has collected data on

FOCUS ON ETHICS

Global Corporate Social Responsibility Strategy

A survey of opinion leaders by Edelman, the world's largest independent public relations firm, found that trust in business "to do what is right," after falling to its lowest points in the middle of the 2007–2009 financial crisis, was still below 50 percent in the United States, United Kingdom, France, and Germany, while being much stronger in India (75 percent) and China (60 percent) where economic growth rates were much stronger. In India and China, a large majority of respondents described the overall reputation of large global businesses as good or excellent, while most respondents in the United States, United Kingdom, and France indicated poor or fair. Among the study's conclusions were the following:

- Trust plays a key role in brand choices.
- Business should play a broader role in society.
- Business should balance investor interests with customer and employee interests.
- Business should square mutual social responsibility and shared purpose with profit-making strategy.

Government and societal expectations of the role that global corporations should play in the multiple and individual communities in which they operate and market are increasing, especially given corporate size and the interrelationship between business and large global problems such as commodity prices, carbon emissions, and water quality. A comparison of annual corporate revenues with country GDP data would find corporations like ExxonMobil, Walmart, Royal Dutch Shell, and BP among the largest economies in the world.

Of course, defining expectations of what corporate social responsibility encompasses and what consumers believe that it means can be challenging. Many consumers equate corporate social responsibility with how a company treats its employees or how it helps the communities in which it operates, while others view the concept in relation to sustainable environmental practices. At the same time, there is no true clarity about what "sustainability" means. A 2008 Yankelovich research study found that while 37 percent of U.S. respondents felt "highly concerned" about environmental issues, only 25 percent felt "highly knowledgeable."

Most of the largest global companies issue annual reports on corporate social responsibility, corporate citizenship, or sustainability in which they summarize their practices and identify the metrics they use to measure their progress. For example, Heineken focuses and reports on progress in seven areas: energy, water, safety, agriculture, supply chain responsibility, responsible beer consumption, and impact on developing markets. In InBev's Global Corporate Citizenship report, the company identifies responsible drinking and environmental performance (water use, energy and climate change, and by-products and waste) as its major areas of focus.

How effectively companies integrate corporate social responsibility sustainability issues into corporate strategy will be a trend to watch. For example, GE positions itself as "Imagination at work" and "GE people worldwide are dedicated to turning imaginative ideas into leading products and services that help solve some of the world's toughest problems." Considering GE's businesses in water processing and power generation, among others, the company's business is closely aligned with its stated citizenship approach: "A full-time commitment with the same goals, strategies, and accountabilities that drive any other part of our business, GE applies its long-standing spirit of innovation and unique set of capabilities to take on tough challenges in our communities." In its annual Ecoimagination sustainability report, GE sets five major commitments: (1) increased revenues from Ecoimagination products, (2) doubled investment in R&D, (3) reduced greenhouse gas emissions and improved energy efficiency, (4) reduced water use and improved water reuse, and (5) keeping the public informed.

There are considerable internal company reasons for these kinds of commitments as well. Employees do not want to work for companies that have no social conscience, suppliers and customers do not want to do business with companies that pollute the environment or are notorious for shoddy products and practices, and communities do not welcome companies that are not good citizens. Increasingly, shareholders are also holding companies more accountable for improved corporate social responsibility practices.

Sources: Edelman Trust Barometer 2009, http://www.edelman.com/, accessed GE 2008 Ecoimagination annual report, "Ecoimagination Is GE"; Joel Makower, *Strategies for the Green Economy* (New York: McGraw-Hill, 2009); AB InBev, http://www.ab-inbev.com, accessed December 10, 2009; Heineken Sustainability Report 2008.

corporate activities since its creation in 1969 and publishes reports on corporate behavior. Fourth-party certification involves government or multilateral agencies. The United Nations' Global Compact, for instance, lists environmental, labor, and human rights principles for companies to follow; participating corporations must submit online updates of their progress for NGOs to scrutinize.[85]

SUMMARY

The task of the international marketer is to seek new opportunities in the world marketplace and satisfy emerging needs through creative management of the firm's good, pricing, distribution, and promotional policies. By its very nature, marketing is the most sensitive of business functions to environmental effects and influences.

The analysis of target markets is the first of the international marketer's challenges. Potential and existing markets need to be evaluated and priorities established for each, ranging from rejection to a temporary holding position to entry. Decisions at the level of the overall marketing effort must be made with respect to the selected markets, and a plan for future expansion must be formulated. The closer that potential target markets are in terms of their geographical,

cultural, and economic distance, the more attractive they typically are to the international marketer.

A critical decision in international marketing concerns the degree to which the overall marketing program should be standardized or localized. The ideal is to standardize as much as possible without compromising the basic task of marketing: satisfying the needs and wants of the target market. Many multinational marketers are adopting globalization strategies that involve the standardization of good ideas, while leaving the implementation to local entities.

The technical side of marketing management is universal, but environments require adaptation within all of the mix elements. The degree of adaptation will vary by market, good, or service marketed, and overall company objectives.

KEY TERMS

income elasticity of demand   481
market audit   481
analogy   481
longitudinal analysis   481
gap analysis   483
concentration strategy   484
diversification   484
positioning   490

reverse innovation   490
global brands   492
standard worldwide pricing   495
dual pricing   495
cost-plus method   495
marginal cost method   495
market-differentiated pricing   495
price escalation   495

dumping   495
gray market   497
arm's length price   498
channel design   498
e-commerce   502
m-commerce   503
media strategy   505

QUESTIONS FOR DISCUSSION

1. Many rational reasons exist for rejecting a particular market in the early stages of screening. Such decisions are made by humans, thus some irrational reasons must exist as well. Suggest some.

2. If, indeed, the three dimensions of distance are valid, to which countries would U.S. companies initially expand? Consider the interrelationships of the distance concepts.

3. Is globalization ever a serious possibility, or is the regional approach the closest the international marketer can ever hope to get to standardization?

4. What are the possible exporter reactions to extreme foreign exchange rate fluctuations?

5. Argue for and against gray marketing.

6. What courses of action are open to an international marketer who finds all attractive intermediaries already under contract to competitors?

INTERNET EXERCISES

1. The software industry is the hardest hit by piracy. Using the web site of the Business Software Alliance (http://www.bsa.org), assess how this problem is being tackled.

2. The global advertising industry has experienced significant consolidation with a few giant communications companies owning most of the major advertising, branding, public relations, digital marketing, marketing research, and other marketing services agencies. Visit the web sites of the four largest communications groups:

http://www.wpp.com
http://www.omnicom.com
http://www.interpublic.com
http://www.publicis.com

From the information they provide about their companies, create a short list of five to ten global advertising agencies that a global marketer might consider working with to create a global advertising campaign and provide advertising services in most major countries.

TAKE A STAND

Apple's iPhone is one of the most globally recognized and popular brands in the world. The company has marketed its product through exclusive deals with telecom providers in the United States, Britain, France, Germany, and, most recently, China. However, even before the iPhone's official launch in the People's Republic, that country already had more than 2 million "unofficial" users—beneficiaries of the thriving iPhone gray market. Some believe that this is the manifestation of pent-up demand for a wildly popular device, produced by a company that places strict regulations on where and how its product is sold and used. Others question whether, in today's environment of rapid global technological innovation, it is even possible to implement effective brand management and control. There are thousands of providers, mostly operating in the gray economy, with the technological capability to unlock the iPhone so that it can be used on networks unauthorized by Apple.

This trend is cutting into the company's bottom line. For example, China is the world's largest mobile market, with almost 700 million users. When Apple finalized its deal with China Unicom to distribute the iPhone, sales expectations ran high. However, the device offered by the official carrier is about twice the price of those available on the gray market ($880 to $1,170, compared with $500 to $800). Additionally, as per Apple's agreement with the Chinese government, the official iPhone does not have WiFi capabilities. Unsurprisingly, consumers have continued to gravitate towards the cheaper "jailbroken" iPhones.

Apple has previously tried to control the unauthorized use of its product, because it costs its authorized partners (such as AT&T, O2, Orange, and Deutsche Telekom) hundreds of dollars per subscriber in monthly fees. However, as soon as Apple develops a possible solution (like the software update it implemented in 2007) intended to make unlocked iPhones useless, unauthorized consumers and gray market providers find a way around it. Some analysts estimate that one out of every four iPhones sold around the world have been unlocked.

For Discussion

1. What can Apple do about unauthorized iPhones, and more importantly, should it do anything?

© REUTERS/STR/Landov LLC

2. The iPhone has become China's best-selling smartphone, countering skepticism by analysts who say the handset is too expensive. What can a business do to recapture market share?

Sources: Juliet Ye, "Behind the Scenes of China's iPhone Apps," *The Wall Street Journal*, November 11, 2009; Kathrin Hille, "iPhone Hits the Shelves Officially in China," *Financial Times*, October 31, 2009; and Peter Burrows, "Inside the iPhone Gray Market," *BusinessWeek*, February 12, 2008.

CHAPTER 15

Services

CHAPTER CONTENTS & LEARNING OBJECTIVES

DIFFERENCES BETWEEN SERVICES AND GOODS

1. To examine the important role of services in international business

THE ROLE OF SERVICES IN THE U.S. ECONOMY

2. To understand why trade in services is more complex than trade in goods

THE ROLE OF GLOBAL SERVICES IN THE WORLD ECONOMY

3. To appreciate the heightened sensitivity required for international service success

GLOBAL TRANSFORMATIONS IN THE SERVICES SECTOR

4. To learn that stand-alone services are becoming more important to world trade

PROBLEMS IN SERVICE TRADE

5. To examine the competitive advantage of firms in the service sector

CORPORATIONS AND SERVICES TRADE

6. To analyze the strategic options available for corporations in the global service market

Globalization has had major implications for international business—from the worldwide spread of information technology and resulting productivity gains to the increased pace of internationalization and the appearance of "born global" firms. Analysts point to labor mobility as the last remaining bastion of preglobalization economics. Workers have tended to move around at a far slower pace than all the other factors of production. There are two reasons that are cited most often: (1) people are culturally embedded, that is, they have connections to their communities and familial networks, which trump the pursuit of better-paying jobs overseas, and (2) would-be migrants are faced with a slew of government regulations and restrictions that block their free movement across borders. However, information technology and the gradual liberalization of international markets are changing the patterns of labor mobility around the globe.

The most powerful motivator for worker migration is financial. Studies have demonstrated that an increase of approximately $1,000 (in 2000 prices) in the purchasing power parity gap between two locations increases migration flows by about 10 percent. Demographic trends represent another contributing factor. Much of the developed world is characterized by aging populations and negative population growth. Meanwhile, many developing countries boast high birthrates and an ever-increasing pool of young, college-educated men and women. For example, the Philippines graduates 380,000 college students trained in U.S. accounting standards *per year*. Clearly, that is a major impetus for firms to both outsource jobs overseas and to import cheap labor.

From a theoretical standpoint, increased labor mobility has numerous potential benefits. Companies benefit through savings on labor costs, which are then passed on to consumers in the form of lower prices on goods and services. Immigrants enjoy better wages and a higher standard of living, while their home countries receive remittances. Concerns over depressed wages and large-scale job losses by natives of countries that are net recipients of migrants have been countered by statistics that suggest that immigration has no effects on average wages or on the return to capital in the receiving country. It simply leads to an increase in total employment, even during bad economic times. However, due to domestic political pressure from interested constituent groups in the developed world, many governments have adopted strict entry laws.

Studies have demonstrated that each reform that introduced tighter rules of entry for immigrants decreases immigration flows by 6 percent to 10 percent. Despite efforts by international organizations like the World Trade Organization to promote liberalization and labor mobility, most Organization for Economic Cooperation and Development member-countries have actually been introducing new legislation to stem the tide of global outsourcing. For example, a new bill in Washington aims to tighten the rules for U.S. companies that hire skilled workers from abroad.

Despite such measures, the new global job shift is certain to continue. Analysts from Forrester Research predict that 3.3 million white-collar jobs, with $136 billion in wages, will shift from the United States to lower-cost countries by 2015. European firms from England, France, and Germany are joining the trend by hiring in Russia, the Baltics, eastern Europe, China, and India. The worker of the future is likely to be increasingly footloose, and the workplace of tomorrow is likely to be truly global.

Sources: Francese Ortega and Giovanni Peri, "The Causes and Effects of International Labor Mobility," Human Development Research Paper, United Nations Development Program, April 2009; "Economist Debates: International Migration," *The Economist*, http://www.economist.com/debate/days/view/371, accessed December 12, 2009; "Work Visa Bill Threatens Indian Outsourcers," *BusinessWeek*, June 2, 2009.

Services are a major component of world trade. This chapter will highlight international business dimensions that are specific to services. A definition of services will be provided, and trade in services and in goods will be differentiated. The role of services in the world economy will then be explained. The chapter will discuss the opportunities and new problems that have arisen because of increasing service trade, with particular focus on the worldwide transformations of industries as a result of profound changes in the environment and in technology. The strategic responses to the transformations by both governments and firms will be explained. Finally, the chapter will outline the initial steps that firms need to undertake to offer services internationally and will look at the future of service trade.

 ## DIFFERENCES BETWEEN SERVICES AND GOODS

1. To examine the important role of services in international business

We rarely contemplate or analyze the precise role of services in our lives. Services often accompany goods, but they are also, by themselves, an increasingly important part of the economy. One author has contrasted services and products by stating that "a good is an object, a device, a thing; a service is a deed, a performance, an effort."[1] That definition, although quite general, captures the essence of the difference between goods and services. Services tend to be more intangible, personalized, and custom-made than goods. Services also are typically using a different approach to customer satisfaction. It has been stated that "service firms do not have products in the form of preproduced solutions to customer's problems; they have processes as solutions to such problems."[2] Services are the fastest growing sector in world trade, and as this chapter's opening vignette shows, employment in the services sector is becoming increasingly global. These major differences add dimensions to services that are not present in goods.

LINK BETWEEN SERVICES AND GOODS

Services may complement goods; at other times, goods may complement services. The offering of goods that are in need of substantial technological support and maintenance may be useless if no proper assurance for service can be provided. For this reason, the initial contract of sale often includes important service dimensions. This practice is frequent in aircraft sales. When an aircraft is purchased, the buyer contracts not only for the physical good—namely, the plane—but often for the training of personnel, maintenance service, and the promise of continuous technological updates. Similarly, the sale of computer hardware depends on the availability of proper servicing and software.

In an international setting, the proper service support can often be crucial. Particularly for newly opening markets or for goods new to market, providing the good alone may be insufficient. The buyer wants to be convinced that proper service backup will be offered for the good before making a commitment. On a smaller scale, individual consumers' selection of a household appliance from a particular vendor is often motivated by the quality of after-purchase service—ease of delivery and haulaway, technical support in case of malfunction, and so forth. Retailers need to recognize that the quality of a product is just as important as the quality of the service system in which it is embedded.

This is especially true in the case of e-commerce, which will be discussed in further detail later in this chapter. As the number of online vendors has exploded in recent years, offering a superior product no longer guarantees a competitive edge. As Figure 15.1 demonstrates, customer satisfaction and e-loyalty can be a function of many tangible and intangible elements, such as physical elements of the vendor site's perceived security (e.g., secure checkout). With rising concerns about identity theft, this last element is likely to only increase in importance.

Figure 15.1　Customer Perceptions of Online Service Providers

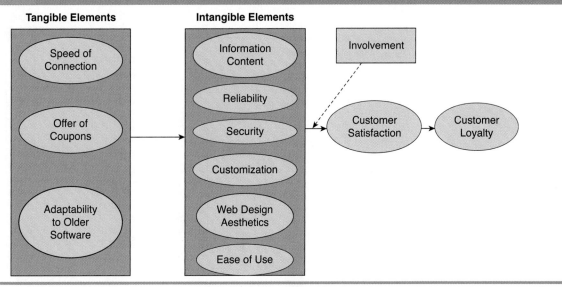

Source: Adapted from Woody G. Kim, "Examining the Relationship among Tangible, Intangible e-SERVQUAL, Online Customer Satisfaction, and Loyalty," paper presented at the International CHRIE Conference, University of Massachusetts–Amherst, 2009, 3.

The link between goods and services often brings a new dimension to international business efforts. A foreign buyer, for example, may want to purchase helicopters and contract for service support over a period of ten years. If the sale involves a U.S. firm, both the helicopter and the service sale will require an export license. Such licenses, however, are issued only for an immediate sale. Therefore, over the ten years, the seller will have to apply for an export license each time service is to be provided. The issuance of a license is often dependent on the political climate; therefore, the buyer and the seller are haunted by uncertainty. As a result, sales may go to firms in countries that can unconditionally guarantee the long-term supply of support services.

The knowledge that services and goods interact, however, is not enough. Successful managers must recognize that different customer groups will frequently view the service-good combination differently. The type of use and the usage conditions will affect evaluations of the market offering. For example, the intangible dimension of "on-time arrival" by airlines may be valued differently by college students than by business executives. Similarly, a 20-minute delay will be judged differently by a passenger arriving at his or her final destination than by one who has just missed an overseas connection. As a result, adjustment possibilities in both the service and the goods areas emerge that can be used as a strategic tool to stimulate demand and increase profitability. As Figure 15.2 shows, service and goods elements may vary substantially in any market offering. The manager must identify the role of each and adjust all of them to meet the desires of the target customer group. By rating the offerings on their dominant (in)tangibility, the manager can compare offerings and also generate information for subsequent market positioning strategies.

STAND-ALONE SERVICES

Services do not have to come in unison with goods. They can compete against goods and become an alternative offering. For example, rather than buy an in-house computer, the business executive can contract computing work to a local or foreign service firm. Similarly, the purchase of a car (a good) can be converted into the purchase of a service by leasing the car from an agency. Services therefore can transform the ownership of a good into its possession or use. This transformation can greatly affect business issues such as distribution, payment structure and flows, and even recycling.

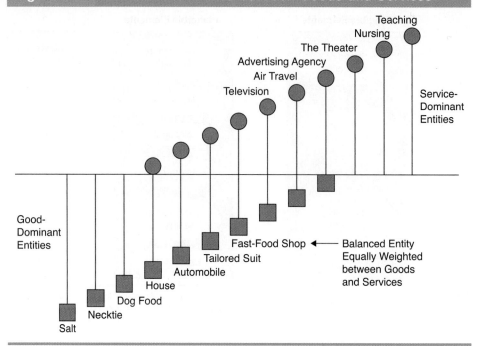

Figure 15.2 Scale of Dominance between Goods and Services

Teaching

Nursing

The Theater

Advertising Agency

Air Travel

Television

Service-Dominant Entities

Good-Dominant Entities

Fast-Food Shop ← Balanced Entity Equally Weighted between Goods and Services

Tailored Suit

Automobile

House

Dog Food

Necktie

Salt

Source: Reprinted with permission from *Marketing of Services*, eds. J. Donnelly and W. George; G. Lynn Shostack, "How to Design a Service," 1981, p. 222, published by the American Marketing Association, Chicago, IL 60606.

Services by themselves can satisfy needs and wants of customers. Entertainment services such as movies or music offer leisure time enjoyment. Insurance services can protect people from financial ruin in case of a calamity.

Services may also compete against one another. As an example, a store may have the option of offering full service to customers or of converting to the self-service format. With automated checkout services, customers may have to be self-sufficient with other activities such as selection, transportation, packaging, and pricing.

Services differ from goods most strongly in their **intangibility**: they are frequently consumed rather than possessed. Though the intangibility of services is a primary differentiating criterion, it is not always present. For example, publishing services ultimately result in a tangible good—namely, a book or a computer disk. Similarly, construction services eventually result in a building, a subway, or a bridge. Even in those instances, however, the intangible component that leads to the final good is of major concern to both the producer of the service and the recipient of the ultimate output, because it brings with it major considerations that are nontraditional to goods.

Another major difference concerns the storing of services. Due to their nature, services are difficult to inventory. If they are not used, the "brown around the edges" syndrome tends to result in high **perishability**. Unused capacity in the form of an empty seat on an airplane, for example, becomes nonsalable quickly. Once the plane has taken off, selling an empty seat is virtually impossible—except for an in-flight upgrade from coach to first class—and the capacity cannot be stored for future use. The difficulty of keeping services in inventory makes it troublesome to provide service back-up for peak demand. To maintain **service capacity** constantly at levels necessary to satisfy peak demand would be very expensive. The business manager must therefore attempt to smooth out demand levels through pricing or promotional tools in order to optimize overall use of capacity.

For the services offering, the time of production is usually very close to or even simultaneous with the time of consumption. This often means close **customer involvement**

intangibility The inability to be seen, tasted, or touched in a conventional sense; the characteristic of services that most strongly differentiates them from products.

perishability Susceptibility to deterioration; the characteristic of services that makes them difficult to store.

service capacity The maximum level at which a service provider is able to provide services to customers.

customer involvement Active participation of customers in the provision of services they consume.

Table 15.1   Examples of Cultural Service Gaps

Manifestations of the Service Provider Performance Gap	Example: Japanese Guests in a German Restaurant
Provider's physical environment gap	Customers cannot read the menu or they mix up the restrooms because they cannot read the signs
Provider's personnel gap	Customers feel uneasy because waiter maintains eye contact while taking the order
Provider's system gap	Customers are irritated because they are neither greeted at the door nor seated
Provider's co-customer gap	Customer feels uneasy because other guests greet them with a handshake when joining their table

Source: Bernd Stauss and Paul Mang, "'Culture Shocks' in Inter-cultural Service Encounters?" *Journal of Services Marketing 13, no. 4/5 (1999): 329–346.*

in the production of services. Customers frequently either service themselves or cooperate in the delivery of services. As a result, the service provider may need to be physically present when the service is delivered. This physical presence creates both problems and opportunities, and introduces a new constraint that is seldom present in the marketing of goods. For example, close interaction with the customer requires a much greater understanding of and emphasis on the cultural dimension of each market. A good service delivered in a culturally unacceptable fashion is doomed to failure. Even in a domestic setting, international exposure can make a service culturally controversial, as Table 15.1 shows. A common pattern of internationalization for service businesses is therefore to develop stand-alone business systems in each country.[3]

The close interaction with customers also points to the fact that services often are custom-made. This contradicts the desire of the firm to standardize its offering; yet at the same time, it offers the service provider an opportunity to differentiate the service. The concomitant problem is that, in order to fulfill customer expectations, **service consistency** is required. For anything offered online, however, consistency is difficult to maintain over the long run. Therefore, the human element in the service offering takes on a much greater role than in the offering of goods. Errors may enter the system, and unpredictable individual influences may affect the outcome of the service delivery. The issue of quality control affects the provider as well as the recipient of services. Efforts to increase control through service uniformity may sometimes be perceived by customers as the limiting of options. Since research has shown that the relative importance of the serviced quality dimensions varies from one culture to another,[4] one single approach to service quality may therefore have a negative market effect.

Buyers have more difficulty observing and evaluating services than goods. This is particularly true when the shopper tries to choose intelligently among service providers. Even when sellers of services are willing and able to provide more **market transparency**, the buyer's problem is complicated: customers receiving the same service may use it differently. Because production lines cannot be established to deliver an identical service each time, and the quality of a service cannot be tightly controlled, the problem of **service heterogeneity** emerges,[5] meaning that services may never be the same from one delivery to another. For example, the counseling by a teacher, even if it is provided on the same day by the same person, may vary substantially depending on the student. But over time, even for the same student, the counseling may change. As a result, service offerings are not directly comparable, which makes quality measurements quite challenging. Therefore, service quality may vary for each delivery. Nonetheless, maintaining service quality is vitally important, since the reputation of the service provider plays an overwhelming role in the customer's choice process.

Services often require entirely new forms of distribution. Traditional channels frequently are multitiered and long and therefore slow. They often cannot be used at

service consistency Uniform quality of service.

market transparency Availability of full disclosure and information about key market factors such as supply, demand, quality, service, and prices.

service heterogeneity The difference from one delivery of a product to another delivery of the same product as a result of the inability to control the production and quality of the process.

all because of the perishability of services. A weather news service, for example, either reaches its audience quickly or rapidly loses value. As a result, direct delivery and short distribution channels are required for international services. When they do not exist, service providers need to be distribution innovators to reach their market.

Increasingly, many services are "footloose," in that they are not tied to any specific location. Advances in technology make it possible for firms to separate production and consumption of services. As a result, labor-intensive service performance can be moved anywhere around the world where qualified, low-cost labor is plentiful. As communication technology further improves, services such as teaching, medical diagnosis, or bank account management can originate from any point in the world and reach customers around the globe.

The unique dimensions of services exist in both international and domestic settings, but their impact has greater importance for the international manager. For example, the perishability of a service, which may be a mere obstacle in domestic business, may become a major barrier internationally because of the longer distances involved. Similarly, quality control for international services may be much more difficult because of different service uses, changing expectations, and varying national regulations.

Services are delivered directly to the user and are therefore frequently much more sensitive to cultural factors than are products. Their influence on the individual abroad may be welcomed or greeted with hostility. For example, countries that place a strong emphasis on cultural identity have set barriers inhibiting market penetration by foreign films. France is leading a major effort within the European Union, for instance, to cap the volume of U.S.-produced films to obtain more playing time for French movies.

THE ROLE OF SERVICES IN THE U.S. ECONOMY

2. To understand why trade in services is more complex than trade in goods

Since the Industrial Revolution, the United States has seen itself as a primary international competitor in the production of goods. In the past decades, however, the U.S. economy has increasingly become a service economy, as Figure 15.3 shows. Transformations in society, such as increased specialization, employment by family

Figure 15.3   Employment in Industrial Sectors as a Percentage of the Total Labor Force

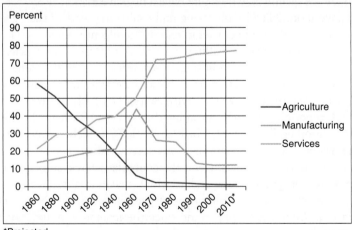

*Projected

Sources: Bureau of Labor Statistics, Occupational Employment Statistics, http://www.bls.gov/oes/#tables, accessed December 13, 2009; Statistical Abstracts Archive, U.S. Census Bureau, http://www.census.gov/compendia/statab/past_years.html, accessed March 23, 2010.

members, scarcity of time, and a constantly growing desire for convenience are some of the factors which have led to the rapid growth in services.[6] The U.S. service sector now produces approximately 80 percent of GDP and employs 77 percent of the workforce.[7] The major segments that comprise the service sector are communications, transportation, public utilities, finance, insurance and real estate, wholesale and retail businesses, government, and "services" (a diverse category including business services, personal services, and professional and health services). The service sector accounts for all of the growth in total nonfarm employment.

Only a limited segment of the total range of U.S. services is sold internationally. Federal, state, and local government employees, for example, sell few of their services to foreigners. U.S. laundries and restaurants only occasionally service foreign tourists. Many service industries that do sell abroad often have at their disposal large organizations, specialized technology, or advanced professional expertise. Strength in these characteristics has enabled the United States to become the world's largest exporter of services. Total U.S. services exported grew from $15 billion in 1970 to almost $509 billion in 2009.[8]

Global service trade has had very beneficial results for many U.S. firms. Most of the large management consulting firms derive more than half of their revenue from international sources. The largest law firms serve customers around the globe, some of them in over a hundred countries. Table 15.2 shows that 12 of the largest 20 law firms in the world are headquartered in the United States, and up to 82 percent of their lawyers reside outside their home country. These facts demonstrate that many service firms and industries have become truly international and formidable in size. Focus on Politics explains the growth of international education and posits some of the key policy issues faced by this industry.

Table 15.2 World's Largest Law Firms

Rank	Firm	Web Site	Number of Lawyers/Fee Earners	Lawyers Outside Home Country (%)	Countries in Which Firms Have Offices
1	Baker & McKenzie International (U.S.)	www.bakernet.com	3,949	82%	39
2	Clifford Chance International (U.K.)	www.cliffordchance.com	2,837	69	21
3	DLA Piper International (U.K.)	www.dlapiper.com	2,459	60	28
4	Linklaters International (U.K.)	www.linklaters.com	2,367	68	19
5	Jones Day National (U.S.)	www.jonesday.com	2,348	27	13
6	Freshfields Bruckhaus Deringer International (U.K.)	www.freshfields.com	2,263	65	15
7	Latham & Watkins National (U.S)	www.lw.com	2,147	25	12
8	Allen & Overy International (U.K.)	www.allenovery.com	2,122	61	22
9	White & Case International (U.S.)	www.whitecase.com	2,120	65	25
10	Skadden Arps Slate Meagher & Flom National (U.S.)	www.skadden.com	1,995	16	13
11	Mayer Brown International (U.S.)	www.mayerbrown.com	1,841	43	9
12	Garrigues (Spain)	www.garrigues.com	1,835	11	9
13	Sidley Austin National (U.S.)	www.sidley.com	1,777	16	9
14	Greenberg Traurig National (U.S.)	www.gtlaw.com	1,760	5	5
15	K & L Gates National (U.S.)	www.klgates.com	1,569	15	6
16	Reed Smith National (U.S.)	www.reedsmith.com	1,482	30	7
17	Lovells International (U.K.)	www.lovells.com	1,421	82	18
18	Fidal National (France)	www.fidal.fr	1,420	<1	2
19	DLA Piper US National (U.S.)	www.dlapiper.com	1,386	0	1
20	Kirkland & Ellis National (U.S.)	www.kirkland.com	1,383	8	4

Source: "The Global 100: Most Lawyers 2009," American Lawyer, http://www.law.com/jsp/tal/PubAlticleTAL.jsp?id=1202433981635, accessed December 6, 2009.

FOCUS ON POLITICS

Medical Tourism as an Alternative to Domestic Health Care

Consumers of medical services in the developed world have started to look for alternatives to high-priced care in their home countries. They are traveling in ever-increasing numbers to exotic destinations like Brazil and Thailand in search of high-quality care at a fraction of the cost. The medical tourism industry has grown by about 14 percent from 2007 to 2009 and is predicted to expand at a rate of 35 percent annually by 2010. By 2012, it is predicted to serve more than 1.6 million international patients.

The rationale behind the industry's development is straightforward—customers search for convenience and cost-effectiveness. A medical procedure at an Indian or Chinese hospital can cost 70 percent less than a patient would pay in the West. For patients from countries with public health care systems like Canada and the United Kingdom, medical travel is often motivated by the desire to avoid long wait periods before their procedures. Additionally, the global spread of technological innovation and international accreditation standards lets patients have increased confidence in the quality of care they receive abroad.

The growth in medical tourism is a boon for health care providers in the developing world. For example, in India, the sector is projected to expand by 30 percent annually from 2009 to 2015 and be worth $4.4 billion. More internationally accredited medical centers are emerging in countries such as the Philippines and Mexico, eager to accommodate the ever-growing stream of Western patients. Governments in the developing world are beginning to invest in support infrastructure in order to promote their health care services internationally.

New companies are also springing up to assist patients with scheduling their procedures overseas. They help clients with planning their trips and offer in-country support, such as airport transfers, after-care arrangements, hospital liaisons, and dispute mediation. Most of these companies started out catering to individual clients. However, several are expanding to offer their services to meet businesses' demand. With the rising costs of providing employee health care, more corporations are beginning to search for alternatives to home-country care.

As medical costs in mature markets continue to soar and demand for elective procedures such as cosmetic and dental surgery rises, medical tourism is rapidly evolving into a viable health care alternative.

Sources: Sara Murray, "Travel Sickness," *Financial Times*, December 8, 2009, 40–43; "Medical Travel Quality Alliance to Certify Medical Tourism Agents for Safer, Quality Health Care for Traveling International Patients," *CNBC*, December 9, 2009, http://bx.businessweek.com/medical-tourism/view?url=http%3A%2F%2Fc.moreover.com%2Fclick%2Fhere.pl%3Fr2389618739%26f%3D9791, accessed December 12, 2009.

However, dramatic global growth is not confined to U.S. firms. Imports of services into the United States are also increasing dramatically. In 2009, the United States imported more than $371 billion worth of services.[9] Competition in global services is rising rapidly at all levels. Hong Kong, Singapore, and western Europe are increasingly active in service industries such as banking, insurance, and advertising. Years ago, U.S. construction firms could count on a virtual monopoly on large-scale construction projects. Today, firms from South Korea, Italy, and other countries are taking a major share of the international construction business.

THE ROLE OF GLOBAL SERVICES IN THE WORLD ECONOMY

3. To appreciate the heightened sensitivity required for international service success

The rise of the service sector is a global phenomenon. Services account for 65 percent of GDP in Jordan, 60 percent in Uruguay, 52 percent in Zambia, and 54 percent in India.[10] Even in the least developed countries, services typically contribute at least 45 percent of GDP. With growth rates higher than other sectors, such as agriculture and manufacturing, services are instrumental in job creation in these countries.[11] In addition, service exports are very important to developing and transitional economies. On average, 20 percent of developing and transitional economy exports are service exports, accounting for more than 29 percent of the world's total services exports combined.

The economies of developing countries have traditionally first established a strong agricultural and then a manufacturing sector to meet basic needs such as food and shelter before venturing into the services sector. Some countries, such as

Mexico, Singapore, Hong Kong, Bermuda, and the Bahamas, are steering away from the traditional economic development pattern and are concentrating on developing strong service sectors.[12] The reasons vary from a lack of natural resources with which to develop agricultural and/or manufacturing sectors to recognition of the strong demand for services and the ability to provide them through tourism and a willing, skilled, and inexpensive labor force. As a result, it is anticipated that services trade will continue to grow. However, as more countries enter the sector, the global services business will become more competitive.

GLOBAL TRANSFORMATIONS IN THE SERVICES SECTOR

Major changes in the environment and technology account for the dramatic rise in services trade. One key environmental change has been the reduction of **government regulation** of service industries. In the early 1980s, many governments adopted the view that reduced government interference in the marketplace would enhance competition. As a result, new players have entered the marketplace. Some service sectors have benefited and others have suffered from this withdrawal of government intervention. Regulatory changes were initially thought to have primarily domestic effects, but they have rapidly spread internationally. For example, the 1984 **deregulation** of the U.S. telecommunication giant AT&T gave rise to the deregulation of Japan's telecommunication monopoly NT&T in 1985. European deregulation followed in the mid-1990s.

Similarly, deregulatory efforts in the transportation sector have had international repercussions. New air carriers have entered the market to compete against established trunk carriers and have done so successfully by pricing their services differently, both nationally and internationally. Obviously, a Dutch airline can count only to a limited extent on government support to remain competitive with new, low-priced fares offered by other carriers from abroad also serving the Dutch market. The deregulatory movement has fostered new competition and new competitive practices. Many of these changes resulted in lower prices, stimulating demand and leading to a rise in the volume of international services trade.

There also has been decreased regulation of service industries by their service groups. For example, business practices in fields such as health care, law, and accounting are becoming increasingly competitive and aggressive. New economic realities require firms in these industries to search for new ways to attract market share and expand their markets. International markets are one frequently untapped possibility for market expansion and have therefore become a prime target for such firms.

Technological advancement is a second major change that has taken place. Technology offers new ways of doing business and permits businesses to expand their horizons internationally. Through computerization, for instance, service exchanges that previously would have been prohibitively expensive are now easily feasible. As an example, Adidas uses one major computer system to coordinate product design from its nearly 200 international subsidiaries around the world.[13] This practice allows not only for better inventory forecasting and utilization of existing equipment, but it also allows design teams based in different countries to interact closely, resulting in a product that can be successful in multiple markets. Technology innovations have also spilled over into the small businesses arena, allowing for

4. To learn that stand-alone services are becoming more important to world trade

government regulation Interference in the marketplace by governments.

deregulation Removal of government interference.

© AFP PHOTO/Andrew Ross/Getty Images, Inc.

Communications reach into all corners of the world.

cost of communication The cost of communicating electronically or by telephone with other locations. These costs have been drastically reduced through the use of fiberoptic cables.

online access to the same kind of planning, management, and accounting tools that the big companies use. Of course, this development could take place only after advances in data transmission procedures. Technology has also sharply reduced the **cost of communication**. Fiberoptic cables have made the cost of international links trivial. A minute on a transatlantic cable laid 40 years ago cost $2.44, but now the same amount of time costs barely more than one cent.

The Internet and web technology have improved the transaction economics of services and succeeded in making many formerly location-bound services tradable.[14] At the same time, the increased use of outsourcing by firms has led to a greater need for global service performance. For example, more use of just-in-time inventory systems has created the need to better coordinate the supply-chain function and has resulted in the creation of more service intermediaries.[15]

Service industry expansion is not confined to those services that are labor intensive and is therefore better performed in areas of the world where labor possesses a comparative advantage. Technology-intensive services are becoming the sunrise industries of this century. Increasingly, firms in a variety of industries can use technology to offer a presence without having to be there physically. Banks, for example, can offer their services through automatic teller machines or telephone and Internet banking. Consultants can advise via videoconferences and teachers can teach the world through multimedia classrooms. Physicians can advise and even perform operations in a distant country if proper computer links can drive roboticized medical equipment.

Due to the growth of corporate web sites, some firms—particularly in the service sector—can quickly become unplanned participants in the international market. For example, potential customers from abroad can visit a web site and require the firm to deliver internationally as well. Of course the firm can choose to ignore foreign interests and lose out on new markets. Alternatively, it can find itself unexpectedly an international service provider. Specialty retailing such as book stores and fitness equipment are examples of services that in this way have become international.[16]

Many service providers have the opportunity to become truly global players. To them, the traditional international market barrier of distance no longer matters. Knowledge, the core of many service activities, can offer a global reach without requiring a local presence. Service providers therefore may have only a minor need for local establishment, because they can operate without premises. You don't have to be there to do business! The effect of such a shift in service activities will be major. Insurance and bank palaces in the downtowns of the world may soon become obsolete. Talented service providers will see the demand for their performance increase, while less capable ones will suffer from increased competition. Most importantly, consumers and society will have a much broader range and quality of service choices available, often at a lower cost.

PROBLEMS IN SERVICE TRADE

5. To examine the competitive advantage of firms in the service sector

Together with the increase in the importance of service trade, new problems have emerged in the service sector. Many of these problems have been characterized as affecting mainly the negotiations between nations, but they are of sufficient importance to firms engaged in international activities to merit a brief review.

DATA COLLECTION PROBLEMS

The data collected on service trade are sketchy. Service transactions are often invisible statistically as well as physically. For example, the trip abroad of a consultant for business purposes may be hard to track and measure. The interaction of variables such as citizenship, residency, location of the transaction, and who or what (if anything) crosses national boundaries further contributes to the complexity of services transactions. Imagine that an Irish citizen working for a Canadian financial consulting firm headquartered in Sweden advises an Israeli citizen living in India on the management of funds deposited in a Swiss bank. Determining the export and import dimensions of such a services transaction is not easy.[17]

SERVICES AS A PERCENTAGE OF GDP

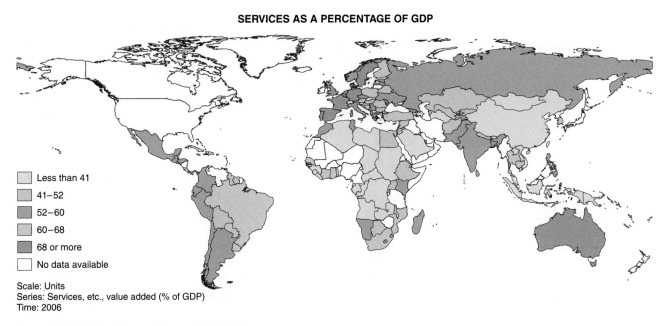

Less than 41
41–52
52–60
60–68
68 or more
No data available

Scale: Units
Series: Services, etc., value added (% of GDP)
Time: 2006

Source: 2008 World Development Indicators, World Bank.

The fact that governments have precise data on the number of trucks exported down to the last bolt but little information on reinsurance flows reflects past governmental inattention to services. Consequently, estimates of services trade vary. Total actual volume of services trade is likely to be larger than the amount shown by official statistics.

Consider the problem of services data collection in industrialized countries, with their sophisticated data gathering and information systems. Now imagine how many more problems are encountered in countries lacking such elaborate systems and unwilling to allocate funds for them. Insufficient knowledge and information have led to a lack of transparency, which makes it difficult for nations either to gauge or to influence services trade. As a result, regulations are often put into place without precise information as to their repercussions on actual trade performance.

GLOBAL REGULATIONS OF SERVICES

Global obstacles to service trade can be categorized into two major types: barriers to entry and problems in performing services abroad.

Barriers to entry are often explained by reference to "**national security**" and "**economic security**." For example, the impact of banking on domestic economic activity is given as a reason why banking should be carried out only by nationals or indeed should be operated entirely under government control. Sometimes the protection of service users is cited, particularly of bank depositors and insurance policyholders. Another justification used for barriers is the **infant-industry** argument: "With sufficient time to develop on our own, we can compete in world markets."

national security The ability of a nation to protect its internal values from external threats.

economic security Perception of a business activity as having an effect on a country's financial resources, often used to restrict competition from firms outside the country.

infant-industry A new type of business which requires some time to get started.

Often, however, this argument is used simply to prolong the ample licensing profits generated by restricted entry. Yet, defining a barrier to services is not always easy. For example, Taiwan gives an extensive written examination to prospective accountants (as do most countries) to ensure that licensed accountants are qualified to practice. The examination is given in Chinese. The fact that few German accountants, for example, read and write Chinese and hence are unable to pass the examination does not necessarily constitute a barrier to trade in accountancy services.

Service companies also encounter difficulties once they have achieved access to the local market. One reason is that rules and regulations based on tradition may inhibit innovation. A more important reason is that governments pursue social objectives through national regulations. The distinction between **discriminatory** and **nondiscriminatory regulations** is of primary importance here. Regulations that impose larger operating costs on foreign service providers than on the local competitors, that provide subsidies to local firms only, or that deny competitive opportunities to foreign suppliers are a proper cause for international concern. The problem of discrimination becomes even more acute when foreign firms face competition from government-owned or government-controlled enterprises. On the other hand, nondiscriminatory regulations may be inconvenient and may hamper business operations, but they offer less cause for international criticism. Yet, such national regulations can be key inhibitors for service innovations. For example, in Japan, pharmaceuticals cannot be sold outside of a licensed pharmacy. Similarly, travel arrangements can only be made within a registered travel office and banking can only be done during banking hours. As a result, innovations offered by today's communications technology cannot be brought to bear in these industries.[18]

All of these regulations make it difficult for international services to penetrate world markets. At the governmental level, services frequently are not recognized as a major facet of world trade or are viewed with suspicion because of a lack of understanding, and barriers to entry often result. To make progress in tearing them down, much educational work needs to be done.

In a major breakthrough in the Uruguay Round, the major GATT participants agreed to conduct services trade negotiations parallel with goods negotiations. The negotiations resulted in 1995 in the forging of a **General Agreement on Trade in Services (GATS)** as part of the World Trade Organization, the first multilateral, legally enforceable agreement covering trade and investment in the services sector. Similar to earlier agreements in the goods sector, GATS provides for most-favored-nation treatment, national treatment, transparency in rule making, and the free flow of payments and transfers. Market-access provisions restrict the ability of governments to limit competition and new-market entry. In addition, sectoral agreements were made for the movement of personnel, telecommunications, and aviation. However, in several sectors, such as entertainment, no agreement was obtained. In addition, many provisions, due to their newness, are very narrow. Therefore, future negotiations have been agreed upon, which will attempt to improve free trade in services.

discriminatory regulations Impose larger operating costs on foreign service providers than on local competitors, that provide subsidies to local firms only, or that deny competitive opportunities to foreign suppliers.

nondiscriminatory regulations Rules which do not differentiate between domestic and foreign firms all are affected alike.

General Agreement on Trade in Services (GATS) A legally enforceable pact among WTO participants that covers trade and investments in the services sector.

6. To analyze the strategic options available for corporations in the global service market

CORPORATIONS AND SERVICES TRADE

SERVICES AND E-COMMERCE

Electronic commerce has opened up new horizons for global services reach, and has drastically reduced the meaning of distance. For example, when geographic obstacles make the establishment of retail outlets cumbersome and expensive, firms can approach their customers via the World Wide Web. Government regulations that might be prohibitive to a transfer of goods may not have any effect on the international marketing of services. Also, regardless of size, companies are finding it increasingly easy to appeal to a global marketplace. The Internet can help service firms in developing and transitional economies overcome two of the biggest barriers they face: gaining credibility in international markets and saving on travel costs. Little-known firms can become instantly "visible" on the Internet. Even a small firm can develop a polished and sophisticated web presence and promotion strategy. Customers are less concerned about geographic location if they feel the firm is electronically accessible. An increasing number of service providers have never met their foreign customers except "virtually" online.[19] A quantitative assessment conducted by the WTO's Electronic Commerce Council indicated that the share of value added that potentially lends itself to electronic commerce exceeds 30 percent of GDP, most importantly distribution, finance, travel, and business services.[20]

Nonetheless, several notes of caution must be kept in mind. First, the introduction of the Internet has occurred at different rates in different countries. There are still many businesses and consumers who do not have access to electronic business media. Unless they are to be excluded from a company's focus, more traditional ways of reaching them must be considered. Also, firms need to prepare their Internet presence for global visitors. For example, the language of the Internet is English, accounting for approximately 40 percent of all web sites. Yet, many of the visitors coming to web sites either may not have English as their first language or may not speak English at all. As a matter of fact, the number of Chinese and Spanish speakers using the Internet has increased dramatically over the past decade (1,087 percent for Chinese and 650 percent for Spanish).[21] Companies need to respond to such visitor language trends.

According to the World Bank, a company's "default" English-language site reaches 36 percent of the world's cumulative gross national product (GNP) audience (approximately $17.6 trillion). Translating a web site in three languages alone—German, Italian, and French—adds an additional 17 percent of the world's GNP (approximately $7.9 trillion). A Japanese-enabled site grants access to an additional 10 percent—$4.8 trillion of the world's buying power. A Spanish-language site delivers 8 percent of the world's GNP. A combination of all these languages (English, German, Italian, French, Japanese, and Spanish) reaches more than 70 percent—nearly $34.5 trillion—of the cumulative GNP audience.[22] Many companies do not permit any interaction on their web sites, thus missing out on feedback or even order placement from visitors. Some web sites are so culture bound that they often leave their visitors bewildered and disappointed due to the cultural assumptions made. However, over time, increasing understanding of doing business in the global marketplace will enable companies to be more refined in their approach to their customers.

TYPICAL INTERNATIONAL SERVICES

Although many firms are active in the international service arena, others do not perceive their existing competitive advantage. Numerous services that are efficiently performed in the home market may have great potential for internationalization.

Financial institutions can offer some functions very competitively internationally in the field of banking services. U.S. banks possess advantages in fields such as mergers and acquisitions, securities sales, credit cards, and asset management. Banks in Europe and Japan are boosting their leadership through large assets and capital bases.

Construction, design, and **engineering services** also have great international potential. Providers of these services can achieve economies of scale not only for machinery and material but also in areas such as personnel management and the overall management of projects. Particularly for international projects that are large scale and long term, the experience advantage weighs heavily in favor of international firms.

Insurance services can be sold internationally by firms knowledgeable about underwriting, risk evaluation, and operations. Firms offering legal and accounting

engineering services Services that are provided in the areas of construction, design, and engineering.

insurance services Services that are provided in underwriting, risk evaluation, and operations.

Environmental concerns take on a major role for both consumers and producers.

Figure 15.4   Global Cooperation

© CORTESIA/COR/INT/NewsCom

services can aid their clients abroad through support activities; they can also help firms and countries improve business and governmental operations. Knowledge of computer operations, data manipulations, data transmission, and data analysis is insufficiently exploited internationally by many small and medium-sized firms.

communication services
Services that are provided in the areas of videotext, home banking, and home shopping, among others.

Similarly, **communication services** have substantial future international opportunities. For example, firms experienced in the areas of videotext, home banking, and home shopping can find international success, particularly where geographic obstacles make the establishment of retail outlets cumbersome and expensive. In addition, global communication services can lead to collaboration, which greatly expands the capability of corporations as shown in Figure 15.4.

teaching services Services that are provided in the areas of training and motivating as well as in teaching of operational, managerial, and theoretical issues.

Many institutions in the educational and corporate sectors have developed expertise in **teaching services**. They are very knowledgeable in training and motivation as well as in the teaching of operational, managerial, and theoretical issues, yet have largely concentrated their work in their domestic markets. It is time to take education global! Too much good and important knowledge is not made available to broad audiences. More knowledge must be communicated, be it through distance learning, study and teaching abroad, or attracting foreign students into the domestic market. The latter option can spur a service industry in itself.

consulting services Services that are provided in the areas of management expertise on such issues as transportation, logistics, and politics.

Management **consulting services** can be provided by firms and individuals to the many countries and corporations in need of them. Of particular value is management expertise in areas where many developing economies need the most help, such as transportation and logistics. Major opportunities also exist for industries that deal with societal problems. For example, firms that develop environmentally safe products or produce pollution-control equipment can find new markets, as nations around the world increase their awareness of and concern about the environment and tighten their laws. Similarly, advances in health care or new knowledge in combating AIDS offer major opportunities for global service success.

tourism The economic benefit of money spent in a country or region by travelers from outside the area.

Tourism also represents a major service export. Every time foreign citizens come to a country and spend their funds, the Current Account effect is that of an export. World travel and tourism generated US$944 billion in 2008.[23] The United Nations' World Tourism Organization (UNWTO) forecasts that international tourism will continue to grow at the average annual rate of 4 percent, partly due to the global rise of e-commerce. For example, due to the explosion of Internet usage in China, the online travel booking market in that country has developed rapidly; 66.7 percent of Chinese consumers use the Internet as their primary source for tourism information, and 70.7 percent of all air travel in the country is booked online.[24] This volume makes tourism one of the most important services in the world. However, this growing exchange of people has also led to greater interdependence and dependence between nations. As Focus on Policy shows, the widespread outbreak of illnesses can now have quicker and deeper repercussions than ever before.

An attractive international service mix can also be achieved by pairing the strengths of different partners. For example, information technology from one country can be combined with the financial resources of other countries. The strengths of the partners can then be used to offer maximum benefits to the international community.

Combining international advantages in services may ultimately result in the development of an even more drastic comparative lead. For example, if a firm has an international head start in such areas as high technology, information gathering, information processing, information analysis, and teaching, the major thrust of its international services might not be to provide these service components individually but

---

FOCUS ON POLITICS

H1N1 and the Global Tourism Industry

The spread of influenza A (H1N1) around the world had a palpable impact on the tourism industry. According to the United Nations' World Tourism Organization (UNWTO), destination travel dropped by nearly 10 percent between 2008 and 2009. "Results reflect the severe impact of the global economic crisis and all the associated causes and effects, exacerbated in some regions by concerns about the outbreak of the influenza A (H1N1) virus," UNWTO said in a statement.

The latest data prompted UNWTO to downscale its 2009 growth forecast for the global tourism industry to a range of −4 to −6 percent. In January 2009, the UNWTO's projection had been between a flat growth and a 2 percent contraction. This was partly attributed to the sharp reduction in global business activity, decreasing disposable income, and associated increased unemployment.

Within the period of the study, the Middle East posted an 18 percent drop in tourist arrivals, while Europe suffered a 10 percent decline. Arrivals in the Americas and Asia-Pacific saw contractions of 5 and 6 percent, respectively. Africa, meanwhile, was the only region to buck the downward trend with a 3 percent growth. Among the Southeast Asian countries, the UN body said only Malaysia reported a growth in arrivals during the same time.

The H1N1 outbreak has, in essence, created a "perfect storm" for the tourism industry in the midst of the global economic downturn. However, most analysts are optimistic that a rebound should be in the works, with the increased production and distribution of the H1N1 vaccine and global economic recovery.

Source: "Global Tourism Slows Due to Crisis," *abs-cbnNEWS.com*, July 8, 2009, http://www.abs-cbnnews.com/07/08/09/global-tourism-slows-due-crisis-ah1n1-scare-un, accessed December 11, 2009; *UNWTO World Tourism Barometer* 7, no. 2 (June 2009): 1–9.

Larger planes can make international shipments more easily and more efficiently.

© AFP/Stringer/Getty Images, Inc.

rather to enable clients, based on a combination of competitive resources, to make better decisions.

For many firms, participation in the Internet will offer the most attractive starting point in marketing their services internationally. The setup of a web site will allow visitors from any place in the globe to come see the offering. Of course, the most important problem will be how to communicate the existence of one's site and how to entice visitors to come. For that, often very traditional advertising and communication approaches need to be used. In some countries, for example, one can find rolling billboards announcing web sites and their benefits. Overall, however, one needs to keep in mind that not everywhere do firms and individuals have access to or make use of the new e-commerce opportunities.

STARTING TO OFFER SERVICES INTERNATIONALLY

For services that are delivered mainly in support of or in conjunction with goods, the most sensible approach for the international novice is to follow the path of the good. For years, many large accounting and banking firms have done this by determining where their major multinational clients have set up new operations and then following them. Smaller service providers who supply manufacturing firms can determine where the manufacturing firms are operating internationally. Ideally, of course, it would be possible to follow clusters of manufacturers abroad to obtain economies of scale internationally while simultaneously looking for entirely new client groups.

Service providers whose activities are independent from goods need a different strategy. These individuals and firms must search for market situations abroad that are similar to the domestic market. Such a search should be concentrated in their area of expertise. For example, a design firm learning about construction projects abroad can investigate the possibility of rendering its design services. Similarly, a management consultant learning about the plans of a country or firm to computerize its operations can explore the possibility of overseeing a smooth transition from manual to computerized activities. What is required is the understanding that similar problems are likely to occur in similar situations.

Another opportunity consists of identifying and understanding points of transition abroad. If, for example, new transportation services are introduced in a country, an expert in containerization may wish to consider whether to offer his or her service to improve the efficiency of the new system.

Leads for international service opportunities can also be gained by staying informed about international projects sponsored by domestic organizations such as the U.S. Agency for International Development or the Trade and Development Agency, as well as international organizations such as the United Nations, the International Finance Corporation, or the World Bank. Frequently, such projects are in need of support through services. Overall, the international service provider needs to search for similar situations, similar problems, or scenarios requiring similar solutions to formulate an effective international expansion strategy.

STRATEGIC INDICATIONS

To be successful in the international service offering, the manager must first determine the nature and the aim of the services-offering core—that is, whether the service will be aimed at people or at things and whether the service act in itself will result in tangible or intangible actions. Figure 15.5 provides examples of such a classification strategy that will help the manager to better determine the position of the services effort.

During this determination, the manager must consider other tactical variables that have an impact on the preparation of the service offering. For example, in conducting research for services, the measurement of capacity and delivery efficiency

Figure 15.5   Understanding the Service Act

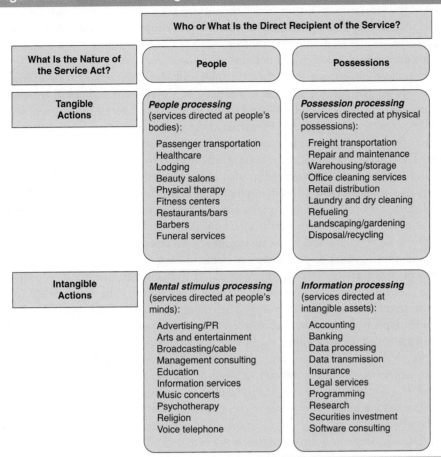

Source: Christopher Lovelock and Jochen Wirtz, *Services Marketing: People–Technology–Strategy*, 5th ed. (Upper Saddle River, NJ: Pearson Publishing, 2005).

often remains highly qualitative rather than quantitative. In communication and promotional efforts, the intangibility of the service reduces the manager's ability to provide samples. This makes communicating the service offered much more difficult than communicating an offer for a good. Brochures or catalogs explaining services often must show a proxy for the service to provide the prospective customer with tangible clues. A cleaning service, for instance, can show a picture of an individual removing trash or cleaning a window. However, the picture will not fully communicate the performance of the service.

Service exporters have three ways to gain credibility abroad: (1) providing objective verification of their capabilities—perhaps through focusing on the company's professional license or certification by international organizations; (2) providing personal guarantees of performance, including referrals and testimonials by satisfied customers; and (3) cultivating a professional image through public appearances at international trade events or conferences and promotional materials such as a web site.[25] Due to the different needs and requirements of individual consumers, the manager must also pay attention to the two-way flow of communication. In the service area, mass communication often must be supported by intimate one-on-one follow-up.

The role of personnel deserves special consideration in international service delivery. The customer interface is intense, therefore, proper provisions need to be made for training of personnel both domestically and internationally. Major emphasis must be placed on appearance. Most of the time the person delivering the service—rather than the service itself—will communicate the spirit, value, and attitudes of the service corporation. Since the service person is both the producer as well as the marketer of the service, recruitment and training techniques must focus on dimensions such as customer relationship management and image projection as well as competence in the design and delivery of the service.[26]

This close interaction with the consumer will also have organizational implications. While tight control over personnel may be desired, the individual interaction that is required points toward the need for an international decentralization of service delivery. This, in turn, requires delegation of large amounts of responsibility to individuals and service "subsidiaries" and requires a great deal of trust in all organizational units. This trust, of course, can be greatly enhanced through proper methods of training and supervision. Sole ownership also helps strengthen this trust. Research has shown that service firms, in their international expansion, tend to greatly prefer the establishment of full-control ventures. Only when costs escalate and the company-specific advantage diminishes will service firms seek out shared-control ventures.[27]

The areas of pricing and financing require special attention. Because services cannot be stored, much greater responsiveness to demand fluctuation must exist, and therefore greater pricing flexibility must be maintained. At the same time, flexibility is countered by the desire to provide transparency for both the seller and the buyer of services in order to foster an ongoing relationship. The intangibility of services also makes financing more difficult. Frequently, even financial institutions with large amounts of international experience are less willing to provide financial support for international services than for products. The reasons are that the value of services is more difficult to assess, service performance is more difficult to monitor, and services are difficult to repossess. Therefore, customer complaints and difficulties in receiving payments are much more troublesome for a lender to evaluate in the area of services than for goods.

Finally, the distribution implications of international services must be considered. Usually, short and direct channels are required. Within these channels, closeness to the customer is of overriding importance to understand what the customer really wants, to trace the use of the service, and to aid the customer in obtaining a truly tailor-made service.

SUMMARY

Services are taking on an increasing importance in international trade. They need to be considered separately from trade in merchandise because they no longer simply complement goods. Often, goods complement services or are in competition with them. Service attributes such as their intangibility, their perishability, their custom design, and their cultural sensitivity frequently make international trade in services more complex than trade in goods.

Services play a growing role in the global economy. International growth and competition in this sector have begun to outstrip that of merchandise trade and are likely to intensify in the future. Even though services are unlikely to replace production, the sector will account for the shaping of new competitive advantages internationally, particularly in light of new facilitating technologies which encourage electronic commerce.

The many service firms now operating only domestically need to investigate the possibility of going global. Historical patterns of service providers following manufacturers abroad have become partially obsolete as stand-alone services become more important to world trade. Management must therefore assess its vulnerability to service competition from abroad and explore opportunities to provide its services internationally.

KEY TERMS

intangibility   520
perishability   520
service capacity   520
customer involvement   520

service consistency   521
market transparency   521
service heterogeneity   521
government regulation   525

deregulation   525
cost of communication   526
national security   527
economic security   527

infant-industry   527
discriminatory regulations   528
nondiscriminatory regulations   528

General Agreement on Trade
    in Services (GATS)   528
engineering services   529
insurance services   529

communication services   530
teaching services   530
consulting services   530
tourism   530

QUESTIONS FOR DISCUSSION

1. How has the Internet affected you as a service consumer?

2. Discuss the future of service internationalization. Which services do you expect to migrate abroad and why?

3. How does the international sale of services differ from the sale of goods?

4. Discuss the benefits and drawbacks of service internationalization for companies in both the developed and the developing worlds.

INTERNET EXERCISES

1. Find the most current data on the five leading export and import countries for commercial services. The information is available on the World Trade Organization site http://www.wto.org—click the statistics button.

2. What are the key services exports and imports of your country? What is the current services trade balance? (for the United States: http://www.bea.gov)

TAKE A STAND

Governments in the developed world have long been pressured to put limits on the outsourcing of service jobs. Some have even implemented tax penalties for companies that engage in offshoring. However, cheaper labor leads to lower costs for both goods and services, which benefits many consumers at home. At the same time, there are domestic losers of outsourcing, such as those who have either lost their jobs or were unable to find new ones when the industry moved offshore. They are often very vocal and well-organized through unions and industry groups, which allows them to apply targeted political pressure to keep companies from going abroad.

For Discussion

1. Do lower costs for businesses and consumers make up for lost jobs in those countries that are departure points for outsourcing?

2. Should governments impose penalties and restrictions to keep services from moving overseas?

SUGGESTED READINGS

Simon Chesterman and Angelina Fisher, *Private Security, Public Order: The Outsourcing of Public Services and Its Limits* (Oxford, MA: Oxford University Press, 2010).

Aaditya Mattoo, Robert M. Stem, and Gianni Zanini, eds., *A Handbook of International Trade in Services* (Oxford, U.K: Oxford University Press, 2007).

Paul P. Maglio, Cheryl A. Kieliszewski, and James C. Spohrer, eds., *Handbook of Service Science (Service Science: Research and Innovations in the Service Economy)* (New York: Springer, 2010).

Faridah Djellal and Faiz Gallouj, *Measuring and Improving Productivity in Services: Issues, Strategies and Challenges (Services, Economy and Innovation)* (Gloucestershire, UK: Edward Elgar Publishing, 2009).

Adrian Palmer, *Principles of Services Marketing*, 5th ed. (New York: McGraw-Hill Higher Education, 2007).

CHAPTER 16

Logistics and Supply-Chain Management

CHAPTER CONTENTS & LEARNING OBJECTIVES

INTERNATIONAL LOGISTICS DEFINED

1. To understand the escalating importance of logistics and supply-chain management as crucial tools for competitiveness

SUPPLY-CHAIN MANAGEMENT

2. To learn about materials management and physical distribution

THE NEW DIMENSIONS OF INTERNATIONAL LOGISTICS

3. To learn why international logistics is more complex than domestic logistics

INTERNATIONAL INVENTORY ISSUES

4. To see how the transportation infrastructure in host countries often dictates the options open to the manager

INTERNATIONAL PACKAGING ISSUES

5. To learn why international inventory management is crucial for success

INTERNATIONAL STORAGE ISSUES

6. To learn about interactions between different logistics components

MANAGEMENT OF INTERNATIONAL LOGISTICS

7. To decide who should be in charge of logistics

THE SUPPLY CHAIN AND THE INTERNET

8. To appreciate how information and data exchange are pivotal for supply-chain management

LOGISTICS AND SECURITY

9. To understand the vulnerability and support of logistics

LOGISTICS AND THE ENVIRONMENT

10. To see and consider the linkages between logistics and sustainability

Supply-Chain Management Logistics in China

The importance of the trade relationship between China and the United States has been steadily rising. In 2000, China was fourth on the list of the top ten U.S. trading partners, following Canada, Mexico, and Japan. Its trade volume with the United States has since more than quadrupled ($94 billion to $408 billion), making it America's second largest trading partner and supplanting Mexico, which historically has held the number two spot. However, some analysts claim that these figures are not market-optimal, pointing to China's inadequate transportation and monitoring infrastructure as a continued impediment to international trade.

The government of the People's Republic has been paying attention. China has budgeted $440 billion over the next 30 years, earmarked for upgrading highways and railroads. This is good news for U.S.-based logistics and transportation companies, such as Schneider Logistics and YRC Worldwide, both of which have started to aggressively develop China-based networks. Both companies believe that China's planned investment should improve supply-chain management in the country, which has long been plagued by antiquated infrastructure systems, fragmented road networks, and limited transportation alternatives.

Jim Ritchie, president of YRC, states: "From a ground-transportation standpoint, the environment in China continues to be highly fragmented, with limited visibility." However, logistics providers, encouraged by Beijing's promised infrastructure investments, have sought to develop cooperative agreements with Chinese transportation suppliers in order to create greater potential synergy in the supply chain. For example, Ritchie remarked that a year ago, it was almost impossible to track freight in China, from the time it was dispatched to a consolidator, until it arrived at port and was loaded back onto a container. However, since YRC has developed direct working relationships with suppliers, the company has been able to better monitor the whereabouts of its customers' cargo. YRC has also dispatched 70 of its own trucks on Chinese roads and has developed 39 joint ventures with local transportation companies, allowing them to provide inland transport for approximately 200 shippers.

Schneider Logistics President Tom Escott also believes that supply-chain reliability in China is improving. According to him, Chinese companies are gradually gaining a better understanding of end-to-end supply-chain management. "Supply-chain functionality in North America includes national distribution, warehousing, and long-haul trucking," said Escott. "These things are still evolving in China, where customers' needs tend to be more localized, with smaller shipping patterns. Suddenly, we are seeing a whole evolution of thinking in the [Chinese] market about distribution and managing supply chains." Schneider Logistics opened its first Chinese office in 2005. It recently received government authorization to establish itself as a domestic carrier and logistics service provider, making it the first (and so far only) North American operator to establish a domestic truckload business in China.

Considering the enormous size of the country's consumer market, its WTO accession, and the gradual liberalization of its government's attitudes toward trade, China is positioned to enjoy economic expansion well into the future. Planned improvements to its supply-chain infrastructure are likely to remove one of the key remaining barriers on the road to prosperity.

Sources: Jeff Burman, *Logistics Management* (March 2007): 22; John J. Coyle, Edward J. Bardi, and C. John Langley, *Supply Chain Management: A Logistics Perspective*, 8th ed. (Mason, OH: South-Western College Publishing, 2008); "Foreign Trade Statistics–China," U.S. Bureau of the Census, http://www.census.gov/foreign-trade/balance/c5700.html#2009, accessed October 22, 2009; "Top Ten Countries with Which the U.S. Trades," U.S. Bureau of the Census, http://www.census.gov/foreign-trade/top/dst/2009/08/balance.html, accessed October 22, 2009; "Moving Goods in China," McKinsey & Co., February 2002, http://www.mckinsey.de, accessed October 21, 2009.

For the international firm, customer locations and sourcing opportunities are widely dispersed. The firm can attain a strategically advantageous position only if it is able to successfully manage complex international networks consisting of its vendors, suppliers, other third parties, and its customers. Neglect of links within and outside of the firm brings not only higher costs but also the risk of eventual noncompetitiveness, due to diminished market share, more expensive supplies, or lower profits. As discussed in the opening vignette, effective international logistics and supply-chain management can produce higher earnings and greater corporate efficiency, which are the cornerstones of corporate competitiveness.

This chapter will focus on international logistics and supply-chain management. Primary areas of concentration will be the links between the firm, its suppliers, and its customers, as well as transportation, inventory, packaging, and storage issues. The logistics management problems and opportunities that are peculiar to international business will also be highlighted.

INTERNATIONAL LOGISTICS DEFINED

1. To understand the escalating importance of logistics and supply-chain management as crucial tools for competitiveness

International logistics is the design and management of a system that controls the forward and reverse flow of materials, services, and information into, through, and out of the international corporation. It encompasses the total movement concept by covering the entire range of operations concerned with movement, including therefore both exports and imports. By taking a systems approach, the firm explicitly recognizes the links among the traditionally separate logistics components within and outside a corporation. By incorporating the interaction with outside organizations and individuals such as suppliers and customers, the firm is able to build on jointness of purpose by all partners in the areas of performance, quality, and timing.

As a result of implementing these systems considerations successfully, the firm can develop just-in-time (JIT) delivery for lower inventory cost, electronic data interchange (EDI) for more efficient order processing, and early supplier involvement (ESI) for better planning of goods development and movement. In addition, the use of such a systems approach allows a firm to concentrate on its core competencies and to form outsourcing alliances with other companies. For example, a firm can choose to focus on manufacturing and leave all aspects of order filling and delivery to an outside provider. By working closely with customers such as retailers, firms can also develop efficient customer response (ECR) systems, which can track sales activity on the retail level. As a result, manufacturers can precisely coordinate production in response to actual shelf replenishment needs, rather than based on forecasts.

materials management The timely movement of raw materials, parts, and supplies into and through the firm.

Two major phases in the movement of materials are of logistical importance. The first phase is **materials management**, or the timely movement of raw materials, parts, and supplies into and through the firm. The second phase is **physical distribution**, which involves the movement of the firm's finished product to its customers. In both phases, movement is seen within the context of the entire process. Stationary periods (storage and inventory) are therefore included. The basic goal of logistics management is the effective coordination of both phases and their various components to result in maximum cost effectiveness while maintaining service goals and requirements.

physical distribution The movement of finished products from suppliers to customers.

systems concept A view of logistics based on the notion that materials-flow activities are so complex that they can be considered only in the context of their interaction.

Key to business logistics are three major concepts: (1) the systems concept, (2) the total cost concept, and (3) the trade-off concept. The **systems concept** is based on the notion that materials-flow activities within and outside of the firm are so extensive and complex that they can be considered only in the context of their interaction. Instead of each corporate function, supplier, and customer operating with the goal of individual optimization, the systems concept stipulates that some components may have to work suboptimally to maximize the benefits of the system as a whole. The systems concept intends to provide the firm, its suppliers, and its customers, both domestic and foreign, with the benefits of synergism expected from the coordinated application of size.

In order for the systems concept to work, information flows and partnership trust are instrumental. Logistics capability is highly information dependent, because information availability is key to planning and to process implementation. Long-term partnership and trust are required in order to forge closer links between firms and managers.

A logical outgrowth of the systems concept is the development of the **total cost concept**. To evaluate and optimize logistical activities, cost is used as a basis for measurement. The purpose of the total cost concept is to minimize the firm's overall logistics cost by implementing the systems concept appropriately.

Implementation of the total cost concept requires that the members of the system understand the sources of costs. To develop such understanding, a system of activity-based costing has been developed, which is a technique designed to more accurately assign the indirect and direct resources of an organization to the activities performed based on consumption.[1] In the international arena, the total cost concept must also incorporate the consideration of total after-tax profit, by taking the impact of national tax policies on the logistics function into account. The objective is to maximize after-tax profits rather than minimizing total cost.

The **trade-off concept**, finally, recognizes the links within logistics systems that result from the interaction of their components. For example, locating a warehouse near the customer may reduce the cost of transportation. However, additional costs are associated with new warehouses. Similarly, a reduction of inventories will save money but may increase the need for costly emergency shipments. Managers can maximize performance of logistics systems only by formulating decisions based on the recognition and analysis of such trade-offs.

A trade-off of costs may go against one's immediate interests. Consider a manufacturer building several different goods. The goods all use one or both of two parts, A and B, which the manufacturer buys in roughly equal amounts. Most of the goods produced use both parts. The unit cost of part A is $7, of part B, $10. Part B has more capabilities than part A; in fact, B can replace A. If the manufacturer doubles its purchases of part B, it qualifies for a discounted $8 unit price. For products that incorporate both parts, substituting B for A makes sense to qualify for the discount, since the total parts cost is $17 using A and B, but only $16 using Bs only. Part B should therefore become a standard part for the manufacturer. But departments building products that only use part A may be reluctant to accept the substitute part B because, even discounted, the cost of B exceeds that of A. Use of the trade-off concept will solve the problem.[2]

SUPPLY-CHAIN MANAGEMENT

The integration of these three concepts has resulted in the new paradigm of **supply-chain management**, where a series of value-adding activities connects a company's supply side with its demand side. It has been defined by the Ohio State University Global SMC forum as "the integration of business processes from end user through original suppliers, that provide products, services, and information that add value for customers."[3] This approach views the supply chain of the entire extended enterprise, beginning with the supplier's suppliers and ending with consumers or end users. The perspective encompasses the entire flow of funds, products and information that form

total cost concept A decision framework that uses cost as a basis for measurement in order to evaluate and optimize logistical activities.

trade-off concept A decision paradigm that recognizes linkages within the decision system.

2. To learn about materials management and physical distribution

supply-chain management Results where a series of value-adding activities connect a company's supply side with its demand side.

one cohesive link to acquire, purchase, convert/manufacture, assemble, and distribute goods and services to the ultimate consumers. The implementation effects of such supply-chain management systems can be major.

Export supply-chain management skills facilitate the identification of attractive sources of supply and help firms develop a low-cost competitive supply position in export markets. They also help develop good relationships with suppliers and ensure increased quality and efficiency. The automobile industry was the first to adopt a comprehensive view of supply-chain management with an emphasis on supplier relations. BMW began to incorporate its suppliers' ideas into its own designs in order to capture their specialized knowledge. Ford Motor Company, which had previously been the most vertically integrated American automotive company, stopped making its own glass and purchased a share in a glass producer. This allowed Ford to use the glass producer's design and technology expertise, while still dictating specifications. This is an example of the so-called **extended enterprise**, where companies consider the entire supply chain to be a single organization that needs to be managed for purposes of both efficiency and effectiveness.[4]

Advances in information technology (IT) have been crucial to progress in supply-chain management and supplier coordination. For example, TaylorMade—Adidas' golfing branch—uses supply-chain planning and execution software in order to optimize performance. In the demand planning phase, sales representatives capture data from retail customers using bar code technology at the point of sale, which is then transmitted in real time to the warehouse. The warehouse is able to compare orders with existing stock and alert vendors of future demand trends. This allows suppliers to plan ahead and improve their delivery schedules, which in turn leads to less inventory and higher levels of customer satisfaction. TaylorMade's successful use of data management software has led to improved performance across the supply chain, including higher inventory turnover rates (33 percent) and a 25 percent reduction in the overall cost of goods sold. On-time delivery of products has gone from 70 percent to more than 95 percent. There are many companies that have followed the TaylorMade model and have benefited from the introduction of IT to their supply-chain management systems.[5] In most cases, the positive impact has become manifest rather quickly. Three years after communications giant Motorola implemented an integrated system of IT supply-chain management, it was able to achieve customer on-time deliveries of 85 to 92 percent (from a previous 30 to 40 percent), and an 18 percent improvement in inventory turnover.[6] In the future, the strategic use of information technology will become increasingly crucial for international managers seeking to develop and maintain key competitive advantages. An overview of the international supply chain is shown in Figure 16.1.

extended enterprise When companies consider the entire supply chain to be a single organization that needs to be managed for purposes of both efficiency and effectiveness.

THE IMPACT OF INTERNATIONAL LOGISTICS

Logistics costs comprise between 10 and 30 percent of the total landed cost of an international order.[7] International firms already have achieved many of the cost reductions that are possible in financing and production, and are now using international logistics as a competitive tool. The environment facing logistics managers in the next ten years will be dynamic and explosive. Technological advances and progress in communication systems and information-processing capabilities are particularly significant in the design and management of logistics systems.

For example, close collaboration with suppliers is required to develop a just-in-time inventory system, which in turn may be crucial to maintaining manufacturing costs at globally competitive levels. Yet, without electronic data interchange, such collaborations or alliances are severely handicapped. While most industrialized countries can offer the technological infrastructure for such computer-to-computer exchange

Figure 16.1   The International Supply Chain

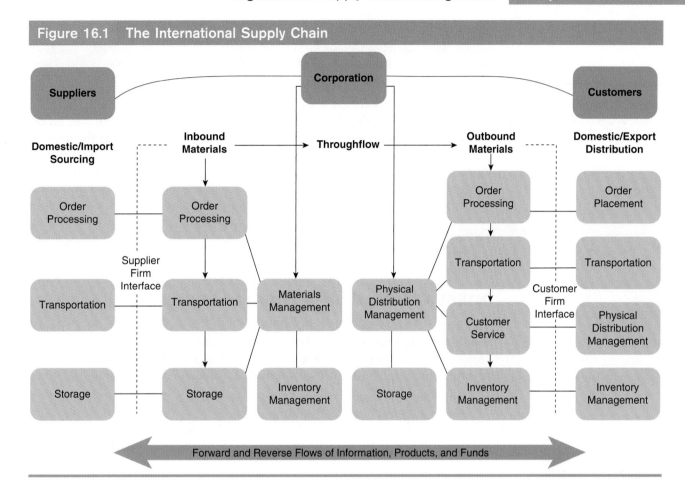

of business information, the application of such a system in the global environment may be severely restricted. It may not be just the lack of technology that forms the key obstacle to modern logistics management, but rather the entire business infrastructure, ranging from ways of doing business in fields such as accounting and inventory tracking, to the willingness of businesses to collaborate with each other.

Inventory carrying costs and transportation costs are also a function of the general health of the global economy. For example, a record spike in fuel prices and drops in consumer demand in 2008 drove logistics costs for American businesses to a record $1.4 trillion, or 10.1 percent of GDP, a percentage unseen since 2000. Up to that point, the U.S. economy had enjoyed a gradual rise in logistics efficiency and productivity, due to increased supply-chain synergies. For example, in 1985, logistics cost 12.3 percent of GDP. Two decades later that figure had dropped to 8.6 percent.[8]

The fundamentals of a country's logistics system remain the best predictor of cost and efficiency. For example, Russia's distribution costs have hovered around 30 percent of GNP, irrespective of the global economic climate, due to a combination of space constraints, poor lines of supply, and inadequate transportation. This makes transactions slow and expensive.[9] Even in countries that have a similar departure point in terms of logistics costs, government policies, infrastructure investment, and accumulation of managerial know-how can make a big difference. For example, since the ratification of NAFTA, Mexico's logistics efficiencies as a percentage of GNP have improved considerably, following the American example, while Brazil's have remained relatively stagnant at an average of 13 percent.[10] Logistics and supply-chain management increasingly are the key dimensions by which firms gain competitiveness in the international marketplace.

THE NEW DIMENSIONS OF INTERNATIONAL LOGISTICS

3. To learn why international logistics is more complex than domestic logistics

In domestic operations, logistics decisions are guided by the experience of the manager, possible industry comparisons, an intimate knowledge of trends, and discovered heuristics—or rules of thumb. The logistics manager in the international firm, on the other hand, frequently has to depend on educated guesses to determine the steps required to obtain a desired service level. Variations in locale mean variations in environment. Lack of familiarity with such variations leads to uncertainty in the decision-making process. By applying decision rules based only on the environment encountered at home, the firm will be unable to adapt well to new circumstances, and the result will be inadequate profit performance. The long-term survival of international activities depends on an understanding of the differences inherent in the international logistics field.

INTERNATIONAL TRANSPORTATION ISSUES

Transportation determines how and when goods will be received. Focus on Entrepreneurship details some of the problems that can be encountered in the transportation process. The transportation issue can be divided into three components: infrastructure, the availability of modes, and the choice of modes among the given alternatives.

FOCUS ON ENTREPRENEURSHIP

Late, Lost, and Damaged Goods

No shipper would want to win Roberts Express "Shipments from Hell" contest. "Winners" have nightmare tales of late, lost, broken, or even burned shipments, demonstrating just about everything that could possibly go wrong in transit. Judges from *Industry Week* and *Transportation and Distribution* magazines gave the top award to a shipment of auto parts that needed to be at an assembly plant in a few hours, since the factory operated on a just-in-time basis. But a misunderstanding over the chartered plane's arrival time and the time the parts needed to arrive kept the freight on the ground for hours. The entire production line was forced to shut down, costing thousands of dollars a minute. Then a thunderstorm delayed the plane's take-off by another half-hour, adding more dollars to the cost of the late shipment.

In another 'Shipment from Hell,' attention to detail could have averted a sticky disaster. A Danish company arranged to send a shipment by rail from New York to Washington State, but forgot to mention that the cargo needed refrigeration. After a week's journey in a railcar, the shipment of imported margarine was a gooey yellow mess. At the opposite end of the spectrum, there is the delivery driver who ignored the warning that his cargo should be protected from sub-zero temperatures, resulting in a truckload of frozen solid adhesive.

Instances of damaged or destroyed goods abound in the contest. One "winner" found its custom-made products at the bottom of Houston Harbor. Another company's million-dollar computer system was smashed as it rolled off the delivery truck. In an ironic twist on the damaged goods problem, one shipment was found burned and melted inside a forty-foot ocean container. It turned out the goods were firefighting equipment, sprinklers, and valves.

Some of the stories involve old-fashioned brazen theft, such as $30,000 in missing beer that the delivery driver had been selling to a convenience store, blocks away from the customer's warehouse.

The stories behind the "Shipments from Hell" illustrate that a host of bizarre circumstances can turn an ordinary shipment into a comedy of errors. If a merchant finds itself on the receiving end of a damaged shipment and decides to pursue legal action, the laws governing international transportation are many and complex. In one classic case (*Raymond Burke* v. *Mersey Docks and Harbour Board*), a container of motorcycles was waiting to be loaded when a harbor truck ran it over. The judge determined that the carrier's contractual responsibility would not begin until loading of the goods in question had actually begun, and the company could not recoup its losses.

Sources: Gregory S. Johnson, "Damaged Goods: Hard-Luck Tales of '97," *The Journal of Commerce*, January 9, 1998, IA, accessed October 21, 2009; Simon Baughen, *Shipping Law*, 4th ed. (New York: Routledge-Cavendish, 2009), 61.

Transportation Infrastructure

In industrialized countries, firms can count on an established transportation network. Around the globe, however, major infrastructural variations will be encountered. Some countries may have excellent inbound and outbound transportation systems but weak internal transportation links. This is particularly true in former colonies, where the original transportation systems were designed to maximize the extractive potential of the countries. In such instances, shipping to the market may be easy, but distribution within the market may represent a very difficult and time-consuming task. Infrastructure problems can also be found in countries where most transportation networks were established between major ports and cities in past centuries. The areas lying outside the major transportation networks will encounter problems in bringing their goods to market.

New routes of commerce have also opened up, particularly between the former East and West political blocs. Yet, without the proper infrastructure, the opening of markets is mainly accompanied by major new bottlenecks. On the part of the firm, it is crucial to have wide market access to be able to appeal to sufficient customers. The firm's **logistics platform**, which is determined by a location's ease and convenience of market reach under favorable cost circumstances, is a key component of a firm's competitive position. Because different countries and regions may offer alternative logistics platforms, the firm must recognize that such alternatives can be the difference between success and failure. Policymakers in turn must recognize the impact they have on the quality of infrastructure. It is governmental planning that enables supply-chain capabilities and substantially affects logistics performance on the corporate level. In an era of foreign direct investment flexibility, the public sector's investment priorities, safety regulations, tax incentives, and transport policies can have major effects on the logistics decisions of firms.[11] In the first nine months of 2009, 114 vessels were boarded, 34 vessels hijacked, and 88 vessels fired upon. A total of 661 crewmembers were taken hostage, 12 kidnapped, 6 killed, and 8 reported missing.[12] For example, whether or not a country has a strong navy can become very meaningful for the logistician in light of the fact that piracy against the world's shipping keeps rising rapidly.

logistics platform Vital to a firm's competitive position, it is determined by a location's ease and convenience of market reach under favorable cost circumstances.

The logistics manager must therefore learn about existing and planned infrastructures abroad and at home and factor them into the firm's strategy. In some countries, for example, railroads may be an excellent transportation mode, far surpassing the performance of trucking, while in others the use of railroads for freight distribution may be a gamble at best. The future routing of pipelines must be determined before any major commitments are made to a particular location if the product is amenable to pipeline transportation. The transportation methods used to carry cargo to seaports or airports must be investigated. Mistakes in the evaluation of transportation options can prove to be very costly. One researcher reported the case of a food processing firm that built a pineapple cannery at the delta of a river in Mexico. Because the pineapple plantation was located upstream, the company planned to float the ripe fruit down to the cannery on barges. To its dismay, however, the firm soon discovered that at harvest time the river current was far too strong for barge traffic. Because no other feasible alternative method of transportation existed, the plant was closed and the new equipment was sold for a fraction of its original cost.[13]

Extreme variations also exist in the frequency of transportation services. For example, a particular port may not be visited by a ship for weeks or even months. Sometimes only carriers with particular characteristics, such as small size, will serve a given location.

All of these infrastructural concerns must be taken into account in the planning of the firm's location and transportation framework. The opportunity of a highly competitive logistics platform may be decisive for the firm's investment decision,

land bridge Transfer of ocean freight on land among various modes of transportation.

sea bridge The transfer of freight among various modes of transportation at sea.

intermodal movements The transfer of freight from one mode or type of transportation to another.

ocean shipping The forwarding of freight by ocean carrier.

liner service Ocean shipping characterized by regularly scheduled passage on established routes.

bulk service Ocean shipping provided on contract either for individual voyages or for prolonged periods of time.

tramp service Ocean shipping via irregular routes, scheduled only on demand.

container ships Ships designed to carry standardized containers, which greatly facilitate loading and unloading as well as intermodal transfers.

roll-on-roll-off (RORO) Transportation vessels built to accommodate trucks, which can drive on in one port and drive off at their destinations.

because it forms a key component of the cost advantages sought by multinational corporations. If a location loses its logistics benefits, due to, for example, a deterioration of the railroad system, a firm may well decide to move on to another, more favorable locale. Business strategist Michael Porter addressed the importance of infrastructure as a determinant of national competitive advantage and highlighted the capability of governmental efforts to influence this critical issue.[14] Governments must keep the transportation dimension in mind when attempting to attract new industries or trying to retain existing firms.

Availability of Modes

International transportation frequently requires ocean or airfreight modes, which many corporations only rarely use domestically. In addition, combinations such as **land bridges** or **sea bridges** may permit the transfer of freight among various modes of transportation, resulting in **intermodal movements**. The international logistics manager must understand the specific properties of the different modes to be able to use them intelligently.

Ocean Shipping　Water transportation is a key mode for international freight movement. Three types of vessels operating in **ocean shipping** can be distinguished by their service: liner service, bulk service, and tramp or charter service. **Liner service** offers regularly scheduled passage on established routes. **Bulk service** mainly provides contractual services for individual voyages or for prolonged periods of time. **Tramp service** is available for irregular routes and scheduled only on demand.

In addition to the services offered by ocean carriers, the type of cargo a vessel can carry is also important. Most common are conventional (break bulk) cargo vessels, container ships, and roll-on-roll-off vessels. Conventional cargo vessels are useful for oversized and unusual cargoes but may be less efficient in their port operations. **Container ships** carry standardized containers that greatly facilitate the loading and unloading of cargo and intermodal transfers. As a result, the time the ship has to spend in port is reduced as are the port charges. **Roll-on-roll-off (RORO)** vessels are essentially oceangoing ferries. Trucks can drive onto built-in ramps and roll off at the destination. Another vessel similar to the RORO vessel is the LASH (lighter aboard ship) vessel. LASH vessels consist of barges stored on the ship and lowered at the point of destination. The individual barge can then operate on inland waterways, a feature that is particularly useful in shallow water.

The availability of a certain type of vessel, however, does not automatically mean that it can be used. The greatest constraints in international ocean shipping are the lack of ports and port services. For example, modern container ships cannot serve some ports because the local equipment cannot handle the resulting traffic. The problem is often found in developing countries, where local authorities lack the funds to develop facilities. In some instances, governments may purposely limit the development of **ports** to impede the inflow of imports. Increasingly, however, governments have begun to recognize the importance of an appropriate port facility structure and are developing such facilities in spite of the large investments necessary.

Air Shipping　**Airfreight** is available to and from most countries. This includes the developing world,

© YOSHIKAZU TSUNO/Getty Images/NewsCom

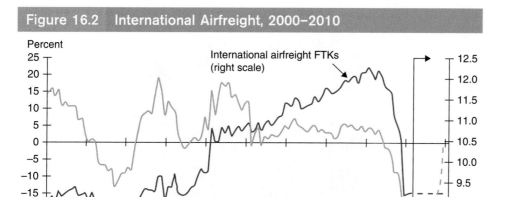

Figure 16.2 International Airfreight, 2000–2010

Note: FTK = Freight tonne-kilometers

Sources: Based on data supplied by member states of the International Air Transport Association (IATA); IATA Economic Briefing, April 2009, www.iata.org/economics, accessed October 21, 2009.

where it is often a matter of national prestige to operate a national airline. The growth and occasional declines in international airfreight are shown in Figure 16.2. The total volume of airfreight in relation to total shipping volume in international business remains quite small. Approximately 20 percent of the world's manufactured exports by weight travel by air. The figure is higher for advanced economies, which export more high-value items. Those are likelier to be shipped by air, particularly if they have a high density, that is, a high weight-to-volume ratio. However, when the global economy experiences a downturn, airfreight tends to lose customers to cheaper modes of transport. For example, amid the global recession in 2008, cargo air traffic declined by more than 20 percent. Airlines, particularly in the United States, responded with aggressive capacity adjustments, but many were not able to keep pace with the precipitous fall in demand, or were caught with fuel hedges higher than spot prices, and were forced to either consolidate or shut down.[15]

Airlines continue to make major efforts to increase the volume of airfreight. Many of these activities have concentrated on developing better, more efficient ground facilities, automating air waybills, introducing airfreight containers, and providing and marketing a wide variety of special services to shippers. In addition, some airfreight companies and ports have specialized and become partners in the international logistics effort.

Changes have also taken place within the aircraft. As an example, 40 years ago, the holds of large propeller aircraft could take only about 10 tons of cargo. Today's jumbo jets can load up to 148 metric tons of cargo, and can therefore transport bulky products,[16] such as locomotives, as shown in Figure 16.3. In addition, aircraft manufacturers have responded to industry demands by developing both jumbo cargo planes and combination passenger and cargo aircraft. The latter carry passengers in one section of the main deck and freight in another. These hybrids can be used by carriers on routes that would be uneconomical for passengers or freight alone.

From the shipper's perspective, the products involved must be appropriate for air shipment in terms of their size. In addition, the market situation for any given product must be evaluated. Airfreight may be needed if a product is perishable or if, for other reasons, it requires a short transit time. The level of customer service needs and expectations can also play a decisive role. For example, the shipment of an industrial product that is vital to the ongoing operations of a customer may be much more urgent than the shipment of packaged consumer products.

ports Harbor towns or cities where ships may take on or discharge cargo; the lack of ports and port services is the greatest constraint in ocean shipping.

airfreight Transport of goods by air; accounts for less than one percent of the total volume of international shipments, but more than 20 percent of value.

Employees of Lufthansa Cargo load freight onto a Boeing 747 at Frankfurt Airport. The 747 fleet has flown 3.5 billion people, equivalent to half the world's population.

Figure 16.3   Large Planes Offer Unprecedented Loading Capacity

Source: *The Guardian*, February 11, 2009, http://www.guardian.co.uk/artanddesign/gallery/2009/feb/11/40th-anniversary-jumbo-jet?picture=343114913, accessed October 19, 2009.

SELECTING A MODE OF TRANSPORT

The international logistics manager must make the appropriate selection from the available modes of transportation. The decision will be heavily influenced by the needs of the firm and its customers. The manager must consider the performance of each mode on four dimensions: transit time, predictability, cost, and noneconomic factors.

Transit Time

transit time The period between departure and arrival of a carrier.

The period between departure and arrival of the carrier varies significantly between ocean freight and airfreight. For example, the 45-day **transit time** of an ocean shipment can be reduced to 24 hours if the firm chooses airfreight. The length of transit time can have a major impact on the overall operations of the firm. As an example, a short transit time may reduce or even eliminate the need for an overseas depot. Also, inventories can be significantly reduced if they are replenished frequently. As a result, capital can be freed up and used to finance other corporate opportunities. Transit time can also play a major role in emergency situations. For example, if the shipper is about to miss an important delivery date because of production delays, a shipment normally made by ocean freight can be made by air. Overall, it has been estimated that each day that goods are in transit adds about 0.8 percent to the cost of the goods. Therefore, an extra twenty-day period spent at sea adds the equivalent of a 16 percent tariff on those goods, drastically reducing their competitiveness.[17]

Perishable products require shorter transit times. Transporting them rapidly prolongs the shelf life in the foreign market. Air delivery may be the only way to enter foreign markets successfully with products that have a short life span. International sales of cut flowers have reached their current volume only as a result of airfreight.

The interaction among selling price, market distance, and form of transportation is not new. Centuries ago, Johann von Thünen, a noted German economist, developed models for the market reach of agricultural products that incorporated these factors. These models informed farmers as to what product could be raised profitably at different distances from its market. Yet, given the forms of transportation available today, the factors no longer pose the rigid constraints experienced by von Thünen; capability of transport creates new opportunities in international business.

At all times, the logistics manager must understand the interactions between different components of the logistics process and their effect on transit times. Unless a smooth flow throughout the supply chain can be assured, bottlenecks will deny any timing benefits from specific improvements. For example, Levi Strauss, the blue jeans manufacturer, offers customers in some of its stores the chance to be measured by a body scanner. Less than an hour after such measurement, a Levi factory has begun to cut the jeans of their choice. Unfortunately, it then takes ten days to get the finished jean to the customer.[18]

Predictability

Providers of both ocean freight and airfreight service wrestle with the issue of reliability. Both modes are subject to the vagaries of nature, which may impose delays. Yet, because **reliability** is a relative measure, the delay of one day for airfreight tends to be seen as much more severe and 'unreliable' than the same delay for ocean freight. However, delays tend to be shorter in absolute time for air shipments. As a result, arrival time via air is more predictable. This attribute has a major influence on corporate strategy. For example, because of the higher predictability of airfreight, inventory safety stock can be kept at lower levels. Greater predictability also can serve as a useful sales tool, since it permits more precise delivery promises to customers. If inadequate port facilities exist, airfreight may again be the better alternative. Unloading operations for oceangoing vessels are more cumbersome and time-consuming than for planes. Merchandise shipped via air is likely to suffer less loss and damage from exposure of the cargo to movement. Therefore, once the merchandise arrives, it is more likely to be ready for immediate delivery—a fact that also enhances predictability.

reliability Dependability; the predictability of the outcome of an action. For example, the reliability of arrival time for ocean freight or airfreight.

An important aspect of predictability is also the capability of a shipper to track goods at any point during the shipment. **Tracking** becomes particularly important as corporations increasingly obtain products from and send them to multiple locations around the world. Being able to coordinate the smooth flow of a multitude of interdependent shipments can make a vast difference in a corporation's performance.[19] Tracking allows the shipper to check on the functioning of the supply chain and to take remedial action if problems occur. Cargo also can be redirected if sudden demand surges so require. However, such enhanced corporate response to the predictability issue is only possible if an appropriate information system is developed by the shipper and the carrier, and is easily accessible to the user. Due to rapid advances in information technology, the ability to know where a shipment is has increased dramatically, while the cost of this critical knowledge has declined. Focus on e-Business explains this further.

tracking The capability of a shipper to obtain information about the location of the shipment at any time.

Studies of customs data have demonstrated that transportation costs (both explicit and in terms of transit time) pose a barrier to trade at least as large as, and frequently larger than, tariffs. Global trade negotiations have steadily reduced tariff rates. As tariffs become a less important barrier to trade, the impact of transportation expenses on total

Product Tracking

Whenever Dawn Pabst of Las Vegas, Nevada, orders a pizza from Domino's, she does not wait for it to arrive at her doorstep. She tracks. She monitors the second-by-second status of her pizza at Dominos.com. Dawn is one of millions of customers who electronically track everything from order accuracy to the moment their pizza is prepared and sent for delivery. This is an example of a powerful new trend. Advances in information technology are transforming America into a nation of "track-a-holics." It would appear that everyone, from logistics managers at large multinational companies to customers like Dawn Pabst, want the ability to electronically track the whereabouts of the products they order or ship. Marketers are keenly aware of this growing consumer demand. When online package tracking was implemented in December 1995, UPS had about 100,000 track requests for the entire month. In December 2009, that number was 27.3 million requests per day.

According to one marketing analyst, "Data is money. The more information you have, the more interesting you are." This realization could explain why Domino's started Pizza Tracker; UPS and FedEx send constant location updates to consumers; cities like Chicago and Washington, DC, have introduced real-time tracking for their transit systems; and a growing number of Web services are offering to monitor everything from flights, to a sleeping baby, to government spending. The growing importance of tracking could reflect consumers' desire for a greater sense of control. Barry Glassner, sociology professor at the University of Southern California, endorses this theory: "I'd much rather know if I'm secure in my job," he says. "But if I can't know that, at least I can know the status of my pizza."

Beyond the marketing psychology of individual consumers, transportation service providers realize that for their corporate clients, a "greater sense of control" translates into calculations of predictability, reliability, and, ultimately, competitiveness and cost. For example, Texas Industries Inc. (TXI)—a large Dallas-based building supply company recently introduced a product tracking system called ReadyTrac. It allows TXI's customers to increase productivity by accessing real-time truck locations from any computer with Internet access. GPS tracking provides information regarding delivery status, including whether trucks have been loaded or are in route to any jobsite. However, ReadyTrac goes a step beyond simple location tracking. Planned program enhancements include the ability to monitor jobsite crew productivity and profitability. The majority of TXI's customers are large construction companies that count labor costs among their biggest expenditures. If ReadyTrac is successful in allowing them to increase crew oversight, this would translate into cost savings for the customer and a strong competitive edge for TXI.

In a case of business innovation spilling over into the policy world, governments and regulatory agencies have started to take notice of developments in product tracking technology. One area, where product tracking could be especially beneficial, is in the incorporation of data into drug packaging in order to protect patients from dangerous counterfeits. Countries have begun to implement laws that require pharmaceutical companies to use tracking technologies. For example, since January 2009, all drugs sold in Turkey have to be packaged with track-and-trace barcode identifiers. Governments are also supporting research in tracking technology. The European Union has sponsored several studies aimed at developing end-to-end traceability for medication, such as the one carried out at the National Centre for Hereditary Coagulation Disorders in Ireland. China and India, which are often identified as the biggest culprits, but whose citizens are also the biggest victims of counterfeit pharmaceuticals, have launched exploratory studies on tracking. Whether contributing to a company's bottom line, appeasing impatient customers, or protecting patients, it looks like product tracking is here to stay.

Sources: Bruce Horovitz, "Tracking Deliveries of all Kinds is on Everyone's Radar," *USA Today*, July 26, 2009; "TXI Ready-Mix Introduces Delivery Tracking System," *The Wall Street Journal*, August 26, 2009; "Tracking the Drug Trail," PharmaceuticalTechnology.com, May 12, 2008, http://www.pharmaceutical-technology.com/features/feature1906/, accessed November 6, 2009.

---

trade costs is on the rise. Nowadays, for the average import shipment to the United States, shippers pay $9 in transportation costs for every $1 paid in tariffs. Even at this level, the United States is actually an outlier, because it pays considerably less for transportation than other countries. For example, aggregate transportation spending for Latin America is 1.5 to 2.5 times higher than for the United States.[20] Transportation costs for a product depend on the distance it is shipped, the type of transport service selected, and the weight-to-value ratio of the good. Because these three factors vary considerably across shipments, transportation costs have a significant influence on prices and patterns of trade.[21]

Cost of Transportation   International transportation services are usually priced on the basis of both the cost of the service provided and the value of the service to the shipper. Due to the high value of the products shipped by air, airfreight is often priced according to the value of the service. In this instance, of course, price becomes a function of market demand and the monopolistic power of the carrier.

The manager must decide whether the clearly higher cost of airfreight can be justified. In part, this will depend on the cargo's properties. The physical density and the value of the cargo will affect the decision. Bulky products may be too expensive to ship by air, whereas very compact products may be more appropriate for airfreight transportation. High-priced items can absorb transportation costs more easily than low-priced goods because the cost of transportation as a percentage of total product cost will be lower. As a result, sending diamonds by airfreight is easier to justify than sending coal. Alternatively, a shipper can decide to mix modes of transportation in order to reduce overall cost and time delays. For example, part of the shipment route can be covered by air, while another portion can be covered by truck or ship.

Most important, however, are the supply-chain considerations of the firm. The manager must determine how important it is for merchandise to arrive on time, which, for example, will be different for standard garments versus high fashion dresses. The effect of transportation cost on price and the need for product availability abroad must also be considered. Simply comparing transportation modes on the basis of price alone is insufficient. The manager must factor in all corporate, supplier, and customer activities that are affected by the modal choice and explore the full implications of each alternative. For example, some firms may want to use airfreight as a new tool for aggressive market expansion. Airfreight may also be considered a good way to begin operations in new markets without making sizable investments for warehouses and distribution centers. The final selection of a mode will be the result of the importance of different modal dimensions to the markets under consideration. A useful overall comparison of different modes of transportation is provided in Table 16.1.

Noneconomic Factors   The transportation sector, nationally and internationally, both benefits and suffers from government involvement. Even though transportation carriers are one prime target in the sweep of privatization around the globe, many carriers are still owned or heavily subsidized by governments. As a result, governmental pressure is exerted on shippers to use national carriers, even if more economical alternatives exist. Such **preferential policies** are most often enforced when government cargo is being transported. Restrictions are not limited to developing countries. For example, in the United States, the federal government requires that all travelers on government business use national flag carriers when available.

For balance of payment reasons, international quota systems of transportation have been proposed. The United Nations Convention on the Code of Conduct for Liner Conferences, which was enacted in 1983, established the "40/40/20" rule in maritime transport. The main provision was that cargo shipments between two

preferential policies Government policies that favor certain (usually domestic) firms; for example, the use of national carriers for the transport of government freight even when more economical alternatives exist.

Table 16.1   Evaluating Transportation Choices

Characteristics of Mode	Mode of Transportation				
	Air	Pipeline	Highway	Rail	Water
Speed (1=fastest)	1	4	2	3	5
Cost (1=highest)	1	4	2	3	5
Loss and Damage (1=least)	3	1	4	5	2
Frequency[1] (1=best)	3	1	2	4	5
Dependability (1=best)	5	1	2	3	4
Capacity[2] (1=best)	4	5	3	2	1
Availability (1=best)	3	5	1	2	4

[1]Frequency: number of times mode is available during a given time period.
[2]Capacity: ability of mode to handle large or heavy goods.

Source: Ronald H. Ballou, *Business Logistics Management*, 5th ed. (Upper Saddle River, NJ: Prentice-Hall, 2004).

countries had to be shared in the following way: 40 percent for ship owners in the country of origin, 40 percent for ship owners in the destination country, and 20 percent for ship owners from third countries (cross-traders). The Liner Code attempted to stimulate local shipping industries, but proved to be counterproductive. It generated market distortions that led to an increase in maritime transport prices. Additionally, the rule created national shipping companies that had no ships and would sell their country's share of cargo to foreign lines, without any responsibility for the subsequent quality or cost of service. In 1992, the European Court ruled that the liner conferences were illegal monopolies and the '40/40/20' rule was lifted.[22]

EXPORT DOCUMENTATION

A firm must deal with numerous forms and documents when exporting to ensure that all goods meet local and foreign laws and regulations. In the simplest form of exporting, the only documents needed are a bill of lading and an export declaration. In most countries, these documents are available either from the government or from transportation firms. For example, an export declaration can be obtained in the United States from the Census Bureau (http://www.census.gov/foreign-trade/regulations/forms). A bill of lading can be obtained in Canada from a shipper, for example, Manitoulin Transport (http://www.manitoulintransport.com).

export declaration A shipping document detailing the type, destination, shipping, timing, and value of an export shipment.

The shipper's **export declaration** provides proper authorization for export and serves as a means for governmental data collection efforts. A **bill of lading** is a contract between the exporter and the carrier indicating that the carrier has accepted responsibility for the goods and will provide transportation in return for payment. The bill of lading can also be used as a receipt and to prove ownership of the merchandise. There are two types of bills, negotiable and nonnegotiable. **Straight bills of lading** are nonnegotiable and are typically used in prepaid transactions. The goods are delivered to a specific individual or company. **Shipper's order** bills of lading are negotiable; they can be bought, sold, or traded while the goods are still in transit and are used for letter of credit transactions. The customer usually needs the original or a copy of the bill of lading as proof of ownership to take possession of the goods.

bill of lading A contract between an exporter and a carrier indicating that the carrier has accepted responsibility for the goods and will provide transportation in return for payment.

straight bill of lading A nonnegotiable bill of lading usually used in prepaid transactions in which the transported goods involved are delivered to a specific individual or company.

A **commercial invoice** is a bill for the goods stating basic information about the transaction, including a description of the merchandise, total cost of the goods sold, addresses of the shipper and seller, and delivery and payment terms. The buyer needs the invoice to prove ownership and to arrange payment. Some governments use the commercial invoice to assess customs duties.

shipper's order A negotiable bill of lading that can be bought, sold, or traded while the subject goods are still in transit and that is used for letter of credit transactions.

Other export documents that may be required include export licenses, consular invoices (used to control and identify goods, they are obtained from the country to which the goods are being shipped), certificates of origin, inspection certification, dock and/or warehouse receipts, destination control statements (serve to notify the carrier and all foreign parties that the item may only be exported to certain destinations), insurance certificates, shipper's export declarations (used to control exports and compile trade statistics), and export packaging lists.[23]

commercial invoice A bill for transported goods that describes the merchandise and its total cost and lists the addresses of the shipper and seller and delivery and payment terms.

The documentation required depends on the merchandise in the shipment and its destination. The number of documents required can be quite cumbersome and costly, creating a deterrent to trade. For example, businesses in Germany spend more than €47 billion annually on administrative costs, in order to comply with close to 10,000 legal obligations under national, European, and international law. The German government was so concerned about this bureaucratic burden that it established the National Regulatory Control Council, which checks all new legislative projects for necessity and administrative costs. Since its establishment in 2006, the Council has checked 900 draft laws and prevented an estimated €3.3 billion in additional costs to businesses.[24] The documentation burden is even more critical for developing economies. In a 2008 survey of informal firms, 67 percent in Côte d'Ivoire and 57 percent in Madagascar pointed to registration fees as a major or very severe obstacle to formally registering their businesses. Consequently, 80 percent of reforms in low- and lower-middle income economies over the past decade were aimed at reducing the administrative burden for firms, mostly by easing business start-up and trade costs.[25]

To ensure that all documentation required is accurately completed and to minimize potential problems, firms just entering the international market should consider using **freight forwarders**, who specialize in handling export documentation. Freight forwarders increasingly choose to differentiate themselves through the development of sophisticated information management systems, particularly with electronic data interchange (EDI).

TERMS OF SHIPMENT AND SALE

The responsibilities of the buyer and the seller should be spelled out as they relate to what is and what is not included in the price quotation and when ownership of goods passes from seller to buyer. **Incoterms** are the internationally accepted standard definitions for terms of sale set by the International Chamber of Commerce (ICC) since 1936.[26] The Incoterms 2000 went into effect on January 1, 2000, with significant revisions to reflect international traders' growing reliance on intermodal transport and the increased use of electronic communications. The new Incoterms also clarify the loading and unloading requirements of both buyers and sellers.[27] Although the same terms may be used in domestic transactions, they gain new meaning in the international arena. The terms are grouped into four categories, starting with the term whereby the seller makes the goods available to the buyer only at the seller's own premises (the "E"-terms), followed by the group whereby the seller is called upon to deliver the goods to a carrier appointed by the buyer (the "F"-terms). Next are the "C"-terms, whereby the seller has to contract for carriage but without assuming the risk of loss or damage to the goods or additional costs after the dispatch, and finally the "D"-terms, whereby the seller has to bear all costs and risks to bring the goods to the destination determined by the buyer. The most common of the Incoterms used in international marketing are summarized in Figure 16.4.

Prices quoted **ex-works (EXW)** apply only at the point of origin, and the seller agrees to place the goods at the disposal of the buyer at the specified place on the date or within the fixed period. All other charges are for the account of the buyer.

One of the new Incoterms is **free carrier (FCA)**, which replaced a variety of FOB terms for all modes of transportation except vessel. FCA (named inland point) applies only at a designated inland shipping point. The seller is responsible for loading goods into the means of transportation; the buyer is responsible for all subsequent expenses. If a port of exportation is named, the costs of transporting the goods to the named port are included in the price.

Free alongside ship (FAS) at a named U.S. port of export means that the exporter quotes a price for the goods, including charges for delivery of the goods alongside a vessel at the port. The seller handles the cost of unloading and wharfage; loading, ocean transportation, and insurance are left to the buyer.

Free on board (FOB) applies only to vessel shipments. The seller quotes a price covering all expenses up to, and including, delivery of goods on an overseas vessel provided by or for the buyer.

Under **cost and freight (CFR)** to a named overseas port of import, the seller quotes a price for the goods, including the cost of transportation to the named port of debarkation. The cost of insurance and the choice of insurer are left to the buyer.

With **cost, insurance, and freight (CIF)** to a named overseas port of import, the seller quotes a price including insurance, all transportation, and miscellaneous charges

freight forwarders Specialists in handling international transportation by contracting with carriers on behalf of shippers.

incoterms International Commerce Terms. Widely accepted terms used in quoting export prices.

ex-works (EXW) Price quotes that apply only at the point of origin; the seller agrees to place the goods at the disposal of the buyer at the specified place on a date or within a fixed period.

free carrier (FCA) Applies only at a designated inland shipping point. Seller is responsible for loading goods into the means of transportation; buyer is responsible for all subsequent expenses.

free alongside ship (FAS) Exporter quotes a price for the goods, including charges for delivery of the goods alongside a vessel at a port. Seller handles cost of unloading and wharfage; loading, ocean transportation, and insurance are left to the buyer.

free on board (FOB) Applies only to vessel shipments. Seller quotes a price covering all expenses up to and including delivery of goods on an overseas vessel provided by or for the buyer.

cost and freight (CFR) Seller quotes a price for the goods, including the cost of transportation to the named port of debarkation. Cost and choice of insurance are left to the buyer.

cost, insurance, and freight (CIF) Seller quotes a price including insurance, all transportation, and miscellaneous charges to the point of debarkation from the vessel or aircraft.

Figure 16.4   Selected Trade Terms

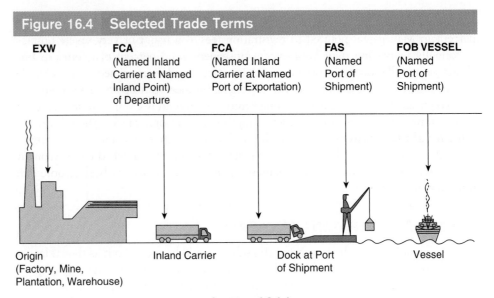

| EXW | FCA (Named Inland Carrier at Named Inland Point) of Departure | FCA (Named Inland Carrier at Named Port of Exportation) | FAS (Named Port of Shipment) | FOB VESSEL (Named Port of Shipment) |

Origin (Factory, Mine, Plantation, Warehouse)   Inland Carrier   Dock at Port of Shipment   Vessel

Country of Origin

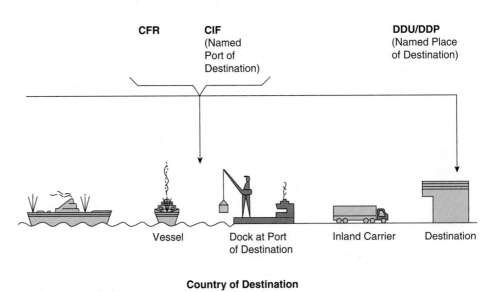

| CFR | CIF (Named Port of Destination) | DDU/DDP (Named Place of Destination) |

Vessel   Dock at Port of Destination   Inland Carrier   Destination

Country of Destination

carriage paid to (CPT)
The price quoted by an exporter for shipments not involving waterway transport, not including insurance.

delivered duty paid (DDP)
Seller delivers the goods, with import duties paid, including inland transportation from import point to the buyer's premises.

delivered duty unpaid (DDU) Only the destination customs duty and taxes are paid by the consignee.

to the point of debarkation from the vessel. If other than waterway transport is used, the terms are **CPT (carriage paid to)** or CIP (carriage and insurance paid to).

With **delivered duty paid (DDP)**, the seller delivers the goods, with import duties paid, including inland transportation from import point to the buyer's premises. With **delivered duty unpaid (DDU)**, only the destination customs duty and taxes are paid by the consignee. Ex-works signifies the maximum obligation for the buyer; delivered duty paid puts the maximum burden on the seller.

Careful determination and clear understanding of terms used, and their acceptance by the parties involved, are vital to avoid misunderstandings and disputes. These terms are also powerful competitive tools. The exporter should therefore learn what importers usually prefer in the particular market and what the specific transaction may require. An inexperienced importer may be discouraged by a quote such as "ex-plant Jessup, Maryland," whereas "CIF Helsinki" will assure the Finnish importer that many additional costs will only be in the familiar home environment.

Increasingly, exporters are quoting more inclusive terms. The benefits of taking charge of the transportation on either a CIF or DDP basis include the following: (1) exporters can offer foreign buyers an easy-to-understand "delivered cost" for the deal; (2) by getting discounts on volume purchases for transportation services, exporters cut shipping costs and can offer lower overall prices to prospective buyers; (3) control of product quality and service is extended to transport, enabling the exporter to ensure that goods arrive to the buyer in good condition; and (4) administrative procedures are cut for both the exporter and the buyer.[28]

When taking control of transportation costs, however, the exporter must know well in advance what impact the additional costs will have on the bottom line. If the approach is implemented incorrectly, exporters can be faced with volatile shipping rates, unexpected import duties, and restive customers. Most exporters do not want to go beyond the CIF quotation because of uncontrollables and unknowns in the destination country. Whatever terms are chosen, the program should be agreed to by the exporter and the buyer(s) rather than imposed solely by the exporter.

INTERNATIONAL INVENTORY ISSUES

Inventories tie up a major portion of corporate funds. Capital used for inventory is not available for other corporate opportunities. Annual **inventory carrying costs** (the expense of maintaining inventories) are heavily influenced by the cost of capital and industry-specific conditions. A company with a 36 percent inventory carrying cost will pay for its inventory twice in two years: once to purchase it, and a second time to carry it for about 25 months. Therefore, inventory managementis critical for make/buy, make-to-order/make-to-stock, and other top-level decisions.[29]

In addition, **just-in-time inventory** policies, which minimize the volume of inventory by making it available only when it is needed, are increasingly required by multinational manufacturers and distributors engaging in supply-chain management. They choose suppliers on the basis of their delivery and inventory performance and their ability to integrate themselves into the supply chain. Proper inventory management may therefore become a determining variable in obtaining a sale.

The purpose of establishing **inventory** systems—to maintain product movement in the delivery pipeline and to have a cushion to absorb demand fluctuations—is the same for domestic and international operations. The international environment, however, includes unique factors such as currency exchange rates, greater distances, and duties. At the same time, international operations provide the corporation with an opportunity to explore alternatives not available in a domestic setting, such as new sourcing or location alternatives. In international operations, the firm can make use of currency fluctuation by placing varying degrees of emphasis on inventory operations, depending on the stability of the currency of a specific country. Entire operations can be shifted to different nations to take advantage of new opportunities. International inventory management can therefore be much more flexible in its response to environmental changes.

In deciding the level of inventory to be maintained, the international manager must consider three factors: the order cycle time, desired customer service levels, and use of inventories as a strategic tool.

ORDER CYCLE TIME

The total time that passes between the placement of an order and the receipt of the merchandise is referred to as **order cycle time**. Two dimensions are of major

4. To see how the transportation infrastructure in host countries often dictates the options open to the manager

inventory carrying costs The expense of maintaining inventories.

just-in-time inventory Materials scheduled to arrive precisely when they are needed on a production line.

inventory Materials on hand for use in the production process; also finished goods on hand.

order cycle time The total time that passes between the placement of an order and the receipt of the product.

importance to inventory management: the length of the total order cycle and its consistency. In international business, the order cycle is frequently longer than in domestic business. It comprises the time involved in order transmission, order filling, packing and preparation for shipment, and transportation. Order transmission time varies greatly internationally depending on the method of communication. Supply-chain driven firms use electronic data interchange (EDI) rather than facsimile, telex, telephone, or mail.

EDI is the direct transfer of information technology between computers of trading partners.[30] The usual paperwork the partners send each other, such as purchase orders and confirmations, bills of lading, invoices, and shipment notices, are formatted into standard messages and transmitted via a direct link network or a third-party network. EDI can streamline processing and administration and reduce the costs of exchanging information.

The order-filling time may also increase because lack of familiarity with a foreign market makes the anticipation of new orders more difficult. Packing and shipment preparation require more detailed attention. Finally, of course, transportation time increases with the distances involved. Larger inventories may have to be maintained both domestically and internationally to bridge the time gaps.

Consistency, the second dimension of order cycle time, is also more difficult to maintain in international business. Depending on the choice of transportation mode, delivery times may vary considerably from shipment to shipment. The variation may require the maintenance of larger safety stocks to be able to fill demand in periods when delays occur.

CUSTOMER SERVICE LEVELS

customer service A corporate effort aimed at customer satisfaction; customer service levels measure the responsiveness that inventory policies permit for a given situation.

The level of **customer service** denotes the responsiveness that inventory policies permit for any given situation. A customer service level of 100 percent would be defined as the ability to fill all orders within a set time—for example, three days. If, within the same three days, only 70 percent of the orders can be filled, the customer service level is 70 percent. The choice of customer service level for the firm has a major impact on the inventories needed. In highly industrialized nations, firms frequently are expected to adhere to very high levels of customer service. Corporations are often tempted to design international customer service standards to similar levels.

Yet, service levels should not be oriented primarily around cost or customary home-country standards. Rather, the international service level should be based on expectations encountered in each market. These expectations are dependent on past performance, product desirability, customer sophistication, and the competitive status of the firm.

Because high customer service levels are costly, the goal should not be the highest customer service level possible, but rather an acceptable level. Different customers have different priorities. Some will be prepared to pay a premium for speed, some may put a higher value on flexibility, and another group may see low cost as the most important issue. Flexibility and speed are expensive, so it is wasteful to supply them to customers who do not value them highly.[31] If, for example, foreign customers expect to receive their merchandise within 30 days, it does not make sense for the international corporation to promise delivery within 10 or 15 days. Indeed, such delivery may result in storage problems. In addition, the higher prices associated with higher customer service levels may reduce the competitiveness of a firm's product. By contrast, in a business-to-business setting, sometimes even a few-hour delay in the delivery of a crucial component may be unacceptable, since the result may be a shutdown of the production process.

In such instances, strategically placed depots in a region must ensure that near instantaneous response becomes possible. For example, Amazon.com rents

11.9 million square feet worldwide, mostly warehouse and fulfillment operation facilities. This allows for speedier deliveries and increased customer satisfaction. Amazon's location decisions are symptomatic of larger trends in the digital economy. While global and regional management headquarters are located in first-tier business cities, fulfillment facilities, call centers, and warehouses are often located in third-tier cities. This distribution is motivated by the search for lower costs (salaries, taxes, and real estate) and better airfreight accessibility.[32]

INVENTORY AS A STRATEGIC TOOL

Inventories can be used by the international corporation as a strategic tool in dealing with currency valuation changes or to hedge against inflation. By increasing inventories before an imminent devaluation of a currency instead of holding cash, the corporation may reduce its exposure to devaluation losses. Similarly, in the case of high inflation, large inventories can provide an important inflation hedge. In such circumstances, the international inventory manager must balance the cost of maintaining high levels of inventories with the benefits accruing from hedging against inflation or devaluation. Many countries, for example, charge a property tax on stored goods. If the increase in tax payments outweighs the hedging benefits to the corporation, it would be unwise to increase inventories before a devaluation.

 ## INTERNATIONAL PACKAGING ISSUES

Packaging is instrumental in getting the merchandise to the ultimate destination in a safe, maintainable, and presentable condition. Packaging that is adequate for domestic shipping may be inadequate for international transportation because the shipment will be subject to the motions of the vessel on which it is carried. Added stress in international shipping also arises from the transfer of goods among different modes of transportation. Figure 16.5 provides examples of some sources of stress in intermodal movement that are most frequently found in international transportation.

The responsibility for appropriate packaging rests with the shipper of goods. The U.S. Carriage of Goods by Sea Act of 1936 states: "Neither the carrier nor the ship shall be responsible for loss or damage arising or resulting from insufficiency of

5. To learn why international inventory management is crucial for success

Figure 16.5   Stresses in Intermodal Movement

| Acceleration Retardation Centrifugal Forces when Driving in Curves Vibrations | Acceleration Retardation Dropping Impact | Acceleration Retardation Shunting Impact Centrifugal Forces in Curves Vibrations | Acceleration Dropping Impact | Heaving Pitching Rolling Centrifugal Forces Yawing Swaying Vibrations |

Note: Each transportation mode exerts a different set of stresses and strains on containerized cargoes. The most commonly overlooked are those associated with ocean transport.
Source: James L. Bossert, ed., *Supplier Management Handbook*, 6th ed, (Milwaukee, WI: American Society for Quality, 2004).

packing." The shipper must therefore ensure that the goods are prepared appropriately for international shipping. This is important because it has been found that "the losses that occur as a result of breakage, pilferage, and theft exceed the losses caused by major maritime casualties, which include fires, sinkings, and collision of vessels. Thus the largest of these losses is a preventable loss."[33]

Packaging decisions must also take into account differences in environmental conditions—for example, climate. When the ultimate destination is very humid or particularly cold, special provisions must be made to prevent damage to the product. The task becomes even more challenging when one considers that, in the course of long-distance transportation, dramatic changes in climate can take place. Still famous is the case of a firm in Taiwan that shipped drinking glasses to the Middle East. The company used wooden crates and padded the glasses with hay. Most of the glasses, however, were broken by the time they reached their destination. As the crates traveled into the dry Middle East, the moisture content of the hay dropped. By the time the crates were delivered, the thin straw offered almost no protection.[34]

The weight of packaging must also be considered, particularly when airfreight is used, as the cost of shipping is often based on weight. At the same time, packaging material must be sufficiently strong to permit stacking in international transportation. Another consideration is that, in some countries, duties are assessed according to the gross weight of shipments, which includes the weight of packaging. Obviously, the heavier the packaging, the higher the duty will be.

The shipper must pay sufficient attention to instructions provided by the customer for packaging. For example, requests by the customer that the weight of any one package should not exceed a certain limit or that specific package dimensions should be adhered to, usually are made for a reason. Often they reflect limitations in transportation or handling facilities at the point of destination.

Although the packaging of a product is often used as a form of display abroad, international packaging can rarely serve the dual purpose of protection and display. Therefore double packaging may be necessary. The display package is for future use at the point of destination; another package surrounds it for protective purposes.

One solution to the packaging problem in international logistics has been the development of intermodal containers—large metal boxes that fit on trucks, ships, railroad cars, and airplanes and ease the frequent transfer of goods in international shipments. Developed in different forms for both sea and air transportation, containers also offer better utilization of carrier space because of standardization of size. The shipper therefore may benefit from lower transportation rates. In addition, containers can offer greater safety from pilferage and damage. Of course, at the same time, the use of containers allows thieves to abscond with an entire shipment, rather than just parts of it. The rise in cargo theft and pilferage has given birth to a whole new industry of "risk consultancies," which are contracted by exasperated ship owners to safeguard their vessels. In addition to providing armed guards on ships and offering their own crafts as escorts, "consultancies" are responsible for parleying with pirates, paying ransoms, and outfitting ships with barbed or electric wires and water cannons to make it hard for pirates to clamber aboard.[35]

A single cargo ship can transport up to 11,000 containers.

© Image Source/Bjoern Holland/Getty Images, Inc.

Container traffic is heavily dependent on the existence of appropriate handling facilities, both domestically and internationally. In addition, the quality of inland transportation must be considered. If transportation for containers is not available and the merchandise must be unpacked and reloaded the expected cost reductions may not materialize.

In some countries, rules for the handling of containers may be designed to maintain employment. For example, U.S. union rules obligate shippers to withhold containers from firms that do not employ members of the International Longshoremen's Association for the loading or unloading of containers within a fifty-mile radius of Atlantic or Gulf ports. Such restrictions can result in an onerous cost burden.

Overall, cost attention must be paid to international packaging. The customer who ordered and paid for the merchandise expects it to arrive on time and in good condition. Even with replacements and insurance, the customer will not be satisfied if there are delays. Dissatisfaction will usually translate directly into lost sales.

INTERNATIONAL STORAGE ISSUES

6. To learn about interactions between different logistics components

Although international logistics is discussed as a movement or flow of goods, a stationary period is involved when merchandise becomes inventory stored in warehouses. Heated arguments can arise within a firm over the need for and utility of warehousing internationally. On the one hand, customers expect quick responses to orders and rapid delivery. Accommodating the customer's expectations would require locating many distribution centers around the world. On the other hand, warehouse space is expensive. In addition, the larger volume of inventory increases the inventory carrying cost. Fewer warehouses allow for consolidation of transportation and therefore lower transportation rates to the warehouse. However, if the warehouses are located far from customers, the cost of outgoing transportation increases. The international logistician must consider the tradeoffs between service and cost to the supply chain in order to determine the appropriate levels of warehousing.

STORAGE FACILITIES

The **location decision** addresses how many distribution centers to have and where to locate them. The availability of facilities abroad will differ from the domestic situation. For example, while public storage is widely available in some countries, such facilities may be scarce or entirely lacking in others. Also, the standards and quality of facilities can vary widely. As a result, the storage decision of the firm is often accompanied by the need for large-scale, long-term investments. Despite the high cost, international storage facilities should be established if they support the overall logistics effort. In many markets, adequate storage facilities are imperative to satisfy customer demands and to compete successfully. For example, since the establishment of a warehouse connotes a visible presence, in doing so a firm can convince local distributors and customers of its commitment to remain in the market for the long term.

Once the decision is made to use storage facilities abroad, the warehouse conditions must be carefully analyzed. As an example, in some countries warehouses have low ceilings. Packaging developed for the high stacking of products is therefore

location decision A decision concerning the number of facilities to establish and where they should be situated.

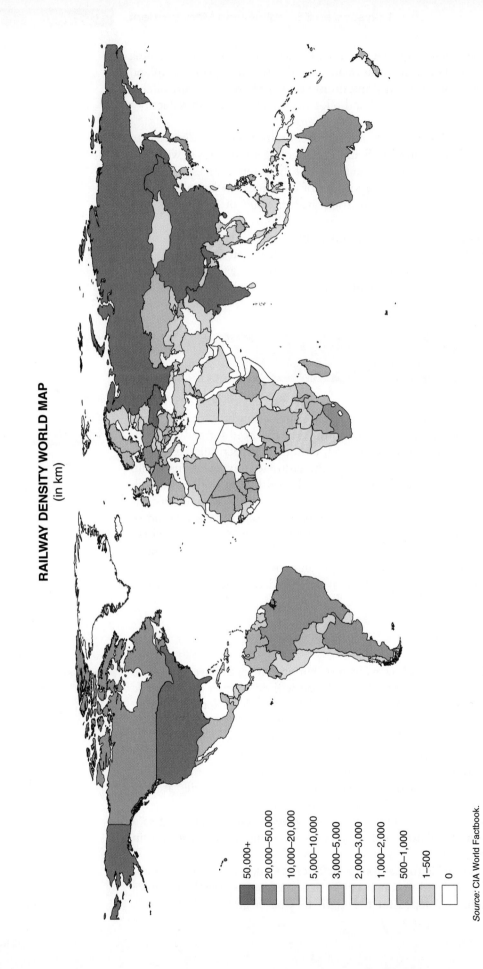

RAILWAY DENSITY WORLD MAP
(in km)

	50,000+
	20,000–50,000
	10,000–20,000
	5,000–10,000
	3,000–5,000
	2,000–3,000
	1,000–2,000
	500–1,000
	1–500
	0

Source: CIA World Factbook.

unnecessary or even counterproductive. In other countries, automated warehousing is available. Proper bar coding of products and the use of package dimensions acceptable to the warehousing system are basic requirements. In contrast, in warehouses still stocked manually, weight limitations will be of major concern. And, if no forklift trucks are available, palletized delivery is of little use.

To optimize the logistics system, the logistician should analyze international product sales and then rank order products according to warehousing needs. Products that are most sensitive to delivery time might be classified as "A" products. "A" products would be stocked in all distribution centers, and safety stock levels would be kept high. Alternatively, the storage of products can be more selective, if quick delivery by air can be guaranteed. Products for which immediate delivery is not urgent could be classified as "B" products. They would be stored only at selected distribution centers around the world. Finally, products for which there is little demand would be stocked only at headquarters. Should an urgent need for delivery arise, airfreight could again assure rapid shipment. Classifying products enables the international logistician to substantially reduce total international warehousing requirements and still maintain acceptable service levels.

SPECIAL TRADE ZONES

Areas where foreign goods may be held or processed and then reexported without incurring duties are called **foreign trade zones** The zones can be found at major ports of entry and also at inland locations near major production facilities. For example, Kansas City, Missouri, has one of the largest foreign trade zones in the United States.

The existence of trade zones can be quite useful to the international firm. For example, in some countries, the benefits derived from lower labor costs may be offset by high duties and tariffs. As a result, location of manufacturing and storage facilities in these countries may prove uneconomical. Foreign trade zones are designed to exclude the impact of duties from the location decision. This is done by exempting merchandise in the foreign trade zone from duty payment. The international firm can therefore import merchandise; store it in the foreign trade zone; and process, alter, test, or demonstrate it—all without paying duties. If the merchandise is subsequently shipped abroad (that is, reexported), no duty payments are ever due. Duty payments become due only if the merchandise is shipped into the country from the foreign trade zone. An interesting example of tax reductions and industrial development incentives is offered by the Shanghai Waigaoqiao Free Trade Zone in China. This facility was established in 1990 on a plot of 10,000 square kilometers. Companies located within the zone are given five years of preferential tax treatment. Instead of paying the corporate tax rate of 15 percent, the tax rate starts at 8 percent and increases over the five-year period to the full 15 percent. This policy has attracted a slew of companies, such as Intel, Hewlett-Packard, Phillip, IBM, and Emerson Electric, creating a technology hub in the heart of China.[36]

Trade zones can also be useful as transshipment points to reduce logistics cost and redesign marketing approaches. For example, Audiovox was shipping small quantities of car alarms from a Taiwanese contract manufacturer directly to distributors in Chile. The shipments were costly and the marketing strategy of requiring high minimum orders stopped distributors from buying. The firm resolved the dilemma by using a Miami trade zone to ship the alarms from Taiwan and consolidate the goods with other shipments to Chile. The savings in freight costs allowed the Chilean distributors to order whatever quantity they wanted and allowed the company to quote lower prices. As a result, sales improved markedly.[37]

foreign trade zones Special areas where foreign goods may be held or processed without incurring duties and taxes until they enter the country outside the zone.

All parties to the arrangement benefit from foreign trade zones. The government maintaining the trade zone achieves increased employment and investment. The firm using the trade zone obtains a spearhead in the foreign market without incurring all of the costs customarily associated with such an activity. As a result, goods can be reassembled, and large shipments can be broken down into smaller units. Also, goods can be repackaged when packaging weight becomes part of the duty assessment. Finally, goods can be given domestic "made-in" status if assembled in the foreign trade zone. Thus, duties may be payable only on the imported materials and component parts rather than on the labor that is used to finish the product.

In addition to foreign trade zones, governments also have established export processing zones and special economic areas. The common dimensions for all the zones are that special rules apply to them when compared with other regions of the country, and that the purpose of these special rules lies in the government's desire to stimulate the economy, particularly the export side of international trade.

Export processing zones usually provide tax- and duty-free treatment for production facilities whose output is destined abroad. The maquiladoras of Mexico are one example of a program that permits firms to take advantage of sharp differentials in labor costs. Firms can carry out the labor-intensive part of their operations in Mexico, while sourcing raw materials or component parts from other nations.

special economic zones
Areas in which there are substantial tax incentives, low prices for land and labor, and no tariffs, created by a country to attract foreign investors.

One country that has used trade zones very successfully for its own economic development is China. Through the creation of **special economic zones**, in which there are substantial tax incentives, low prices for land and labor, and no tariffs, the government has attracted many foreign investors bringing in billions of dollars. The investors have brought new equipment, technology, and managerial know-how and have increased local economic prosperity substantially. The job generation effect has been so strong that the central Chinese government has expressed concern about the overheating of the economy and the inequities between regions with and without trade zones.[38]

For the logistician, the decision whether to use such zones mainly is framed by the overall benefit for the supply-chain system. Clearly, additional transport and retransport are required, warehousing facilities need to be constructed, and material handling frequency will increase. However, the costs may well be balanced by the preferential government treatment or by lower labor costs.

 ## MANAGEMENT OF INTERNATIONAL LOGISTICS

7. To decide who should be in charge of logistics

The very purpose of a multinational firm is to benefit from system synergism and a persuasive argument can be made for the coordination of international logistics at corporate headquarters. Without coordination, subsidiaries will tend to optimize their individual efficiency but jeopardize the efficiency of the overall performance of the supply chain.

CENTRALIZED LOGISTICS MANAGEMENT

A significant characteristic of the centralized approach to international logistics is the existence of headquarters staff that retains decision-making power over logistics activities affecting international subsidiaries. If headquarters exerts control, it must also take the primary responsibility for its decisions. Clearly, ill will may arise if local managers are appraised and rewarded on the basis of a performance they do not control. This may be particularly problematic if headquarters staff suffers from a lack of information or expertise.

To avoid internal problems, both headquarters staff and local management should report to one person. This person, whether the vice president for international logistics or the president of the firm, can then become the final arbiter to decide the firm's priorities. Of course, the individual should also be in charge of determining appropriate rewards for managers, both at headquarters and abroad, so that corporate decisions that alter a manager's performance level will not affect the manager's appraisal and evaluation. Further, the individual can contribute an objective view when inevitable conflicts arise in international logistics coordination. The internationally centralized decision-making process leads to an overall supply-chain management perspective that can dramatically improve profitability.

DECENTRALIZED LOGISTICS MANAGEMENT

When a firm serves many international markets that are diverse in nature, total centralization might leave the firm unresponsive to local adaptation needs. If each subsidiary is made a profit center in itself, each one carries the full responsibility for its performance, which can lead to greater local management satisfaction and to better adaptation to local market conditions. Yet often such decentralization deprives the logistics function of the benefits of coordination. For example, while headquarters, referring to its large volume of overall international shipments, may be able to extract bottom rates from transportation firms, individual subsidiaries by themselves may not have similar bargaining power. The same argument applies also to the sourcing situation, where the coordination of shipments by the purchasing firm may be much more cost-effective than individual shipments from many small suppliers around the world.

Once products are within a specific market, however, increased input from local logistics operations should be expected and encouraged. At the very least, local managers should be able to provide input into the logistics decisions generated by headquarters. Ideally, within a frequent planning cycle, local managers can identify the logistics benefits and constraints existing in their particular market and communicate them to headquarters. Headquarters can then either adjust its international logistics strategy accordingly or explain to the manager why system optimization requires actions different from the ones recommended. Such a justification process will help greatly in reducing the potential for animosity between local and headquarters operations.

OUTSOURCING LOGISTICS SERVICES

A third option, used by some corporations, is the systematic outsourcing of logistics capabilities. By collaborating with transportation firms, private warehouses, or other specialists, corporate resources can be concentrated on the firm's core product.

Many firms whose core competency does not include logistics find it more efficient to use the services of companies specializing in international shipping. This is usually true for smaller shipping volumes, for example in cases when smaller import–export firms or smaller shipments are involved. Such firms prefer to outsource at least some of the international logistics functions, rather than detracting from staff resources and time. Some logistical services providers carve specific niches in the transnational shipping market, specializing for example in consumer goods forwarding.

The resulting lower costs and better service make such third parties the preferred choice for many firms. On the other hand, when hazardous or other strictly regulated materials are involved, some firms may choose to retain control over handling and storing activities, in view of possible liability issues.[39]

one-stop logistics Allows shippers to buy all the transportation modes and functional services from a single carrier.

Going even further, **one-stop logistics** allows shippers to buy all the transportation modes and functional services from a single carrier, instead of going through the pain of choosing different third parties for each service. One-stop logistics ensures a more efficient global movement of goods via different transportation modes. Specialized companies provide EDI tracking services and take care of cumbersome customs procedures; they also offer distribution services, such as warehousing and inventory management. Finally, third parties may even take some of the international shipper's logistical functions. This rapidly growing trend provides benefits to both carriers and shippers.[40] The latter enjoy better service and simplified control procedures and claims settlement. On the other hand, one-stop logistics can help carriers achieve economies of scale and remain competitive in a very dynamic market. The proliferation of one-stop logistics practices is facilitated by the wider acceptance of EDI and the growing importance of quality criteria versus cost criteria in shipping decisions.

While the cost savings and specialization benefits of such a strategy seem clear, one must also consider the loss of control for the firm, its suppliers, and its customers that may result from such outsourcing. Yet, contract logistics does not and should not require the handing over of control. Rather, it offers concentration on one's specialization—a division of labor. The control and responsibility toward the supply chain remain with the firm, even though operations may move to a highly trained outside organization.

THE SUPPLY CHAIN AND THE INTERNET

8. To appreciate how information and data exchange are pivotal for supply-chain management

The Internet has been instrumental in transforming supply-chain management. Firms are now able to conduct many more global comparisons among suppliers and select from a wide variety of choices. At the same time, firms can be much more informed in the structure of their supplier network. In consequence, the supply base of many firms has become much broader, but includes fewer participants.

Many firms use their web sites as a marketing and advertising tool and are expanding them to include order-taking capabilities. The development of new technologies and digital processes has led to a dramatic growth in net e-commerce revenue. In the United States, Internet sales have grown from $995.0 billion in 1999 to $3,333 billion in 2007 and are projected to increase by 9.0 percent annually through 2012.[41]

Companies wishing to enter e-commerce will not have to do so on their own. Hub sites (also known as virtual malls or digital intermediaries) bring together buyers, sellers, distributors, and transaction payment processors in a single marketplace, making convenience the key attraction. Business-to-business (B2B) activity, transactions by manufacturers and merchant wholesalers, account for most e-commerce (93 percent). However, the acceptance of e-commerce is not uniform.[42] The presence of cultural and social factors, which makes customers from some countries more reluctant to shop on-line than others.[43] The future is also growing brighter for hubs in the consumer-to-consumer market, where companies like eBay are setting high standards of profitability.

When customers have the ability to access a company through the Internet, the company has to be prepared for 24-hour order-taking and customer service, and to have the regulatory and customs-handling expertise for international delivery. The instantaneous interactivity that users experience will also be translated into an expectation of expedient delivery of answers and products ordered. Firms must remember that web sites should encourage business, not preclude it. If prospective customers cannot easily and rapidly find what they are looking for on a web site, they are likely to move on and find another site that makes its information and interactivity more apparent.[44]

Some companies elect to build their own international distribution networks. Both QVC, a televised shopping service, and Amazon.com, an online retailer of books, have distribution centers in Britain and Germany to take advantage of the European Internet audience and to fulfill more quickly and cheaply the orders generated by their web sites. Transactions and the information they provide about the buyers will also allow for more customization and service by region, market, or even individual customer.

For industries such as music and motion pictures, the Internet is both an opportunity and a threat. The Web provides a new, efficient method of distribution and customization of products. At the same time, it can be a channel for intellectual property violation through unauthorized posting on other web sites where these products can be downloaded. For example, the music industry is very concerned about a shift in the balance of economic power: If artists can deliver their works directly to customers via technologies such as MP3, what will be the role of labels and distributors?

A number of hurdles and uncertainties may keep companies out of global markets or from exploiting them to their full potential. Some argue that the World Wide Web does not yet live up to its name, because it is mostly a tool for the United States and Europe. For all countries, but particularly developing nations, the issue of universal access to the Internet is crucial. Such access depends on the speed with which governments end their monopolistic structures in telecommunications and open their markets to competition. The 1997 World Trade Organization agreement on telecommunications accelerated the process of liberalization through the establishment of new companies, foreign direct investment in existing companies, and cross-border transmission of services. The Doha Round of service negotiations, which commenced in 2000, has sought to identify additional market openings and areas of further liberalization in telecommunications. Meanwhile, access to the Internet is undergoing major expansion through new technologies such as NetTV and Web phone.[45] As Internet penetration levels increase due to technological advances, improvements in many countries' Web infrastructures, and customer acceptance, e-business will become truly global.

LOGISTICS AND SECURITY

The entire field of supply-chain management and logistics has been thoroughly affected by newly emerging security concerns. After the terrorist attacks of 2001, companies have had to learn that the pace of international transactions has slowed down and that formerly routine steps will now take longer. While in decades past many governmental efforts were devoted to speeding up transactions across borders, national security reasons are now forcing governments to erect new barriers and

9. To understand the vulnerability and support of logistics

FOCUS ON POLITICS

Logistics and National Security

The Department of Homeland Security (DHS) is a cabinet-level agency designed to coordinate U.S. efforts in the war against terror. Twenty-two federal agencies are united in this new department. Some of these agencies affect international shippers, including the Customs Service, Coast Guard, Transportation Security Administration, and the import inspection services of the Food and Drug Administration. Additionally, DHS has implemented a number of antiterror regulations, in an effort to keep the country safe in the post – 9/11 environment.

Importers to the United States and the customs brokers who serve them are feeling the pressure to help secure U.S. borders. For example, a recent Homeland Security screening law, commonly referred to as 10+2, requires shippers and carriers to capture 12 additional data elements than previously required for shipments being imported into the United States. Few firms have systems in place that can capture and disseminate this information. The necessary capital investment is driving up trade costs. Beyond advanced data reporting, importers have also complained about bureaucratic inefficiencies, generated by conflicting agency mandates. For example, shippers have occasionally found themselves caught in a struggle between the Transportation Security Administration and Customs over which agency makes the final decisions regarding cargo security.

During the 2009 NAFTA summit, participants identified border security regulations as one of the most pressing areas of concern and called for harmonizing security requirements across the NAFTA bloc. Some supported customs preclearance throughout all the NAFTA countries, pointing out that a single secure entry/exit point creates a competitive disadvantage for all members. Prior to the terrorist attacks on the World Trade Center, Canada and the United States had taken steps in that direction, issuing a Smart Border report that defined areas beyond the border, where shippers could preclear cargo. However, 9/11 ushered in a more stringent security regime, with some unintended consequences for trade. For example, Canadian transport providers have complained about situations where a cargo shipment is cleared, but the truck driver is not, or cases of critical or perishable cargo lingering in Custom's limbo for weeks, sometimes months, awaiting clearance. Some Canadian suppliers have begun sending two trucks with the same critical cargo across the border to make sure that at least one gets through in the required time period.

Border slowdowns cost North America billions of dollars. However, security liberalization is difficult, because of DHS's superseding mandate to ensure the safety of the United States. DHS operates from a law enforcement standpoint, with trade considerations taking a backseat to security. Despite all the new regulations and increased oversight, it is very difficult to completely secure cargo. Even if the truck, ship, or train is cleared at the point of origin, contamination could occur in transit. It is technologically impossible to monitor every transport shipment from beginning to end.

This has left some analysts wondering whether the cost is worth the price, and whether there can be such a thing as absolute security.

Sources: Inbound Logistics NAFTA Summit Report, "Growing Together, Insider Perspectives on the NAFTA Nations' Economies." January 2009; C. John Langley Jr. and Capgemini U.S. LLC "The State of Logistics Outsourcing: 2008 Third-Party Results and Findings of the 13th Annual Study," 2008, http://www .scl.gatech.edu/research/supply-chain/20083PLReport.pdf.

conduct new inspections. Logistics is one of the business activities most affected,[46] as Focus on Politics shows.

Modern transportation systems have proved to be critical to terrorist activities. They provide the means for the perpetrators to quickly arrive at, and depart from, the sites of attacks. On occasion, terrorists have even used transportation systems themselves to carry out their crimes.

Logistics systems are often the targets of attacks. Consider the vulnerability of pipelines used for carrying oil, natural gas, and other energy sources. Logistics systems also serve as the conduit for the weapons or people who are planning to carry out attacks. These systems are the true soft spots of vulnerability for both nations and firms. Take the issue of sea ports: there are 361 ports in the United States, 126 of which have waters deep enough to accommodate ocean going ships. With the exception of land trade with Mexico and Canada, 95 percent of all international trade shipments to the United States arrive by ship.[47] Thousands of additional shipments arrive by truck and rail. In most instances, the containers are secured by nothing more than a 10¢ seal that can easily be broken.

The need to institute new safeguards for international shipments will affect the ability of firms to efficiently plan their international shipments. There is now more uncertainty and less control over the timing of arrivals and departures. There is also a much greater need for internal control and supervision of shipments. Cargo security will increasingly need not only to ensure that nothing goes missing, but also that nothing has been added to a shipment.

Firms with a just-in-time regimen are exploring alternative management strategies. Planning includes the shift of international shipments from air carriage to sea. Some U.S. firms are thinking about replacing international shipments with domestic ones, where transportation via truck would replace transborder movement altogether and eliminate the use of vulnerable ports. Further down the horizon are planning scenarios in which firms consider the effects of substantial and long-term interruptions of supplies or operations. Still, any actual move away from existing JIT systems is likely to be minor unless new large-scale interruptions occur.

LOGISTICS AND THE ENVIRONMENT

The logistician plays an increasingly important role in allowing the firm to operate in an environmentally conscious way. Environmental laws, expectations, and self-imposed goals set by firms are difficult to adhere to without a logistics orientation that systematically takes such concerns into account. Because laws and regulations differ across the world, the firm's efforts need to be responsive to a wide variety of requirements. One logistics orientation that has grown in importance due to environmental concerns is the development of **reverse distribution** systems. Such systems are instrumental in ensuring that the firm not only delivers the product to the market, but also can retrieve it from the market for subsequent use, recycling, or disposal. To a growing degree the ability to develop such reverse logistics is a key determinant for market acceptance and profitability.

Society also recognizes that retrieval should not be restricted to short-term consumer goods, such as bottles. Rather, it may be even more important to devise systems that enable the retrieval and disposal of long-term capital goods, such as cars, refrigerators, air conditioners, and industrial goods, with the least possible burden on the environment. In Germany, for example, car manufacturers are required to take back their used vehicles for dismantling and recycling purposes. Focus on e-Business presents some of the major issues connected to the design of a reverse logistics system.

Managers are often faced with the trade-offs between environmental concerns and logistical efficiency. Companies increasingly need to learn how to simultaneously achieve environmental and economic goals. Esprit, the apparel maker, and The Body Shop, the well-known British cosmetics producer, screen their suppliers for environmental and social responsibility practices. The significance of this trend is reaffirmed in the rules issued by the International Organization of Standardization (ISO). The ISO 14000 standards target international environmental practices by evaluating companies both at the organization level (management systems, environmental performance, environmental auditing, and communication) and product level (life-cycle assessment, labeling, and product standards). The ISO is continuously introducing new recommendations, with the most recent being ISO 14064 and 14065 for supporting greenhouse gas reduction and emissions trading. Its standards are implemented in 138 countries and are thoroughly integrated with the global economy.[48]

10. To see and consider the linkages between logistics and sustainability

reverse distribution A system responding to the need for product returns that ensures a firm can retrieve a product from the market for subsequent use, recycling, or disposal.

From the perspective of materials management and physical distribution, environmental practices are those that bring about fewer shipments, less handling, and more direct movement. Such practices are to be weighted against optimal efficiency routines, including just-in-time inventory and quantity discount purchasing.

On the transportation side, logistics managers will need to expand their involvement in carrier and routing selection. For example, shippers of oil or other potentially hazardous materials increasingly will need to ensure that the carriers used have excellent safety records and use only double-hulled ships. Society may even expect corporate involvement in choosing the route that the shipment will travel, preferring

---

FOCUS ON BUSINESS

Reverse Logistics, or "Turning Trash into Cash"

Reverse logistics concerns the handling and disposition of returned products and use of related materials and information. U.S. companies pay more than an estimated $35 billion annually for handling, transporting, and processing of returned products—and this figure does not include the costs of disposing or recycling of unwanted items. Nor does it factor in lost administrative time. With the gradual rise of oil and other commodity prices, companies are beginning to see used products less as trash and more as the sum of their raw materials, energy, and labor. This new attitude has intensified the search for innovative ways to extract maximum value from product returns.

More and more companies are entering the reverse logistics business. For example, Genco, a Pittsburgh-based consultancy, specializes in helping retailers, such as Best Buy, Sears, and Target, find buyers for products that were returned as defective and would otherwise be discarded.

One recent study suggests that this allows companies to recover up to 0.3 percent of annual sales (that translates into approximately $100 million in the case of Best Buy). Business has been so brisk that Genco developed its own wholesale brokerage business (Genco Marketplace) that connects sellers and buyers with rejected goods and liquidates about $5 million per day. The next step was the launching of NoBetterDeal.com—a direct-to-consumer Web store. According to Robert R. Auray Jr., Genco Marketplace CEO, "What makes this Web store different is that we source our products from the secondary market. Each year, billions of dollars worth of surplus. inventory and returns are liquidated at a small fraction of their retail value, even though a majority of the goods are high-quality, fully functional items."

Some companies choose to keep the reverse logistics effort in-house. For example, carpet makers Interface and Shaw Industries collect leftover materials and reenter them into production. This frugal approach should result in cost advantages over competitors that produce from scratch. There is also an environmental component to applying the reuse-reduce-recycle principle to reverse logistics that is appealing to eco-conscious consumers. Outdoor gear maker Patagonia has a particularly ambitious reverse logistics program. The company uses recycled fibers from old fleeces and T-shirts to produce its line of Synchilla Vests. Customers can leave their old garments, irrespective of where they were purchased, in a Patagonia store or mail them to a distribution center. About 90 percent of the fabric is spun into new garments and any by-products are used to make a cement additive. The final product is more expensive than virgin polyester, but it fulfills an environmental mandate that is appealing to Patagonia's consumer base.

Whatever the motivation behind the recycling of returned products, the real value of reverse logistics-is in "turning trash into cash," according to Curtis Greve, a senior vice president at Genco. A comprehensive strategy for extracting value from returns results in a competitive advantage and a larger bottom line—two of the fundamental requirements for any successful business. Additionally, remanufactured products cost 40 to 60 percent less to produce and deliver than new products. This is because most of the raw materials already exist in their final form and only a portion goes through added fabrication. Given the finite supply of valuable resources, such as steel, copper, aluminum, and petroleum that are extensively used in many manufacturing sectors, recycling makes not only environmental but also economic sense. Commercial recycling is already an established industry in many developing countries and could be a future source of economic growth for them. Brazil and India, for example, are the world's leading recyclers of aluminum. As resources become ever more scarce, reverse logistics is likely to become not just a choice, but a necessity for global manufacturing.

Sources: Brian Hindo, "Reverse Logistics: From Trash to Cash," *BusinessWeek*, July 24, 2008; "The Footprint Chronicles," Patagonia, http://www.patagonia .com/web/us/patagonia.go?slc=en_US&sct=US&assetid=23429&ln=66, accessed October 27, 2009; "GENCO Marketplace Launches Online Store for Bargain Shoppers–NoBetterDeal.com," March 3, 2009, http://www.genco .com/Press-Releases/2009/090303_GENCO-Marketplace-Launches-On-line-Store.php, accessed October 27, 2009; Sameer Kumar and Valora Putnam, "Cradle to Cradle: Reverse Logistics Strategies and Opportunities across Three Industry Sectors," *International Journal of Production Economics* 115, no. 2 (October 2008): 305–315.

routes that are far from ecologically important and sensitive zones. Firms will need to assert leadership in such consideration of the environment to provide society with a better quality of life.

SUMMARY

As competitiveness is becoming increasingly dependent on efficiency, international logistics and supply-chain management are becoming of major importance.

International logistics is concerned with the flow of materials into, through, and out of the international corporation and therefore includes materials management as well as physical distribution. The logistician must recognize the total systems demands on the firm, its suppliers, and customers to develop trade-offs between various logistics components. By taking a supply-chain perspective, the manager can develop logistics systems that are supplier- and customer-focused and highly efficient. Implementation of such a system requires close collaboration between all members of the supply chain.

International logistics differs from domestic activities in that it deals with greater distances, new variables, and greater complexity because of national differences. One major factor to consider is transportation. The international manager needs to understand transportation infrastructures in other countries and modes of transportation such as ocean shipping and airfreight. The choice among these modes will depend on the customer's demands and the firm's transit time, predictability, and cost requirements. In addition, noneconomic factors such as government regulations weigh heavily in this decision.

Inventory management is another major consideration. Inventories abroad are expensive to maintain yet often crucial for international success. The logistician must evaluate requirements for order cycle times and customer service levels to develop an international inventory policy that can also serve as a strategic management tool.

International packaging is important because it ensures arrival of the merchandise at the ultimate destination in safe condition. In developing packaging, environmental conditions such as climate and handling conditions must be considered.

The logistics manager must also deal with international storage issues and determine where to locate inventories. International warehouse space will have to be leased or purchased and decisions will have to be made about utilizing foreign trade zones.

International logistics management is increasing in importance. Implementing the logistics function with an overall supply-chain perspective that is responsive to environmental demands will increasingly be a requirement for successful global competitiveness.

KEY TERMS

materials management   538
physical distribution   538
systems concept   538
total cost concept   539
trade-off concept   539
supply-chain management   539
extended enterprise   540
logistics platform   543
land bridge   544
sea bridge   544
intermodal movements   544
ocean shipping   544
liner service   544

bulk service   544
tramp service   544
container ships   544
roll-on-roll-off (RORO)   544
ports   545
airfreight   545
transit time   546
reliability   547
tracking   547
preferential policies   549
export declaration   550
bill of lading   550
straight bill of lading   550

shipper's order   550
commercial invoice   550
freight forwarders   551
incoterms   551
ex-works (EXW)   551
free carrier (FCA)   551
free alongside ship (FAS)   551
free on board (FOB)   551
cost and freight (CFR)   551
cost, insurance, and freight (CIF)   551
carriage paid to (CPT)   552
delivered duty paid (DDP)   552

delivered duty unpaid
    (DDU)   552
inventory carrying costs   553
just-in-time inventory   553

inventory   553
order cycle time   553
customer service   554
location decision   557

foreign trade zones   559
special economic zones   560
one-stop logistics   562
reverse distribution   565

QUESTIONS FOR DISCUSSION

1. Explain the key aspects of supply-chain management.

2. Contrast the use of ocean shipping and airfreight.

3. Explain the meaning and impact of transit time in international logistics.

4. How and why do governments interfere in "rational" freight carrier selection?

5. How can an international firm reduce its order cycle time?

6. What role can the international logistician play in improving the environmental friendliness of the firm?

INTERNET EXERCISES

1. What types of information are available to the exporter on The Transport Web? Go to U.S. Department of Transportation, Office of International Transportation and Trade, http://ostpxweb.dot.gov/aviation/intradetransprog.htm, and give examples of transportation links that an exporter would find helpful and explain why.

2. Use an online database to select a freight forwarder. (Refer to http://www.freightnet.com or http://forwarders.com, directories of freight forwarders.)

TAKE A STAND

With the rapid development of information technology, companies are able to collect an increasingly large amount of data about their consumers. Many believe that this is a positive trend that benefits both customers through speedier service and companies through targeted product marketing. However, some observers are growing increasingly concerned about the erosion of individual privacy. If companies know more and more about their customers' tastes, preferences, and lives, how will they use the information?

For Discussion

1. Should there be more legislation to determine how and for how long information is stored, as well as its specific uses?

2. Should consumers be concerned about their privacy amid the rapid growth of information technology?

SUGGESTED READINGS

Donald J. Bowersox, David J. Closs, and M. Bixby Cooper, *Supply Chain Logistics Management*, 3rd ed (New York: McGraw-Hill Higher Education, 2009).

Michael H. Hugos, *Essentials of Supply Chain Management*, 2nd ed (Hoboken, NJ: Wiley, 2006).

Robert M. Monczka, Robert B. Handfield, Larry C. Giunipero, and James L. Patterson. *Purchasing and Supply Chain Management*, 4th ed (Mason, OH: South-Western Cengage Learning, 2008).

Daniel Pollock, *Precipice* (Oak Brook, IL: Council of Logistics Management, 2001).

Tage Skjott-Larsen, Philip B. Schary, Juliana H. Mikkola, and Herbert Kotzab. *Managing the Global Supply Chain*, 3rd ed (Copenhagen Business School Press, 2007).

George A. Zsidisin, and Bob Ritchie, eds., *Supply Chain Risk: A Handbook of Assessment, Management, and Performance (International Series in Operations Research & Management Science)* (New York: Springer, 2008).

CHAPTER 17

Financial Management

CHAPTER CONTENTS & LEARNING OBJECTIVES

WHAT IS THE GOAL OF MANAGEMENT?

1. To understand how value is measured and managed across the multiple units of the multinational firm

IMPORT–EXPORT TRADE FINANCING

2. To examine how international business and investment activity alters and adds to the traditional financial management activities of the firm

MULTINATIONAL INVESTING

3. To understand the primary decision methods used to evaluate the potential risks and returns of a proposed investment in a foreign country

INTERNATIONAL CASH FLOW MANAGEMENT

4. To explore how both operating and financing cash flows are managed within the multinational firm

FOREIGN EXCHANGE EXPOSURE

5. To understand the three primary currency exposures that confront the multinational firm

COUNTERTRADE

6. To analyze the process of using goods and services as a medium of exchange in addition to money in international business

INTERNATIONAL TAXATION

7. To examine the primary differences in the taxation of business internationally, and how governments tax firms operating in their markets

G.M. has become the second-largest automaker in China mainly through a 50-50 venture with S.A.I.C. that makes a wide range of G.M.-designed cars. Under the deal being completed, G.M. would sell a 1 percent stake in the venture to S.A.I.C., raising the Chinese automaker's share to 51 percent, although G.M. would retain equal voting rights in company decisions and have an option to buy back the stake later, people with knowledge of the transaction said. Michael Dunne, an auto consultant specializing in Asian markets, said that for G.M. to accept a minority holding in its main joint venture marked an inevitable decline in G.M.'s influence in China, which has overtaken the United States as the world's largest auto market.

—"G.M. to Sell Stakes to China Partner," *Reuters*, December 3, 2009

The years 2008 and 2009 were obviously traumatic for General Motors. The global financial crisis had led to a global depression in automobile sales, and GM had been hit worse than most. But GM was a very different company in different regions of the world. GM North America and GM Europe were both clearly in crisis, as sales had plummeted and government bailouts (United States) and unit sales (Europe) were required for survival. But GM's activities across Asia, particularly in mainland China, were positive and profitable. The company's sales and competitiveness in China were remarkable, with GM surpassing Toyota and other major global competitors in the highly competitive and rapidly growing Chinese market. So why was GM selling portions of its Chinese and Indian businesses?

The answer was complicated. GM Asia held major corporate interests in a variety of countries and companies, including Daewoo Auto. GM had acquired control of Daewoo's automobile operations in 2001 (Daewoo was a major South Korean multinational conglomerate). The following years had been very good for the Daewoo business unit, and by 2009, GM's Daewoo unit was selling automobile components and vehicles to more than 100 countries.

Daewoo's success meant that it had expected sales (receivables) from buyers all over the world. What was even more remarkable was that the global automobile industry had increasingly used the U.S. dollar as its currency of contract for the multitude of cross-border transactions. All multinational companies must choose a currency for global tracking and control, and for GM, the dollar was obviously the currency of interest and consolidated reporting.

This meant that Daewoo did not really have dozens of foreign currencies to manage, just one, the U.S. dollar. So Daewoo of Korea had, in late 2007 and early 2008, entered into a series of *forward exchange contracts*. These currency contracts locked-in the Korean won value of the many dollar-denominated receivables the company expected to receive from international automobile sales in the coming year. In the eyes of many, this was a conservative and responsible currency hedging policy, that is until the global financial crisis and the following collapse of global automobile sales.

The problem for Daewoo was not that the Korean won per U.S. dollar exchange rate had moved dramatically; it had not. The problem was that Daewoo's sales, like all other automobile industry participants, had collapsed. The sales had not taken place, and therefore the underlying exposures, the expected receivables in dollars by Daewoo, had not happened. But the forward contracts did still happen, and delivering on the contracts had cost GM Daewoo billion—won 2,300 billion to be exact. GM's Daewoo unit was now broke, its equity wiped out by currency hedging gone bad. GM Asia needed money, quickly, and selling interests in its highly successful Chinese and Indian businesses was the only solution found.

Sources: "G.M. to Sell Stakes to China Partner," *Reuters*, December 3, 2009; Paul Betts, Song Jung-a and Louise Lucas, "Calmness in the Face of Adversity at Troubled GM," *Financial Times*, October 30, 2009, 18; Song Jung-a, "Korea Challenge," *Financial Times*, October 20, 2009, 23; "Corporate News: GM's China Sales Grow 78%," *The Wall Street Journal* (Eastern edition), August 4, 2009, B.2.

What exactly is the leadership of the multinational firm attempting to achieve? *Profit maximization*—the first words that leap from the lips—is the simplest answer. But as is the case with much of global business, it is not quite that simple. Should leadership be maximizing the profits in the short run, the long run, for stockholders alone, or for all of the stakeholders of the multinational organization?

WHAT IS THE GOAL OF MANAGEMENT?

1. To understand how value is measured and managed across the multiple units of the multinational firm

The Anglo-American markets, primarily the United States and the United Kingdom, are characterized by many publicly traded companies that seek to maximize shareholder wealth—so-called *stockholder wealth maximization*. Stockholder wealth maximization dictates that the management of the company should actively seek to maximize the returns to stockholders by working to push share prices up and to continually grow the dividends paid out to those same shareholders. This implies in the extreme, however, that management is not seeking to build value or wealth for the other stakeholders in the multinational enterprise: the creditors, management itself, employees, suppliers, the communities in which these firms reside, and even government itself. Clearly the modern concept of free market capitalism is a near sole focus on building wealth for stockholders alone, and has been frequently interpreted as extremely short-run in focus.

But this is not an accepted universal truth in global business. Continental European and Japanese firms have long pursued a wider definition of wealth maximization—*corporate wealth maximization*—that directs management to consider the financial and social health of all stakeholders, and not to focus exclusively on the financial returns of the multinational firm alone. This is not to say that the firm is not driven to maximize its profitability, but it does direct the firm to consider and balance short-term financial goals against long-term societal goals of continued employment, community citizenship, and public welfare needs—an extremely difficult task, at best.

These two different philosophies are not necessarily exclusive, and many firms—in all markets—attempt to find some balance between the two. The stockholder wealth maximization is in many ways much simpler and easier to pursue, having a single objective and in many ways a single client. Although simplistic, and sometimes leading to the abuses that have been so widely reported in recent years (Enron, Worldcom, and Tyco, to name but a few), it has led to the development of the relatively more competitive global business. The Focus on Ethics that follows, highlighting the story of Enron, is but one example of how a lack of ethical balance may lead to ruin.

Although in many ways a kinder and gentler philosophy, corporate wealth maximization has the unenviable charge of attempting to meet the desires of multiple stakeholders. Decision making becomes slower, less decisive, and frequently results in organizations that cannot meet the constantly growing pressures of a global marketplace that rewards innovation, speed, and lower costs. The concerns of social impacts, environmental responsibility, and sustainable development—while sounding good on the public relations releases—impose heavy burdens on organizations trying to compete in a wireless, Internet-based marketplace. The successful multinational enterprises of the coming century will be those that find the unique balance of financial objectives that works for them and their own corporate culture.

GLOBAL FINANCIAL GOALS

The multinational firm, because it is a conglomeration of many firms operating in a multitude of economic environments, must determine for itself the proper balance between three primary financial objectives:

Stockholder Wealth Maximization and Corporate Culture: The Enron Debacle

Enron may be the classic tale of how the singular pursuit of one philosophy, in the absence of consideration of other interests or beliefs, can lead to ruin.

The company's origins were humble: a simple natural gas pipeline operator that saw considerable growth in the 1980s. As the 1980s drew to a close, however, the company's new management team saw new opportunities to build additional shareholder value in making markets in natural gas using the information that flowed naturally to the firm from its existing operations. The Enron story was the subject of countless business school case studies, many news stories, and much Wall Street admiration.

Although now a global player, building and operating pipelines and power plants all over the world, the firm now found itself creating enormous profits through market-making, primarily in North America. As the firm hired more and more of the young best and brightest—paying premium salaries and signing bonuses to the new graduates of the best MBA programs—it built a corporate culture that was singularly focused on profits and greed. Without the healthy balance of wisdom and experience from a time-tested corporate culture, it in many ways became a naive and blind pursuer of stockholder wealth maximization.

By the late 1990s it became increasingly clear to many at the top of Enron that the story itself was losing steam, and profits could not be sustained. Many believe that it was the company's own corporate culture, one based on nothing other than earnings-per-share growth, that led to many of the questionable ethical decisions and ultimately to its demise.

1. Maximization of consolidated, after-tax, income
2. Minimization of the firm's effective global tax burden
3. Correct positioning of the firm's income, cash flows, and available funds

These goals are frequently inconsistent, in that the pursuit of one goal may result in a less desirable outcome in regard to another goal. Management must make decisions about the proper trade-offs between goals about the future (which is why people are employed as managers, not computers).

GENUS CORPORATION

A sample firm aids in illustrating how the various components of the multinational firm fit together, and how financial management must make decisions regarding trade-offs. Genus Corporation is a U.S.-based manufacturer and distributor of extremity-stimulus medical supplies.[1] The firm's corporate headquarters and original manufacturing plant are in New Orleans, Louisiana.

Genus currently has three wholly owned foreign subsidiaries located in Brazil, Germany, and China. In addition to the parent company selling goods in the domestic (U.S.) market and exporting goods to Mexico and Canada, each of the foreign subsidiaries purchases subassemblies (transfers) from the parent company. The subsidiaries then add value in the form of specific attributes and requirements for the local-country market, and distribute and sell the goods in the local market (Brazil, Germany, and China).

The three countries where Genus has incorporated subsidiaries pose very different challenges for the financial management of the firm. These challenges are outlined in Figure 17.1.

Tax Management

Genus, like all firms in all countries, would prefer to pay less taxes rather than more. Whereas profits are taxed at relatively low to moderate rates in China and Brazil, Germany's income tax rate is relatively high (though currently equal to that in the United States). If Genus could "rearrange" its profits among its units, it would prefer to make more of its profits in China and Brazil, given the lower tax burden placed on profits in those countries.

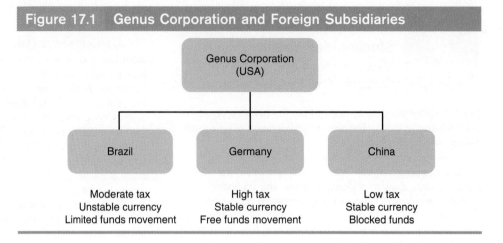

Figure 17.1   Genus Corporation and Foreign Subsidiaries

Currency Management

Ultimately, for valuation purposes, the most important attribute of any of the three country currencies is its ability to maintain its value versus the U.S. dollar, the reporting currency of the parent company. In 2001, the euro replaced the German mark and eleven other European currencies. Although the value of the euro has fluctuated, it is one of the world's primary currencies and is expected to maintain its value well over time. The Chinese renminbi (or *yuan* as it is sometimes called) is not freely convertible into other currencies without governmental approval, and its value is therefore highly controlled and maintained. The Brazilian real, however, is of particular worry. In previous years the value of the Brazilian currency has been known to fall dramatically, wiping out the value of profits generated in Brazil when converted to any other currency, like the dollar. As opposed to what tax management would recommend, Genus would prefer to "rearrange" its profits into Germany and euros for currency management purposes.

Funds Flow Management

The ability to move funds with relative ease and timeliness in a multinational firm is extremely important. For Genus, the German subsidiary experiences no problems with funds movements, as the German financial system is highly developed and open. Although Brazil possesses a number of bureaucratic requirements for justifying the movement of funds in and out of the country, it is still relatively open for moving funds cross-border. Genus's problems lie in China. The Chinese government makes it nearly impossible for foreign corporations to move funds out of China with any frequency, although bringing capital into China is not a problem. For funds management purposes, Genus would like to "rearrange" its profits and cash flows to minimize having funds blocked up in China.

The challenge to financial management of the global firm is management's ability to find the right trade-off between these often conflicting goals and risks.

MULTINATIONAL MANAGEMENT

A number of helpful reminders about multinational companies aid in describing the financial management issues confronting Genus:

- The primary goal of the firm, domestic or multinational, is the maximization of consolidated profits, after tax.

Table 17.1   Genus Corporation's Consolidated Gross Profits (in thousands)

Unit (currency)	Local Currency	Profit (local currency)	Tax Rate (percent)	Taxes Payable (local currency)	Profit After-Tax (local currency)	Exchange Rate (currency/US$)	Profit (US$)
U.S. parent company	Dollar (US$)	4,500	35%	1,575	2,925	—	$2,925
Brazilian subsidiary	Real (R$)	6,250	25	1,563	4,688	R$1.75/$	$2,679
German subsidiary	Euro (€)	3,000	35	1,050	1,950	$1.50/€	$1,300
Chinese subsidiary	Renminbi (Rmb)	2,500	30	750	1,750	Rmb 6.82/$	$ 257
Consolidated Results							
Profits after-tax (000s of US$)							**$7,160**
Shares outstanding (000s)							**10,000**
Earnings per share, EPS (US$)							**$ 0.72**

Notes:
1. Each individual unit of the company maintains its own financial books in local currency required by host governments.
2. The Brazilian real and Chinese renminbi are expressed as local currency per U.S. dollar. The euro, however, as is common practice, is quoted in U.S. dollars per euro.
3. Each individual unit's profits are translated into U.S. dollars for reporting purposes using the average exchange rate for the period (a quarter or a year).
4. United States parent company sales are derived from both sales to unrelated parties as well as intrafirm sales with the three individual foreign subsidiaries.
5. Tax calculations assume profits are derived from the active conduct of goods or service trade in the individual country, and that all profits are retained in the foreign subsidiaries (no dividend payments to the parent company in the United States).

- *Consolidated profits* are the profits of all the individual units of the firm originating in many different currencies as expressed in the currency of the parent company, in this case, the U.S. dollar. Consolidated profits are *not* limited to those earnings that have been brought back to the parent company (repatriated), and in fact these profits may never be removed from the country in which they were earned.

- Each of the incorporated units of the firm (the U.S. parent company and the three foreign subsidiaries) has its own set of traditional financial statements: statement of income, balance sheet, and statement of cash flows. These financial statements are expressed in the local currency of the unit for tax and reporting purposes to the local government.

Table 17.1 provides an overview of the current year's profits before and after tax on both the individual unit level and on the consolidated level, in both local currency and U.S. dollar value.

- The owners of Genus, its shareholders, track the firm's financial performance on the basis of its earnings per share (EPS). EPS is simply the consolidated profits of the firm, in U.S. dollars, divided by the total number of shares outstanding:

$$\text{EPS} = \frac{\text{Consolidated profits after tax}}{\text{Shares outstanding}} = \frac{\$7,160,000}{10,000,000} = \$0.72/\text{share}$$

- Each affiliate is located within a country's borders and is therefore subject to all laws and regulations applying to business activities within that country. These laws and regulations include specific practices as they apply to corporate income and tax rates, currency of denomination of operating and financial cash flows, and conditions under which capital and cash flows may move into and out of the country.

Multinational financial management is not a separate set of issues from domestic or traditional financial management, but the additional levels of risk and complexity introduced by the conduct of business across borders. Business across borders introduces different laws, different methods, different markets, different interest rates, and most of all, different currencies.

The many dimensions of multinational financial management are most easily explained in the context of a firm's financial decision-making process in evaluating a potential foreign investment. Such an evaluation includes:

- Capital budgeting, which is the process of evaluating the financial feasibility of an individual investment, whether it be the purchase of a stock, real estate, or a firm
- Capital structure, which is the determination of the relative quantities of debt capital and equity capital that will constitute the funding of the investment
- Working capital and cash flow management, which is the management of operating and financial cash flows passing in and out of a specific investment project

Changes in interest and exchange rates will affect each of the above steps in the international investment process. All firms, no matter how "domestic" they may seem in structure, are influenced by exchange rate changes. The financial managers of a firm that has any dimension of international activity, imports or exports, or foreign subsidiaries or affiliates, must pay special attention to these issues if the firm is to succeed in its international endeavors. The discussion begins with the difficulties of simply getting paid for international sales: import-export financing.

IMPORT-EXPORT TRADE FINANCING

2. To examine how international business and investment activity alters and adds to the traditional financial management activities of the firm

Unlike most domestic business, international business often occurs between two parties that do not know each other very well. Yet, in order to conduct business, a large degree of financial trust must exist. This financial trust is basically the trust that the buyer of a product will actually pay for it on or after delivery. For example, if a furniture manufacturer in South Carolina receives an order from a distributor located in Cleveland, Ohio, the furniture maker will ordinarily fill the order, ship the furniture, and await payment. Payment terms are usually 30 to 60 days. This is trade on an "open account basis." The furniture manufacturer has placed a considerable amount of financial trust in the buyer but normally is paid with little problem.

Internationally, however, financial trust is pushed to its limit. An order from a foreign buyer may constitute a degree of credit risk (the risk of not being repaid) that the producer (the exporter) cannot afford to take. The exporter needs some guarantee that the importer will pay for the goods. Other factors that tend to intensify this problem include the increased lag times necessary for international shipments and the potential risks of payments in different currencies. For this reason, arrangements that provide guarantees for exports are important to countries and companies wanting to expand international sales. This can be accomplished through a sequence of documents surrounding the letter of credit.

TRADE FINANCING USING A LETTER OF CREDIT

A lumber manufacturer in the Pacific Northwest of the United States, Vanport, receives a large order from a Japanese construction company, Endaka, for a shipment of old-growth pine lumber. Vanport has not worked with Endaka before and therefore seeks some assurance that payment for the lumber will actually be made. Vanport ordinarily does not require any assurance of the buyer's ability to pay (sometimes a

Figure 17.2   Trade Financing with a Letter of Credit (L/C)

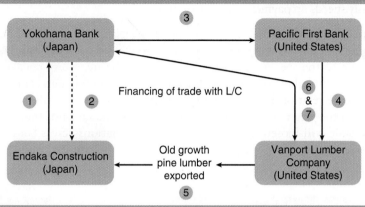

small down payment or deposit is made as a sign of good faith), but an international sale of this size is too large a risk. If Endaka could not or would not pay, the cost of returning the lumber products to the United States would be prohibitive. Figure 17.2 illustrates the following sequence of events that will complete the transaction.

1. Endaka Construction (JAP) requests a letter of credit (L/C) to be issued by its bank, Yokohama Bank.

2. Yokohama Bank will determine whether Endaka is financially sound and capable of making the payments as required. This is a very important step because Yokohama Bank simply wants to guarantee the payment, not make the payment.

3. Yokohama Bank, once satisfied with Endaka's application, issues the L/C to a representative in the United States or to the exporter's bank, Pacific First Bank. The L/C guarantees payment for the merchandise if the goods are shipped as stipulated in accompanying documents. Customary documents include the commercial invoice, customs clearance and invoice, the packing list, certification of insurance, and a bill of lading.

4. The exporter's bank, Pacific First, assures Vanport that payment will be made after evaluating the letter of credit. At this point the credit standing of Yokohama Bank has been substituted for the credit standing of the importer itself, Endaka Construction.

5. When the lumber order is ready, it is loaded onboard the shipper (called a common carrier). When the exporter signs a contract with a shipper, the signed contract serves as the receipt that the common carrier has received the goods, and it is termed the bill of lading.

6. Vanport draws a **draft** against Yokohama Bank for payment. The draft is the document used in international trade to effect payment and explicitly requests payment for the merchandise, which is now shown to be shipped and insured consistent with all requirements of the previously issued L/C. (If the draft is issued to the bank issuing the L/C, Yokohama Bank, it is termed a **bank draft**. If the draft is issued against the importer, Endaka Construction, it is a **trade draft**.) The draft, L/C, and other appropriate documents are presented to Pacific First Bank for payment.

7. If Pacific First Bank (U.S.) had confirmed the letter of credit from Yokohama Bank, it would immediately pay Vanport for the lumber and then collect from the issuing bank, Yokohama. If Pacific First Bank had not confirmed the letter of credit, it would only pass the documents to Yokohama Bank for payment

draft The document used in international trade to require payment for goods from a buyer.

bank draft A financial document drawn against a bank.

trade draft A withdrawal document drawn against a company.

(to Vanport). The confirmed, as opposed to unconfirmed, letter of credit obviously speeds up payment to the exporter.

Regardless, with the letter of credit as the financial assurance, the exporter or the exporter's bank is collecting payment from the importer's bank, not from the importer itself. It is up to the specific arrangements between the importer (Endaka) and the importer's bank (Yokohama) to arrange the final settlement at that end of the purchase.

If the trade relationship continues over time, both parties will gain faith and confidence in the other. With this strengthening of financial trust, the trade financing relationship will loosen. Sustained buyer–seller relations across borders eventually end up operating on an open account basis similar to domestic commerce.

MULTINATIONAL INVESTING

3. To understand the primary decision methods used to evaluate the potential risks and returns of a proposed investment in a foreign country

Any investment, whether it be the purchase of stock, the acquisition of real estate, or the construction of a manufacturing facility in another country, is financially justified if the present value of expected cash inflows is greater than the present value of expected cash outflows; in other words, if it has a positive **net present value (NPV)**. The construction of a **capital budget** is the process of projecting the net operating cash flows of the potential investment to determine if it is indeed a good investment.

net present value (NPV) The sum of the present values of all cash inflows and outflows from an investment project discounted at the cost of capital.

capital budget The financial evaluation of a proposed investment to determine whether the expected returns are sufficient to justify the investment expenses.

CAPITAL BUDGETING

All capital budgets are only as good as the accuracy of the cost and revenue assumptions. Adequately anticipating all of the incremental expenses that the individual project imposes on the firm is critical to a proper analysis.

A capital budget is composed of three primary cash flow components:

1. **Initial expenses and capital outlays.** The initial capital outlays are normally the largest net cash outflow occurring over the life of a proposed investment. Because the cash flows occur up front, they have a substantial impact on the net present value of the project.
2. **Operating cash flows.** The operating cash flows are the net cash flows the project is expected to yield once production is underway. The primary positive net cash flows of the project are realized in this stage; net operating cash flows will determine the success or failure of the proposed investment.
3. **Terminal cash flows.** The final component of the capital budget is composed of the salvage value or resale value of the project at its end. The terminal value will include whatever working capital balances can be recaptured once the project is no longer in operation (at least by this owner).

The financial decision criterion for an individual investment is whether the net present value of the project is positive or negative.[2] The net cash flows in the future are discounted by the average cost of capital for the firm (the average of debt and equity costs). The purpose of discounting is to capture the fact that the firm has acquired investment capital at a cost (interest). The same capital could have been used for other projects of other investments. It is therefore necessary to discount the future cash flows to account for this foregone income of the capital, its opportunity cost. If NPV is positive, then the project is an acceptable investment. If the project's NPV is negative, then the cash flows expected to result from the investment are insufficient to provide an acceptable rate of return, and the project should be rejected.

A PROPOSED PROJECT INVESTMENT

The capital budget for a manufacturing plant in Singapore serves as a basic example. Quorum, a U.S. manufacturer of household consumer products, is considering the construction of a plant in Singapore in 2010. It would cost US$1,660,000 to build and would be ready for operation on January 1, 2011. Quorum would operate the plant for three years and then would sell the plant to the Singapore government.

To analyze the proposed investment, Quorum must estimate what the sales revenues would be per year, the costs of production, the overhead expenses of operating the plant per year, the depreciation allowances for the new plant and equipment, and the Singapore tax rate on corporate income. The estimation of all net operating cash flows is very important to the analysis of the project. Often, the entire acceptability of a foreign investment may depend on the sales forecast for the foreign project.

Telecom's titan, AT&T Corporation, launched China's first foreign telecom venture with Telecom's Shanghai branch after seven years of negotiation.

But Quorum needs U.S. dollars, not Singapore dollars. The only way the stockholders of Quorum would be willing to undertake the investment is if it would be profitable in terms of their own currency, the U.S. dollar. This is the primary theoretical distinction between a domestic capital budget and a multinational capital budget. The evaluation of the project in the viewpoint of the parent will focus on whatever cash flows, either operational or financial, will find their way back to the parent firm in U.S. dollars.

Quorum must, therefore, forecast the movement of the Singapore dollar (S$) over the four-year period as well. The spot rate on January 1, 2010, is S$1.4000/US$. Quorum concludes that the rate of inflation will be roughly 4 percent higher per year in Singapore than in the United States. If the theory of purchasing power parity holds, as described in Chapter 7, it should take roughly 4 percent more Singapore dollars to buy a U.S. dollar per year. Using this assumption, Quorum forecasts the exchange rate from 2011 to 2013.

After considerable study and analysis, Quorum estimates that the net cash flows of the Singapore project, in Singapore dollars, would be those on line 1 in Table 17.2. Line 2 lists the expected exchange rate between Singapore dollars and U.S. dollars over the four-year period, assuming it takes 2 percent more Singapore dollars per U.S. dollar each year (the Singapore dollar is, therefore, expected to depreciate versus

Table 17.2 Multinational Capital Budgeting: Quorum's Evaluation of a Singapore Project

Line #	Description	2010	2011	2012	2013
1	Net cash flow in Singapore dollars (S$)	(1,660,000)	300,000	600,000	1,500,000
2	Exchange rate, S$/US$ (at 4%)	1.4000	1.4560	1.5142	1.5748
3	Expected net cash flow (US$)	(1,185,714)	206,044	396,238	952,496
4	Present value factor (at 12%)	1.0000	0.8929	0.7972	0.7118
5	Present value of cash flow in US$	(1,185,714)	183,968	315,879	677,968
6	Net present value (US$)	(7,900)			
7	Net present value (S$)	153,844			

Notes:

1. The spot exchange rate of S$1.4000/$ is assumed to change by 4 percent per year. S$1.4000 × 1.04 = S$1.4560/$.
2. The present value factor assumes a weighted average cost of capital, here used as the discount rate, of 12 percent. The present value discount factor is then found using the standard formula of $1/(1 + 0.12)^t$, where t is the number of years in the future (1, 2, or 3).

the U.S. dollar). Combining the net cash flow forecast in Singapore dollars with the expected exchange rates, Quorum can now calculate the net cash flow per year in U.S. dollars. Quorum notes that although the initial expense is sizable, the project produces positive net cash flows in its very first year of operations (2011) and remains positive every year after.

Quorum estimates that its cost of capital, both debt and equity combined (the weighted average cost of capital), is about 12 percent per year. Using this as the rate of discount, the discount factor for each of the future years is found. Finally, the net cash flow in U.S. dollars multiplied by the present value factor yields the present values of each net cash flow. The net present value (NPV) of the Singapore project is negative US$7,900. Quorum may decide not to proceed with the project because, according to financial theory it does not create value for the firm.

RISKS IN INTERNATIONAL INVESTMENTS

The risks associated with international investments are substantial, but here we will focus on two—exchange rate risk and interest rate risk—and how they are viewed by investors. How is the Quorum capital budget different from a similar project constructed in Bangor, Maine? It is riskier, at least from the standpoint of cross-border risk. The higher risk of an international investment arises from the different countries, their laws, regulations, potential for interference with the normal operations of the investment project, and obviously currencies—all of which are unique to international investment.

The risk of international investment is considered greater because the proposed investment will be within the jurisdiction of a different government. Governments have the ability to pass new laws, including the potential nationalization of the entire project. The typical problems that may arise from operating in a different country are changes in foreign tax laws, restrictions placed on when or how much in profits may be repatriated to the parent company, and other types of restrictions that hinder the free movement of merchandise and capital among the proposed project, the parent, and any other country relevant to its material inputs or sales.

The other major distinction between a domestic investment and a foreign investment is that the viewpoint or perspective of the parent and the project are no longer the same. The two perspectives differ because the parent only values cash flows it derives from the project. So, for example, in Table 17.2 the project generates sufficient net cash flows in Singapore dollars that the project is acceptable from the *project's viewpoint*, but not from the *parent's viewpoint*. Assuming the same 12 percent discount rate, the NPV in Singapore dollars is +S$153,844, while the NPV to the U.S. parent is −US$7,900 as noted previously. But what if the exchange rate were not to change at all, but would remain fixed for the 2010–2013 period? The NPV would then be positive from both viewpoints. Or what if the Singapore government were to restrict the payment of dividends back to the U.S. parent firm or somehow prohibit the Singapore subsidiary from exchanging Singapore dollars for U.S. dollars (capital controls)? Without cash flows in U.S. dollars, the parent would have no way of justifying the investment. And all of this could occur while the project itself is sufficiently profitable when measured in local currency (Singapore dollars). This split between project and parent viewpoint is a critical difference in international investment analysis.

COMBINING INTEREST-RATE AND EXCHANGE-RATE RISKS

If there is one mistake made more often than any other in international financial management, it is understanding what borrowing or investing in a foreign currency really means. For example, many companies and investors have borrowed in Japan for many years because Japanese yen interest rates are some of the lowest in the world. This

Figure 17.3 The Japanese Yen Carry Trade

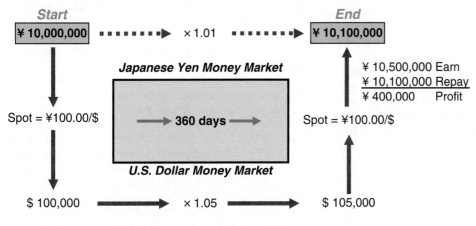

Investors borrow yen at 1.00% per annum

Start		End
¥ 10,000,000	···· ► × 1.01 ···· ►	¥ 10,100,000

¥ 10,500,000 Earn
¥ 10,100,000 Repay
¥ 400,000   Profit

Japanese Yen Money Market

Spot = ¥100.00/$ ► 360 days ►   Spot = ¥100.00/$

U.S. Dollar Money Market

$ 100,000 ──────► × 1.05 ──────► $ 105,000

Invest dollars at 5.00% per annum

An investor borrows ¥10 million at 1 percent interest. The ¥10 million is then exchanged for U.S. dollars and invested at a higher interest rate for one year. At the end of the year, the U.S. dollars are exchanged back into yen in order to repay the yen loan and realize profit. As long as the spot exchange rate is close to the same at the end of the box as it was at the front of the box, the investor profits. But if the yen appreciated against the dollar to, say, ¥95/$, the investor would actually lose money on the speculation.

practice, called the *Japanese Carry Trade*, relies on being able to borrow cheaply and reinvest somewhere else in the world to make a greater return. So what could go wrong?

Consider an international investor who borrows ¥10 million at 1.00 percent interest per annum, which is incredibly cheap. At the end of one year, the investor will need to repay the loan in full, principal and interest, of ¥10.1 million. The money borrowed is exchanged for U.S. dollars at the current spot rate of, say, ¥100/$, yielding $100,000. This $100,000 is then invested in U.S. dollar securities earning 5.00 percent interest for one year. At the end of one year the investor has $105,000, and has earned 5 percent while borrowing the funds at 1 percent. All that is left is to repay the loan and calculate the profits. But that's where things can go wrong.

The entire investment's return is dependent on what the exchange rate is at the end of the period. If the spot rate is still ¥100/$, then the investor exchanges dollars for yen and locks in a profit of ¥400,000 on the investment. This is shown in Figure 17.3. But if the Japanese yen's value has risen against the dollar over that year, to, say, ¥95/$, the $105,000 yields only ¥9,975,000, which is not enough to even repay the loan. Of course if the yen depreciates in value against the dollar, to, say, ¥105/$, the investor's return is even greater. It all depends on the ending spot rate of exchange.

This type of international investment or debt is actually extremely common in global business. A few examples:

- A Norwegian citizen is buying a new home. She can acquire a mortgage for the home's purchase in Norwegian krone for 7.00 percent, or in euros for 5.00 percent. Although the euro is obviously a lower interest rate, she has no real idea of what the rate of exchange between the Norwegian krone and the euro will be in coming years. The mortgage payments may end up being anything, higher, lower, or the same.

- A Thailand based company needs to borrow $20 million or the Thai baht equivalent in order to make a new acquisition. U.S. dollar interest rates offered the company are 8 percent, while the corresponding loan in Thai baht is 18 percent. The Thai company, although it knows it is taking a currency

Brazil Fighting the Rise of the Real

Brazil's government will apply a tax on Brazilian stocks traded as American depository receipts (ADRs) another effort to stem the rapid flow of capital into Brazilian securities that has sent the country's currency soaring against the U.S. dollar. The move came after a 2 percent tax on foreign-exchange inflows was levied and, economists suspect, likely won't do much to rein in the Brazilian real's advance.

Market participants in Brazil said the move was an effort by the government to close a loophole that allowed investors to buy Brazilian shares overseas and avoid a 2 percent tax on foreign investments adopted in the fall of 2009. Brazilian Finance Minister Guido Mantega said the 1.5 percent tax on ADRs was effective immediately. He called it part of a broader effort to halt the appreciation of the real, which has gained 36 percent against the dollar by the end of 2009.

Mantega noted in late 2009, the dollar traded at 1.71 reais and that foreign-exchange volatility has since eased. "We managed to give stability to the exchange rate," he said.

Finance Ministry chief economist Nelson Barbosa said that when Brazilian companies sell ADRs to investors overseas, they are obliged to deposit the shares with Brazil's Cetip custodial agency. Under the new rule, Cetip will charge the issuing company 1.5 percent at the moment the shares are deposited.

Brazilian companies will presumably pass on the 1.5 percent tax to overseas buyers of the shares, which may discourage inflows. The Bank of New York Mellon Brazil ADR Index ended the lay down 1.5 percent. The Bank of New York Mellon Emerging Market ADR finished 0.9 percent lower. New York–based ADR traders suggested the new law was "bad news." Economists were also skeptical the latest measure would work.

"The goal is to prevent investors from taking exposure to Brazilian equities offshore," said Douglas Smith, head of research at Americas Global Research at Standard Chartered Bank. He said Brazil's high interest rates, its robust economy, and broad dollar weakness support the real—undermining such fixes.

Source: John Kolodziejski, "International Finance: Brazil Taxing ADRs to Rein in Real," *The Wall Street Journal* (Eastern edition), November 19, 2009, C.2.

risk, borrows dollars at 8 percent because the difference between interest rates appears so great. This worked fine until the summer of 1997 when the Asian crisis caused the fall of the Thai baht from B25/$ to B40/$. The effective interest rate ends up being 72.85 percent, not 8 percent.

- A London-based money market fund exchanges British pounds for Icelandic krona in early 2006 in order to reap the benefits of extremely high short-term interest rates in Iceland. Unfortunately, as a result of a rapidly rising rate of inflation in Iceland, the Icelandic krona's value versus the British pound (and many other major currencies) plummets in a matter of months, destroying the value of the funds invested in Iceland. Once the money found its way back home to the British pound, the returns were negative, not positive!

The problem is of course that borrowing or investing in foreign currencies includes foreign exchange risk. Unless the borrower or the investor knows with certainty what the exchange rate will be at all future dates of repayment or returns, the currency risk is always present.

cash management The management of cash balances owned by the firm held by banking and other financial institutions.

4. To explore how both operating and financing cash flows are managed within the multinational firm

INTERNATIONAL CASH FLOW MANAGEMENT

Cash management is the financing of short-term or current assets, but the term is used here to describe all short-term financing and financial management of the firm. Even a small multinational firm will have a number of different cash flows moving throughout its system at one time. The maintenance of proper liquidity, the monitoring of payments, and the acquisition of additional capital when needed—all of these require a great degree of organization and planning in international operations.

Figure 17.4 Operating and Financing Cash Flows of a U.S.-Based Multinational Firm

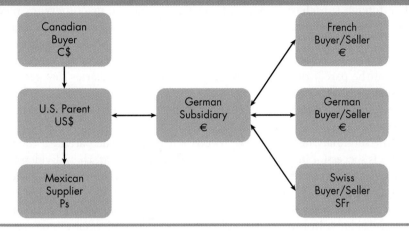

OPERATING CASH FLOWS AND FINANCING CASH FLOWS

Firms possess both operating cash flows and financing cash flows. **Operating cash flows** arise from the everyday business activities of the firm such as paying for materials or resources (accounts payable) or receiving payments for items sold (accounts receivable). In addition to the direct cost and revenue cash flows from operations, there are a number of indirect cash flows. The indirect cash flows are primarily license fees paid to the owners of particular technological processes and royalties to the holders of patents or copyrights.

Financing cash flows arise from the funding activities of the firm. The servicing of existing funding sources, interest on existing debt, and dividend payments to shareholders constitute potentially large and frequent cash flows. Periodic additions to debt or equity through new bank loans, new bond issuances, or supplemental stock sales may also add to the volume of financing cash flows in the multinational firm.

Figure 17.4 provides an overview of how operational and financial cash flows may appear for a U.S.-based multinational firm. In addition to having some export sales in Canada, it may import some materials from Mexico. The firm has gained access to several different European markets by first selling its product to its German subsidiary, which then provides the final touches necessary for sales in Germany, France, and Switzerland. Sales and purchases by the parent with Canada and Mexico give rise to a continuing series of accounts receivable and accounts payable, which may be denominated in Canadian dollars, Mexican pesos, or U.S. dollars.

INTRAFIRM CASH FLOWS AND TRANSFER PRICES

Cash flows between the U.S. parent and the German subsidiary will be both operational and financial in nature. The sale of the major product line to the German subsidiary creates intrafirm accounts receivable and payable. The payments may be denominated in either U.S. dollars or euros. The intrafirm sales may, in fact, be two-way if the German subsidiary is actually producing a form of the product not made in the United States but needed there.

One of the most difficult pricing decisions many multinational firms must make concerns the price at which they sell their products to their own subsidiaries and affiliates. These prices, called **transfer prices**, theoretically are equivalent to what the same product would cost if purchased on the open market. However, it is often impossible to find such a product on the open market; it may be unique to the firm and its product

operating cash flows The cash flows arising from the firm's everyday business activities.

financing cash flows The cash flows of a firm related to the funding of its operations; debt and equity related cash flows.

transfer prices The prices at which a firm sells its products to its own subsidiaries and affiliates.

line. The result is a price that is set internally and may result in the subsidiary being more or less profitable. This, in turn, has impacts on taxes paid in host countries.

The foreign subsidiary may also be using techniques, machinery, or processes that are owned or patented by the parent firm and so must pay royalties and license fees. The cash flows are usually calculated as a percentage of the sales price in Germany. Many multinational firms also spread the overhead and management expenses incurred at the parent over their foreign affiliates and subsidiaries that are using the parent's administrative services.

There are also a number of financing cash flows between the U.S. parent and the German subsidiary. If the subsidiary is partially financed by loans extended by the parent, the subsidiary needs to make regular payments to the parent. If the German subsidiary is successful in its operations and generates a profit, then dividends will be paid back to the parent. If, at some point, the German subsidiary needs more capital than what it can retain from its own profits, it may need additional debt or equity capital. These obviously would add to the potential financial cash flow volume.

The subsidiary, in turn, is dependent on its sales in Germany (euro revenues), France (euro revenues), and Switzerland (Swiss franc revenues) to generate the needed cash flows for paying everyone else. This "map" of operating and financing cash flows does not even attempt to describe the frequency of the various foreign currency cash flows, or to assign the responsibility for managing the currency risks. The management of cash flows in a larger multinational firm, one with possibly 10 or 20 subsidiaries, is obviously complex. The proper management of the cash flows is, however, critical to the success of the multinational business.

CASH MANAGEMENT

The structure of the firm dictates how cash flows and financial resources can be managed. The trend in the past decade has been for the increasing centralization of most financial and treasury operations. The centralized treasury often is responsible for both funding operations and cash flow management. It also may enjoy significant economies of scale, offering more services and expertise to the various units of the firm worldwide than the individual units themselves could support. However, regardless of whether the firm follows a centralized or decentralized approach, there are a number of operating structures that help the multinational firm manage its cash flows.

Netting

Figure 17.5 expands our firm to two European subsidiaries, one in Germany and one in France. The figure illustrates how many of the cash flows between units of a

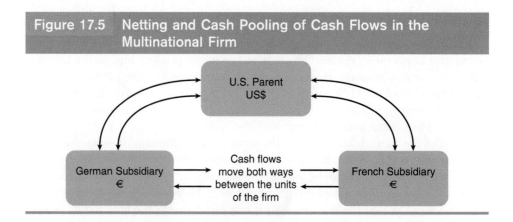

Figure 17.5   Netting and Cash Pooling of Cash Flows in the Multinational Firm

multinational firm are two-way and may result in unneeded transfer costs and transaction expenses. Coordination between units simply requires planning and budgeting of intrafirm cash flows so that two-way flows are "netted" against one another, with only one smaller cash flow as opposed to two having to be undertaken.

Netting can occur between each subsidiary and the parent, and between the subsidiaries themselves (it is often forgotten that many of the activities in a multinational firm occur between subsidiaries, and not just between individual subsidiaries and the parent). Netting is particularly helpful if the two-way flow is in two different currencies, as each would be suffering currency exchange charges for intrafirm transfers.

> **netting** Cash flow coordination between a corporation's global units so that only one smaller cash transfer must be made.

Cash Pooling

A large firm with a number of units operating both within an individual country and across countries may be able to economize on the amount of firm assets needed in cash if one central pool is used for **cash pooling**. With one pool of capital and up-to-date information on the cash flows in and out of the various units, the firm spends much less in terms of foregone interest on cash balances, which are held in safekeeping against unforeseen cash flow shortfalls.

> **cash pooling** Used by multinational firms to centralize individual units' cash flows, resulting in less spending or foregone interest on unnecessary cash balances.

For example, for the firm described in Figure 17.5, the parent and German and French subsidiaries may be able to consolidate all cash management and resources in one place—for example, New York (associated with the U.S. parent). One cash manager for all units would be in a better position for planning intercompany payments, including controlling the currency exposures of the individual units. A single large pool also may allow the firm to negotiate better financial service rates with banking institutions for cash-clearing purposes. In the event that the cash manager would need to be closer to the individual units (both proximity and time zone), the two European units could combine to run cash from one or the other for both.

Leads and Lags

The timing of payments between units of a multinational is somewhat flexible. Again, this allows the management of payments between the French and German subsidiaries and between the parent and the subsidiaries to be much more flexible, allowing the firm not only to position cash flows where they are needed most, but also to help manage currency risk. A foreign subsidiary that is expecting its local currency to fall in value relative to the U.S. dollar may try to speed up or **lead** its payments to the parent. Similarly, if the local currency is expected to rise versus the dollar, the subsidiary may want to wait, or **lag**, payments until exchange rates are more favorable.

> **lead** Paying a debt early to take advantage of exchange rates.

> **lag** Paying a debt late to take advantage of exchange rates.

Reinvoicing

Multinational firms with a variety of manufacturing and distribution subsidiaries scattered over a number of countries within a region may often find it more economical to have one office or subsidiary taking ownership of all invoices and payments between units.

For example, Figure 17.6 illustrates how our sample firm could be restructured to incorporate a **reinvoicing** center. The site for the reinvoicing center in this case is Luxembourg, a country that is known to have low taxes and few restrictions on income earned from international business operations. The Luxembourg subsidiary buys from one unit and sells to a second unit, therefore taking ownership of the goods and reinvoicing the sale to the next unit. Once ownership is taken, the sale/purchase

> **reinvoicing** The policy of buying goods from one unit and selling them to a second unit and reinvoicing the sale to the next unit, to take advantage of favorable exchange rates.

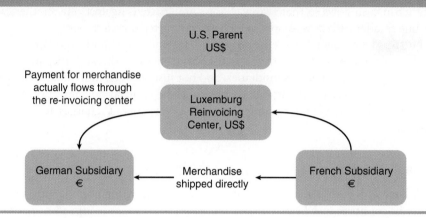

Figure 17.6   Establishing a Reinvoicing Center in the Multinational Firm

can be redenominated in a different currency, netted against other payments, hedged against specific currency exposures, or repriced in accordance with potential tax benefits of the reinvoicing center's host country.

Internal Banks

Some multinational firms have found that their financial resources and needs are becoming either too large or too sophisticated for the financial services that are available in many of their local subsidiary markets. One solution to this has been the establishment of an **internal bank** within the firm. The internal bank actually buys and sells payables and receivables from the various units, which frees the units of the firm from struggling for continual working capital financing and lets them focus on their primary business activities.

All of these structures and management techniques often are combined in different ways to fit the needs of the individual multinational firm. Some techniques are encouraged or prohibited by laws and regulations (e.g., many countries limit the ability to lead and lag payments), depending on the host country's government and stage of capital market liberalization. Multinational cash flow management requires flexibility in thinking—artistry in some cases—as much as technique on the part of managers.

internal bank A multinational firm's financial management tool that actually acts as a bank to coordinate finances among its units.

FOREIGN EXCHANGE EXPOSURE

5. To understand the three primary currency exposures that confront the multinational firm

Companies today know the risks of international operations. They are aware of the substantial risks to balance sheet values and annual earnings that interest rates and exchange rates may inflict on any firm at any time. Financial managers, international treasurers, and financial officers of all kinds are expected to protect the firm from such risks. Firms have, in varying degrees, three types of foreign currency exposure:

transaction exposure The potential for currency losses or gains during the time when a firm completes a transaction denominated in a foreign currency.

1. **Transaction exposure.** This is the risk associated with a contractual payment of foreign currency. For example, a U.S. firm that exports products to France will receive a guaranteed (by contract) payment in French francs in the future. Firms that buy or sell internationally have **transaction exposure** if any of the cash flows are denominated in foreign currency.

2. **Economic exposure.** This is the risk to the firm that its long-term cash flows will be affected, positively or negatively, by unexpected future exchange rate changes. Although many firms that consider themselves to be purely domestic may not realize it, all firms have some degree of **economic exposure**.

3. **Translation exposure.** This risk arises from the legal requirement that all firms consolidate their financial statements (balance sheets and income statements) of all worldwide operations annually. Therefore, any firm with operations outside its home country, operations that will be either earning foreign currency or valued in foreign currency, has **translation exposure**.

Transaction exposure and economic exposure are "true exposures" in the financial sense. This means they both present potential threats to the value of a firm's cash flows over time. The third exposure, translation, is a problem that arises from accounting.

TRANSACTION EXPOSURE

Transaction exposure is the most commonly observed type of exchange rate risk. Only two conditions are necessary for a transaction exposure to exist: (1) a cash flow that is denominated in a foreign currency and (2) the cash flow that will occur at a future date. Any contract, agreement, purchase, or sale that is denominated in a foreign currency that will be settled in the future constitutes a transaction exposure.

The risk of a transaction exposure is that the exchange rate might change between the present date and the settlement date. The change may be for the better or for the worse. For example, suppose that an American firm signs a contract to purchase heavy rolled-steel pipe from a South Korean steel producer for 21,000,000 Korean won. The payment is due in 30 days upon delivery. The 30-day account payable, so typical of international trade and commerce, is a transaction exposure for the U.S. firm. If the spot exchange rate on the date the contract is signed is Won 700/$, the U.S. firm would expect to pay

$$\frac{\text{Won } 21,000,000}{\text{Won } 700/\$} = \$30,000$$

But the firm is not assured of what the exchange rate will be in 30 days. If the spot rate at the end of 30 days is Won 720/$, the U.S. firm would actually pay less. The payment would then be $29,167. If, however, the exchange rate changed in the opposite direction, for example to Won 650/$, the payment could just as easily increase to $32,308. This type of price risk, transaction exposure, is a major problem for international commerce.

TRANSACTION EXPOSURE MANAGEMENT

Management of transaction exposures usually is accomplished by either **natural hedging** or **contractual hedging**. Natural hedging is the term used to describe how a firm might arrange to have foreign currency cash flows coming in and going out at roughly the same times and same amounts. This is referred to as natural hedging because the management or hedging of the exposure is accomplished by matching offsetting foreign currency cash flows and, therefore, does not require the firm to undertake unusual financial contracts or activities to manage the exposure. For example, a Canadian firm that generates a significant portion of its total sales in U.S. dollars may acquire U.S. dollar debt. The U.S. dollar earnings from sales could then be used to service the dollar debt as needed. In this way, regardless of whether the C$/US$ exchange rate goes up or down, the firm would be naturally hedged against the movement. If the U.S. dollar went up in value against the Canadian dollar, the U.S. dollars needed for

economic exposure The potential change in the value of a firm from unexpected changes in exchange rates. Also called "operating exposure" and "strategic exposure."

translation exposure The potential effect of a change in currency values on a firm's financial statements.

natural hedging The structuring of a firm's operations so that cash inflows and outflows by currency are matched.

contractual hedging A multinational firm's use of contracts to minimize its transaction exposure.

debt service would be generated automatically by the export sales to the United States. U.S. dollar inflows would match U.S. dollar cash outflows.

Contractual hedging is when the firm uses financial contracts to hedge the transaction exposure. The most common foreign currency contractual hedge is the **forward contract**, although other financial instruments and derivatives, such as currency futures and options, are also used. The forward contract (see Chapter 7) would allow the firm to be assured a fixed rate of exchange between the desired two currencies at the precise future date. The forward contract would also be for the exact amount of the exposure.

A **hedge** is an asset or a position whose value moves in the equal but opposite direction of the exposure. This means that if an exposure experienced a loss in value of $50, the hedge asset would offset the loss with a gain in value of $50. The total value of the position would not change. This would be termed a perfect hedge.

But perfect hedges are hard to find, and many people would not use them if they were readily available. Why? The presence of a perfect hedge eliminates all downside risk, but also eliminates all upside potential. Many businesses accept this two-sided risk as part of doing business. However, it is generally best to accept risk in the line of business, not in the cash-payment process of settling the business.

RISK MANAGEMENT VERSUS SPECULATION

The distinction between managing currency cash flows and speculating with currency cash flows is sometimes lost among those responsible for the safekeeping of the firm's treasury. If the previous description of currency hedging is followed closely (the selection of assets or positions only to counteract potential losses on existing exposures), few problems should arise. Problems arise when currency positions or financial instruments are purchased (or sold) with the expectation that a specific currency movement will result in a profit, termed speculation.

There are a number of major multinational firms that treat their international treasury centers as "service centers," but rarely do they consider financial management a "profit center". One of the most visible examples of what can go wrong when currency speculation is undertaken for corporate profit occurred in Great Britain in 1991. A large British food conglomerate, Allied-Lyons, suffered losses of £158 million ($268 million) on currency speculation after members of its international treasury staff suffered losses on currency positions at the start of the Persian Gulf War and then doubled-up on their positions in the following weeks in an attempt to recover previous losses. They lost even more.[3]

TRANSACTION EXPOSURE CASE: LUFTHANSA

In January 1985, the German airline Lufthansa purchased 20 Boeing 737 jet aircraft. The jets would be delivered to Lufthansa in one year, in January 1986. Upon delivery of the aircraft, Lufthansa would pay Boeing (U.S.) $500 million. This constituted a huge transaction exposure for Lufthansa. (Note that the exposure falls on Lufthansa not Boeing. If the purchase agreement had been stated in deutsche marks, the transaction exposure would have been transferred to Boeing.)

The Exposure

The spot exchange rate in January 1985, when Lufthansa signed the agreement, was DM 3.2/$. The expected cost of the aircraft to Lufthansa was then

$$\$500,000,000 \times DM3.2/\$ = DM1,600,000,000.$$

---

forward contracts Agreements between firms and banks which permit the firm to either sell or buy a specific foreign currency at a future date at a known price.

hedge To counterbalance a present sale or purchase with a sale or purchase for future delivery as a way to minimize loss due to price fluctuations; to make counterbalancing sales or purchases in the international market as protection against adverse movements in the exchange rate.

Figure 17.7   Lufthansa's Transaction Exposure: Alternatives for Managing the Purchase of $500 Million in Boeing 737s

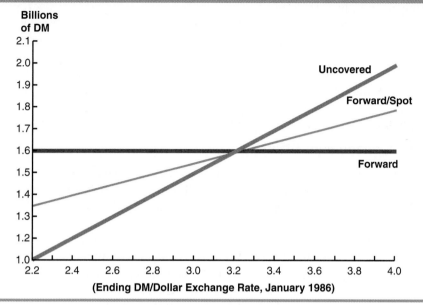

Figure 17.7 illustrates how the expected total cost of $500 million changes to Lufthansa with the spot exchange rate. If the deutsche mark continued to fall against the U.S. dollar as it had been doing for more than four years, the cost to Lufthansa of the Boeing jets could skyrocket easily to more than DM 2 billion.

But the most important word here is expected. There was no guarantee that the spot exchange rate in effect in January of the following year would be DM 3.2/$. The U.S. dollar had been appreciating against the deutsche mark for more than four years at this point. Senior management of Lufthansa was afraid the appreciating dollar trend might continue. For example, if the U.S. dollar appreciated over the coming year from DM 3.2/$ to DM 3.4/$, the cost of the aircraft purchased from Boeing would rise by DM 100 million. Figure 17.8 shows how the DM/$ exchange rate had

Figure 17.8   The DM/$ Spot Exchange Rate: Where Was It Headed?

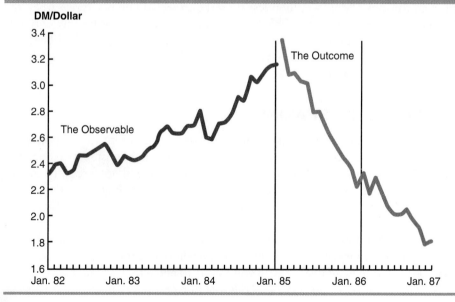

continued to trend upward for several years. By looking at graphics such as this, it was hard to believe that the U.S. dollar would do anything but continue to rise. It takes the truly brave to buck the trend.

But at the same time many senior members of Lufthansa's management believed that the U.S. dollar had risen as far as it would go. They argued that the dollar would fall over the coming year against the deutsche mark (see Figure 17.8). If, for example, the spot rate fell to DM 3.0/$ by January 1986, Lufthansa would pay only DM 1,500 million, a savings of DM 100 million. This was true currency risk in every sense of the word.

The Management Strategy

After much debate, Lufthansa's management decided to use forward contracts to hedge one half of the $500 million exposure. This was obviously a compromise. First, because the exposure was a single large foreign currency payment, to occur one time only, natural hedging was not a realistic alternative. Second, although management believed the dollar would fall, the risk was too large to ignore. It was thought that by covering one half of the exposure, Lufthansa would be protected against the U.S. dollar appreciating, yet still allow Lufthansa some opportunity to benefit from a fall in the dollar. Lufthansa signed a one-year forward contract (sold $250 million forward) at a forward rate of DM 3.2/$. The remaining $250 million owed Boeing was left unhedged.

The Outcome

By January 1986, the U.S. dollar not only fell, it plummeted versus the deutsche mark. The spot rate fell from DM 3.2/$ in January 1985 to DM 2.3/$ in January 1986. Lufthansa had therefore benefited from leaving half the transaction exposure uncovered. But this meant that the half that was covered with forward contracts "cost" the firm DM 225 million!

The total cost to Lufthansa of delivering $250 million at the forward rate of DM 3.2/$ and $250 million at the ending spot rate of DM 2.3/$ was

$$[\$250,000,000 \times DM3.2/\$] + [\$250,000,000 \times DM2.3/\$] = DM\ 1,375,000,000.$$

Although this was DM 225 million less than the expected purchase price when the contract was signed in January 1985, Lufthansa's management was heavily criticized for covering any of the exposure. If the entire transaction exposure had been left uncovered, the final cost would have been only DM 1,150 million. The critics, of course, had perfect hindsight.

CURRENCY RISK SHARING

Firms that import and export on a continuing basis have constant transaction exposures. If a firm is interested in maintaining a good business relationship with one of its suppliers, it must work with that supplier to assure it that it will not force all currency risk or exposure off on the other party on a continual basis. Exchange rate movements are inherently random; therefore some type of risk-sharing arrangement may prove useful.

If Ford (U.S.) imports automotive parts from Mazda (Japan) every month, year after year, major swings in exchange rates can benefit one party at the expense of the other. One solution would be for Ford and Mazda to agree that all purchases by Ford will be made in Japanese yen as long as the spot rate on the payment date is between

¥120/$ and ¥130/$. If the exchange rate is between these values on the payment dates, Ford agrees to accept whatever transaction exposure exists (because it is paying in a foreign currency). If, however, the exchange rate falls outside of this range on the payment date, Ford and Mazda will "share" the difference. If the spot rate on settlement date is ¥110/$, the Japanese yen would have appreciated versus the dollar, causing Ford's costs of purchasing automotive parts to rise. Because this rate falls outside the contractual range, Mazda would agree to accept a total payment in Japanese yen that would result from a "shared" difference of ¥10. Thus, Ford's total payment in Japanese yen would be calculated using an exchange rate of ¥115/$.

Risk-sharing agreements like these have been in use for nearly 50 years on world markets. They became something of a rarity during the 1950s and 1960s, when exchange rates were relatively stable (under the Bretton Woods Agreement). But with the return to floating exchange rates in the 1970s, firms with long-term customer-supplier relationships across borders returned to some old ways of keeping old friends. And sometimes old ways work very well.

ECONOMIC EXPOSURE

Economic exposure, also called operating exposure, is the change in the value of a firm arising from unexpected changes in exchange rates. Economic exposure emphasizes that there is a limit to a firm's ability to predict either cash flows or exchange rate changes in the medium to long term. All firms, either directly or indirectly, have economic exposure.

It is customary to think only of firms that actively trade internationally as having any type of currency exposure (such as Lufthansa described previously). But actually all firms that operate in economies affected by international financial events, such as exchange rate changes, are affected. A barber in Ottumwa, Iowa, seemingly isolated from exchange rate chaos, is still affected when the dollar rises as it did in the early 1980s. If U.S. products become increasingly expensive to foreign buyers, American manufacturers such as John Deere & Co. in Iowa are forced to cut back production and lay off workers, and businesses of all types decline—even the business of barbers. The impacts are real, and they affect all firms, domestic and international alike.

How exposed is an individual firm in terms of economic exposure? It is impossible to say. Measuring economic exposure is subjective, and for the most part it is dependent on the degree of internationalization present in the firm's cost and revenue structure, as well as potential changes over the long run. But simply because it is difficult to measure does not mean that management cannot take some steps to prepare the firm for the unexpected.

Impact of Economic Exposure

The impacts of economic exposure are as diverse as are firms in their international structure. Take the case of a U.S. corporation with a successful British subsidiary. The British subsidiary manufactured and then distributed the firm's products in Great Britain, Germany, and France. The profits of the British subsidiary are paid out annually to the American parent corporation. What would be the impact on the profitability of the British subsidiary and the entire U.S. firm if the British pound suddenly fell in value against all other major currencies (as it did in September and October 1992)?

One woman works this shift at a dish factory.

If the British firm had been facing competition in Germany, France, and its own home market from firms from those other two continental countries, it would now be more competitive. If the British pound is cheaper, so are the products sold internationally by British-based firms. The British subsidiary of the American firm would, in all likelihood, see rising profits from increased sales.

But what of the value of the British subsidiary to the U.S. parent corporations? The same fall in the British pound that allowed the British subsidiary to gain profits would also result in substantially fewer U.S. dollars when the British pound earnings are converted to U.S. dollars at the end of the year. It seems that it is nearly impossible to win in this situation. Actually, from the perspective of economic exposure management, the fact that the firm's total value, subsidiary and parent together, is roughly a wash as a result of the exchange rate change is desirable. Sound financial management assumes that a firm will profit and bear risk in its line of business, not in the process of settling payments on business already completed.

Economic Exposure Management

Management of economic exposure is being prepared for the unexpected. A firm such as Hewlett-Packard (HP), which is highly dependent on its ability to remain cost competitive in markets both at home and abroad, may choose to take actions now that would allow it to passively withstand any sudden unexpected rise of the dollar. This could be accomplished through diversification: diversification of operations and diversification of financing.

Diversification of operations would allow the firm to be desensitized to the impacts of any one pair of exchange rate changes. For example, a multinational firm such as Hewlett-Packard may produce the same product in manufacturing facilities in Singapore, the United States, Puerto Rico, and Europe. If a sudden and prolonged rise in the dollar made production in the United States prohibitively expensive and uncompetitive, HP is already positioned to shift production to a relatively cheaper currency environment. Although firms rarely diversify production location for the sole purpose of currency diversification, it is a substantial additional benefit from such global expansion.

Diversification of financing serves to hedge economic exposure much in the same way as it did with transaction exposures. A firm with debt denominated in many different currencies is sensitive to many different interest rates. If one country or currency experiences rapidly rising inflation rates and interest rates, a firm with diversified debt will not be subject to the full impact of such movements. Purely domestic firms, however, are actually somewhat captive to the local conditions and are unable to ride out such interest rate storms as easily.

It should be noted that, in both cases, diversification is a passive solution to the exposure problem. This means that without knowing when or where or what the problem may be, the firm that simply spreads its operations and financial structure out over a variety of countries and currencies is prepared.

COUNTERTRADE

6. To analyze the process of using goods and services as a medium of exchange in addition to money in international business

General Motors exchanged automobiles for a trainload of strawberries. Control Data swapped a computer for a package of Polish furniture, Hungarian carpet backing, and Russian greeting cards. Uzbekistan is offering crude venom of vipers, toads, scorpions, black widows, and tarantulas, as well as growth-controlling substances from snakes and lizards, in countertrade.[4] These are all examples of countertrade activities carried out around the world.

A DEFINITION OF COUNTERTRADE

Countertrade is a sale that encompasses more than an exchange of goods, services, or ideas for money. In the international market, countertrade transactions "are those transactions that have as a basic characteristic a linkage, legal or otherwise, between exports and imports of goods or services in addition to, or in place of, financial settlements."[5] Historically, countertrade was mainly conducted in the form of **barter**, which is a direct exchange of goods of approximately equal value between parties, with no money involved. Such transactions were the very essence of business at times during which no money—that is, no common medium of exchange—existed or was available. Over time, money emerged as a convenient medium that unlinked transactions from individual parties and their joint timing and therefore permitted greater flexibility in trading activities. Repeatedly, however, we can see returns to the barter system as a result of environmental circumstances. For example, because of the tight financial constraints of both students and the institution, Georgetown University during its initial years of operation after 1789 charged part of its tuition in foodstuffs and required students to participate in the construction of university buildings. During periods of high inflation in Europe in the 1920s, goods such as bread, meat, and gold were seen as much more useful and secure than paper money, which decreased in real value by the minute. In the late 1940s, American cigarettes were an acceptable medium of exchange in most European countries, much more so than any particular currency except for the dollar.

Countertrade transactions have therefore always arisen when economic circumstances made it more acceptable to exchange goods directly rather than use money as an intermediary. Conditions that encourage such business activities are lack of money, lack of value of or faith in money, lack of acceptability of money as an exchange medium, or greater ease of transaction by using goods.

Increasingly, countries and companies are deciding that, sometimes, countertrade transactions are more beneficial to them than transactions based on financial exchange alone. One reason is that the world financial crisis has made ordinary trade financing very risky. Many countries, particularly in the developing world, simply cannot obtain the trade credit or financial assistance necessary to pay for desired imports. Heavily indebted countries, faced with the possibility of not being able to afford imports at all, hasten to use countertrade to maintain at least some product inflow. However, it should be recognized that countertrade does not reduce commercial risk. Countertrade transactions will therefore be encouraged by stability and economic progress. Research has shown that countertrade appears to increase with a country's creditworthiness, because good credit encourages traders to participate in unconventional trading practices.[6]

The use of countertrade permits the covert reduction of prices and therefore allows the circumvention of price and exchange controls.[7] Particularly in commodity markets with cartel arrangements, such as oil or agriculture, this benefit may be very useful to a producer. For example, by using oil as a countertraded product for industrial equipment, a surreptitious discount (by using a higher price for the acquired products) may expand market share.

Countertrade is also often viewed by firms and nations alike as an excellent mechanism to gain entry into new markets. When a producer believes that marketing is not its strong suit, the producer often hopes that the party receiving the goods will serve as a new distributor, opening up new international marketing channels and ultimately expanding the original market. For example, the actor Bruce Willis signed a barter deal with Sobieski Vodka. Willis will help promote the vodka, which features a simple and no frills approach. In exchange he will receive a 3.3 percent equity stake in the firm.[8]

barter A direct exchange of goods of approximately equal value, with no money involved.

Because countertrade is highly sought after in many large markets such as China, the former Eastern bloc countries, as well as South America, engaging in such transactions can provide major growth opportunities for firms. In increasingly competitive world markets, countertrade can be a good way to attract new buyers. By providing countertrade services, the seller is in effect differentiating its product from those of its competitors.[9]

Countertrade also can provide stability for long-term sales. For example, if a firm is tied to a countertrade agreement, it will need to source the product from a particular supplier, whether or not it wants to do so. This stability is often valued very highly because it eliminates, or at least reduces, vast swings in demand and thus allows for better planning. Countertrade, therefore, can serve as a major mechanism to shift risk from the producer to another party. In that sense, one can argue that countertrade offers a substitute for missing forward markets.[10] Finally, under certain conditions, countertrade can ensure the quality of an international transaction. In instances where the seller of technology is paid in output produced by the technology delivered, the seller's revenue depends on the success of the technology transfer and maintenance services in production. Therefore, the seller is more likely to be concerned about providing services, maintenance, and general technology transfer.[11]

In spite of all the apparent benefits of countertrade, there are strong economic arguments against the activity. The arguments are based mainly on efficiency grounds. As Paul Samuelson stated, "Instead of there being a double coincidence of wants, there is likely to be a want of coincidence; so that, unless a hungry tailor happens to find an undraped farmer, who has both food and a desire for a pair of pants, neither can make a trade."[12] Clearly, countertrade ensures that instead of balances being settled on a multilateral basis, with surpluses from one country being balanced by deficits with another, accounts must now be settled on a country-

Table 17.3 A Sample of Barter Agreements

Country		Exported Commodity	
A	**B**	**A**	**B**
U.S.	Russia	• Pepsi products	• 17 submarines, 1 cruiser, 1 frigate, 1 destroyer (for scrap metal)
Hungary	Ukraine	• Foodstuffs • Canned foods • Pharmaceuticals	• Timber
Austria	Ukraine	• Power station emissions control equipment	• 800 megakilowatts/year for 15 years
U.S. (Chrysler)	Jamaica	• 200 pickup trucks	• Equivalent value in iron ore
Ukraine	Czech Republic	• Iron ore	• Mining equipment
U.S. (Pierre Cardin)	China	• Technical advice	• Silks and cashmeres
U.K. (Raleigh Bicycle)	CIS	• Training CIS scientists in mountain bike production	• Titanium for 30,000 bike frames per year
Indonesia	Uzbekistan	• Indian tea • Vietnamese rice • Miscellaneous Indonesian products	• 50,000 tons of cotton/year for three years
Zaire	Italy	• Scrap iron	• 12 locomotives
China	Russia	• 212 railway trucks of mango juice	• Passenger jet
Morocco	Romania	• Citrus products	• Several large ports/small harbors

Sources: "Countertrade Examples," *BarterNews*, March 29, 2010, p. 5; American Countertrade Association, December 1996; Aspy P. Palia and Oded Shenkar, "Countertrade Practices in China," *Industrial Marketing Management*, 1991: 58; http://www.i-trade.com.

by-country or even transaction-by-transaction basis. Trade then results only from the ability of two parties or countries to purchase specified goods from one another rather than from competition. As a result, uncompetitive goods may be traded. In consequence, the ability of countries and their industries to adjust structurally to more efficient production may be restricted. Countertrade can therefore be seen as eroding the quality and efficiency of production and as lowering world consumption.

These economic arguments notwithstanding, however, countries and companies increasingly see countertrade as an alternative that may be flawed but worthwhile to undertake, since some trade is preferable to no trade. Both industrialized and developing countries exchange a wide variety of goods via countertrade. And as Table 17.3 shows, countertrade knows few limits across goods.

INTERNATIONAL TAXATION

Governments alone have the power to tax. Each government wants to tax all companies within its jurisdiction without placing burdens on domestic or foreign companies that would restrain trade. Each country will state its jurisdictional approach formally in the tax treaties that it signs with other countries. One of the primary purposes of tax treaties is to establish the bounds of each country's jurisdiction to prevent double taxation of international income. Focus on Politics shows the effect of taxes on U.S. competitiveness.

7. To examine the primary differences in the taxation of business internationally, and how governments tax firms operating in their markets

TAX JURISDICTIONS

Nations usually follow one of two basic approaches to international taxation: a residential approach or a territorial or source approach. The residential approach to international taxation taxes the international income of its residents without regard to where the income is earned. The territorial approach to transnational income taxes all parties, regardless of country of residency, within its territorial jurisdiction.

Most countries in practice must combine the two approaches to tax foreign and domestic firms equally. For example, the United States and Japan both apply the residential approach to their own resident corporations and the territorial approach to income earned by nonresidents within their territorial jurisdictions. Other countries, such as Germany, apply the territorial approach to dividends paid to domestic firms from their foreign subsidiaries; such dividends are assumed taxed abroad and are exempt from further taxation.

Within the territorial jurisdiction of tax authorities, a foreign corporation is typically defined as any business that earns income within the host country's borders but is incorporated under the laws of another country. The foreign corporation usually must surpass some minimum level of activity (gross income) before the host country assumes primary tax jurisdiction. However, if the foreign corporation owns income-producing assets or a permanent establishment, the threshold is automatically surpassed.

© Clive Sawyer PCL/SuperStock

Accounting practices for the costs of environmental contamination, treatment and restoration, such as in the case of the Rye Sand Dunes, is an evolving issue in international business.

How High Taxes Make the United States Uncompetitive

One of the biggest challenges facing the U.S. economy in the coming decade is that it is now a high corporate income tax country. Although the U.S. possessed one of the lowest corporate tax rates for many years, it has stayed relatively constant while most of the major industrialized countries have continually cut their corporate income tax rates over the past twenty years. As illustrated by the graphic, the average effective corporate U.S. tax rate is now considerably higher than the average corporate tax rate of the other 29 members of the Organization for Economic Cooperation (OECD). The "effective corporate tax rate" combines the federal corporate income tax rate of 35 percent with the average state and local taxes applicable to companies operating in the U.S. for an average rate just above 39 percent.

This higher tax rate has made the U.S. an unattractive country in which to invest. Foreign corporations from around the globe are increasingly reluctant to invest in businesses in the U.S. where they will have to pay a higher tax rate than that same business would if it was formed in Mexico or Canada or France or Germany. In fact, Canada, the Czech Republic, Iceland, Italy, Germany, New Zealand, Spain, Switzerland, and the United Kingdom all reduced their corporate income tax rates in 2008 and 2009. Among the 30 industrialized countries in the OECD, only Japan at 40 percent has a higher tax rate than the U.S.

Many critics of U.S. corporate tax policy argue that foreign companies will now choose to invest their capital in other countries, rather than in the U.S. Foreign investment in the U.S. has actually been quite large in the past 20 years, providing added stimulus to both U.S. economic growth and its expanding productivity. Without that foreign investment, the U.S. economy may start to lose some of its global competitiveness.

And the higher tax rate does not influence just foreign multinationals. Many U.S. based companies may now consider investing their capital outside the U.S. more frequently, in countries which have corporate tax rates of only 28 percent or 29 percent, allowing them to conduct their business and retain more of their profits for reinvestment than they would inside the U.S. (Foreign subsidiaries of U.S. corporations generally do not have to pay U.S. taxes on profits made outside the U.S. unless they choose to bring the profits back to the U.S.) Eventually, critics argue, the U.S. could experience declining international competitiveness and even suffer a growing "hollowing-out" of the domestic economy because companies choose to invest and operate elsewhere.

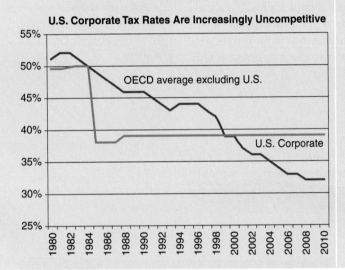

U.S. Corporate Tax Rates Are Increasingly Uncompetitive

OECD average excluding U.S.

U.S. Corporate

Sources: Randy Myers, "Taxed to the Max: Hefty Tax Rates Continue to Penalize U.S. Companies, and the Calls for Reform are Growing Louder," *CFO Magazine*, March 1, 2009; "Tumbling Tax Rates," *The Economist*, March 5, 2010.

---

direct taxes Taxes applied directly to income.

indirect taxes Taxes applied to non-income items, such as value-added taxes, excise taxes, tariffs, and so on.

value-added tax (VAT) A tax on the value contributed at each stage of the production and distribution process; a tax assessed in most European countries and also common among Latin American countries.

TAX TYPES

Taxes are generally classified as direct and indirect. **Direct taxes** are calculated on actual income, either individual or firm income. **Indirect taxes**, such as sales taxes, severance taxes, tariffs, and value-added taxes, are applied to purchase prices, material costs, quantities of natural resources mined, and so forth. Although most countries still rely on income taxes as the primary method of raising revenue, tax structures vary widely across countries.

The **value-added tax (VAT)** is the primary revenue source for the European Union. A value-added tax is applied to the amount of product value added by the production process. The tax is calculated as a percentage of the product price less the cost of materials and inputs used in its manufacture, which have been taxed previously. Through this process, tax revenues are collected literally on the value added by that specific stage of the production process. Under the existing General

Table 17.4 Corporate Income Tax Rates for Selected Countries

Country	2008	Country	2008	Country	2008
Afghanistan	20%	Guatemala	31%	Papua New Guinea	30%
Albania	10	Honduras	30	Paraguay	10
Angola	35	Hong Kong	17	Peru	30
Argentina	35	Hungary	16	Philippines	35
Aruba	28	Iceland	15	Poland	19
Australia	30	India	34	Portugal	25
Austria	25	Indonesia	30	Qatar	35
Bahrain	0	Iran	25	Romania	16
Bangladesh	30	Ireland	13	Russia	24
Barbados	25	Israel	27	Saudi Arabia	20
Belarus	24	Italy	31	Serbia	10
Belgium	34	Jamaica	33	Singapore	18
Bolivia	25	Japan	41	Slovak Republic	19
Bosnia and Herzegovina	10	Jordan	35	Slovenia	22
Botswana	25	Kazakhstan	30	South Africa	35
Brazil	34	Korea, Republic of	28	Spain	30
Bulgaria	10	Kuwait	55	Sri Lanka	35
Canada	33.5	Latvia	15	Sudan	35
Cayman Islands	0	Libya	40	Sweden	28
Chile	17	Lithuania	15	Switzerland	19
China	25	Luxembourg	30	Syria	28
Colombia	33	Macau	12	Taiwan	25
Costa Rica	30	Malaysia	26	Thailand	30
Croatia	20	Malta	35	Tunisia	30
Cyprus	10	Mauritius	15	Turkey	20
Czech Republic	21	Mexico	28	Ukraine	25
Denmark	25	Montenegro	9	United Arab Emirates	55
Dominican Republic	25	Mozambique	32	United Kingdom	28
Ecuador	25	Netherlands	26	United States	40
Egypt	20	Netherlands Antilles	35	Uruguay	25
Estonia	21	New Zealand	30	Venezuela	34
Fiji	31	Norway	28	Vietnam	28
Finland	26	Oman	12	Yemen	35
France	33.33	Pakistan	35	Zambia	35
Germany	29.51	Palestine	16		
Greece	25	Panama	30		

Source: "KPMG's Corporate and Indirect Tax Rate Survey, 2008," KPMG.com; tax rates as of April 1, 2008.

Agreement on Tariffs and Trade (GATT), the legal framework under which international trade operates, value-added taxes may be levied on imports into a country or group of countries (such as the European Union) in order to treat foreign producers entering the domestic markets equally with firms within the country paying the VAT. Similarly, the VAT may be refunded on export sales or sales to tourists who purchase products for consumption outside the country or community. For example, an American tourist leaving London may collect a refund on all value-added taxes paid on goods purchased within the United Kingdom. The refunding usually requires documentation of the actual purchase price and the amount of tax paid.

INCOME CATEGORIES AND TAXATION

There are three primary methods used for the transfer of funds across tax jurisdictions: royalties, interest, and dividends. Royalties are under license for the use of intangible assets such as patents, designs, trademarks, techniques, or copyrights. Interest is the payment for the use of capital lent for the financing of normal business activity. Dividends are income paid or deemed paid to the shareholders of the corporation from the residual earnings of operations. When a corporation declares the percentage of residual earnings that is to go to shareholders, the dividend is declared and distributed.

Taxation of corporate income differs substantially across countries. Table 17.4 provides a summary of corporate tax rates around the world. Of the countries shown, the average tax rate is approximately 26 percent.

withholding taxes Taxes applied to the payment of dividends, interest, or royalties by firms.

Royalty and interest payments to nonresidents are normally subject to **withholding taxes**. Corporate profits are typically double taxed in most countries, through corporate and personal taxes. Corporate income is first taxed at the business level with corporate taxes, then a second time when the income of distributed earnings is taxed through personal income taxes. Withholding tax rates also differ by the degree of ownership that the corporation possesses in the foreign corporation. Minor ownership is termed *portfolio*, while major or controlling influence is categorized as *substantial holdings*. In the case of dividends, interest, or royalties paid to nonresidents, governments routinely apply withholding taxes to their payment in the reasonable expectation that the nonresidents will not report and declare such income with the host-country tax authorities. Withholding taxes are specified by income category in all bilateral tax treaties.

SUMMARY

Multinational financial management is both complex and critical to the multinational firm. Beginning with the very objective of management, stockholder wealth maximization or corporate wealth maximization, all traditional functional areas of financial management are affected by the internationalization of the firm. Capital budgeting, firm financing, capital structure, and working capital and cash flow management, all traditional functions, are made more difficult by business activities that cross borders and oceans, not to mention currencies and markets.

In addition to the traditional areas of financial management, international financial management must deal with the three types of currency exposure: (1) transaction exposure, (2) economic exposure, and (3) translation exposure. Each type of currency risk confronts a firm with serious choices regarding its exposure analysis and its degree of willingness to manage the inherent risks.

This chapter described not only the basic types of risk, but also outlined a number of the basic strategies employed in the management of the exposures. Some of the solutions available today have only arisen with the development of new types of international financial markets and instruments, such as the currency swap. Others, such as currency risk-sharing agreements, are as old as exchange rates themselves.

KEY TERMS

draft   577
bank draft   577
trade draft   577
net present value (NPV)   578
capital budget   578
cash management   582
operating cash flows   583
financing cash flows   583
transfer prices   583

netting   585
cash pooling   585
lead   585
lag   585
reinvoicing   585
internal bank   586
transaction exposure   586
economic exposure   587
translation exposure   587

natural hedging   587
contractual hedging   587
forward contracts   588
hedge   588
barter   593
direct taxes   596
indirect taxes   596
value-added tax (VAT)   596
withholding taxes   598

QUESTIONS FOR DISCUSSION

1. What are the pros and cons of the two different theories of wealth maximization?

2. Why is it important to identify the cash flows of a foreign investment from the perspective of the parent rather than from just the project?

3. Is currency risk unique to international firms? Is currency risk good or bad for the potential profitability of the multinational?

4. Which type of currency risk is the least important to the multinational firm? Should resources be spent to manage this risk?

5. Are firms with no direct international business (imports and exports) subject to economic exposure?

6. What would you have recommended that Lufthansa do to manage its transaction exposure if you had been the airline's chief financial officer in January 1985?

7. Why do you think Lufthansa and Boeing did not use some form of "currency risk sharing" in their 1985–1986 transaction?

8. Which type of firm do you believe is more "naturally hedged" against exchange rate exposure, the purely domestic firm (the barber) or the multinational firm (subsidiaries all over the world)?

9. What are some of the causes for the resurgence of countertrade?

10. What forms of countertrade exist and how do they differ? What are their relative advantages and drawbacks?

11. How consistent is countertrade with the international trade framework?

12. How do differences in corporate income tax rates across countries affect investment by multinational companies?

INTERNET EXERCISES

1. Although major currencies like the U.S. dollar and the Chinese renminbi dominate the headlines, there are nearly as many currencies as countries in the world. Many of these currencies are traded in extremely thin and highly regulated markets, making their convertibility suspect. Finding quotations for these currencies is sometimes very difficult. Using some of the Web pages listed below, see how many African currency quotes you can find. See Emerging Markets at http://emgmkts.com/.

2. Use the *Economist*'s web site to find the latest version of the Big Max Index of Currency over- and under-valuation. See http://www.economist.com.

3. The single unobservable variable in currency option pricing is the volatility, since volatility inputs are an expected standard deviation of the daily spot rate for the coming period of the option's maturity. Using the following web site, pick one currency volatility and research how its value has changed in recent periods over historical periods. See Philadelphia Stock Exchange at http://www.phlx.com/.

4. Using the following major periodicals as starting points, find a current example of a firm with a substantial operating exposure problem. To aid in your search, you might focus on businesses having major operations in countries with recent currency crises, either through devaluation or major home currency appreciation. Sources are *Financial Times* at http://www.ft.com/; *The Economist* at http://www.economist.com/; *Wall Street Journal* at http://www.wsj.com/.

5. In the World Trade Organization's Agreement on Government Procurement, how are *offsets* defined and what stance is taken toward them (refer to the government procurement page on the web site http://www.wto.org)?

TAKE A STAND

Many multinational companies believe that *hedging* is really nothing other than formalized *speculation*. Since many firms use the same complex financial instruments and derivatives that arbitragers and speculators use, they argue that companies are endangering their own future by allowing individuals within the organization to gamble with the company's own funds—for profit. And the profit only arises from the ability of the individual to "beat the market."

For Discussion

1. Multinationals should accept foreign currency risks as part of doing business internationally, and therefore should not spend precious resources and take unnecessary risks related to the use of financial derivatives for hedging. The cure is more harmful than the disease.

2. Multinationals must protect all of their stakeholders—stockholders, creditors, employees, and community—from the risks associated with conducting business in a global marketplace using currencies that bounce up and down in value. Although some hedging techniques may introduce new types of risks for the firm, it is in the entire firm's interest that it hedge significant cash flow risks and add certainty to the conduct of the firm's total business.

CHAPTER 18

Human Resource Management*

CHAPTER CONTENTS & LEARNING OBJECTIVES

MANAGING MANAGERS

1. *To assess the effects of culture on managers and management policies*

SOURCES FOR MANAGEMENT RECRUITMENT

2. *To examine the sources, qualifications, and compensation of international managers*

MANAGING LABOR PERSONNEL

3. *To illustrate the different roles of labor in international markets, especially that of labor participation in management*

*This chapter was contributed by Susan C. Ronkainen.

In today's economic environment of globalization and rapid product innovation, companies are beginning to focus on their human capital as a means of gaining a competitive advantage. Large multinationals, such as ThyssenKrupp and the Wachovia Corporation, as well as small start-ups, like India's Satyam Computer Services, are searching for creative new ways to attract and retain top talent. They are experimenting with advertising campaigns, training, and unorthodox incentive packages. In the absence of generally accepted standards of "what works" in the field of human resources (HR) management, companies are testing out a variety of strategies. There is an increasing urgency to get it right, considering that some of the most pressing global business challenges of the day are directly related to issues of human capital.

There are two potential problem areas that companies need to address. However, if they are successful in the development of new and effective HR management strategies, both of these challenges could prove to be a blessing in disguise. The first potential problem stems from shifting demographic trends. Developed economies are typically characterized by aging populations and low birth rates. As experienced employees retire, the pool of available replacements is getting progressively smaller. Therefore, companies will have to develop strategies for coping with talent shortages. Among them should be the development of corporate cultures that are more accepting of ethnic and gender diversity, given the prevalent global demographic trends. Top U.S.-based multinationals have already started to adopt policies aimed at diversifying their management ranks. Their primary motivation is to attract managerial talent from developing countries with rapidly expanding markets, such as India and China, because of their specific local knowledge and understanding of foreign consumers. Large companies, such as Alcoa, Colgate-Palmolive, Coca-Cola, and United Technologies, generate 60 to 80 percent of their sales outside the United States, and that trend is likely to accelerate.

Colgate is a good example of how to implement a successful HR internationalization strategy. Industry analysts have determined that the company has institutionalized a "process that encourages, rewards, moves around, provides incentives, and closely manages the careers of the best performers worldwide, no matter their national origin." One strategy in Colgate's arsenal is the establishment of a talent-tracking program. The company has operations in 200 countries around the world and has developed a comprehensive database that records information about the capabilities and potential of key international employees. According to one Colgate HR executive, "It gives us a global warehouse of data about our people systems. It's important to us to understand equally the leadership pipeline in Vietnam and in Venezuela." This approach gives the company a competitive edge, because it is able to capitalize on the value of its best employees, irrespective of their national origin.

Colgate's HR internationalization strategy also addresses the second pervasive challenge facing global business—skill deficits. In many parts of the world, young people are not receiving the kind of education that would prepare them for work. As a result, employers are forced to spend extra money and time on training. For example, *Newsweek* reported that companies in the United States spend $1.3 billion annually to teach their employees basic writing skills. In the absence of comprehensive educational reforms, which are the purview of governments, and hence outside the control of business, the ability to tap into international sources of talent should allow enterprises to alleviate the skills problem. Analysts have identified India, where the school system is focused on math and science, as one potential source of skilled employees for U.S. companies, as U.S. science and math programs fall short of worldwide benchmarks.

However, the ideal of a company that is completely foot-loose in its HR practices and able to identify and attract top international talent is compromised by one simple economic/human reality—the relative immobility of labor (as a factor of production). Simply put, individuals have ties to their communities, families, and neighbors, which often make them reluctant to move internationally. For example, U.S. companies have been actively trying to assimilate more Chinese executives into their managerial ranks. However, this has proven to be a difficult task, even in light of increased compensation, because Chinese nationals are often reluctant to deal with the cultural and familial turmoil of a long-term assignment in the United States. One proposed strategy for overcoming labor "stickiness" is the application of "market segmentation" in HR. The basic premise is that companies need to create a set of customized career alternatives for an increasingly diverse workforce. In the words of Shannon Brown, senior human resources executive at FedEx, "people want different opportunities at different phases in their lives. . . . I think our work is going to be more reflective of the individual." Additionally, companies would have to modify their corporate cultures in order to better accommodate employees from different nationalities. Colgate, for example, has developed short-term assignments of up to six months for its international executives, which allows them to gain experience at the company's U.S. headquarters, while minimizing the disruption of their personal lives back at home. If companies are successful in implementing such strategies and nurturing talented employees, regardless of background, they should be able to gain a long-term competitive advantage over their competitors.

Sources: William J. Holstein, "It's Getting Diverse at the Top," *Strategy and Business*, January 6, 2009, 1–5; Richard Rawlinson, Walter McFarland, and Laird Post, "A Talent for Talent," *Strategy and Business*, August 26, 2008, 20–26; Meagan C. Dietz, Gordon Orr, and Jane Xing, "How Chinese Companies Can Succeed Abroad," *The McKinsey Quarterly*, May 2008, 23–32; Kevin Lane and Florian Pollner, "How to Address China's Growing Talent Shortage," *The McKinsey Quarterly*, May 2008, 33–40.

Organizations have two general human resource objectives. The first is the recruitment and retention of a workforce made up of the best people available for the jobs to be done. The recruiter in international operations will need to keep in mind both cross-cultural and cross-national differences in productivity and expectations when selecting employees. Once they are hired, the firm's best interest lies in maintaining a stable and experienced workforce.

The second objective is to increase the effectiveness of the workforce. This depends to a great extent on achieving the first objective. Competent managers or workers are likely to perform at a more effective level if proper attention is given to factors that motivate them.

To attain the two major objectives, the activities and skills needed include:

1. Personnel planning and staffing, the assessment of personnel needs, and recruitment
2. Personnel training to achieve a perfect fit between the employee and the assignment
3. Compensation of employees according to their effectiveness
4. An understanding of labor-management relations in terms of how the two groups view each other and how their respective power positions are established

All of this means that human resource management must become a basic element of a company's expansion strategy. Eighty companies (covering a broad cross-section of company sizes and industries) surveyed have stated that their mission and vision (55.8 percent) and strategies and plans (50.8 percent) are set by global headquarters. The majority of companies have implemented one single global HR system (57.5 percent). The top competency that companies indicated as contributing to global success was having a global mind-set (54.5 percent) signaling an understanding that the ability to work globally is different from working domestically in one's own country. The next top critical competencies for global success are risk tolerance (44 percent), cultural intelligence (44 percent), accommodation/flexibility (38 percent), and being adaptable to change (36 percent).[1] However, the majority reported that they had only moderate involvement in their company's overall business strategy. The task is, therefore, to establish human resources as not only a tactical element to fill needed positions but one whose programs affect overall business results.

Each passes through three crucial areas of impact: (1) personnel control (task-oriented items such as payroll processing and administering compensation and benefits plans), (2) people development (more value is brought to the enterprise by managing talent to be highly effective, thereby universally increasing the quality of output), and (3) talent multiplication (value ladder takes efficiency and quality gains and spreads them upward through the organization).[2] However, by working in a strategic context—including the human resource role in coaching, connecting, and empowering a new generation of executives—human resources can make a direct impact on the bottom line and drive high performance.

 ## MANAGING MANAGERS

The importance of the quality of the workforce in international business cannot be overemphasized, regardless of the stage of internationalization of the firm. Those in early stages of internationalization focus on understanding cultural differences, while those more advanced are determined to manage and balance cultural diversity and eventually to integrate differences within the overall corporate culture. As seen in

1. To assess the effects of culture on managers and management policies

the chapter's opening vignette, international business systems are complex and dynamic and require competent people to develop and direct them.

EARLY STAGES OF INTERNATIONALIZATION

The marketing or sales manager of the firm typically is responsible for beginning export activities. As foreign sales increase, an export manager will be appointed and given the responsibility for developing and maintaining customers, interacting with the firm's intermediaries, and planning for overall market expansion. The export manager also must champion the international effort within the company because the general attitude among employees may be to view the domestic market as more important. Another critical function is the supervision of export transactions, particularly documentation. The requirements are quite different for international transactions than for domestic ones, and sales or profits may be lost if documentation is not properly handled. The first task of the new export manager, in fact, often is to hire a staff to handle paperwork that typically had previously been done by a facilitating agent, such as a freight forwarder.

The firm starting international operations will usually hire an export manager from outside rather than promote from within. The reason is that knowledge of the product or industry is less important than international experience. The cost of learning through experience to manage an export department is simply too great from the firm's standpoint. Further, the inexperienced manager would be put in the position of having to demonstrate his or her effectiveness almost at once.

The manager who is hired will have obtained experience through Foreign Service duty or with another corporation. In the early stages, a highly entrepreneurial spirit with a heavy dose of trader mentality is required. Even then, management should not expect the new export department to earn a profit for the first few years.

ADVANCED STAGES OF INTERNATIONALIZATION

As the firm progresses from exporting to an international division to foreign direct involvement, human resources-planning activities will initially focus on need vis-à-vis various markets and functions. Existing personnel can be assessed and plans made to recruit, select, and train employees for positions that cannot be filled internally. The four major categories of overseas assignments are (1) CEO, to oversee and direct the entire operation; (2) functional head, to establish and maintain departments and ensure their proper performance; (3) troubleshooters, who are utilized for their special expertise in analyzing, and thereby preventing or solving, particular problems; and (4) white- or blue-collar workers.[3] Many technology companies have had to respond to shortages in skilled employees by globalized recruitment using web sites or by hiring headhunters in places such as China and India. For example, of the 120 different nationalities working at Nokia, 45 percent are represented in senior management as coming from a non-Finnish ethnicity.

One of the major sources of competitive advantage of global corporations is their ability to attract talent around the world. The corporations need systematic management-development systems, with the objective of creating and carefully allocating management personnel. An example of this is provided in Figure 18.1. Increasingly, plans call for international experience as a prerequisite for advancement. Aside from having an Englishman as CEO, Colgate (with 75 percent of its sales outside the United States) has eight non-native Americans in its brain trust of nine top operating executives—including people from India and Colombia. More than half of the 200 people in its senior management ranks, including those in staff and support roles, are not originally from the United States.[4]

Figure 18.1   International Management Development

Worldwide recruiting for talent	International experience (through short-term assignments)/ cross-cultural training	Companywide screening for talent identification and promotion across countries and business units	Opportunities for international experience (through long-term assignments) in managing business units	International experience as a precondition for promotion to top management

0   1   2   3   4   5   6   7   8   9   10

Years

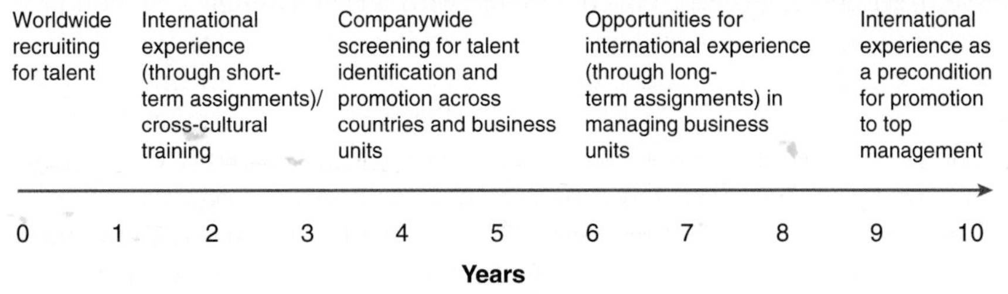

Source: Adapted from Ingo Theuerkauf, "Reshaping the Global Organization," *McKinsey Quarterly* 3, 1991, 104; and Paul Evans, Vladimir Pucik, and Jean-Louis Barsoux, *The Global Challenge: Frameworks for International Human Resource Management* (New York: McGraw-Hill/Irwin, 2002), Chapters 2–4.

In global corporations, there is no such thing as a universal global manager, but a network of global specialists in four general groups of managers has to work together.[5] Global business (product) managers have the task of furthering the company's global-scale efficiency and competitiveness. Country managers have to be sensitive and responsive to local market needs and demands but, at the same time, be aware of global implications. Functional managers have to make sure that the corporation's capabilities in technical, manufacturing, marketing, human resource, and financial expertise are linked and can benefit from each other. Corporate executives at headquarters have to manage interactions among the three groups of managers as well as identify and develop the talent to fill the positions.

As an example of this planning, a management review of human resources is conducted twice a year with each general manager operating Heineken companies, which are located in such countries as Canada, France, Ireland, and Spain. The meeting is attended by the general manager, the personnel manager, the regional coordinating director in whose region the operating company is located, and the corporate director of management development. Special attention is given to managers "in the fast lane," the extent to which they are mobile, what might be done to foster their development, and where they fit into succession planning.[6] In the best examples, the human resources function can become a change leader. For example, Saudi Telecom Company decided to rotate the general managers, sending each of them for short periods of time to take on the job of a peer in another HR function.[7]

Companies should show clear career paths for managers assigned overseas and develop the systems and the organization for promotion.[8] This approach serves to eliminate many of the perceived problems and thus motivates managers to seek out foreign assignments. Furthermore, when jobs open up, the company can quickly determine who is able and willing to take them. Foreign assignments can occur at various stages of the manager's tenure. In the early stages, assignments may be short-term, such as a membership in an international task force for six to twelve months at headquarters in a staff function. Later, an individual may serve as a business-unit manager overseas. Many companies use cross-postings to other countries or across product lines to further an individual's acculturation to the corporation.[9] A period in a head office department or a subsidiary will not only provide an understanding of different national cultures and attitudes but also improve an individual's "know-how" and therefore establish unity and common sense of purpose necessary for the proper implementation of global programs.

At the most advanced stages of globalization, companies need to coordinate and leverage resources across borders. One of the most effective tools in achieving this is cross-border teams consisting of members of multiple nationalities.[10] For these teams to work, members need to have had the necessary experience to appreciate both global synergies and national/regional differences. Without assignments abroad, this is impossible. IBM uses high-tech tools to grapple with an increasingly common problem: making far-flung teams work well together. A growing number and variety of companies divide work globally. Semiconductor maker Intel designs chips in Israel and India as well as in the United States. Carpet maker Tai Ping Carpets International Ltd. recently asked design directors in New York, Paris, and Hong Kong to jointly choose colors for residential carpets. Managers and experts offer these keys for productive global teamwork: have a common understanding of the task, clarify roles and responsibilities, set firm ground rules, get to know other team members, and communicate often.[11]

INTERFIRM COOPERATIVE VENTURES

Global competition is forging new cooperative ties between firms from different countries, thereby adding a new management challenge for the firms involved. Although many of the reasons cited for these alliances (described in Chapter 11) are competitive and strategic, the human resource function is critical to their implementation. As a matter of fact, some of the basic reasons so many of these ventures fail relate to human resource management; for example, managers from disparate venture partners cannot work together, or managers within the venture cannot work with the owners' managers.[12] As more ventures are created in newly emerging markets, the challenge of finding skilled local managers is paramount. If such talent is not secured, developing loyalty to the company may be difficult.[13]

While the ingredients for success of the human resource function will differ with the type of cooperative venture, two basic types of tasks are needed.[14] The first task is to assign and motivate people in appropriate ways so that the venture will fulfill its set strategic tasks. This requires particular attention to such issues as job skills and compatibility of communication and other work styles. For example, some cooperative ventures have failed due to one of the partners assigning relatively weak management resources to the venture or due to managers finding themselves with conflicting loyalties to the parent organization and the cooperative venture organization. The second task is the strategic management of the human resources, that is, the appropriate use of managerial capabilities not only in the cooperative venture but in other later contexts, possibly back in the parent organization. An individual manager needs to see that an assignment in a cooperative venture is part of his or her overall career development.

 SOURCES FOR MANAGEMENT RECRUITMENT

2. To examine the sources, qualifications, and compensation of international managers

expatriate One living in a foreign land; a corporate manager assigned to a location abroad.

The location and the nationality of candidates for a particular job are the key issues in recruitment. A decision will have to be made to recruit from within the company or, in the case of larger corporations, within other product or regional groups, or to rely on external talent. Similarly, decisions will have to be made whether to hire or promote locally or use **expatriates**; that is, home-country nationals or third-country nationals (citizens of countries other than the home or host country). Typically, 43 percent of expatriates are posted in subsidiaries, while the remaining 57 percent have assignments in their company's headquarter's country (i.e., they are inpatriates).[15] The major advantages and disadvantages of expatriates are summarized in Table 18.1. Hampered in their global aspirations by a lack of managerial talent, Chinese companies and multinationals operating in China alike have intensified their competition for capable global managers. In general, the choice process between expatriates and locals is driven by (1) the availability and quality of the talent pool; (2) corporate policies and their cost; as well as (3) environmental constraints on the legal, cultural, or economic

Table 18.1 The Major Advantages and Disadvantages of Expatriates

The advantages of appointing a national of the headquarters country in an overseas post are that the expat:

1. Knows the company's products and culture.
2. Relates easily and efficiently to corporate headquarters; speaks the verbal and cultural language.
3. Has technical or business skills not available locally.
4. May have special transferable capabilities, for example, opening operations in emerging markets.
5. Will protect and promote the interests of headquarters in international joint ventures and acquisitions and other situations requiring tight financial control.
6. Is unlikely to steal proprietary knowledge and set up competing businesses.
7. Does not put the country ahead of the company (unless he or she "goes native").
8. Fits the company's need to develop future leaders and general managers with international experience.

The disadvantages of appointing an expat include:

1. High costs—covering relocation, housing, education, hardship allowance—often exceeding 200 percent of the home-country base.
2. Black-outs; 25 percent of expats have to be called home early.
3. Brown-outs: another 30 percent to 50 percent stay but underperform, leading to lost sales, low staff morale, and a decline in local goodwill.
4. Prolonged start-up and wind-down time: in a typical three-year assignment the first year is spent unpacking and the third year is spent packing and positioning for the next move.
5. A shortsighted focus: expats with a three-year assignment tend to focus on the next career rather than on building the local company.
6. Difficulty in finding experienced managers willing to move because of spouse's career, child's schooling or life-style and security concerns (for example, in Middle Eastern countries).
7. Expat's concern about negative out-of-sight, out-of-mind impact on career development.
8. Re-entry problems: a high percentage of expats leave their companies after overseas assignments because jobs with similar breadth of responsibility are either not available or not offered.
9. Division of senior managers to overseas markets is difficult especially for smaller companies that do not yet have a lock on their domestic markets.

Source: John A. Quelch and Helen Bloom, "Ten Steps to a Global Human Resources Strategy," *Strategy and Business* (First Quarter, 1999): 18–29.

front. Many countries still resist letting jobs go abroad but there is increasing pressure to source employment globally. In the new economy in which the physical location of work may not matter, the choice of becoming an expatriate may be the employee's. A new breed of telecommuters live in countries or even continents apart from their companies' home offices.[16] The biggest issues are managing between multiple time zones from Spain to the United States to Japan, making sure that all employees understand each other and are on the same page.

The recruitment approach changes over the internationalization process of the firm. During the export stage, outside expertise is sought at first, but the firm then begins to develop its own personnel for international operations. With expanded and more involved foreign operations, the firm's reliance on home-country personnel will be reduced as host-country nationals are prepared for management positions. The use of home-country and third-country nationals may be directed at special assignments, such as transfer of technology or expertise. The use of expatriates will

Hiroto Tokusei, left, and his brother Kentaro are Stanford graduates working for Google Japan with an eye on localization.

continue as a matter of corporate policy to internationalize management and to foster the infusion of a particular corporate culture into operations around the world.

When international operations are expanded, a management development dilemma may result. Through internal recruitment, young managers will be offered interesting new opportunities. However, some senior managers may object to the constant drain of young talent from their units. Selective recruitment from the outside will help to maintain a desirable combination of inside and fresh talent. Furthermore, with dynamic market changes or new markets and new business development, outside recruitment may be the only available approach. For example, there is a cultural shift under way at LG. The company, once among the most Korean of Korea's conglomerates, is pushing to diversify its management and become truly global. Many veteran Westerners of IBM, Hewlett-Packard, Procter & Gamble, Unilever, and elsewhere have been lured into the executive suite. The foreigners now represent a quarter of LG's leadership and have taken over key positions, including purchasing, supply-chain management, and human resources.[17]

Currently, most managers in subsidiaries are host-country nationals. The reasons include an increase in availability of local talent, corporate relations in the particular market, and the economies realized by not having to maintain a corps of managers overseas. Local managers are generally more familiar with environmental conditions and how they should be interpreted. Outsourcing, or using a local subcontractor recruitment department, allows a firm to focus on candidates who meet its specific recruiting needs and translate them into specific corporate recruiting needs.[18] (Leaders such as Accenture and IBM and niche companies such as Convergys and Logica are known for their deep-technology leveraging and above-average customer experience.[19]) Local companies can better understand the local educational systems and former corporate experiences. By employing local management, the multinational is responding to host-country demands for increased localization and providing advancement as an incentive to local managers. In this respect, however, localization can be carried too far. If the firm does not subscribe to a global philosophy, the manager's development is tied to the local operation or to a particular level of management in that operation.

Local managers, if not properly trained and indoctrinated, may see things differently from the way they are viewed at headquarters. As a result, both control and the overall coordination of programs may be jeopardized. For the corporation to work effectively, of course, employees must first of all understand each other. Most corporations have adopted a common corporate language, with English as the **lingua franca**; that is, the language habitually used among people of diverse speech to facilitate communication. At most global companies, all top-level meetings are conducted in English. In some companies, two languages are officially in use; for example, at Nestlé both English and French are corporate languages. However, corporate training should focus on a broad spectrum of international communication skills rather than just a systematic knowledge of any one or two languages, and should include such areas as cultural appreciation.[20]

A second goal is to avoid overemphasis on localization, which would prevent the development of an internationalized group of managers with a proper understanding of the impact of the environment on operations. To develop language skills and

lingua franca The language habitually used among people of diverse speech to facilitate communication.

promote an international outlook in their management pools, multinational corporations are increasingly recruiting among foreign students at business schools in the United States, western Europe, and the Far East. When these young managers return home following an initial assignment at corporate headquarters, they will have a command of the basic philosophies of multinational operations.

The decision as to whether to use home-country nationals in a particular operation depends on such factors as the type of industry, the life-cycle stage of the product, the availability of managers from other sources, and the functional areas involved. The number of home-country managers is typically higher in the service sector than in the industrial sector, and overseas assignments may be quite short term. For example, many international hotel chains have established management contracts in China with the understanding that home-country managers will train local successors within three to five years. In the start-up phase of an endeavor, headquarters involvement is generally substantial. This applies to all functions, including personnel. Especially if no significant pool of local managers is available or their competence levels are not satisfactory, home-country nationals may be used. For control and communication reasons, some companies always maintain a home-country national as manager in certain functional areas, such as accounting or finance. On occasion, the need to control may be more specific. For example, expatriates may be used in joint ventures to ascertain the proper use of funds or technologies by the local partner.[21]

The number of home-country nationals in an overseas operation rarely rises above 10 percent of the work force and is typically only 1 percent. The reasons are both internal and external. In addition to the substantial cost of transfer, a manager may not fully adjust to foreign working and living conditions. Good corporate citizenship today requires multinational companies to develop the host country's workforce at the management level. Legal impediments to manager transfers may exist, or other difficulties may be encountered. Many U.S.-based hotel corporations, for example, have complained about delays in obtaining visas to the United States not only for managers but also for management trainees.

The use of third-country nationals is most often seen in large multinational companies that have adopted a global philosophy. The practice of some companies, such as Philips, is to employ third-country nationals as managing directors in subsidiaries. An advantage is that third-country nationals may contribute to the firm's overall international expertise. However, many third-country nationals are career international managers, and they may become targets for raids by competitors looking for high levels of talent. They may be a considerable asset in regional expansion; for example, established subsidiary managers in Singapore might be used to start up a subsidiary in Malaysia. On the other hand, some transfers may be inadvisable for cultural or historical reasons, with transfers between Turkey and Greece as an example.

The ability to recruit for international assignments is determined by the value an individual company places on international operations and the experience gained in working in them. In 2009 1,003 top executives around the world were surveyed for the International Executive Panel. Small and medium-sized businesses as well as major corporations across many different industries were represented on this panel. The survey found that responsibility, latitude for decision making, and regular feedback are much stronger motivators than money. In German companies in particular, but also in Switzerland and Japan, this blend of drivers is considered highly effective. Being invited to join a group of high potentials is a major motivator for Japanese executives especially, while pointing out managers' future prospects is a very effective driver in Indian companies. Almost one top manager in three does not believe that the incentives offered by their companies are suitable for attracting high potentials.

Swiss, Canadian, and French executives are particularly pessimistic in this respect. In Germany, Japan, and India, by contrast, one executive in five is convinced that his or her company is well placed to succeed in the battle for the best and brightest. Corporations have to accept that top managers will join foreign companies in order to earn a higher salary (in Germany and Argentina, no less than 77 percent would approve such a move).[22]

In an era of regional integration, many companies are facing a severe shortage of managers who can think and operate regionally or even globally. Very few companies—even those characterizing themselves as global—have systematically developed international managers by rotating young executives through a series of assignments in different parts of the world. Executives can team with Ernst & Young across the United States or around the world, without ever leaving home to leverage their skills on a short-term assignment as a corporate responsibility fellow or take themselves completely out of their comfort zones by living and working abroad for an extended period of time. Such assignments allow executives to apply their skills and experience across geographies (both nationally and internationally), service lines, and industries.[23] To help find the best cross-border talent, executive search firms such as A. T. Kearney and Heidrick & Struggles can be used.

SELECTION CRITERIA FOR OVERSEAS ASSIGNMENTS

The traits that have been suggested as necessary for the international manager range from the ideal to the real. One characterization describes "a flexible personality, with broad intellectual horizons, attitudinal values of cultural empathy, general friendliness, patience and prudence, impeccable educational and professional (or technical) credentials—all topped off with immaculate health, creative resourcefulness, and respect of peers. If the family is equally well endowed, all the better."[24] In addition to flexibility and adaptability, they have to be able to take action where there is no precedent. Traits typically mentioned in the choosing of managers for overseas assignments are listed in Table 18.2. Their relative importance may vary dramatically, of course, depending on the firm situation, as well as where the choice is being made. The United States is particularly good at business literacy, while Latin Americans have developed the ability to cope with complex social relations.[25]

Competence Factors

An expatriate manager usually has far more responsibility than a manager in a comparable domestic position and must be far more self-sufficient in making decisions and conducting daily business. To be selected in the first place, the manager's technical competence level has to be superior to that of local candidates; otherwise,

Table 18.2 Criteria for Selecting Managers for Overseas Assignment

Competence	Adaptability	Personal Characteristics
Technical knowledge	Interest in overseas work	Age
Leadership ability	Relational abilities	Education
Experience, past performance	Cultural empathy	Sex
Area expertise	Appreciation of new management styles	Health
Language	Appreciation of environmental constraints	Marital relations
	Adaptability of family	Social acceptability

the firm would in most cases have chosen a local person. The manager's ability to do the job in the technical sense is one of the main determinants of ultimate success or failure in an overseas assignment.[26] However, management skills will not transfer from one culture to another without some degree of adaptation. This means that, regardless of the level of technical skills, the new environment still requires the ability to adapt the skills to local conditions. Technical competence must also be accompanied by the ability to lead subordinates in any situation or under any conditions.

Especially in global-minded enterprises, managers are selected for overseas assignments on the basis of solid experience and past performance. Many firms use the foreign tour as a step toward top management. By sending abroad internally recruited, experienced managers, the firm also ensures the continuation of corporate culture—a set of shared values, norms, and beliefs and an emphasis on a particular facet of performance. Two examples are IBM's concern with customer service and 3M's concentration on innovation.

The role of **factual cultural knowledge** in the selection process has been widely debated. **Area expertise** includes a knowledge of the basic systems in the region or market for which the manager will be responsible—such as the roles of various ministries in international business, the significance of holidays, and the general way of doing business. None of these variables is as important as language, although language skill is not always highly ranked by firms themselves. The biggest challenges faced by expatriates in their country of residence is learning the local language.[27] A manager who does not know the language of the country may get by with the help of associates and interpreters but is not in a position to assess the situation fully. Of the Japanese and Korean employees representing their companies in the United States, for example, almost all speak English. Of the Americans representing U.S. companies in China, Japan, or Korea, however, few speak the local language well. Some companies place language skills or aptitude in a larger context; they see a strong correlation between language skill and adaptability. Another reason to look for language competence in managers considered for assignments overseas is that all managers spend most of their time communicating. Even when expatriates have Chinese language capabilities, it is extremely unlikely for them to be able to manage China operations. Knowledge of local employees is also critical to being successful in doing business in China.[28]

factual cultural knowledge Knowledge obtainable from specific country studies published by governments, private companies, and universities and also available in the form of background information from facilitating agencies such as banks, advertising agencies, and transportation companies.

area expertise A knowledge of the basic systems in a particular region or market.

Adaptability Factors

The manager's own motivation to a great extent determines the viability of an overseas assignment and consequently its success. The manager's interest in the foreign culture must go well beyond that of the average tourist if he or she is to understand what an assignment abroad involves. In most cases, the manager will need counseling and training to comprehend the true nature of the undertaking.

Adaptability means a positive and flexible attitude toward change. The manager assigned overseas must progress from factual knowledge of culture to interpretive cultural knowledge, trying as much as possible to become part of the new scene, which may be quite different from the one at home. The work habits of middle-level managers may be more lax, productivity and attention to detail less, and overall environmental restrictions far greater. The manager on a foreign assignment is part of a multicultural team, in which both internal and external interactions determine the future of the firm's operations. For example, a manager from the United States may be used to an informal, democratic type of leadership that may not be applicable in countries such as India, Japan, or Mexico, where employees expect more authoritarian leadership. Yahoo Japan is a Japanese company, and most of its employees are Japanese people who fluently understand how the Japanese mind-set and business work. But Google is still a foreigner that is learning how to speak some Japanese.[29]

Adaptability does not depend solely on the manager. Firms look carefully at the family situation because a foreign assignment often puts more strain on other family members than on the manager. As an example, a U.S. engineering firm had problems in Italy that were traced to the inability of one executive's wife to adapt. She complained to other wives, who began to feel that they too suffered hardships and then complained to their husbands. Morale became so low that the company, after missing important deadlines, replaced most of the Americans on the job.[30] As a response, networks intended for expatriate spouses have been developed on corporate intranets to allow for exchange of advice and ideas.[31]

The characteristics of the family as a whole are important. Historically, family adjustment, children's education, partner resistance, difficult location, and partner's career have been the top five priorities.[32] Screeners look for family cohesiveness and check for marital instability or for behavioral difficulties in children. Abroad, the need to work together as a family often makes strong marriages stronger and causes the downfall of weak ones. Further, commitments or interests beyond the nuclear family affect the adjustment of family members to a new environment. Some firms use earlier transfers within the home country as an indicator of how a family will handle transfer abroad. With the dramatic increase in two-career households, foreign assignments may call for one of the spouses to sacrifice a career or, at best, to put it on hold. Increasingly transferees are requesting for spouse re-employment assistance.[33] As a result, corporations are forming a consortia to try to tackle this problem. Members of the group interview accompanying spouses and try to find them positions with other member companies. In an effort to improve the job search routine for trailing spouses of expatriates, eight member companies formed www.partnerjob.com in 2000. Headquartered in Paris, the nonprofit organization now has more than 40 member companies, with between 170 and 200 openings listed at any one time.[34] Increasingly, this means also male expatriate spouses who accompany their partners abroad.[35]

Personal Characteristics

Despite all of the efforts made by multinational companies to recruit the best person available, demographics still play a role in the selection process. Due to either a minimum age requirement or the level of experience needed, many foreign assignments go to managers in their mid-30s or older. Normally, companies do not recruit candidates from graduating classes for immediate assignment overseas. They want their international people first to become experienced and familiar with the corporate culture, and this can best be done at the headquarter's location.

Although the number of women in overseas assignments is only 20 percent according to one count, women are as interested as men are in the assignments.[36] In a 2006 *Women in Finance* survey sponsored by Citigroup, males were somewhat more likely to accept jobs abroad in the next 12 months (55 percent versus 30.9 percent for females), mainly for family reasons.[37] Corporate hiring practices may be based on the myth that women will not be accepted in the host countries. Many of the relatively few women managers report being treated as foreign business people and not singled out as women. These issues are highlighted in Focus on Culture.

In the selection process, firms are concerned about the health of the people they may send abroad. Some assignments are in host countries with dramatically different environmental conditions from the home country, and they may aggravate existing health problems. Moreover, if the candidate selected is not properly prepared, foreign assignments may increase stress levels and contribute to the development of peptic ulcers, colitis, or other problems.

When candidates are screened, being married is usually considered a plus. Marriage brings stability and an inherent support system, provided family relations are in

The GLOW Network at Siemens

Siemens has embraced diversity as a fundamental perspective for its business objectives. Diversity is the inclusion and creative interplay of different modes of thinking, experiences, types of expertise, and individual qualities across all organizational levels. The company that nurtures diversity can spot opportunities for growth more quickly and have a better understanding of its customers. Siemens has initiated a four-prong initiative, including a Diversity Day, GLOW, the Global Leadership Organization of Women; a cross-generational dialogue, which promotes exchanges between experienced and young employees; and the appointment of 100 Diversity Ambassadors throughout the workforce.

The Global Leadership Organization of Women is a network dedicated to enlarging the contribution of women to Siemens's business. The launch event, held in Munich, drew the 100 most senior women from across the company and from all parts of the world. It marked the first step in the rollout of an ambitious change agenda that encompasses mentoring, establishing flexible working conditions, on- and off-ramping for parental leave, and developing ways to expand the external visibility of women in the company.

Siemens created GLOW because it wants to proactively recruit and retain highly qualified women. Siemens believes this will greatly enhance its talent pool. Throughout the world, women deliver outstanding academic and professional performance, and they represent an important resource for companies. Against the backdrop of demographic change and globalization, companies cannot afford to leave this resource untapped.

GLOW is not an isolated initiative. It is part of the ongoing development of Siemens's corporate culture. In the future, Siemens's management will reflect the diversity of its customers. This is the only way Siemens can satisfy the needs and requirements of more than 2 million customers. Siemens experiences the benefits of diversity again and again. For example,

Japanese, Chinese, or Arab customers prefer to communicate in their own language. If decision makers at Siemens speak that language, a real competitive advantage is realized.

Having a diverse group of senior leaders in place will help develop a better understanding of customer needs. The potential for networking is enormous: innovative ideas can be channeled back to Siemens R&D centers in Germany or used in different parts of the world. Take, for example, the entry-level CT scan device called the Somatom Spirit. It was originally designed, engineered, and manufactured in China exclusively for Chinese hospitals. But because Siemens teams are increasingly global, the company soon realized that this product has potential outside China, as well. It is ideally suited for community hospitals in the United States that cannot afford more expensive high-end models. Today, 75 percent of the Somatom Spirits are sold outside China.

Approximately 80 percent of Siemens's revenues are generated outside Germany; it operates in 190 countries. Yet the representation of women and many nationalities, ethnic groups, and cultures within the management ranks could be stronger. For example, currently only slightly more than one-third of top management is non-German and only 7 percent are women. Siemens's diversity initiative reflects the commitments and beliefs of senior executives and the management board, and it has the highest priority within the company. However, Siemens is not interested in establishing rigid quotas for gender, nationality, and ethnicity. Rather, Siemens wants to unleash the enormous potential of its employees—their cultural and personal backgrounds, their broad range of experience, their special skills—for their benefit and for the benefit of the company. Diverse teams are more creative, and creativity drives innovation.

Sources: DeAnne Aguirre, Laird Post, and Sylvia Ann-Hewlett, "The Talent Innovation Imperative," *Strategy+Business,* August 27, 2009; Peter Loscher, and Jill Lee, "The Glow Network at Siemens," *Strategy+Business,* August 27, 2009; "Interview–Jill Lee," *BPW-Congress,* September 4–6, 2009; http://www .bpw-european-congress.org/, Press Round Table Diversity, Jill Lee, Chief Diversity Officer, Siemens *AG,* Munich, March 16, 2009; http://w1.siemens .com/responsibility/en/index.php.

order. It may also facilitate adaptation to the local culture by increasing the number of social functions to which the manager is invited.

Social acceptability varies from one culture to another and can be a function of any of the other personal characteristics. Background, religion, race, and sex usually become critical only in extreme cases in which a host environment would clearly reject a candidate based on one or more of these variables. The Arab boycott of the state of Israel, for example, puts constraints on the use of managers of Jewish and Arab origin. Women cannot negotiate contracts in many Middle Eastern countries. This would hold true even if the woman were president of the company.

The Selection and Orientation Challenge

Due to the cost of transferring a manager overseas, many firms go beyond standard selection procedures and use **adaptability screening** as an integral part of the

adaptability screening A selection procedure that usually involves interviewing both the candidate for an overseas assignment and his or her family members to determine how well they are likely to adapt to another culture.

Figure 18.2   Companies Offering Cultural Training

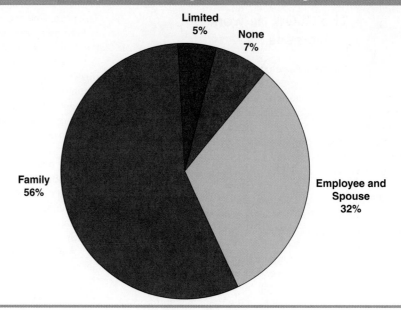

Limited
5%

None
7%

Family
56%

Employee and
Spouse
32%

Source: "Global Relocation Trends," Brookfield Global Relocation Services, 2009.

process. During the screening phase, the method most often used involves interviewing the candidate and the family. The interviews are conducted by senior executives, human relations specialists within the firm, or outside firms. Interviewers ask the candidate and the family to consider the personal issues involved in the transfer; for example, what each will miss the most. In some cases, candidates themselves will refuse an assignment. In others, the firm will withhold the assignment on the basis of interviews that clearly show a degree of risk.

orientation program A program that familiarizes new workers with their roles; the preparation of employees for assignment overseas.

The candidate selected will participate in an **orientation program** on internal and external aspects of the assignment. Internal aspects include issues such as compensation and reporting. External aspects are concerned with what to expect at the destination in terms of customs and culture. The extent and level of the programs will vary; currently, 56 percent offered family training for their executives, 32 percent offered employee and spouse only training, and 5 percent offered only limited training. As shown in Figure 18.2, of companies surveyed worldwide, only 7 percent offered no cultural training currently (but in 1994 as many as 42 percent offered no training).[38] If the company is still in the export stage, the emphasis in this training will be on interpersonal skills and local culture. With expatriates, the focus will be on both training and interacting with host-country nationals. Actual methods vary from area studies to sensitivity training. For a discussion of these methods, see Chapter 5.

Considering the cost of a transfer, catching even one potentially disastrous situation pays for the program for a full year. Some companies have no program at all, however, and others provide programs for higher level management positions only. Companies that have the lowest failure rates typically employ a four-tiered approach to expatriate use (1) clearly stated criteria, (2) rigorous procedures to determine the suitability of an individual across the criteria, (3) appropriate orientation, and (4) constant evaluation of the effectiveness of the procedures.[39]

In this context, it is also important to make the length of the overseas appointment make sense for the individual, the family, and the company. Three-year assignments are typical; however, in some cases when culture gaps are significant (as is in the case of Western and Eastern countries), it may be prudent to have longer tours. More than half of expatriates (58 percent) questioned in 2009 have lived abroad for more than five years. The top three countries for settling down are South Africa, Thailand, and Canada, where 55 percent, 53 percent, and 52 percent respectively, have lived there for more than five years. Male expatriates also tend to live abroad for longer than their female counterparts, with two-thirds (63 percent) of men versus 46 percent of women having lived abroad for more than five years, possibly linked to work versus family commitments.[40]

It is important that the expatriate and his or her family feel the support continuing during their tour. A significant share of the dissatisfaction expressed pertains to perceived lack of support during the international experience, especially in cases of dual-career households.[41] The dual-career households, where the other spouse is not willing to put his or her career on hold and lessen the financial support for the family can cause a major reluctance toward accepting international assignments. Furthermore, as baby boomers retire, companies are sending Generation X and Y employees abroad, many of whom have spouses/partners with their own careers and who are unwilling to give up not only their jobs but also the income associated with their positions.[42]

CULTURE SHOCK

The effectiveness of orientation procedures can be measured only after managers are overseas and exposed to security and socio-political tensions, health, housing, education, social network and leisure activities, language, availability of products and services, and climate. **Culture shock** is the term used for the pronounced reactions to the psychological disorientation that is experienced in varying degrees when spending an extended period of time in a new environment.[43]

culture shock Reactions to the psychological disorientation that most people feel when they move for an extended period of time into a markedly different culture.

One 2008 survey identifies those cities with the highest personal safety ranking based on internal stability, crime, effectiveness of law enforcement, and relationships with other countries. Luxembourg is top, followed by Bern, Geneva, Helsinki, and Zurich, all equally placed at number two. Auckland is ranked fifth in the Asia-Pacific with the best quality of living, followed by Sidney in the 10 spot and Wellington at 12. Honolulu, San Francisco, and Chicago are amongst the safest cities in the United States. Baghdad (215) is the world's least safe city along with Kinshasa (214), Karachi (213), Nairobi (212), and Bangui (211). Luxembourg scores 131.4 on the index, while Baghdad scores 3.8.[44]

Causes and Remedies

The culture shock cycle for an overseas assignment may last about 14 months. Often, goals set for a subsidiary or a project may be unrealistic or the means by which they are to be reached may be totally inadequate. All of these lead to external manifestations of culture shock, such as bitterness and even physical illness. In extreme cases, they can lead to hostility toward anything in the host environment.

The culture shock cycle for an overseas assignment is presented in Figure 18.3. Four distinct stages of adjustment exist during a foreign assignment. The length of the stages is highly individual. The four stages are:

1. **Initial euphoria.** Enjoying the novelty, largely from the perspective of a spectator.
2. **Irritation and hostility.** Experiencing cultural differences, such as the concept of time, through increased participation.
3. **Adjustment.** Adapting to the situation, which in some cases leads to biculturalism and even accusations from corporate headquarters of "going native."
4. **Re-entry.** Returning home to face a possibly changed home environment.

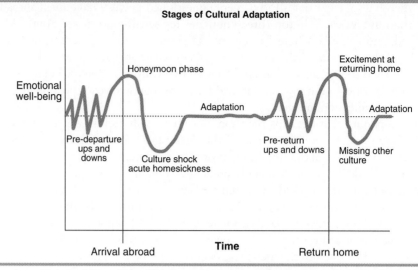

Figure 18.3   Culture Shock Cycle for an Overseas Assignment

Source: Lynne Mitchell and Wayne Myles, "Risk Sense: Developing and Managing International Education Activities with Risk in Mind," Centre for International Programs, University of Guelph, 2010.

The manager may fare better at the second stage than other members of the family, especially if their opportunities for work and other activities are severely restricted. The fourth stage may actually cause a reverse culture shock when the adjustment phase has been highly successful and the return home is not desired. The home environment that has been idealized during the tour abroad may not be perfect after all, and the loss of status and benefits enjoyed abroad may generate feelings of frustration.[45]

Firms themselves must take responsibility for easing one of the causes of culture shock: isolation. By maintaining contact with the manager beyond business-related communication, some of the shock may be alleviated. ExxonMobil, for example, assigns each expatriate a contact person at headquarters to share general information. This helps top management to keep tabs on the manager's progress especially in terms of management succession.

Terrorism: Tangible Culture Shock

International terrorists have frequently targeted corporate facilities, operations, and personnel for attack.[46] Corporate reactions have ranged from letting terrorism have little effect on operations to abandoning certain markets. Some companies try to protect their managers in various ways by fortifying their homes and using local-sounding names to do business in troubled parts of the world. Of course, insurance is available to cover key executives; the cost ranges from a few thousand dollars to hundreds of thousands a year depending on the extent and location of the company's operations. Leading insurers include American International Underwriters, Chubb & Son, and Lloyd's of London. The threat of terrorist activity may have an effect on the company's operations beyond the immediate geographic area of concern. Travel may be banned or restricted in times of threat or areas threatened. An array of organizations have emerged to service companies with employees in the world's hot spots. For example, Rapid Air Support provides in-depth, up-to-the-minute information on government, security, and military situations in various countries and are ready to pull out clients' employees when emergencies arise.[47]

REPATRIATION

Returning home may evoke mixed feelings on the part of the expatriate and the family. Their concerns are both professional and personal. Even in two years, dramatic changes may have occurred not only at home but also in the way the individual and the family perceive the foreign environment. At worst, reverse culture shock may emerge.

The most important professional issue is finding a proper place in the corporate hierarchy. If no provisions have been made, a returning manager may be caught in a holding pattern for an intolerable length of time. The majority of corporations (70 percent) offer a written repatriation policy. For this reason, Dow Chemical, for example, provides each manager embarking on an overseas assignment with a letter that promises a job at least equal in responsibility upon return. Furthermore, because of their isolation, assignments abroad mean greater autonomy and authority than similar domestic positions. Both financially and psychologically, many expatriates find the overseas position difficult to give up. Many executive perks, such as club memberships, will not be funded at home.

The family, too, may be reluctant to give up their special status. In India and Vietnam, for example, expatriate families have servants for most of the tasks they perform themselves at home. Many longer-term expatriates are shocked by increases in the prices of housing and education at home. For the many managers who want to stay abroad, this may mean a change of company or even career—from employee to independent business person. Estimates of global expatriate "failures" range from 16 to 40 percent, resulting in corporate losses estimated between $200,000 and $1.2 million per expatriate failure.[48]

This alternative is not an attractive one for the company, which stands to lose valuable individuals who could become members of an international corps of managers. Therefore, planning for repatriation is necessary.[49] A four-step process can be used for this purpose. The first step involves an assessment of foreign assignments in terms of environmental constraints and corporate objectives, making sure that the latter are realistically defined. The second stage is preparation of the individual for an overseas assignment, which should include a clear understanding of when and how repatriation takes place. During the actual tour, the manager should be kept abreast of developments at headquarters, especially in terms of career paths. Finally, during the actual reentry, the manager should receive intensive organizational reorientation, reasonable professional adjustment time, and counseling for the entire family on matters of, for example, finance. A program of this type allows the expatriate to feel a close bond with headquarters regardless of geographical distance.

COMPENSATION

A Japanese executive's salary in cash is quite modest by U.S. standards, but he is comfortable in the knowledge that the company will take care of him. Compensation is paternalistic; for example, a manager with two children in college and a sizable mortgage would be paid more than a childless manager in a comparable job. As this example suggests, Japanese compensation issues go beyond salary comparisons. They include exchange rates, local taxes, and what the money will buy in different countries. Many compensation packages include elements other than cash.

A firm's expatriate compensation program has to be effective in the following areas: home-country salary, shows the basic level of each category at home; assignment-location costs indicate that expenditures for income taxes, housing, and goods and services are typically higher abroad; assignment-location costs paid by employer and from salary demonstrate that expatriates pay the same amount as their domestic counterparts, with the employer making up the difference; and home-country equivalent purchasing power illustrates that expatriates have the same purchasing power as typical domestic peers, and that they may also receive incentives.[50] To achieve these objectives, firms pay a high premium beyond base salaries to induce managers to accept overseas assignments. The costs to the firm are 2 to 2.5 times the cost of maintaining a manager in a comparable position at home. For example, the average compensation package of a U.S. manager in Hong Kong is $225,500 (base salary is 47 percent of this figure) and for the British manager $170,500 (57 percent). U.S. firms traditionally offer their employees more high-value perks, such as bigger apartments.[51]

The compensation of the manager overseas can be divided into two general categories: (1) base salary and salary-related allowances and (2) non-salary-related allowances. Although incentives to leave home are justifiable in both categories, they create administrative complications for the personnel department in tying them to packages at home and elsewhere. As the number of transfers increases, firms develop general policies for compensating the manager rather than negotiating individually on every aspect of the arrangement.

Base Salary and Salary-Related Allowances

base salary Salary not including special payments such as allowances paid during overseas assignments.

A manager's **base salary** depends on qualifications, responsibilities, and duties, just as it would for a domestic position. Furthermore, criteria applying to merit increases, promotions, and other increases are administered as they are domestically. Equity and comparability with domestic positions are important, especially in ensuring that repatriation will not cause cuts in base pay. For administrative and control purposes, the compensation and benefits function in multinational corporations is most often centralized.

cost-of-living allowance (COLA) An allowance paid during assignment overseas to enable the employee to maintain the same standard of living as at home.

The cost of living varies considerably around the world, as can be seen in Table 18.3. The purpose of the **cost-of-living allowance (COLA)** is to enable the manager to maintain as closely as possible the same standard of living that he or she would have at home. COLA is calculated by determining a percentage of base salary that would be spent on goods and services at the foreign location. (Figures around 50 percent are typical.) The ratios will naturally vary as a function of income and family size. COLA tables for various U.S. cities (of which Washington, DC, is the most often used) and locations worldwide are available through the U.S. State Department Allowances Staff and various consulting firms, such as Business International Corporation. Fluctuating exchange rates will, of course, have an effect on the COLA as well, and changes will call for reviews of the allowance. As an example, assume that living in Helsinki costs the manager 49 percent more than living in Washington, DC. The manager's monthly pay is $10,000, and for his family of four, the disposable income is $5,375 (53.75 percent). Further assume that the dollar weakens from €1.50 to €1.45. The COLA would be:

$$\$5,375 \times 171/100 \times 1.50/1.45 = \$9,508$$

Similarly, if the local currency depreciated, the COLA would be less. When the cost of living is less than in the United States, no COLA is determined.

foreign service premium A financial incentive to accept an assignment overseas, usually paid as a percentage of the base salary.

The **foreign service premium** is actually a bribe to encourage a manager to leave familiar conditions and adapt to new surroundings. Although the methods of paying the premium vary, as do its percentages, most firms pay it as a percentage of the base salary. The percentages range from 10 to 25 percent of base salary. One variation of the straightforward percentage is a sliding scale by amount—15 percent of the first $20,000, then 10 percent, and sometimes a ceiling beyond which a premium is not paid. Another variation is by duration, with the percentages decreasing with every year the manager spends abroad. Despite the controversial nature of foreign service premiums paid at some locations, they are a generally accepted competitive practice.

The environments in which a manager will work and the family will live vary dramatically. For example, consider being assigned to London or Brisbane versus Dar

Table 18.3   International Cost Comparisons

Living cost comparisons of Americans residing in foreign areas are developed four times a year by the U.S. Department of State, Office of Allowances. For each post, two measures are computed: (1) a government index to establish post allowances for U.S. government employees and (2) a local index for use by private organizations. The government index takes into consideration prices of goods imported to posts and price advantages available only to U.S. government employees.

The local index is used by many business firms and private organizations to determine the cost of living allowance for their American employees assigned abroad. Local index measures of 18 key countries around the world are shown here. Maximum housing allowances, calculated separately, are also given. Also included are cost-of-living hardship and differential rate percent. (Danger pay for Kabul, Afghanistan; Algiers, Algeria; and Port-au-Prince, Haiti, can also be found.)

The reports are issued four times annually under the title "U.S. Department of State Indexes of Living Cost Abroad, Quarters Allowances and Hardship Differentials."

Cost of Living Index (Washington, DC = 100)			Maximum Annual Housing Allowance		
Location	Cost of Living Survey Date	Index	Family of 2	Cost of Living Hardship	Differential Rate Percent
Buenos Aires	Mar 2009	111	$46,100	0	0
Canberra	May 2008	139	21,100	20	0
Brussels	May 2009	179	46,400	50	0
Brasilia	Jun 2009	149	46,000	10	0
Shanghai	Aug 2007	132	16,000	30	15
Cairo	Mar 2006	96	22,900	0	15
New Delhi	Nov 2008	107	16,000	5	20
Paris	Apr 2008	190	82,600	70	0
Frankfurt	Jan 2008	167	42,300	35	0
Hong Kong	Jun 2009	156	114,300	42	0
Tokyo	Nov 2008	191	101,100	60	0
Mexico City	Mar 2009	99	44,000	0	15
The Hague	Apr 2009	152	63,000	42	0
Moscow	Feb 2009	154	90,900	25	15
Cape Town	Oct 2008	135	16,000	5	10
Geneva	Nov 2008	235	76,000	90	0
London	Apr 2009	159	82,900	42	0
Hanoi	May 2008	113	46,800	5	25

Source: http://aoprals.state.gov.

es Salaam or Port Moresby or even Bogota or Buenos Aires. Some locations may require little, if any, adjustment. Some call for major adaptation because of climatic differences; political instability; inadequacies in housing, education, shopping, or recreation; or overall isolation. For example, children can attend an international school, where tuition is afforded mainly by employees of multinational corporations who pay compensation packages that include children's education, or be enrolled in Chinese schools, where classes are taught solely in Mandarin. Expatriates whose companies or organizations do not cover children's education, may feel that they have no choice but to home school.[52]

To compensate for this type of expense and adjustment, firms pay **hardship allowances**. The allowances are based on U.S. State Department Foreign Post Differentials. The percentages vary from zero (e.g., the manager in Helsinki) to 35 percent (as in Karachi). The higher allowances typically include a danger pay extra added to any hardship allowance.[53]

Housing costs and related expenses are typically the largest expenditure in the expatriate manager's budget. Firms usually provide a **housing allowance** commensurate with the manager's salary level and position. When the expatriate is the

hardship allowances A premium paid during an assignment to an overseas area that requires major adaptation.

housing allowance A premium paid during assignment overseas to provide living quarters.

country manager for the firm, the housing allowance will provide for suitable quarters in which to receive business associates. In most cases, firms set a range within which the manager must find housing. For common utilities, firms either provide an allowance or pay the costs outright.

One of the major determinants of the manager's lifestyle abroad is taxes. A U.S. manager earning $100,000 in Canada would pay nearly $40,000 in taxes—in excess of $10,000 more than in the United States. For this reason, 90 percent of U.S. multinational corporations have **tax equalization** plans. When a manager's overseas taxes are higher than at home, the firm will make up the difference. However, in countries with a lower rate of taxation, the company simply keeps the difference. The firms' rationalization is that it does not make any sense for the manager in Hong Kong to make more money than the person who happened to land in Singapore. Tax equalization is usually handled by accounting firms that make the needed calculations and prepare the proper forms. Managers can exclude a portion of their expatriate salary from U.S. tax; in 2009, the amount was $87,600.[54] Each U.S. person who has a financial interest in or has signature or other authority over any foreign financial accounts (including banks, securities, or other types of financial accounts) in a foreign country—if the aggregate value of these financial accounts exceeds $10,000 at any time during the calendar year—must report that relationship each calendar year.

Base-salary and nonsalary allowances are categorized in Table 18.4.

tax equalization Reimbursement by the company when an employee in an overseas assignment pays taxes at a higher rate than if he or she were at home.

Non-Salary-Related Allowances

Other types of allowances are made available to ease the transition into the period of service abroad. Typical allowances during the transition stage include (1) a relocation allowance to compensate for the additional expense of a move, such as purchase of electric converters; (2) a mobility allowance as an incentive to managers to go overseas, usually paid in a lump sum and as a substitute for the foreign service premium (some companies pay 50 percent at transfer, 50 percent at repatriation); (3) allowances related to housing, such as home sale or rental protection, shipment and storage of household goods, or provision of household furnishings in overseas locations; (4) automobile protection in terms of covering possible losses on the sale of a car or cars at transfer and having to buy others overseas, usually at a higher cost; (5) travel expenses, using economy-class transportation except for long flights (e.g., from Washington to Taipei); and

Table 18.4

The Benefits of Being an Expatriate

1. Financial benefits (including tax breaks, ability to save, expat packages): 32%
2. Better quality of life (including lifestyle, work/life balance, and greater freedom): 25%
3. Cultural opportunities (including food, language, new experiences): 19%
4. Career development (including gaining international experience, better prospects, greater job security): 17%
5. Travel (including adventure): 14%

Challenges of Being an Expatriate

1. Missing family and friends, being unable to look after elderly relatives, difficulty keeping in touch, loneliness: 23%
2. Language barriers/poor communication: 18%
3. Adapting to culture: 16%
4. Reestablishing a social life, being accepted into the community, making friends: 12%
5. Loss of identity, lack of stability, constantly being a foreigner: 10%

Source: HSBC Bank International, Expat Explorer Survey 2009, Report Two: Expat Experience, www.offshore.hsbc.com.

(6) temporary living expenses, which may become substantial if housing is not immediately available. Companies are also increasingly providing support to make up for income lost by the accompanying spouse.

Education for children is one of the major concerns of expatriate families. Free public schooling may not be available and the private alternatives are expensive. In many cases, children may have to go to school in a different country. Firms will typically reimburse for such expenses in the form of an **education allowance**. In the case of college education, firms reimburse for one round-trip airfare every year, leaving tuition expenses to the family.

Finally, firms provide support for medical expenses, especially to provide medical services at a level comparable to the expatriate's home country. In some cases, this means traveling to another country for care; for example, from Malaysia to Singapore, where the medical system is the most advanced in southeast Asia. Other health-related allowances are in place to allow the expatriate to leave the challenging location periodically for rest and relaxation. Some expatriates in Mexico City get $300 to $500 per family member each month to cover a getaway from the pollution of the city.[55] Leaves from hardship posts such as Port Moresby are routine.

Other issues should be covered by a clearly stated policy. Home leave is provided every year, typically after 11 months overseas, although some companies require a longer period. Home leaves are usually accompanied by consultation and training sessions at headquarters. At some posts, club memberships are necessary because (1) the status of the manager requires them and (2) they provide family members with access to the type of recreation they are used to in the home environment. Because they are extremely expensive—for example, a "mandatory" golf club membership in Tokyo might cost thousands of dollars—the firm's assistance is needed. Benefits and allowances are extended to "significant others" in 24 percent of the companies. Of these, 85 percent recognize nonmarried opposite-sex partners and 84 percent recognize same-sex partners.

> **education allowance**
> Reimbursement by company for dependent educational expenses incurred while a parent is assigned overseas.

Method of Payment

The method of payment, especially in terms of currency, is determined by a number of factors. The most common method is to pay part of the salary in the local currency and part in the currency of the manager's home country. Host-country regulations, ranging from taxation to the availability of foreign currency, will influence the decision. Firms themselves look at the situation from the accounting and administrative point of view and would like, in most cases, to pay in local currencies to avoid burdening the subsidiary. The expatriate naturally will want to have some of the compensation in his or her own currency for various reasons; for example, if exchange controls are in effect, to get savings out of the country upon repatriation may be very difficult.

Compensation of Host-Country Nationals

The compensation packages paid to local managers—cash, benefits, and privileges—are largely determined as a function of internal equity and external competitiveness. Internal equity may be complicated because of cultural differences in compensation; for example, in Japan a year-end bonus of an additional month's salary is common. On the other hand, some incentive programs to increase productivity may be unknown to some nationals. Chinese who have headed overseas for study or employment opportunities sometimes return to China and set up businesses or take on senior management positions in local companies. Furthermore, in many countries, the state provides benefits that may be provided by the firm elsewhere. Since the firm and its employees contribute to the programs by law, the services need not be duplicated.

External competitiveness depends on the market price of trained individuals and their attraction to the firm. External competitiveness is best assessed through surveys of compensation and benefits levels for a particular market. The firm must keep its local managers informed of the survey results to help them realize the value of their compensation packages.

MANAGING LABOR PERSONNEL

None of the firm's objectives can be realized without a labor force, which can become one of the firm's major assets or one of its major problems depending on the relationship that is established. Because of local patterns and legislation, headquarters' role in shaping the relations is mainly advisory, limited to setting the overall tone for the interaction. However, many of the practices adopted in one market or region may easily come under discussion in another, making it necessary for multinational corporations to set general policies concerning labor relations. Often multinational corporations have been instrumental in bringing about changes in the overall work environment in a country. And as decisions are made as to where to locate and how to streamline operations, education and training become important criteria for both countries and companies.

At many companies, educational programs are a means of leveraging valuable company resources. General Electric made a big and potentially risky bet on China's aerospace industry when it struck an agreement with leading Chinese aircraft company Aviation Industry Corp. of China to jointly supply avionics systems for jetliner makers globally. GE defines its avionics systems as the "brains" of the aircraft, helping pilots navigate and operate the plane. The joint venture creates approximately 200 jobs in the United States, in addition to creating bilateral industrial cooperation with China.[56]

Labor strategy can be viewed from three perspectives: (1) the participation of labor in the affairs of the firm, especially as it affects performance and well-being; (2) the role and impact of unions in the relationship; and (3) specific human resource policies in terms of recruitment, training, and compensation.

LABOR PARTICIPATION IN MANAGEMENT

Over the past quarter century, many changes have occurred in the traditional labor–management relationship as a result of dramatic changes in the economic environment and the actions of both firms and the labor force. The role of the worker is changing both at the level of the job performed and in terms of participation in the decision-making process. To enhance workers' role in decision making, various techniques have emerged: self-management, codetermination, minority board membership, and works councils. In striving for improvements in the quality of work life, programs that have been initiated include flextime, quality circles, and work-flow reorganization. Furthermore, employee ownership has moved into the mainstream.

Labor Participation in Decision Making

The degree to which workers around the world can participate in corporate decision making varies considerably. Rights of information, consultation, and codetermination develop on three levels:

1. The shop-floor level, or direct involvement; for example, the right to be consulted in advance concerning transfers.
2. The management level, or through representative bodies; for example, works council participation in setting of new policies or changing of existing ones.
3. The board level; for example, labor membership on the board of directors.[57]

Table 18.5 Degree of Worker Involvement in Decision Making of Firms

	Direct Involvement of Workers[a]	Involvement of Representative Bodies[a]	Board Representation Standing[b]	Overall Standing[c]
Germany	3	1	1	A
Sweden	4	2	1	A
Norway	1	10	1	B
Netherlands	9	4	2	C
France	7	3	2	C
Belgium	5	6	3	D
Finland	2	9	3	D
Denmark	8	7	1	D
Israel	11	5	3	D
Italy	6	8	3	E
Great Britain	10	11	3	E

Source: Susanne Pernicka, "Working Society and Industrial Democracy in Future Europe," *Frontiers of Sociology,* Stockholm, Sweden, 5–9 July, 2005; adapted from Industrial Democracy in Europe International Research Group, *Industrial Democracy in Europe* (Oxford, England: Clarendon Press, 1981), 291; and Industrial Democracy in Europe International Research Group, *Industrial Democracy in Europe Revisited* (Oxford, England: Oxford University Press, 1993), chapter 3.

[a] Involvement is rated on an 11-point scale, where 1 stands for the greatest degree of involvement and 11 for almost no involvement.

[b] All cases without any kind of board participation are coded 3; the right to appoint two or more members, 1; the in-between category, 2.

[c] Rankings are from high (A) to low (E).

The extent of worker participation in decision making in 11 countries is summarized in Table 18.5. Germany has the highest amount of worker participation in any country; **self-management** is standard through workers' councils, which decide all major issues, including the choice of managing director and supervisory board. Currently, the greatest amount of cooperation between labor and capital in participative leadership exists in the Germanic group of European countries (Austria, Germany, Holland, and Switzerland).[58]

In some countries, employees are represented on the supervisory boards to facilitate communication between management and labor by giving labor a clearer picture of the financial limits of management and by providing management with a new awareness of labor's point of view. The process is called **codetermination**. In Germany, companies have a two-tiered management system with a supervisory board and the board of managers, which actually runs the firm. In a firm with 20,000 employees, for example, labor would have 10 of the 20 supervisory board slots divided in the following way: three places for union officials and the balance to be elected from the workforce. At least one member must be a white-collar employee and one a managerial employee.[59] The supervisory board is legally responsible for the managing board. In some countries, labor has **minority participation**. In the Netherlands, for example, works councils can nominate (not appoint) board members and can veto the appointment of new members appointed by others. In other countries, such as the United States, codetermination has been opposed by unions as an undesirable means of cooperation, especially when management–labor relations are confrontational.

A tradition in labor relations, especially in Britain, is **works councils**. They provide labor a say in corporate decision making through a representative body, which may consist entirely of workers or of a combination of managers and workers.

self-management Independent decision making; a high degree of worker involvement in corporate decision making.

codetermination A management approach in which employees are represented on supervisory boards to facilitate communication and collaboration between management and labor.

minority participation Participation by a group having less than the number of votes necessary for control.

works councils Councils that provide labor a say in corporate decision making through a representative body that may consist entirely of workers or of a combination of managers and workers.

LABOR UNION MEMBERSHIP

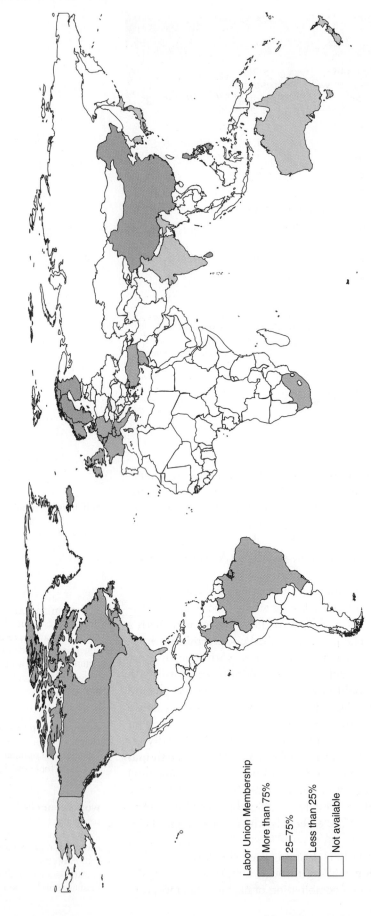

Labor Union Membership

More than 75%

25–75%

Less than 25%

Not available

Source: International Labor Organization.

The councils participate in decisions on overall working conditions, training, transfers, work allocation, and compensation. In some countries, such as Finland and Belgium, workers' rights to direct involvement, especially as it involves their positions, are quite strong. The European Union's works council directive will ultimately require over 1,000 multinational companies, both European and non-European, to negotiate works council agreements. The agreements will provide for at least one meeting per year to improving dialogue between workers and management. Around 10 million workers across the EU have the right to information and consultation on company decisions at European level through their European Works Councils (EWCs). The Works Council Directive applies to companies with 1,000 or more employees, including at least 150 in two or more member-states. Of these, 841 companies have EWCs in operation, covering around 60 percent of workers in the EU.[60]

The countries described are unique in the world. In many countries and regions, workers have few, if any, of these rights. The result is long-term potential for labor strife in those countries and possible negative publicity elsewhere. Over a ten-year period from 1996 to 2006, Canada (186), Spain (170), Denmark (164), Italy (88), and Finland (75) are the countries leading in days lost in all industries and services.[61]

In addition to labor groups and the media, investors and shareholders also are scrutinizing multinationals' track records on labor practices. As a result, a company investing in foreign countries should hold to international standards of safety and health, not simply local standards. This can be achieved, for example, through the use of modern equipment and training. Local labor also should be paid adequately. This increases the price of labor, yet ensures the best available talent and helps avoid charges of exploitation.[62] Companies subcontracting work to local or joint-venture factories need to evaluate industrial relations throughout the system not only to avoid lost production due to disruptions such as strikes, but to ensure that no exploitation exists at the facilities. Several large firms, such as Nike and Reebok, require subcontractors to sign agreements saying they will abide by minimum wage standards.[63] Area of labor compliance is captured by reference to seven core standards (dealing with forced labor, child labor, discrimination, wages and benefits, working hours, freedom of association, and disciplinary practices). While companies have been long opposed to linking free trade to labor standards, the business community is rethinking its strategy mainly to get trade negotiations moving.[64]

Improvement of Quality of Work Life

The term **quality of work life** has come to encompass various efforts in the areas of personal and professional development. Its two clear objectives are to increase productivity and to increase the satisfaction of employees. Of course, programs leading to increased participation in corporate decision making are part of the programs; however, this section concentrates on individual job-related programs: work redesign, team building, and work scheduling.[65]

By adding both horizontal and vertical dimensions to the work, **work redesign programs** attack undesirable features of jobs. Horizontally, task complexity is added by incorporating work stages normally done before and after the stage being redesigned. Vertically, each employee is given more responsibility for making the decisions that affect how the work is done. Toyota does not modify its automobiles to local needs; it customizes both products and operations to the level of consumer sophistication in each country. This strategy pushes Toyota out of Japan, where it is dominant, and into overseas markets, where it has often been the underdog. Following the strategy increases operational complexity, but it maximizes employees' creativity because they have to develop new technologies, new ways of marketing, and

quality of work life Various corporate efforts in the areas of personal and professional development undertaken with the objectives of increasing employee satisfaction and increasing productivity.

work redesign programs Programs that alter jobs to increase both the quality of the work experience and productivity.

new supply chains. Nissan and Honda follow the same strategy, but less rigorously: Toyota offered 94 models in Japan—almost three times as many as Nissan's 35 and Honda's 30 models. Pursuing local customization also exposes Toyota to the sophistication of local tastes.[66] Toyota has such a major challenge on its hands because this crisis strikes at the essence of its reputation.

Closely related to work redesign are efforts aimed at **team building**. For example, in car plants, work is organized so that groups are responsible for a particular, identifiable portion of the car, such as interiors. Each group has its own areas in which to pace itself and to organize the work. The group must take responsibility for the work, including inspections, whether it is performed individually or in groups. The group is informed about its performance through a computer system. The team-building effort includes job rotation to enable workers to understand all facets of their jobs. Another approach to team building makes use of **quality circles**, in which groups of workers regularly meet to discuss issues relating to their productivity. Team building efforts have to be adapted to cultural differences. In cultures that are more individualistic, incentive structures may have to be kept at the individual level and discussions on quality issues should be broad-based rather than precise. Together with the University of Toyota, established four years earlier in Torrance, California by Toyota Motor Sales, these formal mechanisms support Toyota's communication networks by disseminating best practices and company values. In addition, employees are encouraged to join a wide variety of informal groups. Every employee belongs to several committees, self-organizing study groups, and other social groups, of which there are close to 20 in the company. This helps create a multilayered communication network at Toyota.[67]

Flexibility in **work scheduling** has led to changes in when and how long workers are at the workplace. **Flextime** allows workers to determine their starting and ending hours in a given workday; for example, they might arrive between 7:00 and 9:30 a.m. and leave between 3:00 and 5:30 p.m. The idea spread from Germany to the European Union and to other countries such as Switzerland, Japan, New Zealand, and the United States. Some 40 percent of the Dutch working population holds flex- or part-time positions.[68] Despite its advantages in reducing absenteeism, flextime is not applicable to industries using assembly lines. Flexible work scheduling has also led to compressed workweeks—for example, the four-day week—and job sharing, which allows a position to be filled by more than one person. In January 2009, accounting giant KPMG unveiled its new Flexible Futures program for its 11,000 UK-based employees. The options include a four-day workweek and a 20 percent reduction in base pay, a 4- to 12-week sabbatical at 30 percent base pay, a combination of the two options, or sticking with the status quo.[69]

Firms around the world also have other programs for personal and professional development, such as career counseling and health counseling. All of them are dependent on various factors external and internal to the firm. Of the external factors, the most important are the overall characteristics of the economy and the labor force. Internally, either the programs must fit into existing organizational structures or management must be inclined toward change. In many cases, labor unions have been one of the major resisting forces. Their view is that firms are trying to prevent workers from organizing by allowing them to participate in decision making and management.

THE ROLE OF LABOR UNIONS

When two of the world's largest producers of electrotechnology, Swedish Asea and Switzerland's Brown Boveri, merged to remain internationally competitive in a market dominated by a few companies such as General Electric, Siemens, Hitachi, and Toshiba, not everyone reacted positively to the alliance. For tax reasons,

team building A process that enhances the cohesiveness of a department or group by helping members learn how to organize their work and assume responsibility for it.

quality circles Groups of workers who meet regularly to discuss issues related to productivity.

work scheduling Preparing schedules of when and how long workers are at the workplace.

flextime A modification of work scheduling that allows workers to determine their own starting and ending times within a broad range of available hours.

headquarters would not be located in Sweden, and this caused the four main Swedish labor unions to oppose the merger. They demanded that the Swedish government exercise its right to veto the undertaking because Swedish workers would no longer have a say in their company's affairs if it were headquartered elsewhere.

The incident is an example of the role labor unions play in the operation of a multinational corporation. It also points up the concerns of local labor unions when they must deal with organizations directed from outside their national borders.

The role of labor unions varies from country to country, often because of local traditions in management–labor relations. The variations include the extent of union power in negotiations and the activities of unions in general. In Europe, especially in the northern European countries, collective bargaining takes place between an employers' association and an umbrella organization of unions, on either a national or a regional basis, establishing the conditions for an entire industry. On the other end of the spectrum, negotiations in Japan are on the company level, and the role of larger-scale unions is usually consultative. Another striking difference emerges in terms of the objectives of unions and the means by which they attempt to attain them. In the United Kingdom, for example, union activity tends to be politically motivated and identified with political ideology. In the United States, the emphasis has always been on improving workers' overall quality of life. In China, the objective of the All China Federation of Trade Unions, the only legal union umbrella group, is to build a harmonious society.[70]

Investment decisions can also be guided by union considerations. For example, of the more than 30 automobile plants in the United States owned by foreign companies, none have been organized by the United Auto Workers. Foreign car makers have located plants in southern states where the UAW has little presence and where right-to-work laws prevent unions from forcing employees to join and pay dues. In northern states, they have mostly chosen locations in rural areas away from UAW strongholds.[71]

Internationalization of business has created a number of challenges for labor unions. The main concerns that have been voiced are (1) the power of the firm to move production from one country to another if attractive terms are not reached in a particular market; (2) the availability of data, especially financial information, to support unions' bargaining positions; (3) insufficient attention to local issues and problems while focusing on global optimization; and (4) difficulty in being heard by those who eventually make the decisions.[72] This has been countered by new activism to secure core labor standards as fundamental human rights, including freedom of association and the right to organize and bargain collectively.[73]

Although the concerns are valid, all of the problems anticipated may not develop. For example, transferring production from one country to another in the short term may be impossible, and labor strife in the long term may well influence such moves. To maintain participation in corporate decision making, unions are taking action individually and across national boundaries as seen in Focus on Ethics. Individual unions refer to contracts signed elsewhere when setting the agenda for their own negotiations. Supranational organizations such as the as the AFL-CIO—which is affiliated with the International Trade Union Confederation (ITUC), the worldwide union network (based in Brussels, Belgium, the ITUC has more than 230 affiliated union federations in 152 countries representing 150 million workers)—and industry-specific organizations such as the International Metal Workers' Federation exchange information and discuss bargaining tactics. The goal is also to coordinate bargaining with multinational corporations across national boundaries. The International Labor Organization, a specialized agency of the United Nations, has an information bank on multinational corporations' policies concerning wage structures, benefits packages, and overall working conditions.

Labor Unions Attack Nestlé in Russia

Workers at the Swiss firm's factory in the Ural city of Perm have come all the way to the Russian capital to stage a protest. They are complaining about a refusal on the part of factory management to engage in negotiations to increase real wages. Despite the public protests, however, Nestlé is refusing to meet the workers' demands. Over the past 14 years, Nestlé has built up a strong presence in Russia with more than 11,000 employees and 14 production units. However, only four of those are unionized and the workers in Perm are particularly organized. Two-thirds of the plant's staff (of 1,000) are members of a labor union. Hundreds have taken part in the protest actions.

According to a company spokeswoman, Nestlé wages are "above the industry average in the city." She says the average wage at the Nestlé plant is $680, but that is counting management wages. According to the union, the base monthly wage is just $236, with the maximum bonus being $520, including night shifts. Nestlé has increased wages in Perm three times over the past year, by 9, 10, and then 15 percent in January. However, these hikes have not been enough to keep up with the high rate of inflation in the region, which is officially 16.5 percent. In late 2007, the trade union demanded a wage increase of 40 percent, but management reacted by completely pulling out of negotiations with the union. Even when it reduced its demand to 21.5 percent, the bosses refused to come back to the negotiating table, saying the request was not "economically justified."

The Federation of Independent Trade Unions of Russia (FNPR) mobilized to support the Perm protest. At a press conference in Moscow, FNPR fiercely attacked the multinational, saying an "anti-worker" company like Nestlé had no place in Russia. The workers are also finding support for their cause outside of Russia, for example, from Germany's NGG union and the International Union of Food Workers. Larisa Selivanova, chairperson of the trade union committee at the Perm Nestlé factory, thanked SEIU Local 1877 (California Cleaners) for its support: "It is very important for us as we are only beginning to join the global process of struggle for the best life of working people." These international organizations fear that Nestlé will move more of its production to Russia if it can push through its low-wage policy in Perm. However, it is the local workers who are leading the fight.

Finally, in June 2008, Nestlé agreed to formally recognize the union's fundamental right to negotiate wages. The agreement, signed between the union and company representatives, states that wages and wage scales will be an integral part of the collective bargaining process, which is to be conducted annually. It took six months of marching, picketing, leafleting, and international solidarity actions to persuade the company to respect a basic worker right, union officials said. Their campaign has been an important component of the struggle for Nestlé workers globally. Nestlé's Corporate Business Principles state that their business practices are designed to establish a constructive dialogue with unions. As of the fall of 2010, "Nespressure"—squeezing workers and suppressing rights—is being applied again at Nestlé Russia.

Sources: "Spiegel Online International," April, 24, 2008; http://talkingunion .wordpress.com/2008/04/24/seiu-california-cleaners-show-solidarity-with- nestle-russia-workers-struggle/; http://www.youtube.com/watch?v=IK2H1ZB- dqc; http://cms.iuf.org/?q=node/264.

The relations between companies and unions can be cooperative as well. Alliances between labor and management have emerged to continue providing well-paying factory jobs in the face of global competition. Continuing net benefits are reported both by managers and by union representatives in workplaces where cooperative relationships boost quality and cut costs. The benefits come primarily from the informal consultative processes and levels of trust that are engendered.[74]

HUMAN RESOURCE POLICIES

The objectives of a human resource policy pertaining to workers are the same as for management: to anticipate the demand for various skills and to have in place programs that will ensure the availability of employees when needed. For workers, however, the firm faces the problem on a larger scale and does not have, in most cases, an expatriate alternative. This means that, among other things, when technology is transferred for a plant, it has to be adapted to the local work force.

Although most countries have legislation and restrictions concerning the hiring of expatriates, many of them—for example, some of the EU countries and some oil-rich Middle Eastern countries—have offset labor shortages by importing large numbers of workers from countries such as Turkey and Jordan. The EU by design allows free movement of labor. A mixture of backgrounds in the available labor pool can put a strain on personnel development. As an example, the firm may incur considerable expense to provide language training to employees. In Sweden, a certain minimum amount of language training must be provided for all "guest workers" at the firm's expense.

Bringing a local labor force to the level of competency desired by the firm may also call for changes. Russia was one of the fastest growing auto markets in the world, but few Western carmakers were willing to risk a partnership. Renault purchased a 25 percent stake in AvtoVaz, whose Lada brand was famous for the wrong reasons: its plants were fitted with Soviet-era production equipment, and its 100,000 employees produced just 130,000 cars annually. Sales were down 44 percent from 2009 and top executives have said they need to cut 27,000 jobs, almost a third of the total work force, to become even marginally competitive. The company is moving workers toward the exit, cutting typical monthly salaries to 8,000 rubles, roughly $275 (from around 20,000 rubles) a year ago.[75] France car giant Renault and Russia's major car manufacturer started talks in 2010 pertaining to the launching of new projects.

Compensation of the work force is a controversial issue. Payroll expenses must be controlled for the firm to remain competitive; on the other hand, the firm must attract in appropriate numbers the type of workers it needs. The compensation packages of U.S.-based multinational companies have come under criticism, especially when their level of compensation is lower in developing countries than in the United States. Criticism has occurred even when the salaries or wages paid were substantially higher than the local average.

Comparisons of compensation packages are difficult because of differences in the packages that are shaped by culture, legislation, collective bargaining, taxation, and individual characteristics of the job. In northern Europe, for example, new fathers can accompany their wives on a two-week paternity leave at the employer's expense.

SUMMARY

A business organization is the sum of its human resources. To recruit and retain a pool of effective people for each of its operations requires (1) personnel planning and staffing, (2) training activities, (3) compensation decisions, and (4) attention to labor–management relations.

Firms attract international managers from a number of sources, both internal and external. In the earlier stages of internationalization, recruitment must be external. Later, an internal pool often provides candidates for transfer. The decision then becomes whether to use home-country, host-country, or third-country nationals. If expatriate managers are used, selection policies should focus on competence, adaptability, and personal traits. Policies should also be set for the compensation and career progression of candidates

selected for out-of-country assignments. At the same time, the firm must be attentive to the needs of local managers for training and development.

Labor can no longer be considered as simply services to be bought. Increasingly, workers are taking an active role in the decision making of the firm and in issues related to their own welfare. Various programs are causing dramatic organizational change, not only by enhancing the position of workers but by increasing the productivity of the work force as well. Workers employed by the firm usually are local, as are the unions that represent them. Their primary concerns in working for a multinational firm are job security and benefits. Unions therefore are cooperating across national boundaries to equalize benefits for workers employed by the same firm in different countries.

KEY TERMS

expatriate 606
lingua franca 608
factual cultural knowledge 611
area expertise 611

adaptability screening 613
orientation program 614
culture shock 615
base salary 618

cost-of-living allowance (COLA) 618
foreign service premium 618
hardship allowances 619
housing allowance 619

tax equalization 620	minority participation 623	team building 626
education allowance 621	works councils 623	quality circles 626
self-management 623	quality of work life 625	work scheduling 626
codetermination 623	work redesign programs 625	flextime 626

QUESTIONS FOR DISCUSSION

1. Is a "supranational executive corps," consisting of cosmopolitan individuals of multiple nationalities who would be an asset wherever utilized, a possibility for any corporation?

2. Comment on this statement by Lee Iacocca: "If a guy wants to be a chief executive 25 or 50 years from now, he will have to be well rounded. There will be no more of 'Is he a good lawyer, is he a good marketing guy, is he a good finance guy?' His education and his experience will make him a total entrepreneur in a world that has really turned into one huge market. He better speak Japanese or German, he better understand the history of both of those countries and how they got to where they are, and he better know their economics pretty cold."

3. What additional benefit is brought into the expatriate selection and training process by adaptability screening?

4. A manager with a current base salary of $100,000 is being assigned to Lagos, Nigeria. Assuming that you are that manager, develop a compensation and benefits package for yourself in terms of both salary-related and non-salary-related items.

5. What accounts for the success of Japanese companies with both American unions and the more ferocious British unions? In terms of the changes that have come about, are there winners or losers among management and workers? Could both have gained?

6. Develop general policies that the multinational corporation should follow in dealing (or choosing not to deal) with a local labor union.

INTERNET EXERCISES

1. ExpatWomen.com is a comprehensive, global web site helping women living overseas (http://www.expatwomen.com/about_us.php). Real-life expatriate stories are an essential part of this site. What advice can you add for women who want to pursue an overseas experience?

2. Using the web site of Monster, the world's leading career network (http://content.comcast.monster.com/get-the-job/work-abroad/home.aspx), describe the unique challenges of careers in cities outside one's home country.

TAKE A STAND

Asia is home to among the highest paid expatriates in the world, while their poorer counterparts can be found in Australia and western Europe. The highest proportion of expatriates earning more than US$250,000 are in Russia (30 percent), followed by Hong Kong (27 percent), Japan (26 percent), Switzerland (25 percent), and India (25 percent), compared with a global average of 16 percent. The lowest-paid expatriates live in Australia and Belgium, with the majority (63 percent and 61 percent, respectively, versus 35 percent overall) of expatriates earning less than US$100,000.

As well as commanding high salaries, expatriates in Asia further recession-proof themselves by scaling back on the luxuries. Expatriates in Japan (ranking first, 54 percent), Thailand (second, 51 percent) and Hong Kong (third, 49 percent) scale down their spending on luxury items, such as holidays and leisure activities.

Asian countries are among the cheapest for accommodation, with expatriates in Malaysia, China, and India finding accommodation much cheaper than they did living in their countries of origin (50, 49, and 43 percent, respectively, allocating much less of their income toward accommodation, compared with 26 percent among expatriates globally).

For Discussion

1. You have the opportunity to become an expatriate to gain new corporate experience and to see the world. To also save some money, which country would you pick: Singapore, United Arab Emirates (UAE) or India? Why?

2. The opportunities to try new food and cultural dining experiences are often reasons cited as motivators to travel, but what about when you are an expatriate?

Source: HSBC Bank International, *Expat Explorer Survey 2009*, Report One: *Expat Economics*, http://www.offshore.hsbc.com.

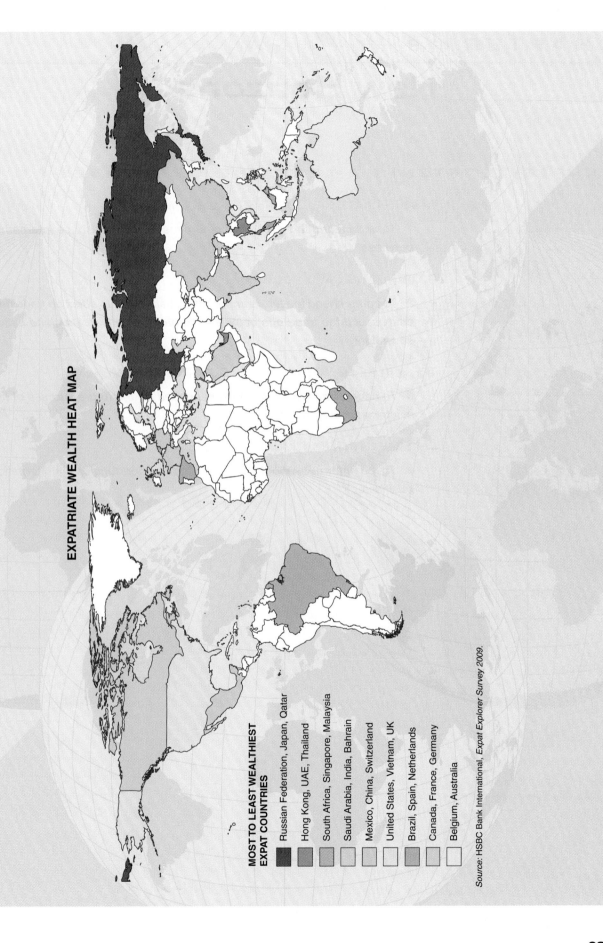

EXPATRIATE WEALTH HEAT MAP

MOST TO LEAST WEALTHIEST EXPAT COUNTRIES

- Russian Federation, Japan, Qatar
- Hong Kong, UAE, Thailand
- South Africa, Singapore, Malaysia
- Saudi Arabia, India, Bahrain
- Mexico, China, Switzerland
- United States, Vietnam, UK
- Brazil, Spain, Netherlands
- Canada, France, Germany
- Belgium, Australia

Source: HSBC Bank International, *Expat Explorer Survey 2009.*

631

New Horizons

CHAPTER CONTENTS & LEARNING OBJECTIVES

THE INTERNATIONAL BUSINESS ENVIRONMENT

1. To understand the many changing dimensions that shape international business

GLOBALIZATION AND FRICTION

2. To comprehend the future impact of globalization, its effect on trade negotiations, and the trade-offs between international collaboration and national sovereignty

THE FUTURE OF INTERNATIONAL BUSINESS MANAGEMENT

3. To understand the various factors needed for the future success of firms in international markets

CAREERS IN INTERNATIONAL BUSINESS

4. To be informed about different career opportunities in international business

Bankers See Scrooge Alive in London

Bankers in London received a lump of coal in their Christmas stockings in 2009 when Alistair Darling, the U.K. finance minister announced a 50 percent tax on all U.K. bank bonuses above £25,000 (about US$40,000). The "supertax," scheduled to be applied in 2010, affects about 20,000 bankers employed by British banks and all foreign banks operating in the United Kingdom. Perhaps the bankers who make such large bonuses might not be the modern equivalents of Bob Cratchit, but they reacted to Darling's announcement as if Ebenezer Scrooge had taken away the Christmas goose from Tiny Tim. Bankers in "The City of London" were maddened by the announcement, and rumors immediately began to fly that bankers would be leaving London in droves. This raised the issue that the United Kingdom government might be sacrificing the golden eggs that banking brings to England over years just for a juicy morsel in the short term.

Many bankers viewed the action as being unfair and pandering to public anger against the banking industry, which realized significant profits in 2009 while the economy was still in recession. Criticism immediately arose that the "supertax" would damage the city's attractiveness as a financial center, creating a stimulus for banks and bankers to look at other centers such as New York, Hong Kong, Singapore, Geneva, and Zurich. The British chairman of KPMG in Europe, the Middle East, and Africa criticized the tax as a "cheap shot" that might prevent talented people from coming to work in London. The CEO of the British Bankers Association stated: "Viewed from abroad, London may well look now like a significantly less attractive place to build a business."

Concerned over the already increasing role of government, London banks reacted to the tax with strategy as well as fury. Undoubtedly, U.K. leaders have been hearing from top bankers about the negative implications of the tax. Goldman Sachs tasked a team of executives to examine strategies regarding where to locate business units. Brokerage firm Tullett Prebon informed its staff that they would have the option of moving overseas to avoid the tax. Those options, however, may be limited as other governments, including France and the United States, also consider taxes on bank bonuses.

The U.K. government rejected the criticisms as humbug. It justified the move with the argument that banks were able to realize profits, and subsequently pay large bonuses, in large part due to the government's "bailout" of the banking system. In a joint article in *The Wall Street Journal*, former British Prime Minister Gordon Brown and French President Nicolas Sarkozy stated: "We agree that a one-off tax in relation to bonuses should be considered a priority, due to the fact that bonuses for 2009 have arisen partly because of government support for the banking system."

Working to ease the feelings of their top-performing executives, banks unrepentantly began looking for ways to mitigate the effects of the tax on their executives, such as adjusting the structure of overall salary and incentives compensation. Understanding how and where to operate in the face of rising government involvement will play a larger role in bank strategy in the next decade. Whether the "supertax" will help Geneva's rue du Rhône, or other financial boulevards, to surpass the twisting lanes of the city remains to be seen. One thing is for certain, Scrooge is a lot more popular among London bankers than Gordon Brown and Alistair Darling.

Sources: Gordon Brown and Nicolas Sarkozy, "For Global Finance, Global Regulation," *The Wall Street Journal*, December 9, 2009; Francesco Guerrera, Justin Baer, and Megan Murphy, "Fears Over Reach of UK Bonus 'Supertax,'" *Financial Times*, December 14, 2009; Patrick Jenkins, Brooke Masters, and Francesco Guerrera, "Bankers Furious at UK Bonus Supertax," *Financial Times*, December 9, 2009; Helia Ebrahimi, "Goldman Sachs Teams Could Quit the City Over Taxes and Regulations," *The Daily Telegraph*, January 4, 2010.

All international businesses face constantly changing world economic conditions. This is not a new situation or one to be feared, because change provides the opportunity for new market positions to emerge and for managerial talent to improve the competitive position of the firm. Recognizing change and adapting creatively to new situations are the most important tasks of the international business executive, as this chapter's opening vignette shows.

Recently, changes are occurring more frequently, more rapidly, and have a more severe impact. Due to growing real-time access to knowledge about and for customers, suppliers, and competitors, the international business environment is increasingly characterized by high speed bordering on instantaneity.[1] In consequence, the past has lost much of its value as a predictor of the future. What occurs today may not only be altered in short order but be completely overturned or reversed. For example, political stability in a country can be completely disrupted suddenly or in a short period, as was the case in Honduras in 2009, when President Manuel Zelaya was removed in an unexpected military coup. The months of confusion that followed showed a 38 percent drop in textile and apparel trade between Honduras and the United States. Companies became nervous over increased international pressure on the new government of Honduras as governments and multilateral institutions suspended aid and financing support until new elections were held.[2]

International businesses are always challenged by this kind of suspense because they prefer to quantify risk. A major, sudden decline in world stock markets leaves corporations, investors, and consumers with strong feelings of uncertainty. Overnight currency declines result in an entirely new business climate for international suppliers and their customers. Changes in weather patterns can result in dramatic spikes and troughs in commodity prices. The shockwaves of the financial crisis that began in 2007 will continue to reverberate globally as systemic vulnerabilities come to light. In all, international business managers today face complex and rapidly changing economic and political conditions.

This chapter will discuss possible future developments in the international business environment, highlight the implications of the changes for international business management, and offer suggestions for a creative response to the changes. The chapter will also explore the meaning of strategic changes as they relate to career choice and career path alternatives in international business.

THE INTERNATIONAL BUSINESS ENVIRONMENT

1. To understand the many changing dimensions that shape international business

This section analyzes the international business environment by looking at political, financial, societal, and technological conditions of change and by providing scenarios of possible future developments as envisioned by an international panel of experts.[3] The impact of these factors on doing business abroad, on international trade relations, and on governmental policy is of particular interest to the international manager. International businesses will need to deal with a complicated scenario: the increased role of governments, the challenges of terrorism and corruption, societal pressures resulting from globalization, the reshaping of existing political blocs, the formation of new groupings, the breakup of old coalitions, and the growing influence of emerging nations.

THE INCREASED ROLE OF GOVERNMENT

International trade activity now affects domestic policy more than ever. For example, trade flows can cause major structural shifts in employment. Links between industries spread these effects throughout the economy. Fewer domestically produced automobiles will affect the activities of the steel industry. Shifts in the sourcing of textiles will affect the cotton industry. Global productivity gains and competitive pressures will force many industries to restructure their activities. In such circumstances, industries are likely to ask their governments to help in their restructuring efforts. Often, such assistance includes a built-in tendency toward protectionist action.

Today, there is a substantial transformation characterized by the response of governments to the failures and weaknesses in the global economy and financial system that triggered the economic crisis in 2007. Public anger and frustrations arising from the crisis led to massive government interventions to prevent systemic collapse, stabilize financial markets, and reinvigorate economic activity. Policy and regulatory efforts to "reform" the system to correct the mistakes and abuses that were seen as causing the crisis will have major implications for the private sector in the coming years. Governments will move to increase regulation of complex financial instruments and require greater securitization for banks. There will be limitations on the size of banks, and overall government control over financial markets will sharply rise in the United States and the European Union. Political pressures to correct currency and trade imbalances will also increase. Government is now a key player in the international business environment, much more than in the past several decades, and is likely to remain that way.

Ironically, while the financial and economic crisis caused a loss of confidence in "American-style capitalism", it may have also worked to demonstrate the resilience and underlying strength of market economics. It certainly revealed the importance of emerging markets and showed the extent of interconnectedness among markets worldwide. Emerging markets and developing countries will have a "greater say" in the global economic system. When leaders of the G-20 nations gathered in London in 2009 and later that year in Pittsburgh, they pledged to work together to strengthen international systems and institutions. They promised to avoid the mistakes made during the Great Depression of the 1930s, when protectionist legislation in the United States led to similar actions by other countries and escalating trade restrictions.

Governments have taken economic actions that may contravene existing market liberalization agreements. Some nations, including the United States and China, have implemented initiatives that include "buy domestic" provisions for goods and services to stimulate local economies. Some of the reform efforts that are being proposed, such as limiting the size of financial services companies, may be in violation of commitments that signatory countries have made to the WTO. Efforts to complete the Doha Round of trade negotiations will be complicated by moves to increase regulation of markets.

Increased government involvement will also be manifested in interrelated efforts to tackle climate change, energy consumption, environmental damage, poverty, malnutrition, and food security. A potential "cap-and-trade" system, which would incent the reduction of emissions through bartering, will create both opportunities and limitations for businesses. The same will hold true for government actions to encourage development of alternative forms of energy. In the United States, agencies such as the Food and Drug Administration and Consumer Protection Agency saw their budgets double in 2009 in order to protect American consumers from unsafe products. In China, where milk tainted with chemicals resulted in death and sickness, the government has executed executives of the milk producers.

Governments cannot be expected, for the sake of the theoretical ideal of "free trade," to sit back and watch the effects of deindustrialization on their countries. The most that can be expected from the executive branch and from legislators is that they will permit an open-market orientation subject to the needs of domestic policy. An open market orientation will be maintained only if governments can provide reasonable assurances to their own firms and citizens that the openness applies to foreign markets as well. Therefore, unfair trade practices such as governmental subsidization, dumping, and industrial targeting will be examined more closely, and retaliation for such activities is likely to be swift and harsh.

Increasingly, governments will need to coordinate policies that affect the international business environment. The development of international indexes and **trigger mechanisms**, which precipitate government action at predetermined intervention points, will be a useful step in that direction. Yet, for them to be effective, governments will need to muster the political fortitude to implement the policies necessary for cooperation. For example, international monetary cooperation will work in the long term only if domestic fiscal policies are responsive to the achievement of the coordinated goals.

At the same time as the need for collaboration among governments grows, it will become more difficult to achieve a consensus. In the western world, the time from 1945 through 1990 was characterized by a commonality of purpose. The common defense against the Communist enemy relegated trade relations to second place and provided a bond that encouraged collaboration. With the common threat gone, however, the bonds diminished and the priority of economic performance increased. More often, economic security and national security were seen as competing with each other, rather than as complementary dimensions of national welfare that can operate in parallel.[4]

Policymakers also need a better understanding of the nature of international trade issues confronting them. Most countries today face both short-term and long-term trade problems. Trade balance issues, for example, are short term in nature, while competitiveness issues are much more long term. All too often, however, short-term issues are attacked with long-term **trade policy measures**, and vice versa. In the United States, for example, the desire to "level the international playing field" with mechanisms such as vigorous enforcement of import restrictions or voluntary restraint agreements may serve long-term competitiveness well, but it does little to alleviate the publicly perceived problem of the trade deficit. For the sake of the credibility of policymakers, it therefore becomes imperative to precisely identify the nature of the problem and to design and use policy measures that are appropriate for its resolution.

In the years to come, governments will be faced with an accelerating technological race and with emerging problems that seem insurmountable by individual firms or even countries alone, such as pollution of the environment and global warming. As market gaps emerge and time becomes crucial, both governments and the private sector will find that even if the private sector knows that a lighthouse is needed, it may still be difficult, time-consuming, and maybe even impossible to build one with private funds alone. As a result, it becomes increasingly important for government to work closely with the business sector to identify market gaps and to devise market-oriented ways of filling them. The international manager in turn will have to spend more time and effort dealing with governments and with macro rather than micro issues.

TERRORISM

The challenges resulting from the continuing threat of terrorism are among the highest priority issue for global marketing decision makers. Combating terrorism is regarded by international businesses as a regrettable fact of life and history, resulting in a continuous job for push-back to be conducted multilaterally and without compromise. Approaches proposed to address the root causes of terrorism include education, improved nourishment, and the ability to control one's own destiny. But there will also be a growing emphasis on national interests accompanied by limited readiness for multilateral solutions to terrorism. It will be a key challenge for governments to avoid coddling to temporary popular demands. Only with the collaboration of all parties concerned can local and regional protectionism and deglobalization be avoided. The greatest imperative will be to develop and maintain the power to execute peace.

trigger mechanisms Specific acts or stimuli that set off reactions.

trade policy measures Mechanisms used to influence and alter trade relationships.

While terrorism is universal in its detrimental effects on nations, it may have exaggerated consequences in developing nations, particularly in the Middle East, Africa, and central Asia. Corporations are likely to revive ethnocentric and polycentric policies and use export activities, rather than foreign direct investment, as the dominant form of dealing with certain foreign markets. They will either pull out from countries that lack law and order or service them only at a very high risk premium. In more developed markets, consumers appear willing to forgo dealings with unproved spaces and are even prepared to change their consumption patterns if needed for security considerations.[5]

CORRUPTION

Corruption is a major detractor from global welfare and local economic development as the enrichment of a privileged few robs from the hopes and aspirations of many. Its consequences are unsafe products, shoddily built roads, structures that collapse, and clinics with equipment purchased at high prices. The heavy human toll of the 2010 earthquake in Haiti was largely due to shoddy construction of housing stock with public funds. In such circumstances, vast public expenditures do not achieve the envisioned use and local interests suffer. While corruption tends to affect high-value government purchasing, it can also play havoc with consumer-goods supply chains. For example, product safety issues have closed several Asian markets to some consumer goods produced in China.[6]

Globally, corruption is estimated to comprise between 5 and 20 percent of contract amounts. There are two major kinds of payments in the corruption context; one consists of paying a foreign government (official) to do something they should not be doing (letting a contract on special terms, etc.); the second is to pay someone to do something they are supposed to do (facilitating payments). It is the first type of payment that really matters in terms of distortion of markets and economic benefits. This is not a victimless crime. Such corruption causes reduction of competition; lessening of quality; increases in prices; and the deprivation of those who lose out on goods, services, or funding. Poor countries suffer the most from bribery schemes because their citizens and companies have few, if any, alternatives. That is what makes rules against corruption so important. They help equalize the playing field and let all capable players participate.

There remains much work to be done, but over the past ten years, the extent of corruption has been reduced on a global level. The United States looked unrealistic, and perhaps even eccentric, when the U.S. Congress passed the Foreign Corrupt Practices Act (FCPA) in 1977, making it illegal for publicly held companies to bribe foreign officials. Many U.S. firms complained about this law, arguing that in many countries the payment of bribes was commonplace and tax deductible. They also claimed that the law hindered their efforts to compete internationally against companies from countries that had no such antibribery laws. Research at the time supported this claim, by indicating that in the years after the antibribery legislation was enacted, U.S. business activity declined precipitously in those countries in which government officials routinely received bribes.

Since then, the issue of bribery has taken on new momentum. Thirty-eight countries (8 more than its membership of 30 nations) are now subscribing to the OECD rules that prohibit the bribery of public officials, among them South Korea, Japan, Mexico, South Africa, and Argentina. Large companies such as Siemens have been taken to court and punished for paying bribes. Increasingly, companies state that the antibribery drive now gives them a clear rationale to say "no" when bribes are requested.

There has been progress, but bribery still exists. Here are several questions that remain: Should rules across borders be the same, particularly when it comes to the allocation of expenses and the treatment of family members, or should there be an acknowledged role for cultural differences? What is a realistic level of how low we can expect to drive this pernicious waste? Should we develop a time table to drive down corruption even further—either in absolute figures (down from the annual $1 trillion that Transparency International estimates) or down to, say, less than 3 percent of contract value? What should the punishment be for those who continue to engage in bribery? Should one just drive the companies and politicians who violate the public trust out of business? Would such steps be fair to most of the employees of these firms who had no inkling of illegal activities? Should there be a statute of limitations for prosecution, or should firms and individuals be forever exposed to the consequences of wrongful behavior in the past? Who should be given any disgorgement of ill-gotten proceeds: the party whose money was misappropriated or the one that did not receive the benefits to which it was entitled?

The bottom line: honesty and trustworthiness are highly important. For their implementation there is still much to be done. Decreased corruption levels will benefit countries, firms, and individuals.[7]

PLANNED VERSUS MARKET ECONOMIES

Much of the last century was shaped by the political, economic, and military competition between the United States and the Soviet Union, which resulted in the creation of two virtually separate economic systems. This key adversarial posture has now largely disappeared, with market-based economic thinking emerging as the front-runner. Virtually all of the former centrally planned economies are working on becoming market-oriented.

International business has made important contributions to this transition process. Trade and investment have offered the populace in these nations a new perspective, new choices, new jobs, and new alternatives for marketing their products and services. At the same time, the bringing together of two separate economic and business systems has resulted in new, and sometimes devastating competition, a loss of government-ordained trade relationships, and substantial dislocations and pain during the adjustment process.

Despite the particularly harsh effects of the world financial crisis and global recession, Russia and the countries of eastern and central Europe will continue to be attractive for international investment due to relatively low labor costs, low-priced input factors, large underused production capacities, and rising consumer power. This attractiveness should result in continued growing investment from western Europe for reasons of geographic proximity, attractive outsourcing opportunities, and the desire to offer economic hope to the populations of new EU countries.

There is newly emerging attention to the issue of whether market activities alone are sufficient to ensure the achievement of individual happiness. Many have begun to question key tenets of capitalism such as competition, risk, property, and profit. Therefore, companies cannot just reuse old approaches but must respond to changing societal requirements. Innovative and comprehensive responses to these requirements in products, packaging, pricing, distribution, and promotion are necessary.

GLOBAL FRICTIONS

The North–South Relationship

The distinction between developed and less-developed countries (LDCs) is unlikely to change. The ongoing disparity between developed and developing nations will continue to be based, in part, on continuing debt burdens and problems with satisfying basic needs. As a result, political uncertainty may well result in increased polarization between the haves and have-nots, with growing potential for political and economic conflict. Demands for political solutions to economic problems are likely to increase. With an estimated one-third of the world population living below the poverty line, many developing countries have been very adversely affected by commodity shortages and increases in food and fuel prices, as well as by the global economic downturn since 2007. The World Bank estimated that the recession will set back much of the progress that had been made in reducing poverty in developing countries and has also estimated that 40 percent of the world's 107 developing countries were "highly exposed" to the global economic crisis. The World Bank has encouraged the more developed countries to allocate at least a small portion of their bailout programs to help poorer nations. The president of the World Bank, Robert Zoellick, stated that "poor people in Africa should not pay the price for a crisis that originated in America."[8] After a summit of the G-8 nations in July 2009, the leaders of those developed nations pledged $20 billion in farm aid to help poor nations feed themselves, but African nations reminded the rich of a need to honor past commitments that had not been fulfilled.[9]

The World Trade Organization states that 2.6 billion people live on less than $2 per day.[10] Some countries may consider migration as a key solution to population-growth problems, yet many emigrants may encounter government barriers to their plans.

The developing countries of Africa continue as a very cool region for international business purposes. Given its size and diversity, it is unreasonable to expect similar economic conditions across all the nations of Africa. At any one time, some countries, their governments, their firms, and the well-being of their citizens will differ sharply from others on the same continent. Nonetheless, there is an overwhelming forecast of the growing plight of Africa. There will continue to be a lack of any realistic debate on regime change and while virtually all African governments want enhanced trade opportunities to earn their own way, they do not have the technical wherewithal to carry out such plans. Ongoing crises triggered by the HIV/AIDS pandemic and by weak infrastructure continue to inhibit the capability of many governments to run their economies. They require not just investment programs but also technical assistance on implementation procedures. International organizations need to go beyond the role of think tanks and become policy initiators. Nongovernmental organizations and private firms attend to some of the most desperate needs caused by poor world gaps, but can offer only a temporary bridging rather than a permanent filling in of such an abyss.

State-owned companies are seen mostly as inefficient, high-cost enterprises that are hotbeds of patronage and corruption. They typically are slow to adapt new technologies and, due to monopoly conditions and a lack of reward for excellence, provide a very low level of service. Similar shortcomings are likely to continue in the financial sector. Foreign investments continue to be largely in the extractive industries, such as oil, gold, iron ore, copper, and chromium, even though there are substantial new opportunities in other industries. Corruption, a lack of transparency, and the absence of equal treatment under law all impair confidence, commitment, and trust among potential investors from developed nations and have acted to dampen significant increases in investments. There must also be an emphasis on education and training since that triggers where the investments and jobs go.[11] It is not enough to expect a rising tide to raise all boats. There must also be significant effort expended to ensure the seaworthiness of the boat, the functioning of its sails, and the capability of its crew. Market-oriented performance will be critical to success in the longer run.

A new factor working in the favor of Southern Hemisphere nations has been the increased demand for minerals and commodities from China. In Africa, China has been reported to have investment activities in 48 countries, mostly aimed at extraction industries. China's strategic need for access to critical resources available in Africa and South America will lead to increased political linkages. China provides badly needed capital, arms deals, and, perhaps more importantly, does not lecture the African governments on their democratic lackings.[12]

environmental protection
Actions taken by governments to protect the environment and resources of a country.

The issue of **environmental protection** will also be a major force shaping the relationship between the developed and the developing world. In light of the need and desire to grow their economies, however, there may be much disagreement on the part of the industrializing nations as to what approaches to take. Of key concern will be the answer to the question: who pays? For example, placing large areas of land out of bounds for development will be difficult for nations that intend to pursue all options for further economic progress. Corporations in turn are likely to be more involved in protective measures if they are aware of their constituents' expectations and the repercussions of not meeting those expectations. Corporations recognize that by being environmentally responsible, a company can build trust and improve its image—therefore becoming more competitive. For example, in the early 1990s the first annual corporate environmental report was published; now, for many international companies, it has become established custom to publish such reports annually.

While some smaller companies may not have fully accepted the necessity of this kind of reporting, it will be increasingly more common for international businesses to take corporate responsibility very seriously, often in the form of a core strategy. Corporations are now openly setting measurements to assess their progress on the areas of their most significant impact, ranging from environmental areas like energy consumption, carbon emissions, clean water, chemical residues, and recycling to social areas such as labor practices, responsible consumption, nutrition, and health concerns.[13]

In light of divergent trends by different groups, three possible scenarios emerge. One scenario is that of continued international cooperation. The developed countries could relinquish part of their economic power to less-developed ones, thus contributing actively to their economic growth through a sharing of resources and technology. Although such cross-subsidization will be useful and necessary for the development of LDCs, it may reduce the rate of growth of the standard of living in the more developed countries. It would, however, increase trade flows between developed and less-developed countries and precipitate the emergence of new international business opportunities.

A second scenario is that of confrontation. Due to an unwillingness to share resources and technology sufficiently (or excessively, depending on the point of view), the developing and the developed areas of the world may become increasingly hostile toward one another. As a result, the volume of international business, both by mandate of governments and by choice of the private sector, could be severely reduced.

A third scenario is that of isolation. Although there may be some cooperation between them, both groups, in order to achieve their domestic and international goals, may choose to remain economically isolated. This alternative may be particularly attractive if each region believes that it faces unique problems and therefore must seek its own solutions.

Emerging Markets

The economic crisis that was triggered in 2007 dramatized the extent and impact of globalization and the integration of international economic activity. It also revealed key differences in economic vitality among countries. After precipitous slides, global companies looked to regain traction in new markets outside the developed economies, where consumer spending can drive new business growth. Business cycles inevitably move from troughs to new peaks. Yet the 2007–2009 trough for the developed nations has been significantly deeper than that for the developing Asian economies. Though curtailed, Asia grew. While most western nations experienced actual economic decline in 2009, China and India delivered gross domestic product growth in the range of 5 to 7 percent.[14]

Businesses in search of economic vitality (and most of them are), look to Asia and other developing regions for growth. For example, in early 2009, China overtook the United States as the largest auto market, and General Motors has identified China as its most important growth market. China is currently the number two market for shipments of personal computers, and Hewlett-Packard is in talks with mobile carriers in China about offering small, portable mini-notebook computers. India seems a likely market for that as well. Philips generated 30 percent of its revenues in emerging markets in 2008–2009.

Converts to market economics like China and India will continue to increase their impact on the world. Economic power will shift globally to Asia, in terms of investment, output, and the integration of eastern business practices. The CEO of Philips put this in a business perspective: "I could easily see that by 2015 around half of our revenue will come from these economies. That would put the center of gravity much more in emerging markets than it is today."[15]

Asian players will have a major role, but they will pursue differentiated paths. China will continue to be the player to watch. Success in China will be the crucial indicator of global competitiveness. "If you can make it there, you can make it anywhere" will be the guiding anthem for businesses seeking global competitive advantage. Chinese firms themselves will become more aggressive in pursuit of global ambitions. The Forbes 2000 list included 89 Chinese companies in 2009, and their share will keep on growing. The challenge for Chinese firms will be in adapting business strategies to become more consumer-driven with greater branding power.

India will continue to be the other major player. In its efforts to rival China for rapid growth, India will look for competitive advantage in services and technology. As India reduces its barriers to trade and investment, companies are likely to see it both as a primary place for process outsourcing and as an important market for goods. The country's linkages in the communications and information sectors are likely to soar. With an enduring democratic tradition, close alignment with the rule of law, and widespread facility with the English language, India will be a must for marketers. Understanding how to bridge the divide between the growing class of affluent urban Indians and the lagging bulk of the population in rural markets will be a challenge to new-market entrants. For example, Harley-Davidson opened sales in India in 2010, but most Indians will not be able to afford its starting price of Rs700,000 ($15,000). The bulk of the market is at the lower end, which is dominated by Hero Honda and the local Bajaj Auto.[16]

Trying to avoid being left behind by their larger neighbors, ASEAN nations have recognized the benefits of economic integration and have pursued trade liberalization initiatives with other countries. Signed at the end of 2009 the China-ASEAN free trade agreement established the world's third largest economic bloc behind the European Union and NAFTA. The benefits of removing tariffs in trade with ASEAN's third largest trading partner outweighed the fears by some, particularly in Indonesia, of Chinese products being dumped and local jobs being lost. ASEAN had already negotiated free trade agreements with India, Australia, and New Zealand.

In the western hemisphere, Brazil's continued economic growth and progress in trade liberalization has also attracted the attention of international businesses. In 2008, 26 percent of Volkswagen's sales came from China and Brazil alone.[17] Also, local Brazilian companies like aircraft manufacturer Embraer and beef producer Marfrig Alimentos are strong contenders in international business.

Overall the growth potential of these emerging economies may be threatened by uncertainty in terms of international relations and domestic policies, as well as social

Export Control Reform Is Necessary

Export controls are a principal means of defending a nation's high technology advantage over its potential adversaries. It is incumbent upon each nation to keep up with constantly evolving technology and adapt its export control system. As of late, the practices of many countries are ineffective and lacking efficiency. Without reform of their export control systems nations may not only lose competitiveness, but may also endanger their national security.

During the Cold War, export controls were successfully implemented in order to isolate the Soviet Union and deny or at least delay its acquisition of the high technology necessary to strengthen its military. Soviet strategy had to depend on brute force, while the Western allies were able to rely on their superior technology to defend their interests. The inability to develop technologically led General Secretary Gorbachev to open up his own country and to allow more freedom in eastern Europe, thus making dissolution inevitable.

Since the end of the Cold War, times, adversaries, and conditions have changed. Nowadays, many argue that export controls are no longer relevant. There is no unanimity among high technology countries about the nature of the threats they face. There is no longer a single nation in possession of a veto that can be wielded when there is disagreement. The current export control forum, the Wassenaar Group, is mostly concerned with keeping dangerous technology out of the hands of terrorists and rogue states.

However, many potential adversaries do not fit the profile of the Wassenaar Group. For example, China and Russia are certainly not rogue states. However, the U.S. Government retains a restrictive licensing policy towards them. The U.S. Government is consistently more limited than its European allies with regard to licenses for products and technologies destined for markets like China. Delays combined with foreign availability of products have meant lost business for U.S. firms and trade frictions with China.

To take but one example, China is the largest and fastest growing machine tool market in the world. The U.S. still tightly licenses five-axis machine tools, because they are considered to be the most sophisticated. These licenses can take from six months to a year to gain government approval.

The Swiss, Germans, and Italians license products with identical capabilities in weeks. Over the past decade the U.S. has lost 50 percent of its share in this fast-growing market. At the same time, the domestic U.S. market has shrunk by 50 percent.

Similar problems occur for semiconductor manufacturing equipment and scientific instruments. Without the cooperation and enthusiastic support between allies, the current export control system does not work. Unilateralism is dead. It costs jobs and does not accomplish its objectives.

There are important reasons to limit the export of one's technology. There are nations capable of substantial minacity—both economically and politically. A strengthening of their power could adversely affect the strategic balance. So, the issue is then, how can a country develop an export control system that receives support from other nations?

The Obama Administration is expected to issue a number of regulatory reforms regarding the way in which the U.S. administers export controls. It is expected that these reforms will provide a better definition of which items belong on the military-oriented munitions list and which items ought to be treated as dual use technologies. There are likely to be other reforms dealing with the mechanics of license processing, with the objective of speeding up licensing time and, most importantly, shortening the list of controlled products that require an individual validated license.

These national reforms are a good first step in what needs to be a global movement. Export controls can be made more relevant and effective if they are more targeted and administered more efficiently. But more needs to be done.

1. Nations need a defined reason and purpose for export controls.

2. Nations need to clarify why it is of interest for their allies to support controls, even if they'd prefer not to do so – and help their allies to adjust their perceptions and rules accordingly.

3. Nations need to expand the list of countries to which they have few or no controls.

4. Nations need to take steps that increase the chance that bad actors will be caught if they violate the rules.

National security and economic interests demand that export control reform becomes a priority. No nation can afford to go more years without addressing this issue.

Note: Paul Freedenberg served as Under Secretary of Commerce for Export Administration under President Reagan and is Chairman of MK Technology in Washington, DC. Michael Czinkota is a former senior advisor for export controls in the Commerce Department. He is a professor at Georgetown University's McDonough School of Business and the University of Birmingham in the U.K.

Source: Adapted from Michael R. Czinkota and Paul Freedenberg, *The Korea Times*, March 30, 2010.

and political dimensions, particularly those pertaining to income distribution. Concerns also exist about infrastructural inadequacies, both physical—such as transportation—and societal—such as legal systems. The consensus of experts is, however, that growth in these countries will be significant. In fact, with emerging economies dramatically outpacing their developed counterparts in growth rates, some international business leaders are looking to develop radically new strategies and products specifically designed to capture market share before global and local competitors preempt them.[18]

Values: Assimilation or Divergence?

Cultures around the globe will continue to become more similar to each other, particularly in the area of macro issues such as accountability, performance expectations, freedom accorded within society, and product preferences. Such cultural assimilations will be profoundly influenced by the United States, threatening less-dominant cultures. At the same time, it will be more difficult to impose overwhelmingly uniform ways of thinking due to an increase in regional and local sovereignty and calls for cultural protectionism even by multilateral organizations.[19]

History indicates that cultures rise and fall over time, with conflict in the process, regardless of information flows, insights, and learning. Otherwise, the world would now be speaking Greek, Latin, or Arabic. Already today, the use of English as a business language can create resentment and hostility. Companies are discovering that language also conveys cultural norms, which, in turn, reduce the creativity and local connections of their employees. It appears to be quite likely that firms will increasingly develop a norm stating, "we did not hire you for your English," which will introduce a new multipolarity to global management.[20]

Businesses will shift from western-dominated management approaches to more inclusive and integrated ones that include Asian cultural elements. Perhaps rule-based firms can add more "family feeling" and relation-based dimension to their organizational culture in order to provide more unity in far flung global organizations. There will be an increased value placed on charismatic leadership to unify global companies behind strategic vision. Firms with a charismatic leader—someone who has the ability to earn trust, who has good interpersonal skills, who is good at cultivation relations, and who is generous in his or her treatment of loyal friends and employees—may have a competitive advantage.[21]

On the micro level, however, ongoing culture clashes will continue, often giving a boost to fundamentalism. In many regions of the world, different cultural groups will increase their contacts as immigration increases. For example, it will be a new experience for many Americans to be exposed to large groups of Latinos and, perhaps even be confronted with becoming a regional minority. Similarly, "western" Europeans will become exposed to the influx and major competition from what used to be communist neighbors. A 2008 survey in South Korea found that 42 percent of the population had never spoken to a foreigner.[22] Some might find this advent of new neighbors unacceptable. All these moves will not leave cultures unchanged. Culture is the result of learned behavior and adjustment to new conditions. Opening up to others on a such a gigantic scale, as the world has done within a relatively short time, will bring some individual xenophobia, but also the reward of growing flexibility, better understanding, and rising tolerance levels. Mobility may well create a new generation of innovators and risk takers.[23]

THE INTERNATIONAL FINANCIAL ENVIRONMENT

The global financial and economic crisis that began in 2007 revealed major vulnerabilities in the functioning of global financial markets, errors in the common wisdom about financial instruments and risk management, and weaknesses in regulatory structures. Securitization had become rife with abuses; rating agencies, along with many others, failed to understand the risks involved in new and old financial instruments; and newer products such as credit default swaps created new stresses on the system. Firms that were "too big to fail" failed anyway. Executive compensation was not structured appropriately and did not provide the right incentives for systemic benefit.

Dramatic efforts to stimulate economic recovery and stabilize financial markets were made by the major economies in the world, sometimes in concert with each other but mostly independently. Global political leaders recognized the need to support large financial institutions, in both the private and public sectors, in order to restore order, prevent financial panic, and increase the flows of financial credit to businesses. In the midst of the crisis, however, when public anger against banks and financial institutions reached dramatic levels, there was common recognition that the situation was out of balance. Greed, excessive compensation, poor judgment about risks, and corruption among the wealthy few were jeopardizing the broader benefits that the financial system provides to societies—and reforms were needed.

In September 2009, Georgetown University and the *Financial Times* hosted the Future of Global Finance Conference to examine lessons learned from the financial and economic crisis that began in 2007 and what kinds of reforms were needed to prevent another global financial crisis. As the participants in that conference discussed the need and prospects for improved regulation and restructuring of global financial markets, the president of Georgetown stated: "We need to remember that free market wealth creation, economic relations between individuals and nations, and the distribution of profit and wealth must be conducted in concert with concern for the common good. If we forget this, then all of our work means little."[24]

At the same Georgetown conference, President Obama's director of the National Economic Council, Lawrence Summers, laid out a vision for a new economic order that would be less vulnerable to future instability and more in tune with broader American interests: "The new American economy needs to be more export-oriented and less consumption-oriented, more environmentally-oriented and less energy production-oriented, more bio and civil engineering-oriented, and less financial engineering-oriented, and more oriented to the interests of the middle class. I would suggest that a stronger, better regulated financial system is crucial for all of that."[25]

The global financial system has experienced dramatic change. Emerging markets play a much larger role in global finance. The basis of global economic decision making shifted from the narrow G-7 to the broader G-20 countries. The Chinese government and sovereign wealth funds have emerged as major institutional investors and sources of capital in the west. Governments around the world have vastly increased their roles in the financial system with the emergence of increased regulations to address the weaknesses in the regulatory structure of financial markets.

Amid calls for a "rebalancing of the global economy," there is a common expectation that returning the global economy to a stronger and broader pattern of growth may take years. While recovery may be more robust in emerging markets than in the developed nations, there are still concerns about financial bubbles remaining in those markets and that their commitment to financial markets may be fragile. The financial crisis revealed high levels of debt among nations that had embraced open markets as well as among developing nations. Developed nations have a strong incentive to help the debtor nations. The G-20 acted in 2009 to strengthen the role of international financial institutions like the International Monetary Fund and World Bank in assisting those nations.

The dollar will remain one of the major international currencies with little probability of gold returning to its former status in the near future. However, some international transaction volume in both trade and finance is increasingly likely to be denominated in nondollar terms, using particularly the euro. The system of floating currencies will likely continue, with occasional attempts by nations to manage exchange rate relationships or at least reduce the volatility of swings in currency values. However, given the vast flows of financial resources across borders, it would appear that market forces rather than government action will be the key determinant of a currency's value. Factors such as investor trust, economic conditions, earnings perceptions, and political stability are therefore likely to have a much greater effect on the international value of currencies than domestic monetary and fiscal experimentation.

Given the close links among financial markets, shocks in one market quickly translate into rapid shifts in others and easily overpower the financial resources of individual governments. Even if there should be a decision by governments to pursue closely coordinated fiscal and monetary policies, they are unlikely to be able to negate long-term market effects in response to changes in economic fundamentals.

A looming concern in the international financial environment will be the **international debt load** of the United States. Both domestically and internationally, the United States is incurring debt that would have been inconceivable only a few decades ago. For example, in the 1970s the accumulation of financial resources by the Arab nations was of major concern in the United States. Congressional hearings focused on whether Arab money was "buying out America." At that time, however, Arab holdings in the United States were $10 billion to $20 billion. Today the accumulation of foreign dollar holdings has reached much higher levels. As of 2009, total foreign ownership of U.S. Treasury securities had reached almost $3.5 trillion. China alone owned $799 billion and Japan owned $747 billion.[26] If one adds the private-sector debt held internationally, China might just become a leading retail banker to the world.

In 1985, the United States became a net negative investor internationally. A temporary weakening of the dollar is not to be confused with a long-term downward trend, particularly with a hands-off government policy. As a result, there are only short-term currency value advantages for new market opportunities abroad for U.S. exporters. Unless there are strong productivity gains, there will be continued losses of manufacturing capabilities and increased dependence on outsourcing. Yet, in light of highly competitive growth of the U.S. market, foreign funds will continue to finance U.S. trade deficits. While large and growing trade imbalances are unsustainable over the long term, the coming decade will still see the United States as a major market, and therefore growth engine, for the world. This debt level makes the United States the largest debtor nation in the world, owing more to other nations than all the developing nations combined. Yet this accumulation of foreign debt may very well introduce entirely new dimensions into the international business relationships of individuals and nations. Once debt has reached a certain level, the creditor as well as the debtor is hostage to the loans.

Foreign holders of dollars may choose to convert their financial holdings into real-property and investments in the United States. This will result in an entirely new pluralism in U.S. society. It will become increasingly difficult and, perhaps, even unnecessary to distinguish between domestic and foreign products—as is already the case with Kias made in Georgia. Senators and members of Congress, governors, municipalities, and unions will gradually be faced with conflicting concerns in trying to develop a national consensus on international trade and investment. National security issues may also be raised as major industries become majority owned by foreign firms.

Industrialized countries are likely to attempt to narrow the domestic gap between savings and investments through fiscal policies. Without concurrent restrictions on international capital flows, such policies are likely to meet with only limited success. Lending institutions can be expected to become more conservative in their financing, a move that may hit smaller firms and developing countries the hardest. At the same time, the entire financial sector is likely to face continuous integration, ongoing bank acquisitions, and a reduction in financial intermediaries. Customers will be able to assert their independence by increasingly being able to present their financial needs globally and directly to financial markets, thus obtaining better access to financial products and providers.

international debt load
Total accumulated negative net investment of a nation.

THE EFFECTS OF POPULATION SHIFTS

The population discrepancy between less-developed nations and the industrialized countries will continue to increase. In the industrialized world, a population increase will become a national priority, given the fact that in many countries, particularly in western Europe, the population is shrinking. The shrinkage may lead to labor shortages and to major societal difficulties when a shrinking number of workers has to provide for a growing elderly population.

population stabilization An attempt to control rapid increases in population and ensure that economic development exceeds population growth.

In the developing world, **population stabilization** will continue to be one of the major challenges of governmental policy. In spite of well-intentioned economic planning, continued rapid increases in population will make it more difficult to ensure that the pace of economic development exceeds population growth. If the standard of living of a nation is determined by dividing the GDP by its population, any increase in the denominator will require equal increases in the numerator to maintain the standard of living. With an annual increase in the world population of 100 million people, the task is daunting. It becomes even more complex when one considers that within countries with high population increases, large migration flows take place from rural to urban areas.

Asia is projected to see its urban population increase by 1.8 billion and Africa by 0.9 billion by 2050. The pace of urbanization has already accelerated in the last decade. As of 2009, half of the world's population lives in urban areas and that urban population "is expected nearly to double by 2050, increasing from 3.3 billion in 2007 to 6.4 billion in 2050. By mid-century the world urban population will likely be the same size as the world's total population in 2004."[27] Such movements and concentrations of people are likely to place significant stress on economic activity and the provision of services but will also make it easier for marketers to direct their activities toward customers.

The Coca-Cola Company puts these trends in perspective: "Estimates show that over the next 12 years, the worldwide population will grow by more than 800 million people. One billion new people will have entered the middle class, and nearly 900 million people will have migrated to urban centers. That means more consumers with more money, who have the ability to purchase more ready-to-drink beverages."[28]

population balance A concern in some countries where the population is being skewed by a preference for male children.

Of key concern in some countries is **population balance**. Technology has made it possible to predict with high accuracy the gender of a child. In many countries where family growth has been restricted, parents have developed a preference for male heirs. Over time, the result has been a skewed population in which males substantially outnumber females. Particularly for younger generations, this development has led to much greater difficulties in finding a partner for marriage. In consequence, some key cultural dimensions have changed. For example, it has been reported that in the state of Haryana, India, there are just 820 girls born for every 1,000 boys. Girls of marriageable age are in such short supply that some parents are not only dropping their demands for wedding dowries (which have a centuries-old cultural tradition) but are offering a "bride price" to families of prospective mates for their sons.[29] One can also argue that over time such imbalances can drive a society to develop family models such as polyandry—in which one woman may have more than one husband. It might also be possible that societies with a large surplus of young men are more prone to engage in wars.

Shifts in demographics are very important to international businesses. A trend to watch is the growth of elderly populations in Asia and Latin America, matching the trend in North America and Europe. "These older populations will become a growing customer segment for the financial-services sector as well as to providers of health care and appropriate household products. In particular, the lack of public support for the disabled and needy—often the result of cultural traditions—will create problems for generations caught in transition. At the same time, there will be major opportunities as older generations will expect more education, entertainment and involvement to enjoy their increased leisure time. As baby-boomer societies experience waves of retirement, companies will shift to increase employee longevity and loyalty. New and substantial incentives will be designed to maintain expertise within and to reduce the need to find specialists outside the firm."[30]

Mobility of the workforce is also an important area. "In a world of permeable borders, there will be more of an opportunity to pick up and move. The ability to prove and improve oneself as well as to access new resources is a powerful motivator for migration. The young and the not-so-well off are primary groups to be involved. The moves and behavior of the young will become an informational signal for others. A tremendous opportunity exists for regions to enrich their quality of life, through the acquisition of young, upwardly mobile immigrants."[31]

THE TECHNOLOGICAL ENVIRONMENT

The concept of the global village is commonly accepted today and indicates the importance of communication. Worldwide, the estimated number of people online in 2009 was 1.7 billion plus.[32] The United States and Canada have the highest percentage of their populations online with 253 million people (74.2 percent). However, Asia now has the highest online population with 738 million users (19.4 percent), followed by Europe with 418 million users (52 percent). While the global digital divide is closing, some areas lag. Africa has only 67 million users (6.8 percent), and some nations are far behind, such as Yemen, where only 370,000 people (1.6 percent) are hooked up to the Internet.[33]

For both consumer services and business-to-business relations, the Internet is democratizing global business. It has made it easier for new global retail brands—like **Amazon.com**—to emerge. The Internet is also helping specialists like Australia's high sensitivity hearing aids manufacturer Cochlear to reach target customers around the world without having to invest in a distribution network in each country. The ability to reach a worldwide audience economically via the Internet spells success for niche marketers who could never make money by just servicing their niches in the domestic market. The Internet permits customers, especially those in emerging markets, to access global brands at more competitive prices than those offered by exclusive national distributors.[34]

Amazon.com Large Internet-based service firm.

Starting a new business will be much easier, allowing a far greater number of suppliers to enter a market. With support from large multinational corporations, small- and medium-sized enterprises can now also be full participants in the global marketplace. Businesses in developing countries can now overcome many of the obstacles of infrastructure and transport that limited their economic potential in the past. The global services economy will be a knowledge-based economy and its most precious resource will be information and ideas. Unlike the classical factors of production—land, labor, and capital—information and knowledge are not bound to any region or country but are almost infinitely mobile and infinitely capable of expansion.[35] This wide availability, of course, also brings new risks to firms. For example, unlike the past, today one complaint can easily be developed into millions of complaints by e-mail and social networking sites.[36] In consequence, firms are subject to much more scrutiny

© NewsCom

Greenpeace activists protest against Genetically Modified Organisms and customer feedback on an international level. Overall, these new technologies offer exciting new opportunities to conduct international business.

High technology will also be one of the more volatile and controversial areas of economic activity internationally. Developments in biotechnology are already transforming agriculture, medicine, and chemistry. Genetically engineered foods, patient-specific pharmaceuticals, gene therapy, and even genetically engineered organs are on the horizon. Innovations such as these will change what we eat, how we treat illness, and how we evolve as a civilization.[37] However, skepticism of such technological innovations is rampant. In many instances, people are opposed to such changes due to religious or cultural reasons, or simply because they do not want to be exposed to such "artificial" products. Achieving agreement on what constitutes safe products and procedures, of defining the border between what is natural and what is not, will constitute one of the great areas of debate in the years to come. Firms and their managers must remain keenly aware of popular perceptions and misperceptions and of government regulations in order to remain successful participants in markets.

Even firms and countries that are at the leading edge of technology will find it increasingly difficult to marshal the funds necessary for further advancements. For example, investments in semiconductor technology are measured in billions rather than millions of dollars and do not bring any assurance of success. Not to engage in the race, however, will mean falling behind quickly in all areas of manufacturing when virtually every industrial and consumer product is "smart" due to its chip technology.

Advancements of information technology and convergence of new technologies will increasingly allow sophisticated new products at lower costs. Even though companies will be willing to adopt these new technologies faster than ever before, doing so will only provide a competitive edge if it is not done at the expense of ease to user and customer friendliness. While youth markets will be quick to use new capabilities, more mature buyers will be reluctant to invest in products that require a high degree of additional learning. From a consumer's perspective, simply excelling in technology has little intrinsic value. It is the application of technology to satisfy human needs and values, at a profit, that will matter for business success.[38]

GLOBALIZATION AND FRICTION

2. To comprehend the future impact of globalization, its effect on trade negotiations, and the trade-offs between international collaboration and national sovereignty

Globalization will continue. However, globalization issues will increasingly be understood to go far beyond the economic dimension and be much broader than "Americanization." One key question will be whether it is possible to compartmentalize globalization and whether some subcomponents can be adhered to while others are excluded. For example, if one discusses trade relations, must human rights, environmental commitments, and conservation of culture necessarily be part of such discussions? Similarly, do open trade relations with the outside require a country to simultaneously fully adhere to a market economy inside the nation? Clearly, there are linkages between all these dimensions, some of them more direct than others. The question is where to draw the boundaries between international collaboration and national sovereignty.

Trade negotiations continue to be fraught with difficulties. The differences between 153 member-nations in the WTO may simply be too great to be bridged in traditional ways. It has been said that nations can be differentiated between those that feed the world, those that fight the world, and those that provide the funding for the feeding and fighting. Such a trichotomy, however, seems to be oriented along the problems of yesteryear. From the perspective of national strategy, funding, feeding, and fighting are temporary symptomatic actions that reflect the needs of the moment.

More long-term actions may be a differentiation of countries and firms into four categories: those who grow; those who make; those who create; those who coordinate. Each category has very distinct needs, concerns, and desires when it comes to trade and investment. For some, the purity of their agricultural production is paramount. Others require a focus on skills and manufacturing employment. Innovators insist on the protection of intellectual property rights while the coordinators place major emphasis on free and open communication.

Initially, the discovery of this wide disparity of goals will act as a damper to negotiations and reduce the simplification of trade and investment flows. There will appear to be too much contradiction to achieve closer cooperation, leading to quite substantial delays in any international agreement. However, over time, a better understanding of trade-off capabilities between national or bloc objectives, as well as the pressure emanating from new bilateral and regional negotiations, will reinvigorate the activities of multilateral institutions. To some degree, the search for differences and disagreements will be replaced by the identification of commonalities. The willingness to share burdens and to do so with those resources that are most available in each nation may then provide the forward pedal power of the trade negotiation bicycle.

A key question will be whether nations are willing to abrogate some of their sovereignty even during difficult economic times. An affirmative answer will strengthen the multilateral trade system and enhance the flow of trade. However, if key trading nations resort to the development of insidious nontariff barriers, unilateral actions, and bilateral negotiations, protectionism will increase on a global scale and the volume of international trade is likely to decline. The danger is real. Popular support for international trade agreements appears to be on the wane. Frequent public demonstrations during WTO meetings indicate that there is much ambivalence by individuals and nongovernmental organizations about trade. It is here where international business academics are, or should be, the guardians who separate fact from fiction in international trade policy discussions. Qualified not by weight of office but by expertise, international business academics are the indirect guarantors of and guides toward free and open markets. Without their input and impact, public apathy and ignorance may well result in missteps in trade policy.[39]

International trade negotiations also will be shaped by restructured composition of global trade. For example, players with exceptionally large productive potential, such as the People's Republic of China, will substantially alter world trade flows. And while governments and firms will be required to change many trading policies and practices as a result, they will also benefit in terms of market opportunities and sourcing alternatives.

Finally, the efforts of governments to achieve self-sufficiency in economic sectors, particularly in agriculture and heavy industries, have ensured the creation of long-term, worldwide oversupply of some commodities and products, many of which historically had been traded widely. As a result, after some period of intense market share competition aided by subsidies and governmental support, a gradual and painful restructuring of these economic sectors will have to take place. This will be particularly true for agricultural cash crops such as wheat, corn, and dairy products and industrial sectors such as steel, chemicals, and automobiles.

The key to remember is that trade waits for no round. International business transactions will continue even without the conclusion of international negotiations. However, having an international agreement is likely to make world trade more efficient, more transparent, and more profitable for all participants. Through international negotiations, the greatest benefits for most people can be achieved. The large players will always be able to take care of their needs. It is the middle rank and the poorer nations that, absent rules, will continue to be fully exposed to the vagaries of power rather than the foreseeable outcome of rule-based trade decisions.

THE FUTURE OF INTERNATIONAL BUSINESS MANAGEMENT

3. To understand the various factors needed for the future success of firms in international markets

Global change results in an increase in risk. One shortsighted alternative for risk-averse managers would be the termination of international activities altogether. However, businesses will not achieve long-term success by engaging only in risk-free actions. Further, other factors make the pursuit of international business mandatory.

International markets are increasingly a source of revenue and profits for firms, as a look at the annual reports and investor presentations of multinational firms (available on their web sites) will show. International markets are vital to a firm's success because they provide sources of new customers, sharpen competitive skills, help cushion slack in sales resulting from recessionary or adverse domestic conditions, and provide long-term competitive advantage. Success in international markets may be crucial to the very survival of the firm. The experience gained will also help companies compete more successfully with foreign firms in their domestic market.

An indicator of this importance is the Edelman Trust Barometer which measures the degree to which educated audiences in 20 countries trust business. If trust in business reaches very low levels, as it did in western Europe and the United States in early 2009, public audiences will probably be more receptive to an increased governmental role in business issues.[40]

Companies must approach CSR in a strategic manner and define their roles in particular issues and the extent of their commitment and involvement in relation to the importance that the issue poses for their business. For example, TOMS Shoes has a program in Argentina that demonstrates best practices in supplier management and was recognized by the U.S. State Department with its 2009 Award for Corporate Excellence (ACE). The company provides shoes to disadvantaged people including children and disaster victims, aiding in the prevention of foot-borne infections, and providing mobility for children to obtain education.[41]

INTERNATIONAL PLANNING AND RESEARCH

Firms must continue to serve customers well to be active participants in the international marketplace. One major change that will come about is that the international manager will need to respond to general governmental concerns to a greater degree when planning a business strategy. Further, societal concern about macro problems needs to be taken into account directly and quickly because societies have come to expect more corporate social responsibility (CSR) from corporations. Taking on a leadership role regarding social causes may also benefit corporations' bottom lines, since consumers appear more willing than ever to act as significant pressure points for policy changes and to pay for their social concerns. Therefore, reputation management, or the art of building reputation as a corporate asset, is likely to gain prominence in the years ahead as the pressure on corporations to be good corporate citizens grows.[42]

Increased competition in international markets will create a need for more niches in which firms can create a distinct international competence. As a result, increased specialization and segmentation will let firms fill very narrow and specific demands or resolve very specific problems for their international customers. Identifying and filling the niches will be easier in the future because of the greater availability of international research tools and information. The key challenge to global firms will be to build and manage decision-making processes that allow quick responses to multiple changing environmental demands. This capability is important since firms face a growing need for worldwide coordination and integration of internal activities, such as logistics and operations, while being confronted with the need for greater national differentiation and responsiveness at the customer level.[43]

In spite of the frequent short-term orientation by corporations and investors, companies will need to learn to prepare for long-term horizons. Particularly in an environment of heated competition and technological battles, of large projects and slow payoffs, companies, their stakeholders, and governments will need to find avenues that not only permit but encourage the development of strategic perspectives.

Governments both at home and abroad will demand that private business practices not increase public costs and that businesses serve customers equally and indiscriminately. The concept directly counters the desire to serve first the markets that are most profitable and least costly. International executives will therefore be torn in two directions. To provide results acceptable to governments, customers, and to the societies they serve, they must walk a fine line, balancing the public and the private good.

© Ted S. Warren/AP Photo

The spotlight is on the first Boeing 777-200LR Worldliner as it is presented to employees and press Tuesday, Feb. 15, 2005 at the Boeing Co. assembly facility in Everett, Wash. The aircraft can carry 301 passengers up to 9,420 nautical miles and is considered to be the company's answer to the Airbus 380 super jumbo airplane.

INTERNATIONAL PRODUCT POLICY

One key issue affecting product planning will be environmental concern. Major growth in public attention paid to the natural environment, environmental pollution, and global warming will provide many new product opportunities and affect existing products to a large degree. For example, manufacturers will increasingly be expected to take responsibility for their products from cradle to grave, and be intimately involved in product disposal and recycling. For example, in the European Union, companies selling electrical goods products must conform to WEEE (the Waste Electrical and Electronic Equipment Directive) and provide methods for the collection and recycling of equipment, including such things as ink cartridges for printers. Those same companies must also conform to RoHS (Restriction of Use of Certain Hazardous Substances Directive), which governs the use of specific chemicals like lead and cadmium in products.

Firms will therefore have to plan for a final stage in the product life cycle, the "post-mortem" stage, during which further corporate investment and management attention are required, even though the product may have been terminated some time ago.[44]

sustainability The interaction of factors in nature and society which determine the longevity and continuity of an approach. Often used in the context of the environment, life styles, and corporate social responsibility.

Businesses can expect increased public attention to **sustainability** issues such as efficient energy use, reduced greenhouse gas emissions, and improved water use and reuse. Many companies are embracing their responsibility to address these issues and to keep the public informed about how they are doing in those efforts. Although some consumers show a growing interest in "sustainable" and truly "natural" products, even if they are less convenient and slightly more expensive, there is still substantial consumer confusion and a need for better information in those areas. In most developed economies, consumers will prefer products that are environmentally friendly but at the same time do not require too much compromise on performance and value.

Worldwide introduction of products will occur much more rapidly in the future. Already, international product life cycles have accelerated substantially. Whereas product introduction could previously be spread out over several years, firms now must prepare for product life cycles that can be measured in months or even weeks. As a result, firms must design products and plan their domestic marketing strategies with the international product cycle in mind. Product introduction will grow more complex, more expensive, and more risky, yet the rewards to be reaped from a successful product will have to be accumulated more quickly.

Early incorporation of the global dimension into product planning, however, does not point toward increased standardization. On the contrary, companies will have to be ready to deliver more mass customization. Customers are no longer satisfied with simply having a product: they want it to precisely meet their needs and preferences. **Mass customization** requires working with existing product technology, often in modular form, to create specific product bundles for a particular customer, resulting in tailor-made jeans or a customized car.

mass customization Working with existing product technology to create specific product bundles, resulting in a customized product for a particular customer.

Factor endowment advantages have a significant impact on the decisions of international executives. Nations with low production costs will be able to replicate products more quickly and cheaply. Countries such as China, India, Israel, and the Philippines offer large pools of skilled people at labor rates much lower than in Europe, Japan, or the United States. All this talent also results in a much wider dissemination of technological creativity, a factor that will affect the innovative capability of firms. For example, in 2009, almost half of all the patents in the United States were granted to foreign entities. Table 19.1 provides an overview of U.S. patents granted to foreign inventors.

Table 19.1   U.S. Patents Granted to Foreign Inventors in 2009

State/Country	Totals	State/Country	Totals	State/Country	Totals
Andorra	4	Germany	25,202	Peru	6
Arab Emirates	34	Greece	105	Philippines	69
Argentina	138	Guatemala	1	Poland	138
Armenia	6	Honduras	1	Portugal	89
Australia	3,976	Hungary	198	Romania	44
Austria	1,418	Iceland	39	Russian Federation	547
The Bahamas	18	India	2,879	Saudi Arabia	111
Barbados	4	Indonesia	13	Singapore	1,266
Belarus	12	Israel	4,550	Slovakia	29
Belgium	1,609	Italy	3,805	Slovenia	68
Bermuda	11	Jamaica	12	South Africa	205
Bolivia	5	Japan	82,396	South Korea	7,173
Bosnia and Herzegovina	3	Jordan	5	Spain	1,216
Brazil	422	Kazakhstan	1	Sri Lanka	12
Bulgaria		Kenya	2	Sweden	3,265
Canada	10,307	Kuwait	22	Switzerland	3,353
Cayman Islands	5	Lebanon	12	Syria	1
Chile	75	Liechtenstein	39	Taiwan	18,001
China, Hong Kong	1,027	Lithuania	14	Thailand	96
China, People Rep.	4,455	Luxembourg	86	Tunisia	10
Colombia	34	Macau		Turkey	85
Costa Rica	13	Malaysia	297	Turks and Caicos	1
Croatia	38	Malta	10	Ukraine	45
Cuba	39	Mexico	243	United Kingdom	9,771
Cyprus	9	Monaco	14	Uruguay	23
Czech Rep.	190	Netherlands Antilles	1	Venezuela	22
Denmark	1,439	Netherlands	3,883	Vietnam	0
Dominican Rep.	2	New Guinea	0	British Virgin Islands	9
Egypt	54	New Zealand	433	Zimbabwe	2
Estonia	24	Nigeria	1		
Finland	2,621	Norway	827		
France	8,561	Pakistan	13		
Georgia (Rep.)	3	Panama	6		

	Totals
Total patents issued in U.S. in 2009	456,321
Total patents issued to U.S. inventors	231,588
Total patents issued to foreign inventors	224,733
Foreign holders as a percentage of total	49.2%

Source: United States Patent and Trademark Office, Office of Electronic Information Productions/Patent Technology Monitoring Division. *Patent Counts by Country/State and Year All Patents—All Types, January 1, 1977–December 31, 2008.* Washington, DC, 2010, http://www.uspto.gov.

This indicates that firms need to make nondomestic know-how part of their production strategies, or they need to develop consistent comparative advantages in production technology in order to stay ahead of the game. Similarly, workers engaged in the productive process must attempt, through training and skill enhancement, to stay ahead of foreign workers who are willing to charge less for their time. Furthermore, we increasingly see that an organization's ability and willingness to learn and to transfer knowledge is becoming the most critical key to multinational success. Developing the nexus between people and processes is therefore a crucial corporate activity.

strategic alliances A new term for collaboration among firms, often similar to joint ventures.

An increase will occur in the trend toward **strategic alliances**, or partnerings, permitting the formation of collaborative arrangements between firms. These alliances will enable firms to take risks that they could not afford to take alone, facilitate technological advancement, and ensure continued international market access. These partners do not need to be large in order to make a major contribution. Depending on the type of product, even small firms can serve as coordinating subcontractors and collaborate in product and service development, production, and distribution.

On the production management side, security concerns now make it imperative to identify and manage one's dependence on international inputs. Industrial customers, in particular, are often seen as pushing for local sourcing. A domestic source simply provides a greater feeling of comfort.

Some firms also report a new meaning associated with the *made-in* dimension in country-of-origin labeling. In the past, this dimension was viewed as enhancing products, such as perfumes made in France or cars made in Germany. Lately, the made-in dimension of some countries may create an exclusionary context by making both industrial customers and consumers reject products from specific regions. As a result, negative effects may result from geographic proximity to terrorists, as has been claimed by some about textile imports from Pakistan.

The bottom line still matters. After all, money needs to be made and international business tends to be quite profitable. However, the issue of dependability of supplies is raised at many senior-management meetings, and a premium is now associated with having a known and long-term supplier. In the future, foreign suppliers may have to be recommended by existing customers or partners and be able to cope with contingencies before their products are even considered.

INTERNATIONAL COMMUNICATIONS

The advances made in international communications will also have a profound impact on international management. Entire industries are becoming more footloose in their operations; that is, they are less tied to their current location in their interaction with markets. Most affected by communications advances will be members of

Communication has become globalized, allowing the direct exchange of ideas and the building of relationships to an unprecedented degree.

the services sector. Companies now look to other countries to outsource key communications activities. Communications for worldwide operations, for example, could easily be located in Africa or Asia without impairing international corporate activities. India—with its highly educated and English-speaking work force, as well as a growing information technology infrastructure—has been particularly effective in establishing itself as an attractive location for outsourced communications activities.

For manufacturers, staff in different countries can not only talk together but can also share pictures and data on their computer screens. These simultaneous interactions with different parts of the world will strengthen research and development efforts. Faster knowledge transfer will allow for the concentration of product expertise, increased division of labor, and a proliferation of global operations.

DISTRIBUTION STRATEGIES

Traditional distributors are finding new ways to expand their offerings. For example, television's QVC has created a shopping mall available to more than 166 million homes worldwide.[45]

Even more important are the new distribution alternatives that are becoming available through changes in technology. Self-sustaining consumer distributor relationships emerge through, say, refrigerators that report directly to grocery store computers that they are running low on supplies and require a home delivery billed to the customer's account. Firms that are not part of such systems will simply not be able to have their offer considered for the transaction.

The link to distribution systems is also crucial to international firms on the business-to-business level. As large retailers use sophisticated inventory tracking and reordering systems, only the firms able to interact with such systems will remain eligible suppliers. Increasingly, firms create their own proprietary distribution systems.

More sophisticated distribution systems will, at the same time, introduce new uncertainties and fragilities into corporate planning. For example, just-in-time delivery systems make firms more efficient yet, on an international basis, also exposes them to more risk due to distribution interruptions. A strike in a faraway country may therefore be newly significant for a company that depends on the timely delivery of supplies.

In the past, cargo security measures concentrated on reducing theft and pilferage from a shipment. Now, international cargo security starts well before the shipping even begins. One result—perhaps unintended—of these changes is a better description of shipment content and a more precise assessment of duties and other shipping fees.

Carriers with sophisticated hub-and-spoke systems have discovered that transshipments between the different spokes adds to delays because of the time needed to re-scrutinize packages. While larger "clean areas" within ports may help reduce this problem, a redesign of distribution systems may lead to fewer hubs and more direct connections.

INTERNATIONAL PRICING

International price competition becomes increasingly heated. Many products will take on commodity characteristics, as semiconductors did in the 1980s. Therefore, small price differentials per unit may become crucial in making an international sale. However, because many new products and technologies will address completely new needs, **forward pricing**, which distributes development expenses over the planned or anticipated volume of sales, will become increasingly difficult and controversial as demand levels are impossible to predict with any kind of accuracy.

forward pricing Setting the price of a product based on its anticipated demand before it has been introduced to the market.

Even for consumer products, price competition will be substantial. The firm that introduces a product will no longer be able to justify higher prices for long; competitors' products will soon be of similar quality. As a result, exchange-rate movements may play more significant roles in maintaining the competitiveness of the international firm. Firms can be expected to prevail on their government to manage the country's currency to maintain a favorable exchange rate. Technology also allows much more interaction on pricing between producer and customer. Electronic commerce providers such as eBay (http://www.ebay.com) or Priceline (http://www.priceline.com) demonstrate how auctioning and bidding offer new global price mechanisms.

Through subsidization, targeting, government contracts, or other hidden forms of support, nations attempt to stimulate their international competitiveness. Due to the price sensitivity of many products, the international manager will be forced to identify such unfair practices quickly, communicate them to his or her government, and insist on either similar benefits or government action to create an internationally level playing field.

At the same time, many firms will work hard to reduce the price sensitivity of their customers. By developing relationships with their markets rather than just carrying out transactions, other dimensions such as loyalty, consistency, the cost of shifting suppliers, and responsiveness to client needs may become much more important than price alone.

CAREERS IN INTERNATIONAL BUSINESS

4. To be informed about different career opportunities in international business

By studying this book, you have learned about the intricacies, complexities, and thrills of international business. Of course, a career in international business is more than jet-set travel between New Delhi, Tokyo, Frankfurt, and New York. It is hard work and requires knowledge and expertise. Yet, in spite of the difficulties, international business expertise may well become a key ingredient for corporate advancement. Preparing for such expertise is, however, not easy, as Focus on Culture shows.

FOCUS ON CULTURE

Ensuring Student Safety Abroad

After the terrorist attacks of September 11, 2001, student safety has become a more vivid concern for many universities. International outreach has long been seen as an important element in undergraduate education. Today, universities must spend time and resources to ensure that those international experiences are safe. A generation ago students primarily studied abroad in western Europe. Now they are literally scattered around the globe, often in remote and isolated places. More than 154,000 U.S. students are studying abroad for college credit, twice the number a decade ago. Varying degrees of perceived anti-American sentiment worldwide has made university administrators very security conscious.

Kroll Inc., a New York–based global risk-management company with offices all over the world, has seen its security consulting business for colleges and universities double since September 11. Today, universities are developing contingency plans for their students studying overseas with planned responses for crises ranging from the breakout of war to students being taken hostage.

Many emergency response strategies include a complete extraction plan should all students studying abroad need to be brought back to the home campus. Before September 11 only about 10 percent of universities had contingency plans for students studying abroad. Now such plans are standard fare. Also common are predeparture orientation programs where students are informed about risky conditions abroad and how those risks vary from site to site. For example, Georgetown University's Office of International Programs advises students not to visit high-risk areas such as Zimbabwe or Somalia while traveling abroad and will not enter into formal agreements to send students to these locations.

Here are a few tips from the Georgetown University Office of Overseas Studies for students studying abroad:

- Keep a sense of humor and learn to laugh at yourself.
- Try not to pass judgment on the host country or culture.
- Learn from your mistakes.
- Take care of yourself: exercise, sleep, eat properly, and do things you enjoy.
- Join clubs, societies, religious affiliations, or other groups of interest.
- Adjust to the host-culture schedule.
- Make friends in the host culture and learn from them. Avoid trying to re-create America abroad.
- Learn key phrases in the local language in order to ask for assistance when needed.
- Try not to look and sound like a tourist. Walk and interact with confidence and an awareness of the surrounding environment in the host city and while traveling.
- Try not to attract attention to yourself as an American (baseball caps, T-shirts, speaking English in large groups in non-English-speaking countries, speaking loudly, etc.)
- Dress, speak, and behave conservatively to avoid misunderstandings. U.S. standards of dress, language, and behavior at home are not always appropriate overseas.

Sources: http://www.overseasstudies.georgetown.edu, accessed January 15, 2010; Annie Gowen, "Caution Tops Syllabus for US Students Abroad: Schools Seek Strategies to Counter Threats," *Washington Post*, June 21, 2003, B1.

To prepare, you should be well versed in a specific functional business area and take summer internships abroad. You should take language courses and travel, not simply for pleasure but to observe business operations abroad and gain a greater appreciation of different peoples and cultures. The following pages provide an overview of further key training and employment opportunities in the international business field.

FURTHER TRAINING

One option for the student in search of more international involvement is to obtain further in-depth training by enrolling in graduate business school programs that specialize in international business education. A substantial number of universities specialize in training international managers. According to the Institute of International Education, the number of U.S. students studying for a degree at universities abroad rose to 240,000 students in 2008. Furthermore, American students increasingly go abroad to complete business and economics degrees, not just for a semester or two. At the same time, business and management are the most popular fields of study for the 623,000 international students at American universities.[46] A review of college catalogs and of materials from groups such as the Academy of International Business will be useful here.

In addition, as the world becomes more global, more organizations are able to assist students interested in studying abroad or in gathering international work experience. For example, http://www.iiepassport.org, http://www.studyabroad.com, http://www.overseasjobs.com, and http://www.egide.asso.fr provide rich information about programs and institutions.

For those ready to enter or rejoin the "real world," different employment opportunities need to be evaluated.

EMPLOYMENT WITH A LARGE FIRM

One career alternative in international business is to work for a large multinational corporation. These firms constantly search for personnel to help them in their international operations. Table 19.2 lists web sites that can be useful in obtaining employment internationally.

Many multinational firms, while seeking specialized knowledge such as languages, expect employees to be firmly grounded in the practice and management of business. Rarely, if ever, will a firm hire a new employee at the starting level and immediately place him or her in a position of international responsibility. Usually, a new employee is expected to become thoroughly familiar with the company's internal operations before being sent abroad. Companies send managers abroad to reflect the corporate spirit, to be tightly wed to the corporate culture, and to be able to communicate well with both local and corporate management personnel. In this liaison position, the manager needs to be exceptionally sensitive to both headquarters and local operations. As an intermediary, the expatriate must be empathetic, understanding, and yet fully prepared to implement the goals set by headquarters.

It is very expensive for companies to send an employee overseas. The annual cost of maintaining a manager overseas is a multiple of the cost of hiring a local manager. Companies want to be sure that the expenditure is worth the benefit. Failure not only affects individual careers, but also sets back the business operations of the firm. Therefore, firms increasingly use training programs for employees destined to go abroad.

Even if a position opens up in international operations, there is some truth in the saying that the best place to be in international business is on the same floor as the

Table 19.2 Web Sites Useful in Gaining International Employment

Careers United
Web site: http://careersunited.org/
Bringing together employers and job seekers in
international development and humanitarian relief.

Council Exchanges
Council on International Educational Exchange
633 3rd Avenue
New York, NY 10017
USA
Telephone: (212) 822-2600
Fax: (212) 822-2649
Web site: http://www.ciee.org
Paid work and internships overseas for college
students and recent graduates. Also offers international
volunteer projects, as well as teaching positions.

Datum Online
91 Charlotte Street
London W1P1LB
UK
Telephone: 44 171 255 1313/1314/1320
Fax: 44 (0) 171 255 1316
E-mail: admin@dutumeurope.com
Web site: http://www.datumeurope.com/
Online database providing all the resources to find IT,
sales, and accountancy jobs across Europe.

Ed-U-Link Services
PO Box 2076
Prescott, AZ 86302
USA
Telephone: (520) 778-5581
Fax: (520) 776-0611
Web site: http://www.edulink.com/JobOpeningsMain
.html
Provides listings of and assistance in locating
teaching jobs abroad.

The Employment Guide's CareerWeb
150 West Brambleton Avenue
Norfolk, VA 23510
USA
Telephone: (800) 871-0800
Fax: (757) 616-1593
Web site: http://www.employmentguide.com
Online employment source with international listings,
guides, publications, etc.

Escape Artist
EscapeArtist.com Inc.
Suite 832-1245
World Trade Center

Panama
Republic of PANAMA
Fax: (011) 507 317 0139
Web site: http://www.escapeartist.com
Web site for U.S. expatriates. Contains links on
overseas jobs, living abroad, offshore investing, free
magazine, etc.

EuroJobs
Heathefield House
303 Tarring Rd.
Worthing
West Sussex BN115JG
UK
Telephone: 44 (0) 1260 223144
Fax: 44(0) 1260 223145
E-mail: medialinks@eurojobs.com
Web site: http://www.eurojobs.com
Lists vacant jobs all over Europe. Also includes the
possibility of submitting CV to recruiters; employment
tips and other services.

Expat Network
International House
500 Purley Way
Croydon
Surrey CRO 4NZ
UK
Telephone: (44) 20 8760 5100
Fax: (44) 20 8760 0469
Web site: http://www.expatnetwork.com
Dedicated to expatriates worldwide, linking to
overseas jobs, country profiles, healthcare,
expatriate gift and bookshop, plus in-depth articles
and industry reports on issues that affect
expatriates. Over 5,000 members. Access is
restricted for nonmembers.

Federation of European Employers (FedEE)
Superla House
127 Chiltern Drive
Surbiton
Surrey, KT5 8LS
UK
Telephone: (44) 20 8339 4134
Fax: (44) 13 5926 9900
Web site: http://www.fedee.com
FedEE's European Personnel Resource Centre
is the most comprehensive and up-to-date
source of pan-European national pay,
employment law, and collective-bargaining data
on the Web.

(continued)

Table 19.2 (Continued)

The Federation of International Trade Associations
11654 Plaza America Drive #120
Reston, VA 20190
+1-703-929-3672
Web site: http://www.fita.orig/jobs/
Job seekers with compliance and international skills.

HotJobs.com
Hotjobs.com, Ltd.
406 West 31st Street
New York, NY 10001
USA
Telephone: (212) 699-5300
Fax: (212) 944-8962
Web site: http://hotjobs.yahoo.com
Contains international job listings, including Europe.

iHipo International High Potential Network
iHipo Pte. Ltd.
185A/3 Joo Chiat Road
Singapore 427456
Web site: http://www.ihipo.com/
A leading international graduate careers website. The social network enables users (students and graduates) to find internship, jobs and graduate programs abroad.

Jobs 2 Me
Web site: http://www.jobs2me.net/job1.htm
Tips for international employment in how to obtain proper documentation.

Jobs.ac.uk
University of Warwick
Coventry CV4 7AL
UK
Telephone: 44 (0) 24 7657 2839
Fax: 44 (0)24 7657 2946
Web site: http://www.jobs.ac.uk/
Search jobs in science, research, academic, and related employment in the UK and abroad.

Medacs Healthcare UK Head Office
Medacs Healthcare Group
5th Floor
41-44 Great Queens Street
Covent Garden
London
WC2B 5AD
Web site: http://www.internationalhealthiobs.com/internationaljobs/
Health care recruitment in the UK has a number of vacancies for different professions.

Monster.com
TMP Worldwide Global Headquarters
1633 Broadway
33rd Floor
New York, NY 10019
USA
Telephone: 1 800 MONSTER or (212) 977-4200
Fax: (212) 956-2142
Web site: http://www.monster.com
Global online network for careers and working abroad.
Career resources (including message boards and daily chats). Over 800,000 jobs.

Nigel Frank International
The Stamp Exchange, Westgate Road
Newcastle Upon Tyne, NE1 1SA
UK
Web site: http://www.nigelfrank.com/microsoft-dynamics-crm-jobs-14.htm?page=1
A leading supplier of CRM recruitment solutions across Europe.

Organization of Women in International Trade
Web site: http://www.owit.org
Offers networking and opportunities in international trade. Has chapters worldwide.

OverseasJobs.com
Aboutjobs.com Network
12 Robinson Road
Sagamore Beach, MA 02562
USA
Telephone: (508) 888-6889
Web site: http://www.overseasjobs.com
Job seekers can search the database by keywords or locations and post a resume online for employers to view.

The Riley Guide
Margaret F. Dikel
11218 Ashley Drive
Rockville, MD 20852
USA
Telephone: (301) 984-4229
Fax: (301) 984-6390
Web site: http://www.rileyguide.com
It is a directory of employment and career information sources and services on the Internet, providing instruction for job seekers and recruiters on how to use the Internet to their best advantage. Includes a section on working abroad, including in Europe.

(continued)

Table 19.2   (Continued)

SCI-IVS USA
814 NE 40th Street
Seattle, WA 98105
USA
Telephone: (206) 545-6585
Fax: (206) 545-6585
Web site: http://www.sci-ivs.org
Through various noncommercial partner organizations worldwide and through SCI international, national, and regional branch development, the U.S. branch of SCI participates in the SCI network, which exchanges over 5,000 volunteers each year in short-term (2–4 week) international group work camps and in long-term (3–12 months) volunteer postings in over 60 countries.

Transitions Abroad Online: Work Abroad
PO Box 1300
Amherst, MA 01004-1300
Telephone: (800) 293-0373 or (413) 256-3414
Fax: (413) 256-0373
Web site: http://www.transitionsabroad.com
Contains articles from its bimonthly magazine; a listing of work abroad resources (including links); lists of key employers, internship programs, volunteer programs, and English-teaching openings.

Twin Employment and Training
2nd Floor
67-71 Lewisham High Street
Lewisham
London SE13 5JX
UK
Web site: http://www.twinemployment.com/

candidates/international.html
Work UK team organizes UK-based work experience and internship programs. The programs offer a great combination of English study and work skills training and then put them into practice in real-life host company placements.

Vacation Work Publications
9 Park End Street
Oxford, OXI 1HJ
UK
Web site: http://www.vacationwork.co.uk
Lists job openings abroad, in addition to publishing many books on the topic. Has an information exchange section and a links section.

Upseek.com
Telephone: (877) 587-5627
Web site: http://www.upseek.com
A global search engine that empowers job seekers in the online job search market. Provides job opportunities from the top career and corporate sites with some European listings.

WWOOF International
PO Box 2675
Lewes BN7 1RB,
UK
Web site: http://www.wwoof.org
WWOOF International is dedicated to helping those who would like to work as volunteers on organic farms internationally.

Source: European Union, http://www.eurunion.org.

chief executive at headquarters. Employees of firms that have taken the international route often come back to headquarters to find only a few positions available for them. After spending time in foreign operations, where independence is often high and authority significant, a return to a regular job at home, which sometimes may not even call on the many skills acquired abroad, may turn out to be a difficult and deflating experience. Such encounters lead to some disenchantment with international activities as well as to financial pressures and family problems, all of which may add up to significant executive stress during re-entry.[47]

OPPORTUNITIES FOR WOMEN IN GLOBAL MANAGEMENT

As firms become more involved in global business activities, the need for skilled global managers is growing. Concurrent with this increase in business activity is the ever growing presence and managerial role of women in international business. Even in regions where, because of cultured conditions, women might struggle to succeed as managers; expatriates are not seen as local women, but rather as "foreigners who happen to be women."

There appear to be some distinct advantages for a woman in a management position overseas. Among them are the advantages of added visibility and increased access to clients. Foreign clients tend to assume that "expatriate women must be excellent, or else their companies would not have sent them."

It also appears that companies that are larger in terms of sales, assets, income, and employees send more women overseas than smaller organizations. Further, the number of women expatriates is not evenly distributed among industries. Industry groups that utilize greater numbers or percentages of women expatriates include banking, electronics, petroleum, publishing, diversified corporations, pharmaceuticals, and retailing and apparel.

EMPLOYMENT WITH A SMALL OR MEDIUM-SIZED FIRM

A second alternative is to begin work in a small or medium-sized firm. Very often, such firms have only recently developed an international outlook, and the new employee will arrive on the "ground floor." Initial involvement will normally be in the export field—evaluating potential foreign customers, preparing quotes, and dealing with activities such as shipping and transportation. With a very limited budget, the export manager will only occasionally visit international markets to discuss business strategies with distributors abroad. Most of the work will be done by e-mail, by video conference, or by telephone. The hours are often long because of the need, for example, to reach a contact during business hours in Hong Kong. Yet the possibilities for implementing creative business transactions are virtually limitless. It is also gratifying and often rewarding that one's successful contribution will be visible directly through the firm's growing export volume.

Alternatively, international work in a small firm may involve importing. Decisions often must be based on limited information, and the manager is faced with many uncertainties. Often things do not work out as planned. Shipments are delayed, letters of credit are canceled, and products almost never arrive in exactly the form and shape anticipated. Yet the problems are always new and offer an ongoing challenge.

As a training ground for international activities, there probably is no better starting place than a small or medium-sized firm. Later on, the person with some experience may find work with a trading or export management company, resolving other people's problems and concentrating almost exclusively on the international arena.

SELF-EMPLOYMENT

A third alternative is to hang up a consultant's shingle or to establish a trading firm. Many companies are in need of help for their international business efforts and are prepared to part with a portion of their profits in order to receive it. Yet it requires in-depth knowledge and broad experience to make a major contribution from the outside or to successfully run a trading firm.

Specialized services that might be offered by a consultant include international market research, international strategic planning, or, particularly desirable, beginning-to-end assistance for international entry or international negotiations. The advantage of this career option is the opportunity to become a true international entrepreneur. Consultants and those who conduct their own export-import or foreign direct investment activities work at a higher degree of risk than those who are not self-employed, but they have an opportunity for higher rewards.

THE COST PER DIEM IN THE WORLD'S MAJOR BUSINESS CITIES
(in U.S. Dollars)

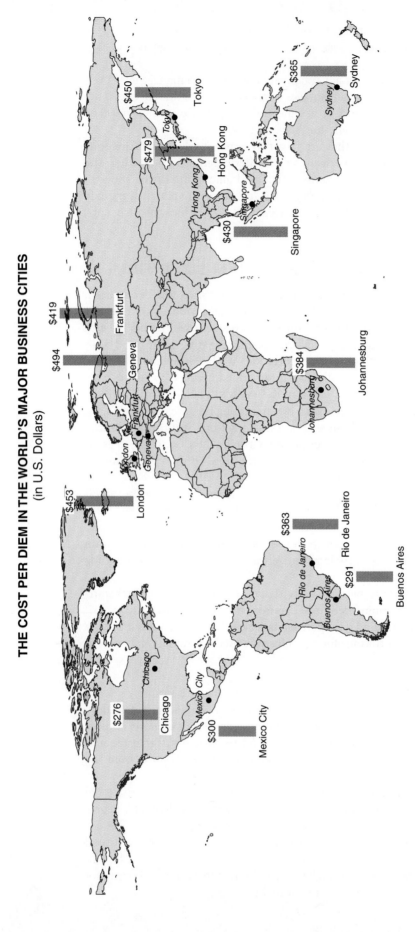

$453 London

$494 Geneva

$419 Frankfurt

$450 Tokyo

$479 Hong Kong

$430 Singapore

$365 Sydney

$384 Johannesburg

$276 Chicago

$300 Mexico City

$363 Rio de Janeiro

$291 Buenos Aires

Source: U.S. Department of State

This concludes the text portion of this book. We hope you have worked with it, learned from it, and enjoyed it. It is important for us to also learn from our customers. Please provide us with feedback, both praise and suggestions for improvement by contacting us:

czinkotm@georgetown.edu
ronkaii@georgetown.edu.
moffettm@t-bird.edu

You can also find regular updates and often discussion contributions on michaelczinkota.com

Thank you for being an international business student!

SUMMARY

This final chapter has provided an overview of the environmental changes facing international managers and alternative managerial responses to the changes. International business is undergoing continuous and complex changes. It affords many challenges and opportunities. "May you live in interesting times" is an ancient Chinese curse. For the international manager, this curse is a call to action. Observing changes and analyzing how best to incorporate them into the international business mission is the bread and butter of the manager. The frequent changes make international business so fascinating to those active in the field. International business managers could well have been the subjects of the old Native American proverb: "When storms come about, little birds seek to shelter while eagles soar." May you be an eagle!

KEY TERMS

trigger mechanisms   636
trade policy measures   636
environmental protection   640
international debt load   645

population stabilization   646
population balance   646
Amazon.com   647
sustainability   652

mass customization   652
strategic alliances   654
forward pricing   655

QUESTIONS FOR DISCUSSION

1. For many developing countries, debt repayment and trade are closely linked. What does protectionism mean to them?

2. Should one worry about the fact that the United States is a debtor nation?

3. How would our lives and our society change if imports were banned?

4. How have security concerns changed the way international firms do business?

INTERNET EXERCISES

1. Find the web sites of international organizations that promote business development. Identify five corporate members with whom you might seek future employment. Why are you particularly interested in them? What regions might interest you? Possible web sites Include Council of the Americas (http://coa.counciloftheamericas.org/), U.S.–India Business Council (http://www.usibc.com), U.S.–China Business Council (http://www.uschina.org/), U.S.-ASEAN Business Council (http://www.us-asean.org/) U.S.–Russia Business Council (http:// www.usrsbc .org), and TransAtlantic Business Dialogue (http://www.tabd.com/).

2. The web site http://www.overseasjobs.com provides valuable information for those interested in jobs overseas. What skills do international employers seem to value most? Peruse the job listings and find several jobs that you might be interested in. Also take a look at the profiles of several international companies that you might be interested in working for. What characteristics do the international firms listed here possess?

TAKE A STAND

It is virtually impossible to be totally protected from terrorism. However, some safety measures can be developed. For example, to reduce the exposure of students to terrorist attacks, it helps to keep them all at home. Another reduction of risk can be achieved by not letting them be exposed to anyone outside their familiar groups. Say goodbye to study abroad programs; forget about international students and scholars!

For Discussion

1. Does such an approach make things better?

2. What do you propose?

NOVA INTERNATIONAL (MACEDONIA)

The summer of 2003 in Skopje, Macedonia, had been one of the hottest on record. Ivan Novakovski, however, was not out enjoying the cool of the evening and the lively nightlife of the sidewalk cafés of Skopje, but sat in his office at the Nova International School. As both the Assistant Director of Nova and a son of the founding family, Ivan was concerned that the school was making a mistake by continuing to price and invoice all customers in U.S. dollars. As the glow of the Millennium Cross—the largest free-standing cross in the world—shone from the top of Vodno Mountain overlooking Skopje, he returned to his analysis.

MACEDONIA AND NOVA INTERNATIONAL

Macedonia is a landlocked country on the Balkan Peninsula in southeastern Europe. Formerly the southernmost part of the Socialist Federated Republic of Yugoslavia, the country's 2 million inhabitants gained their independence from Yugoslavia on September 8, 1991. The country had long been the poorest of the Yugoslavian provinces, and the years following independence were difficult as the economy stumbled into market economics while suffering the ravages of a region wracked by war. Macedonian businesses were no longer protected competitors in the Yugoslavian marketplace, and many found themselves unprepared for the shock of open markets and competition.

The war in nearby Bosnia, the imposition of international sanctions on Serbia, and the neighboring Kosovo crisis in 1999 all delivered successive shocks to Macedonia's struggling trade-based economy at the end of the millennium. In 2001 economic conditions worsened again, this time as a result of an ethnic Albanian uprising with the country. Gross domestic product shrank 4.5 percent, borders were periodically closed, and government spending spiraled into deficit as security expenditures rose. Finally, with an unusual degree of quiet, 2002 and 2003 had brought two full years of relative calm and slow economic recovery.

Venera Novakovski opened the Nova Language Institute in Skopje in late 1991, immediately following Macedonian independence. Like many markets throughout eastern

and southern Europe, the movement towards free market economics had created a number of international business opportunities, one of which was language training. The language institute's growing reputation led to the expansion of the school in 1996 from language training only to become the first private school in Macedonia, providing both primary and secondary educational services. Because Nova was the first private educational institution in Macedonia, it found itself classified as a for-profit company, complete with tax liabilities. Macedonia had not developed a not-for-profit institutional and legal structure which most educational institutions worldwide depend upon.

In the early years Nova was categorized as the "American School," where foreign expatriates sent their children to school while stationed in Macedonia. These expatriates were often in Macedonia for extended stays (two to five years, typically), and finding educational services which were both English-language and accredited outside of Macedonia was very valuable. The expatriate

Exhibit 1   Macedonia and Its Neighbors

© Central Intelligence Agency Factbook

Exhibit 2　　Nova International Macedonia's Income Statement, 2000–2004e (denar)

Nova Revenues	2000	2001	2002	2003	2004e
Tuition per student (US$)	$2,000	$2,200	$2,400	$2,400	$2,400
Avg spot rate (Den/US$)	65.904	68.037	64.350	54.322	50.000
Tuition per student (Den)	131,808	149,681	154,440	130,373	120,000
Percent change (y-o-y)	*11.0%*	*13.6%*	*3.2%*	*−15.6%*	*−8.0%*
Student enrollment	152	163	188	193	202
Total revenues (Den)	20,034,816 ден.	24,398,068 ден.	29,034,720 ден.	25,161,950 ден.	24,240,000 ден.
Percent change (y-o-y)	*16.3%*	*21.8%*	*19.0%*	*−13.3%*	*−3.7%*
Nova Costs					
Faculty costs:	5,836,890	6,101,752	6,310,143	6,518,420	6,709,444
Local faculty (Den)	2,397,560	2,529,426	2,574,955	2,605,855	2,644,943
Foreign faculty (euros)	56,688	58,672	61,606	63,762	66,631
Avg spot rate (Den/euro)	60.67	60.89	60.63	61.36	61.00
Foreign faculty (Den)	3,439,330	3,572,327	3,735,188	3,912,565	4,064,501
General & administrative expenses	764,280	806,315	820,829	830,679	843,139
Energy costs	1,325,898	1,458,488	1,553,290	1,749,004	1,871,434
Materials and consumables	1,187,246	1,252,545	1,275,090	1,290,391	1,309,747
Total operating costs	9,114,314	9,619,100	9,959,352	10,388,494	10,733,765
Percent change in op costs	*4.7%*	*5.5%*	*3.5%*	*4.3%*	*3.3%*
EBITDA (operating profit)	10,920,502	14,778,968	19,075,368	14,773,456	13,506,235
Operating margin	*54.5%*	*60.6%*	*65.7%*	*58.7%*	*55.7%*
Less depreciation	3,235,000	3,568,000	3,946,500	2,647,060	3,325,000
EBIT	7,685,502	11,210,968	15,128,868	12,126,396	10,181,235
Less interest	7,654,800	10,370,000	5,169,000	6,753,000	5,975,000
Earnings Before Taxes	30,702	840,968	9,959,868	5,373,396	4,206,235
Less taxes @ 15%	4,605	126,145	1,493,980	806,009	630,935
Net income	26,096	714,823	8,465,888	4,567,387	3,575,300
Return on revenue	*0.1%*	*2.9%*	*29.2%*	*18.2%*	*14.7%*
Financial Notes (all values for 2004 are forecasts):					
Consumer prices, Macedonia	100.0	105.5	107.4	108.7	109.6
Percent change in CPs	5.8%	5.5%	1.8%	1.2%	0.8%
Percent change in Macedonian costs	5.8%	5.5%	1.8%	1.2%	1.5%
Percent change in Euro Faculty costs	2.5%	3.5%	5.0%	3.5%	4.5%
Percent change in Energy costs	16.0%	10.0%	6.5%	12.6%	7.0%
Avg spot rate (US$/euro)	0.9206	0.8949	0.9422	1.1296	1.2426
Faculty/Total Costs	64.0%	63.4%	63.4%	62.7%	62.5%
Financing Expenses/Sales	38.2%	42.5%	17.8%	26.8%	24.6%

community was growing rapidly as more and more multinational companies were investing in Macedonia, and as a result more foreign governments were increasing their presence and delegations in the former Yugoslavian state.

The Novakovski family was particularly proud of the multitude of accreditation hurdles which they had been able to overcome in a short period of time. Nova was now accredited by the Northwest Association of Accredited Schools in the United States and the U.S. Department of State, and had been a facilitator for the SAT and ACT tests used in North America for student educational advancement for a number of years. Student enrollment growth was strong and steady. By 2003 there were 193 students enrolled in Nova. Roughly 25 percent of the high school students (grades 9–12) and 50 percent of the primary school students (grades 1–8) were international. It was expected that if the school were to actually expand some specific programs and recreational facilities, it could easily be looking at more than 400 students in three to four years. The school's core educational facilities were capable of supporting 450 students on a full time basis.

As illustrated by Exhibit 2, Nova's income statement for the 2000–2004 period, the school had seen its financial results finally brighten in recent years. Although marginally profitable in 2000 and 2001, the school had finally shown substantial profits in 2002 and 2003. Profitability had seemingly peaked in 2002 with a 29 percent return on revenue. The Novakovski family's many years of sacrifice and commitment was finally starting to pay off.

But 2003 had proven a bit of disappointment, as revenues fell and costs rose. The school had closed 2003 with 4.5 million Macedonian denar (Den or MKD) in profit, down considerably from the year before. Ivan believed the problem to be in the school's revenue structure, not its cost structure. Costs had been tightly controlled for many years, and 2003 was no different. But the school's revenues had fallen two years running, and it was largely a result of the rising value of the Macedonian denar. This alone caused a bit of chuckle on Ivan's part; the denar had long been the subject of ridicule, but was now rising against the downtrodden U.S. dollar. The Macedonian denar had been introduced in April of 1992 immediately following independence. (Its name was derived from the ancient Roman monetary unit, the *denarius*.) If Ivan's estimates for the coming year were correct, 2004 would show little improvement.

NOVA'S CURRENCY

Because of its origins as a language institute and its early relationship with both the U.S. State Department and a number of major American companies, tuition was priced and paid in U.S. dollars. This was true for all students, domestic or international, and had never really met with any significant opposition. As an English language school, the payment of tuition in dollars was in many ways considered just another indicator of the school's more global culture.

The Macedonian denar (Den) was now pegged within a small band to the euro. Macedonia was officially classified as a European Union Candidate Country, which meant that it had no guaranteed membership date, but that it was expected to move toward membership in the foreseeable future. As a result, the Macedonian government managed the value of the denar versus the euro—it had hovered around Den60/€ for years, but largely ignored value changes against the U.S. dollar. The denar had weakened steadily against the dollar from 1995 to mid-2002. But since then the direction had

changed, with the denar closing in on Den50/$. Although not shown, the dollar itself had fallen considerably against the euro in recent years. The dollar had fallen to $1.17/€ in June of 2003. Although it had recovered a bit in the last two months, trading at $1.13/€, the magnitude of its fall had been very unsettling. Dollar tuition was now resulting in fewer and fewer euros and Macedonian denar.

Ivan's worry was that Nova's currency of cash flows was not really being well-served by tuition priced, stated, and paid in U.S. dollars. It was the currency of tradition at Nova, and it was the preferred currency of the American expatriate customer base. Although this expatriate segment was not more than 20 percent of all students, it had been the primary growth segment in the past few years.

Nova's cash inflows were simple: receipts from tuition made up 99 percent of the school's net revenues (individual and corporate contributions occasionally yielded some income). The expense side, however, was a bit more diverse. Roughly half of operating expenses were faculty cost, both salary and benefits. Of that, most were paid in euros. This was a result of many faculty members being visitors from many other European countries. In addition to the operating expenses, financing costs—interest—were paid in euros as a result of recent debt extended by the World Bank to Nova for facilities renewal and expansion.[1]

With 75 percent of all revenues coming from Macedonian residents, domestic residents, Ivan wondered whether the tuition should not be paid in denar or euros rather than dollars. But where was the school's future growth really based? Many of the Macedonian students were now moving on to educational and job opportunities

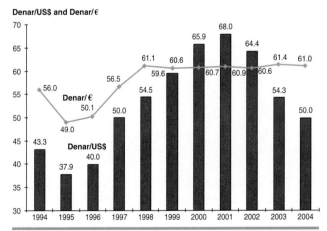

Exhibit 3   Macedonian Denar Exchange Rates, 1994–2004

Source: International Financial Statistics, IMF. All rates are annual average. 2004 values are forecasts.

in western Europe. And the Macedonian government had continued to pursue EU membership aggressively, arguing that the true economic future of the country rested with the EU. EU membership meant the euro as the currency of choice.

Case Questions

1. Why has Nova International used the U.S. dollar as the currency of invoice since its inception? Would it make sense to change this to either the Macedonian denar or the euro?

2. Take a hard look at the income statement presented in Exhibit 2. What is your assessment of the school's business prospects? Why have revenues seemingly fallen in recent years? What costs have the greatest impact on the school's financial results over the period shown?

3. What would you recommend that Ivan Novakovski do about tuition? If you believe Nova should change to the euro or denar, at what rate would you set the new tuition payment?

Note

1. One of the negative accoutrements of having a large expatriate consumer base, one containing the children of many foreign government and business officials, was that security measures in the post–9/11 world were extensive. For example, all of Nova's glass window exterior had been replaced with bullet-proof glass as an added precaution. Although Nova had never had a single criminal or terrorist event, the investment was considered necessary by the Novakovski family to assure parents that their children were in a safe and secure environment.

PORSCHE CHANGES TRACK

Yes, of course we have heard of shareholder value. But that does not change the fact that we put customers first, then workers, then business partners, suppliers and dealers, and then shareholders.
— Dr. Wendelin Wiedeking, CEO, Porsche,
Die Zeit, April 17, 2005

Porsche had always been different. Statements by Porsche leadership, like the one above, always made Veselina (Vesi) Dinova nervous about the company's attitude about creating shareholder value. The company was a paradox. Porsche's attitudes and activities were like that of a family owned firm, but it had succeeded in creating substantial shareholder value for more than a decade. Porsche's CEO, Dr. Wendelin Wiedeking, had been credited with clarity of purpose and sureness of execution. As one colleague described him: "He grew up PSD: poor, smart, and driven."

Porsche's management had created confusion in the marketplace as to which value proposition Porsche presented. Was Porsche continuing to develop an organizational focus on *shareholder value*, or was it returning to its more traditional German roots of *German cronyism*? Simply put, was Porsche's leadership pursuing family objectives at the expense of the shareholder?

PORSCHE AG

Porsche AG was a publicly traded closely held German-based auto manufacturer. Dr. Wendelin Wiedeking, had returned the company to both status and profitability since taking over the company in 1993. Immediately after taking over Porsche, he had killed the 928 and 968 model platforms to reduce complexity and cost, although at the time this left the company with only one platform, the 911. Wiedeking had then brought in a group of Japanese manufacturing consultants, in the Toyota tradition, who led a complete overhaul of the company's manufacturing processes.

Although Porsche was traded on the Frankfurt Stock Exchange (and associated German exchanges), control of the company remained firmly in the hands of the founding families, the Porsche and Piëch families. Porsche had two classes of shares, *ordinary* and *preference*.

The two families held all 8.75 million *ordinary shares*— the shares which held all voting rights. The second class of share, *preference shares*, participated only in profits. All 8.75 million preference shares were publicly traded. Approximately 50 percent of all preference shares were held by large institutional investors in the United States, Germany, and the United Kingdom; 14 percent were held by the Porsche and Piëch families; and 36 percent were held by small private investors. As noted by the chief financial officer, Holger Härter, "As long as the two families hold on to their stock portfolios, there won't be any external influence on company-related decisions. I have no doubt that the families will hang on to their shares."

Porsche was somewhat infamous for its independent thought and occasional stubbornness when it came to disclosure and compliance with reporting requirements—the prerequisites of being publicly traded. In 2002 the company had chosen not to list on the New York Stock Exchange after the passage of the Sarbanes-Oxley Act. The company pointed to the specific requirement of Sarbanes-Oxley that senior management sign off on the financial results of the company personally as inconsistent with German law (which it largely was) and illogical for management to accept. Management had also long been critical of the practice of quarterly reporting, and had in fact been removed from the Frankfurt exchange's stock index in September 2002 because of its refusal to report quarterly financial results.

But, after all was said and done, the company had just reported record profits for the tenth consecutive year (see Exhibit 1). Returns were so good and had grown so steadily that the company had paid out a special dividend of €14 per share in 2002, in addition to increasing the size of the regular dividend. There was a continuing concern that management came first. In the words of one analyst " . . . we think there is the potential risk that management may not rate shareholders' interests very highly." The compensation packages of Porsche's senior management team were nearly exclusively focused on current year profitability (83 percent of executive board compensation was performance-related pay), with no management incentives or stock option awards related to the company's share price.

Exhibit 1   Porsche's Growth in Sales, Income and Margin

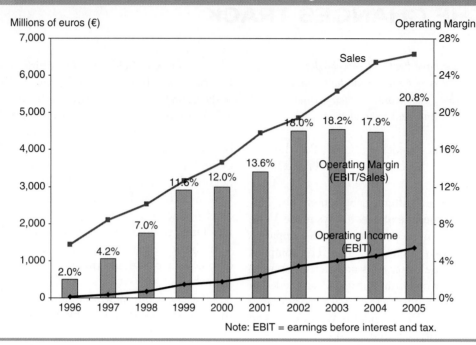

Note: EBIT = earnings before interest and tax.

PORSCHE'S GROWING PORTFOLIO

Porsche had three major vehicle platforms: the premier luxury sports car, the *911*; the competitively priced *Boxster* roadster; and then the off-road sport utility vehicle, the *Cayenne*. Porsche had also announced in 2005 that it would be adding a fourth platform, the *Panamera*, which would be a high-end sedan to compete with Jaguar, Mercedes, and Bentley.

911

The 911 series was still the focal point of the Porsche brand, but many believed that it was growing old and due for replacement. Sales had seemingly peaked in 2000–2001, and fallen back more than 15 percent in 2002–2003. The 911 had always enjoyed nearly exclusive ownership of its market segment. Prices continued to be high, and margins some of the very highest in the global auto industry for production models. The 911 was the only Porsche model which was manufactured and assembled in-house.

Boxster

The Boxster roadster had been introduced in 1996 as Porsche's entry into the lower price end of the sports car market. The Boxster was also considered an anti-cyclical move because the traditional 911 was so high-priced. The Boxster's lower price made it affordable and

less sensitive to the business cycle. It did, however, compete in an increasingly competitive market segment. Boxster sales volumes had peaked in 2000–2001.

Cayenne

The third major platform innovation was Porsche's entry into the sports utility vehicle (SUV) segment, the Cayenne. Clearly at the top end of the market (2002–2003 Cayenne sales averaged more than $70,000 each), the Cayenne had been a very quick success, especially in the SUV-crazed American market at the time. It was considered the most successful new product launch in auto history. The Cayenne's success had been even more dramatic given much pre-launch criticism that the market would not support such a high-priced SUV, particularly one which shared a strong blood-line with the Volkswagen (VW) Touareg. The Porsche Cayenne and VW Touareg shared a common chassis, and in fact were both manufactured at the same factory in Bratislava, Slovakia. Porsche shipped the Cayenne chassis to its facility in Leipzig where the engine, drive train, and interior were combined in final assembly.

Panamera

On July 27, 2005, Porsche announced that it would proceed with the development and production of a fourth major model—the *Panamera*. The name was

Exhibit 2   Return on Invested Capital (ROIC) for European Automakers, 2004

European Automaker	Sales (millions)	Operating Margin			Invested Capital			Capital Turnover	ROIC
		EBIT	Taxes	EBIT After-Tax	Interest Bearing Debt	Stockholders' Equity	Invested Capital		
BMW	€ 44,335	€ 3,745	€ 1,332	€ 2,413	€ 1,555	€ 17,517	€ 19,072	2.32	12.65%
DaimlerChrysler	€ 142,059	€ 4,612	€ 1,177	€ 3,435	€ 9,455	€ 33,541	€ 42,996	3.30	7.99%
Fiat	€ 46,703	€ 22	−€ 29	€ 51	€ 24,813	€ 5,946	€ 30,759	1.52	0.17%
Peugeot	€ 56,797	€ 1,916	€ 676	€ 1,240	€ 6,445	€ 13,356	€ 19,801	2.87	6.26%
Porsche	€ 6,359	€ 1,141	€ 470	€ 671	€ 2,105	€ 2,323	€ 4,428	1.44	15.15%
Renault	€ 40,715	€ 2,148	€ 634	€ 1,514	€ 7,220	€ 16,444	€ 23,664	1.72	6.40%
Volkswagen	€ 88,963	€ 1,620	€ 383	€ 1,237	€ 14,971	€ 23,957	€ 38,928	2.29	3.18%

Source: "European Autos," Deutsche Bank, July 20, 2005; "Porsche," Deutsche Bank, September 26, 2005; Thomson Analytics; author estimates. "Invested Capital" = total stockholders' equity + gross interest-bearing debt. Capital turnover = sales/Invested capital. ROIC (return on invested capital) = EBIT − taxes/invested capital.

derived from the legendary *Carrera Panamericana* long-distance road race held for many years in Mexico. The Panamera would be a premium class four-door four-seat sports coupe, and would compete with the premium sedan models. Pricing was expected to begin at $125,000, rising to $175,000. Production was scheduled to begin in 2009 at a scale of 20,000 units per year.

THE MOST PROFITABLE AUTOMOBILE COMPANY IN THE WORLD

Porsche's financial performance and health, by auto manufacturer standards, European or elsewhere, was excel-

lent. It was clearly the smallest of the major European-based manufacturers with total sales of €6.4 billion in 2004. But, as illustrated in Exhibit 2, Porsche was outstanding by all metrics of profitability and return on invested capital. Porsche's EBITDA, EBIT, and net income margins were the highest among all European automakers in 2004.

Foreign exchange

Porsche's financial results, however, had been the subject of substantial debate in recent years as upwards of 40 percent of operating earnings were thought to be

Exhibit 3   Porsche's Velocity, Margin & ROIC

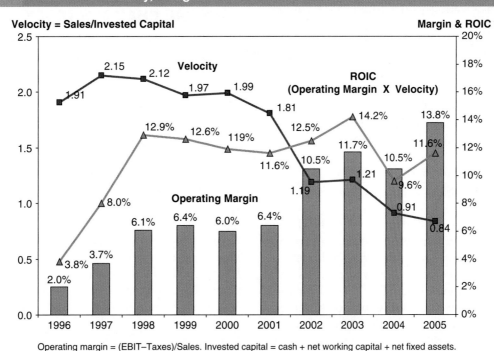

Operating margin = (EBIT−Taxes)/Sales. Invested capital = cash + net working capital + net fixed assets.

derived from currency hedging. Porsche's cost-base was purely European euro; it produced in only two countries, Germany and Finland, and both were euro area members. Porsche believed that the quality of its engineering and manufacturing were at the core of its brand, and it was not willing to move production beyond Europe (BMW, Mercedes, and VW had all been manufacturing in both the United States and Mexico for years). Porsche's sales by currency in 2004 were roughly 45 percent European euro, 40 percent U.S. dollar, 10 percent British pound sterling, and 5 percent other (primarily the Japanese yen and Swiss franc).

Porsche's leadership had undertaken a very aggressive currency hedging strategy beginning in 2001 when the euro was at a record low against the U.S. dollar. In the following years these financial hedges (currency derivatives) proved extremely profitable. For example, nearly 43 percent of operating earnings in 2003 were thought to have been derived from hedging activities. Although profitable, many analysts argued that the company was increasingly an investment banking firm rather than an automaker, and was heavily exposed to the unpredictable fluctuations between the world's two most powerful currencies, the dollar and the euro.

ROIC

It was Porsche's return on invested capital (ROIC), however, which had been truly exceptional over time. The company's ROIC in 2004—following Deutsche Bank's analysis presented in Exhibit 2, was 15.15 percent. This was clearly superior to all other European automakers.

This ROIC reflected Porsche's two-pronged financial strategy: (1) superior margins on the narrow but selective product portfolio; and (2) leveraging the capital and capabilities of manufacturing partners in the development and production of two of its three products. The company had successfully exploited the two primary drivers of the ROIC formula:

$$ROIC = \frac{\text{EBIT After Tax}}{\text{Sales}} \times \frac{\text{Sales}}{\text{Invested Capital}}$$

The first component, operating profits (EBIT, earnings before interest and taxes) after-tax as a percent of sales—operating margin—was exceptional at Porsche due to the premium value pricing derived from its global brand of quality and excellence. This allowed Porsche to charge premium prices and achieve some of the largest of margins in the auto industry. As illustrated in Exhibit 2, Porsche's operating profits after-tax of €671 million

produced an operating margin after tax of 10.55 percent (€671 divided by €6,359 in sales), the highest in the industry in 2004.

The second component of ROIC, the capital turnover ratio (sales divided by invested capital)—velocity—reflected Porsche's manufacturing and assembly strategy. By leveraging the Valmet and VW partnerships in the design, production and assembly of both the Boxster (with Valmet of Finland) and the Cayenne (with Volkswagen of Germany), Porsche had achieved capital turnover ratios which dwarfed those achieved by any other European automaker.

In recent years, however, invested capital had risen faster than sales. But Porsche was not adding fixed assets to its invested capital basis, but cash. The rising cash balances were the result of retained profits (undistributed to shareholders) and new debt issuances (raising more than €600 million in 2004 alone). As a result, fiscal 2003–2004 had proven to be one of Porsche's poorest years in ROIC. Porsche's minimal levels of invested capital resulted from some rather unique characteristics. Invested capital is defined a number of ways, but Vesi used her employer's standardized definition of cash plus net working capital plus net fixed assets. Porsche's invested capital was growing primarily because of its accumulation of cash. Vesi was concerned that using this measure of 'invested capital' led to a distorted view of the company's actual performance. Porsche's minimal fixed asset capital base resulted from the explicit strategy of the company as executed over the past decade.

PORSCHE CHANGES TRACK

The summer and fall of 2005 saw a series of surprising moves by Porsche. First, Porsche announced that the €1 billion investment to design and manufacture the new Panamera would be largely funded by the company itself. Although the introduction of the Panamera had been anticipated for quite some time, the market was surprised that Porsche intended to design and build the car—and its manufacturing facility—nearly totally in-house. The new sports coupe was to be produced in Leipzig, Germany, at the existing Porsche facility, although a substantial expansion of the plant would be required. As opposed to the previous new product introductions, the Boxster and the Cayenne, there would be no major production partner involved. Porsche CEO Wendelin Wiedeking specifically noted this in his press release: "There are no plans for a joint venture with another car maker. But to ensure the profitability of this new model series we will cooperate more closely than so far with selected system suppliers." The German share of the value of the

Panamera would be roughly 70 percent. Like the 911, Boxster, and Cayenne, the Panamera would bear the *Made in Germany* stamp. The second surprise occurred on September 25, 2005, with the announcement to invest € 3 billion in VW.

> *Porsche AG, Stuttgart, seeks to acquire a share of approximately 20 percent in the stock capital of Volkswagen AG, Wolfsburg, entitled to vote. Porsche is taking this decision because Volkswagen is now not only an important development partner for Porsche, but also a significant supplier of approximately 30 percent of Porsche's sales volume. In the words of Porsche's President and CEO: "Making this investment, we seek to secure our business relations with Volkswagen and make a significant contribution to our own future plans on a lasting, long-term basis." Porsche is in a position to finance the acquisition of the planned share in Volkswagen through its own, existing liquidity. After careful examination of this business case, Porsche is confident that the investment will prove profitable for both parties.*
>
> *. . . The planned acquisition is to ensure that . . . there will not be a hostile takeover of Volkswagen by investors not committed to Volkswagen's long-term interests. In the words of Porsche's President and CEO: "Our planned investment is the strategic answer to this risk. We wish in this way to ensure the independence of the Volkswagen Group in our own interest. This "German solution" we are seeking is an essential prerequisite for stable development of the Volkswagen Group and, accordingly, for continuing our cooperation in the interest of both Companies."*
>
> —"Acquisition of Stock to Secure Porsche's Business," Porsche AG (press release), September 25, 2005

Porsche would spend approximately €3 billion to take a 20 percent ownership position in VW. This would make Porsche VW's single largest investor, slightly larger than the government of Lower Saxony.[1] It clearly eliminated any possible hostile acquisitions which may have been on the horizon (DaimlerChrysler was rumored to have been interested in raiding VW.) The announcement was met by near universal opposition.

The family linkages between the two companies were well known. Ferdinand K. Piëch, one of the most prominent members of the Piëch family which along with the Porsche family controlled Porsche, was the former CEO (he retired in 2002) and still Chairman of Volkswagen. He was the grandson of Ferdinand Porsche, the founder of Porsche. Accusations of conflict of interest were immediate, as were calls for his resignation, and the denial of Porsche's request for a seat on VW's board. Although VW officially welcomed the investment by Porsche, Christian Wulff, VW's board member representing the State of Lower Saxony where VW was headquartered, publicly opposed the investment by Porsche. In the eyes of many, the move by Porsche was a return to German corporate cronyism.

> *For years, "Deutschland AG" was emblematic of the cosy network of cross-shareholdings and shared non-executive directorships that insulated Germany from international capitalism. Wendelin Wiedeking, Porsche's chief executive, himself invoked the national angle, saying this "German solution" was essential to secure VW, Europe's largest carmaker, against a possible hostile takeover by short-term investors."*
>
> —"Shield for Corporate Germany or a Family Affair? VW and Porsche Close Ranks," *Financial Times*, Tuesday September 27, 2005, p. 17

Germany, although long known for complex networks of cross-shareholdings, had effectively unwound most of these in the 1990s. This move by Porsche and VW was seen as more of a personal issue—Ferdinand Piëch—rather than a national issue of German alliances. Many Porsche investors had agreed, arguing that if they had wanted to invest in VW they would have done it themselves.

Shareholders in Porsche—the non-family member shareholders—were both surprised and confused by this dramatic turn of events. Although the arguments for solidifying and securing the Porsche/VW partnership were rational, the cost was not. At €3 billion, this was seemingly an enormous investment in a non-performing asset. Analysts concluded that the potential returns to shareholders, even in the form of a special dividend, were now postponed indefinitely.

The announcement of Porsche's intention to take a 20 percent equity interest in VW was greeted with outright opposition on the part of many shareholders in both VW and Porsche. Major investment banks immediately downgraded Porsche from a *buy* to a *sell*, arguing that the returns on the massive investment, some €3 billion, would likely never accrue to shareholders. Although Porsche had explained its investment decision to be one which would assure the stability of its future cooperation with VW, many critics saw it as a choice of preserving the stakes of the Porsche and Piëch families at the expense of non-family shareholders.

Why should a small and highly-profitable maker of sports cars suddenly hitch its fortunes to a lumbering and struggling mass-producer? That was the question that some alarmed shareholders asked this week when Porsche, the world's most profitable carmaker, announced plans to buy 20% stake in Volkswagen (VW), Europe's biggest carmaker. To some critics of the deal, Porsche's move looked like a return to cosy, German corporatism at its worst. Since January 2002, when a change in the law encouraged German companies to sell their cross-shareholdings in each other, free of capital gains tax, new foreign shareholders have often shaken up fossilised German management. A deal with friendly compatriots from Porsche might rescue VW from this distasteful fate, particularly since foreign hedge funds and corporate raiders have been rumored to be circling VW.

—"Business: Keeping It in the Family," *The Economist*, October 1, 2005

Case Questions

1. What strategic decisions made by Porsche over recent years had given rise to its extremely high return on invested capital?

2. Vesi wondered if her position on Porsche might have to distinguish between the company's *ability* to generate results for stockholders versus its *willingness* to do so. What do you think?

3. Is pursuing the interests of Porsche's controlling families different from maximizing the returns to its public share owners?

Note

1. The resulting ownership structure of Volkswagen in October 2005 was: 18.53 percent Porsche; 18.2 percent State of Lower Saxony; 13.0 percent Volkswagen; 8.58 percent Brandes Investment Partners; 3.5 percent Capital Group; and 38.19 percent widely distributed. Porsche still possessed the option to purchase another 3.4 percent.

THE MARKET ENTRY STRATEGY SOCIAL APPROACH

Selena Cuffe did not plan to find the business project of her life in Africa when visiting the First Annual Soweto Wine Festival in Johannesburg, South Africa, in 2005. Until that moment, Selena only related that town with the historical events that led to apartheid. When she went to the wine festival, she was impressed by the high quality of the wines showcased and the stories behind them; vintners trying to thrive within an industry where they were underrepresented. One wine caught her attention and she wanted to know if it was sold in the U.S. but the exhibitor, Vivian Kleynhans, director of African Roots Wine Brands told her that they were already struggling to have distribution within South Africa, let alone the United States.

Selena felt compelled to call her husband in the United States with the promise of a business opportunity. The wines were good and so was the cause of helping these entrepreneurs succeed. Selena's husband, Khary, listened carefully but reminded her that they needed to work out the numbers to see if it was feasible. A month later the Cuffes founded Heritage Link Brands with an office in Massachusetts, and started importing South African wines from indigenous producers.

The couple financed the company with savings from their corporate lives and credit card debt; Selena became CEO and Khary became CFO. "We've had a dozen people ask about becoming investors, but we want to bootstrap as long as we can," he says.[1]

The Cuffes had their mind clear right from the start about the focus of the company: it was not only going to educate consumers about the delicious wines Africa has to offer, but also provide the intriguing stories behind the wines.[2] Their second office was established in California in February 2006. They conducted blind taste tests and packaging reviews all across the U.S. to adapt the product to the market while making contact with stores. Their first distribution deal was with Whole Foods Market, which allowed them to place the brand at the reach of their target audience: (1) African-Americans, (2) socially conscious consumers, and (3) young adults between the ages of 21 and 30 (the millennial consumers).

They worked to obtain licenses to transact alcohol-related business in other states and find warehouses to store the wine. Importing a product like wine or any alcoholic beverage into the U.S. is not as easy as many

© Central Intelligence Agency Factbook

would think, and the Cuffes found an obstacle that endangered the project: each state had different licensing requirements. Some even required supplier signatures, which Selena collected for the first batch of wine during a December 2006 visit to South Africa.[3]

Their main supplier in Africa was the South African Black Vintners Alliance; they started selling the Bowland brand and then the Seven Sisters (from African Roots Wine Brands). New additions came with time. Results for 2007 were not encouraging, forcing the couple to rethink whether the venture was viable or not; they decided to give it more time. It did not take long until they landed another major order: United Airlines requested 10,000 cases of Heritage Link Brands in mid-2008. As time passed the Cuffes widened their focus, to be not only about selling black-owned and produced South African wines, but to also expand their offer to wines made elsewhere by people of African descent.

They have divided their brands into collections:

1. The Continent Collection, which comprises wines produced by African people. Within this collection they sell the Seven Sisters, M'Hudi,

Source: Juan Carlos Schiappa-Pietra (member of the British-Peruvian Chamber of Commerce and external expert at the Center for the Promotion of Imports from Developing Countries CBI, Netherlands), and Guadalupe Amesquita (Universidad Nacional Mayor de San Marcos, Lima, Peru).

Bowland, Women in Wine, and One World by Koopmanskloof Vineyard, this last one is a Fair Trade[4] certified wine.

2. The Diaspora collection, for wine produced by people of African descent throughout the world. Brands such as Divas Uncorked and Passages are sold under this category.

Heritage Link Brands is not only selling wine but the stories behind the wines. They are getting involved in the process of connecting the South African and North American cultures by becoming key participants in the promotion of business relationships or, as Leigh Buchanan from *Inc.* magazine described the Cuffes' business mission statement: "to promote cross-cultural understanding and economic opportunity for disadvantaged populations."[5]

The company's strategy includes training sessions with the wine producers, because most of them are small producers, as well as potential new suppliers throughout the Western Cape, South Africa, in order to strengthen relations and develop commitment from the producers to attain deadlines. To assure this, they travel to South Africa two to three times a year. And so far, all efforts have paid off; with distributors in 41 states. Nowadays Heritage Link Brands' wines are being served on American Airlines flights; sold at retailers such as Whole Foods, Albertsons, and Jewel Osco; and even served in restaurants at Disneyland.[6]

But Heritage Link Brands is not referred to by Selena as a social enterprise, "It's not a thought that comes across our minds. My training is really about how to run a successful business and how to get the most profit you can out of something. People label the tenets upon which I live my life 'socially conscious' but it's just the core of who I am. I want to do things that are taking things to the next level in a way that touches me,"[7] she said when being interviewed by *Black Enterprise* magazine after receiving the *Black Enterprise Next of the Year Award* for the Cuffes' work.

SELLING THE STORIES BEHIND THE WINES: SEVEN SISTERS AND M'HUDI

The Brutus family lived in Pater Noster, a small fishing village on the western coast of South Africa. The Brutus sisters and their baby brother left their town at a very early age when the family was evicted from their home, shortly after their father got fired from his job. Being separated and sent to live with nearby family members, they yearned to return but were not able to do so, given the unfavorable circumstances of the time, with apartheid ruling the country. Twenty years later, after reuniting

with her sisters, Vivian Kleynhans established African Roots Wine Brands and launched the Seven Sisters brand, with a wine named after each sister, made to match the styles and personalities of each of them. Starting youngest to oldest, the range consists of a Bukettraube, Odelia; Pinotage, Rose-Twena; Chenin Blanc, Yolanda; Sauvignon Blanc, Vivian; Pinotage/Shiraz, Dawn; Merlot, June; and Cabernet, Carol.[8]

Vivian oversees the production and management of her brands in collaboration with the Swartland Winery, one of the largest co-operative cellars in South Africa. She also serves as the chairperson of the South African Black Vintners Alliance (SABVA).[9]

It was Vivian's booth that Selena first visited at the Soweto Wine Festival in 2005. Their story became widespread not only because it represented the chance for the Brutus sisters to thrive, but also, like Vivian explains, "We are working toward a legacy for our families that our parents never left behind for us"[10] (http://www.youtube.com/watch?v=9SBsKN_HE3s).

The name M'hudi is derived from the Setswana word "mohudi" meaning "harvester." It is also the name given to a heroine of a great African story. M'hudi fled her war-ravaged village in search of a new beginning. The story is one of courage, determination against seemingly impossible odds, and the relentless pursuit of one's dreams and aspirations. The Rangaka family are the founders of the M'hudi Brand and the main characters in the M'hudi Wines adventure.[11]

When apartheid ended, the majority of South African businesses were owned by white people, and the wine industry was no exception. In 2003, Malmsey Rangaka, a clinical psychologist, and her husband Diale Rangaka, a higher education administrator who lived in the North-West Province, decided to give up their successful careers and move to the Western Cape. Once there, they settled on a 42-hectare wine-grape and fruit producing farm in the Koelenhof area just 15 km from Stellenbosch.

In their own words, this was the first step to participation in a lifestyle, culture, and economic sector few black people had the opportunity to partake in.[12] Until that moment they were not related at all with wine and the process of making it, but with the acquisition of the vineyard, they became the first black family to own one in South Africa. They had to rely on all sources of information to become knowledgeable about the wine-making process. With the help of their neighbors of Villiera Wines, the Grier family led by Jeff Grier who mentored them, they launched the M'hudi brand in 2005. The wine was named after the heroine of Sol Plaatje's novel, who inspired the whole family when making the decision to move to Western Cape.

Their wines have received accolades, and they are currently selling in the U.S. through Heritage Link brands and in the U.K. through Marks and Spencer.

IDENTIFYING THE TRENDS AND THE UNITED STATES

There are few alcoholic beverages served with food that also are beneficial to your health. Wine's health benefits (under moderate consumption), are one of the reasons its consumption is increasing each year in many countries. Companies and distributors are including this feature as part of their marketing strategies to boost their sales. It is becoming part of the trend toward a healthy lifestyle, and the United States is not oblivious to this fact; the U.S domestic exports[13] have increased steadily within the last few years,[14] and China is becoming a promising target for this product.

But local consumption has grown too; in 2007, 269 million cases were sold in U.S.[15] The American market surpassed Italy, a key world consumer, in terms of wine consumption in 2007, and had been on pace to overtake France and become the world's largest wine consumer within five years, according to the U.S. Wine Market: Impact Databank Review and Forecast, 2008 Edition report.[16]

Changing demographic trends are also explaining this phenomenon with an attractive market segment such as the "millennial" generation (ages 21 to 30).[17] According to experts, these millennial consumers base their purchasing decisions more on convenience than price,[18] and this represents a good opportunity for companies that want to get the most out of it.

With over 7,000 wine brands being sold in the United States, but less than 300 labels selling more than 100,000 cases annually,[19] 26 percent of the market was covered by international brands in 2007,[20] and small brands were the ones showing a better performance. But this does not mean consumers are just thinking of buying cheaper brands; they are also paying attention to quality and getting their money's worth.

According to Federico Castellucci from the International Organization of Vine and Wine (OIV), cheaper wines are much more palatable than they were 20 years ago due to the improved winemaking technologies.[21] It is predicted that the American market will continue showing growth of volumes purchased, but decrease in average purchase prices.[22]

How can a marketing strategy based on the stories behind a wine be a decisive factor for consumers? According to expert Robert Smiley, director of the Wine Industry Programs at the Graduate School of Management from UC Davis, aiming at socially conscious consumers is not sufficient to sell much wine: "By and large, the wine has to stand on its own two feet as far as quality goes. If it's good and priced right, it will sell."[23]

However, it's being suggested by Wine Market Council research that new generations have shown a marked interest in wines with a story as well as imported wines. They also are more interested in finding out about wine online, via user reviews or even the winery's own web site, than they are in wine critic scores.[24]

Then again, much of the market's growth in the last decade has come from new brands and from producers barely noticed just a short time ago,[25] and foreign brands seem to be taking advantage of this, with Chilean, Argentinean, and New Zealander brands coming onto the scene as a new alternative to traditional players such as the French, Italian, or Australian wines.

With prices ranging within the US$ 10–20 range, Selena Cuffe's Heritage Link Brands seems to be tapping into this market, with consumers who are thirsty for trying new tastes with interesting stories behind them.

THE BELIEVER

What sets Cuffe apart from most Westerners doing business in Africa is the extent to which, in heart and mind as well as ethnicity, she makes sense in both worlds. "I envision all of you as my brothers and sisters, and being able to share your story is like sharing my own story," Cuffe tells her audience, making explicit the connection she implies in every conversation. "There's a feeling of home, a feeling of family. So that's what motivates me-the feeling that I'm doing something with my family every day."

Questions for Discussion

1. What do you think about Selena Cuffe's market-entry strategy? For what other cases would such a strategy be feasible to use for exports to the United States?

2. Please estimate the U.S. per capita market size of millennials (born between 1982 and 2001; please take only consumers within the legal age for drinking into account). Afterward, using the Internet, estimate how many bottles of wine they buy per year. Finally, what would be your reasonable estimate of the market size of this segment in U.S. dollars?

3. If you were a French, Italian, or Australian wine producer and you were exporting wine to the United States, what defensive international marketing strategy would you follow to prevent market share reduction to new competitive wines?

Notes

1. http://www.inc.com/magazine/20071201/the-believer_pagen_3.html

2.   http://www.heritagelinkbrands.com/assets/client/File/epk-HeritageLinkBrands.pdf

3.   Maya Payne Smart, "A Closer Look: African Roots Wine Brands," *PM Network*, May 2009.

4.   Fair trade is a social movement focused on the promotion of better prices, decent working conditions, local sustainability, and fair terms of trade for producers, farmers, and workers in the developing world.

5.   http://www.inc.com/magazine/20071201/the-believer_pagen_2.html

6.   http://www.blackenterprise.com/entrepreneurs/entrepreneurs-news/2009/05/18/small-business-awards-winners/4

7.   http://www.blackenterprise.com/entrepreneurs/entrepreneurs-news/2009/05/18/small-business-awards-winners/4

8.   http://www.sevensisters.co.za

9.   http://hbsafricaconference.com/2007/panels_entrepreneurship.html

10.   Maya Payne Smart, "A Closer Look: African Roots Wine Brands," *PM Network*, May 2009.

11.   http://www.mhudi.com

12.   http://mhudiwines.blogspot.com/

13.   Domestic exports include commodities, which are grown, produced, or manufactured in the United States, and commodities of foreign origin, which have been changed in the United States, including U.S. Foreign Trade Zones, or which have been enhanced in value. Taken from: www.bis.doc.gov/defenseindustrialbaseprograms/osies/defmarket researchrpts/bearinghandbookfiles/g.-definitions---imports-and-exports.doc

14.   http://www.ita.doc.gov/td/ocg/expwine.htm

15.   http://www.winemarketcouncil.com/research_slideview.asp?position=1

16.   http://www.winespectator.com/webfeature/show/id/US-Wine-Consumption-Grows-for-a-Record-15th-Consecutive-Year-but-Momentum-Slows_4417

17.   http://www.reuters.com/article/idUS117338+14-Sep-2009+PRN20090914

18.   "Maturing with the Millennials: Are Organizations Prepared for the Millennial Consumer?" Economist Intelligence Unit, *The Economist*, 2008.

19.   http://www.winespectator.com/webfeature/show/id/Smaller-Brands-Lead-Growth-in-US-Wine-Consumption_4490

20.   http://www.trade.gov/td/ocg/wine2008.pdf

21.   http://articles.sfgate.com/2009-11-27/business/17181552_1_wine-consumption-global-wine-wine-growers

22.   OIV, "World Vitivinicultural Economic Data Available as of the Beginning of October 2009," report.

23.   http://www.latimes.com/business/la-fi-smallbiz-wine15-2009sep15,0,6949358,full.story

24.   http://palatepress.com/2009/10/do-you-recognize-the-new-wine-consumer/

25.   Barbara Insel, "The U.S Wine Industry," *Business Economics*, January 2008.

WHEN DIAMONDS WEEP

The ancient Greeks called diamonds the tears of the gods. Today, we know that natural diamonds consist of highly compressed carbon molecules. They have become a symbol of beauty, power, wealth, and love. Nevertheless, diamonds and the diamond trade are plagued by a sad reality: the exploitation of populations for diamond extraction and the use of diamond profits to fund terrorist activity and rebel groups.

Trade in diamonds is highly profitable. They are readily convertible to cash, small and easily transportable, not detectable by dogs, nor do they set off metal detectors. Unfortunately, these virtues also make them an easy target for money laundering activities by terrorist and rebel groups. In addition, their high value encourages some diamond-producing countries to employ means of extraction which may violate human rights. Consider the case in Botswana where a rich diamond deposit was discovered on the land belonging to a tribal group, the Bushmen. The government forcibly resettled the 2,500 Bushmen.

THE DIAMOND PRODUCTION PROCESS: FROM MINE TO MARKET

Diamonds are mined in several different ways: from open pits, underground, in alluvial mines (mines located in ancient creek beds where diamonds were deposited by streams), and coastal and marine mines. Despite advances in technology, diamond excavation remains a labor intensive process in most areas of the world. Over 156 million carats of diamonds are mined annually (one carat is the equivalent of 0.2 grams).

Once diamonds have been excavated, they are sorted, by hand, into grades. While there are thousands of categories and subcategories based on the size, quality, color, and shape of the diamonds, there are two broad categories of diamonds—gem-grade and industrial-grade. On average, close to 60 percent of the annual production is of gem-quality. In addition to jewelry, gem-quality stones are used for collections, exhibits, and decorative art objects. Industrial diamonds, because of their hardness and abrasive qualities, are often used in the medical field, in space programs, and for diamond tools.

After the diamonds have been sorted, they are transported to one of the world's four main diamond trading centers—Antwerp, Belgium (which is the largest), New York, United States; Tel Aviv, Israel; and Mumbai,

India. Daily, between 5 and 10 million individual stones pass through the Antwerp trading center. After they have been purchased, the diamonds are sent off to be cut, polished, and/or otherwise processed. Five countries currently dominate the diamond processing industry—India, which is the largest (processing 9 out of every 10 diamonds); Israel; Belgium; Thailand; and the United States, with China emerging as a new processing center. Finally, the polished diamonds are sold by manufacturers, brokers, and dealers to importers and wholesalers all over the world, who in turn, sell to retailers. The total timeframe from the time of extraction to the time at which the diamond is sold to the end consumer is called the "pipeline" and usually takes about two years.

THE NOT SO DAZZLING SIDE OF THE DIAMOND TRADE

While women across the world may hope for a diamond on their finger, the industry's sparkling reputation has been tarnished. Reports have shown that profits from the diamond trade have financed deadly conflicts in African nations such as Angola, Sierra Leone, Congo, Côte d'Ivoire, and Liberia. In addition, reports by the *Washington Post* and Global Witness, a key organization in

AFRICA

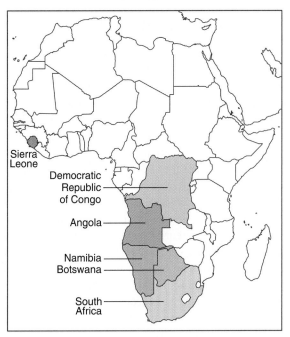

Source: This case was prepared by Daria Cherepennikova under the supervision of Professor Michael R. Czinkota of Georgetown University.

monitoring the global diamond trade, revealed that Al Qaeda used smuggled diamonds from Sierra Leone, most likely obtained via Liberia, to fund its terrorist activities. Diamonds that have been obtained in regions of the world plagued by war and violence have thus been nicknamed "conflict diamonds" or "blood diamonds."

The use of diamonds for illicit activities has been widespread. During the Bush War of Angola in 1992, Jonas Savimbi the head of a rebel movement called UNITA (National Union for the Total Independence of Angola), extended his organization into the vast diamond fields of Angola. In less than one year, UNITA's diamond smuggling network became the largest in the world—netting hundreds of millions of dollars a year with which it purchased weapons. Diamonds were also a useful tool for buying friends and supporters and could be used as a means for stockpiling wealth.

Soon warring groups in other countries such as Sierra Leone, Liberia, and the Democratic Republic of Congo adopted the same strategy. For example, the RUF (Revolutionary United Front) in Sierra Leone, a group that achieved international notoriety for hacking off the arms and legs of civilians and abducting thousands of children and forcing them to fight as soldiers, controlled the country's alluvial diamond fields.

According to current diamond industry estimates, conflict diamonds make up between 2 and 4 percent of the annual global production of diamonds. However, human rights advocates disagree with that number. They argue that up to 20 percent of all diamonds on the market could be conflict diamonds.

THE KIMBERLEY PROCESS

Diamonds are generally judged on the "Four Cs": cut, carat, color, and clarity; the international community has recently pushed for the addition of a "fifth C": conflict. On November 5, 2002, representatives from 52 countries along with mining executives, diamond dealers, and members from advocacy groups met in Interlaken, Switzerland to sign an agreement that they hoped would eliminate conflict diamonds from international trade. The agreement was called the Kimberley Process and took effect on January 1, 2003.

The Kimberley Process is a United Nations-backed certification plan created to ensure that only legally mined rough diamonds, untainted by conflicts, reach established markets around the world. According to the plan, all rough diamonds passing through or into a participating country must be transported in sealed, tamper-proof containers and accompanied by a government-issued certificate guaranteeing the container's contents and origin. Customs officials in importing countries are

required to certify that the containers have not been tampered with and are instructed to seize all diamonds that do not meet the requirements.

The agreement also stipulates that only those countries that subscribe to the new rules will be able to trade legally in rough diamonds. Countries that break the rules will be suspended and their diamond trading privileges will be revoked. Furthermore, individual diamond traders who disobey the rules will be subject to punishment under the laws of their own countries.

CRITICS SPEAK OUT

Several advocacy groups have voiced concerns that the Kimberley Process remains open to abuse and that it will not be enough to stop the flow of conflict diamonds. Many worry that bribery and forgery are inevitable and that corrupt governments officials will render the scheme inoperable. Furthermore, even those diamonds with certified histories attached may not be trustworthy. Alex Yearsley of Global Witness, an advocacy group trying to raise global awareness about conflict diamonds, predicts that firms will "be a bit more careful with their invoices" as a result of the implementation of the Kimberley Process, but warns, "if you're determined, you can get around this process." A 2005 report published by Global Witness highlighted shortcomings of the Kimberley Process and made specific recommendations for its improvement. For example, the report urges governments to implement stricter policies of internal control, advocates for the diamond industry to publicize names of individuals in companies found to be involved in the conflict trade, and pushes for the United Nations to consider implementing sanctions against diamonds from Côte d'Ivoire.

The General Accountability Office, the investigative arm of the U.S. Congress, also voiced concerns in a report: "[T]he period after rough diamonds enter the first foreign port until the final point of sale is covered by a system of voluntary industry participation and self-regulated monitoring and enforcement. These and other shortcomings provide significant challenges in creating an effective scheme to deter trade in conflict diamonds."

Government organizations and policy groups are not the only ones bringing the problem of conflict diamonds to light. Rapper Kanye West released a song entitled "Diamonds from Sierra Leone" after hearing about the atrocities of conflict diamonds in Africa. "This ain't Vietnam still/People lose hands, legs, arms for real," he raps. A Hollywood movie, *The Blood Diamond*, starring Leonardo DiCaprio, also features an ethical dilemma about buying and trading diamonds.

THE DIAMOND INDUSTRY REACTS

Recently, a number of new technologies have emerged that, if adopted by the diamond industry worldwide, could change the way that diamonds are produced, traded, and sold. Several U.S. companies, using machines produced by Russian scientists, have been able to make industrial and gem-grade diamonds artificially. In terms of industrial-grade diamonds, which comprise at least 40 percent of all annual diamond production, this could mean tremendous cost savings for industries using industrial diamonds and the elimination of conflict diamonds from industrial uses. For gem-grade diamonds the viability of synthetic diamonds is questionable. This is largely due to the success of past diamond marketing campaigns—most consumers see synthetic diamonds as inferior to natural ones.

Another emerging technology is laser engraving. Lasers make it possible to mark diamonds—either in their rough or cut stage—with a symbol, number, or bar code that can help to permanently identify that diamond. Companies that adopt the technology have an interesting marketing opportunity to create diamond brands. For example, Intel, a manufacturer of computer chips, launched a mass marketing campaign "Intel Inside" to create brand awareness in the previously homogenous computer chip market. While consumers don't buy the chips directly, they have positive associations with computers using Intel chips—they may even only consider computers who have "Intel inside." Likewise, establishing brand awareness and building equity in its name could add value to the diamond and help increase consumer confidence. Sirius Diamonds, a Vancouver-based cutting and polishing company, now microscopically laser engraves a polar bear logo and an identification number on each gem it processes. Another company, 3Beams Technologies of the United States, is currently working on a system to embed a bar code inside a diamond (as opposed to on its surface) that would make it much more difficult to remove.

Another option is the "invisible fingerprint" invented by a Canadian security company called Identex. The technology works by electronically placing an invisible information package on each stone. The fingerprint can include any information that the producer desires such as the mine source and production date. The data can only be read by Identex's own scanners. Unfortunately, if the diamond is re-cut, the fingerprint will be lost, although it can be reapplied at any time. Though this represents a major drawback of the technology, the re-cutting of a diamond is expensive and typically reduces its size and value. Nevertheless, the technology's creators believe that it will soon become an industry standard because it is a quick and cost-effective away to analyze a stone. The technology may supplement or even replace paper certification.

Lastly, processes are being developed to read a diamond's internal fingerprint—its unique diamond sparkle and combination of impurities. The machine used to do this is called a Laser Raman Spectroscope (LRS). A worldwide database could identify a diamond's origin and track its journey from the mine to end-consumer. However, creation of such a database requires large investments for equipment to cope with the volume of diamonds. Such investment will only happen if customers are willing to pay for such identification.

Questions for Discussion

1. In light of the conflict diamond issue, would you buy a diamond? Why or why not?

2. Do you think the diamond industry as a whole has an ethical responsibility to combat the illicit trade in diamonds?

3. What actions, if any, should the international community take towards nations or corporations found to be trading conflict diamonds?

Sources

"A Crook's Best Friend," The Economist, January 4, 2003.

"Al Qaeda Cash Tied to Diamond Trade," Washington Post, November 2, 2001.

"Conflict and Security; Conflict Diamonds Are Forever," Africa News, November 8, 2002.

Cowell, Alan. "40 Nations in Accord on 'Conflict Diamonds'," The New York Times, November 6, 2002.

DeBeers Group, http://www.debeersgroup.com.

Duke, Lynne. "Diamond Trade's Tragic Flaw," Washington Post, April 29, 2001.

Finlayson, David. "Preserving Diamond's Integrity," Vancouver Sun, December 23, 2002.

Fowler, Robert R. "Final Report of the UN Panel of Experts on Violations of Security Council Sanctions Against UNITA," (S/2000/203) March 10, 2000.

Jha, Amarendra. "Diamond Pact Hits Surat Cutters," The Times of India, December 28, 2002.

Jones, Lucy. "Diamond Industry Rough to Regulate; Central African Republic Works to Monitor Gem Trade," The Washington Times, August 22, 2002.

"Making It Work: Why the Kimberley Process Must Do More to Stop Conflict Diamonds," Global Witness, November 2005.

O'Ferrall, Rory M. "De Beers O'Ferrall Calls Kimberley End of Beginning," December 2, 2002, http://www.diamonds.net (accessed March 28, 2003).

Olson, Donald W. "Diamond, Industrial," *U.S. Survey Minerals Yearbook*, 2001, http://minerals.usgs.gov/minerals/pubs/ (accessed March 28, 2003).

Olson, Donald W. "Gemstones," *U.S. Survey Minerals Yearbook*, 2001, http://minerals.usgs.gov/minerals/pubs/ (accessed March 28, 2003).

Reeker, Philip T. "Implementing the Kimberley Process," January 2, 2003, http://www.diamonds.net (accessed March 28, 2003).

Smillie, Ian. "The Kimberley Process: The Case for Proper Monitoring," Partnership Africa Canada, September 2002, http://www.partnershipafricacanda.org, (accessed March 28, 2003).

Sparshott, Jeffrey. "WTO Targets 'Conflict Diamonds,'" *The Washington Times*, March 1, 2003.

Watson, Andrea. "Tribes Face Death in Diamond Bonanza," *Sunday Express*, January 17, 2006.

"U.S.: Blood Diamond Plan Too Soft," *Associated Press Online*, June 18, 2002.

Chapter 1

1. William J. Bernstein, *A Splendid Exchange, How Trade Shaped the World* (New York: Grove Press, 2008), 10–11.

2. Ibid, 78–79.

3. Paul R. Krugman, "What Do Undergraduates Need to know about Trade?" *AEA Papers and Proceedings,* Mayu, 1193: 23–26.

4. Margaret P. Doxey, *Economic Sanctions and International Enforcement (New York: Oxford University Press, 1980), 10.*

5. World Trade Organization, World Trade Report 2009, www.wto.org/english/ res_e/booksp . . . /world_trade_ report09_e.pdf, accessed August 18, 2009.

6. UNCTAD, World Investment Report 2008, http://www.unctad.org/en/docs/ wir2008_en.pdf, accessed August 18, 2009.

7. Ibid.

8. Ibid.

9. World Trade Organization, World Trade Report 2009, www.wto.org/english/res_e/ booksp . . . /world_trade_ report09_e .pdf, accessed August 18, 2009.

10. Ibid.

11. Eugene H. Fram and Riad Ajami, "Globalization of Markets and Shopping Stress: Cross-Country Comparisons," *Business Horizons,* Jan–Feb 1994, 17–23.

12. U.S. Department of Commerce, Bureau of Economic Analysis, news release, http://www.bea.gov/ newsreleases/international/intinv/intinv-newsrelease.htm, accessed August 19, 2009.

13. U.S. Department of Commerce, International Trade Administration, http://ita.doc.gov/td/industry/otea/ttp/ Top_ Trade_Partners.pdf, accessed August 19, 2009.

14. Michael R. Czinkota and Sarah McCue, *The STAT-USA Companion to International Business, Economics, and Statistics Administration* (Washington, DC: U.S. Department of Commerce, Washington, 2001) 16.

15. Lee LeFever, "Social Networking in Plain English," CommonCrafts Show 2007, http://www.youtube.com/watch? va=6a_KF7TYKVc, accessed August 19, 2009.

16. U.S. Department of Labor, Bureau of Labor Statistics, economic news release, "Employment Situation Summary," August 9, 2009.

17. Richard Deitz and James Orr, "A Leaner, More Skilled U.S. Manufacturing Workforce," *Current Issues in Economics and Finance* 12, 2 (February/March 2006).

18. Michael R. Czinkota, "An Analysis of the Global Position of U.S. Manufacturing," *Thunderbird International Business Review*, October 2003: 505–519.

19. *Characteristics of Business Owners* Washington, DC: U.S. Bureau of the Census, (November 5, 1997).

20. U.S. Trade Promotion Coordinating Committee, 2008 National Export Strategy.

21. Michael R. Czinkota, "How Government Can Help Increase U.S. Export Performance," Testimony for the House Committee on Small Business, One Hundred and Eleventh Congress, Second Session, April 28, 2010.

22. U.S. Department of Commerce, International Trade Administration, http://ita.doc.gov/td/industry/otea/ttp/ Top _Trade_Partners.pdf.

23. Remarks by the President at the Export-Import Bank's Annual Conference, The White House, Office of the Press Secretary, March 11, 2010.

24. Howard Lewis III and J. David Richardson, *Why Global Commitment Really Matters,* Washington DC: Institute for International Economics, 2001.

25. Michael R. Czinkota, Ilkka A. Ronkainen, and Bob Donath, *Mastering Global Markets: Strategies for Today's Trade Globalist,* Mason, OH: South-Western, 2004.

26. Footwear Distributors and Retailers Association, interview with President Matt Priest, July 22, 2009.

Chapter 2

1. New Zealand Ministry of Foreign Affairs and Trade, http://www.mfat.govt.nz, accessed August 21, 2009.

2. Michael R. Czinkota, "The World Trade Organization: Perspectives and Prospects," *Journal of International Marketing 3,* 1 (1995), 85–92.

3. Thomas R. Graham, "Global Trade: War and Peace," *Foreign Policy* 50 (Spring 1983): 124–127.

4. Edwin L. Barber III, "Investment-Trade Nexus," in *U.S. International Policy,* ed. Gary Clyde Hufbauer (Washington DC: The International Law Institute, 1982), 9–4.

5. Matthew Adler, Claire Brunel, Gary Clyde Hufbauer, and Jeffrey J. Schott, Institute for International Economics, "What's on the Table? The Doha Round as of August 2009," 2009.

6. Jessica T. Mathews, "Power Shift," *Foreign Affairs,* January/February 1997, 50–66.

7. U.S. Trade Promotion Coordinating Committee, 2008 National Export Strategy.

8. The Panama Canal Authority, press release, "Leaders of Multilateral Agencies and the Panama Canal Sign Agreement for $2.3 Billion to Finance the Canal Expansion Program," December 9, 2008.

9. Organization for International Investment, www.ofii.org, accessed August 25, 2009.

10. Jason Folkmanis, "Vietnam's Rice Exports May Surge to Record, U.S. Says," *Bloomberg.net*, August 20, 2009.

11. Michael R. Czinkota and Charles J. Skuba, "GM in Asian Auto Market," *Korea Times,* June 14, 2009.

12. "BIS Confirms Sharp Increase of FX Volume," e-FOREX Bank for International Settlements (BIS), Basel, Switzerland, January 2008: p 18–19.

13. Leaders' Statement, "The Global Plan for Recovery and Reform 2 April 2009," www.g20.org.

14. Michael R. Czinkota and Charles J. Skuba, "The American Taxpayer's Global Investment," *Roll Call,* June 9, 2009.

15. Ibid.

16. Michael R. Czinkota, "The World Trade Organization, Perspectives and Prospects," 85–92.

17. Leaders' Statement, "The Global Plan for Recovery and Reform 2 April 2009," www.g20.org.

18. Chris Sewell, "The World Bank Controversy Explained," Medill News Service, February 8, 2001.

19. "What Are the Main Concerns and Criticism about the World Bank and IMF?," http://www.brettonwoodsproject.org.

20. Michael R. Czinkota and Masaaki Kotabe, "A Marketing Perspective of the U.S. International Trade Commission's Antidumping Actions–An Empirical Inquiry," *Journal of World Business* 32, no. 2 (1997): 169–187.

21. Michael R. Czinkota, "Export Promotion: A Framework for Finding Opportunity in Change," *Thunderbird International Business Review* 44, no. 3 (2002): 315–324.

22. Masaaki Kotabe and Michael R. Czinkota, "State Government Promotion of Manufacturing Exports: A Gap Analysis," *Journal of International Business Studies* (Winter 1992): 637–658.

23. Investment Canada Act, http://investcan.ic.gc.ca, July 27, 2003.

24. Jaclyn Fierman, "The Selling Off of America," *Fortune*, December 22, 1986, 35.

25. Organization for International Investment, Washington, DC, http://www.ofii.org/insourcing-stats.htm, accessed September 1, 2009.

26. Ibid.

27. *Statistical Abstract of the United States* (Washington, DC: U.S. Government Printing Office, 2003): 868.

28. Siemens Press Release, "Siemens Opens First Corporate R&D Center in South East Asia" Singapore, October 30, 2008, http://www.siemens.com, accessed September 1, 2009.

29. Stephen Guisinger, "Attracting and Controlling Foreign Direct Investment," *Economic Impact* (Washington, DC: United States Information Agency, 1987), 18.

30. Stephen Guisinger, "Attracting and Controlling Foreign Direct Investment," *Economic Impact* (Washington, DC: United States Information Agency, 1987), 20.

31. Laura Wood, "Research and Markets: China's Guidebook for Pharmaceutical Patent Protection", Reuters, June 22, 2009, http://www.researchandmarkets.com accessed September 1, 2009.

32. Michael R. Czinkota, "Academic Freedom for All in Higher Education: The Role of the General Agreement on Trade in Services," *Journal of World Business,* 41, 2 (2006): 149–160.

33. Michael R. Czinkota, "Time for a North American Trade Policy," *Roll Call,* August 7, 2009.

34. Donald Manzullo and Michael R. Czinkota, "Exports and Imports: For U.S. Manufacturers, It is a Difficult Balancing Act," *The Washington Times*, May 27, 2003, A17.

35. Michael R. Czinkota, ed., *Proceedings of the Conference on the Feasibility of a Protection Cost Index*, August 6, 1987 (Washington, DC: Department of Commerce, 1987), 7.

Chapter 3

1. Adam Smith, *An Inquiry into the Nature and Causes of the Wealth of Nations* (New York, E. P. Dutton & Company, 1937), 4–5.

2. Wassily Leontief, "Domestic Production and Foreign Trade: The American Capital Position Re-Examined," *Proceedings of the American Philosophical Society* 97, no. 4 (September 1953), as reprint in Wassily Leontief, *Input-Output Economics* (New York, Oxford University Press, 1966), 69–70.

3. In Leontief's own words: "These figures show that an average million dollars' worth of our exports embodies considerably less capital and somewhat more labor that would be required to replace from domestic production an equivalent amount of our competitive imports . . . The widely held opinion that–as compared with the rest of the world–the United States' economy is characterized by a relative surplus of capital and a relative shortage of labor proves to be wrong. As a matter of fact, the opposite is true." Leontief, 1953, 86.

4. If this were true, it would defy one of the basic assumptions of the factor proportions theory, that all products are manufactured with the same technology (and therefore same proportions of labor and capital) across countries. However, continuing studies have found this to be quite possible in our imperfect world.

5. For a detailed description of these theories see Elhanan Helpman and Paul Krugman, *Market Structure and Foreign Trade* (Cambridge, MA: MIT Press, 1985).

6. This leads to the obvious debate as to what constitutes a "different product" and what is simply a cosmetic difference. The most obvious answer is found in the field of marketing: if the consumer believes the products are different, then they are different.

7. There are a variety of potential outcomes from external economies of scale. For additional details see Paul R. Krugman and Maurice Obstfeld, *International Economics: Theory and Policy*, 3rd ed. (New York: Harper-Collins, 1994).

8. Michael E. Porter, "The Competitive Advantage of Nations," *Harvard Business Review* (March-April 1990): 73–74.

9. Michael E. Porter, "Clusters and the New Economics of Competition," *Harvard Business Review* November-December 1998, pp. 77–90.

10. The term *international investment* will be used in this chapter to refer to all nonfinancial investment. International financial investment includes a number of forms beyond the concerns of this chapter, such as the purchase of bonds, stocks, or other securities issued outside the domestic economy.

Chapter 4

1. The official terminology used throughout this chapter, unless otherwise noted, is that of the International Monetary Fund (IMF). Because the IMF is the primary source of similar statistics for balance of payments and economic performance worldwide, it is more general than other terminology forms, such as that employed by the U.S. Department of Commerce.

2. All balance of payments data used in this chapter are drawn from the International Monetary Fund's *Balance of Payments Statistics Yearbook.* This source is used because the IMF presents the balance of payments statistics for all member countries on the same basis and in the same format, allowing comparison across countries.

3. The magnitude of the economic devastation in Asia is still largely unappreciated by Westerners. At a conference sponsored by the Milken Institute in Los Angeles, a speaker noted that the preoccupation with the economic problems of Indonesia was incomprehensible because "the total gross domestic product of Indonesia is roughly the size of North Carolina." The following speaker provided a rebuttal, noting that the last time he had checked, "North Carolina did not have a population of 220 million people."

4. Obstfeld, M., and Taylor, A.M., "Globalization and Capital Markets," *NBER Conference Paper*, May 4–5, 2001, p. 6.

Chapter 5

1. Pankaj Ghemawat, "Distance Still Matters," *Harvard Business Review* 79 (September 2001): 137–147.

2. Piet Levy, "Live Like Locals," *Marketing News*, August 30, 2009, 14.

3. Alonso Martinez, Ivan De Souza, Francis Liu, "Multinationals vs. Multilatinas," *Strategy and Business* (Fall, 2003): 56–67.

4. Alfred Kroeber and Clyde Kluckhohn, *Culture: A Critical Review of Concepts and Definitions* (New York: Random House, 1985), 11.

5. Geert Hofstede, "National Cultures Revisited," *Asia-Pacific Journal of Management* 1 (September 1984): 22–24.

6. Edward T. Hall, *Beyond Culture* (Garden City, NY: Anchor Press, 1976), 15.

7. See http://www.mcdonalds.com.

8. Marita von Oldenborgh, "What's Next for India?" *International Business* (January 1996): 44–47; and Ravi Vijh, "Think Global, Act Indian," *Export Today* (June 1996): 27–28.

9. "French Movies," http://www.understandfrance.org/France/FrenchMovies.html; "Subsidy Wars," *The Economist*, February 24, 2005, 76.

10. "India Digitizes Age-Old Wisdom," *The Washington Post,* January 8, 2006, A22.

11. "Information Minister Aims to Throw Cultural Vulgarians Out of the Game," *The Washington Post*, February 2, 1999, A16.

12. "Asian Pop Stars Struggle to Find Cross-Cultural Groove," *The Wall Street Journal,* March 31, 2005, B1, B2.

13. George P. Mundak, "The Common Denominator of Cultures," in *The Science of Man in the World*, ed. Ralph Linton (New York: Columbia University Press, 1945), 123–142.

14. Robert Moran, Philip Harris, and Sarah Moran, *Managing Cultural Differences* (Burlington, MA: Elsevier Inc., 2007), 203.

15. "Euroteen Market Grabs U.S. Attention," *Marketing News*, October, 22, 2001, 15.

16. http://www.ethnologue.com.

17. David A. Ricks, *Blunders in International Business*, 3rd edition (Maiden, MA: Blackwell, 2000), 4.

18. David A, Hanni, John K. Ryans, and Ivan R. Vernon, "Coordinating International Advertising: The Goodyear Case Revisited for Latin America," *Journal of International Marketing* 3, no. 2 (1995): 83–98.

19. "French Snared in Web of English," *The Washington Post*, September 27, 2000, A19; and "France: Mind Your Language," *The Economist*, March 23, 1996, 70–71.

20. "A World Empire by Other Means," *The Economist*, December 22, 2001,65.

21. Rory Cowan, "The e Does Not Stand for English," *Global Business.* March 2000, L/22.

22. "Russian Government Wants to Introduce Cyrillic Version of the Internet," *Reuters*, January 4, 2008.

23. Margareta Bowen, "Business Translation," *Jerome Quarterly* (August–September 1993): 5–9.

24. "Nokia Veti Pois Mainoskampanjansa," *Uutislehti 100,* June 15, 1998, 5.

25. "Sticky Issue," *The Economist*, August, 24, 2002, 51.

26. Edward T. Hall, "The Silent Language of Overseas Business," *Harvard Business Review* 38 (May–June 1960): 87–96.

27. "Anywhere, Anytime," *The Wall Street Journal,* November 21, 2005, R6.

28. *World Almanac and the Book of Facts 2009* (Mahwah, NJ: Funk & Wagnalls, 2008), 707.

29. Carla Power, "Faith in the Market," *Foreign Policy*, January/February 2009, 70–75;" Profit versus the Prophet: Islamic Law has Transformed Some Muslims into Creative Bankers." *Los Angeles Times*, February 10, 2008, M11.

30. "Out from Under," *Marketing News* July 21, 2003, 1, 9.

31. T. Edwards, P. Almond, I. Clark, and T. Colling, "Reverse Diffusion in US Multinationals: Barriers from the American Business System," *The Journal of Management Studies* 42, no. 6 (September 2005): 1261–1286.

32. Douglas McGray, "Japan's Gross National Cool," *Foreign Policy*, May/June 2002, 44.

33. Y.H. Wong and Ricky Yee-kwong, "Relationship Marketing in China: Guanxi, Favoritism and Adaptation," *Journal of Business Ethics* 22, no. 2 (1999): 107–118.

34. Earl P. Spencer, "EuroDisney–What Happened? "*Journal of International Marketing* 3, no. 3 (1995): 103–114.

35. Sergey, Frank, "Global Negotiations: Vive Les Differences!" *Sales and Marketing Management* 144 (May 1992): 64–69.

36. See, for example, Terri Morrison, *Kiss, Bow, or Shake Hands: How to Do Business In Sixty Countries* (Holbrook, MA.: Adams Media, 1994) or Roger Axtell, *Do's and Taboos Around the World* (New York: John Wiley & Sons, 1993). For holiday observances, see http://www.religioustolerance.org/main_day.htm#cal and http://www.dir.yahoo.com/society_and_culture/holidays_and_observances, accessed 9/1/03.

37. James A. Gingrich, "Five Rules for Winning Emerging Market Consumers," *Strategy and Business* (second quarter, 1999): 68–76.

38. "Feng Shui Strikes Chord," available at http://www.money.cnn.com/1999/09/11/life/q_fengshui; and "Fung Shui Man Orders Sculpture Out of Hotel," *South China Morning Post*, July 27, 1992, 4.

39. "Year of the Mouse," *The Economist,* September 30, 2005, 58; "The Feng Shui Kingdom," *The New York Times,* April 25, 2005, A14.

40. "U.S. Superstores Find Japanese Are a Hard Sell," *The Wall Street Journal*, February 14, 2000, B1, B4.

41. The results of the Gallup study are available at http://www.fortune.com.

42. Kenichi Ohmae, "Managing in a Borderless World," *Harvard Business Review* 67 (May–June 1989): 152–161.

43. Peter McGinnis, "Guanxi or Contract: A Way to Understand and Predict Conflict Between Chinese and Western Senior Managers in China-Based Joint Ventures," in *Multinational Business Management and Internationalization of Business Enterprises*, ed. Daniel E. McCarthy and Stanley J. Hille (Nanjing, China: Nanjing University Press, 1993), 345–351.

44. Tim Ambler, "Reflections in China: Re-Orienting Images of Marketing, *Marketing Management* 4 (summer 1995): 23–30.

45. "Why State Farm Tries to be a Good Neighbor to Asian-American Community," *Advertising Age*, September 1, 2009, 8.

46. Jagdish N. Sheth and S. Prakash Sethi, "A Theory of Cross-Cultural Buying Behavior," in *Consumer and Industrial Buying Behavior*, eds. Arch G. Woodside, Jagdish N. Sheth, and Peter D. Bennett (New York: Elsevier North-Holland, 1977), 369–386.

47. Geert Hofstede, *Culture's Consequences: International Differences in Work-Related Values* (Beverly Hills, CA.: Sage Publications, 1984), Chapter 1.

48. Geert Hofstede and Michael H. Bond, "The Confucius Connection: From Cultural Roots to Economic Growth," *Organizational Dynamics* 16 (spring 1988): 4–21.

49. Simcha Ronen and Oded Shenkar, "Clustering Countries on Attitudinal Dimensions: A Review and Synthesis," *Academy of Management Journal* 28 (September 1985): 440–452.

50. Sanna Sundqvist, Lauri Frank, and Kaisu Puumalainen, "The Effects of Country Characteristics, Cultural Similarity and Adoption Timing on the Diffusion of Wireless Communications," *Journal of Business Research* 58, no. 1 (2005), 107–110.

51. "Building a 'Cultural Index' to World Airline Safety," *The Washington Post*, August 21, 1994, A8.

52. Sengun Yenijurt and Janell Townsend, "Does Culture Explain Acceptance of New Products in a Country? An Empirical Investigation, *International Marketing Review* 20, no. 4 (2003): 377–397.

53. "Is E-Commerce Boundary-less? Effects of Individualism-Collectivism and Uncertainty Avoidance on Internet Shopping," *Journal of International Business Studies* 35, no. 6 (2004): 545–560.

54. "Exploring Differences in Japan, U.S. Culture," *Advertising Age International*, September 18, 1995, 1–8.

55. James A. Lee, "Cultural Analysis in Overseas Operations," *Harvard Business Review* 44 (March–April 1966): 106–114.

56. Peter Liesch, John Steen, Gary Knight, and Michael Czinkota, "Problematizing the Internationalization Decision: Terrorism-induced Risk," *Management Decision* 44, no. 6 (2006), 809–823.

57. W. Chan Kim and R. A. Mauborgne, "Cross-Cultural Strategies," *Journal of Business Strategy* 7 (Spring 1987): 28–37.

58. Rosalie Tung, "Selection and Training of Personnel for Overseas Assignments," *Columbia Journal of World Business* 16 (Spring 1981): 68–78.

59. Simcha Ronen, "Training the International Assignee," in *Training and Career Development*, ed. I. Goldstein (San Francisco: Jossey-Bass 1989), 426–440.

60. Nadeem Firoz and Taght Ramin, "Understanding Cultural Variables Is Critical to Success in International Business," *International Journal of Management* 21, no. 3 (2004): 307–324.

61. See for example Johnson & Johnson credo at http://www.jnj.com/our_company/our_credo/index.htm.

62. "World News: Chinese Village Hopes for a Disney Windfall," *The Wall Street Journal*, August 24, 2009, A8; "Main Street, H.K.," *The Wall Street Journal*, January 23, 2008, B1–B2; "Disney Rewrites Script to Win Fans in India," *The Wall Street Journal*, June 11, 2007, A1, A10; Ibsen Martinez, "Romancing the Globe," *Foreign Policy*, November/December 2005, 48–56.

Chapter 6

1. Quoted in Philippe Dollinger, *The German Hansa* (Stanford, CA: Stanford University Press, 1970), 49.

2. Robin Renwick, *Economic Sanctions* (Cambridge, MA: Harvard University Press, 1987), 11.

3. Margaret P. Doxey, *Economic Sanctions and International Enforcement* (New York: Oxford University Press, 1987), 10.

4. George E. Shambaugh, *States, Firms, and Power: Successful Sanctions in United States Foreign Policy* (Albany, NY: State University of New York Press, 1999), 202.

5. G. Scott Erickson, "Export Controls: Marketing Implications of Public Policy Choices," *Journal of Public Policy and Marketing* 16, no. 1 (spring 1997): 83.

6. Michael R. Czinkota and Erwin Dichtl, "Export Controls and Global Changes," *DerMarkt* 35, no. 3, (1996): 148–155.

7. Robert M. Springer Jr., "New Export Law an Aid to International Marketers," *Marketing News*, January 3, 1986, 10, 67.

8. U.S. Department of Commerce, Bureau of Industry and Security, http://www.bis.doc.gov/, accessed October 29, 2009.

9. Donald Kirk, "Clinton says North Korea missile tests won't affect talks", *The Christian Science Monitor*, October 12, 2009.

10. Allen S. Krass, "The Second Nuclear Era: Nuclear Weapons in a Transformed World," in *World Security: Challenges for a New Centtny*, 2d ed., M. Klare and D. Thomas, eds. (St. Martin's Press, 1994), 85-105.

11. Craig Barrett, President Intel, Speech to the American Management Association, Spring 2002, Phoenix

12. E. M. Hucko, *Aussenwirtschaftsrecht-Kriegswaffenkontrollrecht, Textsammlung mit Einführung*, 4th ed. (Cologne, 1993).

13. Michael R. Czinkota, "From Bowling Alone to Standing Together," *Marketing Management*, March/April 2002, 12–16.

14. http://comerhouse.icaap.org/briefings/19.html, accessed July 15, 2003.

15. Habib Mohsin and Leon Zurawicki, "Corruption and Foreign Direct Investment," *Journal of International Business Studies*, 33, 2:291–307.

16. George Moody, *Grand Corruption: How Business Bribes Damage Developing Countries* (Oxford: World View Publishing, 1997): 23.

17. U.S. Department of Justice, press release, "Chiquita Brands International, Inc., Pleads Guilty to Making Payments to a Designated Terrorist Organization and Agrees To Pay a $25 Million Fine," March 19, 2007.

18. Michael R. Czinkota, Ilkka A. Rohkainen, and Bob Donath, *Mastering Global Markets*, (Cincinnatt: Thomson, 2004), 362.

19. Michael G. Harvey, "A Survey of Corporate Programs for Managing Terrorist Threats," *Journal of International Business Studies* (Third Quarter 1993): 465–478.

20. Harvey J. Iglarsh, "Terrorism and Corporate Costs," *Terrorism* 10 (1987): 227–230.

21. G. Hart and W. Rudman, *America Still Unprepared—America Still in Danger* (New York: Council on Foreign Relations, 2002), 14.

22. Gary A. Knight, Michael R. Czinkota, and Peter W. Liesch, "Terrorism and the International Firm," Proceedings: Annual meeting of the Academy of International Business, Honolulu, HI: Academy of International Business, 2003.

23. Frank Jack Daniels, Saul Hudson, and Eric Walsh, *Reuters*, FACTBOX: "Venezuela's nationalizations under Hugo Chavez", Mar 5, 2009

24. Tina Hodges, "Bolivia's Gas Nationalization: Opportunity and Challenges," *Petroleum World*, November 25, 2007; Steven Mufson, "Bolivian Gas Takeover Sets a Familiar Scene," *Washington Post*, May 4, 2006.

25. Shengliang Deng, Pam Townsend, Maurice Robert, and Normand Quesnel, "A Guide to Intellectual Property Rights in Southeast Asia and China," *Business Horizons* (November–December 1996): 43–50.

26. TRIPS, a more detailed overview of the TRIPS agreement, www.wto.org, February 1,2001.

27. Associated Press, "Brazil to break Merck AIDS drug patent, government wants lower price on anti-retroviral medication," May 4, 2007.

28. "Risky Returns," *The Economist*, May 25, 2000, http://www.economist.com.

29. Paul Blustein, "Kawasaki to Pay Additional Taxes toU.S.," *The Washington Post*, December 11, 1992, D1.

30. http://www.opic.gov, Washington, DC: Overseas Private Investment Corporation, May 2, 2001.

31. Federal News Service, *Hearing of the House Judiciary Committee*, April 23, 1997; American Bar Association, *Business Law Today* 11, no. 1 (September/October 2001) http://www.abanet.org/buslaw/blt/bltsept01_snap.html

32. Surya Prakash Sinha, *Wlmt Is Law? The Differing Theories of Jurisprudence* (New York: Paragon House, 1989).

33. New Rule Project, http://www.newrules.org/retail/rules/pharmacy-ownership-laws/pharmacy-ownership-laws-europe. accessed Oct. 29, 2009.

34. Michael R. Czinkota and Jon Woronoff. *Unlocking Japan's Market* (Chicago: Probus Publishing, 1991).

35. http://www.tdctrade.com/mktprof/europe/mprussia.htm, accessed June 30, 2003.

36. Timothy P. Blumentritt and Douglas Nigh, "The Integration of Subsidiary Political Activities in Multinational Corporations," *Journall of International Business Studies*, 33, 1, 2002, 57–77.

37. Michael R. Czinkota, "The Policy Gap in International Marketing," *Journal of International Marketing*, 8, 1, 2000: 99–111.

38. Bruce D. Keillor, G. Tomas M. Hult, Deborah Owens, "An Empirical Investigation of Market Barriers and the Political Activities of Individual Firms," *International Journal of Commerce and Management*, 12, 2, 2002, 89–106.

39. Michael R. Czinkota, "International Information Needs for U.S. Competitiveness," *Business Horizons* 34, 6 (November/December 1991): 86–91.

40. Eric Lipton and Steven R. Weisman, "Wide Net Cast by Lobby for Colombia Trade Pact", *New York Times*, April 8, 2008.

41. Najmeh Bozorgmehr and Stefan Wagstyl, "European Business Sees New

Area of Potential," *Financial Times*, February 6, 2002. http://www.ft.com.

42. International Court of Arbitration (Paris, International Chamber of Commerce), www.iccwbo.org, accessed May 25, 2010.

Chapter 7

1. Liquidity is not widely understood. A relevant example would be the ability of homeowners to sell their home for cash today. Although they could do it, they would most likely receive a cash payment that is far below the asset's true value–the fair market value.

Chapter 8

1. Global Business Policy Council, *Globalization Ledger* (Washington, DC: A. T. Kearney, 2000), 3.

2. Vitaly Klintsov, Irene Shvakman, and Yermolai Solzhenitsyn, "How Russia Could be More Productive," *McKinsey Quarterly*, September 2009.

3. C. K. Prahalad and Stuart L. Hart, "The Fortune at the Bottom of the Pyramid," *Strategy and Business*, (first quarter, 2002): 35–47.

4. www2.goldmansachs.com/ideas/brics/book/BRICs-Chapter9.pdf.

5. "African Debt, European Doubt" *Economist*, April 8, 2000, 46.

6. The discussion of economic integration is based on the pioneering work by Bela Balassa, *The Theory of Economic Integration* (Homewood, IL: Richard D. Irwin, 1961).

7. http://www.ustr.gov/trade-agreements/free-trade-agreements.

8. *The European Union: A Guide for Americans* (Washington, DC: Delegation of the European Commission to the United States, 2009), Chapter 2. See http://www.eurunion.org/infores/euguide/euguide.htm.

9. Jacob Viner, *The Customs Union Issue* (New York: Carnegie Endowment for International Peace, 1950).

10. "Japan Seeks Compensation from EU for Post-EU Expansion Tariff Rise," *Fiji Press English News Service*, July 1, 2003, 1.

11. J. Waelbroeck, "Measuring Degrees of Progress in Economic Integration," in *Economic Integration, Worldwide, Regional, Sectoral*, ed. F. Machlop (London: Macmillan, 1980).

12. "Nokia Closes Bochum, But Opens Cluj Factory," *Softpedia News*, January 15, 2008.

13. "Reverse Brain Drain Threatens U.S. Economy," *USA Today*, February 23, 2004.

14. "EU-Swiss Trade Opening Up," *World Trade*, September 2000, 20. See also http://secretariat.efta.int.

15. "EU-wide Migration Policy 'Needed,'" *BBC News*, March 26, 2008.

16. "EU Trade Deals Will Not Hang on Doha," *Financial Times*, July 10, 2006, 9.

17. "The Cancun Challenge," *The Economist*, September 6, 2003, 59–61.

18. *The European Union: A Guide for Americans* (Washington, DC: Delegation of the European Commission to the United States, 2009), ch. 2.

19. "Summary of the U.S.–Canada Free Trade Agreement," *Export Today* 4 (November–December 1988): 57–61.

20. Gary C. Hufbauer and Jeffrey J. Schott, *NAFTA: An Eight-Year Appraisal* (Washington, DC: Institute for International Economics, 2003), Chapter 1.

21. Sidney Weintraub, *NAFTA at Three: A Progress Report* (Washington, DC: Center for Strategic and International Studies, 1997): 17–18.

22. John Cavanagh, Sarah Anderson, Jaime Serra, and J. Enrique Espinosa, "Happily Ever NAFTA," *Foreign Policy* (September/ October 2002): 58–65.

23. For annual trade information, see http://www.census.gov/foreign-trade

24. "U.S. Trade with Mexico during the Third NAFTA Year," *International Economic Review* (Washington, DC: International Trade Commission, April 1997): 11.

25. "Fox and Bush, for Richer, for Poorer," *The Economist*, February 3, 2001, 37–38.

26. "Aerospace Industry Migrating to Mexico in Greater Numbers, *Republic*, April 2, 2008.

27. Laura Heller, "The Latin Market Never Looked So Bueno," *DSN Retailing Today*, June 10, 2002, 125–126.

28. "Retail Oasis," *Business Mexico*, April 2001, 15.

29. Lara Sowinki, "NAFTA: Two Sides of the Coin," *World Trade*, August 2009; "Mexico: Business Is Standing Its Ground," *BusinessWeek*, April 20, 2009.

30. "Americas: Critics Aside, NAFTA Has Been a Boon to Mexico," *The Wall Street Journal*, January 9, 2004, A.11; "NAFTA's Scorecard: So Far, So Good; *BusinessWeek*, July 9, 2001, 54–56.

31. "Democrats Likely to Run Cross-Border Trucking Project Off the Road," *The Washington Post*, March 3, 2009, 3.

32. "Localizing Production," *Global Commerce*, August 20, 1997, 1.

33. Congressional Research Service, MERCOSUR: Evolution and Implications for U.S. Trade Policy, (Washington, DC: January 5, 2007).

34. Office of the United States Trade Representative, *Third Report to the Congress of the Operations of the Andean Trade Preferences Act as Amended* (Washington, DC.: Author, April 30, 2007).

35. http://www.aseansec.org/64.htm.

36. http://www.apec.org/etc/medialib/apec_media_library/downloads/sec/pubs/2009.Par.0009.File.tmp/09_APEC@Glance.pdf.

37. "Profile: African Union," *BBC News*, March 26, 2009.

38. Ibrahim El-Husseini, Fadi Majdalani, and Alessandro Borgogna, "Filling the Gulf States' Infrastructure Gap," *Strategy & Business*, September 22, 2009.

39. Mohsin S. Khan, "The GCC Monetary Union: Choice of Exchange Rate Regime," Peterson Institute for International Economics, April, 2009.

40. Ayesha Daya, "OPEC May Cut Output to Defend $80 Oil," *Bloomberg.com*, February 8, 2008.

41. http://www.emdirectory.com.

42. James A. Gingrich, "Five Rules for Winning Emerging Market Consumers," *Strategy and Business* (second quarter, 1999): 19–33.

43. Steve Hamm, Manjeet Kripalani, Bruce Einhorn, Andy Reinhardt in Paris, and bureau reports, "Tech's Future," *BusinessWeek*, September 27, 2004.

44. "GE Pins Hopes on Emerging Markets," *The Wall Street Journal*, April 14, 2005, A3, A10.

45. United Nations Conference on Trade and Development, World Investment Prospects Survey, 2009–2011 Survey, September 1, 2009, available at: http://www.area development.com/article_pdf/id75040_Worldinv Prospects002.pdf

46. "Resilient Asia Poised to Lead Recovery from Global Slowdown, Says ADB," Asian Development Bank press release, September 22, 2009.

47. "Weak Exports Hit China's Growth," *BBC News*, April 16, 2009, http://news.bbc.co.uk/2/hi/8001315.stm, accessed October 8, 2009.

48. Press Conference by Prime Minister Dr. Manmohan Singh following G-20 Summit in Pittsburgh, PA, September 25, 2009, Embassy of India, http://www.indianembassy.org/newsite/press_release/2009/Sept/14.asp, accessed October 8, 2009.

49. Long Yongtu, Former Vice Minister, Foreign Trade and Economic Cooperation of the People's Republic of China, speech at the Institute for International Economics May 23, 2005, http://www.iie.com/publications/papers/paper.cfm?ResearchID=529, accessed October 8, 2009.

50. Robyn Meredith, "The Elephant and the Dragon: The Rise of India and China and What It Means for All of Us," WW Norton & Company, New York and London, 2007: 59.

51. Michael R. Czinkota and Charles J. Skuba, "GM in Asian Auto Market," *Korea Times*, June 14, 2009.

52. Ibid.

53. Alan Rosling, Executive Director, Tata Sons, "Mantras for Emerging Markets," January 2005, http://www.tata.com/media/Speeches/inside.aspx, accessed October 9, 2009.

54. World Bank, India Country Overview 2009, http//www.worldbank.org, accessed October 9, 2009.

55. Gurcharan Das, "The India Model," *Foreign Affairs* 85, no. 4 (July/August 2006): 2.

56. FedEx India Reference Guide, http://offer.van.fedex.com/m/p/fdx/index.asp, accessed October 11, 2009.

57. World Bank, Brazil Country Brief 2009, http://www.worldbank.org, accessed October 9, 2009.

58. UNCTAD Survey World Investment Prospects 2009–2011, 54.

59. Christine M. Manna, Director, Corporate Communications, Embraer, September 2, 2009.

60. Carlos M. Gutierrez, U.S. Secretary of Commerce, speech to the American Chamber of Commerce, Rio de Janeiro, October 8, 2008. This speech is available at http://www.commerce.gov/NewsRoom/SecretarySpeeches/PROD01-007350

61. "Doing Business 2010," World Bank 2009, 4.

62. Zhan Lisheng, "TNT Sees Little Impact on Business from Postal Law Changes," *China Daily*, September 24, 2009.

63. Office of the U.S. Trade Representative, *The 2009 National Trade Estimate Report on Foreign Trade Barriers*, 105–108. This report is available at: http://www.ustr.gov/sites/default/files/uploads/reports/2009/NTE/asset_upload_file405_15451.pdf.

64. Ibid., 112–113.

65. Yeo, Vivian "China 'Green Dam' Enforcement Faces Hurdles," *C-Net News*, October 9, 2009.

66. "Issues of Importance to American Business in the U.S.–China Commercial Relationship," the United States Chamber of Commerce, 2007, 13.

67. Medical News Today, "Brazilian President Silva Issues Compulsory License For Merck's Antiretroviral Efavirenz," May 9, 2007, http://www.medicalnewstoday.com/articles/70154.php.

68. 2008 Piracy Study, Business Software Alliance, 5.

69. The Coca-Cola Company, press release, September 29, 2006, http://www.thecoca-colacompany.com/ourcompany/wn20060929_kerala.html.

70. Rovito, Rich "Next Stop–India: Harley-Davidson Preparing Strategy for Indian Market," *The Business Journal of Milwaukee*, January 16, 2009.

71. Transparency International, Global Corruption Report 2009, 397–402.

72. "China's Other Face: The Red and the Black," *The Economist*, October 1, 2009.

73. Heather Timmons, "In India, New Crusade on Corruption," *The New York Times*, July 30, 2009.

74. YouTube, http://www.youtube.com/watch?v=I-IvjXnkHwA, accessed October 11, 2009.

75. Meredith, Robyn, "The Elephant and the Dragon," 129.

76. World Bank, *Private Participation in Infrastructure Database*, http://ppi.worldbank.org/resources/ppi_methodology.aspx, accessed October 12, 2009.

77. Don Belt, "India's Highway: Fast Lane to the Future," *National Geographic*, October 2009.

78. Ministry of Industry and Trade of the Czech Republic, Foreign Trade of the Czech Republic–1-8/2009, http://www.mpo.cz/dokument56901.html, accessed October 12, 2009.

79. Steve LeVine, "Putin's Natural Gas Offers to Shell, Total," *BusinessWeek.com*, July 1, 2009.

80. Paul Abelsky and Lucian Kim, "Russia Remains Committed to Free Market Amid Crisis, Putin Says," *Bloomberg.com*, September 29, 2009.

81. LeVine, Steve, "Putin's Natural Gas Offers to Shell, Total."

82. "50 Years of Pepsi in Russia," *Beverage World*, August 15, 2009.

83. The World Bank considers $2,000 per year to be the minimum to sustain a decent life.

84. Dana James, "B2-4B" Spells Profits," *Marketing News*, November 5, 2001, 1, 11–12.

85. http://www.hp.com/hpinfo/newsroom/press/2000/001012a.html?jumpid=reg_R1002_USEN.

86. This framework is adapted from C.K. Prahalad and Stuart L. Hart, "The Fortune at the Bottom of the Pyramid," *Strategy and Business* (first quarter, 2002): 35–47.

87. "Cell Phones Reshaping Africa," *CNN.com*, October 17, 2005; "Calling Across the Divide," *The Economist*, March 12, 2005, 74.

88. "Major Victories for Micro-Finance," *Financial Times*, May 18, 2005, 10. See also http://www.planetfinance.org.

89. Cait Murphy, "The Hunt for Globalization That Works," *Fortune*, October 28, 2002, 163–176.

90. "And the Winners Are . . . ," *The Economist*, September 18, 2004, 60–62; Arundhati Parmar, "Indian Farmers Reap Web Harvest," *Marketing News*, June 1, 2004, 27, 31.

91. Muhammad Yunus, *Creating a World without Poverty, Social Business and the Future of Capitalism*, 2007, (page 92) http://www.publicaffairsbooks.com/public affairsbooks-cgi-bin/display?book=9781586484934.

92. "Making the Web Worldwide," *The Economist*, September 28, 2004, 76.

93. "Laptop Program for Kids in Poor Countries Teams Up with Microsoft Windows," *The Wall Street Journal*, May 16, 2008, B1.

94. "Cell Phones for the People," *BusinessWeek*, November 14, 2005, 65.

95. C. K. Prahalad and Allen Hammond, "Serving the World's Poor, Profitably," *Harvard Business Review* 80 (September 2002): 48–59.

96. "Drinks for Developing Countries," *The Wall Street Journal*, November 27, 2001, B1, B3.

97. Eric Friberg, Risto Perttunen, Christian Caspar, and Dan Pittard, "The Challenges of Europe 1992," *The McKinsey Quarterly* 21, no. 2 (1988): 3–15.

98. Ronald Haddock and John Jullens, "The Best Years of the Auto Industry Are Still to Come," *Strategy and Business*, May 26, 2009.

99. "City Focus: Tesco Takes on China," *Daily Mail*, August 12, 2008.

100. Gianluigi Guido, "Implementing a Pan-European Marketing Strategy," *Long Range Planning* 24, no. 5 (1991): 23–33.

101. http://www.forum.nokia.com/.

102. "EU and US Approaches to Lobbying," *Euractiv.com*, February 15, 2005.

Chapter 9

1. Global Business Policy Council, *Globalization Ledger*, Washington, DC: A.T. Kearney, April 2000, 3; and Jane Fraser and Jeremy Oppenheim, "What's New About Globalization?" *The McKinsey Quarterly* 2 (1997): 168–179.

2. Michael R. Czinkota and Ilkka A. Ronkainen, "A Forecast of Globalization, International Business and Trade: Report from a Delphi Study," *Journal of World Business* 40 (Winter 2005): 111–123.

3. Jonathan Sprague, "China's Manufacturing Beachhead," *Fortune*, October 28, 2002, 1192A–J.

4. Patricia Jiayi Ho, "GM Discusses India Venture with China Partner," *The Wall Street Journal Digital Network*, October 18, 2009.

5. Bruce Greenwald and Judd Kahn, "All Strategy Is Local," *Harvard Business Review* 83 (September 2005): 94–107.

6. Pankaj Ghemawat, "Regional Strategies for Global Leadership," *Harvard*

Business Review 83 (December 2005): 98–108.

7. The section draws heavily from George S. Yip, *Total Global Strategy II* (Englewood cliffs, NJ: Prentice Hall, 2002), Chapters 1 and 2; Jagdish N. Sheth and Atul Parvatiyar, "The Antecedents and Consequences of Integrated Global Marketing," *International/ Marketing Review* 18 2001: 16–29.

8. Ernst Dichter, "The World Customer," *Harvard Business Review* 40 (July–August 1962): 113–122.

9. Kenichi Ohmae, *The Invisible Continent: Four Strategic Imperatives of the New Economy* (New York: Harper Business, 2001), Chapter 1; Kenichi Ohmae, *The Borderless World Power and Strategy in the Interlinked Economy* (New York: Harper Business, 1999), Chapter 1; Kenichi Ohmae, *Triad Power–The Coming Shape of Global Competition* (New York: Free Press, 1985), 22–27.

10. "BRICs and the Mobile Web," *BusinessWeek*, October 13, 2008, 72.

11. Luciano Catoni, Nora Förisdal Larssen, James Nayor, and Andrea Zocchi, "Travel Tips for Retailers," *The McKinsey Quarterly* 38, no. 3 (2002): 88–98.

12. "Bharti, Wal-Mart Open First Joint Store in India," *The Times of India*, May 30, 2009.

13. The Nielsen Company, "Trends in Online Shopping, A Global Nielsen Consumer Report," February 2008, http://th .nielsen.com/site/documents/Global Online ShoppingReportFeb08.pdf.

14. Catherine George and J. Michael Pearson, "Riding the Pharma Roller Coaster," *The McKinsey Quarterly* 38, no. 4, (2002): 89–98.

15. Nicholas Mockett, "Global M&A Trends in Paper, Packaging and Printing: 2003–2004," PriceWaterhouseCoopers Forest & Paper Industry Practice, available at www.pwc.com/forestry.

16. "Will GE's Appliances Suffer Under a New Owner?" *The Wall Street Journal*, June 16, 2008, A11; William Patalon III, "GE Home Appliance Unit Sale Underscores Again That Corporations and Investors Alike Must Go Global to Succeed," *Money Morning*, May 29, 2008, available at www .moneymorning.com.

17. Stuart Crainer, "And the New Economy Winner Is . . . Europe, *Strategy and Business* 6 (second quarter, 2001): 40–47.

18. "The 2009 CIO 100 Winners: Driving Future Business Growth with Technology Innovation," *CIO Magazine*, June 1, 2009.

19. "Telecommunications," *The Economist*, April 4, 2002, 102.

20. Daniel J. Isenberg, "The Global Entrepreneur," *Harvard Business Review* 86 (December 2008): 107–111.

21. Gary Knight, Tage Koed Madsen, and Per Servais, "An Inquiry into Born-Global Firms in Europe and the USA," *International Marketing Review* 21 no. 6 (2004): 645–666; Oystein Moen and Per Servais, "Born Global or Gradual Global?" *Journal of International Marketing* 10 no. 3 (2002): 49–72.

22. www.cochlear.com.

23. PepsiCo 2008 Annual Report, Indra K. Nooyi, chairman and chief executive officer, Letter to Shareholders, 2.

24. Jordan D. Lewis, *Trusted Partners: How Companies Build Mutual Trust and Win Together* (New York: The Free Press, 2000): 157.

25. "Sara Lee Receives Binding Offer of 1.275 Euros Billion from Unilever for Its Global Body Care Business," Sara Lee Corporation, September 25, 2009.

26. David Goldman, "Microsoft and Yahoo: Search Partners", *CNNMoney .com*, July 29, 2009.

27. Cait Murphy, "The Hunt for Globalization that Works," *Fortune*, October 28, 2002, 67–72.

28. http://www.grameencreativelab.com/ live-examples/grameen-danone-foods .html.

29. Nestlé presentation, "Bernstein Pan-European Strategic Conference," by James Singh, September 2009, http:// www.nestle.com/NestleResearch/ Innovations/Present/Present.htm, accessed October 22, 2009.

30. Myung-Su Chae and John S. Hill "Determinants and Benefits of Global Strategic Planning Formality," *International Marketing Review* 17, no. 6 (2000): 538–562.

31. Marcus Alexander and Harry Korine, "When You Shouldn't Go Global," *Harvard Business Review*, 86 (December 2008): 70–77.

32. Douglas MacMillan, Peter Burrows, and Spencer Ante, "*The APP Economy,*" *BusinessWeek*, November 2, 2009, 45–49.

33. C. Samuel Craig and Susan P. Douglas, "Configural Advantage in Global Markets," *Journal of International Marketing* 8, no. 1 (2000): 6–26.

34. Michael E. Porter, *Competitive Strategy* (New York: Free Press, 1998), Chapter 1.

35. "TMC's Hybrid Vehicles Sold 2 Million," Toyota, September 18, 2009.

36. "A Magic Moment for Ford of Europe," *BusinessWeek*, July 6, 2009.

37. "Nokia Market Share Dives in Asia-Pacific," *Reuters*, December 4, 2008.

38. Pankaj Ghemawat and Thomas Hout, "Tomorrow's Global Giants? Not the Usual Suspects," *Harvard Business Review* 86 (November 2008): 80–89.

39. Michael Porter, *Competitive Advantage* (New York: The Free Press, 1987), Chapter 1.

40. Robert M. Grant, *Contemporary Strategy Analysis: Concepts, Techniques, Applications* (Oxford, England: Blackwell, 2002) Chapter 8.

41. George S. Yip, *Total Global Strategy II* (Upper Saddle River, N J: Prentice-Hall, 2002), Chapter 10.

42. The models referred to are GE/McKinsey, Shell International, and A.D. Little portfolio models and Kevin Coyne, "Enduring Ideas: The GE–McKinsey Nine-Box Matrix," *McKinsey Quarterly*, September 2008.

43. www.generalmills.com/corporate/ company/joint_ ventures.aspx.

44. Richard Tomlinson, "Europe's New Computer Game," *Fortune*, February 21, 2000, 219–224.

45. Saeed Samiee and Kendall Roth, "The Influence of Global Marketing Standardization on Performance," *Journal of Marketing* 56 (April 1992): 1–17.

46. "Euroteen Market Grabs U.S. Attention," *Marketing News*, October 22, 2001, 15.

47. "The American Connection," *The Washington Post*, May 25, 2002, E1–E2.

48. Aruna Chandra and John K., Ryans, "Why India Now?" *Marketing Management*, March/April 2002, 43–45.

49. Imad B. Baalbaki and Naresh K. Malhotra, "Marketing Management Bases for International Market Segmentation: An Alternate Look at the Standardization/Customization Debate," *International Marketing Review* 10, no. 1 (1993): 19–44.

50. Alonso Martinez, Ivan de Souza, and Francis Liu, "Multinationals vs. Multilatinas: Latin America's Great Race," *Strategy and Business*, Fall 2003, 45–58.

51. Pankaj Ghemawat, "Managing Differences: The Central Challenge of Global Strategy," *Harvard Business Review* 85 (March 2007): 59–68.

52. Pascal Cagni, "Think Global, Act European," *Developments in Strategy and Business*, August 30, 2004, available at www.bah.com.

53. Pankaj Ghemawat, "Regional Strategies for Global Leadership," *Harvard Business Review* 83 (December 2005): 98–104.

54. "Shania Reigns," *Time*, December 9, 2002, 80–85.

55. http://www.nokia.com/NOKIA_ COM_1/About_Nokia/Sidebars_new_ concept/Nokia_in_brief/InBrief_08.pdf.

56. Larry Greenemeier, "Offshore Outsourcing Grows to Global Proportions," *Information Week*, February 2002, 56–58.

57. "Philips Electronics to Make China One of Three Big Research Centers," *The Wall Street Journal*, December 20, 2002, B4.

58. W. Chan Kim, and Renee Mauborgne, "Blue Ocean Strategy," *Harvard Business Review*, 82 (October 2004): 76–84.

59. Gary Hamel and C. K. Prahalad, "Do You Really Have a Global Strategy?" *Harvard Business Review* 63 (July–August 1985): 75–82.

60. Edward Tse, Andrew Cainey, and Ronald Haddock, "Evolution on the Global Stage," *Leading Ideas On Line*, October 9, 2007, available at http://www.strategy-business.com/li/leading ideas/li00046?pg=all.

61. Andreas F. Grein, C. Samuel Craig, and Hirokazu Takada, "Integration and Responsiveness: Marketing Strategies of Japanese and European Automobile Manufacturers," *Journal of International Marketing* 9, no. 2 (2001): 19–50.

62. James A. Gingrich, "Five Rules for Winning Emerging Market Consumers," *Strategy and Business* (Second Quarter, 1999): 19–33.

63. "Does Globalization Have Staying Power?" *Marketing Management*, March/April 2002, 18–23.

64. Kamran Kashani, "Beware the Pitfalls of Global Marketing," *Harvard Business Review* 67 (September– October 1989): 91–98.

65. http://www-935.ibm.com/services/us/gbs/bus/html/bcs_whatwethink.html.

66. Larry Huson, and Nabil Sakkab, "Connect and Develop: Inside Procter and Gamble's New Model For Innovation," *Harvard Business Review*, 84 (March 2006): 46–58.

67. George Yip and Audrey Bink, "Managing Global Accounts," *Harvard Business Review* 85 (September 2007): 103–111.

68. David B. Montgomery and George S. Yip, "The Challenge of Global Customer Management," *Marketing Management*, Winter 2000, 22–29.

69. Julian Birkinshaw, "Global Account Management: New Structures, New Tasks," *FT Mastering Management*, 2001, available at www.ftmastering.com/mmo/mmo 05_2.htm.

70. Ikujiro Nonaka and Hirotaka Takeuchi, *The Knowledge Creating Company*, (New York: Oxford University Press, 1995), 115.

71. John A. Quelch and Helen Bloom, "Ten Steps to Global Human Resources Strategy," *Strategy and Business* 4 (first quarter, 1999): 18–29.

72. Available at http://www.whirlpoolcorp.com.

73. Pablo Haberer and Adrian Kohan, "Building Global Champions in Latin America," *The McKinsey Quarterly*, March 2007, 35–41.

74. Meagan Dietz, Gordon Orr, and Jane Xing, "How Chinese Companies Can Succeed Abroad," *The McKinsey Quarterly*, May 2008, 23–31.

75. This section draws from Niraj Dawar and Tony Frost, "Competing with the Giants: Survival Strategies for Local Companies in Emerging Markets," *Harvard Business Review* 77 (March–April 1999): 119–129; and Güliz Ger, "Localizing in the Global Village: Local Firms Competing in Global Markets," *California Management Review* 41 (Summer 1999): 64–83.

76. John H. Roberts, "Defensive Marketing: How a Strong Incumbent Can Protect Its Position," *Harvard Business Review* 83 (November 2005): 150–163.

77. Jonathan Ledgard, "Škoda Leaps to Market," *Strategy and Business* 10 (Fall 2005): 1–12.

78. Guillermo D'Andrea, E. Alejandro Stengel, and Anne Goebel-Krstelj, "6 Truths About Emerging-Market Consumers," *Strategy and Business* 10 (Spring 2004): 59–69.

79. Alonso Martinez, Ivan De Souza, and Francis Liu, "Multinationals vs. Multilatinas," *Strategy and Business* 9 (Fall 2003): 56–67.

80. "The Little Aircraft Company That Could," *Fortune*, November 14, 2005, 201–208.

81. "Chasing Desi Dollars," *Time Inside Business*, August 2005, A22–A24.

82. Ibsen Martínez, "Romancing the Globe," *Foreign Policy*, November/December 2005, 48–56.

83. www.jollibee.com.ph/corporate/international.htm.

84. Arindan Bhattacharya and David Michael, "How Local Companies Keep Multinationals at Bay," *Harvard Business Review*, 86 (March 2008): 85–95.

85. Douglas Ready, Linda Hill, and Jay Conger, "Winning the Race for Talent in Emerging Markets," *Harvard Business Review*, 86 (November 2008): 62–71.

86. Sharon O'Donnell and Insik Jeong, "Marketing Standardization within Global Industries," *International Marketing Review* 17, 1 (2000): 19–33.

Chapter 10

1. Corporations are actually given a charter by government to undertake a business activity. The original corporate charters often established limits for the life span and nature of the corporation's activities.

2. The stakeholder analysis of the corporation is often credited to Edward Freeman, *Strategic Management: A Stakeholder Perspective* (Upper Saddle River, NJ: Prentice-Hall, 1984).

3. Peter Drucker, *The Practice of Management*, (New York: Harper & Row Publishers, 1954).

4. Dr. Wendelin Wiedeking, CEO, Porsche, *Die Zeit*, April 17, 2005.

5. Students of business have, for many years, studied the same companies—ABB, General Electric, BP, IBM, UBS, for example—all of which are publicly traded. They have been the subject of academic study because of the high degree of reporting and disclosure that they provide as a result of being publicly traded. Unfortunately, although they may sometimes be relatively more successful and more recognizable, they are a small minority of the hundreds of thousands of businesses operating globally.

6. Mara Faccio and Larry H. P. Lang, "The Ultimate Ownership of Western European Corporations," *Journal of Financial Economics* 65 (2002): 365. See also Torben Pedersen and Steen Thomsen, "European Patterns of Corporate Ownership," *Journal of International Business Studies* 28, no. 4 (fourth quarter, 1997): 759–778.

7. A basic tenet of most fiduciary responsibilities is that the party with the fiduciary duty—in this case, the management of the corporation—cannot have any conflict of interest when operating on behalf of its party. In effect, the management of the corporation must operate first and foremost, without compromise, in the interests of stockholders.

8. Michael Jensen and W. Meckling, "Theory of the Firm: Managerial Behavior, Agency Costs, and Ownership Structure," *Journal of Financial Economics* 3 (1976); and Michael C. Jensen, "Agency Cost of Free Cash Flow, Corporate Finance and Takeovers," *American Economic Review* 76 (1986): 323–329.

9. This definition of the corporate objective is based on that supported by the International Corporate Governance Network (ICGN), a nonprofit organization committed to improving corporate governance practices globally.

10. "OECD Principles of Corporate Governance," Organization for Economic Cooperation and Development, 1999, revised 2004.

11. For a summary of comparative corporate governance, see R. La Porta, F. Lopez-de-Silanes, and A. Schleifer, "Corporate Ownership Around the World," *Journal of Finance* 54 (1999): 471–517. See also A. Schleifer and R. Vishny, "A Survey of Corporate Governance," *Journal of Finance* 52 (1997): 737–783; and the Winter 2007 issue (vol. 19 no. 1) of the *Journal of Applied Corporate Finance*.

12. There is considerable detail and depth in the multitude of ways in which the operations of the corporation may be made more sustainable, including the recent adoptions of a series of International Organization for Standardization (ISO) standards on sustainability. These new ISO standards now cover areas such as greenhouses gases, the carbon footprint of products and services, environmental management and communication, and environmental labeling and

production declarations. Visit www.iso.org for additional detail.

Chapter 11

1. Jonathan D. Day, "Organizing for Growth," *McKinsey Quarterly*, May 2001, 4–5.

2. Lawrence M. Fischer, "Thought Leader," *Strategy and Business*, 7 (fourth quarter, 2002), 115–123.

3. Robert J. Flanagan, "Knowledge Management in the Global Organization in the 21st Century," *HR Magazine* 44, no. 11 (1999): 54–55.

4. "Partners in Wealth," *The Economist*, January 21, 2006, 16–17.

5. http://www.licensing.org/.

6. Jay R. Galbraith, *Designing the Global Corporation* (New York: Jossey-Bass, 2000), Chapter 3.

7. http://www.timberland.com/corp/index.jsp?page= international.

8. See, for example, Samuel Humes, *Managing the Multinational Confronting the Global-Local Dilemma* (London: Prentice-Hall, 1993), Chapter 1.

9. Vijay Govindarajan, Anil K. Gupta, and C. K. Prahalad, *The Quest for Global Dominance Transforming Global Presence into Global Competitive Advantage* (New York: Jossey-Bass, 2001), Chapter 1 and 2.

10. Michael J. Mol, *Ford Mondeo: A Model T World Car?* (Hershey, PA: Idea Group Publishing, 2001), 1–21.

11. Dura Automotive Systems, Inc., press release, "DURA Automotive Systems Announces Global Reorganization and Other Business Updates," October 13, 2008.

12. Philippe Lasserre, "Regional Headquarters: the Spearhead for Asia Pacific Markets," *Long Range Planning* 29 (February, 1996): 30–37, and John D. Daniels, "Bridging National and Global Marketing Strategies Through Regional Operations," *International Marketing Review* 4 (autumn 1987): 29–44.

13. "Boeing's Defense Unit to Divide Its Operations into 3 Segments," *The Wall Street Journal*, January 28, 2006, A5.

14. "The New Organization," *The Economist*, January 21, 2006, 3–5.

15. Christopher A. Bartlett and Sumantra Ghoshal, *Managing Across Borders* (Cambridge, MA: Harvard Business School Press, 2002), Chapter 10.

16. www.dow.com.

17. Milton Harris and Artur Raviy, "Organization Design," *Management Science*, 48 (July, 2002): 852–865.

18. John P. Workman Jr., Christian Homburg and Kjell Gruner, "Marketing Organization: Framework of Dimensions and Determinants," *Journal of Marketing* 62 (July, 1998): 21–41; and Chuck U. Farley,

"Looking Ahead at the Marketplace It's Global and It's Changing," Donald R. Lehman and Katherine E. Jocz, eds., *Reflections on the Futures of Marketing* (Cambridge, MA: Marketing Science Institute, 1995), 15–35.

19. William Taylor, "The Logic of Global Business," *Harvard Business Review* 68 (March–April 1990): 91–105.

20. Mohanbir Sawhney, "Don't Homogenize, Synchronize," *Harvard Business Review* 79 (July–April 2001): 100–108.

21. Gerard Fairtlough, *The Three Ways of Getting Things Done* (London: Triarchy Press, 2005), Chapters 3 and 4.

22. Ilkka A. Ronkainen. "Thinking Globally, Implementing Successfully", *International Marketing Review* 13, no. 3 (1996): 4–6.

23. "Why Multiple Headquarters Multiply," *The Wall Street Journal*, November 19, 2007, B1, B3.

24. Jack Neff, "Unilever Reorganization Shifts P&L Responsibility," *Advertising Age*, February 28, 2005, 13; "Despite Revamp, Unwieldy Unilever Falls Behind Rivals," *The Wall Street Journal*, January 3, 2005, A1, A5.

25. Russell Eisenstat, Nathaniel Foote, Jay Galbraith, Danny Miller, "Beyond the Business Unit," *TheMcKinsey Quarterly* 37, no. 1, (2001): 180–195.

26. "Country Managers," *Business Europe*, October 16, 2002, 3; John A. Quelch and Helen Bloom, "The Return of the Country Manager," *International Marketing Review* 13, no. 3, (1996): 31–43.

27. Rodman Drake and Lee M. Caudill, "Management of the Large Multinational: Trends and Future Challenges," *Business Horizons* 24 (May–June 1981): 83–91.

28. http://www.halliburton.com/.

29. http://www.yum.com.

30. Sanjay Khosla, Kraft International presentation at Lehman Brothers Back-to-School Consumer Conference, September 3, 2008; Mike Gambrell, Dow Chemical Company, speech at Emerging Markets Summit 2008, September 23, 2008.

31. Christopher A. Bartlett and Sumantra Ghoshal, "Matrix Management: Not a Structure, a Frame of Mind," *Harvard Business Review* 68 (July–August 1990): 138–145.

32. "Big and No Longer Blue," *The Economist*, January 21, 2006, 15; "Beyond Blue," *BusinessWeek*, April 18, 2005, 68–76.

33. The Coca-Cola Company, 2008 Annual Review; Nestlé, http://www.nestle.com/.

34. http://www.jwtinside.com/case-studies.php?pid=25.

35. Carlos Ghosn, "Saving the Business Without Losing the Company" *Harvard*

Business Review 80 (January 2002): 37–45.

36. Gary L Neilson, Karla L Martin, and Elizabeth Powers "The Secrets to Successful Strategy Execution," *Harvard Business Review*, 86 (June 2008): 61–70.

37. Procter & Gamble, 2009 annual report, http://annualreport.pg.com/annualreport2009/leadership/index.shtml, accessed November 22, 2009.

38. General Electric, http://www.ge.com/company/leadership/executives.html, accessed November 22, 2009.

39. Beth Stackpole, "Boeing's Global Collaboration Environment Pioneers Groundbreaking 787 Dreamliner Development Effort, *Design News*, May 14, 2007.

40. The ABB Group, http://www.abb.com/ accessed November 22, 2009.

41. Richard Benson-Armer and Tsun-Yan Hsieh. "Teamwork Across Time and Space." *The McKinsey Quarterly* 33, no. 4 (1997): 18–27.

42. David A. Griffith and Michael G. Harvey, "An Intercultural Communication Model for Use in Global Interorganizational Networks," *Journal of International Marketing* 9, no. 3 (2001): 87–103.

43. Laurel Wentz, "TBWA Worldwide: How to Behave as a Network," *Advertising Age*, January 9, 2009.

44. Ingo Theuerkauf, David Ernst, Amir Mahini, "Think Local, Organize . . . ," *International Marketing Review* 13, no. 3 (1996): 7–12.

45. C.K. Prahalad, "Globalizaation, Digitization, and the Multinational Enterprise," paper presented at the Annual Meetings of the Academy of International Business, November 1999.

46. Keith Epstein Grow and Chi-Dhu Tschang, "The New E-spionage Threat", *BusinessWeek*, April 10, 2008.

47. Gary A. Curtis, Kelly Dempski, and Catherine S. Farley, "Does Your Company Have an IT Generation Gap?" Accenture report, October 2009.

48. Christopher A. Bartlett and Sumantra Ghoshal, "Tap Your Subsidiaries for Global Reach," *Harvard Business Review* 64 (November–December 1986): 87–94.

49. "Mercedes-Benz Advanced Design Studio–Irvine, California," *Car Body Design* 2, June 2008.

50. http://www.zurich.ibm.com/news/09/pentacene.html.

51. P&G 2009 Sustainability Review, "Designed to Matter."

52. David A. Aaker and Erich Joachimsthaler, "The Lure of Global Branding," *Harvard Business Review* 77 (November/December 1999): 137–144.

53. Cyril Bouquet, Julian Birkinshaw "Weight versus Voice: How Foreign

Subsidiaries Gain Attention from Corporate Headquarters," *Academy of Management Journal* 51 (June 2008): 577–601.

54. "A European Electronics Giant Races to Undo Mistakes in the U.S.," *The Wall Street Journal*, January 7, 2004, A1, A10.

55. "India's First Wal-Mart Draws Excitement, Not Protest Venture Comes With Limits That Protect Merchants," *Washington Post*, July 13, 2009.

56. Julian Birkinshaw and Neil Hood, "Unleash Innovation in Foreign Subsidiaries," *Harvard Business Review* 79 (March 2001): 131–137; and Julian Birkinshaw and Nick Fry, "Subsidiary Initiatives to Develop New Markets," *Sloan Management Review* 39 (Spring 1998): 51–61.

57. Vijay Govindarajan and Robert Newton, *Management Control Systems* (New York: McGraw-Hill/Irwin, 2000), Chapter 1.

58. Anil Gupta and Vijay Govindarajan, "Organizing for Knowledge Within MNCs," *International Business Review* 3, no. 1 (1994): 443–457.

59. William G. Ouchi, "The Relationship Between Organizational Structure and Organizational Control," *Administrative Science Quarterly* 22 (March 1977): 95–112.

60. Laurent Leksell, *Headquarters-Subsidiary Relationships in Multinational Corporations* (Stockholm, Sweden: Stockholm School of Economics, 1981), Chapter 5.

61. Henry P. Conn and George S. Yip, "Global Transfer of Critical Capabilities," *Business Horizons* 38 (January/February 1997): 22–31.

62. Anant R. Negandhi and Martin Welge, *Beyond Theory Z* (Greenwich, CT: JAI Press, 1984), 16.

63. http://www.nokia.com/A4433643.

64. Michael R. Czinkota and Ilkka A. Ronkainen, "International Business and Trade in the Next Decade: Report from a Delphi Study," *Journal of International Business Studies* 28, no. 4 (1997): 676–694.

65. Tsun-Yuan Hsieh, Johanne La Voie, and Robert A. P. Samek, "Think Global, Hire Local," *The McKinsey Quarterly* 35, no. 4 (1999): 92–101.

66. Introduced by Chairman and CEO Irene Rosenfeld, "Inside the Kraft Foods Transformation," August 27, 2009, 56.

67. "Thinking for a Living," *The Economist*, January 21, 2006, 9–12.

68. R. J. Alsegg, *Control Relationships Between American Corporations and Their European Subsidiaries*, AMA Research Study No. 107 (New York: American Management Association, 1971), 7.

69. Ron Edwards, Adlina Ahmad, and Simon Moss, "Subsidiary Autonomy:

The Case of Multinational Subsidiaries in Malaysia," *Journal of International Business Studies* 33, no. 1 (2002): 183–191.

70. John J. Dyment, "Strategies and Management Controls for Global Corporations," *The Journal of Business Strategy* 7 (spring 1987): 20–26.

71. Alfred M. Jaeger, "The Transfer of Organizational Culture Overseas: An Approach to Control in the Multinational Corporation." *Journal of International Business Studies* 14 (fall 1983): 91–106.

72. Michael Goold and Andrew Campbell, "Do You Have a Well-Designed Organization?" *Harvard Business Review* 80 (March 2002): 117–124.

73. Michael C. Mankins, and Richard Steele, "Turning Great Strategy into Great Performance," *Harvard Business Review* 83 (July–August 2005): 65–72.

Chapter 12

1. David A. Ricks, *Blunders in International Business,* 4th ed. (Maiden, MA: Wiley-Blackwell, 2006).

2. Attila Yaprak, "Culture Study in International Marketing: A Critical Review and Suggestions for Future Research," *International Marketing Review* 25, no. 2 (2008): 215–229.

3. C. Samuel Craig and Susan P. Douglas, *International Marketing Research,* 3rd ed. (New York: Wiley, 2005).

4. For an excellent diagnostics tool see, Prof. Tamer Cavusgil's "Company Readiness to Export" (CORE), Michigan State University, http://globaledge.msu.edu/diagtools/core .asp, accessed May 25, 2010.

5. Internet World Stats, https:www .internetworldstats.com/stats1.htm, accessed November 17, 2009; CIA–The World Factbook, https://www.cia .gov/library/publications/the-world-factbook/rankorder/2004rank.html, accessed November 17, 2009.

6. "The National Trade Data Bank," http://www.stat-usa.gov/tradtest.nsf, accessed May 25, 2010.

7. Michael R. Czinkota, "International Information Cross-Fertilization in Marketing: An Empirical Assessment" *European Journal of Marketing* 34, no. 11/12 (2000): 1305–1314.

8. Abraham L. Newman, "Building Transnational Civil Liberties; Transgovernmental Entrepreneurs and the European Data Privacy Directive," *International Organization* 62, no. 1 (2008): 103–130.

9. Ricks, *Blunders in International Business.*

10. Michael R. Czinkota, "Russia's Transition to a Market Economy: Learning About Business," Journal of International Marketing 5, 4 (fall 1997): 73–93.

11. Michael R. Czinkota and Masaaki Kotabe, "Product Development the Japanese Way," in M. Czinkota and M Kotabe, *Trends in International Business: Critical Perspectives* (Oxford: Blackwell Publishers, 1998), 153–158.

12. Peter Landwher, "Empathic Design vs. Empathetic Design: A History of Confusion," November 2007, http:// privacy.cs.cmu.edu/dataprivacy/ projects/dialectics/designmethods/ plandweh.pdf, accessed November 2009.

13. Martijn G. de Jong, Jan-Benedict E. M. Steenkamp, Jean-Paul Fox, Hans Baumgartner, "Using Item Response Theory to Measure Extreme Response Style in Marketing Research: A Global Investigation," *Journal of Marketing Research* 45, no. 1 (2008): 104–115.

14. Jeff Miller, "Online Marketing Research," Rajiv Grover and Marco Vriens, eds., *The Handbook of Marketing Research: Uses, Misuses, and Future Advances* (London: Sage, 2006): 110–132.

15. Janet Ilieva, Steve Baron, and Nigel M. Healey, "On-line Surveys in Marketing Research: Pros and Cons," *International Journal of Marketing Research* 44, no. 3 (2002): 361–376.

16. Martine Van Selm and Nicholas W. Jankowski, "Conducting Online Surveys," *Quality and Quantity* 40, no. 3 (June 2006): 435–456.

17. William D. Neal, "Still Got It: Shortcomings Plague the Industry," *Marketing News*, September 16, 2002, 37.

18. Reena Jana, "Mining Virtual Worlds for Market Research," *BusinessWeek*, August 13, 2007.

19. Naresh K. Malhotra and David F. Birks, *Marketing Research: An Applied Approach*, 3rd ed. (Upper Saddle River, NJ: FT Press, 2008).

20. For details on the symposium and additional research studies, see http:// databases.si.umich.edu/reputations, accessed November 14, 2004.

21. Dan Frommer, "Google's Free GPS Service Crushes Garmin, TomTom Shares (GOOG, GRMN, NOK, AAPL)," *Business Insider*, October 28, 2009.

22. Albert Caruana and Michael T. Ewing, "How Corporate Reputation, Quality, and Value Influence Online Loyalty," *Journal of Business Research* 26 (August 2009): 1–8.

23. Mark E. A. Danielson, "Economic Espionage: A Framework for a Workable Solution," *Minnesota Journal of Law, Science, and Technology*, no. 2, (2009): 503–549.

24. C-SPAN: Report on Chinese Espionage, http://www.christusrex.org/www2/ china/acquisition/acqpagel.html. accessed November 15, 2009.

25. Andrel Delbecq, Andrew H. Van de Ven, and David H. Gustafson, *Group Techniques for Program Planning* (Glenview, IL: Scott Foresman, 1975), 83.

26. Duen-Ren Liu, Meng-Jung Shih, Churn-Jung Liau, and Chin-Hui Lai, "Mining the Change of Event Trends for Decision Support in Environmental Scanning," *Expert Systems with Applications* 36, no. 2, Pt. 1 (March 2009): 972–984.

Chapter 13

1. Masaaki Kotabe and Crystal X. Jiang, "Ch. 17: Contemporary Research Trends in International Marketing–the 2000s," in *The Oxford Handbook of International Business (Oxford Handbooks in Business & Management)* 2nd ed., Alan M. Rugman (ed.). (New York: Oxford University Press, 2009), 462.

2. Geoffrey Bankunda, "Corporate Managers' International Orientation and the Export Performance of Firms in Uganda," *Eastern Africa Social Science Research Review* 20, no. 1 (January 2004): 27–50.

3. Taewon Suh, Mueun Bae, and Sumit K. Kundu, "Antecedents to smaller firms' perceived cost and attractiveness in going abroad," in *Enhancing Knowledge Development in Marketing*, (B. Money and R. Rose, eds.) Chicago: American Marketing Association, 2003.

4. S. Cavusgil and G. Knight, "Innovation, Organizational Capabilities and the Born-Global Firm," *Journal of International Business Studies*, 35 no. 2. (2004): 124–141, S. Cavusgil, G. Knight, and J. Riesenberger, *International Business: Strategy, Management*, and the New Realties (Upper Saddle Rever, NJ: Prentice-Hall, 2007).

5. Masaaki Kotabe and Kristiaan Helsen, *The SAGE Handbook of International Marketing* (London: Sage Publications, 2009).

6. Michael R. Czinkota, I. Ronkainen, and M. Ortiz-Buonafina, *The Export Marketing Imperative*, (Cincinnati: Thomson, 2005).

7. Michael Kutschker and Iris Bäuerle, "Three Plus One: Multidimensional Strategy of Internationalization," *Management International Review* 37, 2 (1997): 103–125.

8. Alex Coad, *The Growth of Firms: A Survey of Theories and Empirical Evidence (New Perspectives on the Modem Corporation* (Northampton, MA: Edward Elgar Publishing, 2009), 25–39.

9. Richard D. Hadley and Heather I. M. Wilson, "The Network Model of Internationalization and Experiential Knowledge," *International Business Review* 12, no. 6, (December 2003): 697–717.

10. S. Cavusgil, L. Hui Shi, C. White, and S. Zou, "Global Account Management Strategies: Drivers and Outcomes," *Journal of International Business Studies*, May 21, 2009.

11. Alan Bevan, Saul Estrin, and Klaus Meyer, "Foreign Investment Location and Institutional Development in Transition Economies," *International Business Review* 13, no. 1 (February 2004): 43–64.

12. Czinkota, Ronkainen, and Ortiz-Buonafina, *The Export Marketing Imperative*, Thomson/AMA, 2004.

13. M. Ángeles Gallego, Encarnación Ramos Hidalgo, Francisco J. Acedo, José C. Casillas, and Ana M. Moreno, "The Relationship Between Timing of Entry into a Foreign Market, Entry Mode Decision and Market Selection," *Time & Society*, 18, no. 2–3 (2009): 306–331.

14. Michael R. Czinkota, *International Marketing and Accessibility* (Washington D.C.: U.S. Department of Commerce, 2007).

15. WTO News: 2004 News Items, available online: http://www.wto.org/english/news_e/news04_e/dsb_30nov04_ e.htm, accessed October 11, 2009.

16. Chang-Ing Hsu and Hui-Chieh Li, "An Integrated Plant Capacity and Production Planning Model for High-tech Manufacturing Firms with Economies of Scale," *International Journal of Production Economics*, 118, no. 2 (April 2009): 486–500.

17. Stanley J. Paliwoda and John K. Ryans eds., *International Marketing: Modern and Classic Papers*, (Northampton, MA: Edward Elgar Publishing, 2008), 226.

18. Isobel Doole and Robin Lowe, *International Marketing Strategy: Analysis, Development and Implementation*, 5th ed. (London: Cengage Learning, 2008), 22–34.

19. Michael R. Czinkota, "A National Export Development Policy for New and Growing Businesses," in *The Future of Global Business: A Reader*, M. Czinkota, M. Kotabe and I. Ronkainen, eds. (Oxford: Routledge, 2011).

20. Jane W. Lu and Paul W. Beamish, " SME Internationalization and Performance: Growth vs. Profitability," *Journal of International Entrepreneurship*, 4, no. 1 (March 2006): 27–48.

21. O.E. Williamson. *The Economic Institutions of Capitalism*, New York: Free Press, 1985.

22. Michael R. Czinkota and Masaaki Kotabe, "Entering the Japanese Market: A Reassessment of Foreign Firms' Entry and Distribution Strategies," *Industrial Marketing Management*, 29 (2000): 483–491.

23. Tobias Kollmann, "What Is E-entrepreneurship?—Fundamentals of Company Founding in the Net Economy," *International Journal of Technology Management*, 33, no. 4 (2006): 322–340.

24. E. Reiljan, "The Role of Cooperation and Innovation in Reducing the Likelihood of Export Withdrawals: The Case of the Estonian Wood Sector," *Journal of East West Business* 13, no. 2/3 (2007): 243–261.

25. S. Tamer Cavusgil and Gary Knight, *Born Global Firms: A New International Enterprise* (New York: Business Expert Press, 2009).

26. Oystein Moen and Per Servais, "Born Global or Gradual Global? Examining the Export Behavior of Small and Medium-Sized Firms," *Journal of International Marketing*, 10, no. 2 (2002): 49–72.

27. Mike W. Peng, Yuanyuan Zhou, and Anne S. York, "Behind Make or Buy Decisions in Export Strategy: A Replication and Extension of Trabold," *Journal of World Business* 41, no. 3 (September 2006): 289–300.

28. Dong-Sung Cho, *The General Trading Company. Concept and Strategy* (Lexington, MA: Lexington Books, 1987), 2.

29. R. Larke and K. Davies, "Recent Changes in the Japanese Wholesale System and the Importance of the Sogo Shosha," *The International Review of Retail, Distribution and Consumer Research*, 17 no. 4 (2007): 377.

30. Masanori Ono, "Trading Companies as Financial Intermediaries in Japan," working paper presented at the 2009 Pacific Rim Conference of the Western Economic Association International. Available online at http://mpra.ub.uni-muenchen .de/17331/1/Ono2009 Sept.pdf, accessed October 5, 2009.

31. Alice Amsden, "The Wild Ones: Industrial Policies in the Developing World," in *The Washington Consensus Reconsidered: Towards a New Global Governance*, Narcis Serra and Joseph E. Stiglitz, eds. (New York: Oxford University Press, 2008).

32. Current Export Trade Certificate of Review Holders, available online, http://www.ita.doc.go, accessed October 5, 2009.

33. William A. Kerr, "International Trade Education: Do We Need a New Model for the Global Market?" *The Estey Centre Journal of International Law and Trade Policy* 8, no. 1 (2007): 1–11.

34. Donald W. Hackett, "The International Expansion of U.S. Franchise Systems," in *Multinational Product Management*, Warren J. Keegan and Charles S. Mayer, eds. (Chicago: American Marketing Association, 1979), 61–81.

35. "Franchise Businesses Prepare for Economic Challenges," *International Franchise Association*, Washington, DC, January 7, 2009, available online: http://www.franchise.org, accessed October 5, 2009.

36. Lance E. Brouthers and Jason P. McNicol, "International Franchising and Licensing," *The SAGE Handbook of International Marketing*, Masaaki Kotabe

and Kristiaan Helsen, eds. (Newbury Park, CA: Sage Publications, 2009).

37. Waheedan Jariwalla, "The Starbucks Trademark Prevails," *Law Society of England and Wales*, January 12, 2007; Linda Huan, "Commercial Franchising in China," *Franchise Council of Australia*, September 19, 2008.

38. Gary A. Knight, "The New Global Marketing Realities," in *Marketing in the 21st Century: New World Marketing*, Timothy J. Wilkinson and Andrew R. Thomas, eds. (Santa Barbara, CA: Greenwood Publishing Group, 2007), 3–25.

39. Dong Chen, Seung Ho Park, and William Newburry, "Parent Contribution and Organizational Control in International Joint Ventures," *Strategic Management Journal* 30, no. 11 (2009): 1133–1156.

40. Rodney McAdam, Tom O'Hare, and Sandra Moffett, "Collaborative Knowledge Sharing in Composite New Product Development: An Aerospace Study," *Technovation*, 28, no. 5 (May 2008): 245–256.

41. Xiaohua Sun and Lin Hu, "Game Analysis of Strategic Partner Selection of Chinese and Foreign Technology Alliance," *International Business Research* 2, no. 4 (2009): 46–49.

42. Susanne Royer and Roland Simons, "Evolution of Cooperation and Dynamics of Expectations–Implications for Strategic Alliances," *International Journal of Strategic Business Alliances*, 1, no. 1 (2009): 73–88.

43. Christian Homburg, Joseph P. Cannon, Harley Krohmer, and Ingo Kiedaisch, "Governance of International Business Relationships: A Cross-Cultural Study on Alternative Governance Modes," *Journal of International Marketing* 17, no. 3 (September 2009): 1–20.

44. Sonja J. Dickinson and B. Ramaseshan, "Maximising Performance Gains from Cooperative Marketing: Understanding the Role of Environmental Contexts," *Journal of Marketing Management*, 24, nos. 5–6 (July 2008): 541–566.

45. David Murphy, *Understanding Risk: The Theory and Practice of Financial Risk Management*, (London, MA: Chapman & Hall/Crc. Financial Mathematics Series, 2008).

46. Bradley Sugars, *Successful Franchising*, (Columbus, OH: McGraw-Hill, 2005), 17.

47. Hana Alberts, "China Unicorn and Telefonica Reach Deal," *Forbes.com*, September 7, 2009, available online; http://www.forbes.com/2009/09/07/china-unicom-telefonica-markets-equity-deal.html, accessed October 2, 2009; Ameya Karve, "India's OnMobile Global Signs Pacts With Spain's Telefonica," *The Wall Street Journal*, July 14, 2009.

48. Srinivasan Balakrishnan and Mitchell P. Koza, "Information Asymmetry, Adverse Selection, and Joint Ventures: Theory and Evidence," in *Strategic Alliances: Theory and Evidence*, Jeffrey J. Reuer, ed. (New York: Oxford University Press, 2004), 120.

49. Andrew C. Inkpen, "Knowledge Transfer and International Joint Ventures: The Case of NUMMI and General Motors," *Strategic Management Journal*, 29, no. 4 (October 24, 2007): 447–453.

50. Marc Lifsher, "California Panel Delays Vote on NUMMI's Request for Training Pay," *Los Angeles Times*, September 26, 2009.

51. http://www.eads.com/1024/en/Homepage1024.html, accessed October 3, 2009.

52. Jorge Walter, Christoph Lechner, and Franz W. Kellermanns, "Disentangling Alliance Management Processes: Decision Making, Politicality, and Alliance Performance," *Journal of Management Studies* 45, no. 3 (May 2008): 530–560.

53. United Nations, *Guidelines for Foreign Direct Investment* (New York: United Nations, 1975), 65–76.

54. Li Dong and Keith W. Glaister, "National and Corporate Culture Differences in International Strategic Alliances: Perceptions of Chinese Partners," *Asia Pacific Journal of Management* 24, no. 2 (June 2007): 191–205.

55. Harumi Ito and Darin Lee, "Domestic Code Sharing, Alliances, and Airfares in the U.S. Airline Industry," *The Journal of Law and Economics* 50, no. 2 (May 2007): 355–380.

56. "Starbucks Acquires Full Ownership of Starbucks Coffee France SAS," *Forbes.com*, available online, http://www.forbes.com/feeds/businesswire/2009/09/01/businesswire128500452.html, accessed October 6, 2009.

57. Jing Li, Changhui Zhou, and Edward J. Zajac, "Control, Collaboration, and Productivity in International Joint Ventures: Theory and Evidence," *Strategic Management Journal* 30, no. 8, (April 3, 2009): 865–884.

58. John M. Mezias, "How to Identify Liabilities of Foreignness and Assess Their Effects on Multinational Corporations," *Journal of International Management*, 8, no. 3 (2002): 265–282.

59. Chiung-Hui Tseng, "Exploring Location-Specific Assets and Exploiting Firm-Specific Advantages: An Integrative Perspective on Foreign Ownership Decisions," *Canadian Journal of Administrative Sciences* 24, no. 2 (June 13, 2007): 120–134.

Chapter 14

1. American Marketing Association, http://www.marketing power.com, 2007.

2. Robert Barrels, "Are Domestic and International Marketing Dissimilar?" *Journal of Marketing* 36 (July 1968): 56–61.

3. Pankaj Ghemawat, "Distance Still Matters: The Hard Reality of Global Expansion," *Harvard Business Review*, 79 (September 2001): 137–147.

4. For one of the best summaries, see Country Monitor, *Indicators of Market Size for 195 Countries* (New York: EIU, 2009).

5. Philip Kotler and Kevin Lane Keller, *A Framework for Marketing Management*, 4th ed. (Upper Saddle River, NJ: Prentice-Hall, 2009), 153.

6. James A. Gingrich, "Five Rules for Winning Emerging Market Consumers," *Strategy and Business* (second quarter, 1999): 68–76.

7. The Coca-Cola Company 2008 Annual Review, 8.

8. https://www.cia.gov/library/publications/the-world-factbook/fields/2047.html?countryName=&countryCode=&regionCode=V.

9. Samuel Craig and Susan P. Douglas, "Conducting Market Research in the Twenty First Century," *International Marketing Review*, 18 (2001): 80–90.

10. Van R. Wood, John R. Darling, and Mark Siders, "Consumer Desire to Buy and Use Products in International Markets: How to Capture It, How to Sustain It," *International Marketing Review*, 16, no. 3 (1999): 231–242.

11. "Feast and Famine," *The Economist*, October 1, 2009; and "Russian Auto Market to Be Third Largest Worldwide by 2012," *Frost*, January 29, 2009.

12. Yuval Atsmon and Vinay Dixit, "Understanding China's Wealthy," *The McKinsey Quarterly*, July 2009, 32–33.

13. Igal Aval and Jehiel Zif, "Marketing Expansion Strategies in Multinational Marketing," *Journal of Marketing* 43 (spring 1979): 84–94.

14. C. K. Prahalad and Hrishi Bhattacharyya, "Twenty Hubs and No HQ", *Strategy and Business*, Spring 2008, 1–6.

15. The Advertising Standards Authority, United Kingdom, http://www.asa.org.uk/asa/adjudications/Public/TF_ADJ_45250.htm, accessed November 26, 2009.

16. http://www.logitech.com/.

17. Carl A. Sohlberg, "The Perennial Issue of Adaptation or Standardization of International Marketing Communication: Organizational Contingencies and Performance," *Journal of International Marketing* 10, no. 3 (2002): 1–21.

18. "Barbie in China: Mattel to Open Barbie Superstore in Shanghai," *Huffington Post*, March 3, 2009.

19. "Haier India Forays into New Business Category—Launches Stylish, Sleek and Safest Range of Haier Spa Water Heater," *India PR Wire*, August 13, 2009.

20. Jean-Noel Kapferer, *Survey Among 210 European Brand Managers* (Paris: Euro-RSCG, 1998).

21. http://www.murray-europe.com/uk_pages/landing_pages/contact_us.html; and Davis Goodman, "Thinking Export? ISO 9000," *Export Today*, August 1998, 48–49.

22. http://www.iso.org, accessed November 27, 2009.

23. "Krispy Kreme: Sweet on Britain," *USA Today*, August 12, 2003, 6A, 7A.

24. "Taking a Bite Out of China, *Nation's Restaurant News*, October 15, 2007, S20–S22.

25. Nader Tavssoli and Jin K. Han, "Auditory and Visual Brand Identifiers in Chinese and English," *Journal of International Marketing* 10, no. 2 (2002): 13–28.

26. Erika Morphy, "Cutting the Cost of Compliance," *Export Today* 12 (January 1996): 14–18.

27. Owen Fletcher, "Lenovo, HP Lead Way into Rural China PC Market," *PC World*, November 2, 2009.

28. Jeffrey R. Immelt, Chris Trimble, and Vijay Govindarajan, "How GE Is Disrupting Itself," *Harvard Business Review* 87 (October 2009): 56–63.

29. "Indian Firms Shift Focus to the Poor," *The Wall Street Journal*, October 20, 2009, A1, 18.

30. "Waste Not," *Business Europe*, February 20, 2002, 4.

31. Johny K. Johansson, Ilkka A. Ronkainen, and Michael R. Czinkota, "Negative Country-of-Origin Effects: The Case of the New Russia," *Journal of International Studies* 25, no. 1 (1994): 1–21.

32. Philip Kotler and David Gertner, "Country as Brand, Product, and Beyond: A Place Marketing and Brand Management Pespective," *Journal of Brand Management* 9 (April 2002): 249–261.

33. Edwin Colyer, "India: A Hot Brand Climate?" *BusinessWeek*, May 31, 2006.

34. "Global Brands," *BusinessWeek*, August 1, 2005, 45–46.

35. Johny K. Johansson and Ilkka A. Ronkainen, "Are Global Brands the Right Choice for Your Company?" *Marketing Management*, March/April 2004, 53–56.

36. Jean-Noël Kapferer, "The Post-Global Brand," *Journal of Brand Management* 12, no. 5 (2005): 319–324.

37. Douglas B. Holt, John A. Quelch, and Earl L. Taylor, "How Global Brands Compete," *Harvard Business Review* 82 (September 2004): 68–75.

38. Interbrand, *Going Global: Global Branding-Risks and Rewards* (New York: Interbrand, October 2005), 1–7, available at www.interbrand.com.

39. Johny K. Johansson and Ilkka A. Ronkainen, "The Esteem of Global Brands," *Journal of Brand Management* 12, no. 5 (2005): 339–354.

40. www.uschamber.com/ncf/initiatives/counterfeiting.htm.

41. Ilkka A. Ronkainen and Jose-Luis Guerrero-Cusumano, "Correlates of Intellectual Property Violation," *Multinational Business Review* 9, no. 1 (2001): 59–65.

42. Matthew Myers, S. Tamer Cavusgil, and Adamantios Diamantopoulos, "Antecedents and Actions of Export Pricing Strategy: A Conceptual Framework and Research Propositions," *European Journal of Marketing* 36, no. 1/2 (2002): 159–189.

43. "Marketers Pursue the Shallow-Pocketed," *The Wall Street Journal*, January 26, 2007, B3.

44. *Avon Products*, Third Quarter 2009 Earnings report, October 29, 2009, accessed November 27, 2009.

45. Swee Hoon Ang, Siew Meog Leong, and Philip Kotler, "The Asian Apocalypse: Crisis Marketing for Consumers and Businesses," *Long Range Planning* 33 (February 2000): 97–119.

46. Kent B. Monroe, *Pricing: Making Profitable Decisions* (New York: McGraw-Hill, 2003), 12.

47. Johan Ahlberg, Nicklas Garemo, and Tomas Naucler, "The Euro: How to Keep Your Prices Up and Your Competitors Down," *The McKinsey Quarterly*, 2 (1999): 112–118; and "Even After Shift to Euro, One Price Won't Fit All," *The Wall Street Journal Europe*, December 28, 1998, 1.

48. Stephen A. Butscher, "Maximizing Profits in Euroland," *Journal of Commerce*, May 5, 1999, 5.

49. www.agmaglobal.org.

50. Ilkka A. Ronkainen and Linda Van de Gucht, "Making a Case for Gray Markets," *Journal of Commerce*, January 6, 1987, 13A.

51. Jen-Hung Huang, Bruce C. Y. Lee, and Shu Hsun Ho, "Consumer Attitude toward Gray Market Goods," *International Marketing Review* 21, no. 6 (2004): 598–614.

52. Higinbotham, Chun W. Y., "International Transfer Pricing: Practical Solutions for Intra-Company Pricing," *International Tax Journal* 28 (fall 2002): 1–22.

53. Internal Revenue Service, "Announcements and Report Concerning Advance Pricing Agreements," March 27, 2009, http://www.irs.gov/pub/irs-utl/2008apa032709.pdf, accessed December 12, 2009.

54. Mohammad F. Al-Eryani, Pervaiz Alam, and Syed H. Akhter, "Transfer Pricing Determinants of U.S. Multinationals," *Journal of International Business Studies* 21 (fall 1990): 409–425.

55. http://www.oecd.org/document/34/0,3343,en_2649_33753_1915490_1_1_1_1,00.html.

56. Todd Guild, "Think Regionally, Act Locally: Four Steps to Reaching the Asian Consumer," *McKinsey*, September 2009, 25–35.

57. Michael R. Czinkota, "Distribution of Consumer Products in Japan," in *International Marketing Strategy: Environmental Assessment and Entry Strategies*, Michael R. Czinkota and Ilkka A. Ronkainen, eds. (Ft. Worth, TX: The Dryden Press, 1994), 293–307.

58. Scott Kirsner, "The Customer Experience," *Fast Company.com*, December 2007.

59. Internet World Stats, http://www.internetworldstats.com/stats.htm, accessed December 10, 2009.

60. http://www.export.gov/sellingonline/eg_main_o2o784.asp.

61. UPS Fact Sheet, http://www.ups.com, accessed December 9, 2009.

62. http://www.dell.com/downloads/global/casestudies/2005_iglu.pdf.

63. Hope Katz Gibbs, "Taking Global Local," *Global Business*, December 1999, 44–50.

64. http://www.export.gov/sellingonline/eg_main_020781.asp.

65. "Music Piracy Poses a Threat to Regional Artists," *The Wall Street Journal*, June 4, 2002, B10.

66. Anne Austin, Jonathon Barnard, and Nicky Hutcheon, "Advertising Expenditure Forecasts," *ZenithOptimedia*, October 2009.

67. Laurel Wentz and Bradley Johnson, "Top 100 Global Advertisers Heap Their Spending Abroad," *Advertising Age*, November 30, 2009.

68. Austin, Barnard, and Hutcheon, "Advertising Expenditure Forecasts."

69. Wentz and Johnson, "Top 100 Global Advertisers Heap Their Spending Abroad."

70. Austin, Barnard, and Hutcheon, "Advertising Expenditure Forecasts."

71. http://ec.europa.eu, Audiovisual and Media Policies, accessed December 8, 2009.

72. Allied Media, http://www.allied-media.com/aljazeera/JAZdemog.html, accessed December 9, 2009.

73. Abbey Klaasen, "Search Marketing," *Advertising Age*, November 2, 2009.

74. Hiroko Tabuchi, "In Japan, an Odd Perch for Google: Looking Up at the Leader," *The New York Times*, November 30, 2009.

75. Tom Warren, "T-Mobile Invades Busy London Rail Station," http://www.neowin.net, January 17, 2009.

76. Rocky Fu, "China Online Shopping Statistics 2009 Part 1—Penetration Rate by City," *Online Shopping*, December 9, 2009.

77. Lulu Raghavan, "Lessons from the Maharaja Mac," *Landor*, December 2007.

78. http://motherjones.com/politics/2009/09/fiji-spin-bottle.

79. http://adage.com/images/random/datacenter/2008/globalaccounts2008.pdf.

80. Authur Baldauf, David W. Cravens, and Nigel F. Piercy, "Examining the Consequences of Sales Management Control Strategies in European Field Sales Organization," *International Marketing Review* 18, no. 5 (2001): 474–508.

81. Joseph A. Lawton, "Kodak Penetrates the European Copier Market with Customized Marketing Strategy and Product Changes," *Marketing News*, August 1984, 1, 6, See also http://www.kodak.com.

82. "Fuel and Freebies," *The Wall Street Journal*, June 10, 2002, B1, B6.

83. Michael E. Porter and Mark R. Kramer, "The Competitive Advantage of Corporate Philanthropy, *Harvard Business Review* 80 (December 2002): 56–68.

84. "Business Scales World Summit," *The Wall Street Journal*, August 28, 2002, A12, A13.

85. Gary Gereffi, Ronnie Garcia-Johnson, and Erika Sasser, "The NGO-Industrial Complex," *Foreign Policy*, July/August 2001, 56–66.

Chapter 15

1. Leonard L. Berry and A. Parasuraman, "Listening to the Customer: The Concept of a Service-Quality Information System," in Christopher H. Lovelock, *Services Marketing*, 6th ed. (Upper Saddle River, NJ: Prentice Hall, 2006): 182.

2. Christian Grönroos, "Adopting a Service Logic for Marketing," *Marketing Theory* 6, no. 3 (2006): 317–333.

3. Michael R. Czinkota, D. Grossman, R. Javalgi, and N. Nugent, "Foreign Market Entry Mode of Service Firms," *Journal of World Business* 44, no. 3 (July 2009): 274–286.

4. Lawrence Cunningham, Clifford Young, Moonkyu Lee, and Wolfgang Ulaga, "Customer Perceptions of Service Dimensions: Cross-Cultural Analysis and Perspective," *International Marketing Review* 23, no. 2 (2006): 192–210.

5. David A. Schweidel, Peter S. Fader, and Eric T. Bradlow, "Understanding Service Retention Within and Across Cohorts Using Limited Information," *Journal of Marketing* 72, no. 1 (January 2008): 82–94.

6. Richard G. Lipsey and Alice Nakamura, *Services Industries and the Knowledge-Based Economy*, (Calgary, CA: University of Calgary Press, 2006), 513.

7. CIA, *The World Factbook*, https://www.cia.gov/library/publications/the-world-factbook/geos/us.html, accessed December 5, 2009.

8. "U.S. Export Factsheet," Department of Commerce, International Trade Administration, http://www.trade.gov/press/press_releases/2009/export-factsheet_021109.pdf, accessed December 5, 2009.

9. U.S. Census Bureau, Bureau of Economic Analysis, December 10, 2009, http://www.bea.gov/, accessed December 16, 2009.

10. U.S. Department of State, "Background Notes," http://www.state.gov/r/pa/ei/bgn/index.htm, accessed December 7, 2009.

11. Barry Bosworth and Susan M. Collins, "Accounting for Growth: Comparing China and India," *Journal of Economic Perspectives* 22, no. 1 (2008): 45–66.

12. Janet Y. Murray, Masaaki Kotabe, and Stanford A. Westjohn, "Global Sourcing Strategy and Performance of Knowledge-Intensive Business Services: A Two-Stage Strategic Fit Model," *Journal of International Marketing* 17, no. 4 (December 2009): 90–105.

13. Adidas Group Annual Report 2009, http://adidas-group.corporate-publications.com/2008/gb/en/adidas-gruppe-kompakt/major-locations-and-promotion-partnerships.html, accessed December 6, 2009.

14. Timothy J. Sturgeon and Gary Gereffi, "Measuring Success in the Global Economy: International Trade, Industrial Upgrading, and Business Function Outsourcing in Global Value Chains," *Transnational Corporations* 18, no. 2 (August 2009): 1–36.

15. Joel D. Wisner, Keah-Choon Tan, and G. Keong Leong, *Principles of Supply Chain Management: A Balanced Approach*, 2nd ed. (New York: Cengage Learning, 2008), 339.

16. David M. Brock, Michael J. Powell, and C. R. Hinings, "Archetypal Change and the Professional Service Firm," *Research in Organizational Change and Development* 16 (2007): 221–251.

17. Ruth N. Bolton, Dhruv Grewal, and Michael Levy, "Six Strategies for Competing through Service: An Agenda for Future Research," *Journal of Retailing* 83, no. 1 (2007): 1–4.

18. S. Alam, M. Noor, and M. Kamal, "ICT Adoption in Small and Medium Enterprises," *International Journal of Business and Management* 4, no. 2 (February 2009): 112–126.

19. Emin M. Dinlersoz and Pedro Pereira, "On the Diffusion of Electronic Commerce," *International Journal of Industrial Organization* 25, no. 3 (June 2007): 541–574.

20. WTO Electronic Commerce Gateway, http://www.wto.org/english/tratop_E/ecom_e/ecom_e.htm, accessed December 12, 2009.

21. "Top Ten Internet Languages," *Internet World Statistics*, http://www.internetworldstats.com/stats7.htm, accessed December 10, 2009.

22. "Nine, Ninety, Ninety: Add 9 Languages and Reach 90% of the World Market in 90 Days" http://www.motionpoint.com/company/motionpoint-news/archived-news-2008/223-add-9-languages-and-reach-90-percent-of-the-world-market-in-90-d.html, accessed March 23, 2010 this refers to 2006 World Bank GNI which = GNP

23. *UNWTO World Tourism Barometer* 7, no. 2 (June 2009): 1–9.

24. *China Hospitality News*, http://www.chinahospitality news.com/en, accessed December 17, 2009.

25. Paul G. Patterson and Muris Cicic, "A Typology of Service Firms in International Markets: An Empirical Investigation," *Journal of International Marketing* 3, no. 4 (1995): 57–83.

26. World Bank Ecommerce Publications, http://publications.worldbank.org/ecommerce/, accessed December 17, 2009.

27. Michael R. Czinkota, D. Grossman, R. Javalgi, and N. Nugent, Foreign Market Entry Mode of Service Firms: The Case of U.S. MBA Programs," *Journal of World Business* 44, no. 3 (2009): 274–286.

Chapter 16

1. Rajiv D. Banker, Indranil R. Bardhan, and Tai-Yuan Chen, 'The Role of Manufacturing Practices in Mediating the Impact of Activity-based Costing on Plant Performance,' *Accounting, Organizations and Society* 33, no. 1 (January 2008): 1–19.

2. Donald Waters, ed. *Global Logistics: New Directions in Supply Chain Management,* 5th ed. (Philadelphia, PA: Kogan Page, 2007), 148.

3. P. C. Nolan, www.pcnolan.com . accessed October 13, 2009; Council of Supply Chain Management Professionals, www.cscmp.org, accessed October 13, 2009.

4. James B. Ayers, *Handbook of Supply Chain Management (Resource Management)*, 2nd ed. (London, UK: Auerbach Publications, 2006), Ch. 2, p. 13; John J. Coyle, Edward J. Bardi, and C. John Langley, *Supply Chain Management: A Logistics Perspective.* 8th ed. (Mason, OH: South-Western Cengage Learning, 2008), Ch. 9, 376.

5. Nathalie Fabbe-Costes and Jacques Colin, 'Formulating Logistics Strategy,' in *Global Logistics: New Directions in Supply Chain Management*, 5th ed., Donald Waters, ed. (Philadelphia, PA: Kogan Page, 2007).

6. Robert M. Monczka, Robert B. Handfield, and Larry Giunipero, *Purchasing and*

Supply Chain Management, 5th ed. (Philadelphia, PA: Kogan Page, 2007), 148.

7. Interview with Marcio Stewart, Latin America analyst for Inbound Logistics, in *Latin American Logistics: A New World Venture*, June 2008, 4, http://www.inboundlogistics.com/digital/latinamerica_digital08.pdf, accessed October 20, 2009.

8. John D. Schulz, "Logisticians 'Survive the Slump,' but Costs Hit 10.1 percent of GDP," Annual Council of Supply Chain Management Professionals Report, *Logistics Management*, June 19, 2008.

9. Coyle, Bardi, and Langley, *Supply Chain Management*, Ch. 9, 376.

10. Interview with Marcio Stewart.

11. Fabbe-Costes and Colin, "Formulating Logistics Strategy."

12. "Unprecedented Increase in Somali Pirate Activity, ICC Reports," International Chamber of Commerce, http://www.iccwbo.org/, Kuala Lumpur, October 21, 2009, accessed October 13, 2009.

13. David A. Ricks, *Blunders in International Business*, 4th ed. (Hoboken, NJ: Wiley-Blackwell, 2006).

14. *On Competition, Updated and Expanded Edition* (Cambridge, MA: Harvard Business School Press, 2008).

15. *Review of Maritime Transport 2008*, United Nations Conference on Trade and Development, http://www.unctad.org/Templates/Page.asp?intItemID=4658&lang=1, accessed October 20, 2009.

16. Boeing company web site, http://www.boeing.com/commercial/freighters/index.html, accessed October 18, 2009.

17. Douglas H. Brooks and David Hummels (eds.), *Infrastructure's Role in Lowering Asia's Trade Costs: Building for Trade* (Northampton, MA: Edward Elgar Publishing, 2009).

18. Robert M. Monczka, Robert B. Handfield, and Larry Giunipero, *Purchasing and Supply Chain Management*, 4th ed. (Mason, OH: Cengage Learning, 2009), 357.

19. J. F. Arvis, M. A. Mustra, J. Panzer, L. Ojala, and T. Naula, "Connecting to Compete: Trade Logistics in the Global Economy," in *The Global Enabling Trade Report*, 2008 World Economic Forum (Washington, DC: The World Bank, 2008), 54.

20. Brooks and Hummels, *Infrastructure's Role in Lowering Asia's Trade Costs*.

21. David Hummels, "Transportation Costs and International Trade in the Second Era of Globalization," *Journal of Economic Perspectives* 21, no. 3 (2007): 131–154.

22. Supee Teravaninthorn and Gael Raballand, *Transport Prices and Costs in Africa: A Review of the Main International Corridors* (Washington, DC: The World Bank, 2009): 52.

23. U.S. Department of Commerce, *A Basic Guide to Exporting*, 10th ed. (Washington, DC: International Trade Administration, 2008).

24. Christine Kronz and Christian Zipse, Statistisches Bundesamt Deutschland, "Too Much Bureaucracy?" *Destatis*, August 3, 2009.

25. World Bank, *Doing Business Report 2010: Reforming Through Difficult Times* (Houndmills, UK: Palgrave Macmillan, 2009).

26. International Chamber of Commerce, "What Are Incoterms," available online, http://www.iccwbo.org/incoterms/id3042/index.html, accessed October 20, 2009.

27. International Chamber of Commerce, "The 13 Incoterms," available online, http://www.iccwbo.org/incoterms/id3038/index.html, accessed October 20, 2009.

28. Carl A. Nelson, *Import/Export: How to Take Your Business Across Borders*, 4th ed. (New York: McGraw-Hill, 2009), 28–30.

29. J. E. Holsenback and H. J. McGill, "A Survey of Inventory Holding Cost Assessment and Safety Stock Allocation," *Academy of Accounting and Financial Studies Journal* 11, no. 1 (2007): 111–120.

30. Ven Sriram and Snehamay Banerjee, "Electronic Data Interchange: Does Its Adoption Change Purchasing Policies and Procedures?" *Journal of Supply Chain Management* 30, no. 1994: 30–40.

31. Duncan R. Shaw, "Why Smart Business Networks Continue and Develop: A Structural and Processual Model of Value Flows," in *The Network Experience: New Value from Smart Business Networks*, Peter H. M. Vervest and Diederik W. van Liere (eds.) (Berlin, Germany: Springer, 2008), 305–327.

32. Edward J. Malecki and Bruno Moriset, *The Digital Economy: Business Organization, Production Processes, and Regional Developments* (New York, Routledge, 2008), 109–110.

33. Charles A. Taft, *Management of Physical Distribution and Transportation*, 7th ed. Homewood, IL: Irwin, 184: 324.

34. David A. Ricks, *Blunders in International Business* (Oxford, UK: Blackwell Publishing, 2006).

35. "Splashing, and Clashing, in Murky Waters," *The Economist*, August 20, 2009.

36. Coyle, Bardi, and Langley, *Supply Chain Management*, 533.

37. "69th Annual Report of the Foreign-Trade Zones Board to the Congress of the United States," International Trade Administration, U.S. Foreign Trade Zones Board: 24, available online: http://ia.ita.doc.gov/ftzpage/annualreport/ar-2007.pdf, accessed October 21, 2009.

38. Masahisa Fujita, Satoru Kumagai, and Koji Nishikimi, (eds.), *Economic Integration in East Asia: Perspective from Spatial and Neoclassical Economics* (Cheltenham, UK: Edward Elgar Publishing, 2008), 83.

39. Top Ten Outsourcing Survey, The Outsourcing Institute, www.outsourcing.com, accessed October 21, 2009.

40. Michael R. Czinkota and Ilkka Ronkainen, "A Forecast of Globalization, International Business, and Trade: Report from a Delphi Study," *Journal of International Business* 40 (2005): 111–123.

41. U.S. Bureau of the Census, E-Stats, May 28, 2009, http://www.census.gov/econ/estats/2007reportfinal.pdf, accessed October 19, 2009.

42. "US Online Retail Forecast, 2008 to 2013," Forrester Research, February 2009, updated March 2009; "Must-Haves for Manufacturer Web Sites," Forrester Research, July 2007.

43. Miklos Vasarhelyi and Michael Alles, "Electronic Commerce," in *Encyclopedia of Business and Finance*, 2nd ed. (Thomson Gale, 2007).

44. D. Vrontis, D. Ktoridou, and Y. Melanthiou, "Website Design and Development as An Effective and Efficient Promotional Tool: A Case Study in the Hotel Industry in Cyprus," *Journal of Website Promotion* 2, 3/4 (2008): 125–139.

45. "Telecommunication Services," World Trade Organization, http://www.wto.org/english/tratop_e/serv_e/telecom_e.htm, accessed October 19, 2009.

46. Michael R. Czinkota, Georg Knight, Peter Liesch, John Stern, Terrorism and International Business: A research agenda, *Journal of International Business Studies*, 45, 1, 2010.

47. David Hummels, Volodymyr Lugovskyy, and Alexandre Skiba, "The Trade Reducing Effects of Market Power in International Shipping," *Journal of Development Economics* 89, no. 1 (May 2009): 84–97.

48. Internal Organization for Standardization, www.ico.ch, accessed October 20, 2009; Robert Malone, "Reverse Side of Logistics: The Business of Returns," *Forbes*, November 2005.

Chapter 17

1. Extremity stimulus medical appliances are electrically charged sheaths that are fit over the hands, feet, or other extremities of the human subject where

increased blood flow and nerve tissue regeneration is desired. This is a fictional product.

2. There are, of course, other traditional decision criteria used in capital budgeting, such as the internal rate of return, payback period, and so forth. For the sake of simplicity, NPV is used throughout the analysis in this chapter. Under most conditions, NPV is also the most consistent criterion for selecting good projects, as well as selecting among projects.

3. A note of particular irony in this case was that the chief currency trader for Allied-Lyons had authored an article in the British trade journal *The Treasurer* only a few months before. The article had described the proper methods and strategies for careful corporate foreign currency risk management. He had concluded with the caution to never confuse "good luck with skillful trading."

4. *Trade Finance*, May 1992, 13.

5. "Current Activities of International Organizations in the Field of Barter and Barter-Like Transactions," *Report of the Secretary General*, United Nations General Assembly, 1984, 4.

6. Jean-Francois Hennart and Erin Anderson, "Countertrade and the Minimization of Transaction Costs, An Empirical Examination," *The Journal of Law, Economics, and Organization*, September 2, 1993, 307.

7. Jean-Francois Hennart, "Some Empirical Dimensions of Countertrade," *Journal of International Business Studies* 21 second quarter, (1990): 243–270.

8. "Bruce Willis Signs Major Barter Deal," *The Tuesday Barter Report*, December 29, 2009, p. 2.

9. Jong H. Park, "Is Countertrade Merely a Passing Phenomenon? Some Public Policy implications," in *Proceedings of the 1988 Conference,* ed. R. King, Charleston, SC, Academy of International Business, Southeast Region, 1988, 67–71.

10. Hennart, "Some Empirical Dimensions of Countertrade."

11. Rolf Mirus and Bernard Yeung, "Why Countertrade? An Economic Perspective," *The International Trade Journal* 7, no. 4 (1993): 409–433.

12. Paul Samuelson, *Economics*, 11th ed., (New York, McGraw-Hill, 1980), 260.

Chapter 18

1. "Preliminary Finding of Going Global Readiness Report Released", *HR.com*, July 25, 2008; www.jeitosa.com.

2. John Higgins, "The Innovation Imperative: How HR Can Elevate Its Business Impact to Enable High Performance," *Accenture*, 2009.

3. Mark Mendendall, Edward Dunbar, and Gary Oddou, "Expatriate Selection Training and Career- Pathing: A Review and Critique," *Human Resource Management*, 26, no. 3, (2006): 331–354; Richard D. Hays, "Expatriate Selection: Insuring Success and Avoiding Failure," *Journal of International Business Studies* 5 (summer 1974): 25–37.

4. J. Holstein, "It's Getting Diverse at the Top," Strategy and Business, January 06, 2009, 1-5.

5. Christopher A. Bartlett and Sumantra Ghoshal, "What Is a Global Manager" *Harvard Business Review*, 81(August 2003): 99–107.

6. "Waking Up Heineken," *BusinessWeek*, September 8, 2003, 68–72, Jan van Rosmalen, "Internationalising Heineken Human Resource Policy in a Growing International Company," *International Management Development* (summer 1985): 11–13.

7. Richard Rawlinson, Walter McFarland, and Laird Post, "A Talent for Talent," *Strategy and Business*, August 26, 2008, 20–26.

8. John A. Quelch and Helen Bloom, "Ten Steps to a Global Human Resources Strategy," *Strategy and Business* (first quarter, 1999): 18–29.

9. Floris Majlers, "Inside Unilever: The Evolving Transnational Company," *Harvard Business Review* 70 (September/October 1992): 46–52.

10. Vijay Govindarajan and Anil K. Gupta, "Building an Effective Global Business Team," *Sloan Management Review* 42 (summer 2001):63–72.

11. Phred Dvorak, "Theory & Practice: How Teams Can Work Well Together From Far Apart," *The Wall Street Journal*, September 17, 2007, B3.

12. Dong Chen, Seung Ho Park, and William Newburry, "Parent Contribution and Organizational Control in International Joint Ventures," *Strategic Management Journal*, 30, no. 11 (2009): 1133–1156.

13. Yu-Ching Chiao, Chwo-Ming Joseph Yu, and Ju-Tzu Ann Peng "Partner Nationality, Market-Focus and IJV Performance: A Contingent Approach," *Journal of World Business* 44, no. 3 (July 2009): 238–249.

14. Farok J. Contractor and Peter Lorange, *Cooperative Strategies and Alliances* (New York: Pergamon, 2002).

15. http://www.brookfieldgrs.com/insights_ideas/grts/.

16. "For 'Extreme Telecommuters,' Remote Work Means Really Remote," *The Wall Street Journal*, January 31, 2001, B1, B7.

17. "The Foreigners at the Top of LG," *BusinessWeek*, December 22, 2008, 56–57.

18. Alex Dakotta, "Building an International Recruiting Department," *Dakotta.com*, April 16, 2009.

19. Robert Brown, "Magic Quadrant for Comprehensive HR BPO," Gartner RAS Core, November 25, 2008.

20. Mirjaliisa Charles and Rebecca Marschan-Piekkari, "Language Training for Enhanced Horizontal Communication: A Challenge for MNCs," *Business Communication Quarterly* 65, no. 2 (2002): 9–30.

21. David Ahlstrom, Gary Bruton, and Eunice S. Chan, "HRM of Foreign. Firms in China: The Challenge of Managing Host Country Personnel," *Business Horizons* 44 (May 2001): 57–62.

22. "Reward—Seeking the Ideal Blend of Financial Compensation and Fulfillment," Egon Zehnder International 6th International Executive Panel, June 2009.

23. Thomas J. Delong, John J. Gabarro, Robert, J. Lees, "Why Mentoring Matters in a Hypercompetitive World," *Harvard Business Review*, 86 (January 2008): 115–118.

24. "Selecting International Business Managers Effectively; Assessment Methods and Core Competencies for Success," *Human Resource Management International Digest* 15, no. 3 (2007): 334–343.

25. Rober Rosen, *Global Literacies: Lessons on Business Leadership and National Cultures* (New York: Simon & Schuster, 2000).

26. Susan Schneider and Rosalie Tung, "Introduction to the International Human Resource Management Special Issue", *Journal of World Business* 36 (winter 2001): 341–346.

27. HSBC Bank International, Expat Explorer Survey 2009, Report Two: Expat Experience, www.offshore.hsbc.com.

28. "Helping You Do Business in China," China-Britain Business Council, 2009.

29. "In Japan, an Odd Perch for Google: Looking Up at the Leader," *New York Times*, November 29, 2009.

30. "Expat Spouses: It Takes Two," *Financial Times*, March 1, 2002, 35; Margaret A. Schaffer and David A. Harrison, "Forgotten Partners of International Assignments: Development and Test of a Model of Spouse Adjustment," *Journal of Applied Psychology* 86, 2 (2001): 238–252.

31. "Have Wife, Will Travel," *The Economist*, December 16, 2002, 70.

32. "Global Relocation Trends," Brookfield Global Relocation Services, 2009; Bronwyn Fryer, "The Problem with Short-Term Overseas Assignments," *Harvard Business Review*, July 20, 2009.

33. Henrik Holt Larson, "Global Career as Dual Dependency Between the Organization and the Individual," *Journal of Management Development* 23, no. 9 (2004): 860–869.

34. http://www.expatica.com/hr/story/dual-careers-or-duelling-careers-10544.html?ppager=3#.

35. Jan Seliner and Alicia Leung, "Provision and Adequacy of Corporate Support to Male Spouse An Exploratory Study," *Personal Review* 32, no. 1 (2003): 9–14.

36. Kevin Ibeh, Sara Carter, Deborah Poff, and Jim Hamill, "How Focused Are the World's Top-Rated Business Schools on Educating Women for Global Management?" *Journal of Business Ethics* 83, no 1 (November 2008): 65–83; Linda Stroh, Arup Verma, and Stacey Valy-Durbin, "Why Are Women Left at Home: Are They Willing to Go on International Assignments?", *Journal of World Business* 35 (fall 2000): 238–245.

37. Elizabeth Johns, Erika Dorman, "Stay or Go: What Globalization Means for Women in Finance," *AFP Exchange*, October 2006, 66-69.

38. "Global Relocation Trends," Brookefield Global Relocation Services, 2009.

39. J. Stewart Black and Hal B. Gregsen, "The Right Way to Manage Expats," *Harvard Business Review* 77 (March/April 1999): 52–61; Rosalie Tung, " Selection and Training of Personnel for Overseas Assignments," *Columbia Journal of World Business* 16 (spring 1981): 68–78.

40. http://www.offshore.hsbc.com/1/2/international/expat/expat-survey/expat-experience-report-2009.

41. Michael G. Harvey, "Dual-Career Expatriates: Expectations, Adjustment and Satisfaction with International Relocation," *Journal of International Business Studies* 28, no. 3 (1997): 627–658.

42. Dual-Career Issues for Expatriates: Benefits Threatened by Economic Woes?" ORC Worldwide, January 23, 2009.

43. L. Robert Kohls, *Survival Kit for Overseas Living* (Yarmouth, ME: Intercultural Press, 1979), 62–68.

44. "Quality of Living Global City Ranking 2008," *Mercer Survey*, June 10, 2008.

45. C. Delia Contreras and Fabio Bravo, "Should You Accept an International Assignment?" *Chemical Engineering Progress* (August 2003): 67–76.

46. Michael Czinkota and G. Suder, "Towards an Understanding of Terrorism Risk in the MNE," *Multinational Business Review* 13, no. 3 (April 2007).

47. http://www.airpartner.com/en-us/why-air-partner/a-commitment-to-safety/.

48. Irene Chiotis-Leskowich, "The Family as a Developmental Issue in Expatriate Assignments," *Development and Learning in Organizations* 23, no. 6 (2009): 4–7.

49. Robert Miner, "Preparation of Expatriates for Global Assignments Revisited," *Journal of Diversity* 3, no. 2 (second quarter, 2009).

50. http://www.orcworldwide.com/compensation/mobility/balance.php.

51. Karen E. Thuerner, "Asia Adds Up," *Global Business* (June 2000): 51–55.

52. "Pricy Tuition Turns Expats to Home Schooling," *China Daily*, September 7, 2009.

53. U.S. Department of State, *Indexes of Living Costs-Abroad, Quarters Allowances, and Hardship Differentials*.

54. Courtesy of Thomas B. Cooke, Esq.

55. "Expat Life Gets Less Cushy," *The Wall Street Journal*, October 26, 2007, W1, W10.

56. "Corporate News: GE Agrees to Supply *China* Aircraft Industry," *The Wall Street Journal*, November 16, 2009, B.3.

57. Industrial Democracy in Europe International Research Group, *Industrial Democracy in Europe* (Oxford, UK: Clarendon Press, 1981), ch. 14; Industrial Democracy in Europe International Research Group, *Industrial Democracy in Europe Revisited* (Oxford, UK: Oxford University Press, 1993), ch. 3.

58. Erna Szabo, Felix C. Brodbeck, Deanne N. Den Hartog, and Gerhard Reber, "The Germanie Europe Cluster: Where Employees Have a Voice," *Journal of World Business* 37 (spring 2002): 55–67.

59. John Addison, "Non-Union Representation in Germany," *Journal of Labor Research* 20 (winter 1999): 73–91.

60. "European Works Councils," European Trade Union Confederation (ETUC), 2008.

61. "International Comparisons of Labour Disputes in 2006," *Economic & Labour Market Review* 2, no. 2 (April 2008).

62. http://www.ilo.org/global/What_we_do/InternationalLabour Standards/lang–en/index.htm.

63. http://www.adidas-group.com/en/SER2008/Progress-and-targets/Progress-and-targets-Supply-Chain-Labour.asp; and Gary Gereffi, Ronie Garcia-Johnson, Erika Sasser, "The NGO-Industrial Complex," *Foreign Policy*, July/August 2001, 56–66.

64. "Firms Rethink Hostility of Linking Trade, Labor Rights," *The Wall Street Journal*, February 2, 2001, A12.

65. http://www.artemismanagement.com/work-redesign.html.

66. Hirotaka Takeuchi, Emi Osono, and Norihiko Shimizu, "The Contradictions that Drive Toyota's Success," *Harvard Business Review* 86 (June 2008): 96–105.

67. Paul Desmond, "Laying the Groundwork for Tomorrow's Teams," Smartenterprise Exchange, 2008.

68. "Hour by Hour," *Global Business* (November 2000): 25.

69. Sylvia Hewlett, "FlexTime: A Recession Triple Win," *Harvard Business Review*, August 2009.

70. "China Union Expands at McDonald's," *The Wall Street Journal*, April 7–8, 2007, A3.

71. "Honda and UAW Clash Over New Factory Jobs," *The Wall Street Journal*, October 10, 2007, A1, A19.

72. S. B. Prasad and Y. Kirshna Shetty, *An Introduction to Multinational Management* (Englewood Cliffs, NJ: Prentice Hall, 1976), Appendix 8-A.

73. Jay Mazur, "Labor's New Internationalism," *Foreign Affairs* (January/February 2000): 79–93.

74. Sarah Oxenbridge and William Brown "Achieving a New Equilibrium? The Stability of Cooperative Employer-Union Relationships," *Industrial Relations Journal* 35, no. 5 (September 2004): 388–403.

75. "Corporate News: Avtovaz Bumps Up Against Kremlin–Barred from Layoffs, Car Maker Slashes Pay and Urges Retirements," *The Wall Street Journal*, November 2, 2009, B3.

Chapter 19

1. William Lazer and Eric H. Shaw, "Global Marketing Management: At the Dawn of the New Millennium," *Journal of International Marketing*, 8, 1, (2000): 65–77.

2. Kevin Bogardus, "U.S. Business Sees Honduran Elections as Solutions to Crisis," *The Hill*, October 28, 2009.

3. The information presented here is based largely on an original Delphi study by Michael R. Czinkota and Ilkka A. Ronkainen utilizing an international panel of experts.

4. Michael R. Czinkota, "Rich Neighbors, Poor Relations," *Marketing Management*, Spring 1994, 46–52.

5. Michael R. Czinkota and Ilkka Ronkainen, "Urgent Matters," *Marketing Management*, July/August 2009.

6. Ibid.

7. Michael R. Czinkota, "The End of Corruption," *Japan Today*, December 21, 2009.

8. Steve Schifferes, "Crisis 'to Trap 53m in Poverty,'" *BBC News*, February 12, 2009.

9. Phil Stewart and Gernot Heller, "G8 Pledges $20bn Farm Aid to Poor Nations," *Reuters*, July 10, 2009.

10. Mike Moore, "Preparations for the Fourth WTO Ministerial Conference," Paris, October 9, 2001, http://www.wto.org.

11. Davos, "Business and Political Leaders Discuss Digital Divide," *World*

Economic Forum, http://www.wforum.org, February 2, 2001.

12. Llewllyn King, "China's Investment in Africa," Hearst Newspapers, *www.Timesunion.com*, November 20, 2009.

13. Michael R. Czinkota and Charles J. Skuba, "Business Not as Usual," *Marketing Management*, Summer 2010.

14. Michael R. Czinkota and Charles J. Skuba, "Sources of New Growth," *Marketing Management*, Spring 2010.

15. Richard Milne, "European Companies to Focus on Emerging Markets," *Financial Times*, November 20, 2009.

16. Joe Leahy and James Fontanella-Khan, "Harley Revs Up to Attract Indian Fans," *Financial Times*, January 3, 2010.

17. Richard Milne, "European, Companies to Focus on Emerging Markets," *Financial Times*, November 20, 2009.

18. Jefrey R. Immelt, Vijay Govindarajan, and Chris Trimble, "How GE Is Disrupting Itself," *Harvard Business Review*, October 2009.

19. M. U. N. Moore, "Body Endorses Cultural Protectionism," *Washington Post*, October 21, 2008, A14.

20. Michael R. Czinkota and Ilkka A. Ronkainen, "Trends and Indications in International Business—Topics for Future Research," *Management International Review*, 2009.

21. Shaomin Li, Managing International Business in Relation-Based versus Rule Based Countries," New York, *Business Expert Press*, 2010.

22. "The Others," *The Economist*, December 17, 2009.

23. Czinkota and Ronkainen, ibid.

24. John J. DeGioia, remarks at Georgetown University's McDonough School of Business, Future of Global Finance Conference, September 18, 2009.

25. Lawerence H. Summers, remarks at Georgetown University's McDonough School of Business, Future of Global Finance Conference, September 18, 2009.

26. U.S. Treasury Department, http://treas.gov/tic/mfh.txt, accessed January 12, 2010.

27. UN Population Division, World Urbanization Prospects—the 2007 Revision, http://www.un.org/esa/population, accessed January 5, 2009.

28. The Coca-Cola Company, 2008 Annual Review.

29. John Lancaster, "The Desperate Bachelors," *Washington Post*, December 2, 2002, A1, A17.

30. Czinkota and Ronkainen, "Trends and Indications in International Business."

31. Ibid.

32. http://www.internetworldstats.com, accessed January 6, 2010.

33. Ibid.

34. John Ouelch, "Global Village People," *Worldlink magazine*, January/February 1999, http://www.worldlink.co.uk.

35. Renato Ruggiero, "The New Frontier," *WorldLink*, January/February 1998, http://www.worldlink.co.uk.

36. Minoru Makihara, Co-Chairman of the Annual Meeting of the World Economic Forum, Davos 2010, www.weforum.org.

37. Polly Campbell, "Trend Watch 2003," *The Edward Lowe Report*, January 2003, 1–3.

38. Czinkota and Ronkainen, "Trends and Indications in International Business."

39. Michael R. Czinkota, "The Policy Gap in International Marketing," *Journal of International Marketing*, 8, 1 (2000): 99–111.

40. http://www.Edelman.com/trust

41. U.S. State Department press release, "Secretary Clinton Presents Awards for Corporate Excellence," December 9, 2009, http://www.state.gov, accessed January 14, 2010.

42. "The Corporation and the Public: Open for Inspection," World Economic Forum, http://www.weforum.org, February 2, 2001.

43. Benn R. Konsynski and Jahangir Karimi, "On the Design of Global Information Systems," in *Globalization, Technology, and Competition: The Fusion of Computers and Telecommunication's in the 1990s*, ed. S. Bradley, J. Hausman, and R. Nolan (Boston: 1993), 81–108.

44. Michael R. Czinkota and Masaaki Kotabe, *Marketing Management*, 2nd ed. (Cincinnati: South-Western College Publishing, 2001), 234–235.

45. Corporate facts, http://www.qvc.com, accessed January 14, 2010.

46. Institute of International Education, *Open Doors*, http://www.iie.org, accessed January 15, 2010.

47. Michael G. Harvey, "Repatriation of Corporate Executives: an Empirical Study," *Journal of International Business Studies* 20 (spring, 1989): 131–144.

A

abandoned product ranges   The outcome of a firm narrowing its range of products to obtain economies of scale, which provides opportunities for other firms to enter the markets for the abandoned products.

absolute advantage   The ability to produce a good or service more efficiently than it can be produced elsewhere.

accidental exporters   Firms which participate in international trade due to initiative of active outside demand rather than based on gradual inside planning.

accounting diversity   The range of differences in national accounting practices.

acculturation   The process of adjusting and adapting to a specific culture other than one's own.

adaptability screening   A selection procedure that usually involves interviewing both the candidate for an overseas assignment and his or her family members to determine how well they are likely to adapt to another culture.

administrative shelter   Protecting firms through laws and regulations.

agency theory   The question of whether the principals of an organization, ownership, and management may not be aligned in terms of strategy, interests, and risk-taking.

agent   A representative or intermediary for the firm that works to develop business and sales strategies and that develops contacts.

airfreight   Transport of goods by air; accounts for less than one percent of the total volume of international shipments, but more than 20 percent of value.

allocation mentality   The tradition of acquiring resources based not on what is needed but on what the plan makes available.

Amazon.com   Large Internet-based service firm.

American terms   Quoting a currency rate as the U.S. dollar against a country's currency (e.g., U.S. dollars/yen).

analogy   A method for estimating market potential from similar products when data for the specific products do not exist.

antidumping   Laws that many countries use to impose tariffs on foreign imports. They are designed to help domestic industries that are injured by competition from abroad due to imported products being sold at low prices.

antitrust laws   Laws that prohibit monopolies, restraint of trade, and conspiracies to inhibit competition.

applied tariffs   Duty level actually charged at border crossing.

arbitration   The procedure for settling a dispute in which an objective third party hears both sides and makes a decision; a procedure for resolving conflict in the international business arena through the use of intermediaries such as representatives of chambers of commerce, trade associations, or third-country institutions.

area expertise   A knowledge of the basic systems in a particular region or market.

area structure   An organizational structure in which geographic divisions are responsible for all manufacturing and marketing in their respective areas.

area studies   Training programs that provide factual preparation prior to an overseas assignment.

arm's length price   A price that unrelated parties would have reached.

autarky   Self-sufficiency: a country that is not participating in international trade.

average cost method   An accounting principle by which the value of inventory is estimated as the average cost of the items in inventory.

B

backtranslation The retranslation of text to the original language by a different person than the one who made the first translation.

backward innovation The development of a drastically simplified version of a product.

balance of payments (BOP) A statement of all transactions between one country and the rest of the world during a given period; a record of flows of goods, services, and investments across borders.

bank draft A financial document drawn against a bank.

barter A direct exchange of goods of approximately equal value, with no money involved.

base salary Salary not including special payments such as allowances paid during overseas assignments.

bearer bond A bond owned officially by whoever is holding it.

best practice An idea which has saved money or time, or a process that is more efficient than existing ones.

bilateral negotiations Negotiations carried out between two nations focusing only on their interests.

bill of lading A contract between an exporter and a carrier indicating that the carrier has accepted responsibility for the goods and will provide transportation in return for payment.

black hole The situation that arises when an international marketer has a low-competence subsidiary—or none at all—in a highly strategic market.

born global Newly founded firm that, from its inception, is established as an international business.

bound tariffs Duties agreed upon in international negotiations, often higher than those duties actually charged.

boycott An organized effort to refrain from conducting business with a particular country of origin or seller of goods or services; used in the international arena for political or economic reasons.

brain drain A migration of professional people from one country to another, usually for the purpose of improving their incomes or living conditions.

Bretton Woods Agreement An agreement reached in 1944 among finance ministers of 45 Western nations to establish a system of fixed exchange rates.

bribery The use of payments or favors to obtain some right or benefit to which the briber has no legal right; a criminal offense in the United States but a way of life in many countries.

Buddhism A religion that extends through Asia from Sri Lanka to Japan and has 360 million followers, emphasizing spiritual attainment rather than worldly goods.

buffer stock Stock of a commodity kept on hand to prevent a shortage in times of unexpected demand; under international commodity and price agreements, the stock controlled by an elected or appointed manager for the purpose of managing the price of the commodity.

bulk service Ocean shipping provided on contract either for individual voyages or for prolonged periods of time.

buy-back A refinement of simple barter with one party supplying technology or equipment that enables the other party to produce goods, which are then used to pay for the technology or equipment that was supplied.

C

capital account An account in the BOP statement that records transactions involving borrowing, lending, and investing across borders.

capital budget The financial evaluation of a proposed investment to determine whether the expected returns are sufficient to justify the investment expenses.

capital flight The rapid flow of private funds abroad because investors believe that the return on investment or the safety of capital is not sufficiently ensured in their own countries.

capital gains Profits that arise from the increase in the value of an asset, such as a publicly traded share, over what was paid for that same asset.

Caribbean Basin Initiative (CBI) Extended trade preferences to Caribbean countries granting them special access to the markets of the United States.

carriage and insurance paid to (CIP) The price quoted by an exporter for shipments not involving waterway transport, including insurance.

carriage paid to (CPT) The price quoted by an exporter for shipments not involving waterway transport, not including insurance.

cartel An association of producers of a particular good, consisting either of private firms or of nations, formed for the purpose of suppressing the market forces affecting prices.

Cash management The management of cash balances owned by the firm held by banking and other financial institutions.

cash pooling Used by multinational firms to centralize individual units' cash flows, resulting in less spending or foregone interest on unnecessary cash balances.

center of excellence The location of product development outside the home country because of an advantage of skills.

central plan The economic plan for the nation devised by the government of a socialist state; often a five-year plan that stipulated the quantities of goods to be produced.

centralization The concentrating of control and strategic decision making at headquarters.

change agent A person or institution who facilitates change in a firm or in a country.

channel design The length and width of the distribution channel.

Christianity The largest organized world religion with over 2 billion followers; Protestantism encourages work and accumulation of wealth.

code law Law based on a comprehensive set of written statutes.

codetermination A management approach in which employees are represented on supervisory boards to facilitate communication and collaboration between management and labor.

commercial invoice A bill for transported goods that describes the merchandise and its total cost and lists the addresses of the shipper and seller and delivery and payment terms.

Commercial Service A department of the U.S. Department of Commerce that gathers information and assists U.S. business executives in conducting business abroad.

Committee on Foreign Investments in the United States (CFIUS) A federal committee, chaired by the U.S. Treasury, with the responsibility to review major foreign investments to determine whether national security or related concerns are at stake.

commodity price agreement An agreement involving both buyers and sellers to manage the price of a particular commodity, but often only when the price moves outside a predetermined range.

common agricultural policy (CAP) An integrated system of subsidies and rebates applied to agricultural interests in the European Union.

common law Law based on tradition and depending less on written statutes and codes than on precedent and custom—used in the United States.

common market A group of countries that agree to remove all barriers to trade among members, to establish a common trade policy with respect to nonmembers, and also to allow mobility for factors of production—labor, capital, and technology.

communication services Services that are provided in the areas of videotext, home banking, and home shopping, among others.

comparative advantage The ability to produce a good or service more cheaply, relative to other goods and services, than is possible in other countries.

competitive advantage The ability to produce a good or service more cheaply than other countries due to favorable factor conditions and demand conditions, strong related and supporting industries, and favorable firm strategy, structure, and rivalry conditions.

competitive assessment A research process that consists of matching markets to corporate strengths and providing an analysis of the best potential for specific offerings.

composition of trade The ratio of primary commodities to manufactured goods in a country's trade.

concentration strategy The market expansion policy that involves concentrating on a small number of markets.

confiscation The forceful government seizure of a company without compensation for the assets seized.

Confucianism A code of conduct with 150 million followers throughout Asia, stressing loyalty and relationships.

consulting services Services that are provided in the areas of management expertise on such issues as transportation, logistics, and politics.

container ships Ships designed to carry standardized containers, which greatly facilitate loading and unloading as well as intermodal transfers.

contender A local company whose assets are transferable, allowing it to compete head-on with established global players worldwide.

content analysis Systematic evaluation of communication for frequency of expressions.

contract manufacturing Outsourcing the actual production of goods so that the corporation can focus on research, development, and marketing.

contractual hedging A multinational firm's use of contracts to minimize its transaction exposure.

contributor A national subsidiary with a distinctive competence, such as product development.

control Refers to legal restraints on what a foreign investor may own or control in another country.

coordinated decentralization Direction of overall corporate strategy by headquarters while granting subsidiaries the freedom to implement strategy within established ranges.

coordinated intervention A currency value management method whereby the central banks of the major nations simultaneously intervene in the currency markets, hoping to change a currency's value.

corporate governance The relationship among stakeholders used to determine and control the strategic direction and performance of the corporation.

corporate income tax A tax applied to all residual earnings, regardless of what is retained or what is distributed as dividends.

corporate social responsibility (CSR) To operate an organization in a manner which will both assure a profitable and sustainable future for the organization's primary stakeholders while having positive and managed impacts on both society and the environment. (Also frequently referred to as *corporate responsibility*.)

corporate sustainability The corporate pursuit of long-term profitability and viability while making positive contributions to both society and the environment.

corporation The most common form of business organization which has all of the rights and responsibilities as that of an individual, while possessing limited liability to its owners.

corruption Payments or favors made to officials in return for services.

correspondent banks Banks located in different countries and unrelated by ownership that have a reciprocal agreement to provide services to each other's customers.

cost and freight (CFR) Seller quotes a price for the goods, including the cost of transportation to the named port of debarkation. Cost and choice of insurance are left to the buyer.

cost, insurance, and freight (CIF) Seller quotes a price including insurance, all transportation, and miscellaneous charges to the point of debarkation from the vessel or aircraft.

cost leadership A pricing tactic where a company offers an identical product or service at a lower cost than the competition.

cost of communication The cost of communicating electronically or by telephone with other locations. These costs have been drastically reduced through the use of fiber-optic cables.

cost-of-living allowance (COLA) An allowance paid during assignment overseas to enable the employee to maintain the same standard of living as at home.

cost-plus method A pricing policy in which there is a full allocation of foreign and domestic costs to the product.

counterpurchase A refinement of simple barter that unlinks the timing of the two transactions, but still matches the value.

coups d'état A forced change in a country's government, often resulting in attacks of foreign firms and policy changes by the new government.

critical commodities list Governmental information about products that are either particularly sensitive to national security or controlled for other purposes.

cross-marketing activities A reciprocal arrangement whereby each partner provides the other access to its markets for a product.

cross rates Exchange rate quotations which do not include the U.S. dollar as one of the two currencies quoted.

cross-subsidization The use of resources accumulated in one part of the world to fight a competitive battle in another.

cultural assimilator A program in which trainees for overseas assignments must respond to scenarios of specific situations in a particular country.

cultural convergence Increasing similarity among cultures accelerated by technological advances.

cultural imperialism The imposition of a foreign viewpoint, non-local perspective, or civilization on a people.

cultural risk The risk of business blunders, poor customer relations, and wasted negotiations that results when firms fail to understand and adapt to the differences between their own and host countries' cultures.

cultural universals Similarities in the total way of life of any group of people.

culture shock Reactions to the psychological disorientation that most people feel when they move for an extended period of time in to a markedly different culture.

cumulative transaction adjustment (CTA) The equity account entry on the consolidated balance sheet of multinational companies that is created to account for the translation of the foreign currency denominated balance sheets of foreign subsidiaries. Its value related to any individual foreign subsidiary only impacts the consolidated income of the company upon sale or liquidation of the subsidiary itself.

currency flows The movement of currency from nation to nation, which in turn determines exchange rates.

current account An account in the BOP statement that records the results of transactions involving merchandise, services, and unilateral transfers between countries.

current transfer A current account on the Balance of Payments statement that records gifts from the residents of one country to the residents of another.

customer involvement Active participation of customers in the provision of services they consume.

customer service A total corporate effort aimed at customer satisfaction; customer service levels measure the responsiveness that inventory policies permit for a given situation.

customer structure An organizational structure in which divisions are formed on the basis of customer groups.

Customs union Collaboration among trading countries in which members dismantle trade barriers among members and also establish a common trade policy with respect to nonmembers.

D

data privacy Electronic information security that restricts secondary use of data according to laws and preferences of the subjects.

decentralization The granting of a high degree of autonomy to subsidiaries.

deemed exports Addresses people rather than products where knowledge transfer could lead to a breach of export restrictions.

defender A local company that has assets that give it a competitive advantage only in its home market.

delivered duty paid (DDP) Seller delivers the goods, with import duties paid, including inland transportation from import point to the buyer's premises.

delivered duty unpaid (DDU) Only the destination customs duty and taxes are paid by the consignee.

Delphi studies A research tool using a group of experts to rank major future developments.

density Weight-to-volume ratio; often used to determine shipping rates.

deregulation Removal of government interference.

differentiation Takes advantage of the company's real or perceived uniqueness on elements such as design or after-sales service.

direct intervention The process governments used in the 1970s if they wished to alter the current value of their currency. It was done by simply buying or selling their own currency in the market using their reserves of other major currencies.

direct investment account An account in the BOP statement that records investments with an expected maturity of more than one year and an investor's ownership position of at least 10 percent.

direct involvement Participation by a firm in international business in which the firm works with foreign customers or markets to establish a relationship.

direct quotation A foreign exchange quotation that specifies the amount of home country currency needed to purchase one unit of foreign currency.

direct taxes Taxes applied directly to income.

discriminatory regulations Impose larger operating costs on foreign service providers than on local competitors, that provide subsidies to local firms only, or that deny competitive opportunities to foreign suppliers.

distributed earnings The proportion of a firm's net income after taxes which is paid out or distributed to the stockholders of the firm.

distributor A representative or intermediary for the firm that purchases products from the firm, takes title, and assumes the selling risk.

diversification A market expansion policy characterized by growth in a relatively large number of markets or market segments.

dividend yield The dividend paid per share to shareholders as a percent of the current share price.

division of labor The premise of modern industrial production where each stage in the production of a good is performed by one individual separately, rather than one individual being responsible for the entire production of the good.

dodger A local company that sells out to a global player or becomes part of an alliance.

Doha Round Currently (2010) ongoing international trade and investment liberalization negotiations within the World Trade Organization (WTO) initiated in 2001 in Doha, Qatar.

domestication Government demand for partial transfer of ownership and management responsibility from a foreign company to local entities, with or without compensation.

double-entry bookkeeping Accounting methodology where each transaction gives rise to both a debit and a credit of the same currency amount. It is used in the construction of the balance of payments.

draft The document used in international trade to require payment for goods from a buyer.

dual pricing Price-setting strategy in which the export price and domestic price are differentiated.

dual-use items Goods and services that are useful for both military and civilian purposes.

dumping Selling goods overseas at a price lower than in the exporter's home market, or at a price below the cost of production, or both.

E

eclectic paradigm Representing a collection of forces or drivers.

e-commerce The ability to offer goods and services over the Web.

economic and monetary union (EMU) The ideal among European leaders that economic integration should move beyond the four freedoms; specifically, it entails (1) closer coordination of economic policies to promote exchange rate stability and convergence of inflation rates and growth rates, (2) creation of a European central bank, and (3) replacement of national monetary authorities by the European Central Bank and adoption of the euro as the European currency.

economic exposure The potential change in the value of a firm from unexpected changes in exchange rates. Also called "operating exposure" and "strategic exposure."

economic infrastructure The transportation, energy, and communication systems in a country.

economic security Perception of a business activity as having an effect on a country's financial resources, often used to restrict competition from firms outside the country.

economic union A union among trading countries that has the characteristics of a common market and also harmonizes monetary policies, taxation, and government spending and uses a common currency.

economies of scale Production economies made possible by the output of larger quantities.

education allowance Reimbursement by company for dependent educational expenses incurred while a parent is assigned overseas.

effective tax rate Actual total tax burden after including all applicable tax liabilities and credits.

embargo A governmental action, usually prohibiting trade entirely, for a decidedly adversarial or political rather than economic purpose.

empathic design A user-centered design approach that observes customers in their normal environment in order to see how they use products and better identify their needs.

engineering services Services that are provided in the areas of construction, design, and engineering.

environmental protection Actions taken by governments to protect the environment and resources of a country.

environmental scanning Obtaining ongoing data about a country.

ethnocentric Tending to regard one's own culture as superior; tending to be home-market oriented.

ethnocentrism The regarding of one's own culture as superior to others'.

euro A single currency used by the European Union that replaced all the individual currencies of the participating member states.

eurocurrency A bank deposit in a currency other than the currency of the country where the bank is located; not confined to banks in Europe.

eurodollars U.S. dollars deposited in banks outside the United States; not confined to banks in Europe.

Euromarkets Money and capital markets in which transactions are denominated in a currency other than that of the place of the transaction; not confined to Europe.

European terms Quoting a currency rate as a country's currency against the U.S. dollar (e.g., yen/U.S. dollars).

European Union An economic union between 15 leading European countries.

exchange controls Controls on the movement of capital in and out of a country, sometimes imposed when the country faces a shortage of foreign currency.

expatriate One living in a foreign land; a corporate manager assigned to a location abroad.

experiential knowledge Knowledge acquired through involvement as opposed to information, which is obtained through communication, research, and education.

experimentation A research tool to determine the effects of a variable on an operation.

export complaint systems   Allow customers to contact the original supplier of a product in order to inquire about products, make suggestions, or present complaints.

export-control system   A system designed to deny or at least delay the acquisition of strategically important goods to adversaries; in the United States, based on the Export Administration Act and the Munitions Control Act.

export declaration   A shipping document detailing the type, destination, shipping, timing, and value of an export shipment.

export license   A license provided by the goverment which permits the export of sensitive goods or services.

export management companies (EMCs)   Domestic firms that specialize in performing international business services as commission representatives or as distributors.

export trading company (ETC)   The result of 1982 legislation to improve the export performance of small- and medium-sized firms, the export trading company allows businesses to band together to export or offer export services. Additionally, the law permits bank participation in trading companies and relaxes antitrust provisions.

expropriation   The government takeover of a company with compensation frequently at a level lower than the investment value of the company's assets.

extended enterprise   When companies consider the entire supply chain to be a single organization that needs to be managed for purposes of both efficiency and effectiveness.

extender   A company that is able to exploit its success at home as a platform for expansion elsewhere.

external economies of scale   Lower production costs resulting from the free mobility of factors of production in a common market.

extraterritoriality   An exemption from rules and regulations of one country that may challenge the national sovereignty of another. The application of one country's rules and regulations abroad.

ex-works (EXW)   Price quotes that apply only at the point of origin; the seller agrees to place the goods at the disposal of the buyer at the specified place on a date or within a fixed period.

F

factor intensity   The proportion of capital input to labor input used in the production of a good.

factor mobility   The ability to freely move factors of production across borders, as among common market countries.

factor proportions theory   Systematic explanation of the source of comparative advantage.

factors of production   All inputs into the production process, including capital, labor, land, and technology.

factual cultural knowledge   Knowledge obtainable from specific country studies published by governments, private companies, and universities and also available in the form of background information from facilitating agencies such as banks, advertising agencies, and transportation companies.

fiduciary responsibility   A relationship between two parties whereby one party has the trust and legal and ethical duty to act in the best interests of the other.

field experience   Experience acquired in actual rather than laboratory settings; training that exposes a corporate manager to a different cultural environment for a limited amount of time.

FIFO   Method of valuation of inventories for accounting purposes, meaning First-In-First-Out. The principle rests on the assumption that costs should be charged against revenue in the order in which they occur.

financial account   An account in the BOP statement that records transactions involving borrowing, lending, and investing across borders.

financial incentives   Monetary offers intended to motivate; special funding designed to attract foreign direct investors that may take the form of land or buildings, loans, or loan guarantees.

financial infrastructure   Facilitating financial agencies in a country; for example, banks.

financial mercantilism   Government policy to protect and promote the home-country financial and non-financial companies first.

financing cash flows   The cash flows of a firm related to the funding of its operations; debt and equity related cash flows.

fiscal incentives   Incentives used to attract foreign direct investment that provide specific tax measures to attract the investor.

fixed-exchange-rate   The government of a country officially declares that its currency is convertible into a fixed amount of some other currency.

flextime   A modification of work scheduling that allows workers to determine their own starting and ending times within a broad range of available hours.

floating-exchange-rate   Under this system, the government possesses no responsibility to declare that its currency is convertible into a fixed amount of some other currency; this diminishes the role of official reserves.

focus group   A research technique in which representatives of a proposed target audience contribute to market research by participating in an unstructured discussion.

foreign availability   The degree to which products similar to those of a firm can be obtained in markets outside the firm's home country. Crucial to export determination.

foreign bond   Bonds issued in national capital markets by borrowers (private companies or sovereign states) from other countries.

Foreign Corrupt Practices Act   A 1977 law making it a crime for U.S. executives of publicly traded firms to bribe a foreign official in order to obtain business.

foreign currency exchange rate   The price of one country's currency in terms of another country's currency.

foreign direct investment   The establishment or expansion of operations of a firm in a foreign country. Like all investments, it assumes a transfer of capital.

foreign market opportunity analysis   Broad-based research to obtain information about the general variables of a target market outside a firm's home country.

foreign policy   The area of public policy concerned with relationships with other countries.

foreign service premium   A financial incentive to accept an assignment overseas, usually paid as a percentage of the base salary.

foreign tax credit   Credit applied to home-country tax payments due for taxes paid abroad.

foreign trade zones   Special areas where foreign goods may be held or processed without incurring duties and taxes until they enter the country outside the zone.

Fortress Europe   Concern that the integration of the European Union may result in increased restrictions on trade and investment by outsiders.

forward contracts   Agreements between firms and banks which permit the firm to either sell or buy a specific foreign currency at a future date at a known price.

forward pricing   Setting the price of a product based on its anticipated demand before it has been introduced to the market.

forward rates   Contracts that provide for two parties to exchange currencies on a future date at an agreed-upon exchange rate.

franchising   A form of licensing that allows a distributor or retailer exclusive rights to sell a product or service in a specified area.

free alongside ship (FAS)   Exporter quotes a price for the goods, including charges for delivery of the goods alongside a vessel at a port. Seller handles cost of unloading and wharfage; loading, ocean transportation, and insurance are left to the buyer.

free carrier (FCA)   Applies only at a designated inland shipping point. Seller is responsible for loading goods into the means of transportation; buyer is responsible for all subsequent expenses.

free on board (FOB)   Applies only to vessel shipments. Seller quotes a price covering all expenses up to and including delivery of goods on an overseas vessel provided by or for the buyer.

free trade area   An area in which all barriers to trade among member countries are removed, although sometimes only for certain goods or services.

Free Trade Area of the Americas (FTAA)   A hemispheric trade zone covering all of the Americas. Organizers hope for it to be operational by 2005.

freight forwarders   Specialists in handling international transportation by contracting with carriers on behalf of shippers.

functional structure   An organizational structure in which departments are formed on the basis of functional areas such as production, marketing, and finance.

G

gap analysis   Analysis of the difference between market potential and actual sales.

General Agreement on Tariffs and Trade (GATT)   An international code of tariffs and trade rules signed by 23 nations in 1947; headquartered in Geneva, Switzerland; now part of the World Trade Organization with 148 members.

General Agreement on Trade in Services (GATS)   A legally enforceable pact among WTO participants that covers trade and investments in the services sector.

glasnost   The Soviet policy of encouraging the free exchange of ideas and discussion of problems, pluralistic participation in decision making, and increased availability of information.

global account management   Global customers of a company may be provided with a single point of contact for domestic and international operations and consistent worldwide service.

global brands   Brands that reach the world's megamarkets and are perceived as the same brand by consumers and internal constituents.

globalization   The increased mobility of goods, services, labor, technology, and capital throughout the world.

glocal   Refers to an individual, group, division, unit, organization, or community that is willing and able to think globally and act locally.

glocalization   A term coined to describe the networked global organization approach to an organizational structure.

gold standard   A standard for international currencies in which currency values were stated in terms of gold.

goods trade   An account of the BOP statement that records funds used for merchandise imports and funds obtained from merchandise exports.

government regulation   Interference in the marketplace by governments.

gray market   Marketing of products through unauthorized channels.

Group of Five   Name given to the five industrialized nations that meet periodically to achieve a cooperative effort on international economic and monetary issues. The **Group of Seven**, the **Group of Ten**, and the **Group of Twenty** are forums for member nations to discuss key issues related to the global economy.

H

hardship allowance   A premium paid during an assignment to an overseas area that requires major adaptation.

hedge   To counterbalance a present sale or purchase with a sale or purchase for future delivery as a way to minimize loss due to price fluctuations; to make counterbalancing sales or purchases in the international market as protection against adverse movements in the exchange rate.

high-context cultures   Cultures in which behavioral and environmental nuances are an important means of conveying information.

Hinduism   With 860 million followers, a way of life rather than a religion, with economic and other attainment dictated by the caste into which its followers are born.

housing allowance   A premium paid during assignment overseas to provide living quarters.

I

implementer   The typical subsidiary role, which involves implementing strategy that originates with headquarters.

import substitution A policy for economic growth adopted by many developing countries that involves the systematic encouragement of domestic production of goods formerly imported.

income elasticity of demand A means of describing change in demand in relative response to a change in income.

incoterms International Commerce Terms. Widely accepted terms used in quoting export prices.

in-depth studies Market research tools that gather detailed data used to study consumer needs across markets.

indirect involvement Participation by a firm in international business through an intermediary, in which the firm does not deal with foreign customers or firms.

indirect quotation Foreign exchange quotation that specifies the units of foreign currency that could be purchased with one unit of the home currency.

indirect taxes Taxes applied to non-income items, such as value-added taxes, excise taxes, tariffs, and so on.

infant-industry A new type of business which requires some time to get started.

information system Can provide the decision maker with basic data for most ongoing decisions.

infrastructure shortages Problems in a country's underlying physical structure, such as transportation, utilities, and so on.

initial public offering (IPO) The first sale or issuance of shares of ownership (stock) in an organization to the market. A private firm which issues its shares to the public market would henceforth be classified as publicly traded.

input-output analysis A method for estimating market activities and potential that measures the factor inflows into production and the resultant outflow of products.

insurance services Services that are provided in underwriting, risk evaluation, and operations.

intangibility The inability to be seen, tasted, or touched in a conventional sense; the characteristic of services that most strongly differentiates them from products.

intellectual property right (IPR) Legal right resulting from industrial, scientific, literary, or artistic activity.

interbank interest rates The interest rate charged by banks to banks in the major international financial centers.

intermodal movements The transfer of freight from one mode or type of transportation to another.

internal bank A multinational firm's financial management tool that actually acts as a bank to coordinate finances among its units.

internal economies of scale Lower production costs resulting from greater production for an enlarged market.

internalization Occurs when a firm establishes its own multinational operation, keeping information that is at the core of its competitiveness within the firm.

international bond Bond issued in domestic capital markets by foreign borrowers (foreign bonds) or issued in the Eurocurrency markets in currency different from that of the home currency of the borrower (Eurobonds).

international competitiveness The ability of a firm, an industry, or a country to compete in the international marketplace at a stable or rising standard of living.

international debt load Total accumulated negative net investment of a nation.

international law The body of rules governing relationships between sovereign states; also certain treaties and agreements respected by a number of countries.

International Monetary Fund (IMF) A specialized agency of the United Nations established in 1944. An international financial institution for dealing with balance of payment problems; the first international monetary authority with at least some degree of power over national authorities.

International Trade Organization (ITO) A forward-looking agreement on the approach to international trade and investment embodied in the 1948 Havana Charter; due to disagreements among sponsoring nations, its provisions were never ratified.

interpretive cultural knowledge   An acquired ability to understand and appreciate the nuances of foreign cultural traits and patterns.

interview   A face-to-face research tool to obtain in-depth information.

intra-industry trade   The simultaneous export and import of the same good by a country. It is of interest due to the traditional theory that a country will either export or import a good, but not do both at the same time.

intranet   A process that integrates a company's information assets into a single accessible system using Internet-based technologies such as e-mail, news groups, and the World Wide Web.

inventory   Materials on hand for use in the production process; also finished goods on hand.

inventory carrying costs   The expense of maintaining inventories.

investment income   The proportion of net income that is paid back to a parent company.

Islam   A religion that has over 1 billion followers from the west coast of Africa to the Philippines, as well as in the rest of the world and is supportive of entrepreneurism but not of exploitation.

J

joint occurrence   Occurrence of one or several shifts affecting the business environment in several locations simultaneously.

Joint Research and Development Act   A 1984 law that allows both domestic and foreign firms to participate in joint basic-research efforts without fear of U.S. antitrust action.

just-in-time inventory   Materials scheduled to arrive precisely when they are needed on a production line.

K

knowledge transfer   The movement, communication, and implementation of insights and information across international borders between individuals, organizations, or corporate units.

L

lag   Paying a debt late to take advantage of exchange rates.

land bridge   Transfer of ocean freight on land among various modes of transportation.

Law of One Price   The theory that the relative prices of any single good between countries, expressed in each country's currency, is representative of the proper or appropriate exchange rate value.

lead   Paying a debt early to take advantage of exchange rates.

Leontief Paradox   The general belief that the United States, as a capital-abundant country, should be exporting capital-intensive products whereas its exports are labor intensive.

LIBOR   The London InterBank Offer Rate. The rate of interest charged by top-quality international banks on loans to similar quality banks in London. This interest rate is often used in both domestic and international markets as the rate of interest on loans and other financial agreements.

licensing   A firm gives a license to another firm to produce, package, or market its product.

licensing agreement   An agreement in which one firm permits another to use its intellectual property in exchange for compensation.

LIFO   Method of valuation of inventories for accounting purposes, meaning Last-In-First-Out. The principle rests on the practice of recording inventory by "layer" of the cost at which it was incurred.

liner service   Ocean shipping characterized by regularly scheduled passage on established routes.

lingua franca The language habitually used among people of diverse speech to facilitate communication.

lobbyist Typically, a well-connected person or firm that is hired by a business to influence the decision making of policymakers and legislators.

local content Regulations to gain control over foreign investment by ensuring that a large share of the product is locally produced or a larger share of the profit is retained in the country.

location decision A decision concerning the number of facilities to establish and where they should be situated.

logistics platform Vital to a firm's competitive position, it is determined by a location's ease and convenience of market reach under favorable cost circumstances.

longitudinal analysis A longitudinal analysis that involves repeated observations of the same items over long periods of time.

low-context cultures Cultures in which most information is conveyed explicitly rather than through behavioral and environmental nuances.

M

Maastricht Treaty The agreement signed in December 1991 in Maastricht, the Netherlands, in which European Community members agreed to a specific timetable and set of necessary conditions to create a single currency for the EU countries.

macroeconomic level Level at which trading relationships affect individual markets.

management contract An international business alternative in which the firm sells its expertise in running a company while avoiding the risk or benefit of ownership.

managerial commitment The desire and drive on the part of management to act on an idea and to support it in the long run.

maquiladoras Mexican border plants, with lower labor costs, make goods and parts or process food for export back to the United States.

marginal cost method This method considers the direct costs of producing and selling goods for export as the floor beneath which prices cannot be set.

market audit A method of estimating market size by adding together local production and imports, with exports subtracted from the total.

market-differentiated pricing Price-setting strategy based on demand rather than cost.

market segment Group of customers that share characteristics and behaviors.

market transparency Availability of full disclosure and information about key market factors such as supply, demand, quality, service, and prices.

marketing infrastructure Facilitating marketing agencies in a country; for example, market research firms, channel members.

mass customization Working with existing product technology to create specific product bundles, resulting in a customized product for a particular customer.

materials management The timely movement of raw materials, parts, and supplies into and through the firm.

matrix structure An organizational structure that uses functional and divisional structures simultaneously.

maximization of shareholder value The pursuit of the interests of corporate shareholders, primarily the profitability of the organization, over and above the interests of other stakeholders. (Also commonly referred to as *shareholder wealth maximization*.)

m-commerce Any transaction involving the transfer of ownership or rights to use goods and services, which is initiated and/or completed by using mobile access to computer-mediated networks with the help of an electronic device.

media strategy Strategy applied to the selection of media vehicles and the development of a media schedule.

mercantilism Political and economic policy in the seventeenth and early eighteenth centuries aimed at increasing a nation's wealth and power by encouraging the export of goods in return for gold.

microeconomic level Level of business concerns that affects an individual firm or industry.

microfinance The provision of financial services to low-income clients, including consumers and the self-employed, who traditionally lack access to banking and related services.

mininationals Newer companies with sales between $200 million and $1 billion that are able to serve the world from a handful of manufacturing bases.

minority participation Participation by a group having less than the number of votes necessary for control.

mixed aid credits Credits at rates composed partially of commercial interest rates and partially of highly subsidized developmental aid interest rates.

mixed structure An organizational structure that combines two or more organizational dimensions; for example, products, areas, or functions.

most-favored nation (MFN) A term describing a GATT clause that calls for member countries to grant other member countries the same most favorable treatment they accord any country concerning imports and exports. In the U.S. now called Normal Trade Relations (NTR).

multidomestic strategy A business strategy where each individual country organization is operated as a profit center.

multilateral negotiations Trade negotiations among more than two parties; the intricate relationships among trading countries.

multinational corporations Companies that invest in countries around the globe.

N

national security The ability of a nation to protect its internal values from external threats.

national sovereignty The supreme right of nations to determine national policies; freedom from external control.

natural hedging The structuring of a firm's operations so that cash inflows and outflows by currency are matched.

net errors and omissions account Makes sure the balance of payments (BOP) actually balances.

net present value (NPV) The sum of the present values of all cash inflows and outflows from an investment project discounted at the cost of capital.

netting Cash flow coordination between a corporation's global units so that only one smaller cash transfer must be made.

1992 White Paper A key document developed by the EC Commission to outline the further requirements necessary for a successful integration of the European Union.

nondiscriminatory regulations Rules which do not differentiate between domestic and foreign firms; all are affected alike.

nonfinancial incentives Nonmonetary offers intended to motivate; special offers designed to attract foreign direct investors that may take the form of guaranteed government purchases, special protection from competition, or improved infrastructure facilities.

nontariff barriers Barriers to trade, other than tariffs. Examples include buy-domestic campaigns, preferential treatment for domestic bidders, and restrictions on market entry of foreign products such as involved inspection procedures.

not-invented-here (NIH) syndrome A defensive, territorial attitude that, if held by managers, can frustrate effective implementation of global strategies.

O

observation A research tool where the subject's activity and behavior are scrutinized.

ocean shipping The forwarding of freight by ocean carrier.

official reserves account An account in the BOP statement that shows (1) the change in the amount of funds immediately available to a country for making international payments and (2) the borrowing and lending that has taken place between the monetary authorities of different countries either directly or through the International Monetary Fund.

offshore banking   The use of banks or bank branches located in low-tax countries, often Caribbean islands, to raise and hold capital for multinational operations.

one-stop logistics   Allows shippers to buy all the transportation modes and functional services from a single carrier.

operating cash flows   The cash flows arising from the firm's everyday business activities.

operating or service lease   A lease that transfers most but not all benefits and costs inherent in the ownership of the property to the lessee. Payments do not fully cover the cost of purchasing the asset or incurring the liability.

operating risk   The danger of interference by governments or other groups in one's corporate operations abroad.

opportunity costs   The returns foregone on any resource or asset from using it in its next best use. The principle emphasizes that most assets or resources have alternative uses that have real value.

order cycle time   The total time that passes between the placement of an order and the receipt of the product.

orientation program   A program that familiarizes new workers with their roles; the preparation of employees for assignment overseas.

ownership risk   The risk inherent in maintaining ownership of property abroad. The exposure of foreign owned assets to governmental intervention.

P

Patent Cooperations Treaty (PCT)   An agreement that outlines procedures for filing one international patent application rather than individual national applications.

Pax Americana   An American peace since 1945 that led to increased international business transactions.

Pax Romana   Two relatively peaceful centuries in the Roman Empire leading to a successful expansion of business.

pension liabilities   The accumulating obligations of employers to fund the retirement or pension plans of employees.

perestroika   An attempt to fundamentally reform the Soviet economy by improving the overall technological and industrial base and the quality of life for Soviet citizens through increased availability of food, housing, and consumer goods.

perishability   Susceptibility to deterioration; the characteristic of services that makes them difficult to store.

physical distribution   The movement of finished products from suppliers to customers.

Plaza Agreement   An accord reached in 1985 by the Group of Five that held that the major nations should join in a coordinated effort to bring down the value of the U.S. dollar.

podcasts   A series of digital media files that are released episodically and often downloaded through web syndication.

political risk   The risk of loss by an international corporation of assets, earning power, or managerial control as a result of political actions by the host country.

political union   A group of countries that have common foreign policy and security policy and that share judicial cooperation.

population balance   A concern in some countries where the population is being skewed by a preference for male children.

population stabilization   An attempt to control rapid increases in population and ensure that economic development exceeds population growth.

portfolio investment account   An account in the BOP statement that records investments in assets with an original maturity of more than one year and where an investor's ownership position is less than 10 percent.

portfolio models   Tools that have been proposed for use in market and competitive analysis. They typically involve two measures—internal strength and external attractiveness.

ports   Harbor towns or cities where ships may take on or discharge cargo; the lack of ports and port services is the greatest constraint in ocean shipping.

positioning   The perception by consumers of a firm's product in relation to competitors' products.

preferential policies   Government policies that favor certain (usually domestic) firms; for example, the use of national carriers for the transport of government freight even when more economical alternatives exist.

price controls   Regulation of the prices of goods and services.

price escalation   The establishing of export prices far in excess of domestic prices—often due to a long distribution channel and frequent markups.

primary data   Data obtained directly for a specific research purpose through interviews, focus groups, surveys, observation, or experimentation.

private placement   The sale of debt securities to private or institutional investors without going through a public issuance like that of a bond issue or equity issue.

privatization   A policy of shifting government operations to privately owned enterprises to cut budget costs and ensure more efficient services.

process structure   A variation of the functional structure in which departments are formed on the basis of production processes.

product cycle theory   A theory that views products as passing through four stages: introduction, growth, maturity, decline; during which the location of production moves from industrialized to lower-cost developing nations.

product differentiation   The effort to build unique differences or improvements into products.

product structure   An organizational structure in which product divisions are responsible for all manufacturing and marketing.

production possibilities frontier   A theoretical method of representing the total productive capabilities of a nation used in the formulation of classical and modern trade theory.

promotional message   The content of an advertisement or a publicity release.

protectionistic legislation   A trade policy that restricts trade between (to or from) one country and another.

proxy information   Data used as a substitute for more desirable data that are unobtainable.

psychological distance   A mental measure resulting form the combination of physical and mental distance.

punitive tariff   A tax on an imported good or service intended to punish a trading partner.

purchasing power parity (PPP)   The theory that the price of internationally traded commodities should be the same in every country, and hence the exchange rate between the two currencies of those countries should be the ratio of prices in the two countries.

Q

qualitative information   Data that are not amenable to statistical analysis, but provide a better understanding, description, or prediction of given situations, behavioral patterns, or underlying dimensions.

quality circles   Groups of workers who meet regularly to discuss issues related to productivity.

quality of life   The standard of living combined with environmental factors, it determines the level of well-being of individuals.

quality of work life   Various corporate efforts in the areas of personal and professional development undertaken with the objectives of increasing employee satisfaction and increasing productivity.

quantitative data   Information based on numeric and statistical relationships.

quotas Legal restrictions on the import quantity of particular goods, imposed by governments as barriers to trade.

R

reference groups Groups such as the family, co-workers, and professional and trade associations that provide the values and attitudes that influence and shape behavior, including consumer behavior.

reinvoicing The policy of buying goods from one unit and selling them to a second unit and reinvoicing the sale to the next unit, to take advantage of favorable exchange rates.

reliability Dependability; the predictability of the outcome of an action. For example, the reliability of arrival time for ocean freight or airfreight.

representative office An office of an international bank established in a foreign country to serve the bank's customers in the area in an advisory capacity; does not take deposits or make loans.

retaliation The trade or investment policy response to one nation's or group of nations' trade actions or restrictions, undertaken by another nation or group of nations in order to demonstrate displeasure or to seek retribution and change for this action.

reverse distribution A system responding to the need for product returns that ensures a firm can retrieve a product from the market for subsequent use, recycling, or disposal.

reverse innovation Refers to an innovation seen first, or likely to be used first, in the developing world before spreading to the industrialized world.

roll-on-roll-off (RORO) Transportation vessels built to accommodate trucks, which can drive on in one port and drive off at their destinations.

royalty The compensation paid by one firm to another under an agreement.

S

sanction A governmental action, usually consisting of a specific coercive trade measure, that distorts the free flow of trade for an adversarial or political purpose rather than an economic one.

scale economies The increasing efficiency gains from greater size or scale, often described as lower cost per unit of output.

scenario building The identification of crucial variables and determining their effects on different cases or approaches.

sea bridge The transfer of freight among various modes of transportation at sea.

secondary data Data originally collected to serve another purpose than the one in which the researcher is currently interested.

self-management Independent decision making; a high degree of worker involvement in corporate decision making.

self-reference criterion The unconscious reference to one's own cultural values.

sensitivity training Training in human relations that focuses on personal and interpersonal interactions; training that focuses on enhancing an expatriate's flexibility in situations quite different from those at home.

service capacity The maximum level at which a service provider is able to provide services to customers.

service consistency Uniform quality of service.

service heterogeneity The difference from one delivery of a product to another delivery of the same product as a result of the inability to control the production and quality of the process.

services trade The international exchange of personal or professional services, such as financial and banking services, construction, and tourism.

shipper's order A negotiable bill of lading that can be bought, sold, or traded while the subject goods are still in transit and that is used for letter of credit transactions.

Single European Act The legislative basis for the European Integration.

Smoot-Hawley Act A 1930 act that raised import duties to the highest rates ever imposed by the United States; designed to promote domestic production, it resulted in the downfall of the world trading system.

social infrastructure The housing, health, educational, and other social systems in a country.

social stratification The division of a particular population into classes.

soft power The ability to obtain what one wants through co-option and attraction.

sogoshosha A large Japanese general trading company.

sovereign wealth fund Investment vehicle containing only government financial assets, which are invested globally.

special economic zones Areas in which there are substantial tax incentives, low prices for land and labor, and no tariffs, created by a country to attract foreign investors.

specie Gold and silver.

spot rates Contracts that provide for two parties to exchange currencies with delivery in two business days.

stakeholder capitalism The operation of a firm or organization in a manner which attempts to balance the interests of all stakeholders of the organization (stockholders, employees, creditors, suppliers, customers, and community).

stakeholders All persons or groups which may affect or be affected by the activities of an organization like a corporation.

standard of living The level of material affluence of a group or nation, measured as a composite of quantities and qualities of goods.

standard worldwide pricing Price-setting strategy based on average unit costs of fixed, variable, and export-related costs.

state-owned enterprise A corporate form that has emerged in non-Communist countries, primarily for reasons of national security and economic security.

straight bill of lading A nonnegotiable bill of lading usually used in prepaid transactions in which the transported goods involved are delivered to a specific individual or company.

strategic alliances A new term for collaboration among firms, often similar to joint ventures.

strategic leader A highly competent firm located in a strategically critical market.

supply-chain management Results where a series of value-adding activities connect a company's supply side with its demand side.

surveys The use of questionnaires to obtain quantifiable research information.

sustainability The interaction of factors in nature and society which determine the longevity and continuity of an approach. Often used in the context of the environment, life styles, and corporate social responsibility.

systems concept A concept of logistics based on the notion that materials-flow activities are so complex that they can be considered only in the context of their interaction.

T

tariffs Taxes on imported goods and services, instituted by governments as a means to raise revenue and as barriers to trade.

tax equalization Reimbursement by the company when an employee in an overseas assignment pays taxes at a higher rate than if he or she were at home.

tax policy A means by which countries may control foreign investors.

teaching services Services that are provided in the areas of training and motivating as well as in teaching of operational, managerial, and theoretical issues.

team building A process that enhances the cohesiveness of a department or group by helping members learn how to organize their work and assume responsibility for it.

technology transfer The transfer of systematic knowledge for the manufacture of a product, the application of a process, or the rendering of a service.

"tentative U.S. tax" The calculation of U.S. taxes on foreign source incomes to estimate U.S. tax payments.

terrorism   Illegal and violent acts toward property and people.

theocracy   A legal perspective based on religious practices and interpretations.

total cost concept   A decision framework that uses cost as a basis for measurement in order to evaluate and optimize logistical activities.

tourism   The economic benefit of money spent in a country or region by travelers from outside the area.

tracking   The capability of a shipper to obtain information about the location of the shipment at any time.

trade creation   A benefit of economic integration; the benefit to a particular country when a group of countries trade a product freely among themselves but maintain common barriers to trade with nonmembers.

trade diversion   A cost of economic integration; the cost to a particular country when a group of countries trade a product freely among themselves but maintain common barriers to trade with nonmembers.

trade draft   A withdrawal document drawn against a company.

trademark licensing   Providing someone the right to use an established brand symbol in exchange for payment

trade-off concept   A decision concept that recognizes linkages within the decision system.

trade policy measures   Mechanisms used to influence and alter trade relationships.

trade promotion authority   The right of the U.S. president to negotiate trade treaties and agreements with the U.S. Congress' authority to accept or reject, but not amend.

trading blocs   Formed by agreements among countries to establish links through movement of goods, services, capital, and labor across borders.

tramp service   Ocean shipping via irregular routes, scheduled only on demand.

transaction cost theory   The thought that the carrying out of an interaction (typically in business and exchange) takes resources and will cause expenses.

transaction exposure   The potential for currency losses or gains during the time when a firm completes a transaction denominated in a foreign currency.

transfer prices   The prices at which a firm sells its products to its own subsidiaries and affiliates.

transfer risk   The danger of having one's ability to transfer profits or products in and out of a country inhibited by governmental rules and regulations.

transit time   The period between departure and arrival of a carrier.

translation exposure   The potential effect of a change in currency values on a firm's financial statements.

transparency   The open and public disclosure and reporting of the activities of an organization, including financial, civil, and environmental impacts and concerns.

Treaty of Rome   The original agreement that established the foundation for the formation of the European Economic Community.

triangular arbitrage   The exchange of one currency for a second currency, the second for a third, and the third for the first in order to make a profit.

trigger mechanisms   Specific acts or stimuli that set off reactions.

turnkey operation   A specialized form of management contract between a customer and an organization to provide a complete operational system together with the skills needed for unassisted maintenance and operation.

U

undistributed earnings   The proportion of a firm's net income after taxes which is retained within the firm for internal purposes.

unsolicited order   An unplanned business opportunity that arises as a result of another firm's activities.

unstructured data   Information collected for analysis with open-ended questions.

V

value-added tax (VAT) A tax on the value contributed at each stage of the production and distribution process; a tax assessed in most European countries and also common among Latin American countries.

virtual team A team of people who are based at various locations around the world and communicate through intranet and other electronic means to achieve a common goal.

voluntary restraint agreements Trade-restraint agreements resulting in self-imposed restrictions not covered by WTO rules; used to manage or distort trade flows. For example, Japanese restraints on the export of cars to the United States, often the direct result of trade measure threats.

W

Webb-Pomerene Act A 1918 statute that excludes from antitrust prosecution U.S. firms cooperating to develop foreign markets.

webcast A media file distributed over the Internet using streaming media technology to distribute a single content source to many simultaneous listeners/viewers.

withholding taxes Taxes applied to the payment of dividends, interest, or royalties by firms.

works councils Councils that provide labor a say in corporate decision making through a representative body that may consist entirely of workers or of a combination of managers and workers.

work redesign programs Programs that alter jobs to increase both the quality of the work experience and productivity.

work scheduling Preparing schedules of when and how long workers are at the workplace.

working capital management The coordination of a firm's current assets (cash, accounts receivable, inventories) and current liabilities (accounts payable, short-term debt).

World Bank An international financial institution created in 1944 to facilitate trade.

world-class competitors Multinational firms that can compete globally with domestic products.

World Trade Organization (WTO) The institution that supplanted GATT in 1995 to administer international trade and investment accords.

A. C. Nielsen, 512
A. T. Kearney, 258, 610
Aaker, David A., 691
ABB Group, 378
Abbott Laboratories, 189
ABB Stromberg, 376
Abelsky, Paul, 688
ABN Amro, 120
Abtibi-Consolidated, 307
Accenture, 379, 608
Acedo, Francisco J., 693
Acer, 316
Acker, Olaf, 156
Action Cameras, 427
Adam, Karla, 197
Adcock, F. E., 175
Addison, John, 699
Adelphia, 347
Adidas, 391, 525
Adler, Matthew, 683
Advanced Micro Devices, 181
Aero Engines, 446
Aerospatiale Matra, 450
AES, 448
African Roots Wine Brands, 676
Aguirre, DeAnne, 613
Ahlberg, Johan, 695
Ahlstrom, David, 698
Ahmad, Adlina, 692
Aida, 331
AIG, 225, 226, 352
Airbus Industrie, 247, 328, 450
Air France, 447
AIRINC, 159
Ajami, Riad, 683
Aker Yards, 330, 331
Akhter, Syed H., 695
Alam, Pervaiz, 695
Alam, S., 696
Alberts, Hana, 694
Albertson's, 248
Alcatel Lucent, 373, 445
Alcoa, 601
ALDI, 306
Alexander, David, 47
Alexander, Marcus, 689
Alibaba.com, 274
Al Jazeera, 508
Allen, Paul, 334
Allen & Overy International, 523
Alles, Michael, 697
Allied-Lyons, 216, 588

Almond, P., 685
Alsegg, R. J., 692
Alstom, 331
Altman, Roger, 21
Amarendra, Jha, 681
Amazon.com, 329, 503, 504, 554, 555, 563, 647
Ambler, Tim, 685
America Movil, 10
American Airlines, 447
American Chung Nam Incorporated (ACN), 295, 296, 298
American Express, 493
American International Group. See AIG
American International Underwriters, 616
American Jewish Congress, 147
Amésquita, Guadalupe, 678
Amsden, Alice, 693
AmWay, 501
Anderson, Robert, 331
Anderson, Ronald C., 339
Anderson, Sarah, 687
Andreff, Wladimir, 478
Andrews, Edmund, 76
Anheuser-Busch InBev NV, 477–478, 513
Ante, Spencer, 689
Antweiler, Werner, 112
Apple, 493, 515
Aranoff, Shara L., 125
Arcelik Anonim Sirketi, 307
Arcor, 328
Arthur Anderson (auditing firm), 347, 349
Arthur D. Little, 156
Arvis, J. F., 697
Asea AB, 626
Ashoka foundation, 309
Asian Development Bank, 258
Atari, 14
Atkins, Charles, 189
Atsmon, Yuval, 694
AT&T, 325, 515, 525, 579
Atthipat Kulapngvanich, 469
Audiovox, 559
Auray, Robert R., 566
Austin, Anne, 695
Aval, Igal, 694
Aviation Industry Corp of China, 622
Avon, 495, 507
AvtoVAZ, 286–291, 629
Axtell, Roger, 685
Ayal, Igal, 485
Ayers, James B., 696

Baalbaki, Imad B., 317, 689
Babalola, Joseph Yai Olabiyi, 171
Badr, Badr al, 270
Bae, Mueun, 693
Baer, Justin, 633
Baerwald, Thomas J., 24
Baidu, 501, 506
Bailey, David, 284
Bain Capital, 464
Bajaj Auto, 641
Baker & McKenzie International, 523
Balakrishnan, Srinivasan, 694
Balassa, Bela, 687
Baldauf, Authur, 696
Baliga, B. R., 382
Ballou, Ronald H., 549
Banerjee, Snehamay, 697
Banker, Rajiv D., 696
Bank of England, 217, 226
Bank of New York, 122
Bank of Tokyo-Mitsubishi, 309
Bankunda, Geoffrey, 693
Barbarossa, 187
Barber, Edwin L., III, 683
Barbosa, Nelson, 582
Bardhan, Indranil R., 696
Bardi, Edward J., 537, 696
Barnard, Jonathon, 695
Barrels, Robert, 694
Barrera, Adriana, 47
Barrett, Craig, 686
Barry, Doug, 433
Barsoux, Jean-Louis, 605
Bartlett, Christopher A., 371, 379, 698, 691
Bäuerle, Iris, 693
Baughen, Simon, 542
Bay, The, 146
Beagrie, Neil, 402
Beagrie, Robert, 402
Beamish, Paul W., 693
Bear Stearns, 224, 225, 352
Bechtel, 96
Becker, Elizabeth, 135
Becket, Thomas, 197
Behrman, Jack N., 52
Belot, Stanislas, 189
Belt, Don, 688
Benedict XVI, 3
Benetton, 306, 500
Benson-Armer, Richard, 691
Bentley, Ross, 168

Bernstein, William J., 175, 683
Berry, Leonard L., 646
Best Buy, 389, 566
Best Price Modern Wholesale, 306
Betts, Paul, 571
Bevan, Alan, 693
Bharti, 306, 689
Bhattacharya, Arindan, 690
Bhattacharyya, Hrishi, 371, 694
Bink, Audrey, 690
Bin Laden, Tarek, 90
Birkinshaw, Julian, 376, 690, 691, 692
Bizet, Jean-Pierre, 372
BJ&B, 19
Black, J. Stewart, 166, 699
Black & Decker, 311–312, 365
Blackwell, Norman, 372
Bleeke, Joel, 446
Blinder, Alan, 130, 131
Bloom, David, 120
Bloom, Helen, 607, 690, 691, 698
Blumentritt, Timothy P., 686
Blustein, Paul, 686
BMW AG, 9, 484, 493, 540
Body Shop, The, 567
Boeing Airplane Company, 41, 82, 164,
    247, 327–328, 361, 377, 378, 511,
    588–590, 599, 651
Boel, Mariann Fisher, 143
Bogardus, Kevin, 699
Bolton, Ruth N., 696
Bombardier, 328
Bonaparte, Napoleon, 262
Bond, Michael H., 685
Boon, Dany, 139
Boot, Max, 187
Borden, Jeff, 271
Borgogna, Alessandro, 687
Bossert, James L., 555
Boston Consulting Group, 431
Bosworth, Barry, 696
Bouquet, Cyril, 691
Bové, José, 11
Bowater, 307
Bowen, Margareta, 685
Bowersox, Donald J., 569
Bozorgmehr, Najmeh, 686
BP plc, 9, 266, 386, 467, 513, 595
Bradlow, Eric T., 696
Bradsher, Keith, 130
Brasher, Philip, 135
Bravo, Fabio, 699
Briand, Xavier, 47
British Airways, 447
British Bankers Association, 633
British East India Company, 64–65, 438
Brock, David M., 696
Brodbeck, Felix C., 699
Brooks, Douglas H., 697
Brouthers, Lance E., 693
Broux, Bill, 443
Brown, Gordon, 197, 633
Brown, Robert, 698

Brown, Shannon, 601
Brown, Tim, 135
Brown, Tom J., 414
Brown, William, 699
Brown Boveri, 626
Brunel, Claire, 683
Bruton, Gray, 698
Buckley, P., 90
Buffett, Warren, 221
Burger King, 11, 170
Burman, Jeff, 537
Burrows, Peter, 271, 515, 689
Bury, J. B., 175
Bush, George W., 47, 130, 132, 194, 431
Bushell-Embling, Dylan, 181
Bussman, Johannes, 156
Butscher, Stephen A., 695

C. Itoh & Company, Ltd., 439
Cadbury-Schweppes, 147, 303, 365
Caesar, Julius, 187
Cagni, Pascal, 689
Caimler-Chrysler Aerospace AG, 450
Cainey, Andrew, 690
Calderon, Felipe, 47
California Pizza Kitchen, 11
Callaghan, James, 52
Camera, Nina, 122
Campbell, Andrew, 692
Campbell, Polly, 700
Cannon, Joseph P., 694
CANTV Telefonos de Venezuela D, 123,
    124
Capell, Kerry, 459
Capitaland Limited, 10
Caplan, Jessica, 168
Cargill Incorporated, 187, 334
Carnival Cruise Lines, 331
Carphone Warehouse, 389
Carrefour, 250, 328
Carter, Sara, 699
CASA, 450
Casillas, José C., 693
Caspar, Christian, 688
Casson, M., 90
Castaldi, Richard M., 437
Castellucci, Federico, 677
Castro, Arachu, 402
Caterpillar, 47, 310, 446
Catoni, Luciano, 689
Caudill, Lee M., 691
Cavanagh, John, 687
Caves, Richard E., 89
Cavusgil, S. Tamer, 392, 692, 693, 695
Cederholm, Lars, 375
Cemex S.A., 10, 187
Cereal Partners Worldwide, 315–316
Cerebus Capital Management, 464
Chad-Cameroon Petroleum Development,
    468
Chae, Myung-Su, 689
Chaffin, Joshua, 61
Chalaby, Jean K., 443

Chambers, John, 270, 271
Champion International, 307
Chan, Eunice S., 698
Chandra, Aruna, 689
Changhui Zhou, 694
Chang-Ing Hsu, 693
Chapin, Caroline, 284
Chaquita Brands International, 182,
    278–279
Charles, Mirjaliisa, 698
Chavez, Hugo, 122–124, 187
Cheatham, Owen, 464
Chedraui, 248
Chen, Dong, 694, 698
Chen, Ivy S. N., 437
Chen, Tai-Yuan, 696
Chesterman, Simon, 535
Cheung, J., 351
Cheung Yan, 295–299
Chevron Corporation, 9, 467
Chi-Dhu Tschang, 691
Child, Peter, 372
China Film Group, 169
China Inner Mongolia Forestry Industry
    Company, 298
China National Petroleum Corporation, 10
China Ocean Shipping (Group) Company, 10
China State Construction Engineering
    Corporation, 10
China Unicom, 515
Chiotis-Leskowich, Irene, 699
Chiung-Hui Tseng, 694
Chwo-Ming Joseph Yu, 698
Chubb & Sib, 616
Chuetsu Pulp & Paper, 307
Churchill, Gilbert A., 414
Ciba, 387
Cicic, Muris, 696
Cifra, 247
Cisco, 270, 271, 493, 512
CITIC Group, 10
Citigroup (includes Citibank & Citicorp),
    268, 380, 389, 612
Clark, I., 685
Clarke, Michael, 321
Clifford Chance International, 523
Clinton, Bill, 47
Closs, David J., 569
CLP Holdings, 10
CNN, 11, 508
Coad, Alex, 693
Coca-Cola, 58, 143, 152, 265, 269, 304,
    311, 482, 500, 601, 646
Cochlear, 308, 647
Coghill and Beery International, 168
Cohen, Margot, 135
Colgate Palmolive, 324, 376, 507, 601,
    602, 604
Colin, Jacques, 696
Colling, T., 685
Collings, David G., 326
Collins, Susan M., 696
Columbia Pictures, 102

Columbus, Christopher, 24
Colyer, Edwin, 695
Comcast, 283
Comerci, 248
Companhia Vale do Rio Doce, 10
Compartamos, 268
Conger, Jay, 690
Conn, Henry P., 383, 692
Connally, John B., 210
ConocoPhillips, 9, 187
Conrad Hotels, 153
Consolidated Papers, 307
Consulting Trends International, 132
Contoladora Mabe, 307
Contractor, Farok J., 698
Contreras, C. Delia, 699
Convergys, 608
Converse, 391
Cook, James, 24
Cooke, Thomas B., 699
Cooper, M. Bixby, 569
Cooperrider, David, 454
Corder, C. K., 407
Corning Incorporated, 376, 386,
    446, 591
Correl, A. D. "Pete," 463
Cowan, Rory, 685
Coyle, John J., 537, 696
Craig, C. Samuel, 414, 689
Crainer, Stuart, 689
Cravens, David W., 696
Credit Suisse, 483
Cuffe, Khary, 675
Cuffe, Selena, 675–678
Cultural Savvy, 170
Cunard, 331
Cunningham, Lawrence, 696
Curtis, Gary A., 691
Curves International Inc., 145
Czinkota, Michael R., 434, 642, 683, 684,
    685, 686, 688, 692, 693, 695, 696, 697,
    699, 700

Daewoo Motor, 448, 571
Daewoo Shipbuilding, 331
Daihatsu, 492
Daimler-Chrysler, 91, 92
Dakotta, Alex, 698
Dalton, Matthew, 61
D'Andrea, Guillermo, 690
Dangdang, 329
Daniels, Frank Jack, 686
Daniels, John D., 691
Danone, 303, 304, 310, 328, 496
Darling, Alistair, 633
Darling, John R., 694
Das, Gurcharan, 262, 688
Da Silva, Lula, 263
David, Finlayson, 681
Davies, K., 693
Da Vinci, Leonardo, 453
Dawar, Niraj, 328, 690
Day, Jonathan D., 691

Daya, Ayesha, 687
DBRS, 398
Debrowski, Thomas, 292
De Châo, Fogo, 11
De Gama, Vasco, 24
DeGioia, John J., 700
Deitz, Richard, 683
De la Torre, José, 184
Dell, 56, 316, 501, 504
Del Monte, 279
Deloitte Consulting, 283
DeLong, Thomas J., 698
Delta Airlines, 447
De Margerie, Christophe, 267
Dempski, Kelly, 691
Deng, Shengliang, 686
Deng Xiao Ping, 260, 261
De Noble, Alex F., 437
DEP Corporation, 491
Desmond, Paul, 699
De Souza, Ivan, 684, 689
Deutsche Bundesbank, 7
Deutsche Telekom AG, 9, 515
Diamantopoulos, Adamantios, 695
Dichter, Ernst, 306, 686, 689
Dichtl, Erwin, 686
Dickinson, Sonja J., 694
Dietrich, Niklas, 156
Dietz, Meagan, 602, 690
Di Gregorio, Dante, 248
Dinlersoz, Emin M., 696
Disney. See Walt Disney Company
Dixit, Vinay, 694
Djellal, Faridah, 535
DKSH, 470, 473
DLA Piper International, 523
DLA Piper US National, 523
Dole Food Company, 279
Dollinger, Philippe, 686
Domino's, 548
Donath, Bob, 686
Dong-Sung Cho, 693
Donohue, Inc., 307
Doole, Isobel, 693
Dorfman, Brad, 304
Dorman, Erika, 699
Douglas, Susan P., 414, 689
Dow Chemical Company, 368–370,
    375, 617
Doxey, Margaret P., 683, 685
Drake, Rodman, 691
Drucker, Peter, 336, 690
Duke, Lynn, 681
Duley, Gunter, 87
Dunbar, Edward, 698
Dun & Bradstreet, 9, 10, 501
Dung, Nguyen Huu, 134
Dunkin' Donuts, 488
Dunne, Michael, 571
Dunning, John, 88, 90
Dura Automotive Systems, 365
Dvorak, Phred, 698
Dyment, John J., 692

Early Light Industrial Company, 292
Eastman Kodak, 511
eBay, 503, 563, 655
Ebrahimi, Helia, 633
Eckert, Robert, 292
Edelman, 355, 513, 650
Edmunds, Joseph Edsel, 278
Edwards, Ron, 692
Edwards, T., 685
Einhorn, Bruce, 687
Eisenstat, Russell, 691
EIU.com, 401
Electricite De France, 9
Electrolux AB, 146, 307
Elesselly, Mona, 506
7-Eleven, 469, 471
El-Husseini, Ibrahim, 687
Eller, Claudia, 139
Ellis, Guy, 276
Embraer, 263, 264, 328, 641
Emerson Electric, 559
Endaka Construction, 576–578
Enrol, 572
Enron, 342, 347, 349–351, 356, 573
Ensign, Prescott, 376
E.On, 9
Erickson, G. Scott, 686
Ericsson, 155, 241, 445, 446, 450
Ernst, David, 446, 691
Ernst & Young, 283, 610
Erste Bank der Oesterreichischen
    Sparkassen AG, 424
Eryani, Mohammad F. al-, 695
Escott, Tom, 537
Espinosa, J. Enrique, 687
Espirit, 567
Estrin, Saul, 693
Eunjung Cha, Ariana, 130
European Aeronautic Defence and Space 4,
    50
European Bank for Reconstruction and
    Development (EBRD), 287, 289
European Central Bank, 7, 33, 38
Euro RSCG Worldwide, 510, 511
Evans, Paul, 605
Evans, Scott, 385
Exportadora Bananera Noboa, 279
ExxonMobil Corporation, 9, 20, 187, 266,
    353, 467, 513, 616

Fabbe-Costes, Nathalie, 696
Faccio, Mara, 690
Facebook, 14, 312, 508
Facker, Martin, 39
Fader, Peter S., 696
Fair Labor Association, 19
Fairtlough, Gerard, 691
Fannie Mae, 225, 226
Farley, Catherine S., 691
Farley, Chuck U., 691
Fauth, Rebecca, 284
FedEx, 262, 264, 504, 548, 601
FEDOTRAZONAS, 19

Ferraris, Carol J., 133
Fiat, 250, 446
Fidal National, 523
Field, Alan M., 276
Fierman, Jaclyn, 684
Fincantieri, 331
Firoz, Nadeem, 686
First Data, 229
First Light, 293
Fischer, Lawrence M., 691
Fishback, Bo, 309
Fisher-Price, 293, 294
Fitch, Inc., 297
Flanagan, Robert J., 691
Fletcher, Owen, 695
Fletcher Challenge Paper, 307
Folkmanis, Jason, 683
Fontanella-Khan, James, 700
Foote, Nathaniel, 691
Foote, Virginia, 134
Ford Motor Company, 9, 365, 483, 492, 540, 590, 591
Formosa Plastic Group, 10
Fowler, Robert R., 681
Fram, Eugene H., 683
France Telecom, 321
Franco Telecom, 9
Frank, Lauri, 163, 685
Fraser, Jane, 311, 688
Freddie Mac, 225, 226
Freedenberg, Paul, 642
FreeScale, 229
French Telecom, 250
Fresh Del Monte Produce, 279
Freshfields Bruckhaus Deringer International, 523
Friberg, Eric, 688
Friedman, Milton, 339
Friedman, Thomas, 280
Friedrich, Roman, 156
Frito-Lay Thailand Co. Ltd., 470
Frost, Tony, 328, 376, 690
Fry, Ronald, 454
Fryer, Bronwyn, 698
Fu, Rocky, 695
Fuggers, 438
Fuji, 322
Fujita, Masahisa, 697
Fujitsu, 445, 448
Fung, Patrick K. O., 437
Fyffes, 279

Gabarro, John J., 698
Galbraith, Jay, 691
Gallego, M. Angeles, 693
Gallouj, Faiz, 535
Gandhi, Mahatma, 33
Gandhi, Rajiv, 262
Garcia-Johnson, Ronnie, 696, 699
Garemo, Nicklas, 695
Garmin, 410
Garrigues, 523
Gates, Bill, 334

Gazprom, 267
Genco, 566
General Electric (GE), 9, 154, 307, 374, 377, 490, 512, 513
General Foods, 511
General Mills, 315, 447
General Motors (GM), 38, 39, 262, 305, 448, 571
Gen Tek, 229
Genus Corporation, 572–575
George, Catherine, 689
Georgia Hardwood Lumber Company, 464
Georgia Pacific, 307, 339, 463–465
Ger, Güliz, 690
Gerard, Leo, 126
Gereffi, Gary, 696, 699
Gergely, Andras, 56
Gertner, David, 695
Gettleman, Jeffrey, 90
GfK Roper Consulting, 319
Ghemawat, Pankaj, 684, 688, 689
Ghoshal, Sumantra, 379, 691, 696
Ghosn, Carlos, 691
Gibbs, Hope Katz, 695
Gibbs, Richard, 454
Gigante. See Grupo Gigante
Gillette, 310, 321, 493
Gingrich, James A., 685, 687
Giunipero, Larry C., 569, 696, 697
GKN Aerospace, 249
Glaister, Keith W., 694
Glassner, Barry, 548
GlaxoSmithKline, 512
Global Crossing, 347
Globo TB, 329
GM Daewoo, 305
Godrej Consumer Products Ltd., 310, 490
Goebel-Krstelj, Anne, 690
Goldman, David, 689
Goldman Sachs, 633
Gol Transportes Aéreos, 329
Gonzalez de Castilla, Fernan, 248
Goodman, Davis, 695
Goodyear, 146
Google, 310, 410, 493, 508, 509, 608, 611
Goold, Michael, 692
Gorbachev, Mikhail, 642
Gould, Jens Erik, 47
Governance Metrics International (GMI), 347, 348
Govindarajan, Vijay, 248, 691, 692, 695, 698, 700
Gowen, Annie, 656
Graham, Thomas R., 683
Grameen Bank, 268
Grameen Group, 310
Grameen Phone Ltd., 268, 269
Grant, Robert M., 689
Greenberg Traurig National, 523
Greenemeier, Larry, 689
Greenhouse, Steven, 19
Greenwald, Bruce, 688
Gregsen, Hal B., 699

Grein, Andreas F., 690
Greve, Curtis, 566
Grewal, Dhruv, 696
Grier, Jeff, 677
Griffith, David A., 691
Grönroos, Christian, 696
Gross, Daniel, 11
Gross, Thomas, 375
Grossman, D., 696
Grow, Keith Epstein, 691
Gruma, 489
Gruner,. Kjell, 691
Grupo Elektra, 329
Grupo Gigante, 247, 248
Grupo Noboa, 279
Guerrera, Francesco, 633
Guerrero-Cusumano, Jose-Luis, 695
Guido, Gianluigi, 688
Guild, Todd, 695
Guisinger, Stephen, 684
Gupta, Anil K., 248, 691, 692, 698
Gutierrez, Carlos M., 688

Haberer, Pablo, 690
Hackett, Donald W., 693
Haddock, Ronald, 489, 688
Hadley, Richard D., 693
Haier Appliances, 307, 487
Hall, Edward T., 141, 685
Halliburton, 374
Hamel, Gary, 690
Hamill, Jim, 699
Hamm, Steve, 687
Hammond, Allen, 688
Hammurabi, King of Babylon, 191
Han, Jin K., 695
Handfield, Robert B., 569, 696, 697
Hanni, David A., 685
Hannibal, 173
Hanrahan, Charles E., 61
Harley-Davidson, 46, 265, 641
Harman Group, 353
Harris, Milton, 691
Harris, Philip R., 151, 685
Harrison, David A., 698
Hart, G., 686
Hart, Stuart L., 688
Hartog, Deanne N. Den, 699
Harvey, Michael G., 686
Hayes Company, Inc., 294
Hays, Richard D., 698
HealthSouth, 347
Heckscher, Eli, 66, 72–74
Heidrick & Struggles, 610
Heineken, 513, 605
Heller, Gernot, 699
Heller, Laura, 687
Helpman, Elhanan, 684
Helsen, Kristiaan, 693, 694
Hemus, Jonathan, 385
Henderson, Fritz, 262
Henkel, 155, 325, 377
Hennart, Jean-Francois, 698

Henry II (king), 197
Hensley, David, 372
Herbst, Moira, 280
Heritage Link Brands, 675–678
Hermes Kreditanstalt, 191
Hero Honda Motors, 641
Hershey, 328
Hewlett, Sylvia Ann, 613, 699
Hewlett-Packard, 68, 268, 310, 316, 325,
    446, 493, 559, 592
  in China, 490, 641
Hidalgo, Encarnación Ramos, 693
Hiebert, Murray, 135
Higgins, John, 698
Higinbotham, Chun W. Y., 695
Hilco Corp., 293
Hill, John S., 689
Hill, Linda, 690
Hille, Kathrin, 515
Hilton Hotels, 153, 154
Hindo, Brian, 566
Hinings, C. R., 696
Hipp, Laura, 56
Hira, Ron, 280
H&M, 493, 499
Ho, Patricia Jiayi, 688
Hodges, Tina, 686
Hofstede, Geert, 141, 684, 685
Holcim, 187
Holland America Line, 331
Holsenback, J. E., 697
Holstein, J., 698
Holstein, William J., 602
Holt, Douglas B., 695
Holtbrügge, Dirk, 454
Homburg, Christian, 691, 694
Honda Motor Co Ltd, 9, 46, 56, 96, 221,
    493, 626
Honeyland, 455–458
Honeywell, 247, 325, 381
Hong Kong and Shanghai Banking
    Corporation (HSBC), 120, 159, 197
Hong Li Da, 293
Hon Hal Precision Industries, 10
Hood, Neil, 692
Horovitz, Bruce, 548
Hout, Thomas, 689
Hu, Wayne W., 189
Huan, Linda, 694
Hucko, E. M., 686
Hudson, Henry, 24
Hudson, Saul, 686
Hufbauer, Gary Clyde, 683, 687
Hugos, Michael H., 569
Hui-Chieh Li, 693
Hult, Tomas M., 686
Humes, Samuel, 691
Hummels, David, 697
Humphries, Andrew, 454
Huson, Larry, 690
Huston, Larry, 376
Hutcheon, Nicky, 695
Hutchison (mobile operator), 485

Hutchison Wampoa Limited, 9, 10
Hyatt, 453
Hymall, 272
Hymer, Stephen, 89
Hyundai Heavy Industries Co., 331
Hyundai Motor Company, 10, 445, 508

IAT Group, 279
Ibeh, Kevin, 699
IBM, 283, 308, 324, 445, 559, 606, 608,
    611
Iglarsh, Harvey J., 686
IKEA, 306, 314, 381, 459–462, 499
Immelt, Jeffrey R., 695, 700
Infosys Technologies, 283
Inkpen, Andrew C., 694
Intel, 91, 154, 181, 283, 354, 493, 504,
    559, 606
International Paper Company, 307
INVISTA, 380
Isenberg, Daniel J., 309, 689
Ishikawajima Heavy Industries, 446
Ito, Harumi, 694
Ivanchuk, Sergei, 153

J. P. Morgan & Co., 224
Jackson, John H., 36
Jaeger, Alfred M., 382, 692
Jaeger, Sabina, 455
Jahangir, Nuruddin Salim, 65
James, Dana, 688
Japan External Trade Organization
    (JETRO), 51
Jardine Matheson Holdings Ltd, 10
Jariwalla, Waheedan, 694
Javalgi, R., 696
Jen-Hung Huang, 695
Jenkins, Patrick, 633
Jensen, Michael, 690
Jeong, Insik, 690
Jeter, Derek, 321
Jhai Foundation, 269
Jhooti, Sab, 427
Jiang, Crystal X., 693
Jiangsu Five Star Appliance, 389
Jing Li, 694
Joachimsthaler, Erich, 691
Jo-Anne Stroes, 294
Joby, 486
Johansson, Johny K., 695
John Deere & Co., 591
Johns, Elizabeth, 699
Johnson, Bradley, 695
Johnson, Gregory S., 542
Johnson, Nicholas, 47
Johnson, Renee, 61
Johnson & Johnson, 375, 505, 512
Johnston, Lauren, 39
Joko, Inc., 268
Jollibee Foods Corporation, 329
Jones, Gareth, 56
Jones, Lucy, 681
Jones Day National, 523

Jullens, John, 688
Jung-a, Song, 571
Ju-Tzu Ann Peng, 698

Kadannikov, Vladimir, 286–289
Kahn, Judd, 688
Kaka, 321
Kamal, M., 696
Kamprad, Ingvar, 459
Kantor, Jeffrey, 437
Kantor, Mickey, 278
Kao Corporation, 309
Kapferer, Jean-Noel, 695
Karimi, Jahangir, 700
Karve, Ameya, 694
Kashani, Kamran, 690
Kasyanov, Mikhail, 286
Kauffman Foundation, 282
Kawasaki, 46
Kawasaki Heavy Industries, 446
Keah-Choon Tan, 696
Keegan, Sheila, 414
Keillor, Bruce D., 686
Keller, Kevin Lane, 694
Kellermanns, Franz W., 694
Kelley, Dan, 433
Kellogg Co., 165, 406
Kentucky Fried Chicken (KFC), 142, 143,
    488, 489
Kerr, William A., 693
Keynes, John Maynard, 211
Khan, Mohsin S., 687
Khosla, Sanjay, 303, 691
Kia Motors, 10, 645
Kidger, Peter J., 382
Kiedaisch, Ingo, 694
Kieliszewski, Cheryl A., 535
Kim, Lucian, 688
Kim, W. Chan, 686
Kim, Woody G., 519
Kindleberger, Charles P., 89
King, Llewllyn, 700
Kirk, Donald, 686
Kirkland & Ellis National, 523
Kirsner, Scott, 695
Klaasen, Abbey, 695
Klayman, Ben, 478
Kleinhans, Vivian, 675, 676
K & L Gates National, 523
Klintsov, Vitaly, 687
Kluckhohn, Clyde, 140, 684
Kmart, 248
Knight, Gary, 686, 689, 694
Knight, Georg, 693, 697
Koch, Charles, 465
Koch, Fred, 464
Koch Industries, 307, 339, 463–465
Kodak, 322, 366
Kohan, Adrian, 690
Kohls, L. Robert, 699
Kohut, Andrew, 406
Kollmann, Tobias, 693
Kolodziejsk, John, 582

Komatsu, 310, 446
Kone Corporation, 146
Konigsberg, Alexander S., 454
Konsynski, Benn R., 700
Korine, Harry, 689
Korth, Christopher M., 52, 57
Kotabe, Masaaki, 684
Kotler, Philip, 694, 695
Kotzab, Herbert, 569
Kovach, Gretel C., 47
Koxinga. *See* Zheng Chenggong
Koza, Mitchell P., 694
KPMG, 626, 633
Kraft Foods International, 140, 303, 365,
　　375, 386, 511
Kramer, Mark R., 696
Krass, Allen S., 686
Kripalani, Manjeet, 687
Kroeber, Alfred, 140, 684
Krohmer, Harley, 694
Kroll, Inc., 656
Kronz, Christine, 697
Krugman, Paul, 66, 80–82, 683, 684
KTF, 156
Ktoridou, D., 697
Kumar, Sameer, 566
Kundu, Sumit K., 693
Kutschker, Michael, 693
Kyd, Stewart, 333, 334

La Baie, 146
La bottega del Caffè, 11
La Campagnie des Indes, 438, 439
Lafaive, Michael D., 131
Lafarge, 187
Lafley, A. G., 359
Lam, Leona, 293
Lamy, Pascal, 33
Lancaster, John, 700
Lancóme, 501
Lane, Charlotte R., 125
Lane, Kevin, 602
Lang, Larry H. P., 690
Langley, C. John, 537, 564, 696
Lapdesk Company, 309
La Porta, R., 690
Larke, R., 693
Larsen & Toubro Infotech, 283
Larson, Henrik Holt, 698
Larssen, Nora Förisdal, 689
Lasserre, Philippe, 691
Lassiter, James, 139
Latham & Watkins National, 523
La Voie, Johanne, 692
Lawton, Joseph A., 696
Layne, Kingsley A., 278
Lazer, William, 696
Leahy, Joe, 700
Lebedyansky, 310
Lechner, Christoph, 694
Leconcepts Holdings, 293
Ledgard, Jonathan, 690
Lee, Bruce C. Y., 695

Lee, James A., 685
Lee, Jill, 613
Lee, Moonkyu, 696
Lee Der Industrial, 292–294
Lee & Man Paper Manufacturing Limited, 298
Lees, Robert J., 698
LeFever, Lee, 683
Lego A/S, 323
Lehman Brothers, 225, 226, 352
Leksell, Laurent, 692
Lenovo, 372, 490
Leong, G. Keong, 696
Leontief, Wassily, 66, 74–75, 91, 684
Leung, Alicia, 699
Lever. *See* Unilever
Lever, Lord, 52
LeVine, Steve, 688
Levi Strauss & Co., 317, 378, 391, 446, 547
Levy, Michael, 696
Levy, Piet, 684
Lewis, Carl, 453
Lewis, Howard, III, 683
Lewis, Jordan D., 689
LG Corp., 10, 56, 307, 608
LG Telecom, 156
Li, Shaomin, 700
Li Dong, 694
Liesch, Peter, 686
Life Is Good, Inc., 294
Lifsher, Marc, 694
Linder, Staffan Burenstam, 66, 76–77, 89
Lin Hu, 694
LinkedIn, 508
Linklaters International, 523
Lipsey, Richard G., 696
Lipton, Eric, 686
Little, Arthur D., 156
Liu, Francis, 684, 689
Livius (Livy), Titus, 175
Lloyd's of London, 616
Lloyd Werft, 331
Loctite, 501
Logica, 608
Logitech, 486
Long Yongtu, 687
Lopez-de-Silanes, F., 690
Lorange, Peter, 698
L'Oréal, 505
Loscher, Peter, 613
Louis Vuitton, 152, 493
Lovells International, 523
Lovelock, Christopher, 533
Lowe, Robin, 693
Lu, Jane W., 693
Lucas, Louise, 571
Lufthansa, 447, 546, 588–591, 599
Lugovskyy, Volodymyr, 697
Lund, Susan, 189
Lynn, Matthew, 197

MacKenzie, Angus, 385
MacMillan, Douglas, 689
Madsen, Tage Koed, 689

Maggi, 492
Maglio, Paul P., 535
Mahini, Amir, 691
Majdalani, Fadi, 687
Majlers, Floris, 698
Makita, 365
Makower, Joel, 513
Malecki, Edward J., 697
Malhotra, Naresh K., 689
Malone, Robert, 697
Mang, Paul, 521
Manitoulin Transport, 550
Mankins, Michael C., 692
Manna, Christine, 688
Mantega, Guido, 582
Manzullo, Donald, 684
Marfrig Alimentos, 641
Marlboro, 493
Marriott International Corporation, 184,
　　453, 510
Mars, 328
Marschan-Peikkari, Rebecca, 698
Martenson, Rita, 461
Martin, Karla L., 691
Martinez, Alonso, 489, 684, 689, 690
Martinez, Ibsen, 139, 686, 690
Mary Kay Cosmetics, 47
Mascon Global, 322
MasterCard, 322
Masters, Brooke, 633
Mathews, Jessica T., 683
Mathotra, Naresh K., 317
Matsushita, Konosuke, 384
Matsushita Electric, 310
Mattel, 292–294, 487
Mattoo, Aaditya, 535
Mauborgne, R. A., 686
Maxdata, 316
Mayer Brown International, 523
Mazda, 590, 591
Mazur, Jay, 699
McAdam, Rodney, 694
MCC, 450
McCann Worldgroup, 510, 511
McCormack, Heidi, 288, 290
McCormick, Fergus, 398
McCue, Sarah, 683
McDonalds Corporation, 11, 13, 142, 143,
　　152, 170, 221, 306
McFarland, Walter, 602, 698
McGill, H. J., 697
McGinnis, Peter, 685
McGray, Douglas, 685
McKinsey Global Institute, 230, 348, 355
McNicol, Jason P., 693
3M Company, 325, 611
Mead Corporation, 307
MeadWestvaco, 307
Meckling, W., 690
Melanthiou, Y., 697
Mendenhall, Mark, 166, 698
Mengniu, 329
Mercedes-Benz, 56, 380, 493

Merck, 189, 264, 512
Meredith, Robyn, 687
Merkel, Angela, 42
Meyer, Klaus, 693
MG Rover, 284, 285
Michael, David, 690
Microfinance International (MFI), 309
Microsoft, 181, 269, 283, 306, 310, 334,
    493, 504
Mikkola, Juliana H., 569
Miller, Danny, 691
Miller, John W., 276
Milne, Richard, 700
Mimore, Andrew, 19
Miner, Robert, 699
Minoru Makihara, 700
Mirus, Rolf, 87, 698
Mitchell, Lynne, 616
Mitsubishi, 446
Mitsubishi Corporation (general trading
    company), 439
Mitsubishi Heavy Industries, 446
Mitsubishi Motors, 91, 216
Mitsubishi Paper, 307
Mitsui & Co., Ltd., 439
Mobile Telecommunications Company, 10
Mockett, Nicholas, 689
Moen, Oystein, 689, 693
Moffett, Michael H., 122, 131, 292, 463, 466
Moffett, Sandra, 694
Mohammad (prophet of Islam), 197
Mohsin, Habib, 686
Mol, Michael J., 691
Monczka, Robert M., 569, 696, 697
Monroe, Kent B., 695
Montgomery, David B., 690
Moody, George, 686
Moody's, 118
Moore, Karl J., 376
Moore, M. U. N., 700
Moore, Mike, 699
Moore, Molly, 171
Morales, Evo, 188
Moran, Robert T., 151, 685
Moran, Sarah, 151, 685
Moreno, Ana M., 693
Morgan Stanley Capital International
    (MSCI), 124, 229
Morgenthau, Henry, Jr., 211
Mori Building Corporation, 156
Moriset, Bruno, 697
Morley, Michael J., 326
Morphy, Erika, 695
Morrison, Terri, 685
MOS Burger, 11
Moss, Simon, 692
Motoren-und-Turbinen Union, 446
Motorola, 155, 269, 314, 446, 450, 481, 540
Mountford, Paul, 270
M-Real, 307
Mufson, Steven, 686
Mundak, George P., 685
Murphy, Cait, 688, 689

Murphy, David, 694
Murphy, Kate, 153
Murphy, Megan, 633
Murray, Janet Y., 696
Murray, Sara, 524
Murray Manufacturing, 488
Mustra, M. A., 697
Myers, Matthew, 695
Myers, Randy, 596
Myles, Wayne, 616
Myung-bak, Lee, 39
Myung-Su Chae, 689

Nacional de Chocolates, 328
Nakamura, Alice, 696
National Geographic Society (NGS), 509
National Steel Car, 56
NATO, 96
Naucler, Tomas, 695
Naula, T., 697
Navarro, Gladys, 276
Nayor, James, 689
Neal, Molly, 478
Neckar, David H., 184
Neff, Jack, 691
Negandhi, Anant R., 692
Neilson, Gary L., 691
Nelson, Carl A., 697
Nestle SA, 9, 91, 159, 303, 304, 310, 447,
    495, 512, 608
Newburry, William, 694, 698
Newton, Robert, 692
New United Motor Manufacturing Inc.
    (NUMMI), 449
New World Development Co., Ltd, 10
Nguyen, Thanh, 122
Nielsen Company, 306
Nigh, Douglas, 686
Nike, 152, 311, 391, 430, 454, 625
Nikolova, Dafina, 280
Nine Dragons Paper (Holdings) Limited,
    295–299
Nissan, 56, 158, 375, 380, 626
Nixon, Richard M., 210
NoBetterDeal.com, 566
Nobriega, Tobias, 124
Nokia, 147, 155, 241, 269, 272, 314, 326,
    391, 450, 492, 499
Nolan, P. C., 696
Nonaka, Ikujiro, 690
Noor, M., 696
Nooyi, Indra K., 689
Norfield, Tony, 120
Norman, Richard, 460
Norske Skogindustrier, 307
Northern Rock, 226
Northrop Grumman, 511
Nova International, 665–668
Novakovski, Ivan, 665, 666
Novakovski, Venera, 665
Novartis, 386
Novatek, 267
NT&T, 525

NTT DoCoMo, 156
Nugent, N., 696

O2, 515
Obama, Barack, 39, 47, 127, 128, 130, 265,
    643
Obstfeld, Maurice, 113, 114, 684
Oddou, Gary, 698
O'Donnell, Sharon, 690
O'Ferrall, Rory M., 682
Office Depot, 154
Oglivy Group, 510
O'Hare, Tom, 694
Ohlin, Bertil, 66, 72–74
Ohmae, Kenichi, 306, 685, 689
Ojala, L., 697
Okun, Deanna Tanner, 126
O'Laughlin, Peg, 130
Olgivy & Mather, 470
Oliver, Jamie, 427
Olson, Donald W., 682
Oneworld, 447
Ono, Masanori, 693
Onuoha, Austin, 466
Oost-Indische Compagnie, 438
Opera Software ASA, 312
Oppenheim, Jeremy, 311, 688
Oracle Corporation, 493, 508
Orange, 156, 515
Orr, Gordon, 602, 690
Orr, James, 683
Ortega, Francese, 517
Ortiz-Buonafina, M., 693
Osono, Emi, 385, 699
Ouchi, William G., 692
Overbrook Entertainment, 139
Overseas Private Investment Corporation
    (OPIC), 191
Owens, Deborah, 686
Oxenbridge, Sarah, 694
Oxford Economic Forecasting, 15

Pabst, Dawn, 548
Pacific First Bank, 577
Palia, Aspy P., 594
Paliwoda, Stanley J., 693
Palmer, Adrian, 535
Panasonic, 326, 450
Panzer, L., 697
Parasuraman, A., 696
Park, Jong H., 698
Park, Seung Ho, 694, 698
Parkatiyar, Atul, 311
Parker, Robin, 427
Park Ji-sung, 321
Parmalat, 347
Parmar, Arundhati, 688
Parvatiyar, Atul, 689
Patagonia, 566
Patalon, William, III, 689
Patni Americas, 283
Patterson, James L., 569
Patterson, Paul G., 696

Payforit, 156
PayPal, 503
Pearson, Daniel R., 126
Pearson, J. Michael, 689
Pedersen, Torben, 690
Peng, Mike W., 693
People's Bank of China, 7
PepsiCo, 47, 143, 170, 265, 267, 303, 309, 310, 446
Pereira, Pedro, 696
Peri, Giovanni, 517
Perman, Stacy, 309
Pernicka, Susanne, 623
Pernod Ricard, 507
Perttunen, Risto, 688
Petran, Meredith, 135
Petroleo Brasiliero S.A. - Petrobras, 10, 188
Petroleos De Venezeula, 10
Petronas - Petroliam Nasional Bhd, 10
Pew Reasearch Center for the People and the Press, 406
Philips, 374, 380, 384, 446, 609, 641
Philips Electronics, 322
Phung, Le Cong, 134
Piaf, Edith, 139
Piazza's Seafood World, 133
Piderit, Sandy, 454
Piëch, Ferdinand, 333
Piëch, Ferdinand K., 673
Pierce, Moira S., 189
Piercy, Nigel F., 696
Pier1 Imports, 461
Pinkert, Dean A., 125
Pittard, Dan, 688
Pizza Hut, 488, 489
P&O, 331
Poff, Deborah, 699
Poliner, Florian, 602
Pollock, Daniel, 569
Polo, Marco, 24
Porche, Ferdinand, 673
Porsche, 333, 336, 669–674
Porter, Michael, 66, 80, 82–86, 89, 91, 544, 684, 689
Portucel, 307
Post, Laird, 602, 613, 698
Powell, Michael J., 696
Power, Carla, 685
Powers, Elizabeth, 691
Poynder, John, 341
Poynter, Thomas A., 57
Prahalad, C. K., 371, 687, 688 690, 691, 694
Prasad, S. B., 699
Pressley, Sue Anne, 56
Preston, Julia, 280
Pret a Manger, 11
Priceline, 655
Priest, Matt, 683
Princess Cruises, 331
Proctor & Gamble, 9, 47, 148, 164, 243, 262, 309, 310, 318, 321, 325, 608
Prusu, Tom, 127
Psion, 450

Pucik, Vladimir, 605
Puck, Jones F., 454
Puck, Wolfgang, 11
Putin, Vladimir, 267
Putnam, Valora, 566
Puumalainen, Kaisu, 163, 685

Qahtani, Yasser Saeed al-, 321
Qualcomm, 181
Quanta Computer, 269
Quelch, John A., 607, 690, 691, 695, 698
Quesnel, Normand, 686
Quorum, 579, 580
QVC, 563, 655

Raballand, Gael, 697
Raghavan, Lulu, 695
Raiffeisen Zentralbank AG, 424
Rakuten Inc., 506
Raleigh America, Inc., 294
Raman, Anand P., 385
Ramaseshan, B., 695
Ramin, Taght, 686
Ramirez, Rafael, 460
Ramnarayan, Abhinav, 168
Rangaka, Diale, 676
Rangaka, Malmsey, 676
Rapid Air Support, 616
Raviy, Artur, 691
Rawlinson, Richard, 602, 698
RDA Advantage West Midlands, 285
Ready, Douglas, 690
Reagan, Ronald, 642
Reber, Gerhard, 699
Reeb, David M., 339
Reebok, 311, 391, 625
Reed Smith National, 523
Reeker, Philip T., 682
Reiljan, E., 693
Reinhardt, Andy, 687
Renault, 290, 483, 629
Renwick, Robin, 686
RepsolYPF, 188
Reusser, Beverly, 280
Reyes, Roselio, 19
Ribaud, Franck, 496
Ricardo, David, 66, 67–68, 72, 90, 91
Richardson, J. David, 683
Richardson-Vicks, 310
Ricks, David A., 406, 685
Riesenberger, J., 693
Ritchie, Bob, 569
Ritchie, Jim, 537
Robert, Maurice, 686
Roberts, John H., 690
Robinson, James Harvey, 65
Robust Group, 327–328
Roche, 402
Rodriguez, Kenia, 19
Rohm and Haas, 370
Rolls-Royce, 446
Ronen, Simcha, 685, 686
Ronkainen, Ilkka A., 276, 280, 459, 686, 688
Rooney, Wayne, 478

Root, Franklin R., 480
Rosburgh, Charles, 199
Rosemann, Michael, 414
Rosen, Rober, 698
Rosenberg, Mica, 47
Rosenfeld, Irene, 692
Rosling, Alan, 262, 688
Rosmalen, Jan van, 698
Rosneft, 267, 333
Rosoboronexport, 288–290
Rosson, Philip J., 503
Roth, Kendall, 689
Rovell, Darren, 478
Rovito, Rich, 688
Rowlands, Ian, 402
Rowntree Mackintosh, 325
Roya, Weid, 56
Royal Caribbean, 331
Royal Dutch/Shell Group, 9, 467, 513
Royer, Susanne, 446, 694
Rudman, W., 686
Ruggiero, Renato, 700
Rushkoff, Douglas, 392
Russell Athletic, 19
RWE Group, 9
Ryans, John K., 685, 689

SAIC Motor Corp., 305, 571
Saint Gobain, 96
Sakkab, Nabil, 376, 690
Samek, Robert A. P., 692
Samiee, Saeed, 689
Samsung Electronics Co., Ltd, 10, 166, 314, 450, 493
Samsung Heavy Industries Co., 331
Samuelson, Paul, 594, 698
Samuelson, Robert J., 3
Sandoz, 386
Sang-Hun, Choe, 39
San SeSan Global, 472
Sappi Ltd., 307
Sara Lee, 310
Sarkozy, Nicolas, 275, 633
Sasol Limited, 10
Sasser, Erika, 696, 699
Satyam Computer Systems, 265, 601
Saudi Aramco, 467
Saudi Telecom Company, 605
Savimbi, Jonas, 680
Sawhney, Mohanbir, 691
Schaffer, Margaret A., 698
Schary, Philip B., 569
Schiappa-Pietra, Juan Carlos, 678
Schifferes, Steve, 699
Schleifer, A., 690
Schneider, Susan, 698
Schneider Electric, 367
Schneider Logistics, 537
Schott, Jeffrey J., 683, 687
Schulz, John D., 697
Schumpeter, Joseph, 3
Schweidel, David A., 696
Scullion, Hugh, 326

Sears, 160, 248, 566
Seleco, 470
Seliner, Jan, 699
Selivanova, Larisa, 628
Semapa, 307
Sematech, 450
Sengupta, Jati K., 454
Senise, Jairo, 489
Sergey, Frank, 685
Serra, Jaime, 687
Servais, Per, 689
Sethi, S. Prakash, 161, 685
Sewell, Chris, 683
Shambaugh, George E., 686
Shaw, Duncan R., 697
Shaw, Eric H., 699
Shaw Industries, 566
Shell, 266
Shenkar, Oded, 594, 685
Shenon, Philip, 47
Sheraton Corporation, 448, 453
Sherriff, Lucy, 156
Sheth, Jagdish N., 161, 311, 685, 689
Shetty, Y. Kirshna, 699
Shi, L. Hui, 693
Shieh, T., 345
Shimizu Norihiko, 385, 699
Shvakman, Irene, 687
Siders, Mark, 694
Sidley Austin National, 523
Siecor, 386
Siemens AG, 9, 55, 349, 386, 446, 448, 450, 637
Siew Meog Leong, 695
Sigla S.A. (Grupo Vips), 451
Simonim, Bernard L., 447
Simons, Roland, 446, 694
SIMPAY, 156
Singer, Eleanor, 402
Singh, James, 304, 689
Singh, Manmhohan, 258, 262, 687
Singh, Sonoo, 359
Singtel Ltd, 10
Sinha, Surya Prakash, 686
Sirius Diamonds, 681
Skadden Arps Slate Meagher & Flom National, 523
Skiba, Alexandre, 697
Skjott-Larsen, Tage, 569
Skoda, 327
SK Telecom, 156
Skuba, Charles J., 683, 688, 700
Sky Team, 447
Smiley, Robert, 677
Smillie, Ian, 682
Smith, Adam, 66–67, 72, 90, 684
Smith, Douglas, 582
Smith, Will, 139
Smithfield Foods, 47
Smurfir-Stone, 307
Sobieski Vodka, 594
Sogou, 506
Sohlberg, Carl A., 694

Solzhenitsyn, Yermolai, 687
Sony, 102, 156, 322, 450
Sony BMG, 143
Soriana, 248
Soros, George, 468
Sorrell, Martin, 3
Soto, Steven, 248
Sowinki, Lara, 687
Sparshott, Jeffrey, 682
Spencer, Earl P., 685
Spire Research and Consulting, 371
Spohrer, James C., 535
Sprague, Jonathan, 688
Springer, Robert M., Jr., 686
Spring Windows Fashions, 294
Sriram, Ven, 697
St. Laurent Paperboard, 307
Stackpole, Beth, 691
Standard Chartered Bank, 582
Stanley Works, 321
Star Alliance, 447
Starbucks Coffee Company, 11, 152, 445, 451, 500
Star Cruises/NCL, 331
State Farm, 160
Stauss, Bernd, 521
Steele, Richard, 692
Steen, John, 686
Steinberger, Mike, 11
Stem, Robert M., 535
Stengel, E. Alejandro, 690
Stern, John, 697
Sterrett, David, 304
STET, 250
Stewart, Marcio, 697
Stewart, Phil, 699
Stewart, Thomas A., 385
ST Microelectronics, 349
Stora Enso, 307
Stovitz, Ken, 139
Stroh, Linda, 699
Sturgeon, Timothy J., 696
STX Group, 331
Subway, 306
Suder, G., 699
Suez, 9
Sugars, Bradley, 694
Suh, Taewon, 693
Summers, Lawrence, 643, 700
Sundqvist, Sanna, 163, 685
Susman, Gerald I., 454
Suter, Tracy A., 414
Swedwood Group, 459
Swee Hoon Ang, 695
Symbian, 450
Szabo, Erna, 699

Tabuchi, Hiroko, 695
Tai Ping Carpets International Ltd., 606
Takada, Hirokazu, 690
Takeuchi, Hirotaka, 385, 690, 699
TAL Group, 362, 363
Tandy Corporation, 149

TaoBao, 501
Tao Kae Noi, 469–474
Target, 461, 566
Tata Motors, 274, 490
Tata Sons, 262
Tavssoli, Nader, 695
Taylor, Alan M., 113, 114, 684
Taylor, Earl L., 695
Taylor, William, 691
TaylorMade, 540
TBWA Worldwide, 378
Telefonica de Espana, 250, 449
Telefónica Mòviles, 156
Telefónica SA, 9, 326
Telenor, 389
Televisa, 329
Telfonos De Mexico S.A. De C.V., 10
Teravaninthorn, Supee, 697
Térisse, Peter Andre, 496
Tesco, 272, 389
Tetra-Pak, 326
Texas Industries, 445, 548
Theuerkauf, Ingo, 605, 691
Thomas, Douglas, 248
Thomasch, Paul, 478
Thomsen, Steen, 690
Thuerner, Karen E., 699
Thurlow, Edward, 341
ThyssenKrupp, 56
Thyssen Krupp, 601
Tierra Dynamic Company, 433
Timberland, 363, 364
Tim Hortons, 11
Timmons, Heather, 688
Tiny Computers Ltd., 316
T-Mobile, 156, 485, 508
Tochisako, Atsumasa, 309
Toedman, James, 135
Tokusel, Hiroto, 608
Tokusel, Kentaro, 608
Tomlinson, Richard, 689
TOMS Shoes, 650
Tom Tom, 410
Toshiba, 446
Total, 9, 267
Townsend, Janell, 685
Townsend, Pam, 686
Toyota Motor Corporation, 9, 56, 146, 290, 385, 405
Toys "R" Us, 306, 318
Trimble, Chris, 695, 700
Trumpf, 367
Tse, Edward, 690
Tsui, J., 345
Tsun-Yuan Hsieh, 691, 692
Tullett Prebon, 633
Tung, Rosalie, 686
Türk Telekom, 270
Turner, Ernie, 375
Twain, Shania, 321
Twitter, 14, 508
Tyco, 347, 572
Tz'u-hsi, Empress Dowager, 7

Ulaga, Wolfgang, 696
Unicom, 449
Unilever, 250, 268, 303, 309, 310, 318, 321, 349, 512, 608
Unisource Worldwide, 464
UNITE, 19
United Airlines, 447
United Fruit Company, 277
United Technologies, 321
UPM-Kymmene, 307
UPS, 264, 271, 504, 548
UST Global, 283

Valy-Durbin, Stacy, 699
Van de Gueht, Linda, 695
Vanport Lumber Company, 576–578
Vasarhelyi, Miklos, 697
Venevision, 329
Verma, Arup, 699
Verne, Jules, 28
Vernon, Ivan R., 685
Vernon, Raymond, 66, 77–80, 88
Vernon-Wortzel, H., 184
Viner, Jacob, 687
Vishny, R., 690
Vodafone Group Plc, 9, 156, 321, 485
Volkswagen Group, 9, 250, 327, 333, 380, 641
Volvo, 384
Von Brocke, Jan, 414
Von Oldenborgh, Marita, 685
Von Thünen, Johann, 29, 547
Vrontis, D., 697
V Water, 310

Wachovia Corporation, 601
Waelbroeck, J., 687
Wagstyl, Stefan, 686
Walker, Sue, 455–458
Walmart, 9, 20, 247, 248, 294, 306, 503, 513
Walsh, Eric, 686
Walt Disney Company, 91, 143, 154, 167–169, 493
Walter, Jorge, 694
Wanxiang, 329
Ward, Jay, 122
Warner Bros., 139
Warren, Hugh, 132
Warren, Tom, 695

Waters, Donald, 696
Watson, Andrea, 682
Weintraub, Sidney, 687
Weisman, Steven R., 686
Welch, Jack, 377
Welge, Martin, 692
Wen Jiabao, 262
Wentz, Laurel, 691, 695
West, Kanye, 680
Westerhaus, Michael, 402
Westjohn, Stanford A., 696
Weyerhauser, 229, 307
Weyer Werft, 331
Whirlpool, 326, 380
White, C., 693
White, Harry D., 211
White, Michael, 267
White & Case International, 523
Wiedeking, Wendelin, 669, 690
Wielaard, Robert, 181
Willamette Industries, 307
Williams, Rowan, 197
Williamson, Irving A., 125
Williamson, O. E., 693
Willis, Bruce, 593, 594
Wilson, Harold, 52
Wilson, Heather I. M., 693
Wilson, Richard, 56
Wipro, 283
Wirtz, Jochen, 533
Wisner, Joel D., 696
Wolf, Martin, 33
Wong, Y. H., 685
Wongtada, Nittaya, 469
Wood, Laura, 684
Wood, Van R., 694
Wood River Oil & Refining, 464
Workers Rights Consortium (WRC), 19
Workman, John P., Jr., 691
World Bank, 16, 20, 33, 35, 42, 61, 117, 209, 211, 264, 413
WorldCom, 347, 572
Woronoff, Jon, 686
Wortzel, L., 184
Wulff, Christian, 673

Xerox, 382
Xiaohua Sun, 694

Xing, Jane, 602, 690
Xinling, Liu, 515
Xu, Mary, 126

Yahoo!, 310, 506, 508, 611
Yandex, 506
Yankelovich, 513
Ye, Juliet, 515
Yearsley, Alex, 680
Yee-kwong, Ricky, 685
Yenijurt, Sengun, 685
Yeo, Vivian, 688
Yesipovsky, Igor, 290
Yeung, Bernard, 698
Yili, 329
Yip, George S., 305, 383, 689
Yip, Leslie S. C., 437
Yokohama Bank, 577, 578
Yorio, V., 488
York, Anne S., 693
Youaaou n'Dour, 268
Young, Clifford, 696
Young, Tata, 143
YouTube, 508
Youtube.com, 170
YRC Worldwide, 537
Yu, Jiang, 128, 130
Yuanyuan Zhou, 693
Yu-Ching Chiao, 698
Yum Brands, 374, 489, 507
Yunus, Muhammad, 688
Yurchenko, Olga, 145

Zahn Lisheng, 688
Zajac, Edward J., 694
Zanini, Gianni, 535
Zelaya, Manuel, 633
Zhang Shuhong, 294
Zheng Chenggong, 187
Zheng Xiaoyu, 294
Zif, Jehiel, 485, 694
Zipse, Christian, 697
Zocchi, Andrea, 689
Zoellick, Robert, 630
Zou, S., 693
Zsidisin, George A., 569
Zurawicki, Leon, 686

Abandoned product ranges, 81
Absolute advantage, 66–67
Access, 89
Accidental exporters, 429
Account deficits, 120
Accounting, 350
Accounting firms, 440
Account management programs, 325
Acculturation, 141
Acquisitions, 87, 88
Adaptability, 612
Adaptability screening, 613
Adaptation, 486–487
Administrative shelter, 49
Adoption tendency, 164
Advertising, 505–511
    cultural issues and, 508, 510
    deception in, 192
    and foreign languages, 145–147, 406
    on Internet, 507, 508
    media regulations and, 507
    print, 507–508
    promotional message for, 508, 510
    radio expenditures for, 507
    sex and, 155
    spending on, 506–507
    television expenditures for, 507
Advertising agencies, 510–511
Aerospace industry, 247
Aesthetics, 155–156
Africa, 639
    diamond trade, 679–681
    economic integration in, 253
    poverty in, 639
    sub-Saharan, 157
    wine production in, 675–678
African Industrial Property Office
    (ARIPO), 195
African Intellectual Property Organization
    (OAPI), 195
African Union (AU), 253
Agency theory, 340
Agent, 437
Agriculture, 648
    China and, 48
    climate and, 25–26
    employment and, 649
    European Union and, 244
    regions and, 29
    and trade, 240
    United States and, 244
Aircraft industry, 26, 41

Airfreight, 544, 547, 549
Airline industry, 519
Air transportation, 556
    refueling points, 28
Alabama, 56
Algeria, 253, 257
Al Qaeda
    funding of, 680
Aluminum industry, 25
Amazon.com, 647
American corporations, and international
    experience, 609
American Depositary Receipts (ADRs), 123
American depository receipts (ADRs),
    220
Americans. See United States
American terms, 202
Amsterdam Treaty, 245
Analogy, 481
Andean Common Market (ANCOM), 250,
    254
Andean Trade Preference Act (ATPA),
    251
Angola, 257, 679, 680
Antidumping laws, 46
Antitrust laws, 180
Appliance industry, 155, 491
Applied tariffs, 43
Aquaculture, 132–134
Arab countries, 163. See also specific
    countries
    cultural dimensions scores for, 163
    franchising in, 444
    and Israel, 180, 613
    and Jewish executives, 613
    and women executives, 613
Arab culture, 147, 153
Arab League, 176, 257
Arab Maghreb Union, 253
Arbitration, 196
Area expertise, 611
Area structure, 365, 367–368, 375, 498
Area studies, 166
Argentina, 26, 153
    commercial law in, 192
    economic integration of, 250
    Pampas, 26
Arm's length price, 498
ASEAN Free Trade Area (AFTA), 235,
    252
    map of, 255
    members of, 254

Asia. See also specific countries in
    cultural lifestyles and, 161–163
    current account balances of, 111
    dollar index of, 112
    economic crisis in, 109–113, 116
    free trade in, 252
    and North American trade, 249
Asian Free Trade Area (AFTA), 235
Asia Pacific Economic Cooperation
    (APEC), 235, 252, 254
Asia Pacific region, 639, 641
Assets, 200
Association of Southeast Asian Nations
    (ASEAN), 252
Attitudes, 152–154
Auditing, 350–351
Auditors, 344–345
Australia, 252
Australia New Zealand Food Authority, 192
Austria
    and European integration, 243
    labor and management in, 623
Autarky, 64, 69
Automotive industry, 28, 56, 241
    in China, 261–262
    in Eastern Europe, 327
    globalization and, 313, 323
    GM-AVTOVAZ joint venture, 286–291
    in Japan, 492
    in Korea, 305
    labor costs of, 627
    in U.S. South, 56
"Axis of Evil," 194

Backtranslation, 147
Bahamas, service industry in, 525
Bahrain, 28, 253
Balance of payments (BOP), 96, 104, 106
    current account, 98–101
    and economic crises, 109–113
    as flow statement, 97
    fundamentals of, 96–98
    problems with, 95
    of United States, 104, 107–108
Balance of trade (BOT), 99
Banana industry, 276–279
Bangladesh, 252, 268
Bank-based regimes, 346
Bank draft, 577
Banking industry, 526, 586
    and Asian economic crisis, 112–113
    history of, 218

Banking industry (*Continued*)
  international lending, 218–219
  liquidity and management, 112–113
  as trade intermediaries, 439–440
Banking liquidity, 112–113
Bank of England, 217
Bank of International Settlements (BIS), 205
Bank of Japan, 210
Barter, 593, 594
Base salary, 618
B2B (business-to-business) e-commerce,
  562, 655
Bearer bond, 219
Belarus, 236
Belgium
  bilingualism in, 491
  and European integration, 242
Bermuda, 525
Berne Convention, 188
Best practice, 140
Best practice, 377
Beverage industry, 443, 446
Bhutan, 252
Big Mac Index, 213, 214
Bilateral negotiations, 59
Bilateral Trade Agreement (BTA)
  (U.S-Vietnam), 132
Bilingualism, 491, 608
Bill of lading, 550, 577
Biotechnology, 192, 648
Black hole, 380
Board of Directors, 343–344
  compensation for, 349–350
  responsibilities of, 342
Body language, 147–148
Bolivia, 250, 251
Bond market, 219, 268
Bonds, 219
Bookkeeping, 97–98
Born global, 308, 436
Born global companies, 308
Botswana, 269, 679
"Boundarylessness," 377
Bound tariffs, 43
Bovine Spongiform Encephalopathy (BSE),
  39
Boycotts, 180
Boycotts, 180
Brain drain, 54, 241, 242
Brand aesthetics, 490, 492–493
Brand identification (Branding), 155, 512
Brand names, 488, 489
Brand strategy decisions, 492–494
Brazil, 160
  breakfast in, 488
  cultural dimensions scores for, 163
  currency in, 574
  customs of, 153
  economic integration of, 250
  as emerging market, 263–264
  foreign direct investment policy of, 53
  iron ore industry in, 28
  rainforest, 183

resources of, 25
  style in, 491
Breast-milk substitutes, 195
Bretton Woods Agreement, 114, 209, 210, 591
Bribery, 637
Bribery, 181, 182
BRIC nations, 271
"Bridgehead" expansion, 429
Brigham Young University, Center for
  International and Area Studies, 159
British Columbia, natural resources in, 25
Broadcast media, 507. *See also* Radio;
  Television
Brown University, 19
Brunei, 252
Buddhism, 151
Budget, controls of, 383
Buffalo, New York, 28
Buffer stock, 257
Built environment, 26
Bulk service, 544
Bundesbank (Germany), 210
Bureaucracy, and controls, 383–384
Business ethics, 182–183
Business Profile Series, 159
Business stakeholders, 336
Business startups, 647
Business travel, 159
Buy-domestic campaigns, 47

CACM. *See* Central American Common
  Market (CACM)
CADIVI, 122–123
CAFTA (U.S-Central American Free
  Trade Agreement), 194, 235
California, 85
Cambodia, 142
  economic integration and, 252
  mobile phone use in, 155
Canada
  bilingualism in, 491
  economic integration and, 252
  and European Union, 240
  export promotion, 50
  foreign direct investment and, 54
  Foreign Investment Review Agency, 54
  investment policy of, 51
  iron ore industry in, 28
  language laws in, 146
  product sophistication range, 76
  and trade with U.S, 246
CANTV ADRs, 123
Capital
  business evolution and capital access, 215
  mobility of, 230
Capital account, 96, 98, 101
Capital budget, 578–579
Capital budgeting, 576
Capital (financial), and channel design, 500
Capital flight, 55, 109, 113–116
Capital flow, 109, 113
  and European Union, 244
  foreign direct investment and, 52

Capital gains, 338
Capital inflow, 103, 113, 115–116
Capital markets, 200, 217–219
Capital mobility, 86, 113
Capital outflow. *See* Capital flight
Capital structure, 576
Career opportunities overseas, 604–606,
  610–615, 656–663
  and self-employment, 661
  web sites for, 658–660
Caribbean Basin Initiative, 238
Caribbean Basin Initiative (CBI), 251
Caribbean Common Market, 251
Caribbean Community (CARICOM), 251,
  254, 255
Caribbean countries, 251
  NAFTA and, 251
  tourism and, 54
Carriage and insurance paid to (CIP), 552
Carriage paid to (CPT), 552
Cartels, 257
Cash flow, and transfer prices, 583–584
Cash management, 582, 584–586
Cash pooling, 585
Catfish industry, 132–134
Cattle industry, 35
CD-ROMs (Compact Disk/Read-Only
  Memory), 401
Cell phones, 81, 313
Centers of Excellence, 376
Central America. *See also* countries of
  NAFTA and, 251
Central American Common Market
  (CACM), 251, 254
Central Europe, 194, 638. *See also* countries
  of
Centralization, 372
  of logistics management, 561
Centralized treasury, 584
Chad-Cameroon Petroleum Development,
  468
Chairman of the Board, 343, 344. *See also*
  Chief Executive Officer (CEO)
Chambers of commerce, 440
Change, propensity to, 161
Change agents, 54
Channel design, 498–501
Character, and channel design, 500
Chicago, 27
Chief Executive Officer (CEO), 343, 344,
  348. *See also* Chairman of the Board
Chief Financial Officer (CFO), 344
Chief Operating Officer (COO), 344
Chile, 88
  economic integration of, 250
  mobile phone use in, 155
  resources of, 25
  and trade with U.S., 238
China, 252, 560
  agriculture in, 48
  and American culture, 484
  APEC and, 252
  and Asian financial crisis, 110, 111

automotive industry in, 261–262
banking in, 380
brand names in, 489
capital inflow to, 115–116
car financing in, 261–262
cell phone usage in, 81
Chinese Postal Law, 264
consumer products in, 316
consumers in, 155, 484
corporate governance in, 351
cultural attitudes of, 151
currency in, 208, 261–262, 574
current and financial account balance
   in, 115
economic potential of, 641, 649
as emerging market, 260–262
export of rubber tires to U.S.,
   125–130
foreign direct investment in, 260
gift giving in, 153
gross domestic product of, 261
hotel management in, 609
household income in, 258
imports, 261–262
and incentive packages for industry, 56
individualism in, 163
intellectual property rights in, 188
Internet issues, 264
liberalization in, 260
management logistics in, 537
market segments and, 484
natural resources in, 25
online sales in, 508
paper industry, 295–299
political change in, 260, 261
prison labor in, 183
product adaptation in, 169
and regional trade areas, 235
shipping costs in, 537
telecommunications in, 308
toy exports, 292–294
transportation in, 537
and United States, 48
and WTO, 193, 258, 537, 639
Christianity, 148
Cities
   cost per diem in, 662
   migration patterns and, 26
Civil disturbance, 184
Classical trade theory, 65–72, 88
Class issues. *See* Social stratification
Climate, 25–26
Coalition building, 193
Cocoa, 257
Code law, 191, 191
Code Napoleon, 346
Codetermination, 623
Coffee, 257
Cold War, 194, 636, 642
Collateralized debt obligations
   (CDOs), 224
Colombia, 250
Color, 155

Columbia river valley, 25
Comision de Administracion de Divisas
   (CADIVI), 122–123
Commercial codes, 191
Commercial invoice, 550
**Committee on Foreign Investments in the
   United States (CFIUS), 51**
Commodity price agreements, 254, 257.
   See also Cartels
Common agricultural policy (CAP), 244
Common law, 191, 192
Common Market, 239
Common Market for Eastern and Southern
   Africa (COMESA), 253, 256
Common markets, 29, 239
Commonwealth nations, map of, 255
Communications, 27–29
   about innovation, 164
   and channel design, 501
   and management, 654–655
Communication services, 530
Comparative advantage, 67, 72, 73–74
Compensation
   of Boards of Directors, 349–350
   and host country nationals, 621
   of labor force, 627, 629
   method of payment, 621
   for overseas assignments, 617–622
   and tax equalization, 620
Competition, 84–86, 394, 431
   and channel design, 499
   and economic integration, 241
   globalization and, 308–310, 312–314,
      324–325
   international, 174
   monitoring of, 490
Competitive advantage of nations theory,
   66, 84–85
Competitive assessment, 396
Competitive clusters, 85
Complementary marketing, 447
Composition of trade, 14
Computer industry, 312, 316
Concentration, 484, 485
Confirmed, 577
Confiscation, 187–188
Confucianism, 151
Congo, 679
Consistency, 554
Consolidated profits, 575
Consortia, 450
Construction industry, 524
Construction services, 529
Consular invoices, 550
Consulting firms, as trade intermediaries,
   440
Consulting services, 530
Consumers
   globalization, 305–306
   and Internet, 655
   socialization of, 157
Consumption per capita, 481
Container (intermodal) shipping, 555

Container ships, 544
Contender, 328
Content analysis, 410
Continuity, and channel design, 501
Contract manufacturing, 448
Contractual hedging, 587
Contributor, 380
Control, 102
Control, and channel design, 500–501
Control, of local units, 383
Control policies, 51
Controls, 381–387
   behavioral, 383–385
   budgetary, 383
   bureaucratic (formalized), 383–384
   cultural, 384–386
   definition of, 381
   and function, 386
   from headquarters, 381
   management and, 387
   output, 382
   rewards or sanctions and, 387
   self-emerging, 382
Convertibility, 209, 210
Cool hunters. *See* Trend spotters
Coordinated decentralization, 373
Coordinated decentralization, 373
Coordinated intervention, 210
Copper resources, 88
Copyright piracy, 188
Corporate culture, 326–327, 385
   interfirm cooperation, 446–451
   and wealth maximization, 573
Corporate governance, 110, 112, 333–337,
   345–346
   auditing, 350–351
   in China, 351
   comparative regimes of, 345
   executive pay, 352
   external forces, 343
   failures in, 347
   goals of, 334–335
   legal system, historical development of,
      346
   market for corporate control, 352
   public perspective, 337
   reform of, 348–352
   and reputation, 347–348
   structure of, 343–345
Corporate income tax, 597
Corporate objective, 337–341
   operational goals, 338
   publicly traded or privately held, 338–
      339
   separation of ownership from
      management, 340–341
   shareholder wealth maximization,
      339–340
   stakeholder capitalism, 341
Corporate philanthropy, 512
Corporate responsibility and sustainability,
   352–356
   differing perceptions on, 355

Corporate responsibility and sustainability (*Continued*)
  ranking of issues, 355
  trust, 355–356
Corporate socialism, 110
Corporate social responsibility (CSR), 353, 650
Corporate stakeholders, 335–337
Corporate sustainability, 353
Corporate taxes, 597
Corporate vision, 375
Corporate wealth maximization, 572
Corporate web sites, 526
Corporations, 333. *See also* Firms
  and import restrictions, 49
Correspondent bank, 218
Corruption, 181, 182. *See also* Bribery
  in international business environment, 637–638
Cost, and channel design, 500
Cost, insurance, and freight, 551
Cost and freight (CFR), 551
Cost leadership, 314
Cost of communication, 526
Cost of living allowance (COLA), 618, 619
Cost-plus method of pricing, **495**
Cote d'Ivoire, 679
Cotenou Agreement, 238
Countertrade, 592–595
Country Commercial Guides, 401
Country Commercial Guides, 159
Country managers, 604
Country of origin, 373, 491, 654
Country organizations, 379–381, 383
Country Reports, 159
Coup d'état, 185
Coverage, and channel design, 500
Credit default swaps, 225–226
Creditors, 335
Credit quality, 222
Critical commodities list, 177
Cross-cultural
  behavior, 161
  differences, 141
Cross-licensing, 447
Cross-market activities, 447–448
Cross-national strategies, 486
Cross rates, 203, 204
Cross-subsidization, 322
Cuba
  and Nicaragua, 185
  and United States, 175
Cultural analysis, 161–165
  embracing local culture, 167
  manners and customs, 152–154
  performance analysis, 151
Cultural assimilator, 167
Cultural attitudes, 151–152
Cultural bias, 165
Cultural competence, 140, 610–612
Cultural consultants, 160
Cultural controls, 383–387
Cultural convergence, 155

Cultural differences, 141
  and executive recruitment, 609
Cultural dimensions, 160, 161–163
Cultural dominance, 141–142
Cultural imperialism, 142
Cultural knowledge, 158–160, 612
Cultural lifestyle. *See* Lifestyle
Cultural risk, 140
Cultural sensitivity training, 165
Cultural training, 613–615
Cultural universals, 144
Cultural universals, 144
Cultural values, 317, 385
Culture, 169. *See also* Popular culture
  business blunders, 160
  and business success, 167–169
  and channel design, 499
  and corporations, 326–327
  definition of, 140–141
  elements of, 144
  and service gaps, 521
Culturegrams, 159
Cultures, high and low context, 141
Culture shock, 615–616
Currency. *See also* Foreign currency
  big three (four), 207
  black market in Venezuela, 122–124
  collapse of, 110
  global trading, 207
  value of, 212–213
  world guide to, 205
Currency flows, 38
Currency management, 574
Currency markets, 201–208. *See also*
  Currency trading; Foreign currency
  exchange and cross rate tables, 204
  global turnover of, 206
  Iceland, 119–121
  intervention in, 210
  online, 207
  and risk, 211
  size and composition of, 205–207
  structure of, 207
  technology and, 207
Currency rates
  American terms, 202
  European terms, 202
  quotations for, 201–205
Currency risk sharing, 590–591
Currency symbols, 201
Currency trading, linguistics of, 201–205.
  See also Currency markets
Current account, 96, 98–101, 104
  balances, 96
  and gross domestic product, 71
Current and financial account, 104
Current income, 98–99
Current transfers, 99
Curse of oil, 466
Customer involvement, 520
Customers, and channel design, 499
Customer service, 365, 368, 512, 554–555
  outsourcing of, 322

Customer structure, 365, 368
Customs, 152–154
Customs Union, 238–239

Damaged goods, 542
Data, sources of, 403–404
Data privacy, 402–403
Debt, 42, 103, 229
Debt markets, 344
Decentralization, 372–373, 561
Deceptive advertising, 192
Decision making, 372–373
Deemed exports, 179
Defender, 328
Deglobalization, 636
Deindustrialization, 635
Delivered duty paid (DDP), 552
Delivered duty unpaid (DDU), 552
Delphi studies, 411
Demand conditions, 84
Denmark, 211, 243
Depression of 1930s, 33
Deregulation, 230, 525
Derivatives
  regulation of, 229–230
  securitization of, 223–224
Desertification, 44
Design services, 529
Detergent industry, 309
Developing countries
  and industrialized countries, 42–43
  trade and, 43
  World Bank and, 42
Developing markets, 267–271
  creative buying power, 268
  improving access, 268–269
  research, 268
  shaping aspirations, 269
  tailoring local solutions, 268
Developmental gap, 42
Diamond trade, 679–681
Differentiation, 314
Direct intervention, 210
Direct investment, 102–103, 109
Direct involvement, 435
Directories, 399, 501
Direct taxes, 596
Disclosure, 342, 346
Discriminatory (nondiscriminatory) regulations, 528
Distributed earnings, 598
Distribution, 498–505, 655. *See also* Shipping
  channels and, 498–501
  globalization and, 306
  home delivery, 655
  hub and spoke systems, 655
  and Internet, 655
  joint ventures and, 450
  just-in-time systems, 655
  security issues of, 655
  of services, 534
Distributor, 437, 440

Diversification, **484,** 485
  of financing, 592
  of operations, 592
Dividends, 598
Dividend yield, 338
Division of labor, 66–**67,** 72
Dodger, 327
"Doing Business 2010" report, 264
Domestication, 188
Domestic International Sales Corporation
  (DISC), 431
Domestic policy
  and global policy, 37–43
  and international trade, 37–40, 43
  and quality of life, 34
  and standard of living, 34
  trade and investment policies and, 59
Dominican Republic, 25
Double-entry bookkeeping, 97–98
Draft, 577
Dual pricing, 495
Dual use items, 177, 179
Duke University, 19
Dumping, 495, 636
Dutch Disease, 466

Early supplier involvement (ESI), 538
East African Community (EAC), 253
Eastern Europe, 327, 638
E-business, 326, 329, 566
  training programs, 168
Eclectic paradigm, 88
E-commerce, 306, **502,** 503
  B2B (business-to-business), 562
  in Europe, 562
  revenues of, 503
  service industry and, 528–529
  value of, 562
Economic Community of Central African
  States (CEEAC), 253
Economic Community of the Great Lake
  Countries, 253
Economic Community of West African
  States (ECOWAS), 253, 254, 255
Economic crises, 109. *See also* Financial
  crisis of 2007–2009
  balance of payments and, 109–113
  global, 33
  revitalizing international institutions,
    40–42
Economic exposure, 587, 592–595
Economic infrastructure, 154
Economic integration, 235, 238–239, 253
  in Africa, 253
  in Asia, 251–253
  and competition, 241
  dissatisfaction with, 243
  and economies of scale, 241
  in Europe, 242–245
  and factor productivity, 241
  history of, 242–244
  Indian subcontinent, 252
  and international manager, 271–273

  in Latin America, 250–251
  levels of, 238–239
  lobbying and, 272–273
  maps of, 255–256
  in the Middle East, 253
  in North America, 245–250
  reasons for, 239–242
Economic planning, multinational
  corporations, 54
Economic rent, 83
Economic risk, 189–190
Economic security, 527
Economic union, 239
Economies of scale, 243, 584
  and economic integration, 241
  and imperfect competition, 80–82
Ecuador, 250, 257
Education, 157, 523
Educational institutions, as trade
  intermediaries, 441
Education allowance, 621
Efficient customer response (ECR) systems,
  538
Electric power, 491
Electronic data interchange (EDI), 538,
  554, 562
Electronic discussion groups, 378
Electronic information services, 399–401
Electronic mail. *See* E-mail
Electronics, 305, 307
Elephants, 173
E-mail, 28, 146
Embargo, 43, **175**
Emerging markets, 257–264, 308, 640–643
  as barriers to business, 264–266
  Brazil as, 263–264
  China as, 260–262
  economic integration and international
    manager, 271–273
  globalization and, 305
  India as, 262–263
  infrastructure problems, 265–266
  and organizational structures, 378
Empathic design, 405
Employment policy, and local workers, 169,
  190
Employment/unemployment, 34, 243. *See
  also* Career opportunities overseas
  and foreign direct investment, 53–55
  globalization and, 517
  NAFTA and, 249
  service industry and, 522
Energy resources, 25
Engineering services, 529
English language, 145–147
Entertainment industry, 142–143, 494
Entrepreneurship, 433
Environmental awareness, 42–45, 572
  and product policy, 652
Environmental factors, to strategic
  planning, 308
Environmental issues, 183, 636, 640
  global map of, 44–45

Environmental laws, 565
Environmental protection, 640
Environmental scanning, 410–411
Equality, 161
Equity alliances, 446–447
Equity markets, 219–220, 344, 345
Equity participation, 448–449
Estonia, 316
Ethiopia, 185
Ethnocentrism, 165
EU. *See* European Union
EUREKA project, 54
Euro, 207–208, 211, 239, 243
  and dollar, 217
  exchange rates of, 212
  Sweden and, 211
  value of, 212, 217
Eurobonds, 217
Eurocurrency, 217
  exchange rates of, 217, 218
  interest rates of, 217–218
  LIBOR rates, 218
Eurocurrency, 217
Eurodollars, 217
"Euroland," 239
Euromarkets, 215, 218
Europe, 524. *See also* specific country in
  cultural segmentation and, 162, 163
  e-commerce in, 562
  and international monetary system,
    207–208
  labor unions in, 626
  management goals in, 572
  research and development projects in,
    55
  social customs of, 148
European Aeronautic Defense and Space
  Company (EADS), 450
European Commission, 244, 245
European Court of Justice, 245
European Currency Unit (ECU), 211
European Economic and Monetary Union
  (EMU), 211, 239
European Economic Area (EEA), 235,
  243, 244, 488
European Economic Community (EEC),
  241
  tax havens and, 597
European Free Trade Association (EFTA),
  238, 242–244, 254
European Monetary System (EMS),
  211–212
European Parliament, 245
European Patent Office, 195
European Space Agency, 26
European terms, 202
European Union Candidate Country, 667
European Union (EU), 143, 235, 244–245,
  254, 255, 258
  and agricultural trade, 35, 240, 244
  capital flow and, 244
  consortia and, 450
  Council of Ministers, 244, 245

European Union (EU) (*Continued*)
  Court of Justice, 245
  currency of, 211
  and data privacy, 402–403
  dual use items for export, 177–178
  Economic and Monetary Union (EMU)
    within, 211
  and Euro, 211, 239
  European Constitution, 245
  European Council, 245
  European Parliament, 245
  and genetically modified crops, 648
  government contracts and, 244
  history of, 242–244
  immigration policy and, 243
  incentive packages in, 56
  labor in, 624, 628
  map of, 255
  megaprojects of, 450
  members of, 211, 239, 242, 243
  organization of, 244–245
  and regional food names, 143
  and regional trade areas, 235
  security issues of, 402–403
  and tariffs, 240–241
  television programming and, 142
  Turkey and, 275
  and weapon components, 179
  and wireless communications, 241
  work benefits in, 626
Excess capacity, 430
Exchange controls, 189
Exchange-Rate Mechanism (ERM), 212
Exchange rates, 201, 230, 576, 592
  bilateral, 212
  dollars per Euro, 217
  Euro and, 201, 212
  floating, 210
  and interest rates, 217
  purpose of, 212–214
  quotations, terminology of, 201–205
  table, 204
Executives. *See also* Management; Managers
  compensation of, 352
  culture shock and, 615–616
  as global leaders, 601
  international experience of, 609
  overseas assignments, 604–606, 610–615
  recruitment of, 610
  talent pool of, 601
Expansion strategy, 484–486
Expatriates, 606–610
  advantages/disadvantages of, 606–607
  compensation for, 617–622
Experiential knowledge, 158–159
Export Administration Act, 177
Export complaint systems, 409
Export controls, 178–180
  deemed exports, 179
  national interests and, 179–180
  third world and, 178
  United States and, 178
Export-control system, 176, 177

Export declaration, 550
Export department, 362
Export documentation, 550–551
Export-Import Bank, 440
Export license, 177
Export management companies (EMCs),
    437–438
  compensation for, 437–438
  power conflicts and, 437–438
Export manager, 604–606
Export processing zones, 560
Export promotion agencies, 441
Exports and exporting, 49–51, 435–436
  bureaucratic red tape and, 50
  competition and, 51
  and economic integration, 244
  financing of, 576–578
  government regulations and, 397
  government subsidies for, 50
  and jobs, 38
  national security controls, 49
  pricing of, 494–496
  promotion of, 49–51, 58–60
  public funds for, 51
  research for, 395–397
  restrictions on, 49
  supply chain management of, 540
  United States and, 100
Export service programs, 50
Export Trading Company Act of 1982, 181,
    439
Export trading company (ETCs), 439, 440
Expropriation, 187
Extended enterprise, 540
Extenders, 328
External economies of scale, 82, 241
Externalities, 83–84
Extractive industries, 647
Extractive Industries Transparency
    Initiative (EITI), 468
Extra-territorial Income Tax Exclusion
    (ETI), 431
Extra-territoriality, 174
Ex-works (EXW), 551

Facsimile transmission (FAX), 28
Factor conditions, 84
Factor endowments, 73–74
Factor intensities (proportions), 72
Factor mobility, 89, 239
Factor prices, 73–74
Factor productivity, 241
Factor proportions theory, 66, 72, 73, 76
Factors of production, 72
Factual cultural knowledge, 611
Factual information, 158
False invoicing, 115
Families, 157–158, 617
  and overseas assignments, 612, 620, 621
Family-based systems, 345
Family-owned firms, 339
Federal Corrupt Practices Act, 182
Federal Reserve Bank, of New York, 210

Federation of International Trade
    Associations, 399
Fiber optic cables, 526
Fiduciary responsibility, 340
Field experience, 167
Financial account, 101, 104
Financial assets, 97
Financial centers, 205, 217
Financial crisis of 2007–2009, 221–231
  collateralized debt obligations (CDOs),
    224
  credit default swaps, 225–226
  global contagion, 227–228
  remedy, 228–231
  securitization of derivatives, 223–224
  subprime debt, 221–223
Financial derivatives, 102
Financial environment, 634–648
Financial incentives, 56
Financial industry, 29
Financial infrastructure, 154
Financial markets, 221, 346. *See also* Global
    financial markets
Financial mercantilism, 228
Financial services, 529
Financial stakeholders, 335
Financial Times, 204
Financing, international, 215–217
  domestic borrower/domestic currency,
    216
  domestic borrower/foreign currency, 216
  foreign borrower/domestic currency, 216
  foreign borrower/foreign currency, 217
Financing cash flows, 583
Finland
  bilingualism in, 491
  and European integration, 243
  and European Union, 240
  foreign direct investment in, 102
  shipbuilding in, 316
Firms, 88–90. *See also* Multinational
    corporations
  and channel design, 499–500
  effects of international expansion, 435–
    436
  and European Union, 243, 244
  and international business, 435–436,
    452–453
  international companies, 325
  local presence of, 324–327, 445–452
  marketing and, 486–487
  motives for international expansion, 433–
    435
  reorganization of, 257
  staffing of, 601–602
  startup issues and, 435–436
  strategy, structure and rivalry, 85
  and trade, 85–86
Fiscal incentives, 56
Fiscal policy, 645
Fixed exchange rate, 106, 114
Flextime, 626
Floating exchange rates, 106, 114, 210

Flow statement, 97
Focus groups, 154, 404–405
  product research and, 154
Focus on Technology, 269
Food industry, 244, 315, 469–474
Footwear industry, 72, 89
Foreign aid, 34
Foreign availability, 178
Foreign bonds, 219
Foreign Corrupt Practices Act, 181, 182, 637
Foreign currency market, 212–213. See also
    Currency
  currency market exchange rate of, 202,
    203–205
  Venezuela, 122–124
Foreign direct investment, 12, 52–55, 60,
    64, 86–87
  capital out-flows and, 55
  control of, 102
  costs and benefits of, 52, 55
  decision sequences of, 87
  and domestic investment, 579–580
  full ownership and, 451–452
  government promotion of, 54–56
  government restrictions on, 55
  home country perspective of, 54–55
  host country perspective on, 52–54
  incentive packages for, 54–56
  jobs and, 54
  profit and, 102
  and technological sensitive industry, 54
  theory of, 88
Foreign exchange exposure, 586–591
Foreign language skills. See also Language
  in Japan, 166
  in United States, 165
Foreign market opportunity analysis, 395
Foreign policy, 34
Foreign service premium, 618
Foreign trade zones, 560
Forest products industry, 463–465
40/40/20 rule, 549, 550
Forward contract, 588
Forward pricing, 655
Forward rates, 203–205
France
  breakfast cereals in, 165
  cultural dimensions score for, 163
  export promotion, 50
  and foreign video recorders, 47
  and international monetary system, 210
Franchising, 444–445
Frankfurt stock exchange, 219
Free alongside ship (FAS), 551
Free carrier (FCA), 551
Free movement of labor, 628
Free on board (FOB), 551, 552
Free trade, 244, 635, 643, 649
  areas, 29, 238
  in Asia, 252
  barriers to, 46
  benefits of, 235
  jobs and, 249

Free Trade Area of the Americas
    (FTAA), 235, 251
Freight forwarders, 551
Full ownership, 451–452
Functional managers, 604
Functional structure, 365, 368
Funds flow, 574
Funny faces scale, 407
Furniture industry, 459–462

Gander, Newfoundland, 28
Gap analysis, 483
GATT. See General Agreement on Tariffs
    and Trade (GATT)
GCC. See Gulf Cooperation Council
    (GCC)
Gender roles, 161, 646
General Agreement on Tariffs and Trade
    (GATT), 36, 276
General Agreement on Tariffs and Trade
    (GATT), 35–36
  Annecy Round, 36
  Dillon Round, 36
  Doha Round, 36, 37
  Geneva Round, 36
  Kennedy Round, 36
  negotiations in, 36
  taxation and, 596–597
  Tokyo Round, 36
  Torquay Round, 36
  Uruguay Round, 36, 189, 528
General Agreement on Trade in Services
    (GATS), 36
Generally accepted accounting principles,
    344
Genetically engineered foods, 648
Genetically modified (GM) crops, 648,
    655
Genetically modified organisms (GMOs),
    647
Genetically modified products, 192
Geography, 24–29
  built environment and, 26
  climate and, 25–26
  explorations and, 24
  history of, 24
  human population and, 26
  interaction and, 26–27
  location, 24–25
  movement and, 27–29
  place and, 25–26
  regions, 29
  rivers and, 27–28
  soils and, 26, 27
Geology, 25
Georgetown University, 19
Germany, 163, 175
  and armament exports, 176
  corporate tax rates in, 597
  current and financial account
    relationships, 104, 105
  export promotion, 50
  immigration policy of, 243

  incentive packages for industry, 56
  and international monetary system, 210
  labor and management in, 623
  negotiating styles in, 162
  and protection of language, 146
  recycling in, 565
  resources of, 26
  risk insurance in, 191
  Ruhr Valley, 26
  stakeholder practices in, 341
  and worker benefits, 626
Ghana, 185, 406
Gift giving, 153
Glass-Steagall Act, repeal of, 222
Global account management, 325, 379
Global cooperation, 530
Global economic crisis, 33
Global financial markets
  assets, instruments, and institutions, 200–
    201
  capital markets, 214–221
  currency market, 201–208
  evolution of global monetary system, 208
  exchange rates, 212–214
  new era of, 199
Globalization, 18, 305–311, 327. See also
    International business;
    Internationalization
  business opportunities and, 647
  competitive factors in, 308–310,
    322–323
  and country-market choice, 315–316
  and customer service, 322
  decision-making and, 324
  entertainment and, 142–143
  by industry and market, 308–311
  international firms and, 325
  local factors and, 324–328
  motivational drivers for, 306–311
  organization structures and, 325
  outsourcing of jobs and, 517–518
  and service industry, 525–526
  strategy planning for, 305, 311–329
  and trade negotiations, 648–650
Global leaders. See Executives
Global links, 11
Global Manufacturing Principles (Mattel),
    292
Global networks, 317
Global policy, 35–43
  domestic influences on, 37–43
  market forces and, 37–38
Global programs, 323–324
Global tourism, and H1N1, 531
Global trade regulation, 35–37
Global village, 647
Global warming, 44
Glocal, 374
Glocalization, 321
Gold standard, 208–209, 210
Goods and services, 518–519. See also
    Service
Goods and services (Continued)

compared, 518–522
definition of, 518
scale of dominance between, 520
tangible and intangible elements of, 518–520
Good trade, 98–101
Government
data collection and, 527–528
and interfirm cooperation, 450
and multinational corporations, 450, 451
and product counterfeiting, 494
and service industry, 528–529
as trade intermediaries, 439–440
Government-based regimes, 346
Government policy, 34, 634–636. *See also* Domestic policy
and e-commerce, 504–505
franchising and, 445
and incentive packages for industry, 56
industrial, 83, 84
multinational corporations and, 54
and service industry, 527–528
short and long-term goals of, 43, 59, 634–636
Government regulation, 525
GPS tracking, 548
Graduate education, 159
Gray markets, 497
Great Britain. *See also* United Kingdom
cultural dimensions scores for, 163
Great Depression of 1930s, 33
"Greenfield investment," 88
Greenhouse gas emissions, 45
Gross domestic product (GDP)
current account balances and, 71
service industry and, 523, 527
tourism and, 530–531
Group of Five, 210, 237
Group of Seven, 237
Group of Ten, 210
Group of Twenty, 237
Growth hormone controversy, 35
Guanxi, 158
Guerrilla warfare, 184
"Guest workers," 629
Gulf Cooperation Council (GCC), 253–255

Hardship allowances, 619, 620
Harvard University, 19
H-1B temporary worker visa program, 280–283
Headhunting recruiting firms, 604
Health care industry and Internet, 526
Hedge, 588
Hierarchy, management and, 157–158
High-context cultures, 141
High technology products, 178. *See also* Technology
Highway routes, map of, 558
Hinduism, 149
Hiring practices, and nationals, 165
H1N1 and global tourism, 531

Holland, labor and management in, 623
Holocaust, 147
Holy Cross University, 19
Home countries. *See* Host (home) countries
Home furnishings, 459–462
Home leave, 621
Honey, 455–458
Hong Kong, 153–154, 252, 524, 525
Asian financial crisis and, 110
compensation in, 618
cultural dimensions score for, 163
economic integration and, 252
and protection of language, 146
social customs in, 147
as transportation hub, 27
Host (home) countries, 621–622
and business regulations, 174–175
and foreign direct investment, 52–55
hiring from, 606
multinational corporations and, 54–55
politics and laws of, 191–192
Hotel chains, 609
Household income, 318
Housing allowance, 619
Housing sector, 222
Houston, Texas, 27, 28
Human resource management, 603, 628–629
Human resources, 601
Hungary
account deficit, 120
and countertrade, 592
Hydrology, 25

Iceland, 119–121
Illiquid markets, 230–231
Immigrants, 243
Immigration, and H-1B temporary worker visa program, 280–283
Imperfections, 89
Imperfect markets and strategic trade theory, 66, 80–82, 89
Implementers, 380
Imports and importing, 43, 46–49, 435–436
barriers to, 48–49
circumvention of laws, 49
financing of, 576–578
import controls, 48–49
import restrictions, 43, 46, 48–49, 636
promotion of, 51
reduced prices on, 240–241
research for, 396–397
United States and, 100
Import substitution, 89
Incentive packages, 56
Income, 98–99
investment income, 98
Income elasticity of demand, 481
Incoterms, 551
In-depth studies, 155
India, 58, 153, 252, 641
advertising in, 147
Bhopal disaster, 196
customer service operations in, 322

as emerging market, 262–263, 265
expatriate families in, 617
and export limits, 397
and foreign cultures, 142
gender imbalance in, 646
middle-class in, 318
service industry in, 524
Indirect involvement, 435
Indirect tax, 596
Individualism, 161, 163, 164
Indonesia, 258
Asian currency crisis and, 111
cultural dimensions score for, 163
economic integration and, 252
intellectual property rights in, 188
Industrialized countries, 42, 645
Industrial policy, 83, 84
Industrial sector, 51. *See also* Manufacturing sector
Industry-specific organizations, 627
Infant-industry, 527
Information system, 408
Information technology (IT) industry, 540
Infrastructure, 154, 305–306
transportation, 543–544
Initial expenses and capital outlays, 578
Initial public offering (IPO), 339
Innovation, 164
Input-output analysis, 75
Institute of International Education, 657
Institutions, 200
Insurance, against risk, 190–191
Insurance industry, 616
Insurance services, 529
Intangibility, 520, 533
Intellectual property protection, 494
in emerging markets, 264
Intellectual property right (IPR), 58, 188–189
trade-related, 189
Interactions (human activity), 26–27
Inter-American Development Bank, 433
Interbank interest rates, 217
Interest payments, 598
Interest rates, 576, 580
of eurocurrency, 217, 218
and exchange rates, 217
Interfirm cooperation, 445–451, 606
contractual agreements, 447
full ownership and, 451–452
informal, 447
Intermediaries, 501–502, 510, 512. *See also* International intermediaries
Intermodal movements, 544
Internal analysis, 313
Internal bank, 586
Internal economies of scale, 80–82, 241
Internal education, 166, 377–379
Internal forces, 343
Internalization, 90
Internal stakeholders, 336

International Air Transport Association (IATA), 399
International asset values, 222
International banking, 218–219
International bond, 219
International bond market, 219
International business. *See also* Globalization
  as change agent, 141
  codes and guidelines for, 195
  company reorganization and, 272
  defined, 5
  entry and development strategies for, 435–436, 451–452
  exporting and, 395–396
  firms motives for, 433–435
  geographic perspectives on, 24–29
  global links, 11–15
  history of, 6–10
  impact of, on U.S., 16
  importing and, 396–397
  management and, 428–429
  need for, 4–5
  new challenges for managers, 3
  opportunities in, 428
  politics and, 174
  preparation and information for, 393
  profit and risk in, 434
  regulations of, 174–175, 180–183
  research for, 393–395, 410, 412
  rules and regulations for, 180–183
  strategic effects of, 433–435
International capital markets, 217–218
International competitiveness, 174
International debt load, 103, 109, 645
International Finance Corporation, 532
International financial centers (IFC). *See* Financial centers
International financial markets, 221
International financing, 215–217
International information system, 408–412
International intermediaries, 436–445
  private sector facilitators, 438–439, 452
  public sector facilitators as, 440–441
Internationalization. *See also* Globalization
  executive recruitment for, 604–606
  motives for, 430–431
International Labor Organization (ILO), 627
International law, 195–196
  arbitration or litigation in, 196
  jurisdiction in, 195–196
International logistics. *See* Logistics
International Monetary cooperation, 636
International Monetary Fund (IMF), 33, 42, 210, 399
  and Asian economic crisis, 110
  net errors and omissions account of, 104
  rules and regulations of, 41
International money markets, 217–218
International Organization of Standardization, 567
International politics, 194–195

International relations, 194–196
International security markets, 219–220
International Standards Organization (ISO), 201, 488
International Stock Exchange (ISE), 220
International taxation, 595–598
International trade, 64
  gains of, 69, 70, 72
  since 1945, 35–37
  value of, 38
International Trade Center, 399
International Trade Commission (ITC), 46, 125
International Trade Organization (ITO), 35
International transactions, 97
Internet, 647–648. *See also* World Wide Web
  advertising on, 507
  in China, 264
  customer feedback and, 408–409
  and distribution strategies, 655
  e-commerce and, 502–505
  education and, 378
  global penetration of, 503
  language and, 529
  in Laos, 269
  research and, 408–409
  security and, 505
  service industry and, 526–527, 531–532
  and supply chain, 562–563
  taxes and, 504–505
Interpretive cultural knowledge, 160, 611
Interpretive knowledge, 160
Interviews, 404
Intracultural differences, 141
Intrafirm financing, 583–584
Intra-industry trade, 81, 82
Intranets, 378
Inventory, 553–555, 567
Inventory carrying costs, 553
Investment
  assets and liabilities, 102
  domestic and foreign, 579–580
  government policy on, 51, 58–60
  promotion, 55–57
  restrictions, 55
  risks of, 580
Investment Canada, 51
Investment income, 98
Invoicing, over and under, 69–70
Iran, 194, 237, 257
Iraq, 194, 257
Islam, 149
Israel
  and Arab countries, 180
  and trade with U.S., 238
Italy, 50, 85, 89, 524
Ivory Coast, 185

Jamaica, 25
Japan, 153, 310, 322, 323, 324
  automotive industry in, 492
  consortia and, 450

  consumers in, 324
  corporate culture in, 385
  corporate tax rates in, 597
  cultural dimension scores for, 163
  culture of, 141, 157
  current and financial account relationships, 104, 105
  diet products in, 490
  distribution system in, 164
  education in, 157
  and European Union, 240
  executive compensation in, 617
  exports and, 50, 51
  foreign corporations in, 652–653
  and foreigners, 152
  honey imports, 456–458
  intellectual property rights in, 189
  and international monetary system, 210
  International Trade Commission and, 46
  language skills in, 166
  legal culture of, 191
  management goals in, 572
  manners in, 152
  multinational corporations in, 54
  oil refineries in, 28
  pharmaceutical industry in, 528
  sogoshosha in, 439
  technical dominance of, 54
  telecommunications industry, 525
  transfer price abuse in, 581
  and United States, 40, 252
  work benefits in, 626
  worker productivity in, 26
  work rules in, 54
Japanese Carry Trade, 581
Japanese companies in United States, 611
Japan External Trade Organization (JETRO), 51
Jhai Foundation, 269
Jobs, in service industry, 524. *See also* Career opportunities overseas
Joint occurrences, 412
Joint Research and Development Act of 1984, 450
Joint ventures, 286–291, 447, 449–451
Jordan, 238, 524
Judaism, 147
Just-in-time (JIT) delivery system, 28, 538, 655
Just-in-time (JIT) inventory, 553

Kazakhstan, 236
Kenya, 154
Kimberley Process, 680
Kinship, 157
Knowledge industry, 525–526
Knowledge transfer, 52
Kuwait, 253, 257

Labor, 629
  global sourcing, 292–294
  H-1B temporary worker visa program, 280–283

Labor (*Continued*)
  occupations, map of, 624
  participation in management by,
    622–623, 625, 626
Labor law, 188
Labor personnel, 622–629
Labor unions, 449, 626–628
Lag, 585
Land bridges, 544
Language, 144–147, 608, 611. *See also*
    Foreign language
  bilingualism, 491, 608
  courses in, 657
  and culture, 406
  and executive hiring, 608
  historic context of, 147
  Internet and, 529
  laws regarding, 146
  nonverbal, 147–148
  slang and, 145–146
  and use of English, 145–147, 608, 611
  and World Wide Web, 504, 510
  and written exams, 528
Language barrier, 528
Laos, 252
Laser Raman Spectroscope (LRS), 681
Latin America, 511
  banana industry, 276–279
  and limits on exports, 397
Latin America Integration Association
  (LAIA), 254
Latvia, 316
Law. *See also* Trade laws
  influencing of politics and, 192–194
  and international relations, 194–196
  legal differences and restraints, 191–192
Law firms, 523
Law of one price, 213–214
Lead, 585
League of Nations, 175–176
Leather fashion industry, 85
Leontief paradox, 66, 74–75
Less-developed countries (LDCs), 638,
  640
Letter of credit (L/C), 576–578
Liberia, 679
LIBID (London Interbank Bid Rate),
  218
LIBOR (London Interbank Offer Rate),
  217
  Eurocurrency, 218
  U.S. dollar and Japanese Yen, 227
Libya, 253, 257, 269
Licensing, 442–444, 447, 452
  research & development and, 363
Licensing agreements, 87, 442
Lifestyle, 161–163
Limited liability, 334
Liner service, 544
Lingua franca, 608
Linkages, between financial institutions,
  201
Lithuania, 316

Lobbying, 193–194, 272–273
Local content, 188
Local content regulations, 188
Local culture, 167–168, 323–324, 493
Local (native) employees, 169, 190
Location decision, 557
Logistics, 542–553, 567. *See also*
    Transportation
  centralized management of, 561–562
  costs of, 541
  decentralized management of, 561
  definition of, 538–539
  outsourcing of, 561–562
  reverse, 565
  security and, 563–564
Logistics platform, 543
Lomé Convention, 276
London, as financial center, 205, 217
London Interbank Offer Rate. *See* LIBOR
  (London Interbank Offer Rate)
London stock exchange, 219
Longitudinal analysis, 481
Los Angeles, water in, 25
Low-context cultures, 141
Loyalty, 157
Luxembourg, 585

Maastricht Treaty, 211, 239, 245
Macedonia, 665–668
Macroeconomic level, 16
Mad cow disease, 39
Maintenance, service and repair, 491
Malaysia, 82, 85, 386
  Asian economic crisis and, 111
  economic integration and, 252
  intellectual property rights in, 188
Maldives, 252
Management, 344, 572–576. *See also*
    Executives; Managers
  communication advances and, 654–655
  control system and, 387
  corporate culture and, 326–327
  and cultural values, 152
  of currency, 574
  of distribution channels, 502
  financial goals of, 572–573
  and flow of information, 324–325
  of funds flow, 574
  future of, 650–656
  and headquarters staff, 323–325
  imperfections in, 89
  and interfirm cooperation, 450–451
  joint ventures and, 451
  labor and, 622–623, 625, 626
  logistics and, 560–562, 567
  of marketing, 486–514
  overseas development of, 605
  planning and research, 650–656
  of product line, 492–494
  separation from ownership, 346
  short and long-term priorities, 429, 651
  taxes and, 574
  training programs for, 387

Management contracts, 448
Managerial commitment, 428
Managers, 140, 603–622. *See also*
    Executives; Management
  economic integration and, 254
  expertise of, 159
  export, 604
  and foreign cultures, 147–148, 167
  and foreign languages, 145, 146–147
  functional, 604
  from host country, 167
  and international business expansion,
    452–453
  and international knowledge, 158–159,
    429, 430
  and laws and politics of host country,
    193–196
  and local politics, 167–169, 190–191
  for logistics, 543, 567
  marketing, 477–478
  and negotiations, 167
  and organizational structures, 367
  overseas assignments, 604–606,
    610–615
  personal characteristics of, 612–613
  and political action, 192–194
  and political risk, 190–191
  precareer experience of, 158
  religion and, 613
  and research, 394–395
  and service industry, 532–534
  for single country, 373, 604
  standards of behavior, 183
  and strategic planning, 327, 328
  and subordinates, 157–158
  talent pool of, 601
  training of, 165–167
Manners, 152–154
Mano River Union, 253
Manufacturing sector, 292–294, 524
Maps
  environmental problems, 44–45
  global terrorism, 186
  international groupings, 255–256
  international trade organizations,
    255–256
  labor force occupations, 624
  major cities, living costs in, 661
  trade and travel networks, 558–559
  world religions, 150
Maquiladoras, 249, 560
Marginal cost method, 495
Market analysis, 312–313
Market audit, 481
Market barriers, 47–49
Market-based regimes, 345–346
Market behavior, 140
Market concentration, 484
Market-differentiated pricing, 495
Market diversification/segment
  concentration, 484
Market economy *versus* planned economy,
  638

Market entry strategy social approach, 675–678
Market factors, 305–306
Market forces, 183
Marketing, 316–317, 321, 479–486
  area characteristics, 488–490
  company-related factors in, 486, 492
  complementary (piggybacking), 447
  consistency and, 493
  country specific factors in, 479–480
  estimating potential, 481–483
  identifying and screening, 479–484
  and income distribution, 481–482
  management of, 477–478
  and overseas development, 488–490
  preliminary screening, 480–481
  pricing policy and, 494–498
  product policy and, 487–494
  promotional policy and, 505–514
  public relations, 512–514
  sales potential and, 483
  segmentation and, 483–484
  standardization in, 486–487
  standardization vs. adaptation in, 486–487
  strategies for, 314–318
Marketing infrastructure, 154
Marketing mix variables, 316–318
Market portfolio, 315
Market research, and foreign languages, 146–147
Market segments, 77. See also Segmentation
Market transparency, 521
Marriage, 612, 621
Marshall Plan, 34, 242
Marxism-Leninism, 148
Masculinity, 161, 163
Massachusetts Institute of Technology (MIT), 410
Mass customization, 652
Mass production, 78
Material culture, 154–155
Material elements, 154–155
Materials management, 538
Matrix structure, 365, 368, 369
Mauritania, 253
Maximization of shareholder value, 337
M-commerce, 503
Media strategy, 505
Megaprojects, 450
Mentoring, 166
Mercantilism, 64–65
MERCOSUR (Mercado Comun del Sur), 235, 250
  map of, 255
  members of, 254
Mergers and acquisitions, 303, 307
Mexico, 75, 153
  cultural dimensions score for, 163
  incentive packages for industry, 56
  microfinance in, 268
  NAFTA and, 47, 89, 246, 247, 249, 323

negotiating styles in, 162
  oil industry, 467
  product sophistication range, 76–77
  retail stores in, 247–248
  service industry in, 525
  trade agreements of, 238
  and trade with United States, 246, 249
  worker safety in, 183
MIBOR (Madrid Interbank offer rate), 217
Microeconomic level, 17
Microfinance, 268
Microwave sales, 318
Middle-class family, 318
Middle East, 88
  economic integration in, 253
  labor shortages in, 628
  manners in, 152
Migration, rural to urban, 26
Minimum-wage legislation, 174
Mininationals, 308
Minority participation, 623
Missionary work, 159
Mississippi, 56
Mixed aid credits, 50
Mixed (hybrid) structures, 365
Mixed structure, 368
Mobile phone industry, 313
Modernization, 152
Monetary policy, 222
Monetary systems, 208–212
Money laundering, 115
Money markets, international, 217–218
Monopolies, 82, 83
Morocco, 253
Mortgage lending, 222
Most-Favored Nation (MFN), 36, 193
Motorcycle industry, 46
Movement, 27–29. See also Communications; Transportation
Movie industry, 171
MP3 technology, 564
Multidomestic strategy, 305–306
Multilateral negotiations, 59
Multinational corporations, 8, 57, 574–576
  business practices and, 54
  capital budget of, 578–579
  as change agents, 54
  and communication technology, 28–29
  financial management of, 574–576, 588
  and foreign direct investment, 57–58
  full ownership and, 451–452
  in host countries, 57, 324–327, 445–452
  and in-house advertising, 510
  interfirm cooperation and, 445–452
  investments of, 578–582
  and local support systems, 55–56
  recruitment of managers, 606–610
  research and development and, 52, 53
Munitions Control Act, 177
Myanmar, 252

NAFTA. See North American Free Trade Agreement (NAFTA)

National Basketball Association, 477
Nationalism, 242
National prosperity, 84
National Science Foundation, 410
National security, 49, 527
  exports and, 49
  and sharing research, 402
National sovereignty, 34, 656
National Trade Data Bank (NTDB), 401
Nation-states, 38
Natural hedging, 587
"Natural" products, 652
Negotiations, 36, 59, 167, 648–650
  manners and, 152
  styles of, 162
Nepal, 252
Net errors and omissions account, 104
Netherlands
  cultural dimensions scores for, 163
  labor and management in, 623
  oil industry in, 28
Net present value (NPV), 578
Netting, 584
Network, 378
Newsletters, 399
New York
  as financial center, 205, 217
  as transportation hub, 27–28
New York stock exchange, 219
New Zealand, 252, 626
  account deficit, 120
  honey industry, 455–458
Niche markets, 183
Nigeria, 257, 406
Night-shift workers, 626
NLR ("no license required") conditions, 177
Nondiscriminatory (discriminatory) regulations, 528
Nonfinancial incentives, 56
Nontariff barriers, 46, 488
Normal trade relations (NTR), 193
North American Commission on Labor Cooperation (NAALC), 246
North American Free Trade Agreement (NAFTA), 47, 235, 238, 246–250, 272, 323, 367, 432
  commission on environmental compliance, 246
  map of, 255
  members of, 254
  opposition to, 246
  retail trade and, 247
  statistical discrepancies and, 75
  trade increases and, 249
North American population shifts, 646
North Carolina, 85
North Korea, 194
North-South relationship, 638–640
Norway, 28, 175, 243
Not-invented-here syndrome (NIH), 324, 375
Nova International School, 665–668
Nuclear weapons, 178

Objective information, 158
Observation (research tool), 405
Ocean shipping, 544, 547, 561
Officers, 344
Official reserves account, 105
Offshore centers, 595
Offshore financial centers (IOFCs). *See*
    Financial centers
Oil industry, 88, 466–468. *See also*
    Organization of Petroleum Exporting
    Countries (OPEC)
    environmental safely and, 567
    and global cooperation, 530
    prices and, 257
    refineries and, 28
Oman, 253
One-stop logistics, 562
*On the Principles of Political Economy and
    Taxation* (Ricardo), 66
OPEC. *See* Organization of Petroleum
    Exporting Countries (OPEC)
Open account basis, 576
Open-market orientation, 635
Operating cash flows, 578, 583
Operating exposure, 591
Operating risk, 184
Opportunity costs, 70
Order cycle time, 553–554
Ordinary shares, 669
Organizational memory, 382
Organizational structures, 361–381, 387
    black hole situation and, 380
    contributor and, 380
    and country organizations, 379–381
    and emerging markets, 378
    evolution of, 370–372
    implementation of, 372–381
    implementers and, 380
    informal, 363, 365
    international division, 363–365
    markets and, 370
    networks and, 374–376
    product divisions and, 370
Organization for Economic Cooperation
    and Development (OECD), 182, 237,
    252–253, 342, 399
    tax havens and, 596
    transfer pricing guidelines of, 498
Organization for European Economic
    Cooperation (OEEC), 242
Organization of African Unity, 176
Organization of American States (OAS),
    176, 182
Organization of Petroleum Exporting
    Countries (OPEC), 237, 257, 467
Organizations. *See also* Organizational
    structures
    functions of, 361–372
    internal cooperation within, 377–379
    networked, 374–376
Orientation program, 614
Outsourcing, 562–563, 645, 646

Overlapping product ranges theory, 66, 76–77
Overproduction, 430
Overseas assignments, 615–616
    attrition rate for, 615
    compensation for, 617–622
    culture shock and, 615–616
    and families, 612, 620, 621
    good and bad locations, 615
    home leave, 621
    and medium-sized firm, 661
    recruitment for, 606–610
    repatriation from, 617
    self-employment and, 661
    terrorism and, 616
    Web site for job opportunities, 658–660
Overseas Private Investment Corporation
    (OPIC), 191
Ownership risk, 184

Packaging, 488, 555–557, 567
    climate and, 556
    as display, 556
    promotional aspect of, 491
    weight of, 556
Pakistan, 185
    economic integration and, 252
    economy of, 654
    and textile industry, 654
Paper industry, 295–299, 307, 310, 463–465
Paradox of plenty, 466
Paraguay, 250
Parallel importation. *See* Gray markets
Paris, as financial center, 217
Patent Cooperation Treaty (PCT), 195
Patent law, 195
Patent protection, 188
Patents and foreign inventors, 653
Pax Americana, 7
Pax Romana, 6
Payment terms, 576
Peace Corps, 159
Percentage change calculations, 205
Performance requirements, 51
Perishability, 520
Personal selling, 511
Personnel services, 533–534
Peru, 251, 511
Petroleum. *See* Oil industry
Pharmaceutical industry, 305, 307, 494, 528
Philippines
    Asian financial crisis and, 111
    economic integration and, 252
    intellectual property rights in, 188
Phone service, mobile, 154
Physical distribution, 538
PIBOR (Paris Interbank offer rate), 217
Piggybacking, 447
Piracy, 187, 543, 556
Planned economy *versus* market economy,
    638
Plans, 383
Plaza Agreement, 210

Podcasts, 378
Poland
    and countertrade, 592
    and protection of language, 146
Political environment, 638–643
Political risk, 183–189
    management of, 190–191
Political union, 239
Politics
    indoctrination sessions, 405
    influencing of politics and laws, 192–194
    lobbying, 192–194
    terminology of, 191
Popular culture, 142–143
Population, 26, 646–647
Population balance, 646
Population increase, 646
Population stabilization, 646
Portfolio investment, 102
Portfolio models, 315
Portugal, 243
Positioning, 507
Positioning, 490
Poverty, 638–639
Power distance, 163
Power structure, 157–158
Preference shares, 669
Preferential policies, 549
Price controls, 190
Price coordination, 497–498
Price escalation, 495
Price sensitivity, 318
Pricing, 82–83, 655–656
    and affordability, 318
    and foreign market, 496–497
    of services, 534
Primary data, 403
Primary research, 403–408
Princeton University, 19
Privacy
    data and, 402–403
    and Internet, 505
Private placement, 220
Privatization, in transport sector, 549
Process structure, 368
Product adaptation, 169
Product characteristics, 491–492
Product counterfeiting, 494
Product cycle, 66, 88
    stages of, 77–78
    trade implications of, 78–80
Product differentiation, 81
Production possibilities frontiers, 68–70
Production sharing agreements, 466
Product policy, 487–494, 652–654
Products
    and cultural attitudes, 154
    positioning of, 507
    research and, 154
    tracking of, 548
Product sophistication range, 76
Product structure, 365–367, 368

Profit, 102
   joint ventures and, 450
Program development, 318–323
Promotional message, 508
Protectionism, 58–59. *See also* Tariffs
Protectionist legislation, 58
Proximity to customers, 430
Proxy information, 401
Psychological distance, 432
Publicly traded companies, 344, 572
Public relations, 512–514
Publish What You Pay (PYP) program,
   468
Puerto Rico, 75
Punitive tariffs, 40, 49
Purchasing power parity (PPP), 212
"Putting Your Best Foot Forward"
   (publication), 159

Qatar, 253, 257
Qualitative information, 405
Quality circles, 626
Quality of life, 34
Quality of work life, 625–626
Quantitative data, 405
Quebec
   language laws in, 146
   natural resources in, 25
Quotas, 46

Radio, 507. *See also* Broadcast media
Railroad industry, 28
Railroads, map of, 558
Rainforest destruction, 45
Real assets, 97
Reciprocal quotations, 203
Recruitment, 628–629, 656–657, 660–661
   adaptability factors, 611–612
   and competence factors, 610–611
   and cultural attitudes, 609
   family issues and, 612–613
   of host country nationals, 606–610
   for overseas jobs, 604–606, 610–615
   and personal characteristics, 612–613
   and selection and orientation, 613–615
   sources for, 606–610
   of third country nationals, 609
   of women, 612, 660–661
Recycling, 491, 566
   of capital goods, 565
Reference groups, 157
Refinancing, 229
Refineries, 28
Refrigerators, 318
Regional integration, 235, 251, 367, 610
Regionalism, 242
Regional protectionism, 636
Regions, 169
   foreign direct investment in, 52–53
   patterns of movement and, 29
   and world trade, 235–236
Regulators, 345
Reinvoicing, 585–586

Related industries, 84–85
Relative price, 70
Reliability, 547
Religion. *See also* specific religions
   and international business, 148
   map of, 150
   sensitivities, 148–151
Repetition, 83
Representative office, 218
Reputation Research Network, 410
Research
   attributes of, 407–409
   critical information for, 396–397
   and data privacy, 402–403
   foreign market potentials, 396
   government sources of, 399
   importing and, 396–397
   for international business, 393–394,
     410, 412
   international information, 397, 399,
     408–412
   national security and, 402
   objectives for, 395–397
   primary, 403–408
   relevance of, 407
   secondary sources of, 396–397
   techniques of, 403–408
   and terrorism, 403
Research and development (R & D), 53,
   322, 372, 652, 654
   in Europe, 55
   foreign direct investment and, 54
   and licensing, 363
   multinational corporations and, 52, 53
Residential patterns, 26
Resource refining, 28
Retail trade, 247, 248, 655
   globalization and, 306
Returned products, 566
Reverse distribution, 565
Reverse innovation, 490
Reverse logistics, 565–566
Revolutionary United Front (Sierra Leone),
   680
Risk, 183–184, 195–196, 588
   financial markets and, 211
   and international business, 434
Risk management, speculation and, 588
Risk sharing, 592
RoHS (Restriction of Use of Certain
   Hazardous Substances Directive),
   652
Roll-on-roll-off, 544
Royalty, 442, 598
Rubber industry, 257
Rules and regulations, 41, 161, 180–183
Russia, 152, 236. *See also* Soviet Union
   automotive industry in, 286–291, 483
   distribution costs in, 541
   natural resources in, 25
   new markets in, 323
   as transition economy, 266–267
   value-added tax in, 192

SAARC. *See* South Asian Association for
   Regional Cooperation (SAARC)
SACU. *See* Southern African Customs
   Union (SACU)
Safe harbor, 505
Safety standards, 183
Sales
   decline in, 430
   as motive for internationalization, 430
   terms of, 551–553
Sales potential, 483
Sales promotion, and intermediaries,
   511–512
Same-sex partners, 621
Sanction, 175
   history of, 176
   problems with, 176
   unilateral or multilateral, 176
Sarbanes-Oxley Act, 348–349, 669
Satellite TV, 317
Saudi Arabia, 253, 257
   culture of, 141
   and intellectual property law, 195
   modernization and, 152
   water in, 25
Scale economies, 83. *See also* Economies of
   scale
Scenario building, 411–412
Sea bridges, 544
Seaweed snacks, 469–474
Secondary data, 397
Secondary data, 397, 401–402
Secularism, 148
Securitization, 223–224, 229
Security, 655
   and logistics, 563–565
   and shipping, 655
Segmentation, 316–318, 483–484
Self-employment, 661
Self-management, 622, **623**
Self-reference criterion, 164
Semiconductor industry, 82, 85
Sensitivity training, 167
Service, 533. *See also* Goods and Services;
   Service industry
   custom-made, 520–521
   definition of, 518
   distribution of, 520–521
   and goods compared, 518–522
   and maintenance, 322
   repair and maintenance, 491
   stand-alone, 519–522
Service capacity, 520
Service consistency, 521
Service heterogeneity, 521
Service industry, 98, 520, 529–534. *See also*
   Service
   classifications within, 532–534
   corporations and, 529–534
   cultural factors in, 521, 522
   data collection problems in, 526–528
   education and, 523
   as export, 530–531

Service industry (*Continued*)
  and GDP, 523, 527
  and global economy, 525–528
  government policy and, 527–529
  international projects and, 532
  Internet and, 526–527, 531–532
  and labor force, 522
  language barrier in, 528
  portability of, 522
  pricing and financing of, 534
  startup approach, 532
  in United States, 522–524
Service organization, 399
Services trade, 98
Sex, marketing and, 155
Shannon, Ireland, 28
Shareholder rights, 335, 342, 351
Shipper's order, 550
Shipping. *See also* Distribution
  and e-commerce, 504
  port security and, 655
  security and, 655
  and terms of sales, 551–553
SIBOR (Singapore Interbank offer rate), 217
Sierra Leone, 679, 680
Singapore, 524, 525, 579
  Asian financial crisis and, 111
  economic integration and, 252
  as financial center, 206, 217
  intellectual property rights in, 188
  and trade with U.S., 238
Single European Act, 235, **244,** 245
Small Business Administration, 440
Smoot-Hawley Act, 7
Snack food industry, 469–474
Social causes, 41
Social customs, 147–148
Social infrastructure, 154
Social institutions, 157–158
Social media, 508
Social organization, 157
Social responsibility, 354, 572
Social stakeholders, 336–337
Social stratification, 157
Soft power, 322
Software industry, 494
Sogoshosha, 439
Soil, 26, 28
South Africa, 25
South African Black Vintners Alliance, 675–678
South African Customs Union, 253, 254
South Asian Association for Regional Cooperation (SAARC), 252, 254
South Carolina, 85
Southern African Customs Union (SACU), 239, 254
Southern African Development Community (SADC), 253, 255
South Korea, 307, 524
  economic integration and, 252
  education in, 157

incentive packages for industry, 56
  mobile phone use in, 155
  official reserves account of, 106
  and regional trade areas, 235
  worker productivity and, 26
Sovereign wealth funds, 12
Soviet Union. *See also* Russia
  break-up of, 178
  disintegration of, 178
  and nuclear weapons, 178–179
  and United States, 638
Spain
  and European integration, 243
  and European Union, 240
Special economic zones, 560
Specialization
  and capital and labor factors, 73
  of production, 69
Specie, 65
Speculation, 588
Sponsorships, 477–478
Sports, commercial sponsorship of, 477–478
Spot rates, 203, 205
Sri Lanka, 252
St. Louis, Missouri, 28
Stakeholder capitalism, 338
Stakeholders, 335–337, 342
  business, 336
  corporate, 335–337
  financial, 335
  internal, 336
  public perspective of, 337–338
  social, 336–337
Stand-alone services, 519–522
Standardization, 316, 318, 486–487, 511
Standard of living, 34
Standards, national *vs.* international, 48
Standard worldwide pricing, 495
State enterprise, 639
Statistical Yearbook, 398
Statistics, discrepancies in, 75
Steel industry, 241
Stock exchanges, 344
Stockholder wealth maximization, 573
Stock market. *See* Stock exchanges
Storage, 557, 559
Store location strategy, 26
Straight bills of lading, 550
Strategic alliances, 445, 451, 654
Strategic business unit (SBU), 311
Strategic leader, 380
Strategic planning, 325, 327, 328
  environmental factors, 308
  and international manager, 272
  local company in the global environment, 327–329
Strategic trade, 80–86, **82,** 84
Students abroad, 656
Subprime debt, 221–223
Sugar industry, 257
Supply and demand, 183
Supply chain, 550–551, 562–563
Supply-chain management, 539, 567

Supporting industries, 84–85
Supranational organizations, 627
Surveys, 405–407, 408
Sustainability, 652
Sustainable development, 572
Sweden, 629
  and Euro, 211
  and European integration, 211, 240, 243
  and foreign direct investment, 54
  home furnishings, 459–462
  labor unions in, 626, 627
  as repair center, 322
Switzerland, 626
  and European integration, 243
  labor and management in, 623
Systems concept, 538–539

Taiwan, 160
  Asian financial crisis and, 110
  economic integration and, 252
  intellectual property rights in, 188
  and regional trade areas, 235
Tariffs, 41, 46
  and agriculture, 240
  applied, 43
  on bananas, 276–279
  as barriers in emerging markets, 265
  bound, 43
  on Chinese rubber tires, 125–130
  cost per job implications, 130
  punitive, 40, 49
  on Vietnamese catfish, 132–134
  and WTO, 41
Taxation, 595–598
  of corporate income, 597
  direct taxes, 596
  e-commerce and, 504–505
  income categories and, 598
  indirect taxes, 596
  international, 595–598
  labor unions and, 626
  and trade policy, 50
  value-added tax (VAT), 596, 597
  withholding taxes, 598
Tax equalization, 620
Tax havens, 596
Tax jurisdiction, 595
Tax law, 189–190, 431
Tax management, 573–574
Tax policy, 189
Tax shelters, 595
Teaching services, 530
Team building, 626
Teams (councils), 377
Technological advances, 155, 525, 647–648
Technological innovation, 77
Technology, 89. *See also* High technology products
  cost efficiency of, 207
  subsidized imports of, 54
Technology-intensive industries, foreign direct investment, 54
Technology transfer, 52

Teenagers, 391–392
Telecommunications industry, 28, 308, 563
Telegraph, 28
Television and television programs, 155.
    See also Broadcast media
    licensing of, 443
    reality shows, 443
Temporary worker visa program, 280–283
Tennessee, 56
Tennessee River Valley, 25
Terminal cash flows, 578
Terms of sales, 551–553
Terms of shipping, 551–553
Terrain, 25
Terrorism, 184
    and American business, 184–185
    and critical research, 403
    funding, 679–680
    global, map of, 186
    against industry, 184
    insurance against, 616
    and international students, 656
    and overseas assignments, 616
    security against, 616
    September 11, 2001, 165, 180, 184–185,
        636–637
    State Sponsors of, 323
    transportation and, 564
Textile industry, 85, 654
Thailand
    economic crisis in, 109, 111
    economic integration and, 252
    exports in, 38
    intellectual property rights in, 188
    marketing techniques in, 159
    snack food industry, 469–474
Theocracy, 191
Theories of trade, 89
    absolute advantage, 66–67
    classical, 65–72, 88
    comparative advantage, 66, 67
    competitive advantage of nations, 66,
        84–85
    factor proportions, 66, 72–77
    foreign direct investment, 87–88
    imperfect markets and strategic trade, 66,
        82–84
    international investment, 86–90
    Leontief paradox, 66, 74–75
    overlapping product ranges, 66, 76–77
    product cycle, 66, 77–78, 88
Third-party logistics (3PL) providers, 537
Third world, export controls and, 178
Tin, 257
Tire tariffs, 125–130
Tobacco products, 183
Tokyo, as financial center, 206, 217
Tombouctou, 27
Total cost concept, 539
Tourism, 25, 530–531
    Caribbean countries and, 54
    and GDP, 530–531
    H1N1 scare and, 531

Toy industry, 292–294
Tracking, 547, 548
Trade, 86–87
    cost, 83
    and domestic policy, 634–636
    international perspective on, 59–60
    negotiations, 36, 59–60, 648–649
    promotion of, 59
    regions and, 235–236
    tax legislation and, 50
Trade Act of 1974, 125
Trade Act of 1988, 182
Trade Adjustment Assistance programs,
    59
Trade associations, 399
Trade barriers, 43, 46–49
Trade creation, 240
Trade directories, 501
Trade disputes, 40
    and hormone-fed cattle, 35
    U.S. and Japan, 46
Trade diversion, 240
Trade draft, 577
Trade financing, 576–578
Trade flows, 38
Trade intermediary, 436. See also
    International intermediaries
Trade laws, 191–194, 196. See also Law
    and deceptive advertising, 192
    and entrepreneurial activity, 192
    history of, 191
Trademark licensing, 443
Trade-off concept, 539
Trade policies
    management of, 57–58
    U.S. imports of Chinese rubber tires,
        125–130
    U.S. imports of Vietnamese catfish and,
        132–134
Trade policy measures, 58–60, 110, 636
Trade promotion, 512
Trade promotion authority, 59
Trade regulation, global, 35–37
Trade statistics, 75
Trade terms, 552
Trade zones, 559–560
Trading bloc, 235, 238
Trading companies, 438–440
Training programs, 159, 657
    cross-cultural, 166
    in cultural understanding, 165–168
    online, 168
    for overseas employment, 614
Tramp service, 544
Transaction cost theory, 435
Transaction exposure, 586, 588–590
Transatlantic Free Trade Area (TAFTA),
    235
Transfer pricing, 498, 583–584
Transfer risk, 184
Transition economies, 266–267. See also
    Emerging markets
Transit time, 546

Translation exposure, 587
Translators, 167, 406
Transparency, 342, 346, 350
Transportation, 27–29, 550
    air shipping (airfreight), 544–545
    cost of, 548–549
    and geography, 24–25
    infrastructure of, 543–544
    international issues, 542–546
    map of, 558
    ocean shipping, 544
    predictability of, 547–550
    privatization, 549
    security and, 563–564, 655
    selecting a mode of, 546–550
    and travel time, 559
    trucking, 246, 249, 250
Treasury securites, top holders of, 129
Treaties of Friendship, Commerce, and
    Navigation (FCN), 195
Treaty of Managua, 251
Treaty of Rome, 242, 244
Trend spotters, 391–392
Triangular arbitrage, 203
Tribalism, 157
Trigger mechanisms, 636
TRIPS (trade-related aspects of intellectual
    property rights), 189
Trucking industry, 246, 249, 250
Tunisia, 253
Turkey, 116, 275
Turnkey operations, 448

Uganda, mobile phone use in, 155
Ukraine, 266
Uncertainty avoidance, 161
Undergraduate courses, 159
Unemployment, 284–285
UNICEF, 512
UNITA (National Union for the Total
    Independence of Angola), 680
UNITE, 19
United Arab Emirates, 257
United Kingdom, 145, 572
    and eurodollar accounts, 217
    and European integration, 243
    and European Union, 211
    export promotion, 50
    industrial failures, 284–285
    and international monetary system, 210
    labor in, 623, 627
    television programs in, 443
United Nations, 195
    Code of Conduct for Transnational
        Corporations, 195
    Conference on Trade and Development
        (UNCTAD), 399
    economic sanctions and, 176
    and multinationals, 512
    and service industry, 531
United Nations Convention on the Code
    of Conduct for Liner Conferences,
    549, 550

United Nations World Tourism
    Organization (UNWTO), 531
United States, 75, 142, 152–153, 163, 171
    account deficit, 120
    and advertising expenditures, 506, 507
    agricultural trade and, 240
    and Asia, 100
    balance of payments, 107–108
    and Canada, 246, 432
    and China, 48, 205
    comprehension of foreign culture in,
        165
    corporate tax rates in, 596, 597
    and Cuba, 175
    cultural dimensions score for, 163
    cultural values, 152–153
    current and financial account balances,
        99, 104
    customs union and, 242
    and data privacy, 402
    as debtor nation, 104, 645
    direct investment and, 102–103
    economic integration and, 252
    entertainment industry of, 142, 144
    and European Union, 35, 242
    exports and, 100, 176–177, 249
    financial account of, 101, 103
    foreign investment and, 51, 55
    and foreign trade, 50, 58, 240, 262
    gray market in, 497
    imports and, 39–40, 100
    and incentive packages for industry, 55
    individualism and, 163
    intellectual property rights in, 188
    international monetary system and, 210
    and international trade, 39
    and Japan, 40, 152, 252
    job loss in, 246, 249
    labor unions in, 627
    management goals in, 572
    manufacturing in, 100
    and Mexico, 246, 249
    and NAFTA, 47, 246
    national security and, 402, 563–564
    natural resources of, 25–26
    New Federalism, 58
    and nuclear weapons, 178–179
    product sophistication range, 76
    and regional trade areas, 235
    risk insurance in, 191
    sanctions and, 176
    service industry in, 522–524
    and Soviet Union, 638
    steel industry in, 28
    technical dominance of, 54
    trade deficits of, 645
    trade laws and, 176, 177, 183, 191
    trade policies of, 58–59, 125–130
    trading companies in, 439
    and United Kingdom, 433
    work benefits in, 626
    youth culture in, 152

United States export control system, 177–
    178
United States Federal Reserve System, 210
Unsolicited orders, 429
Unstructured data, 404
Urbanization, 646
Uruguay, 250, 524
U.S. Agency for International Development
    (USAID), 532
U.S.-Canada Free Trade Agreement, 246
U.S. Carriage of Goods by Sea Act, 555
U.S. Customs Service, 564
U.S. Department of Commerce, 439, 440
    critical commodities list, 177
    Economics and Statistics Administration,
        401
    and exports controls, 177
    and intermediaries, 501
    nontariff barriers and, 488
    publications of, 159
    statistical discrepancies and, 75
U.S. Department of Energy, and export
    controls, 177
U.S. Department of Homeland Security,
    564
U.S. Department of State, 177
    Allowances Staff, 618, 619
U.S. dollar, 202, 644
    and Asian currencies, 112
    and Euro, 217
U.S. International Trade Commission
    (ITC), 125
U.S. Labor Department, 249
U.S. Securities and Exchange Commission,
    345
U.S. Trade and Development Agency, 532

Value-added-activities, 321–322
Value-added tax, 505, 596, 597
Values, 152–154, 643
Venezuela, 257, 405
    black market for foreign currencies,
        122–124
    economic integration and, 250
    mobile phone use in, 155
    oil industry, 467
Verne, Jules, 28
Vietnam, 235, 252
    catfish industry in, 132–134
    expatriate families in, 617
    new markets in, 322
Virgin Islands, 75
Virtual teams, 378
Voluntary restraint agreements, 46, 48, 636

Wages, 623
Wall Street Journal, 478
Warehousing, 439–440, 557, 559–560, 562
Warranties, 492
Wealth of Nations, The (Smith), 66, 67
Webb-Pomerene Act, 180, 439
Webcasts, 378

WEEE (Waste Electrical and Electronic
    Equipment Directive), 652
Western countries. See also specific
    countries
    cultural lifestyles of, 161–163
Western Europe. See Europe
Wine industry, 85, 675–678
Wireless communication industry, 241
Withholding taxes, 598
Women
    in Arab countries, 613
    and corporate ladder, 612
    in overseas assignments, 612, 660–661
Worker safety, 183
Workers Rights Consortium (WRC), 19
Working capital, 576
Work redesign programs, 626
Work rules, 54
Work scheduling, 626
Works councils, 623
World Atlas (World Bank), 399
World Bank, 42, 211
    and AIDS, 512
    in developing world, 42
    and service industry, 532
    World Atlas, 399
World Cup, 477
World Economic Outlook, 399
World e-Inclusion, 268
World Factbook, 150
World Health Organization (WHO), 195
World Investment Report 2002, 9
World Trade, 159
World Trade Organization (WTO), 40–42,
    648, 649
    bribery rules of, 182
    and China, 193, 258, 635
    and cultural dominance, 143
    difficulties of, 41
    e-commerce and, 528
    and hormone-fed beef dispute, 35
    international law and, 195
    and right to establishment, 41
    social causes and, 42
    as source of information, 399
    tax subsidies and, 431
    telecommunications and, 563
World War I, 175
World Wide Web, 408, 528–529. See also
    Internet
    corporations and, 526
    e-commerce and, 502–505
    hub sites on, 502
    language and, 504, 510
    and service industry, 526–529
    and sites for international employment,
        658–660
    and supply chain, 563

Xenophobia, 643

Zambia, 524